Rock Song Index

BY BRUCE POLLOCK

Nonfiction

In Their Own Words: Lyrics & Lyricists, 1955–1974

The Face of Rock & Roll: Images of a Generation

When Rock Was Young: A Nostalgic Review of the Top 40 Era

When the Music Mattered: Rock in the 1960s

The Disco Handbook

Housework for Men

The Rock & Roll Fun Book

Hipper Than Our Kids

The Rock Song Index

Working Musicians

Fiction

Playing for Change

Me, Minsky & Max

It's Only Rock and Roll

Edited Works

Popular Music: An Annotated Index to American Popular Songs, Vols. 7–24 (1983–1999)

GUITAR: For the Practicing Musician, issues 1–100 (1983–1992**)**

Selected Liner Notes

Troubadours of the Folk Era (1993)

Richie Havens Anthology (1994)

Best of Sha Na Na (1995)

The Lovin' Spoonful: Platinum & Gold (2002)

Rock Song Index

2nd Edition

The 7500 Most Important Songs
of the Rock and Roll Era: 1944–2000

Bruce Pollock

Routledge
Taylor & Francis Group
New York   London

Published in 2005 by
Routledge
Taylor & Francis Group
270 Madison Avenue
New York, NY 10016

Published in Great Britain by
Routledge
Taylor & Francis Group
2 Park Square
Milton Park, Abingdon
Oxon OX14 4RN

© 2005 by Taylor & Francis Group, LLC
Routledge is an imprint of Taylor & Francis Group

Printed in the United States of America on acid-free paper
10 9 8 7 6 5 4 3 2 1

International Standard Book Number-10: 0-415-97073-3 (Hardcover)
International Standard Book Number-13: 978-0-415-97073-0 (Hardcover)
Library of Congress Card Number 2005014085

Library of Congress Cataloging-in-Publication Data

Pollock, Bruce.
   The rock song index : the 7500 most important songs of the rock and roll era : 1944-2000 / Bruce Pollock.-- 2nd ed.
     p. cm.
   Includes bibliographical references (p.   ) and indexes.
   ISBN 0-415-97073-3 (hardback : alk. paper)
   1. Rock music--Bibliography. I. Title.

ML128.R6P65 2005
016.78242166--dc22

2005014085

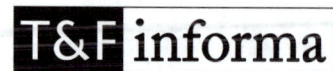

Taylor & Francis Group is the Academic Division of T&F Informa plc.

Visit the Taylor & Francis Web site at
http://www.taylorandfrancis.com

and the Routledge Web site at
http://www.routledge-ny.com

CONTENTS

INTRODUCTION TO THE REVISED EDITION

Rather than revised, this edition of the original 1997 volume of *The Rock Song Index* has been dramatically overhauled. It has been turned inside out, like an old briefcase, one with many hidden interior pockets and zippered compartments, and its contents have been subjected to a new and inspired scrutiny. Most of the old commentaries have been rewritten as have some central precepts that accounted for a song's inclusion in the book. The only remaining constant is the figure of 7,500 defining songs as necessary and crucial to illustrate and populate the literature of rock and roll, from its earliest rumblings, circa 1944, to its state of the art at the end of the millennium.

But, in order to accommodate approximately 400 new songs from 1997–2000, an equal number had to be dropped. And, to highlight perhaps 1,000 more essential songs my research and listening led me to in the past five years, new rules for exclusion had to be created. The most obvious and satisfying one was the ability I gave myself to eliminate songs that peaked on the pop charts between numbers 6 and 10. Hundreds of nominal "hit" songs that added nothing to an artist's credibility and were usually there at the tail end of a career as gifts of one sort or another (but not necessarily to the listener) fell by the wayside with a pleasing crunch, to be replaced by vital tunes that I was horrified to realize had missed my attention the first time around.

I am aware that this new set of 7,500 songs, much more prominently arranged by title in this edition, for easy artist, year, songwriter, album, label, and producer reference, could seem similarly riddled with omissions five years (or five minutes) hence. In some ways, like learning an instrument, researching the history of rock and roll through individual songs is a lifetime study and a daunting task. As challenging as it is to keep current, as one generation of songwriters recycles another, it is even more arrogant to feel certain that you've scoured every hidden zippered compartment and yellowed notebook on the map for sources of amazing and influential material. On the other hand, having been for nine years the editor in chief of a song-oriented magazine for rock guitarists that often held popularity surveys, I came to realize that approximately 20 percent of the songs on a given survey usually accounted for 80 percent of the votes, with one or two (i.e., "Stairway to Heaven") running far ahead of the pack. The remaining 80 percent of the songs received one or two votes apiece. This knowledge has pretty well shielded me from the presumption that the average reader is apt to find his or her own obscure favorite song detailed in these pages. Otherwise, I would have had to stretch the book to 20,000 songs, at which point I might as well have turned it into one of those telephone-sized reference books I've seen around (and own) that simply include or try to include everything ever released by anyone—which, to me, would have vitiated the whole idea of the book.

The whole idea of the book, as it was in the first edition, is to combine many different sources in making my selection—singles and album cuts, chart positions and critical acclaim, noted cover versions and historic movie usages, respected personal confessions of professional music listeners and more unforgiving chart positions—with my own half-century journey as a radio addict in the 1950s, to a much published author and record reviewer in the 1970s, to the editor of an annual reference book on the year's five hundred most important songs through the 1980s and 1990s, and to my present position as a prolific compilation producer at one of the remaining major record labels in New York City. It is also to combine, or compile as it were, the best information from dozens of existing research entities, each with their function, but each serving only their own constituencies—fans of hit singles; fans of albums; fans of R&B, country music, or British hits; underground fanatics; early rock and roll, punk, or rap enthusiasts—and rarely crossing over. Here, I hope, is where it all comes together into a unity that is objective, varied, scintillating, and, of paramount importance, easy to dance to.

But, actually, a dance groove is only one of the elements necessary to distinguish a good song from a great one, to say nothing of an important or an influential one. Rightly, many critics refuse to separate a song from its performance, and just as many, from Steve Allen on, dismiss lyrics outright. Surely, a #1 designation on the pop charts confers—if nothing else—a lifetime of repeat airplay on the oldies circuit, but given the vagaries of record company politics and payola, the herdlike limited mentality of the nation's radio programmers, the influence of TV and film, focus groups, call-in research, call-out research, tour support, expensive videos, and other mitigating priorities, what separates a #1 from a #5 (or, for that matter, a hit from a stiff) is impossible to quantify, let alone justify. And while, especially since the 1990s, most chart positions have to be regarded with the baseball equivalent of an asterisk, it is nevertheless true that a rock and roll song worldview without hit singles would be as skewed and chaotic as one comprised solely of hits, even if that has meant, on occasion, the inclusion of certain songs that were personally offensive to my own taste. But, as a radio programmer told me once when I was writing an article on the subject, "Taste has nothing to do with it." Thus, I can promise, less than 1 percent of the titles in this book have been put there solely due to my own taste (which nevertheless accounts for seventy-five songs, a pretty decent afternoon of eclectic listening).

This doesn't mean that personal taste hasn't been involved in some way or other in many more of these selections, even if it's someone else's personal taste. Given that there are a vast number of songs in here that never made any chart, but yet have been deemed to imply an historical relevance, it is fair to question what is meant by relevance and what is meant by history (or what is meant by deemed to imply, for that matter). Considering, too, that record reviewers, as a breed, are often as sheep-like as the radio programmers they feel they are an

idealistic alternative to, following the lead of a few New York or Ann Arbor or San Francisco–based pop potentates who claim to have listened to and rated every song released, in order to parrot their opinions, one must be aware of biases from this area as well, sometimes even more insidious than the commercial implications of chart positions (the name Alex Chilton springs to mind). But, to me at least, it is a comfort to note that any reaction to a song, on first listening or tenth listening, even one known to have launched a thousand imitators as well as punk rock in England or folk rock in Greenwich Village, is based on so many variables that to give it its due here is an act of faith that must of necessity thumb its nose at quantification. The competing agendas of art and business, time of exposure, age, circumstance, memory, genius, luck, and happy accident are exactly what make these 7,500 songs stand up so proudly, having survived so many if not all of the tests that have rendered the also-rans to their deserved obscurity.

Not all songs are created equal, of course; some were the product of a writer or an artist on an unconscious hot streak, or a flashing moment never to be repeated. Some had a line, a hook, a groove, a catchphrase so totally of the moment that no one not living in that moment can understand or appreciate what it meant to those who first experienced its unique power in the backseat of a car, on a crowded dance floor, in the middle of a public rally, or sitting alone on the roof dialing in a station in Pittsburgh, the only station in the nation to play it, on a clear night, wrapped in unrequited lust for a girl named Diana or Denise or Gloria, Sherry, Peggy Sue, Iris, Sara, or Claudette, or a boy named Johnny. In this regard, as you will see from the sources listed in the bibliography, I have based these discriminating determinations on the work of not one but many experts whose lives, if not livings (and vice-versa), put them in a position to have their judgments on albums, artists, and songs (often in that order) taken seriously.

In this book, however, it is the song that predominates as the music's prime mover through history, with each of the three indexes serving a distinct purpose in illustrating that movement. For that reason, in this revision particularly, the Song Title Index forms the core of the text. And as much as it has been written to be read straight through, it's much more likely to be used instead as a tool for someone who needs to find out, once and for all, who sang, wrote, or covered a given song, when and in what album it first appeared, and, if he or she has a second to spare, what the reasoning was behind its inclusion. Rest assured, however, that a linear reading of these pages has its own rewards, as much through the occasional serendipitous segue as anything else. But to me the Yearly Index and the Artist Index are by far more critical in sustaining the book's most compelling subplot. While the alphabetical Artist Index is self-explanatory, it is by no means designed to be an exhaustive account of every song or even every hit by the given subject. For the most part, I have attempted to weigh selections in favor of earlier, breakthrough hits, at the expense of later ones, as in most cases the later hits rode on the backs of the earlier ones at the same time as they were dilutions of the vision that inspired the artist in the first place. I have also tried to select the most important songs as well as the biggest. In some cases, I have been forced into including great percentages of material by certain superstars who just wouldn't stop dominating their era. But that's why they're superstars.

In the Yearly Index, because songs have for the most part been designated by their year of introduction, there is a good chance that a song's original year of appearance will differ considerably from the year in which it achieved its height of popularity. My feeling in this matter is that once a song has been released on an album available to the public, its journey commences, through critics, record label officials, artist and repertoire agents searching for material, publishing magnates compiling samples of their wares for commercials and movie soundtracks, and/or friendly contemporaries of the artist who may have heard the song in previous incarnations and have just been waiting for the artist to release it before they could put out their own versions. Once out in the wider world anything can happen. The original version can become a stiff or a hit, a B-side or a neglected album cut. It can emerge in concert where the headline act takes a shine to it, or the headline act's manager snags it for their new up-and-coming thrush. Clive Davis might take note of it to launch a diva or a record label six years later. For these reasons, the date of first release is more important to me than the date of ultimate success, especially if the originating artist has any kind of a career based on that song.

It has long been my contention that, as important as image and attitude and video and internal politics are in establishing singers and bands, without a key song, they're not going to acquire a dedicated following beyond a thirty-mile radius of their hometown. These key songs, usually but not always hits, are the fuel that drives the business, and that drives the vehicle of rock and roll around the corner of Surf Avenue to the crossroads of folk and acid rock. The songs create careers, movements, indelible memories, radio formats, and national magazines. In the Yearly Index I have noted with an asterisk the key songs of each year during the year they were released, in the hopes of fueling a larger debate. When was the first rock and roll record, how did Motown grow, what kind of havoc did the Beatles wreak? Here you can chart the year-to-year evolution of folk to folk rock to the laid back mellow singer/songwriter, and blues to R&B to blues rock to heavy metal. You can watch an underground movement grow, flourish, and then devour itself, to be replaced by the natural opposite reaction. As U2 guitarist Dave "The Edge" Evans once said at a Rock and Roll Hall of Fame ceremony, "We spent many years in a garage trying not to sound anything like Jimmy Page."

My original thought may have been that these 7,500 songs would form an ideal radio station, one that would connect all the pieces of this intriguing art form and present them in one place with amazing and informative segues. But even as this fantasy has become more and more of a remote as well as a financially ruinous proposition, the technology has emerged so that it is now literally possible that all of these 7,500 songs could be placed on one's own iPod, or whatever descendant or competing product takes over the turf, making the entire development of rock and roll, in the form of the greatest songs

this generation of writers and musicians has produced, according to those who experienced them,
those who sang them, heard them, played them, and
recorded them again and again, available to the ear
on demand, in something less than four hundred
hours. For that real opportunity, I give thanks to the
Internet pioneers who have broken radio's elitist
demographic typecasting and given everyone a
chance to become a true music fan. Not tangen-
tially, I also have to thank the lifelong song scholars
and magazines and books devoted to the subject that
keep the dialogue alive, giving everyone a hunger to
hear what they've missed even as they keep tabs on
what's next.

TITLE INDEX

A

A.B.C.'S OF LOVE, THE

Artist: Frankie Lymon and the Teenagers
Written by: George Goldner, Richard Barrett
From the album: *The Teenagers*
Label: Gee
Produced by: George Goldner
Year: 1956
The Teenagers were the original subteen hearthrobs of doo-wop. A generation later the Jackson 5 would sing "ABC" (Motown, '70).

A.D.I./THE HORROR OF IT ALL

Artist: Anthrax
Written by: Anthrax
From the album: *Return of the Living Dead, Part II Soundtrack*
Label: Island
Year: 1986
Comic book metal meets its horror movie destiny.

ABACAB

Artist: Genesis
Written by: Phil Collins, Tony Banks, Mike Rutherford
From the album: *Abacab*
Label: Atlantic
Produced by: Hugh Padgham
Year: 1981
Essential progressive rhyme scheme.

ABC

Artist: The Jackson 5
Written by: Freddie Perren, Berry Gordy Jr., Deke Richards, Fonce Mizell
From the album: *ABC*
Label: Motown
Produced by: Freddie Perren, Berry Gordy Jr., Deke Richards, Fonce Mizell
Year: 1970
Frankie Lymon and the Teenagers for a new generation. The second of four straight smashes for the family group. An impressive enough debut to start, in and of itself, a new dance era, perfectly timed to the start of a new decade.

ABILENE

Artist: George Hamilton IV
Written by: John D. Loudermilk, Bob Gibson, Lester Brown, Albert Stanton
From the album: *Abilene*
Label: RCA
Produced by: Chet Atkins
Year: 1963
#1 country/Top 20 crossover indicating Hamilton's drift from rockabilly to country music, a sojourn many original and/or played-out rockers would be taking in the decades to come.

ABOUT A BOY

Artist: Patti Smith
Written by: Patti Smith
From the album: *Gone Again*
Label: Arista
Produced by: Lenny Kaye, Malcolm Burn
Year: 1996
The bohemian icon of a previous era returns to form after the deaths of her husband and her brother, to eulogize a kindred spirit, Kurt Cobain.

ABOUT A GIRL

Artist: Nirvana
Written by: Nirvana
From the album: *Bleach*
Label: Sub Pop
Produced by: Butch Vig
Year: 1991
After a night listening to the Beatles.

ABRACADABRA

Artist: Steve Miller Band
Written by: Steve Miller
From the album: *Abracadabra*
Label: Capitol
Produced by: Steve Miller, Gary Mallaber
Year: 1982
Space cowboy R&B in the video age.

ABRAHAM, MARTIN AND JOHN

Artist: Dion
Written by: Dick Holler
From the album: *Dion*
Label: Laurie
Produced by: Phil Gernhard
Year: 1968
Poignant easy listening social protest about Lincoln, King, and Kennedy in an era of much more violent expression. Covered by Smokey Robinson and the Miracles (Tamla, '69).

ABSOLUTE BEGINNERS

Artist: David Bowie
Written by: David Bowie
From the album: *Absolute Beginners Soundtrack*
Label: EMI-America
Produced by: Clive Langer, David Bowie, Alan Winstanley
Year: 1986

ACCIDENTS WILL HAPPEN

Artist: Elvis Costello
Written by: Declan McManus (Elvis Costello)
From the album: *Armed Forces*
Label: Columbia
Produced by: Nick Lowe
Year: 1979
A cynical mouthful from the guy who once insulted Ray Charles and slugged Bonnie Bramlett in the same evening.

ACE OF SPADE

Artist: O.V. Wright
Written by: Deadric Malone
From the album: *A Nickel and a Nail/Ace of Spades*
Label: Backbeat
Produced by: Willie Mitchell
Year: 1970
Biggest crossover hit for an R&B master.

ACE OF SPADES

Artist: Motorhead
Written by: Ian Kilmeister (Lemmy), Philthy Taylor, (Fast) Eddie Clarke
From the album: *Ace of Spades*
Label: Mercury
Produced by: Vic Maile
Year: 1980
One of their most monumental metal onslaughts.

ACHILLES LAST STAND

Artist: Led Zeppelin
Written by: Jimmy Page, Robert Plant, John Paul Jones, John Bonham
From the album: *Led Zeppelin*
Label: Atlantic
Produced by: Jimmy Page
Year: 1976
Landmark ten-minute performance opus.

ACHIN' TO BE

Artist: The Replacements
Written by: Paul Westerberg
From the album: *Don't Tell a Soul*
Label: Sire
Produced by: Matt Wallace, the Replacements
Year: 1989
His ultimate punk folk ballad—Westerberg achin' to be mainstream.

ACID QUEEN

Artist: The Who
Written by: Pete Townshend
From the album: *Tommy*
Label: Decca
Produced by: Kit Lambert
Year: 1969
From the all-purpose deaf, dumb, and blind boy pinball epic, remade in the movie as a camp masterpiece by Tina Turner (Polydor, '76).

ACID TRAX

Artist: Phuture
Written by: Earl Smith Jr., Pierre Nathanial Jones, Herb J.
Produced by: Marshall Jefferson
Label: Trax
Year: 1987
Seminal house music anthem, paving the way for electronica and trance.

ACROSS THE GREAT DIVIDE

Artist: The Band
Written by: Robbie Robertson
From the album: *The Band*
Label: Capitol
Produced by: John Simon, the Band
Year: 1968
Bedrock Americana: the root of the coming roots rock movement.

ACT NATURALLY

Artist: Buck Owens
Written by: Vonie Morrison, Johnny Russell
From the album: *The Best of Buck Owens*
Label: Capitol
Produced by: Ken Nelson
Year: 1963
Buck's first #1 country hit (followed by four more in a row), covered by the Beatles (Capitol, '66), with Ringo in the lead. B-side of "Yesterday."

ADD SOME MUSIC TO YOUR DAY

Artist: The Beach Boys
Written by: Brian Wilson, Mike Love, Joe Knott
From the album: *Sunflower*
Label: Reprise
Produced by: Brian Wilson
Year: 1970
In the autumn of their career.

ADDICTED TO LOVE

Artist: Robert Palmer
Written by: Robert Palmer
From the album: *Riptide*
Label: Atlantic
Produced by: Bernard Edwards
Year: 1986
Soundcheck favorite of many a guitar band, from Van Halen to Sonic Youth. Palmer's only #1 is

attached to one of the all-time great videos. Covered by Ciccone Youth (Sonic Youth) (Enigma/Blast First, '89).

ADIA

Artist: Sarah McLachlan
Written by: Sarah McLachlan
From the album: *Surfacing*
Label: Arista
Produced by: Pierre Marchand
Year: 1997
Defining "Lilith" rock.

ADORABLE

Artist: The Drifters
Written by: Buck Ram
Label: Atlantic
Produced by: Neshui Ertegun
Year: 1955
Easing the transition from doo-wop to R&B with a lilting ballad. Ram would perfect this niche with the Platters.

ADULT EDUCATION

Artist: Hall & Oates
Written by: Daryl Hall, John Oates, Sara Allen
From the album: *Rock 'N Soul (Part I)*
Label: RCA
Produced by: Hall & Oates, Bob Clearmountain
Year: 1984

ADVENTURES OF GRANDMASTER FLASH ON THE WHEELS OF STEEL, THE

Artist: Grandmaster Flash and the Furious Five
Written by: Various
From the album: *The Great Rap Hits*
Label: Sugarhill
Produced by: Sylvia Robinson, Joey Robinson Jr.
Year: 1980
The gang's all here for this epic and pioneering demonstration of the fine art of sampling. Heard mainly in New York City, this incredible mixed tape featuring everyone from Blondie to Chic had history written all over it. It also had lawsuit written all over it.

AFFAIR OF THE HEART

Artist: Rick Springfield
Written by: Rick Springfield, Blaise Tosti, Danny Tate
From the album: *Living in Oz*
Label: RCA
Produced by: Rick Springfield, Bill Drescher
Year: 1983

AFRICA

Artist: Toto
Written by: David Paich, Jeff Porcaro
From the album: *Toto IV*

Label: Columbia
Produced by: Toto
Year: 1982
Their biggest hit accomplishes the hitherto improbable feat of fitting Kilimanjaro into the lyric without missing a beat or messing with the meter.

AFRO

Artist: Jon Spencer Blues Explosion
Written by: Jon Spencer
From the album: *Extra Width*
Label: Matador
Produced by: Jon Spencer and Muff Winwood
Year: 1993
Something like the blues.

AFTER MIDNIGHT

Artist: Eric Clapton
Written by: John J. Cale
From the album: *Eric Clapton*
Label: Atco
Produced by: Delaney Bramlett
Year: 1970
Clapton begins his post-God singing career by switching to a Stratocaster. Covered by the author, J. J. Cale (Shelter, '72).

AFTER THE FIRE

Artist: Pete Townshend
Written by: Pete Townshend
From the album: *Deep End—Live*
Label: Atlantic
Year: 1985
Emotionally taut commentary on Northern Ireland; covered by Roger Daltrey (Atlantic, '85). Suggested segues: "Where the Streets Have No Name" by U2, "Zombie" by the Cranberries, "The Troubles" by the Roches, "Invisible Sun" by Sting.

AFTER THE GOLDRUSH

Artist: Neil Young
Written by: Neil Young
From the album: *After the Goldrush*
Label: Reprise
Produced by: David Briggs, Neil Young, Kendall Pacios
Year: 1970
A loner again after a stint with Crosby, Stills & Nash, Young hits his solo stride with this classic history of San Francisco.

AFTER THE LOVE HAS GONE

Artist: Earth, Wind & Fire
Written by: David Foster, Jay Graydon, Bill Champlin
From the album: *I Am*
Label: ARC
Produced by: Maurice White
Year: 1979
Funk crossover presages New Jack Swing.

AFTER THE RAIN

Artist: Nelson
Written by: Gunnar Nelson, Matt Wilson, Marc Tanner, Rick Wilson
From the album: *After the Rain*
Label: DCG
Produced by: Marc Tanner, David Thoener
Year: 1990
A smash by the twin sons of Rick Nelson, coming in the same year that produced hits by Wilson Phillips, the scions of California legends Brian Wilson and John Phillips.

AFTERNOON DELIGHT

Artist: Starland Vocal Band
Written by: Bill Danoff
From the album: *Starland Vocal Band*
Label: Windsong
Produced by: Milt Okun
Year: 1976
Harmonious folk rock dalliance in the fading heyday of the sunshine era.

AGAIN

Artist: Janet Jackson
Written by: James Harris III, Terry Lewis, Janet Jackson
From the album: *janet*
Label: A&M
Produced by: James Harris III, Terry Lewis, Janet Jackson
Year: 1993
An actress/singer now, in the Diana Ross mold, this is Janet's Oscar-nominated breathless ballad from the film *Poetic Justice*, costarring Tupac Shakur.

AGAINST ALL ODDS (TAKE A LOOK AT ME NOW)

Artist: Phil Collins
Written by: Phil Collins
From the album: *Against All Odds Soundtrack*
Label: Atlantic
Produced by: Arif Mardin
Year: 1984
Capping Collins' ascent to the peak of the middle-of-the-road.

AGAINST THE WIND

Artist: Bob Seger
Written by: Bob Seger
From the album: *Against the Wind*
Label: Capitol
Produced by: Bill Szymczyk
Year: 1980
Seger returns to his favorite theme, charting his heroic course from Midwestern working-man to superstar and back again.

AGE OF CONSENT

Artist: New Order
Written by: New Order
From the album: *Low Life*
Label: Qwest
Produced by: New Order
Year: 1985
The openly gay duo, Bronski Beat, named their first album after this track.

AHAB THE ARAB

Artist: Ray Stevens
Written by: Ray Stevens
From the album: *1,837 Seconds of Humor*
Label: Mercury
Year: 1962
Politically incorrect novelty now even more so.

AIN'T EVEN DONE WITH THE NIGHT

Artist: John (Cougar) Mellencamp
Written by: John Cougar Mellencamp
From the album: *Nothing Matters and What If It Did*
Label: Riva
Year: 1981
In the midst of skinny-tie new wave, a rootsy, arena rock anthem.

AIN'T GOT NO HOME

Artist: Clarence "Frogman" Henry
Written by: Clarence Henry
Label: Argo
Produced by: Paul Gayten
Year: 1956
Deep-throated New Orleans R&B novelty, literally earning Henry his nickname.

AIN'T IT A SHAME

Artist: Fats Domino
Written by: Fats Domino, Dave Bartholomew
From the album: *Rock and Rollin' with Fats Domino*
Label: Imperial
Produced by: Dave Bartholomew
Year: 1955
Domino's first crossover hit, after eleven R&B hits in five years; gentleman crooner Pat Boone had the bigger cover (Dot, '55). For the next two years, Fats' tunes would spend a total of 153 weeks on the R&B charts (41 at #1).

AIN'T IT FUN

Artist: The Dead Boys
Written by: Cheetah Chrome, Peter Laughner
From the album: *We Have Come for Your Children*
Label: Sire
Produced by: Felix Pappalardi
Year: 1978
Composed with a prime instigator of the mid-'70s Akron Indie Punk rock scene; Laughner played in Pere Ubu before it was Pere Ubu.

AIN'T NO MOUNTAIN HIGH ENOUGH

Artist: Marvin Gaye and Tammi Terrell
Written by: Nick Ashford, Valerie Simpson
From the album: *United*
Label: Tamla
Produced by: Harvey Fuqua, Johnny Bristol
Year: 1967
Motown inspirational peak, great career move for three of the label's more perfect couples. Cover by Diana Ross was a #1 R&B/#1 crossover.

AIN'T NO NIGGA

Artist: Jay Z featuring Foxy Brown
Written by: Jonathan Burks, Shawn Carter, Inga Moorehead, Dennis Lambert and Brian Potter
From the album: *Reasonable Doubt*
Label: Priority
Year: 1996
Transforming the Four Tops' "Ain't No Woman Like the One I've Got" into pungent protest.

AIN'T NO STOPPIN' US NOW

Artist: McFadden and Whitehead
Written by: Gene McFadden, John Whitehead
From the album: *McFadden and Whitehead*
Label: Philadelphia International
Produced by: Gene McFadden, John Whitehead, Jerry Cohen
Year: 1979
#1 R&B/Top 20 crossover from Philly. After that, they stopped.

AIN'T NO SUNSHINE

Artist: Bill Withers
Written by: Bill Withers
From the album: *Just as I Am*
Label: Sussex
Produced by: Bill Withers
Year: 1971
His first hit started as the B-side of "Harlem." Stephen Stills on guitar.

AIN'T NO WAY

Artist: Aretha Franklin
Written by: Carolyn Franklin
From the album: *Lady Soul*
Label: Atlantic
Produced by: Jerry Wexler
Year: 1967
B-side of "(Sweet Sweet Baby) Since You've Been Gone."

AIN'T NO WOMAN (LIKE THE ONE I GOT)

Artist: The Four Tops
Written by: Dennis Lambert, Brian Potter
From the album: *Keeper of the Castle*
Label: Dunhill
Produced by: Dennis Lambert, Brian Potter
Year: 1973

AIN'T NOBODY

Artist: Rufus and Chaka Khan
Written by: David Wolinski

From the album: *Live—Stompin' at the Savoy*
Label: Warner Brothers
Produced by: Russ Titelman
Year: 1983
Pioneering use of the Linn drum machine gives Chaka Kahn's band their fourth #1 R&B hit.

AIN'T NOBODY HERE BUT US CHICKENS

Artist: Louis Jordan and His Tympani Five
Written by: Joan Whitney, Alex Kramer
Label: Decca
Produced by: Milt Gabler
Year: 1946
#1 R&B crossover. Pretty soon all those R&B chickens would come home to roost, with the pioneering Jordan opening the barn door.

AIN'T NOBODY HOME

Artist: Howard Tate
Written by: Jerry Ragavoy
Label: Verve
Produced by: Jerry Ragavoy
Year: 1966
His biggest crossover hit became more of a signature for B. B. King and Bonnie Raitt.

AIN'T NOTHIN' GOIN' ON BUT THE RENT

Artist: Gwen Guthrie
Written by: Gwen Guthrie
From the album: *Good to Go Lover*
Label: Polydor
Produced by: Gwen Guthrie
Year: 1986
Borrowing a phrase from her grandfather and a bass line from Grandmaster Flash, the former Aretha Franklin backup singer constructs a domestic equality masterpiece.

AIN'T NOTHIN' YOU CAN DO

Artist: Bobby Bland
Written by: Deadric Malone, Joe Scott
From the album: *Ain't Nothin' You Can Do*
Label: Duke
Produced by: Joe Scott
Year: 1964
A powerful statement of the blues, from a time when the blues could still hit Top 20 on the pop charts.

(AIN'T NOTHING BUT A) HOUSE PARTY

Artist: Show Stoppers
Written by: Dell Sharh, Joseph Thomas
Label: Heritage
Produced by: Del Sharh
Year: 1968
Classic frat house soul shouter, covered by the J. Geils Band (Atlantic, '73).

AIN'T NOTHING LIKE THE REAL THING

Artist: Marvin Gaye and Tammi Terrell
Written by: Nick Ashford, Valerie Simpson
From the album: *You're All I Need*
Label: Tamla
Produced by: Nick Ashford, Valerie Simpson
Year: 1968
Their first #1 R&B/Top 10 crossover. Covered by Aretha Franklin (Atlantic, '74). Later an anthem for Coca-Cola.

AIN'T TALKIN' 'BOUT LOVE

Artist: Van Halen
Written by: Eddie Van Halen, Alex Van Halen, Michael Anthony, David Lee Roth
From the album: *Van Halen*
Label: Warner Brothers
Produced by: Ted Templeman
Year: 1978
Early metal noodlings from the Pasadena titan's monster debut album; Eddie on hyper guitar.

AIN'T THAT JUST LIKE A WOMAN?

Artist: Louis Jordan and His Tympani Five
Written by: Fleecie Moore, Claude Demetrius
Label: Decca
Produced by: Milt Gabler
Year: 1949
Another funky, cheeky, blues rocker. Covered by a big Jordan fan, Fats Domino (Imperial, '61). Suggested segue: Chuck Berry's guitar intro to "Johnny B. Goode."

AIN'T THAT LOVIN' YOU BABY

Artist: Jimmy Reed
Written by: Jimmy Reed
Label: Vee-Jay
Year: 1955
Deceptively simple, influential, and hypnotic R&B hit. Covered by the Youngbloods (RCA, '67), Elvis Presley (RCA, '68).

AIN'T THAT PECULIAR

Artist: Marvin Gaye
Written by: Smokey Robinson, Warren Moore, Marv Tarplin, Robert Rogers
From the album: *Greatest Hits (Vol. 2)*
Label: Tamla
Produced by: Smokey Robinson
Year: 1965
Gaye's second #1 R&B/Top 10 crossover comes from the Miracles stable. Suggested segue: "Honky Tonk" by Bill Doggett.

AIN'T TOO PROUD TO BEG

Artist: The Temptations
Written by: Eddie Holland, Norman Whitfield
From the album: *Gettin' Ready*

Label: Gordy
Produced by: Norman Whitfield
Year: 1966
Rare Whitfield-Holland collaboration results in a #1 R&B/Top 20 crossover. Establishes David Ruffin's brand of soul-baring intensity.

AIN'T WASTIN' TIME NO MORE

Artist: Allman Brothers
Written by: Greg Allman
From the album: *Eat a Peach*
Produced by: Tom Dowd
Label: Capricorn
Year: 1972
Written about the death of brother Duane, this was the opening track on their first album without him.

AIR THAT I BREATHE, THE

Artist: Albert Hammond
Written by: Albert Hammond, Mike Hazelwood
From the album: *It Never Rains in Southern California*
Label: Mums
Produced by: Don Altfeld, Albert Hammond
Year: 1972
Cover by the Hollies (Epic, '74) was the hit. Written in L.A., where just breathing the air is an adventure.

ALADDIN SANE

Artist: David Bowie
Written by: David Bowie
From the album: *Aladdin Sane*
Label: RCA
Produced by: Ken Scott, David Bowie
Year: 1973
Pouty pyrotechnics from the master, a battle plan for mope rock. Covered by Bauhaus (4AD, '80).

ALBATROSS

Artist: Fleetwood Mac
Written by: Peter Green
From the album: *English Rose*
Produced by: Mike Vernon
Label: Epic
Year: 1969
Instrumental hit in England, Peter Green on guitar.

ALEX CHILTON

Artist: The Replacements
Written by: Paul Westerberg, Tom Stinson, Chris Mars
From the album: *Pleased to Meet Me*
Label: Sire
Produced by: Jim Dickinson
Year: 1987
Elegizing a minor deity of alt-rock culture, and becoming ones themselves in the process.

ALICE'S RESTAURANT

Artist: Arlo Guthrie
Written by: Arlo Guthrie

From the album: *Alice's Restaurant*
Label: Reprise
Produced by: Van Dyke Parks, Lenny Waronker
Year: 1967
The epic endless folkie tone poem of the alternate culture, basis for the Arthur Penn movie and still played religiously by certain FM stations every Thanksgiving.

ALISON

Artist: Elvis Costello
Written by: Declan McManus (Elvis Costello)
From the album: *My Aim Is True*
Label: Columbia
Produced by: Nick Lowe
Year: 1977
Rapier wordplay, Costello at his caustic best. Covered by Linda Ronstadt (Asylum, '80).

ALIVE

Artist: Pearl Jam
Written by: Eddie Vedder, Stone Gossard
From the album: *Ten*
Label: Epic
Produced by: Nick Parashar, Pearl Jam
Year: 1991
Early dysfunctional stirrings from the Seattle co-chairmen of grunge, Eddie Vedder.

ALIVE AND KICKING

Artist: Simple Minds
Written by: Simple Minds
From the album: *Once upon a Time*
Label: A&M
Produced by: Jimmy Iovine, Bob Clearmountain
Year: 1985
Symbolizing their Earth-bound, chart-bound incarnation.

ALL ALONE AM I

Artist: Brenda Lee
Written by: Arthur Altman, Manos Hadjidakis, Jean Ioannidis
From the album: *All Alone Am I*
Label: Decca
Produced by: Owen Bradley
Year: 1962
Brenda's post-rockabilly balladeering peak. Imported from Greece.

ALL ALONG THE WATCHTOWER

Artist: Bob Dylan
Written by: Bob Dylan
From the album: *John Wesley Harding*
Label: Columbia
Produced by: Bob Johnston
Year: 1968
One of the few echoes of the volatile and metaphorically abundant "old" Dylan on this spare and severe album. Incendiary cover by Jimi Hendrix (Reprise, '68) effectively claimed the song. But Dave Matthews does a great live version, too.

ALL-AMERICAN BOY, THE

Artist: Bill Parsons
Written by: Bill Parsons, Orville Lunsford
From the album: *Detroit City and 11 Other Hits by Bobby Bare*
Label: Fraternity
Year: 1958
Sung by Bobby Bare but credited to the writer, Parsons, who did a lip-sync tour behind it, while Bare was in the service. Bare got the last laugh, however, with a long and prosperous country music career; Parsons went on to record "Hot Rod Volkswagon," which stiffed (Starday, '60). Suggested segues: "Johnny B. Goode" by Chuck Berry, "So You Wanna Be a Rock and Roll Star" by the Byrds.

ALL APOLOGIES

Artist: Nirvana
Written by: Kurt Cobain
From the album: *In Utero*
Label: DGC
Produced by: Steve Albini
Year: 1993
Sometimes seen as Cobain's advance suicide note.

ALL AROUND THE WORLD

Artist: The Jam
Written by: Paul Weller
From the album: *This Is the Modern World*
Label: Polydor
Year: 1977
Stellar single from these postmod, premodern English rockers.

ALL AROUND THE WORLD

Artist: Lisa Stansfield
Written by: Lisa Stansfield, Ian Devaney, Andy Morris
From the album: *Affection*
Label: Arista
Produced by: Ian Devaney, Andy Morris
Year: 1990
Stansfield, with her postmodern disco soul and Euro style, was the first white female from England to top the R&B charts; tune was also a #1 UK crossover.

ALL AROUND THE WORLD

Artist: Titus Turner
Written by: Titus Turner
Label: Wing
Year: 1955
Cover by Little Willie John was his first Top 10 hit (King, '55). Cover by Little Milton was called "Grits Ain't Groceries" (Checker, '69).

ALL BY MYSELF

Artist: Eric Carmen
Written by: Eric Carmen
From the album: *Eric Carmen*
Label: Arista
Produced by: Jimmy Ienner
Year: 1976
First solo effort from the former Raspberry establishes his overly sensitive solo persona.

ALL COME TRUE

Artist: World Party
Written by: Karl Wallinger
From the album: *Private Revolution*
Label: Chrysalis
Produced by: Karl Wallinger
Year: 1986
Ex-Waterboy Wallinger's debut hit with his own band echoes the Stones.

ALL CRIED OUT

Artist: Lisa Lisa and Cult Jam
Written by: Full Force
From the album: *Lisa Lisa and Cult Jam with Full Force*
Label: Columbia
Produced by: Full Force
Year: 1985
Completing the trip from the street to the stage with a #1 R&B/#1 crossover.

ALL DAY AND ALL OF THE NIGHT

Artist: The Kinks
Written by: Ray Davies
From the album: *Kinks Size*
Label: Reprise
Produced by: Shel Talmy
Year: 1964
The British invasion, Music Hall division. Feisty, rollicking, and slightly risqué for its day.

ALL FOR LOVE

Artist: Bryan Adams, Rod Stewart, and Sting
Written by: Bryan Adams, Robert John "Mutt" Lange and Michael Kamen
From the album: *Three Musketeers Soundtrack*
Produced by: Mutt Lange
Label: Hollywood
Year: 1993
Adams's big movie ballad times three, with his middle-of-the-road musketeers.

ALL 4 LOVE

Artist: Color Me Badd
Written by: Howard Thompson, Color Me Badd
From the album: *C.M.B.*
Label: Giant
Produced by: Hamza Lee, Royal Bayyan
Year: 1991

ALL GROWN UP

Artist: The Crystals
Written by: Jeff Barry, Ellie Greenwich, Phil Spector

From the album: *Uptown Twist*
Label: Philles
Produced by: Phil Spector
Year: 1964
The girl-group swan song—nowhere to go but middle-class. Suggested seque: "Almost Grown" by Chuck Berry.

ALL HER FAVORITE FRUIT

Artist: Camper Van Beethoven
Written by: David Lowery, Victor Krummenacher, Greg Lisher, Chris Pedersen
From the album: *Key Lime Pie*
Label: Virgin
Produced by: Dennis Herring
Year: 1989
Powered by Lowery's loopy conviction, these moderately happy Campers finish their legendary careers in typically elliptical Bakerstown-on-downs fashion.

ALL I COULD DO WAS CRY

Artist: Etta James
Written by: Gwen Gordy, Berry Gordy Jr., Roquel Davis (Tyran Carlo)
From the album: *At Last*
Label: Argo
Year: 1960
First lady of the blues has her first Top 10 R&B/Top 40 crossover. More money in the bank toward the Gordy's future Detroit startup, Motown.

ALL I EVER NEED IS YOU

Artist: Sonny and Cher
Written by: Jimmy Holiday, Eddie Reeves
From the album: *All I Ever Need Is You*
Label: Kapp
Produced by: Snuff Garrett
Year: 1971
They would be divorced three years later.

ALL I HAVE TO DO IS DREAM

Artist: The Everly Brothers
Written by: Boudleaux Bryant
From the album: *The Everly Brothers Best*
Label: Cadence
Produced by: Archie Bleyer
Year: 1958
In the blissful heyday of their ethereal harmonies, they accomplished the rare triple #1 pop/country/R&B crossover. In fact, on the morning of May 4, 1957, this tune topped all seven of *Billboard*'s then-operating charts, the only time this has ever been done.

ALL I KNOW

Artist: Art Garfunkel
Written by: Jimmy Webb
From the album: *Angel Clare*
Label: Columbia
Produced by: Roy Halee, Art Garfunkel

Year: 1973
Looking to a master craftsman of the romantic ballad for his solo best-seller.

ALL I NEED

Artist: The Temptations
Written by: Eddie Holland, Frank Wilson, R. Dean Taylor
From the album: *With a Lot o Soul*
Label: Gordy
Produced by: Norman Whitfield
Year: 1967
Top 10 R&B/Top 40 crossover.

ALL I NEED IS A MIRACLE

Artist: Mike & the Mechanics
Written by: Mike Rutherford, Christopher Neil
From the album: *Mike & the Mechanics*
Label: Atlantic
Produced by: Christopher Neil
Year: 1985
Mid-tempo rocker from the formerly progressive Mike Rutherford.

ALL I NEED TO KNOW (DON'T KNOW MUCH)

Artist: Bette Midler
Written by: Barry Mann, Cynthia Weil, Tom Snow
From the album: *No Frills*
Label: Atlantic
Produced by: Chuck Plotkin
Year: 1983
Mann regains his mid-'60s songwriting chops on this smouldering ballad. Best-selling cover retitled "Don't Know Much" by Linda Ronstadt and Aaron Neville (Elektra, '88).

ALL I REALLY WANT TO DO

Artist: Bob Dylan
Written by: Bob Dylan
From the album: *Another Side of Bob Dylan*
Label: Columbia
Produced by: Tom Wilson
Year: 1964
Dylan at his most accommodating, during his least-accommodating phase. Lent itself well to more commercially viable versions by the Byrds (Columbia, '65) and Cher (Imperial, '65).

ALL I WANNA DO

Artist: Sheryl Crow
Written by: Sheryl Crow, Bill Bottrell, David Baerwald, Kevin Gilbert, Wyn Cooper
From the album: *Tuesday Night Music Club*
Label: A&M
Produced by: Bill Bottrell
Year: 1994
Picturesque and picaresque multi-Grammy folk/rocker, happily detailing the bleak, sun-sploched antics of a couple of L.A. daytime drinkers.

ALL I WANNA DO IS MAKE LOVE TO YOU

Artist: Heart
Written by: Robert John "Mutt" Lange
From the album: *Brigade*
Label: Capitol
Produced by: Richie Zito
Year: 1990
Launching Mutt Lange's superstar-'90s period. But by then this band knew their soap-opera formula by heart.

ALL I WANT

Artist: Joni Mitchell
Written by: Joni Mitchell
From the album: *Blue*
Produced by: Joni Mitchell
Label: Reprise
Year: 1971
Investigating her maturing hungers.

ALL I WANT

Artist: Toad The Wet Sprocket
Written by: Dean Dinning, Randy Guss, Todd Nichols, Glen Phillips
From the album: *Fear*
Label: Columbia
Produced by: Gavin Mackillop
Year: 1992
Early alt-pop/rock chart breakthrough.

ALL IS LONELINESS

Artist: Big Brother and the Holding Company
Written by: Louis Hardin
From the album: *Big Brother and the Holding Company*
Label: Mainstream
Produced by: Bob Shad
Year: 1968
San Francisco psychedelic blues, courtesy of Port Arthur Texas—Janis Joplin.

ALL MY LOVE

Artist: Led Zeppelin
Written by: John Paul Jones, Robert Plant
From the album: *In through the Out Door*
Label: Swan Song
Produced by: Jimmy Page
Year: 1979
Plant at his most mock-anguished.

ALL MY LOVING

Artist: The Beatles
Written by: John Lennon, Paul McCartney
From the album: *Meet the Beatles*
Label: Capitol
Produced by: George Martin
Year: 1964
One of their smoothest ballads. Featured in their groundbreaking, image-making docu-farce, *A Hard Day's Night*.

ALL NIGHT LONG (ALL NIGHT)

Artist: Lionel Richie
Written by: Lionel B. Richie
From the album: *Can't Slow Down*
Label: Motown
Produced by: Lionel Richie, James Carmichael
Year: 1983
Mild-mannered ska-lite pop crossover was Motown's then-top-selling single of all time. Sung at the 1984 Olympic games in L.A.

ALL OR NOTHING

Artist: Milli Vanilli
Written by: Frank Farian, Dietman Kawohl, Harold Baierl
From the album: *Girl, You Know It's True*
Label: Arista
Produced by: Fred Farian
Year: 1989
At first all, and then nothing, as the members of the group were stripped of their New Artist Grammy for not actually performing on their hit songs.

ALL RIGHT NOW

Artist: Free
Written by: Paul Rodgers, Andy Fraser
From the album: *Fire and Water*
Label: Atlantic
Produced by: John Kelly, Free
Year: 1970
Out of Bad Company, Free's melodic metal reigned briefly as a sophisticated respite to Zeppelin's mainstream frenzy.

ALL SHE WANTS TO DO IS DANCE

Artist: Don Henley
Written by: Danny Kortchmar
From the album: *Building the Perfect Beast*
Label: Geffen
Produced by: Don Henley, Danny Kortchmar, Greg Ladanyi
Year: 1985
Henleyesque vitriol.

ALL SHE WANTS TO DO IS ROCK

Artist: Wynonie Harris
Written by: Teddy McRea, Beatrice Harris
Label: King
Year: 1949
The first #1 R&B hit of the rock and roll era Harris helped create with his version of Roy Brown's "Good Rockin' Tonight."

ALL SHOOK UP

Artist: Elvis Presley
Written by: Otis Blackwell, Elvis Presley
From the album: *Just for You*
Label: RCA
Produced by: Steve Sholes
Year: 1957
One of the King's most essential shivery early rockers, his second of four number one hits of '57, the number one single of the year (for the second year in a row) and tied for his all-time #1.

ALL STAR

Artist: Smash Mouth
Written by: Gregory Camp
From the album: *Astro Lounge*
Label: Interscope
Year: 1999
In a cynical age, a somewhat affirmative anthem, from the Ben Stiller movie *Mystery Men*.

ALL SUMMER LONG

Artist: The Beach Boys
Written by: Brian Wilson
From the album: *All Summer Long*
Label: Capitol
Produced by: Brian Wilson
Year: 1964
Beach music in its original form.

ALL THAT JAZZ

Artist: Echo and the Bunnymen
Written by: Jamie McCullough, Leslie Pattinson, Will Sergeant, Pete De Freitas
From the album: *Crocodiles*
Label: Sire
Produced by: David Balse, Bill Drummond
Year: 1980
Second-wave punk protest with a reggae lilt.

ALL THAT SHE WANTS

Artist: Ace of Base
Written by: Jonas (Joker) Berggren, Ulf (Buddha) Edberg, Jenny Berggren, Marla Berggren
From the album: *The Sign*
Produced by: Joker, Denniz Pop, Buddha
Label: Arista
Year: 1993
Easy-listening ska meets pop, wherein Abba meets Sally from "Sally Go Round the Roses" by the Jaynetts.

ALL THAT YOU DREAM

Artist: Little Feat
Written by: Billy Payne, Paul Barrere
From the album: *Waiting for Columbus*
Label: Warner Brothers
Produced by: Lowell George
Year: 1978
Covered by Linda Ronstadt (Asylum, '78).

ALL THE KING'S HORSES

Artist: The Firm
Written by: Paul Rodgers
From the album: *Mean Business*
Label: Atlantic
Year: 1986

ALL THE MAN I NEED

Artist: Sister Sledge
Written by: Dean Pitchford, Tom Snow
From the album: *The Sisters*
Label: Cotillion
Year: 1978
Another Clive Davis song-casting coup. Whitney Houston's version, called "All the Man That I Need" (Arista, '90) was a #1 R&B/#1 crossover.

ALL THE SMALL THINGS

Artist: Blink 182
Written by: Tom Delong, Mark Hoppus
From the album: *Enema of the State*
Label: MCA
Year: 1999
State of the art of post-punk.

ALL THE WAY FROM MEMPHIS

Artist: Mott the Hoople
Written by: Ian Hunter
From the album: *The Hoople*
Label: Columbia
Produced by: Ian Hunter, Dave Griffin, Pete Watts
Year: 1973
Searing glam-bam metal monster, Top 10 in England; in New York City, the Dolls were preparing their response.

ALL THE YOUNG DUDES

Artist: Mott the Hoople
Written by: David Bowie
From the album: *All the Young Dudes*
Label: Columbia
Produced by: David Bowie
Year: 1972
Mott's only US hit and biggest UK hit is one of glam's glitziest moment, with nods to the Velvet Underground, defining, in the waning days of the hippie, the angry opposition, fomenting in England.

ALL THIS AND MORE

Artist: The Dead Boys
Written by: Jimmy Zero
From the album: *Young and Loud and Snotty*
Produced by: Genya Raven
Label: Sire
Year: 1977
Turning to an urban legend, the former Goldy Zelkowitz, Akron's angry young punks create a new scene and a new dream.

ALL THIS TIME

Artist: Sting
Written by: Gordon Sumner (Sting)
From the album: *The Soul Cages*
Label: A&M
Produced by: Hugh Padgham, Sting
Year: 1991

ALL THIS USELESS BEAUTY

Artist: Elvis Costello
Written by: Elvis Costello
From the album: *All This Useless Beauty*
Label: Warner Brothers
Year: 1996
Still smouldering after all these years.

ALL THOSE YEARS AGO

Artist: George Harrison
Written by: George Harrison
From the album: *Somewhere in England*
Label: Dark Horse
Produced by: George Martin
Year: 1981
In the wake of the John Lennon tragedy, Harrison took a turn at summing things up, with Ringo, Paul, and Linda on the track.

ALL TOGETHER NOW

Artist: The Beatles
Written by: John Lennon, Paul McCartney
From the album: *Yellow Submarine*
Label: Apple
Produced by: George Martin
Year: 1968
The Beatles as a barbershop quartet.

ALL TOMORROW'S PARTIES

Artist: The Velvet Underground
Written by: Lou Reed
From the album: *The Velvet Underground and Nico*
Label: Verve
Produced by: Andy Warhol
Year: 1967
The former Long Island staff songwriter derides the fashionably chic, while in the process becoming fashionably chic himself, thanks in part to Nico's voice, decadence personified and wrapped in velvet.

ALL WOMAN

Artist: Lisa Stansfield
Written by: Lisa Stansfield, Ian Devaney, Andy Morris
From the album: *Real Love*
Label: Arista
Produced by: Ian Devaney
Year: 1991
Defying the odds, Stansfield nabs another #1 R&B/Top 10 crossover.

ALL YOU NEED IS LOVE

Artist: The Beatles
Written by: John Lennon, Paul McCartney
From the album: *Magical Mystery Tour*
Label: Capitol
Produced by: George Martin
Year: 1967
Opening with the strains of the French National Anthem, this best-selling credo of '68 stood in blissful opposition to the many ringing declamations of the counterculture. Featured in the last episode of the cult TV classic *The Prisoner*.

ALLENTOWN

Artist: Billy Joel
Written by: Billy Joel
From the album: *The Nylon Curtain*
Label: Columbia
Produced by: Phil Ramone
Year: 1982
Entering his Woody Guthrie phase. Suggested segues: "Youngstown" by Bruce Springsteen; "My City Was Gone" by the Pretenders.

ALLERGIES

Artist: Paul Simon
Written by: Paul Simon
From the album: *Hearts and Bones*
Label: Warner Brothers
Produced by: Roy Halee, Paul Simon, Russ Titelman
Year: 1983
Symptomatic of his ingrained urban malaise. Neat solo by guitarist Al DiMeola.

ALLEY CAT

Artist: Bent Fabric
Written by: Jack Harlen, Frank Bjorn
From the album: *Alley Cat*
Label: Atco
Year: 1962
Instrumental from wonderful Copenhagen.

ALLEY OOP

Artist: The Hollywood Argyles
Written by: Dallas Frazier
From the album: *Hollywood Argyles*
Label: Lute
Produced by: Gary Paxton, Kim Fowley
Year: 1960
The endearing comic-book dinosaur comes to rock and roll life in a legendary one-shot. Several of the Hollywood Argyles went on to future careers in the music business, including Gary Paxton and Kim Fowley; the competing (and more authentic) Dante and the Evergreens (Madison) as well as the Dyno-Sores (Rendezvous) went nowhere.

ALMOST GROWN

Artist: Chuck Berry
Written by: Chuck Berry
From the album: *Chuck Berry Is on Top*
Label: Chess
Produced by: Leonard Chess, Phil Chess
Year: 1959
Typically cogent, wise, empathetic and uplifting analysis of the eternal adolescent experience: in its subtle way, it was more penetrating than many of the works of Leiber and Stoller, his chief rivals in mining this turf, whose "Yakety Yak" was released a month later.

ALMOST PARADISE (LOVE THEME FROM *FOOTLOOSE*)

Artist: Mike Reno and Ann Wilson
Written by: Dean Pitchford, Eric Carmen
From the album: *Footloose Soundtrack*
Label: Columbia
Year: 1984
Big movie ballad, sung by the lead singers of Loverboy and Heart, respectively.

ALMOST SATURDAY NIGHT

Artist: John Fogerty
Written by: John C. Fogerty
From the album: *John Fogerty*
Label: Asylum
Produced by: John C. Fogerty
Year: 1975
Defying the loneliest night of the week with an appropriately rockabillyesque charmer. Covered by Dave Edmunds (Swan Song, '81).

ALONE

Artist: Heart
Written by: Billy Steinberg, Tom Kelly
From the album: *Bad Animals*
Label: Capitol
Produced by: Ron Nevison
Year: 1987
In capable corporate hands, Heart reach the peak of their well-earned formula.

ALONE AGAIN (NATURALLY)

Artist: Gilbert O'Sullivan
Written by: Raymond O'Sullivan
From the album: *Gilbert O'Sullivan Himself*
Label: MAM
Produced by: Gordon Mills
Year: 1972
Convoluted, most certainly disturbed, seemingly autobiographical tale that invented nerd rock.

ALONE AGAIN OR

Artist: Love
Written by: Arthur Lee
From the album: *Forever Changes*
Label: Elektra
Produced by: Bruce Botnick, Arthur Lee
Year: 1967
His soul's been psychedelicized.

ALONE AT LAST

Artist: Jackie Wilson
Written by: Johnny Lehmann (words and adaptation of music)
Label: Brunswick
Produced by: MDL
Year: 1960
Based on the first Movement of Tchaikovsky's Piano Concerto in B-flat minor.

ALONG CAME JONES

Artist: The Coasters
Written by: Jerry Leiber, Mike Stoller
Label: Atco
Produced by: Jerry Leiber, Mike Stoller
Year: 1959
More of the good-natured novelty formula; not as biting as some others.

ALPHABET STREET

Artist: Prince
Written by: Prince Rogers Nelson
From the album: *Lovesexy*
Label: Paisley Park
Produced by: Prince
Year: 1988

ALREADY GONE

Artist: Eagles
Written by: Bob Strandlund, Jack Tempchin
From the album: *On the Border*
Label: Asylum
Produced by: Bill Szymczyk
Year: 1974
Celebrating the commitment-phobic male.

ALRIGHT

Artist: Janet Jackson
Written by: James Harris III, Terry Lewis, Janet Jackson
From the album: *Rhythm Nation 1814*
Label: A&M
Produced by: Jimmy Jam, Terry Lewis
Year: 1989
Jackson's patented teenybop chick-hop, a genre she helped make the dominant chartbeat of the late-'80/early '90s.

ALWAYS

Artist: Bon Jovi
Written by: Jon Bon Jovi
From the album: *Cross Roads*
Label: Mercury
Produced by: Peter Collins
Year: 1994
Opens with six lyrical clichés in a row.

ALWAYS BE MY BABY

Artist: Mariah Carey
Written by: Mariah Carey, Jermaine Dupri, Manuel Seal
From the album: *Daydream*
Label: Columbia
Produced by: Jermaine Dupri
Year: 1995
The last of her five #1 R&B/#1 crossovers completes the journey from thrush to diva.

ALWAYS ON MY MIND

Artist: Elvis Presley
Written by: Johnny Christopher, Wayne Carson Thompson, Mark James
From the album: *Separate Ways*
Label: RCA
Year: 1970
Stirring ballad of love's forgetfulness, suitable for all manufactured holidays from Valentine's Day through Secretary's Day. Introduced as the B-side of "Separate Ways." A hit on the country charts for Brenda Lee (Decca, '72). #1 pop hit by Willie Nelson (Columbia, '82); #1 UK by the Pet Shop Boys (EMI-Manhattan, '88).

ALWAYS THE SUN

Artist: The Stranglers
Written by: The Stranglers
From the album: *Dreamtime*
Label: Columbia
Year: 1987
Melodic breakthrough of sorts for notorious English punks.

ALWAYS WITH ME, ALWAYS WITH YOU

Artist: Joe Satriani
Written by: Joe Satriani
From the album: *Surfing with the Alien*
Label: Relativity
Produced by: John Cuniberti, Joe Satriani
Year: 1987
The S.F. guitar teacher (Kirk Hammett, Steve Vai) as hero.

AM I EVIL

Artist: Diamond Head
Written by: Sean Harris, Brian Tatler
From the album: *Lightning to the Nations*
Produced by: Sean Harris, Brian Tatler
Label: Earmark
Year: 1982
Monster British metal track favored by Metallica, who covered it (Elektra, '88). They also covered "Helpless."

AMANDA

Artist: Boston
Written by: Tom Scholz
From the album: *Third Stage*
Label: MCA
Produced by: Tom Scholz
Year: 1986
Scholz is still the master of high-tech, corporate arena rock after an extended writer's block. For their only #1, he used his own creation, the Rockman amp.

AMAZING

Artist: Aerosmith
Written by: Steven Tyler, Richard Supa
From the album: *Get a Grip*
Produced by: Bruce Fairbairn
Label: Geffen
Year: 1993
A toned and tuneful, hit-bound, autobiographical career summation.

AMAZING JOURNEY

Artist: The Who
Written by: Pete Townshend
From the album: *Tommy*
Label: Decca
Produced by: Kit Lambert
Year: 1969
Marking the beginning of one of rock's more amazing journeys from rock opera to movie to ballet, to hit album, finally and ultimately, twenty years later, to Broadway itself.

AMBROSE (PART V)

Artist: Linda Laurie
Written by: Linda Gertz (Linda Laurie)
Label: Glory
Year: 1959
Perhaps the oddest novelty record to ever crack the Bottom 40, by the author of the Helen Reddy hit "Leave Me Alone (Ruby Red Dress)," which explains a lot.

AMELIA

Artist: Joni Mitchell
Written by: Joni Mitchell
From the album: *Hejira*
Label: Asylum
Produced by: Joni Mitchell
Year: 1976
Mitchell's most striking metaphor for flight.

AMEN

Artist: The Impressions
Written by: Curtis Mayfield, John W. Pate Sr.
From the album: *Keep on Pushing*
Label: ABC-Paramount
Produced by: Johnny Pate
Year: 1964
With their gospel fervor and flavor intact, the Impressions presoul civil rights anthem.

AMERICA

Artist: Simon and Garfunkel
Written by: Paul Simon
From the album: *Bookends*
Label: Columbia
Produced by: Roy Halee, Paul Simon, Art Garfunkel
Year: 1968
Wistful and cloistered as a Greyhound bus heading East, with Kathy out of cigarettes and Mrs. Wagner pies. Covered in a progressive version by England's the Nice (Mercury, '72).

AMERICAN BEAT

Artist: The Fleshtones
Written by: Peter Zaremba
From the album: *Blast Off*
Label: RIOR

Year: 1979
Underground roots rock.

AMERICAN CITY SUITE

Artist: Cashman and West
Written by: Dennis Minogue (Terry Cashman),
Thomas Picardo (Tommy West)
From the album: *A Song or Two*
Label: Dunhill
Produced by: Terry Cashman, Tommy West
Year: 1972
As opposed to their paean to baseball ("Whitey,
Mickey and the Duke"), this three-part opus casts
a jaundiced eye on its equally declining subject.
Consists of "Sweet City Song," "All around the
Town" and "A Friend Is Dying."

AMERICAN DREAMER

Artist: Laura Nyro
Written by: Laura Nyro
From the album: *Nested*
Label: Columbia
Produced by: Laura Nyro, Roscoe Harring
Year: 1978
Returning from the walking wounded of the '60s,
Nyro reclaims a bit of her past penchant for unre-
pentant urban romanticism.

AMERICAN GIRL

Artist: Tom Petty and the Heartbreakers
Written by: Tom Petty
From the album: *Tom Petty & the Heartbreakers*
Label: Shelter
Produced by: Tom Petty
Year: 1977
Rejuvenating the ghost of folk/rock with a ringing
anthem, this ringer for Roger McGuinn wound up
garnering a cover version of this tune from his
mentor; neither cracked the charts.

AMERICAN LOVERS

Artist: Thomas Jefferson Kaye
Written by: Donald Fagen, Walter Becker
From the album: *First Grade*
Label: ABC/Dunhill
Produced by: Gary Katz
Year: 1974
The great, lost Steely Dan track.

AMERICAN MUSIC

Artist: The Blasters
Written by: Dave Alvin
From the album: *American Music*
Label: Slash
Produced by: Ron Weiser
Year: 1980
Roots rock anthem and cause.

AMERICAN MUSIC

Artist: Violent Femmes
Written by: Gordon Gano

From the album: *Why Do Birds Sing*
Label: Slash
Produced by: Michael Bienhorn
Year: 1991
Perennial staple on Los Angeles rock radio.

AMERICAN PIE

Artist: Don McLean
Written by: Don McLean
From the album: *American Pie*
Label: United Artists
Produced by: Ed Freeman
Year: 1971
Celebrating either rock's death or its continued
resilience, this folk/rock epic effectively defined
and confined McLean's pop career.

AMERICAN TUNE

Artist: Paul Simon
Written by: Paul Simon
From the album: *There Goes Rhymin' Simon*
Label: Columbia
Produced by: Paul Samwell-Smith
Year: 1973
Saying goodbye to the counter-culture of the
'60s—and good riddance.

AMERICAN WOMAN

Artist: The Guess Who
Written by: Randall Bachman, Burton Cummings,
Garry Peterson, Jim Kale
From the album: *American Woman*
Label: RCA
Produced by: Jack Richardson
Year: 1970
This anti-female, anti-American rockin' rant from
Canada went to #1, possibly inspiring the answer
song, "I Am Woman" by Australia's Helen Reddy,
two years later. Covered by Lennie Kravitz in the
'99 movie *Austin Powers*.

AMIE

Artist: Pure Prairie League
Written by: Craig Fuller
From the album: *Bustin' Out*
Label: RCA
Produced by: Robert Alan Ringe
Year: 1975
Folk/rock goes country; country/rock goes pop—
middle-of-the-dirt-road music is born.

AMOS MOSES

Artist: Jerry Reed
Written by: Jerry Reed
From the album: *Georgia Sunshine*
Label: RCA
Produced by: Chet Atkins
Year: 1971
Reed creates an enduring country character and
gains a pop crossover.

AN EVERLASTING LOVE

Artist: Andy Gibb
Written by: Barry Gibb
From the album: *Shadow Dancing*
Label: RSO
Produced by: Karl Richardson, Albhy Galuten,
Barry Gibb
Year: 1978
After leaping into pop rock history with three
straight #1 singles, this middling hit started the
youngest Gibb's inexorable decline toward Broad-
way, bankruptcy, and early death.

AN INNOCENT MAN

Artist: Billy Joel
Written by: Billy Joel
From the album: *An Innocent Man*
Label: Columbia
Produced by: Phil Ramone
Year: 1983
One of the highlights of Billy's album-length trib-
ute to the soul-based rock of the mid-'60s—and his
newfound, if short-lived, requited teenage lust for
the model Christie Brinkley.

AN OLD FASHIONED LOVE SONG

Artist: Three Dog Night
Written by: Paul Williams
From the album: *Harmony*
Label: Dunhill
Produced by: Gabriel Mekler
Year: 1971
In the era of the self-contained group, Three Dog
Night were comparable to Judy Collins and Tom
Rush in their talent for discovering songwriters.
This was their seventh Top 10 hit with an outside
song. In this case, the songwriter was the diminu-
tive popster Paul Williams, who wrote "You and
Me against the World" for Helen Reddy, among
others.

AN OPEN LETTER TO MY TEENAGE SON

Artist: Victor Lundberg
Written by: Robert Thompson
Label: Sun
Year: 1967
At the height of the rebellious '60s, the reaction
sets in.

ANA NG

Artist: They Might Be Giants
Written by: John Flansburgh, John Linnell
From the album: *Lincoln*
Label: Restless
Produced by: Bill Kraus
Year: 1988
From a repertoire that defines the Berklee/
Berkeley/Beserkley school of collegiate eclectic
cross-genre irony, an inspirational modern rock

classic, sped-up, zany, and as inscrutable as the title character.

ANARCHY IN THE UK

Artist: The Sex Pistols
Written by: Steve Jones, Paul Cook, Glen Matlock, John Lydon (Johnny Rotten)
From the album: *Never Mind the Bollocks, Here's the Sex Pistols*
Label: Warner Brothers
Produced by: Chris Thomas, Bill Price
Year: 1976
Launching the good ship punk rock (actually a garbage scow) in London with a Molotov Cocktail instead of champagne. Every angry young band within earshot on two continents was suitably impressed and depressed.

ANCHORAGE

Artist: Michelle Shocked
Written by: Michelle Shocked
From the album: *Short Sharp Shocked*
Label: Mercury
Produced by: Pete Anderson
Year: 1988
Out of Austin, a tribute to the continuing wandering spirit of the musician class.

AND FOOLS SHINE ON

Artist: Brother Cane
Written by: Marti Frederickson and Damon Johnson
From the album: *Seeds*
Produced by: Marti Frederickson
Label: Virgin
Year: 1995
Arena rock in the studio.

AND I LOVE HER

Artist: The Beatles
Written by: John Lennon, Paul McCartney
From the album: *A Hard Day's Night*
Label: Capitol
Produced by: George Martin
Year: 1964
Pure McCartney ballad formula that would age but never get old. Sung in *A Hard Day's Night*.

AND I'M TELLING YOU I'M NOT GOING

Artist: Jennifer Holliday
Written by: Tom Eyen, Henry Krieger
From the album: *Dreamgirls Original Cast LP Album*
Label: Geffen
Produced by: David Foster
Year: 1982
This booming ballad from the Supremesesque musical was a #1 R&B/Top 25 R&B crossover.

AND IT STONED ME

Artist: Van Morrison
Written by: Van Morrison

From the album: *Moondance*
Label: Warner Brothers
Produced by: Van Morrison
Year: 1970
Ethereal and earthy, Morrison describes his emotional weather, exquisitely.

AND SHE WAS

Artist: Talking Heads
Written by: David Byrne, Chris Frantz, Tina Weymouth, Jerry Harrison
From the album: *Little Creatures*
Label: Sire
Produced by: Talking Heads
Year: 1985
Steely Dan for the Video Age; punk rock for intellectuals.

AND THE CRADLE WILL ROCK

Artist: Van Halen
Written by: Eddie Van Halen, Alex Van Halen, Michael Anthony, David Lee Roth
From the album: *Women and Children First*
Label: Warner Brothers
Produced by: Ted Templeman
Year: 1980
Ferocious metal showpiece.

AND WHEN I DIE

Artist: Laura Nyro
Written by: Laura Nyro
From the album: *More Than a New Discovery*
Label: Verve/Forecast
Produced by: Milt Okun
Year: 1967
Prime exponent of Nyro's Broadway soul with a Bronx cheer, covered by Okun's other proteges, Peter, Paul and Mary (Warner Brothers, '66), and turned into a hit by Blood, Sweat & Tears (Columbia, '69).

AND YOU AND I

Artist: Yes
Written by: Jon Anderson, Chris Squire, Bill Bruford, Steve Howe
From the album: *Close to the Edge*
Label: Atlantic
Produced by: Eddie Offord, Yes
Year: 1972
Early magnum opus.

AND YOUR BIRD CAN SING

Artist: The Beatles
Written by: John Lennon and Paul McCartney
From the album: *Yesterday and Today*
Produced by: George Martin
Label: Capitol
Year: 1965
As compared to the monkey and the dog, the bird metaphor in rock simply does not have legs (even if the bird is an English chick). Suggested segue:

"Rockin' Robin" by Bobby Day, "I'm Like a Bird" by Nelly Furtado.

ANGEL

Artist: Aerosmith
Written by: Steven Tyler, Desmond Child
From the album: *Permanent Vacation*
Produced by: Bruce Fairbairn
Label: Geffen
Year: 1987
The biggest hit from their comeback album was this showcase ballad for Steven Tyler's quivering emotions.

ANGEL

Artist: Aretha Franklin
Written by: Carolyn Franklin, Sonny Saunders
From the album: *Hey Now Hey (The Other Side of the Sky)*
Label: Atlantic
Produced by: Quincy Jones, Aretha Franklin
Year: 1973
#1 R&B/Top 20 crossover. Moving on from Jerry Wexler and Arif Mardin to another studio genius.

ANGEL

Artist: Madonna
Written by: Steve Bray, Madonna Ciccone
From the album: *Like a Virgin*
Label: Warner Brothers
Produced by: Nile Rodgers
Year: 1984
Her sixth of eleven Top 10 singles in a row, demonstrating her undeniable grip on the hot button of an adolescent subculture.

ANGEL

Artist: Sarah McLachlan
Written by: Sarah McLachlan
From the album: *Surfacing*
Label: Arista
Produced by: Pierre Marchand
Year: 1997
At her funereal best.

ANGEL BABY

Artist: Rosie and the Originals
Written by: Rose Hamlin
Label: Highland
Year: 1960
Heavenly echoes of early girl group innocence, after which Rosie Hamlin was lured into a solo career, from which she never emerged.

ANGEL EYES

Artist: The Jeff Healey Band
Written by: John Hiatt, Fred Koller
From the album: *See the Light*
Label: Arista
Produced by: Greg Ladanyi
Year: 1989

Blues rocking ballad hit; an anomaly in the catalogue of its mondo quirky writers as well as the Canadian, heavy-blues, bar band performing it.

ANGEL FROM MONTGOMERY

Artist: John Prine
Written by: John Prine
From the album: *John Prine*
Label: Atlantic
Produced by: Arif Mardin
Year: 1971
Powerful folk/rock portrait of middle-American emptiness. Covered by Bonnie Raitt (Warner Brothers, '74). Sung, for some unknown reason, by Meg Ryan in the movie *Courage under Fire* ('96).

ANGEL OF DEATH

Artist: Slayer
Written by: Jeff Hanneman
From the album: *Reign in Blood*
Label: Def Jam/Geffen
Produced by: Rick Rubin
Year: 1986
A staple of the death metal repertoire, the soundtrack of the subterranean mall. Sampled by Public Enemy in "She Watches Channel O" (Def Jam, '88).

ANGEL OF HARLEM

Artist: U2
Written by: Paul Hewson (Bono), Dave Evans (Edge), Adam Clayton, Larry Mullen
From the album: *Rattle and Hum*
Label: Island
Produced by: Jimmy Iovine
Year: 1988
Dedicated to Billie Holiday.

ANGEL OF MINE

Artist: Monica
Written by: Ron Lawrence, Travon Potts
From the album: *The Boy Is Mine*
Label: Arista
Produced by: Rodney Jerkins
Year: 1998
#2 R&B/#1 crossover.

ANGEL OF THE MORNING

Artist: Merrilee Rush
Written by: Chip Taylor
From the album: *Angel of the Morning*
Label: Bell
Produced by: Chips Moman, Tommy Cogbill
Year: 1967
In the late '60s free-love mode, the one-night stand from the female point of view, written, however, by the same guy who wrote "Wild Thing" for the Troggs. Covered by Juice Newton (Capitol, '81), whose version was a big hit in South America, leading to its later appearance on a car radio in the Oliver Stone movie *Salvador*. In 1995, Chrissie

Hynde covered it in her acting debut on the TV show *Friends*. She was no Leather Tuscadero (AKA Suzy Quatro).

ANGELES

Artist: Elliot Smith
Written by: Elliot Smith
From the album: *Either/Or*
Label: Kill Rock Stars
Year: 1997
A lover's leaving prompts this introspective transcontinental lament, sung by Smith on the *Good Will Hunting* soundtrack.

ANGELIA

Artist: Richard Marx
Written by: Richard Marx
From the album: *Repeat Offender*
Label: EMI
Produced by: David Cole, Richard Marx
Year: 1989
His seventh straight Top 5 single.

ANGELS LISTENED IN, THE

Artist: The Crests
Written by: Billy Dawn Smith, Sid Faust
From the album: *The Angels Listened In*
Label: Coed
Year: 1959
Essential blue-eyed doo-wop, otherwise known as Italian soul.

ANGELS OF THE SILENCES

Artist: Counting Crows
Written by: Adam Duritz, Charles Gillingham, Counting Crows
From the album: *Recovering the Satellites*
Label: DGC
Produced by: Gil Norton
Year: 1996
Modern rock dramatics.

(ANGELS WANNA WEAR MY) RED SHOES, THE

Artist: Elvis Costello
Written by: Declan McManus (Elvis Costello)
From the album: *My Aim Is True*
Label: Columbia
Produced by: Nick Lowe
Year: 1977
Nerd rock disguised as pub rock from his earliest sessions with backup band Clover.

ANGI

Artist: Davey Graham
Written by: Davey Graham
From the album: *¾ A.D*
Label: Topic
Year: 1962
Acoustic guitar instrumental by a major influence on Jimmy Page. Covered by Bert Jansch (Vanguard, '65), who went on to form Pentangle with

John Renbourn. Covered by Simon and Garfunkel (Columbia, '65).

ANGIE

Artist: The Rolling Stones
Written by: Mick Jagger, Keith Richards
From the album: *Goat's Head Soup*
Label: Rolling Stones
Produced by: Jimmy Miller
Year: 1972
Jagger at his most convincingly heartfelt, lusting after another man's wife.

ANGIE BABY

Artist: Helen Reddy
Written by: Alan O' Day
From the album: *Free and Easy*
Label: Capitol
Produced by: Joe Wissert
Year: 1974
She was no Ruby from "Ruby Red Dress" even though she was quirky enough to hit #1.

ANGRY EYES

Artist: Loggins and Messina
Written by: Jim Messina, Kenny Loggins
From the album: *Loggins and Messina*
Label: Columbia
Produced by: Jim Messina
Year: 1972
Prime folk/rock under-reaction.

ANIMAL

Artist: Pearl Jam
Written by: Dave Abbruzzese, Jeff Ament, Stone Gossard, Mike McCready, Eddie Vedder
From the album: *VS*
Label: Epic
Produced by: Brendan O'Brien, Pearl Jam
Year: 1993
Entering their Pearl Jam against the world phase.

ANNA (GO TO HIM)

Artist: Arthur Alexander
Written by: Buzz Cason, Tony Moon
Label: Dot
Produced by: Noel Ball
Year: 1963
R&B favorite was an early Beatles performing choice. Covered by Marshall Crenshaw, who played John Lennon in *Beatlemania*.

ANNETTE'S GOT THE HITS

Artist: Red Cross
Written by: Steve McDonald, Jeff McDonald
From the album: *Red Cross*
Label: Posh Boy
Produced by: Red Cross
Year: 1980
Low-fi, underground punk staple of L.A. radio.

ANNIE HAD A BABY

Artist: The Midnighters
Written by: Henry Glover, Syd Nathan (Lois Mann)
From the album: *The Midnighters*
Label: Federal
Produced by: Henry Glover
Year: 1954
Classic R&B sequel to the notorious "Work with Me, Annie," reached #1 R&B four months after its conception.

ANNIE, HE'S NOT YOUR DADDY

Artist: Kid Creole and the Coconuts
Written by: August Darnell
From the album: *Wise Guy*
Label: Sire/Ze
Produced by: August Darnell
Year: 1982
A poignant, disco-era, lost classic that hit it big in England.

ANNIE'S AUNT FANNY

Artist: The Midnighters
Written by: Hank Ballard
From the album: *The Midnighters*
Label: Federal
Produced by: Henry Glover
Year: 1954
Concluding the Annie trilogy.

ANNIE'S SONG

Artist: John Denver
Written by: H. J. Deutschendorf Jr. (John Denver)
From the album: *Back Home Again*
Label: RCA
Produced by: Milt Okun
Year: 1974
Pristine folk/rock smash dedicated to his then-wife was his second #1.

ANODYNE

Artist: Uncle Tupelo
Written by: Jay Farrar, Jeff Tweedy
From the album: *Anodyne*
Label: Sire
Produced by: Brian Paulson
Year: 1993
Edgy latter-day folk/rock. Wilco was in the wind.

ANOTHER BRICK IN THE WALL

Artist: Pink Floyd
Written by: Roger Waters
From the album: *The Wall*
Label: Columbia
Produced by: Roger Waters, David Gilmour, Bob Ezrin
Year: 1979

The voice of the English preppie. All in all, another major statement, as Pink Floyd reinvents itself for the arena era.

ANOTHER DAY

Artist: Paul McCartney and Wings
Written by: Paul McCartney, Linda McCartney
From the album: *Wings' Greatest*
Label: Apple
Produced by: Paul McCartney, Linda McCartney
Year: 1971
Another era; Paul has his first post-Beatles hit with another band.

ANOTHER DAY IN PARADISE

Artist: Phil Collins
Written by: Phil Collins
From the album: *… But Seriously Folks*
Label: Atlantic
Produced by: Hugh Padgham, Phil Collins
Year: 1989
Taking on homelessness, with a middle-of-the-road backbeat, Collins garners his sixth #1 and a recurring part on *Miami Vice* and MTV as the aging, everyman of rock and roll.

ANOTHER GIRL

Artist: The Beatles
Written by: John Lennon, Paul McCartney
From the album: *Help!*
Label: Capitol
Produced by: George Martin
Year: 1965
From their second movie, this was a neo-psychedelic stiff.

ANOTHER GIRL, ANOTHER PLANET

Artist: The Only Ones
Written by: Peter Perrett
From the album: *Special View*
Label: Epic
Produced by: Vengeance Productions
Year: 1979
Legendary deep cut, known only to other bands and critics.

ANOTHER NAIL IN MY HEART

Artist: Squeeze
Written by: Chris Difford, Glenn Tilbrook
From the album: *Argybargy*
Label: A&M
Produced by: Squeeze and John Wood
Year: 1980
Progressive pop.

ANOTHER NIGHT

Artist: Real McCoy

Written by: Jai Winding, Patricia Peterson, Olaf Jeglitza
From the album: *Real McCoy*
Label: Arista
Produced by: J. Wind, Quickmix, Ojay
Year: 1994
Massive '90s Euro-disco-groove.

ANOTHER ONE BITES THE DUST

Artist: Queen
Written by: John Deacon
From the album: *The Game*
Label: Elektra
Produced by: Queen
Year: 1980
Deacon's favorite dance hall mode results in Queen's second US #1.

ANOTHER PART OF ME

Artist: Michael Jackson
Written by: Michael Jackson
From the album: *Bad*
Label: Epic
Produced by: Quincy Jones
Year: 1987
Which we wouldn't hear about for another few years, and which we would try to avoid hearing about ever since.

ANOTHER SATURDAY NIGHT

Artist: Sam Cooke
Written by: Sam Cooke
From the album: *Ain't That Good News*
Label: RCA Victor
Produced by: Hugo and Luigi
Year: 1964
#1 R&B/ Top 10 crossover typifying his sad-edged crooning style. Covered by Cat Stevens (A&M, '74).

ANTHRAX

Artist: Gang of Four
Written by: Jon King, Andy Gill, Hugo Burnham
From the album: *Entertainment*
Label: Warner Brothers
Produced by: Andy Gill, Jon King, Rob Warr
Year: 1980
Doctrinaire rock tract from England. A line like "Feel like a beetle on its back" spoke to collegiate rockers on both sides of the Atlantic who wanted to break from the influence of the Fab Four.

ANTICIPATION

Artist: Carly Simon
Written by: Carly Simon
From the album: *Anticipation*
Label: Elektra
Produced by: Paul Samwell-Smith
Year: 1971

Stentorian show-folk rock-turned-catsup commercial, defining the stopped-up hopes of an impatient generation.

ANTS MARCHING

Artist: Dave Matthews Band
Written by: Dave Matthews
From the album: *Under the Table and Dreaming*
Label: RCA
Produced by: Steve Lillywhite
Year: 1995
In the wake of the Dead, a jam band comes creeping out of North Carolina.

ANY DAY NOW

Artist: Chuck Jackson
Written by: Bob Hilliard, Burt Bacharach
From the album: *Greatest Hits*
Label: Wand
Produced by: Luther Dixon
Year: 1962
Dramatic R&B ballad was Chuck's biggest hit.

ANY MAJOR DUDE WILL TELL YOU

Artist: Steely Dan
Written by: Donald Fagen, Walter Becker
From the album: *Pretzel Logic*
Label: ABC
Produced by: Gary Katz
Year: 1974
At the peak of their tongue-in-cheek angst.

ANY TIME AT ALL

Artist: The Beatles
Written by: John Lennon, Paul McCartney
From the album: *A Hard Day's Night*
Label: Capitol
Produced by: George Martin
Year: 1964

ANY WAY YOU WANT IT

Artist: Journey
Written by: Steve Perry, Neil Schon
From the album: *Departure*
Label: Columbia
Produced by: Geoff Workman, Kevin Elson
Year: 1980
Defining their arena power pop, defined by Steve Perry's soaring vocal chops.

ANY WAY YOU WANT ME (THAT'S HOW I WILL BE)

Artist: Elvis Presley
Written by: Aaron Schroeder, Cliff Owens
From the album: *Any Way You Want Me*
Label: RCA
Produced by: Steve Sholes
Year: 1956
B-side of "Love Me Tender."

ANY WORLD (THAT I'M WELCOME TO)

Artist: Steely Dan
Written by: Donald Fagen, Walter Becker
From the album: *Katy Lied*
Label: ABC
Produced by: Gary Katz
Year: 1975
Swinging at the edge of doom.

ANYTHING THAT'S PART OF YOU

Artist: Elvis Presley
Written by: Don Robertson
From the album: *Elvis' Golden Records (Vol. III)*
Label: RCA
Produced by: Steve Sholes
Year: 1962
B-side of "Good Luck Charm."

ANYTIME, ANY PLACE

Artist: Janet Jackson
Written by: James Harris III, Terry Lewis, Janet Jackson
From the album: *janet*
Label: Virgin
Produced by: James Harris III, Terry Lewis, Janet Jackson
Year: 1993
#1 R&B/#1 crossover, with "And On and On" on the B-side.

ANYWAY, ANYHOW, ANYWHERE

Artist: The Who
Written by: Pete Townshend, Roger Daltrey
From the album: *The Who Sing My Generation*
Label: Decca
Produced by: Kit Lambert
Year: 1966
Following up "I Can't Explain," this tune was, according to Townshend, an attempt to explain in three words how Charlie Parker plays the sax. It became the theme for the influential UK dance show, *Ready, Steady, Go*. Note the rare Daltrey credit.

APACHE

Artist: The Shadows
Written by: Jerry Lordan
Label: Columbia
Year: 1960
#1 UK instrumental by Cliff Richard's legendary backing band, the Shadows, with guitar hero Hank Marvin, an early influence on the Ventures, and Mark Knopfler of Dire Straits. US hit by Jorgen Ingmann (Atco, '61). Introduced by the UK studio musician Bert Weedon.

APEMAN

Artist: The Kinks
Written by: Ray Davies

From the album: *Lola vs. the Powerman and the Moneygoround (Part I)*
Label: Reprise
Produced by: Ray Davies
Year: 1970
Taking the monkey motif to the next level. Suggested segue: "Monkey Man" by the Rolling Stones, "One Monkey Don't Stop No Show" by Honey Cone, "Monkey Gone to Heaven" by the Pixies.

APPETITE

Artist: Prefab Sprout
Written by: Paddy McAloon
From the album: *Two Wheels Good*
Label: Epic
Produced by: Thomas Dolby
Year: 1985
Jazzy post-punk English cabaret charmer.

APPLE, PEACHES, PUMPKIN PIE (READY OR NOT)

Artist: Jay and the Techniques
Written by: Maurice Irby Jr.
From the album: *Apples, Peaches, Pumpkin Pie*
Label: Smash
Produced by: Jerry Ross
Year: 1967
Feel good one-shot from Long Island.

APRIL FOOLS

Artist: Rufus Wainwright
Written by: Rufus Wainwright
From the album: *Rufus Wainwright*
Label: Dream Works
Produced by: Jon Brion
Year: 1998
The sensitive post-new age male emerges, with the voice of a choirboy.

AQUA BOOGIE (A PSYCHOALPHADISCOBETA BIOAQUADULOOP)

Artist: Parliament
Written by: George Clinton, William "Bootsie" Collins, Bernie Worrell
From the album: *Motor Booty Affair*
Label: Casablanca
Produced by: George Clinton
Year: 1978
#1 R&B/crossover culminates a breakout year. Then it was back to Funkadelic.

AQUALUNG

Artist: Jethro Tull
Written by: Ian Anderson
From the album: *Aqualung*
Label: Reprise
Produced by: Ian Anderson, Terry Ellis
Year: 1971
Ian Anderson's flute-driven thing; the ultimate progressive FM radio twisted standard.

AQUARIUS/THE FLASH FAILURES (LET THE SUN SHINE IN)

Artist: Melba Moore, James Rado and Gerome Radni
From the album: *Hair*
Label: RCA
Produced by: Andy Wiswell
Year: 1968
The original downtown hippie rock musical makes it to Broadway and the charts, big time. Covered by the 5th Dimension (Soul City '69) went to #1.

ARCH GODLINESS AND PURPLEFUL MAGIC

Artist: Essra Mohawk
Written by: Essra Mohawk
From the album: *This Is Sandy's Album*
Produced by: Frank Zappa
Label: Warner Brothers
Year: 1970
Concerning the dilemma, relevant back then, of trying to persuade a potential lover to ingest a certain purple tab as if it were a truth serum. This was the showcase solo from her days as Uncle Meat with Frank Zappa's Mothers of Invention.

ARE FRIENDS ELECTRIC

Artist: Gary Numan and Tubeway Army
Written by: Gary Numan
From the album: *Replicas*
Label: Atco
Produced by: Gary Numan
Year: 1979
Leading the British synth wave with his first #1 UK

ARE YOU A BOY OR ARE YOU A GIRL?

Artist: The Barbarians
Written by: Doug Morris, Elliot Greenberg, Barbara Baer, Robert Schwartz
From the album: *Are You a Boy or Are You a Girl*
Label: Laurie
Produced by: Robert Schwartz
Year: 1965
A classic garage band era, working-class protest that appeared when long hair on men was strictly a middle-class collegiate fad.

ARE YOU EXPERIENCED?

Artist: Jimi Hendrix
Written by: Jimi Hendrix
From the album: *Are You Experienced?*
Label: Reprise
Produced by: Chas Chandler
Year: 1967
Electric, space-age blues: amplified, psychedelicized, and funkdafied. Every guitarist within earshot went back to the woodshed, demoralized.

ARE YOU GONNA GO MY WAY

Artist: Lennie Kravitz
Written by: Lenny Kravitz, Craig Ross
From the album: *Are You Gonna Go My Way*
Label: Virgin
Produced by: Lenny Kravitz
Year: 1993
Biggest rock track for the reformed TV brat, son of Roxy Roker from *The Jeffersons*, and married to Lisa Bonet of *The Cosby Show*.

ARE YOU HAPPY NOW

Artist: Richard Shindell
Written by: Richard Shindell
From the album: *Sparrow's Flight*
Label: Philo
Year: 1992
Witty and biting folk/rock word play about breaking up on Halloween and taking a picture. Soon he'd move on from such brilliant pettiness to write for Joan Baez.

ARE YOU LONESOME TONIGHT

Artist: Elvis Presley
Written by: Roy Turk, Lou Handman
From the album: *Elvis' Golden Records (Vol. III)*
Label: RCA
Produced by: Steve Sholes
Year: 1960
Taking on a pop cult soulmate, Al Jolson, who originated this song in '26, Elvis spent six weeks at #1 with it, primarily by virtue of his finely mumbled, nearly Shakespearean mid-song recitation, one of the greatest in rock history. Peaked at #22 on the country charts, his last appearance there for eight years.

ARE YOU READY

Artist: Pacific Gas and Electric
Written by: Charlie Allen, John Hill
From the album: *Are You Ready*
Label: Columbia
Produced by: John Hill
Year: 1970
One-shot bar band crossover.

ARIEL

Artist: Dean Friedman
Written by: Dean Friedman
From the album: *Dean Friedman*
Label: Lifesong
Produced by: Rob Stevens
Year: 1977
Deft and ineffable portrait of latter-day hippie love affair is one of the cutest songs ever to hit Top 40.

ARMEGEDDON IT

Artist: Def Leppard
Written by: Steve Clark, Joe Elliot, Robert John "Mutt" Lange, Phil Collen, Rick Savage

From the album: *Hysteria*
Label: Mercury
Produced by: Mutt Lange
Year: 1987
Lite-metal explodes with their fourth Top 10 hit from the monster album.

ARMS OF MARY

Artist: Sutherland Brothers and Quiver
Written by: Iain Sutherland
From the album: *Reach for the Sky*
Label: Columbia
Produced by: Howard Albert, Ron Albert
Year: 1976
Winsome coming of age saga was their commercial and evocative peak. Covered by Chilliwack (Mushroom, '78), the Everly Brothers (Mercury, '86).

ARMY OF ME

Artist: Bjork
Written by: Bjork, Graham Massey
From the album: *Post*
Label: Elektra
Produced by: Bjork, Nellee Hooper
Year: 1995
Strikingly weird debut from the Nordic chanteuse.

ARNOLD LAYNE

Artist: Pink Floyd
Written by: Syd Barrett
From the album: *Piper at the Gates of Dawn*
Label: Columbia
Produced by: Norman Smith, Joe Boyd
Year: 1967
Floyd's first single: a tale of a transvestite, told by a basket case.

AROUND AND AROUND

Artist: Chuck Berry
Written by: Chuck Berry
From the album: *Chuck Berry Is on Top*
Label: Chess
Produced by: Leonard Chess, Phil Chess
Year: 1959
Early Jagger and Richards bonding experience. Covered by the Animals (MGM, '64) and the Rolling Stones (London, '64) on the legendary *T.A.M.I Show* music documentary.

AROUND THE CLOCK

Artist: Wynonie Harris
Written by: Wynonie Harris, Jimmy Witherspoon
Label: King
Year: 1945
Bill Haley might have been listening, or at least his writers, Max Freedman and Jimmy DeKnight were.

AROUND THE WAY GIRL

Artist: LL Cool J
Written by: James Todd Smith, Marlon Williams, Rick James

From the album: *Mama Said Knock You Out*
Label: Def Jam
Produced by: Marley Marl
Year: 1990
With samples from funk superstar Rick James, this was label Def Jam's biggest hit.

AS COOL AS I AM

Artist: Dar Williams
Written by: Dar Williams
From the album: *Mortal City*
Label: Razor & Tie
Produced by: Steven Miller
Year: 1996
The new evolution of folk/rock as collegiate sexual empowerment.

AS TEARS GO BY

Artist: Marianne Faithfull
Written by: Mick Jagger, Andrew Loog-Oldham, Keith Richards
From the album: *Marianne Faithfull*
Label: London
Produced by: Andrew Loog-Oldham
Year: 1964
Delicate pop/rock semi-hit would define Faithfull as the ultimate lost waif of the decade. Covered by its authors, the Rolling Stones (London, '64), it became an even bigger hit in '66.

AS THE YEARS GO PASSING BY

Artist: Albert King
Written by: Deadric Malone
Label: Atlantic
Year: 1969
Estbablishing Malone as one of the foremost writers of the genre. Covered by the Animals (MGM, '69), George Thorogood (EMI-America, '82), Gary Moore (Charisma, '90).

ASCENSCION

Artist: Maxwell
Written by: Musze and Itall Shur
From the album: *Maxwell's Urban Hang Suite*
Label: Columbia
Produced by: Stewart Matthewman, Musze, PM
Year: 1996
Leading the ascenscion of modern R&B in its epic battles with hip hop.

ASHES ARE BURNING

Artist: Renaissance
Written by: Michael Dunford, Betty Mary Thatcher
From the album: *Ashes Are Burning*
Label: Sovereign
Produced by: Dick Plant
Year: 1973
Folk/rock breakthrough for the traditional English folk sound.

ASHES TO ASHES

Artist: David Bowie
Written by: David Bowie
From the album: *Scary Monsters*
Label: RCA
Produced by: Tony Visconti, David Bowie
Year: 1980
#1 UK hit is a sequel to "Space Oddity" and came with a trend-setting and very expensive pre-MTV music video.

ASTRAL PLANE

Artist: Modern Lovers
Written by: Jonathan Richman
From the album: *The Modern Lovers*
Label: Beserkley
Produced by: John Cale
Year: 1971
A rock original—childlike and childish, charming and charmed—like its unabashed author, lead singer Jonathan Richman. From sessions produced by ex-Velvet Underground cofounder, John Cale, dating back to the '60s.

ASTRONOMY DOMINE

Artist: Pink Floyd
Written by: Syd Barrett
From the album: *Ummagumma*
Label: Harvest
Produced by: Norman Smith, Pat Peard
Year: 1970
Floyd's (and Barrett's) psychedelic-era swansong, covered by underground metal contenders, Viovod (Mechanic, '89).

AT LAST

Artist: Etta James
Written by: Mack Gordon, Harry Warren
From the album: *At Last*
Label: Argo
Produced by: Leonard Chess
Year: 1961
Etta's signature ballad, a Top 10 R&B/Top 50 crossover, received new life when it was used at a climactic moment in the '89 Dustin Hoffman/Tom Cruise film *Rain Man*. Subsequently immortalized in a Cadillac commercial as the ultimate high-class luxury song. Introduced by Glenn Miller in the '42 film *Orchestra Wives*.

AT MY FRONT DOOR (CRAZY LITTLE MAMA SONG)

Artist: The El Dorados
Written by: John C. Moore, Ewart Abner
From the album: *Crazy Little Mama*
Label: Vee Jay
Year: 1955
Groundbreaking crossover covered by Pat Boone (Dot, '55). Pat would take six more R&B tunes to the Top 10 through the '50s. The El Dorados would have an oldies magazine named after their

only other semi-hit, "Bim Bam Boom." Doesn't quite equate.

AT SEVENTEEN

Artist: Janis Ian
Written by: Janis Ian
From the album: *Between the Lines*
Label: Columbia
Produced by: Brooks Arthur
Year: 1975
Nerd rock standard of the self-absorbed confessional mode is at odds with Ian's earlier career as a protest singer.

AT THE HOP

Artist: Danny and the Juniors
Written by: Artie Singer, John Medora, Dave White
Label: ABC Paramount
Produced by: Arthur Singer
Year: 1957
Dick Clark-inspired anthem of the *American Bandstand* generation, originally entitled "Do the Bop," represented the first acknowledgment of rock and roll's original dance era, extolling the virtues of the Lindy, the Slop, the Bop, the Stroll, the Chicken, the Calypso, and so on. "The Twist" and the next dance era was right around the corner.

AT THIS MOMENT

Artist: Billy and the Beaters
Written by: Billy Vera
From the album: *Billy and the Beaters*
Label: Alfa/Rhino
Produced by: Jeff Baxter
Year: 1981
An archetype R&B-influenced slow dance number that was revived on the TV show *Family Ties* in 1986, and went to #1 five years after it originally flopped as a single. Shown twice in one season as Michael J. Fox's wedding song, this was an early indicator that such high-profile product placement could work wonders on the pop charts.

AT YOUR BEST YOU ARE LOVE

Artist: The Isley Brothers
Written by: Ronald Isley, Rudolph Isley, O'Kelly Isley, Ernest Isley, Marvin Isley, Chris Jasper
From the album: *Harvest for the World*
Label: T-Neck
Produced by: Isley Brothers, Chris Jasper
Year: 1976
Covered by Aaliyah (Blackground, '94).

ATLANTIC CITY

Artist: Bruce Springsteen
Written by: Bruce Springsteen
From the album: *Nebraska*
Label: Columbia
Produced by: Bruce Springsteen
Year: 1982

Moody film-noir study in desolation and redemption was Springsteen's first (B&W) video. Stands as a companion piece to but not in the Burt Lancaster/ Susan Sarandon movie of the same name.

ATLANTIS

Artist: Donovan
Written by: Donovan Leitch
From the album: *Barabajagal*
Label: Epic
Produced by: Mickie Most
Year: 1969
Typical other-worldly folk/rock from the crown prince of the genre.

ATOMIC DOG

Artist: George Clinton
Written by: George Clinton, Garry Shider, David Spradley
From the album: *Computer Games*
Label: Capitol
Produced by: George Clinton
Year: 1983
A nod to the original rock and roll animal by the legendary producer of Parliament/Funkadelic/ Brides of Funkenstein, et al. The contemporary rock and roll animal, Snoop Doggy Dogg sampled this in his debut single, "What's My Name."

ATTICS OF MY LIFE

Artist: Grateful Dead
Written by: Jerry Garcia, Robert Hunter
From the album: *American Beauty*
Label: Warner Brothers
Produced by: Grateful Dead
Year: 1970
Psychedelic bluegrass; moonshine meets Sunshine.

AUDIENCE IS LISTENING, THE

Artist: Steve Vai
Written by: Steve Vai
From the album: *Passion and Warfare*
Label: Relativity
Produced by: Steve Vai
Year: 1990
Virtuoso guitar from the former Frank Zappa and David Lee Roth sideman.

AUTHORITY SONG, THE

Artist: John (Cougar) Mellencamp
Written by: John Cougar Mellencamp, Don Gehman
From the album: *Uh-Huh*
Label: Riva
Produced by: Don Gehman, Little Bastard
Year: 1983
Not quite "I Fought the Law," but carrying a similar message.

AUTOBAHN

Artist: Kraftwerk
Written by: Ralf Hutter, Florean Schneider
From the album: *Autobahn*
Label: Vertigo
Produced by: Ralf Hutter, Florian Schneider
Year: 1975
Introducing the industrialized sound of the new German dancehall.

AUTOMATIC

Artist: Pointer Sisters
Written by: Brock Walsh, Mark Goldenberg
From the album: *Break Out*
Label: Planet
Produced by: Richard Perry
Year: 1984
Dance track of the year, presaging another dance era on the charts for the rest of the decade.

AVALON

Artist: Roxy Music
Written by: Bryan Ferry
From the album: *Avalon*
Label: Warner Brothers
Produced by: Rhett Davies, Roxy Music
Year: 1982
Mood music for the age of decadence.

AVENGING ANNIE

Artist: Andy Pratt
Written by: Andy Pratt
From the album: *Andy Pratt*
Label: Columbia
Produced by: John Nagy
Year: 1973
Smart-mouthed New England folk/rock one-shot, covered by Roger Daltrey (Atlantic, '77).

AWARD TOUR

Artist: A Tribe Called Quest
Written by: Ali Shaheed Muhammed, Phife Dawg, Q-Tip, Bryan Higgins
From the album: *Midnight Marauders*
Label: Jive
Year: 1993
Where hip hop meets bebop and rap meets scat on the corner of Queens Boulevard and Utopia Parkway.

AWAY

Artist: The Feelies
Written by: Glen Mercer
From the album: *Only Life*
Label: A&M
Year: 1988
Critic/cult band classic from New Jersey.

B

BABA O'RILEY

Artist: The Who
Written by: Pete Townshend
From the album: *Who's Next*
Label: Decca
Produced by: The Who

Year: 1971
The seeker and the seekee find each other. This was reputedly an early performance milestone for the young Madonna.

BABALU'S WEDDING DAY

Artist: The Eternals
Written by: Charlie Girona, Bill Martin, Alex Miranda
Label: Hollywood
Year: 1959
More of the Ricky Ricardo influence that pervaded '59.

BABE

Artist: Styx
Written by: Dennis DeYoung
From the album: *Cornerstone*
Label: A&M
Produced by: Styx
Year: 1979
Their biggest hit.

BABE, I'M GONNA LEAVE YOU

Artist: Joan Baez
Written by: Anne Bredon
Label: Vanguard
Year: 1962
Folk classic covered by Quicksilver Messenger Service in the hippie movie *Revolution* (United Artists, '69). Was also one of the earliest influences on the eclectic folk/rock/blues direction pursued by Led Zeppelin, who covered it on their first album (Atlantic, '69).

BABOOSHKA

Artist: Kate Bush
Written by: Kate Bush
From the album: *Never Forever*
Label: EMI-America
Produced by: Kate Bush, Jon Kelly
Year: 1980
Improbable tale redeemed by Kate's ineffable warbling of the title. Suggested segue: "Escape (the Piña Colada Song)" by Rupert Holmes.

B-A-B-Y

Artist: Carla Thomas
Written by: Isaac Hayes, David Porter
From the album: *Carla*
Label: Stax
Produced by: Isaac Hayes, David Porter
Year: 1966
The daughter of R&B great Rufus Thomas gets her biggest R&B hit.

BABY BABY BABY

Artist: TLC
Written by: Kenny Edmunds (Babyface), Antonio Reid (L.A. Reid), Daryl Simmons
From the album: *Oooooooohhh ... on the TLC Tip*

Label: LaFace
Produced by: Dallas Austin
Year: 1992
#1 R&B/Top 10 crossover for the preeminent chick-hop trio.

BABY BABY DON'T CRY

Artist: The Miracles
Written by: Smokey Robinson, Pete Moore, Terry Johnson
From the album: *Time out for Smokey Robinson and the Miracles*
Label: Tamla
Produced by: Smokey Robinson, Al Cleveland, Terry Johnson
Year: 1969
Their last big hit with Smokey, a Top 10 R&B/Top 10 crossover.

BABY BLUE

Artist: The Echoes
Written by: Val Lageux, Sam Guilino
Label: Seg-Way
Produced by: Jack Gold
Year: 1961
Farewell to Italian soul's Golden Era, acknowledged as such, almost, by Bob Dylan in "It's All Over Now Baby Blue."

BABY BOOM CHÉ

Artist: John Trudell
Written by: John Trudell, Jesse Ed Davis
From the album: *Aka Graffiti Man*
Label: Rykodisc
Produced by: Jackson Browne
Year: 1992
Amazing tone poem about the coming of age of the rock and roll generation.

BABY BOY

Artist: Mary Kay Place
Written by: Mary Kay Place
Label: Columbia
Produced by: Brian Ahern
Year: 1976
A #1 country/Bottom 40 R&R crossover from the ultra-hip, late-night, Norman Lear soap opera parody *Mary Hartman, Mary Hartman.*

BABY COME BACK

Artist: Player
Written by: Peter Beckett, John Crowley
From the album: *Player*
Label: RSO
Produced by: Dennis Lambert, Brian Potter
Year: 1978
L.A. studio soul.

BABY DON'T FORGET MY NUMBER

Artist: Milli Vanilli

Written by: Frank Farian, Franz Reuter, Brad Howell, Roger Dalton
From the album: *Girl, You Know It's True*
Label: Arista
Produced by: Fred Farian
Year: 1989
First #1 single for the fabricated duo.

BABY DON'T GET HOOKED ON ME

Artist: Mac Davis
Written by: Mac Davis
From the album: *Baby Don't Get Hooked on Me*
Label: Columbia
Produced by: Rick Hall
Year: 1972
Preening country folk pop. Kenny Rogers would perfect this groove.

BABY DON'T GO

Artist: Sonny and Cher
Written by: Sonny Bono
From the album: *Baby Don't Go*
Label: Reprise
Produced by: Sonny Bono
Year: 1964
Taking the quintessential doo-wop couplet of the '50s—"I love you so/never let you go"—and turning it mournful, cosmic, and photogenic all at once. Was a West Coast hit (recorded as Caesar and Cleo) before it was rereleased after they hit big with "I Got You Babe."

BABY DON'T YOU DO IT

Artist: Marvin Gaye
Written by: Eddie Holland, Lamont Dozier, Brian Holland
From the album: *How Sweet It Is (to Be Loved by You)*
Label: Tamla
Produced by: Brian Holland, Lamont Dozier
Year: 1964
Covered by the Band as "Don't Do It" (Capitol, '72).

BABY FALL DOWN

Artist: T-Bone Burnette
Written by: T-Bone Burnette
From the album: *Proof through the Night*
Label: Warner Brothers
Produced by: Jeff Eyrich
Year: 1983
The future roots-rock producer goes solo with a folk/rock morality tale.

BABY GET LOST

Artist: Dinah Washington
Written by: Billy Moore Jr.
Label: Mercury
Year: 1949
This Billie Holiday tune was the first #1 R&B hit for the Queen of the Harlem Blues.

BABY GOT BACK

Artist: Sir Mix-a-Lot
Written by: Anthony Ray (Sir Mix-a-Lot)
From the album: *Mack Daddy*
Label: Def American
Produced by: Sir Mix-a-Lot
Year: 1992
Seattle rapper and friend of Public Enemy hits #1 with a backhand tribute to the female anatomy. Suggested segue: "Dunkie Butt" by 12 Gauge, "Da Butt" by E.U., "Rump Shaker" by Wreckx N Effect.

BABY HOLD ON

Artist: Eddie Money
Written by: Eddie Mahoney (Eddie Money), Johnny Lyon
From the album: *Eddie Money*
Label: Columbia
Produced by: Bruce Botnick
Year: 1978
A San Francisco/New Jersey collaboration with bar band affinities.

BABY I LOVE YOU

Artist: Aretha Franklin
Written by: Ronnie Shannon
From the album: *Aretha Arrives*
Label: Atlantic
Produced by: Jerry Wexler
Year: 1967
A big year for the Queen of Soul—and soul in general.

BABY I LOVE YOUR WAY

Artist: Peter Frampton
Written by: Peter Frampton
From the album: *Frampton*
Label: A&M
Produced by: Peter Frampton
Year: 1975
Lite metal from the former Humble Pie front man. Covered by Big Mountain in the movie *Reality Bites* (RCA, '94).

BABY I'M A-WANT YOU

Artist: Bread
Written by: David Gates
From the album: *Baby I'm a-Want You*
Label: Elektra
Produced by: David Gates
Year: 1971
A couple of years later, they were toast.

BABY I'M YOURS

Artist: Barbara Lewis
Written by: Van McCoy
From the album: *Baby I'm Yours*
Label: Atlantic
Produced by: Ollie McLaughlin
Year: 1963

Warm and comforting soul in the Dionne Warwick mold.

BABY JANE

Artist: Rod Stewart
Written by: Rod Stewart, Jay Davis
From the album: *Body Wishes*
Label: Warner Brothers
Produced by: Tom Dowd, Rod Stewart
Year: 1983
His sixth and last #1 UK.

BABY LET ME FOLLOW YOU DOWN

Artist: Bob Dylan
Written by: Bob Dylan (Arranged)
From the album: *Bob Dylan*
Label: Columbia
Produced by: John Hammond
Year: 1962
Borrowing freely from folk and blues (and in this case, Westport, Connecticut folk artist Eric Von Schmidt), Dylan would represent a reaction not only against the pop operatics of the post-Army Elvis, but of the collegiate harmonies of the Kingston Trio and their homogenized ilk. Covered by Jackie DeShannon (Liberty, '63).

BABY LET'S PLAY HOUSE

Artist: Arthur Gunter
Written by: Knox Phillips, Jerry Phillips
Label: Excello
Year: 1954
Covered by Elvis, for his first appearance on the country charts (Sun, '54). Suggested segue: "I Wanna Play House with You," by Eddy Arnold (RCA, '51).

BABY LOVE

Artist: The Supremes
Written by: Eddie Holland, Lamont Dozier, Brian Holland
From the album: *Where Did Our Love Go*
Label: Motown
Produced by: Brian Holland, Lamont Dozier
Year: 1964
The biggest American made song of the year.

BABY OH BABY

Artist: The Shells
Written by: Hiram Johnson, Nathaniel Banknight, Walter Coleman
Label: Johnson
Year: 1957
Classic New York doo-wop rescued from obscurity in '61, when it became the group's only hit.

BABY ONE MORE TIME

Artist: Britney Spears
Written by: Max Martin
From the album: *Baby One More Time*

Produced by: Max Martin
Label: Jive
Year: 1998
Heralding the return of the eternal teen good girl/bad girl. The Ronettes and the Shangri-Las, to say nothing of Tiffany and Samantha Fox, weren't impressed. But Madonna was, maybe.

BABY PLAYS AROUND

Artist: Elvis Costello
Written by: Declan McManus (Elvis Costello), Cait O'Riordan
From the album: *Spike*
Label: Warner Brothers
Produced by: T-Bone Burnette, Kevin Killen
Year: 1989
Supper club infidelity.

BABY STOP CRYING

Artist: Bob Dylan
Written by: Bob Dylan
From the album: *Street Legal*
Label: Columbia
Produced by: Don DeVito
Year: 1978
Song to himself.

BABY TALK

Artist: Jan and Dean
Written by: Melvin H. Schwartz
From the album: *Jan and Dean's Golden Hits*
Label: Dore
Produced by: Lou Adler, Herb Albert
Year: 1958
Post doo-wop beach music from California.

BABY, DON'T DO IT

Artist: The 5 Royales
Written by: Lowman Pauling
From the album: *The Rockin' 5 Royales*
Label: Apollo
Year: 1953
First R&B hit for a major force in '50s writing, playing, and producing, Lowman Pauling.

BABY, I LOVE YOU

Artist: The Ronettes
Written by: Jeff Barry, Ellie Greenwich, Phil Spector
From the album: *... introducing the Fabulous Ronettes featuring Ronnie*
Label: Philles
Produced by: Phil Spector
Year: 1963
Girl-group passion at its most abject and symphonic. Covered by the quintessential dispassionate boy-group, the Ramones (Sire, '80), its irony appreciated only in England.

BABY, I NEED YOUR LOVING

Artist: The Four Tops

Written by: Eddie Holland, Lamont Dozier, Brian Holland
From the album: *Four Tops*
Label: Motown
Produced by: Brian Holland, Lamont Dozier
Year: 1964
First chart single for the Detroit veterans.

BABY, I'M FOR REAL

Artist: The Originals
Written by: Marvin Gaye, Anna Gaye
From the album: *Baby, I'm for Real*
Label: Soul
Produced by: Marvin Gaye
Year: 1969
#1 R&B/Top 20 crossover, written by Marvin Gaye and his then-wife, Berry Gordy's sister, Anna.

BABY, IT'S YOU

Artist: The Shirelles
Written by: Burt Bacharach, Mack David, Barney Williams
From the album: *Baby, It's You*
Label: Scepter
Produced by: Burt Bacharach
Year: 1961
Their abortive pop move under the watchful, disapproving eye of Brill Building icon Burt Bacharach. Mack's brother Hal was listening. Covered by the Smith (Dunhill, '69).

BABY, NOW THAT I'VE FOUND YOU

Artist: The Foundations
Written by: John Macleod, Tony Macaulay
From the album: *Baby, Now That I've Found You*
Label: Uni
Produced by: Tony Macaulay
Year: 1967
Multiracial British soul group was the first to crossover to the US R&B charts with this pop breakthrough. Prelude to the British Invasion of the '70s and '80s, featuring the soul and reggae-influenced stylings of the Clash, Elvis Costello, Roxy Music, the Jam, the Style Council, Culture Club, Spandau Ballet, Simply Red, and the Christians.

BABY, SCRATCH MY BACK

Artist: Slim Harpo
Written by: James Moore (Slim Harpo)
From the album: *Baby, Scratch My Back*
Label: Excello
Produced by: Jay Miller
Year: 1966
#1 R&B crossover.

BABY, WHAT A BIG SURPRISE

Artist: Chicago
Written by: Peter Cetera

From the album: *Chicago XI*
Label: Columbia
Produced by: James William Guercio
Year: 1977
The Big Rock Band sound by now contains no surprises.

BABY, WHAT YOU WANT ME TO DO

Artist: Jimmy Reed
Written by: Jimmy Reed
From the album: *New Jimmy Reed Album*
Label: Vee-Jay
Produced by: Calvin Carter, Jimmy Bracken, Ewart Abner
Year: 1960
Reed's simplified country blues soul strikes a chord in a new generation. Covered by the Everly Brothers (Warner Brothers, '60), Etta James (Argo, '64), the Righteous Brothers (Moonglow, '65), Carla Thomas (Stax, '66), Arthur Conley (Atco, '67), Elvis Presley (RCA, '68), the Byrds (Columbia, '69), Ike and Tina Turner (United Artists, '71), Jerry Lee Lewis (Mercury, '73), Johnny and Edgar Winter (Blue Sky, '76).

BABY, WORKOUT

Artist: Jackie Wilson
Written by: Jackie Wilson, Alonzo Tucker
From the album: *Baby, Workout*
Label: Brunswick
Year: 1963
His biggest rocker, a #1 R&B/Top 10 crossover.

BABY, YOU'RE A RICH MAN

Artist: The Beatles
Written by: John Lennon, Paul McCartney
From the album: *Magical Mystery Tour*
Label: Capitol
Produced by: George Martin
Year: 1967
The B-side of "All You Need Is Love," written for their manager, Brian Epstein. Suggested segue: "Taxman" by George Harrison.

BABY (YOU'VE GOT WHAT IT TAKES)

Artist: Brook Benton and Dinah Washington
Written by: Clyde Otis, Murray Stein
From the album: *The Two of Us*
Label: Mercury
Produced by: Clyde Otis
Year: 1960
A classic soul duet that was the #1 R&B song of the year and a Top 10 crossover. Marvin and Tammy were listening.

BABY'S IN BLACK

Artist: The Beatles
Written by: John Lennon, Paul McCartney

From the album: *Beatles '65*
Label: Capitol
Produced by: George Martin
Year: 1965

BABYDOLL

Artist: Hole
Written by: Hole
From the album: *Pretty on the Inside*
Label: Caroline
Produced by: Kim Gordon, Don Fleming
Year: 1991
In the nascent era of the Riot Grrrl, Courtney Love is the prototype.

BABYLON

Artist: David Gray
Written by: David Gray
From the album: *White Ladder*
Produced by: Keith Olson
Label: ATO
Year: 2000
Debut of a soulful Irish singer/songwriter.

BACK & FORTH

Artist: Aaliyah
Written by: Robert Kelly
From the album: *Age Ain't Nothin' but a Number*
Produced by: Robert Kelly
Label: Blackground
Year: 1994
Junior high-school chick-hop.

BACK FOR GOOD

Artist: Take That
Written by: Gary Barlow
From the album: *Back for Good*
Produced by: Chris Porter, Gary Barlow
Label: Arista
Year: 1995
Perhaps the track that made the world safe for the Backstreet Boys and all the reemergent "boy" bands to follow.

BACK HOME AGAIN

Artist: John Denver
Written by: H. J. Deutschendorf Jr. (John Denver)
From the album: *Back Home Again*
Label: RCA
Produced by: Milt Okun
Year: 1974
Returning to a familiar theme for a #1 country/Top 10 crossover.

BACK IN BLACK

Artist: AC/DC
Written by: Angus Young, Malcolm Young, Brian Johnson
From the album: *Back in Black*
Produced by: Mutt Lange
Label: Atlantic

Year: 1980
A tribute to departed lead singer Bon Scott, sung by the highly charged Brian, and backed by Angus and Malcolm, their preppies-on-acid Bermuda shorts and orchestra.

BACK IN MY ARMS AGAIN

Artist: The Supremes
Written by: Eddie Holland, Lamont Dozier, Brian Holland
From the album: *More Hits*
Label: Motown
Produced by: Brian Holland, Lamont Dozier
Year: 1965
Their first #1 R&B/#1 crossover. Only the Beatles had a better year at the top of the charts.

BACK IN THE DAY

Artist: Ahmad
Written by: Ahmad Lewis, Stefan Gordy
From the album: *Ahmad*
Produced by: Ahmad
Label: Giant
Year: 1994
A catalogue of urban nostalgia for the mid-'80s.

BACK IN THE HIGH LIFE AGAIN

Artist: Steve Winwood
Written by: Steve Winwood, Will Jennings
From the album: *Back in the High Life*
Label: Island
Produced by: Steve Winwood, Russ Titleman
Year: 1986
The best beer commercial he never made. Fellow pubstalkers, Eric Clapton and the men of Genesis, took note.

BACK IN THE SADDLE

Artist: Aerosmith
Written by: Steven Tyler, Joe Perry
From the album: *Rocks*
Produced by: Jack Douglas, Aerosmith
Label: Columbia
Year: 1976
One of their more enduring war horses.

BACK IN THE USA

Artist: Chuck Berry
Written by: Chuck Berry
From the album: *Twist*
Label: Chess
Produced by: Leonard Chess, Phil Chess
Year: 1959
Covered by the Beatles as "Back in the USSR" (Apple, '68).

BACK NINE, THE

Artist: Loudon Wainwright III
Written by: Loudon Wainwright III

From the album: *More Love Songs*
Label: Rounder
Year: 1987
A bogey in the game of life.

BACK OF A CAR

Artist: Big Star
Written by: Alex Chilton
From the album: *Radio City*
Label: Ardent
Produced by: John Fry
Year: 1974
Make-out music for Generation X.

BACK OFF BOOGALOO

Artist: Ringo Starr
Written by: Richard Starkey (Ringo Starr)
From the album: *Blasts from Your Past*
Label: Apple
Produced by: George Harrison
Year: 1972
In an effort to keep in step with the current dance crazes, this was about six years late.

BACK ON THE CHAIN GANG

Artist: The Pretenders
Written by: Chrissie Hynde
From the album: *Learning to Crawl*
Label: Sire
Produced by: Chris Thomas
Year: 1984
The Pretenders' biggest hit was an ode to guitarist James Honeyman Scott, who'd recently died of a drug overdose. Featured in the soundtrack album to Martin Scorsese's *The King of Comedy*.

BACK STABBERS

Artist: The O'Jays
Written by: Kenny Gamble, Leon Huff, John Whitehead
From the album: *Back Stabbers*
Label: Philadelphia International
Produced by: Kenny Gamble, Leon Huff
Year: 1972
After a variety of stiffs on Neptune, Bell, and Imperial, the O'Jays come home to a theme, a team, and a locale that suits them, Philadelphia, home of urban paranoia. Featured in the '77 movie *Looking for Mr. Goodbar*.

BACK STREET GIRL

Artist: The Rolling Stones
Written by: Mick Jagger, Keith Richards
From the album: *Flowers*
Label: London
Produced by: Andrew Loog-Oldham
Year: 1967
Reportedly, the only song Jagger liked on the album, which included "Ruby Tuesday," "Lady Jane," "Have You Seen Your Mother Baby (Standing in the Shadows)." Now that's a tough critic.

BACK TO LIFE

Artist: Soul II Soul
Written by: Romeo
From the album: *Keep on Movin'*
Label: Virgin
Produced by: Nellee Hooper, Jazzie B.
Year: 1989
Soulful reggae, big on the dance floors of England, featuring the voice of Caron Wheeler.

BACK UP, TRAIN

Artist: Al Green
Written by: Curtis Rogers, Palmer E. James
From the album: *Al Green*
Label: Hot Line
Produced by: Willie Mitchell
Year: 1967
Introducing the heir apparent to Sam Cooke, Otis Redding, and Smokey Robinson in an early stiff.

BACKFIELD IN MOTION

Artist: Mel and Tim
Written by: Herbert T. McPherson, Melvin Harden
Label: Bamboo
Produced by: Gene Chandler
Year: 1969
Kiddie soul precursor to all the rump songs to follow. Produced by the Duke of Earl.

BACKSTREETS

Artist: Bruce Springsteen
Written by: Bruce Springsteen
From the album: *Born to Run*
Label: Columbia
Produced by: Jon Landau, Mike Appel, Bruce Springsteen
Year: 1975
Expanding his urban mythology state; New Jersey as the national teenage psyche and all-night parking lot personified.

BAD

Artist: Michael Jaskson
Written by: Michael Jaskson
From the album: *Bad*
Label: Epic
Produced by: Quincy Jones
Year: 1987
First of four #1 R&B crossovers from the *Thriller* followup, as Michael enters his self-annointed King of Pop phase.

BAD, BAD LEROY BROWN

Artist: Jim Croce
Written by: Jim Croce
From the album: *Life and Times*
Label: ABC
Produced by: Terry Cashman, Tommy West
Year: 1973
Chicago's mean streets, the unplugged rendition. Covered by Hoboken's Frank Sinatra (Reprise, '74).

BAD BLOOD

Artist: Neil Sedaka
Written by: Phil Cody, Neil Sedaka
From the album: *Overnight Success*
Label: Rocket
Produced by: Robert Appere, Neil Sedaka
Year: 1975
With Elton John on backing vocals, Neil goes to England to get his biggest hit. But most of the bad blood still remained back in Brooklyn.

BAD BOY

Artist: Miami Sound Machine
Written by: Larry Dermer, Joe Galdo, Rafael Vigil
From the album: *Primitive Love*
Label: Epic
Produced by: Emilio Estefan
Year: 1986
The unadulterated beat of South Beach.

BAD BOY

Artist: Clarence Palmer and The Jive Bombers
Written by: Lil Armstrong
Label: Savoy
Produced by: Fred Mendelsohn
Year: 1956
One of the more memorable falsetto performances of rock and roll's golden age. Originated by the blues singer Lil Armstrong.

BAD BOYS

Artist: Inner Circle
Written by: Inner Circle
From the album: *Inner Circle*
Label: Big Beat/Atlantic
Produced by: Ian Lewis
Year: 1993
Reggae-influenced theme from the TV show *Cops*.

BAD CASE OF LOVIN' YOU

Artist: Robert Palmer
Written by: John Martin
From the album: *Secrets*
Label: Island
Produced by: Robert Palmer
Year: 1979
Modern blue-eyed soul from Britain.

BAD GIRL

Artist: The Miracles
Written by: Smokey Robinson, Berry Gordy Jr.
From the album: *Greatest Hits from the Beginning*
Label: Chess/Tamla
Produced by: Berry Gordy Jr.
Year: 1959
Emphasizing his doo-wop roots, this is Smokey's tribute to Barrett Strong's cousin Nolan of Detroit's seminal Diablos.

BAD GIRLS

Artist: Donna Summer
Written by: Donna Summer, Bruce Sudano, Joe Esposito, Edward Hokenson
From the album: *Bad Girls*
Label: Casablanca
Produced by: Giorgio Moroder, Pete Bellotte
Year: 1978
Her first #1 R&B/#1 crossover. Suggested segue: "I'm Livin' in Shame" by the Supremes.

BAD INFLUENCE

Artist: Robert Cray
Written by: Robert Cray, Mike Vannice
From the album: *Bad Influence*
Label: Hightone
Produced by: Bruce Bromberg, Dennis Walker
Year: 1983
The emergence of a new blues guitar hero. Covered by Cray's hero Eric Clapton (Duck, '86).

BAD LOVE

Artist: Eric Clapton
Written by: Eric Clapton, Mick Jones
From the album: *Journeyman*
Label: Duck
Produced by: Mick Jones
Year: 1989
A latter-day guitar highlight.

BAD MEDICINE

Artist: Bon Jovi
Written by: Jon Bon Jovi, Richie Sambora, Desmond Child
From the album: *New Jersey*
Label: Mercury
Produced by: Bruce Fairbairn
Year: 1988
Representing the apex of the second great corporate arena metal heyday.

BAD MOON RISING

Artist: Creedence Clearwater Revival
Written by: John C. Fogerty
From the album: *Green River*
Label: Fantasy
Produced by: John C. Fogerty
Year: 1969
Forecasting the new political climate, without a weatherman, Creedence earns their only #1 single in the UK; in the US it was their second of four #2s.

BAD REPUTATION

Artist: Joan Jett
Written by: Joan Jett, Kenny Laguna, Ritchie Cordell, Martin Kupersmith
From the album: *Joan Jett*
Label: Blackheart/Ariola
Produced by: Ritchie Cordell, Kenny Laguna
Year: 1981
Former teeny punk goddess with the Runaways burnishes her image. In real life, she was a poster girl for clean living, at least until she shaved her head and joined the Broadway revival cast of *The Rocky Horror Picture Show.*

BAD REPUTATION

Artist: Freedy Johnston
Written by: Freedy Johnston
From the album: *Perfect World*
Label: Elektra
Produced by: Butch Vig
Year: 1994
Prime Midwestern folk/rock; the sound of the '90s college campus, catches Vig on a creative furlough between Nirvana and Garbage. He'd use this furlough to produce the folkie Firetown as well.

BAD SNEAKERS

Artist: Steely Dan
Written by: Donald Fagen, Walter Becker
From the album: *Katy Lied*
Label: ABC
Produced by: Gary Katz
Year: 1975
Mentioning piña colada in a song four years before Rupert Holmes, and in a more properly citified context, too.

BAD TIME

Artist: Grand Funk Railroad
Written by: Mark Farner
From the album: *All the Girls in the World Beware*
Label: Capitol
Produced by: Jimmy Ienner
Year: 1975
Their last big hit; Ienner would move on to the ultimate retro soundtrack album, *Dirty Dancing.*

BAD TO ME

Artist: Billy J. Kramer and the Dakotas
Written by: John Lennon, Paul McCartney
From the album: *Bad to Me*
Label: Imperial
Produced by: George Martin
Year: 1963
#1 in the UK, Top 10 in the US a year later for manager Brian Epstein's other band.

BAD TO THE BONE

Artist: George Thorogood
Written by: George Thorogood
From the album: *Bad to the Bone*
Label: EMI-America
Year: 1982
The Delaware retro-rocker establishes a persona: half-cartoon, half-romance, with a stutter.

BAD TRIP

Artist: Camper Van Beethoven
Written by: Camper Van Beethoven
From the album: *Telephone Free Landslide Victory*
Label: Independent Project
Produced by: Camper Van Beethoven
Year: 1985
Just your typical Southern California cowboys on acid, complaining.

BADGE

Artist: Cream
Written by: Eric Clapton, George Harrison
From the album: *Goodbye*
Label: RSO
Produced by: Felix Pappalardi
Year: 1969
Clapton rocks out and moves on.

BADLANDS

Artist: Bruce Springsteen
Written by: Bruce Springsteen
From the album: *Darkness on the Edge of Town*
Label: Columbia
Produced by: Jon Landau, Bruce Springsteen
Year: 1978
New Jersey as the Old West. Bon Jovi would ride that particular horse straight to the glue factory.

BAKER STREET

Artist: Gerry Rafferty
Written by: Gerry Rafferty
From the album: *City to City*
Label: United Artists
Produced by: Hugh Murphey, Gerry Rafferty
Year: 1978
Mellow song of coming home. Best sax part since "Born Too Late" in 1958. Kenny G may have been listening.

BALD HEAD

Artist: Roy Byrd and His Blues Jumpers
Written by: Henry Roeland Byrd
Label: Mercury
Year: 1950
Introducing the classic New Orleans keyboard style of the good Professor Longhair, rapping about a girl with the opposite sense of tonsorial fashion. Everyone from Fats Domino to Dr. John to Sinead O'Connor took note.

BALL AND CHAIN

Artist: Big Brother and the Holding Company
Written by: Willa Mae Thornton
From the album: *Cheap Thrills*
Label: Columbia
Produced by: John Simon
Year: 1968
Janis Joplin's Monterey signature. Introduced by Big Mama Thorton.

BALL OF CONFUSION (THAT'S WHAT THE WORLD IS TODAY)

Artist: The Temptations
Written by: Norman Whitfield, Barrett Strong

From the album: *Greatest Hits (Vol. II)*
Label: Motown
Produced by: Norman Whitfield
Year: 1970
Entering their politically aware phase. Suggested segue: "What's Goin' On" by Marvin Gaye, "War" by Edwin Starr.

BALLAD OF A TEENAGE QUEEN

Artist: Johnny Cash
Written by: Jack Clement
From the album: *Johnny Cash Sings the Songs That Made Him Famous*
Label: Sun
Produced by: Sam Phillips
Year: 1958
Convincingly empathetic country crossover.

BALLAD OF A THIN MAN

Artist: Bob Dylan
Written by: Bob Dylan
From the album: *Highway 61 Revisited*
Label: Columbia
Produced by: Tom Wilson
Year: 1965
Introducing the antibohemian everyman, Mr. Jones, later to reappear in "Mr. Jones" by Counting Crows. When Dylan sang this at the Newport Folk Festival, everyone thought he was talking about them—but he says he was actually talking about Stones' guitarist Brian Jones.

BALLAD OF AN EASY RIDER

Artist: The Byrds
Written by: Roger McGuinn
From the album: *Easy Rider Soundtrack*
Label: Columbia
Produced by: Terry Melcher
Year: 1969
The price of freedom, '60s style, with help from an uncredited Bob Dylan, the waning counter culture, Phil Spector, Peter Fonda, and Jack Nicholson (who came to *Easy Rider* right after making the nearly equally ineffable films *Psych-Out* and *Head*)!

BALLAD OF BONNIE AND CLYDE, THE

Artist: Georgie Fame
Written by: Mitch Murray, Peter Callender
From the album: *The Ballad of Bonnie and Clyde*
Label: Epic
Produced by: Manney Kellem
Year: 1968
Suggested segue: "The Ballad of John and Yoko" by the Beatles.

BALLAD OF IRA HAYES

Artist: Johnny Cash
Written by: Peter LaFarge
From the album: *Bitter Tears*

Label: Columbia
Produced by: Don Law, Frank Jones
Year: 1964
Folk tune about the downfall of a Native-American vet, also hauntingly sung by Native American folk singer Patrick Sky (Vanguard, '65).

BALLAD OF JOHN AND YOKO, THE

Artist: The Beatles
Written by: John Lennon, Paul McCartney
From the album: *Hey Jude*
Label: Apple
Produced by: George Martin
Year: 1969
Establishing their cause as modern folk heroes, even if they never got out of bed.

BALLAD OF LUCY JORDAN

Artist: Marianne Faithfull
Written by: Shel Silverstein
From the album: *Broken English*
Label: Island
Produced by: Mark Miller Mundy
Year: 1980
From the pen of another raspy soulmate. Featured in the '91 movie *Thelma and Louise*.

BALLAD OF PETER PUMPKINHEAD

Artist: XTC
Written by: Andy Partridge
From the album: *Nonsuch*
Label: Geffen
Produced by: Gus Dudgeon
Year: 1992
Breakthrough track for the artsy British band is the story of a hero coming to a bad end, as heroes often do. Covered by Crash Test Dummies in the movie *Dumb and Dumber* (RCA, '94).

BALLAD OF THE GREEN BERETS, THE

Artist: Staff Sergeant Barry Sadler
Written by: Barry Sadler, Robin Moore
From the album: *Ballads of the Green Berets*
Label: RCA
Produced by: Andy Wiswell
Year: 1966
The opposition responds to "Eve of Destruction." Not surprisingly, it was a #1 country/#1 crossover, followed up soon after by "The A Team" and "I Won't Be Home for Christmas."

BALLOON MAN

Artist: Robyn Hitchcock & the Egyptians
Written by: Robyn Hitchcock
From the album: *Globe of Frogs*
Label: A&M
Produced by: the Egyptians
Year: 1988

BALLROOM BLITZ

Artist: The Sweet
Written by: Mike Chapman, Nicky Chinn
From the album: *Desolation Boulevard*
Label: Capitol
Produced by: Mike Chapman, Nicky Chinn
Year: 1975
Frenetic pop metal smash featured in *Wayne's World*.

BALTIMORE

Artist: Five Chinese Brothers
Written by: Tom Meltzer
From the album: *Singer, Songwriter, Beggarman, Thief*
Label: 1-800-Prime
Produced by: Don Peterkofsky
Year: 1992
Bittersweet alt-country tribute to the kind of a town that names its sports teams after doo-wop groups (i.e., the Ravens and the Orioles).

BANANA BOAT SONG, THE

Artist: The Tarriers
Adapted by Erik Darling, Alan Arkin, Bob Carey
Label: Glory
Year: 1957
The folk sound goes calypso; several trips later this same boat would bring us the infinitely more scintillating sound of reggae. Harry Belafonte's version of this Irving Burgee song was subtitled "Day-O" (RCA, '57).

BANANA SPLITS (TRA LA SONG)

Artist: The Dickies
Written by: Mark Barkan, Richie Adams
From the album: *The Incredible Shrinking Dickies*
Label: A&M
Produced by: John Hewlett
Year: 1979
Theme from the TV cartoon gets the suburban punk treatment.

BAND OF GOLD

Artist: Freda Payne
Written by: Ronald Dunbar, Edyth Wayne
From the album: *Band of Gold*
Label: Invictus
Produced by: Greg S. Perry
Year: 1970
From the new label home of Motown graduates, Holland-Dozier-Holland, this was the first song by a solo black female singer to top the pop charts in England.

BAND ON THE RUN

Artist: Paul McCartney and Wings
Written by: Paul McCartney, Linda McCartney
From the album: *Band on the Run*
Label: Apple
Produced by: Paul McCartney
Year: 1974

Suggested segue: "Homeward Bound" by Simon and Garfunkel, "Leaving on a Jet Plane" by Peter, Paul and Mary.

BANG A GONG (GET IT ON)

Artist: T. Rex
Written by: Marc Feld (Marc Bolan)
From the album: *Electric Warrior*
Label: Reprise
Produced by: Tony Visconti
Year: 1972
Lite metal hit from England, where it was taken more seriously. Suggested segue: "So Alive" by Love and Rockets. Mott the Hoople was listening.

BANG AND BLAME

Artist: R.E.M.
Written by: Michael Stipe, Peter Buck, Bill Berry, Mike Mills
From the album: *Monster*
Label: Reprise
Produced by: Scott Litt, R.E.M.
Year: 1994
One of their hardest rockers, tailor made for the Alternative arena they now presided over.

BANG BANG (MY BABY SHOT ME DOWN)

Artist: Cher
Written by: Sonny Bono
From the album: *The Sonny Side of Cher*
Label: Imperial
Produced by: Sonny Bono
Year: 1966
Prophetic role reversal.

BANG THE DRUM ALL DAY

Artist: Todd Rundgren
Written by: Todd Rundgren
From the album: *The Ever Popular Tortured Artist Effect*
Label: Bearsville
Produced by: Todd Rundgren
Year: 1983
Devoted to the fine art of sloth.

BANGLA-DESH

Artist: George Harrison
Written by: George Harrison
From the album: *Concert for Bangala-Desh*
Label: Apple
Produced by: Phil Spector, George Harrison
Year: 1971
Theme song for the first of the all-world, rock-charity-song event.

BANK ROBBER

Artist: The Clash
Written by: John Mellor (Joe Strummer), Mick Jones
From the album: *Black Market Clash*
Label: Epic/Nu Disc

Produced by: Mikey Dread
Year: 1980
The record company said it sounded like "all of David Bowie's records played backwards at once." Eventually became a big hit in England.

BARBARA ANN

Artist: The Regents
Written by: Fred Fassert
From the album: *Barbara Ann*
Label: Gee
Produced by: Morris Diamond, Lou Cicchetti
Year: 1961
From Dion and the Belmonts' Bronx neighborhood, quintessential white doo-wop. Covered on the West coast by the Beach Boys (Capitol, '65).

BARBIE GIRL

Artist: Aqua
Written by: Soren Rasted, Claus Noreen, Rene Dif, Lene Grawford Nystrom
From the album: *Aquarium*
Label: MCA
Year: 1997
Adhering to the era's litigious zeitgeist, once this became a hit, Barbie tried to sue.

BAREFOOTIN'

Artist: Robert Parker
Written by: Robert Parker
From the album: *Barefootin'*
Label: Nola
Produced by: Wherly-Burly Productions
Year: 1966
Only hit for the venerable New Orleans sax man.

BARGAIN

Artist: The Who
Written by: Pete Townshend
From the album: *Who's Next*
Label: Decca
Produced by: The Who
Year: 1971
A ripping rocker, now Madison Avenue bargaining chip.

BARRACUDA

Artist: Heart
Written by: Ann Wilson, Nancy Wilson, Michael Derosier, Roger Fisher
From the album: *Little Queen*
Label: Portrait
Produced by: Mike Flicker
Year: 1977
A feminist rocker with teeth.

BASKET CASE

Artist: Green Day
Written by: Billy Joe Armstrong, Green Day
From the album: *Dookie*
Label: Reprise

Produced by: Rob Cavallo, Green Day
Year: 1994
Making punk rebellion palatable for the suburban subteens of the '90s.

BATDANCE

Artist: Prince
Written by: Prince Rogers Nelson
From the album: *Batman Soundtrack*
Label: Warner Brothers
Produced by: Prince
Year: 1989
Fourth #1 R&B/#1 crossover for the caped crusader.

BATMAN'S THEME

Artist: The Marketts
Written by: Neil Hefti
From the album: *Out of Limits!*
Label: Warner Brothers
Produced by: Dick Glaser
Year: 1966
Surf band's cover of the TV theme is their enduring legacy.

BATTLE HYMN OF LIEUTENANT CALLEY

Artist: C Company featuring Terry Nelson
Written by: Julian Wilson, Jane Smith
Label: Plantation
Year: 1971
A folk antihero emerges from the killing fields of Vietnam and hits the Top 40.

BATTLE OF NEW ORLEANS, THE

Artist: Johnny Horton
Written by: Jimmy Driftwood
Label: Columbia
Produced by: Don Law
Year: 1959
Based on the fiddle tune "Bonaparte's Retreat," with lyrics added by country singer Driftwood, who did his own version (RCA, '59). Horton's version was a rare #1 country/#1 crossover.

BE-BOP-A-LULA

Artist: Gene Vincent
Written by: Gene Vincent, Sheriff Tex Davis
Label: Capitol
Produced by: Ken Nelson
Year: 1956
Introducing another crack rockabilly guitar band, from Norfolk, Virginia, the Blue Caps, featuring Galluping Cliff Gallup on lead, Wee Willie Williams on rhythm, Jumping Jack Neal on bass, and Gene Vincent handling the vocals and songwriting, with the suspicious aid of the deejay Sheriff Tex. Originally the B-side of "Woman Love," this echoing epic went Top 5 country/Top 10 pop.

BE BOP BABY

Artist: Ricky Nelson
Written by: Pearl Lendhurst
From the album: *Ricky*
Label: Imperial
Produced by: Ricky Nelson, Jimmy Haskell, Ozzie Nelson
Year: 1957
Early example of the power of TV to move rock and roll product to the teens of America. Also, there was Barney Kessel's guitar.

BE CAREFUL WITH A FOOL

Artist: B. B. King
Written by: B. B. King, Jules Taub
Label: RPM
Year: 1952
Hit the pop charts in '57, introducing Lucille to the masses. Covered by Johnny Winter (Columbia, '69).

BE MY BABY

Artist: The Ronettes
Written by: Jeff Barry, Ellie Greenwich, Phil Spector
From the album: *… introducing the fabulous Ronettes featuring Ronnie*
Label: Philles
Produced by: Phil Spector
Year: 1963
Spector at his creative and romantic peak, romancing Ronnie. The Ronettes's only Top 10 hit.

BE MY GUEST

Artist: Fats Domino
Written by: Fats Domino, Tommy Boyce, John Marascalco
Label: Imperial
Produced by: Dave Bartholomew
Year: 1959
A New Orleans welcome. Boyce, like Rodgers, would find his Hart for a string of 1960s gems.

BE MY YOKO ONO

Artist: Barenaked Ladies
Written by: Stephen Page, Ed Robertson
From the album: *Gordon*
Label: Sire
Produced by: Scott Dibbie, Barenaked Ladies
Year: 1992
Canadian folk rock mythologizing.

BE NEAR ME

Artist: ABC
Written by: Martin Fry, Mark White
From the album: *how to be a…. Zillionaire*
Produced by: Martin Rushent
Label: Mercury
Year: 1985
Glossy post-disco English soul.

BE THANKFUL FOR WHAT YOU GOT

Artist: William Devaughn
Written by: William DeVaughn
From the album: *Be Thankful for What You Got*
Label: Roxbury
Produced by: Frank Floavanti
Year: 1974
#1 R&B bedroom ballad.

BE TRUE TO YOUR SCHOOL

Artist: The Beach Boys
Written by: Brian Wilson
From the album: *Little Deuce Coupe*
Label: Capitol
Produced by: Brian Wilson
Year: 1963
Branching out from the beach, this single contains a bit of "On Wisconsin," although Brian himself probably never left his bedroom.

BEACH BABY

Artist: Danny Hutton
Written by: John Carter, Gil Shakespeare
Label: HBR
Year: 1966
Eternal summertime anthem, for some reason never rereleased by Hutton's band, Three Dog Night. Cover by First Class (UK, '74) went to #4 in the UK and the US.

BEACON FROM MARS

Artist: Kaleidoscope
Written by: Kaleidoscope
From the album: *A Beacon from Mars*
Label: Epic
Produced by: Stu Eisen, Mike Goldberg
Year: 1968
Mega Middle Eastern rock extravaganza for David Linley's psychedelic unit. Led Zeppelin and Camper Van Beethoven would profit from the experience.

BEAR CAT

Artist: Rufus Thomas
Written by: Sam Phillips
Label: Sun
Produced by: Sam Phillips
Year: 1953
So blatant a copy of Leiber and Stoller's "Hound Dog" that the author was sued to take it off the market. A year later, Sam's protégé Elvis would take on the real thing.

BEASLEY STREET

Artist: John Cooper Clarke
Written by: John Cooper Clark, Martin Hannett, Steve Hopkins
From the album: *Snap, Crackle and Bop*
Label: Epic
Year: 1980
Ranting poetics of a would-be English Dylan.

BEAST OF BURDEN

Artist: The Rolling Stones
Written by: Mick Jagger, Keith Richards
From the album: *Some Girls*
Label: Rolling Stones
Produced by: Glimmer Twins
Year: 1978
In rock mythology, the donkey would never replace the monkey. Covered by Bette Midler (Atlantic, '83), where a suave Mick appears in the very cool video.

BEAT GOES ON, THE

Artist: Sonny and Cher
Written by: Sonny Bono
From the album: *In Case You're in Love*
Label: Atco
Produced by: Sonny Bono
Year: 1967
Sonny's stab at the great American rock and roll saga five years before "American Pie."

BEAT IT

Artist: Michael Jackson
Written by: Michael Jackson
From the album: *Thriller*
Label: Epic
Produced by: Quincy Jones, Michael Jackson
Year: 1983
A #1 R&B/#1 crossover from Jackson's mega-selling mega-opus album and video, launching the MTV-era as a major factor in the marketplace of ideas and dollars. Title taken from the first words in the musical *West Side Story*, which also formed the basis of the video concept. Guitar solo taken by Eddie Van Halen left Michael a wide window of rock scene credibility.

BEAT ON THE BRAT

Artist: The Ramones
Written by: Douglas Colvin, John Cummings, Jeff Hyman, Thomas Erdelyi
From the album: *The Ramones*
Label: Sire
Produced by: Craig Leon
Year: 1976
Stellar antifolk/rock rant begets a new teen revolution of the working class.

BEAT SURRENDER

Artist: The Jam
Written by: Paul Weller
From the album: *Beat Surrender*
Label: Polydor
Year: 1982
Their last record together was their fourth #1 UK hit. Weller moved on to the more soulful Style Council.

BEAT THE RETREAT

Artist: Richard and Linda Thompson
Written by: Richard Thompson
From the album: *Pour Down Like Silver*
Label: Island
Produced by: Richard Thompson, John Wood
Year: 1975
The peerless folk duo is still obsessed by their death motif.

BEAT(EN) GENERATION, THE

Artist: The The
Written by: Matt Johnson
From the album: *Mind Bomb*
Label: Epic
Produced by: Wayne Livesey, Rolli Mossiman, Matt Johnson
Year: 1989
Suggested segues: "The Blank Generation" by Richard Hell & the Voidoids, "My Generation" by the Who, "My Generation, Part 2" by Todd Snider and "I Hate My Generation" by Cracker.

BEATSTREET

Artist: Grandmaster Flash and the Furious Five with Mr. Ness and Cowboy
Written by: Melvin Glover, Reggie Griffin
From the album: *Beatstreet*
Label: Sugarhill
Year: 1984
From the breakdance movie, *Beatstreet*.

BEAUTIFUL DAY

Artist: U2
Written by: Bono and U2
From the album: *All That You Can't Leave Behind*
Label: Island
Year: 2000
The most relevant band on the planet is still anthemic after all these years.

BEAUTIFUL DELILAH

Artist: Chuck Berry
Written by: Chuck Berry
From the album: *Chuck Berry's Golden Decade (Vol. III)*
Label: Chess
Produced by: Leonard Chess, Phil Chess
Year: 1958
A droll metaphor from the former hairdresser.

BEAUTIFUL LOSER

Artist: Bob Seger
Written by: Bob Seger
From the album: *Beautiful Loser*
Label: Capitol
Produced by: Punch Andrews, Bob Seger
Year: 1975
His early-years signature, which he must have thought would be his epitaph. Title of Leonard Cohen's first novel.

BEAUTIFUL MORNING, A

Artist: The Rascals
Written by: Felix Cavaliere, Edward Brigati Jr.
From the album: *Rascals Greatest Hits (Time Peace)*
Label: Atlantic
Produced by: The Rascals
Year: 1968
Blissed-out summation of mid-'60s euphoria, much of it chemically induced.

BEAUTIFUL PEOPLE

Artist: Melanie
Written by: Melanie Safka
From the album: *Melanie*
Label: Buddah
Produced by: Peter Schekeryk
Year: 1969
The Edith Piaf of Brooklyn gets started with a yearning flower plaint. Covered by the New Seekers (Elektra, '71).

BEAUTIFUL PEOPLE, THE

Artist: Marilyn Manson
Written by: Brian (Marilyn Manson) Warner
From the album: *Antichrist Superstar*
Label: Nothing
Produced by: Trent Reznor, Marilyn Manson
Year: 1996
Morose post-mope post-mortem.

BEAUTY AND SADNESS

Artist: The Smithereens
Written by: Pat DiNizio
From the album: *Beauty and Sadness*
Label: D-Tone
Produced by: Don Dixon
Year: 1982
Perfect pop, like perfect love, unrequited.

BEAUTY IS ONLY SKIN DEEP

Artist: The Temptations
Written by: Eddie Holland, Norman Whitfield
From the album: *Temptations' Greatest Hits*
Label: Gordy
Produced by: Norman Whitfield
Year: 1966
Their biggest hit of '66 and most relevant message.

BEAUTY SCHOOL DROPOUT

Artist: Alan Paul, Marya Small and Choir
Written by: Jim Jacobs, Warren Casey
From the album: *Grease Original Cast Album*
Label: MGM
Produced by: Arnold Maxin
Year: 1972
The only song from the '50s parody that really cuts close to the scalp. "There Are Worse Things I Could Do" is a close second.

BECAUSE

Artist: The Beatles
Written by: John Lennon, Paul McCartney
From the album: *Abbey Road*
Label: Apple
Produced by: George Martin
Year: 1969
In the midst of personal and social turmoil, another effortless love ballad.

BECAUSE

Artist: Dave Clark Five
Written by: Dave Clark
From the album: *American Tour*
Label: Epic
Produced by: Dave Clark
Year: 1964
The poppiest of the first Invasion army.

BECAUSE I LOVE YOU (THE POSTMAN SONG)

Artist: Stevie B.
Written by: W. Allen Brooks
From the album: *Love and Emotion*
Label: LMR
Produced by: Stevie B.
Year: 1990
#1 one-shot dance track.

BECAUSE OF YOU

Artist: 98 Degrees
Written by: Anders Bagge, Aentor Birgisson, Christian Karlsson, Patrick Tucker
From the album: *98 Degrees and Rising*
Label: Motown
Year: 1998
Unrepentant harmonizing as only the Swedes can write it.

BECAUSE THE NIGHT

Artist: Patti Smith
Written by: Bruce Springsteen, Patti Smith
From the album: *Easter*
Label: Arista
Produced by: Jimmy Iovine
Year: 1978
A meeting of the East Coast titans of poetic romantic angst produces the epic single Phil Spector might have made with Dylan. Covered by a succeeding generation's bohemian ideals, 10,000 Maniacs (Elektra, '94).

BECAUSE THEY'RE YOUNG

Artist: Duane Eddy
Written by: Aaron Schroeder, Don Costa, Wally Gold
From the album: *$1,000,000.00 Worth of Twang*
Label: Jamie
Produced by: Lee Hazelwood
Year: 1960

His biggest hit, title tune from the Dick Clark/ Tuesday Weld film, *Because They're Young*, in which James Darren sings a vocal version.

BECK'S BOLERO

Artist: Jeff Beck Group
Written by: Jimmy Page
From the album: *Truth*
Produced by: Mickey Most, Jeff Beck
Label: Epic
Year: 1968
Beck joins the British guitar pantheon occupied by Clapton and Page.

BED OF ROSES

Artist: Bon Jovi
Written by: Jon Bon Jovi
From the album: *Keep the Faith*
Label: Mercury
Produced by: Bob Rock
Year: 1992

BEDS ARE BURNING

Artist: Midnight Oil
Written by: Midnight Oil
From the album: *Diesel and Dust*
Label: Columbia
Produced by: Wayne Livesey, Midnight Oil
Year: 1987
Biggest US hit for the politically-oriented Australian rock band.

BEECHWOOD 4-5789

Artist: The Marvelettes
Written by: Marvin Gaye, Berry Gordy Jr., William Stevenson
From the album: *Playboy*
Label: Tamla
Produced by: William Stevenson
Year: 1962
Having taken on the post office in their first hit, the Marvelettes move on to the phone company.

BEEN AROUND THE WORLD

Artist: Puff Daddy
Written by: David Bowie, Lisa Stansfield, Andy Morris, Ian Devaney, Christopher Wallace, Ron Lawrence, Deric Angelettie, Mason Betha, Sean (Puffy) Combs
From the album: *No Way Out*
Label: Bad Boy
Produced by: Sean Combs, Ron Lawrence, Deric Angelettie
Year: 1998
And stolen riffs from every corner of it. This one is from the Lisa Stansfield hit, "All around the World."

BEEN CAUGHT STEALING

Artist: Jane's Addiction
Written by: Jane's Addiction

From the album: *Ritual de lo Habitual*
Label: Warner Brothers
Produced by: Dave Jerden, Perry Farrell
Year: 1991
Breakthrough rock track for the semioutrageous L.A. band.

BEEN ON A TRAIN

Artist: Laura Nyro
Written by: Laura Nyro
From the album: *Christmas and the Beads of Sweat*
Label: Columbia
Produced by: Arif Mardin, Felix Cavaliere
Year: 1971
Laura gets off the Top 40 train for a long and worried journey past confession into torment.

BEEP, BEEP

Artist: The Playmates
Written by: Donald Claps, Carl Cicchetti
From the album: *At Play with the Playmates*
Label: Roulette
Produced by: Hugo and Luigi
Year: 1958
Novelty answer song to "Maybellene" was their biggest hit.

BEESWING

Artist: Richard Thompson
Written by: Richard Thompson
From the album: *Mirror Blue*
Label: Capitol
Produced by: Mitchell Froom
Year: 1993
Post-folk ballad that could have been written in 1693.

BEFORE I LET YOU GO

Artist: BlackStreet
Written by: Teddy Riley, Leon Sylvers, Melvin Riley, Chauncey Hannibal, Dave Hollister
From the album: *This Is Me*
Label: Warner Brothers
Produced by: Teddy Riley
Year: 1994
The Riley Brothers find their supergroup, briefly.

BEFORE THE DELUGE

Artist: Jackson Browne
Written by: Jackson Browne
From the album: *Late for the Sky*
Label: Asylum
Produced by: Jackson Browne, Al Schmidt
Year: 1974
One of the few alternate culture survival anthems that has actually survived, along with its author.

BEFORE YOU ACCUSE ME

Artist: Bo Diddley
Written by: Ellas McDaniel (Bo Diddley)
From the album: *Bo Diddley*
Label: Checker

Produced by: Willie Dixon
Year: 1957
The man who invented paranoia (as well as, if you ask him, rock and roll). Covered by Eric Clapton (Duck, '89).

BEGGAR'S DAY

Artist: Crazy Horse
Written by: Nils Lofgren
From the album: *Crazy Horse*
Label: Reprise
Produced by: Jack Nitzsche, Bruce Botnick
Year: 1971
From the legendary Danny Whitten-era version of Neil Young's once-and-future backing band, a great Lofgren cut, covered by Nils (A&M, '77).

BEGINNINGS

Artist: Chicago
Written by: Robert Lamm
From the album: *Chicago Transit Authority*
Label: Columbia
Produced by: James William Guercio
Year: 1969
The Chicago Big Rock Band sound wafts in off the lake.

BEHIND BLUE EYES

Artist: The Who
Written by: Pete Townshend
From the album: *Who's Next*
Label: Decca
Produced by: The Who
Year: 1971
One of Townshend's most tortured ballads.

BEHIND THE WALL

Artist: Tracy Chapman
Written by: Tracy Chapman
From the album: *Tracy Chapman*
Label: Elektra
Produced by: David Kershenbaum
Year: 1988
Urban folktale of domestic violence.

BEHIND THE WALL OF SLEEP

Artist: The Smithereens
Written by: Pat DiNizio
From the album: *Especially for You*
Label: Enigma
Produced by: Don Dixon
Year: 1986
Brooding post-modern rockabilly from Hoboken.

BEING FOR THE BENEFIT OF MR. KITE

Artist: The Beatles
Written by: John Lennon, Paul McCartney
From the album: *Sgt. Pepper's Lonely Hearts Club Band*

Label: Capitol
Produced by: George Martin
Year: 1967
From the concept album to begin all concept albums, the Beatles betray their skiffle roots.

BEING WITH YOU

Artist: Smokey Robinson
Written by: Smokey Robinson
From the album: *Being with You*
Label: Tamla
Produced by: George Tobin
Year: 1981
Biggest solo hit for the future Motown veep; a smooth sailing, mellow #1 R&B/#2 crossover.

BELA LUGOSI'S DEAD

Artist: Bauhaus
Written by: Bauhaus
Label: Small Wonder (UK)
Produced by: Bauhaus
Year: 1979
Debut single for the progenitors of gothic rock. The Jam, the Cure, New Order, the Jesus and Mary Chain, and the Smiths would mine the turf.

BELIEVE

Artist: Cher
Written by: Brian Higgins, Stuart McLennan, Walter Collins, Steve Torch, Timothy Powell, Matthew Gray, Paul Barry
From the album: *Believe*
Label: Warner Brothers
Produced by: Todd Terry, Junior Vasquez, Brian Rawling
Year: 1999
Cher regains her dance floor credibility with this affirmative statement, although nonbelievers might claim it was the vocoder solo rather than the seven (!) collaborators that put it over the top.

BELIEVE IT OR NOT (THEME FROM *THE GREATEST AMERICAN HERO*)

Artist: Joey Scarbury
Written by: Stephen Geyer, Mike Post
From the album: *The Greatest American Hero*
Label: Elektra
Produced by: Mike Post
Year: 1981
Inescapable TV theme. But shouldn't be mentioned in the same breath as Post's "Theme from *Hill Street Blues*."

BELIEVE ME

Artist: The Royal Teens
Written by: Joe Villa, Tom Austin
Label: Capitol
Year: 1959
The heartbreak of suburban high school romance, in the declining days of Italian soul.

BELIEVE WHAT YOU SAY

Artist: Ricky Nelson
Written by: Johnny Burnette, Dorsey Burnette
From the album: *Ricky Sings Again*
Label: Imperial
Produced by: Ricky Nelson, Jimmy Haskell, Ozzie Nelson
Year: 1958
Rockabillyesque.

BELL BOTTOM BLUES

Artist: Derek and the Dominoes
Written by: Eric Clapton, Derek and the Dominoes
From the album: *Layla*
Label: Atco
Produced by: Tom Dowd
Year: 1970
Easy blues listening.

BELLS, THE

Artist: Lou Reed
Written by: Lou Reed
From the album: *The Bells*
Label: Arista
Produced by: Lou Reed
Year: 1979
One of Reed's personal all-time favorites.

BELLS OF RHYMNEY, THE

Artist: The Byrds
Written by: Idris Davies, Pete Seeger
From the album: *Mr. Tambourine Man*
Label: Columbia
Produced by: Jim Dickson
Year: 1965
Ringing antiwar song is a showcase for McGuinn's 12 string Rickenbacker. Introduced by Pete Seeger.

BEN

Artist: Michael Jackson
Written by: Walter Schart, Don Black
From the album: *Ben*
Label: Motown
Produced by: Freddie Perren, Berry Gordy Jr., Deke Richards, Fonce Mizell
Year: 1972
Before Willy the whale, there was Ben the rat. Michael's first big movie ballad from the movie *Willard*.

BEND ME, SHAPE ME

Artist: American Breed
Written by: Scott English, Laurence Weiss
From the album: *Bend Me, Shape Me*
Produced by: Bill Traut
Label: Atca
Year: 1967
Good-time, Frat rock one-shot. Writer English would be back as the author of "Brandy," which record exec Clive Davis would change to "Mandy"

for Barry Manilow when he launched his new label, named after the Brooklyn high school honor society, Arista. Drummer Andre Fisher went on to Rufus.

BENEATH A FESTERING MOON

Artist: Guided by Voices
Written by: Robert Pollard
From the album: *The Lounge Ax Defense and Relocation Compact Disc*
Label: Touch and Go
Produced by: Guided by Voices
Year: 1996
From the prolific indie legend.

BENNIE AND THE JETS

Artist: Elton John
Written by: Elton John, Bernie Taupin
From the album: *Goodbye Yellow Brick Road*
Label: MCA
Produced by: Gus Dudgeon
Year: 1973
Elton's biggest R&B crossover. Some New York football fans used to refer to it as "Vinnie and the Jets." But no more.

BENT

Artist: Matchbox Twenty
Written by: Rob Thomas
From the album: *Mad Season*
Produced by: Matt Serletic
Label: Atlantic
Year: 2000
The twisted shape of arena rock in the new millennium.

BERLIN

Artist: Lou Reed
Written by: Lou Reed
From the album: *Lou Reed*
Label: RCA
Produced by: Bob Ezrin
Year: 1973
Lou visits the spiritual home of glam rock on one of his more critically reviled efforts.

BERNADETTE

Artist: The Four Tops
Written by: Eddie Holland, Lamont Dozier, Brian Holland
From the album: *Reach Out*
Label: Motown
Produced by: Brian Holland, Lamont Dozier
Year: 1967
Perfecting their anguished groove.

BERNADETTE

Artist: Paul Simon
Written by: Paul Simon, Derek Wolcott
From the album: *Songs from the Capeman*
Label: Warner Brothers

Year: 1997
Introduced by Mark Anthony and Maria Salguero in Simon's Latino Broadway musical, which opened and closed within a few short weeks (and a few short blocks from his Brill Building beginnings).

BESIDE YOU

Artist: Van Morrison
Written by: Van Morrison
From the album: *Astral Weeks*
Produced by: Lewis Merenstein
Label: Warner Brothers
Year: 1968

BEST DISCO IN TOWN, THE

Artist: The Ritchie Family
Written by: Henri Belolo, Jacques Morali, Phil Hurtt, Richard Rome
From the album: *Arabian Nights*
Label: Marlin
Produced by: Jacques Morali, Ritchie Rome
Year: 1976
By the people behind the Village People.

BEST OF MY LOVE

Artist: The Eagles
Written by: Don Henley, Glenn Frey, John David Souther
From the album: *On the Border*
Label: Asylum
Produced by: Bill Szymczyk
Year: 1974
The first of their five #1s.

BEST OF MY LOVE

Artist: The Emotions
Written by: Maurice White, Albert McKay
From the album: *Rejoice*
Label: Columbia
Produced by: Maurice White
Year: 1977
#1 R&B/#1 crossover for the former gospel singers and former Earth, Wind & Fire backup group.

BEST OF TIMES, THE

Artist: Styx
Written by: Dennis DeYoung
From the album: *Paradise Theater*
Label: A&M
Produced by: Styx
Year: 1981
Second-biggest single from their best-selling album.

BEST THING THAT EVER HAPPENED TO ME

Artist: Gladys Knight & the Pips
Written by: Jim Weatherly
From the album: *Imagination*

Label: Buddah
Produced by: Tony Camillo
Year: 1973
Warm and mellow anthem of a soul surivivor.

BEST THINGS IN LIFE ARE FREE, THE

Artist: Janet Jackson with Luther Vandross, Bell Biv Devoe, and Ralph Tresvant,
Written by: James Harris III, Terry Lewis, Ralph Tresvant, Michael Bivins, Ronnie DeVoe
From the album: *Mo' Money Soudtrack*
Label: Perspective/A&M
Produced by: Jimmy Jam, Terry Lewis
Year: 1992
But all the collaborators have to get their piece.

BETCHA BY GOLLY WOW

Artist: The Stylistics
Written by: Thom Bell, Linda Creed
From the album: *The Stylistics*
Label: Avco
Produced by: Thom Bell
Year: 1971
Philly soul's songwriting odd couple on a major roll.

BETH

Artist: Kiss
Written by: Peter Criscuola (Peter Criss), Stanley Penridge, Bob Ezrin
From the album: *Destroyer*
Label: Casablanca
Produced by: Bob Ezrin
Year: 1976
A ballad gains this cartoon metal band their biggest hit.

BETTE DAVIS EYES

Artist: Jackie Deshannon
Written by: Jackie DeShannon, Donna Weiss
From the album: *New Arrangement*
Label: Columbia
Year: 1975
Portrait of a modern she-devil. Cover by Kim Carnes (EMI-America, '81) was the top song of '75—except for "Physical" by Olivia Newton-John (who has Debbie Reynolds' eyes)—winning Grammys for both Song and Record of the Year. While Kim disappeared, Olivia got a chance to act in some major films. But she was no Debbie Reynolds.

BETTER BE GOOD TO ME

Artist: Tina Turner
Written by: Mike Chapman, Nicky Chinn, Holly Knight
From the album: *Private Dancer*
Label: Capitol
Produced by: Carter
Year: 1984
An affirmative statement of life, love, and career after Ike.

BETTER BY YOU, BETTER THAN ME

Artist: Spooky Tooth
Written by: Gary Wright
From the album: *Spooky Two*
Label: A&M
Year: 1969
Prime sludge from the moors of England.

BETTER MAN

Artist: Pearl Jam
Written by: Eddie Vedder, Stone Gossard, Jeff Ament, Mike McCready, Dave Abbruzzese
From the album: *Vitalogy*
Label: Epic
Produced by: Brendan O'Brien, Pearl Jam
Year: 1994
Lives of unquiet desperation, made almost exquisitely unbearable by one of PJ's most poignant melodies.

BETTER THAN I'VE EVER BEEN

Artist: Cindy Bullens
Written by: Cindy Bullens
From the album: *Somewhere Between Heaven and Earth*
Label: Blue Lobster/Artemis
Year: 1999
One-time "female Bruce Springsteen" turns to alt-country to help her recover from the death of her daughter.

BETTER THINGS

Artist: The Kinks
Written by: Ray Davies
From the album: *Give the People What They Want*
Label: Arista
Year: 1981
Ray Davies in a rare conciliatory mood. Covered by folk singer Dar Williams (Razor & Tie, '97). Covered to devastating effect by fountains of Wayne in *The Manchurian Candidate*, '04.

BETTY AND DUPREE

Artist: Chuck Willis
Written by: Chuck Willis
From the album: *King of the Stroll*
Label: Atlantic
Produced by: Ahmet Ertegun, Jerry Wexler
Year: 1958
Tackling the "Frankie & Johnny" myth.

BETWEEN TRAINS

Artist: Robbie Robertson
Written by: Robbie Robertson
From the album: *The King of Comedy Soundtrack*
Label: Warner Brothers
Produced by: Robbie Robertson
Year: 1983
His best post-Band ramblin' song.

BEYOND THE SEA

Artist: Bobby Darin
Written by: Jack Lawrence, Charles Trenet
From the album: *That's All*
Label: Atco
Produced by: Ahmet Ertegun
Year: 1960
Introduced by Charles Trenet in France, '47. Darin makes his pop move, anticipated by "Mack the Knife" in '59. The Copa beckoned.

BICYCLE RACE

Artist: Queen
Written by: Freddie Mercury
From the album: *Jazz*
Label: Elektra
Produced by: Roy Thomas Baker, Queen
Year: 1978
Arena rock for a sport without an arena and, specifically, background music for a topless photo op that many in the press were thrilled to attend.

BIG BAD JOHN

Artist: Jimmy Dean
Written by: Jimmy Dean
From the album: *Big Bad John and Other Fabulous Songs and Tales*
Label: Columbia
Produced by: Don Law
Year: 1961
The tale of the heroic minor who saves his buddies at the cost of his own life was a #1 country/#1 crossover. Suggested segue: "The Springhill Mining Disaster" by Ewan MacColl and Peggy Seeger.

BIG BANG BABY

Artist: Stone Temple Pilots
Written by: Robert DeLeo, Scott Weiland
From the album: *Tiny Music… Songs from the Vatican Gift Shop*
Label: Atlantic
Produced by: Brendan O'Brien
Year: 1996
Epitomizing the faux alternative sound that dominated the radio in the aftermath of grunge.

BIG BEAT, THE

Artist: Fats Domino
Written by: Fats Domino, Dave Bartholomew
Label: Imperial
Produced by: Dave Bartholomew
Year: 1958
Title song from the film, costarring Gogi Grant.

BIG BOSS MAN

Artist: Jimmy Reed
Written by: Al Smith, Luther Dixon
From the album: *New Jimmy Reed Album*
Label: Vee-Jay
Produced by: Calvin Carter
Year: 1961

One of Reed's grittiest antiauthority statements. Covered by John Hammond Jr. (Vanguard, '65), Elvis Presley (RCA, '67), and the Grateful Dead (Warner Brothers, '71).

BIG BOTTOM

Artist: Spinal Tap
Written by: Christopher Guest, Michael McKean, Rob Reiner, Harry Shearer
From the album: *This Is Spinal Tap Soundtrack*
Produced by: Christopher Guest and Michael McKean
Label: Polydor
Year: 1984
After eviscerating heavy metal, the actor/songwriting team would be back to take on folk music in *A Mighty Wind*.

BIG BOY PETE

Artist: Don and Dewey
Written by: Don Harris, Dewey Terry
From the album: *Jungle Hop*
Label: Specialty
Produced by: Harold Battiste
Year: 1959
Great track from the New Orleans soul songwriting duo. Covered by the Olympics (Arvee, '60).

BIG BREAK, THE

Artist: Richard Berry
Written by: Richard Berry, Joe Josea
From the album: *Richard Berry and the Dreamers*
Label: Crown
Year: 1954
Another jailhouse classic from the man who sang "Riot in Cell Block #9" (and wrote "Louie Louie").

BIG EMPTY

Artist: Stone Temple Pilots
Written by: Dean DeLeo, Scott Weiland
From the album: *The Crow Soundtrack*
Label: Interscope
Produced by: Brendan O'Brien
Year: 1994
From the alt-rock soundtrack of the year.

BIG EYED BEANS FROM VENUS

Artist: Captain Beefheart
Written by: Van Don Vliet
From the album: *Clear Spot*
Label: Reprise
Produced by: Ted Templeman
Year: 1972
Rocks out, curiously.

BIG GIRLS DON'T CRY

Artist: The Four Seasons
Written by: Bob Gaudio, Bob Crewe
From the album: *Sherry and 11 Others*
Label: Vee Jay

Produced by: Bob Crewe
Year: 1962
Following "Sherry," a falsetto take on the dynamics of high school dating.

BIG HUNK O'LOVE, A

Artist: Elvis Presley
Written by: Aaron Schroeder, Sid Wyche
From the album: *50,000,000 Elvis Fans Can't Be Wrong: Elvis' Gold Records (Vol. II)*
Label: RCA
Produced by: Steve Sholes, Sid Jaxon, Chet Atkins
Year: 1959
The twelfth and last #1 of the '50s for Elvis, recorded in Nashville in June of the year, while on leave from the army. By the author of the Toppers' notorious "Baby Let Me Bang Your Box."

BIG HURT, THE

Artist: Miss Toni Fischer
Written by: Wayne Shanklin
From the album: *The Big Hurt*
Label: Signet
Year: 1959
This early example of the popular phasing guitar effect gave Miss Fischer her biggest hit.

BIG LOG

Artist: Robert Plant
Written by: Jezz Woodruffe, Robbie Blunt, Robert Plant
From the album: *The Principle of Moments*
Label: Es Paranza
Produced by: Pat Moran
Year: 1983
His biggest solo hit.

BIG LOVE

Artist: Fleetwood Mac
Written by: Lindsay Buckingham
From the album: *Tango in the Night*
Label: Warner Brothers
Produced by: Richard Dashut, Lindsay Buckingham
Year: 1987
Hail and farewell to Mac's last golden era.

BIG MAN

Artist: The Four Preps
Written by: Glen Larson, Bruce Belland
From the album: *The Things We Did Last Summer*
Label: Capitol
Year: 1958
Stradding the surf and folk markets.

BIG MAN IN TOWN

Artist: The Four Seasons
Written by: Bob Crewe
From the album: *Rag Doll*
Label: Philips
Produced by: Bob Crewe
Year: 1964
Sadness behind the high-pitched bravado.

BIG MAN ON MULBERRY STREET

Artist: Billy Joel
Written by: Billy Joel
From the album: *The Bridge*
Label: Columbia
Produced by: Phil Ramone
Year: 1986
Served as the basis for an episode of the TV series *Moonlighting*.

BIG ME

Artist: Foo Fighters
Written by: Dave Grohl
From the album: *Foo Fighters*
Label: RossWell
Produced by: Foo Fighters. Barett Jones
Year: 1995
Picking up the pieces, Dave Grohl moves on from Nirvana.

BIG PIMPIN

Artist: Jay Z
Written by: Butler, Shawn (Jay Z) Carter, B.Freeman, Kyambo Joshua, Tim Mosley
From the album: *Volume 3: Life and Times of S. Carter*
Label: Roc-a-fella
Year: 2000
Thug life still appeals to the suburban set.

BIG POPPA

Artist: Notorious B.I.G.
Written by: Biggie Smalls, the Isley Brothers
From the album: *Ready to Die*
Produced by: Sean Puffy Combs
Label: Bad Boy
Year: 1994
Soon after someone shot Biggie, a huge, incredibly gorgeous, spray-painted mural sprang up in his home-town neighborhood in the Bronx, folk art almost the equal of this rapper's legacy.

BIG SHOT

Artist: Billy Joel
Written by: Billy Joel
From the album: *52nd Street*
Label: Columbia
Produced by: Phil Ramone
Year: 1978
Perhaps his most revealing hit.

BIG SKY, THE

Artist: Kate Bush
Written by: Kate Bush
From the album: *Hounds of Love*
Label: EMI-America
Produced by: Kate Bush
Year: 1985
Lush and spacious as all outdoors.

BIG TIME

Artist: Peter Gabriel
Written by: Peter Gabriel
From the album: *Birdy*
Label: Geffen
Produced by: Peter Gabriel, Daniel Lanois
Year: 1986
First Top 10 hit from the most progressive member of Genesis.

BIG TIME SENSUALITY

Artist: Bjork
Written by: Bjork
From the album: *Debut*
Produced by: Nellee Hooper
Label: Elektra
Year: 1993
As a vocalist, let alone a sex symbol, Bjork is definitely an acquired taste.

BIG TRAIN FROM MEMPHIS

Artist: John Fogerty
Written by: John C. Fogerty
From the album: *Centerfield*
Label: Warner Brothers
Produced by: John C. Fogerty
Year: 1985
Squarely in the rockabilly tradition. Covered by the Class of '55: Carl Perkins, Jerry Lee Lewis, Roy Orbison and Johnny Cash (American, '86).

BIG YELLOW TAXI

Artist: Joni Mitchell
Written by: Joni Mitchell
From the album: *Ladies of the Canyon*
Label: Reprise
Produced by: Joni Mitchell
Year: 1970
Ecological whimsy. B-side is her version of "Woodstock." Suggested Segue: "Nothing but Flowers" by Talking Heads. Covered by Counting Crows (Geffen, '03).

BIGELOW 6–200

Artist: Brenda Lee
Written by: Don Woody, Paul Simmons
Label: Decca
Produced by: Paul Cohen
Year: 1956
Brenda's smokin' rockabilly debut was the B-side of her first single, "Jambalaya."

BIGGEST NIGHT OF HER LIFE, THE

Artist: Harper's Bizarre
Written by: Randy Newman
From the album: *Anything Goes*
Label: Warner Brothers
Produced by: Lenny Waronker
Year: 1967
An early-teen dream epic from Newman's days as a relatively sincere senior-prom songwriting advocate.

BIGGEST PART OF ME, THE

Artist: Ambrosia
Written by: David Pack
From the album: *One Eighty*
Produced by: Freddie Piro, Ambrosia
Label: Warner Brothers
Year: 1980
The lilting sound of studio rock.

BIGMOUTH STRIKES AGAIN

Artist: The Smiths
Written by: Stephen Morrissey, Johnny Marr
From the album: *The Queen Is Dead*
Label: Sire
Produced by: Stephen Morrissey, Johnny Marr
Year: 1986
Often referred to as their version of "Jumping Jack Flash."

BIKINI DRAG

Artist: The Pyramids
Written by: Gary Usher
Label: Best
Produced by: John Hodge
Year: 1964
Legendary surf instrumental, featured in and undoubtedly the best part of the Frankie & Annette film *Bikini Beach*. Subsequently covered by neo-Surf diehards like the Phantom Surfers, the Finks, and the Boardwalkers.

BIKO

Artist: Peter Gabriel
Written by: Peter Gabriel
From the album: *Peter Gabriel*
Label: Mercury
Produced by: Steve Lillywhite
Year: 1980
Tribute to the South African martyr Stephen Biko brings Gabriel into the worldbeat arena. Covered by Joan Baez (Gold Castle, '87).

BILLIE JEAN

Artist: Michael Jackson
Written by: Michael Jackson
From the album: *Thriller*
Label: Epic
Produced by: Quincy Jones, Michael Jackson
Year: 1983
First #1 R&B/#1 crossover from the world's all-time top-selling album, from which Jackson emerges as a mysterious, sylph-like, ambisexual figure, in a great hat.

BILLS, BILLS, BILLS

Artist: Destiny's Child
Written by: Kandi Burruss, LeToya Luckett, Beyonce Knowles, Kevin Briggs, Kelendria Rowland

From the album: *The Writing Is on the Wall*
Produced by: Kevin "Shekspere" Briggs
Label: Columbia
Year: 1999
Following up their debut hit "No No No (Part 2)," with an even bigger one.

BILLY, DON'T BE A HERO

Artist: Bo Donaldson and the Heywoods
Written by: Peter Callendar, Mitch Murray
From the album: *Bo Donaldson and the Heywoods*
Label: ABC
Produced by: Steve Barri
Year: 1974
Antiwar ditty was a trans-Atlantic #1 crossover. UK version was by Paper Lace (Bus Stop, '74).

BIRD DOG

Artist: The Everly Brothers
Written by: Boudleaux Bryant
From the album: *The Everly Brothers Best*
Label: Cadence
Produced by: Archie Bleyer
Year: 1958
Their most overt country lyric still went Top 5 R&B. It would take several years for the R&B charts to be revised to prevent this kind of thing from happening too often.

BIRD IS THE WORD, THE

Artist: The Rivingtons
Written by: Al Frazier, Turner Wilson Jr., Carl White, John Harris
From the album: *Doing the Bird*
Label: Liberty
Produced by: Jack Levy, Adam Ross, Al Frazier
Year: 1963
Frat rock at its frothiest.

BIRD ON THE WIRE

Artist: Judy Collins
Written by: Leonard Cohen
From the album: *Who Knows Where the Time Goes*
Label: Elektra
Produced by: David Anderle
Year: 1968
Leonard Cohen balances rock and poetry, poetry and fiction, melody and monotone, performance and seduction. Judy Collins transcends most of those discrepancies. Recorded by Cohen (Columbia, '69); covered by Joe Cocker (A&M, '70).

BIRDHOUSE IN YOUR SOUL

Artist: They Might Be Giants
Written by: John Flansburgh, John Linnell
From the album: *Flood*
Produced by: Clive Langer, Alan Winstanley
Label: Elektra
Year: 1990
The Brooklyn wordsmiths wax particularly inane on their commercial breakthrough.

BIRDIES

Artist: Pere Ubu
Written by: David Thomas, Allen Ravenstine, Tony Maimone, Scott Krauss, Mayo Thompson
From the album: *Urgh! A Music War Soundtrack*
Label: A&M
Produced by: Ken Hamann, Pere Ubu
Year: 1981
Clever underground song usage. Suggested segue: "If You Wanna Be a Bird" by the Holy Modal Rounders.

BIRDLAND

Artist: Weather Report
Written by: Joe Zawinul
From the album: *Heavy Weather*
Label: Columbia
Produced by: Joe Zawinul, Jaco Pastorius
Year: 1977
Biggest track from the biggest album by the definers and defenders of the short-lived jazz/rock fusion genre. Jaco would have called it punk jazz. Covered by Manhattan Transfer (Atlantic, '79).

BIRDS AND THE BEES, THE

Artist: Jewel Akens
Written by: Herb Newman
From the album: *The Birds & the Bees*
Label: Era
Year: 1960
Post-rockabilly philosophizing from Texas.

BIRMINGHAM BOUNCE

Artist: Hard rock Gunter and the Pebbles
Written by: Sid Gunter
Label: Bama
Year: 1950
Ushering in another early '50s mini-dance craze. Covered by Amos Milburn (Aladdin, '50), Red Foley (Decca, '50).

BIRMINGHAM SUNDAY

Artist: Joan Baez
Written by: Richard Fariña
From the album: *Joan Baez/5*
Label: Vanguard
Year: 1964
About the bombing of a black church in Alabama, written by her sister's husband—Richard Fariña—and based on the English folk tune, "I Loved a Lass."

BIRTH, SCHOOL, WORK, DEATH

Artist: The Godfathers
Written by: The Godfathers
From the album: *Birth, School, Work, Death*
Label: Epic
Produced by: Vic Maile
Year: 1988
Gangsta rock, the working-class white British version of gangsta rap.

BIRTHDAY

Artist: The Beatles
Written by: John Lennon, Paul McCartney
From the album: *The Beatles*
Label: Apple
Produced by: George Martin
Year: 1968

BIRTHDAY

Artist: The Sugarcubes
Written by: Sugarcubes
From the album: *Life's Too Good*
Label: Elektra
Produced by: R. Sholman, P. Burkett
Year: 1988
First single from the exotic neurotics from Iceland, featuring lead singer Bjork, who makes Kate Bush sound like Petula Clark.

BITCH

Artist: Meredith Brooks
Written by: Meredith Brooks, Shelly Peiken
From the album: *Blurring the Edges*
Produced by: Geza
Label: Capitol
Year: 1997
Exploiting a feminist moment on the Top 40, in the shadow of Alanis.

BITCH

Artist: The Rolling Stones
Written by: Mick Jagger, Keith Richards
From the album: *Sticky Fingers*
Label: Rolling Stones
Produced by: Jimmy Miller
Year: 1971
One of their hornier rockers.

BITCH IS BACK, THE

Artist: Elton John
Written by: Elton John, Bernie Taupin
From the album: *Caribou*
Label: MCA
Produced by: Gus Dudgeon
Year: 1974
Provocative wordplay, back then.

BITS AND PIECES

Artist: The Dave Clark Five
Written by: Dave Clark, Mike Smith
From the album: *Coast to Coast*
Label: Epic
Produced by: Dave Clark
Year: 1964

BITTEREST PILL (I EVER HAD TO SWALLOW), THE

Artist: The Jam
Written by: Paul Weller

From the album: *The Bitterest Pill*
Label: Polydor
Year: 1982

BITTERSWEET SYMPHONY

Artist: The Verve
Written by: Richard Ashcroft, Mick Jagger, Keith Richards
From the album: *Urban Hymns*
Label: Virgin
Produced by: John Leckie
Year: 1997
Rough and ragged British garage rock, with a nod (and a royalty check) to the masters, Jagger and Richards. Suggested segue: "The Last Time" by the Rolling Stones.

BIZARRE LOVE TRIANGLE

Artist: New Order
Written by: Bernard Summer, Stephen Morris, Peter Hook, Gillian Gilbert
From the album: *Brotherhood*
Label: Qwest
Produced by: New Order
Year: 1986
Covered by Frente (Mammoth, '94).

BLACK

Artist: Pearl Jam
Written by: Pearl Jam
From the album: *Ten*
Label: Epic
Produced by: Nick Parashar, Pearl Jam
Year: 1991
Beautiful and painful ballad of lost love.

BLACK AND BLUE

Artist: Van Halen
Written by: Eddie Van Halen, Alex Van Halen, Michael Anthony, Sammy Hagar
From the album: *OU812*
Label: Warner Brothers
Produced by: Van Halen, Don Landee
Year: 1988
Rocking harder, enjoying it less.

BLACK AND WHITE

Artist: Three Dog Night
Written by: David Arkin, Earl Robinson
From the album: *Seven Separate Fools*
Label: Dunhill
Produced by: Richard Polodor
Year: 1972
Their third and last #1 was composed in 1955 in response to the Supreme Court's decision banning segregation and introduced in the US by Sammy Davis Jr. Robinson also wrote several other American classics, including "Joe Hill," "Ballad for Americans," and "The House I Live In."

BLACK ANGEL'S DEATH SONG

Artist: The Velvet Underground
Written by: Lou Reed
From the album: *The Velvet Underground and Nico*
Label: Verve
Produced by: Andy Warhol
Year: 1967
Laying waste to Beatlemania, and putting a torch to Dylan's garbage pail, the Velvet Underground's influence would rival that of Led Zeppelin, who did pretty much the same thing to the blues, with a whole other set of power chords.

BLACK CAT

Artist: Janet Jackson
Written by: Janet Jackson
From the album: *Rhythm Nation 1814*
Label: A&M
Produced by: Jimmy Jam, Terry Lewis
Year: 1989
#1 hit from the monster album that gave a nation of young girls its dancing orders via MTV.

BLACK COFFEE IN BED

Artist: Squeeze
Written by: Chris Difford, Glenn Tilbrook
From the album: *Sweets from a Stranger*
Label: A&M
Produced by: Phil McDonald
Year: 1982
Suggested segue: "Brown Sugar" by the Rolling Stones, "Brother Louie" by Stories.

BLACK DENIM TROUSERS AND MOTORCYCLE BOOTS

Artist: The Cheers
Written by: Jerry Leiber, Mike Stoller
Label: Capitol
Produced by: Jerry Leiber, Mike Stoller
Year: 1955
The patented Leiber and Stoller patter, adapted for a white audience fearful of the impending rock and roll onslaught, typified, at the time, by Marlon Brando and his denim-and-leather brethren, as seen in *The Wild Ones*, in which Lee Marvin's rival gang was named the Beetles.

BLACK DIAMOND

Artist: Kiss
Written by: Paul Stanley, Gene Simmons
From the album: *Kiss*
Label: Casablanca
Produced by: Bob Ezrin
Year: 1974
Easily the most influential track from their debut album. Covered by the Replacements (Twin Tone, '84).

BLACK DOG

Artist: Led Zeppelin

Written by: Jimmy Page, Robert Plant, John Paul Jones
From the album: *Led Zeppelin IV (Untitled)*
Label: Atlantic
Produced by: Jimmy Page
Year: 1971
Return of the dog, to a new, jam packed arena, filled with horny guys.

BLACK FRIDAY

Artist: Steely Dan
Written by: Donald Fagen, Walter Becker
From the album: *Katy Lied*
Label: ABC
Produced by: Gary Katz
Year: 1975
Anticipating the coming crash.

BLACK GOLD

Artist: Soul Asylum
Written by: Dave Pirner
From the album: *Grave Dancers Union*
Label: Columbia
Produced by: Michael Beinhorn
Year: 1992
Minneapolis cohorts of Hüsker Dü and the Replacements reclaim their alt-rock credibility.

BLACK HOLE SUN

Artist: Soundgarden
Written by: Chris Cornell
From the album: *Superunknown*
Label: A&M
Produced by: Michael Beinhorn, Soundgarden
Year: 1994
From Seattle, a perfectly gorgeous answer to the Beatles's "Good Day Sunshine." A year later Beatle clones from England would be all over the place.

BLACK IS BLACK

Artist: Los Bravos
Written by: Tony Hayes, Steve Wadey, M. Grainger
From the album: *Black Is Black*
Label: Parrot
Produced by: Ivor Ramonde
Year: 1966
Gene Pitneyesque garage rock one-shot from Italy.

BLACK MAGIC WOMAN

Artist: Fleetwood Mac
Written by: Peter Green
From the album: *English Rose*
Label: Epic
Produced by: Mike Vernon
Year: 1969
Showcasing Peter Green, one of the finest of English blues guitarists. Covered by Santana (Columbia, '71).

BLACK MOUNTAIN SIDE

Artist: Led Zeppelin
Written by: Jimmy Page

From the album: *Led Zeppelin*
Label: Atlantic
Produced by: Jimmy Page
Year: 1969
Adapted from the British folk guitarist Davey Graham's "She Moved through the Fair." Suggested segue: "White Summer," Page's Yardbirds instrumental.

BLACK NIGHT

Artist: Charles Brown
Written by: Jessie Mae Robinson
From the album: *Mood Music*
Label: Aladdin
Year: 1951
Third and final segment of Brown's dark trilogy of the urban blues that began with "Drifting Blues" and continued with "Trouble Blues." Covered by Bobby Bland (Duke, '65).

BLACK OR WHITE

Artist: Michael Jackson
Written by: Michael Jackson, Bill Bottrell
From the album: *Dangerous*
Label: Epic
Produced by: Michael Jackson, Bill Bottrell
Year: 1991
A socially minded message from Michael shortly before he began to vividly become the answer to his own question.

BLACK PEARL

Artist: Sonny Charles and the Checkmates, Ltd.
Written by: Irwin Levine, Toni Wine, Phil Spector
Label: A&M
Produced by: Phil Spector
Year: 1969
The boy genius Spector comes out of retirement to work with some bubblegum masters.

BLACK SABBATH

Artist: Black Sabbath
Written by: Tony Iommi, Geezer Butler, Ozzy Osbourne, Bill Ward
From the album: *Black Sabbath*
Label: Warner Brothers
Produced by: Rodger Rain
Year: 1971
Perennially indomitable sludge personified.

BLACK SLACKS

Artist: Joe Bennett and the Sparkletones
Written by: Joe Bennett, Jimmy Denton
Label: ABC Paramount
Year: 1957
Essential rock and roll attire.

BLACK STAR

Artist: Yngwie Malmsteen
Written by: Yngwie Malmsteen
From the album: *Rising Force*
Label: Polydor
Produced by: Yngwie Malmsteen
Year: 1985
Swedish metal guitar God no longer waiting.

BLACK STEEL IN THE HOUR OF CHAOS

Artist: Public Enemy
Written by: Carlton Ridenhour, James Boxley, Eric Sadler
From the album: *It Takes a Nation of Millions to Hold Us Back*
Label: Def Jam
Produced by: Hank Shocklee, Carl Ryder
Year: 1988
Militant rap finds it moment. Covered by Tricky (Island, '95).

BLACK VELVET

Artist: Alannah Myles
Written by: David Tyson, Christopher Ward
From the album: *Alannah Myles*
Label: Atlantic
Produced by: David Tyson
Year: 1990
Elvis-inspired one-shot. Suggested segue: "Walking in Memphis" by Marc Cohn.

BLACK WATER

Artist: The Doobie Brothers
Written by: Pat Simmons
From the album: *What Were Once Vices Are Now Habits*
Label: Warner Brothers
Produced by: Ted Templeman
Year: 1974
B-side of "Another Park, Another Sunday" was their biggest hit. Suggested Mississippi River segue: "Proud Mary" by Creedence Clearwater Revival.

BLACKBERRY WAY

Artist: The Move
Written by: Roy Wood
From the album: *Looking On*
Produced by: Roy Wood, Jeff Lynne
Label: Capitol
Year: 1969
Melodic metal approaching the epiphany of "Do Ya."

BLACKBIRD

Artist: The Beatles
Written by: John Lennon, Paul McCartney
From the album: *The Beatles*
Label: Apple
Produced by: George Martin
Year: 1968
One of their prettiest acoustic efforts.

BLAME IT ON THE RAIN

Artist: Milli Vanilli
Written by: Diane Warren
From the album: *Girl, You Know It's True*
Label: Arista
Produced by: Fred Farian
Year: 1989
Third of three straight #1s. The group may have been phony, but Diane Warren didn't have to apologize, or return any royalties.

BLANCHE

Artist: The Three Friends
Written by: Frank Stropoli, Anthony Grochowski, Joseph Francavilla (Joe Villa), Nick Cutrone
Label: Lido
Year: 1956
Celebrating a neighborhood girl, distant cousin of "Florence," if not "Gloria."

BLANK GENERATION

Artist: Richard Hell and the Voidoids
Written by: Michael Meyers (Richard Hell)
From the album: *Blank Generation*
Label: ORK
Produced by: Richard Gottehrer, Richard Hell
Year: 1976
From the CBGB's proving ground that spawned New York's version of punk rock, this was an anthem for post-flower-power youth derived from the repertoire of Hell's first band, Television. Hell would eventually overcome his own malaise and fill in enough personal blanks to marry the quintessentially funky Patti Smyth of Scandal. It wouldn't last.

BLAZE OF GLORY

Artist: Jon Bon Jovi
Written by: Jon Bon Jovi
From the album: *Blaze of Glory Soundtrack*
Label: Polygram
Produced by: Danny Kortchmar, Jon Bon Jovi
Year: 1990
Returning to their profitable gunslinger motif.

BLEECKER STREET

Artist: Simon and Garfunkel
Written by: Paul Simon
From the album: *Wednesday Morning, 3 A.M.*
Label: Columbia
Produced by: Tom Wilson
Year: 1964
Simon shifts neighborhoods in the mid-'60s, from Tin Pan Alley to Greenwich Village. Shortly he would move uptown again.

BLESS YOU

Artist: Tony Orlando
Written by: Barry Mann, Cynthia Well
From the album: *Bless You and 11 Other Hits*
Label: Epic
Produced by: Al Nevins, Don Kirshner
Year: 1961
Introducing another pair of Kirshner-discovered songwriters, Barry and Cynthia. Orlando would make his fortune with his next concept, Dawn.

BLIND

Artist: Korn
Written by: Korn
From the album: *Follow the Leader*
Label: Immortal
Produced by: Ross Robinson
Year: 1998
With the popular turf now dominated by rap and hip hop, hard rock concedes, buys in, sells out.

BLINDED BY THE LIGHT

Artist: Bruce Springsteen
Written by: Bruce Springsteen
From the album: *Greetings from Asbury Park*
Label: Columbia
Produced by: Jim Cretecos, Mike Appel
Year: 1973
First single from the Boss of Asbury Park sparked immediate comparisons in the *New York Times* to Bob Dylan, Van Morrison, the Band, Allen Ginsberg, and the cult movie *El Topo*. But none of the comparisons would have meant a thing to the record company if not for Manfred Mann's truncated version of the track (Polydor, '73), which went to #1 (like the Byrds similar *Reader's Digest* rendering of Dylan's "Mr. Tambourine Man"), whetting the appetite of a waiting nation. But the wait would be longer than anyone expected.

BLING BLING

Artist: B.G.
Written by: Manny Fresh, Lil Wayne, Baby
From the album: *Chopper City in the Ghetto*
Label: Cash Money
Year: 1999
What the well dressed rapper shouldn't be caught dead without.

BLISTER IN THE SUN

Artist: Violent Femmes
Written by: Gordon Gano
From the album: *Violent Femmes*
Label: Slash
Produced by: Mark Van Hecke
Year: 1982
Trademark angst from Minneapolis, with a nasal accent.

BLITZKRIEG BOP

Artist: The Ramones
Written by: Douglas Colvin, John Cummings, Jeff Hyman, Thomas Erdelyi
From the album: *The Ramones*
Label: Sire
Produced by: Craig Leon
Year: 1976
A three-chord band statement, anthem, and world view to do "Louie Louie" proud.

BLOCK ROCKIN' BEATS

Artist: The Chemical Brothers
Written by: Tom Rowlands, Ed Simons, Jesse Weaver
From the album: *Dig Your Own Hole*
Label: Caroline
Produced by: The Chemical Brothers
Year: 1997
Prime mover in the year's almost big electronica movement.

BLOCKBUSTER

Artist: The Sweet
Written by: Mike Chapman, Nicky Chinn
From the album: *The Sweet*
Label: Bell
Produced by: Mike Chapman, Nicky Chinn
Year: 1973
Their biggest UK hit stiffed stateside.

BLONDE IN THE BLEACHERS

Artist: Joni Mitchell
Written by: Joni Mitchell
From the album: *For the Roses*
Label: Asylum
Produced by: Joni Mitchell
Year: 1972
Trying out for the Susan Sarandon part in *Bull Durham*.

BLOOD AND ROSES

Artist: The Smithereens
Written by: Pat DiNizio
From the album: *Especially for You*
Label: Enigma
Produced by: Don Dixon
Year: 1986
Their breakthrough single, from the film *Dangerously Close*.

BLOW UP THE OUTSIDE WORLD

Artist: Soundgarden
Written by: Chris Cornell
From the album: *Down on the Upside*
Label: A&M
Produced by: Soundgarden, Adam Kasper
Year: 1996
Seattle reacts, as grunge comes tumbling down.

BLOWIN' IN THE WIND

Artist: Bob Dylan
Written by: Bob Dylan
From the album: *The Freewheelin' Bob Dylan*
Label: Columbia
Produced by: John Hammond
Year: 1963
Like Hank Ballard ("The Twist") and Freddy Parris ("In the Still of the Nite") before him, Bob Dylan has been accused of not writing one of his most famous works, this anthem of the Civil Rights Era. Though the case has largely disappeared from anyone's radar, never adequately researched was what other songs the supposed real writer of "Blowin' in the Wind" went on to write—as compared to Dylan's output over the next thirty or so years. Covered by Peter, Paul and Mary (Warner Brothers, '63) in the career-launching version, and Stevie Wonder, in the #1 R&B version (Tamla, '69).

BLUE

Artist: Joni Mitchell
Written by: Joni Mitchell
From the album: *Blue*
Label: Reprise
Produced by: Joni Mitchell
Year: 1971
For a painterly songwriter entering her most vulnerable period, a perfectly appropriate title for this battle report from the aftermath of the sexual revolution. Covered by Sarah McLachlan (Arista, '95) for a new generation of post-romantics.

BLUE ANGEL

Artist: Roy Orbison
Written by: Roy Orbison, Joe Melson
From the album: *Roy Orbison's Greatest Hits*
Label: Monument
Produced by: Fred Foster
Year: 1960
As a diva, Marlene Deitrich had nothing on Roy.

BLUE BAYOU

Artist: Roy Orbison
Written by: Roy Orbison, Joe Melson
From the album: *In Dreams*
Label: Monument
Produced by: Fred Foster
Year: 1963
This melancholy ode was the B-side of Roy's biggest R&B hit, "Mean Woman Blues." Cover was a million-selling single for Linda Ronstadt (Asylum, '77). Suggested segue: "Coconut Grove" by the Lovin' Spoonful.

BLUE HOTEL

Artist: Chris Isaak
Written by: Chris Isaak
From the album: *Chris Isaak*
Label: Warner Brothers
Produced by: Erik Jacobsen
Year: 1987
The man with the studied Orbisonian twang takes a walk down Lonely Street.

BLUE JAY WAY

Artist: The Beatles
Written by: George Harrison
From the album: *Magical Mystery Tour*
Label: Capitol
Produced by: George Martin
Year: 1967
Entering Mr. Harrison's quasi-spiritual neighborhood.

BLUE JEAN

Artist: David Bowie
Written by: David Bowie
From the album: *Tonight*
Label: EMI-America
Produced by: Nile Rodgers, David Bowie
Year: 1984

BLUE MONDAY

Artist: Fats Domino
Written by: Fats Domino, Dave Bartholomew
From the album: *This Is Fats Domino*
Label: Imperial
Produced by: Dave Bartholomew
Year: 1957
Fats' fifth #1 R&B, fourth Top 10 crossover is from the motion picture *The Girl Can't Help It*.

BLUE MONDAY

Artist: New Order
Written by: New Order
From the album: *Power, Corruption and Lies*
Label: Factory
Produced by: New Order
Year: 1983
This monster 12" topped the UK charts. Re-recorded (Qwest, '88).

BLUE MONEY

Artist: Van Morrison
Written by: Van Morrison
From the album: *His Band and Street Choir*
Label: Warner Brothers
Produced by: Van Morrison
Year: 1971
In the Caledonia soul groove.

BLUE MOON

Artist: The Marcels
Written by: Richard Rodgers, Lorenz Hart
From the album: *Blue Moon*
Label: Colpix
Produced by: Stu Phillips
Year: 1961
The 1934 standard was covered by Elvis Presley on *The Sun Sessions* (RCA, '56). But it was the Marcels' perfect doo-wop #1 R&B/#1 crossover that really had the aspiring bass men lining up on the corners of urban America for years to come. Suggested segue: "Zoom Zoom Zoom" by the Collegians.

BLUE MOON OF KENTUCKY

Artist: Bill Monroe
Written by: Bill Monroe
Label: Columbia
Year: 1947
Bluegrass classic was the B-side of Elvis' first single, "That's All Right, Mama" (Sun, 1954).

BLUE ON BLACK

Artist: Kenny Wayne Shepherd
Written by: Kenny Wayne Shepherd

From the album: *Blue on Black*
Produced by: Kenny Wayne Shepherd, Jerry Harrison
Label: Giant
Year: 1998
Blistering guitar rocker.

BLUE SHADOWS

Artist: Lowell Fulson
Written by: Lloyd Glenn
From the album: *Hung down Head*
Label: Swing Time
Year: 1950
First hit for the L.A. bluesman and Ray Charles's employer.

BLUE SKY

Artist: Allman Brothers
Written by: Dickie Betts
From the album: *Eat a Peach*
Produced by: Tom Dowd
Label: Capricorn
Year: 1972
Betts' lilting signature piece.

BLUE SUEDE SHOES

Artist: Carl Perkins
Written by: Carl Perkins
From the album: *Dance Album*
Label: Sun
Produced by: Sam Phillips
Year: 1956
First anthem of the newly discovered teenage market (i.e., rock and roll). The big issues would be style, territory, and attitude, as put forth in this, the first triple crossover record, entering the country charts two weeks ahead of Elvis' "Heartbreak Hotel," then beating it to the R&B charts by a month in March, and the pop charts by a month (again) in April. Presley's cover of "Blue Suede Shoes" (RCA, '56) peaked well below Perkins' (and didn't chart R&B or country). Oddly enough, and setting the tone for Perkins' later career, his record stopped at #2 on all three charts. Revived in the classic teen-frustration movie *Porky's Revenge*.

BLUE VELVET

Artist: The Clovers
Written by: Bernie Wayne, Lee Morris
Label: Atlantic
Produced by: Ahmet Ertegun, Jerry Wexler
Year: 1955
Introduced by Tony Bennett (Columbia, '51), popularized by Bobby Vinton (Epic, '63), but tailor-made for reverse crossover doo-wop legendhood by the Clovers.

BLUEBERRY HILL

Artist: Fats Domino
Written by: Al Lewis, Larry Stock, Vincent Rose
From the album: *This Is Fats Domino*
Label: Imperial
Produced by: Dave Bartholomew

Year: 1956
Fats' pop breakthrough after twenty R&B hits was initially a cowboy song, popularized by Gene Autry in the '41 movie *The Singing Hills*.

BLUEBIRD

Artist: Buffalo Springfield
Written by: Stephen Stills
From the album: *Buffalo Springfield Again*
Label: Atco
Produced by: Turk-Pila
Year: 1967
Influential folk/rock hit, laying the groundwork for Crosby, Stills, Nash & Young; Souther, Hillman and Furay; and Poco, Firefall, et al. Suggested segue: "If You Were a Bluebird" by Joe Ely.

BLUEJEAN BOP

Artist: Gene Vincent
Written by: Gene Vincent, Hal Levy
From the album: *Bluejean Bop*
Label: Capitol
Produced by: Ken Nelson
Year: 1956
Rockabilly standard, revived by Paul McCartney (Capitol, '99).

BLUES FOR BUDDAH, A

Artist: The Silencers
Written by: Jimmie O'Neill
From the album: *A Blues for Buddah*
Label: RCA
Produced by: Flood, the Silencers
Year: 1990
U2esque plaint from Ireland about the Middle East.

BLUES HAD A BABY AND THEY NAMED IT ROCK AND ROLL

Artist: Muddy Waters
Written by: McKinley Morganfield (Muddy Waters), Brownie McGhee
From the album: *Hard Again*
Produced by: Johnny Winter
Label: Blue Sky
Year: 1977
Eloquently restating the obvious.

BLUES POWER

Artist: Eric Clapton
Written by: Eric Clapton, Leon Russell
From the album: *Blues Power*
Label: RSO
Produced by: Jon Astley
Year: 1980
Still his defining credo.

BO DIDDLEY

Artist: Bo Diddley
Written by: Ellas McDaniel (Bo Diddley)

From the album: *Bo Diddley's a Twister*
Label: Checker
Produced by: Willie Dixon
Year: 1955
Introducing the beat that would infiltrate the repertoires of a thousand frat-house rock bands and a lyric that would encourage a generation of rappers to use their own names as a focal point in song.

BOA CONSTRICTOR

Artist: Shel Silverstein
Written by: Shel Silverstein
From the album: *Inside Folk Songs*
Label: Atlantic
Produced by: Roy Halee
Year: 1962
The advent of a twisted talent. As an author, Silverstein has brought endearing quirkiness to the Top-40, as a crooner, he makes Tom Waits sound like Johnny Mathis. Covered by Johnny Cash (Columbia, '69).

B.O.B. (BOMBS OVER BAGHAD)

Artist: OutKast
Written by: Andre Benjamin, Antwan Andre Patton and David Sheats
From the album: *Stankonia*
Produced by: OutKast
Label: Arista
Year: 2000
Early indication of OutKast's explosive potential.

BOBBY JEAN

Artist: Bruce Springsteen
Written by: Bruce Springsteen
From the album: *Born in the USA.*
Label: Columbia
Produced by: Jon Landau, Bruce Springsteen, Steve Van Zandt, Chuck Plotkin
Year: 1984
The Boss's tribute to his departed guitarist, Miami Steve, who moved back to New Jersey to work for another boss, Tony Soprano.

BOBBY'S GIRL

Artist: Marcie Blane
Written by: Henry Hoffman, Gary Klein
Label: Seville
Produced by: Marv Holtzman
Year: 1962
Quintessential teen anthem, written by two swell guys. Covered in England by Susan Maugham (Phillips, '62).

BOBBYSOX TO STOCKINGS

Artist: Frankie Avalon
Written by: Richard Dicicco, Russ Faith
From the album: *A Whole Lotta Frankie*
Label: Chancellor
Year: 1959
The *American Bandstand* worldview.

BODHISATTVA

Artist: Steely Dan
Written by: Donald Fagen, Walter Becker
From the album: *Countdown to Ecstasy*
Label: ABC
Produced by: Gary Katz
Year: 1973
Artsy collegiate answer to the collected works of Kahlil Gibran.

BOHEMIAN RHAPSODY

Artist: Queen
Written by: Freddie Mercury
From the album: *A Night at the Opera*
Label: Elektra
Produced by: Roy Thomas Baker
Year: 1975
As befitting their arty record label, Queen exhibits their light operatic leanings in one of the biggest UK hits of all time. Lovingly resurrected by Wayne (Mike Myers) and the boys in the car in the movie *Wayne's World*.

BOMBER

Artist: Motorhead
Written by: Ian Kilmeister (Lemmy), Philthy Taylor, (Fast) Eddie Clarke
From the album: *Bomber*
Label: Bronze
Produced by: Jimmy Miller
Year: 1979
London during the blitz was their largest influence.

BONE MACHINE

Artist: The Pixies
Written by: Charles Francis (Black Francis)
From the album: *Surfer Rosa*
Label: 4AD/Rough Trade
Produced by: Steve Albini
Year: 1988
By way of the legendary Fort Apache Studio, the noisy beginnings of the Boston alternative sound that would include Dinosaur Jr., Throwing Muses, the Breeders (featuring the Pixies' Kim Deal), and the Lemonheads.

BONG BONG I LOVE YOU MADLY

Artist: Vince Castro
Written by: Vince Castro Jr., Charles Merenstein
Label: ABC Paramount
Year: 1958
Cited by *Stormy Weather*, the magazine for oldies fanatics, as one of the greatest rock and roll achievements. Go figure.

BONGO ROCK

Artist: Preston Epps
Written by: Preston Epps, Arthur Egnoian
From the album: *Bongo, Bongo, Bongo*
Label: Original Sound

Year: 1959
Most famous use of bongos in pop history, outside of an early Ricky Ricardo performance on *I Love Lucy*. Maynard G. Krebs was listening.

BONITA APPLEBUM

Artist: A Tribe Called Quest
Written by: Jonathan Davis, Ali-Shaheed Muhammed, Malik Taylor
From the album: *People's Instinctive Travels and Paths of Rhythm*
Label: Jive
Produced by: A Tribe Called Quest
Year: 1990
Experimental and invigorating new direction in hip hop.

BONY MORONIE

Artist: Larry Williams
Written by: Larry Williams
Label: Specialty
Produced by: Artie Rupe
Year: 1957
Learning his rhyming lessons from Little Richard.

BOOBS A LOT

Artist: The Fugs
Written by: Peter Stampfel
From the album: *First Album*
Label: ESP
Produced by: Harry Smith
Year: 1965
Stretching the envelope on pop propriety, the Fugs briefly gave scatology a good name.

BOOGALOO DOWN BROADWAY

Artist: Fantastic Johnny C.
Written by: Jesse James
From the album: *Boogaloo down Broadway*
Label: Phil L.A. of Soul
Produced by: Jesse James
Year: 1967
Still dancing, while the rest of the Youth Culture was nodding off.

BOOGIE CHILLEN

Artist: John Lee Hooker
Written by: John Lee Hooker
Label: Modern
Year: 1949
#1 R&B tune that led to the chooglin' boogie blues groove favored by Creedence Clearwater Revival and Canned Heat.

BOOGIE DOWN!

Artist: Eddie Kendricks
Written by: Anita Poree, Frank Wilson, Leonard Caston
From the album: *Boogie Down!*
Label: Tamla

Produced by: Frank Wilson, Leonard Caston
Year: 1974
#1 R&B crossover presaging disco.

BOOGIE FEVER

Artist: The Sylvers
Written by: Freddie Perren, Keni St. Lewis
From the album: *Showcase*
Label: Capitol
Produced by: Freddie Perren
Year: 1976
Dance floor affliction.

BOOGIE NIGHTS

Artist: Heatwave
Written by: Rod Temperton
From the album: *Too Hot to Handle*
Label: Epic
Produced by: Barry Blue
Year: 1977
Characterizing a generation's night life heyday.

BOOGIE ON REGGAE WOMAN

Artist: Stevie Wonder
Written by: Stevie Wonder
From the album: *Fulfillingness First Finale*
Label: Tamla
Produced by: Stevie Wonder
Year: 1974
Cross-cultural dance move.

BOOGIE OOGIE OOGIE

Artist: A Taste of Honey
Written by: Janice Johnson, Perry Kibble, Larry Mizell
From the album: *A Taste of Honey*
Label: Capitol
Produced by: Fonce Mizell
Year: 1978
Apogee of this particular groove. Group won a Grammy for Best New Artist and promptly disappeared.

BOOGIE WONDERLAND

Artist: Earth, Wind and Fire with the Emotions
Written by: John Lind, Allee Willis
From the album: *I Am*
Label: ARC
Produced by: Maurice White, Al McKay
Year: 1979
Entering the disco arena.

BOOK OF LOVE

Artist: The Monotones
Written by: Warren Davis, George Malone, Charles Patrick
Label: Argo
Year: 1957
The eternal rock and roll question was inspired by a toothpaste commercial for Pepsodent.

BOOM BOOM

Artist: John Lee Hooker
Written by: John Lee Hooker
Label: VeeJay
Year: 1962
Given its original impetus and title by a bar maid in Detroit named Luilla. Covered by the Animals (MGM, '65).

BOOT EM UP

Artist: The Du Droppers
Written by: Charles Singleton, Rose Marie McCoy
Label: RCA
Year: 1954
Prime rhythm rocker, following up their revealing chartmakers of '53: "I Wanna Know," succeeded by "I Found Out."

BOOTS OF SPANISH LEATHER

Artist: Bob Dylan
Written by: Bob Dylan
From the album: *The Freewheelin' Bob Dylan*
Label: Columbia
Produced by: John Hammond
Year: 1963
An international rambling song. In this case, it's the girl who's rambling, by boat.

BOOTZILLA

Artist: Bootsy's Rubber Band
Written by: George Clinton, William Collins
From the album: *Bootsy? Player of the Year*
Label: Warner Brothers
Produced by: George Clifton
Year: 1978
Life after disco, courtesy of James Brown's famous bassist and Clinton collaborator, William "Bootsy" Collins.

BOP GUN (ENDANGERED SPECIES)

Artist: Parliament
Written by: George Clinton, Gary Shider, Walter Morrison
From the album: *Funkentelechy vs. the Placebo Syndrome*
Label: Casablanca
Produced by: George Clinton
Year: 1977
Updated by Ice Cube as "Bop Gun (One Nation)" (Priority, '94) as a new anthem of the disaffected.

BOPPIN' THE BLUES

Artist: Carl Perkins
Written by: Carl Perkins, Howard Griffin
From the album: *Dance Album*
Label: Sun
Produced by: Sam Phillips
Year: 1956
Following up "Blue Suede Shoes," but with not nearly the same impact.

BOP-TING-A-LING

Artist: LaVern Baker
Written by: Winfield Scott
From the album: *LaVern Baker*
Label: Atlantic
Produced by: Ahmet Ertegun, Jerry Wexler
Year: 1955
Baker's rockin' soul owned the '50s.

BORDER RADIO

Artist: The Blasters
Written by: Dave Alvin
From the album: *The Blasters*
Label: Slash
Produced by: The Blasters
Year: 1981
On which the voice of Wolfman Jack shall be heard forever. Suggested segue: "Mexican Radio" by Wall of Voodoo.

BORDER SONG (HOLY MOSES)

Artist: Elton John
Written by: Elton John, Bernie Taupin
From the album: *Elton John*
Label: MCA
Produced by: Gus Dudgeon
Year: 1970
Crossing the border to the lucrative US market, on the brink of a singer/songwriter/piano man resurgence. Covered by Aretha Franklin (Atlantic, '70).

BORDERLINE

Artist: Camper Van Beethoven
Written by: David Lowery, Victor Krummenacher, Greg Lisher, Chris Pedersen
From the album: *Key Lime Pie*
Label: Virgin
Produced by: Dennis Herring
Year: 1989
Obliterating the borders between cow-punk and antifolk, a new world beat for a new flannel world.

BORDERLINE

Artist: Madonna
Written by: Reggie Lucas
From the album: *Madonna*
Label: Sire
Produced by: Reggie Lucas, Jellybean Benitez
Year: 1983
First hit single for the displaced Detroit dancehall diva, a compelling return to girl-group yearning, spiced up with interracial innuendo for the jaded '80s.

BORN AT THE RIGHT TIME

Artist: Paul Simon
Written by: Paul Simon
From the album: *The Rhythm of the Saints*
Label: Warner Brothers

Produced by: Paul Simon
Year: 1990
Visiting one of the key ports of entry for rock and roll, New Orleans, Simon prepares for the big five-oh.

BORN IN CHICAGO

Artist: The Paul Butterfield Blues Band
Written by: Nick Gravenites
From the album: *The Paul Butterfield Blues Band*
Label: Elektra
Produced by: Paul Rothchild
Year: 1965
Heartland blues rock with a feeling … and several stellar instrumentalists, including Paul Butterfield on the amplified harp, and Mike Bloomfield and Elvin Bishop on guitars. Like the Yardbirds and the Rolling Stones in England, they covered Muddy Waters and Willie Dixon tunes with gusto, dexterity, passion, and aplomb. But lacking their teeny-bop sex appeal, they failed to become America's answer to either of them, thus making Cream and the Jimi Hendrix Experience necessary and Led Zeppelin inevitable.

BORN IN THE USA

Artist: Bruce Springsteen
Written by: Bruce Springsteen
From the album: *Born in the USA.*
Label: Columbia
Produced by: Jon Landau, Bruce Springsteen, Chuck Plotkin
Year: 1984
His most rousing protest song was co-opted as a campaign slogan by Ronald Reagan. Suggested segue: "Kill for Peace" by the Fugs.

BORN ON THE BAYOU

Artist: Creedence Clearwater Revival
Written by: John C. Fogerty
From the album: *Bayou Country*
Label: Fantasy
Produced by: John C. Fogerty
Year: 1969
Staking out their swamp-rock turf.

BORN ON THE WRONG PLANET

Artist: The String Cheese Incident
Written by: Bill Nershi
From the album: *Born on the Wrong Planet*
Label: Love Lights
Year: 1997
Title track on the tireless alt-country jam band's first album has become a live performing favorite.

BORN SLIPPY

Artist: (Nuxx) Underworld
Written by: Darren Emerson, Karl Hyde, Rick Smith
From the album: *Born Slippy*
Label: TVT

Produced by: Underworld
Year: 1995
Insidiously catchy techno-dance groove was popularized in the 1996 film *Trainspotting*.

BORN TO BE MY BABY

Artist: Bon Jovi
Written by: Jon Bon Jovi, Richie Sambora, Desmond Child
From the album: *NewJersey*
Label: Mercury
Produced by: Bruce Fairbairn
Year: 1989
Pseudo-Springsteenian, fake Spectoresque concoction.

BORN TO BE WILD

Artist: Steppenwolf
Written by: Mars Bonfire
From the album: *Steppenwolf*
Label: Dunhill
Produced by: Gabriel Mekler
Year: 1968
Ultimate biker anthem. Heard the next year in *Easy Rider*.

BORN TO LOSE

Artist: The Heartbreakers
Written by: John Genzale (Johnny Thunders)
From the album: *L.A.M.F.*
Label: Track
Produced by: Speedy Keen, Daniel Secunda
Year: 1977
Signature number and credo for the former New York Doll and his band.

BORN TO RUN

Artist: Bruce Springsteen
Written by: Bruce Springsteen
From the album: *Born to Run*
Label: Columbia
Produced by: Mike Appel, Bruce Springsteen
Year: 1975
Arriving at the Top 40 as if it were his missed senior prom, in a tux and dungarees, on a Harley with a harlot, his head exploding, and only the occasional pothole to stop him.

BORN TOO LATE

Artist: The Poni Tails
Written by: Fred Tobias, Charles Strouse
Label: ABC Paramount
Produced by: Don Costa
Year: 1958
Previewing the yearning girl-group sound of the next decade, with a sax solo for the ages. Suggested segue: "Jo-Ann" by the Playmates.

BORN UNDER A BAD SIGN

Artist: Albert King
Written by: Booker T. Jones, William Bell

From the album: *King of the Blues Guitar*
Label: Stax
Produced by: Jim Stewart
Year: 1967
He wasn't B.B. or even Freddie. But Albert was the King of Memphis Soul on this future standard. Covered by Booker T. and the MGs (Stax, '68), the Paul Butterfield Blues Band (Elektra, '68), and Cream (RSO, '68).

BOTH SIDES NOW

Artist: Judy Collins
Written by: Joni Mitchell
From the album: *Wildflowers*
Label: Elektra
Produced by: Mark Abramson
Year: 1968
Joni's wise and winsome folk/rock classic was Judy's first Top 10 hit covered by Joni Mitchell (Reprise, '69).

BOTTLE OF WINE

Artist: Tom Paxton
Written by: Tom Paxton
From the album: *Ain't That News*
Label: Elektra
Year: 1963
Folk-flavored sing-along drinking song, covered by the Fireballs (Atco, '68).

BOTTLE, THE

Artist: Gil Scott-Heron
Written by: Gil Scott-Heron, Brian Jackson
From the album: *First Minute of a New Day*
Label: Arista
Year: 1975
A former Last Poet reclaims his protest turf. Suggested segue: "1 Million Bottlebags" by Public Enemy.

BOULDER TO BIRMINGHAM

Artist: Emmylou Harris
Written by: Bill Danoff, Emmylou Harris
From the album: *Pieces of the Sky*
Produced by: Brian Aherne
Label: Reprise
Year: 1975
Maiden venture into songwriting for the Queen of alt-country finds her knee-deep in Americana.

BOUND FOR GLORY

Artist: Phil Ochs
Written by: Phil Ochs
From the album: *All the News That's Fit to Sing*
Label: Elektra
Produced by: Paul Rothchild, Jac Holzman
Year: 1964
A tribute to the folk patron saint, Woody Guthrie, originally the title of Woody's semi-autobiography.

BOX OF RAIN

Artist: Grateful Dead
Written by: Jerry Garcia, Robert Hunter
From the album: *Workingman's Dead*
Label: Warner Brothers
Produced by: Bob Matthews, Betty Cantor, the Grateful Dead
Year: 1970

BOXCARS

Artist: Joe Ely
Written by: Butch Hancock, Joe Ely
From the album: *Honky Tonk Masquerade*
Label: MCA
Produced by: Chip Young
Year: 1978
Haunting Austin-bred country rocker, written with Joe's favorite hometown collaborator.

BOXER, THE

Artist: Simon and Garfunkel
Written by: Paul Simon
From the album: *Bridge over Troubled Water*
Label: Columbia
Produced by: Roy Halee, Paul Simon, Art Garfunkel
Year: 1969
Simon moves past the lightweight sparring of his Top 40 folk/rock adolescence into the welterweight ranks of FM album-oriented rock. Great punching bag effects.

BOXING

Artist: Ben Folds Five
Written by: Ben Folds
From the album: *The Ben Folds Five*
Produced by: Caleb Southern
Label: Passenger
Year: 1995
Early effort got the songwriter's coveted seal of approval from Bette Midler (Warner Brothers, '98).

BOY IN THE BUBBLE, THE

Artist: Paul Simon
Written by: Paul Simon
From the album: *Graceland*
Label: Warner Brothers
Produced by: Paul Simon
Year: 1986
Writing from rhythm tracks brought back from Africa, Simon comes up with a free-associative gem of modern-day disassociation.

BOY IS MINE, THE

Artist: Brandy and Monica
Written by: Rodney Jerkins, Fred Jerkins, Brandy Norwood, LeShawn Daniels, Japhe Tejeda
From the album: *Never S-A-Y Never*
Label: Atlantic
Produced by: Dallas Austin, Fred Jerkins, Rodney Jerkins, LaShawn Daniels
Label: Arista

Year: 1998
Also released at the same time on the Monica album, *The Boy Is Mine* (Arista)

BOY NAMED SUE, A

Artist: Shel Silverstein
Written by: Shel Silverstein
From the album: *A Boy Named Sue and His Other Country Songs*
Label: RCA
Produced by: Chet Atkins, Felton Jarvis
Year: 1969
Coming from a boy named Shel, this obviously painful autobiographical tale of fathers and sons and the fragile male psyche was by far Johnny Cash's biggest all-time crossover hit (Columbia, '69).

BOY WITH A PROBLEM

Artist: Elvis Costello
Written by: Declan McManus (Elvis Costello), Chris Difford
From the album: *Imperial Bedroom*
Label: Columbia
Produced by: Geoff Emerich
Year: 1982
A UK songwriting super session, with a familiar theme.

BOYS

Artist: The Shirelles
Written by: Luther Dixon, Wes Farrell
From the album: *Tonight's the Night*
Label: Scepter
Produced by: Luther Dixon
Year: 1960
B-side of "Will You Love Me Tomorrow." Covered by the Beatles (Vee-Jay, '64).

BOYS ARE BACK IN TOWN, THE

Artist: Thin Lizzy
Written by: Phil Lynott
From the album: *Jailbreak*
Label: Mercury
Produced by: John Alcock
Year: 1976
The Springsteen sound reaches the streets of Ireland, where Phil Lynott gives it a black eye.

BOYS DON'T CRY

Artist: The Cure
Written by: Robert Smith, Laurence Tolhurst, Michael Dempsey
From the album: *Boys Don't Cry*
Label: Fiction/PVC
Produced by: Chris Parry
Year: 1979
First critical success for the gloomiest of gothic rockers.

BOYS OF SUMMER, THE

Artist: Don Henley
Written by: Don Henley, Mike Campbell

From the album: *Building the Perfect Beast*
Label: Geffen
Produced by: Don Henley, Danny Kortchmar, Greg Ladanyi
Year: 1985
Evocative tale of a painful breakup of an even more painful relationship has all the details right, from Mike Campbell's indelible opening guitar figure to the vision of a "Deadhead sticker on a Cadillac." When it was covered by the Ataris in '03, the line was changed to "Black Flag sticker …" Just wasn't the same thing at all.

BOYS TO MEN

Artist: New Edition
Written by: James Harris III, Terry Lewis
From the album: *Heart Break*
Label: MCA
Produced by: Jimmy Jam, Terry Lewis
Year: 1988
Somewhere in Philly, a neo-doo-wop harmony group would be forming around this title. They would have bigger hits than New Edition, but not a bigger influence.

BRAIN DAMAGE

Artist: Pink Floyd
Written by: Roger Waters
From the album: *Dark Side of the Moon*
Label: Harvest
Produced by: Pink Floyd
Year: 1973

BRAND NEW KEY

Artist: Melanie
Written by: Melanie Safka
From the album: *Gather Me*
Label: Neighborhood
Produced by: Peter Schekeryk
Year: 1971
Bubblicious #1 hit that would stall her efforts to escape a lightweight tag.

BRANDY (MANDY)

Artist: Scott English
Written by: Scott English, Richard Kerr
Label: Janus
Year: 1972
Three years after it first stiffed, Clive Davis changed the title of this song and gave it to Bette Midler's former keyboard player Barry Manilow (Bell, '75) to launch his new record label, Arista. Just in case classic pop wasn't the right formula for '75, Clive backed himself up by also signing punk poet Patti Smith.

BRANDY (YOU'RE A FINE GIRL)

Artist: Looking Glass
Written by: Elliot Lurie
From the album: *Looking Glass*

Label: Epic
Produced by: Mike Gershman, Bob Lifton, Looking Glass
Year: 1972
Lilting seafaring throwback to a calmer time, in the early '60s, when the AM radio sound still ruled. Suggested segue: "A Taste of Honey" by Bobby Scott.

BRASS IN POCKET (I'M SPECIAL)

Artist: The Pretenders
Written by: Chrissie Hynde, James Honeyman Scott
From the album: *The Pretenders*
Label: Sire
Produced by: Chris Thomas
Year: 1980
#1 UK introduction to a tough-minded independent rocker in self-imposed exile from Ohio. As a waitress in the video, she could've been auditioning to be the next Rita Tushingham, who starred in the movie *A Taste of Honey*.

BREAD AND BUTTER

Artist: The Newbeats
Written by: Larry Parks, Jay Turnbow
From the album: *Bread and Butter*
Label: Hickory
Year: 1964
An awesome falsetto. Suggested segue: "Peanut Butter" by the Marathons.

BREAK IT DOWN AGAIN

Artist: Tears For Fears
Written by: Roland Orzabel, Alan Griffiths
From the album: *Elemental*
Label: Mercury
Produced by: Tony Palmer, Alan Griffiths, Roland Orzabel
Year: 1993
Synth pioneer Orzabel moves into Duran Duran territory.

BREAK IT TO ME GENTLY

Artist: Aretha Franklin
Written by: Marvin Hamlisch, Carole Bayer Sager
From the album: *Sweet Passion*
Label: Atlantic
Produced by: Marvin Hamlisch, Carole Bayer Sager
Year: 1977
Aretha gives M.O.R.'s leading songwriting couple their first #1 R&B hit.

BREAK IT TO ME GENTLY

Artist: Brenda Lee
Written by: Diane Lampert, Joe Seneca
From the album: *Let Me Sing!*
Label: Decca
Produced by: Owen Bradley
Year: 1961

Rock's original Little Girl with the Big Voice utilizes it on this tailor-made ballad.

BREAK MY MIND

Artist: The Box Tops
Written by: Gram Parsons
From the album: *The Box Tops*
Label: Bell
Produced by: Dan Penn
Year: 1967
Launching the career of three legends in the making. Gram Parsons would join the Byrds the following year and help create country rock. Alex Chilton would graduate from the Box Tops into cult status and influence almost all of alt-rock, starting with the Replacements. Dan Penn, meanwhile, would become one of soul's top songwriters. Covered by Parsons's band, the Flying Burrito Brothers (A&M, '72).

BREAK MY STRIDE

Artist: Matthew Wilder
Written by: Matthew Wilder, Greg Prestopino
From the album: *I Don't Speak the Language*
Label: Private
Produced by: Pete Bunetta, Rick Chudacoff, Bill Elliott
Year: 1983
Pleasant, pulsing empowering pop/rock one-shot.

BREAK ON THROUGH

Artist: The Doors
Written by: Jim Morrison, Robbie Krieger, John Densmore
From the album: *Strange Days*
Label: Elektra
Produced by: Paul Rothchild
Year: 1967
Their first single, inspired by Aldous "Doors of Perception" Huxley, was an organ propelled rush.

BREAK STUFF

Artist: Limp Bizkit
Written by: Wes Borland, Fred Durst, John Otto, Sam Rivers
From the album: *Significant Other*
Label: Flip
Produced by: Limp Bizkit, Terry Date
Year: 1999
A rallying cry, of a sort, at the Woodstock 30TH Anniversary Festival, where lots of folks took the title literally.

BREAK UP TO MAKE UP

Artist: The Stylistics
Written by: Thom Bell, Linda Creed, Kenny Gamble
From the album: *Round 2: The Stylistics*
Label: Avco
Produced by: Thom Bell
Year: 1972
Bell and Creed deliver another Philly soul classic.

BREAKDOWN

Artist: The Buzzcocks
Written by: Pete Shelley, Howard DeVoto
From the album: *Spiral Scratch*
Label: New Hormones
Produced by: Martin Rushent
Year: 1978
In the wake of the Sex Pistols, perfect pop for agitated people.

BREAKDOWN

Artist: Tom Petty and the Heartbreakers
Written by: Tom Petty
From the album: *Tom Petty & the Heartbreakers*
Label: Shelter
Produced by: Tom Petty
Year: 1977
Patented tense, taut showstopper became his first Top 40 hit. Covered by Suzi Quatro (RSO, '79).

BREAKFAST AT TIFFANYS

Artist: Deep Blue Something
Written by: Todd Pipes
From the album: *Home*
Label: Interscope
Year: 1995
A small epic of conversational epiphanies, dedicated to the memory of Holly Golightly.

BREAKIN' … THERE'S NO STOPPING US

Artist: Ollie and Jerry
Written by: Ollie E. Brown, Jerry Knight
From the album: *Breakin'*
Label: Polydor
Produced by: Ollie Brown
Year: 1984
From the breakdance exploitation film.

BREAKIN' MY HEART (PRETTY BROWN EYES)

Artist: Mint Condition
Written by: Larry Waddell, Stokely Williams, Jeffrey Allen
From the album: *Meant to Be Mint*
Label: Perspective
Produced by: Jellybean Johnson, Mint Condition
Year: 1992
Modern funk, Top 40 style.

BREAKING UP IS HARD TO DO

Artist: Neil Sedaka
Written by: Howard Greenfield, Neil Sedaka
From the album: *Neil Sedaka Sings His Greatest Hits*
Label: RCA Victor
Produced by: Al Nevins Don Kirshner
Year: 1962
Reputedly inspired by rock and roll classic "It Will Stand" by the Showmen, this was Sedaka's biggest

hit of the '60s. Years later, he recorded it again, slower (Rocket, '76).

BREAKOUT

Artist: Foo Fighters
Written by: Foo Fighters
From the album: *There Is Nothing Left to Lose*
Produced by: Adam Kasper, Foo Fighters
Label: RCA
Year: 2000

BREAKS, THE

Artist: Kurtis Blow
Written by: James Moore, Lawrence Smith, Kurt Walker, Robert Ford Jr., Russell Simmons
From the album: *Kurtis Blow*
Label: Mercury
Produced by: James Moore, Robert Ford
Year: 1980
Classic rap track, dedicated to the art of break dancing and the whims of fate.

BREAKUP SONG (THEY DON'T WRITE 'EM), THE

Artist: The Greg Kihn Band
Written by: Greg Kihn, Steven Wright, Gary Philips
From the album: *Rockihnroll*
Label: Beserkley
Produced by: Matthew King Kaufman
Year: 1987
Jonathan Richman's label mates show a knack for the power pop move that was more pronounced a little further down the coastline in L.A.

BREATHE AGAIN

Artist: Toni Braxton
Written by: Kenny Edmunds (Babyface)
From the album: *Toni Braxton*
Label: LaFace/Arista
Produced by: Babyface
Year: 1993
A new soul diva emerges to take up where Anita Baker left off.

BREATHING

Artist: Kate Bush
Written by: Kate Bush
From the album: *Never Forever*
Label: EMI-America
Produced by: Kate Bush, Jon Kelly
Year: 1980
A passionate ode to the life-force on the morning after annihilation.

BREATHLESS

Artist: Jerry Lee Lewis
Written by: Otis Blackwell
Label: Sun

Produced by: Sam Phillips
Year: 1958
With his keyboard chops from Ike Turner and his gospel fervor from his cousin Jimmy Swaggart, Jerry Lee reaches his pumping peak with his third and final triple crossover. Covered by X in the '84 remake of the Godard movie *Breathless*.

BRIAN WILSON

Artist: Barenaked Ladies
Written by: Stephen Page
From the album: *Gordon*
Label: Sire
Produced by: Michael Philip-Wojewoda
Year: 1992
Satirizing the deleterious effects of hero worship.

BRICK

Artist: Ben Folds Five
Written by: Ben Folds, Darren Jesse
From the album: *Whatever and Ever, Amen*
Produced by: Ben Folds
Label: 550 Music/Caroline
Year: 1997
A mid-'90s collegiate relationship sinks like a stone but a keyboard-bashing star emerges.

BRICK HOUSE

Artist: The Commodores
Written by: Lionel B. Richie Jr., Ronald La Pread, Thomas McClary, Walter Orange, William King Jr., Milan Williams
From the album: *Commodores*
Label: Motown
Produced by: James Carmichael, the Commodores
Year: 1977
Funk powerhouse.

BRIDGE OF SIGHS

Artist: Robin Trower
Written by: Robin Trower
From the album: *Bridge of Sighs*
Label: Chrysalis
Produced by: Matthew Fisher
Year: 1974
Guitarist Trower transcends his Hendrix fixation.

BRIDGE OVER TROUBLED WATER

Artist: Simon and Garfunkel
Written by: Paul Simon
From the album: *Bridge over Troubled Water*
Label: Columbia
Produced by: Roy Halee, Paul Simon, Art Garfunkel
Year: 1969
Simon returns to the 59TH Street bridge of his youth (and early hit single), this time crossing it from the New York City side, with a touch of gospel, and a smile for Art. Cover by Aretha Franklin (Atlantic, '71) was a #1 R&B/Top 10 crossover.

BRIGHT LIGHTS, BIG CITY

Artist: Jimmy Reed
Written by: Jimmy Reed
Label: Vee-Jay
Year: 1961
Chasing the muse of the blues into the deadly era of "The Twist," Reed gets his biggest R&B hit. Suggested segue: "Detroit City" by Bobby Bare. Covered by the Animals (MGM, '65), Neil Young (Reprise, '83).

BRILLIANT DISGUISE

Artist: Bruce Springsteen
Written by: Bruce Springsteen
From the album: *Tunnel of Love*
Label: Columbia
Produced by: Jon Landau, Bruce Springsteen, Chuck Plotkin
Year: 1985
All grown up, but hardly settled down.

BRIMFUL OF ASHA

Artist: Cornershop
From the album: *When I Was Born for the 7th Time*
Produced by: Tjinder Singh, The Automator
Label: Luaka Bop
Year: 1997
A tribute to Bollywood, with the sound everybody was looking for in 1968, the last time the sitar was thought to be rock's secret weapon. Heard almost in its entirety in the 1996 movie, *The Pallbearer*.

BRING IT ON HOME TO ME

Artist: Sam Cooke
Written by: Sam Cooke
From the album: *The Best of Sam Cooke*
Label: RCA Victor
Produced by: Hugo and Luigi
Year: 1962
Covered by the Animals (MGM, '65); Eddie Floyd's biggest hit (Stax, '68). Suggested segue: "I Want to Go Home" by Charles Brown and Amos Milburn (Ace, '59).

BRING THE BOYS HOME

Artist: Freda Payne
Written by: Angelo Bond, General Johnson, Greg S. Perry
From the album: *Contact*
Label: Invictus
Produced by: Greg S. Perry
Year: 1971
General Johnson notwithstanding, one of the year's best protest songs. In civilian life, Johnson was the former lead singer of the Showmen ("It Will Stand").

BRING THE NOISE

Artist: Public Enemy
Written by: Carlton Ridenhour, Hank Shocklee, Eric Sadler
From the album: *It Takes a Nation of Millions to Hold Us Back*

Label: Def Jam
Produced by: Hank Shocklee, Carl Ryder
Year: 1988
Bringing the threatening noise of R&B up to a decibel level loud enough to be heard above the din of modern anomie. Featured in the film *Less Than Zero*. Covered by Anthrax (Megaforce, '91).

BRINGIN' ON THE HEARTBREAK

Artist: Def Leppard
Written by: Steve Clark, Joe Elliott, Pete Willis
From the album: *High N' Dry*
Label: Mercury
Produced by: Steve Clark, Joe Elliott, Pete Willis
Year: 1981
Scions of Zeppelin start a new Metal Age in England with Iron Maiden, Judas Priest, and Motorhead among the troops.

BRISTOL STOMP, THE

Artist: The Dovells
Written by: Dave Appell
From the album: *The Bristol Stomp*
Label: Parkway
Year: 1961
Another twist in the continuing saga of the baby boom's first dance craze. Before it was through, a solid couple of years of this groove would all but shake out the remaining original R&B pioneers, paving the way for a new jangly guitar sound and white hope to replace Elvis Presley, called the Beatles.

BROKEN ARROW

Artist: Buffalo Springfield
Written by: Neil Young
From the album: *Buffalo Springfield Again*
Label: Atco
Produced by: Turk-Pila
Year: 1967
Neil's earthy poetics take root in the old West.

BROKEN ARROW

Artist: Robbie Robertson
Written by: Robbie Robertson
From the album: *Robbie Robertson*
Label: Geffen
Produced by: Robbie Robertson, Daniel Lanois
Year: 1987
Borrowing Neil Young's title, fellow Canadian guitarist takes it in a moodier direction, befitting his Indian roots. Covered by Rod Stewart (Warner Brothers, '92).

BROKEN ENGLISH

Artist: Marianne Faithfull
From the album: *Broken English*
Produced by: Mark Miller Mundy
Label: Island
Year: 1980
Listen to what time has wrought on Faithfull's once demure and wistful voice, and worldview.

BROKEN HEARTED MELODY

Artist: Sarah Vaughan
Written by: Hal David, Sherman Edwards
Label: Mercury
Year: 1959
A Top 10 R&B/Top 10 crossover brings mainstream success to one of the great jazz singers of all time. Wasn't too shabby a credit for the lyricist either.

BROKEN WINGS

Artist: Mr. Mister
Written by: Richard Page, Steven George, Robert John "Mutt" Lange
From the album: *Welcome to the Real World*
Label: RCA
Produced by: Mutt Lange
Year: 1985
Middle-of-the-road pop rock from the Air Supply warehouse, forecasting producer Lange's seamless shift into country music with Shania Twain.

BRON Y' AUR STOMP

Artist: Led Zeppelin
Written by: Jimmy Page, Robert Plant, John Paul Jones, John Bonham
From the album: *Led Zeppelin III*
Label: Atlantic
Produced by: Jimmy Page
Year: 1970
Revealing their jug-band sympathies.

BROTHER LOUIE

Artist: Hot Chocolate
Written by: Errol Brown, Anthony Wilson
From the album: *Cicero Park*
Label: Big Tree
Produced by: Mickie Most
Year: 1973
This pop reggae story of interracial romance was one of their 13 UK hits. The cover by New York City rock band Stories (Kama Sutra, '73) went to #1 for their only hit.

BROTHERS

Artist: Stevie Ray Vaughan and Jimmie Vaughan
Written by: Stevie Ray Vaughan, Jimmie Vaughan
From the album: *Family Style*
Label: Epic
Produced by: Nile Rodgers
Year: 1990
The long-awaited duet by the Austin based bluesy brothers, released posthumously.

BROTHERS GONNA WORK IT OUT

Artist: Public Enemy
Written by: Charles Ridenhour, Keith Shocklee, Eric Sadler
From the album: *Fear of a Black Planet*

Label: Def Jam
Produced by: Stuart Robertz, Cerwin Depper, Gary G. Wiz, the JBL
Year: 1990
Hitting the R&B Top 20 with a protest song.

BROTHERS IN ARMS

Artist: Dire Straits
Written by: Mark Knopfler
From the album: *Brothers in Arms*
Label: Warner Brothers
Produced by: Neil Dorfsman, Mark Knopfler
Year: 1985
Acoustic anthem.

BROWN EYED GIRL

Artist: Van Morrison
Written by: Van Morrison
From the album: *Blowin' Your Mind*
Label: Bang
Produced by: Bert Berns
Year: 1967
Coming of age fable is Van's first hit. Used in the background of the enema scene in Oliver Stone's *Born on the Fourth of July*.

BROWN EYED HANDSOME MAN

Artist: Chuck Berry
Written by: Chuck Berry
From the album: *After School Sessions*
Label: Chess
Produced by: Leonard Chess, Phil Chess
Year: 1957
Not above self-promotion, Berry was just better at it than most.

BROWN SHOES DON'T MAKE IT

Artist: The Mothers of Invention
Written by: Frank Zappa
From the album: *Absolutely Free*
Label: Verve
Produced by: Tom Wilson
Year: 1967
Symphonic social satire. Bach (P.D.Q.) meets *Mad Magazine*.

BROWN SUGAR

Artist: D'Angelo
Written by: D'Angelo
From the album: *Brown Sugar*
Label: EMI
Year: 1995
Emergent R&B in a hip hop world.

BROWN SUGAR

Artist: The Rolling Stones
Written by: Mick Jagger, Keith Richards
From the album: *Sticky Fingers*
Label: Rolling Stones

Produced by: Jimmy Miller
Year: 1971
One of their all-time signature riffs introduce their sixth US #1.

BROWNSVILLE GIRL

Artist: Bob Dylan
Written by: Bob Dylan, Sam Shepard
From the album: *Knocked out Loaded*
Label: Columbia
Year: 1986
Two bohemian giants in decline.

BRUISED VIOLET

Artist: Babes in Toyland
Written by: Babes in Toyland
From the album: *Fontanelle*
Label: Reprise
Produced by: Lee Ranaldo
Year: 1990
The Riot Grrrrl sound as produced by a Riot boy from Sonic Youth. Segues: "Violet" by Hole, "Flower" by Liz Phair.

BUBBLEGUM

Artist: Kim Fowley
Written by: Kim Fowley
From the album: *Outrageous*
Label: Imperial
Year: 1969
Legendary track from a quintessentially infamous rock-and-roll character. Covered by Sonic Youth (SST, '86).

BUBBLEGUM FACTORY

Artist: Red Kross
Written by: Jeff McDonald
From the album: *Third Eye*
Label: Atlantic
Produced by: Red Kross
Year: 1990
Major label debut of the West Coast indie punks. To avoid conflict with the real Red Cross, their name was changed to protect the innocent.

BUDDY HOLLY

Artist: Weezer
Written by: Rivers Cuomo
From the album: *Weezer*
Label: DGC
Produced by: Ric Ocasek
Year: 1994
Alt-rock on the kitschy pop tip, aided by *Happy Days*'s own Al Molinaro in the video. The Replacements were a lot more serious about "Alex Chilton."

BUFFALO SOLDIER

Artist: The Flamingos
Written by: David Barnes, Myra Smith, Margaret Lewis

Label: Polydor
Year: 1970
About a legendary brigade of black soldiers. Bob Marley wrote about them, too.

BUFFALO STANCE

Artist: Neneh Cherry
Written by: Neneh Cherry, Booga Bear, Phil Ramacon, Jamie Morgan
From the album: *Raw like Sushi*
Label: Virgin
Produced by: T. Simenon, M. Saunders
Year: 1989
Reggae flavored one-shot by the daughter of jazz trumpeter Don and sister of rock one-shot Eagle Eye ("Save Tonight"). Originated in the UK by Morgan McVey. Remixed by Bomb the Bass. Featured in the '89 movie *Slaves of New York*.

BUILD ME UP, BUTTERCUP

Artist: The Foundations
Written by: Tony Macaulay, Michael D'Abo, John McLeod
From the album: *Build Me up, Buttercup*
Label: Uni
Produced by: Tony Macaulay
Year: 1969
Pop singalong prominently featured in *There's Something about Mary*.

BUILDING A MYSTERY

Artist: Sarah McLachlan
Written by: Sarah McLachlan, Pierre Marchand
From the album: *Surfacing*
Produced by: Pierre Marchand
Label: Arista
Year: 1997
Coffeehouse confessional inspired by Laura Nyro, Joni Mitchell, and Kate Bush.

BULLET THE BLUE SKY

Artist: U2
Written by: Paul Hewson (Bono), Dave Evans (Edge), Adam Clayton, Larry Mullen
From the album: *The Joshua Tree*
Label: Island
Produced by: Brian Eno, Daniel Lanois
Year: 1987
After a trip to San Salvador. Suggested segue: "They Dance Alone" by Sting.

BUMP AND GRIND

Artist: R. Kelly
Written by: Robert Kelly
From the album: *12 Play*
Label: Jive
Produced by: Robert Kelly
Year: 1994
Hip hop reduced to its essentials, #1 R&B /#1 crossover.

BUNGLE IN THE JUNGLE

Artist: Jethro Tull
Written by: Ian Anderson
From the album: *War Child*
Label: Chrysalis
Produced by: Terry Ellis, Ian Anderson
Year: 1974
Their second biggest hit, a flute thing.

BURDEN IN MY HAND

Artist: Soundgarden
Written by: Chris Cornell
From the album: *Down on the Upside*
Label: A&M
Year: 1996
Seattle scenesters suffering, like Cobain, from survivor's guilt.

BURN

Artist: Deep Purple
Written by: Ritchie Blackmore, David Coverdale, Jon Lord, Ian Paice
From the album: *Burn*
Label: Warner Brothers
Produced by: Deep Purple
Year: 1974
Basic Blackmore burning on guitar.

BURN ON, BIG RIVER

Artist: Randy Newman
Written by: Randy Newman
From the album: *Sail Away*
Label: Reprise
Produced by: Russ Titelman, Lenny Waronker
Year: 1972
Newman on ecology, celebrating Cleveland's polluted Cuyahoga River. Suggested segues: "Cuyahoga" by R.E.M., "My City Was Gone" by the Pretenders, "Cleveland Rocks" by Ian Hunter, "The Heart of Rock and Roll" by Huey Lewis and the News.

BURN THAT CANDLE

Artist: Bill Haley and His Comets
Written by: Winfield Scott
From the album: *Rock around the Clock*
Label: Decca
Produced by: Milt Gabler
Year: 1955
From one of the genre's best writers, Haley snags a Top 10 hit in the aftermath of "Rock around the Clock."

BURNIN' FOR YOU

Artist: Blue Oyster Cult
Written by: Donald Roeser (Buck Dharma), Richard Meltzer
From the album: *Fire of Unknown Origin*
Label: Columbia
Produced by: Martin Birch
Year: 1981

Completing their journey from the in-joke of master rock journalist Richard Meltzer, to the rock mainstream they once mocked.

BURNING BRIDGES

Artist: Jack Scott
Written by: Melvin Miller
From the album: *Burning Bridges*
Produced by: Ed Carlton
Year: 1960
Second-biggest hit for one of rockabilly's most underrated voices.

BURNING DOWN ONE SIDE

Artist: Robert Plant
Written by: Jezz Woodruffe, Robert Plant, Robbie Blunt
From the album: *Pictures at Eleven*
Label: Swan Song
Produced by: Robert Plant
Year: 1982
Led Zeppelin icon carries forward his trademark moan.

BURNING DOWN THE HOUSE

Artist: Talking Heads
Written by: David Byrne, Chris Frantz, Tina Weymouth, Jerry Harrison
From the album: *Speaking in Tongues*
Label: Sire
Produced by: Talking Heads
Year: 1983
Chanelling their nerdbeat into their biggest hit.

BURNING HEART

Artist: Survivor
Written by: Frankie Sullivan, Jim Peterik
From the album: *Rocky IV Soundtrack*
Label: Scotti Brothers
Produced by: Frank Sullivan, Jim Peterik
Year: 1985
Striking arena-Rocky pay dirt again.

BURNING LOVE

Artist: Elvis Presley
Written by: Dennis Linde
From the album: *Burning Love and Hits from His Movies, Volume 2*
Label: RCA
Year: 1969
Elvis's 38TH and last Top 10 single was introduced by stellar R&B journeyman Arthur Alexander.

BURY MANILOW

Artist: Trotsky Icepick
Written by: Trotsky Icepick
From the album: *Baby*
Label: SST

Year: 1987
Alternative cynicism. Suggested segue: "Debbie Gibson Is Pregnant with My Two-Headed Love Child" by Mojo Nixon and Skid Roper.

BURY MY HEART AT WOUNDED KNEE

Artist: Buffy Sainte-Marie
Written by: Buffy Sainte-Marie
From the album: *Coincidence & Likely Stories*
Label: Ensign/Chrysalis
Year: 1992
Of a piece with her other Native American anthem, "My Country 'Tis of Thy People, You're Dying." Covered by the Indigo Girls (Epic, '95).

BURY MY LOVELY

Artist: October Project
Written by: Julie Flanders, Emil Adler
From the album: *October Project*
Label: Epic
Produced by: Glen Rosenstein
Year: 1993
The Renaissance of the '90s, featuring the ethereal voice of Mary Fahl.

BUS STOP

Artist: The Hollies
Written by: Graham Gouldman
From the album: *Stop, Stop, Stop*
Label: Imperial
Produced by: Ron Richards
Year: 1966
Meeting cute. The ubiquitous Gouldman provides the Hollies with their second biggest hit.

BUST A MOVE

Artist: Young MC
Written by: Marvin Young (Young MC), Matt Dike, Michael Ross
From the album: *Stone Cold Rhymin'*
Label: Delicious
Produced by: Michael Ross, Matt Dike
Year: 1989
Crossover rap—street-smart, but not dangerous.

BUSTED

Artist: Johnny Cash
Written by: Harlan Howard
From the album: *Blood, Sweat and Tears*
Label: Columbia
Produced by: Don Law, Frank Jones
Year: 1963
Broke, not arrested. Top 20 country hit by Cash. Cover by Ray Charles (ABC Paramount, '63) was a Top 10 R&B/Top 10 crossover.

BUSY CHILD

Artist: Crystal Method
Written by: Ken Jordan, Scott Kirkland
From the album: *Outpost*
Produced by: Crystal Method

Label: Geffen
Year: 1997
Studio wizardry epitomizing the new pyschedelica propelled by Ecstacy.

BUT ANYWAY

Artist: Blues Traveler
Written by: Chan Kinchla, John Popper
From the album: *Blues Traveler*
Label: A&M
Produced by: Justin Niebank
Year: 1991
Post-Butterfield harmonica histrionics. Revived in '96.

BUT I DO

Artist: Clarence "Frogman" Henry
Written by: Robert Guidry, Paul Gayten
From the album: *You Always Hurt the One You Love*
Produced by: Allen Toussaint
Label: Argo
Year: 1960
Producer Toussaint stokes his legendary resumé.

BUTTA LOVE

Artist: Next
Written by: Lance Alexander, Tony Tolbert, Roger Huggar, Arkieda Clowers, Darren Lighty
From the album: *Rated Next*
Produced by: KayGee, Darren Lighty
Label: Arista
Year: 1997
A hip hop love song of appreciation, right down to her pretty toes.

BUTTERFLY

Artist: Charlie Gracie
Written by: Cal Mann, Bernie Lowe
Label: Cameo
Year: 1957
Dance groove from Philly, the dance capitol of '50s America and the land of Dick Clark's *American Bandstand*.

BUZZIN' FLY

Artist: Tim Buckley
Written by: Tim Buckley
From the album: *Happy/Sad*
Label: Elektra
Produced by: Jerry Lester
Year: 1969
Bravura performance from a one man jazz/rock/folk/blues fusion.

BY THE TIME I GET TO PHOENIX

Artist: Glen Campbell
Written by: Jimmy Webb
From the album: *By the Time I Get to Phoenix*
Label: Capitol
Produced by: Al DeLory

Year: 1967

Breakup classic is part of the essential cabaret repertoire, mostly in the male division. Reba McEntyre did cover it (MCA, '95), but she was going in the other direction, from Nashville to L.A. to star in her own sitcom.

BYE BYE BABY

Artist: Big Brother and the Holding Company
Written by: R. Powell St. John
From the album: *Big Brother and the Holding Company*
Label: Mainstream
Produced by: John Riney
Year: 1968
Introducing their new lead singer, a salty belter from Texas named Janis Joplin.

BYE BYE BABY

Artist: Mary Wells
Written by: Mary Wells
Label: Motown
Produced by: Smokey Robinson
Year: 1961
Mary's audition tune, which she had written for Jackie Wilson, became her first single (Motown 1003), a Top 10 R&B/Top 50 crossover. Motown 1001 was "My Beloved" by the Sanitones.

BYE BYE BABY (BABY GOODBYE)

Artist: The Four Seasons
Written by: Bob Crewe, Bob Gaudio
From the album: *The Four Seasons Entertain You*
Label: Phillips
Produced by: Bob Crewe
Year: 1965
Ten years later, a cover by the Bay City Rollers (Arista, '75) was the top song of the year in the UK.

BYE BYE BYE

Artist: *NSYNC
Written by: Andreas Carlsson, Kristian Lindin, Jacob Schulze
From the album: *No Strings Attached*
Label: Jive
Year: 2000
Saying goodbye to the boy band era of the late '90s.

BYE BYE LOVE

Artist: The Everly Brothers
Written by: Boudleaux Bryant, Felice Bryant
From the album: *The Everly Brothers*
Label: Cadence
Produced by: Archie Bleyer
Year: 1957
Pristine country harmonies in rockabilly drag; a perfect fit for the new rock and roll market. After dozens of rejections, both the Everly Brothers and this Felice and Boudleaux Bryant tune make the big time.

BYE, BYE, JOHNNY

Artist: Chuck Berry
Written by: Chuck Berry
From the album: *Rockin' at the Hops*
Label: Chess
Produced by: Leonard Chess, Phil Chess
Year: 1960
A live staple of the early Rolling Stones (London, '72).

C

C. C. RIDER

Artist: Chuck Willis
Written by: Ma Rainey, Chuck Willis
Label: Atlantic
Produced by: Ahmet Ertegun, Jerry Wexler
Year: 1957
First crossover hit for the influential R&B singer/songwriter/King of the Stroll. Originated by Blues legend Ma Rainey. Covered by the Animals (MGM, '64).

C.R.E.A.M. (CASH RULES EVERYTHING AROUND ME)

Artist: Wu Tang Clan
From the album: *Enter the Wu-Tang: 36 Chambers*
Written by: Robert Diggs, Jason Hunter, Clifford Smith, Lamont Hawkins, Corey Woods, Dennis Coles, Russell Jones, Gary Grice
Produced by: RZA
Label: Loud
Year: 1993
Downscale rap autobiography, scathing and relentless.

C U WHEN YOU GET THERE

Artist: Coolio and 40 Thevz
Written by: Artis Ivey Jr., Dominick Aldridge, Henry Straughter, Maleek Straughter
From the album: *Nothing to Lose Soundtrack*
Produced by: Romeo
Label: Tommy Boy
Year: 1997
A poetic rap exhortation to his troubled brothers, for the most part unheeded.

ÇA PLANE POUR MOI

Artist: Plastic Bertrand
Written by: Lou Deprijck, Yves Lacomblez, Alan Ward
From the album: *Ça Plane Pour Moi*
Label: Sire
Produced by: Lou Deprijck
Year: 1978
Punk disco novelty from Belgium sung in French.

CADILLAC WALK

Artist: Mink Deville
Written by: John "Moon" Martin
From the album: *Mink DeVille*

Label: Capitol
Year: 1977
Rockabilly redux, in a pink zoot suit. Covered by the writer, John "Moon" Martin (Capitol, '78).

CALENDAR GIRL

Artist: Neil Sedaka
Written by: Howard Greenfield, Neil Sedaka
From the album: *Neil Sedaka Sings His Greatest Hits*
Label: RCA Victor
Produced by: Al Nevins, Don Kirshner
Year: 1961
The kind you see in the dentist's office, rather than *Playboy*. Made into a movie in '94.

CALIFORNIA DREAMIN'

Artist: The Mamas and the Papas
Written by: John Phillips, Michelle Gilliam
From the album: *If You Can Believe Your Eyes and Ears*
Label: Dunhill
Produced by: Lou Adler
Year: 1966
Written in New York City, pondering a Westward move that would symbolize the drift of the culture for the remainder of the decade. Almost recorded by Barry McGuire as the follow-up to "Eve of Destruction," which might have changed everything.

CALIFORNIA GIRLS

Artist: The Beach Boys
Written by: Brian Wilson
From the album: *Shutdown (Vol. II)*
Label: Capitol
Produced by: Brian Wilson
Year: 1964
Their ultimate picture postcard. Covered by the ultimate California man, David Lee Roth (Warner Brothers, '85), with an entirely different sort of girl in mind.

CALIFORNIA LOVE

Artist: 2PAC featuring Dr. Dre and Roger Troutman
Written by: Tupac Shakur, Dr. Dre, Roger Troutman, Larry Troutman, Joe Cocker, Chris Stainton, Michael Hooks, Ronald Hudson
From the album: *All Eyez on Me*
Produced by: Dr. Dre
Label: Death Row
Year: 1995
California as a battleground state in rap's eventually fatal East-West divide. Tupac Shakur was shot and killed in New York in 1996.

CALIFORNIA SUN

Artist: Joe Jones
Written by: Henry Glover, Morris Levy
From the album: *Let's Have a Party*
Label: Roulette
Year: 1961
A couple of the most notorious titans of the early rock and roll era acquire writing credits for this

escapist ditty. The New Orleans soul man, Jones, gets a week on the pop charts. In 1964, the Rivieras, from Indiana, turned it into a major surf classic (Riviera, '64). Covered by a couple of notorious East coast bands, the Dictators (Epic, '75) and the Ramones (Sire, '77).

CALIFORNIA ÜBER ALLES

Artist: Dead Kennedys
Written by: Eric Boucher (Jello Biafra), John Greenway, Michael Franti, Gene Pistel
From the album: *Fresh Fruit for Rotting Vegetables*
Label: I.R.S./Cherry Red
Produced by: East Bay Ray, Jim K.
Year: 1980
First single for the San Francisco hard-core legends; an attack on California governor Jerry Brown.

CALIFORNICATION

Artist: Red Hot Chili Peppers
Written by: Michael (Flea) Balzary, John Frusciante, Anthony Kiedis, Chad Smith
From the album: *Californication*
Produced by: Rick Rubin
Label: Warner Brothers
Year: 2000
Moody rocker about sex, drugs, and Hollywood peaked on the Top 100 at #69.

CALL IT STORMY MONDAY

Artist: T-Bone Walker
Written by: T-Bone Walker
Label: Black & White
Produced by: Ralph Bass
Year: 1947
Barn-burning blues by a guitar monument, who influenced Jimi Hendrix and the rest of the electric blues aristocracy (Clapton, Beck, Page, Bloomfield, Allman, et al). Covered by the Allman Brothers—with Duane (Capricorn, '71).

CALL ME

Artist: Blondie
Written by: Giorgio Moroder, Deborah Harry
From the album: *The Best of Blondie*
Label: Chrysalis
Produced by: Giorgio Moroder
Year: 1980
Debbie does disco. From the Richard Gere movie, *American Gigolo*.

CALL ME

Artist: Aretha Franklin
Written by: Aretha Franklin
From the album: *This Girl's in Love with You*
Label: Atlantic
Produced by: Tom Dowd, Jerry Wexler, Arif Mardin
Year: 1969
#1 R&B/Top 20 crossover. Covered by Phil Perry (Capitol, '91).

CALL ME (COME BACK HOME)

Artist: Al Green
Written by: Al Green, Willie Mitchell, Al Jackson
From the album: *Call Me*
Label: Hi
Produced by: Willie Mitchell
Year: 1973
After a banner '72, Green's effortless soul reaches a creative peak that would not be reflected on the singles chart, which had him moving downhill from there.

CALL ME THE BREEZE

Artist: J. J. Cale
Written by: John J. Cale
From the album: *Naturally*
Label: Shelter
Year: 1972
Covered by Lynyrd Skynyrd (MCA, '74)

CALL ME UP IN DREAMLAND

Artist: Van Morrison
Written by: Van Morrison
From the album: *His Band and Street Choir*
Label: Warner Brothers
Produced by: Van Morrison
Year: 1971
New Orleans revisited by the mystic Irishman.

CALLING DR. LOVE

Artist: Kiss
Written by: Gene Simmons
From the album: *Rock and Roll Over*
Label: Casablanca
Produced by: Eddie Kramer
Year: 1976
Early example of the under-explored Three Stooges influence on rock and roll. Segue: "Walk This Way" by Aerosmith, "The Curly Shuffle" by Jump N the Saddle.

CALLING OCCUPANTS OF INTERPLANETARY CRAFT

Artist: Klaatu
Written by: Terry Draper, John Woloschuk
From the album: *Klaatu*
Label: Capitol
Produced by: Klaatu
Year: 1977
Semi-notorious Beatle hoax netted this obscure Canadian band a cover by the Carpenters (A&M, '77).

CALLING TO YOU

Artist: Robert Plant
Written by: Otis Blackwell, Robert Plant
From the album: *Fate of Nations*
Label: Es Paranza/Atlantic

Year: 1993
Teaming up with a crafty old rock and roll hand.

CAMELLIA

Artist: Hall & Oates
Written by: Daryl Hall, John Oates
From the album: *Daryl Hall and John Oates*
Label: RCA
Produced by: Chris Bond
Year: 1975
Early single set in Atlanta is still one of their all-time best stiffs.

CAN I CHANGE MY MIND

Artist: Tyrone Davis
Written by: Barry Despenza, Carl Wolfolk
From the album: *Can I Change My Mind?*
Label: Dakar
Produced by: Willie Henderson
Year: 1968
Easygoing #1 R&B/Top 10 crossover. Robert Cray was listening.

CAN I GET A WITNESS

Artist: Marvin Gaye
Written by: Eddie Holland, Lamont Dozier, Brian Holland
From the album: *Marvin Gaye/Greatest Hits*
Label: Tamla
Produced by: Brian Holland, Lamont Dozier
Year: 1963
A triumph of Gaye's raw soul. Covered by the Rolling Stones (London, '64), Lee Michaels (A&M, '69).

CAN I KICK IT

Artist: A Tribe Called Quest
Written by: Lou Reed
From the album: *People's Instinctive Travels and the Paths of Rythm*
Label: Jive
Year: 1993
Borrowing a lick and a mood from "A Walk on the Wild Side," Lou Reed's song about the hip white elite's brief flirtation with the drug culture, the new hip hop tribalists kick off their debut album by remaining at the scene of the crime.

CAN I PLAY WITH MADNESS

Artist: Iron Maiden
Written by: Bruce Dickenson, Steve Harris, Adrian Smith
From the album: *Seventh Son of a Seventh Son*
Label: Capitol
Year: 1988
Riding the new wave of metal they helped create.

CAN THE CAN

Artist: Suzi Quatro
Written by: Mike Chapman, Nicky Chinn
From the album: *Suzi Quatro*

Label: Bell
Produced by: Mike Chapman, Nicky Chinn
Year: 1973
#1 UK debut of the petite leather rock goddess stiffed in US.

CAN WE STILL BE FRIENDS

Artist: Todd Rundgren
Written by: Todd Rundgren
From the album: *Hermit of Mink Hollow*
Label: Bearsville
Produced by: Todd Rundgren
Year: 1978
Rock's original auteur at his most Beatlesque.

CAN WE TALK

Artist: Tevin Campbell
Written by: Kenny Edmunds (Babyface), Daryl Simmons
From the album: *I'm Ready*
Label: Qwest
Produced by: Babyface, Daryl Simmons
Year: 1993
New teen hip hop sensation hits sophomore year with not a blemish in sight.

CAN YOU PLEASE CRAWL OUT YOUR WINDOW?

Artist: Bob Dylan
Written by: Bob Dylan
Label: Columbia
Produced by: Tom Wilson
Year: 1965
Forerunner of "Sooner or Later (One of Us Must Know)," the Dylan approach to antiromance, released as a single, which naturally stiffed. First recorded by the Vacels (Kama Sutra, '65), which didn't do half as well.

CAN'T BUY ME LOVE

Artist: The Beatles
Written by: John Lennon, Paul McCartney
From the album: *A Hard Day's Night*
Label: Capitol
Produced by: George Martin
Year: 1964
The third of their six #1 singles of '64.

CAN'T FIGHT THIS FEELING

Artist: Reo Speedwagon
Written by: Kevin Cronin
From the album: *Wheels Are Turning*
Label: Epic
Produced by: Kevin Cronin Jr., Gary Richrath, Alan Gratzer
Year: 1985
Their biggest hit, an arena ballad.

CAN'T FIND MY WAY HOME

Artist: Blind Faith

Written by: Steve Winwood
From the album: *Blind Faith*
Label: Atco
Produced by: Jimmy Miller
Year: 1969
Top track for the British blues/rock supergroup (Clapton, Winwood, Baker, Grech).

CAN'T GET ENOUGH

Artist: Bad Company
Written by: Mick Ralphs
From the album: *Bad Co.*
Label: Swan Song
Produced by: Bad Company
Year: 1974
Their biggest hard rock hit.

CAN'T GET ENOUGH OF YOUR LOVE, BABE

Artist: Barry White
Written by: Barry White
From the album: *Can't Get Enough*
Label: 20TH Century
Produced by: Barry White
Year: 1974
Big in the boudoir; a #1 R&B/#1 crossover.

CAN'T GET IT OUT OF MY HEAD

Artist: Electric Light Orchestra (ELO)
Written by: Jeff Lynne
From the album: *Eldorado*
Label: United Artists
Produced by: Jeff Lynne
Year: 1974
First US Top 10 by the progenitors of the Move.

CAN'T GET THERE FROM HERE

Artist: R.E.M.
Written by: Michael Stipe, Peter Buck, Bill Berry, Mike Mills
From the album: *Fables of the Reconstruction*
Label: IRS
Produced by: Joe Boyd
Year: 1985
Evolving from amateur to semipro, with their jangly alternative to Van Halen. The Blasters and X on one coast, the Smithereens on the other, and Matthew Sweet somewhere in between took heart. In Florida, Tom Petty was smiling.

CAN'T HARDLY WAIT

Artist: The Replacements
Written by: Paul Westerberg
From the album: *Pleased to Meet Me*
Label: Sire
Produced by: Jim Dickinson
Year: 1987
Major label polish and decline.

CAN'T HELP FALLING IN LOVE

Artist: Elvis Presley
Written by: George Weiss, Luigi Creatore, Hugo Peretti
From the album: *Blue Hawaii*
Label: RCA
Produced by: Steve Sholes
Year: 1961
From *Blue Hawaii*, one of his most enduring ballads, covered by UB40 (Virgin, '92). Also covered by Bono in the Elvis-cover crazy film soundtrack of *Honeymoon in Vegas* (Epic Soundtrax, '92).

(CAN'T LIVE WITHOUT YOUR) LOVE AND AFFECTION

Artist: Nelson
Written by: Matt Nelson, Gunnar Nelson, Marc Tanner
From the album: *After the Rain*
Label: Geffen
Produced by: Marc Tanner, David Thoener
Year: 1990
#1 pop rocker for the sons of the late Rick.

CAN'T NOBODY HOLD ME DOWN

Artist: Puff Daddy
Written by: Sean Combs, Steve Jordan, Carlos Brody, Nashiel Myrick, Mason Betha, Greg Prestopino, Matthew Wilder, Sylvia Robinson
From the album: *No Way Out*
Label: Arista
Year: 1997
Early excitement of the sampling form has given way to a Cliff Notes vision of the songwriting craft. The beneficiary here is "Break My Stride" by Matthew Wilder.

CAN'T SEEM TO MAKE YOU MINE

Artist: The Seeds
Written by: Sky Saxon
From the album: *The Seeds*
Label: GNP-Crescendo
Produced by: Marcus Tybalt
Year: 1967
A favorite cut by the cult band's cult band. Covered by Big Star (PVC, '68), the Ramones (Warner Brothers, '94).

CAN'T STAND LOSING YOU

Artist: The Police
Written by: Gordon Summer (Sting)
From the album: *Outlandos D'Amour*
Label: A&M
Produced by: The Police
Year: 1978

Their first UK hit when rereleased in '79, ushering in new wave—the measured, intellectual response to punk.

CAN'T STOP

Artist: After 7
Written by: Kenny (Babyface) Edmunds, Antonio (L.A.) Reid
From the album: *After 7*
Produced by: Babyface, L.A. Reid
Label: Virgin
Year: 1989
#1 R&B hit, with a vocal by Kenny's brother Kevon, who'd later have a solo hit "24/7" (RCA, '99).

CAN'T STOP THIS THING WE STARTED

Artist: Bryan Adams
Written by: Bryan Adams, Robert John "Mutt" Lange
From the album: *Waking up the Neighbors*
Produced by: Mutt Lange
Label: A&M
Year: 1991
Called in Mutt to restore his rock cred; didn't work.

CAN'T TRUSS IT

Artist: Public Enemy
Written by: Carlton Ridenhour, Hank Shocklee, Gary Rinaldo
From the album: *Apocalypse '91 … The Enemy Strikes Black*
Label: Def Jam
Produced by: Stuart Robertz, Cerwin Depper, Gary G. Wiz, the JBL
Year: 1991
Their biggest hit.

CAN'T YOU HEAR MY HEARTBEAT?

Artist: Herman's Hermits
Written by: John Carter, Ken Lewis
From the album: *Hold On*
Label: MGM
Produced by: Mickie Most
Year: 1965
A first British invasion classic.

CAN'T YOU SEE THAT SHE'S MINE

Artist: Dave Clark Five
Written by: Dave Clark, Mike Smith
From the album: *Dave Clark Five Return*
Label: Epic
Produced by: Dave Clark
Year: 1964
Coming in on the coattails of the Beatles.

CANDIDA

Artist: Dawn
Written by: Irwin Levine, Tony Wine
From the album: *Candida*
Label: Bell
Produced by: Hank Medress, Dave Appell
Year: 1970
Most famous Candida other than Candida Donadio, legendary literary agent for Thomas Pynchon, Don Delillo, and others.

CANDLE IN THE WIND

Artist: Elton John
Written by: Elton John, Bernie Taupin
From the album: *Goodbye Yellow Brick Road*
Label: MCA
Produced by: Gus Dudgeon
Year: 1973
Elton and Bernie's Hollywood Fixation Part I, written about Marilyn Monroe. Live version released as a single (MCA, '87). Rewritten as a tribute to Princess Diana after her death and sung at the funeral on television. Went on to become the best-selling single of all time (A&M, '97).

CANDY EVERYBODY WANTS

Artist: 10,000 Maniacs
Written by: Natalie Merchant, Dennis Drew
From the album: *Our Time in Eden*
Label: Elektra
Produced by: Paul Fox
Year: 1993
Sung at the Clinton '92 inaugural along with the Lulu classic, "To Sir with Love."

CANDY GIRL

Artist: The Four Seasons
Written by: Larry Santos
From the album: *Ain't That a Shame and 11 Others*
Label: Vee Jay
Produced by: Bob Crewe
Year: 1963

CANDY GIRL

Artist: New Edition
Written by: Larry Johnson (Maurice Starr), Michael Jonzun
From the album: *Candy Girl*
Label: Streetwise
Produced by: Maurice Starr, Michael Jonzun
Year: 1983
#1 UK/#1 R&B debut for the Boston-based "Next Jackson 5," featuring Bobby Brown, Ralph Tresvant, Ricky Bell, Michael Bivins, and Ronald DeVoe, all future R&B/hip hop legends, including Johnny Gill who replaced Brown in '86. Soon Starr would create the white New Edition and name them New Kids on the Block.

CANDY MAN

Artist: Roy Orbison
Written by: Fred Neil, Beverly Ross
From the album: *Roy Orbison's Greatest Hits*
Label: Monument
Produced by: Fred Foster
Year: 1961
The session guitarist Fred Neil puts a down payment on a condo in Coconut Grove.

CANNONBALL

Artist: The Breeders
Written by: Kim Deal
From the album: *Last Splash*
Label: 4AD/Elektra
Produced by: Kim Deal
Year: 1993
Typifying the hard edge and the soft center of the neo-folk/rock sound of the '90s, Kim Deal's Pixies's side project hits it big.

CANTALOOP (FLIP FANTASIA)

Artist: US3
Written by: Herbie Hancock, Geoff Wilkinson, Mel Simpson
From the album: *Hand on the Torch*
Label: Blue Note
Produced by: Geoff Wilkinson, Mel Simpson
Year: 1993
Nifty hip bop concoction, based on Hancock's jazz classic "Cantalope Island" (Columbia, '76).

CAPPUCINO

Artist: MC Lyte
Written by: MC Lyte (Lana Moorer), Aquil Davidson, Markel Riley, Walter Scott
From the album: *Eyes on This*
Label: First Priority
Year: 1989
Spunky Brooklyn rapper visits the next world.

CAPTAIN FOR DARK MORNINGS

Artist: Laura Nyro
Written by: Laura Nyro
From the album: *New York Tendaberry*
Label: Columbia
Produced by: Roy Halee, Laura Nyro
Year: 1969
Nyro at the extremes of her melodic, romantic, spaced-out urban soul is the missing link between Carole King and Janis Joplin.

CAPTAIN JACK

Artist: Billy Joel
Written by: Billy Joel
From the album: *Billy Joel*
Label: Columbia
Produced by: Phil Ramone
Year: 1971
The angry young man from Long Island rants about the alternate culture.

CAPTAIN'S DEAD

Artist: Guided By Voices
Written by: Robert Pollard
From the album: *Devil Between My Toes*
Label: Schwa
Year: 1987
Introducing a quirky new voice on the underground lo-fi scene.

CAR ON A HILL

Artist: Joni Mitchell
Written by: Joni Mitchell
From the album: *Court and Spark*
Label: Asylum
Produced by: Joni Mitchell
Year: 1974
After-hours cocktail jazz for survivors of the folk/rock and sexual revolutions.

CAR WASH

Artist: Rose Royce
Written by: Norman Whitfield
From the album: *I Wanna Get Next to You*
Label: MCA
Produced by: Norman Whitfield
Year: 1977
#1 R&B/#1 crossover from the movie *Car Wash*.

CAR WHEELS ON A GRAVEL ROAD

Artist: Lucinda Williams
Written by: Lucinda Williams
From the album: *Car Wheels on a Gravel Road*
Produced by: Roy Bittan, Lucinda Williams
Label: Mercury
Year: 1998
Atmospheric middle-of-the-dirt-road classic.

CARA MIA

Artist: Jay and the Americans
Written by: Bunny Lewis (Tulio Tropani), Annunzio Mantovani (Lee Lange)
From the album: *Blockbusters*
Label: United Artists
Year: 1965
Introduced in England by David Whittield and Mantovani (London, '54). Buoyed by Elvis's and Jackie Wilson's forays into the light-opera realms, Jay Black plumbs to the roots of Italian soul with this cover of the British million seller.

CARAVAN

Artist: Van Morrison
Written by: Van Morrison
From the album: *Astral Weeks*
Label: Warner Brothers
Produced by: Lee Merenstein
Year: 1969
A rambling song, for born-again gypsies.

CARAVAN OF LOVE

Artist: Isley/Jasper/Isley
Written by: Ernest Isley, Marvin Isley, Chris Jasper
From the album: *Caravan of Love*
Label: CBS Associated
Produced by: Ernest Isley, Marvin Isley, Chris Jasper
Year: 1985
#1 R&B/Top 10 crossover. Cover by the Housemartins went to #1 UK (Elektra, '86).

CARBONA NOT GLUE

Artist: The Ramones
Written by: Douglas Colvin, John Cummings, Jeff Hyman, Thomas Erdelyi
From the album: *Leave Home*
Label: Sire
Produced by: Tony Bongiovi, Thomas Erdelyi
Year: 1977
Reviving the art of getting high on the sly. Suggested segue: "Mellow Yellow" by Donovan.

CAREFREE HIGHWAY

Artist: Gordon Lightfoot
Written by: Gordon Lightfoot
From the album: *Sundown*
Label: Reprise
Produced by: Lenny Waronker
Year: 1974
Rambling song for folks who prefer to do their rambling in an SUV.

CAREFUL THERE'S A BABY IN THE HOUSE

Artist: Loudon Wainwright III
Written by: Loudon Wainwright III
From the album: *Album II*
Label: Atlantic
Year: 1971
The James Thurber of folk rock, knocking around the house of domesticity.

CARELESS WHISPER

Artist: Wham!
Written by: George Michael, Andrew Ridgeley
From the album: *Make It Big*
Label: Columbia
Produced by: George Michael
Year: 1984
Listed as Wham! on the label in the US, George Michael in the UK. Who could tell the difference?

CAREY

Artist: Joni Mitchell
Written by: Joni Mitchell
From the album: *Blue*
Label: Reprise
Produced by: Joni Mitchell
Year: 1971
Her uncharactistically lighthearted travelogue of a second single was a bigger stiff than the first, "Big Yellow Taxi."

CARIBBEAN QUEEN (NO MORE LOVE ON THE RUN)

Artist: Billy Ocean
Written by: Keith Diamond, Billy Ocean
From the album: *Suddenly*
Label: Jive
Produced by: Keith Diamond
Year: 1984
From England by way of Trinidad, Ocean relaunches his career with a #1 R&B/#1 crossover that was originally called "European Queen."

CARMELITA

Artist: Warren Zevon
Written by: Warren Zevon
From the album: *Warren Zevon*
Label: Asylum
Produced by: Jackson Browne
Year: 1976
Mythologizing the romance of drugs, something which he'd never outgrow. Covered by Linda Ronstadt (Asylum, '77), Counting Crows (DGC, '99).

CARNIVAL

Artist: Natalie Merchant
Written by: Natalie Merchant
From the album: *Tigerlily*
Label: Elektra
Produced by: Natalie Merchant
Year: 1995
Nasal nocturnal celebration from the former leader of 10,000 Maniacs is at odds with the earthier, angrier chants issued by many other female singers this year.

CAROL

Artist: Chuck Berry
Written by: Chuck Berry
From the album: *Chuck Berry Is on Top*
Label: Chess
Produced by: Leonard Chess, Phil Chess
Year: 1958
One of his hardest rockers; covered by the Rolling Stones (London, '64).

CAROLINA IN MY MIND

Artist: James Taylor
Written by: James Taylor
From the album: *James Taylor*
Label: Apple
Produced by: Peter Asher
Year: 1969
Previewing the laid-back mellow sound of the '70s, New England's Sweet Baby James dreams of the Southland while recording in London on the Beatles label with the brother of Paul's old girlfriend, Jane Asher, producing. Covered by the Everly Brothers (Warner Brothers, '69), Melanie (Buddah, '70).

CAROLINE, NO

Artist: The Beach Boys
Written by: Brian Wilson
From the album: *Pet Sounds*
Label: Capitol
Produced by: Brian Wilson

Year: 1966
Homemade recording, complete with barking dogs, is beautiful and anguished, like its composer, who, years later in an interview, suggested that his intended title was "Carol I Know."

CARRIE-ANNE

Artist: The Hollies
Written by: Allan Clarke, Graham Nash, Tony Hicks
From the album: *Evolution*
Label: Epic
Produced by: Ron Richards
Year: 1967
Harmonizing in the tube station.

CARRY IT ON

Artist: Judy Collins
Written by: Gil Turner
From the album: *5th*
Label: Elektra
Produced by: Mark Abramson, Jac Holzman
Year: 1965
Civil-rights-era standard bearer.

CARRY ON

Artist: Crosby, Stills, Nash & Young
Written by: Stephen Stills
From the album: *Déjà Vu*
Produced by: Crosby, Stills, Nash & Young
Label: Atlantic,
Year: 1970
Crusading for justice, top down on the L.A. Freeway.

CARRY ON WAYWARD SON

Artist: Kansas
Written by: Kerry Livgren
From the album: *Leftoverture*
Label: Kirshner
Produced by: Jeff Glixman
Year: 1976
Inspirational arena-sized folk/rocker was their first hit.

CARRY THAT WEIGHT

Artist: The Beatles
Written by: John Lennon, Paul McCartney
From the album: *Abbey Road*
Label: Apple
Produced by: George Martin
Year: 1969
Part of the legendary "Medley" that concludes with "and in the end the love you make/is equal to the love you take."

CARS

Artist: Gary Numan
Written by: Gary Numan
From the album: *The Pleasure Principal*
Label: Atco
Produced by: Gary Numan
Year: 1980
His lone American hit presages the coming Euro invasion of the Eurythmics and A Flock of Seagulls.

CASANOVA

Artist: Levert
Written by: Reggie Calloway
From the album: *The Big Throwdown*
Label: Atlantic
Produced by: Reggie Calloway
Year: 1987
#1 R&B/Top 10 crossover for the second generation O'Jays.

CASE OF YOU, A

Artist: Joni Mitchell
Written by: Joni Mitchell
From the album: *Blue*
Produced by: Joni Mitchell
Label: Reprise
Year: 1971
From her first magnum opus, gleefully revealing her copious needs.

CASEY JONES

Artist: Grateful Dead
Written by: Jerry Garcia
From the album: *Workingman's Dead*
Label: Warner Brothers
Produced by: Bob Matthews, Betty Cantor, the Grateful Dead
Year: 1970
Updating an epic American cautionary folk tale originally recorded by Billy Murray and the American Quartet (Victor, '10).

CASSIDY

Artist: Bob Weir
Written by: John Barlow
From the album: *Ace*
Label: Warner Brothers
Year: 1972
Immortalizing the Kerouac hero, Neil Cassidy. Suggested segues: "On the Road" by Aztec Two-Step, "Hey Jack Kerouac" by 10,000 Maniacs.

CAST YOUR FATE TO THE WIND

Artist: Vince Guaraldi Trio
Written by: Vince Guaraldi
From the album: *Jazz Impressions of Black Orpheus*
Label: Fantasy
Year: 1962
Evocative jazz/rock classic spawned a generation of hitchhikers.

CASTLES MADE OF SAND

Artist: Jimi Hendrix
Written by: Jimi Hendrix
From the album: *Axis: Bold as Love*
Label: Reprise
Produced by: Chas Chandler
Year: 1968
Gentle lament pondering the verities of nature. Segue: "The Tide Is High" by Blondie.

CASUAL LOOK, A

Artist: The Six Teens
Written by: Ed Wells
Label: Flip
Year: 1956
A passing doo-wop glance.

CAT SCRATCH FEVER

Artist: Ted Nugent
Written by: Ted Nugent
From the album: *Cat Scratch Fever*
Label: Epic
Produced by: Tom Werman, Lew Futterman, Cliff Davies
Year: 1977
The traditional arena rock itch as performed by a master marksman. Suggested segues: "Stray Cat Blues" by the Rolling Stones, "Hot Blooded" by Foreigner.

CAT'S IN THE CRADLE

Artist: Harry Chapin
Written by: Harry Chapin, Sandra Chapin
From the album: *Verities and Balderdash*
Label: Elektra
Produced by: Paul Leka
Year: 1974
Moralizing tale of a father and son too busy for each other. Covered by Ugly Kid Joe (Mercury, '94).

CATCH THE WIND

Artist: Donovan
Written by: Donovan Leitch
From the album: *Catch the Wind*
Label: Hickory
Produced by: Steve Hoffman
Year: 1965
Gossamer folk/rock standard, covered by the Blues Project at their most gossamer (Verve/Folkways, '66).

CATCH US IF YOU CAN

Artist: Dave Clark Five
Written by: Dave Clark, Lenny Davidson
From the album: *Having a Wild Weekend*
Label: Epic
Produced by: Dave Clark
Year: 1965
Popcorn from the film.

CATFISH

Artist: Joe Cocker
Written by: Bob Dylan
From the album: *Stingray*

Label: A&M
Year: 1976
An ode to baseball's pioneering free agent, Catfish Hunter. Recorded by Dylan (Columbia, '91).

CATHOLIC SCHOOL GIRLS RULE

Artist: Red Hot Chili Peppers
Written by: Anthony Kiedis, Michael Balzary (Flea), Hirth Martinez
From the album: *Freaky Styley*
Label: Enigma
Produced by: George Clinton
Year: 1985
The notorious S.F. posers get off to a funking good start, courtesy of their mentor in crime, George Clinton. Suggested segue: "Only the Good Die Young" by Billy Joel.

CATHY'S CLOWN

Artist: The Everly Brothers
Written by: Don Everly, Phil Everly
From the album: *A Date with the Everly Brothers*
Label: Warner Brothers
Produced by: Wesley Rose
Year: 1960
After signing with Warner Brothers for a cool million, they launched the label with the biggest hit of their career, Don's magnum opus, inspired by an old girlfriend. Went to #1 in the US and the UK.

CAUGHT IN A MOSH

Artist: Anthrax
Written by: Joey Belladonna, Frank Bello, Charles Benante, Ian Rosenfeld, Dan Spitz
From the album: *Among the Living*
Produced by: Eddie Kramer
Label: Megaforce
Year: 1987
Defining the new speedcore dance floor scrum.

CAUGHT UP IN YOU

Artist: .38 Special
Written by: Jeff Carlisi, Don Barnes, Jim Peterik, Frankie Sullivan
From the album: *Special Forces*
Label: A&M
Produced by: Rodney Mills
Year: 1982
Mellowing their Southern rock sound for a chart run. Sullivan and Peterik would move on to Survivor.

CAUSE WE'VE ENDED AS LOVERS

Artist: Syreeta
Written by: Stevie Wonder
From the album: *Stevie Wonder Presents Syreeta*
Label: Motown
Produced by: Stevie Wonder
Year: 1974

Stevie's heartbreaking farewell to his soon-to-be ex-wife, Syretta Wright. Covered by Jeff Beck (Epic, '75).

CAUSING A COMMOTION

Artist: Madonna
Written by: Steve Bray, Madonna Ciccone
From the album: *Who's That Girl Soundtrack*
Label: Sire
Produced by: Steve Bray, Madonna
Year: 1987
The only good thing to come out of the movie.

C'EST LA VIE

Artist: Robbie Nevil
Written by: Robbie Nevil
From the album: *Robbie Nevil*
Label: Manhattan
Year: 1987
In a Richard Marx L.A. studio groove.

C'EST LA VIE (YOU NEVER CAN TELL)

Artist: Chuck Berry
Written by: Chuck Berry
From the album: *St. Louis to Liverpool*
Label: Chess
Produced by: Leonard Chess, Phil Chess
Year: 1964
Philosophizing over a boogie beat. Covered by Emmylou Harris (Warner Brothers, '77). Featured in the movie *Pulp Fiction*.

CEASE TO EXIST

Artist: Red Cross
Written by: Charles Manson
From the album: *Born Innocent*
Label: Smoke 7
Year: 1982
Taking their Los Angelino punk mythology too far with a song from the pen of the demonic killer.

CECILIA

Artist: Simon and Garfunkel
Written by: Paul Simon
From the album: *Bridge over Troubled Water*
Label: Columbia
Produced by: Roy Halee, Paul Simon, Art Garfunkel
Year: 1969
A no-account street girl encountered on the stoop. Julio was loitering nearby.

CELEBRATE

Artist: Three Dog Night
Written by: Garry Bonner, Alan Gordon
From the album: *Suitable for Framing*
Label: Dunhill
Produced by: Gabriel Mekler
Year: 1970
All-time frat-party anthem.

CELEBRATED SUMMER

Artist: Hüsker Dü
Written by: Bob Mould
From the album: *New Day Rising*
Label: SST
Produced by: Bob Mould
Year: 1985
Midwestern Sonic Youth, with a Dead Boys attitude and Richard Thompson leanings.

CELEBRATION

Artist: Kool & the Gang
Written by: Robert Bell, Kool & the Gang, Eumir Deodato
From the album: *Celebrate*
Label: De-Lite
Produced by: Eumir Deodato
Year: 1980
Their only #1 R&B/#1 crossover; disco is dead, long live funk.

CELEBRITY SKIN

Artist: Hole
Written by: Hole
From the album: *Live through This*
Produced by: Michael Beinhorn
Label: Geffen
Year: 1998
As only celebrity-like Courtney Love could experience it.

CELLULOID HEROES

Artist: The Kinks
Written by: Ray Davies
From the album: *Everybody's in Showbiz, Everybody's a Star*
Label: RCA
Produced by: Ray Davies
Year: 1972
Purging his movie obsessions. Suggested segue: "Candle in the Wind" by Elton John.

CENTERFIELD

Artist: John Fogerty
Written by: John C. Fogerty
From the album: *Centerfield*
Label: Warner Brothers
Produced by: John C. Fogerty
Year: 1985
Aching to get off the bench and return to the show. The antidote to Cashman and West's baseball odes. Cast perfectly into the *Bull Durham* soundtrack (Capitol, '88).

CENTERFOLD

Artist: The J. Geils Band
Written by: Seth Justman
From the album: *Freeze-Frame*
Label: EMI-America
Produced by: Seth Justman
Year: 1982

The Boston bar band gains a long-awaited #1 in the video age with a perfectly appropriate—if patently unbelievable—storyline.

CENTRAL RESERVATION

Artist: Beth Orton
Written by: Beth Orton
From the album: *Central Reservation*
Label: DeConstruction
Produced by: Ben Watt
Year: 1999
Evoking British folk enchantresses like Maggie Haslip and Sandy Denny in a treatise on deviance.

CERTAIN GIRL, A

Artist: Ernie K-Doe
Written by: Allen Toussaint (Naomi Neville)
Label: Minit
Produced by: Allen Toussaint
Year: 1961
Early New Orleans classic treasured in England. Covered by the Final Gear (Pye, '64), Jimmy Page, and the Yardbirds (Epic, '65) as the B-side of "I Wish You Would," as well as Warren Zevon (Asylum, '80).

CHAIN GANG

Artist: Sam Cooke
Written by: Sam Cooke
From the album: *The Best of Sam Cooke*
Label: RCA
Produced by: Hugo & Luigi
Year: 1960
First hit on RCA and biggest since "You Send Me" could have been a metaphor for all indentured servitude, from professional recording to professional sports. But rocked better than most; a #2 R&B/#2 crossover for the ultimate soul man.

CHAIN GANG

Artist: Bobby Scott
Written by: Sol Quasha, Herb Yakus
From the album: *Scott Free*
Label: ABC Paramount
Year: 1956
Early taste of jazz/rock.

CHAIN OF FOOLS

Artist: Aretha Franklin
Written by: Don Covay
From the album: *Lady Soul*
Label: Atlantic
Produced by: Jerry Wexler
Year: 1967
Paying her respects to the masters, Wexler and Covay, Aretha notches her fourth #1 R&B/Top 10 crossover of the year. This was the tune playing during John Travolta's second greatest dance sequence, in the movie *Michael*.

CHAIN, THE

Artist: Fleetwood Mac
Written by: Lindsay Buckingham, Stephanie Nicks, Christine McVie, John McVie, Mick Fleetwood
From the album: *Rumours*
Label: Warner Brothers
Produced by: Richard Dashut, Ken Caillat, Fleetwood Mac
Year: 1977
From their double breakup breakout album, a dire chant.

CHAINS

Artist: The Cookies
Written by: Gerry Goffin, Carole King
Label: Dimension
Produced by: Gerry Goffin
Year: 1962
A good day at the office for the stellar songwriting team of Goffin and King. Covered by the Beatles (Veejay, '64) as a token of their Brill Building esteem.

CHAINS OF LOVE

Artist: Erasure
Written by: Andy Bell, Vince Clarke
From the album: Innocents
Produced by: Stephen Hague
Label: Sire
Year: 1988
Europop disco smash.

CHAINS OF LOVE

Artist: Joe Turner
Written by: Ahmet Ertegun, Van Walls
Label: Atlantic
Year: 1951
Big R&B hit for the honey-throated Kansas City blues man. Covered by Pat Boone (Dot, '56), Bobby Bland (Duke, '69).

CHAMPAGNE SUPERNOVA

Artist: Oasis
Written by: Noel Gallagher
From the album: *What's the Story, Morning Glory*
Produced by: Owen Morris
Label: Epic
Year: 1995
A toast to the Beatles.

CHANGE IS GONNA COME, A

Artist: Sam Cooke
Written by: Sam Cooke
From the album: *Ain't That Good News*
Label: RCA Victor
Produced by: Hugo and Luigi
Year: 1964
The B-side of "Shake," Sam's enduring hopeful anthem, a soulful, pointed response to "Blowin' in the Wind," was released as a single only after his death in December, '64. Covered by Aretha Franklin (Atlantic, '67).

CHANGE OF HEART

Artist: Cyndi Lauper
Written by: Essra Mohawk
From the album: *True Colors*
Label: Portrait
Produced by: Lenny Petze, Cyndi Lauper
Year: 1986
The campy Brooklyn diva meets Philly's Secret Diva, the former Zappa chorus girl, AKA Uncle Meat, who achieved a long-awaited songwriting mini-epiphany, nearly equal to when the Shangri-Las recorded her "I'll Never Learn" (Mercury, '66).

CHANGE THE WORLD

Artist: Eric Clapton and Babyface
Written by: Tommy Sims, Gordon Kennedy, Wayne Kirkpatrick
From the album: *Phenomenom Soundtrack*
Produced by: Babyface
Label: Reprise
Year: 1996
Originally recorded by country singer Wynonna (Curb, '96).

CHANGE YOUR MIND

Artist: Neil Young with Crazy Horse
Written by: Neil Young
From the album: *Sleeps with Angels*
Label: Reprise
Produced by: David Briggs, Neil Young
Year: 1994
Neil dedicated this tune to his surrogate rock and roll heir, the late Kurt Cobain of Nirvana.

CHANGED THE LOCKS

Artist: Lucinda Williams
Written by: Lucinda Williams
From the album: *Lucinda Williams*
Produced by: Lucinda Williams, Dusty Wakeman
Label: Rough Trade
Year: 1988
Early cow/punk portrait of the artist as a woman scorned. Covered by Tom Petty (Warner Brothers, '96).

CHANGES

Artist: David Bowie
Written by: David Bowie
From the album: *Hunky Dory*
Label: RCA
Produced by: Ken Scott
Year: 1971
Rock's first fashion guru identifies change as a concept, a niche, a trend, a market, with a stutter borrowed from Roger Daltrey.

CHANGES

Artist: Phil Ochs
Written by: Phil Ochs
From the album: *Phil Ochs in Concert*
Label: Elektra

Produced by: Paul Rothchild
Year: 1966
Nailing the generational malaise, and almost getting a hit single. Covered by Crispian St. Peters (Janus, '66), Jim and Jean (Elektra, '66). Suggested segue: "Urge for Going" by Tom Rush.

CHANGES

Artist: 2PAC
Written by: Tupac Shakur, Bruce Hornsby
From the album: *Best Of*
Label: Amaru Death Row
Year: 1999
Posthumous release, utilizing Bruce Hornsby's "The Way It Is" as part of an updated tale of greater caution.

CHANTILLY LACE

Artist: The Big Bopper
Written by: J. P. Richardson
From the album: *Chantilly Lace*
Label: Mercury
Year: 1958
How Wolfman Jack might have sounded had he decided to cut a record of his act.

CHAPEL OF LOVE

Artist: The Dixie Cups
Written by: Jeff Barry, Ellie Greenwich, Phil Spector
From the album: *Chapel of Love*
Label: Red Bird
Produced by: Jerry Leiber, Mike Stoller, Jeff Barry
Year: 1964
Grasping the last Brill Building sure thing: girl-group innocence and wedded bliss.

CHARITY BALL

Artist: Fanny
Written by: June Millington, Jean Millington, Alice DeBuhe
From the album: *Charity Ball*
Label: Reprise
Produced by: Richard Perry
Year: 1971
Femme rock with balls.

CHARLIE BROWN

Artist: The Coasters
Written by: Jerry Leiber, Mike Stoller
From the album: *Yakety Yak*
Label: Atco
Produced by: Jerry Leiber, Mike Stoller
Year: 1959
If not their most enduring novelty, certainly their most cartoonish.

CHARLIE FREAK

Artist: Steely Dan
Written by: Donald Fagen, Walter Becker
From the album: *Pretzel Logic*

Label: ABC
Produced by: Gary Katz
Year: 1974
An ode to those who didn't survive the '60s.

CHEATING IN THE NEXT ROOM

Artist: Z. Z. Hill
Written by: George Jackson, Robert Alton Miller
From the album: *Down Home*
Label: Malaco
Year: 1981
Bluesy breakthrough nearly 20 years into a soulful career.

CHECK YO SELF

Artist: Ice Cube
Written by: O' Shea Jackson (Ice Cube)
From the album: *The Predator*
Label: Priority
Produced by: DJ Pooh
Year: 1992
#1 R&B/Top-20 crossover statement of rap priorities from the founding lyricist of NWA, one of the most outspoken of gangsta rap groups.

CHEESEBURGER IN PARADISE

Artist: Jimmy Buffett
Written by: Jimmy Buffett
From the album: *Son of a Son of a Sailor*
Label: ABC
Produced by: Norbert Putnam
Year: 1978
Celebrating the simple joys of sloth. A nice career if you could get it, and he did.

CHELSEA GIRL

Artist: Nico
Written by: Lou Reed, Sterling Morrison
From the album: *Chelsea Girl*
Label: Verve
Produced by: Tom Wilson
Year: 1967
Title song from the Andy Warhol cult classic film about sleazy living, from which Lou Reed derived a lifetime of material.

CHELSEA HOTEL #2

Artist: Leonard Cohen
Written by: Leonard Cohen
From the album: *New Skin for an Old Ceremony*
Label: Columbia
Produced by: Leonard Cohen, John Lissauer
Year: 1974
Evoking the bohemian ghost of the '60s, when poets and blues singers briefly ruled over beautiful long-haired guitarists, and Janis Joplin and Leonard Cohen made the Chelsea New York's version of Hollywood's Sunset Marquis. Covered by Lloyd Cole (Atlantic, '91).

CHELSEA MORNING

Artist: Joni Mitchell
Written by: Joni Mitchell
From the album: *Clouds*
Label: Reprise
Produced by: Joni Mitchell
Year: 1969
Painterly cityscape. Future favorite song of future President Bill Clinton. Covered by Judy Collins (Elektra, '69).

CHEMICALS BETWEEN US, THE

Artist: Bush
Written by: Gavin Rossdale
From the album: *The Science of Things*
Label: Trauma
Year: 1999
Caustic post-modern commentary.

CHEREE

Artist: Suicide
Written by: Alan Vega, Martin Rev
From the album: *Suicide*
Label: Red Star
Produced by: Craig Leon, Marty Thau
Year: 1977
Experimental Bowery cult band expands on Lou Reed's bleak Manhattan vision.

CHERISH

Artist: The Association
Written by: Terry Kirkman
From the album: *And Then … Along Comes the Association*
Label: Valiant
Year: 1966
Enduring folk/rock love ballad.

CHERISH

Artist: Kool & the Gang
Written by: Ronald Bell, Kool & the Gang, James Bonneford
From the album: *Emergency*
Label: De-Lite
Produced by: Ronald Bell, Kool & the Gang, James Bonneford
Year: 1984
Their 9TH #1 R&B and 6TH Top 10 crossover.

CHERISH

Artist: Madonna
Written by: Patrick Leonard, Madonna Ciccone
From the album: *Like a Prayer*
Label: Sire
Produced by: Patrick Leonard, Madonna
Year: 1989
Finishing the '80s with her 16TH Top 5 single in a row.

CHERRY BOMB

Artist: John (Cougar) Mellencamp
Written by: John Cougar Mellencamp
From the album: *The Lonesome Jubilee*
Label: Mercury
Produced by: Don Gehman, John Mellencamp
Year: 1987
Heartland nostalgia. Suggested Segue: "Night Moves" by Bob Seger.

CHERRY BOMB

Artist: The Runaways
Written by: Joan Jett, Kim Fowley
From the album: *The Runaways*
Label: Mercury
Produced by: Kim Fowley
Year: 1976
Jailbait anthem for the all-girl metal band featuring future guitar goddesses Joan Jett and Lita Ford. Covered by Joan Jett with L7 (Epic, '95).

CHERRY OH BABY

Artist: Eric Donaldson
Written by: Eric Donaldson
Label: Trojan
Produced by: Tommy Cowan, Bunny Lee
Year: 1971
Reggae classic, covered by the Rolling Stones (Rolling Stones, '76), UB40 (A&M, '83).

CHERRY PIE

Artist: Marvin and Johnny
Written by: Marvin Phillips, Joe Josea
Label: Modern
Produced by: Art Rupe
Year: 1954
Doo-wop mouthful, covered by Skip and Flip (Brent, '60).

CHERRY PIE

Artist: Warrant
Written by: Jani Lane
From the album: *Cherry Pie*
Label: Columbia
Produced by: Beau Hill
Year: 1990
From the Kiss School of Euphemism.

CHERRY, CHERRY

Artist: Neil Diamond
Written by: Neil Diamond
From the album: *The Feel of Neil Diamond*
Label: Bang
Produced by: Jeff Barry, Ellie Greenwich
Year: 1966
First big hit for the missing link between Gary Lewis and Gary Puckett.

CHERRY-COLOURED FUNK

Artist: Cocteau Twins
Written by: Cocteau Twins
From the album: *Heaven or Las Vegas*
Label: 4AD/Capitol
Produced by: Cocteau Twins
Year: 1990
A breath of artistic life into this moody, meandering band that previously made the Cowboy Junkies seem like speedcore thrashers.

CHEST FEVER

Artist: The Band
Written by: Robbie Robertson
From the album: *Music from Big Pink*
Label: Capitol
Produced by: John Simon, the Band
Year: 1968
Organic rock.

CHESTNUT MARE

Artist: The Byrds
Written by: Roger McGuinn, Jacques Levy
From the album: *The Byrds (Untitled)*
Label: Columbia
Produced by: Terry Melcher, Jim Dickson
Year: 1970
A hootenanny hoedown. Levy would collaborate with Dylan and Leonard Cohen.

CHEVY VAN

Artist: Sammy Johns
Written by: Sammy Johns
From the album: *Sammy Johns*
Label: GRC
Produced by: Larry Knechtel
Year: 1975
#1 country crossover for the first anticlassic car song. Suggested segues: "Convoy" by C. W. McCall, "Like a Rock" by Bob Seger.

CHEYENNE

Artist: The Del Lords
Written by: Scott Kempner
From the album: *Based on a True Story*
Label: Enigma
Produced by: Neil Giraldo
Year: 1988
The garage band sound of some New York City dreamers.

CHICAGO

Artist: Graham Nash
Written by: Graham Nash
From the album: *Songs for Beginners*
Label: Atlantic
Produced by: Graham Nash
Year: 1971
Outside agitating at the Democratic convention of '68, where the Baby Boom electorate, at their first official gathering, helped to ensure the election of their nemesis, Richard M. Nixon.

CHICKEN SHACK BOOGIE

Artist: Amos Milburn
Written by: Amos Milburn
Label: Aladdin
Year: 1948
The first #1 R&B hit for the pioneering stylist (reissued in '56). Fats Domino was listening. The Rolling Stones were listening to Milburn's cover of the '40 Don Raye classic, "Down the Road Apiece," which they would cover in '65.

CHILD OF MINE

Artist: Carole King
Written by: Carole King
From the album: *Carole King: Writer*
Label: Ode
Produced by: John Fischbach
Year: 1971
Preparing for the keyboard playing singer/songwriter era she, Billy Joel, and Elton John would usher in.

CHILDHOOD

Artist: Michael Jackson
Written by: Michael Jackson
From the album: *HISstory*
Label: Epic
Year: 1995
According to Jackson, his defining lyric and mea culpa. Theme from the movie *Free Willy 2*.

CHILDREN OF GOD

Artist: The Swans
Written by: Michael Gira, Jarboe
From the album: *Children of God*
Label: Caroline
Year: 1987
Peak moment from the experimental New York art/rock droners.

CHILDREN OF THE FUTURE

Artist: Steve Miller Band
Written by: Steve Miller
From the album: *Children of the Future*
Label: Capitol
Produced by: Glyn Johns, Steve Miller
Year: 1968
They would all live happily ever after in San Francisco and play the Chicago blues.

CHILDREN OF THE GRAVE

Artist: Black Sabbath
Written by: Tony Iommi, Geezer Butler, Ozzy Osbourne, Bill Ward
From the album: *Master of Reality*
Label: Warner Brothers
Produced by: Rodger Bain
Year: 1971
Reinventing the Addams Family as a rock concert conceit. Covered by Ozzy Osbourne (Jet, '82) and on his tribute album to his legendary late guitarist Randy Rhoads (CBS Associated, '87).

CHILDREN OF THE REVOLUTION

Artist: T. Rex
Written by: Marc Bolan
Label: EMI
Produced by: Tony Visconti
Year: 1972
Nonalbum rarity hit #2 in England.

CHIMES OF FREEDOM

Artist: Bob Dylan
Written by: Bob Dylan
From the album: *Another Side of Bob Dylan*
Label: Columbia
Produced by: Tom Wilson
Year: 1964
A freedom song, of a personal sort, for "every strung out person in the whole wide universe." Covered by the Byrds (Columbia, '65), Bruce Springsteen (Columbia, '86).

CHINA CAT SUNFLOWER

Artist: Grateful Dead
Written by: Jerry Garcia, Robert Hunter
From the album: *Aoxomoxoa*
Label: Warner Brothers
Produced by: Bob Matthew, Betty Cantor
Year: 1969
A mystical, translucent ball of twine.

CHINA GIRL

Artist: Iggy Pop
Written by: David Bowie
From the album: *The Idiot*
Label: RCA
Produced by: David Bowie
Year: 1977
Covered by David Bowie (EMI-America, '83).

CHINA GROVE

Artist: The Doobie Brothers
Written by: Tom Johnston
From the album: *What Were Once Vices Are Now Habits*
Label: Warner Brothers
Produced by: Ted Templeman
Year: 1973
Pastoral, almost ballpark rock.

CHINESE ROCKS

Artist: The Heartbreakers
Written by: Douglas Colvin (Dee Dee Ramone), Richard Meyer (Richard Hell)
From the album: *L.A.M.F.*
Label: Track
Year: 1977
Documenting the heyday of American glam, written by two punk legends.

CHLOE DANCER/CROWN OF THORNS

Artist: Mother Love Bone

Written by: Andrew Wood, Mother Love Bone
From the album: *Shine*
Label: Stardog
Year: 1989
Crucial Seattle scene track. Included in the Cameron Crowe movie homage *Singles* (Epic, '92).

CHOICE OF COLORS

Artist: The Impressions
Written by: Curtis Mayfield
From the album: *Young Mods' Forgotten Story*
Label: Curtom
Produced by: Curtis Mayfield
Year: 1969
#1 R&B/Top 20 crossover.

CHOKIN' KIND, THE

Artist: Waylon Jennings
Written by: Harlan Howard
From the album: *Hangin' On*
Label: RCA
Produced by: Chet Atkins
Year: 1967
Top 10 country hit for the former Cricket turned country outlaw. Cover by Joe Simon was his first #1 R&B/Top 20 crossover (Sound Stage 7, '69).

CHOO CHOO CH'BOOGIE

Artist: Louis Jordan and His Tympani Five
Written by: Vaughan Horton, Denver Darling, Milt Gabler
Label: Decca
Produced by: Milt Gabler
Year: 1946
One of the biggest R&B hits of all time, and a Top 10 crossover for the pioneering jump blues legend. Chuck Berry was reevaluating his options.

CHRISTINE SIXTEEN

Artist: Kiss
Written by: Gene Simmons
From the album: *Love Gun*
Label: Casablanca
Produced by: Eddie Kramer, Kiss
Year: 1977
Gene got tongue. Suggested segue: "Stray Cat Blues" by the Rolling Stones, "Hot Blooded" by Foreigner.

CHRISTO REDENTOR

Artist: Donald Byrd
Written by: Duke Pearson
From the album: *A New Perspective*
Label: Blue Note
Year: 1963
Introduced by jazz pianist Duke Pearson. Byrd's version was used to haunting effect in the Robert De Niro film *A Bronx Tale* in 1993. Covered by harp demigod Charlie Musselwhite (Vanguard, '67), Harvey Mandel (Philips, '69).

CHUCK E.'S IN LOVE

Artist: Rickie Lee Jones

Written by: Rickie Lee Jones
From the album: *Rickie Lee Jones*
Label: Warner Brothers
Produced by: Russ Titelman, Lenny Waronker
Year: 1979
Colorful portrait of an L.A. character introduces a new Bohemian B-girl. Made the world safe for Sheryl Crow, a decade and a half later. Undoubtedly part of the essential Norah Jones collection.

CHURCH BELLS MAY RING

Artist: The Willows
Written by: Tony Middleton, Richard Davis, Ralph Martin, Joe Martin, Morty Craft
Label: Melba
Produced by: Morty Craft
Year: 1956
Perfectly embodying the eternal blissful harmony of doo-wop, the anti-blues.

CHURCH OF LOGIC, SIN AND LOVE

Artist: The Men
Written by: Jef Scott
From the album: *The Men*
Produced by: David Leonard
Label: Polydor
Year: 1992
On the road in the '90s and smelling the coffee.

CINDERELLA'S BIG SCORE

Artist: Sonic Youth
Written by: Sonic Youth
From the album: *Goo*
Label: Geffen
Produced by: Nicholas Sansone, Sonic Youth
Year: 1990
Major label splash, a bellyflop.

CINDY INCIDENTALLY

Artist: The Faces
Written by: Rod Stewart, Ron Wood, Ian McLachan
From the album: *Ooh La La*
Label: Warner Brothers
Produced by: Glyn Johns
Year: 1973
Smiling Faces.

CINDY TELLS ME

Artist: Brian Eno
Written by: Brian Eno
From the album: *Here Come the Warm Jets*
Label: Antilles
Produced by: Brian Eno
Year: 1974
Brainy, quirky pop rock for the progressive sound painter.

CINEMA SHOW

Artist: Genesis
Written by: Peter Gabriel, Tony Banks, Phil Collins, Steve Hackett

From the album: *Selling England by the Pound*
Label: Charisma
Produced by: John Burns, Genesis
Year: 1973
Burnishing their art/rock legend.

CINNAMON GIRL

Artist: Neil Young with Crazy Horse
Written by: Neil Young
From the album: *Everybody Knows This Is Nowhere*
Label: Reprise
Produced by: David Briggs, Neil Young
Year: 1970
Contains the notable spastic guitar part that the entire city of Seattle was probably weaned on.

CIRCLE GAME, THE

Artist: Buffy Sainte-Marie
Written by: Joni Mitchell
From the album: *Fire and Fleet and Candlelight*
Label: Vanguard
Year: 1967
Folkie life cycle, written by Mitchell in response to Neil Young's "Sugar Mountain." Covered by Tom Rush (Elektra, '68). Featured in the youth cult movie *The Strawberry Statement* (MGM, '70). Mitchell's version is on *Ladies of the Canyon* (Reprise, '70).

CISCO KID

Artist: War
Written by: Sylvester Allen, Lee Oscar Levitin, Morris Dickerson, Leroy "Lonnie" Jordan, Howard Scott, Charles W. Miller, Harold R. Brown
From the album: *The World Is a Ghetto*
Label: United Artists
Produced by: Jerry Goldstein
Year: 1972
Biggest hit for the Latino funk band. Duncan Reynoldo would have been proud. Antonio Banderas was listening.

CITIES ON FLAME WITH ROCK AND ROLL

Artist: Blue Oyster Cult
Written by: Sandy Pearlman, Donald Roeser (Buck Dharma), Jack Bouchard
From the album: *Blue Oyster Cult*
Label: Columbia
Produced by: Sandy Pearlman
Year: 1972
Opening heavy metal's door to the glitterati. The New York Dolls would shortly tramp on through.

CITY OF NEW ORLEANS, THE

Artist: Steve Goodman
Written by: Steve Goodman
From the album: *Steve Goodman*
Label: Buddah
Produced by: Norbert Putnam, Kris Kristofferson

Year: 1971
A vivid cross-country railroad love song. Covered by Arlo Guthrie (Reprise, '72), Willie Nelson (Columbia, '84).

CIVIL WAR

Artist: Guns N' Roses
Written by: Guns N' Roses
From the album: *Use Your Illusion II*
Label: Geffen
Produced by: Mike Clink, Guns N' Roses
Year: 1991
Previewing their double-price-tag double-album set as well as the eventual Slash and Izzy split.

CLAIR

Artist: Gilbert O'Sullivan
Written by: Raymond O'Sullivan
From the album: *Back to Front*
Label: MAM
Produced by: Gordon Mills
Year: 1972
The Irish Jonathan Richman.

CLAP FOR THE WOLFMAN

Artist: The Guess Who
Written by: Burton Cummings, Bill Wallace, Kurt Winter
From the album: *Road Food*
Label: RCA
Produced by: Jack Richardson
Year: 1974
Their last big hit celebrates an American icon, deejay Wolfman Jack, who used to broadcast from Del Rio, Texas, but could obviously be heard in Bannatyne, Canada.

CLAP, THE

Artist: Yes
Written by: Steve Howe
From the album: *The Yes Album*
Produced by: Yes and Eddie Offord
Label: Atlantic
Year: 1971
Brilliant instrumental by guitarist Howe.

CLASH CITY ROCKERS

Artist: The Clash
Written by: John Mellor (Joe Strummer), Mick Jones
From the album: *The Clash*
Label: Epic
Produced by: Mickey Foote
Year: 1977
What could a poor boy in London do in the late '70s except to sing in a politically driven, reggae-influenced band? This single was added to the US version of their first album when it was finally released in '79, after their second.

CLASSICAL GAS

Artist: Mason Williams
Written by: Mason Williams
From the album: *Mason Williams' Phonograph Record*
Label: Warner Brothers
Produced by: Mike Post
Year: 1968
Guitar showpiece, as heard on *The Smothers Brothers Comedy Hour*.

CLAUDETTE

Artist: Roy Orbison
Written by: Roy Orbison
Label: Sun
Produced by: Sam Phillips
Year: 1958
Written about Orbison's then-wife, Claudette, who would soon be killed in a motorcycle accident. Covered by the Everly Brothers on the B-side of "All I Have to Do Is Dream" (Cadence, '58).

CLEAN UP WOMAN

Artist: Betty Wright
Written by: Willie Clarke, Clarence Reid
From the album: *I Love the Way You Love*
Label: Alston
Produced by: Willie Clarke, Clarence Reid
Year: 1971
Before Helen Reddy sang "I Am Woman," 19-year-old R&B belter Betty, from Miami, could already see right through it.

CLEVELAND ROCKS

Artist: Ian Hunter
Written by: Ian Hunter
From the album: *You're Never Alone with a Schizophrenic*
Label: Chrysalis
Produced by: Mick Ronson, Ian Hunter
Year: 1979
Obviously a visitor's anthem, featured in the '87 Cleveland movie *Light of Day* and theme for the '90s Cleveland-based sitcom, *The Drew Carey Show*, with the entire cast in a dancing video that put Dr. Pepper to shame.

CLIFFS OF DOVER

Artist: Eric Johnson
Written by: Eric Johnson
From the album: *Ah Via Musicom*
Label: Capitol
Year: 1991
New guitar virtuouso on the block.

CLIMB TO SAFETY

Artist: Widespread Panic
Written by: Jerry Joseph, Glenn Esparza
From the album: *Til the Medicine Takes*
Label: Capricorn
Year: 1999
The jam band concept survives and thrives.

CLOCK, THE

Artist: Johnny Ace
Written by: John Alexander
From the album: *Memorial Album: For Johnny Ace*
Label: Duke
Year: 1953
First R&B hit for the Charles Brown influenced crooner. Same clock Bill Haley would shortly rock around.

CLOSE MY EYES FOREVER

Artist: Lita Ford with Ozzy Osbourne
Written by: Lita Ford, Ozzy Osbourne
From the album: *Lita*
Label: RCA
Produced by: Mike Chapman
Year: 1989
The king and queen of hell's senior prom (soon to be supplanted by Kurt and Courtney).

CLOSE THE DOOR

Artist: Teddy Pendergrass
Written by: Kenny Gamble, Leon Huff
From the album: *Life Is a Song Worth Singing*
Label: Philadelphia International
Produced by: Kenny Gamble, Leon Huff
Year: 1978
The ultimate bedroom ballad for the former lead singer of Harold Melvin & the Blue Notes.

CLOSE TO THE EDGE

Artist: Yes
Written by: Jon Anderson, Steve Howe, Yes
From the album: *Close to the Edge*
Label: Atlantic
Produced by: Eddie Offord
Year: 1972
Bach and roll bacchanal.

CLOSE TO YOU

Artist: Maxi Priest
Written by: Gary Benson, Winston Sela, Max Elliott
From the album: *Bonafide*
Label: Charisma
Produced by: Sly & Robbie
Year: 1990
Reggae track tops the charts.

CLOSE YOUR EYES

Artist: The Five Keys
Written by: Chuck Willis
Label: Capitol
Year: 1955
One of doo-wop's finest moments. Covered by Peaches and Herb (Polydor, '67).

CLOSER

Artist: Nine Inch Nails
Written by: Trent Reznor
From the album: *The Downward Spiral*
Label: TVT

Produced by: Trent Reznor, Flood
Year: 1994
Profoundly disturbing, in a horror movie sort of way.

CLOSER TO FINE

Artist: Indigo Girls
Written by: Emily Saliers
From the album: *Indigo Girls*
Label: Epic
Produced by: Scott Litt
Year: 1989
New folk-harmony duo's breakthrough effort.

CLOSER TO HOME

Artist: Grand Funk Railroad
Written by: Mark Farner
From the album: *Closer to Home*
Label: Capitol
Produced by: Terry Knight
Year: 1970
First big hit for the monster trucks of middle American metal.

CLOSER TO THE HEART

Artist: Rush
Written by: Gary Lee Weinrib (Geddy Lee), Alex Zivojinovich (Alex Lifeson), Neil Peart, Peter Talbot
From the album: *A Farewell to Kings*
Label: Mercury
Produced by: Terry Brown, Rush
Year: 1977
Virtuosic Canadian metal trio produces its first arena anthem.

CLOSER YOU ARE, THE

Artist: The Channels
Written by: Earle Lewis, Morgan C. Robinson
Label: Whirlin' Disc
Year: 1956
Classic New York doo-wop.

CLOSING TIME

Artist: Leonard Cohen
Written by: Leonard Cohen
From the album: *The Future*
Label: Virgin
Produced by: Steve Lindsay, Bill Ginn, Leanne Ungar, Rebecca DeMornay, Yoav Goren
Year: 1992
An idol in Europe and a cult figure in the US, Cohen shows no signs of retiring.

CLOSING TIME

Artist: Semisonic
Written by: Dan Wilson
From the album: *Feeling Strangely Fine*
Produced by: Nick Launday
Label: MCA
Year: 1998

Philosophizing at the senior prom; Wilson's post-graduate thesis after Trip Shakespeare.

CLOUD NINE

Artist: The Temptations
Written by: Norman Whitfield, Barrett Strong
From the album: *Cloud Nine*
Label: Gordy
Produced by: Norman Whitfield
Year: 1968
Preaching an antidrug message to earn Motown its first Grammy.

CLOUDBUSTING

Artist: Kate Bush
Written by: Kate Bush
From the album: *Hounds of Love*
Label: EMI-America
Produced by: Kate Bush
Year: 1985
Deep in the web of her unique technology, something good is preparing to happen. Sampled by the Utah Saints (London/PLG, '93).

CLOUDY

Artist: Simon and Garfunkel
Written by: Paul Simon
From the album: *Parsley, Sage, Rosemary and Thyme*
Label: Columbia
Produced by: Bob Johnston
Year: 1966
Atmospheric folk/rock, heard in *The Graduate*.

C'MON AND GET MY LOVE

Artist: Cathy Dennis
Written by: Danny Poku, Cathy Dennis
From the album: *A Little Bit of This, a Little Bit of That*
Label: Polygram
Produced by: Danny D.
Year: 1990
Squarely in the '90s dance pocket.

C'MON AND RIDE IT (THE TRAIN)

Artist: Quad City DJs
Written by: C.C. Lemonhead, Jay McGowan, Barry White, Michael Phillips
From the album: *Get on up and Dance*
Label: Big Beat
Year: 1996
Unstoppable engine of energy.

C'MON AND SWIM

Artist: Bobby Freeman
Written by: Sylvester Stewart
From the album: *C'mon and S-w-i-m*
Label: Autumn
Produced by: Cougar Productions
Year: 1964
Briefly popular move that unaccountably remained in the dance floor repertoire of 45 percent of those

who originally learned it, even thirty years later. Luckily, Sly would soon find his own groove, with his Family Stone.

C'MON EVERYBODY

Artist: Eddie Cochran
Written by: Eddie Cochran, Jerry Capehart
From the album: *Eddie Cochran*
Label: Liberty
Produced by: Eddie Cochran, Jerry Capehart
Year: 1958
One of Cochran's most convincing rockers; a much bigger hit in the UK, where he was touring when he was killed in a car crash in 1960.

COCA COLA DOUCHE

Artist: The Fugs
Written by: Tuli Kupferberg, Ed Sanders
From the album: *Virgin Fugs*
Label: ESP
Produced by: Harry Smith
Year: 1965
Bringing a poetic eye and a tin ear to the camps of rock and roll decadence. For a time in '67 they played in the same neighborhood (actual and metaphorical) as Frank Zappa's Mothers of Invention.

COCAINE

Artist: J.J. Cale
Written by: John Cale
From the album: *Troubadour*
Produced by: Audie Ashworth
Label: Shelter
Year: 1976
Can't live with it, can't live without it ode to the power of the evil powder. Covered by Eric Clapton (RSO, '77). Dave Van Ronk's version of the blues classic with the same title was much more powerful.

COCONUT

Artist: Nilsson
Written by: Harry Nilsson
From the album: *Nilsson Schmilsson*
Label: RCA
Produced by: Richard Perry
Year: 1971
A reggae-inflected romp, now a staple number for the all-inclusive vacationing class.

COCONUT GROVE

Artist: The Lovin' Spoonful
Written by: John Sebastian, Zal Yanovsky
From the album: *Hums of the Lovin' Spoonful*
Label: Kama Sutra
Produced by: Erik Jacobsen
Year: 1966
Autoharp heaven. Tribute to the mellow essence of Freddy Neil's southern hideaway.

COD'INE

Artist: Buffy Sainte-Marie
Written by: Buffy Sainte-Marie
From the album: *It's My Way*
Label: Vanguard
Produced by: Elmer Jared Gordon
Year: 1964
Striking antidrug lament made chilling by Sainte-Marie's quaking, quavery wail. Covered by Quicksilver Messenger Service, in the movie *Revolution* (United Artists, '69).

CODEX

Artist: Pere Ubu
Written by: David Thomas, Allen Ravenstine, Tony Maimone, Scott Krauss, Tom Herman
From the album: *Dub Housing*
Label: Chrysalis
Produced by: Pere Ubu, Ken Hamman
Year: 1978
Personifying the urban, mid-century, white, young, American blues, with the eerie howl of a heartland Captain Beefheart.

COLD AS ICE

Artist: Foreigner
Written by: Lou Grammatico (Lou Gramm), Mick Jones
From the album: *Foreigner*
Label: Atlantic
Produced by: John Sinclair, Gary Lyons, Mick Jones
Year: 1977
Looking no further than the arena for inspiration.

COLD BLOODED

Artist: Rick James
Written by: James Johnson Jr. (Rick James)
From the album: *Cold Blooded*
Label: Motown
Produced by: Rick James
Year: 1983
Funk stalwart's third #1 R&B/Top 40 crossover.

COLD BLUE STEEL AND SWEET FIRE

Artist: Joni Mitchell
Written by: Joni Mitchell
From the album: *For the Roses*
Label: Asylum
Produced by: Joni Mitchell
Year: 1972
Reaching a poetic peak.

COLD, COLD HEART

Artist: Hank Williams
Written by: Hank Williams
Label: MGM
Produced by: Fred Rose
Year: 1951
Turning his Audrey-inspired pain into the stuff of a major career move. Mitch Miller appropriated the tune for Tony Bennett's #1 pop cover (Columbia, '51).

COLD-HEARTED

Artist: Paula Abdul
Written by: Elliot Wolff
From the album: *Forever Your Girl*
Produced by: Elliot Wolff, K. Cohen
Label: Virgin
Year: 1988
Third straight #1 for Janet Jackson's choreographer began as the B-side of her first #1 "Straight Up."

COLD ROCK A PARTY

Artist: MC Lyte
Written by: (Lana Moorer) MC Lyte, Rashad Smith
From the album: *Bad As I Wanna B*
Label: EastWest
Produced by: Sean Combs
Year: 1996
Uninvited guest makes a splash. Lil Kim was polishing her elocution.

COLD SWEAT

Artist: James Brown and the Famous Flames
Written by: James Brown, Alfred Ellis
From the album: *Cold Sweat*
Label: King
Produced by: James Brown, Alfred Ellis
Year: 1967
Funk personified.

COLD TURKEY

Artist: John Lennon with the Plastic Ono Band
Written by: John Lennon
From the album: *The Plastic Ono Band, Live Peace in Toronto 1969*
Label: Apple
Produced by: Phil Spector, John Lennon, Yoko Ono
Year: 1969
Coming down from the Beatles, the first stage.

COLORADO

Artist: Chevy Chase
Written by: Christopher Guest, Sean Kelly, Tony Hendra
From the album: *Lemmings Original Cast Album*
Label: Banana
Produced by: Tony Hendra
Year: 1973
Chevy perfects his John Denver, in the musical that spawned the *National Lampoon* as well as all those vacation movies.

COLORADO

Artist: The Flying Burritto Brothers
Written by: Rick Roberts
From the album: *Flying Burrito Brothers*
Label: Asylum
Year: 1971
Moving from country/rock to folk/rock. Covered by Linda Ronstadt (Asylum, '73).

COLORS

Artist: Ice-T
Written by: Tracy Morrow (Ice-T), Africa Islam
From the album: *Colors Soundtrack*
Label: Warner Brothers
Produced by: Ice-T, Africa Islam
Year: 1988
A lecture on the essence of gang identity.

COMBINATION OF THE TWO

Artist: Big Brother and the Holding Company
Written by: Sam Andrew
From the album: *Cheap Thrills*
Label: Columbia
Produced by: John Simon
Year: 1968
Kicking off their psychedelic blues/rock career at the Monterey Rock and Pop Festival.

COME A LITTLE BIT CLOSER

Artist: Jay and the Americans
Written by: Tommy Boyce, Bobby Hart, Wes Farrell
From the album: *Come a Little Bit Closer*
Label: United Artists
Year: 1964
Biggest hit for the semi-operatic New Yorkers.

COME AND GET IT

Artist: Badfinger
Written by: Paul McCartney
From the album: *Magic Christian Music*
Label: Apple
Produced by: Paul McCartney
Year: 1969
Their first hit, from the movie *The Magic Christian*, starring Ringo Starr and Peter Sellers.

COME AND GET THESE MEMORIES

Artist: Martha and the Vandellas
Written by: Eddie Holland, Lamont Dozier, Brian Holland
From the album: *Come and Get These Memories*
Label: Gordy
Produced by: Brian Holland, Lamont Dozier
Year: 1963
First hit for Motown's hungriest sounding group.

COME AND GET YOUR LOVE

Artist: Redbone
Written by: Lolly Vegas
From the album: *Wouoka*
Label: Epic
Produced by: Pat Vegas, Lolly Vegas
Year: 1974
The '70s AM radio sound. Covered by Real McCoy (Arista '95).

COME AND STAY WITH ME

Artist: Marianne Faithfull
Written by: Jackie DeShannon
From the album: *Marianne Faithfull*
Label: London
Produced by: Tony Calder
Year: 1965
Jagger discovery and protégé gets soulful. Covered by Cher (Imperial, '65), Jackie DeShannon (Imperial, '67).

COME AND TALK TO ME

Artist: Jodeci
Written by: Devante Swing
From the album: *Forever My Lady*
Label: Uptown
Produced by: Andre Harrell, Steve Lucas
Year: 1991
#1 R&B/Top 20 crossover in the year's back to doo-wop flavor.

COME AS YOU ARE

Artist: Nirvana
Written by: Kurt Cobain, Krist Novaselic, Dave Grohl
From the album: *Nevermind*
Label: DGC
Produced by: Butch Vig
Year: 1991
The big lie, as one DJ put it: "He did have a gun." Suggested segue: "Eighties" by Killing Joke. Blink 182 were listening.

COME BACK BABY

Artist: Ray Charles
Written by: Ray Charles
From the album: *The Ray Charles Story*
Label: Atlantic
Produced by: Ahmet Ertegun, Jerry Wexler
Year: 1954
Putting his rhythm to the blues.

COME BACK TO ME

Artist: Janet Jackson
Written by: James Harris III, Terry Lewis, Janet Jackson
From the album: *Rhythm Nation 1814*
Label: A&M
Produced by: Jimmy Jam, Terry Lewis
Year: 1989

COME BACK WHEN YOU GROW UP

Artist: Bobby Vee
Written by: Martha Sharp
From the album: *Come Back When You Grow Up*
Label: Liberty
Produced by: Snuff Garrett
Year: 1966
Suggested segue: "Born Too Late" by The Poni Tails.

COME DANCING

Artist: The Kinks
Written by: Ray Davies
From the album: *State of Confusion*
Label: Arista
Produced by: Ray Davies
Year: 1983
Tearing the dance hall down; the Kinks's biggest hit in nearly twenty years.

COME GO WITH ME

Artist: The Dell Vikings
Written by: C. E. Quick
From the album: *Come Go with the Dell Vikings*
Label: Dot
Produced by: Joe Averbach
Year: 1957
Interracial harmony group records first of two Top 10 R&B/Top 10 crossovers. The other was "Whispering Bells."

COME GO WITH ME

Artist: Expose
Written by: Lewis Martinee
From the album: *Exposure*
Label: Arista
Produced by: Lewis Martinee
Year: 1987
Debut hit for the Miami-based girl group.

COME IN FROM THE COLD

Artist: Joni Mitchell
Written by: Joni Mitchell
From the album: *Night Ride Home*
Label: Geffen
Produced by: Joni Mitchell, Larry Klein
Year: 1991
Signing with David Geffen's record company, Mitchell finally moves past her distancing jazz phase of the '80s.

COME IN NUMBER-51, YOUR TIME IS UP

Artist: Pink Floyd
Written by: Roger Waters, David Gilmour, Nick Mason, Rick Wright
From the album: *Music from the Motion Picture Zabriskie Point*
Label: Columbia
Year: 1969
Psychedelic credibility for *Antonioni's* high-profile counter-cultural dud.

COME MONDAY

Artist: Jimmy Buffett
Written by: Jimmy Buffett
From the album: *Living and Dying in 3/4 Time*
Label: Dunhill
Produced by: D. Gant
Year: 1974

Welcome to Margaritaville, the lazy, hazy Key West of the mind that Jimmy Buffett populated and popularized like Springsteen did New Jersey.

COME ON

Artist: Chuck Berry
Written by: Chuck Berry
From the album: *Twist*
Label: Chess
Produced by: Leonard Chess, Phil Chess
Year: 1961
First UK single for the Rolling Stones (London, '64).

COME ON, BABY

Artist: Jo-Ann Campbell
Written by: Jo-Ann Campbell
Label: Eldorado
Year: 1957
For the offending phrase "drive on baby," Alan Freed's "Blonde Bombshell" was stricken from the airwaves of repressive America.

COME ON EILEEN

Artist: Dexy's Midnight Runners
Written by: Kevin Rowland, Jim Paterson, Kevin Adams
From the album: *Too-Rye-Ay*
Label: Mercury
Produced by: Clive Langer, Alan Winstanley
Year: 1983
Rousing, beer soaked #1 US/UK one-shot.

COME ON, LET'S GO

Artist: Ritchie Valens
Written by: Ritchie Valens
From the album: *Richie Valens*
Label: Del-Fi
Produced by: Bob Keane
Year: 1958
His first hit; a Buddy Holly-inspired, Tex-Mex rocker.

COME ON OVER BABY (ALL I WANT IS YOU)

Artist: Christina Aguilera
Written by: Johan Aberg, Paul Rein
From the album: *Christina Aguilera*
Label: RCA
Year: 2000
Voice of a new generation of shameless hussies. But what a voice.

COME OUT AND PLAY

Artist: Offspring
Written by: Dexter Holland, Greg K., Noodles, Ron Welty
From the album: *Smash*
Label: Epitaph
Produced by: Thom Wilson
Year: 1994
Alternative rock takes on racism and gang warfare.

COME SAIL AWAY

Artist: Styx
Written by: Dennis DeYoung
From the album: *The Grand Illusion*
Label: A&M
Produced by: Styx
Year: 1977
Pomp rock.

COME SEE ABOUT ME

Artist: The Supremes
Written by: Eddie Holland, Lamont Dozier, Brian Holland
From the album: *Where Did Our Love Go*
Label: Motown
Produced by: Brian Holland, Lamont Dozier
Year: 1964
Perfecting their girl-group formula with their third #1 in a row.

COME SOFTLY TO ME

Artist: The Fleetwoods
Written by: Gary Troxel, Gretchen Christopher, Barbara Ellis
From the album: *Come Softly to Me*
Label: Dolton
Produced by: Bob Reisdorff
Year: 1959
The leading edge of the new soft sound in rock. Frank Sinatra, and other concerned citizens, thought they had beaten the beast back. But everyone was only momentarily tuned out, too busy reading the good parts of *Lady Chatterly's Lover* and *Peyton Place*.

COME TO BUTT-HEAD

Artist: Beavis and Butt-Head
Written by: Mike Judge, Nile Rodgers
From the album: *Beavis and Butt-Head Experience*
Label: Geffen
Produced by: Nile Rodgers
Year: 1993
The '90s experience: dumb and dumber.

COME TO ME

Artist: Marv Johnson
Written by: Marvin Johnson, Berry Gordy Jr.
From the album: *Marvelous Marv Johnson*
Label: United Artists
Produced by: Berry Gordy
Year: 1958
Early echoes of the coming Detroit sound of Motown, the first release on Berry Gordy's label, which was then licensed to United Artists.

COME TO MY WINDOW

Artist: Melissa Etheridge
Written by: Melissa Etheridge
From the album: *Yes I Am*
Label: Island
Produced by: Hugh Padgham, Melissa Etheridge
Year: 1994

Tortured love relationship that dared not speak its name, at least not until *Rolling Stone* sent a reporter over. Suggested segue: "I Kissed a Girl" by Jill Sobule.

COME TO THE SUNSHINE

Artist: Harper's Bizarre
Written by: Van Dyke Parks
From the album: *Feelin' Groovy*
Label: Warner Brothers
Produced by: Lenny Waronker
Year: 1966
Showcasing the work of the noted L.A. eccentric and friend of Brian Wilson, Van Dyke Parks.

COME TOGETHER

Artist: The Beatles
Written by: John Lennon, Paul McCartney
From the album: *Abbey Road*
Label: Apple
Produced by: George Martin
Year: 1969
Restating their ultimate theme for their eighteenth #1. Covered by Aerosmith (Columbia, '78). Segue: "You Can't Catch Me" by Chuck Berry.

COME TOMORROW

Artist: Manfred Mann
Written by: Bob Elgin, Frank Augustus, Dolores Phillips
From the album: *Five Faces of Manfred Mann*
Label: Ascot
Year: 1965
Antiwar rocker.

COME WITH ME

Artist: Puff Daddy
Written by: Jon Bonham, Sean Puffy Combs, Mark Curry, Jimmy Page, Robert Plant
From the album: *No Way Out*
Label: Bad Boy
Produced by: Sean Combs
Year: 1998
The amazingly versatile clothing designer Sean Combs shows an affinity for Led Zep's "Kashmir." Featured in the movie *Godzilla*.

COMES A TIME

Artist: Neil Young
Written by: Neil Young
From the album: *Comes a Time*
Label: Reprise
Produced by: David Briggs, Neil Young, Jim Mulligan, Ben Keith
Year: 1978
Moving back to the folk/rock fold.

COMFORTABLY NUMB

Artist: Pink Floyd
Written by: Roger Waters, David Gilmour
From the album: *The Wall*

Label: Columbia
Produced by: Roger Waters, David Gilmour, Bob Ezrin
Year: 1979
Gilmour steps out on one of his best guitar solos. Last time Waters and Gilmour would collaborate.

COMING AROUND AGAIN

Artist: Carly Simon
Written by: Carly Simon
From the album: *Coming around Again*
Label: Arista
Produced by: Russ Kunkel, Bill Payne, George Massenburg, Paul Samwell-Smith
Year: 1986
This theme for the Nora Ephron film *Heartburn* re-established Carly as the voice of her newly-divorced Baby Boom generation that she'd been purporting to be ever since "That's the Way I Always Heard It Should Be" in 1971.

COMING INTO LOS ANGELES

Artist: Arlo Guthrie
Written by: Arlo Guthrie
From the album: *Running down the Road*
Label: Reprise
Year: 1969
Essential folk/rock subversion back in the days when drug running seemed a fairly innocuous career path.

COMING ON STRONG

Artist: Brenda Lee
Written by: David Wilkins
From the album: *Coming on Strong*
Label: Decca
Produced by: Owen Bradley
Year: 1966
Her last pop hit and latter-day state-fair concert opener.

COMING UP

Artist: Paul McCartney with Wings
Written by: Paul McCartney
From the album: *McCartney II*
Label: Columbia
Produced by: Paul McCartney
Year: 1980
Recorded live in Glasgow, this was his 7TH and last solo #1.

COMMERCIAL RAIN

Artist: Inspiral Carpets
Written by: Inspiral Carpets
From the album: *Life*
Label: Elektra
Year: 1990
Big on the incipient Rave scene in England.

COMMON MAN

Artist: The Blasters

Written by: Dave Alvin
From the album: *Hard Line*
Label: Slash
Produced by: Jeff Eyrich
Year: 1985
Lighting out for John Cougar Mellencamp territory.

COMMON PEOPLE

Artist: Pulp
Written by: Nick Banks, Jarvis Cocker, Candida Doyle, Steve Mackey and Russell Senior
From the album: *Different Class*
Produced by: Chris Thomas
Label: Island
Year: 1995
From a whisper to a scream, this is a dissection of class warfare masquerading as a scathing character portrait, and vice-versa.

COMPARED TO WHAT

Artist: Les McCann and Eddie Harris
Written by: Gene McDaniels
From the album: *Swiss Movement*
Label: Atlantic
Produced by: Neshul Ertegun, Joel Dorn
Year: 1970
Outspoken jazz/R&B groove and philosophy.

COMPLETE CONTROL

Artist: The Clash
Written by: John Mellor (Joe Strummer), Mick Jones
From the album: *The Clash*
Label: Epic
Produced by: Lee Perry
Year: 1977
Fierce autobiographical single was produced by reggae legend Lee Perry and added to the US version of their UK album.

COMPUTER LOVE

Artist: Kraftwerk
Written by: Karl Barios, Ralf Hutter, Emil Schult
From the album: *Computer World*
Produced by: Chris Thomas
Label: Warner Brothers
Year: 1982
Early ode to technology.

CONCENTRATION MOON

Artist: The Mothers of Invention
Written by: Frank Zappa
From the album: *We're Only In It for the Money*
Label: Verve
Produced by: Frank Zappa
Year: 1968
Zappa at his most sweetly cynical.

CONCRETE AND CLAY

Artist: Eddie Rambeau
Written by: Tommy Moeller, Brian Parker

From the album: *Concrete and Clay*
Label: Dyno Voice
Produced by: Bob Crewe
Year: 1965
Evocative cityscape.

CONCRETE JUNGLE

Artist: Bob Marley and the Wailers
Written by: Bob Marley
From the album: *Catch a Fire*
Produced by: Bob Marley, Chris Blackwell
Label: Island
Year: 1972
Inner-city Jamaica, or anywhere.

CONEY ISLAND BABY

Artist: The Excellents
Written by: Vinny Catalano, Peter Alonzo
Label: Blast
Produced by: Vinny Catalano
Year: 1962
Legendary tale of urban fantasy by a Bronx group who'd never seen the Parachute Jump in person. Big winner on DJ Murray the K's Boss-Record-of-the-Week contest on 1010 WINS in New York City.

CONEY ISLAND BABY

Artist: Lou Reed
Written by: Lou Reed
From the album: *Coney Island Baby*
Label: RCA
Produced by: Lou Reed
Year: 1976
Reflecting on high school traumas and the glory of love; Lou's tribute to doo-wop goes out to the kids at the candy store.

CONFESSION, THE

Artist: Laura Nyro
Written by: Laura Nyro
From the album: *Eli and the Thirteenth Confession*
Label: Columbia
Produced by: Laura Nyro, Charlie Calello
Year: 1968
The advent of the confessional mode of rock song-writing, which would come to fruition with Joni Mitchell, before being demolished by Madonna, only to be resurrected by Tori Amos, only to be demolished by Alanis Morrisette.

CONGA

Artist: Miami Sound Machine
Written by: Enrique Garcia
From the album: *Primitive Love*
Label: Epic
Produced by: Emilio Estefan
Year: 1986
Rock and roll reclaims its Latin dance roots. Perez Prado was smiling.

CONNECTED

Artist: Stereo MCS
Written by: Rob Birch, Nick Hallan, Harry Casey, Rick Finch
From the album: *Connected*
Label: Gee Street/Island
Produced by: Stereo MCs
Year: 1993
Techno disco smash, appropriated from K.C. and the Sunshine Band protege Jimmy Bo Horne's R&B hit, "Let Me (Let Me Be Your Lover)" (Sunshine Sound, '78).

CONQUISTADOR

Artist: Procol Harum
Written by: Gary Brooker, Keith Reid
From the album: *Procol Harum*
Label: Deram
Produced by: Chris Thomas
Year: 1967
Progressive rock mainstay, in tap shoes.

CONSTANT CRAVING

Artist: k.d. Lang
Written by: Kathryn Dawn Lang, Ben Mink
From the album: *Ingenue*
Label: Sire
Produced by: Greg Penny, Ben Mink, k.d. Lang
Year: 1992
Patsy Cline reincarnated as Hank Williams.

CONTINUING STORY OF BUNGALOW BILL, THE

Artist: The Beatles
Written by: John Lennon, Paul McCartney
From the album: *The Beatles*
Label: Apple
Produced by: George Martin
Year: 1968
A cartoon for British TV.

CONTORT YOURSELF

Artist: James Chance
Written by: James Chance
From the album: *Buy Contortions*
Label: Ze
Year: 1979
Snarling sax-driven post-punk no-wave anthem.

CONVOY

Artist: C. W. McCall
Written by: William Fries, Louis Davis
From the album: *Black Bear Road*
Label: MGM
Produced by: Don Sears, Chip Davis
Year: 1975
#1 country truckstop crossover.

COO COO

Artist: Big Brother and the Holding Company
Written by: Pete Albin
From the album: *Big Brother and the Holding Company*
Label: Mainstream
Produced by: Bob Shad
Year: 1968
Propelled by a wailing Janis Joplin.

COOL

Artist: Pylon
Written by: Pylon
From the album: *Pylon!!*
Label: Armageddon
Year: 1980
R.E.M. contemporaries forgotten in the Athens gold rush.

COOL FOR CATS

Artist: Squeeze
Written by: Chris Difford, Glenn Tilbrook
From the album: *Cool for Cats*
Label: A&M
Produced by: John Wood, Squeeze
Year: 1979
First UK hit for the singer/songwriters, hailed for their Lennonesque cleverness and McCartneyesque melodies; derided for their McCartneyesque slightness, Lennonesque archness.

COOL IT NOW

Artist: New Edition
Written by: Vincent Brantley, Rick Timas
From the album: *New Edition*
Label: MCA
Produced by: Vincent Brantley, Rick Timas
Year: 1984
Teen idolhood was preferred on Bobby Brown. Whitney Houston was watching.

COOL JERK

Artist: The Capitols
Written by: Donald Storball
From the album: *Dance the Cool Jerk*
Label: Karen
Produced by: Ollie McLaughlin
Year: 1966
What came after the Frug.

COOL METRO

Artist: David Johansen
Written by: David Johansen, Syl Sylvain
From the album: *David Johansen*
Label: Blue Sky
Produced by: Richard Robinson, David Johansen
Year: 1978
The roots of Buster Poindexter.

COOL PLACES

Artist: Sparks and Jane Wiedlin
Written by: Ron Mael, Russel Mael
From the album: *Sparks in Outer Space*
Label: Atlantic
Year: 1983
Biggest hit for the pets of chic L.A., sung with a Go-Go girl.

COP KILLER

Artist: Body Count
Written by: Tracy Morrow (Ice T)
From the album: *Body Count*
Label: Warner Brothers
Produced by: Ernie C., Lee T.
Year: 1992
More explicit than "I Fought the Law" and "I Shot the Sheriff" (and certainly "I Shot Mr. Lee") combined, this track came to symbolize gangsta rap as an antiauthoritarian genre glorifying violence and espousing anarchy under the guise of merely describing it. Tracy Morrow went on to an acting career, most recently on TV, playing a cop.

COPACABANA (AT THE COPA)

Artist: Barry Manilow
Written by: Barry Manilow, Bruce Sussman, Jack Feldman
From the album: *Even Now*
Label: Arista
Produced by: Ron Dante, Barry Manilow
Year: 1976
Bette Midler's former keyboard player and arranger finds his disco niche in this elaborate made-for-Lifetime-TV saga.

COPPERHEAD ROAD

Artist: Steve Earle
Written by: Steve Earle
From the album: *Copperhead Road*
Label: Uni
Produced by: Tony Brown, Steve Earle
Year: 1988
Runs parallel to his "Nowhere Road" and cuts through "Guitar Town" on its way to alt-country nirvana.

COPPERLINE

Artist: James Taylor
Written by: James Taylor, Reynolds Price
From the album: *New Moon Shine*
Label: Columbia
Produced by: Don Grolnick
Year: 1991
Taking on contemporary times in the exurbs, with the help of novelist Price.

CORRINE, CORRINA

Artist: Joe Turner
Written by: Peter Chatman, Mayo J. Williams, Mitchell Parrish
Label: Decca
Year: 1941.
R&B chestnut that Turner recorded originally with Art Tatum, and revived in '56 for his first crossover hit. Covered by Ray Peterson (Dunes, '61), in

Phil Spector's first production after the Teddy Bears.

CORTEZ THE KILLER

Artist: Neil Young
Written by: Neil Young
From the album: *Zuma*
Label: Reprise
Produced by: Neil Young, David Briggs, Tim Mulligan
Year: 1975
One of Young's most popular efforts, covered by Built to Spill, the Church, Government Mule, Henry Kaiser, Dave Matthews Band, Elliot Murphy, Matthew Sweet.

COSMIC SLOP

Artist: Funkadelic
Written by: George Clinton
From the album: *Cosmic Slop*
Label: Westbound
Produced by: George Clinton
Year: 1973
Only a year or so away from when the slop would hit the fan.

COTTONFIELDS

Artist: The Highwaymen
Written by: Huddie Ledbetter (Leadbelly)
From the album: *Standing Room Only*
Label: United Artists
Produced by: Dave Fisher
Year: 1961
The pasteurized sound of early '60s folk harmony. Covered by the Beach Boys (Capitol, '69).

COULD IT BE I'M FALLING IN LOVE

Artist: The Spinners
Written by: Melvin Steals, Mervin Steals
From the album: *The Spinners*
Label: Atlantic
Produced by: Thom Bell
Year: 1972
#1 R&B/Top 10 crossover: Smokey Robinson transplanted to Philadelphia.

COULD THIS BE MAGIC

Artist: The Dubs
Written by: Richard Blandon, Hiram Johnson
Label: Gone
Produced by: George Goldner
Year: 1957
Classic Top 20 doo-wop ballad that never charted R&B.

COULD YOU BE LOVED

Artist: Bob Marley & the Wailers
Written by: Bob Marley
From the album: *Uprising*
Label: Island

Year: 1980
Charted R&B and UK.

COULD'VE BEEN

Artist: Tiffany
Written by: Lois Blaisch
From the album: *Tiffany*
Label: MCA
Produced by: G. E. Tobin
Year: 1987
#1 follow-up to her #1 debut ("I Think We're Alone Now") established her as the teen queen of the mall versus her good girl preppie opposite Debbie Gibson.

COULDN'T GET IT RIGHT

Artist: Climax Blues Band
Written by: Derek Holt, Colin Cooper, John Cuffley, Peter Haycock, Derek Holt, Frederick Jones
From the album: *Gold Plated*
Label: Sire
Produced by: Mike Vernon
Year: 1977
Southern-fried pop rock, with an unstoppable hook.

COULDN'T STAND THE WEATHER

Artist: Stevie Ray Vaughan & Double Trouble
Written by: Stevie Ray Vaughan
From the album: *Couldn't Stand the Weather*
Label: Epic
Produced by: Stevie Ray Vaughan, Double Trouble
Year: 1984
A guitar star rises in Austin, Texas.

COUNT EVERY STAR

Artist: The Ravens
Written by: Bruno Coquatrix, Sammy Gallop
From the album: *Write Me a Letter*
Label: National
Year: 1950
Spotlighting the doo-wop reverse crossover penchant. Hugo Winterhalter had the pop hit (RCA, '50).

COUNT ME IN

Artist: Gary Lewis and the Playboys
Written by: Glen D. Hardin
From the album: *A Session with Gary Lewis and the Playboys*
Label: Liberty
Produced by: Snuff Garrett
Year: 1965
Big on AM radio, when everyone else was preparing for FM.

COUNT ON ME

Artist: Jefferson Starship
Written by: Jesse Barish
From the album: *Earth*
Label: Grunt

Produced by: Larry Cox, Jefferson Starship
Year: 1978
Entering their arena rock phase.

COUNTING BLUE CARS

Artist: Dishwalla
Written by: Scott Alexander, Rodney Browning, Gregory Kolanek, John Richards, George Pendergast
From the album: *Pet Your Friends*
Label: A&M
Produced by: Phil Nicolo
Year: 1995
In which God is pictured as a woman.

COUNTRY ROAD

Artist: James Taylor
Written by: James Taylor
From the album: *Sweet Baby James*
Label: Warner Brothers
Produced by: Peter Asher
Year: 1971
Berkshire country.

COURT OF THE CRIMSON KING

Artist: King Crimson
Written by: Pete Sinfield, Ian McDonald
From the album: *In the Court of the Crimson King*
Label: Atlantic
Produced by: King Crimson
Year: 1969
Opening the gates for progressive rock.

COUSIN DUPREE

Artist: Steely Dan
Written by: Walter Becker, Donald Fagen
From the album: *Two Against Nature*
Produced by: Walter Becker, Donald Fagen
Label: Giant
Year: 2000
Back in the old neighborhood, a jazzbo can't find the action. But the album won a Grammy.

COVER GIRL

Artist: New Kids on the Block
Written by: Larry Johnson (Maurice Starr)
From the album: *Hangin' Tough*
Label: Columbia
Produced by: Maurice Starr
Year: 1988
Cover guys, the new edition of New Edition.

COVER ME

Artist: Bruce Springsteen
Written by: Bruce Springsteen
From the album: *Born in the USA.*
Label: Columbia
Produced by: Jon Landau, Bruce Springsteen, Chuck Plotkin
Year: 1984
A commercial, if not artistic peak.

COVER OF THE *ROLLING STONE*

Artist: Dr. Hook
Written by: Shel Silverstein
From the album: *Sloppy Seconds*
Label: Columbia
Produced by: Ron Haffkine
Year: 1973
Poking fun at the careerist lust that dominated the mid-'70s rock and roll business, written by someone who knew a thing or two about lust.

COWBOY

Artist: Kid Rock
Written by: Robert Ritchie, Earl Shafer, James Trombly, John Travis
From the album: *Devil without a Cause*
Produced by: Kid Rock, John Travis
Label: Top Dog/Lava
Year: 1999
Sounding like the new Gene Vincent, sort of.

COWBOY

Artist: Randy Newman
Written by: Randy Newman
From the album: *Randy Newman Creates Something New under the Sun*
Label: Reprise
Produced by: Van Dyke Parks, Russ Titelman, Lenny Waronker
Year: 1968
Newman exhibits his tender, sentimental side for the first time.

COWBOYS TO GIRLS

Artist: The Intruders
Written by: Kenny Gamble, Leon Huff
From the album: *Cowboys to Girls*
Label: Gamble
Produced by: Kenny Gamble, Leon Huff
Year: 1968
#1 R&B/Top 10 crossover puts Philly soul on the map, reaffirming Philadelphia as the dance capitol of America.

COWGIRL IN THE SAND

Artist: Neil Young
Written by: Neil Young
From the album: *Everybody Knows This Is Nowhere*
Label: Reprise
Produced by: David Briggs, Neil Young
Year: 1969
Young finds his muse.

CRACKERBOX PALACE

Artist: George Harrison
Written by: George Harrison
From the album: *Thirty-Three and 1/3*
Label: Dark House
Produced by: Tom Scott, George Harrison
Year: 1976
Finally, the spirit moves him.

CRACKIN' UP

Artist: Bo Diddley
Written by: Ellas McDaniel (Bo Diddley)
From the album: *Go Bo Diddley*
Label: Chess
Produced by: Leonard Chess
Year: 1959
But not as funny as "Say Man." Covered by the Gants (Liberty, '66).

CRACKLIN' ROSIE

Artist: Neil Diamond
Written by: Neil Diamond
From the album: *Tap Root Manuscript*
Label: Uni
Produced by: Tom Catalano
Year: 1970
Evoking the ghost of the Brill Building.

CRADLE OF LOVE

Artist: Billy Idol
Written by: William Broad (Billy Idol), David Werner
From the album: *Charmed Life*
Label: Chrysalis
Produced by: Keith Forsey
Year: 1990
His biggest hit; from the Andrew Dice Clay movie *Ford Fairlane*.

CRASH INTO ME

Artist: Dave Matthews Band
Written by: Dave Matthews
From the album: *Crash*
Label: RCA
Produced by: Steve Lillywhite
Year: 1996
The mellow and mellifluous musings of a career voyeur and jam band king.

CRAZY

Artist: Patsy Cline
Written by: Willie Nelson
From the album: *Patsy Cline Showcase*
Label: Decca
Produced by: Owen Bradley
Year: 1961
One of the all-time country jukebox classic weepers; #2 country/Top 10 crossover. Ross Perot's '92 presidential theme song.

CRAZY

Artist: Seal
Written by: Sealhenry (Seal) Samuel
From the album: *Seal*
Label: Sire
Produced by: Trevor Horn
Year: 1991
International dance track, with a reggae soul.

CRAZY FOR YOU

Artist: Madonna
Written by: John Bettis, Jon Lind
From the album: *Vision Quest Soundtrack*
Label: Geffen
Produced by: Jellybean Benitez
Year: 1985
Her second #1 hit, from the inspirational wrestling movie

CRAZY LITTLE THING CALLED LOVE

Artist: Queen
Written by: Freddie Mercury
From the album: *The Game*
Label: Elektra
Produced by: Mack, Queen
Year: 1980
Their first #1 and biggest all-time hit, a jaunty little throwaway reportedly written in the bath. It was then supplanted at the top by the much more credible "Another Brick in the Wall" by Pink Floyd.

CRAZY LOVE

Artist: Van Morrison
Written by: Van Morrison
From the album: *Moondance*
Label: Warner Brothers
Produced by: Van Morrison
Year: 1970
B-side of his second single, "Come Running" has become one of his most enduring and enchanting statements. Featured in the '89 film *Always*.

CRAZY MAMA

Artist: J. J. Cale
Written by: Mick Jagger, Keith Richards
From the album: *Naturally*
Label: Shelter
Produced by: Audie Ashworth
Year: 1972
Covered by the Rolling Stones (Rolling Stones, '76).

CRAZY MAN, CRAZY

Artist: Bill Haley and His Comets
Written by: Bill Haley
Label: Essex
Produced by: Milt Gabler
Year: 1953
Killing time between the release and reissue of "Rock around the Clock."

CRAZY MAN MICHAEL

Artist: Fairport Convention
Written by: Richard Thompson, Dave Swarbrick
From the album: *Liege & Lief*
Label: A&M
Produced by: Joe Boyd
Year: 1969
English folksters on a toot.

CRAZY MARY

Artist: Victoria Williams
Written by: Victoria Williams

From the album: *Loose*
Label: Atlantic
Produced by: Paul Fox
Year: 1994
Grim character portrait of the year. Covered by Pearl Jam (Chaos/Columbia, '93).

CRAZY ON YOU

Artist: Heart
Written by: Ann Wilson, Nancy Wilson, Roger Fisher
From the album: *Dreamboat Annie*
Label: Mushroom
Produced by: Mike Flicker
Year: 1976
Top 40 breakthrough for the arena-sized girl-group, fronted by the Wilson sisters.

CRAZY TRAIN

Artist: Ozzy Osbourne
Written by: Ozzy Osbourne, Randy Rhoads, Bob Daisley, Lee Gary Kerslake
From the album: *Blizzard of Ozz*
Label: Jet
Produced by: Max Norman
Year: 1981
The flamboyant Black Sabbath vocalist creates his own metal legacy with his first hit; guitarist Randy Rhoads was about to become a legend.

CREAM

Artist: Prince & the New Power Generation
Written by: Prince Rogers Nelson, New Power Generation
From the album: *Diamonds and Pearls*
Label: Paisley Park
Produced by: Prince, New Power Generation
Year: 1991
Introducing his newest back-up band.

CREEP

Artist: Radiohead
Written by: Radiohead
From the album: *Pablo Honey*
Label: Capitol
Produced by: Sean Slade, Paul Q. Kolderie
Year: 1993
Launching the indie wave of the '90s at Fort Apache studios, outside of Boston, with the future alternative legends from Exeter. Suggested segue: "The Air That I Breathe" by Albert Hammond.

CREEP

Artist: TLC
Written by: Dallas Austin
From the album: *Crazysexycool*
Label: LaFace
Produced by: Dallas Austin
Year: 1994
#1 R&B/#1 crossover establishes the sound of chick hop.

CREEQUE ALLEY

Artist: Mamas & the Papas
Written by: John Phillips, Michelle Gilliam
From the album: *Deliver*
Label: Dunhill
Produced by: Lou Adler
Year: 1967
Autobiography of the folk scene.

CRIMINAL

Artist: Fiona Apple
Written by: Fiona Apple
From the album: *Tidal*
Produced by: Andrew Slater
Label: Work Group
Year: 1996
An anxious warbler, sentenced to hard emotional labor, gains her first and only Top 40 hit and Grammy Award with her first single. A notorious video—resembling soft-core pornography—no doubt helped popularize the song.

CRIMSON AND CLOVER

Artist: Tommy James and the Shondells
Written by: Tommy James, Pete Lucia
From the album: *Crimson and Clover*
Label: Roulette
Produced by: Tommy James
Year: 1969
His biggest hit since "Hanky Panky," in 1966 Covered by Joan Jett (Boardwalk, '82).

CRIPPLED INSIDE

Artist: John Lennon
Written by: John Lennon
From the album: *Imagine*
Label: Apple
Produced by: John Lennon
Year: 1971
Rock therapy.

CROCODILE ROCK

Artist: Elton John
Written by: Elton John, Bernie Taupin
From the album: *Don't Shoot Me, I'm Only the Piano Player*
Label: MCA
Produced by: Gus Dudgeon
Year: 1972
Retro rocker was his first #1.

CROSS-EYED MARY

Artist: Jethro Tull
Written by: Ian Anderson
From the album: *Aqualung*
Label: Reprise
Produced by: Ian Anderson, Terry Ellis
Year: 1971
Typifies the kind of groupies drawn to heavy metal bonds.

CROSSROADS

Artist: Cream
Written by: Robert Johnson
From the album: *Wheels of Fire*
Label: Atco
Produced by: Felix Pappalardi
Year: 1968
The Clapton guitar standard. Originated by legendary bluesman Robert Johnson (Vocalion, '36).

CROSSROADS, THA

Artist: Bone Thugs-n-Harmony
Written by: Steven House, Tim Middleton, Tony Cowan, Charlie Scruggs, Byron McCane, Anthony Henderson, Chris Jasper, The Isley Brothers
From the album: *E.1999 Eternal*
Label: Ruthless
Produced by: DJ U-Neek
Year: 1995
Where doo-wop meets hip hop in a bone-chilling tale of disharmony.

CROSSTOWN TRAFFIC

Artist: Jimi Hendrix
Written by: Jimi Hendrix
From the album: *Electric Ladyland*
Label: Reprise
Produced by: Jimi Hendrix
Year: 1968
Clocking in at #52, this was his second biggest US hit after "All Along the Watchtower" (#20). In the UK he had five Top 10 hits, and "Voodoo Chile" went to #1.

CRUCIFY

Artist: Tori Amos
Written by: Tori Amos
From the album: *Little Earthquakes*
Produced by: Davitt Sigerson
Label: Atlantic
Year: 1992
Melodic confessional from the tortured Laura Nyro school.

CRUEL LITTLE NUMBER

Artist: The Jeff Healey Band
Written by: Jeff Healey, Joe Rockman, Tom Stephen, Carl Marsh, Justis Walker
From the album: *Feel This*
Label: Arista
Produced by: Jeff Healey, Joe Hardy
Year: 1992
#1 rock track from the blind, blues-guitar phenom from Canada.

CRUEL SUMMER

Artist: Bananarama
Written by: Tony Swain, Steve Jolley
From the album: *Bananarama*
Label: London
Produced by: Tony Swain, Steve Jolley
Year: 1984

An incessantly infectious summmertime UK/US Top 10 that established this droll British girl-group as instant successors to the Go-Gos and the Bangles. Video was filmed in the shadows of the Brooklyn Bridge.

CRUEL TO BE KIND

Artist: Nick Lowe
Written by: Nick Lowe, Robert Ian Gomm
From the album: *Labour of Lust*
Label: Columbia
Produced by: Nick Lowe
Year: 1978
His biggest US hit.

CRUISIN'

Artist: Smokey Robinson
Written by: Smokey Robinson, Marvin Tarplin
From the album: *Where There's Smoke*
Label: Tamla
Produced by: Smokey Robinson
Year: 1979
Smokey on cruise control. His biggest solo hit of the '70s.

CRUISIN' FOR BURGERS

Artist: The Mothers of Invention
Written by: Frank Zappa
From the album: *Uncle Meat*
Label: Bizarre
Produced by: Frank Zappa
Year: 1969
Out of the mire that is Los Angeles, some fast food from the '50s.

CRUMBLIN' DOWN

Artist: John (Cougar) Mellencamp
Written by: John Cougar Mellencamp, George Michael Green
From the album: *Uh-Huh*
Label: Riva
Produced by: Don Gehman, Little Bastard
Year: 1983
Crashing through the wall between John Cougar and John Cougar Mellencamp.

CRUNGE, THE

Artist: Led Zeppelin
Written by: Jimmy Page, Robert Plant, John Paul Jones, John Bonham
From the album: *Houses of the Holy*
Label: Atlantic
Produced by: Jimmy Page
Year: 1973
Their mock homage to James Brown. Segue: "Sex Machine" by James Brown.

CRUSH

Artist: Dave Matthews Band
Written by: Dave Matthews
From the album: *Before These Crowded Streets*
Label: RCA

Year: 1998
Never-ending love; never-ending jam.

CRUSH ON YOU

Artist: The Jets
Written by: Jerry Knight, Aaron Zigman
From the album: *The Jets*
Label: MCA
Produced by: Dan Powell, D. Rivkin, Jerry Knight, Aaron Zigman
Year: 1986
New generation Osmond family from Tonga by way of Minneapolis, with appropriately Osmond-flavored teeny dance pop.

CRY

Artist: Johnny Ray
Written by: Churchill Kohlman
Label: Okeh
Produced by: Mitch Miller
Year: 1951
The #1 pop record of '52 was the first example of a white pop song crossing over to the R&B charts (where it was also #1).

CRY BABY

Artist: Garnet Mimms and the Enchanters
Written by: Jerry Ragovoy (Norman Meade), Bert Berns (Bert Russell)
From the album: *Cry Baby and 11 Other Hits*
Label: United Artists
Produced by: Jerry Ragovoy
Year: 1963
#1 R&B/Top 10 crossover. Covered by Janis Joplin (Columbia, '70).

CRY BABY CRY

Artist: The Beatles
Written by: John Lennon, Paul McCartney
From the album: *The Beatles*
Label: Apple
Produced by: George Martin
Year: 1968
Covered by Richard Barone (Passport, '87).

CRY LIKE A BABY

Artist: The Box Tops
Written by: Dan Penn, Spooner Oldham
From the album: *Cry Like a Baby*
Label: Mala
Produced by: Dan Penn
Year: 1968
Blue-eyed Memphis soul. Their second biggest hit.

CRY LIKE A BABY

Artist: Kasey Chambers
Written by: Kasey Chambers
From the album: *The Captain*
Produced by: Nash Chambers
Label: Asylum
Year: 2000

Roots rock from the outbacks of Australia; Kasey was only a couple of years away from an American breakthrough of sorts with the great "Not Pretty Enough."

CRY LIKE A RAINSTORM

Artist: Linda Ronstadt
Written by: Eric Kaz
From the album: *Cry Like a Rainstorm, Howl Like the Wind*
Label: Elektra
Produced by: Peter Asher
Year: 1989
Kaz's most famous song after "Love Has No Pride."

CRY TO ME

Artist: Solomon Burke
Written by: Bert Berns (Bert Russell)
From the album: *Best of Solomon Burke*
Label: Atlantic
Produced by: Bert Berns, Jerry Wexler
Year: 1961
Soul gem, covered by Betty Harris (Jubilee, '63), Garnett Mimms and the Enchanters (United Artists, '65), The Rolling Stones (London, '65), Freddy Scott (Shout, '67).

CRYIN'

Artist: Aerosmith
Written by: Steven Tyler, Joe Perry and Taylor Rhodes
From the album: *Get a Grip*
Produced by: Bruce Fairbairn
Label: Geffen
Year: 1987
A timeless ode to the yin and yang of the old in and out. Video features the debut performance of future film star Alicia Silverstone.

CRYING

Artist: Roy Orbison
Written by: Roy Orbison, Joe Melson
From the album: *Crying*
Label: Monument
Produced by: Fred Foster
Year: 1961
An impossibly ecstatic series of closing crescendos define Roy Orbison as rock's Pagliacci.

CRYING GAME, THE

Artist: Dave Berry
Written by: Geoff Stephens
Label: Decca
Year: 1964
Moody mid-tempo UK hit. Covered by Brenda Lee (Decca, '65) and revived by Boy George for the film, *The Crying Game* (SBK, '93).

CRYING IN THE CHAPEL

Artist: The Orioles
Written by: Artie Glenn

Label: Jubilee
Year: 1953
Pop gospel gem with mass appeal was a triple cross-over by three different artists. The Orioles had the #1 R&B/Top 20 crossover. June Valli had the pop Top 10 hit (RCA). Covered on the country charts by the author's son, Darrell Glenn (Valley), as well as Rex Allen (Decca). Later cover by Elvis Presley went to #3 (RCA, '65).

CRYING IN THE RAIN

Artist: The Everly Brothers
Written by: Howard Greenfield, Carole King
From the album: *Golden Hits of the Everly Brothers*
Label: Warner Brothers
Produced by: Wesley Rose
Year: 1962
One of their defining swan songs. By 1964, while the Beatles were dominating the American charts, minds, and radio waves with the Everly sound, the Brothers' best effort was called "Gone Gone Gone."

CRYING TIME

Artist: Buck Owens
Written by: Buck Owens
From the album: *I've Got a Tiger by the Tail*
Label: Capitol
Year: 1965
In the wake of the Beatles' success with "Act Naturally" came Ray Charles's #1 R&B/Top 10 cover of this Owens tune (ABC Paramount, '66), recorded by Buck on the B-side of his long-running #1 country/Top 30 crossover "I've Got a Tiger by the Tail" (Capitol, '65).

CRYSTAL BLUE PERSUASION

Artist: Tommy James and the Shondells
Written by: Tommy James, Mike Vale, Ed Gray
From the album: *Crimson and Clover*
Label: Roulette
Produced by: Tommy James
Year: 1969
Thinly veiled pyschedelic bubblegum.

CRYSTAL SHIP

Artist: The Doors
Written by: Jim Morrison, Robbie Krieger, John Densmore
From the album: *Strange Days*
Label: Elektra
Produced by: Paul Rothchild
Year: 1967
B-side of "Light My Fire," a comparatively tranquil ride. Covered by Duran Duran (Capitol, '95).

CULT OF PERSONALITY

Artist: Living Colour
Written by: Vernon Reid, Will Calhoun, Cary Glover, Muzz Skillings
From the album: *Vivid*

Label: Epic
Produced by: Ed Stasium
Year: 1989
Driven by Reid's avant guitar, a true anomaly, black heavy metal.

CUM ON FEEL THE NOIZE

Artist: Slade
Written by: Noddy Holder, Jim Lea
From the album: *Slayed*
Label: Polydor
Produced by: Chas Chandler
Year: 1973
Barely literate frat rock for soccer fans. Entered UK charts at #1. Covered for American football fans by L.A.'s post-Randy Rhoads Quiet Riot (Epic, '83).

CUMBERSOME

Artist: Seven Mary Three
Written by: John Pollock, John Ross
From the album: *American Standard*
Produced by: Tom Morris
Label: Mammoth
Year: 1995

CUP OF LIFE, THE

Artist: Ricky Martin
Written by: Robi Rosa, Desmond Child, Luis Escolar
From the album: *Music of the World Cup*
Label: Columbia
Year: 1998
Bolstered by a world-beating performance on the Grammy Award telecast, flooring Rosie O'Donnell, this theme from soccer's World Cup created a window for Latin rock and pop a mile wide and a foot deep. The primary beneficiary, aside from Martin himself, would be Carlos Santana.

CUPID

Artist: Sam Cooke
Written by: Sam Cooke
From the album: *The Best of Sam Cooke*
Label: RCA Victor
Produced by: Hugo and Luigi
Year: 1961
A tribute to the first Love Man. Future successors, from Smokey Robinson to Otis Redding to Al Green to Babyface to Usher, might refer to this as chapter one in the Book of Love.

CUPID'S BOOGIE

Artist: Johnny Otis, Mel Walker & Little Esther
Written by: Johnny Otis, Herman Lubinsky
Label: Savoy
Year: 1950
Otis' third #1 R&B hit of the year, with Little Esther (Phillips) in devilishly angelic form.

CURLY SHUFFLE, THE

Artist: Jump 'N' the Saddle

Written by: Peter Quinn
Label: Atlantic
Year: 1983
Suggested segue: Aerosmith's ode to the Three Stooges, "Walk This Way."

CUT ACROSS SHORTY

Artist: Eddie Cochran
Written by: Wayne Walker, Marijohn Wilkin
Label: Liberty
Produced by: Snuff Garrett
Year: 1958
Something special about that running man. Carl Smith had the country hit (Columbia, '60). Also covered by Rod Stewart alone (Mercury, '70), and with the Faces (Warner Brothers, '74).

CUT YOUR HAIR

Artist: Pavement
Written by: Stephen Malkmus
From the album: *Crooked Rain, Crooked Rain*
Label: Matador
Produced by: Pavement
Year: 1994
Defining low-fi slacker anthem.

CUTS LIKE A KNIFE

Artist: Bryan Adams
Written by: Bryan Adams, Jim Vallance
From the album: *Cuts Like a Knife*
Label: A&M
Produced by: Bob Adams, Bob Clearmountain
Year: 1983
From Canada, the new Neil Young, but without the angst or verisimilitude.

CUTS YOU UP

Artist: Peter Murphy
Written by: Peter Murphy, Paul Statham
From the album: *Deep*
Label: Beggar's Banquet
Produced by: Simon Rogers, Peter Murphy
Year: 1990
Bowiesque dramaturgy.

CUYAHOGA

Artist: R.E.M.
Written by: Michael Stipe, Peter Buck, Bill Berry, Mike Mills
From the album: *Life's Rich Pageant*
Label: IRS
Produced by: Don Gehman
Year: 1986
Like a good new-generation roots band, their prescription for the future was to start over from the beginning.

CYNICAL GIRL

Artist: Marshall Crenshaw
Written by: Marshall Crenshaw
From the album: *Marshall Crenshaw*

Label: Warner Brothers
Produced by: Richard Gottehrer
Year: 1982
Buddy Holly drops out of college in search of his dream girl. Weezer was listening. Suggested segue: "I've Had It" by the Bellnotes.

CYPRESS AVENUE

Artist: Van Morrison
Written by: Van Morrison
From the album: *Astral Weeks*
Label: Warner Brothers
Produced by: Lee Merenstein
Year: 1969
Setting out on Van's metaphorical creative avenue, with guru Bert Burns the unlikely spiritual guide. Future '70s and '80s icons Bruce Springsteen and Bono were listening.

D

D'YER MAKER

Artist: Led Zeppelin
Written by: John Paul Jones, Robert Plant, John Bonham
From the album: *Houses of the Holy*
Label: Atlantic
Produced by: Jimmy Page
Year: 1973
Heavy reggae.

DA BUTT

Artist: E.U.
Written by: Marcus Miller, Mark Stevens
From the album: *School Daze Soundtrack*
Label: EMI-Manhattan
Produced by: Marcus Miller
Year: 1988
Short-lived new dance craze from the Spike Lee film.

DA DA DA (I DON'T LOVE YOU, YOU DON'T LOVE ME)

Artist: Trio
Written by: Krall Krawinkel, Stephan Remmler
From the album: *Da Da Da*
Label: Mobile Suit Corporiation
Produced by: Klaus Voorman
Year: 1982
Triumph of German engineering.

DA DIP

Artist: Freak Nasty
Written by: Eric Timmons
From the album: *Controversee That's Life…and That's the Way It Is*
Label: Triad
Year: 1997
Neo post-disco moodiness.

DA DOO RON RON

Artist: The Crystals
Written by: Jeff Barry, Ellie Greenwich, Phil Spector
From the album: *The Crystals Sing the Greatest Hits*
Label: Philles
Produced by: Phil Spector
Year: 1963
Borrowing the days of the week motif as well as the tag line from the Shirelles's "I Met Him on a Sunday."

DAD I'M IN JAIL

Artist: Was (Not Was)
Written by: David Weiss (David Was), Donald Fagenson (Don Was)
From the album: *What up, Dog*
Label: Chrysalis
Produced by: Don Was, David Was
Year: 1988
The hilarious and grim results of a misspent youth. Suggested segue: "Liar" by the Henry Rollins Band.

DADDY ROLLING STONE

Artist: Otis Blackwell
Written by: Otis Blackwell
From the album: *All Shook Up*
Produced by: Otis Blackwell
Label: Inner City
Year: 1953
Blackwell would pen seminal rock classics for Elvis Presley and Jerry Lee Lewis.

DADDY'S HOME

Artist: Shep and the Limelites
Written by: James Sheppard, William Miller
From the album: *Our Anniversary*
Label: Hull
Year: 1961
One of the all-time doo-wop sentimental classics, made even more poignant by the fact that James Sheppard never did make it home. He was found dead in his car on the Long Island Expressway in 1970.

DAMN, I WISH I WAS YOUR LOVER

Artist: Sophie B. Hawkins
Written by: Sophie B. Hawkins
From the album: *Tongues and Tails*
Label: Columbia
Produced by: Rick Chertoff, Ralph Schukett
Year: 1992
Updating the Lesley Gore aggressive suburban princess persona.

DANCE AWAY

Artist: Roxy Music
Written by: Bryan Ferry
From the album: *Manifesto*
Label: Atco
Produced by: Roxy Music
Year: 1979
Following up "Love Is the Drug" with another languid epic.

DANCE, DANCE, DANCE (YOWSAH, YOWSAH, YOWSAH)

Artist: Chic
Written by: Nile Rodgers, Bernard Edwards, Kenny Lehman
From the album: *Chic*
Label: Atlantic
Produced by: Nile Rodgers, Bernard Edwards
Year: 1977
Evoking a bygone disco era of zoot suits, dance marathons, and dead horses.

DANCE (DISCO HEAT)

Artist: Sylvester
Written by: Victor Orsborn, Eric Robinson
From the album: *Step II*
Label: Fantasy
Produced by: Harvey Fuqua, Sylvester
Year: 1978
A twisted disco original. RuPaul was waiting in the wings.

DANCE HALL DAYS

Artist: Wang Chung
Written by: Jack Hues
From the album: *Points on the Curve*
Label: Geffen
Produced by: Chris Hughes, Ross Cullum
Year: 1984
Biggest UK hit for the UK techno dance band.

DANCE LITTLE SISTER

Artist: Terence Trent D'Arby
Written by: Terence Trent D'Arby
From the album: Introducing t*he Hardline According to Terence Trent D'Arby*
Label: Columbia
Produced by: Martyn Ware, Terence Trent D'Arby
Year: 1987
Third single from his debut album was much bigger in the UK.

DANCE OF THE ROCK AND ROLL INTERVIEWERS

Artist: Frank Zappa with the Royal Philharmonic Orchestra.
Written by: Frank Zappa
From the album: *Frank Zappa's 200 Motels Soundtrack*
Label: United Artists
Produced by: Frank Zappa
Year: 1971
From Zappa's caustic rock documentary.

DANCE ON

Artist: The Shadows
Written by: V.E. Murtaugh
From the album: *The Shadows Greatest Hits*
Label: Columbia
Year: 1963
Third #1 UK hit for the Hank Marvin-led English guitar band that paved the way for Jimmy Page, Jeff Beck, and Mark Knopfler, but never had a hit in the US.

DANCE THE NIGHT AWAY

Artist: Van Halen
Written by: Eddie Van Halen, Alex Van Halen, Michael Anthony, David Lee Roth
From the album: *Van Halen II*
Label: Warner Brothers
Produced by: Ted Templeman
Year: 1979
First Top 20 single for the L.A. guitar hero Eddie Van Halen and his namesake band.

DANCE THIS MESS AROUND

Artist: The B-52's
Written by: The B-52's
From the album: *The B-52's*
Label: Warner Brothers
Produced by: Chris Blackwell
Year: 1979
Opening the incipient Athens, Georgia, college scene to inquiring minds, the original queens of hairspray chic reinvent grassroots boogie. Michael Stipe stopped applying to out-of-town colleges.

DANCE TO THE BOP

Artist: Gene Vincent
Written by: Gene Vincent, Sheriff Tex Davis
Label: Capitol
Produced by: Ken Nelson
Year: 1957
Last of six chart hits.

DANCE TO THE MUSIC

Artist: Sly & the Family Stone
Written by: Sylvester Stewart
From the album: *Dance to the Music*
Label: Epic
Produced by: Sly Stone
Year: 1968
Injecting the funk into psychedelic soul.

DANCE WITH ME

Artist: Peter Brown with Betty Wright
Written by: Peter Brown, Robert Rans
From the album: *A Fantasy Love Affair*
Label: Drive
Year: 1977
Home-studio made disco smash.

DANCE WITH ME

Artist: The Drifters
Written by: Jerry Leiber (Lewis Lebish), Mike Stoller (Elmo Glick), Irv Nahan, George Treadwell
From the album: *Drifters' Greatest Hits*
Label: Atlantic
Produced by: Jerry Leiber, Mike Stoller
Year: 1959
Top 20 follow up to their Top 10 breakthrough "There Goes My Baby."

DANCE WITH ME HENRY (THE WALLFLOWER)

Artist: Etta James
Written by: Johnny Otis, Hank Ballard, Etta James
Label: Modern
Year: 1955
Part of the "Annie" franchise, also known as "Roll with Me Henry." It was written, largely by the same crew, in answer to "Work with Me Annie." Etta had her biggest R&B hit with it. Covered by Georgia Gibbs (Mercury, '55). Featured prominently in the '85 film *Back to the Future*.

DANCIN' FOOL

Artist: Frank Zappa
Written by: Frank Zappa
From the album: *Sheik Yerbouti*
Label: Zappa
Produced by: Frank Zappa
Year: 1979
When Frank Zappa invades the disco scene you know he's only in it for the money. Sure enough, this was his biggest single.

DANCING DAYS

Artist: Led Zeppelin
Written by: Jimmy Page, Robert Plant
From the album: *Houses of the Holy*
Label: Atlantic
Produced by: Jimmy Page
Year: 1973
B-side of "Over the Hills and Far Away" is their answer to the Lovin' Spoonful.

DANCING IN THE DARK

Artist: Bruce Springsteen
Written by: Bruce Springsteen
From the album: *Born in the USA.*
Label: Columbia
Produced by: Jon Landau, Bruce Springsteen, Chuck Plotkin
Year: 1984
He'd been taking lessons from Crazy Janey, but it was Courtney Cox in the video. Artie Shaw was not amused.

DANCING IN THE MOONLIGHT

Artist: King Harvest
Written by: Sherman Kelly
From the album: *Dancing in the Moonlight*
Label: Perception
Produced by: Berjot Robinson
Year: 1973
Mood music for an eerie tribal ritual, reminiscent of the Band's "King Harvest (Has Surely Come)."

DANCING IN THE STREET

Artist: Martha & the Vandellas
Written by: Marvin Gaye, William Stevenson, Ivy Hunter
From the album: *Dance Party*
Label: Gordy
Produced by: William Stevenson
Year: 1964
In the waning days of safe streets, they get their biggest hit. Covered by the Mamas & the Papas (Dunhill, '67). Suggested Segues: "Street Fighting Man" by the Rolling Stones, "Racing in the Streets" by Bruce Springsteen.

DANCING MACHINE

Artist: The Jackson 5
Written by: Weldon Parks, Hal Davis, Donald Fletcher
From the album: *Get It Together*
Label: Motown
Produced by: Hal Davis
Year: 1974
Last hit as the 5.

DANCING ON THE CEILING

Artist: Lionel Richie
Written by: Lionel B. Richie, Carlos Rios
From the album: *Dancing on the Ceiling*
Label: Motown
Produced by: Lionel Richie, Narada Michael Walden
Year: 1985
Clever video.

DANCING QUEEN

Artist: Abba
Written by: Benny Andersson, Bjorn Ulvaeus, Stig Anderson
From the album: *Arrival*
Label: Atlantic
Produced by: Benny Andersson, Bjorn Ulvaeus
Year: 1977
A #1 US/#1 UK crossover, this frothy and incessant ditty was Abba's biggest international hit.

DANCING WITH MYSELF

Artist: Billy Idol and Generation X
Written by: William Broad (Billy Idol), Tony James
From the album: *Don't Stop*
Label: Chrysalis
Year: 1981
Idol's last hit before going solo.

DANDELION

Artist: The Rolling Stones
Written by: Mick Jagger, Keith Richards

From the album: *Through the Past, Darkly (Big Hits, Vol. II)*
Label: London
Produced by: Andrew Loog-Oldham
Year: 1967
They were never much for flower power.

DANDY

Artist: Herman's Hermits
Written by: Ray Davies
From the album: *Best of Herman's Hermits (Vol. II)*
Label: MGM
Produced by: Mickie Most
Year: 1966
A Ray Davies character portrait. Segue: The Kinks's "Dedicated Follower of Fashion."

DANGER ZONE

Artist: Kenny Loggins
Written by: Giorgio Moroder, Tom Whitlock
From the album: *Top Gun Soundtrack*
Label: Columbia
Produced by: Giorgio Moroder
Year: 1986
From the Tom Cruise film *Top Gun*. Loggins was still living off the goodwill from *Caddyshack*'s "I'm Alright."

DANGEROUS

Artist: Busta Rhymes
Written by: Rashad Smith, Trevor Smith, Henry Stone, Freddy Stonewall, Lawrence Dermer
From the album: *When Disaster Strikes*
Label: Elektra
Year: 1998
Gangsta rap, without the gang.

DANGEROUS

Artist: Roxette
Written by: Per Gessel
From the album: *Look Sharp*
Label: EMI
Produced by: Clarence Ofwerman
Year: 1990
Perfecting the Swedish penchant for perfect pop/rock.

DANGLING CONVERSATION, THE

Artist: Simon and Garfunkel
Written by: Paul Simon
From the album: *Parsley, Sage, Rosemary and Thyme*
Label: Columbia
Produced by: Bob Johnston
Year: 1966
Folk/rock goes to college.

DANIEL

Artist: Elton John
Written by: Elton John, Bernie Taupin
From the album: *Don't Shoot Me, I'm Only the Piano Player*
Label: MCA
Produced by: Gus Dudgeon
Year: 1972
One of Bernie's best and fastest lyrics, even though Elton edited out the final verse. One of a dozen songs the pair wrote over the course of two days.

DANNY

Artist: Elvis Presley
Written by: Fred Wise, Ben Weisman
Label: RCA
Produced by: Steve Sholes
Year: 1957
Recorded in '58 for the film *King Creole* but never used. Conway Twitty covered it (MGM, '60) as "Lonely Blue Boy" for his second biggest hit. The original finally surfaced on *Elvis: A Legendary Performer, Vol. 3* (RGA, '79).

DANNY'S SONG

Artist: Loggins and Messina
Written by: Kenny Loggins
From the album: *Sittin' In*
Label: Columbia
Produced by: Jim Messina
Year: 1971
Folk/rock grows up. Covered by Anne Murray (Capitol, '73).

DARK END OF THE STREET, THE

Artist: James Carr
Written by: Dan Penn, Chips Moman
Label: Goldwax
Produced by: Quinton Claunch, Doc Russell
Year: 1967
An all-time cheatin' classic. Covered by Clarence Carter as "Making Love (at the Dark End of the Street)" (Atlantic, '69), the Flying Burrito Brothers (A&M, '69), Aretha Franklin (Atlantic, '70).

DARK LADY

Artist: Cher
Written by: John Durrill
From the album: *Dark Lady*
Label: MCA
Produced by: Snuff Garrett
Year: 1974
Her third solo #1.

DARK STAR

Artist: Grateful Dead
Written by: Jerry Garcia, Robert Hunter
From the album: *Live/Dead*
Label: Warner Brothers
Produced by: Grateful Dead
Year: 1968
One of the first Hunter/Garcia collaborations, this defining anthem appeared on the B-side of "Born Cross Eyed" in '68, but its defining twenty-three-minute version was captured later in *Live/Dead*. A piece of Jerry's solo is captured in Antonioni's 1970 ersatz psychedelic commentary *Zabriskie Point*.

DARKNESS ON THE EDGE OF TOWN

Artist: Bruce Springsteen
Written by: Bruce Springsteen
From the album: *Darkness on the Edge of Town*
Label: Columbia
Produced by: Jon Landau, Bruce Springsteen
Year: 1978
Leaving the comfortable borders of New Jersey (adolescence) and venturing into the dark unknown (adulthood).

DAUGHTER

Artist: Pearl Jam
Written by: Pearl Jam
From the album: *Vs*
Label: Epic
Produced by: Brendan O'Brien, Pearl Jam
Year: 1991
Funny, familiar, familial tensions.

DAVID WATTS

Artist: The Kinks
Written by: Ray Davies
From the album: *Something Else by the Kinks*
Label: Reprise
Produced by: Shel Talmy
Year: 1968
Dickensian Davies. Covered by the Jam (Polydor, '78).

DAVY THE FAT BOY

Artist: Randy Newman
Written by: Randy Newman
From the album: *Randy Newman Creates Something New under the Sun*
Label: Reprise
Produced by: Van Dyke Parks, Lenny Waronker
Year: 1968
After years as a quirky staff songwriter, Newman's incomparable twisted signature finally appears on a song for himself.

DAWN (GO AWAY)

Artist: The Four Seasons
Written by: Bob Gaudio, Sandy Linzer
From the album: *Dawn (Go Away) and 11 Other Great Songs*
Label: Philips
Produced by: Bob Crewe
Year: 1964
Inaugurating Frankie Valli's holier-than-thou persona.

DAWN OF CORRECTION

Artist: The Spokesmen
Written by: John Madara, David White, Raymond Gilmore

From the album: *Dawn of Correction*
Label: Decca
Year: 1965
Answer song to "Eve of Destruction."

DAY AFTER DAY

Artist: Badfinger
Written by: William Peter Ham
From the album: *Straight Up*
Label: Apple
Produced by: Todd Rundgren, George Harrison
Year: 1971
Beatlesque in extremis.

DAY BY DAY

Artist: Cast of Godspell
Written by: John-Michael Tebelak, Stephen Schwartz
From the album: *Godspell Original Cast*
Label: Bell
Produced by: Stephen Schwartz
Year: 1971
Spirit on the stage.

DAY DREAMING

Artist: Aretha Franklin
Written by: Aretha Franklin
From the album: *To Be Young, Gifted and Black*
Label: Atlantic
Produced by: Tom Dowd, Jerry Wexler, Arif Mardin
Year: 1972
Her ninth #1 R&B/Top 10 crossover.

DAY IN—DAY OUT

Artist: David Bowie
Written by: David Bowie
From the album: *Never Let Me Down*
Label: EMI
Produced by: D. Richards, David Bowie
Year: 1986
Bowie's take on arena rock.

DAY IN THE LIFE, A

Artist: The Beatles
Written by: John Lennon, Paul McCartney
From the album: *Sgt. Pepper's Lonely Hearts Club Band*
Label: Capitol
Produced by: George Martin
Year: 1967
Their major existential statement in a chord: the beckoning void of its final endless note closes the song and the album and opens a new era in album rock and FM radio.

DAY OF THE LOCUSTS

Artist: Bob Dylan
Written by: Bob Dylan
From the album: *New Morning*
Label: Columbia
Produced by: Bob Johnston

Year: 1970
Dr. Bob accepts his honorary degree at Princeton, with a title taken from the famous Nathaniel West novel satirizing Hollywood, in which one of the main characters is named Homer Simpson.

DAY TRIPPER

Artist: The Beatles
Written by: John Lennon, Paul McCartney
From the album: *Yesterday and Today*
Label: Capitol
Produced by: George Martin
Year: 1965
The B-side of "We Can Work It Out."

DAYDREAM

Artist: The Lovin' Spoonful
Written by: John Sebastian
From the album: *Daydream*
Label: Kama Sutra
Produced by: Erik Jacobsen
Year: 1966
Good time street music for the new denizens of the weekday daylight hours, your average middle-class college dropout.

DAYDREAM BELIEVER

Artist: The Monkees
Written by: John Stewart
From the album: *The Birds, the Bees and the Monkees*
Label: Colgems
Produced by: Chip Taylor
Year: 1967
Their third and final #1. Covered by the author, the ex-Kingston Trio replacement John Stewart (Warner Brothers, '72), Anne Murray (Capitol, '79). Rereleased by the Monkees minus Nesmith in 1986.

DAYS BETWEEN

Artist: Grateful Dead
Written by: Jerry Garcia, Robert Hunter
Label: Arista
Year: 1994
One of the last tunes Garcia completed before his death in '95.

DAYS OF WINE AND ROSES

Artist: Dream Syndicate
From the album: *The Days of Wine and Roses*
Label: Rough Trade
Produced by: Chris D.
Year: 1982
An eight-minute tour of the Paisley Underground, L.A.'s new folk/rock scene.

DAYTON, OHIO 1903

Artist: Nilsson
Written by: Randy Newman
From the album: *Nilsson Sings Newman*
Label: RCA

Produced by: Nilsson House Productions
Year: 1970
The universes meet.

DAZED AND CONFUSED

Artist: Led Zeppelin
Written by: Jimmy Page
From the album: *Led Zeppelin*
Label: Atlantic
Produced by: Jimmy Page
Year: 1969
Amps on ten, the new Yardbirds offer their dazed and confused fusion of the Delta blues and teeny-bop metal.

DAZZ

Artist: Brick
Written by: Reginald Hargis, Edward Irons, Ray Ransom Jr.
From the album: *Good High*
Label: Bang
Produced by: Jim Healy, Johnny Duncan, Robert Lee, Brick
Year: 1977
Mating disco and jazz for a #1 R&B/Top 10 crossover.

DE DO DO DO, DE DA DA DA

Artist: The Police
Written by: Gordon Sumner (Sting)
From the album: *Zenyatta Mondatta*
Label: A&M
Produced by: Nigel Gray, the Police
Year: 1980
Their first Top 10 hit in the US.

DEACON BLUES

Artist: Steely Dan
Written by: Donald Fagen, Walter Becker
From the album: *Aja*
Label: ABC
Produced by: Gary Katz
Year: 1977
Masterful career retrospective of every musician.

DEAD END STREET

Artist: The Kinks
Written by: Ray Davies
From the album: *Kinks Kronicles*
Label: Reprise
Produced by: Shel Talmy
Year: 1967
Mr. Davies' favorite neighborhood.

DEAD FLOWERS

Artist: The Rolling Stones
Written by: Mick Jagger, Keith Richards
From the album: *Sticky Fingers*
Produced by: Jimmy Miller
Label: Rolling Stones
Year: 1971

Their commentary on Big Pink and the US roots/rock movement. Covered by Townes Van Zandt, the man who invented this sound.

DEAD MAN WALKING

Artist: Bruce Springsteen
Written by: Bruce Springsteen
From the album: *Music Inspired by the Film Dead Man Walking*
Label: Columbia
Produced by: Bruce Springsteen
Year: 1995
Pass the envelope please. The Boss gets more work in Hollywood after "Streets of Philadelphia" picked up a Golden Globe.

DEAD MAN'S CURVE

Artist: Jan and Dean
Written by: Brian Wilson, Jan Berry, Roger Christian, Artie Komfeld
From the album: *Surf City and Other Swingin' Cities*
Label: Liberty
Produced by: Jan Berry
Year: 1964
Classic (and sadly prophetic) car song: classic cars, Stingray and Jaguar XKE.

DEAD SKUNK

Artist: Loudon Wainwright III
Written by: Loudon Wainwright III
From the album: *Album III*
Label: Columbia
Produced by: Thomas Jefferson Kaye
Year: 1972
His one and only chart hit; a middle-of-the-dirt-road smash.

DEAF FOREVER

Artist: Motorhead
Written by: Ian Kilmeister (Lemmy), Mick Burston, Phil Campbell, Pete Gill
From the album: *Orgasmatron*
Label: GGWR/Profile
Produced by: Bill Laswell
Year: 1986
A nod of empathy toward their loyal fan base.

DEAR ABBY

Artist: John Prine
Written by: John Prine
From the album: *Sweet Revenge*
Label: Atlantic
Produced by: Arif Mardin
Year: 1973
Answering confessional rock.

DEAR GOD

Artist: XTC
Written by: Andy Partridge
From the album: *Skylarking*
Label: Geffen
Produced by: Todd Rundgren

Year: 1987
Atheist anthem. Suggested segue: "One of Us" by Joan Osborne.

DEAR LADY TWIST

Artist: Gary US Bonds
Written by: Frank J. Guida
From the album: *Dance 'Til Quarter to Three*
Label: LeGrand
Produced by: Frank J. Guida
Year: 1961
A twist on the Twist.

DEAR LANDLORD

Artist: Bob Dylan
Written by: Bob Dylan
From the album: *John Wesley Harding*
Label: Columbia
Produced by: Bob Johnston
Year: 1968
Compared to the pre-motorcycle accident, mid-'60s verbose Dylan, this was virtually a haiku. Much harder work for Dylanographers. Covered by Joe Cocker (A&M, '70).

DEAR MR. FANTASY

Artist: Traffic
Written by: Steve Winwood, James Capaldi, Chris Wood
From the album: *Mr. Fantasy*
Label: United Artists
Produced by: Jimmy Miller
Year: 1968
Introducing the blue-eyed British psychedelic jazz rockers to America.

DEAR ONE

Artist: Larry Finnegan
Written by: John Lawrence Finneran, Vincent Finneran
Label: Old Town
Year: 1962
In the agonized Dear John (or dear Del Shannon) mode.

DEAR PRUDENCE

Artist: The Beatles
Written by: John Lennon, Paul McCartney
From the album: *The Beatles*
Label: Apple
Produced by: George Martin
Year: 1968
Dedicated to Mia Farrow's sister, Prudence. Covered by the Five Stairsteps on the B-side of "O-o-h Child." (Buddah, '70). Also a big UK hit for Siouxsie & the Banshees (Wonderland, '83).

DEATH OR GLORY

Artist: The Clash
Written by: John Mellor (Joe Strummer), Mick Jones
From the album: *London Calling*

Produced by: Guy Stevens
Label: Epic
Year: 1979
A strong protest statement and rallying cry. Glory, so to speak, came with "Rock the Casbah" in '83.

DEBASER

Artist: The Pixies
Written by: Charles Francis (Black Francis)
From the album: *Doolittle*
Label: 4AD/Elektra
Produced by: Gil Norton
Year: 1989
The East Coast suburban industrial sound: drudge.

DECEMBER 1963 (OH WHAT A NIGHT)

Artist: The Four Seasons
Written by: Bob Gaudio, Judy Parker
From the album: *Who Loves You*
Label: Warner Brothers
Produced by: Bob Gaudio
Year: 1975
Their biggest international hit, #1 US/#1 UK. Remixed version became another international monster in '94.

DEDE DINAH

Artist: Frankie Avalon
Written by: Bob Marcucci, Pete DeAngelis
From the album: *A Whole Lotta Frankie*
Label: Chancellor
Produced by: Bob Marcucci, Pete DeAngelis
Year: 1958
From the *American Bandstand* assembly line in Philadelphia, a former trumpeter steps up for his solo.

DEDICATED FOLLOWER OF FASHION

Artist: The Kinks
Written by: Ray Davies
From the album: *Kinks Kinkdom*
Label: Reprise
Produced by: Shel Talmy
Year: 1966
Answering his own "Dandy."

DEDICATED TO THE ONE I LOVE

Artist: The 5 Royales
Written by: Lowman Pauling, Ralph Bass
From the album: *Dedicated to You*
Label: King
Produced by: Ralph Bass
Year: 1958
One of the great doo-wop classics, propelled as much by Lowman Pauling's stinging guitar as the timeless sentiments for radio listeners everywhere. Cover by the Shirelles hit the Top 10 (Scepter, '61). The Mamas & the Papas struck similar paydirt (Dunhill, '67).

DEEP DARK TRUTHFUL MIRROR

Artist: Elvis Costello
Written by: Declan MacManus (Elvis Costello)
From the album: *Spike*
Label: Warner Brothers
Produced by: T-Bone Burnette, Kevin Killen
Year: 1989
Almost confessional folk.

DEEP DEEP TROUBLE

Artist: Bart Simpson
Written by: Matt Groening, Jeff Townes (D. J. Jazzy Jeff)
From the album: *The Simpsons Sing the Blues*
Label: Geffen
Produced by: John Boylan, D. J. Jazzy Jeff
Year: 1990
Better than Beavis and Butt-Head's "Come to Butt-Head" (Geffen, '93) and further confirming that Groening must be a fan of satirist Nathaniel West.

DEEP PURPLE

Artist: Nino Tempo and April Stevens
Written by: Mitchell Parrish, Peter De Rose
From the album: *Deep Purple*
Label: Atco
Year: 1963
Doo-wopping the classics, volume LCIV. Originated by Larry Clinton (RCA, '44).

DEEPER AND DEEPER

Artist: Madonna
Written by: Shep Pettibone, Madonna Ciccone, Tony Shimkin
From the album: *Erotica*
Label: Maverick
Produced by: Shep Pettibone, Madonna
Year: 1992
Her answer to "More, More, More" by porn-merchant Andrea True. No relation to the Aretha Franklin quasi-spiritual version from *Sister Act, Part Two*.

DEFROST YOUR HEART

Artist: Charlie Feathers
Written by: Quinton Flaunch, William Cantrell
Label: Sun
Produced by: Sam Phillips
Year: 1955
The legendary rockabilly sideman wrote the famous Presley #1 country B-side, "I Forgot to Remember to Forget."

DELIRIOUS

Artist: Prince
Written by: Prince Rogers Nelson
From the album: *1999*
Label: Warner Brothers
Produced by: Prince
Year: 1982
Following up his first Top 10 hit, "Little Red Corvette," with his second.

DELTA DAWN

Artist: Bette Midler
Written by: Alex Harvey, Larry Collins
From the album: *The Divine Miss M*
Label: Atlantic
Produced by: Joel Dorn
Year: 1972
Rural character portrait, given added character by Bette's suburban swagger. Covered by Tanya Tucker (Columbia, '72), Helen Reddy (Capitol, '72).

DELTA LADY

Artist: Joe Cocker
Written by: Leon Russell
From the album: *Joe Cocker*
Label: A&M
Produced by: Denny Cordell
Year: 1969
The lady was Rita Coolidge. Covered by Leon Russell (Shelter, '70).

DENISE

Artist: Randy and the Rainbows
Written by: Neil Levenson
Label: Rust
Produced by: The Tokens
Year: 1963
Essential Italian soul. Cover by Blondie, in French (Chrysalis, '78), went to #1 UK.

DEPORTEES (THE PLANE WRECK AT LOS GATOS)

Artist: Arlo Guthrie
Written by: Woody Guthrie, Martin Hoffman
From the album: *Arlo Guthrie*
Label: Reprise
Year: 1969
Tapping into the folk tradition of his father, Woody.

DER KOMMISSAR

Artist: After the Fire
Written by: Johann (Falco) Hoelzel, Andrew Piercy, Robert Ponger
From the album: *ATF*
Label: Epic
Produced by: John Eden
Year: 1983
Falco had the original hit in Germany.

DESERIE

Artist: The Charts
Written by: Joseph Grier, Danny Robinson
Label: Everlast
Produced by: Bobby Robinson, Danny Robinson
Year: 1957
In doo-wop 101, the midterm; "Gloria" was the final exam.

DESIRE

Artist: U2

Written by: Paul Hewson (Bono)
From the album: *Rattle and Hum*
Label: Island
Produced by: Jimmy Iovine
Year: 1988
Grammy winner was their first #1 in the UK. Suggested segue: "1969" by the Stooges.

DESOLATION ROW

Artist: Bob Dylan
Written by: Bob Dylan
From the album: *Highway 61 Revisited*
Label: Columbia
Produced by: Tom Wilson
Year: 1965
Postcards of the hanging, East Village style.

DESPERADO

Artist: The Eagles
Written by: Don Henley, Glenn Frey
From the album: *Desperado*
Label: Asylum
Produced by: Glyn Johns
Year: 1973
Latching on to the outlaw country mystique. Covered by their former boss, Linda Ronstadt (Asylum, '73).

DESPERADOS WAITING FOR A TRAIN

Artist: Tom Rush
Written by: Guy Clark
From the album: *Ladies Love Outlaws*
Label: Columbia
Year: 1973
Guy Clark on the life cycle.

DESTINY STREET

Artist: Richard Hell
Written by: Richard (Hell) Meyers, Robert Quine, Fred Maher, Nack
From the album: *Destiny Street*
Produced by: Alan Betrock
Label: Sire
Year: 1982
Sure as hell wasn't 6TH between Avenues C and D.

DESTROYER

Artist: The Kinks
Written by: Ray Davies
From the album: *Give the People What They Want*
Label: Arista
Produced by: Ray Davies
Year: 1981
Detailing his ongoing battle with his personal demon, paranoia.

DETERIORATA

Artist: National Lampoon
Written by: Christopher Guest, Tony Hendra
From the album: *Radio Dinner*
Label: Banana

Produced by: Tony Hendra
Year: 1972
Previewing the *National Lampoon/Lemmings* satiric sensibility that would dominate TV once *Saturday Night Live* arrived on the air in '75.

DETOX MANSION

Artist: Warren Zevon
Written by: Warren Zevon, Jorge Calderon
From the album: *Sentimental Hygiene*
Label: Virgin
Produced by: Warren Zevon, Andrew Slater
Year: 1987
Confessions of a chronic abuser.

DETROIT CITY

Artist: Bobby Bare
Written by: Bobby Bare
From the album: *Detroit City and Other Hits by Bobby Bare*
Label: RCA
Produced by: Chet Atkins
Year: 1963
Introducing the countrypolitan sound—a natural outgrowth of The Everly Brothers' trip to the Brill Building. Soon Nashville would be awash in strings.

DETROIT ROCK CITY

Artist: Kiss
Written by: Stanley Eisen (Paul Stanley), Bob Ezrin
From the album: *Destroyer*
Label: Casablanca
Produced by: Bob Ezrin
Year: 1976
Anthemic hard rocker, B-side of "Beth," and later a the subject of a movie which Marshall Mathers undoubtedly snuck into for free.

DEUCE

Artist: Kiss
Written by: Stanley Eisen (Paul Stanley), Gene Simmons
From the album: *Kiss*
Label: Casablanca
Produced by: Kenny Kerner, Richie Wise
Year: 1974
One of their early concert openers and Ace Frehley's favorite Kiss song. Segue: "Go All the Way" by the Raspberries.

DEVIL GATE DRIVE

Artist: Suzi Quatro
Written by: Mike Chapman, Nicky Chinn
From the album: *Quatro*
Label: Bell
Produced by: Mike Chapman
Year: 1974
#1 in the UK, where a girl from the midwest could still wear leather pants. Chrissie Hynde, in Ohio, started making travel arrangements.

DEVIL IN HIS HEART

Artist: The Donays

Written by: Richard Drapkin
Label: Brent
Year: 1962
Classic girl-group nugget from Detroit, covered by the Beatles (Capitol, '64), thus assuring Drapkin cash enough to buy a VW van.

DEVIL INSIDE

Artist: Inxs
Written by: Andrew Farriss, Michael Hutchence
From the album: *Kick*
Label: Atlantic
Produced by: Chris Thomas
Year: 1987
Australian group led by Michael Hutchence follow up their biggest hit "Need You Tonight."

DEVIL OR ANGEL

Artist: The Clovers
Written by: Blanche Carter
Label: Atlantic
Produced by: Ahmet Ertegun, Jerry Wexler
Year: 1955
#4 R&B hit. Top 10 cover by Bobby Vee (Liberty, '60).

DEVIL WENT DOWN TO GEORGIA, THE

Artist: Charlie Daniels
Written by: Charlie Daniels, Tommy Crain, Taz DiGregorio, Fred Edwards, Charles Hayward, Jim Marshall
From the album: *Million Mile Reflections*
Label: Epic
Produced by: Charlie Daniels
Year: 1979
#1 country/Top 10 crossover story song with Biblical implications. In the similarly themed movie about legendary bluesman Robert Johnson, *Crossroads*, the boy was played by Ralph Maccio, the devil's guitar by former Zappa sideman Steve Vai.

DEVIL WITH A BLUE DRESS ON

Artist: Shorty Long
Written by: Shorty Long, William Stevenson
Label: Soul
Produced by: William Stevenson
Year: 1964
First release on the new Motown subsidiary. Covered by Mitch Ryder & the Detroit Wheels in a medley with "Good Golly, Miss Molly" (New Voice, '66).

DEVIL WOMAN

Artist: Cliff Richard
Written by: Christine Authors, Terry Britten
From the album: *I'm Nearly Famous*
Label: Rocket
Produced by: Bruce Welch
Year: 1976

First big US hit after 18 years and 66 singles on the UK charts.

DEVIL'S HAIRCUT

Artist: Beck
Written by: Beck Hanson, Michael King, John Simpson
From the album: *Odelay*
Produced by: Mario Caldato Jr.
Label: DGC
Year: 1996
Alt-rock's newest cut-up, emulating Robert Johnson, makes his own deal with the devil.

DEVOTED TO YOU

Artist: The Everly Brothers
Written by: Boudleaux Bryant
From the album: *The Everly Brothers Best*
Label: Cadence
Produced by: Archie Bleyer
Year: 1958
B-side of "Bird Dog," a future wedding band classic.

DIAL MY HEART

Artist: The Boys
Written by: Kenny Edmunds (Babyface), Antonio Reid (L. A. Reid), Daryl Simmons
From the album: *Messages from the Boys*
Label: Motown
Produced by: Babyface, L. A. Reid
Year: 1988
#1 R&B/Top 20 crossover.

DIAMOND GIRL

Artist: Seals and Crofts
Written by: James Seals, Darrell Crofts
From the album: *Diamond Girl*
Label: Warner Brothers
Produced by: Louie Shelton
Year: 1973
Everlyesque folk/rock.

DIAMONDS AND PEARLS

Artist: The Paradons
Written by: West Tyler, Charles Weldon, Bill Myers, William Powers, Edward Scott
Label: Milestone
Produced by: Edward Scott
Year: 1960
Your father's bling bling.

DIAMONDS AND PEARLS

Artist: Prince
Written by: Prince Rogers Nelson, New Power Generation
From the album: *Diamonds and Pearls*
Label: Paisley Park
Produced by: Prince, New Power Generation
Year: 1991
Dress down Friday at the offices of Paisley Park.

DIAMONDS AND RUST

Artist: Joan Baez
Written by: Joan Baez
From the album: *Diamonds and Rust*
Label: A&M
Produced by: David Kershenbaum
Year: 1975
Joannie and Bobby, from Joannie's point of view. Bobby's point of view is allegedly stated in "Queen Jane Approximately," but probably boils down to "Love Is Just a Four-Letter Word." Covered by Judas Priest (Columbia, '79).

DIAMONDS ON THE SOLES OF HER SHOES

Artist: Paul Simon
Written by: Paul Simon, Joseph Shabalala
From the album: *Graceland*
Label: Warner Brothers
Produced by: Paul Simon
Year: 1986
The roots of rhythm remain. Written with Joseph Shabalala of the noted African group Ladysmith Black Mambazo.

DIANA

Artist: Paul Anka
Written by: Paul Anka
From the album: *Diana,*
Label: ABC Paramount
Produced by: Don Costa
Year: 1957
This quintessential tale of a young adolescent yearning for the charms of an older woman was the product of the first of the new breed of Tin Pan Alley rock and rollers, who could not only write the lyrics and the music, but also sing the songs, balance the books, and rent an office in the Brill Building. The song was the first by a teenager to go #1 UK.

DIARY, THE

Artist: Neil Sedaka
Written by: Howard Greenfield, Neil Sedaka
From the album: *Neil Sedaka*
Label: RCA Victor
Produced by: Al Nevins
Year: 1958
Rejected by Little Anthony, this tune established Sedaka as a suitable alternate boy soprano.

DID IT IN A MINUTE

Artist: Daryl Hall & John Oates
Written by: Daryl Hall, Janna Allen, Sara Allen
From the album: *Private Eyes*
Label: RCA
Produced by: Hall & Oates
Year: 1981
Sara (Smile) Allen and her sister cement their writing relationship with the duo.

DID YOU EVER HAVE TO MAKE UP YOUR MIND

Artist: The Lovin' Spoonful
Written by: John Sebastian
From the album: *Do You Believe in Magic*
Label: Kama Sutra
Produced by: Erik Jacobsen
Year: 1965
Armed with his autoharp and harmonica belt, converted Greenwich Village folkie John Sebastian reigns briefly as the hip king of the hop.

DID YOU SEE JACKIE ROBINSON HIT THAT BALL

Artist: Buddy Johnson
Written by: Buddy Johnson
Label: Decca
Year: 1949
A jump blues tribute to the pioneering Brooklyn Dodger infielder makes the R&B chart and millions cheered.

DIDDLEY DADDY

Artist: Bo Diddley
Written by: Ellas McDaniel (Bo Diddley)
From the album: *Bo Diddley's 16 All-Time Greatest Hits*
Label: Checker
Produced by: Leonard Chess
Year: 1955
The Rolling Stones almost chose this as their first single. Instead it was Chuck Berry's "Come On."

DIDDY WAH DIDDY

Artist: Bo Diddley
Written by: Ellas McDaniel (Bo Diddley), Willie Dixon
From the album: *Bo Diddley*
Label: Checker
Produced by: Willie Dixon
Year: 1957
The title phrase has a place in the language of folk music equaled only by "Guabi Guabi." Covered by Captain Beefheart as his first single (A&M, '66).

DIDN'T I (BLOW YOUR MIND THIS TIME)

Artist: The Delfonics
Written by: Thom Bell, William Hart
From the album: *The Delfonics*
Label: Philly Groove
Produced by: Stan Watson, Thom Bell
Year: 1970
A defining Philly groove.

DIFFERENCE, THE

Artist: The Wallflowers
Written by: Jakob Dylan
From the album: *Bringing down the Horse*
Label: Interscope

Produced by: T-Bone Burnette
Year: 1996
Following his bloodline to the bank (and a Grammy), with an antilove song.

DIFFERENT CORNER, A

Artist: Wham!
Written by: George Michael
From the album: *Music from the Edge of Heaven*
Label: Columbia
Produced by: George Michael
Year: 1986
Last #1 UK/Top 10 US before George went solo.

DIFFERENT DRUM

Artist: The Stone Poneys
Written by: Mike Nesmith
From the album: *Evergreen (Vol. II)*
Label: Capitol
Produced by: Nik Venet
Year: 1965
The nascent liberated L.A. woman, delivered in the adenoidal tones of an Arizona expatriate, written in the parlance of folk/rock, by the intellectual Monkee.

DIGERIDOO

Artist: Aphex Twin
Written by: Richard D. James
From the album: *Analogue Bubblebath, V. 2*
Produced by: Richard D. James
Label: Rabbit City
Year: 1992
Breakthrough in dance-hall technology.

DIGGING THE DIRT

Artist: Peter Gabriel
Written by: Peter Gabriel
From the album: *Us*
Produced by: Peter Gabriel, Daniel Lanois
Label: Geffen
Year: 1992
For his first recording in six years, Gabriel did research on Death Row.

DIGNITY

Artist: Bob Dylan
Written by: Bob Dylan
From the album: *Greatest Hits III*
Label: Columbia
Year: 1995
Used in the TV series *Touched by an Angel*. Dylan would lose the remainder of his dignity about a decade later when he appeared in an ad for the lingerie company, Victoria's Secret.

DIM ALL THE LIGHTS

Artist: Donna Summer
Written by: Donna Summer
From the album: *Bad Girls*
Label: Casablanca
Produced by: Giorgio Moroder, Pete Bellotte

Year: 1979
Still on a disco tear.

DIM, DIM THE LIGHTS (I WANT SOME ATMOSPHERE)

Artist: Bill Haley and His Comets
Written by: Julius Dixon, Beverly Ross
From the album: *Rock around the Clock*
Label: Decca
Produced by: Milt Gabler
Year: 1954
Making the world a safer place for Elvis, Haley charts his first R&B crossover.

DIMMING OF THE DAY, THE

Artist: Richard and Linda Thompson
Written by: Richard Thompson
From the album: *Pour Down Like Silver*
Label: Island
Produced by: Richard Thompson, John Wood
Year: 1975
Covered by Bonnie Raitt (Capitol, '94).

DIRT

Artist: Lou Reed
Written by: Lou Reed
From the album: *Street Hassle*
Label: Arista
Produced by: Lou Reed, Richard Robinson
Year: 1978

DIRTY BOULEVARD

Artist: Lou Reed
Written by: Lou Reed
From the album: *New York*
Label: Sire
Produced by: Fred Maher, Lou Reed
Year: 1989
Like Neil Diamond (Brooklyn), Dion (the Bronx), or Paul Simon (Queens), Lou sums up his neighborhood (NY's East Village) better than anyone.

DIRTY DEEDS DONE DIRT CHEAP

Artist: AC/DC
Written by: Angus Young, Malcolm Young
From the album: *Dirty Deeds Done Dirt Cheap*
Label: Atlantic
Produced by: Harry Vanda, Malcolm Young
Year: 1981
Bon Scott tour de force. Covered by Joan Jett (Blackheart, '90).

DIRTY DIANA

Artist: Michael Jackson
Written by: Michael Jackson
From the album: *Bad*
Label: Epic
Produced by: Quincy Jones

Year: 1987
Extolling the dark side of his mentor, Ross, with a #1 R&B/#1 crossover, with Steve Stevens playing the Eddie Van Halen part on guitar.

DIRTY DIRTY FEELING

Artist: Elvis Presley
Written by: Jerry Leiber, Mike Stoller
From the album: *Elvis Is Back*
Label: RCA
Produced by: Jerry Leiber, Mike Stoller
Year: 1960
And no wonder, the movie this was written for, *Tickle Me*, features Elvis at an all-girl dude ranch.

DIRTY LAUNDRY

Artist: Don Henley
Written by: Don Henley, Danny Kortchmar
From the album: *I Can't Stand Still*
Label: Asylum
Produced by: Don Henley, Danny Kortchmar
Year: 1982
First solo hit for the former Eagle contains little in the way of backstage revelations.

DIRTY OLD TOWN

Artist: Rod Stewart
Written by: Ewan MacColl
From the album: *The Rod Stewart Album*
Label: Mercury
Produced by: Lou Reizner
Year: 1969
Rod at his grittiest, back when he was still a scuffling homeboy. Suggested segues: "Streets of London" by Ralph McTell, "Gilbert Street" by Sweet Thursday.

DIRTY WATER

Artist: The Standells
Written by: Ed Cobb
From the album: *Dirty Water*
Label: Tower
Produced by: Ed Cobb
Year: 1965
In the "Coney Island Baby" tradition (wherein a Bronx group portrayed themselves as Brooklyn natives), this garage rocker about Boston's Charles River was done by a group from L.A.

DIRTY WORK

Artist: Steely Dan
Written by: Donald Fagen, Walter Becker
From the album: *Can't Buy a Thrill*
Label: ABC
Produced by: Gary Katz
Year: 1972
Former staff songwriters come unglued after reading Joseph Heller and Thomas Pynchon.

DISAPPEAR

Artist: Inxs
Written by: Jon Farriss, Michael Hutchence
From the album: *X*

Label: Atlantic
Produced by: Chris Thomas
Year: 1990
Their last big hit, in which is foretold the disappearance of lead singer Hutchence, who would later commit suicide. In the new century, the group would seek to replace him via televised talent search.

DISAPPOINTED

Artist: Public Image Ltd. (P.I.L.)
Written by: Public Image Ltd.
From the album: *9*
Label: Virgin
Produced by: Stephen Hague, Eric Thorngren
Year: 1989
Following up the Sex Pistols with a pill for impotence.

DISCO INFERNO

Artist: Trammps
Written by: Leroy Green, Ron Kersey
From the album: *Disco Inferno*
Label: Atlantic
Produced by: Norman Harris
Year: 1977
Featured in the disco epic *Saturday Night Fever*.

DISCO LADY

Artist: Johnnie Taylor
Written by: Don Davis, Harvey Scales, Albert Vance
From the album: *Eargasm*
Label: Columbia
Produced by: Don Davis
Year: 1976
The world's first platinum selling single.

DISCO NIGHTS (ROCK FREAK)

Artist: GQ
Written by: Emmanuel Le Blanc, Herbert Lane, Keith Crier, Paul Service
From the album: *Disco Nights*
Label: Arista
Produced by: Jimmy Simpson, Bear Roy Fleming
Year: 1979

DISCOTHEQUE

Artist: U2
Written by: Paul (Bono) Hewson, Dave (The Edge) Evans
From the album: *Pop*
Label: Island
Produced by: Flood, Howie B.
Year: 1997
First single from the album finds them experimenting with electronica. #1 UK.

DISSIDENT

Artist: Pearl Jam
Written by: Eddie Vedder, Stone Gossard, Jeff Ament, Mike McCready, Dave Abbruzzese

From the album: *Vs*
Label: Epic
Produced by: Brendan O'Brien, Pearl Jam
Year: 1993
Flying their flannel freak flag.

DISTANCE, THE

Artist: Cake
Written by: Greg Brown
From the album: *Fashion Nugget*
Label: Capricorn
Year: 1996
Quirk rock.

DIXIE FRIED

Artist: Carl Perkins
Written by: Carl Perkins, Herman Parker
Label: Sun
Produced by: Sam Phillips
Year: 1956
Only two singles past the glory of "Blue Suede Shoes," Carl didn't even make the Top 100 with this country hit.

DIZZY

Artist: Tommy Roe
Written by: Tommy Roe, Freddy Weller
From the album: *12 in a Roe/A Collection of Tommy Roe's Greatest Hits*
Label: ABC
Produced by: Steve Barri
Year: 1969
Like Elvis, Tommy Roe returned to #1 in '69 for the first time since '62.

DJ CULTURE

Artist: Pet Shop Boys
Written by: Neil Tennant, Chris Lowe
From the album: *Discography: The Complete Singles Collection*
Label: EMI
Produced by: Stephen Hague
Year: 1991
They wrote the book.

DO ANYTHING

Artist: Natural Selection
Written by: Frederick Thomas, Elliot Erickson, Ingrid Chaver
From the album: *Natural Selection*
Label: East/West
Year: 1991
Hip-hop one shot.

DO FRIES GO WITH THAT SHAKE?

Artist: George Clinton
Written by: George Clinton, Sheila Washington, Stephen Washington
From the album: *R&B Skeletons in the Closet*
Label: Capitol
Produced by: George Clinton

Year: 1986
One of his more perfect titles.

DO IT

Artist: Pink Faeries
Written by: Mick Farren, John (Twink) Adler
From the album: *Never Never Land*
Label: Polydor
Year: 1971
The early inklings of glam. Covered by Henry Rollins (Texas Hotel, '87).

DO IT ('TIL YOU'RE SATISFIED)

Artist: B.T. Express
Written by: Billy Nichols
From the album: *Do It ('Til You're Satisfied)*
Label: Roadshow
Year: 1974
Inspired by his drum machine, Billy Nichols creates an R&B classic for the Brooklyn Trucking Express.

DO IT AGAIN

Artist: The Beach Boys
Written by: Brian Wilson, Mike Love
From the album: *20/20*
Label: Capitol
Produced by: Brian Wilson
Year: 1968
Rerecorded by Brian and his daughter Carnie for the documentary *I Just Wasn't Made for These Times*, and its soundtrack album (MCA, '95).

DO IT AGAIN

Artist: Steely Dan
Written by: Donald Fagen, Walter Becker
From the album: *Can't Buy a Thrill*
Label: ABC
Produced by: Gary Katz
Year: 1972
Dressing their bohemian jazz ethos in Top-40 garb Fagen and Becker score their first big hit.

DO ME!

Artist: Bell Biv Devoe
Written by: Carl Bourelly, Michael Bivens, Ronnie Devoe, Ricky Bell
From the album: *Poison*
Label: MCA
Produced by: Carl Bourelly, Dr. Freeze
Year: 1990
Post-high school New Edition.

DO RIGHT WOMAN, DO RIGHT MAN

Artist: Aretha Franklin
Written by: Dan Penn, Chips Moman
From the album: *I Never Loved a Man*
Label: Atlantic
Produced by: Jerry Wexler
Year: 1967

B-side of "I Never Loved a Man (the Way I Love You)," this Memphis soul classic is one of her all-time greatest performances. Covered by the Flying Burrito Brothers (A&M, '69).

DO SOMETHING FOR ME

Artist: The Dominoes
Written by: Rose Marks, Billy Wards
From the album: *The Dominoes Featuring Clyde McPhatter*
Label: King
Year: 1950
From their first session a new direction emerges for R&B: the mainstream.

DO THE PUSH AND PULL (PART I)

Artist: Rufus Thomas
Written by: Rufus Thomas
From the album: *Rufus Thomas Live/Doing the Push and Pull at P. J.'s*
Label: Stax
Produced by: Al Bell, Thom Nixon
Year: 1970
A dance for the new post-bliss era is his only #1 R&B hit. If only Jules Feiffer could have choreographed it.

DO THE STRAND

Artist: Roxy Music
Written by: Bryan Ferry
From the album: *For Your Pleasure*
Label: Warner Brothers
Produced by: Chris Thomas, John Astley
Year: 1973
Dance music for people too hip to dance.

DO THEY KNOW IT'S CHRISTMAS?

Artist: Band-Aid
Written by: Bob Geldof, Midge Ure
Label: Columbia
Year: 1984
An all-star charity jam for Ethiopian relief that launched Geldof toward knighthood. This #1 single was the biggest seller in UK history, and hit Top 20 in the US. It led to the famous Live Aid concert, as well as a spate of rock aid events. Cut again in '89 by a new set of all-stars.

DO WAH DIDDY

Artist: The Exciters
Written by: Jeff Barry, Ellie Greenwich
From the album: *Tell Him*
Label: United Artists
Produced by: Jeff Barry, Ellie Greenwich
Year: 1963
Covered by Manfred Mann as "Do Wah Diddy Diddy" (Ascot, '64). It must have been that added "Diddy" that propelled the previous stiff to #1 US/#1 UK, a fact that couldn't have been lost on Sean Combs.

DO YA

Artist: The Move
Written by: Jeff Lynne
From the album: *Split Ends*
Label: United Artists
Produced by: Jeff Lynne
Year: 1972
In some quarters, rock song of the year. Covered by Lynne in ELO (United Artists, '76), Ace Frehley (Megaforce, '89).

DO YA THINK I'M SEXY

Artist: Rod Stewart
Written by: Rod Stewart, Carmine Appice
From the album: *Blondes Have More Fun*
Label: Warner Brothers
Produced by: Tom Dowd
Year: 1979
Rod does disco and vice-versa.

DO YOU BELIEVE IN LOVE

Artist: Huey Lewis and the News
Written by: Robert John "Mutt" Lange
From the album: *Picture This*
Label: Chrysalis
Produced by: Huey Lewis and the News
Year: 1982
Rootsy bar-band rocker, with a dash of Mutt.

DO YOU BELIEVE IN MAGIC

Artist: The Lovin' Spoonful
Written by: John Sebastian
From the album: *Do You Believe in Magic*
Label: Kama Sutra
Produced by: Erik Jacobsen
Year: 1965
Epitomizing the good-time jangly essence of folk/rock, the Spoonful electrify Greenwich Village with this single.

DO YOU FEEL LIKE WE DO?

Artist: Peter Frampton
Written by: Peter Frampton, Michael Gallagher, John Sidmos, Rick Wills
From the album: *Frampton's Camel*
Label: A&M
Produced by: Peter Frampton
Year: 1973
Became a hit when he performed it on *Frampton Comes Alive* in '76, through the magic of the talk box. Segue: "Sweet Emotion" by Aerosmith.

DO YOU KNOW WHERE YOU'RE GOING TO? (THEME FROM *MAHOGANY*)

Artist: Diana Ross
Written by: Gerry Goffin, Michael Masser
From the album: *Diana Ross*
Label: Motown
Produced by: Michael Masser
Year: 1975
Big movie ballad is Diana's third #1 and marks a major return to form for Carole King's former husband and lyricist Gerry Goffin.

DO YOU LOVE ME?

Artist: The Contours
Written by: Berry Gordy Jr.
From the album: *Do You Love Me*
Label: Gordy
Produced by: Berry Gordy Jr.
Year: 1962
Early Motown dance groove is a #1 R&B/Top 10 crossover. Covered by the Dave Clark Five (Epic, '64). Featured in the '87 film *Dirty Dancing*.

DO YOU REALLY WANT TO HURT ME?

Artist: Culture Club
Written by: Roy Hay, Jon Moss, Michael Craig, George O'Dowd
From the album: *Kissing to be Clever*
Label: Epic
Produced by: Steve Levene
Year: 1983
Catchy British soul in lite reggae drag was the first trans-Atlantic hit for crossdressing Boy George.

DO YOU REMEMBER

Artist: Phil Collins
Written by: Phil Collins
From the album: *… But Seriously folks*
Label: Atlantic
Produced by: Hugh Padgham, Phil Collins
Year: 1990
Third Top 10 hit from the album.

DO YOU REMEMBER ROCK AND ROLL RADIO

Artist: The Ramones
Written by: Douglas Colvin, John Cummings, Jeff Hyman
From the album: *End of the Century*
Label: Sire
Produced by: Phil Spector
Year: 1979
Queens boys protest song, produced by the man who arguably created the need for rock and roll radio in the first place.

DO YOU WANNA MAKE LOVE

Artist: Peter McCann
Written by: Peter McCann
From the album: *Peter McCann*
Label: 20TH Century
Produced by: Hal Yoegler
Year: 1977
Top 10 one-shot. B-side is his version of the Jennifer Warnes hit, "Right Time of the Night," which he also wrote.

DO YOU WANNA TOUCH ME

Artist: Gary Glitter
Written by: Gary Glitter, Mike Leander
Label: Bell
Produced by: Mike Leander
Year: 1973
Covered by Joan Jett (Boardwalk, '82).

DO YOU WANT TO DANCE?

Artist: Bobby Freeman
Written by: Bobby Freeman
From the album: *Do You Want to Dance*
Label: Josie
Year: 1958
Sock-hop standard, with a false ending that drove DJs mad.

DO YOU WANT TO KNOW A SECRET

Artist: The Beatles
Written by: John Lennon, Paul McCartney
From the album: *Introducing the Beatles*
Label: Vee Jay
Produced by: George Martin
Year: 1963
A hit in England for Billy J. Kramer & the Dakotas (Parlaphone, '63), which they later sang in the '74 movie *Stardust*. The Beatles's version was George's biggest vocal hit. Suggested segue: "I Really Love You" by the Stereos.

DOCTOR MY EYES

Artist: Jackson Browne
Written by: Jackson Browne
From the album: *Saturate Before Using*
Label: Asylum
Produced by: Richard Orshoff
Year: 1972
In the mellowing year of California folk/rock, Browne's laid-back philosophizing made the Top 10. Cover by the Jackson 5 made the Top 10 in England.

DOCTORIN' THE TARDIS

Artist: The Timelords
Written by: Mike Chapman, Nicky Chinn, Bill Drummond, Jimi Cauty
Label: KLF
Year: 1988
#1 UK dance single by members of the Justified Ancients of Mu Mu, who would evolve into the KLF.

DOES YOUR CHEWING GUM LOSE ITS FLAVOR ON THE BEDPOST OVERNIGHT?

Artist: Lonnie Donegan
Written by: Billy Rose, Marty Bloom, Ernest Breuer

Label: Dot
Year: 1959
Pre-Beatles England skiffle standard, originated by Harry Richman in '24.

DOESN'T REALLY MATTER

Artist: Janet Jackson
Written by: James (Jimmy Jam) Harris, Terry Lewis, Janet Jackson
From the album: *The Nutty Professor II, The Klumps*
Label: Def Jam
Year: 2000
Due to a wardrobe malfunction, this would probably be the last time a song of hers appeared in a family movie.

DOESN'T SOMEBODY WANT TO BE WANTED

Artist: The Partridge Family
Written by: Mike Appel, Wes Farrell, Jim Cretecos
From the album: *Up to Date*
Label: Bell
Produced by: Wes Farrell
Year: 1971
Appel and Cretecos get a major writing credit, finally giving them enough funds to bankroll their new boy, the future Boss, Bruce Springsteen.

DOGGIN' AROUND

Artist: Jackie Wilson
Written by: Lena Agree
From the album: *Jackie Sings the Blues*
Label: Brunswick
Produced by: Dick Jacobs, Nat Tarnopol
Year: 1960
B-side of the operatic "Night" is Jackie at his bluesiest; his third #1 R&B.

DOIN' IT TO DEATH

Artist: JB's
Written by: James Brown
From the album: *Doin' It to Death*
Label: People
Produced by: James Brown
Year: 1973
Funk jam celebrates the return of sax man Maceo Parker to the JB's fold.

DOLL PARTS

Artist: Hole
Written by: Courtney Love, Kristen Pfaff, Eric Erlandson, Patty Schemel
From the album: *Live through This*
Label: DGC
Produced by: Paul Q. Kolderie, Sean Slade
Year: 1994
Commercial breakthrough for Kurt Cobain's feisty widow, Courtney Love.

DOLLY DAGGER

Artist: Jimi Hendrix
Written by: Jimi Hendrix
From the album: *Rainbow Bridge*
Label: Reprise
Produced by: Jimi Hendrix
Year: 1971
Last pre-posthumous single, before the deluge of reissues by the infamous Hendrixologist Alan Douglas.

DOLPHINS, THE

Artist: Fred Neil
Written by: Fred Neil
From the album: *Fred Neil*
Label: Elektra
Produced by: Nik Venet
Year: 1967
Fred Neil's crowning achievment (along with playing guitar on "Dream Lover" and "Diana"), swimming with the Dolphins. Covered by Dion (Laurie, '68), Richie Havens (Stormy Forest, '72), Beth Orton and Terry Callier (Dedicated, '97).

DOMINIQUE

Artist: The Singing Nun
Written by: Jeanine Decker (Soeur Sourire)
Label: Phillips
Year: 1963
Soon after singing this French folk lullabye praising the founder of the Dominican order on *The Ed Sullivan Show* Soeur Sourire left the convent to pursue wider interests, typified by her follow-up stiff "Glory Be to God for the Golden Pill." Debbie Reynolds played her in *The Singing Nun*, the movie, and Sally Fields was undoubtedly inspired by her in *The Flying Nun*, the TV series. Jeanine Decker and her companion both committed suicide in 1985.

DOMINO

Artist: Van Morrison
Written by: Van Morrison
From the album: *His Band and Street Choir*
Label: Warner Brothers
Produced by: Van Morrison
Year: 1970
Aside from "Brown Eyed Girl," his only other hit single.

DON'T

Artist: Elvis Presley
Written by: Jerry Leiber, Mike Stoller
From the album: *Touch of Gold (Vol. I)*
Label: RCA
Produced by: Steve Sholes
Year: 1958
Elvis the sexual predator, '50s style. Does he say "kiss" or "kill" in the first verse?

DON'T ASK ME TO BE FRIENDS

Artist: The Everly Brothers

Written by: Gerry Goffin, Jack Keller
Label: Warner Brothers
Produced by: Wesley Rose
Year: 1962
Third straight stiff of '62 after starting the year with two Top 10 hits.

DON'T ASK ME TO BE LONELY

Artist: The Dubs
Written by: Richard Blandon
From the album: *Meet the Shells*
Label: Gone
Year: 1957
New York doo-wop classic, foretells the glory only four months later of "Could This Be Magic."

DON'T BE A DROP-OUT

Artist: James Brown and the Famous Flames
Written by: James Brown, Nat Jones
From the album: *Raw Soul*
Label: King
Produced by: James Brown
Year: 1966
Public service announcement as crossover hit.

DON'T BE CRUEL

Artist: Bobby Brown
Written by: Kenny Edmunds (Babyface), Antonio Reid (L.A. Reid), Daryl Simmons
From the album: *Don't Be Cruel*
Label: MCA
Produced by: Babyface, L. A. Reid
Year: 1988
Launching his solo career with a surefire title. In fact, Cheap Trick was covering the Elvis tune on the same Top 10 of '88

DON'T BE CRUEL (TO A HEART THAT'S TRUE)

Artist: Elvis Presley
Written by: Otis Blackwell, Elvis Presley
From the album: *Real Elvis*
Label: RCA
Produced by: Steve Sholes
Year: 1956
Accomplishing his first #1 country/R&B/pop crossover, along with the transmogrified, freshly groomed "Hound Dog." He would do this twice more in his career, both times in '57.

DON'T BELIEVE THE HYPE

Artist: Public Enemy
Written by: Carlton Ridenhour, Hank Shocklee, Eric Sadler, Charles Drayton
From the album: *It Takes a Nation of Millions to Hold Us Back*
Label: Def Jam
Produced by: Hank Shocklee, Carl Ryder
Year: 1988
Racist, sexist, and visionary rap, spearheaded by Ridenhour, a Long Island college kid, takes

collegiate America by storm, evoking memories of the Black Panthers and their White Panther sympathizers of the '60s.

DON'T BOGART ME

Artist: Fraternity of Man
Written by: Elliot Ingber, Stash Wagner
From the album: *Fraternity of Man*
Label: ABC
Produced by: Kim Fowley
Year: 1968
Classic '60s dope etiquette period piece featured in the movie *Easy Rider*. Covered by Little Feat (Warner Brothers, '78) under its more appropriate title "Don't Bogart That Joint."

DON'T BOTHER ME

Artist: The Beatles
Written by: George Harrison
From the album: *Meet the Beatles*
Label: Capitol
Produced by: George Martin
Year: 1964
The quiet Beatle finally gets a copyright all his own.

DON'T BREAK THE HEART THAT LOVES YOU

Artist: Connie Francis
Written by: Benny Davis, Ted Murry
From the album: *Connie Francis Sings*
Label: MGM
Produced by: Connie Francis
Year: 1962
Her third #1.

DON'T BRING ME DOWN

Artist: The Animals
Written by: Gerry Goffin, Carole King
From the album: *Animalization*
Label: MGM
Produced by: Mickie Most
Year: 1966
Essential Brill Building folk/rock.

DON'T BRING ME DOWN

Artist: Electric Light Orchestra (ELO)
Written by: Jeff Lynne
From the album: *Discovery*
Label: Jet
Year: 1979
Biggest hit in the US for Jeff Lynne's Beatlesque group.

DON'T CALL ME NIGGER, WHITEY

Artist: Sly and the Family Stone
Written by: Sylvester Stewart
From the album: *Stand!*
Label: Epic
Produced by: Sly Stone

Year: 1969
Message music, ahead of its time.

DON'T CRY

Artist: Guns N' Roses
Written by: Axl Rose, Izzy Stradlin
From the album: *Use Your Illusion II*
Label: Geffen
Produced by: Mike Clink, Guns N' Roses
Year: 1991
Displaying their ballad chops. But it was no "Sweet Child of Mine."

DON'T CRY DADDY

Artist: Elvis Presley
Written by: Mac Davis, Billy Strange
From the album: *Worldwide 50 Gold Award Hits (Vol. I)*
Label: RCA
Produced by: Chips Moman, Felton Jarvis, Elvis Presley
Year: 1969
Recorded at his first Memphis session since '55, this was Elvis's biggest hit on the country charts since '58. Wayne Newton was listening.

DON'T CRY OUT LOUD

Artist: Melissa Manchester
Written by: Peter Allen, Carole Bayer Sager
From the album: *Don't Cry out Loud*
Label: Arista
Produced by: Harry Maslin
Year: 1978
Broadway ballad written by a couple of showbiz kids, one of them the husband of Liza Minnelli, the other the wife of Marvin Hamlisch, though not at the time.

DON'T DISTURB THIS GROOVE

Artist: The System
Written by: Mic Murphy, David Frank
From the album: *Don't Disturb This Groove*
Label: Capitol
Produced by: The System
Year: 1987
Synth-based funk instrumental.

DON'T DO ME LIKE THAT

Artist: Tom Petty and the Heartbreakers
Written by: Tom Petty
From the album: *Damn the Torpedoes*
Label: Backstreet
Produced by: Jimmy Iovine, Tom Petty
Year: 1979
In the funky late 70s, Petty's brand of folk/rock was thought of as alternative.

DON'T DREAM IT'S OVER

Artist: Crowded House
Written by: Neil Finn
From the album: *Crowded House*

Label: Capitol
Produced by: Mitchell Froom
Year: 1987
Biggest hit for the former Split Enz.

DON'T EAT THE YELLOW SNOW

Artist: Frank Zappa
Written by: Frank Zappa
From the album: *Apostrophe*
Label: DiscReet
Produced by: Frank Zappa
Year: 1974
Sage Eskimo wisdom from the solo Mother gains him the first of his three chart singles.

DON'T FALL APART ON ME TONIGHT

Artist: Bob Dylan
Written by: Bob Dylan
From the album: *Infidels*
Label: Columbia
Produced by: Bob Dylan, Mark Knopfler
Year: 1983
Dylan's first appearance on MTV and the end of the world as we knew it (but he felt fine).

(DON'T FEAR) THE REAPER

Artist: Blue Oyster Cult
Written by: Donald Roeser (Buck Dharma)
From the album: *Agents of Fortune*
Label: Columbia
Produced by: Sandy Pearlman
Year: 1976
An arena crowd-pleaser about death is their first hit. Suggested segue: "Dust in the Wind" by Kansas.

DON'T FORBID ME

Artist: Pat Boone
Written by: Charles Singleton
From the album: *Pat's Great Hits*
Label: Dot
Year: 1956
Pat had the hit, but I wouldn't be surprised if it was released first by Elvis Presley with the Million Dollar Quartet: Carl Perkins, Jerry Lee Lewis, and Johnny Cash (Sun, '56).

DON'T FORGET ME WHEN I'M GONE

Artist: Glass Tiger
Written by: Alan Frew, Jim Vallance, Sam Reid
From the album: *The Thin Red Line*
Label: Manhattan
Produced by: Jim Vallance
Year: 1986
Smash from Canada, produced by Bryan Adams's partner.

DON'T GET ME WRONG

Artist: The Pretenders
Written by: Chrissie Hynde
From the album: *Get Close*
Label: Sire
Produced by: Jimmy Iovine
Year: 1986
Midcareer crisis.

DON'T GIVE UP

Artist: Peter Gabriel and Kate Bush
Written by: Peter Gabriel
From the album: *So*
Label: Geffen
Produced by: Peter Gabriel, Daniel Lanois
Year: 1986
With Kate Bush on background harmonies, standing by him, believing in him, urging him on, a man could scale the Matterhorn on one leg.

DON'T GIVE UP ON US

Artist: David Soul
Written by: Tony Macaulay
From the album: *David Soul*
Label: Private Stock
Produced by: Tony Macaulay
Year: 1977
As singing TV detectives go, Hutch was more soulful than Don Johnson, had a better voice than Bruce Willis, but not in the same crooning league as Telly Savalas. He got the only #1 of the bunch, however.

(DON'T GO BACK TO) ROCKVILLE

Artist: R.E.M.
Written by: Michael Stipe, Peter Buck, Bill Berry, Mike Mills
From the album: *Reckoning*
Label: IRS
Produced by: Don Dixon, Mitch Easter
Year: 1983
Place where rock came back from the dead again.

DON'T GO BREAKING MY HEART

Artist: Elton John and Kiki Dee
Written by: Elton John, Bernie Taupin
From the album: *Elton John's Greatest Hits (Vol. II)*
Label: rocket
Produced by: Gus Dudgeon
Year: 1976
His biggest all-time hit save for his latter-day Disney-era pop ballads and funeral songs.

DON'T GO HOME WITH YOUR HARD-ON

Artist: Leonard Cohen
Written by: Leonard Cohen, Phil Spector
From the album: *Death of a Ladies Man*
Label: Warner Brothers
Produced by: Phil Spector
Year: 1977
Legendary mismatch of artist and producer and vernacular.

DON'T HANG UP

Artist: The Orlons
Written by: Dave Appell
From the album: *Not Me*
Label: Cameo
Year: 1963
Philly dance groove, midway between *American Bandstand* and *Soul Train*.

DON'T IT MAKE MY BROWN EYES BLUE

Artist: Crystal Gayle
Written by: Richard Leigh
From the album: *We Must Believe in Magic*
Label: United Artists
Produced by: Allen Reynolds
Year: 1977
In the footsteps of Olivia Newton-John, Loretta Lynn's youngest sister goes pop for a rare #1 country/Top 10 crossover.

DON'T IT MAKE YOU WANT TO GO HOME

Artist: Joe South
Written by: Joe South
From the album: *Don't It Make You Want to Go Home*
Label: Capitol
Produced by: Joe South
Year: 1969
South's version crossed over to country. Brook Benton (Cotillion, '70) crossed over to R&B. Both hit the pop charts.

DON'T JUST STAND THERE (WHAT'S ON YOUR MIND)

Artist: Patty Duke
Written by: Lor Crane, Bernice Ross
From the album: *Don't Just Stand There*
Label: United Artists
Year: 1964
On the TV pop princess scale, she was no Shelley Fabares.

DON'T KNOCK MY LOVE

Artist: Wilson Pickett
Written by: Wilson Pickett, Brad Shapiro
From the album: *Don't Knock My Love*
Label: Atlantic
Produced by: Brad Shapiro, Dave Crawford
Year: 1971
Gold single was his fifth and last #1 R&B.

DON'T LEAVE ME THIS WAY

Artist: Thelma Houston
Written by: Kenny Gamble, Leon Huff, Cary Gilbert
From the album: *Any Way You Like It*
Label: Tamla
Produced by: Hal Davis
Year: 1977
Womanizing the Teddy Pendergrass tune for a #1 R&B/#1 crossover disco smash. The Pendergrass version is on *Wake up Everybody* by Harold Melvin & the Bluenotes (Philadelphia International, '75).

DON'T LET GO

Artist: Roy Hamilton
Written by: Jesse Stone (Charles Calhoun)
Label: Epic
Year: 1958
Prime R&B from the pen of an esteemed veteran. Covered by Commander Cody (Warner Brothers, '75).

DON'T LET GO (LOVE)

Artist: En Vogue
Written by: Andrea Martin, Ivan Matias, Marqueze Etheridge, Organized Noise
From the album: *Set It Off* Soundtrack
Label: East/West
Year: 1996
Biggest hit for the R&B girl group from San Francisco, a #1 R&B/#2 crossover.

DON'T LET GO THE COAT

Artist: The Who
Written by: Pete Townshend
From the album: *Face Dances*
Label: Warner Brothers
Produced by: Bill Szymczyk
Year: 1981
In a mystical mood.

DON'T LET IT BRING YOU DOWN

Artist: Neil Young
Written by: Neil Young
From the album: *After the Goldrush*
Label: Reprise
Produced by: David Briggs, Neil Young, Kendall Pacios
Year: 1970
Neil's prescription for the pervasive post-Woodstock malaise of a generation.

DON'T LET ME BE LONELY TONIGHT

Artist: James Taylor
Written by: James Taylor
From the album: *One Man Dog*
Label: Warner Brothers
Produced by: Peter Asher

Year: 1973
Michael Brecker on sax. Covered by The Isley Brothers (T-Neck, '73), Eric Clapton (Reprise, '01).

DON'T LET ME BE MISUNDERSTOOD

Artist: The Animals
Written by: Benny Benjamin, Gloria Caldwell, Sol Marcus
From the album: *Animal Tricks*
Label: MGM
Produced by: Mickie Most
Year: 1965
Bridging the gap between folk/rock and garage punk, this is the first Animals single of an incredible 1965, which would also feature, in succession "Bring It on Home to Me," "We Gotta Get out of This Place" and, to cap it off, "It's My Life."

DON'T LET ME DOWN

Artist: The Beatles
Written by: John Lennon, Paul McCartney
From the album: *Hey Jude*
Label: Apple
Produced by: George Martin
Year: 1969
The B-side of "Get Back."

DON'T LET THE GREEN GRASS FOOL YOU

Artist: Wilson Pickett
Written by: Jerry Akines, Johnnie Bellmon, Victor Drayton, Reginald Turner
From the album: *Wilson Pickett in Philadelphia*
Label: Atlantic
Produced by: Marvin Gaye
Year: 1970
First of his two gold singles.

DON'T LET THE JONESES GET YOU DOWN

Artist: The Temptations
Written by: Norman Whitfield, Barrett Strong
From the album: *Puzzle People*
Label: Gordy
Produced by: Norman Whitfield
Year: 1969
More of their down home philosophizing.

DON'T LET THE SUN CATCH YOU CRYING

Artist: Gerry and the Pacemakers
Written by: Gerry Marsden
From the album: *Don't Let the Sun Catch You Crying*
Label: Laurie
Produced by: George Martin
Year: 1964
First and biggest hit for Brian Epstein's other clients.

DON'T LET THE SUN GO DOWN ON ME

Artist: Elton John
Written by: Elton John, Bernie Taupin
From the album: *Caribou*
Label: MCA
Produced by: Gus Dudgeon
Year: 1974
Elton compares himself to the British Empire in this Grammy winning performance. Revived by Sir Elton and George Michael (MCA, '90) in a live performance that topped the charts in the US and UK.

DON'T LET'S START

Artist: They Might Be Giants
Written by: John Flansburgh, John Linnell
From the album: *They Might Be Giants*
Label: Bar/None
Year: 1986
As heard over 1–800-SONG (their Brooklyn dial-a-song number); the auspicious beginnings of a prolific career.

DON'T LIE TO ME

Artist: Big Star
Written by: Alex Chilton, Chris Bell
From the album: *#1 Record*
Label: Ardent
Produced by: John Fry
Year: 1972
Chilton graduates from the Box Tops, but never fulfills his yearbook predictions.

DON'T LOOK BACK

Artist: Boston
Written by: Tom Scholz
From the album: *Don't Look Back*
Label: Epic
Produced by: Tom Scholz, Dave Butler
Year: 1978
Arena monster inspired by Tom's favorite piece of gear.

DON'T LOOK BACK

Artist: Fine Young Cannibals
Written by: David Steele, Roland Gift, Andy Cox
From the album: *The Raw and the Cooked*
Label: IRS
Produced by: David Steele, Roland Gift, Andy Cox
Year: 1989

DON'T LOOK BACK IN ANGER

Artist: Oasis
Written by: Noel Gallagher
From the album: *What's the Story, Morning Glory*
Label: Epic
Produced by: Owen Morris, Noel Gallagher
Year: 1995

The angry young men of the latest British invasion, mainly angry at each other. Segue: "Imagine" by John Lennon.

DON'T LOSE MY NUMBER

Artist: Phil Collins
Written by: Phil Collins
From the album: *No Jacket Required*
Label: Atlantic
Produced by: Hugh Padgham, Phil Collins
Year: 1985
Segue: "Rikki Don't Lose That Number" by Steely Dan.

DON'T MAKE ME OVER

Artist: Dionne Warwick
Written by: Burt Bacharach, Hal David
From the album: *Dionne Warwick's Golden Hits, Part One*
Label: Scepter
Produced by: Burt Bacharach, Hal David
Year: 1963
Warwick's past as a stand-in Shirelle shines through here, especially her independent attitude, which resulted in her biggest R&B hit. Covered by Jennifer Warnes (Arista, '79).

DON'T MAKE ME WAIT

Artist: Peech Boys
Written by: Bernard Fowler, B. Williams
From the album: *Life Is Something Special*
Produced by: Larry Levan
Label: Island
Year: 1983
A gem from the legendary producer Larry Levan, defining the new urban dancefloor after the trauma of disco.

DON'T MEAN NOTHIN'

Artist: Richard Marx
Written by: Richard Marx, Bruce Gaitsch
From the album: *Richard Marx*
Label: Manhattan
Produced by: David Cole, Richard Marx
Year: 1987
Inheriting the soft rock mantle from David Gates with his first single and first Top 10 hit.

DON'T MESS WITH BILL

Artist: The Marvelettes
Written by: Smokey Robinson
From the album: *Greatest Hits*
Label: Tamla
Produced by: Smokey Robinson
Year: 1966
Smokey's touch returns the Marvelettes to the Top 10 for the first time in four years.

DON'T MIND ROCKIN' TONIGHT

Artist: Ducks Deluxe
Written by: Martin Belmont, Nick Garvey

From the album: *Don't Mind Rockin' Tonight*
Label: RCA
Produced by: Dave Bloxham
Year: 1974
Fevered retro rockabilly boogie from the pubs of England. The Motors evolved from this band, as did Sean Tyla. Graham Parker was listening.

DON'T PASS ME BY

Artist: The Beatles
Written by: Richard Starkey (Ringo Starr)
From the album: *The Beatles*
Label: Apple
Produced by: George Martin
Year: 1968
Ringo's first shot as a writer.

DON'T PLAY THAT SONG (YOU LIED)

Artist: Ben E. King
Written by: Ahmet Ertegun, Betty Nelson
From the album: *Ben E. King's Greatest Hits*
Label: Atco
Produced by: Jerry Wexler, Ahmet Ertegun
Year: 1962
Covered by Aretha Franklin (Atlantic, '70).

DON'T PULL YOUR LOVE

Artist: Hamilton, Joe Frank, and Reynolds
Written by: Dennis Lambert, Brian Potter
From the album: *Hamilton, Joe Frank, and Reynolds*
Label: Dunhill
Produced by: Dennis Lambert, Brian Potter
Year: 1971
First hit for the former T-Bones.

DON'T RUN WILD

Artist: The Del Fuegos
Written by: Dan Zanes, Tom Lloyd, James Ralston
From the album: *Boston, Mass*
Label: Slash
Produced by: Mitchell Froom
Year: 1985
The garage band sound returns with a Boston accent.

DON'T SAY GOODNIGHT (IT'S TIME FOR LOVE) (PARTS I AND II)

Artist: The Isley Brothers
Written by: Ronald Isley, Rudolph Isley, O'Kelly Isley, Ernest Isley, Marvin Isley
From the album: *Go All the Way*
Label: T-Neck
Produced by: Isley Brothers, Chris Jasper
Year: 1980
Isleys take it down with the help of a sultry groove.

DON'T SAY NOTHIN' BAD (ABOUT MY BABY)

Artist: The Cookies
Written by: Gerry Goffin, Carole King

Label: Dimension
Produced by: Gerry Goffin
Year: 1963
Aggressively defending her man against the Mean Girls of the era, not so different from the Mean Girls of any era.

DON'T SHAKE ME LUCIFER

Artist: Roky Erickson and the Aliens
Written by: Roky Erickson
From the album: *The Evil One*
Label: 415
Year: 1982
Wigged-out Texas acid rock from the leader of the 13th Floor Elevators.

DON'T SPEAK

Artist: No Doubt
Written by: Gwen Stefani, Eric Stefani
From the album: *Tragic Kingdom*
Label: Trauma
Produced by: Matthew Wilder
Year: 1996
Reinventing the neighborhood tease as fashion role model. Went to #1 in England.

DON'T STAND SO CLOSE TO ME

Artist: The Police
Written by: Gordon Sumner (Sting)
From the album: *Zenyatta Mondatta*
Label: A&M
Produced by: Nigel Gray, the Police
Year: 1980
Sting assumes his most professorial position yet: lusting after a young student.

DON'T STOP

Artist: Fleetwood Mac
Written by: Christine McVie
From the album: *Rumours*
Label: Warner Brothers
Produced by: Richard Dashut, Ken Caillat, Fleetwood Mac
Year: 1977
Bill Clinton campaign theme.

DON'T STOP BELIEVIN'

Artist: Journey
Written by: Steve Perry, Neal Schon, Jonathon Cain
From the album: *Escape*
Label: Columbia
Produced by: Mike Stone, Kevin Elson
Year: 1981
Second hit in a row for the arena giants, after ten stiffs.

DON'T STOP 'TIL YOU GET ENOUGH

Artist: Michael Jackson

Written by: Michael Jackson
From the album: *Off the Wall*
Label: Epic
Produced by: Quincy Jones
Year: 1979
Michael writes his first #1 R&B tune.

DON'T TALK (PUT YOUR HEAD ON MY SHOULDER)

Artist: The Beach Boys
Written by: Tony Asher, Brian Wilson
From the album: *Pet Sounds*
Produced by: Brian Wilson
Label: Capitol
Year: 1966
At his romantic and protective peak.

DON'T TALK TO STRANGERS

Artist: Rick Springfield
Written by: Rick Springfield
From the album: *Success Hasn't Spoiled Me Yet*
Label: RCA
Produced by: Keith Olson, Rick Springfield
Year: 1982
Second-biggest hit for the former soap opera actor.

DON'T TELL ME

Artist: Madonna
Written by: Mirwais Ahmadzai, Madonna
From the album: *Music*
Label: Maverick
Year: 2000

DON'T TELL ME LIES

Artist: Breathe
Written by: Dave Glaspar, Marcus Lillington
From the album: *All That Jazz*
Label: A&M
Produced by: Bob Sergeant
Year: 1986
British Dance track took three years to become a hit.

DON'T TELL ME WHAT LOVE CAN DO

Artist: Van Halen
Written by: Eddie Van Halen, Alex Van Halen, Sammy Hagar, Michael Anthony
From the album: *Balance*
Label: Warner Brothers
Produced by: Bruce Fairbairn
Year: 1994
Hanging on by a chord change.

DON'T THINK TWICE, IT'S ALL RIGHT

Artist: Bob Dylan
Written by: Bob Dylan
From the album: *The Freewheelin' Bob Dylan*

Label: Columbia
Produced by: John Hammond
Year: 1963
Folkie cynic sees beneath the surface sweetness of all those coy *American Bandstand* dancers and the folk music audience. Covered by Peter, Paul and Mary (Warner Brothers, '63), the Wonder Who (aka the Four Seasons) (Philips, '65), Elvis Presley (RCA, '73). Segue: "Understand Your Man" by Johnny Cash.

DON'T TOUCH ME THERE

Artist: The Tubes
Written by: Ron Nagle, Jane Dornacke
From the album: *Young and Rich*
Label: A&M
Produced by: Al Kooper
Year: 1976
Loopy San Francisco soft porn theatrics in the same neighborhood where topless shoeshine stands and Carol Doda once reigned supreme.

DON'T TRY TO LAY NO BOOGIE WOOGIE ON THE KING OF ROCK AND ROLL

Artist: Long John Baldry
Written by: Jeff Thomas
From the album: *It Ain't Easy*
Label: Warner Brothers
Produced by: Rod Stewart
Year: 1971
Stewart's full tilt production of his Steampacket bandmate.

DON'T TURN AROUND

Artist: Tina Turner
Written by: Diane Warren, Albert Hammond
Label: Capitol
Produced by: Bryan Adams, Bob Clearmountain
Year: 1986
As introduced by Tina Turner on the B-side of "Typical Male," a powerful rocking farewell to Ike. Cover by the reggae band Aswad (Mango, '88) was #1 UK. Version by Ace of Base went Top 10 (Arista, '94).

DON'T WALK AWAY

Artist: Jade
Written by: Vassal Benford, Ron Spearman
From the album: *Jade to the Max*
Label: Giant
Produced by: Vassal Benford
Year: 1993

DON'T WANNA FALL IN LOVE

Artist: Jane Child
Written by: Jane Child
From the album: *Jane Child*
Label: Warner Brothers
Produced by: Jane Child
Year: 1990

Former member of the Canadian Opera Company and the Royal Conservatory of Music goes slumming in the land of pop.

DON'T WANT TO BE A FOOL

Artist: Luther Vandross
Written by: Luther Vandross, Marcus Miller
From the album: *Power of Love*
Label: Epic
Produced by: Luther Vandross, Marcus Miller.
Year: 1991
Top 10 R&B/Top 10 crossover.

DON'T WORRY

Artist: Marty Robbins
Written by: Marty Robbins
Label: Columbia
Produced by: Don Law
Year: 1961
#1 country/Top 10 crossover.

DON'T WORRY BABY

Artist: The Beach Boys
Written by: Brian Wilson, Roger Christian
From the album: *Shut Down (Vol. II)*
Label: Capitol
Produced by: Brian Wilson
Year: 1964
This B-side of their biggest hit, "I Get Around," has aged more gracefully than most of their rock and roll fantasies. Covered by the Beach Boys and the Everly Brothers in the '89 movie, *Tequila Sunrise.*

DON'T WORRY, BE HAPPY

Artist: Bobby McFerrin
Written by: Bobby McFerrin
From the album: *Cocktail Soundtrack*
Label: EMI-Manhattan
Produced by: Linda Goldstein
Year: 1987
Jazz-flavored a-cappella jingle perfectly epitomized the sanitized if not etherized Reagan '80s.

DON'T WORRY (IF THERE'S A HELL BELOW WE'RE ALL GONNA GO)

Artist: Curtis Mayfield
Written by: Curtis Mayfield
From the album: *Curtis*
Label: Curtom
Produced by: Curtis Mayfield
Year: 1970
Former leader of the Impressions is still preaching the gospel of soul.

DON'T YOU (FORGET ABOUT ME)

Artist: Simple Minds
Written by: Keith Forsey, Steve Schiff

From the album: *The Breakfast Club Soundtrack*
Label: A&M
Produced by: Keith Forsey
Year: 1985
Getting a big American boost from its appearance in the proto-Generation-X film *The Breakfast Club.*

DON'T YOU JUST KNOW IT

Artist: Huey Smith
Written by: Huey Smith
From the album: *Havin' a Good Time*
Label: Ace
Produced by: Johnny Vincent
Year: 1958
The New Orleans keyboard man's biggest hit was released just after Mardi Gras and was in the Top 10 by April.

DON'T YOU KNOW

Artist: Ray Charles
Written by: Ray Charles
From the album: *The Ray Charles Story*
Label: Atlantic
Produced by: Ahmet Ertegun, Jerry Wexler
Year: 1954
B-side was "Losing Hand." Covered by Fats Domino (Imperial, '55).

DON'T YOU KNOW

Artist: Della Reese
Written by: Bobby Worth
From the album: *Don't You Know*
Label: RCA
Produced by: Hugo & Luigi
Year: 1959
This standard ballad, adapted from "La Bohème," was a #1 R&B/#2 crossover. The following year, label mate Elvis Presley turned "O Sole Mio" into "It's Now or Never."

DON'T YOU KNOW I LOVE YOU

Artist: The Clovers
Written by: Ahmet Ertegun
Label: Atlantic
Produced by: Ahmet Ertegun, Herb Abramson
Year: 1951
Out of the Mills Brothers and the Ink Spots, the Clovers help establish doo-wop as the make-out music of the '50s—at least until the Dominoes and the Drifters came along.

DON'T YOU WANT ME

Artist: Human League
Written by: Jo Callis, Phil Oakey, Adrian Wright
From the album: *Dare*
Label: A&M/Virgin
Produced by: Martin Rushent, Human League
Year: 1982
First of the mid-'80s British techno invasion, synthesized alienation bands; #1 UK (#1 US six months later).

DON'T YOU WORRY 'BOUT A THING

Artist: Stevie Wonder
Written by: Stevie Wonder
From the album: *Innervisions*
Produced by: Stevie Wonder
Label: Tamla
Year: 1973
From the Grammy-winning album, Stevie lets us know he's moved beyond Syreeta.

DON'TCHA THINK IT'S TIME

Artist: Elvis Presley
Written by: Clyde Otis, Willie Dixon
From the album: *50,000,000 Elvis Fans Can't Be Wrong: Elvis' Gold Records (Vol. II)*
Label: RCA
Produced by: Steve Sholes
Year: 1958
B-side of "Wear My Ring."

DONNA

Artist: Ritchie Valens
Written by: Ritchie Valens
From the album: *Richie Valens*
Label: Del-Fi
Produced by: Bob Keane
Year: 1958
His biggest brooding hit, with "La Bamba" on the flip side, straddling the borderline between Tex/Mex and rockabilly.

DONNA THE PRIMA DONNA

Artist: Dion
Written by: Dion DiMucci, Ernie Maresca
From the album: *Donna the Prima Donna*
Label: Columbia
Produced by: Robert Mersey
Year: 1963
Still searching for a girlfriend two years after "Runaround Sue."

DOO WOP (THAT THING)

Artist: Lauryn Hill
Written by: Lauryn Hill
From the album: *The Miseducation of Lauryn Hill*
Produced by: Lauryn Hill
Label: Columbia
Year: 1998
A hip hop tribute to the sound of a previous generation.

DOOR IS STILL OPEN TO MY HEART, THE

Artist: The Cardinals
Written by: Chuck Willis
Label: Atlantic
Year: 1955
Covered by Dean Martin (Reprise, '64).

DOUBLE DARE YA

Artist: Bikini Kill
Written by: Bikini Kill
From the album: *Bikini Kill*
Label: Kill Rock Stars
Produced by: Ian Mackaye
Year: 1970
The antifeminity movement in its purest, most explosive Riot Grrrl form.

DOUBLE DUTCH BUS

Artist: Frankie Smith
Written by: Frankie Smith, William Bloom
From the album: *Children of Tomorrow*
Label: WMOT
Produced by: Frankie Smith, William Bloom
Year: 1981
From the streets of Philadelphia, the rapping rope-a-dope slang of the '80s.

DOUBLE SHOT (OF MY BABY'S LOVE)

Artist: The Swinging Medallions
Written by: Don M. Smith, Cyril E. Vetter
From the album: *Double Shot (of My Baby's Love)*
Label: Smash
Produced by: John McElrahn
Year: 1966
Frat-house prequel to "Love Me Two Times" by the Doors.

DOUBLE VISION

Artist: Foreigner
Written by: Lou Grammatico (Lou Gramm), Mick Jones
From the album: *Double Vision*
Label: Atlantic
Produced by: Keith Olson
Year: 1978
Their biggest hit that wasn't a ballad.

DOUBLE-CROSSIN' BLUES

Artist: Johnny Otis with Little Esther and the Robins
Written by: Johnny Otis
Label: Savoy
Produced by: Ralph Bass
Year: 1950
Legendary Greek R&B orchestra leader gets his first #1 R&B hit with the cream of L.A. singers.

(DOWN AT) POPPA JOE'S

Artist: The Dixiebelles
Written by: Jerry Dean Smith
From the album: *Down at Poppa Joe's*
Label: Sound Stage 7
Produced by: Bill Justis
Year: 1963
Shindig south of "Sugar Shack."

DOWN BY THE LAZY RIVER

Artist: The Osmonds
Written by: Alan R. Osmond, Merrill Osmond
From the album: *Phase III*
Label: MGM
Produced by: Rick Hall
Year: 1972
Defining AM radio's waning days.

DOWN BY THE RIVER

Artist: Neil Young
Written by: Neil Young
From the album: *Everybody Knows This Is Nowhere*
Label: Reprise
Produced by: David Briggs, Neil Young
Year: 1969
Epic neo-west folk/rock answer to "Hey Joe." Covered by Buddy Miles (Mercury, '70), the Brooklyn Bridge (Buddah, '70). Featured in the '69 film *The Strawberry Statement*.

DOWN BY THE WATER

Artist: P. J. Harvey
Written by: Polly Jean Harvey
From the album: *To Bring You My Love*
Label: Island
Produced by: Flood, P. J. Harvey, John Parish
Year: 1995
Establishing herself as the most unique female blues rocker since Janis Joplin.

DOWN HOME GIRL

Artist: Alvin Robinson
Written by: Jerry Leiber, Artie Butler
Label: Red Bird
Produced by: Jerry Leiber, Mike Stoller
Year: 1964
Covered by the Rolling Stones (London, '64).

DOWN IN MEXICO

Artist: The Coasters
Written by: Jerry Leiber, Mike Stoller
From the album: *The Coasters*
Label: Atco
Produced by: Jerry Leiber, Mike Stoller
Year: 1956
The Coasters slip across the border to Tijuana for their first R&B hit.

DOWN IN THE BOONDOCKS

Artist: Billy Joe Royal
Written by: Joe South
From the album: *Down in the Boondocks*
Label: Columbia
Produced by: Joe South
Year: 1965
White trash anthem was a country hit by Freddy Weller (Capitol, '75). Covered by Joe South (Capitol, '70).

DOWN IN THE BOTTOM

Artist: Howlin' Wolf
Written by: Chester Burnette
From the album: *Tune Box*
Label: Chess
Year: 1950
Introducing the bottomless voice that would entrance a generation of young Chicago blues fanatics, most of them living in England.

DOWN IN THE FLOOD

Artist: Bob Dylan
Written by: Bob Dylan
From the album: *Greatest Hits, Volume 2*
Produced by: Leon Russell
Label: Columbia
Year: 1972

DOWN IN THE TUBE STATION AT MIDNIGHT

Artist: The Jam
Written by: Paul Weller
From the album: *All Mod Cons*
Produced by: Chris Parry, Vic Coppersmith-Heaven
Label: Polydor
Year: 1978
Where English soul meets the ghost of doo-wop.

DOWN LOW (NOBODY HAS TO KNOW)

Artist: R. Kelly featuring Ronald Isley
Written by: Robert Kelly
From the album: *R. Kelly*
Produced by: Robert Kelly
Label: Jive
Year: 1995
Creeping and crawling to the next affair, a Top 10 R&B/Top 10 crossover.

DOWN ON ME

Artist: Big Brother and the Holding Company
Written by: Janis Joplin
From the album: *Big Brother and the Holding Company*
Label: Mainstream
Produced by: Bob Shad
Year: 1968
Janis's updated white-woman blues packs an emotional and sexual double whammy.

DOWN ON THE CORNER

Artist: Creedence Clearwater Revival
Written by: John C. Fogerty
From the album: *Willy and the Poor Boys*
Label: Fantasy
Produced by: John C. Fogerty
Year: 1969
Convincing New Orleansiana, by way of Northern California, where it's at least a mile and a half between corners.

DOWN RIVER

Artist: David Ackles
Written by: David Ackles
From the album: *David Ackles*
Produced by: David Anderle, Russ Miller
Label: Elektra
Year: 1968
Evocative keyboard ballad of lost love and failed reunion. It was Elvis Costello's choice as the song that changed his life.

DOWN SO LOW

Artist: Mother Earth
Written by: Tracy Nelson
From the album: *Living with the Animals*
Label: Mercury
Produced by: Barry Goldberg, Dan Healy, Mark Naftalan
Year: 1968
Perennially third-billed (to Janis Joplin and Grace Slick) San Francisco blues Vesuvius Tracy Nelson achieved a personal and career epiphany on this gospel-inflected classic. The note she hits on the last "down" is justification, by itself, for the multitude of clinkers that she's lent her precious voice to ever since. Covered by Linda Ronstadt (Asylum, '76). Rerecorded by a solo Tracy Nelson (Atlantic, '73).

DOWN THE AISLE OF LOVE

Artist: The Quintones
Written by: The Quintones
Label: Hunt
Produced by: Doc Bagby
Year: 1958
Essential doo-wop monogamy.

DOWN TOWN, THE

Artist: Days of the New
Written by: Travis Meeks
From the album: *Days of the New*
Label: Outpost
Year: 1998

DOWN UNDER

Artist: Men at Work
Written by: Colin Hay, Roy Strykert
From the album: *Business as Usual*
Label: Columbia
Produced by: Peter Mclan
Year: 1982
Ultimate left field hit from and about Australia was #1 in the US, the UK, and Australia.

DOWN WITH DISEASE

Artist: Phish
Written by: Trey Anastasio, Tom Marshall
From the album: *Hoist*
Produced by: Paul Fox
Label: Elektra
Year: 1994
Downhill after the intro. But what a ride.

DOWN WITH THE KING

Artist: Run-D.M.C.
Written by: Pete Phillips, Joseph Simmons, Darryl McDaniels, John Penn, James Rado, Gerome Ragni, Galt McDermott
From the album: *Down with the King*
Label: Profile
Produced by: Pete Rock
Year: 1993
Seminal rap group returns with a kinder and gentler boast, tied to the big ballad from *Hair!* "Where Do I Go."

DOWNTOWN

Artist: Petula Clark
Written by: Tony Hatch
From the album: *Downtown*
Label: Warner Brothers
Produced by: Tony Hatch
Year: 1964
Grammy winner was Clark's first hit. Meanwhile, a generation on the edge of a night life dreamed of Carnaby Street and Mary Quant miniskirts but were stranded in mom's apartment watching cheerleaders patrol the avenue in pedal pushers.

DOWNTOWN TRAIN

Artist: Tom Waits
Written by: Tom Waits
From the album: *Rain Dogs*
Label: Island
Produced by: Tom Waits
Year: 1985
The B, the D, the R? Tom consorts with Brooklyn girls, never recovers. From the movie *Down by Law*. Covered by Mary Chapin-Carpenter (Columbia '86), Patty Smyth (Columbia, '87), Rod Stewart (Warner Brothers, '90).

DR. FEELGOOD

Artist: Mötley Crüe
Written by: Mick Mars, Nikki Sixx
From the album: *Dr. Feelgood*
Label: Elektra
Produced by: Bob Rock
Year: 1989
An ode to perhaps the same nefarious physician once visited by Aretha Franklin. But a different song.

DR. WU

Artist: Steely Dan
Written by: Donald Fagen, Walter Becker
From the album: *Katy Lied*
Label: ABC
Produced by: Gary Katz
Year: 1975
Seeking much-needed help from a wacko shrink.

DRAG CITY

Artist: Jan & Dean
Written by: Brian Wilson, Jan Berry, Roger Christian

From the album: *Drag City*
Label: Liberty
Produced by: Jan Berry
Year: 1963
Racing in the streets could only lead to no good, as any fan of teen exploitation movies could tell you.

DRAGGIN' THE LINE

Artist: Tommy James
Written by: Tommy James, Robert L. King
From the album: *Christian of the World*
Label: Roulette
Produced by: Tommy James
Year: 1971
Frothy summertime tune was his biggest solo hit.

DRAIN YOU

Artist: Nirvana
Written by: Nirvana
From the album: *Nevermind*
Label: DGC
Produced by: Butch Vig
Year: 1991
Cobain's love/hate letter to his fans.

DRE DAY

Artist: Dr. Dre featuring Snoopy Doggy Dogg
Written by: Andre Young (Dr. Dre), Calvin Broadus (Snoop Doggy Dogg), Colin Wolfe
From the album: *The Chronic*
Label: Death Row
Produced by: Dr. Dre
Year: 1992
Sung by the anti-Sam Cooke of the stoop, Snoop, the dog metaphor come to life.

DREAM BABY DREAM

Artist: Alan Vega and Martin Rev
Written by: Alan Vega, Martin Rev
Label: Ze
Produced by: Ric Ocasek
Year: 1980
Legendary 12-inch single, by the provocative Lower East Side New York electronic duo otherwise known as Suicide.

DREAM BABY, HOW LONG MUST I DREAM

Artist: Roy Orbison
Written by: Cindy Walker
From the album: *Roy Orbison's Greatest Hits*
Label: Monument
Produced by: Fred Foster
Year: 1962
A typical Orbisonian tear-drenched ballad of frustration, written by the author of "You Don't Know Me" and other country gems.

DREAM LOVER

Artist: Bobby Darin

Written by: Bobby Darin
From the album: *The Bobby Darin Story*
Label: Atco
Produced by: Ahmet Ertegun
Year: 1959
Hall of Fame soft rocker; the song is dedicated to studio backup and future Angels' lead singer, Peggy Santiglia, whom Darin mentions by name in the closing moments of the outro. Neil Sedaka on piano.

DREAM ON

Artist: Aerosmith
Written by: Steven Tallarico (Tyler)
From the album: *Aerosmith*
Produced by: Adrian Barber
Label: Columbia
Year: 1973
With the power chords to build a dream on, the perfect Top 40 rock ballad. Preparing their own, just out of earshot, were Journey, Boston, Foreigner, Styx, and many many more. This became a hit in '76.

DREAM WEAVER

Artist: Gary Wright
Written by: Gary Wright
From the album: *Dream Weaver*
Label: Warner Brothers
Produced by: Gary Wright
Year: 1976
Spooky toothless.

DREAMIN'

Artist: Johnny Burnette
Written by: Ted Ellis, Barry DeVorzon
From the album: *Dreamin'*
Label: Liberty
Produced by: Snuff Garrett
Year: 1960
Softening rockabilly into country/rock.

DREAMIN'

Artist: Vanessa Williams
Written by: Lisa Montgomary, Geneva Paschal, Michael Forte
From the album: *The Right Stuff*
Label: Wing
Year: 1988
Versatile actress, model, and beauty queen conquers the pop arena with all her clothes on.

DREAMING

Artist: Blondie
Written by: Deborah Harry, Chris Stein
From the album: *Eat to the Beat*
Label: Chrysalis
Produced by: Mike Chapman
Year: 1979
Punk rock pin-up girl achieves pop perfection.

DREAMING OF YOU

Artist: Selena
Written by: Franne Golde, Tom Snow
From the album: *Dreaming of You*
Label: EMI Latin
Year: 1995
Selena's last hit signals the official arrival of Latina pop, whose prime purveyor would be Jennifer Lopez, who played her in the posthumous biopic.

DREAMING, THE

Artist: Kate Bush
Written by: Kate Bush
From the album: *The Dreaming*
Label: EMI-America
Produced by: Kate Bush
Year: 1982
Kate discovers the Fairlight (also the didgeridoo), and England would never be the same.

DREAMS

Artist: The Cranberries
Written by: Noel Hogan, Dolores O'Riordan
From the album: *Everybody Else Is Doing It, So Why Can't We?*
Label: Island
Produced by: Stephen Street
Year: 1993
Ethereal Irish folk harmonies.

DREAMS

Artist: Fleetwood Mac
Written by: Stephanie Nicks
From the album: *Rumours*
Label: Warner Brothers
Produced by: Richard Dashut, Ken Caillat, Fleetwood Mac
Year: 1977
Thoroughly Americanized, utterly Los Angelized, their biggest hit.

DREAMS

Artist: Van Halen
Written by: Eddie Van Halen, Alex Van Halen, Michael Anthony, Sammy Hagar
From the album: *5150*
Label: Warner Brothers
Produced by: Van Halen, Don Landee, Mick Jones
Year: 1986
Coauthored by the new front-man, Sammy "The Red Rocker" Hagar, whom the departing David Lee Roth dubbed just as exciting as "the new Darren on *Bewitched.*"

DREAMTIME

Artist: Daryl Hall
Written by: Daryl Hall, John Beeby
From the album: *Three Hearts and the Happy Ending Machine*
Label: RCA
Produced by: David A. Stewart, T-Bone Wolk

Year: 1986
Blue-eyed solo.

DRESS

Artist: P. J. Harvey
Written by: Polly Jean Harvey, Robert Ellis
From the album: *Dry*
Label: Indigo/Island
Produced by: P. J. Harvey
Year: 1992
Low-fi feminist rage from England.

DRESS REHEARSAL RAG

Artist: Judy Collins
Written by: Leonard Cohen
From the album: *In My Life*
Label: Elektra
Produced by: Mark Abramson
Year: 1966
Collins puts her art-theatre stamp of approval on the Canadian novelist/poet/singer/songwriter. An era of depressing songs would result.

DRESS YOU UP

Artist: Madonna
Written by: Peggy Stanziale, Andrea LaRusso
From the album: *Like a Virgin*
Label: Sire
Produced by: Nile Rodgers
Year: 1984
Fashion statement: prom gown, sneakers, black socks.

DRIFT AWAY

Artist: Dobie Gray
Written by: Mentor Williams
From the album: *Drift Away*
Label: Decca
Produced by: Mentor Williams
Year: 1973
Pining for the lost magic of rock and roll.

DRIFTIN' BLUES

Artist: Johnny Moore and the Three Blazers
Written by: Charles Brown, Johnny Moore, Eddie Williams
Label: Aladdin
Year: 1946
Charles Brown's down-and-out masterpiece of soulful crooning. Covered by Sam Cooke (RCA, '63), Ray Charles (ABC/Paramount, '66), Bobby Bland (Duke, '68), Eric Clapton (RSO, '75).

DRINKING WINE SPO-DEE O-DEE

Artist: Stick McGhee
Written by: Stick McGhee, Mayo Williams
Label: Atlantic
Year: 1949

Atlantic records enters the marketplace with a Top 10 R&B hit. The mythic drinking song was covered by Wynonie Harris (King, '49), Jerry Lee Lewis (Sun, '59; Mercury, '73).

DRIP DROP

Artist: The Drifters
Written by: Jerry Leiber, Mike Stoller
From the album: *Rockin' and Driftin'*
Label: Atlantic
Year: 1958
The old leaky roof blues. Covered by Dion (Columbia, '63).

DRIVE

Artist: The Cars
Written by: Ric Ocasek
From the album: *Heartbeat City*
Label: Elektra
Produced by: Mutt Lange
Year: 1984
Singer Ben Orr's finest moment and the Cars' biggest hit. The emotional ballad was played at Orr's funeral in 2000. Ocasek married the girl in the video.

DRIVE MY CAR

Artist: The Beatles
Written by: John Lennon, Paul McCartney
From the album: *Yesterday and Today*
Label: Capitol
Produced by: George Martin
Year: 1965
Paul McCartney on slide guitar.

DRIVE SOUTH

Artist: John Hiatt
Written by: John Hiatt
From the album: *Slow Turning*
Label: A&M
Produced by: Glyn Johns
Year: 1988
Cover by Suzy Bogguss (Mercury, '93) was a big country hit.

DRIVE-IN SHOW

Artist: Eddie Cochran
Written by: Fred Dexter, Clare Kane
From the album: *Eddie Cochran*
Label: Liberty
Produced by: Snuff Garrett, Eddie Cochran, Jerry Capeheart
Year: 1957
Calculated follow-up to "Sittin' in the Balcony."

DRIVEN TO TEARS

Artist: The Police
Written by: Gordon Sumner (Sting)
From the album: *Zenyatta Mondatta*
Label: A&M

Produced by: Nigel Gray, the Police
Year: 1980

DRIVER 8

Artist: R.E.M.
Written by: Michael Stipe, Peter Buck, Bill Berry, Mike Mills
From the album: *Fables of the Reconstruction*
Label: IRS
Produced by: Joe Boyd
Year: 1985
On the road to a Motel 6.

DRIVING MY LIFE AWAY

Artist: Eddie Rabbitt
Written by: Eddie Rabbitt, Even Stevens, David Malloy
From the album: *Horizon*
Label: Elektra
Produced by: David Malloy
Year: 1980
Greeting the new Reagan era with a #1 country/Top 10 crossover from the Meat Loaf/Blondie movie *Roadie*.

DRIVING WHEEL

Artist: Little Junior Parker
Written by: Roosevelt Sykes
Label: Duke
Year: 1961
His best since "Mystery Train," written by the author of "I'm Your Honeydripper."

DRIVING YOUR GIRLFRIEND HOME

Artist: Morrissey
Written by: Stephen Morrissey, Mark Nevin
From the album: *Kill Uncle*
Label: Sire
Produced by: Clive Langer, Alan Winstantly
Year: 1991
One of his best tracks.

DROWN

Artist: Son Volt
Written by: Jay Farrar
From the album: *Trace*
Produced by: Brian Paulson
Label: Warner Brothers
Year: 1996
The voice of alt country.

DROWN IN MY TEARS

Artist: Ray Charles
Written by: Henry Glover
From the album: *Ray Charles*
Label: Atlantic
Produced by: Ahmet Ertegun, Jerry Wexler
Year: 1956
Big R&B hit. Covered by the early, awesome Richie Havens (Douglas, '66).

DROWING IN THE SEA OF LOVE

Artist: Joe Simon
Written by: Kenny Gamble, Leon Huff
From the album: *Drowning in the Sea of Love*
Label: Spring
Year: 71.
Picking up where Phil Phillips left off in "Sea of Love."

DRUG STORE TRUCK DRIVIN' MAN

Artist: The Byrds
Written by: Roger McGuinn, Gram Parsons
From the album: *Dr. Byrds and Mr. Hyde*
Label: Columbia
Produced by: Gary Usher
Year: 1969
Byrds take the exit for country/rock, a genre in which Parsons would become a legend.

DRUGSTORE ROCK 'N ROLL

Artist: Janis Martin
Written by: Janis Martin
Produced by: Chet Atkins
Label: RCA
Year: 1956
Known as the female Elvis, Janis is one of the lost bad girls of rockabilly. A-side was "Will You Willyum."

DUDE (LOOKS LIKE A LADY)

Artist: Aerosmith
Written by: Steven Tyler, Joe Perry, Desmond Child
From the album: *Permanent Vacation*
Produced by: Bruce Fairbairn
Label: Geffen
Year: 1987
Coming out of involuntary retirement with a modernization of the ancient theme first suggested in "Are You a Boy or Are You a Girl" by the Barbarians. Instead of a hippie, it's a crossdresser.

DUELING BANJOS

Artist: Eric Weissberg and Steve Mandel
Written by: Arthur Smith
From the album: *Dueling Banjos*
Label: Warner Brothers
Produced by: Eric Weisberg
Year: 1972
Three decades worth of banjo on one tune from the movie *Deliverance*. Answered in the Bottom-10 by Martin Mull with "Dueling Tubas" (Capricorn, '73).

DUKE OF EARL

Artist: Gene Chandler
Written by: Earl Edwards, Eugene Dixon (Gene Chandler), Bernie Williams
From the album: *The Duke of Earl*
Label: Vee Jay
Produced by: Carl Davis
Year: 1961
One of the ultimate doo-wop statements and sustaining fantasies, a #5 R&B/#1 crossover. Chandler was originally a member of the Dukays when he recorded this song about comember Earl Edwards.

DUKE OF PRUNES

Artist: The Mothers of Invention
Written by: Frank Zappa
From the album: *Absolutely Free*
Label: Verve
Produced by: Tom Wilson
Year: 1967
Taking on all those dead white men of Europe.

DUM DUM

Artist: Brenda Lee
Written by: Jackie DeShannon, Sharon Sheeley
From the album: *All the Way*
Label: Decca
Produced by: Owen Bradley
Year: 1961
Rockabilly flavor added by Jackie DeShannon, the West Coast leatherette Carole King and Sharon Sheeley, Eddie Cochran's girlfriend, who wrote "Poor Little Fool."

DUMB

Artist: Nirvana
Written by: Kirk Cobain
From the album: *In Utero*
Produced by: Steve Albini
Label: DCG
Year: 1993

DUST IN THE WIND

Artist: Kansas
Written by: Kerry Livgren
From the album: *Point of Know Return*
Label: Kirshner
Produced by: Jeff Glixman
Year: 1977
Delicate acoustic dirge.

DYNAMITE

Artist: Brenda Lee
Written by: Mort Carson, Tom Glazer
From the album: *Brenda Lee*
Label: Decca
Produced by: Paul Cohen
Year: 1957
Spawning a nickname and a career for the first lady of rockabilly. Covered by Dave Edmunds (Swan Song, '79).

DYSLEXIC HEART

Artist: Paul Westerberg
Written by: Paul Westerberg
From the album: *Singles Soundtrack*
Label: Epic Soundtrax
Produced by: Scott Litt, Paul Westerberg
Year: 1992
From the Cameron Crowe epic immortalizing a pre-grunge Seattle, a Minneapolis Replacement.

E

EARLY 1970

Artist: Richard Starkey (Ringo Starr)
Written by: Ringo Starr
From the album: *Ringo*
Produced by: Richard Perry
Label: Apple
Year: 1970
The breakup of the Beatles from the drummer's point of view. B-side of "It Don't Come Easy."

EARLY IN THE MORNING

Artist: The Gap Band
Written by: Lonnie Simmons, Charles Wilson, Rudolph Taylor
From the album: *The Gap Band IV*
Label: Total Experience
Produced by: Lonnie Simmons
Year: 1982
Follow up to "Burn Rubber." Covered by Robert Palmer (EMI-Manhattan '88).

EARLY IN THE MORNING

Artist: The Rinky Dinks
Written by: Bobby Darin
Label: Atlantic
Year: 1958
Recorded pseudonymously by Bobby Darin. Covered by Buddy Holly (Coral, '58).

EARLY MORNING RAIN

Artist: Judy Collins
Written by: Gordon Lightfoot
From the album: *5th*
Label: Elektra
Produced by: Mark Abramson, Jac Holzman
Year: 1965
Early classic for the Canadian folk hero Lightfoot. Covered by Peter, Paul and Mary (Warner Brothers, '65), Ian and Sylvia (Vanguard, '65).

EARN ENOUGH FOR US

Artist: XTC
Written by: Andy Partridge
From the album: *Skylarking*
Label: Geffen
Produced by: Todd Rundgren
Year: 1987
A glorious anomaly: Working-class pop rock.

EARTH ANGEL (WILL YOU BE MINE)

Artist: The Penguins
Written by: Curtis Williams, Gaynel Hodge, Jesse Belvin
From the album: *The Cool Cool Penguins*
Label: Dooto
Produced by: Dootsie Williams
Year: 1954
The B-side of "Hey Senorita" was the first #1 R&B/Top 10 crossover of the rock era and the second after "Sh-Boom" to hit the Top 10. Like "Sh-Boom," it was covered in a higher-charting version by the Canadian pop group, the Crew Cuts (Mercury, '55), who also covered "Koko Mo," "Oop Shoop," "A Story Untold," and "Tell Me Why."

EASIER SAID THAN DONE

Artist: The Essex
Written by: William Linton, Larry Huff
From the album: *Easier Said Than Done*
Label: Roulette
Produced by: Henry Glover
Year: 1963
Responding with rare honesty to the advice dispensed in "Tell Him" by the Exciters earlier in the year.

EAST–WEST

Artist: The Paul Butterfield Blues Band
Written by: Mark Naftalin, Nick Gravenites
From the album: *East West*
Label: Elektra
Produced by: Paul Rothchild, Mark Abramson
Year: 1966
Guitarist Mike Bloomfield's transcontinental transcendental magnum opus. Suggested segue: "Marquee Moon" by Television.

EASY

Artist: The Commodores
Written by: Lionel B. Richie Jr.
From the album: *Commodores*
Label: Motown
Produced by: James Carmichael, the Commodores
Year: 1977
Mellow as a Tuesday afternoon

EASY LIVIN'

Artist: Uriah Heap
Written by: Ken Hensley
From the album: *Demons and Wizards*
Label: Mercury
Year: 1972
The definition of sludge.

EASY LOVER

Artist: Philip Bailey
Written by: Philip Bailey, Phil Collins, Nathan East
From the album: *Chinese Wall*
Label: Columbia
Produced by: Philip Bailey, Phil Collins
Year: 1985
A pair of solo drummers—Bailey from Earth, Wind, and Fire, joined by Collins from Genesis—with a US/UK smash.

EASY TO BE HARD

Artist: Lynn Kellog
Written by: James Rado, Gerome Ragni, Galt MacDermot
From the album: *Hair! A Tribal Rock Musical*
Label: RCA
Produced by: Andy Wiswell
Year: 1967
One of the four hit songs from the original rock musical. Cracks in the façade of the sexual revolution. Covered by Three Dog Night (Dunhill, '69).

EAT THE RICH

Artist: Krokus
Written by: Christian Rohr, Femando Von Arb, Marc Storace, Butch Stone
From the album: *Headhunter*
Label: Arista
Produced by: Tom Allum
Year: 1983
The essential heavy metal philosophy and appeal, also espoused by Motorhead and Aerosmith in different songs with the same title.

EBB TIDE

Artist: Roy Hamilton
Written by: Carl Sigman, Robert Maxwell
Label: Epic
Year: 1954
Dramatic R&B ballad given the appropriate gospel feel by Hamilton, whose previous "You'll Never Walk Alone" topped the R&B charts that year. Introduced by Frank Chacksfield (London, '53). Covered by the Righteous Brothers (Philles, '65).

EBONY AND IVORY

Artist: Paul McCartney and Stevie Wonder
Written by: Paul McCartney
From the album: *Tug of War*
Label: Columbia
Produced by: George Martin
Year: 1982
Two pop icons offer their plan for world harmony.

EBONY EYES

Artist: The Everly Brothers
Written by: John D. Loudermilk
From the album: *The Golden Hits of the Everly Brothers*
Label: Warner Brothers
Produced by: Wesley Rose
Year: 1961
Eleventh out of 14 Top 10 hits and their last appearance as a duo on the country charts for 23 years.

ECHOES OF LOVE

Artist: The Doobie Brothers
Written by: Willie Mitchell, Earl Randle, Pat Simmons
From the album: *Livin' on the Fault Line*
Label: Warner Brothers
Produced by: Ted Templeman
Year: 1977
Ineffable classic in neo doo-wop style. Covered by the Pointer Sisters (Planet, '78).

EDDIE, MY LOVE

Artist: The Teen Queens
Written by: Aaron Collins, Maxwell Davis, Sam Ling
From the album: *Eddie My Love*
Label: RPM
Produced by: Sam Bihari
Year: 1956
From L.A., girl-group doo-wop at its most despairing and compelling.

EDGE OF HEAVEN, THE

Artist: Wham!
Written by: George Michael
From the album: *Music from the Edge of Heaven*
Label: Columbia
Produced by: George Michael
Year: 1986
#1 UK/Top 10 US.

EDGE OF SEVENTEEN (JUST LIKE THE WHITE WINGED DOVE)

Artist: Stevie Nicks
Written by: Stephanie Nicks
From the album: *Bella Donna*
Label: Modern
Produced by: Jimmy Iovine
Year: 1981
Signature move for folk/rock's whirling diva. Natalie Merchant was watching.

EFFIGY

Artist: Creedence Clearwater Revival
Written by: John C. Fogerty
From the album: *Willy and the Poor Boys*
Label: Fantasy
Produced by: John C. Fogerty
Year: 1969
Prototype for alt country. Covered by Uncle Tupelo (Arista, '93).

EFFLOURESCE AND DELIQUESCE

Artist: The Chills
Written by: Martyn Phillips
From the album: *Submarine Bells*
Label: Slash
Produced by: Gary Smith

Year: 1990
Haunting neo-psychedelia from New Zealand.

EGG PLANT (THAT ATE CHICAGO), THE

Artist: Dr. West's Medicine Show and Junk Band
Written by: Norman Greenbaum
Label: GoGo
Produced by: T. Mazer
Year: 1966
Greenbaum would recover to write "Spirit in the Sky."

EGYPTIAN REGGAE

Artist: The Modern Lovers
Written by: Jonathan Richman
From the album: *Rock & Roll with the Modern Lovers*
Produced by: Matthew King Kaufman, Glen Kolodkin
Label: Beskerkley
Year: 1977
Top 5 in England. Suggested segue: "Walk Like an Egyptian" by the Bangles.

EIGHT DAYS A WEEK

Artist: The Beatles
Written by: John Lennon, Paul McCartney
From the album: *Beatles VI*
Label: Capitol
Produced by: George Martin
Year: 1965
After 11 Top 10 hits in '64, they start '65 with the first of five straight #1s, taking them into early '66.

EIGHT MEN AND FOUR WOMEN

Artist: O.V. Wright
Written by: Deadric Malone
From the album: *Eight Men and Four Women*
Label: Back Beat
Produced by: Willie Mitchell
Year: 1967
His biggest R&B hit. Suggested segue: "There Is Something on Your Mind (Part 2)" by Bobby Marchan.

EIGHT MILES HIGH

Artist: The Byrds
Written by: Jim McGuinn (Roger McGuinn), Gene Clark, David Crosby
From the album: *5D (Fifth Dimension)*
Label: Columbia
Produced by: Allen Stanton
Year: 1966
Post-flyte fantasy, inspired by John Coltrane, retired by the US Government. Suggested segues: "Along Comes Mary" by the Association and "I Couldn't Get High" by the Fugs.

867–5309 (JENNY)

Artist: Tommy Tutone

Written by: Alex Call, James Keller
From the album: *Tommy Tutone 2*
Label: Columbia
Produced by: Chuck Plotkin, James Keller, Tommy Tutone
Year: 1982
Frat rock ode to a working girl.

EIGHTEEN

Artist: Alice Cooper
Written by: Vincent Furnier (Alice Cooper), Michael Bruce, Glen Buxton, Dennis Dunaway, Neal Smith
From the album: *Love It to Death*
Label: Straight
Produced by: Bob Ezrin, Jack Richardson
Year: 1971
Frank Zappa's bizarre protege Vincent Furnier creates a legendary nom de plume and an anthem of teenage rage.

EIGHTEEN AND LIFE

Artist: Skid Row
Written by: Dave Sabo, Rachel Bolan
From the album: *Skid Row*
Label: Atlantic
Produced by: Michael Wagener
Year: 1989
If sixteen is the perfect rock and roll age for a girl, for a boy eighteen has got to be the pits.

EIGHTEEN WITH A BULLET

Artist: Pete Wingfield
Written by: Barry Hammond, William Wingfield
From the album: *Breakfast Special*
Label: Island
Produced by: Pete Wingfield, Barry Hammond
Year: 1975
Retro-doo wop novelty from England achieved its title on the charts in November of the year.

88 LINES ABOUT 44 WOMEN

Artist: The Nails
Written by: David Kaufman
From the album: *Hotel for Women*
Label: Jimboco/PVC
Produced by: Gregg Winter, Bruce Harris
Year: 1982
Obscure New York band's masterly couplets about coupling in all its intricate varieties. Later on RCA. Re-rediscovered on EMI in '92, where it was promptly recycled in a car commercial.

EINSTEIN ON THE BEACH (FOR AN EGGMAN)

Artist: Counting Crows
Written by: Adam Duritz, David Bryson, Charlie Gillingham, Matt Malloy, Steve Bowman
From the album: *DGC Rarities (Vol. 1)*

Label: DGC
Produced by: Counting Crows
Year: 1994
Scraping the vaults to capitalize on the success of "Mr. Jones," which was a tribute to Bob Dylan writing about Brian Jones. This seems to be a tribute to classical composer Philip Glass, with a subtitle referencing John Lennon.

EL PASO

Artist: Marty Robbins
Written by: Marty Robbins
From the album: *Gunfighter Ballads and Trail Songs*
Label: Columbia
Produced by: Don Law
Year: 1959
The epic #1 country/#1 crossover story-song, ending in death.

ELEANOR RIGBY

Artist: The Beatles
Written by: John Lennon, Paul McCartney
From the album: *Revolver*
Label: Capitol
Produced by: George Martin
Year: 1966
Peeking out of the studio, a love song to "all the lonely people." Covered by Ray Charles (ABC Paramount, '68), Aretha Franklin (Atlantic, '69).

ELECTED

Artist: Alice Cooper
Written by: Vincent Furnier (Alice Cooper), Michael Bruce, Glen Buxton, Dennis Dunaway, Neal Smith
From the album: *Billion Dollar Babies*
Label: Warner Brothers
Produced by: Bob Ezrin
Year: 1972
From the tour on which columnist Bob Greene played Santa Claus (and was beheaded a hundred times, more or less).

ELECTRIC AVENUE

Artist: Eddy Grant
Written by: Eddy Grant
From the album: *Killer on the Rampage*
Label: Portrait
Produced by: Eddy Grant
Year: 1983
Big reggae dance track from England.

ELENORE

Artist: The Turtles
Written by: Howard Kaylan, Mark Volman, Jim Pons, Al Nichol, John Barbata
From the album: *Battle of the Bands*
Label: White Whale
Produced by: Chip Douglas
Year: 1968
West Coast post-doo-wop rock at its harmonious peak.

ELEVATION

Artist: U2
Written by: Bono, U2
From the album: *All That You Can't Leave Behind*
Label: Island
Year: 2000
Launching a new tour with a Grammy winner for Best Performance.

ELEVATORS (ME AND YOU)

Artist: OutKast
Written by: Andre Benjamin, Antwan Andre Pattan
From the album: *ATLiens*
Label: LaFace
Year: 1996
Spotlighting the Dirty South, Atlanta, the new hip hop hotbed.

ELI'S COMING

Artist: Laura Nyro
Written by: Laura Nyro
From the album: *Eli and the Thirteenth Confession*
Label: Columbia
Produced by: Laura Nyro, Charlie Calello
Year: 1968
If Carole King had gone to Music and Art instead of straight to work for Don Kirshner at 1650 Broadway. Covered by Three Dog Night (Dunhill, '69).

ELUSIVE BUTTERFLY

Artist: Bob Lind
Written by: Bob Lind
From the album: *Don't Be Concerned*
Label: World Pacific
Produced by: Richard Bock
Year: 1965
The effusive downfall of folk/rock.

ELVIS IS DEAD

Artist: Living Colour
Written by: Vernon Reid
From the album: *Time's Up*
Label: Epic
Produced by: Ed Stasium
Year: 1990
Wishful thinking by the black heavy metal band, taking up where Bo Diddley left off.

ELVIS IS EVERYWHERE

Artist: Mojo Nixon and Skid Roper
Written by: Mojo Nixon
From the album: *Bo-Day-Shus*
Label: Enigma
Year: 1987
Preaching the gospel of rock to the converted.

EMBRYONIC JOURNEY

Artist: Jefferson Airplane
Written by: Jorma Kaukonen
From the album: *Surrealistic Pillow*
Label: RCA
Produced by: Rick Jarrard
Year: 1967
Classic early instrumental, revealing Jorma's Reverend Gary Davis proclivities. Featured in the last episode of *Friends*, but having nowhere near the impact of Green Day's "Time of Your Life (Good Riddance)," which was featured in the clips show prior to the last episode of *Seinfeld*.

EMOTION

Artist: Samantha Sang
Written by: Barry Gibb, Robin Gibb
From the album: *Emotion*
Label: Private Stock
Produced by: Albey Galutin, Karl Richardson
Year: 1977
She coulda been the next Olivia Newton-John.

EMOTIONAL RESCUE

Artist: The Rolling Stones
Written by: Mick Jagger, Keith Richards
From the album: *Emotional Rescue*
Label: Rolling Stones
Produced by: Glimmer Twins
Year: 1980
A rock and roll mid-life crisis; their second biggest hit of the '80s.

EMOTIONALLY YOURS

Artist: Bob Dylan
Written by: Bob Dylan
From the album: *Empire Burlesque*
Label: Columbia
Year: 1985
Biding time between his second and third comebacks. Covered by the O'Jays (EMI, '91).

EMOTIONS

Artist: Mariah Carey
Written by: Dave Hall, Mariah Carey
From the album: *Emotions*
Label: Columbia
Produced by: David Cole, Rob Clivilles
Year: 1991
Somewhat of a sophomore slump for the new pop/R&B diva. This would be the only #1 R&B/#1 crossover from the album; her first had two.

EMOTIONS

Artist: Brenda Lee
Written by: Mel Tillis, Ramsey Kearney
From the album: *Emotions*
Label: Decca
Produced by: Owen Bradley
Year: 1961
Pop hit with a country pedigree, but no country crossover.

EMPEROR'S NEW CLOTHES

Artist: Sinead O'Connor
Written by: Sinead O'Connor
From the album: *I Do Not Want What I Haven't Got*
Label: Ensign/Chrysalis
Produced by: Nellee Hooper, Sinead O'Connor
Year: 1990
After covering Prince's "Nothing Compares to U" as a torchy weeper, the shaven-headed Irish troubadour O'Connor torches the charts with a pop rocker. A girl after Elvis Costello's heart, she would next move on to antagonizing the pope, Frank Sinatra, the cast of *Saturday Night Live*, Bob Dylan fans at Madison Square Garden, and the entire country music audience.

EMPIRE OF THE SENSELESS

Artist: The Mekons
Written by: The Mekons
From the album: *The Mekons Rock and Roll*
Label: A&M
Produced by: The Mekons
Year: 1989
This critically revered English punk band achieves partial redemption.

EMPTY ARMS

Artist: Ivory Joe Hunter
Written by: Joe Hunter
Label: Atlantic
Year: 1957
His last of seven Top 10 R&B hits.

EMPTY GARDEN (HEY HEY JOHNNY)

Artist: Elton John
Written by: Elton John, Bernie Taupin
From the album: *Jump Up*
Label: Geffen
Produced by: Chris Thomas
Year: 1982
In memory of John Lennon.

END, THE

Artist: The Beatles
Written by: John Lennon, Paul McCartney
From the album: *Abbey Road*
Label: Apple
Produced by: George Martin
Year: 1969
Suggested segue: "God Save the Queen" by the Sex Pistols.

END, THE

Artist: The Doors
Written by: Jim Morrison, Robbie Krieger, John Densmore, Ray Manzarek
From the album: *The Doors*
Label: Elektra
Produced by: Paul Rothchild
Year: 1967
Oedipal epic: contorted, disturbed, and disturbing poetics. Remixed for use in the film and soundtrack *Apocalypse Now* (Elektra, '79).

END OF THE INNOCENCE, THE

Artist: Don Henley
Written by: Don Henley, Bruce Hornsby
From the album: *The End of the Innocence*
Label: Geffen
Produced by: Don Henley, Bruce Hornsby
Year: 1989
This eloquent and all-encompassing diatribe defines Henley's post-Eagles renaissance. Bruce Hornsby mans the keyboards.

END OF THE ROAD

Boyz II Men
Written by: Kenny Edmunds (Babyface), Antonio Reid (L.A. Reid), Daryl Simmons
From the album: *Boomerang Soundtrack*
Label: Gee Street/LaFace
Produced by: Babyface, L. A. Reid
Year: 1992
High harmony history was made briefly when this title assumed the mantle of the longest-running #1 single of all time, until Whitney Houston swept by it a few weeks later with "I Will Always Love You."

END OF THE WORLD, THE

Skeeter Davis
Written by: Sylvia Dee, Arthur Kent
From the album: *The End of the World*
Label: RCA Victor
Produced by: Chet Atkins
Year: 1963
Rare Top 10 R&B/Top 10 country/Top 10 pop crossover reflected Davis's feelings after losing her best friend and former singing partner Betty Jack Davis (no relation) in a car crash.

ENDLESS FAREWELL

Artist: Soul Asylum
Written by: Dave Pirner
From the album: *Hang Time*
Label: Twin Tone
Produced by: Ed Stasium, Lenny Kaye
Year: 1988
Little brothers to Minneapolis scenesters Hüsker Dü and the Repacements say goodbye to the punk era with a tearful ballad (Pirner on keyboards).

ENDLESS LOVE

Artist: Lionel Richie and Diana Ross
Written by: Lionel B. Richie
From the album: *Endless Love Soundtrack*
Label: Motown
Produced by: Lionel Richie
Year: 1981
As cherished in some quarters as this tune may be as a wedding song, it must be said that it was just this sort of under-the-credits treacle that did almost as much to undermine the brilliance of the Scott Spencer novel from which it derives its title as the casting, directing, and screenwriting of the movie itself.

ENDLESS SLEEP

Artist: Jody Reynolds
Written by: Jody Reynolds, Dolores Nance
Label: Demon
Year: 1958
Reynolds's double-suicide dirge inaugurates a new Bandstand craze: the dance of death. Suggested segue: "Tragedy" by Thomas Wayne, "Tell Laura I Love Her," by Ray Peterson, "Running Bear" by J.P. Richardson.

ENDLESS SUMMER NIGHTS

Artist: Richard Marx
Written by: Richard Marx
From the album: *Richard Marx*
Label: EMI-Manhattan
Produced by: H. Gatica
Year: 1988
Briefly reviving the art of the summer song.

ENGINE NUMBER 9 (GET ME BACK ON TIME)

Artist: Wilson Pickett
Written by: Kenny Gamble, Leon Huff
From the album: *Wilson Pickett in Philadelphia*
Label: Atlantic
Produced by: Kenny Gamble, Leon Huff
Year: 1970
Gold single.

ENJOY THE SILENCE

Artist: Depeche Mode
Written by: Martin Gore
From the album: *Violator*
Label: Sire
Produced by: Depeche Mode, Flood
Year: 1990
Their fashionable angst achieves its antiseptic peak with their first and only Top 10 hit.

ENJOY YOURSELF

Artist: The Jacksons
Written by: Kenny Gamble, Leon Huff
From the album: *The Jacksons*
Label: Epic
Produced by: Kenny Gamble, Leon Huff
Year: 1976
First hit as the Jacksons is a post-pubescent, post-Motown dance groove.

ENTER SANDMAN

Artist: Metallica
Written by: James Hetfield, Lars Ulrich, Kirk Hammett
From the album: *Metallica (The Black Album)*
Label: Elektra
Produced by: Bob Rock, James Hetfield, Lars Ulrich
Year: 1991
The reigning and thundering beast of metal make their semimelodic (commercial) move.

ENTERTAINER, THE

Artist: Billy Joel
Written by: Billy Joel
From the album: *Streetlife Serenader*
Label: Columbia
Produced by: Michael Stewart
Year: 1974
Self-absorbed confessional from the pen and piano of the former L.A. lounge lizard Bill Martin.

EPIC

Artist: Faith No More
Written by: Faith No More
From the album: *The Real Thing*
Label: Slash
Produced by: Matt Wallace, Faith No More
Year: 1990
This sobering rebuke to the ghost of Jim Morrison—"You want it all and you can't have it"—hit a nerve in the nervous '90s.

ERIC B IS PRESIDENT

Artist: Eric B & Rakim
Written by: Eric Barrier, William Griffin
From the album: *Paid in Full*
Label: 4TH & Broadway
Produced by: Eric B & Rakim
Year: 1987
In many minds, the new Commander in Chief of rap. But "Paid in Full" was more invigorating.

EROTICA

Artist: Madonna
Written by: Shep Pettibone, Madonna Ciccone
From the album: *Erotica*
Label: Maverick/Sire
Produced by: Shep Pettibone, Madonna Ciccone
Year: 1992
Shameless shelf promotion for her sex "book."

ERUPTION

Artist: Van Halen
Written by: Eddie Van Halen, Alex Van Halen, Michael Anthony, David Lee Roth
From the album: *Van Halen*
Label: Warner Brothers
Produced by: Ted Templeman
Year: 1978
Early signature two hand tapping guitar solo had a profound effect on the nature of rock guitar playing for the next decade, as well as the guitar equipment industry.

ESCAPADE

Artist: Janet Jackson
Written by: James Harris III, Terry Lewis, Janet Jackson
From the album: *Rhythm Nation 1814*
Label: A&M
Produced by: Jimmy Jam, Terry Lewis
Year: 1989
Her second #1 R&B/#1 crossover.

ESCAPE (THE PIÑA COLADA SONG)

Artist: Rupert Holmes
Written by: Rupert Holmes
From the album: *Partners in Crime*
Label: Infinity
Produced by: Rupert Holmes, Jom Boyer
Year: 1979
O'Henryesque story song of mistaken identity. Suggested segue: the haunting "Babooshka" by Kate Bush.

ETERNAL FLAME

Artist: Bangles
Written by: Billy Steinberg, Tom Kelly, Susannah Hoffs
From the album: *Everything*
Label: Columbia
Produced by: Davitt Sigerson
Year: 1989
Susannah Hoffs goes out on a corporate high note with a #1 US/#1 UK smash. Later she'd be making movies directed by her mother.

ETON RIFLES

Artist: The Jam
Written by: Paul Weller
From the album: *Setting Sons*
Label: Polydor
Produced by: Vic Coppersmith-Heaven
Year: 1979
First hit for the influential UK group, a powerful post-war protest.

EULOGY TO LENNY BRUCE

Artist: Nico
Written by: Tim Hardin
From the album: *Chelsea Girl*
Label: Verve
Produced by: Tom Wilson
Year: 1967
Saying goodbye to a soulmate, the satirist Lenny Bruce. Covered by Tim Hardin as "Lenny's Tune" (Verve Forcast, '69). Suggested segue: "Lenny Bruce" by Bob Dylan.

EUPHORIA

Artist: The Holy Modal Rounders
Written by: Robin Remaily
From the album: *Moray Eels Eat the Holy Modal Rounders*
Label: Paul Rothschild
Produced by: Paul Rothschild
Year: 1967
Encapsulating their subversive acid bluegrass philosophy. Covered by the Nitty Gritty Dirt Band (Liberty, '67), the Youngbloods (RCA, '70).

EUROPEAN SON: TO DELMORE SCHWARTZ

Artist: The Velvet Underground
Written by: Lou Reed
From the album: *The Velvet Underground and Nico*
Label: Verve
Produced by: Andy Warhol
Year: 1967
Like the Fugs, whom they replaced at the Dom, the Velvet Underground were inspired by the beat poets. Eventually Lou Reed, who studied with Delmore Schwartz at Syracuse, would have his poems published in the *Harvard Review*. Unlike the Fugs, the Velvet Underground had the musical ability to embrace rock and roll as a means to saving a few lives, Alex Chilton and Paul Westerberg among them.

EVE OF DESTRUCTION

Artist: Barry McGuire
Written by: Steve Barri, P. F. Sloan
From the album: *Eve of Destruction*
Label: Dunhill
Produced by: Lou Adler
Year: 1965
For anyone seeking P.F. Sloan, this protest anthem is the logical first stop. Covered by the Turtles (White Whale, '65).

EVEN A DOG CAN SHAKE HANDS

Artist: Warren Zevon
Written by: Warren Zevon, Peter Buck, Bill Berry, Mike Mills
From the album: *Sentimental Hygiene*
Label: Virgin
Produced by: Nico Bolas, Andrew Slater, Warren Zevon
Year: 1987
Zevon takes over the Michael Stipe role in R.E.M for a song.

EVEN BETTER THAN THE REAL THING

Artist: U2
Written by: U2
From the album: *Achtung, Baby*
Produced by: Daniel Lanois, Brian Eno
Label: Island
Year: 1991
Adopting a new ironic approach in the new decade.

EVEN FLOW

Artist: Pearl Jam
Written by: Eddie Vedder, Stone Gossard
From the album: *Ten*
Label: Epic
Produced by: Nick Parashar, Pearl Jam
Year: 1991
Making their serious arena move.

EVEN IT UP

Artist: Heart
Written by: Ann Wilson, Nancy Wilson, Sue Ennis
From the album: *Bebe Le Strange*
Label: Portrait
Produced by: Mike Flicker, Gonnie and Howie
Year: 1980
Last hit from their arena rock period is a slight nod to feminism. After this they would be playing with house money, as the ballads rolled in.

EVEN THE LOSERS

Artist: Tom Petty and the Heartbreakers
Written by: Tom Petty
From the album: *Damn the Torpedoes*
Label: Backstreet
Produced by: Jimmy Iovine, Tom Petty
Year: 1979
Early autobiographical anthem of a loser getting lucky.

EVER FALLEN IN LOVE (WITH SOMEONE YOU SHOULDN'T HAVE FALLEN IN LOVE WITH)

Artist: The Buzzcocks
Written by: Pete Shelley
From the album: *Love Bites*
Label: United Artists
Produced by: Martin Rushent
Year: 1978
Pete Shelley takes over and moves the Sex Pistols-influenced band a step closer to modern rock. Covered by the Fine Young Cannibals (Island, '87) in the Jonathan Demme film *Something Wild*.

EVERLASTING LOVE

Artist: Robert Knight
Written by: James Cason, Mac Gayden
Label: Rising Sons
Produced by: Buzz Cason, Mac Gaydon
Year: 1967
Three times a hit in three different decades, the second by Carl Carlton (Backbeat, '74), the third by Rex Smith (Columbia, '81).

EVERLONG

Artist: Foo Fighters
Written by: Dave Grohl
From the album: *The Colour and the Shape*
Label: RossWell
Produced by: Gil Norton
Year: 1997
Pining for his lost Nirvana, Grohl tries to move on in this moving ballad.

EVERY BEAT OF MY HEART

Artist: The Pips
Written by: Johnny Otis
Label: Vee-Jay
Produced by: Ralph Bass
Year: 1961

A #1 R&B/Top 10 crossover, rerecorded under the name of Gladys Knight & the Pips (Fury, '61). Both sides came out at the same time and competed with each other; the Vee-Jay version won the battle, but lost the war. Covered by James Brown (King, '65).

EVERY BREATH I TAKE

Artist: Gene Pitney
Written by: Gerry Goffin, Carole King
From the album: *World-Wide Winners*
Label: Musicor
Produced by: Phil Spector
Year: 1961
A notable stiff, with Spector at the helm. Pitney would recover to become the East Coast Roy Orbison.

EVERY BREATH YOU TAKE

Artist: The Police
Written by: Gordon Sumner (Sting)
From the album: *Synchronicity*
Label: A&M
Produced by: Hugh Padgham, the Police
Year: 1983
In a very good year for UK bands, this peaen to obsessive love was the biggest hit of the year.

EVERY DAY I HAVE THE BLUES

Artist: Lowell Fulson
Written by: Peter (Memphis Slim) Chatman
Label: Swingtime
Year: 1950
#5 R&B hit version of the Memphis Slim blues standard, covered by Johnny Raye (Okeh, '52), Big Joe Williams with the Count Basie Orchestra (Clef, '55), B. B. King on the legendary album that launched a generation of white electric blues guitarists *Live at the Regal* (RPM, '65), James Brown (King, '70), Fleetwood Mac (Blue Horizon, '71), Chuck Berry (Chess, '72).

EVERY DAY I WRITE THE BOOK

Artist: Elvis Costello
Written by: Declan McManus (Elvis Costello)
From the album: *Punch the Clock*
Label: Columbia
Produced by: Clive Langer, Alan Winstanley
Year: 1983
Motown-flavored rocker nets Costello his first US Top 40.

EVERY DOG HAS HIS DAY

Artist: Let's Active
Written by: Mitch Easter
From the album: *Every Dog Has His Day*
Label: I.R.S.
Produced by: Mitch Easter

Year: 1988
R.E.M. mentor with a cult favorite.

EVERY GRAIN OF SAND

Artist: Bob Dylan
Written by: Bob Dylan
From the album: *Shot of Love*
Label: Columbia
Produced by: Bumps Blackwell, Chuck Plotkin, Bob Dylan
Year: 1981
A Dylan gem from his overlooked "religious" period. Covered by Emmylou Harris (Reprise, '95).

EVERY LITTLE BIT

Artist: Patti Griffin
Written by: Patti Griffin
From the album: *Living with Ghosts*
Label: A&M
Year: 1996
A new poignant folk/rock voice among her shriller sisters.

EVERY LITTLE KISS

Artist: Bruce Hornsby and the Range
Written by: Bruce Hornsby
From the album: *The Way It Is*
Label: RCA
Produced by: E. Scheiner, Bruce Hornsby
Year: 1986
A touch of country soul from the new age jazzbo.

EVERY LITTLE STEP

Artist: Bobby Brown
Written by: Kenny Edmunds (Babyface), Antonio Reid (L. A. Reid)
From the album: *Don't Be Cruel*
Label: MCA
Produced by: Babyface, L. A. Reid
Year: 1989
Child R&B prodigy takes another leap forward with his first #1 R&B/Top 10 crossover.

EVERY LITTLE THING

Artist: The Beatles
Written by: John Lennon, Paul McCartney
From the album: *Beatles VI*
Label: Capitol
Produced by: George Martin
Year: 1965

EVERY LITTLE THING SHE DOES IS MAGIC

Artist: The Police
Written by: Gordon Sumner (Sting)
From the album: *Ghost in the Machine*
Label: A&M
Produced by: Hugh Padgham, the Police
Year: 1981
Their patented reggae lite dents the US Top 5.

EVERY MORNING

Artist: Sugar Ray
Written by: Mark McGrath, David Kahne, Richard Bean, Abel Zarate, Pablo Tellez, Craig Bullock, Charlier Farrier, Joseph Nichol, Rodney Sheppard
From the album: *14:59*
Label: Lava
Produced by: David Kahne
Year: 1998
Following up their #1 debut, "Fly."

EVERY 1'S A WINNER

Artist: Hot Chocolate
Written by: Errol Brown
From the album: *Every 1's a Winner*
Label: Infinity
Produced by: Mickie Most
Year: 1979
Last of three US hits for the UK soul band that had thirteen Top 10 hits in England.

EVERY PICTURE TELLS A STORY

Artist: Rod Stewart
Written by: Rod Stewart, Ron Wood
From the album: *Every Picture Tells a Story*
Label: Mercury
Produced by: Tom Dowd
Year: 1971
Countrified rocker is Rod at his raspin' best.

EVERY ROSE HAS ITS THORN

Artist: Poison
Written by: Bobby Dall, C.C. Deville, Brett Michaels, Rikki Rockett
From the album: *Open up and Say Ahh*
Label: Capitol
Produced by: Tom Werman
Year: 1988
Looking to the arena rock ballad for their biggest hit.

(EVERY TIME I TURN AROUND) BACK IN LOVE AGAIN

Artist: L.T.D.
Written by: Len Hanks, Zane Grey
From the album: *Something to Love*
Label: A&M
Produced by: Bobby Martin
Year: 1977
Turning in a pop direction for their only #1 R&B/Top 10 crossover, with Jeffrey Osbourne on lead vocals.

EVERY TIME YOU GO AWAY

Artist: Daryl Hall & John Oates
Written by: Daryl Hall

From the album: *Voices*
Label: RCA
Produced by: Hall & Oates
Year: 1985
An embarrassment of riches; this soulful ballad was not quite appropriate to extend Hall & Oates' more uptempo hot streak. But the cover by Paul Young (Columbia, '85) went to #1.

EVERYBODY

Artist: Tommy Roe
Written by: Tommy Roe
From the album: *Sweet Pea*
Label: ABC
Produced by: Felton Jarvis
Year: 1963
Buddy Holly-inspired rocker, inspired by Roe's tour with the Beatles. Will forever be remembered as the tune that was interrupted on 1010 WINS in New York for the bulletin announcing the assassination of JFK.

EVERYBODY (BACKSTREET'S BACK)

Artist: Backstreet Boys
Written by: Max Martin, Denniz Pop
From the album: *Backstreet Boys*
Label: Jive
Year: 1997
Third of five Top 10 hits that launched the boy band sound of the premillenium.

EVERYBODY EVERYBODY

Artist: Black Box
Written by: Mirko Limoni, Daniele Davoli, Valerio Semplici
From the album: *Dreamland*
Label: RCA
Produced by: Groove Groove Melody
Year: 1990
Dance sensation from Italy, featuring the uncredited voice of US diva, Martha Wash.

EVERYBODY HAVE FUN TONIGHT

Artist: Wang Chung
Written by: Peter Wolf, Wang Chung
From the album: *Mosaic*
Label: Geffen
Produced by: Peter Wolf
Year: 1986
Completing their US crossover with a Top 10 dance hall smash.

EVERYBODY HURTS

Artist: R.E.M.
Written by: Michael Stipe, Peter Buck, Bill Berry, Mike Mills
From the album: *Automatic for the People*
Label: Warner Brothers
Produced by: Scott Litt, R.E.M.
Year: 1993

Antisuicide lyric was written by drummer Bill Berry before he retired from the band.

EVERYBODY IS A STAR

Artist: Sly and the Family Stone
Written by: Sylvester Stewart
From the album: *Greatest Hits*
Label: Epic
Produced by: Sly Stone
Year: 1970
This B-side of "Thank You (Falettingme Be Mice Elf Agin)" reflects the year's pseudo-empowering communal spirit.

EVERYBODY KNOWS

Artist: Leonard Cohen
Written by: Leonard Cohen
From the album: *I'm Your Man*
Produced by: Roscoe Beck, Michael Robidoux, Jean-Michel Reusser
Label:
Year: 1988
Drier and droller than ever.

EVERYBODY NEEDS SOMEBODY TO LOVE

Artist: Solomon Burke
Written by: Bert Berns, Solomon Burke, Jerry Wexler
From the album: *Best of Solomon Burke*
Label: Atlantic
Produced by: Bern Berns, Jerry Wexler, Bob Porter
Year: 1964
Soul classic, covered by Wilson Pickett (Atlantic, '67).

EVERYBODY PLAYS THE FOOL

Artist: The Main Ingredient
Written by: Kenneth Williams, Rudy Clark, Jim Bailey
From the album: *Bitter Sweet*
Label: RCA
Produced by: Luther Simmons, Tony Sylvester
Year: 1972
A big year for mainstream R&B philosophising. See: "Backstabbers" by the O'Jays, "I Can See Clearly Now" by Johnny Nash, "Freddy's Dead" by Curtis Mayfield.

EVERYBODY WANTS TO RULE THE WORLD

Artist: Tears For Fears
Written by: Roland Orzabal, Ian Stanley, Chris Hughes
From the album: *Songs from the Big Chair*
Label: Mercury
Produced by: Chris Hughes, Roland Orzabel, Ian Stanley
Year: 1985

Wordly and wise synth jam defines the British invasion of the '80s.

EVERYBODY WANTS YOU

Artist: Billy Squier
Written by: Billy Squier
From the album: *Emotions in Motion*
Label: Capitol
Produced by: Billy Squier, Mack
Year: 1982
Reacting to arena success. A few years later, nobody would want him.

EVERYBODY'S BEEN BURNED

Artist: The Byrds
Written by: David Crosby
From the album: *5D (Fifth Dimension)*
Label: Columbia
Produced by: Allen Stanton
Year: 1967
Caustic Crosby just before being burned by the Byrds.

EVERYBODY'S FREE (TO WEAR SUNSCREEN)

Artist: Baz Luhrman
Written by: Tim Cox, Nigel Swanson
From the album: *Something for Everybody*
Label: Capitol
Year: 1999
Hilarious commencement speech/column by journalist Mary Schmich, with music from the movie *Romeo & Juliet*. Probably the first hit record to be derived from an Internet rumor, this one attributing the text to author Kurt Vonnegut.

(EVERYBODY'S GONNA HAVE) A WONDERFUL TIME UP THERE (GOSPEL BOOGIE)

Artist: Pat Boone
Written by: Lee Roy Abernethy
Label: Dot
Year: 1958
B-side of his cover of the Orioles' "It's Too Soon to Know," was a cover of Leroy Abernethy's gospel classic from 1947.

EVERYBODY'S GOT SOMETHING TO HIDE EXCEPT ME AND MY MONKEY

Artist: The Beatles
Written by: John Lennon, Paul McCartney
From the album: *The Beatles*
Label: Apple
Produced by: George Martin
Year: 1968

The legendary monkey motif gets the Beatle treatment: the monkey is Yoko (the walrus is Paul).

EVERYBODY'S HAPPY NOWADAYS

Artist: The Buzzcocks
Written by: Pete Shelley
From the album: *Singles Going Steady*
Label: IRS
Produced by: Martin Rushent
Year: 1978
Power punk.

EVERYBODY'S SOMEBODY'S FOOL

Artist: Connie Francis
Written by: Howard Greenfield, Jack Keller
From the album: *More Greatest Hits*
Label: MGM
Produced by: Joe Sherman, Arnold Maxin
Year: 1960
Connie goes country for her biggest hit, Top 20 country/#1 pop.

EVERYBODY'S TALKIN'

Artist: Fred Neil
Written by: Fred Neil
From the album: *Fred Neil*
Label: Elektra
Produced by: Nik Venet
Year: 1967
Explaining his motives, Fred Neil quits the NY folk/rock scene to take off for Coconut Grove. Covered by Nilsson (RCA, '67). Nilsson's version became his first Top 10 hit after being featured in the '69 film *Midnight Cowboy*, wherein Dustin Hoffman and John Voight take off for Miami as well.

EVERYBODY'S TRYING TO BE MY BABY

Artist: Carl Perkins
Written by: Carl Perkins
From the album: *Dance Album*
Label: Sun
Produced by: Sam Phillips
Year: 1957
Rockabilly performing favorite of the Beatles. Covered by The Beatles (Capitol '65).

EVERYDAY

Artist: Buddy Holly
Written by: Buddy Holly
From the album: *The Buddy Holly Story*
Label: Coral
Produced by: Norman Petty
Year: 1957
B-side of "Peggy Sue."

EVERYDAY IS A WINDING ROAD

Artist: Sheryl Crow
Written by: Sheryl Crow, Jeff Trott, Brian MacLeod
From the album: *Sheryl Crow*
Label: A&M
Produced by: Sheryl Crow, Mitchell Froom
Year: 1996
Perfect post-Eagles L.A. folk/rocker.

EVERYDAY IS LIKE SUNDAY

Artist: Morrissey
Written by: Stephen Morrissey, Stephen Street
From the album: *Viva Hate*
Label: Sire
Produced by: Stephen Street
Year: 1988
Gloomy and grey. Covered by the Pretenders in the film *Boys on the Side* (Arista, '95).

EVERYDAY PEOPLE

Artist: Sly and the Family Stone
Written by: Sylvester Stewart
From the album: *Stand!*
Label: Epic
Produced by: Sly Stone
Year: 1969
Acid funk with a down-home message and a psychedelic soul chaser was their biggest hit and the first of three #1 R&B/#1 crossovers.

EVERYONE IS GOOD

Artist: The Roches
Written by: Terre Roche
From the album: *Another World*
Label: Warner Brothers
Produced by: Jeffrey Lesser, the Roches
Year: 1989
Their most beautiful folk/rock hymn.

EVERYONE'S GONE TO THE MOON

Artist: Jonathan King
Written by: Kenneth King
From the album: *Jonathan King or Then Again*
Label: Parrot
Year: 1965
Novelty commentary by the noted English scenemaker.

EVERYTHING

Artist: Jody Watley
Written by: Gardner Cole, James Newton Howard
From the album: *Larger Than Life*
Label: MCA
Produced by: Andre Cymone
Year: 1989
Third hit From the album; #1 R&B/Top 10 crossover.

EVERYTHING ABOUT YOU

Artist: Ugly Kid Joe
Written by: Klaus Eichstadt, Whitfield Crane
From the album: *As Ugly as They Wanna Be*
Label: Stardog
Produced by: Ryan Dom, Ugly Kid Joe
Year: 1992
Alternative bubblegum rant; featured in *Wayne's World*.

EVERYTHING FALLS APART

Artist: Dog's Eye View
Written by: Peter Stuart
From the album: *Happy Nowhere*
Label: Columbia
Year: 1996
Listening to Mose Allison's jazz locutions.

(EVERYTHING I DO) I DO IT FOR YOU

Artist: Bryan Adams
Written by: Bryan Adams, Robert John "Mutt" Lange and Michael Kamen
From the album: *Robin Hood: Prince of Thieves Soundtrack*
Produced by: Mutt Lange
Label: Morgan Creek
Year: 1991
Big movie ballad.

EVERYTHING I MISS AT HOME

Artist: Cherrelle
Written by: James Harris III, Terry Lewis
From the album: *Affair*
Label: Tabu
Produced by: Jimmy Jam, Terry Lewis
Year: 1988
#1 R&B tale by the Michael Henderson protégé, of a woman on the brink.

EVERYTHING I OWN

Artist: Bread
Written by: David Gates
From the album: *Baby I'm a-Want You*
Label: Elektra
Produced by: David Gates
Year: 1972
Air supply was listening.

EVERYTHING IS BEAUTIFUL

Artist: Ray Stevens
Written by: Ray Stevens
From the album: *Everything Is Beautiful*
Label: Barnaby
Produced by: Ray Stevens
Year: 1970
Uncharactertistically rose-colored perspective from the country satirist.

EVERYTHING IS BROKEN

Artist: Bob Dylan
Written by: Bob Dylan

From the album: *Oh Mercy*
Label: Columbia
Produced by: Daniel Lanois
Year: 1989
Dylan's state of the decade address. In the '90s this function would be served by his cryptic comments accepting a Lifetime Achievement Grammy Award on TV.

EVERYTHING SHE WANTS

Artist: Wham!
Written by: George Michael
From the album: *Make It Big*
Label: Columbia
Produced by: George Michael
Year: 1984
#1 follow-up to a #1 establishes Michael and Ridgeley as the London teen faves of the month, if not the year.

EVERYTHING TO EVERYONE

Artist: Everclear
Written by: Art Alexakis, Everclear
From the album: *So Much for the Afterglow*
Label: Capitol
Produced by: Art Alexakis
Year: 1997

EVERYTHING YOU WANT

Artist: Vertical Horizon
Written by: Mark Ender, Ben Grosse
From the album: *Everything You Want*
Produced by: Matthew Scannell
Label: RCA
Year: 2000
Subverting their jam band roots for a #1 record.

EVERYTHING YOUR HEART DESIRES

Artist: Hall and Oates
Written by: Daryl Hall
From the album: *ooh yeah*
Label: Arista
Produced by: Hall & Oates, T-Bone Wolk
Year: 1988
After a long layoff, they come back with their sixteenth and last Top 10 hit.

EVERYTHING ZEN

Artist: Bush
Written by: Gavin Rossdale
From the album: *Sixteen Stone*
Label: Capitol
Produced by: Clive Langer, Alan Winstanley, Bush
Year: 1994
First single for the British invasion band. Segue: "Rockin' in the Free World" by Neil Young.

EVERYTHING'S ALRIGHT

Artist: Yvonne Elliman
Written by: Tim Rice, Andrew Lloyd Webber

From the album: *Jesus Christ Superstar*
Label: Decca
Produced by: Tim Rice, Andrew Lloyd Webber
Year: 1971
Mid-tempo secular love song from the legendary rock opera.

EVIL

Artist: Howlin' Wolf
Written by: Willie Dixon
From the album: *Moaning in the Moonlight*
Label: Chess
Year: 1954
Naming and personifying an attitude and a sound. Hit the R&B charts in '69 at the height of the urban blues revival spearheaded by the Paul Butterfield Blues Band and undermined by Led Zeppelin.

EVIL EYE

Artist: Alcatrazz
Written by: Yngwie Malmsteen
From the album: *Live Sentence*
Label: Rocshire
Year: 1984
Introducing a new guitar god in the classically-oriented Swede, Yngwie Malmsteen.

EVIL HEARTED YOU

Artist: The Yardbirds
Written by: Graham Gouldman
From the album: *Having a Rave up with the Yardbirds*
Label: Epic
Produced by: Paul Samwell-Smith
Year: 1965
Big hit in the UK.

EVIL THAT MEN DO, THE

Artist: Queen Latifah with KRS-One
Written by: Dana Owens (Queen Latifah), Kris Parker (KRS-One)
From the album: *All Hail the Queen*
Label: Tommy Boy
Produced by: KRS-One
Year: 1989
Queen of Rap duets with the Minister of Information.

EVIL WAYS

Artist: Santana
Written by: Clarence Henry
From the album: *Santana*
Label: Columbia
Produced by: Brent Dangerfield, Santana
Year: 1969
Their biggest early hit except for their cover of Fleetwood Mac's "Black Magic Woman."

EVIL WOMAN

Artist: Electric Light Orchestra (ELO)
Written by: Jeff Lynne
From the album: *Face the Music*
Label: United Artists

Produced by: Jeff Lynne
Year: 1975
Wings lite.

EVOL

Artist: Sonic Youth
Written by: Sonic Youth
From the album: *Evol*
Label: SST
Produced by: Martin Bisi, Sonic Youth
Year: 1986
Recording since '82 (in at least 82 different guitar tunings), the influential art/noise rockers make their move toward accessibility.

EXCITABLE BOY

Artist: Warren Zevon
Written by: Warren Zevon, Leroy Marinell
From the album: *Excitable Boy*
Label: Asylum
Produced by: Jackson Browne, Waddy Wachtel
Year: 1976
Running with scissors. A defining gem of the L.A. singer/songwriter school of the '70s.

EXHALE (THE SHOOP SHOOP SONG)

Artist: Whitney Houston
Written by: Kenny Edmunds (Babyface)
From the album: *Waiting to Exhale*
Label: Arista
Produced by: Babyface
Year: 1995
Whitney's last #1 R&B/#1 crossover (through the millenium), from the movie *Waiting to Exhale*.

EXODUS

Artist: Bob Marley & the Wailers
Written by: Bob Marley
Label: Island
Produced by: Bob Marley & the Wailers, Chris Blackwell
Year: 1963
In 1977 this became their biggest R&B hit, reflecting their long journey out of obscurity to world fame.

EXORCISING THE EVIL SPIRITS FROM THE PENTAGON, OCT. 21, 1967

Artist: The Fugs
Written by: Tuli Kupferberg, Ed Sanders
From the album: *Tenderness Junction*
Label: ESP
Year: 1968
Yippies attempt to levitate the Pentagon, during a high point in the '60s protest movement.

EXPECTING TO FLY

Artist: Buffalo Springfield
Written by: Neil Young

From the album: *Buffalo Springfield Again*
Label: Atco
Produced by: Turk-Pila
Year: 1967
One of Young's most fragile melodies eulogizes a generation's false hopes.

EXPRESS

Artist: B. T. Express
Written by: Louis Risbrook, Barbara Lomas, William Risbrook, Orlando Woods, Richard Thompson, Carlos Ward, Dennis Rowe
From the album: *Do It ('Til You're Satisfied)*
Label: Roadshow
Produced by: Jeff Lane
Year: 1974
Big disco groove is their second #1 R&B/Top 10 crossover, following up "Do It ('Til You're Satisfied").

EXPRESS YOURSELF

Artist: Madonna
Written by: Steve Bray, Madonna Ciccone
From the album: *Like a Prayer*
Label: Sire
Produced by: Steve Bray, Madonna
Year: 1989
Madonna in an Oprah frame of mind. Top video.

EXPRESSWAY TO YOUR HEART

Artist: The Soul Survivors
Written by: Kenny Gamble, Leon Huff
From the album: *When the Whistle Blows Anything Goes*
Label: Crimson
Produced by: Kenny Gamble, Leon Huff
Year: 1967
Last exit to Philly soul.

EXPRESSWAY TO YR SKULL

Artist: Sonic Youth
Written by: Sonic Youth
From the album: *Evol*
Label: SST
Produced by: Martin Bisi, Sonic Youth
Year: 1986
Like a rave up in a hornet's nest.

EYE IN THE SKY

Artist: The Alan Parsons Project
Written by: Eric Woolfson, Alan Parsons
From the album: *Eye in the Sky*
Label: Arista
Produced by: Alan Parsons
Year: 1982
Biggest hit for the legendary recording engineer (*Abbey Road, Dark Side of the Moon*).

EYE OF FATIMA (PARTS I AND II)

Artist: Camper Van Beethoven
Written by: Camper Van Beethoven
From the album: *Our Beloved Revolutionary Sweetheart*
Label: Virgin
Produced by: Dennis Herring
Year: 1988
Camping out on the fine line between whimsy and AOR.

EYE OF THE TIGER (THE THEME FROM *ROCKY III*)

Artist: Survivor
Written by: Frank Sullivan, Jim Peterik
From the album: *Eye of the Tiger*
Label: Scotti Brothers
Produced by: Frank Sullivan, Jim Peterik
Year: 1982
Arena rock, reduced to accommodate a boxing ring, then expanded to fill a movie screen. Suggested segue: "The Boxer" by Simon and Garfunkel.

EYES OF A NEW YORK WOMAN

Artist: Insect Trust
Written by: Thomas Pynchon, Jeff Ogden
From the album: *Hoboken Saturday Night*
Label: Atco
Produced by: Steve Duboff
Year: 1970
A (middle) Eastern hoedown, with lyrics taken straight out of Thomas Pynchon's epic literary novel of 1963, *V.*, as sung in the book by Benny Profane. Suggested segue: "Nice Nice, Very Nice" by Ambrosia, with lyrics by Kurt Vonnegut.

EYES OF A STRANGER

Artist: Queensryche
Written by: Chris DeGarmo, Geoff Tate
From the album: *Operation: Mindcrime*
Label: EMI-Manhattan
Produced by: Peter Collins
Year: 1988
From their magnum metal opera.

EYES WITHOUT A FACE

Artist: Billy Idol
Written by: William Broad (Billy Idol), Steve Stevens
From the album: *Rebel Yell*
Label: Chrysalis
Produced by: Keith Forsey
Year: 1984
Scary Bowiesque denunciations based on a '59 French horror movie.

EYESIGHT TO THE BLIND

Artist: Sonny Boy Williamson

Written by: Aleck Miller (Sonny Boy Williamson)
Label: Trumpet
Year: 1951
First modern genius of the blues harp, paved the way for Junior Wells and Paul Butterfield. Covered by the Larks (Apollo, '51), the Who in *Tommy* (Decca, '69).

F

FA-FA-FA-FA-FA (SAD SONG)

Artist: Otis Redding
Written by: Otis Redding, Steve Cropper
From the album: *Dictionary of Soul*
Label: Volt
Produced by: Otis Redding, Jim Stewart, Steve Cropper
Year: 1966
Elemental soul scatting.

FACE THE FACE

Artist: Pete Townshend
Written by: Pete Townshend
From the album: *White City*
Label: Atco
Produced by: Chris Thomas
Year: 1985
From his album as novel as album, a controversial ode.

FACTORY GIRL

Artist: The Rolling Stones
Written by: Mick Jagger, Keith Richards
From the album: *Beggars Banquet*
Label: London
Produced by: Jimmy Miller
Year: 1968
They return to their element, the bluesy working-class old neighborhood.

FADE TO BLACK

Artist: Metallica
Written by: James Hetfield, Lars Ulrich, Cliff Burton, Kirk Hammett
From the album: *Master of Puppets*
Label: Elektra
Produced by: Mark Whittaker, Metallica
Year: 1984
A new guitarist, Kirk Hammett, replaces Dave Mustaine, but the mission remains the same: complete heavy metal domination.

FADING LIKE A FLOWER

Artist: Roxette
Written by: Per Gessle
From the album: *Joyride*
Label: EMI
Produced by: Clarence Ofwerman
Year: 1991
Swedish pop perfection.

FAIRYTALE OF NEW YORK

Artist: The Pogues
Written by: Shane MacGowan, Jem Finer
From the album: *If I Should Fall from Grace with God*
Label: Island
Produced by: Steve Lillywhite
Year: 1988
One of the all-time great Christmas songs, with Mrs. Lillywhite, Kirsty MacColl, on backing vocals. Closest contender: "2000 Miles" by the Pretenders.

FAITH

Artist: George Michael
Written by: George Michael
From the album: *Faith*
Label: Columbia
Produced by: George Michael
Year: 1987
Top single of 1988.

FAKE

Artist: Alexander O'Neal
Written by: James Harris III, Terry Lewis
From the album: *Hearsay*
Label: Tabu
Produced by: Jimmy Jam, Terry Lewis
Year: 1987
Former Jam and Lewis Minneapolis band-mate in Flyte Tyme gets his biggest US single, a #1 R&B/ Top 25 crossover, after four UK hits.

FALL ON ME

Artist: R.E.M.
Written by: Michael Stipe, Peter Buck, Bill Berry, Mike Mills
From the album: *Life's Rich Pageant*
Label: IRS
Produced by: Don Gehman
Year: 1985
Ready to accept the mantle of folk/rock's next great hope.

FALLEN OUT OF LOVE

Artist: Amy Correia
Written by: Amy Correia
From the album: *Amy Correia*
Produced by: Jeremy Stacey
Label: Capitol
Year: 2000
Singer/songwriter as chanteuse, wearing a gardenia. Norah Jones was ready to take over this niche.

FALLIN' IN LOVE (AGAIN)

Artist: Hamilton, Joe Frank, and Reynolds
Written by: Danny Hamilton, Ann Hamilton
From the album: *Fallin' in Love*
Label: Playboy
Produced by: Jim Price
Year: 1975
Even bigger than their jingle for Alka Seltzer as the T-Bones, a #1 hail and farewell to country/rock.

FALLING

Artist: Julee Cruise
Written by: Angelo Badalamenti, David Lynch
From the album: *Floating into the Night*
Label: Warner Brothers
Year: 1990
Eerie theme for the cult TV classic *Twin Peaks*.

FAME

Artist: David Bowie
Written by: John Lennon, David Bowie, Carlos Alomar
From the album: *Young Americans*
Label: RCA
Produced by: Harry Maslin, David Bowie
Year: 1975
His first US #1. Suggested segue: "Hot" by James Brown, "Foot Stompin'" by the Flares.

FAME

Artist: Irene Cara
Written by: Dean Pitchford, Michael Gore
From the album: *Fame*
Label: RSO
Produced by: Michael Gore
Year: 1980
Title theme from the movie about New York's High School of the Performing Arts. Promising to live forever, the song, as well as the kids, hardly made it past the advent of MTV.

FAME AND FORTUNE

Artist: Elvis Presley
Written by: Fred Wise, Ben Wiseman
From the album: *Elvis' Golden Records (Vol. III)*
Label: RCA
Produced by: Steve Sholes
Year: 1960
B-side of "Stuck on You." One of his most moving performances, revelations.

FAMILY AFFAIR

Artist: Sly and the Family Stone
Written by: Sylvester Stewart
From the album: *There's a Riot Goin' On*
Label: Epic
Produced by: Sly Stone
Year: 1971
Multitextured, many-leveled, drive-time funk is their third and last #1 R&B/#1 crossover.

FAMILY MAN

Artist: Mike Oldfield
Written by: Mike Oldfield, Morris Pert, Tim Cross, Rick Fenn, Mike Frye
From the album: *Five Miles Out*
Label: Caroline
Year: 1982
This was an on-the-bus favorite for Hall & Oates, who made it into their eleventh Top 10 hit (RCA, '83).

FAMOUS BLUE RAINCOAT

Artist: Leonard Cohen
Written by: Leonard Cohen
From the album: *Songs of Love and Hate*
Label: Columbia
Produced by: John Simon
Year: 1971
A letter from Clinton Street, Cohen at his most divinely melancholy. Covered by Jennifer Warnes (Cypress, '87).

FANNIE MAE

Artist: Buster Brown
Written by: Waymon Glasco
From the album: *The New King of the Blues*
Label: Fire
Year: 1960 #1 R&B.

FANTASTIC VOYAGE

Artist: Lakeside
Written by: Fred Alexander, Otis Stokes, Artis Ivey, Brian Dobbs, Norman Beavers, Marvin Craig, Tiemeyer McCain, Thomas Shelby
From the album: *Fantastic Voyage*
Label: Solar
Produced by: Dick Griffey
Year: 1981
Their only #1 R&B hit. Covered by Coolio (Tommy Boy, '94).

FANTASY

Artist: Mariah Carey
Written by: Mariah Carey, Dave Hall, Adrian Belew, Steven Stanley, Chris Franz, Tina Weymouth
From the album: *Daydream*
Label: Columbia
Produced by: Mariah Carey, Dave Hall, Sean Combs
Year: 1995
Borrowing a bit of "Genius of Love" for her ninth #1 and fourth #1 R&B/#1 crossover.

FAR BEHIND

Artist: Candlebox
Written by: Kevin Martin
From the album: *Candlebox*
Label: Maverick/Warner Brothers
Produced by: K. Gray, Candlebox
Year: 1993
Where alt rock meets hard rock: at the tombstone of a friend.

FAREWELL ANGELINA

Artist: Joan Baez
Written by: Bob Dylan
From the album: *Farewell Angelina*
Label: Vanguard
Produced by: Maynard Solomon
Year: 1965
As Annette did for Anka and Warwick for Bacharach and David, Baez gave Dylan's poetry its quintessential female voice.

FAREWELL SONG

Artist: Big Brother and the Holding Company
Written by: Sam Andrew
From the album: *Farewell Song*
Label: Mainstream
Produced by: John Simon
Year: 1968
Finally released on the album *Farewell Song* (Columbia, '82).

FARM HOUSE

Artist: Phish
Written by: Tom Marshall, Trey Anastasio
From the album: *Farmhouse*
Produced by: Trey Anastasio
Label: Elektra
Year: 2000
Out at the woodshed in Vermont, the jam band rehearses for retirement.

FARM YARD CONNECTION, THE

Artist: Fun Boy Three
Written by: Fun Boy Three
From the album: *Waiting*
Label: Chrysalis
Year: 1983
Late reggae entry caught between invasions.

FARMER JOHN

Artist: Don and Dewey
Written by: Don Harris, Dewey Terry
From the album: *Jungle Hop*
Label: Specialty
Produced by: Harold Battiste
Year: 1959
Covered by the Premiers (Warner Brothers, '64).

FARMER'S DAUGHTER

Artist: The Beach Boys
Written by: Brian Wilson
From the album: *Surfin' USA*
Label: Capitol
Produced by: Nik Venet
Year: 1963
Covered by Fleetwood Mac (Reprise, '81).

FARTHER UP THE ROAD

Artist: Bobby Bland
Written by: J. Veasey, Don Robey
Label: Duke
Produced by: Joe Scott
Year: 1957
This #1 R&B crossover was the first of his sixty-three R&B chart singles.

FASHION

Artist: David Bowie
Written by: David Bowie
From the album: *Scary Monsters*
Label: RCA
Produced by: Tony Visconti, David Bowie
Year: 1980
Return to his favorite topic.

FAST AS YOU CAN

Artist: Fiona Apple
Written by: Fiona Apple
From the album: *When the Pawn…*
Produced by: Andrew Slater
Label: Columbia
Year: 1999
Confessions of a junior mess.

FAST CAR

Artist: Tracy Chapman
Written by: Tracy Chapman
From the album: *Tracy Chapman*
Label: Elektra
Produced by: David Kershenbaum
Year: 1988
The debut left-field folkie smash of the year. Classic car song of the post-car-song era; restless youth approaching a dead end.

FAST TIMES AT RIDGEMONT HIGH

Artist: Sammy Hagar
Written by: Sammy Hagar
From the album: *Fast Times at Ridgemont High Soundtrack*
Label: Full Moon
Year: 1982
From the influential post-Slacker, pre-Generation X movie based on a Cameron Crowe book and experience.

FAT MAN, THE

Artist: Fats Domino
Written by: Dave Bartholomew
From the album: *Rock and Rollin' with Fats Domino*
Label: Imperial
Produced by: Dave Bartholomew
Year: 1950
Influenced by Amos Milburn, the Fat Man arrives upon the scene in New Orleans, with his first of 38 Top 10 R&B hits.

FATHER

Artist: LL Cool J
Written by: James Todd Smith, Jean Claude Olivier, Samuel Barnes, George Michael, Geoffrey Overbig
From the album: *Phenomenon*
Label: Def Jam
Year: 1997
An excerpt from his autobiography, uses George Michael's "Father Figure."

FATHER AND SON

Artist: Cat Stevens
Written by: Cat Stevens
From the album: *Tea for the Tillerman*
Produced by: Paul Samwell-Smith
Label: A&M
Year: 1971
Moving folk/rock confessional.

FATHER FIGURE

Artist: George Michael
Written by: George Michael
From the album: *Faith*
Label: Columbia
Produced by: George Michael
Year: 1987
Second of four #1 hits from the album.

FATHER OF MINE

Artist: Everclear
Written by: Art Alexakis, Greg Eclund, Craig Montoya
From the album: *So Much for the Afterglow*
Label: Capitol
Produced by: Art Alexakis
Year: 1997
Talking back to his deadbeat dad.

FEAR IS A MAN'S BEST FRIEND

Artist: John Cale
Written by: John Cale
From the album: *Fear*
Label: Island
Produced by: John Cale
Year: 1974
Disturbing rocker from the cofounder of the Velvet Underground, at the peak of his disturbed form.

FEAR OF A BLACK PLANET

Artist: Public Enemy
Written by: Charles Ridenhour
From the album: *Fear of a Black Planet*
Label: Def Jam
Produced by: Stuart Robertz, Cerwin Depper, Gary G. Wiz, the JBL
Year: 1990
Nailing the urban zeitgeist.

FEED THE TREE

Artist: Belly
Written by: Tanya Donelly
From the album: *Star*
Label: Sire
Produced by: Tracy Chisholm
Year: 1993
Post-Bangles folk/rock allegory of empowerment by a veteran new scenestress.

FEEL LIKE MAKIN' LOVE

Artist: Roberta Flack and Donny Hathaway
Written by: Roberta Flack, Peabo Bryson
From the album: *Feel Like Makin' Love*
Label: Atlantic
Produced by: Roberta Flack

Year: 1974
1 R&B/#1 crossover is the top R&B hit of the year.

FEEL LIKE MAKING LOVE

Artist: Bad Company
Written by: Paul Rodgers, Mick Ralphs
From the album: *Straight Shooter*
Label: Swan Song
Produced by: Bad Company
Year: 1975
Mellow offspring of Free and Mott the Hoople was their second and last Top 10 hit.

FEEL SO GOOD

Artist: Mase
Written by: Deric Angelettie, Robert Bell, Ronald Bell, George Brown, Lawrence Dermer, Joe Galdo, Robert Mickens, Charles Smith, Dennis Thomas, Rafael Vigil, Robert Westfield
From the album: *Harlem World*
Label: Bad Boy
Produced by: Sean Combs
Year: 1997
Strutting his stuff, with help from Kool & the Gang.

FEEL THE PAIN

Artist: Dinosaur Jr.
Written by: Joseph Mascis
From the album: *Without a Sound*
Label: Sire
Produced by: J. Mascis
Year: 1994
Big on the college circuit.

FEELIN' ALRIGHT

Artist: Traffic
Written by: David Mason
From the album: *Traffic*
Label: United Artists
Produced by: Jimmy Miller
Year: 1968
Late psychedelic/early progressive rocker. Covered by Joe Cocker (A&M, '69).

FEELIN' GOOD

Artist: Little Junior's Blue Flames
Written by: Little Junior Parker
Produced by: Sam Phillips
Label: Sun
Year: 1953
First hit for the Howlin' Wolf harmonica player.

FEELS GOOD

Artist: Tony! Toni! Tone!
Written by: Dwayne Wiggins, Ray Wiggins, Timothy Christian, Caron Wheeler
From the album: *The Revival*
Label: Wing
Produced by: Tony! Toni! Tone!
Year: 1990

Second straight #1 R&B from the album subverts a familiar James Brown drum line.

FEELS LIKE THE FIRST TIME

Artist: Foreigner
Written by: Mick Jones
From the album: *Foreigner*
Label: Atlantic
Produced by: John Sinclair, Gary Lyons
Year: 1977
Their first radio ready metal hit.

FEMME FATALE

Artist: The Velvet Underground
Written by: Lou Reed
From the album: *The Velvet Underground and Nico*
Label: Verve
Produced by: Andy Warhol
Year: 1967
At the epicenter of glam: a moody, suppressed, eyewitness account of the rise and fall of Andy Warhol's Factory.

FERRY CROSS THE MERSEY

Artist: Gerry and the Pacemakers
Written by: Gerry Marsden
From the album: *Ferry Cross the Mersey*
Label: Laurie
Produced by: George Martin
Year: 1964
Elegiac snapshot of the land from whence the first British Invasion was plotted and launched.

FEVER

Artist: Little Willie John
Written by: Otis Blackwell (John Davenport), Joe Seneca (Eddie Cooley)
From the album: *Fever*
Label: King
Produced by: Henry Glover
Year: 1956
Little Willie John's much-revered heartbreaking version sets the standard. Peggy Lee's cool cover was a bigger hit (Capitol, '58). Covered by Elvis Presley (RCA, '60), the McCoys (Bang, '65).

FFUN

Artist: Con Funk Shun
Written by: Michael Cooper
From the album: *Secrets*
Label: Mercury
Produced by: Con Funk Shun
Year: 1977
A funk tribute to the Beach Boys.

50 FT. QUEENIE

Artist: P. J. Harvey
Written by: Polly Jean Harvey
From the album: *Rid of Me*
Label: Island
Produced by: P. J. Harvey
Year: 1993

Ingeniously amateurish hard-rocking demo indicates why Harvey became a leading figure in the anti-thrush movement of the early '90s.

54 46 (WAS MY NUMBER)

Artist: Toots and the Maytals
Written by: Frederick Toots Hibbert
From the album: *Toots Live*
Label: Mango
Produced by: Leslie Kong
Year: 1972
Quintessential reggae lament about a quintessential reggae situation: being busted for marijuana.

59TH STREET BRIDGE SONG (FEELIN' GROOVY), THE

Artist: Simon and Garfunkel
Written by: Paul Simon
From the album: *Parsley, Sage, Rosemary and Thyme*
Label: Columbia
Produced by: Bob Johnston
Year: 1966
Atypical Simon at momentary peace, parked on a perch between Queens and Manhattan. Cover by Harper's Bizarre (Warner Brothers, '67) hit the Top 20. Years later, Simon would name his first son Harper. Probably a coincidence.

FIFTY WAYS TO LEAVE YOUR LOVER

Artist: Paul Simon
Written by: Paul Simon
From the album: *Still Crazy After All These Years*
Label: Columbia
Produced by: Phil Ramone, Paul Simon
Year: 1975
Simon's biggest single and only solo #1 typifies his uneasy relationship with relationships.

FIGHT THE POWER (PART I)

Artist: The Isley Brothers
Written by: Ronald Isley, Rudolph Isley, O'Kelly Isley, Ernest Isley, Marvin Isley
From the album: *The Heat Is On*
Label: T-Neck
Produced by: Isley Brothers, Chris Jasper
Year: 1975
#1 R&B/Top 10 crossover from the top-selling album is a scathing critique of the powers that be.

FIGHT THE POWER

Artist: Public Enemy
Written by: Carlton Ridenhour, Hank Shocklee, Keith Shocklee, Eric Sadler
From the album: *Fear of a Black Planet*
Label: Def Jam
Produced by: Stuart Roberz, Cerwin Depper, Gary G. Wiz, the JBL
Year: 1989

After fourteen years with nothing much changed, Public Enemy ramps up the Isleys' charges to include Elvis Presley and John Wayne. Featured in Spike Lee's '89 film *Do the Right Thing*.

FIN

Artist: Pavement
Written by: Stephen Malkmus
From the album: *Brighten the Corners*
Label: Matador
Produced by: Pavement
Year: 1997
Collegiate angst.

FINAL COUNTDOWN, THE

Artist: Europe
Written by: Joey Tempest
From the album: *The Final Countdown*
Label: Epic
Produced by: Kevin Elson
Year: 1986
#1 UK/Top 10 US. Hair guitar.

FINAL SOLUTION

Artist: Pere Ubu
Written by: Craig Bell, Tom Herman, Scott Krause, Tony Maimone, Allen Ravenstine, Dave Thomas
Label: Hearthan
Produced by: Pere Ubu, Ken Hamman, Paul Hamman
Year: 1976
Opening up the Akron scene, with nuclear dissonance.

FINALLY

Artist: Ce Ce Peniston
Written by: Ce Ce Peniston, Felipe Delgado, E. Linnear
From the album: *Finally*
Label: A&M
Produced by: Felipe Delgado
Year: 1991
Hip-hop ballad from the former Miss Black Arizona.

FINALLY GOT MYSELF TOGETHER (I'M A CHANGED MAN)

Artist: The Impressions
Written by: Edward Townshend
From the album: *Finally Got Myself Together*
Label: Curtom
Produced by: Ed Townshend
Year: 1974
Their fourth and last #1 R&B/Top 20 crossover, first sans Curtis Mayfield.

FIND THE COST OF FREEDOM

Crosby, Stills & Nash

Written by: Stephen Stills
From the album: *Four-Way Street*
Label: Atlantic
Year: 1971
Harmonious protest, portending the rise of the singer/songwriter era.

FINE FINE BOY, A

Artist: Darlene Love
Written by: Jeff Barry, Ellie Greenwich, Phil Spector
Label: Philles
Produced by: Phil Spector
Year: 1963
The ubiquitous sessions singer (Crystals, Bob B. Soxx, and the Bluejeans) steps out on her own, with negligible results.

FINE FINE DAY, A

Artist: Tony Carey
Written by: Tony Carey
From the album: *Some Tough City*
Label: MCA
Produced by: Peter Hauke
Year: 1984
One of the year's most poignant story-songs.

FINER THINGS, THE

Artist: Steve Winwood
Written by: Steve Winwood, Will Jennings
From the album: *Back in the High Life*
Label: Island
Produced by: Steve Winwood, Russ Titelman
Year: 1986
Winwood scores with the ladies who lunch.

FINEST WORKSONG

Artist: R.E.M.
Written by: Michael Stipe, Peter Buck, Bill Berry, Mike Mills
From the album: *Document*
Label: IRS
Produced by: Scott Litt, R.E.M.
Year: 1986
New folk directive.

FINGER POPPIN' TIME

Artist: The Midnighters
Written by: Hank Ballard
From the album: *Hank Ballard's Biggest Hits*
Label: King
Year: 1960
Capitalizing on the fallout from Chubby Checker's letter-perfect cover of his tune, "The Twist," Ballard gets his first #1 R&B/Top 10 crossover.

FINGERTIPS

Artist: Steve Wonder
Written by: Henry Cosby, Clarence Paul
From the album: *The Jazz Soul of Little Stevie*
Label: Tamla
Produced by: Berry Gordy Jr.

Year: 1962
Adopting Ray Charles as his honorary uncle, (Little) Stevie would prove to be more than kin to that blind genius of the keyboard. His fourth release on Tamla, a live recording, would be his first #1 R&B/#1 crossover, complete with an encore that surprised the bass player, who didn't know what key to play it in.

FINISH WHAT YA STARTED

Artist: Van Halen
Written by: Eddie Van Halen, Alex Van Halen, Michael Anthony, Sammy Hagar
From the album: *OU812*
Label: Warner Brothers
Produced by: Van Halen, Don Landee
Year: 1988
No easy task; only the Stones and Aerosmith even tried it.

FIRE!

Artist: Arthur Brown
Written by: Arthur Brown, Vincent Crane, Peter Ker, Finesilver
From the album: *The Crazy World of Arthur Brown*
Label: Atlantic
Produced by: Kit Lambert
Year: 1968
Fire-breathing progressive novelty.

FIRE

Artist: Robert Gordon
Written by: Bruce Springsteen
From the album: *Fresh Fish Special*
Label: Private Stock
Produced by: Robert Gordon, Richard Gottehrer
Year: 1978
Catch of the day, rockabilly à la Boss. Covered by the Pointer Sisters (Planet, '79), Bruce Springsteen (Columbia, '86).

FIRE

Artist: Jimi Hendrix
Written by: Jimi Hendrix
From the album: *Are You Experienced?*
Label: Reprise
Produced by: Chas Chandler
Year: 1967
A favorite concert opener, evoking the fire-breathing guitar pyrotechnics of his Monterey-closing "Wild Thing."

FIRE

Artist: Ohio Players
Written by: Leroy Bonner, Ralph Middlebrooks, Marshall Jones, William Beck, Marvin Pierce, Jim Williams, Clarence Satchell
From the album: *Fire*
Label: Mercury
Produced by: Ohio Players
Year: 1974
Four alarm funk smash is their first #1 R&B/#1 crossover.

FIRE AND DESIRE

Artist: Rick James and Teena Marie
Written by: Rick James
From the album: *Street Songs*
Label: Gordy
Year: 1981
Essential funk duet.

FIRE AND RAIN

Artist: James Taylor
Written by: James Taylor
From the album: *Sweet Baby James*
Label: Warner Brothers
Produced by: Peter Asher
Year: 1970
His first hit single charts the depths of his drug problem and the demise of his first band.

FIRE DOWN BELOW

Artist: Bob Seger
Written by: Bob Seger
From the album: *Night Moves*
Label: Capitol
Produced by: Bob Seger, Jack Richardson
Year: 1976
Basic sweaty frat-house metaphor.

FIRE ENGINE

Artist: Thirteenth Floor Elevators
Written by: Roky Erickson
Label: International Artists
Produced by: Gorbyn Productions
Year: 1966
Texas psychedelia. Covered by Television (ROIR, '82).

FIRE LAKE

Artist: Bob Seger
Written by: Bob Seger
From the album: *Against the Wind*
Label: Capitol
Produced by: Bob Seger
Year: 1980
Midwestern equivalent of Springsteen's Greasy Lake. Suggested segue: "Burn on, Big River" by Randy Newman.

FIRESTARTER

Artist: Prodigy
Written by: Liam Howlett, Keith Flint, Trevor Horn, Anne Dudley, Jonathan Jeczalik, Paul Morley, Greg Langan, Kim Deal
From the album: *Fat of the Land*
Label: Warner Brothers
Year: 1997
A raver on the new drug-soaked dance floor.

FIRST CUT IS THE DEEPEST

Artist: Cat Stevens
Written by: Cat Stevens

From the album: *Matthew and Son*
Label: Deram
Year: 1967
Coming of age anthem was a hit in England for P. P. Arnold. Covered by Rod Stewart (Warner Brothers, '77), Sheryl Crow (A&M, '03).

FIRST GIRL I LOVED, THE

Artist: The Incredible String Band
Written by: Robin Williamson
From the album: *Spirits (Layers of the Onion)*
Label: Elektra
Produced by: Joe Boyd
Year: 1967
Existential folk lament, as haunting as it is twisted. Female version by Judy Collins (Elektra, '68).

FIRST I LOOK AT THE PURSE

Artist: The Contours
Written by: Smokey Robinson
Label: Tamla
Produced by: Berry Gordy Jr.
Year: 1965
Streetwise advice from Bob Dylan's favorite poet, Smokey Robinson. Covered by the J. Geils Band (Atlantic, '71).

FIRST NIGHT

Artist: Monica
Written by: Jermaine Dupri, Tamara Savage, Mary McLeo, Pam Sawyer
From the album: *The Boy Is Mine*
Label: Arista
Produced by: Jermaine Dupri
Year: 1998
The new teen prudery, no sex until the second date.

FIRST TIME EVER I SAW YOUR FACE

Artist: Peggy Seeger
Written by: Ewan MacColl
Label: Folkways
Year: 1962
Folk love song written for Peggy by her husband and covered by the Kingston Trio (Capitol, '62), Peter, Paul and Mary (Warner Brothers, '65). It became a hit in '72 after being sung by Roberta Flack in the Clint Eastwood movie *Play Misty for Me*. In the original, the line is I *thought* our joy would last until the end of time. In Roberta's version she sings "I *knew* our joy …" thus making it a pop song.

FIRST TIME, THE

Artist: Surface
Written by: Bernard Jackson, Brian Simpson
From the album: *3 Deep*
Label: Columbia
Produced by: Surface
Year: 1990
Their third #1 R&B/#1 crossover.

FISHERMAN'S BLUES

Artist: The Waterboys
Written by: Mike Scott, Steve Wickham
From the album: *Fisherman's Blues*
Label: Chrysalis
Produced by: John Dunford, Mike Scott
Year: 1988
Dylan Thomas meets Bob Dylan at an Irish pub on MacDougal Street, writes an anthem.

FISHNET

Artist: Morris Day
Written by: James Harris III, Terry Lewis
From the album: *Daydreaming*
Label: Warner Brothers
Produced by: Morris Day
Year: 1988 #1
R&B hit reunites the members of Prince's backing band, the Time. Influential Minneapolis songwriter/producers and the Time members, Harris and Lewis, named their publishing company Flyte Tyme.

FIVE D (FIFTH DIMENSION)

Artist: The Byrds
Written by: Jim McGuinn (Roger McGuinn)
From the album: *5D (Fifth Dimension)*
Label: Columbia
Produced by: Allen Stanton
Year: 1966
Where you wind up after being eight miles high.

FIVE FEET HIGH AND RISING

Artist: Johnny Cash
Written by: Johnny Cash
From the album: *Songs of Our Soul*
Label: Columbia
Produced by: Sam Phillips
Year: 1959
B-side of the protest song, "I Got Stripes."

5:15

Artist: The Who
Written by: Pete Townshend
From the album: *Quadrophenia*
Label: MCA
Produced by: John Entwistle
Year: 1973
From Townshend's second rock opera.

500 MILES AWAY FROM HOME

Artist: Bobby Bare
Written by: Bobby Bare, Charlie Williams, Hedy West
From the album: *500 Miles Away from Home*
Label: RCA
Produced by: Chet Atkins
Year: 1963
Countrypolitan hit with folk/roots.

FIVE LONG YEARS

Artist: Eddie Boyd
Written by: Eddie Boyd
Label: J.O.B.
Year: 1952
#1 R&B hit was a Yardbirds concert staple. Covered by Eric Clapton (Warner Brothers, '94).

FIVE O'CLOCK WORLD

Artist: The Vogues
Written by: Allen Reynolds
From the album: *Five O'Clock World*
Label: Co & Ce
Produced by: Dick Glasser
Year: 1965
Folk music graduates to easy listening, gets an office job.

5-10-15 HOURS

Artist: Ruth Brown and Her Rhythm Makers
Written by: Rudolph Toombs
Label: Atlantic
Year: 1952
Her answer to (and opinion of) "Sixty Minute Man" was her second #1 R&B hit.

FIVE TO ONE

Artist: The Doors
Written by: Jim Morrison, Robbie Krieger, John Densmore, Ray Manzarek
From the album: *Waiting for the Sun*
Label: Elektra
Produced by: Paul Rothchild
Year: 1968
From whence came the title of their biography *No One Here Gets out Alive*.

FIVE YEARS

Artist: David Bowie
Written by: David Bowie
From the album: *The Rise and Fall of Ziggy Stardust and the Spiders from Mars*
Produced by: David Bowie, Ken Scott
Label: RCA
Year: 1972
Setting the scene for his landmark album with a mock autobiographical tale.

FIXING A HOLE

Artist: The Beatles
Written by: John Lennon, Paul McCartney
From the album: *Sgt. Pepper's Lonely Hearts Club Band*
Label: Capitol
Produced by: George Martin
Year: 1967
Fixing their relationship.

FLAME STILL BURNS

Artist: Youth of Today
Written by: Ray Cappo
From the album: *We're Not in This Alone*
Label: Revelation
Year: 1988
Positive core rap by a future devotee of Hari Krishna.

FLAME, THE

Artist: Cheap Trick
Written by: Robert Mitchell, Dick Graham
From the album: *Lap of Luxury*
Label: Epic
Produced by: Ritchie Zito
Year: 1988
Aided by a slick production, Rick Neilsen and crew finally scale the commercial heights, and succeed in sounding just like any other corporate arena band.

FLASHDANCE ... WHAT A FEELING

Artist: Irene Cara
Written by: Keith Forsey, Irene Cara, Giorgio Moroder
From the album: *Flashdance*
Label: Casablanca
Produced by: Giorgio Moroder
Year: 1983
Pulsating title tune from the attempted *Saturday Night Fever* of the '80s.

FLASHLIGHT

Artist: Parliament
Written by: George Clinton, William "Bootsie" Collins, Bernie Worrell
From the album: *Funkentelechy vs. the Placebo Syndrome*
Label: Casablanca
Produced by: George Clinton
Year: 1977
First #1 R&B/Top 20 R&R crossover for the undisco kids.

FLIP, FLOP AND FLY

Artist: Joe Turner
Written by: Jesse Stone (Charles Calhoun), Joe Turner (Lou Willie Turner)
From the album: *Joe Turner*
Label: Atlantic
Produced by: Ahmet Ertegun, Jerry Wexler
Year: 1955
Getting more mileage from his previous hit, "Shake, Rattle and Roll," Turner turns to his favorite collaborator, Jesse Stone.

FLIRTIN' WITH DISASTER

Artist: Molly Hatchet
Written by: David Lawrence Hludeck, Danny Joe Brown, Banner Harvey Thomas
From the album: *Flirtin' with Disaster*
Label: Epic
Produced by: Tom Werman
Year: 1980
Taking the hatchet to the memory of Lynyrd Skynyrd.

FLOAT ON

Artist: The Floaters
Written by: Arnold Ingram, James Mitchell Jr., Marvin Willis
From the album: *Floaters*
Label: ABC
Produced by: Woody Wilson
Year: 1977
Deep in the tech funk pocket, a #1 R&B/Top 5 crossover.

FLORENCE

Artist: The Paragons
Written by: Julius McMichaels, Paul Winley
From the album: *The Paragons Meet the Jesters*
Label: Winley
Year: 1957
By exploiting the hoodlum image engendered by "Rock around the Clock" for maximum sales, the Paragons would predate the Rolling Stones by seven years, Snoop Doggy Dogg by more than thirty. Florence was their only musical legacy, however. And she was no "Gloria," not even "Blanche."

FLOWER

Liz Phair
Written by: Liz Phair
From the album: *Exile in Guyville*
Label: Matador
Produced by: Liz Phair, Brad Wood
Year: 1993
Ushering in the age of female rage, a low-fi Oberlin girl in Stonesian drag. Suggested segues: "Doll Parts" by Hole and "50 Ft. Queenie" by P. J. Harvey.

FLY

Artist: Sugar Ray
Written by: William Maragh, Sugar Ray
From the album: *Floored*
Label: Atlantic
Produced by: David Kahne
Year: 1997
The L.A. rockers start their career with a #1.

FLY AWAY

Artist: Lenny Kravitz
Written by: Lenny Kravitz
From the album: *5*
Label: Virgin
Produced by: Lenny Kravitz
Year: 1998
Hunk rock.

FLY GIRL, A

Artist: Boogie Boys
Written by: Gary Muddbone Cooper, Joe Malloy, William Stroman, Andy Sheriff, David Spradley
Label: Capitol
Year: 1982

Saturday night on the stoop in the early '80s, the black alternative to MTV.

FLY LIKE AN EAGLE

Artist: The Steve Miller Band
Written by: Steve Miller
From the album: *Fly Like an Eagle*
Label: Capitol
Produced by: Steve Miller
Year: 1976
San Francisco blues rock, ten years later, a classic of FM radio, the new AM.

FLY, ROBIN, FLY

Artist: Silver Convention
Written by: Sylvester Levay, Stephen Prager
From the album: *Save Me*
Label: Midland International
Produced by: Michael Kunze
Year: 1975
#1 R&B/#1 crossover from the discos of Germany.

FLYIN' THE FLANNEL

Artist: fIREHOSE
Written by: Mike Watt
From the album: *Flyin' the Flannel*
Label: Columbia
Produced by: Paul Q. Kolderie, fIREHOSE
Year: 1991
The legendary Minuteman survivor paves the way for grunge.

FLYING HIGH AGAIN

Artist: Ozzy Osbourne
Written by: Ozzy Osbourne, Randy Rhoads, Bob Daisley, Lee Gary Kerslake
From the album: *Diary of a Madman*
Label: Jet
Produced by: Max Norman
Year: 1981
This would become guitarist Rhoads's epitaph, when he died in a plane crash a few months after the release of the album.

FLYING SAUCER, THE

Artist: Dickie Goodman
Written by: Mae Boren Axton
Label: Luniverse
Year: 1956
Novelty collage of current popular songs, taking off where even Orson Welles dared not follow—presaging the technique of sampling, but not its intent.

FOGGY NOTION

Artist: The Velvet Underground
Written by: Lou Reed, Maureen Tucker, Sterling Morrison, Doug Yule, Hy Weiss
Label: Verve
Year: 1969
Covered by Jonathan Richman and the Modern Lovers (Rounder, '94).

FOLLOW

Artist: Richie Havens
Written by: Jerry Merrick
From the album: *Mixed Bag*
Label: Verve/Folkways
Produced by: Jerry Schoenbaum
Year: 1967
Early in-concert show-stopper; a ten-minute stream of new consciousness, raised to a higher level by Richie's booming voice. Featured in the 1996 movie *The Pallbearer*.

FOLLOW YOU DOWN

Artist: Gin Blossoms
Written by: Scott Johnson, Bill Leen, Robin Wilson, Jesse Valenzuela, Phillip Rhodes
From the album: *Congratulations, I'm Sorry*
Label: A&M
Produced by: Gin Blossoms, John Hampton
Year: 1996
Folk/rock lament from the film *Empire Records*.

FOLLOW YOU FOLLOW ME

Artist: Genesis
Written by: Phil Collins, Tony Banks, Mike Rutherford
From the album: *And Then There Were Three*
Label: Atlantic
Produced by: D. Hentschel, Genesis
Year: 1978
Minus their founding artists, Gabriel and Hackett, the formerly progressive Genesis begins to proceed without impediment toward the Top 10.

FOLSOM PRISON BLUES

Artist: Johnny Cash
Written by: Johnny Cash
From the album: *Johnny Cash with His Red and Blue Guitar*
Label: Sun
Produced by: Sam Phillips
Year: 1956
The rockabilly rebellion moves forward, with a tale told by an outlaw, in a voice that'd been to hell and back.

FOOL, FOOL, FOOL

Artist: The Clovers
Written by: Ahmet Ertegun
Label: Atlantic
Produced by: Ahmet Ertegun, Herb Abramson
Year: 1951
Their second straight #1 R&B hit. They spent a total of forty-three weeks on the R&B charts in '51.

FOOL (IF YOU THINK ITS OVER)

Artist: Chris Rea
Written by: Chris Rea
From the album: *Whatever Happened to Benny Santini?*

Label: Magnet
Produced by: Gus Dudgeon
Year: 1977
Working-class British rock.

FOOL FOR THE CITY

Artist: Foghat
Written by: Dave Peverett
From the album: *Fool for the City*
Label: Bearsville
Produced by: Nick Jameson
Year: 1975
Exemplary blues rocker.

FOOL FOR YOU, A

Artist: Ray Charles
Written by: Ray Charles
From the album: *Ray Charles*
Label: Atlantic
Produced by: Ahmet Ertegun, Jerry Wexler
Year: 1955
Widely regarded as one of his finest performances, especially at the '58 Newport Jazz Festival. Turned into a ballet by the New York City Ballet Company in '89.

FOOL IN LOVE, A

Artist: Ike and Tina Turner
Written by: Ike Turner
Label: Sue
Produced by: Ike Turner
Year: 1962
Their first hit; a Top 10 R&B/Top 30 crossover.

FOOL IN THE RAIN

Artist: Led Zeppelin
Written by: Jimmy Page, Robert Plant, John Paul Jones
From the album: *In through the Out Door*
Label: Swan Song
Produced by: Jimmy Page
Year: 1979
Answering "Silhouettes on the Shade." You knew then they were running out of gas.

FOOL NUMBER 1

Artist: Brenda Lee
Written by: Kathryn R. Fulton
From the album: *Brenda, That's All*
Label: Decca
Produced by: Owen Bradley
Year: 1961

FOOL ON THE HILL, THE

Artist: The Beatles
Written by: John Lennon, Paul McCartney
From the album: *Magical Mystery Tour*
Label: Capitol
Produced by: George Martin
Year: 1967

Patent proselytizing. Covered by Sergio Mendes and Brazil 66 (A&M, '68).

FOOL TO CRY

Artist: The Rolling Stones
Written by: Mick Jagger, Keith Richards
From the album: *Black and Blue*
Label: Rolling Stones
Produced by: Glimmer Twins
Year: 1976
One of Jagger's best vocals.

FOOL, THE

Artist: Sanford Clark
Written by: Lee Hazelwood
Label: Dot
Produced by: Lee Hazelwood
Year: 1956
Covered by the Gallahads (Jubilee, '56). Producer/author Hazelwood and session guitarist Al Casey would move on to Duane Eddy.

FOOL'S GOLD

Artist: Graham Parker
Written by: Graham Parker
From the album: *Heat Treatment*
Label: Mercury
Produced by: Robert "Mutt" Lange
Year: 1976
Exploding from the pubs, hoisting a pint of stout.

FOOL'S GOLD

Artist: The Stone Roses
Written by: John Squire, Ian Brown
From the album: *The Stone Roses*
Label: Silvertone/Jive
Produced by: John Leckie
Year: 1989
Top 10 UK smash establishes England's droning neopsychedelic rave scene. See: My Bloody Valentine.

FOOLED AROUND AND FELL IN LOVE

Artist: Elvin Bishop
Written by: Elvin Bishop
From the album: *Struttin' My Stuff*
Label: Capricorn
Produced by: Bill Szymczyk, Allen Blazek
Year: 1976
Mike Bloomfield's one-time guitar mate in the Butterfield Blues Band creates a middling, noodling Southern rock hit.

FOOLIN'

Artist: Def Leppard
Written by: Steve Clark, Joe Elliott, Robert John "Mutt" Lange
From the album: *Pyromania*
Label: Mercury

Produced by: Robert "Mutt" Lange
Year: 1983
Processed metal studio-craft.

FOOLISH BEAT

Artist: Debbie Gibson
Written by: Debbie Gibson
From the album: *Out of the Blue*
Label: Atlantic
Produced by: Fred Zarr, Debbie Gibson
Year: 1987
Pubescent prodigy achieves pop perfection with her first #1.

FOOLISH LITTLE GIRL

Artist: The Shirelles
Written by: Howard Greenfield, Helen Miller
From the album: *Baby, It's You*
Label: Scepter
Produced by: Luther Dixon
Year: 1963
Sixth and last Top 10 hit for one of the all-time greatest girl groups.

FOOLS FALL IN LOVE

Artist: The Drifters
Written by: Jerry Leiber, Mike Stoller
Label: Atlantic
Year: 1957.
Top 10 R&B hit achieved latter-day stature in the Leiber & Stoller Broadway production of *Smokey Joe's Café*, '94. Covered by Elvis Presley (RCA, '71).

FOOT TAPPER

Artist: The Shadows
Written by: Hank Marvin, Bruce Welch
From the album: *The Shadows Greatest Hits*
Label: Columbia
Year: 1963
Third #1 UK from the influential British guitar band. In the film *Summer Holiday*.

FOOTLOOSE

Artist: Kenny Loggins
Written by: Dean Pitchford, Kenny Loggins
From the album: *Footloose Soundtrack*
Label: Columbia
Produced by: Kenny Loggins, Lee DeCarlo
Year: 1984
Wherein Kevin Bacon makes his dancing debut. Reprised by Bacon and Eric McCormack in a kicking dance number on *Will & Grace*.

FOR A DANCER

Artist: Jackson Browne
Written by: Jackson Browne
From the album: *Late for the Sky*
Label: Asylum
Produced by: Jackson Browne, Al Schmidt

Year: 1974
Contemplating his first wife's suicide.

FOR ALL WE KNOW

Artist: The Carpenters
Written by: Fred Carlin, Robb Royer, James Griffin
From the album: *The Carpenters*
Label: A&M
Produced by: Jack Daugherty
Year: 1971
Theme from the classic Renee Taylor/Joe Bologna movie *Lovers and Other Strangers* (which was nowhere near as hysterical as their other movie, *Made for Each Other*, which had a poignant theme by Trade Martin).

FOR EMILY (WHEREVER I MAY FIND HER)

Artist: Simon and Garfunkel
Written by: Paul Simon
From the album: *Parsley, Sage, Rosemary and Thyme*
Label: Columbia
Produced by: Bob Johnston
Year: 1966
Probably in England, where she may have seen him as a busker, before the advent of folk/rock. Released as a single in 1972.

FOR EVERYMAN

Artist: Jackson Browne
Written by: Jackson Browne
From the album: *For Everyman*
Label: Asylum
Produced by: Jackson Browne
Year: 1973
Searching folk epic is one of his finest.

(FOR GOD'S SAKE) GIVE MORE POWER TO THE PEOPLE

Artist: The Chi-Lites
Written by: Eugene Record
From the album: *(For God's Sake) Give More Power to the People*
Label: Brunswick
Produced by: Eugene Record
Year: 1971
Part of a significant early '70s black social protest movement set in motion by "The Revolution Will Not Be Televised" by the Last Poets.

FOR LOVIN' ME

Artist: Peter, Paul and Mary
Written by: Gordon Lightfoot
From the album: *A Song Will Rise*
Label: Warner Brothers
Produced by: Albert Grossman, Milt Okun
Year: 1964
Folk reaction to the Beatles philosophy, epitomized in this rambling saga of self-aggrandizing self-destruction.

FOR NO ONE

Artist: The Beatles
Written by: John Lennon, Paul McCartney
From the album: *Revolver*
Label: Capitol
Produced by: George Martin
Year: 1966
Melancholy companion of "Eleanor Rigby." Alan Civil on French horn.

FOR ONCE IN MY LIFE

Artist: Stevie Wonder
Written by: Ronald Miller, Orlando Murden
From the album: *For Once in My Life*
Label: Columbia
Produced by: Henry Cosby
Year: 1968
Stevie in the pop arena, peaks at #2, besting the '67 Tony Bennett original by 89 points, and Tony didn't cross over to R&B, either.

FOR THE GOOD TIMES

Artist: Kris Kristofferson
Written by: Kris Kristofferson
From the album: *Kris Kristofferson*
Label: Monument
Produced by: Fred Foster
Year: 1969
Best new country singer/songwriter since Mickey Newbury. A #1 country/#11 crossover for Ray Price (Columbia, '70).

FOR THE LOVE OF MONEY

Artist: The O'Jays
Written by: Kenny Gamble, Leon Huff
From the album: *Ship Ahoy*
Label: Philadelphia International
Produced by: Kenny Gamble, Leon Huff
Year: 1973
A ripe rock and roll topic for a mix tape. Suggested segues: "Money" by Barrett Strong, "It's Money That Matters" by Randy Newman, "Money Honey" by Clyde McPhatter, "Your Cash Ain't Nothin' but Trash" by the Clovers, "Money" by Pink Floyd, "Money Changes Everything" by Cyndi Lauper.

FOR THE ROSES

Artist: Joni Mitchell
Written by: Joni Mitchell
From the album: *For the Roses*
Label: Asylum
Produced by: Joni Mitchell
Year: 1972
Moving out of folk/rock into art/rock, through jazz.

FOR THE SAKE OF THE SONG

Artist: Townes Van Zandt
Written by: Townes Van Zandt
From the album: *For the Sake of the Song*
Produced by: Jack Clement, Jim Malloy

Label: Poppy
Year: 1968
Alt folk poetry from Texas that influenced several generations of singer/songwriters, from Gram Parsons to Lucinda Williams.

FOR THOSE ABOUT TO ROCK (WE SALUTE YOU)

Artist: AC/DC
Written by: Angus Young, Malcolm Young and Brian Johnson
From the album: *For Those About to Rock (We Salute You)*
Produced by: Mutt Lange
Label: Atlantic
Year: 1981
Flick your Bic.

FOR WHAT IT'S WORTH

Artist: Buffalo Springfield
Written by: Stephen Stills
From the album: *Buffalo Springfield*
Label: Atco
Produced by: Charles Greene, Brian Stone
Year: 1967
This classic protest song about an L.A.-police-vs.-hippie confrontation over loitering on the streets in front of several rock night clubs became an anthem for all such spectacles of youth taking the law into their own hands (and getting their heads handed to them), of which the later '60s would be rife.

FOR WHOM THE BELL TOLLS

Artist: Metallica
Written by: James Hetfield, Lars Ulrich, Cliff Burton
From the album: *Ride the Lightning*
Label: Megaforce
Produced by: Mark Whittaker, Metallica
Year: 1984
Did any of these guys read Hemingway? Fans of original bassist Cliff Burton couldn't care less.

FOR YASGUR'S FARM

Artist: Mountain
Written by: George Gardes, Corky Laing, Felix Pappalardi, Gail Collins, Gary Ship
From the album: *Mountain Climbing*
Label: Windfall
Produced by: Felix Pappalardi
Year: 1970
Elegiac rock tribute to the legendary Woodstock host, Max Yasgur.

FOR YOU

Artist: Bruce Springsteen
Written by: Bruce Springsteen
From the album: *Greetings from Asbury Park*
Label: Columbia
Produced by: Jim Cretecos, Mike Appel
Year: 1973

One of Springsteen's first free associative epics, sets the agony of a suicidal affair into a Spectorian wall of jingle jangle, with Clarence Clemmons as Daddy Gee on the sax. Covered by Greg Kihn (Beserkley, '77), Manfred Mann (Warner Brothers, '81).

FOR YOU BLUE

Artist: The Beatles
Written by: George Harrison
From the album: *Let It Be*
Label: Apple
Produced by: Phil Spector
Year: 1970
As a reward for "Something," George gets the B-side of "The Long and Winding Road."

FOR YOU I WILL

Artist: Monica
Written by: Diane Warren
From the album: *Space Jam Soundtrack*
Label: Warner Sunset
Year: 1997
A big movie ballad from the pen of the reigning master of the form.

FOR YOUR EYES ONLY

Artist: Sheena Easton
Written by: Bill Conti, Mike Leeson
From the album: *For Your Eyes Only Soundtrack*
Label: Liberty
Year: 1981
Title song.

FOR YOUR LOVE

Artist: Ed Townsend
Written by: Ed Townsend
Label: Capitol
Year: 1958
Only hit for the deep-voiced crooner.

FOR YOUR LOVE

Artist: The Yardbirds
Written by: Graham Gouldman
From the album: *For Your Love*
Label: Epic
Produced by: Paul Samwell-Smith
Year: 1965
First trans-Atlantic Top 10 crossover for England's original heavy metal band. Guitar god Eric Clapton quit the band before this tune was released. Jeff Beck replaced him.

FOR YOUR PRECIOUS LOVE

Artist: Jerry Butler and the Impressions
Written by: Arthur Brooks, Richard Brooks, Jerry Butler
Label: Abner
Produced by: Calvin Carter
Year: 1958
Introducing the gospelized soul of the original Impressions, with Jerry Butler and Curtis Mayfield.

Covered by Garnett Mimms and the Enchanters (United Artists, '63), Jackie Wilson and Count Basie (Brunswick, '68).

FOREVER

Artist: Kiss
Written by: Stanley Eisen (Paul Stanley), Michael Bolton
From the album: *Hot in the Shade*
Label: Mercury
Produced by: Gene Simmons, Paul Stanley
Year: 1989
A hired gun helps Kiss get their biggest hit aside from "Beth."

FOREVER MAN

Artist: Eric Clapton
Written by: Jerry Williams
From the album: *Behind the Sun*
Label: Duck
Produced by: Ted Templeman, Lenny Waronker
Year: 1985
"God" in his descendancy.

FOREVER YOUNG (THE WILD ONES)

Artist: The Bodeans
Written by: Sammy Llanas, Kurt Neumann
From the album: *Outside Looking In*
Label: Slash
Produced by: Jerry Harrison, He and He
Year: 1987
Propulsive neo-folk rock with updated Everly Brothers harmonies.

FOREVER YOUNG

Artist: Bob Dylan
Written by: Bob Dylan
From the album: *Planet Waves*
Label: Asylum
Produced by: Bob Dylan
Year: 1973
One of his most accessible and moving messages.

FOREVER YOUNG

Artist: Rod Stewart
Written by: Rod Stewart, Jim Cregan, Kevin Savigar
From the album: *Out of Order*
Label: Warner Brothers
Produced by: Rod Stewart, Andy Taylor
Year: 1988
Rod's Highland hymn.

FOREVER YOUR GIRL

Artist: Paula Abdul
Written by: Oliver Lieber
From the album: *Forever Your Girl*
Produced by: Oliver Leiber
Label: Virgin
Year: 1988
Follow up to "Straight Up" is her second straight #1 and her biggest R&B hit.

FORGET HIM

Artist: Bobby Rydell
Written by: Tony Hatch
From the album: *Forget Him*
Label: Cameo
Produced by: Frank Day
Year: 1964
His sixth and last Top 10 hit. Later they'd name the high school in the movie *Grease* after him; because that movie is on television somewhere in the United States almost every day, he'll never be entirely forgotten.

FORGOT ABOUT DRE

Artist: Dr. Dre featuring Eminem
Written by: Marshall (Eminem) Mathers
From the album: *2001*
Produced by: Dr. Dre
Label: Aftermath
Year: 1999
Younger generation hip hop superstar pays his respects to his elder.

FORTRESS AROUND YOUR HEART

Artist: Sting
Written by: Gordon Sumner (Sting)
From the album: *The Dream of the Blue Turtles*
Label: A&M
Produced by: Pete Smith, Sting
Year: 1985
Hallmark of his recent dip into New Age romanticizing.

FORTUNATE SON

Artist: Creedence Clearwater Revival
Written by: John C. Fogerty
From the album: *Willy and the Poor Boys*
Label: Fantasy
Produced by: John C. Fogerty
Year: 1969
Freedom of choice as a class issue. B-side of "Down on the Corner."

FORTY DAYS

Ronnie Hawkins
Written by: Bernie Roth
From the album: *Ronnie Hawkins*
Label: Roulette
Year: 1959
With Levon Helms, later of the Band, on drums.

FORTY MILES OF BAD ROAD

Artist: Duane Eddy
Written by: Al Casey, Duane Eddy
From the album: *$1,000,000.00 Worth of Twang*
Label: Jamie
Produced by: Lee Hazelwood
Year: 1959
Of the twenty-eight instrumentals to hit the Top-40 in '59 this was the eleventh most popular. But

Duane Eddy as a player would easily have more staying power than the likes of Johnny & the Hurricanes, the Virtues, the Rock-a-Teens, and Santo & Johnny. Only Link Wray could rival him.

FORTY THOUSAND HEADMEN

Artist: Traffic
Written by: Steve Winwood, James Capaldi
From the album: *Traffic*
Label: United Artists
Produced by: Jimmy Miller
Year: 1968
Brooding, funky, acid flashback. Suggested segue: "Under African Skies" by Paul Simon.

FOUND OUT ABOUT YOU

Artist: The Gin Blossoms
Written by: Doug Hopkins
From the album: *New Miserable Experience*
Label: A&M
Produced by: John Hampton, the Gin Blossoms
Year: 1992
Bringing jangly rock back to the charts, and with it an onslaught of '90s alternative bands, which, like the Gin Blossoms, were all second-generation versions of the Grass Roots.

FOUNTAIN OF SORROW

Artist: Jackson Browne
Written by: Jackson Browne
From the album: *Late for the Sky*
Label: Asylum
Produced by: Jackson Browne, Al Schmidt
Year: 1974
Exquisitely painful self-examination.

FOUR DAYS GONE

Artist: Buffalo Springfield
Written by: Stephen Stills
From the album: *Last Time Around*
Label: Atco
Produced by: Charles Greene, Brian Stone
Year: 1968
Suggested segue: "Draft Dodger Rag" by Phil Ochs.

FOUR HUNDRED YEARS

Artist: Bob Marley & the Wailers
Written by: Winston MacKintosh (Peter Tosh)
Label: Island
Produced by: Lee Perry
Year: 1969
The Third-World beat sound of reggae arrives on these shores, with a deep sense of history and outrage.

FOUR IN THE MORNING

Artist: Jesse Colin Young
Written by: Jesse Colin Young
From the album: *Soul of a City Boy*
Label: Capitol
Produced by: Felix Pappalardi
Year: 1964

The East coast folkie answer to "Hey Joe." Covered by Jesse's folk/rock group, the Youngbloods (RCA, '67).

409

Artist: The Beach Boys
Written by: Brian Wilson, Gary Usher
From the album: *Surfin' Safari*
Label: Capitol
Produced by: Nik Venet
Year: 1962
The B-side of "Surfin' Safari" and the Beach Boys' first major label classic car song hit—classic car: the 409 Chevy. The stereo version was produced by Brian Wilson and included on *Little Deuce Coupe* (Capitol, '62).

4 + 20

Artist: Crosby, Stills & Nash
Written by: Stephen Stills
From the album: *Crosby, Stills & Nash*
Produced by: Crosby, Stills & Nash
Label: Atlantic
Year: 1970
Draft-age American youth at the crossroads.

FOUR SEASONS OF LONELINESS

Artist: Boyz 2 Men
Written by: James Harris, Terry Lewis
From the album: *Evolution*
Label: Motown
Produced by: James Harris, Terry Lewis
Year: 1997
Regaining their soft touch for their fifth #1 hit.

FOUR STRONG WINDS

Artist: Ian and Sylvia
Written by: Ian Tyson
From the album: *Four Strong Winds*
Label: Vanguard
Year: 1964
The loneliness and the romance of drifting has never been so eloquently stated. Covered by George Hamilton IV (RCA, '66), Neil Young (Reprise, '78).

FOURTH OF JULY

Artist: Dave Alvin
Written by: Dave Alvin
From the album: *Romeo's Escape*
Produced by: Steve Berlin
Label: Epic
Year: 1987
Landmark of the '80s American roots revival. Covered by X (Elektra, '87).

4TH OF JULY, ASBURY PARK (SANDY)

Artist: Bruce Springsteen
Written by: Bruce Springsteen
From the album: *The Wild, the Innocent and the E Street Shuffle*
Label: Columbia
Produced by: Jim Cretecos, Mike Appel
Year: 1973
Summer night on the Jersey Shore: the answer to the Drifters "Under the Boardwalk" and the Excellents' "Coney Island Baby."

FOX ON THE RUN

Artist: The Sweet
Written by: Brian Connolly, Andrew Scott, Stephen Priest, Michael Tucker
From the album: *Desolation Boulevard*
Label: Capitol
Produced by: Mike Chapman, Nicky Chinn
Year: 1975
English light metal just before the new wave of English heavy metal.

FOXY LADY

Artist: Jimi Hendrix
Written by: Jimi Hendrix
From the album: *Are You Experienced?*
Label: Reprise
Produced by: Chas Chandler
Year: 1967
A salacious come-on for the sexual revolution, unaccountably passed over by the R&B charts.

FRAGILE

Artist: Wire
Written by: Colin Newman, Graham Lewis
From the album: *Pink Flag*
Label: Harvest
Produced by: Mike Thorne
Year: 1977
Experimental minimalists react to arena rock. Sonic Youth was listening.

FRAMED

Artist: The Robins
Written by: Jerry Leiber, Mike Stoller
Label: Spark
Produced by: Jerry Leiber, Mike Stoller
Year: 1954
Funky L.A. R&B track and situation, paving the way for the Coasters.

FRANK MILLS

Artist: Shelly Plympton
Written by: James Rado, Gerome Ragni, Galt MacDermot
From the album: *Hair! A Tribal Rock Musical*
Label: RCA
Produced by: Andy Wiswell
Year: 1967
Solo showstopper from the landmark rock musical.

FRANKENSTEIN

Artist: Edgar Winter Group
Written by: Edgar Winter
From the album: *They Only Come out at Night*
Label: Epic
Produced by: Rick Derringer
Year: 1972
Monster instrumental.

FRANKLIN'S TOWER

Artist: Grateful Dead
Written by: Jerry Garcia, Robert Hunter, Billy Kreutzmann
From the album: *Blues for Allah*
Label: Grateful Dead
Produced by: The Grateful Dead
Year: 1975
Recorded at the Sphinx in Egypt.

FRANTIC MOMENT

Artist: Eddie Hazel
Written by: George Clinton, Bootsy Collins, Bernie Worrell
From the album: *Games, Dames & Guitar Games*
Label: Warner Brothers
Year: 1977
Giving the Funkadelic guitarist some—but it wasn't enough.

FREAK ME

Artist: Silk
Written by: Keith Sweat, Roy Murray
From the album: *Lose Control*
Label: Keia
Produced by: Keith Sweat, T.H.
Year: 1992
#1 R&B/#1 crossover.

FREAK SCENE

Artist: Dinosaur Jr.
Written by: Joseph Mascis
From the album: *Bug*
Label: SST
Produced by: J. Mascis
Year: 1987
Career and (Boston) scene-establishing track.

FREDDY'S DEAD (THEME FROM *SUPERFLY*)

Artist: Curtis Mayfield
Written by: Curtis Mayfield
From the album: *Superfly Soundtrack*
Label: Curtom
Produced by: Curtis Mayfield
Year: 1972
The street-level blaxploitation anthem was his biggest hit.

FREE

Artist: Phish
Written by: Trey Anastasio, Tom Marshall
From the album: *Billy Breathes*
Label: Elektra
Year: 1996

Post-hippie Phish food from the home of Ben & Jerry.

FREE AS A BIRD

Artist: The Beatles
Written by: John Lennon, Paul McCartney, George Harrison, Ringo Starr
From the album: *Anthology I*
Label: Capitol
Produced by: Jeff Lynne
Year: 1995
Previously unreleased 1977 Lennon demo reunites the Beatles.

FREE BIRD

Artist: Lynyrd Skynyrd
Written by: Ronnie Van Zant, Allen Collins
From the album: *Lynyrd Skynyrd (pronounced leh-nerd skin-nerd)*
Label: MCA/Sounds of the South
Produced by: Al Kooper
Year: 1973
Dedicated to Southern soulmate Duane Allman. The '76 live version became an FM radio anthem.

FREE FALLIN'

Artist: Tom Petty and the Heartbreakers
Written by: Tom Petty, Jeff Lynne
From the album: *Full Moon Fever*
Label: MCA
Produced by: Jeff Lynne
Year: 1989
Taking a sabbatical from the Heartbreakers, Tom hires all of the Heartbreakers but the drummer to play on this record.

FREE MAN IN PARIS

Artist: Joni Mitchell
Written by: Joni Mitchell
From the album: *Court and Spark*
Label: Asylum
Produced by: Joni Mitchell
Year: 1974
Joni drops out of the musical rat race a mere three months after her first and only Top 10 single, "Help Me." Rumored to be about media mogul David Geffen.

FREE NELSON MANDELA

Artist: The Specials
Written by: Jerry Dammers, Rhoda Dakar
From the album: *In the Studio*
Label: Chrysalis
Produced by: Elvis Costello
Year: 1985
Taking a political stand, with a reggae beat.

FREE RIDE

Artist: Edgar Winter Group
Written by: Dan Hartman
From the album: *They Only Come out at Night*
Label: Epic

Produced by: Rick Derringer
Year: 1972
Southern rock with a touch of glam.

FREE THE PEOPLE

Artist: Delaney and Bonnie
Written by: Barbara Keith
From the album: *To Bonnie from Delaney*
Label: Atco
Produced by: Delaney Bramlett
Year: 1970
Folk gospel sing-along.

FREE YOUR MIND

Artist: En Vogue
Written by: Thomas McElroy, Denzil Foster
From the album: *Funky Divas of Soul*
Label: Atco/East West
Produced by: Thomas McElroy, Denzil Foster
Year: 1992
Tip of the verbal hat to George Clinton turns into a Curtis-Mayfield-meets-the-Supremes plea for color-blindness.

FREE YOUR MIND AND YOUR ASS WILL FOLLOW

Artist: Funkadelic
Written by: Grace Cook, Eddie Hazel, Tawl Ross
From the album: *Free Your Mind and Your Ass Will Follow*
Label: Westbound
Year: 1970
Ten-minute signature opus paves the way for the funk revolution. Grace Cook was Eddie Hazel's mother.

FREED PIG

Artist: Sebadoh
Written by: Lou Barlow
From the album: *III*
Label: Homestead
Produced by: Sean Slade
Year: 1991
Squealing rant from the modern king of such low-fi low self-esteem confessionals.

FREEDOM

Artist: George Michael
Written by: George Michael
From the album: *Listen without Prejudice (Vol., 1)*
Label: Columbia
Produced by: George Michael
Year: 1990
His second song with this title. The kind of freedom George was referring to here would be revealed when he sued his record company to get out of his contract.

FREEDOM

Artist: Richie Havens
Written by: Richie Havens
From the album: *Woodstock Soundtrack*

Label: Cotillion
Year: 1970
Instant folk gospel jam composed on stage at the 1969 Woodstock Festival, waiting for the other acts to arrive.

FREEDOM

Artist: Jimi Hendrix
Written by: Jimi Hendrix
From the album: *The Cry of Love*
Label: Reprise
Produced by: Jimi Hendrix
Year: 1971
Free at last, from the bounds of the Earth, Hendrix's ghost plays on.

FREEDOM

Artist: Wham!
Written by: George Michael
From the album: *Make It Big*
Label: Columbia
Produced by: George Michael
Year: 1984
Making the world safe for Michael Bolton.

FREEDOM OF SPEECH

Artist: Ice-T
Written by: Tracy (Ice-T) Morrow
From the album: *Freedom of Speech ... Just Watch What You Say*
Label: Sire
Year: 1989
Former NWA founder takes advantage of his rights.

FREEDOM RIDER

Artist: Traffic
Written by: Steve Winwood, James Capaldi
From the album: *John Barleycorn Must Die*
Label: United Artists
Produced by: Chris Blackwell, Steve Winwood
Year: 1970
Accessing American '60s protest references.

FREEWAY JAM

Artist: Jeff Beck
Written by: Max Middleton
From the album: *Jeff Beck with the Jan Hammer Group*
Label: Epic
Produced by: Jan Hammer
Year: 1976
Signature guitar epic from the man who wouldn't be God.

FREEWAY OF LOVE

Artist: Aretha Franklin
Written by: Narada Michael Walden, Jeffrey Cohen
From the album: *Who's Zoomin' Who?*
Label: Arista
Produced by: Narada Michael Walden
Year: 1985

In her biggest hit in over ten years, Aretha loosens up and gets to ride in a pink Cadillac, with the Boss' horn man, Clarence Clemmons, beside her.

FREEWILL

Artist: Rush
Written by: Gary Lee Weinrib (Geddy Lee), Alex Zivojinovich (Alex Lifeson), Neil Peart
From the album: *Permanent Waves*
Label: Mercury
Produced by: Terry Brown, Rush
Year: 1980
With a nod to novelist Ayn Rand.

FREEZE-FRAME

Artist: The J. Geils Band
Written by: Seth Justman, Peter Wolf
From the album: *Freeze-Frame*
Label: EMI-America
Produced by: Seth Justman
Year: 1982
Exploiting the terminology of the new video age.

FREIGHT TRAIN

Artist: Rusty Draper
Written by: Elizabeth Cotten
Label: Mercury
Year: 1957
Hit version of the classic folk tune, originated by Elizabeth Cotton at the turn of the century and recorded by her (Folkways, '58).

FRENZY

Artist: The Fugs
Written by: Tuli Kupferberg, Ed Sanders
From the album: *The Fugs*
Label: ESP
Produced by: Harry Smith
Year: 1965
The sound of Beatnik glory, released as a single—naturally it stiffed.

FRESH

Artist: Kool & the Gang
Written by: Ronald Bell, Kool & the Gang, James Bonneford
From the album: *Emergency*
Label: De-Lite
Produced by: Ronald Bell, Kool & the Gang, James Bonneford
Year: 1984
Eighth #1 R&B hit out of nine.

FRESH AIR

Artist: Quicksilver Messenger Service
Written by: Dino Valenti (Chester Powers), Jesse Farrow
From the album: *Just for Love*
Label: Capitol
Produced by: Quicksilver Messenger Service
Year: 1970

Ecological protest from San Francisco after the Gold Rush. Written by the author of "Get Together."

FRESH GARBAGE

Artist: Spirit
Written by: Jay Ferguson
From the album: *Spirit*
Label: Ode
Produced by: Lou Adler
Year: 1968
Timothy Leary lives.

FRESHMEN, THE

Artist: The Verve Pipe
Written by: Brian Vander Ark
From the album: *Villains*
Label: RCA
Produced by: Jack Joseph Puig
Year: 1997
The dark side of personal irresponsibility. Remade from the 1994 version.

FRIDAY I'M IN LOVE

Artist: The Cure
Written by: Robert Smith, Simon Gallup, Boris Williams, Purl Thompson, Perry Bamonte
From the album: *Wish*
Label: Elektra
Produced by: The Cure, Dave Allen
Year: 1992
After years of moping, their closest thing to an up tune.

FRIDAY ON MY MIND

Artist: The Easybeats
Written by: Harry Vanda, George Young
From the album: *Friday on My Mind*
Label: United Artists
Produced by: Shel Talmy
Year: 1966
Working class folk/rock by the Pomus & Shuman of Australia.

FRIEND OF THE DEVIL

Artist: Grateful Dead
Written by: Jerry Garcia, Robert Hunter, John Dawson
From the album: *American Beauty*
Label: Warner Brothers
Produced by: Grateful Dead
Year: 1970
Outlaw bluegrass.

FRIENDS

Artist: Buzzy Linhart
Written by: Mark Klingman, Buzzy Linhart
Label: Buddah
Produced by: Buzzy Linhart, Bill Takas, Luther Rix
Year: 1970

Greenwich Village party song. Covered by Bette Midler (Atlantic, '70).

FROM A BUICK 6

Artist: Bob Dylan
Written by: Bob Dylan
From the album: *Highway 61 Revisited*
Label: Columbia
Produced by: Tom Wilson
Year: 1965
Dylanized car classic—classic car: a Buick 6.

FROM A DISTANCE

Artist: Nanci Griffith
Written by: Julie Gold
From the album: *Lone Star State of Mind*
Label: MCA
Produced by: Tony Breen, Nanci Griffith
Year: 1987
Protest anthem discovered and published by renegade country folk artist Griffith. Popularized by Bette Midler (Atlantic, '90).

FROM ME TO YOU

Artist: The Beatles
Written by: John Lennon, Paul McCartney
From the album: *Jolly What! The Beatles and Frank Ifield*
Label: Vee Jay
Produced by: George Martin
Year: 1963
England's top song of '63. Covered by Del Shannon (Big Top, '63) who was the first American artist to cover a Beatle tune. It stiffed at lucky # 77. Re-released by the Beatles as the B-side of "Please Please Me" (Vee-Jay, '64).

FROM SMALL THINGS (BIG THINGS ONE DAY COME)

Artist: Dave Edmunds
Written by: Bruce Springsteen
From the album: *DE7th*
Label: Columbia
Year: 1982
Covering one of the Boss' smaller epics.

FROM THE BEGINNING

Artist: Emerson Lake and Palmer (ELP)
Written by: Greg Lake
From the album: *Emerson Lake and Palmer*
Label: Cotillion
Produced by: Greg Lake
Year: 1972
Forming the keyboard basis of classic(al) rock.

FROZEN

Artist: Madonna
Written by: Madonna Cicconne, Patrick Leonard

From the album: *Ray of Light*
Label: Warner Brothers
Year: 1998

FU-GEE-LA

Artist: The Fugees
Written by: Nel Wyclef Jean, Samuel Michel, Lauryn Hill, Allen McGrier, Tina Marie Brockert, Salaam Remi Gibbs
From the album: *The Score*
Label: Ruffhouse
Produced by: LeJam Productions
Year: 1995
Introducing the sound of Afro-Bohemia.

FUCK THA POLICE

Artist: NWA
Written by: M. C. Ren, Ice Cube
From the album: *Straight Outa Compton*
Label: Ruthless
Produced by: Dr. Dre
Year: 1988
Ratching up the anger quotient in South Central L.A.

FUJIYAMA MAMA

Artist: Annisteen Allen
Written by: Earl Burrows
Label: Capitol
Year: 1955
A Korean War story. Covered by label-mate Wanda Jackson a year later in the truly bombs over Nakasaki version.

FULL OF FIRE

Artist: Al Green
Written by: Al Green, Willie Mitchell, Mabon Hodges
From the album: *Full of Fire*
Label: Hi
Produced by: Willie Mitchell
Year: 1975
Green goes disco, with #1 R&B/Top 30 crossover.

FUN FUN FUN

Artist: The Beach Boys
Written by: Brian Wilson, Mike Love
From the album: *Shut Down (Vol. II)*
Label: Capitol
Produced by: Brian Wilson
Year: 1964
Car classic—classic car: the T-Bird. Released a week after the Beatles arrived in the US.

FUNHOUSE

Artist: Kid 'N Play
Written by: Christopher Reid, Christopher Martin
From the album: *Kid 'N Play's Funhouse*
Label: Select
Year: 1990
Featured in their kiddie hip hop film *House Party*.

FUNK #49

Artist: The James Gang
Written by: Joe Walsh, Jim Fox, Dale Peters
From the album: *James Gang Rides Again*
Label: ABC
Produced by: Bill Szymczyk
Year: 1970
Launching Walsh's classic rock guitar career from Cleveland. Walsh would later return to this setting (via Hollywood) for a bit part as himself on the Cleveland based *The Drew Carey Show*.

FUNKDAFIED

Artist: Da Brat
Written by: Jermaine Dupri, Da Brat (Shawntae Harris)
From the album: *Funkdafied*
Label: So So Def
Produced by: Jermaine Dupri
Year: 1994
Mommy could swear as well as daddy.

FUNKIN' FOR JAMAICA

Artist: Tom Browne
Written by: Tom Browne, Toni Smith
From the album: *Love Approach*
Label: GRP
Produced by: Dave Grusin, Larry Rosen
Year: 1980
All star funk jam and street party featuring Dave Grusin, Bernard Wright, Marcus Miller went to #1 R&B.

FUNKY BROADWAY (PART I)

Artist: Dyke & the Blazers
Written by: Arlester Christian
From the album: *The Funky Broadway*
Label: Original Sound
Produced by: Art Barrett, Coleman
Year: 1967
After the original was a moderate hit, Muscle Shoals cover by Wilson Pickett was a #1 R&B/Top 10 crossover.

FUNKY BUT CHIC

Artist: David Johansen
Written by: David Johansen, Syl Sylvain
From the album: *David Johansen*
Label: Blue Sky
Produced by: Richard Robinson, David Johansen
Year: 1977
Statement of purpose from the ex-New York Doll.

FUNKY COLD MEDINA

Artist: Tone Loc
Written by: Marvin Young (Young MC), Michael Ross, Matt Dike
From the album: *Lc-ed After Dark*
Label: Delicious Vinyl
Produced by: Michael Ross, Matt Dike

Year: 1989
New kind of hip hop fly girl, same kind of torture.

FUNKY KINGSTON

Artist: Toots and the Maytals
Written by: Frederick Toots Hibbert
From the album: *Funky Kingston*
Label: Island
Produced by: Chris Blackwell, Warrick Lynn
Year: 1975
One of reggae's defining statements, attitudes, locales.

FUNKY WORM

Artist: Ohio Players
Written by: Leroy Bonner, Ralph Middlebrooks, Marshall Jones, Walter Morrison, Andrew Noland
From the album: *Pleasure*
Label: Westbound
Produced by: Ohio Players
Year: 1973
Following Sly and George Clinton into the upper echelons of funk.

FUNKYTOWN

Artist: Lipps, Inc.
Written by: Steve Greenberg
From the album: *Mouth to Mouth*
Label: Casablanca
Produced by: Steve Greenberg
Year: 1979
Homemade techno dance hit from Prince's Minneapolis. Covered by Pseudo Echo (RCA, '86).

FUTURE'S SO BRIGHT, I GOTTA WEAR SHADES, THE

Artist: Timbuk 3
Written by: Pat MacDonald
From the album: *Greetings from Timbuk 3*
Label: IRS
Produced by: Dennis Herring
Year: 1986
Folk/rock irony from Texas. Herring would make his mark with Camper Van Beethoven.

G

G.T.O.

Artist: Ronny and the Daytonas
Written by: John Wilkin
From the album: *G.T.O.*
Label: Mala
Produced by: Bill Justis
Year: 1964
Growing up under the hood.

GALILEO

Artist: The Indigo Girls
Written by: Emily Saliers

From the album: *Rites of Passage*
Label: Epic
Produced by: Peter Collins
Year: 1992
Thrilling folk/rock contemplation of reincarnation.

GALLOWS POLE

Artist: Led Zeppelin
Written by: Traditional
From the album: *Led Zeppelin III*
Label: Atlantic
Produced by: Jimmy Page
Year: 1970
Betraying their folkie roots with a Leadbelly tune. Revived by the reunited Page and Plant (Atlantic, '94).

GALVESTON

Artist: Glen Campbell
Written by: Jimmy Webb
From the album: *Galveston*
Label: Capitol
Produced by: Al DeLory
Year: 1969
Searching antiwar ballad. His second straight #1 country/Top 10 crossover with a Jimmy Webb tune (following up "Wichita Lineman").

GAMBLER, THE

Artist: Kenny Rogers
Written by: Don Schlitz
From the album: *The Gambler*
Label: United Artists
Produced by: Larry Butler
Year: 1977
#1 country/Top 20 crossover spawned a TV movie.

GAME OF LOVE, THE

Artist: Wayne Fontana and the Mindbenders
Written by: Clint Ballard Jr.
From the album: *The Game of Love*
Label: Fontana
Year: 1964
Reasserting the values of middle America, which would come under assault from '60s folk singers like Gale Garnett and her flower child ilk.

GAMES PEOPLE PLAY

Artist: Joe South
Written by: Joe South
From the album: *Introspect*
Label: Capitol
Produced by: Joe South
Year: 1969
Perceptive and outspoken, this was a rare country/R&B/pop crossover by three different artists. South had the pop hit, Freddie Weller the country Top 10 (Columbia, '69), and Donald Height the R&B version (Jubilee, '69). South had the Top 10 UK version, and the song won a Grammy. Enjoying a reputation as one of the world's hippest songwriters,

South's tune was subsequently covered by singers from many different worlds, including Duane Allman, the Ventures, Tesla, the Flying Burritto Brothers, Inner Circle, Lee Dorsey, Jerry Lee Lewis, Brenda Lee, Conway Twitty, Barbara Mandrell, Wanda Jackson, Waylon Jennings, Lynn Anderson, and Petula Clark.

GAMES WITHOUT FRONTIERS

Artist: Peter Gabriel
Written by: Peter Gabriel
From the album: *Peter Gabriel*
Label: Mercury
Produced by: Steve Lillywhite
Year: 1980
Expanding his progressive world vision.

GANGSTA LEAN

Artist: D.R.S.
Written by: Chris Jackson, E. Jay Turner, Tracy Carter
From the album: *51*
Label: Capitol
Produced by: Chris Jackson, Delaney McGil
Year: 1993
Hoisting a cold one to his fallen neighborhood cronies.

GANGSTA'S PARADISE

Artist: Coolio with T.I.
Written by: Artis Ivey Jr., Larry Sanders, Doug Rasheed, Stevie Wonder
From the album: *Dangerous Minds Soundtrack*
Label: MCA
Year: 1995
Powerful contemporary sermoning on the street-corner, with help from Stevie Wonder's "Pastime Paradise."

GANGSTER OF LOVE

Artist: Johnny Guitar Watson
Written by: Johnny Watson
From the album: *Gangster of Love*
Label: King
Year: 1963
Covered by Steve Miller, who borrowed the glorious phrase, known only to rock and roll addicts, "the pompatus of love," from "The Letter" by the Medallions (Duotone, '54).

GANGSTERS

Artist: The Specials
Written by: Jerry Dammers
From the album: *The Specials*
Label: 2-Tone/Chrysalis
Produced by: Elvis Costello
Year: 1979
US single breakthrough launches the British 2-Tone Ska label, paving the way for the Selecter, Madness, the Beat, and eventually, Fun Boy Three.

GARDEN OF EARTHLY DELIGHTS

Artist: XTC
Written by: Andy Partridge
From the album: *Oranges and Lemons*
Label: Geffen
Produced by: Paul Fox
Year: 1989
Perfecting their Beatlesque psychedelic worldview.

GARDEN PARTY

Artist: Rick Nelson
Written by: Rick Nelson
From the album: *Garden Party*
Label: Decca
Produced by: Rick Nelson
Year: 1972
Snubbing the oldies revival in favor of country rock with the Stone Canyon Band.

GATES OF EDEN

Artist: Bob Dylan
Written by: Bob Dylan
From the album: *Bringing It All Back Home*
Label: Columbia
Produced by: Tom Wilson
Year: 1965
Dylan's sermon of the moment: there are no truths, except his.

GEE!

Artist: The Crows
Written by: Viola Watkins, Daniel Norton, William Davis
Label: Rama
Produced by: George Goldner
Year: 1954
Early R&B standard bearer, crossed over to the Top 20 a year later.

GEE BABY, AIN'T I GOOD TO YOU

Artist: Nat King Cole
Written by: Andy Razaf, Don Redman
Label: Capitol
Year: 1944
Written by Fats Waller's collaborator, Razaf, a #1 R&B/Top 20 crossover. Covered by Ray Charles (ABC/TRC, '67).

GEE WHIZ! (LOOK AT HIS EYES)

Artist: Carla Thomas
Written by: Carla Thomas
From the album: *Gee Whiz!*
Label: Atlantic
Produced by: Jim Stewart
Year: 1961
Early example of Memphis soul is Carla's biggest hit.

GENESIS

Artist: Hot Tuna
Written by: Jorma Kaukonen
From the album: *Quah*
Label: Grunt
Produced by: Jack Cassady
Year: 1974
Melancholy postscript to his old band the Airplane's "Third Week at the Chelsea."

GENIE IN A BOTTLE

Artist: Christina Aguilera
Written by: Steve Kipner, David Frank, Pam Sheyne
From the album: *Christina Aguilera*
Produced by: Guy Roche
Label: RCA
Year: 1999
A new thrush appears on the teen horizon, with pipes.

GENIUS OF LOVE

Artist: Tom Tom Club
Written by: Tina Weymouth, Chris Frantz, Steven Stanley, Adrian Belew
From the album: *Tom Tom Club*
Label: Sire
Produced by: Tom Tom Club
Year: 1981
Influential dance track from the Talking Heads rhythm section.

GENTLE ON MY MIND

Artist: John Hartford
Written by: John Hartford
From the album: *Gentle on My Mind*
Label: RCA
Produced by: Felton Jarvis
Year: 1967
Country folk rambling standard. Glen Campbell (Capitol, '67) had the only Top 40 hit.

GEORGIA ON MY MIND

Artist: Ray Charles
Written by: Hoagy Carmichael, Stuart Gorrell
From the album: *Ray Charles' Greatest Hits*
Label: ABC-Paramount
Produced by: Sid Feller
Year: 1960
Pining for his birthplace. Ray's first pop #1, crosses over to #3 R&B, but not country. Introduced by Mildred Bailey in 1930.

GEORGY GIRL

Artist: The Seekers
Written by: Jim Dale, Tom Springfield
From the album: *Georgy Girl*
Label: Capitol
Produced by: Tom Springfield
Year: 1966
Sprightly folk/rock title tune from the movie, co-authored by the Broadway actor Jim Dale.

GET A JOB

Artist: The Silhouettes
Written by: Richard Lewis, Howard Biggs
From the album: *Get a Job*
Label: Ember
Produced by: Kae Williams
Year: 1957
One of the all-time classic #1 R&B/#1 crossovers, its disturbingly realistic content disguised by its nonsense syllables. Covered by the Mills Brothers (Decca, '57). In response, Berry Gordy Jr. wrote "Got a Job" for the Miracles. In a more delayed but no less appropriate reaction, the '50s parody group Sha-Na-Na named themselves after the song's nonsense syllables.

GET AT ME DOG

Artist: DMX
Written by: Damon Blackman, Samuel Taylor, Earl Simmons
From the album: *It's Dark and Hell Is Hot*
Label: Ruff Riders/Def Jam
Produced by: Grease, PK
Year: 1998
Though musical contexts may come and go, the Dog prevails.

GET BACK

Artist: The Beatles
Written by: John Lennon, Paul McCartney
From the album: *Let It Be*
Label: Apple
Produced by: George Martin
Year: 1969
Their biggest hit of '69 and 17TH #1 (out of 20).

GET CLOSER

Artist: Seals and Crofts
Written by: James Seals, Darrell Crofts
From the album: *Get Closer*
Label: Warner Brothers
Produced by: Louie Shelton
Year: 1976
Placid folk/rocker, better known as a toothpaste commercial.

GET DANCIN'

Artist: Disco Tex and the Sex-O-Lettes
Written by: Bob Crewe, Kenny Nolan Helfman
From the album: *Disco Tex and the Sex-o-Lettes*
Label: Chelsea
Produced by: Bob Crewe
Year: 1974
The continuing adventures of Monte Rock III, the self-made, self-promoting hairdresser, who wound up with a cameo in *Saturday Night Fever*. RuPaul was watching.

GET DOWN GET DOWN (GET ON THE FLOOR)

Artist: Joe Simon
Written by: Raeford Gerald, Joe Simon
From the album: *Get Down*
Label: Spring
Produced by: Raeford Gerald, Joe Simon
Year: 1975
Joe goes disco for his biggest hit.

GET DOWN TONIGHT

Artist: K. C. & the Sunshine Band
Written by: Harry Casey, Richard Finch
From the album: *K. C. and the Sunshine Band*
Label: TK
Produced by: Harry Casey, Richard Finch
Year: 1975
First #1 R&B/#1 crossover by a white-led band since Jimmy Gilmer & the Fireball's "Sugar Shack" in '63.

GET HERE

Artist: Oleta Adams
Written by: Brenda Russell
From the album: *Circle of One*
Label: Fontana
Year: 1991
#1 R&B/Top 10 crossover written by the author of "Piano in the Dark."

GET IT RIGHT

Artist: Aretha Franklin
Written by: Luther Vandross, Marcus Miller
From the album: *Get It Right*
Label: Arista
Produced by: Luther Vandross
Year: 1983
Soulful follow-up to "Jump to It."

GET IT WHILE YOU CAN

Artist: Garnet Mimms and the Enchanters
Written by: Jerry Ragovoy (Norman Meade), Mort Shuman
Label: United Artists
Produced by: Jerry Ragovoy
Year: 1963
Poignant Brill Building soul. Covered by Howard Tate (Verve, '66), Janis Joplin (Columbia, '71).

GET OFF

Artist: Foxy
Written by: Carlos Driggs, Ishmael Ledesma
From the album: *Get Off*
Label: Dash
Produced by: Cory Wade
Year: 1978
Out of the discos of Miami.

GET OFF OF MY CLOUD

Artist: The Rolling Stones
Written by: Mick Jagger, Keith Richards
From the album: *December's Children (and Everybody's)*
Label: London
Produced by: Andrew Loog-Oldham
Year: 1965
Developing their trademark anti-Beatles attitude.

GET ON THE GOOD FOOT, PART I

Artist: James Brown
Written by: James Brown, Fred Wesley, Joe Mims
From the album: *Get on the Good Foot*
Label: Polydor
Produced by: James Brown
Year: 1972
Summertime classic urges hippies and blacks to just get along.

GET OUT OF CONTROL

Artist: Daniel Ash
Written by: Daniel Ash
From the album: *Foolish Thing Desire*
Label: Columbia
Year: 1992
Solo one-shot from a Bauhaus and Love and Rockets graduate.

GET OUT OF MY LIFE WOMAN

Artist: Lee Dorsey
Written by: Allen Toussaint
From the album: *The New Lee Dorsey*
Label: Amy
Produced by: Allen Toussaint
Year: 1965
New Orleans legend Toussaint gives us the new Lee Dorsey, not as mellow as the old.

GET OUTA MY DREAMS, GET INTO MY CAR

Artist: Billy Ocean
Written by: Robert John "Mutt" Lange, Billy Ocean
From the album: *Tear Down These Walls*
Label: Jive
Produced by: Mutt Lange
Year: 1988
The title of his third #1 R&B/#1 crossover may have been based on a Ringo Starr ad-lib in the outro of his version of "You're Sixteen."

GET OVER YOU

Artist: The Undertones
Written by: John O'Neill
From the album: The Undertones
Label: Sire
Produced by: Roger Bechirian
Year: 1979
Reinventing Buddy Holly with a nervous Scottish quiver.

GET READY

Artist: The Temptations
Written by: Smokey Robinson
From the album: *Temptations Sing Smokey*
Label: Gordy
Produced by: Smokey Robinson

Year: 1966
Eddie Kendricks classic, influenced by Jackie Lee's notorious dance of urban paranoia, "The Duck" (Mirwood, '65). Covered by Rare Earth (Motown, '70).

GET RHYTHM

Artist: Johnny Cash and the Tennessee Two
Written by: Johnny Cash
From the album: *Johnny Cash and His Hot and Blue Guitar*
Produced by: Sam Phillips
Label: Sun
Year: 1956
Making a splash in Nashville; B-side of "I Walk the Line." Rereleased in 1969.

GET THAT GASOLINE BLUES

Artist: NRBQ
Written by: Terry Adams, Charlie Craig
From the album: *Workshop*
Label: Kama Sutra
Year: 1974
Topical tune is the only chart hit for the world's best bar band.

GET TOGETHER

Artist: The We Five
Written by: Dino Valenti (Chester Powers)
From the album: *Make Someone Happy*
Label: A&M
Produced by: Frank Werber
Year: 1965
San Francisco peace anthem has a career as checkered as its writer, noted beat rocker Dino Valenti, aka Billy Roberts, aka Chester Powers. After folkie Hamilton (Bob) Camp introduced it, the We Five brought it back to the charts as a follow-up to "You Were on My Mind" (A&M, '65). It was then covered by the San Francisco scenesters, the Jefferson Airplane (RCA, '66). Their San Francisco neighbors, HP Lovecraft, put it on their first album (Philips, '67). The East Coast rag and roll contingent, the Youngbloods, next released it as a single (RCA, '67), at which time it stiffed. In '69, after its initial intent had been all but subverted by its use in a public service announcement for the United Conference of Christians and Jews, it was rereleased by the Youngbloods (RCA, '69) to become a Top 10 hit at last. Valenti, meanwhile, was either in jail, at sea, on drugs, contemplating a variety of lawsuits, or all of the above. He would re-emerge in Quicksilver Messenger Service, another San Francisco band, and they would return Hamilton Camp's favor, by covering one of his tunes, "Pride of Man."

GET UP AND BOOGIE

Artist: Silver Convention
Written by: Sylvester Levay, Stephen Prager
From the album: *Silver Convention*
Label: Midland International

Produced by: Michael Kunze
Year: 1976
Returning to the discos of Germany to follow-up "Fly Robin Fly."

GET UP! (BEFORE THE NIGHT IS OVER)

Artist: Technotronic
Written by: Manuella Kamosi, Thomas De Quincey (Jo Bogaert)
From the album: *Pump up the Jam—the Album*
Label: SBK
Produced by: Jo Bogaert
Year: 1989
Belgian track big on the international techno disco scene.

GET UP (I FEEL LIKE BEING A) SEX MACHINE

Artist: James Brown
Written by: James Brown
From the album: *Sex Machine*
Label: King
Produced by: James Brown
Year: 1970
With this, the son of "Give It up or Turn It a Loose," the hardest-working man in show business showed no signs of flagging.

GET UP, STAND UP

Artist: Bob Marley & the Wailers
Written by: Bob Marley
From the album: *Burnin'*
Label: Island
Produced by: Chris Blackwell, the Wailers
Year: 1973
A call to arms, unheeded.

(GET YOUR KICKS ON) ROUTE 66

Artist: Nat King Cole
Written by: Bobby Troup
Label: Capitol
Year: 1946
A generation that cut its teeth on this essential rambling tune while they were still in their cribs, would reenact its message twenty years later, by Harley, by thumb, and in VW vans all across the continent. Covered by the Rolling Stones (London, '64), Them (Parrot, '65), Depeche Mode (Sire, '87).

GETAWAY

Artist: Earth, Wind & Fire
Written by: Peter Cor, Beloyd Taylor
From the album: *Spirit*
Label: Columbia
Produced by: Maurice White, Charles Stepney
Year: 1976
Setting a standard for funk drumming.

GETTIN' JIGGY WIT IT

Artist: Will Smith
Written by: Will Smith, Samuel Barnes, Bernard Edwards, Nile Rodgers, Joe Robinson, James Alexander, Ben Cauley, Larry Dodson, Willie Hall, Harvey Henderson, Dave Porter, Winston Stewart
From the album: *Big Willie Style*
Label: Columbia
Produced by: Poke & Tone
Year: 1998
And only one of these cowriters can prevent this song from being licensed.

GETTING BETTER

Artist: The Beatles
Written by: John Lennon, Paul McCartney
From the album: *Sgt. Pepper's Lonely Hearts Club Band*
Label: Capitol
Produced by: George Martin
Year: 1967
Recovering from the testiness of their *Revolver* era, with plenty of optimistic homilies.

GHETTO HEAVEN

Artist: The Family Stand
Written by: Peter Lord, V. Jeffrey Smith, Sandra St. Victor
From the album: *Chain*
Label: Atlantic
Produced by: V. Jeffrey Smith, Peter Lord
Year: 1990
The writing trio would move on to Paula Abdul.

GHETTO JAM

Artist: Domino
Written by: Kevin Gilliam, Domino
From the album: *Domino*
Label: RAL/Chaos
Produced by: D. J. Battlecat
Year: 1993
A gangsta rap Sunday confession.

GHETTO SUPASTAR (THAT IS WHAT YOU ARE)

Artist: Pras Michel with Old Dirty Bastard and Mya
Written by: Pras Michel, Wyclef Jean, Barry Gibb, Robin Gibb, Maurice Gibb, Russell Jones
From the album: *Bulworth Soundtrack*
Label: Interscope
Year: 1998
Top 10 R&B/Top 20 crossover from the Warren Beatty political satire *Bulworth*. With a chorus drawn from "Islands in the Stream" by Kenny Rogers and Dolly Parton.

GHOST TOWN

Artist: The Specials
Written by: Jerry Dammers
From the album: *Ghost Town/Why?/Friday Night Saturday Morning*
Label: 2-Tone
Produced by: John Collins
Year: 1981
Their most powerful song; #1 UK.

GHOSTBUSTERS

Artist: Ray Parker Jr.
Written by: Ray Parker Jr.
From the album: *Ghostbusters Soundtrack*
Label: Arista
Produced by: Ray Parker Jr.
Year: 1984
#1 R&B/#1 crossover from the movie. Suggested segue: "I Want a New Drug" by Huey Lewis and the News.

G.I. JIVE

Artist: Louis Jordan
Written by: Donald Kahn, Johnny Mercer
Label: Decca
Year: 1944
Of his 18 #1 R&B hits, this is Jordan's only #1 crossover. The next black male singer to accomplish this feat would be Nat Cole, with "Mona Lisa" in 1950. Thirteen years later, Sam Cooke with "You Send Me" would join the club.

GIMME ALL YOUR LOVIN'

Artist: ZZ Top
Written by: Billy Gibbons, Dusty Hill, Frank Beard
From the album: *Eliminator*
Label: Warner Brothers
Produced by: Bill Ham
Year: 1983
Playing the part of a boogie band on MTV.

GIMME DAT DING

Artist: Pipkins
Written by: Albert Hammond, Mike Hazelwood
From the album: *Gimme Dat Ding*
Label: Capitol
Produced by: John Burgess
Year: 1970
From the irrepressible *Benny Hill Show*.

GIMME GIMME SHOCK TREATMENT

Artist: The Ramones
Written by: Douglas Colvin, John Cummings, Jeff Hyman, Thomas Erdelyi
From the album: *Leave Home*
Label: Sire
Produced by: Tony Bongiovi, Thomas Erdelyi
Year: 1977
Coming a year after "Teenage Lobotomy," an early warning sign that the Ramones might not be able to sustain their brain-draining barrage forever. Nearly twenty years later, however, they would cover Tom Waits' "I Don't Want to Grow Up" as proof that the struggle was still worth the effort.

GIMME INDIE ROCK

Artist: Sebadoh
Written by: Lou Barlow
Label: Homestead
Year: 1991
Representing the '90s low-fi sound and attitude.

GIMME LITTLE SIGN

Artist: Brenton Wood
Written by: Alfred Smith, Joseph Hooven, Jerry Winn
From the album: *Oogum Boogum*
Label: Double Shot
Produced by: Joseph Hooven, Jerry Winn
Year: 1967
Mid-tempo soul in the Brook Benton mold.

GIMME SHELTER

Artist: The Rolling Stones
Written by: Mick Jagger, Keith Richards
From the album: *Let It Bleed*
Label: London
Produced by: Jimmy Miller
Year: 1969
Violence and death, a shot away, as evidenced by the chilling documentary named after it. Covered by the track's backup singer, Merry Clayton (Ode, '70).

GIMME SOME LOVIN'

Artist: Spencer Davis Group
Written by: Steve Winwood, Muff Winwood, Spencer Davis
From the album: *Gimme Some Lovin'*
Label: United Artists
Produced by: Jimmy Miller, Chris Blackwell
Year: 1967
The Hammond B3 organ provides the basis for their biggest hit.

GIMME SOME TRUTH

Artist: John Lennon
Written by: John Lennon
From the album: *Imagine*
Label: Apple
Produced by: John Lennon
Year: 1971
Setting a model that verbose rockers from R.E.M. to Billy Joel would use when they wanted to let it all hang out. Of course, Chuck Berry did it first in "Too Much Monkey Business" and Bob Dylan did it best in "Subterranean Homesick Blues."

GIMME THREE STEPS

Artist: Lynyrd Skynyrd
Written by: Ronnie Van Zant, Allen Collins
From the album: *Lynyrd Skynyrd (pronounced leh-nerd skin-nerd)*
Label: Sounds of the South
Produced by: Al Kooper
Year: 1973
Sophisticated Southern shuffle.

GIMME YOUR LOVE

Artist: Aretha Franklin and James Brown
Written by: Narada Michael Walden, Jeffrey Cohen
From the album: *Gimme Your Love*
Label: Arista
Produced by: Narada Michael Walden
Year: 1989
The Queen of Soul duets with the Godfather, who is the only artist who has more #1 R&B hits than she does.

GIN AND JUICE

Artist: Snoop Doggy Dogg
Written by: Calvin Broadus (Snoop Doggy Dogg)
From the album: *Doggy Style*
Label: Death Row
Produced by: Dr. Dre
Year: 1993
Verbal riff of the year.

GIN-SOAKED BOY

Artist: Tom Waits
Written by: Tom Waits
From the album: *Swordfishtrombones*
Label: Island
Produced by: Tom Waits
Year: 1983
The glorious results of a misspent life.

GIRL

Artist: The Beatles
Written by: John Lennon, Paul McCartney
From the album: *Rubber Soul*
Label: Capitol
Produced by: George Martin
Year: 1965
Expanding into new terrains of complexity.

GIRL CAN'T HELP IT, THE

Artist: Little Richard
Written by: Bobby Troup
From the album: *Little Richard*
Label: Specialty
Produced by: Art Rupe
Year: 1955
Little Richard's coming-out party, as seen in the Jayne Mansfield movie of the same name. Revived in 1981 by Divine in the camp classic film *Polyester*.

GIRL DON'T COME

Artist: Sandie Shaw
Written by: Chris Andrews
From the album: *Sandie Shaw*
Label: Reprise
Year: 1965
Biggest US crossover for the English proto-hippie thrush.

GIRL FROM THE NORTH COUNTRY

Artist: Bob Dylan
Written by: Bob Dylan
From the album: *The Freewheelin' Bob Dylan*
Label: Columbia
Produced by: John Hammond
Year: 1963
In an era of Bandstand dancers from Philly, candystore girl-groups from New York City and Detroit, surfing sun goddesses in L.A. (and Mandy Rice Davies scandalizing England), Dylan defies the stereotypes to extol a decidedly different locale and female persona.

GIRL, I'M GONNA MISS YOU

Artist: Milli Vanilli
Written by: Frank Farian, Dietman Kawohl, Peter Bischof-Fallenstein
From the album: *Girl, You Know It's True*
Label: Arista
Produced by: Fred Farian
Year: 1989
Second of three #1 tunes for the dance duo that was eventually stripped of its new artist Grammy for not singing on their records.

GIRL IN TROUBLE (IS A TEMPORARY THING), A

Artist: Romeo Void
Written by: Debora Iyall, Peter Woods, Frank Zincavage, David Kahne
From the album: *Instincts*
Label: Columbia
Produced by: David Kahne
Year: 1984
Closest thing to a hit for the San Francisco natives.

GIRL IS MINE, THE

Artist: Michael Jackson and Paul McCartney
Written by: Michael Jackson
From the album: *Thriller*
Label: Epic
Produced by: Quincy Jones, Michael Jackson
Year: 1983
With the leadoff single from the album, the former Beatle escorts the former leader of the Jackson 5 past the velvet rope into heavy MTV rotation. A black community stood and cheered.

GIRL OF MY BEST FRIEND

Artist: Elvis Presley
Written by: Sam Bobrick, Beverly Ross
From the album: *Elvis Is Back*
Label: RCA
Produced by: Steve Sholes
Year: 1960
Top 10 in England, with "A Mess of Blues" on the B-side (RCA, '60). Covered in the US by Elvis sound-alike Ral Donner (Gore, '61).

GIRL WATCHER

Artist: The O'Kaysions
Written by: Ronald Killette (Buck Trail)
From the album: *Girl Watcher*
Label: ABC
Year: 1968
Early Philly soul one-shot.

GIRL WHO LIVES ON HEAVEN HILL

Artist: Hüsker Dü
Written by: Grant Hart
From the album: *New Day Rising*
Produced by: Spot, Husker Du
Label: SST
Year: 1985
Minneapolis speedcore punks have a heart.

GIRL YOU NEED A CHANGE OF MIND (PART I)

Artist: Eddie Kendricks
Written by: Leonard Caston, Anita Poree
From the album: *People ... Hold On*
Label: Tamla
Year: 1972
Often cited as the first disco record ... which was not enough to bring it past #87 on the charts.

GIRL, YOU KNOW IT'S TRUE

Artist: Milli Vanilli
Written by: Frank Farian, Peter Bischof-Fallenstein, Dietman Kawohl
From the album: *Girl, You Know It's True*
Label: Arista
Produced by: Fred Farian
Year: 1989
Kicking off their eventually discredited debut album that contained three Top 10 hits by various artists.

GIRL, YOU'LL BE A WOMAN SOON

Artist: Neil Diamond
Written by: Neil Diamond
From the album: *Neil Diamond's Greatest Hits*
Label: Bang
Produced by: Jeff Barry, Ellie Greenwich
Year: 1967
And old enough to attend one of Neil's shows in Las Vegas. Covered by Urge Overkill on the *Pulp Fiction* Soundtrack (MCA, '94).

GIRLFRIEND

Artist: Bobby Brown
Written by: Larry White, Lee Peters, Kirk Crumpler
From the album: *King of Stage*
Label: MCA
Produced by: Larry White
Year: 1986

Introducing the Linn 9000 drum machine—as well as the #1 R&B debut for the former New Edition heartthrob.

GIRLFRIEND

Artist: Modern Lovers
Written by: Jonathan Richman
From the album: *The Modern Lovers*
Label: Beserkley
Produced by: John Cale
Year: 1971
Eternal teenage yearnings from an eternal teenager.

GIRLFRIEND

Artist: Pebbles
Written by: Kenny Edmunds (Babyface), Antonio Reid (L.A. Reid)
From the album: *Pebbles*
Label: MCA
Produced by: Babyface, L.A. Reid
Year: 1988
Producer Edmunds aka Babyface finds his Ronnie Spector in Perri McKissack aka Pebbles. They celebrate with a #1 R&B/Top 10 crossover.

GIRLFRIEND

Artist: Matthew Sweet
Written by: Matthew Sweet
From the album: *Girlfriend*
Label: Zoo
Produced by: Fred Maher, Matthew Sweet
Year: 1991
Breakthrough track for the semi-acoustic singer/songwriter.

GIRLFRIEND IN A COMA

Artist: The Smiths
Written by: Stephen Morrissey, Johnny Marr
From the album: *Strangeways Here We Come*
Label: Sire
Produced by: Stephen Morrissey, Johnny Marr
Year: 1987
Jerry Seinfeld would have understood.

GIRLS AND BOYS

Artist: Blur
Written by: Damon Albarn, Graham Coxon, Alex James, Dave Rountree
From the album: *Parklife*
Label: ERG/SBK
Produced by: Stephen Street
Year: 1994
Blurring the sexuality of the English dancehall of the '90s. Suggested segue: "Lola" by the Kinks.

GIRLS, GIRLS, GIRLS

Artist: Mötley Crüe
Written by: Tommy Lee, Nikki Sixx, Mick Mars
From the album: *Girls, Girls, Girls*
Label: Elektra
Produced by: Tom Werman
Year: 1987
Pamela Anderson invites over some friends.

GIRLS JUST WANT TO HAVE FUN

Artist: Robert Hazard
Written by: Robert Hazard
Label: RCA
Year: 1982
Popularized by Cyndi Lauper in her breathtaking debut album (Portrait, '84).

GIRLS ON FILM

Artist: Duran Duran
Written by: Andy Taylor, John Taylor, Roger Taylor, Simon LeBon, Nick Rhodes
From the album: *Duran Duran*
Label: Harvest/EMI
Produced by: Colin Thurston
Year: 1981
Must-see video for those who don't subscribe to the Playboy Channel.

GIRLS TALK

Artist: Elvis Costello
Written by: Declan McManus (Elvis Costello)
From the album: *Taking Liberties*
Label: Columbia
Produced by: Nick Lowe
Year: 1980
The last word on the opposite sex. Covered by Linda Ronstadt (Asylum, '80).

GIVE HIM A GREAT BIG KISS

Artist: The Shangri-Las
Written by: George Morton
From the album: *The Shangri-Las*
Label: Red Bird
Produced by: Shadow Morton
Year: 1964
New York girl group (and boy group) classic. Covered by the New York Dolls (Mercury, '74).

GIVE IT AWAY

Artist: Red Hot Chili Peppers
Written by: Anthony Kiedis, Michael Balzary (Flea), John Frusciante, Chad Smith
From the album: *Blood Sugar Sex Majik*
Label: Warner Brothers
Produced by: Rick Rubin
Year: 1991
"Summer of Love" sentiments with a '90s snarl.

GIVE IT TO ME

Artist: The J. Geils Band
Written by: Seth Justman, Peter Wolf
From the album: *Bloodshot*
Label: Atlantic
Produced by: Bill Szymczyk
Year: 1973
Following Springsteen and Southside Johnny to the great American East coast bar-band reunion dance and trading card show.

GIVE IT TO ME BABY

Artist: Rick James
Written by: James Johnson Jr. (Rick James)
From the album: *Street Songs*
Label: Gordy
Produced by: Rick James
Year: 1981
Too drunk to score. Reportedly the inspiration for Michael Jackson's "Thriller."

GIVE IT UP

Artist: Public Enemy
Written by: Charles Ridenhour, Hank Shocklee, Keith Shocklee, Gary Rinaldo, Sean DeVore, Alvertis Isbell, Marvell Thomas
From the album: *Muse Sick-N-Hour Mess Age*
Label: Jam/RAL/Island
Produced by: Stuart Robertz, Cerwin Depper, Gary G. Wiz, the JBL
Year: 1994
Their second crossover; Top 30 R&B/Top 40.

GIVE IT UP OR TURN IT LOOSE

Artist: James Brown
Written by: James Brown
From the album: *Ain't It Funky*
Label: King
Produced by: James Brown
Year: 1969
Godfather of all grooves gives up a #1 R&B/Top 20 crossover.

GIVE ME JUST A LITTLE MORE TIME

Artist: The Chairmen of the Board
Written by: Brian Holland, Edythe Wayne
From the album: *Give Me Just a Little More Time*
Label: Invictus
Produced by: The Staff
Year: 1970
Featuring General Johnson, first heard on "It Will Stand" by the Showmen.

GIVE ME JUST ONE NIGHT

Artist: 98 Degrees
Written by: Anders Bagge, Aentor Birgisson, Ogalde
From the album: *Revelation*
Label: Uptown
Year: 2000
Boy band single, imported from Sweden, land of harmony.

GIVE ME LOVE (GIVE ME PEACE ON EARTH)

Artist: George Harrison
Written by: George Harrison

From the album: *Living in the Material World*
Label: Apple
Produced by: George Harrison
Year: 1973
George's mission.

GIVE ME ONE REASON

Artist: Tracy Chapman
Written by: Tracy Chapman
From the album: *New Beginning*
Label: Elektra
Produced by: Don Gehman
Year: 1995
Bluesy comeback for the Boston folkie who hit it
big with "Fast Car."

GIVE ME THE NIGHT

Artist: George Benson
Written by: Rod Temperton
From the album: *Give Me the Night*
Label: Warner Brothers
Produced by: Quincy Jones
Year: 1980
The once and future jazz guitarist gets ready for his
vocal solo. Rod and Quincy get ready for Michael
Jackson.

GIVE PEACE A CHANCE

Artist: John Lennon
Written by: John Lennon, Paul McCartney
From the album: *The Plastic Ono Band, Live Peace in
Toronto 1969*
Label: Apple
Produced by: John Lennon, Yoko Ono
Year: 1969
Lennon's first non-Beatles hit; Yoko-inspired per-
formance art, recorded during a "Bed-in" for peace
at their hotel room in Montreal in June, with a
backup band consisting of, among others, Dr. Tim-
othy Leary and Tommy Smothers. Sung by Pete
Seeger at the Washington Monument during a
peace march later in the year.

GIVE US YOUR BLESSING

Artist: Ray Peterson
Written by: Jeff Barry, Ellie Greenwich
Label: Dunes
Produced by: Jerry Leiber, Mike Stoller
Year: 1963
Teen tragedy, covered by America's most tragic
girl-group, the Shangri-Las (Red Bird, '65).

GIVEN TO FLY

Artist: Pearl Jam
Written by: Mike McCready, Eddie Vedder
From the album: *Yield*
Label: Epic
Produced by: Brendan O'Brien
Year: 1998
Segue: "Going to California" by Led Zeppelin.

GIVING IT ALL AWAY

Artist: Roger Daltrey
Written by: David Courtney, Leo Sayer
From the album: *Daltrey*
Label: Track
Year: 1973
First hit for the Who frontman. Covered by Leo
Sayer (Warner Brothers, '75).

GIVING IT UP FOR YOUR LOVE

Artist: Jerry Lyn Williams
Written by: Jerry Lyn Williams
From the album: *Gone*
Label: Columbia
Year: 1979
Blues rocker popularized by Delbert McClinton
(Capitol, '80).

GIVING YOU THE BENEFIT

Artist: Pebbles
Written by: Kenny Edmunds (Babyface), Antonio
Reid (L.A. Reid)
From the album: *Always*
Label: MCA
Produced by: Babyface, L.A. Reid
Year: 1990
Third #1 R&B/Top 10 R&R crossover for the
then-Mrs. Reid is the producer's favorite Pebbles
song.

GIVING YOU THE BEST THAT I GOT

Artist: Anita Baker
Written by: Anita Baker, Skip Scarborough, Randy
Holland
From the album: *Giving You the Best That I Got*
Label: Elektra
Produced by: Michael Powell
Year: 1988
Where R&B meets jazz, in the stately voice of Anita
Baker and the percussion of Paulinho de Costa.

GLAD ALL OVER

Artist: The Dave Clark Five
Written by: Dave Clark, Mike Smith
From the album: *Glad All Over*
Label: Epic
Produced by: Dave Clark
Year: 1964
They had their moment; this was it.

GLAD TO BE GAY

Artist: Tom Robinson
Written by: Tom Robinson
From the album: *Power in the Darkness*
Label: Harvest
Produced by: Chas Thomas
Year: 1978
Anthem of personal protest, originally on the '76
LP *Rising Free*.

GLAMOUR BOYS

Artist: Living Colour
Written by: Vernon Reid
From the album: *Vivid*
Label: Epic
Produced by: Mick Jagger
Year: 1988
As McCartney did for Michael Jackson, Mick Jag-
ger helps a black act break a tacit color barrier, this
one in the heavy metal arena.

GLAMOROUS LIFE, THE

Artist: Sheila E.
Written by: Prince Rogers Nelson
From the album: *Sheila E. in the Glamourous Life*
Label: Warner Brothers
Produced by: Sheila E., Starr Company
Year: 1984
First and biggest hit for Prince's one-time drum-
mer and protégé.

GLASS ONION

Artist: The Beatles
Written by: John Lennon, Paul McCartney
From the album: *The Beatles*
Label: Apple
Produced by: George Martin
Year: 1968
A coffin for used Beatle titles and characters.

GLORIA

Artist: Laura Branigan
Written by: Trevor Veitch, Giancarlo Bigazzi,
Umberto Tozzi
From the album: *Branigan*
Label: Atlantic
Produced by: Greg Mathieson
Year: 1982
The schizoid '80s Gloria was a big hit in Italy by
Bigazzi.

GLORIA

Artist: Charles Brown
Written by: Leon Rene
Label: Exclusive
Year: 1947
The R&B Gloria. Other, more rocking Glorias
would follow. Covered by the Mills Brothers
(Decca, '48).

GLORIA

Artist: The Cadillacs
Written by: Esther Navarro
Label: Josie
Produced by: Esther Navarro
Year: 1954
The all-time doo-wop Gloria arrives, in this tune
written about singer Gloria Smith, who may or
may not have been a hard-to-get neighborhood
tease. Covered by a generation of kids on the corner, most notable among them the Passions (Audicon, '60).

GLORIA

Artist: Them
Written by: Van Morrison
From the album: *Here Comes the Night*
Label: Parrot
Produced by: Tommy Scott
Year: 1966
The rock and roll Gloria is perhaps the most famous one of all, transposed by Van Morrison's brogue into a midnight goddess of love. Covered by the Shadows of Knight (Dunwich, '65) and the Doors, at a '69 soundcheck (Elektra, '73).

GLORIA

Artist: U2
Written by: Paul Hewson (Bono), Dave Evans (Edge), Adam Clayton, Larry Mullen
From the album: *October*
Label: Island
Produced by: Steve Lillywhite
Year: 1980
The spiritual Gloria is no relation to any other Glorias. Although the Irish band was probably familiar with Van Morrison's main squeeze.

GLORIA (IN EXCELSIUS)

Artist: Patti Smith
Written by: Patti Smith
From the album: *Horses*
Label: Arista
Produced by: John Cale
Year: 1976
Patti the punk poet transforms the girl of Van Morrison's dreams into a raving bisexual bohemian demon out of a Lower East Side rock opera.

GLORY

Artist: Liz Phair
Written by: Liz Phair
From the album: *Exile in Guyville*
Label: Matador
Produced by: Liz Phair, Brad Wood
Year: 1993
Exquisitely moody drone from the Sonic Youth School of Low Art.

GLORY DAYS

Artist: Bruce Springsteen
Written by: Bruce Springsteen
From the album: *Born in the USA.*
Label: Columbia
Produced by: Jon Landau, Bruce Springsteen, Chuck Plotkin
Year: 1984
Fifth of seven Top 10 hits From the album: Suggested segue: "Night Moves" by Bob Seger, "Cherry Bomb" by John Mellencamp.

GLORY OF LOVE (THEME FROM *THE KARATE KID II*), THE

Artist: Peter Cetera
Written by: Peter Cetera, David Foster
From the album: *Solitude / Solitare*
Label: Warner Brothers
Produced by: Michael Omartian
Year: 1986
Big movie song for the former lead singer for Chicago.

GLORY OF LOVE, THE

Artist: The Five Keys
Written by: Billy Hill
Label: Aladdin
Year: 1951
One of the best groups of the doo-wop era. This '36 hit for Benny Goodman was also covered by Otis Redding (Volt, '67).

GO

Artist: Moby
Written by: Angelo Badalamenti, David Lynch
Label: Instinct
Produced by: Richard Melville Hall
Year: 1991
Twin Peaks theme as dance-hall rave, by the techno geek supreme.

GO

Artist: Pearl Jam
Written by: Brendan O'Brien, Pearl Jam
From the album: *Vs*
Label: Epic
Produced by: Brendan O'Brien
Year: 1993
May be about Eddie Vedder's truck.

GO ALL THE WAY

Artist: Raspberries
Written by: Eric Carmen
From the album: *Raspberries*
Label: Capitol
Produced by: Jimmy Ienner
Year: 1972
Frat rock enters the post-liberated '70s.

GO NOW

Artist: Bessie Banks
Written by: Larry Banks, Milton Bennett
Label: Red Bird
Produced by: Jerry Leiber, Mike Stoller
Year: 1963
Popularized by the Moody Blues (London, '65), whose future work would be nothing like this.

GO SEE THE DOCTOR

Artist: Kool Moe Dee
Written by: Moe Dewese
From the album: *I'm Kool Moe Dee*
Label: Jive
Produced by: Moe Dewese, Teddy Riley, Lavaba

Year: 1987
Instructive editorial in the era of AIDS.

GO WHERE YOU WANNA GO

Artist: Mamas & the Papas
Written by: John Phillips
From the album: *If You Can Believe Your Eyes and Ears*
Label: Dunhill
Produced by: Lou Adler
Year: 1966
In the dawning days of free love, a dubious philosophy. Suggested segue: "If You Love Somebody Set Them Free" by Sting (A&M, '85). Cover by the 5th Dimension (Soul City, '67) was their first hit.

GO YOUR OWN WAY

Artist: Fleetwood Mac
Written by: Lindsay Buckingham
From the album: *Rumours*
Label: Warner Brothers
Produced by: Richard Dashut, Ken Caillat, Fleetwood Mac
Year: 1977
Autobiographical soap operatics from their monster album.

GO, JIMMY, GO

Artist: Jimmy Clanton
Written by: Doc Pomus, Mort Shuman
Label: Ace
Produced by: Johnny Vincent
Year: 1959
As an example of the interchangeability of rock and roll parts in the Bandstand era, before Clanton heard this tune it was entitled "Go, Bobby, Go" and pitched by the writers to Bobby Rydell. Bobby's loss was Jimmy's second biggest hit.

GOD

Artist: John Lennon
Written by: John Lennon
From the album: *John Lennon / Plastic Ono Band*
Label: Apple
Produced by: Phil Spector
Year: 1970
Coming down from the Beatles, the second stage.

GOD GAVE ROCK AND ROLL TO YOU

Artist: Argent
Written by: Rod Argent
From the album: *In Deep*
Label: Epic
Produced by: Argent
Year: 1973
As subject matter, rock and roll has spawned many such quasi-religious anthems. Suggested segues: "It Will Stand" by the Showmen, "Rock and Roll Is Here to Stay" by Danny & the Juniors, "For Those

About to Rock (We Salute You)" by AC/DC, "Rock and Roll" by the Velvet Underground.

GOD, LOVE AND ROCK 'N' ROLL

Artist: Teegarden and Van Winkle
Written by: Skip Knape, David Teegarden
Label: Westbound
Year: 1970
Summing up the year's major concerns, with a folk/rock beat, so you couldn't dance to it.

GOD ONLY KNOWS

Artist: The Beach Boys
Written by: Brian Wilson, Tony Asher
From the album: *Pet Sounds*
Label: Capitol
Produced by: Brian Wilson
Year: 1966
Reported to be Paul McCartney's favorite song, which inspired Brian to go head-to-head with him in a creative/ego battle he could never win or recover from.

GOD SAVE THE QUEEN

Artist: The Sex Pistols
Written by: Paul Cook, Steve Jones, Glen Matlock, John Lydon (Johnny Rotten)
From the album: *Never Mind the Bollocks, Here's the Sex Pistols*
Label: Warner Brothers
Produced by: Chris Thomas, Bill Price
Year: 1977
Their first and biggest UK hit, establishing the nihilistic rock and roll attitude that would overtake England for the next three years.

GOD'S COMIC

Artist: Elvis Costello
Written by: Declan McManus (Elvis Costello)
From the album: *Spike*
Label: Warner Brothers
Produced by: T-Bone Burnette, Kevin Killen
Year: 1989

GOD'S SONG (THAT'S WHY I LOVE MANKIND)

Artist: Randy Newman
Written by: Randy Newman
From the album: *Sail Away*
Label: Warner Brothers
Produced by: Russ Titelman, Lenny Waronker
Year: 1972
Randy's feistiest diatribe redefines the era of *Jesus Christ Superstar*. Covered by Etta James (Chess, '72).

GODZILLA

Artist: Blue Oyster Cult
Written by: Donald Roeser (Buck Dharma)

From the album: *Spectres*
Label: Columbia
Produced by: Sandy Pearlman
Year: 1977
Establishing the natural creative leap between heavy metal and horror movies. The various members of Anthrax, Slayer, and White Zombie were captivated by this scintillating premise.

GOIN' BACK

Artist: Dusty Springfield
Written by: Gerry Goffin, Carole King
From the album: *Golden Hits*
Label: Philips
Year: 1966
Goffin and King master folk/rock. Dusty's 7TH Top 10 UK hit. Covered by the Byrds (Columbia, '67), Carole King (Ode, '71), Nils Lofgren (A&M, '75). Suggested segue: "Sugar Mountain" by Neil Young.

GOIN' DOWN TO LIVERPOOL

Artist: Bangles
Written by: Kimberly Rew
From the album: *All over the Place*
Label: Columbia
Produced by: David Kahne
Year: 1984
The girl-group from L.A. ventures across the pond to the Liverpool home of their biggest influence: the Beatles. Covered by Kimberly Rew's band, Katrina & the Waves (Capitol, '85).

GOIN' HOME

Artist: Fats Domino
Written by: Fats Domino, Alvin Young
From the album: *Rock and Rollin' with Fats Domino*
Label: Imperial
Produced by: Dave Bartholomew
Year: 1952
His first #1 R&B hit.

GOIN' MOBILE

Artist: The Who
Written by: Pete Townshend
From the album: *Who's Next*
Label: Decca
Produced by: The Who
Year: 1971
Known primarily for his slashing rhythm (and the occasional trashing of a stage guitar), this tale of a "hippie gypsy" from the aborted Lifehouse Project is enhanced by Townshend's use of an electronic device called an envelope follower on his guitar.

GOIN' OUT OF MY HEAD

Artist: Little Anthony and the Imperials
Written by: Teddy Randazzo, Bobby Weinstein
From the album: *I'm on the Outside (Looking In)*
Label: DCP
Produced by: Teddy Randazzo

Year: 1964
A precursor to the crooning style that would add years to their career in Las Vegas.

GOIN' TO THE RIVER

Artist: Fats Domino
Written by: Dave Bartholomew, Fats Domino
From the album: *Rock and Rollin' with Fats Domino*
Label: Imperial
Produced by: Dave Bartholomew
Year: 1953
The biggest R&B hit of '53.

GOING BACK TO CALI L.L.

Artist: LL Cool J
Written by: James Todd Smith, Rick Rubin
From the album: *Less Than Zero Soundtrack*
Label: Def Jam
Produced by: Rick Rubin
Year: 1987
In rap circles, nowhere near the same kind of a sun and surf place most rockers found it.

GOING TO A GO-GO

Artist: The Miracles
Written by: Smokey Robinson, Warren Moore, Robert Rogers, Marv Tarplin
From the album: *Going to a Go-Go*
Label: Tamla
Produced by: Smokey Robinson
Year: 1965
Covered by the Rolling Stones (Rolling Stones, '82).

GOING TO CALIFORNIA

Artist: Led Zeppelin
Written by: Jimmy Page, Robert Plant
From the album: *Led Zeppelin IV (Untitled)*
Label: Atlantic
Produced by: Jimmy Page
Year: 1971
Too late for the Great Folk Scare.

GOING UNDERGROUND

Artist: The Jam
Written by: Paul Weller
From the album: *Setting Sons*
Label: Polydor
Produced by: Vic Coppersmith-Heaven
Year: 1979
First of four #1 UK singles for the Who-influenced band that never made the US charts.

GOING UP THE COUNTRY

Artist: Canned Heat
Written by: Al Wilson, Canned Heat
From the album: *Living the Blues*
Label: Liberty
Produced by: Skip Taylor
Year: 1968
Basic boogie leads the antipsychedlic back-to-the-roots movement.

GOLD

Artist: John Stewart
Written by: John Stewart
From the album: *Bombs Away Dream Baby*
Label: RSO
Year: 1979
Former Kingston Trio lead singer makes a belated leap to folk/rock.

GOLDEN AGE OF ROCK 'N' ROLL

Artist: Mott the Hoople
Written by: Ian Hunter
From the album: *The Hoople*
Label: Columbia
Produced by: Ian Hunter, Dave Griffin, Pete Watts
Year: 1974
With Bowie, Iggy, Lou Reed, Alice Cooper. Others opted for '54 with Elvis, Bo Diddley, Chuck Berry, and Fats Domino, or '64 with the Beatles, the Stones, Motown, and Bob Dylan, or '84 with Springsteen, Prince, Michael Jackson, and Madonna, or '94 with Pearl Jam, Hole, Tori Amos, Babyface, and Dinosaur Jr.

GOLDEN SLUMBERS

Artist: The Beatles
Written by: John Lennon, Paul McCartney
From the album: *Abbey Road*
Label: Apple
Produced by: George Martin
Year: 1969
Their best lullaby.

GOLDEN YEARS

Artist: David Bowie
Written by: David Bowie
From the album: *Station to Station*
Label: RCA
Produced by: Harry Maslin, David Bowie
Year: 1976
Flirting with soul.

GONE AT LAST

Artist: Paul Simon and Phoebe Snow
Written by: Paul Simon
From the album: *Still Crazy After All These Years*
Label: Columbia
Produced by: Phil Ramone, Paul Simon
Year: 1975
Queens gospel, sung with a Jersey girl.

GONE AWAY

Artist: Offspring
Written by: Bryan Keith Hubbard
From the album: *Ixnay on the Hombre*
Label: Columbia
Year: 1997
Big song on the album is a eulogy.

GONE DEAD TRAIN

Artist: Randy Newman

Written by: Jack Nitzsche, Russ Titelman
From the album: *Performance Soundtrack*
Label: Warner Brothers
Produced by: Jack Nitzsche
Year: 1970
Chilling L.A. blues by a former Phil Spector studio hand, sung in the Mick Jagger movie by Newman. Covered by Crazy Horse (Reprise, '71).

GONE TILL NOVEMBER

Artist: Wyclef Jean
Written by: Wyclef Jean
From the album: *Carnival*
Label: Ruffhouse
Produced by: Jerry Duplesis
Year: 1997
Epic rhyme of the hip hop mariner.

GONNA FLY NOW (THEME FROM *ROCKY*)

Artist: Deetta Little and Nelson Pigford
Written by: Ayn Robbins, Bill Conti, Carol Connors
From the album: *Rocky Soundtrack*
Label: United Artists
Produced by: Bill Conti
Year: 1976
Bill Conti had the hit single (United Artists, '76).

GONNA MAKE YOU SWEAT

Artist: C&C Music Factory
Written by: Rob Clivilles, Freedom Williams
From the album: *Gonna Make You Sweat*
Label: Columbia
Produced by: Rob Clivilles, David Cole
Year: 1991
Heavy MTV dance rotation brought this a #1 R&B/#1 crossover.

GOO GOO MUCK

Artist: The Cramps
Written by: Ronnie Cook, Edgar James
From the album: *Psychedelic Jungle*
Label: I.R.S.
Produced by: the Cramps
Year: 1981
Retro rockabilly.

GOOD

Artist: Better Than Ezra
Written by: Kevin Griffin
From the album: *Deluxe*
Label: Elektra
Produced by: Dan Rothschild
Year: 1995
The pop alternative to grunge.

GOOD DAY SUNSHINE

Artist: The Beatles
Written by: John Lennon, Paul McCartney

From the album: *Revolver*
Label: Capitol
Produced by: George Martin
Year: 1966
Reacting to "Do You Believe in Magic" by the Lovin' Spoonful.

GOOD ENOUGH

Artist: Bobby Brown
Written by: Kenny Edmunds (Babyface), Antonio Reid (L.A. Reid), Daryl Simmons
From the album: *Bobby*
Label: MCA
Produced by: Babyface, L. A. Reid
Year: 1992
From his first real album in four years.

GOOD ENOUGH

Artist: Bonnie Raitt
Written by: John Hall, Johanna Hall
From the album: *Home Plate*
Label: Warner Brothers
Produced by: Paul Rothchild
Year: 1975
Handmade love song, homemade soul.

GOOD GOLLY, MISS MOLLY

Artist: Little Richard
Written by: John Marascalco, Robert Blackwell
Label: Speciality
Produced by: Bumps Blackwell
Year: 1958
His fourth and last Top 10 hit. Covered by Mitch Ryder (New Voice, '66) in a medley with "Devil with the Blue Dress On," Creedence Clearwater Revival (Fantasy, '69), the Meat Puppets (SST, '86). Paul McCartney was taking those screams to heart.

GOOD HEART, A

Artist: Feargal Sharkey
Written by: Maria McKee
From the album: *Feargal Sharkey*
Label: A&M/Virgin
Produced by: Dave Stewart
Year: 1985
Former Undertones lead singer gets his only #1 UK, written by former Lone Justice lead singer.

GOOD LIFE, THE

Artist: Weezer
Written by: Rivers Cuomo
From the album: *Pinkerton*
Produced by: Weezer
Label: Geffen
Year: 1996
Nerd rock gives way to dweeb rock.

GOOD LOVIN'

Artist: The Clovers
Written by: Ahmet Ertegun, Jesse Stone (Charles Calhoun), Leroy Kirkland, Danny Taylor

Label: Atlantic
Produced by: Ahmet Ertegun, Herb Abramson
Year: 1953

GOOD LOVIN'

Artist: The Olympics
Written by: Artie Resnick, Rudy Clark
Label: Loma
Year: 1965
Covered by the Young Rascals (Atlantic, '66).

GOOD LOVIN' AIN'T EASY TO COME BY

Artist: Marvin Gaye and Tammi Terrell
Written by: Nick Ashford, Valerie Simpson
From the album: *Marvin Gaye and His Girls*
Label: Tamla
Produced by: Nick Ashford, Valerie Simpson
Year: 1969
Their last big hit together. Tammi Terrell died in '70. Marvin also sang with Diana Ross, Mary Wells, Kim Weston, and Martha Reeves.

GOOD LUCK CHARM

Artist: Elvis Presley
Written by: Aaron Schroeder, Wally Gold
From the album: *Elvis' Golden Records (Vol. III)*
Label: RCA
Produced by: Steve Sholes
Year: 1962
His seventeenth #1 and last until 1969.

GOOD MORNING CAPTAIN

Artist: Slint
Written by: Slint
From the album: *Spiderland*
Label: Touch & Go
Produced by: Brian Paulson, Slint
Label: Touch & Go
Year: 1991
Rambling, mumbling post-arena rock showpiece.

GOOD MORNING, GOOD MORNING

Artist: The Beatles
Written by: John Lennon, Paul McCartney
From the album: *Sgt. Pepper's Lonely Hearts Club Band*
Label: Capitol
Produced by: George Martin
Year: 1967
As cheery as "A Day in the Life" was dour.

GOOD MORNING, LITTLE SCHOOL GIRL

Artist: Grateful Dead
Written by: H. G. Demarais
From the album: *The Grateful Dead*
Label: Warner Brothers
Produced by: Grateful Dead
Year: 1967
Psychedelicizing the ultimate schoolboy fantasy, the Grateful Dead take the Trips Festival nationwide. Derived from the '37 original by Sonny Boy Williamson. Covered by The Yardbirds (Epic, '69), Ten Years After (Deram, '69), Muddy Waters (Blue Sky, '78).

GOOD MORNING STARSHINE

Artist: Lynn Kellog, Melba Moore, James Rado and Gerome Ragni
Written by: James Rado, Gerome Ragni, Galt MacDermot
From the album: *Hair! A Tribal Rock Musical*
Label: RCA
Produced by: Andy Wiswell
Year: 1967
Covered by Oliver (Jubilee, '70).

GOOD OLD ROCK AND ROLL

Artist: Cat Mother and the All Night Newsboys
Written by: Various
From the album: *Street Giveth … and the Street Taketh Away*
Label: Polydor
Produced by: Jimi Hendrix
Year: 1969
Medley of '50s rock and roll by Hendrix's East Village neighbors. He had more presence as a producer with Eire Apparent.

GOOD RIDDANCE (TIME OF YOUR LIFE)

Artist: Green Day
Written by: Billie Joe Armstrong, Green Day
From the album: *Nimrod*
Label: Reprise
Produced by: Green Day, Rob Cavallo
Year: 1997
Power punk at a pop crossroads; tune made mainstream history with its use in the *Seinfeld* clips show preceding the finale.

GOOD ROCKIN' TONIGHT

Artist: Roy Brown
Written by: Roy Brown
Label: DeLuxe
Year: 1947
Cover by Wynonie Harris went to #1 R&B (King, '48). Cover by Elvis Presley (Sun, '54) actually made people hear the news.

GOOD THING

Artist: Fine Young Cannibals
Written by: David Steele, Roland Gift
From the album: *The Raw and the Cooked*
Label: IRS
Produced by: David Steele, Roland Gift
Year: 1989
Second straight #1 for the UK ska band. Used in the movies *Scandal* and *Tin Men*.

GOOD THING

Artist: Paul Revere and the Raiders
Written by: Terry Melcher, Mark Lindsay, Paul Revere
From the album: *The Spirit of '67*
Label: Columbia
Produced by: Terry Melcher
Year: 1967
Garage rock in revolutionary war drag.

GOOD TIME CHARLIE'S GOT THE BLUES

Artist: Danny O'Keefe
Written by: Danny O'Keefe
From the album: *O'Keefe*
Label: Signpost
Produced by: Arif Mardin
Year: 1972
Poignant folk/rock midlife crisis, originally recorded on Jerden in '67, and again on Atlantic in '70 (Produced by Ahmet Ertegun). Covered by Elvis Presley (RCA, '74).

GOOD TIMES

Artist: Chic
Written by: Nile Rodgers, Bernard Edwards
From the album: *Risque*
Label: Atlantic
Produced by: Nile Rodgers, Bernard Edwards
Year: 1979
Emblematic of the high times of the late '70s, before the low times of the early '80s crept in. Sampled on "Rapper's Delight" by the Sugarhill Gang (Sugarhill, '79).

GOOD TIMES

Artist: Sam Cooke
Written by: Sam Cooke
From the album: *Ain't That Good News*
Label: RCA
Produced by: Hugo and Luigi
Year: 1964

GOOD TIMES ROLL

Artist: The Cars
Written by: Ric Ocasek
From the album: *The Cars*
Label: Elektra
Produced by: Roy Thomas Baker
Year: 1978
Synthesized rockabilly with a Boston accent.

GOOD TIMES, BAD TIMES

Artist: Led Zeppelin
Written by: Jimmy Page, John Bonham, John Paul Jones
From the album: *Led Zeppelin*
Label: Atlantic

Produced by: Jimmy Page

Year: 1969

Their first chart single in an era that would soon make chart singles all but obsolete.

GOOD TIMIN'

Artist: Jimmy Jones

Written by: Clint Ballard Jr., Fred Tobias

From the album: *Good Timin'*

Label: Cub

Produced by: Otis Blackwell

Year: 1960

Frankie Lymon-inspired Top 10 R&B/Top 10 crossover.

GOOD VIBRATIONS

Artist: The Beach Boys

Written by: Brian Wilson, Mike Love

From the album: *Smiley Smile*

Label: Capitol

Produced by: Brian Wilson

Year: 1966

Years in the making and yet eerily at one with the times, this would be Brian's last #1 with the Beach Boys. Also the best rock and roll moment for the Theremin, Lothar & the Hand People notwithstanding.

GOOD VIBRATIONS

Artist: Marky Mark and the Funky Bunch

Written by: Donnie Wahlberg, Spice, Mark Walhberg

From the album: *Music for the People*

Label: Interscope

Produced by: Donnie Wahlberg, Spice

Year: 1991

New Kids on the Block's younger brother. Went on to model underwear and star in movies about rock stars and porn stars.

GOODBYE

Artist: Steve Earle

Written by: Steve Earle

From the album: *Train a Comin'*

Label: winter harvest

Year: 1995

Alt-country masterwork, covered by Emmylou Harris (Warner Brothers, '95).

GOODBYE AND HELLO

Artist: Tim Buckley

Written by: Tim Buckley

From the album: *Goodbye and Hello*

Label: Elektra

Produced by: Jerry Yester

Year: 1967

A tragic folk/rock hero at the dawning of the singer/songwriter age.

GOODBYE CRUEL WORLD

Artist: James Darren

Written by: Gloria Shayne

From the album: *Teenage Triangle*

Label: Colpix

Year: 1963

On some surveys, the worst Top 10 record of all time, despite the prominent calliope.

GOODBYE PORK PIE HAT

Artist: Jeff Beck

Written by: Charles Mingus

From the album: *Wired*

Label: Epic

Produced by: George Martin, Jan Hammer

Year: 1976

The original jazzy Jeff takes on a Mingus masterwork.

GOODBYE TO INNOCENCE

Artist: Madonna

Written by: Shep Pettibone, Madonna Ciccone

From the album: *Just Say Roe*

Label: Sire

Produced by: Shep Pettibone, Madonna

Year: 1994

Track was contributed to a collection released to support Pro Choice.

GOODBYE TO MY HOMIES

Artist: Master P

Written by: Master P, Silkk the Shocker, Sons of Funk, Mo B Dick, Freddie Perren, Christine Perren

From the album: *MP Da Last Don*

Label: No Limit

Year: 1998

Joining forces with Boyz II Men.

GOODBYE TO YOU

Artist: Scandal

Written by: Zack Smith

From the album: *Scandal*

Label: Columbia

Produced by: Vini Poncia

Year: 1983

Early MTV hit with a do-it-yourself attitude and one of the great New York street girl voices of rock and roll, Patty Smyth, who married the similarly legendary Richard Hell. Later on she would divorce Hell, duet with Don Henley, and marry John McEnroe.

GOODBYE YELLOW BRICK ROAD

Artist: Elton John

Written by: Elton John, Bernie Taupin

From the album: *Goodbye Yellow Brick Road*

Label: MCA

Produced by: Gus Dudgeon

Year: 1973

Elton and Bernie's Hollywood fixation, Part II.

GOODNIGHT IRENE

Artist: The Weavers

Written by: Huddie Ledbetter, John Lomax

Label: Decca

Produced by: Milt Gabler

Year: 1950

Performed in prison by Leadbelly in 1933, the B-side of the Weavers' first hit, "Tzena Tzena Tzena," outdid the A-side by reaching #1. Through the '50s, several Leadbelly tunes would achieve visibility through the pioneering work of the Weavers; in the '60s he'd become a generational hero, along with Weavers leader Pete Seeger.

GOODNIGHT MY LOVE

Artist: Jesse Belvin

Written by: George Motola, Jesse Belvin

Label: Modern

Produced by: George Motola

Year: 1951

Out of L.A.'s Compton section—a generation away from spawning gangsta rap—Belvin's ballad would become DJ Alan Freed's closing theme in New York. Belvin's other masterwork, "Earth Angel," would become a doo-wop anthem.

GOODNIGHT SAIGON

Artist: Billy Joel

Written by: Billy Joel

From the album: *The Nylon Curtain*

Label: Columbia

Produced by: Phil Ramone

Year: 1982

Suggested segue: "Still in Saigon" by the Charlie Daniels Band.

GOODNIGHT SWEET JOSEPHINE

Artist: The Yardbirds

Written by: Anthony Hazard

Label: Epic

Year: 1968

Their last single.

GOODNIGHT, SWEETHEART, GOODNIGHT

Artist: The Spaniels

Written by: Calvin Carter, James Hudson

From the album: *Goodnight, It's Time to Go*

Label: Vee-Jay

Produced by: Calvin Carter

Year: 1954

Their biggest R&B hit, a defining doo-wop gem.

GOODNIGHT TONIGHT

Artist: Paul McCartney and Wings

Written by: Paul McCartney, Linda McCartney

From the album: *All the Best*

Label: Capitol

Produced by: Paul McCartney

Year: 1979

11TH of 15 top 5 hits for McCartney's other group.

GOODY GOODY

Artist: Frankie Lymon
Written by: Johnny Mercer, Matt Melneck
From the album: *Rock and Roll*
Label: Gee
Produced by: George Goldner
Year: 1957
The preternaturally gifted boy soprano from Harlem lifts a tune from the catalogue of no-less-an-urban demigod than Frank Sinatra. The beginning and the end of Frankie's (Lymon that is) solo career.

GOODY TWO SHOES

Artist: Adam Ant
Written by: Stuart (Adam Ant) Goddard, Marco Pirroni
From the album: *Friend or Foe*
Label: Epic
Produced by: Adam Ant, Marco Pironi
Year: 1982
Made-for-MTV dance rock with a bad attitude.

GOT A HOLD ON ME

Artist: Christine McVie
Written by: Christine McVie, Todd Sharp
From the album: *Christine McVie*
Label: Warner Brothers
Produced by: Russ Titelman
Year: 1984
Taking a blues sabbatical from Fleetwood Mac.

GOT A JOB

Artist: The Miracles
Written by: Roquel Davis (Tyran Carlo), Berry Gordy Jr.
From the album: *Greatest Hits from the Beginning*
Label: End
Produced by: Berry Gordy Jr.
Year: 1958
A gateway to the Motown era, in which Berry Gordy would provide many fine black performers with gainful employment, none more gainfully than William "Smokey" Robinson.

GOT ME WAITING

Artist: Heavy D and the Boys
Written by: Heavy D, Luther Vandross, Pete Rock, C. L. Smooth.
From the album: *Nuttin' But Love*
Label: Uptown/MCA
Year: 1994
Back to the Top 20 after an absense of three years.

GOT MY MIND SET ON YOU

Artist: James Ray
Written by: Rudy Clark
Label: Dynamic Sound
Year: 1962
Same team that combined for the Top 10 R&B hit, "If You Gotta Make a Fool of Somebody." Covered by George Harrison (Dark Horse, '88).

GOT MY MOJO WORKING

Artist: Muddy Waters
Written by: Preston Foster
From the album: *Trouble No More*
Label: Chess
Year: 1956
Symbolizing the magical power of the blues, the mojo makes its first appearance, obtained by Muddy down in Louisiana, probably New Orleans. Covered by Manfred Mann (Ascot, '64), the Paul Butterfield Blues Band (Elektra, '64), Elvis Presley (RCA, '71).

GOT TO BE REAL

Artist: Cheryl Lynn
Written by: David Foster, Cheryl Lynn, David Paich
From the album: *Cheryl Lynn*
Label: Columbia
Produced by: Marty Paich, David Paich
Year: 1978
#1 R&B/Top 20 crossover for a graduate of *The Gong Show*. Ray Parker Jr. on guitar.

GOT TO BE THERE

Artist: Michael Jackson
Written by: Elliot Willensky
From the album: *Got to Be There*
Label: Motown
Produced by: Freddie Perren, Berry Gordy Jr., Deke Richards, Fonce Mizell
Year: 1971
Michael goes solo with a Top 5 R&B/Top 5 crossover.

GOT TO GET YOU INTO MY LIFE

Artist: The Beatles
Written by: John Lennon, Paul McCartney
From the album: *Revolver*
Label: Capitol
Produced by: George Martin
Year: 1966
First use of horns on a Beatle track.

GOT TO GET YOU OFF MY MIND

Artist: Solomon Burke
Written by: Solomon Burke, Delores Burke, J. B. Moore
From the album: *Best of Solomon Burke*
Produced by: Jerry Wexler
Label: Atlantic
Year: 1965
Breakup tune dedicated to the memory of Sam Cooke is his biggest hit.

GOT TO GIVE IT UP (PART I)

Artist: Marvin Gaye
Written by: Marvin Gaye
From the album: *Marvin Gaye Live at the London Palladium*
Label: Tamla
Produced by: Art Stewart
Year: 1977
Marvin enters the funk arena with a tribal chant.

GOT TO MOVE

Artist: Fleetwood Mac
Written by: Elmore James, Marshall Sehorn
From the album: *Fleetwood Mac*
Label: Reprise
Produced by: Keith Olson, Fleetwood Mac
Year: 1968
Blues standard by the influential guitarist Elmore James, best known for "The Sky Is Crying" and "I Believe I'll Dust My Broom."

GOTHAM CITY (THEME FROM *BATMAN*)

Artist: R. Kelly
Written by: Robert Kelly
From the album: *Batman and Robin Soundtrack*
Label: Warner Sunset
Produced by: R. Kelly
Year: 1997
The infamous love man in a socially conscious mode.

GOTTA HOLD ON TO THIS FEELING

Artist: Jr. Walker and the All-Stars
Written by: Pam Sawyer, Johnny Bristol, Joe Hinton
From the album: *What Does It Take to Win Your Love*
Label: Soul
Year: 1970
Motown horn man's most compelling riff.

GOTTA SERVE SOMEBODY

Artist: Bob Dylan
Written by: Bob Dylan
From the album: *Slow Train Coming*
Label: Columbia
Produced by: Jerry Wexler, Barry Beckett
Year: 1979
Entering his controversial religious phase. But with Dylanology a moribund industry at that point, his every move and verbal nuance no longer causing the world to instantly react and ponder, it was only relatively controversial.

GOTTA TRAVEL ON

Artist: The Weavers
Written by: Pete Seeger, Lee Hayes, Fred Hellerman, Dave Lazar, Ronnie Gilbert, Paul Clayton, Larry Ehrlich
From the album: *Travelin' on with the Weavers*
Label: Vanguard
Produced by: Milt Gabler
Year: 1958

Essential rambling classic from the folk repertoire. Cover by Billy Grammar (Monument, '58) was a rare Top 20 R&B/Top 10 country/Top 10 crossover.

GRACE

Artist: Jeff Buckley
Written by: Jeff Buckley, Gary Lucas
From the album: *Grace*
Produced by: Andy Wallace
Label: Columbia
Year: 1994
Blissful, doomed falsetto, just like his father Tim.

GRACELAND

Artist: Paul Simon
Written by: Paul Simon
From the album: *Graceland*
Label: Warner Brothers
Produced by: Paul Simon
Year: 1986
Simon achieves a state of rock and roll grace, with this father-and-son rambling song.

GRADUATION DAY

Artist: The Four Freshmen
Written by: Joe Sherman, Noel Sherman
From the album: *Freshman Favorites*
Label: Capitol
Year: 1956
Approaching their various graduation days, in high school and junior high school in Hawthorne, California, the Wilson family, aka the Beach Boys, would soon reinvent these ethereal harmonies to apply to the '60s teen dream of surf and turf. Covered by the Arbors (Date, '67).

GRATITUDE

Artist: Ani DiFranco
Written by: Ani DiFranco
From the album: *Not So Soft*
Label: Righteous Babe
Produced by: Ani DiFranco
Year: 1991
New voice of women's lib in the post-lib era.

GRAVITY OF THE SITUATION

Artist: Vic Chesnutt
Written by: Vic Chesnutt
From the album: *Is the Actor Happy*
Produced by: John Keane
Label: Texas Hotel
Year: 1995
From the Southern singer/songwriter's best album.

GRAZING IN THE GRASS

Artist: Hugh Masekela
Written by: Harry Elston, Philemon Hou
From the album: *The Promise of a Future*
Label: Uni
Produced by: Stewart Levine
Year: 1968
#1 R&B/#1 crossover instrumental by the South African trumpeter is based on a Zambian song. Vocal version by the Friends of Distinction (RCA, '69) was a Top 10 R&B/Top 10 crossover, with tongue-twisting lyrics by group member Harry Elston.

GREASE

Artist: Frankie Valli
Written by: Barry Gibb
From the album: *Grease The Original Soundtrack*
Label: RSO
Produced by: Barry Gibb, Albhy Galuten, Karl Richardson
Year: 1978
With the title tune from the movie version of the '50s musical, Valli hits a personal singles peak.

GREASY HEART

Artist: Jefferson Airplane
Written by: Grace Slick
From the album: *Crown of Creation*
Label: RCA
Produced by: Al Schmitt
Year: 1968
Typically antagonistic antilove song helmed by Grace Slick, filled with bile and cholesterol.

GREAT BALLS OF FIRE

Artist: Jerry Lee Lewis
Written by: Otis Blackwell, Jack Hammer
From the album: *Jerry Lee's Greatest Hits*
Label: Sun
Produced by: Sam Phillips
Year: 1957
Following up his #1 country/#1 R&B/Top 5 crossover cover of Roy Hall's (and Big Maybelle's) "Whole Lotta Shakin'," Jerry Lee and his pumping piano get another triple crossover. Covered by Tiny Tim (Reprise, '69).

GREAT BEYOND, THE

Artist: R.E.M.
Written by: Michael Stipe, Peter Buck and Mike Mills
From the album: *Man on the Moon Soundtrack*
Label: Warner Brothers
Produced by: Patrick McCarthy
Year: 1999
Impressionistic tribute to Andy Kauffman and Sir Isaac Newton.

GREAT GIG IN THE SKY, THE

Artist: Pink Floyd
Written by: Roger Waters, Richard Wright
From the album: *Dark Side of the Moon*
Produced by: Pink Floyd
Label: Harvest
Year: 1973
From the album that stayed on the charts longer than 99 percent of all rock star's careers: nearly fifteen years!

GREAT GOSH A MIGHTY

Artist: Little Richard
Written by: Richard Penniman (Little Richard), Billy Preston
From the album: *Lifetime Friend*
Label: Warner Brothers
Produced by: Dan Hartman, Billy Preston
Year: 1986
Out of religious retirement and into heavy makeup, this comeback track was in the movie *Down and Out in Beverly Hills*.

GREAT MANDELLA, THE

Artist: Peter, Paul and Mary
Written by: Peter Yarrow
From the album: *Album 1700*
Label: Warner Brothers
Produced by: Albert Grossman, Milt Okun
Year: 1967
Best of Yarrow's folk/rock philosophizing.

GREAT PRETENDER, THE

Artist: The Platters
Written by: Buck Ram
From the album: *Encore of Golden Hits*
Label: Mercury
Produced by: Buck Ram
Year: 1955
The quintessential R&B love ballad, under the hand of Buck Ram and the vocal chords of Tony Williams, takes on a stately grandeur, gaining the Platters their first #1 R&B/#1 crossover.

GREATEST LOVE OF ALL, THE

Artist: George Benson
Written by: Linda Creed, Michael Masser
From the album: *Weekend in L.A.*
Label: Warner Brothers
Produced by: Michael Masser
Year: 1977
Empowering theme from Muhammed Ali's biopic—*The Greatest*—is a treatise on children, self-respect, and the love of life, with lyrics by a Philly soul songwriting legend, Creed, who died of cancer at the age of thirty-eight, just as Whitney Houston's cover (Arista '85) was peaking at #1.

GREEN

Artist: Throwing Muses
Written by: Kristen Hersh
From the album: *Throwing Muses*
Label: 4AD
Produced by: Gil Norton
Year: 1986
The Paisley Underground, Northeast quadrant.

GREEN DAY

Artist: Green Day
Written by: Billy Joe Armstrong, Green Day
From the album: *1039/Smoothed Out*
Label: Lookout
Produced by: Andy Ernst, Green Day
Year: 1991
Introducing their brand of playful punk posturing.

GREEN DOOR, THE

Artist: Jim Lowe
Written by: Bob Davie, Marvin Moore
From the album: *Songs Behind the Green Door*
Label: Dot
Year: 1956
Suggested segue: "Party Lights" by Claudine Clark.

GREEN EYED LADY

Artist: Sugarloaf
Written by: Jerry Corbetta, J. C. Phillips, David Riordan
From the album: *Sugarloaf*
Label: Liberty
Produced by: Frank Slay
Year: 1970

GREEN GRASS AND HIGH TIDES

Artist: The Outlaws
Written by: Hugh Thomasson
From the album: *Outlaws*
Label: Arista
Produced by: Paul Rothschild
Year: 1975
Southern rock guitar extravaganza.

GREEN MANILISHI (WITH THE TWO PRONGED CROWN), THE

Artist: Fleetwood Mac
Written by: Peter Green
From the album: *Best of British Rock: Live in Concert The Roots of Fleetwood Mac*
Label: Pair
Produced by: Mike Vernon
Year: 1969
Bravura blues excursion, covered by Judas Priest (Epic, 1979).

GREEN ONIONS

Artist: Booker T. and the MG's
Written by: Steve Cropper, Booker T. Jones, Al Jackson Jr., Lewis Steinberg.
From the album: *Green Onions*
Label: Stax
Produced by: Jim Stewart
Year: 1962
Soul food by the house band at Stax.

GREEN RIVER

Artist: Creedence Clearwater Revival
Written by: John C. Fogerty
From the album: *Green River*
Label: Fantasy
Produced by: John C. Fogerty
Year: 1969
Choogling boogie.

GREEN TAMBOURINE

Artist: The Lemon Pipers
Written by: Shelley Pinz, Paul Leka
From the album: *Green Tambourine*
Label: Buddah
Produced by: Paul Leka
Year: 1967
Psychedelic bubblegum ditty spotlights an era when playing music and panhandling were often indistinguishable.

GREENBACK DOLLAR

Artist: The Kingston Trio
Written by: Hoyt Axton, Ken Ramsey
From the album: *New Frontier*
Label: Capitol
Produced by: Voile Gillmore
Year: 1963
Essential anticapitalist folk sentiments that would briefly be taken to the level of lifestyle in the late '60s.

GREENFIELDS

Artist: The Brothers Four
Written by: Terry Gilkyson, Rick Dehr, Frank Miller
From the album: *The Brothers Four*
Label: Columbia
Year: 1960
Ecologically correct folk standard, written by Terry Gilkyson and the Easy Riders, of "Marianne" fame.

GRINDING PROCESS

Artist: The Melvins
Written by: the Melvins
From the album: *Deep Six*
Label: C/Z
Year: 1985
Early echoes of the Seattle scene as it moved from sludge to grunge.

GROOM'S STILL WAITING AT THE ALTAR, THE

Artist: Bob Dylan
Written by: Bob Dylan
Label: Columbia
Produced by: Chuck Plotkin, Bob Dylan
Year: 1981
Passionate non-album cut was the nearest thing to classic Dylan since "Highway 61 Revisited."

GROOVE IS IN THE HEART

Artist: Deee-Lite
Written by: Deee-Lite, Herbie Hancock, John Davis
From the album: *World Clique*
Label: Elektra
Produced by: Deee-Lite
Year: 1990
B-52's of the '90s, transplanted to New York's high-disco society. Q-Tip supplies the rap.

GROOVE ME BABY

Artist: King Floyd
Written by: King Floyd
Label: Chimneyville
Produced by: Quardell Quezerque
Year: 1970
#1 R&B/Top 10 crossover from New Orleans.

GROOVIN'

Artist: The Rascals
Written by: Felix Cavaliere, Edward Brigati Jr.
From the album: *Groovin'*
Label: Atlantic
Produced by: The Rascals
Year: 1967
The Rascals at their grooviest, with a groove based on a Cuban dance rhythm called baion. Covered by Aretha Franklin (Atlantic, '68).

GROOVIN' IS EASY

Artist: Electric Flag
Written by: Nick Gravenites, Ron Polte
From the album: *A Long Time Comin'*
Label: Columbia
Produced by: John Court
Year: 1968
Led by ex-Paul Butterfield blues guitarist, Mike Bloomfield, some prime Chicago noodling.

GROOVY KIND OF LOVE, A

Artist: The Mindbenders
Written by: Toni Wine, Carole Bayer
From the album: *A Groovy Kind of Love*
Label: Fontana
Year: 1966
In the late Brill Building mix and match tradition by two writers who'd achieve considerably more fame collaborating with others. Covered by Phil Collins (Atlantic, '88).

GROUP SEX

Artist: The Circle Jerks
Written by: Jeffrey Pierce, Greg Hetson, Keith Lehrer, Keith Morris, Roger Downing
From the album: *Group Sex*
Label: Frontier
Produced by: Cary Markoff, Circle Jerks
Year: 1980
L.A. Punk confidential.

GROWIN' UP

Artist: Bruce Springsteen
Written by: Bruce Springsteen
From the album: *Greetings from Asbury Park*
Label: Columbia
Produced by: Jim Cretecos, Mike Appel
Year: 1973
An American original strafes his old high school with Dylanesque word play and Spectorian over-statement.

GROWIN' UP IN THE HOOD

Artist: Compton's Most Wanted
Written by: Terry Allen, Andre Manuel, Joe Simon, Aaron Tyler
From the album: *Straight Checkn Em*
Label: Orpheus/Epic
Produced by: Big Beat Productions
Year: 1991
The voice of gangsta rap gets national visibility in the movie *Boyz in the Hood*, the 'hood in question, the Compton section of L.A.

GUANTANAMERA

Artist: The Weavers
Written by: Pete Seeger, Hector Angelo, Jose Marti
From the album: *Reunion at Carnegie Hall*
Label: Vanguard
Produced by: Milt Gabler
Year: 1963
A freedom song, translated by the major voice of the '60s generational conscience, Pete Seeger, and presented in a rousing concert of triumph, by his first group, the Weavers. Covered by the Sandpipers (A&M, '66).

GUDBYE T'JANE

Artist: Slade
Written by: Noddy Holder, Jim Lea
From the album: *Slayed*
Label: Polydor
Produced by: Chas Chandler
Year: 1973
Sludge meets glam outside the arena, gives it a black eye.

GUESS THINGS HAPPEN THAT WAY

Artist: Johnny Cash
Written by: Jack Clement
From the album: *Johnny Cash Sings the Songs That Made Him Famous*
Label: Sun
Produced by: Sam Phillips
Year: 1958
His second straight #1 country/Top 15 crossover.

GUILTY

Artist: Bonnie Raitt
Written by: Randy Newman
From the album: *Takin' My Time*
Label: Warner Brothers
Produced by: John Hall
Year: 1973
Bonnie turns Newman's neuroticism into bar-room blues. Covered by Randy Newman (Warner Brothers, '74).

GUILTY BY ASSOCIATION

Artist: Vic Chesnutt
Written by: Vic Chesnutt
From the album: *Is the Actor Happy*
Produced by: John Keane
Label: Texas Hotel
Year: 1995
Legendary underground poet finds his voice in this dirge.

GUITAR AND PEN

Artist: The Who
Written by: Pete Townshend
From the album: *Who Are You*
Label: MCA
Produced by: Glyn Johns, Jon Astley
Year: 1978
The other side of Pete Townshend.

GUITAR BOOGIE SHUFFLE

Artist: Arthur Smith and His Crackerjacks
Written by: Arthur Smith
Label: Superdisc
Year: 1946
Covered in 1959, the year of the instrumental, by the Virtues (Hunt, '59). Suggested segue: "Guitar Jamboree" by Chris Spedding (RAK, '76).

GUITAR MAN

Artist: Jerry Reed
Written by: Jerry Reed
From the album: *The Unbelievable Guitar and Voice of Jerry Reed*
Label: RCA
Produced by: Chet Atkins
Year: 1967
Stiffed on the country chart, but the cover by Elvis Presley became his last #1 country hit, crossing over to the Top 40 in '68 and '81.

GUITAR TOWN

Artist: Steve Earle
Written by: Steve Earle
From the album: *Guitar Town*
Label: MCA
Produced by: Tony Brown, Emory Gordy Jr.
Year: 1986
An alt-country rocker without peer.

GYPSIES, TRAMPS AND THIEVES

Artist: Cher
Written by: Robert Stone
From the album: *Gypsies, Tramps and Thieves*
Label: Kapp
Produced by: Snuff Garrett
Year: 1971
One of Garrett's favorite productions, originally entitled "Gypsies and White Trash."

GYPSY

Artist: Fleetwood Mac
Written by: Stephanie Nicks
From the album: *Mirage*
Label: Warner Brothers
Produced by: Richard Dashut, Lindsay Buckingham, Ken Caillet, Fleetwood Mac
Year: 1982
Stevie Nicks steps front and center for her defining metaphor.

GYPSY

Artist: Suzanne Vega
Written by: Suzanne Vega
From the album: *Solitude Standing*
Label: A&M
Produced by: Lenny Kaye, Steve Addabbo
Year: 1987
A Washington Square acoustic throwback in '80s dress.

GYPSY, THE

Artist: The Ink Spots
Written by: Billy Reid
Label: Decca
Year: 1946
Landmark single for the landmark black harmony group that would influence a doo-wop generation. It was their second 1 R&B/#1 crossover, spending ten weeks atop the pop charts. Taking special note of Jerry Daniels lead singing were Jimmy Ricks of the Ravens and Sonny Til of the Orioles (as well as Curtis Mayfield of the Impressions). Covered by Sam Cooke (RCA, '65).

GYPSY LIFE, THE

Artist: John Gorka
Written by: John Gorka
From the album: *Temporary Road*
Label: High Street
Produced by: Dawn Atkinson, Steven Miller
Year: 1992
Folk/rock rambling gem, defining the new Americana radio format of the '90s. Backing vocal by Nanci Griffith.

GYPSY MAN

Artist: War
Written by: Sylvester Allen, Lee Oscar Levitin, Morris Dickerson, Leroy "Lonnie" Jordan, Howard Scott, Charles W. Miller, Harold R. Brown
From the album: *Deliver the Word*
Label: United Artists
Produced by: Jerry Goldstein
Year: 1973
Top 10 R&B/Top 10 crossover.

GYPSY WOMAN

Artist: The Impressions
Written by: Curtis Mayfield
From the album: *The Impressions*
Label: ABC-Paramount
Produced by: Curtis Mayfield
Year: 1961
Their first R&B/crossover, inspired by the Ink Spots. Covered by Brian Hyland (Uni, '70).

GYPSY WOMAN (SHE'S HOMELESS)

Artist: Crystal Waters
Written by: Crystal Waters, Neil Conway
From the album: *Surprise*
Label: Mercury
Produced by: The Basement Boys
Year: 1991
Tragic urban scenario that you could dance to.

H

HAIL, HAIL ROCK 'N' ROLL

Artist: Garland Jeffreys
Written by: Garland Jeffreys
From the album: *Don't Call Me Buckwheat*
Label: RCA
Produced by: Garland Jeffreys
Year: 1991
One man's history of rock and roll, and race relations.

HAIR

Artist: James Rado, Gerome Ragni and Company
Written by: James Rado, Gerome Ragni, Galt MacDermot
From the album: *Hair! A Tribal Rock Musical*
Label: RCA
Produced by: Andy Wiswell
Year: 1967
Dominating the charts like no musical before or since, this is one of four Top 5 singles to emerge from the countercultural rock opera in 1969—in a version by the Cowsills (MGM '69)—including the year's number one song, "Aquarius/Let the Sun Shine In" by the Fifth Dimension.

HAIR OF THE DOG

Artist: Nazareth
Written by: Nazareth
From the album: *Hair of the Dog*
Label: A&M
Produced by: Manny Charlton
Year: 1975
The rock and roll condition, personified.

HAIRSPRAY

Artist: Rachel Sweet
Written by: Rachel Sweet, Anthony Battaglea, Willa Bassen
From the album: *Hairspray Soundtrack*
Label: MCA
Produced by: Kenny Vance
Year: 1988
Akron's punk princess finds her milieu, a decade too late, in this classic film about rock and roll and race in Baltimore in the early '60s.

HALF A MIND

Artist: The Holy Modal Rounders
Written by: Peter Stampfel
From the album: *Moray Eels Eat the Holy Modal Rounders*
Label: Elektra
Produced by: Frazier Mohawk
Year: 1965
Legendary old-time good-time folkies' most dangerous concept.

HALF-BREED

Artist: Cher
Written by: Mary Dean, Al Capps
From the album: *Half-Breed*
Label: MCA
Produced by: Snuff Garrett
Year: 1973
Her biggest hit, sans Sonny.

HALF MOON

Artist: Janis Joplin
Written by: John Hall
From the album: *Pearl*
Label: Columbia
Produced by: Paul Rothchild
Year: 1970
Janis at her rock-teasing best.

HALLELUJAH

Artist: Leonard Cohen
Written by: Leonard Cohen
From the album: *Various Positions*
Produced by: John Lissauer
Label: Columbia
Year: 1985
Worth the two years it took to write.

HALLELUJAH, I LOVE HER SO

Artist: Ray Charles
Written by: Ray Charles
From the album: *Ray Charles*
Label: Atlantic
Produced by: Ahmet Ertegun, Jerry Wexler
Year: 1956
One of the great modern gospel performances. Covered by Peggy Lee (Capitol, '59), the Quarrymen (Lost Gold, '60).

HAMMOND SONG

Artist: The Roches
Written by: Maggie Roche
From the album: *The Roches*
Label: Warner Brothers
Produced by: Robert Fripp
Year: 1979
Sisterly harmony trio achieve critical mass with this litany of parental warnings tied to a sojourn at a Kung Fu temple in Hammond, Louisiana. In Atlanta, the Indigo Girls were listening; in San Francisco, so were the Bangles.

HAND IN GLOVE

Artist: The Smiths
Written by: Stephen Morrissey, Johnny Marr
From the album: *The Smiths*
Label: Sire
Produced by: The Smiths
Year: 1984
First single for the British nerd prince of melancholy, Stephen Morrissey and his cohorts. Covered by Sandi Shaw (Rough Trade, '84).

HAND IN MY POCKET

Artist: Alanis Morissette
Written by: Glen Ballard, Alanis Morisette
From the album: *Jagged Little Pill*
Label: Maverick
Produced by: Glen Ballard
Year: 1995
With a trigger finger on a can of Mace.

HAND OF KINDNESS

Artist: Richard Thompson
Written by: Richard Thompson
From the album: *Hand of Kindness*
Label: Hannibal
Produced by: Joe Boyd
Year: 1983
Hiding a razor blade.

HANDBAGS AND GLADRAGS

Artist: Rod Stewart
Written by: Mike D'Abo
From the album: *The Rod Stewart Album*
Label: Mercury
Produced by: Lou Reizner
Year: 1969
Unsparing Rod, with a classic drizzly Limey epic. Suggested segue: "She's Leaving Home" by the Beatles.

HANDLE WITH CARE

Artist: Traveling Wilburys
Written by: The Traveling Wilburys
From the album: *Traveling Wilburys (Vol. I)*
Label: Wilbury
Produced by: Jeff Lynne, George Harrison
Year: 1988
Biggest hit for the inspired one-off consisting of George Harrison, Bob Dylan, Tom Petty and Roy Orbison.

HANDS TO HEAVEN

Artist: Breathe
Written by: Dave Glaspar, Marcus Lillington
From the album: *All That Jazz*
Label: A&M
Produced by: Bob Sergeant
Year: 1988
In the Paul Weller/Spandau Ballet neo-soul groove, this plaintive ballad was their first and biggest hit.

HANDSOME JOHNNY

Artist: Richie Havens
Written by: Richie Havens, Lou Gossett
From the album: *Mixed Bag*
Label: Verve/Forecast
Produced by: Jerry Schoenbaum
Year: 1967
From the Revolutionary War through Vietnam, a ringing protest. Richie got a standing ovation that lasted through two commercial breaks when he sang it on *The Johnny Carson Show*.

HANDY MAN

Artist: Jimmy Jones
Written by: Otis Blackwell, Jimmy Jones
Label: Cub
Produced by: Otis Blackwell
Year: 1960
Marvelous falsetto. Covered by James Taylor (Columbia, '77).

HANG 'EM HIGH

Artist: Booker T. and the MG's
Written by: Jack Gold, Phil Zeller, Dominic Frontiere
From the album: *Soul Limbo*
Label: Stax
Produced by: Booker T. and the MG's
Year: 1968
Spaghetti soul, from the film.

HANG ON IN THERE BABY

Artist: Johnny Bristol
Written by: Johnny Bristol
From the album: *Hang on in There Baby*
Label: MGM
Produced by: Johnny Bristol
Year: 1974
Best-selling solo effort from the former Motown producer/writer.

HANG ON ST. CHRISTOPHER

Artist: Tom Waits
Written by: Tom Waits
From the album: *Frank's Wild Years*
Label: Island
Produced by: Tom Waits
Year: 1987

HANG ON TO YOUR EGO

Artist: The Beach Boys
From the album: *Pet Sounds*
Label: Capitol
Produced by: Brian Wilson
Year: 1966
A picture of Brian, drifting out with the tide. First appears on the album as "I Know There's an Answer." The CD reissue contains the original lyrics.

HANG UP MY ROCK AND ROLL SHOES

Artist: Chuck Willis
Written by: Chuck Willis
Label: Atlantic
Produced by: Zenas "Big Daddy" Sears
Year: 1958
B-side of "What Am I Living For." Not the first rocker to contemplate the choice of selling out, buying in, or going your own way. Would die before he'd get the chance to make that decision.

HANGAR 18

Artist: Megadeth
Written by: Dave Mustaine
From the album: *Maximum Megadeth*
Label: Capitol
Produced by: Maximus
Year: 1991
Where the US government keeps its aliens (and retired heavy metal bands) buried.

HANGIN' ON TO THE GOOD TIMES

Artist: Little Feat
Written by: Bill Payne, Paul Barrere, Fred Tacket, Craig Fuller
From the album: *Let It Roll*
Label: Warner Brothers
Produced by: Billy Payne, George Massenburg
Year: 1988
Poignant reunion song. Suggested segues: "Back Where It All Begins" by the Allman Brothers, "It's Been a Long Time" by Southside Johnny & the Asbury Jukes.

HANGIN' TOUGH

Artist: New Kids on the Block
Written by: Larry Johnson (Maurice Starr)
From the album: *Hangin' Tough*
Label: Columbia
Produced by: Maurice Starr
Year: 1988
Second straight #1. The B-side was a cover of the Delfonics' "Didn't I Blow Your Mind This Time."

HANGINAROUND

Artist: Counting Crows
Written by: Adam Duritz, David Bryson, Dan Vickrey, Ben Mize
From the album: *This Desert Life*
Label: DGC
Produced by: David Lowery, Dennis Herring
Year: 1999

HANGING BY A MOMENT

Artist: Lifehouse
Written by: Jason Wade
From the album: *No Name Face*
Produced by: Ron Aniello
Label: Dreamworks
Year: 2000
Christian rock crossovers, like Creed, with a huge radio track.

HANGING ON THE TELEPHONE

Artist: The Nerves
Written by: Jack Lee
From the album: *Nerves*
Label: Nerves
Year: 1976
A moment of glory for Peter Case's power pop partner, Jack Lee; Blondie's cover (Chrysalis, '79) was their third UK hit.

HANKY PANKY

Artist: Madonna
Written by: Patrick Leonard, Madonna Ciccone
From the album: *I'm Breathless*
Label: Sire
Produced by: Patrick Leonard, Madonna
Year: 1990
Not the same kind of thing Ellie Greenwich had in mind.

HANKY PANKY

Artist: The Raindrops
Written by: Jeff Barry, Ellie Greenwich
From the album: *The Raindrops*
Label: Jubilee
Produced by: Jeff Barry, Ellie Greenwich
Year: 1963
B-side of "That Boy John." Covered by the Shondels (Swap, '63). Re-release by Tommy James & the Shondels (Roulette, '66) was a hit.

HAPPENING, THE

Artist: Diana Ross and the Supremes
Written by: Eddie Holland, Lamont Dozier, Brian Holland
From the album: *Supremes' Greatest Hits*
Label: Motown
Produced by: Brian Holland, Lamont Dozier
Year: 1967
Their tenth #1 hit, and the first as "Diana Ross and the Supremes," is the title song of a lame movie.

HAPPENINGS TEN YEARS TIME AGO

Artist: The Yardbirds
Written by: Keith Relf, James McCarty, Jeff Beck, Jimmy Page

From the album: *Yardbirds' Greatest Hits*
Label: Epic
Produced by: Simon Napier-Bell
Year: 1966
Beck and Page in a rare collaboration.

HAPPIER BLUE

Artist: Chris Smither
Written by: Chris Smither
From the album: *Happier Blue*
Produced by: John Nagy
Label: Flying Fish
Year: 1993
Definer and prime practictioner of smooth blues.

HAPPINESS IS A WARM GUN

Artist: The Beatles
Written by: John Lennon, Paul McCartney
From the album: *The Beatles*
Label: Apple
Produced by: George Martin
Year: 1968
Subversive gem from Lennon. Covered by the Breeders (4AD, '90), Karl Wallinger (Chrysalis, '92).

HAPPY

Artist: The Rolling Stones
Written by: Mick Jagger, Keith Richards
From the album: *Exile on Main Street*
Label: Rolling Stones
Produced by: Jimmy Miller
Year: 1972
Keith writing against title and type.

HAPPY BIRTHDAY

Artist: Altered Images
Written by: Altered Images
From the album: Happy Birthday
Produced by: Martin Rushent
Label: Epic
Year: 1981
Early video age romp from England. In America, Patty Smyth of Scandal was vamping in the wings.

HAPPY BIRTHDAY, SWEET SIXTEEN

Artist: Neil Sedaka
Written by: Howard Greenfield, Neil Sedaka
From the album: *Neil Sedaka Sings His Greatest Hits*
Label: RCA Victor
Produced by: Al Nevins, Don Kirshner
Year: 1961
Quintessential song of the quintessential rock and roll age.

HAPPY DAYS

Artist: Pratt and McLain
Written by: Norman Gimbel, Charles Fox

From the album: *Pratt and McLain Featuring Happy Days*
Label: Reprise
Produced by: Steve Barri, Michael Omartian
Year: 1976
Theme from the '70s TV show celebrating the '50s.

HAPPY GO LUCKY ME

Artist: Paul Evans
Written by: Al Byron, Paul Evans
Label: Guaranteed
Year: 1960
Good time music, a few years too soon.

HAPPY, HAPPY BIRTHDAY BABY

Artist: The Tune Weavers
Written by: Margo Sylvia, Gilbert Lopez
Label: Checker
Year: 1957
Essential doo-wop. Segue: "I Don't Want to Spoil the Party" by the Beatles.

HAPPY HOUR

Artist: The Housemartins
Written by: Paul D. Heaton, Stan Cullimore
From the album: *London 0 Hull 4*
Label: Elektra
Produced by: John Williams
Year: 1986
Lift a glass to the first UK hit for the literate popsters, spiritual cousins of Prefab Sprout, and the Christians.

HAPPY JACK

Artist: The Who
Written by: Pete Townshend
From the album: *Happy Jack*
Label: Decca
Produced by: Kit Lambert
Year: 1967
Creating a semifolk hero.

HAPPY ORGAN, THE

Artist: Dave "Baby" Cortez
Written by: Ken Wood, David Clowney
From the album: *Dave "Baby" Cortez and the Happy Organ*
Label: Clock
Produced by: Dave "Baby" Cortez
Year: 1959
Celebrating the Hammond B-3 sound that would influence a generation of suburban garage bands on two continents.

HAPPY PEOPLE

Artist: The Temptations
Written by: Lionel B. Richie, Jeffrey Bowen, Donald Baldwin
From the album: *A Song for You*

Label: Gordy
Produced by: Norman Whitfield
Year: 1974
Their thirteenth and last #1 R&B hit.

HAPPY TOGETHER

Artist: The Turtles
Written by: Garry Bonner, Alan Gordon
From the album: *Happy Together*
Label: White Whale
Produced by: Joe Wissert
Year: 1967
Their biggest hit; California bubblegum at its finest.

HARD AS A ROCK

Artist: AC/DC
Written by: Angus Young, Malcolm Young
From the album: *Ballbreaker*
Produced by: Rick Rubin
Label: Atlantic
Year: 1995

HARD DAY'S NIGHT, A

Artist: The Beatles
Written by: John Lennon, Paul McCartney
From the album: *A Hard Days Night*
Label: United Artists
Produced by: George Martin
Year: 1964
Title song from the movie that established the Beatles as worthy of attention from the cynical folk/rock-leaning/Jean-Luc-Godard-enthralled intelligentsia.

HARD HABIT TO BREAK

Artist: Chicago
Written by: Stephen Kipner, John Parker
From the album: *17*
Label: Full Moon
Produced by: David Foster
Year: 1984
Full in their easy listening stride; their 14TH Top 10 hit.

HARD KNOCK LIFE

Artist: Jay Z
Written by: Shawn Carter, Mark James, Charles Strouse, Martin Charnin
From the album: *Hard Knock Life*
Label: Roc-A-Fella
Year: 1998
Unlikely urchins unite in the mind of a rapper who is unafraid to reveal his show music proclivities.

HARD LOVE

Artist: Claudia Schmidt
Written by: Bob Franke
From the album: *New Goodbyes, Old Hellos*
Label: Flying Fish
Produced by: Claudia Schmidt, Michael Pasfield
Year: 1983

New folk classic as interpreted by one of the scene's more powerful voices. The writer's version, recorded live at a half-empty coffee house, sounds like Phil Ochs with a head cold.

HARD LOVIN' LOSER

Artist: Richard and Mimi Fariña
Written by: Richard Fariña
From the album: *Reflections in a Crystal Wind*
Label: Vanguard
Year: 1966
The only chart record for the author of the Pynchonesque novel, *Been Down So Long It Looks Like Up to Me*, arrived for a cup of coffee at #97 courtesy of Judy Collins (Elektra, '67) about a year after Fariña had been killed in a motorcycle accident coming home from his book publication party.

HARD LUCK WOMAN

Artist: Kiss
Written by: Stanley Eisen (Paul Stanley)
From the album: *Rock and Roll Over*
Label: Casablanca
Produced by: Eddie Kramer
Year: 1976
Covered by Garth Brooks (Polygram, '94).

HARD RAIN'S A-GONNA FALL, A

Artist: Bob Dylan
Written by: Bob Dylan
From the album: *The Freewheelin' Bob Dylan*
Label: Columbia
Produced by: John Hammond
Year: 1963
About as rabid and riotous (and boisterous and Biblical) a departure from the pop (and antiwar folk singing) norm as you could hear before 1964. Covered by Bryan Ferry (Reprise, '89), Edie Brickell in the movie *Born on the 4th of July* (MCA, '89).

HARD TO HANDLE

Artist: Otis Redding
Written by: Otis Redding, Alvertis Isbell, Booker T. Jones
From the album: *Immortal Otis Redding*
Label: Volt
Produced by: Steve Cropper
Year: 1968
Intense and rocking B-side of "Amen." Covered by the Black Crowes (Def American, '90). Featured in the '92 movie *The Commitments*.

HARD TO SAY I'M SORRY

Artist: Chicago
Written by: Peter Cetera, David Foster
From the album: *16*
Label: Full Moon
Produced by: David Foster
Year: 1982
Their second of three #1 songs. From the film *Summer Lovers*.

HARDEN MY HEART

Artist: Quarterflash
Written by: Marv Ross
From the album: *Quarterflash*
Label: Geffen
Produced by: John Boylan
Year: 1981
One shot hit from Oregon band.

HARDER THEY COME, THE

Artist: Jimmy Cliff
Written by: Jimmy Cliff
From the album: *The Harder They Come Soundtrack*
Label: Mango
Produced by: Jimmy Cliff
Year: 1972
Underclass anthem from the classic reggae movie and sampler.

HARDEST TIME, THE

Artist: Los Lobos
Written by: David Hidalgo, Louie Perez
From the album: *By the Light of the Moon*
Label: Slash
Produced by: T-Bone Burnette
Year: 1987
Ineffable Tex-Mex soul.

HARD-HEADED WOMAN

Artist: Elvis Presley
Written by: Claude De Metrius
From the album: *King Creole*
Label: RCA
Produced by: Steve Sholes
Year: 1958
His first million-selling single, from the Walter Matthau/Carolyn Jones movie *King Creole*. De Metrius had formerly collaborated with another legendary mover and shaker, Louis Jordan.

HARLEM NOCTURNE

Artist: Johnny Otis
Written by: Earl Hagen, Dick Rogers
Label: Savoy
Year: 1946
Haunting sax instrumental, originated by Randy Brooks in '40. Covered by the Viscounts (Madison, '60).

HARLEM SHUFFLE

Artist: Bob and Earl
Written by: Bob Reig, Earl Nelson
From the album: *Harlem Shuffle*
Label: Marc
Year: 1964
Covered by the Rolling Stones (Rolling Stones, '91).

HARPER VALLEY PTA, THE

Artist: Jeannie C. Riley
Written by: Tom T. Hall
From the album: *The Harper Valley PTA*

Label: Plantation
Produced by: Shelby Singleton
Year: 1968
Sudsy classic was a #1 country/#1 crossover, only the second since "Big Bad John" by Jimmy Dean in '61—Bobby Goldsboro having accomplished the same feat with "Honey" barely five months before. Became a movie in '78 and a TV series in '81.

HARVEST MOON

Artist: Neil Young
Written by: Neil Young
From the album: *Harvest Moon*
Label: Reprise
Produced by: David Briggs, Neil Young
Year: 1992
Answering his own earlier acoustic album, *Harvest* (Reprise, '72).

HATS OFF TO LARRY

Artist: Del Shannon
Written by: Del Shannon
From the album: *Little Town Flirt*
Label: Big Top
Produced by: Irving Micahnik, Harry Balk
Year: 1961
His trademark falsetto angst; his second biggest hit.

HAUNTED HOUSE

Artist: Johnny Fuller
Written by: Robert Geddins
Label: Specialty
Year: 1959
Halloween standard. Covered by Jumping Gene Simmons (Hi, '64).

HAVE A CIGAR

Artist: Pink Floyd
Written by: Roger Waters
From the album: *Wish You Were Here*
Label: Columbia
Year: 1975
From whence came "Which One's Pink?"

HAVE I THE RIGHT?

Artist: The Honeycombs
Written by: Alan Blaikley, Hard Blaikley
From the album: *Here Come the Honeycombs*
Label: Interphon
Produced by: Joe Meek
Year: 1965
Big international crossover.

HAVE I TOLD YOU LATELY

Artist: Van Morrison
Written by: Van Morrison
From the album: *Avalon Sunset*
Label: Mercury
Produced by: Van Morrison
Year: 1989
Moving from sacred to earthly heaven. Covered by Rod Stewart (Warner Brothers, '93) and Van in a

Grammy-winning duet with the Chieftains (RCA, '95).

HAVE MERCY BABY

Artist: The Dominoes
Written by: Billy Ward
Label: Federal
Year: 1952
From the stars of Alan Freed's early ground-breaking Cleveland soirees, this #1 R&B hit was the biggest of '52, kicking off a decade of dance music, culminating in the gyrations of "At the Hop" in '58 and "The Twist," '60–'62, which launched the first interracial dance craze of the postwar era. Covered by James Brown (King, '65).

HAVE MERCY JUDGE

Artist: Chuck Berry
Written by: Chuck Berry
From the album: *Back Home*
Label: Chess
Produced by: Leonard Chess, Phil Chess
Year: 1970
Introduced as a bluesman to Chess records by Muddy Waters, Berry displays his chops.

HAVE YOU EVER LOVED A WOMAN

Artist: Freddie King
Written by: Billy Myles
From the album: *Let's Hide Away and Dance Away*
Label: Federal
Produced by: Sonny Thompson
Year: 1962
Blues classic covered by Eric Clapton in Derek and the Dominos (Atco, '70).

HAVE YOU EVER SEEN THE RAIN?

Artist: Creedence Clearwater Revival
Written by: John C. Fogerty
From the album: *Pendulum*
Label: Fantasy
Produced by: John C. Fogerty
Year: 1970
Swamp rock during Biblical times.

HAVE YOU HEARD

Artist: John Mayall's Bluesbreakers
Written by: John Mayall
From the album: *John Mayall's Bluesbreakers*
Label: London
Produced by: Mike Vemon
Year: 1967
Noted British blues maven and bandleader gives Eric Clapton his first major guitar showcase.

HAVE YOU NEVER BEEN MELLOW

Artist: Olivia Newton-John
Written by: John Farrar
From the album: *Have You Never Been Mellow?*
Label: MCA
Produced by: John Farrar
Year: 1975
Top 10 country/#1 crossover ballad by the anti-Helen Reddy.

HAVE YOU SEEN HER

Artist: The Chi-Lites
Written by: Eugene Record
From the album: *(For God's Sake) Give More Power to the People*
Label: Brunswick
Produced by: Eugene Record
Year: 1971
#1 R&B/Top 10 and UK crossover.

HAVE YOU SEEN HER FACE?

Artist: The Byrds
Written by: Chris Hillman
From the album: *Younger Than Yesterday*
Label: Columbia
Produced by: Gary Usher
Year: 1966
The "American Beatles" answer to "I've Just Seen a Face" by the (genuine) Beatles.

HAVE YOU SEEN MY BABY

Artist: Randy Newman
Written by: Randy Newman
From the album: *12 Songs*
Produced by: Lenny Waronker
Label: Reprise
Year: 1970
Kicking off his second revered album. Covered by the Flamin' Groovies (Kama Sutra, '71), Ringo Starr (Apple, '73), the Walker Brothers (GTO, '77).

HAVE YOU SEEN THE SAUCERS?

Artist: Jefferson Airplane
Written by: Paul Kantner
From the album: *Thirty Seconds over Winterland*
Label: Grunt
Year: 1969
Kantner introduces an enduring obsession on a classic single. Suggested segue: "It Came out of the Sky" by Creedence Clearwater Revival.

HAVE YOU SEEN YOUR MOTHER, BABY, STANDING IN THE SHADOW

Artist: The Rolling Stones
Written by: Mick Jagger, Keith Richards
From the album: *Got Live If You Want It*
Label: London
Produced by: Andrew Loog-Oldham
Year: 1966
Their fifth Top 10 single to hit the charts in eleven months.

HAVEN'T GOT TIME FOR THE PAIN

Artist: Carly Simon
Written by: Carly Simon, Jacob Brackman
From the album: *Hotcakes*
Label: Elektra
Produced by: Richard Perry
Year: 1974
A yuppie credo, penned by Brackman, who'd once defined his generation in *Esquire* magazine. Carly would eventually define her generation by writing songs for Nora Ephron movies.

HAVING A PARTY

Artist: Sam Cooke
Written by: Sam Cooke
From the album: *The Best of Sam Cooke*
Label: RCA Victor
Produced by: Hugo and Luigi
Year: 1962
B-side of "Bring It on Home to Me." Covered by Rod Stewart (Warner Brothers, '94).

HAWAII 5-O

Artist: The Ventures
Written by: Mort Stevens
From the album: *Hawaii 5-O*
Label: Liberty
Produced by: Joe Saraceno
Year: 1969
Twangy TV theme returns the legendary surf guitar band to the Top 10 after five years.

HAWK (EL GAVILAN), THE

Artist: Marianne Faithfull
Written by: Kris Kristofferson
From the album: *Trouble in Mind*
Label: Island
Year: 1986
Anguished lament from the movie *Trouble in Mind* is a career peak for the singer and the author.

HAZEY JANE II

Artist: Nick Drake
Written by: Nick Drake
From the album: *Bryter Layer*
Label: Hannibal
Produced by: Joe Boyd
Year: 1970
Moody gem from the morose singer/songwriter. On the same album, "Hazey Jane I" wasn't half as good.

HAZY SHADE OF WINTER, A

Artist: Simon and Garfunkel
Written by: Paul Simon
From the album: *Bookends*
Label: Columbia
Produced by: Roy Halee, Paul Simon, Art Garfunkel
Year: 1968

Covered by the Bangles in the film *Less Than Zero* (Def Jam, '87).

HE AIN'T HEAVY … HE'S MY BROTHER

Artist: The Hollies
Written by: Bob Russell, Bobby Scott
From the album: *He Ain't Heavy … He's My Brother*
Label: Epic
Produced by: Ron Richards
Year: 1970
Flowery post-'60s anthem, with Elton John on piano.

HE GIVES US ALL HIS LOVE

Artist: Randy Newman
Written by: Randy Newman
From the album: *Sail Away*
Label: Reprise
Produced by: Russ Titelman, Lenny Waronker
Year: 1972
Became the theme for the movie *The Great American Smokeout*.

HE HIT ME (AND IT FELT LIKE A KISS)

Artist: The Crystals
Written by: Gerry Goffin, Carole King
From the album: *He's a Rebel*
Label: Philles
Produced by: Phil Spector
Year: 1963
Even the male-dominated atmosphere of "My Boyfriend's Back" and "Don't Say Nothing Bad (About My Baby)" a song like this seems unforgiveable. Covered, not surprisingly, by Hole (DGC, '95).

HE LOVES U NOT

Artist: Dream
Written by: Steve Kipner, David Frank, Pam Sheyne, H. Ousley
From the album: *It Was All a Dream*
Label: Jive
Produced by: David Frank, Steve Kipner
Year: 2000
A gaggle of white chicks at the dance.

HE WAS A FRIEND OF MINE

Artist: Bob Dylan
Written by: Bob Dylan
From the album: *The Freewheelin' Bob Dylan*
Label: Columbia
Produced by: John Hammond
Year: 1963
Eulogy to a rambling man. Covered by the Byrds (Columbia, '65).

HE WAS MY BROTHER

Artist: Simon and Garfunkel
Written by: Paul Simon (Paul Kane)
From the album: *Wednesday Morning 3 A.M.*
Label: Columbia
Produced by: Tom Wilson
Year: 1964
Stepping from his teenage role as a rock and roll entrepreneur, Paul Simon enters the folk/rock generation, although the tune, about the slain civil rights workers in Mississippi, was written under a pseudonym. Segue: "Michael, Andrew and James" by Richard and Mimi Fariña.

HE WAS REALLY SAYING SOMETHING

Artist: The Velvelettes
Written by: Norman Whitfield, Mickey Stevenson, Eddie Holland
Label: V.I.P.
Produced by: Norman Whitfield
Year: 1965
Motown throwaway is a hidden gem. Covered by Bananarama (London, '83).

HE WILL BREAK YOUR HEART

Artist: Jerry Butler
Written by: Curtis Mayfield, Jerry Butler, Calvin Carter
From the album: *Jerry Butler's Golden Hits*
Label: Vee Jay
Produced by: Calvin Carter
Year: 1960
Also known as "He Don't Love You (Like I Love You)." Butler's first post-Impressions hit as a soul solo, written and performed with his old collaborator, Curtis Mayfield. Covered by Tony Orlando and Dawn (Elektra, '75).

HE'LL HAVE TO GO

Artist: Jim Reeves
Written by: Joe Allison, Audrey Allison
From the album: *He'll Have to Go*
Label: RCA
Produced by: Chet Atkins
Year: 1959
#1 country/Top 10 crossover. Answered in "He'll Have to Stay" by Jeanne Black (Capitol, '60). Reeves would remain obsessed with this theme for the rest of his life.

HE'S A BAD BOY

Artist: Carole King
Written by: Gerry Goffin, Carole King
Label: Dimension
Produced by: Carole King
Year: 1963
Her biggest stiff, unless you want to count "Queen of the Beach."

HE'S A REBEL

Artist: The Crystals
Written by: Gene Pitney
From the album: *He's a Rebel*
Label: Philles
Produced by: Phil Spector
Year: 1962
Recreating the sensitive outsider for a new rock and roll generation. Another hit for the great uncredited girl group lead singer of the '60s, Darlene Love.

HE'S GONE

Artist: The Chantels
Written by: Arlene Smith
From the album: *We Are the Chantels*
Label: End
Produced by: George Goldner
Year: 1957
Featuring Arlene Smith singing lead, one of the golden voices of the doo-wop era.

HE'S GOT THE FEVER

Artist: Southside Johnny and the Asbury Jukes
Written by: Bruce Springsteen
From the album: *I Don't Want to Go Home*
Label: Epic
Produced by: Steve Van Zandt
Year: 1976
New Jersey bar-band proteges of the Boss deliver the workman-like goods.

HE'S GOT THE WHOLE WORLD IN HIS HANDS

Artist: Laurie London
Written by: Geoff Love
From the album: *Laurie London*
Label: Capitol
Year: 1957
One-record British invasion that pictured the English as prep-school wimps. That image would soon change.

HE'S SO FINE

Artist: The Chiffons
Written by: Ronnie Mack
From the album: *He's So Fine*
Label: Laurie
Produced by: Mitch Margo, Phil Margo, Hank Medress, Jay Siegel
Year: 1963
Mellow girl group classic was a #1 R&B/#1 crossover.

HE'S SO SHY

Artist: The Pointer Sisters
Written by: Tom Snow
From the album: *Special Things*
Label: Planet
Produced by: Richard Perry
Year: 1980
Suggested segues: "Soft-Spoken Guy" by the Chiffons, "Too Shy" by Kajagoogoo.

HE'S SURE THE BOY I LOVE

Artist: The Crystals
Written by: Barry Mann, Cynthia Weil

From the album: *He's a Rebel*
Label: Philles
Produced by: Phil Spector
Year: 1962
Stellar Darlene Love vocal.

HE'S THE GREATEST DANCER

Artist: Sister Sledge
Written by: Bernard Edwards, Nile Rodgers
From the album: *We Are Family*
Label: Còtillion
Produced by: Bernard Edwards, Nile Rodgers
Year: 1978
#1 R&B/Top 10 crossover.

HEAD LIKE A HOLE

Artist: Nine Inch Nails
Written by: Trent Reznor
From the album: *Pretty Hate Machine*
Label: TVT
Produced by: Trent Reznor
Year: 1990
From the trailblazing mad scientists of '90s techno alternative rage.

HEAD OVER FEET

Artist: Alanis Morissette
Written by: Alanis Morissette, Glen Ballard
From the album: *Jagged Little Pill*
Label: Maverick
Produced by: Glen Ballard
Year: 1995
Fifth hit from the album. Alanis is vunerable after all.

HEAD OVER HEELS

Artist: Tears For Fears
Written by: Roland Orzabal, Ian Stanley, Chris Hughes
From the album: *Songs from the Big Chair*
Label: Mercury
Produced by: Chris Hughes
Year: 1985
A big year for British synth bands, none bigger than Tears for Fears.

HEAD TO TOE

Artist: Lisa Lisa and Cult Jam
Written by: Chick Rains
From the album: *Spanish Fly*
Label: Columbia
Produced by: Full Force
Year: 1987
Her crowning groove; a #1 R&B/#1 crossover for Lisa Velez.

HEAR MY TRAIN A-COMING

Artist: Jimi Hendrix
Written by: Jimi Hendrix

From the album: *Rainbow Bridge*
Label: Reprise
Produced by: Jimi Hendrix
Year: 1971
One of his great performances.

HEARD IT IN A LOVE SONG

Artist: The Marshall Tucker Band
Written by: Toy Caldwell
From the album: *Carolina Dreams*
Label: Capricorn
Produced by: Paul Hornsby
Year: 1977
Biggest hit for the Southern rockers, a lilting cowboy ballad.

HEART AND SOUL

Artist: The Cleftones
Written by: Hoagy Carmichael, Frank Loesser
From the album: *Heart and Soul*
Label: Gee
Produced by: George Goldner
Year: 1961
A scenic highlight along the standards to doo-wop route. Introduced by Larry Clinton and his Orchestra in the 1938 movie, *A Song Is Born*.

HEART AND SOUL

Artist: T'Pau
Written by: Carol Decker, Ronnie Rogers
From the album: *T'Pau*
Label: Virgin
Produced by: Roy Thomas Baker
Year: 1987
Top 10 US/UK one-shot.

HEART ATTACK

Artist: Olivia Newton-John
Written by: Steven Kipner, Paul Bliss
From the album: *Physical*
Label: MCA
Produced by: John Farrar
Year: 1981
13TH Top 10 hit.

HEART COUNTRY

Artist: Firetown
Written by: Paul Davis, Doug Erikson
From the album: *In the Heart of the Heart Country*
Label: Atlantic
Produced by: Butch Vig
Year: 1987
Inspired roots rock one-shot. Vig would move on to alt rock with Nirvana and Garbage.

HEART FULL OF SOUL

Artist: The Yardbirds
Written by: Graham Gouldman
From the album: *Having a Rave up with the Yardbirds*
Label: Epic
Produced by: Paul Samwell-Smith
Year: 1965

On their second and last Top 10 hit, Beck imitates a sitar on his fuzz box. Covered by Chris Isaak (Reprise, '87).

HEART LIKE A WHEEL

Artist: Linda Ronstadt
Written by: Anna McGarrigle
From the album: *Heart Like a Wheel*
Label: Capitol
Produced by: Peter Asher
Year: 1974
Ronstadt at her earthiest. Covered by Kate and Anna McGarrigle (Reprise, '76), whose version of the song was used in the Joan Didion movie *Play It as It Lays*.

HEART NEEDS A HOME, A

Artist: Richard and Linda Thompson
Written by: Richard Thompson
From the album: *Hokey Pokey*
Label: Island
Produced by: Simon Nicol, John Wood
Year: 1974
Ethereal harmonizing.

HEART OF GLASS

Artist: Blondie
Written by: Deborah Harry, Chris Stein
From the album: *Parallel Lines*
Label: Chrysalis
Produced by: Mike Chapman
Year: 1978
#1 US/#1 UK crossover establishes the one-time Max's Kansas City waitress as the sensuously cynical voice of a generation's ennui.

HEART OF GOLD

Artist: Neil Young
Written by: Neil Young
From the album: *Harvest*
Label: Reprise
Produced by: Elliot Mazur, Neil Young
Year: 1972
In search of a simple rhyme and a simpler time, Neil loses his heart, but gains his only #1 single.

HEART OF ROCK AND ROLL, THE

Artist: Huey Lewis and the News
Written by: Johnny Colla, Huey Lewis
From the album: *Sports*
Label: Chrysalis
Produced by: Huey Lewis & the News
Year: 1984
Stumping for Cleveland, future site of the Rock and Roll Hall of Fame.

HEART OF STONE

Artist: The Rolling Stones
Written by: Mick Jagger, Keith Richards
From the album: *Now*

Label: London
Produced by: Andrew Loog-Oldham
Year: 1965
Their signature sound and stance.

HEART OF THE CITY

Artist: Nick Lowe
Written by: Nick Lowe
From the album: *Pure Pop for Now People*
Label: Columbia
Produced by: Nick Lowe
Year: 1978
B-side of "So It Goes," from an album entitled *Jesus of Cool* when it was released in England; this track was done live.

HEART OF THE MATTER, THE

Artist: Don Henley
Written by: Don Henley, Mike Campbell, J. D. Souther
From the album: *The End of the Innocence*
Label: Geffen
Produced by: Don Henley, Danny Kortchmar, Mike Campbell
Year: 1989
It's all about forgiveness; Henley's masterpiece.

HEART OF THE SUNRISE

Artist: Yes
Written by: Jon Anderson, Chris Squire, Bill Bruford
From the album: *Fragile*
Label: Atlantic
Produced by: Eddie Offord, Yes
Year: 1972
The dawning of the age of progressive rock.

HEART SHAPED BOX

Artist: Nirvana
Written by: Nirvana
From the album: *In Utero*
Label: DGC
Produced by: Steve Albini
Year: 1993
Hooking up with Courtney Love.

HEARTACHE TONIGHT

Artist: The Eagles
Written by: Don Henley, Glenn Frey, Bob Seger, John David Souther
From the album: *The Long Run*
Label: Asylum
Produced by: Bill Szymczyk
Year: 1979
Their 5TH and last #1.

HEARTBEAT

Artist: Buddy Holly
Written by: Buddy Holly
From the album: *The Buddy Holly Story*

Label: Coral
Produced by: Norman Petty
Year: 1958
A Holly classic that peaked in the Bottom 20. Holly garnered a mere two Top 10 songs, one solo and one with the Crickets, yet his infuence is immense, starting with the Beatles.

HEARTBEAT—IT'S A LOVEBEAT

Artist: The Defranco Family
Written by: William Gregory Hudspeth, Michael Kennedy
From the album: *Heartbeat—It's a Lovebeat*
Label: 20TH Century
Produced by: Walt Meskell
Year: 1973
Manufactured bubble opus for the preteen set who were too old to appreciate the Partridge Family.

HEARTBEATS ACCELERATING

Artist: Kate and Anna McGarrigle
Written by: Anna McGarrigle
From the album: *Heartbeats Accelerating*
Label: Private Music
Produced by: Peter Marchand
Year: 1990
Carrying the flag of folk/rock to a new generation. Marchand would make his mark producing Sarah McLachlan. Covered by Linda Ronstadt (Elektra, '94).

HEARTBREAK BEAT

Artist: The Psychedelic Furs
Written by: Richard Butler, Tim Butler, John Ashton
From the album: *Midnight to Midnight*
Label: Columbia
Produced by: Chris Kimsey
Year: 1987
Synth rock at its most anthemic.

HEARTBREAK HOTEL

Artist: The Jacksons
Written by: Michael Jackson
From the album: *Triumph*
Label: Epic
Produced by: The Jacksons
Year: 1980
Even before he became the King of pop, and way before he married the King of rock and roll's daughter, Michael was brazen enough to appropriate a hallowed Presley title. A decade later, Whitney Houston would do the same.

HEARTBREAK HOTEL

Artist: Elvis Presley
Written by: Mae Boren, Tommy Durden, Elvis Presley
From the album: *Elvis' Golden Records*

Label: RCA
Produced by: Steve Sholes
Year: 1956
Leading the rockabilly onslaught of '56 onto the previously highly unattainable upper rung of the pop ladder, this is the first rock and roll song to hit #1 since Bill Haley's "Rock around the Clock," nine months before. Although, the four other #1s of '55 were white pop covers of R&B hits: "Sincerely" by the McGuire Sisters, "Hearts of Stone" by the Fontane Sisters, "Dance with Me Henry" by Georgia Gibbs, and "Ain't That a Shame" by Pat Boone. One of the all-time biggest country records as well.

HEARTBREAKER

Artist: Led Zeppelin
Written by: Jimmy Page, Robert Plant, John Paul Jones, John Bonham
From the album: *Led Zeppelin II*
Label: Atlantic
Produced by: Jimmy Page
Year: 1969
The riff that launched a generation of arena rock bands.

HEARTS

Artist: Marty Balin
Written by: Jesse Barish
From the album: *Balin*
Label: EMI-America
Produced by: John Balin
Year: 1981
Airplane's Balin takes off for Journey territory.

HEARTS OF STONE

Artist: The Charms
Written by: Rudy Jackson, Eddie Ray
Label: De Luxe
Year: 1954
#1 R&B. Cover by the Fontane Sisters (Dot, '55) hit #1 pop.

HEAT IS ON, THE

Artist: Glenn Frey
Written by: Keith Forsey, Harold Faltermeyer
From the album: *Beverly Hills Cop Soundtrack*
Label: MCA
Produced by: Keith Forsey, Harold Faltermeyer
Year: 1985
Frey begins his multimedia comeback blitz with a movie song.

HEAT WAVE

Artist: Martha and the Vandellas
Written by: Eddie Holland, Lamont Dozier, Brian Holland
From the album: *Heat Wave*
Label: Gordy
Produced by: Brian Holland, Lamont Dozier
Year: 1963

Motown's most prolific writers anticipate the long hot summers of the mid-'60s, in Detroit, Newark, Watts, and elsewhere.

HEAVEN

Artist: Bryan Adams
Written by: Bryan Adams, Jim Vallance
From the album: *Reckless*
Label: A&M
Produced by: Bryan Adams, Bob Clearmountain
Year: 1984
His best ballad is from the movie *A Night in Heaven*.

HEAVEN

Artist: Warrant
Written by: Jani Lane
From the album: *Dirty Rotten Filthy Stinkin' Rich*
Label: Columbia
Produced by: Beau Hill
Year: 1989
Hair band ballad. Suggested segue: "The Way I Feel Tonight" by the Bay City Rollers.

HEAVEN AND PARADISE

Artist: Meadowlarks
Written by: Don Jullian
Label: Dooto
Year: 1955
Essential doo-wop landscape.

HEAVEN HELP ME

Artist: Deon Estus
Written by: Deon Estus, George Michael
From the album: *Spell*
Label: Mika/Polydor
Produced by: George Michael
Year: 1989
Soul music transported from Detroit, via George Michael's label in England.

HEAVEN HELP US ALL

Artist: Stevie Wonder
Written by: Ronald Miller
From the album: *Signed, Sealed, Delivered*
Label: Tamla
Produced by: Ronald Miller, Tom Baird
Year: 1970
Invoking the religious spirit of the troubled era. Suggested segues: "Instant Karma" by John Lennon, "Put Your Hand in the Hand" by Ocean, "Jesus is Just All Right" by the Byrds, "Spirit in the Sky" by Norman Greenbaum.

HEAVEN IS A PLACE ON EARTH

Artist: Belinda Carlisle
Written by: Rick Nowels, Ellen Shipley
From the album: *Heaven on Earth*
Label: MCA
Produced by: Rick Nowels

Year: 1987
#1 US/UK crossover for the former Go-Go.

HEAVEN KNOWS

Artist: Donna Summer and Brooklyn Dreams
Written by: Giorgio Moroder, Pete Bellotte, Donna Summer, Gregg Mathieson
From the album: *Live and More*
Label: Casablanca
Produced by: Pete Bellotte, Giorgio Moroder
Year: 1978
Disco staple.

HEAVEN KNOWS I'M MISERABLE NOW

Artist: The Smiths
Written by: Stephen Morrissey, Johnny Marr
Label: Sire
Produced by: John Porter
Year: 1984
Stating his defining premise Morrissey provides the Smiths with their first UK hit, not released on LP until '87.

HEAVEN ON THE SEVENTH FLOOR

Artist: Paul Nicholas
Written by: Dominic Bugatti, Frank Musker
Label: RSO
Produced by: Christopher Neil
Year: 1977
From the well-traveled theatrical singer who'd appeared in *Hair!*, *Grease*, *Jesus Christ Superstar* and *Tommy*.

HEAVY MAKES YOU HAPPY (SHA NA-BOOM-BOOM)

Artist: The Staple Singers
Written by: Jeff Barry, Bobby Bloom
From the album: *The Staple Singers*
Label: Stax
Produced by: Steve Cropper
Year: 1970
First Top 10 R&B/Top 30 crossover for the family gospel group.

HEEBY JEEBIES

Artist: Little Richard
Written by: John Marascalco, Maybelle Wade Jackson
From the album: *Little Richard*
Label: Specialty
Produced by: Bumps Blackwell
Year: 1956
B-side of "She's Got It."

HELEN WHEELS

Artist: Paul McCartney and Wings
Written by: Paul McCartney, Linda McCartney

From the album: *Band on the Run*
Label: Apple
Produced by: Paul McCartney
Year: 1973
One of his most convincing post-Beatles rockers.

HELL

Artist: Squirrel Nut Zippers
Written by: Tom Maxwell, Jim Mathus
From the album: *Hot*
Label: Mammoth
Produced by: Brian Paulson
Year: 1997
Capitalizing on the year's biggest musical influence, the rebirth of swing, caused by the use of Brian Setzer's version of "Jump, Jive and Wail" in a Gap commercial.

HELLO

Artist: Lionel Richie
Written by: Lionel B. Richie
From the album: *Can't Slow Down*
Label: Motown
Produced by: Lionel Richie, James Carmichael
Year: 1983
#1 R&B/#1 crossover ballad and answering machine favorite.

HELLO, GOODBYE

Artist: The Beatles
Written by: John Lennon, Paul McCartney
From the album: *Magical Mystery Tour*
Label: Capitol
Produced by: George Martin
Year: 1967
Closing out '67 with their third straight #1. Starting in '66, the Beatles were content to limit their AM output (they didn't release any singles from *Sgt. Pepper*), and devote most of their time to the newly upgraded FM radio dial, which proved much more able to air the bulk of their album cuts.

HELLO, I LOVE YOU

Artist: The Doors
Written by: Jim Morrison, Robbie Krieger, John Densmore, Ray Manzarek
From the album: *Waiting for the Sun*
Label: Elektra
Produced by: Paul Rothchild
Year: 1968
At their teeny boppiest.

HELLO IN THERE

Artist: John Prine
Written by: John Prine
From the album: *John Prine*
Label: Atlantic
Produced by: Arif Mardin
Year: 1971
An American family portrait by the Ansel Adams of folk/rock. Covered by Bette Midler (Atlantic, '72).

HELLO, IT'S ME

Artist: The Nazz
Written by: Todd Rundgren
From the album: *The Nazz*
Label: SGC
Produced by: Todd Rundgren
Year: 1969
Low-Fi Beatle-mongering. Covered by the group's leader, Todd Rundgren (Bearsville, '72).

HELLO, IT'S ME

Artist: Lou Reed and John Cale
Written by: Lou Reed, John Cale
From the album: *Songs for Drella*
Label: Sire
Produced by: John Cale, Lou Reed
Year: 1989
Reuniting fellow Velvets Lou Reed and John Cale, this deathbed homage as performance piece, dedicated to the memory of their mentor, Andy Warhol, debuted at the Brooklyn Academy of Music.

HELLO MARY LOU

Artist: Ricky Nelson
Written by: Gene Pitney
From the album: *Rick Is 21*
Label: Imperial
Produced by: Rick Nelson
Year: 1961
After taking a year off to turn 21, Ricky emerges as Rick, with two of his best sides ever. The A-side was "Travelin' Man." Solo by James Burton turned on a generation of guitarists.

HELLO SKINNY

Artist: The Residents
Written by: Homer Flynn II, Hardy Fox
From the album: *Duck Stab*
Label: Ralph
Year: 1978
Weird even by San Francisco standards.

HELLO STRANGER

Artist: Marianne Faithfull
Written by: Doc Pomus, Mac Rebennack
From the album: *Strange Weather*
Label: Island
Produced by: Mark Miller Mundy
Year: 1987
A scintillating match of composer, lyricist, song, and performer.

HELLO STRANGER

Artist: Barbara Lewis
Written by: Barbara Lewis
From the album: *Baby I'm Yours*
Label: Atlantic
Produced by: Ollie McLaughlin
Year: 1963
Lush #1 R&B/Top 5 crossover was her biggest hit.

HELL'S BELLS

Artist: AC/DC
Written by: Angus Young, Malcolm Young and Brian Johnson
From the album: *Back in Black*
Label: Atlantic
Produced by: Mutt Lange
Year: 1980
They toll for thee in knickers.

HELP!

Artist: The Beatles
Written by: John Lennon, Paul McCartney
From the album: *Help!*
Label: Capitol
Produced by: George Martin
Year: 1965
Movie theme song in which Lennon begins expressing the previously unexpressible. Suggested segue: "Problems" by the Everly Brothers.

HELP I'M A ROCK

Artist: The Mothers of Invention
Written by: Frank Zappa
From the album: *Freak Out*
Label: Verve
Produced by: Tom Wilson
Year: 1966
Inventing psychedelica.

HELP ME

Artist: Joni Mitchell
Written by: Joni Mitchell
From the album: *Court and Spark*
Label: Asylum
Produced by: Joni Mitchell
Year: 1974
Her first and only Top 10 single.

HELP ME MAKE IT THROUGH THE NIGHT

Artist: Kris Kristofferson
Written by: Kris Kristofferson
From the album: *Kris Kristofferson*
Label: Monument
Produced by: Fred Foster
Year: 1969
#1 country/Top 10 crossover for Sammi Smith (Mega, '70).

HELP ME SOMEBODY

Artist: The 5 Royales
Written by: Lowman Pauling
From the album: *The Rockin' Five Royals*
Label: King
Year: 1953
#1 R&B smash for the prototypical rock 'n' rhythm group. B-side "Crazy Crazy Crazy" was a Lowman Pauling guitar showcase.

HELP ME, MARY

Artist: Liz Phair
Written by: Liz Phair
From the album: *Exile in Guyville*
Label: Matador
Produced by: Liz Phair, Brad Wood
Year: 1993
The critically acclaimed debut album yields a hand-crafted tapestry of anguish.

HELP ME, RHONDA

Artist: The Beach Boys
Written by: Brian Wilson
From the album: *Beach Boys Today*
Label: Capitol
Produced by: Brian Wilson
Year: 1965
Their second #1.

HELPLESS

Artist: Crosby, Stills, Nash & Young
Written by: Neil Young
From the album: *Deja Vu*
Label: Atlantic
Produced by: Crosby, Stills, Nash & Young
Year: 1970
Coming down from "Sugar Mountain." Re-recorded by Young (Reprise, '77).

HELPLESS

Artist: Diamond Head
Written by: Sean Harris, Brian Tatler
From the album: *Lightning to the Nations*
Produced by: Sean Harris, Brian Tatler
Label: Earmark
Year: 1982
Scathing British metal that influenced Metallica. Covered by Metallica (Elektra, '87).

HELTER SKELTER

Artist: The Beatles
Written by: John Lennon, Paul McCartney
From the album: *The Beatles*
Label: Apple
Produced by: George Martin
Year: 1968
The Beatles as the Rolling Stones, whose cross to bear was Altamont. This tune was inalterably connected to the Sharon Tate murders as a purported Charles Manson influence. Covered by Siouxsie & the Banshees (Polydor, '79).

HEMORRHAGE (IN MY HANDS)

Artist: Fuel
Written by: Carl Bell
From the album: *Something Like Human*
Produced by: Carl Bell, Ben Grosse
Label: Epic
Year: 2000
New metal.

HENRY'S GOT FLAT FEET

Artist: The Midnighters
Written by: Hank Ballard
From the album: *The Midnighters*
Label: Federal
Produced by: Henry Glover
Year: 1955
An answer song to the Etta James hit, "The Wall-flower," also known as "Roll with Me Henry," also known as "Dance with Me Henry," the Henry in question not Hank Ballard, but producer Henry Glover.

HER TOWN TOO

Artist: James Taylor and J.D. Souther
Written by: James Taylor
From the album: *Dad Loves His Work*
Label: Columbia
Produced by: Peter Asher
Year: 1981
Pleasant folk/rock about the demise of his mythic marriage to Carly Simon.

HERE AND NOW

Artist: Luther Vandross
Written by: Terry Steele, David L. Elliot
From the album: *The Best of Love*
Label: Epic
Produced by: Luther Vandross, Marcus Miller
Year: 1989
His biggest hit, a #1 R&B/Top 10 crossover.

HERE COME THOSE TEARS AGAIN

Artist: Jackson Browne
Written by: Jackson Browne, Nancy Farnsworth
From the album: *The Pretender*
Label: Asylum
Produced by: Jon Landau
Year: 1976
Best-selling single from the album.

HERE COMES A REGULAR

Artist: The Replacements
Written by: Paul Westerberg
From the album: *Tim*
Label: Sire
Produced by: Tommy Erdelyi
Year: 1985
Honing their sloppy-drunk, sad, rebellious image for mass consumption, with the help of a Ramone.

HERE COMES MY GIRL

Artist: Tom Petty and the Heartbreakers
Written by: Tom Petty, Mike Campbell
From the album: *Damn the Torpedoes*
Label: Backstreet
Produced by: Jimmy Iovine, Tom Petty
Year: 1979
Like a Byrd.

HERE COMES SUMMER

Artist: Jerry Keller
Written by: Jerry Keller
From the album: *Here Comes Jerry Keller*
Label: Kapp
Year: 1959
Refining the art of the summer song.

HERE COMES THE HOTSTEPPER

Artist: Ini Kamose
Written by: Ini Kamose, Salaam Gibbs, Chris Kenner, Kenton Nix, Fats Domino, A. Kinley
From the album: *Pret à Porter Soundtrack*
Label: Columbia
Produced by: S. Remi
Year: 1994
Prominence in the Altman high-fashion film boosted this vintage reggae gem to #1. Chorus based on "Land of 1,000 Dances."

HERE COMES THE JUDGE

Artist: Shorty Long
Written by: Billie Jean Brown, Suzanne DePasse, Frederick Long
Label: Soul
Produced by: Shorty Long, Billie Jean Brown
Year: 1968
Top 5 R&B/Top 10 crossover. DePasse took this songwriting credit all the way to a top front office position at Motown. But she was no Smokey Robinson.

HERE COMES THE NIGHT

Artist: Lulu
Written by: Bert Berns
Label: Decca
Year: 1964
Covered by Them (Parrot, '65).

HERE COMES THE RAIN AGAIN

Artist: Eurythmics
Written by: Annie Lennox, Dave Stewart
From the album: *Touch*
Label: RCA
Produced by: Dave Stewart
Year: 1984
Moody blues from an essential couple in the British synth-wave invasion of the mid-'80s.

HERE COMES THE SUN

Artist: The Beatles
Written by: George Harrison
From the album: *Abbey Road*
Label: Apple
Produced by: George Martin
Year: 1969
George finally takes off his shades. Covered by Richie Havens (Stormy Forest, '71).

HERE COMES YOUR MAN

Artist: The Pixies
Written by: Charles Francis (Black Francis)
From the album: *Doolittle*
Label: 4AD/Elektra
Produced by: Gil Norton
Year: 1989
Their closest thing to pop.

HERE I AM (COME AND TAKE ME)

Artist: Al Green
Written by: Chuck Jackson, Marvin Yancy Jr., Lee Charles
From the album: *Call Me*
Label: Hi
Produced by: Willie Mitchell
Year: 1973
Jackson and Yancy would move on to Natalie Cole.

HERE I GO AGAIN

Artist: Whitesnake
Written by: David Coverdale, Bernie Marsden
From the album: *Whitesnake*
Label: Geffen
Produced by: Keith Olsen
Year: 1987
Remixed version of their '82 stiff became the biggest US hit for this aging arena band.

(HERE THEY COME) FROM ALL OVER THE WORLD

Artist: Jan & Dean
Written by: Steve Barri, P. F. Sloan
From the album: *From All over the World*
Label: Liberty
Produced by: Jan Berry
Year: 1965
Theme from the legendary youth cult concert film, *The T.A.M.I. Show*, which starred James Brown, the Rolling Stones, Jan and Dean, Ike and Tina, and others.

HERE, THERE AND EVERYWHERE

Artist: The Beatles
Written by: John Lennon, Paul McCartney
From the album: *Revolver*
Label: Capitol
Produced by: George Martin
Year: 1966
One of their most captivating melodies. Covered by Emmylou Harris (Reprise, '76), George Benson (Warner Brothers, '89).

HERE 'TIS

Artist: Bo Diddley
Written by: Ellas McDaniel (Bo Diddley)
From the album: *Bo Diddley's a Twister*
Label: Chess
Produced by: Willie Dixon

Year: 1955
Covered by the Yardbirds (Epic, '65).

HERE TODAY

Artist: Paul McCartney
Written by: Paul McCartney
From the album: *Tug of War*
Produced by: George Martin
Year: 1982
Dedicated to the memory of John Lennon.

HERE WE GO

Artist: C&C Music Factory featuring Freedom Williams and Zelma Davis
Written by: Rob Clivilles, Freedom Williams
From the album: *Gonna Make You Sweat*
Label: Columbia
Produced by: Rob Clivilles, David Cole
Year: 1991
Into another dance era.

HERE'S TO THE STATE OF MISSISSIPPI

Artist: Phil Ochs
Written by: Phil Ochs
From the album: *I Ain't Marchin' Anymore*
Label: Elektra
Produced by: Paul Rothchild
Year: 1964
Stirring polemic that energized the Civil Rights movement.

HERE'S WHERE THE STORY ENDS

Artist: The Sundays
Written by: David Gavurin, Harriet Wheeler
From the album: *Reading, Writing and Arithmetic*
Label: DGC
Produced by: Ray Shulman, the Sundays
Year: 1990
The voice of Harriet Wheeler—spacey, ethereal, flitting just out of reach—ushers in waif rock with a UK smash. Natalie Merchant was taking notes. Stevie Nicks felt old.

HERO

Artist: Mariah Carey
Written by: Walter Afanasieff, Mariah Carey
From the album: *Music Box*
Label: Columbia
Produced by: Walter Afanasieff
Year: 1993
Affirmative pop psychology.

HERO OF THE DAY

Artist: Metallica
Written by: James Hetfield, Lars Ulrich, Kirk Hammett
From the album: *Load*
Label: Elektra

Produced by: Bob Rock, James Hetfield, Lars Ulrich
Year: 1995
Affirmative metal thrashing.

HEROES

Artist: David Bowie
Written by: David Bowie
From the album: *Heroes*
Label: RCA
Produced by: Tony Visconti, David Bowie
Year: 1977
Venturing into Kraftwerk territory, Bowie wrote this about his spiritual homeland, Berlin. The amazing Robert Fripp on guitar.

HEROES AND VILLAINS

Artist: The Beach Boys
Written by: Brian Wilson, Van Dyke Parks
From the album: *Smiley Smile*
Label: Brother
Produced by: Brian Wilson, Van Dyke Parks
Year: 1967
Beginning to sense he "just wasn't made for these times," Brian finds a soul brother to collaborate with. From the all-time epic, *Smile*, which wasn't completed until 2004.

HEROIN

Artist: The Velvet Underground
Written by: Lou Reed
From the album: *The Velvet Underground and Nico*
Label: Verve
Produced by: Andy Warhol
Year: 1967
The reaction to the "Summer of Love."

HEY! BABY

Artist: Bruce Channel
Written by: Marvin Montgomery, Margaret Cobb, Bruce Channel
From the album: *Hey! Baby (and 11 Other Songs About Your Baby)*
Label: Smash
Produced by: Mayor Bill Smith
Year: 1962
Delbert McClinton's harmonica part inspired John Lennon's harp solo in "Love Me Do."

HEY BO DIDDLEY

Artist: Bo Diddley
Written by: Ellas McDaniel (Bo Diddley)
From the album: *Road Runner*
Label: Checker
Year: 1957
Classic call and response.

HEY BULLDOG

Artist: The Beatles
Written by: John Lennon, Paul McCartney
From the album: *Yellow Submarine*
Label: Apple

Produced by: George Martin
Year: 1969
Revisiting an enduring motif.

HEY DEANNIE

Artist: Shaun Cassidy
Written by: Eric Carmen
From the album: *Born Late*
Label: Warner/Curb
Produced by: Michael Lloyd
Year: 1978
The teen idol trip, scripted by someone who'd been there.

HEY, GIRL

Artist: Freddie Scott
Written by: Gerry Goffin, Carole King
From the album: *Freddie Scott Sings*
Label: Colpix
Produced by: Gerry Goffin
Year: 1963
Previewing uptown soul.

HEY GOOD LOOKIN'

Artist: Hank Williams
Written by: Hank Williams
Label: MGM
Produced by: Fred Rose
Year: 1951
Second biggest of his seven Top 10 country singles of '51.

HEY GRANDMA

Artist: Moby Grape
Written by: Jerry Miller, Don Stevenson
From the album: *Moby Grape*
Label: Columbia
Produced by: David Rubinson
Year: 1967
The great lost San Francisco band's great lost track, an appropriate symbol for a scene, a dream, a moment, a movement, and a revolution up in smoke.

HEY JACK KEROUAC

Artist: 10,000 Maniacs
Written by: Natalie Merchant
From the album: *In My Tribe*
Label: Elektra
Produced by: Peter Asher
Year: 1987
Jazz-flavored folk rock with a Beat-generation protagonist. Suggested segues: "Raining down on Bleecker Street" by Devonsquare, "Cassidy" by Bob Weir, "The Persecution and Resurrection of Dean Moriarity (On the Road)" by Aztec Two Step, and "Zen Coan Rides Again" by Dave Van Ronk.

HEY JEALOUSY

Artist: The Gin Blossoms
Written by: Doug Hopkins
From the album: *New Miserable Experience*

Label: A&M
Produced by: John Hampton, the Gin Blossoms
Year: 1992
First posthumous hit for the band's former guitarist, whose suicide earlier in the year was overshadowed by Nirvana leader Kurt Cobain's similarly self-inflicted death.

HEY JOE

Artist: The Leaves
Written by: Dino Valenti (Billy Roberts)
From the album: *Hey Joe*
Label: Mira
Produced by: Norm Ratner
Year: 1965
First example of outlaw punk. Covered by Love (Elektra, '66), Cher (Imperial, '67), Jimi Hendrix as his first UK single (Reprise, '67). Segue: "I Fought the Law" by the Bobby Fuller Four.

HEY JUDE

Artist: The Beatles
Written by: John Lennon, Paul McCartney
From the album: *Hey Jude*
Label: Capitol
Produced by: George Martin
Year: 1968
Their all-time best-seller and the #1 song of '68. This cautionary ode to Lennon's son Julian scaled the charts in the waning months of a scathing year of political backlash against rock and its musicians—peaking in time to be the song coming on right after the newscast announcing the election of hippie nemesis Richard M. Nixon and the beginning of the end of the Alternate Culture. Covered by Wilson Pickett (Atlantic, '69).

HEY LADIES

Artist: Beastie Boys
Written by: Adam Horovitz, Adam Yauch, Michael Diamond, the Dust Brothers
From the album: *Paul's Boutique*
Label: Capitol
Produced by: Dust Brothers
Year: 1989

HEY LITTLE COBRA

Artist: The Rip Chords
Written by: Marshal Howard Connors, Carol Connors
From the album: *Hey Little Cobra and Other Red Hot Hits*
Label: Columbia
Produced by: Terry Melcher
Year: 1963
Carol Connors is the former Teddy Bear Annette Kleinbard.

HEY MAN, NICE SHOT

Artist: Filter
Written by: Richard Patrick
From the album: *Short Bus*
Label: Reprise
Year: 1995
I saw the news today. Oh boy!

HEY NINETEEN

Artist: Steely Dan
Written by: Walter Becker, Donald Fagen
From the album: *Gaucho*
Label: MCA
Produced by: Gary Katz
Year: 1980
First Top 10 hit in seven years for the aging jazzbos, but is it worth the effort just to be able to communicate with teenage girls who don't remember Aretha Franklin, the Queen of soul?

HEY, PAULA

Artist: Paul and Paula
Written by: Ray Hildebrand
From the album: *Paul and Paula Sing for Young Lovers*
Label: Philips
Produced by: Mayor Bill Smith
Year: 1962
High school sweethearts get married, Texas style (by the mayor?). Bruce Springsteen had a different opinion of the subject in "The River," but then, he's from New Jersey.

HEY PORTER

Artist: Johnny Cash
Written by: Johnny Cash
From the album: *Johnny Cash and His Hot and Blue Guitar*
Produced by: Sam Phillips
Label: Sun
Year: 1958

HEY, SCHOOLGIRL

Artist: Tom and Jerry
Written by: Paul Simon, Art Garfunkel
Label: Big
Year: 1958
An early *American Bandstand* appearance for the future Simon and Garfunkel propelled this cut to the Top 50.

HEY, THAT'S NO WAY TO SAY GOODBYE

Artist: Leonard Cohen
Written by: Leonard Cohen
From the album: *Songs of Leonard Cohen*
Label: Columbia
Produced by: John Simon
Year: 1968
Song poetry as a concept and a reality; a brooding, country-sounding sing-along dirge. Covered by the Vogues (Reprise, '70).

HEY THERE LONELY BOY

Artist: Ruby and the Romantics
Written by: Earl Shuman, Leon Carr

Label: Kapp
Produced by: Allan Stanton
Year: 1963
Covered by Eddie Holman as "Hey There Lonely Girl" (ABC, '69).

HEY, WESTERN UNION MAN

Artist: Jerry Butler
Written by: Kenny Gamble, Leon Huff, Jerry Butler
From the album: *The Ice Man Cometh*
Label: Mercury
Produced by: Kenny Gamble, Leon Huff
Year: 1968
His first #1 R&B since '60 is another Philly soul building block.

(HEY WON'T YOU PLAY) ANOTHER SOMEBODY DONE SOMEBODY WRONG SONG

Artist: B. J. Thomas
Written by: Larry Butler, Chips Moman
From the album: *Reunion*
Label: ABC
Produced by: Chips Moman
Year: 1975
A good year for #1 country/#1 crossovers with a grand total of five, including "I'm Sorry" and "Thank God I'm a Country Boy" by John Denver, "Before the Next Teardrop Falls" by Freddy Fender, and "Rhinestone Cowboy" by Glen Campbell. And not including "When Will I Be Loved" by Linda Ronstadt (#1 country/#2 crossover) or "Have You Never Been Mellow" by Olivia Newton-John (#3 country/#1 crossover).

HI HI HI

Artist: Paul McCartney and Wings
Written by: Paul McCartney, Linda McCartney
From the album: *Wings over America*
Label: Apple
Produced by: Paul McCartney
Year: 1972
The former cute Beatle at his cutest.

HICKORY WIND

Artist: The Byrds
Written by: Gram Parsons, Bob Bucannan
From the album: *Sweetheart of the Rodeo*
Label: Columbia
Produced by: Gary Usher
Year: 1968
Introduced the drugstore-cowboy legend, Gram Parsons, one of the prime motivating forces behind the return-to-your-country-roots rock revolution espoused by this album and inspired by Bob Dylan's earthy collaborations with the Band in Woodstock. Revived by Gram Parsons (Reprise, '74) and covered by Gram's soulmate, Emmylou Harris (Warner Brothers, '79).

HIDE AWAY

Artist: Freddie King
Written by: Sonny Thompson, Freddie King
From the album: *Let's Hide Away and Dance Away*
Label: Federal
Produced by: Sonny Thompson
Year: 1961
Top 10 R&B/Top 30 crossover by a master of the blues guitar; covered by Eric Clapton, with John Mayall's Bluesbreakers (London, '66).

HIGH AND DRY

Artist: Radiohead
Written by: Colin Greenwood, Jon Greenwood, Ed O'Brien, Phil Selway, Thom Yorke
From the album: *The Bends*
Label: Capitol
Produced by: John Leckie
Year: 1996
Suffering a sophomore slump, until they make friends with the studio.

HIGH COIN

Artist: Harper's Bizarre
Written by: Van Dyke Parks
From the album: *Anything Goes*
Label: Warner Brothers
Produced by: Lenny Waronker
Year: 1967
Big-Surian extravaganza previews Parks's lush epics to come. Covered by the Charlatans (Philips, '69).

HIGH ENOUGH

Artist: Damn Yankees
Written by: Ted Nugent, Tommy Shaw, Jack Blades
From the album: *Damn Yankees*
Label: Warner Brothers
Produced by: Ron Nevison
Year: 1990
All-star arena concoction with a killer hook.

HIGH FLYING BIRD

Artist: Judy Henske
Written by: Billy Edd Wheeler
From the album: *High Flying Bird*
Label: Elektra
Year: 1964
One of folk's great voices mines a country gem. Covered by Richie Havens (Verve-Forecast, '67), the Jefferson Airplane at the Monterey Rock and Pop Festival in '67 (Grunt, '74), H.P. Lovecraft (Phillips, '68).

HIGH ON YOU

Artist: Survivor
Written by: Frankie Sullivan, Jim Peterik
From the album: *Vital Signs*
Label: Epic
Produced by: Ron Nevison
Year: 1984
Arena rock for the jukebox.

HIGH SCHOOL CONFIDENTIAL

Artist: Jerry Lee Lewis
Written by: Ron Hargrave, Jerry Lee Lewis
From the album: *High School Confidential*
Label: Sun
Produced by: Sam Phillips
Year: 1958
As seen opening the Mamie Van Doren/Russ Tamblyn teen exploitation flick of the same name. The same year Jerry Lee would be appearing in the confidential magazines himself, for marrying his thirteen-year-old cousin.

HIGH SCHOOL NIGHTS

Artist: Dave Edmunds
Written by: Dave Edmunds, Sam Gould, John, David
From the album: *Porky's Revenge Soundtrack*
Label: Columbia
Produced by: Dave Edmunds
Year: 1985
Highlight of the movie once thought of as raunchy.

HIGH SCHOOL USA

Artist: Tommy Facenda
Written by: Frank J. Guida
Label: Atlantic
Year: 1959
Sparing no expense or effort, approximately 28 separate versions of this high schoology were tailored to specific markets around the USA; a lot of work for a mere Top-30 showing.

HIGH TIME WE WENT

Artist: Joe Cocker
Written by: Chris Stainton, Joe Cocker
From the album: *Joe Cocker*
Label: A&M
Produced by: Denny Cordell, Leon Russell
Year: 1971
Big concert favorite. John Belushi was watching.

HIGHER

Artist: Creed
Written by: Mark Tremonti, Scott Stapp
From the album: *Human Clay*
Label: Wind-up
Year: 1999
Making their bid to be the arena voice of the new millennium.

HIGHER GROUND

Artist: Stevie Wonder
Written by: Stevie Wonder
From the album: *Innervisions*
Label: Tamla
Produced by: Stevie Wonder
Year: 1973
Secular gospel, a #1 R&B/Top 10 crossover. Covered by Red Hot Chili Peppers (EMI, '89), Aretha Franklin on her second gospel album *One Lord, One Faith, One Baptism* (Arista, '87).

HIGHER LOVE

Artist: Steve Winwood
Written by: Steve Winwood, Will Jennings
From the album: *Back in the High Life*
Label: Island
Produced by: Steve Winwood, Russ Titelman
Year: 1986
With Jennings as his Bernie Taupin, Winwood achieves his first US #1.

HIGHLANDS

Artist: Bob Dylan
Written by: Bob Dylan
From the album: *Time out of Mind*
Label: Columbia
Produced by: Daniel Lanois
Year: 1997
Still capable of a 16-minute opus after all these years.

HIGHWAY 61 REVISITED

Artist: Bob Dylan
Written by: Bob Dylan
From the album: *Highway 61 Revisited*
Label: Columbia
Produced by: Tom Wilson
Year: 1965
Dylan in a Biblical frame of mind and reference. Covered by Johnny Winter (Columbia, '69), P. J. Harvey (Island, '94).

HIGHWAY STAR

Artist: Deep Purple
Written by: Ritchie Blackmore, Ian Gillan, Roger Glover, Jon Lord, Ian Paice
From the album: *Machine Head*
Label: Warner Brothers
Produced by: Deep Purple
Year: 1972
Blackmore's guitar monsterpiece.

HIGHWAY TO HELL

Artist: AC/DC
Written by: Malcolm Young, Angus Young, Bon Scott
From the album: *Highway to Hell*
Label: Atlantic
Produced by: Mutt Lange
Year: 1979
Lead singer and cowriter, Bon Scott, knew the route whereof he preached.

HIGHWAY TOES

Artist: Christopher Guest
Written by: Christopher Guest, Sean Kelly
From the album: *Lemmings Original Cast Album*
Label: Banana
Produced by: Tony Hendra
Year: 1973

Guest dusts off his James Taylor for the landmark rock satire of the Woodstock Generation. *This Is Spinal Tap* was only a decade away, starring Guest (and Hendra). Twenty years after that, Guest would take on folk music with *A Mighty Wind*.

HI-HEEL SNEAKERS

Artist: Tommy Tucker
Written by: Robert Higgenbotham
From the album: *Hi-Heel Sneakers*
Label: Checker
Produced by: Herb Abramson
Year: 1964
As fashion statements go, not as important as "Blue Suede Shoes" but definitely more danceable than "Tan Shoes and Pink Shoelaces." Covered by Jerry Lee Lewis (Smash, '64), Stevie Wonder (Tamla, '65), José Feliciano (RCA, '68).

HIM

Artist: Rupert Holmes
Written by: Rupert Holmes
From the album: *Partners in Crime*
Label: Infinity
Produced by: Rupert Holmes, Jim Boyer
Year: 1979
From here he'd move on to Broadway with *The Mystery of Edwin Drood*.

HIM OR ME, WHAT'S IT GONNA BE

Artist: Paul Revere and the Raiders
Written by: Mark Lindsay, Terry Melcher
From the album: *Revolution*
Label: Columbia
Produced by: Terry Melcher
Year: 1967
Their fourth Top 10 hit.

HIP TO BE SQUARE

Artist: Huey Lewis and the News
Written by: Bill Gibson, Huey Lewis, Sean Hopper
From the album: *Fore!*
Label: Chrysalis
Produced by: Huey Lewis and the News
Year: 1986
New nerd anthem.

HIP-HOP HOORAY

Artist: Naughty by Nature
Written by: Naughty by Nature
From the album: *19 Naughty III*
Label: Tommy Boy
Produced by: Naughty by Nature
Year: 1993
Celebrating hip hop's '90s mainstream ascendancy with a #1 R&B/Top 10 crossover.

HIPPY HIPPY SHAKE

Artist: Chan Romero
Written by: Chan Romero
Label: Del Fi
Produced by: Bob Keane
Year: 1959
Prelude to the garage band revolution only a British invasion away. Covered by the Swinging Blue Jeans (Imperial, '64), the Georgia Satellites in the movie *Cocktail* (Elektra, '87).

HIS LIPS GOT IN THE WAY

Artist: Bernadette Castro
Written by: Howard Greenfield, Helen Miller
Label: Colpix
Year: 1964
Exposure as the daughter of the inventor of the Castro convertible sofa and the star of its TV commercial probably got her this single.

HISTORY LESSON (PART II)

Artist: The Minutemen
Written by: Dennes Boon, Mike Watt
From the album: *Double Nickels on the Dime*
Label: SST
Produced by: Ethan James
Year: 1984
His band became our life. Boon becomes his own Bob Dylan for a new generation, who would go on to repeat his tragic history lesson, down to its saddest riff in the world. Suggested Segue: Dylan's "My Back Pages" as covered by the Byrds.

HISTORY OF UTAH

Artist: Camper Van Beethoven
Written by: David Lowery
From the album: *Camper Van Beethoven*
Label: Pitch a Tent
Produced by: Camper Van Beethoven
Year: 1986
Lowery's epic roots-rock anthem, the roots of which plunge to the depths of the American experience: the pilgrims, the Apaches, "Apache" by the Shadows, gypsies, peyote, and the campfire stories of sixth graders everywhere.

HIT ME WITH YOUR BEST SHOT

Artist: Pat Benatar
Written by: Eddie Schwartz
From the album: *Crimes of Passion*
Label: Chrysalis
Produced by: Keith Olson
Year: 1980
Histrionic belter tempts fate.

HIT ME WITH YOUR RHYTHM STICK

Artist: Ian Dury and the Blockheads
Written by: Ian Dury, Chaz Jankel
From the album: *Do It Yourself*
Label: Stiff
Year: 1979
The original leaping gnome gets a #1 in the UK

HIT THE ROAD, JACK

Artist: Ray Charles
Written by: Percy Mayfield
From the album: *Ray Charles' Greatest Hits*
Label: ABC Paramount
Produced by: Sid Feller
Year: 1961
Ray's first #1 R&B/#1 crossover, written by a great poet of the blues in a playful mood.

HITCH HIKE

Artist: Marvin Gaye
Written by: Clarence Paul, William Stevenson
From the album: *Marvin Gaye/Greatest Hits*
Label: Tamla
Produced by: William Stevenson
Year: 1964
New dance sensation, used mainly by college dropouts thumbing rides to California.

HITCHIN' A RIDE

Artist: Vanity Fair
Written by: Peter Callendar, Mitch Murray
Label: Page One
Year: 1970
Traveling light.

HOCUS POCUS

Artist: Focus
Written by: Jan Akkerman, Theis Van Leen
From the album: *Moving Waves*
Label: Sire
Produced by: Mike Vernon
Year: 1973
Instrumental from the Dutch guitar hero, Jan Akkerman.

HOLD BACK THE NIGHT

Artist: Graham Parker & the Rumour
Written by: Graham Parker
From the album: *Howlin' Wind*
Label: Mercury
Produced by: Mutt Lange
Year: 1976
One of Britain's angrier young men invades the Pub with a band led by guitarist Brinsley Schwarz.

HOLD ME

Artist: Fleetwood Mac
Written by: Christine McVie, Robbie Patton
From the album: *Mirage*
Label: Warner Brothers
Produced by: Richard Dashut, Lindsay Buckingham, Ken Caillet, Fleetwood Mac
Year: 1982
Third biggest hit.

HOLD ME DADDY

Artist: XTC
Written by: Andy Partridge
From the album: *Oranges and Lemons*
Label: Geffen

Produced by: Paul Fox
Year: 1989
The angst-written wordaholic confesses. Suggested segue: "Mother" by John Lennon.

HOLD ME NOW

Artist: Thompson Twins
Written by: Tom Bailey, Alannah Currie, Joe Leeway
From the album: *Into the Gap*
Label: Arista
Produced by: Alex Sadkin, Tom Bailey
Year: 1984
Their biggest hit. But they were no Duran Duran, no Eurythmics. Then again, they weren't twins and they weren't Thompsons, either.

HOLD ME TIGHT

Artist: Johnny Nash
Written by: Johnny Nash
From the album: *Hold Me Tight*
Label: JAD
Produced by: Johnny Nash, Arthur Jenkins
Year: 1968
First Top 10 single for the Hawaiian-born reggae crooner.

HOLD MY HAND

Artist: Hootie and the Blowfish
Written by: Mark Bryan, Dean Felber, Darius Rucker, Jim Sonefeld
From the album: *Cracked Rear View*
Label: Atlantic
Produced by: Don Gehman
Year: 1994
New South bar band breakthrough.

HOLD ON

Artist: En Vogue
Written by: Thomas McElroy, Denzil Foster, En Vogue
From the album: *Born to Sing*
Label: Atlantic
Produced by: Thomas McElroy, Denzil Foster
Year: 1990
First big hit, a #1 R&B/#2 crossover, from the R&B quartet from San Francisco.

HOLD ON

Artist: Lou Reed
Written by: Lou Reed
From the album: *New York*
Label: Sire
Produced by: Fred Maher, Lou Reed
Year: 1989
Critically acclaimed track from his most critically acclaimed album.

HOLD ON

Artist: Wilson Phillips
Written by: Glen Ballard, Chynna Phillips, Camie Wilson
From the album: *Wilson Phillips*

Label: SBK
Produced by: Glen Ballard
Year: 1990
Scions of Beach Boy Brian (Wilson) and Papa John (Phillips) produce their second generation ephemeral pop/rock epiphany. The first of four #1 hits from the album.

HOLD ON, I'M COMIN'

Artist: Sam and Dave
Written by: Isaac Hayes, David Porter
From the album: *Hold on, I'm Comin'*
Label: Stax
Produced by: Jim Stewart
Year: 1966
A definition of soul, #1 R&B/Top 25 crossover.

HOLD ON LOOSELY

Artist: 38 Special
Written by: Jeff Carlisi, Don Barnes, Jim Peterik
From the album: *Wild-Eyed Southern Boys*
Label: A&M
Produced by: Rodney Mills
Year: 1981
Emotionally charged anthem from their early arena days.

HOLD ON TIGHT

Artist: Electric Light Orchestra (ELO)
Written by: Jeff Lynne
From the album: *Time*
Label: Jet
Produced by: Jeff Lynne
Year: 1981
Their last US/UK hit. Lynne would move on to the Traveling Wilburys.

HOLD ON TO THE NIGHTS

Artist: Richard Marx
Written by: David Cole, Richard Marx
From the album: *Richard Marx*
Label: Chrysalis
Produced by: Richard Marx
Year: 1988
Fourth and biggest hit on the album, reaching #1.

HOLD THE LINE

Artist: Toto
Written by: David Paich
From the album: *Toto*
Label: Columbia
Produced by: Toto
Year: 1978
L.A. studio perfection.

HOLD WHAT YOU'VE GOT

Artist: Joe Tex
Written by: Joe Tex
From the album: *Hold What You Got*
Label: Dial
Produced by: Buddy Killen

Year: 1964
After ten years of trying, the first hit for "Soul Brother No. 2."

HOLD YOU TIGHT

Artist: Tara Kemp
Written by: William Hammond, Tuhin Roy, Jake Smith
From the album: *Tara Kemp*
Label: Giant
Produced by: Jake Smith
Year: 1991
Dance pop/R&B one shot.

HOLD YOUR HEAD UP

Artist: Argent
Written by: Rod Argent, Chris White
From the album: *All Together Now*
Label: Epic
Produced by: Argent
Year: 1972
An uplifting rallying cry for rock supporters in a lackluster year.

HOLDING BACK THE YEARS

Artist: Simply Red
Written by: Mick Hucknall, Neil Moss
From the album: *Picture Book*
Label: Elektra
Produced by: Steven Levine
Year: 1986
Blue-eyed English soul. Originally released by Hucknall's first group, the Frantic Elevators (No Waiting, '83).

HOLE HEARTED

Artist: Extreme
Written by: Nuno Bettencourt, Gary Cherone
From the album: *Pornograffiti II*
Label: A&M
Produced by: Michael Wagener
Year: 1990
Scions of Aerosmith tune down for radio consumption.

HOLIDAY

Artist: Madonna
Written by: Curtis Hudson, Lisa Stevens
From the album: *Madonna*
Label: Sire
Produced by: Jellybean
Year: 1983
A stagestruck wannabe from Detroit crashes the big show. Seventeen years and thirty-six Top 10 hits later, she'd still be there, and still singing this catchy track, a Top 25 R&B/Top 20 crossover, which hit the Top 10 in the UK three different times.

HOLIDAY

Artist: Scorpions
Written by: Rudolf Schenker, Klaus Meine

From the album: *Lovedrive*
Label: Mercury
Produced by: Dieter Dierks
Year: 1979

HOLIDAY IN CAMBODIA

Artist: The Dead Kennedys
Written by: Eric Boucher (Jello Biafra), East Bay Ray, Klaus Flouride, Bruce Slesinger
From the album: *Fresh Fruit for Rotting Vegetables*
Label: I.R.S./Cherry Red
Produced by: Geza X, Norm
Year: 1980
US hardcore answer to the Sex Pistols' "Holidays in the Sun." Lead singer/actor/poet Biafra came in fourth out of ten candidates in a San Francisco mayoralty run off in '79 to elect a successor to the murdered Harvey Milk.

HOLIDAYS IN THE SUN

Artist: The Sex Pistols
Written by: Steve Jones, Paul Cook, John Beverly (Sid Vicious), John Lydon (Johnny Rotten)
From the album: *Never Mind the Bollocks, Here's the Sex Pistols*
Label: Warner Brothers
Produced by: Chris Thomas, Bill Price
Year: 1977
In Brighton, where people sit on the beach in their overcoats.

HOLLYWOOD NIGHTS

Artist: Bob Seger & the Silver Bullet Band
Written by: Bob Seger
From the album: *Stranger in Town*
Label: Capitol
Produced by: Bob Seger, Punch Andrews
Year: 1977
Seger predates Billy Joel and Bruce Springsteen as a working-class superstar tempted by a Hollywood cutie.

HOLLYWOOD SWINGING

Artist: Kool & the Gang
Written by: Robert Bell, Ricky West, Charles Smith, George Brown, Ronald Bell, Robert Mickens, Dennis Thomas
From the album: *Wild and Peaceful*
Label: De-Lite
Produced by: Kool & the Gang
Year: 1973
#1 R&B/Top 10 crossover; sax-driven funk.

HOLOCAUST

Artist: Big Star
Written by: Alex Chilton
From the album: *3rd*
Label: PVC
Produced by: Jim Dickinson
Year: 1978

HOME IS ANYWHERE YOU HANG YOUR HEAD

Artist: Elvis Costello
Written by: Declan McManus (Elvis Costello)
From the album: *Blood and Chocolate*
Label: Columbia
Produced by: Nick Lowe, Colin Fairley
Year: 1986
One of his best titles.

HOME IS WHERE THE HATRED IS

Artist: Esther Phillips
Written by: Gil Scott-Heron
From the album: *From a Whisper to a Scream*
Label: Kudu
Produced by: Creed Taylor
Year: 1972
A long way from her boogieing days with Johnny Otis, Esther gives voice to this pointed protest from the pen of a Last Poet. Covered by Gil Scott-Heron and Brian Jackson (Arista, '76).

HOMECOMING QUEEN'S GOT A GUN, THE

Artist: Julie Brown
Written by: Julie Brown, Terrence McNally, Charlie Coffey, Ray Colcord
From the album: *Trapped in the Body of a White Girl*
Label: Sire
Year: 1987
Suburban satire. Suggested segue: "The Sweater" by Meryn Cadell.

HOMEWARD BOUND

Artist: Simon and Garfunkel
Written by: Paul Simon
From the album: *Parsley, Sage, Rosemary and Thyme*
Label: Columbia
Produced by: Bob Johnston
Year: 1966
Written in a tube station in England, awaiting his return to the states and superstardom.

HOMOSAPIEN

Artist: Pete Shelley
Written by: Pete Shelley
From the album: *Homosapien*
Label: Arista
Year: 1982
Dance hit for the former leader of the Buzzcocks.

HONEST I DO

Artist: Jimmy Reed
Written by: Jimmy Reed, Ewart Abner Jr.
Label: Vee-Jay
Year: 1957
His biggest Top 40 hit.

HONEY

Artist: Bobby Goldsboro
Written by: Bobby Russell
From the album: *Honey*
Label: United Artists
Produced by: Bob Montgomery, Bobby Goldsboro
Year: 1968
#1 country/#1 crossover weeper.

HONEY DON'T

Artist: Carl Perkins
Written by: Carl Perkins
From the album: *Dance Album*
Label: Sun
Produced by: Sam Phillips
Year: 1955
B-side of "Blue Suede Shoes." Covered by the Beatles (Capitol, '65).

HONEY HUSH

Artist: Joe Turner
Written by: Joe Turner (Lou Willie Turner)
From the album: *Joe Turner*
Label: Atlantic
Produced by: Ahmet Ertegun, Jerry Wexler
Year: 1954
Top 10 R&B breakthrough; crossed over to Top 40 in a 1960 reissue. Written by Big Joe, under his wife's name.

HONEY LOVE

Artist: The Drifters
Written by: Clyde McPhatter, J. Gerald
Label: Atlantic
Produced by: Ahmet Ertegun, Jerry Wexler
Year: 1954
#1 R&B despite (or more likely because of) being banned around the country for suggestive lyrics. R. Kelly appropriated the title years later to augment his suggestive career.

HONEY PIE

Artist: The Beatles
Written by: John Lennon, Paul McCartney
From the album: *The Beatles*
Label: Apple
Produced by: George Martin
Year: 1968
John Lennon lead guitar.

HONEY (TOUCH ME WITH MY CLOTHES ON)

Artist: Gilda Radner
Written by: Gilda Radner, Paul Shaffer
From the album: *Live in New York*
Label: Warner Brothers
Produced by: Paul Shaffer, Jerry Wexler
Year: 1979
One of the best post-Ronettes Ronettes songs, sung by the original sweetheart of *Saturday Night Live*. Shafer would burnish his musical legend as David

Letterman's smooth sidekick and as coauthor of Billy Crystal's "You Look Mahvelous."

HONEY WHITE

Artist: Morphine
Written by: Mark Sandman
From the album: *Yes*
Label: Rykodisc
Produced by: Paul Kolderie, Sean Slade
Year: 1995
Delicious sax romp.

HONEYCOMB

Artist: Georgia Shaw
Written by: Bob Merrill
Label: Decca
Year: 1954
Cover by Jimmie Rodgers (Roulette, '57). Top 10 country/#1 crossover.

HONEYDRIPPER, THE

Artist: Joe Liggins
Written by: Joe Liggins
Label: Speciality
Produced by: Art Rupe
Year: 1945
Sexually oriented jump blues was the #1 R&B record of the '40s, suggesting a pathway to rock and roll for the Dominoes to exploit at Alan Freed's pioneering Cleveland dances. Covered by Roosevell Sykes (RCA, '46).

HONG KONG GARDEN

Artist: Siouxsie and the Banshees
Written by: Susan Dallion, Steve Severin, John McKay, Kenny Morris
From the album: *The Scream*
Label: Polydor
Produced by: Steve Lillywhite
Year: 1978
Debut single for the inspired punk band hit Top 10 UK.

HONKY CAT

Artist: Elton John
Written by: Elton John, Bernie Taupin
From the album: *Honky Chateau*
Label: Uni
Produced by: Gus Dudgeon
Year: 1972
And his pumping piano. Segue: "Play That Funky Music White Boy" by Wild Cherry.

HONKY TONK

Artist: Bill Doggett
Written by: Henry Glover, Bill Doggett, Billy Butler, Shape Sheppard, Clifford Scott
Label: King
Produced by: Henry Glover
Year: 1956
Blasting sax instrumental; #1 R&B/#2 crossover.

HONKY TONK MASQUERADE

Artist: Joe Ely
Written by: Butch Hancock, Joe Ely
From the album: *Honky Tonk Masquerade*
Label: MCA
Produced by: Chip Young
Year: 1978
The missing link between Buddy Holly and Tom Petty.

HONKY TONK WOMEN

Artist: The Rolling Stones
Written by: Mick Jagger, Keith Richards
From the album: *Through the Past Darkly (Big Hits, Vol. II)*
Label: London
Produced by: Jimmy Miller
Year: 1969
The Stones on the prowl without Brian Jones. A classic #1 US/#1 UK smash, released the day after his funeral.

HOOK

Artist: Blues Traveler
Written by: John Popper
From the album: *Four*
Label: A&M
Produced by: Steve Thompson, Michael Barbiero
Year: 1994
Powered by Popper's blissful harp.

HOOKED ON A FEELING

Artist: B. J. Thomas
Written by: Mark James
From the album: *On My Way*
Label: Scepter
Produced by: Chips Moman
Year: 1968
Covered by Blue Swede (EMI, '74).

HOOTENANNY

Artist: The Replacements
Written by: Paul Westerberg
From the album: *Let It Be*
Produced by: Peter Jasperson, Paul Stark
Label: Twin-Tone
Year: 1984
The voice of Gen X defiance take on the Beatles in the album's title and the essence of the '60s Folk Scare in the song.

HOOVER FACTORY

Artist: Elvis Costello
Written by: Declan McManus (Elvis Costello)
From the album: *Taking Liberties*
Label: Columbia
Produced by: Nick Lowe
Year: 1980

HOPELESSLY DEVOTED TO YOU

Artist: Olivia Newton-John
Written by: John Farrar
From the album: *Grease (Soundtrack)*
Label: RSO
Produced by: John Farrar
Year: 1978
From her miscast epic *Grease*, in which she plays Debbie Reynolds as Sandra Dee. She was closer to Doris Day.

HORSE, THE

Artist: Cliff Nobles & Co.
Written by: Jesse James
From the album: *The Horse*
Label: Phil L.A. of Soul
Produced by: Jesse James
Year: 1968
Top 5 R&B/Top 5 crossover.

HORSE WITH NO NAME, A

Artist: America
Written by: Lee Brunnell
From the album: *America*
Label: Warner Brothers
Produced by: Ian Samwell
Year: 1972
Youngian folk/rock clone.

HORSES

Artist: Rickie Lee Jones
Written by: Rickie Lee Jones, Walter Becker
From the album: *Flying Cowboys*
Label: Geffen
Produced by: Walter Becker
Year: 1989
A meeting of rock's hipster elite.

HOT BLOODED

Artist: Foreigner
Written by: Lou Grammatico (Lou Gramm)
From the album: *Double Vision*
Label: Atlantic
Produced by: Keith Olson, Mick Jones
Year: 1978
Perfecting their randy worldview.

HOT BOYZ

Artist: Missy Elliott, featuring Nas, Eve and Q-Tip
Written by: Melissa (Missy) Elliott, Tim Mosley
From the album: *Da Real World*
Label: The Gold Mind/East West
Produced by: Timbaland & Magoo
Year: 1999
Powerful new rap diva defends her turf.

HOT BURRITO #1

Artist: The Flying Burritto Brothers
Written by: Gram Parsons

From the album: *The Gilded Palace of Sin*
Label: A&M
Produced by: Flying Burrito Brothers, Larry Marks, Henry Levy
Year: 1969
Their signature anthem. Covered by Emmylou Harris (Warner Brothers, '81).

HOT CHILD IN THE CITY

Artist: Nick Gilder
Written by: James McColloch, Nick Gilder
From the album: *City Nights*
Label: Chrysalis
Produced by: Mike Chapman
Year: 1978
Chart-topping one-shot from England.

HOT DOG, THAT MADE HIM MAD

Artist: Wanda Jackson
Written by: Danny Barker, Don Raye
From the album: *Wanda Jackson*
Label: Capitol
Produced by: Ken Nelson
Year: 1956
Introduced by Madonna's favorite sex symbol, Bette Hutton. But to experience Wanda singing the word "hot" is to know the meaning of the word for the first time.

HOT FOR TEACHER

Artist: Van Halen
Written by: Eddie Van Halen, Alex Van Halen, Michael Anthony, David Lee Roth
From the album: *1984*
Label: Warner Brothers
Produced by: Ted Templeman
Year: 1984
Perfecting their eternal adolescent bad-boy image for the age of MTV.

HOT FUN IN THE SUMMERTIME

Artist: Sly and the Family Stone
Written by: Sylvester Stewart
From the album: *Greatest Hits*
Label: Epic
Produced by: Sly Stone
Year: 1969
Summertime classic in an era of riots and looting, war and protest, sun, surf and hippies being shot on rooftops by the San Francisco police.

HOT GIRLS IN LOVE

Artist: Loverboy
Written by: Paul Dean, Bruce Fairbairn
From the album: *Keep It Up*
Label: Columbia
Produced by: Bruce Fairbairn

Year: 1983
Lite metal lite beer fantasy.

HOT! HOT! HOT!

Artist: Buster Poindexter
Written by: Alphonsus Cassell
From the album: *Buster Poindexter*
Label: RCA
Produced by: Hank Medress
Year: 1987
All dolled up and heading to the disco, Buster commits the party anthem of the year.

HOT IN THE CITY

Artist: Billy Idol
Written by: William Broad (Billy Idol)
From the album: *Billy Idol*
Label: Chrysalis
Produced by: Keith Forsey
Year: 1982
Joining the retro rockabilly ranks (X, the Blasters) for his first US hit.

HOT LEGS

Artist: Rod Stewart
Written by: Rod Stewart
From the album: *Footloose and Fancy Free*
Label: Warner Brothers
Produced by: Tom Dowd
Year: 1977
Rod displays his sexist side, with a landmark music video to boot.

HOT LINE

Artist: The Sylvers
Written by: Freddie Perren, Keni St. Lewis
From the album: *Something Special*
Label: Capitol
Produced by: Freddie Perren
Year: 1977
Second biggest hit for the family disco group.

HOT LOVE

Artist: T. Rex
Written by: Marc Feld (Marc Bolan)
From the album: *Beard of Stars*
Label: Regal/Zonophone UK
Year: 1971
Their biggest UK hit. Stalled in the states at a cold #72.

HOT N' NASTY

Artist: Humble Pie
Written by: Steve Marriott, Greg Ridley, Jerry Shirley, Clem Clempson
From the album: *Smokin'*
Label: A&M
Produced by: Humble Pie
Year: 1972
Arena dandy Steve Marriott in an R&B groove.

HOT PANTS (SHE GOT TO USE WHAT SHE GOT TO GET WHAT SHE WANTS)

Artist: James Brown
Written by: James Brown, Fred Wesley
From the album: *Hot Pants*
Label: People
Produced by: James Brown
Year: 1971
#1 R&B/Top 20 crossover. Bridging the gap between "Short Shorts" and "The Thong Song."

HOT PATOOTIE, BLESS MY SOUL

Artist: Meat Loaf
Written by: Richard O'Brien
From the album: *The Rocky Horror Picture Show Cast Album*
Label: Ode
Year: 1975
Exposing his theatrical roots, Marvin Lee Aday aka Meat Loaf partakes of the era's greatest cult musical and social phenomenon.

HOT ROD HEARTS

Artist: Robbie Dupree
Written by: Bill LaBounty, Stephen Geyer
From the album: *Robbie Dupree*
Label: Elektra
Produced by: Peter Bunetta, Rick Chudacoff
Year: 1980
Springsteenian tribute to "Hungry Heart."

HOT ROD LINCOLN

Artist: Johnny Bond
Written by: Charlie Ryan, W. S. Stevenson
Label: Souvenir
Year: 1955
This trusty rockabilly vehicle was originated by Tiny Hill. Covered by author Charlie Ryan (4-Star, '60), Johnny Bond (Republic, '60), Commander Cody (Paramount, '72).

HOT SHIT (COUNTRY GRAMMAR)

Artist: Nelly
Written by: Jayson Epperson, Cornell (Nelly) Hayes
From the album: *Country Grammar*
Label: Uptown
Year: 2000
Out in the cow patch with Sally.

HOT STUFF

Artist: Donna Summer
Written by: Pete Bellotte, Harold Faltermeyer, Keith Forsey
From the album: *Bad Girls*
Label: Casablanca
Produced by: Giorgio Moroder, Pete Bellotte

Year: 1979
Second #1 from the her best-selling album.

HOTEL CALIFORNIA

Artist: Eagles
Written by: Don Henley, Glenn Frey, Don Felder
From the album: *Hotel California*
Label: Asylum
Produced by: Bill Szymczyk
Year: 1977
All-purpose metaphor serves as the vehicle for their most enduring classic (classic guitarist: Joe Walsh).

HOTEL HAPPINESS

Artist: Brook Benton
Written by: Earl Shuman, Leon Carr
From the album: *Golden Hits, Volume 2*
Label: Mercury
Year: 1963
Located up at the top of Lonely Street.

HOUND DOG

Artist: Big Mama Thornton
Written by: Jerry Leiber, Mike Stoller
Label: Peacock
Produced by: Jerry Leiber, Mike Stoller
Year: 1953
Fruition of Leiber and Stoller's R&B infatuation and a #1 R&B track for Big Mama, complete with a chorus of barking dogs. Covered in a semi-lewd, semi-novelty version by Elvis Presley (RCA, '56), which he introduced in a career-enhancing swivel-hipped performance on *The Milton Berle Show* in June of '56. By August it was his second #1 (and his first #1 country/R&B/pop crossover). The rock and roll gold rush was officially on.

HOURGLASS

Artist: Squeeze
Written by: Chris Difford, Glenn Tilbrook
From the album: *Babylon and On*
Label: A&M
Year: 1987
Comeback single was their biggest hit.

HOUSE AT POOH CORNER

Artist: Nitty Gritty Dirt Band
Written by: Kenny Loggins
From the album: *Uncle Charlie and His Dog Teddy*
Label: Liberty
Produced by: Bill McEwen
Year: 1970
Rare representative of the underexplored Winnie-the-Pooh influence on rock and roll. Covered by Loggins and Messina (Columbia, '72).

HOUSE OF BLUE LIGHTS, THE

Artist: Freddie Slack and Ella Mae Morse
Written by: Freddy Slack, Don Raye
Label: Capitol
Year: 1946
Classic R&B boogie (and rap) by the author of "Beat Me Daddy, Eight to the Bar" and "Down the Road a Piece" (Raye) and the singer of "Cow Cow Boogie" (Morse with Slack on keyboards). Sung by Morse in the '46 film *How Do You Do*. Watered down crossover pop hit by Chuck Miller (Mercury, '55). Covered by Chuck Berry (Chess, '74).

HOUSE OF THE RISING SUN

Artist: The Weavers
Written by: Traditional
From the album: *Travelin' on with the Weavers*
Label: Vanguard
Produced by: Milt Gabler
Year: 1958
The legendary American folk classic was performed by Bob Dylan on his first album (Columbia, '61). The Animals covered it in a folk/rock landmark (MGM, '64).

HOUSE THAT JACK BUILT, THE

Artist: Aretha Franklin
Written by: Bobby Lance, Fran Robbins
From the album: *Aretha's Gold*
Label: Atlantic
Produced by: Jerry Wexler
Year: 1968
Top 10 R&B/Top 10 crossover.

HOUSE WHERE NOBODY LIVES

Artist: Tom Waits
Written by: Tom Waits
From the album: *Mule Variations*
Label: Epitaph
Produced by: Tom Waits, Kathleen Brennan
Year: 1999

HOW BIZARRE

Artist: OMC
Written by: Pauly Fuemana, Alan Jansson
From the album: *How Bizarre*
Label: Huh
Year: 1997
Epitomizing the media-saturated new breed of cynically self-aware hipsters. Went to #1 in eight countries.

HOW BLUE CAN YOU GET

Artist: B. B. King
Written by: B. B. King, Joe Josea
Label: Kent
Year: 1962
B.B. and Lucille's enduring signature.

HOW CAN I BE SURE

Artist: The Rascals
Written by: Felix Cavaliere, Edward Brigati Jr.
From the album: *Groovin'*
Label: Atlantic
Produced by: The Rascals
Year: 1967
Society on the brink of chaos, Felix Cavaliere on the brink of marriage, this existential doo-wop number was popular in certain Italian neighborhoods where time had stopped in 1958.

HOW CAN I FALL?

Artist: Breathe
Written by: Dave Glaspar, Marcus Lillington
From the album: *All That Jazz*
Label: A&M
Produced by: Bob Sergeant
Year: 1988
Breathless, blue-eyed British soul.

HOW CAN I MEET HER?

Artist: The Everly Brothers
Written by: Gerry Goffin, Jack Keller
From the album: *The Golden Hits of the Everly Brothers*
Label: Warner Brothers
Produced by: Wesley Rose
Year: 1962
B-side of "That's Old Fashioned."

HOW CAN WE BE LOVERS

Artist: Michael Bolton
Written by: Diane Warren, Desmond Child, Michael Bolton
From the album: *Soul Provider*
Label: Columbia
Produced by: Desmond Child, Michael Bolton
Year: 1990
Corporate soul.

HOW CAN YOU MEND A BROKEN HEART

Artist: Bee Gees
Written by: Barry Gibb, Robin Gibb
From the album: *Trafalgar*
Label: Atco
Produced by: Robert Stigwood, Bee Gees
Year: 1971
Their first #1 US single.

HOW DEEP IS YOUR LOVE

Artist: Bee Gees
Written by: Barry Gibb, Robin Gibb, Maurice Gibb
From the album: *Saturday Night Fever*
Label: RSO
Produced by: Albhy Galutin, Karl Richardson, Bee Gees
Year: 1977
From the classic soundtrack that brought disco home to middle America, this was their fourth #1.

HOW DO I MAKE YOU

Artist: Linda Ronstadt
Written by: Billy Steinberg
From the album: *Mad Love*
Label: Asylum
Produced by: Peter Asher
Year: 1977
First Top 10 hit for Ronstadt that was not a classic rock cover.

HOW DO U WANT IT

Artist: 2Pac featuring K.C. and Jo Jo
Written by: Tupac Shakur, J. Jackson, Bruce Fisher, Quincy Jones
From the album: *All Eyez on Me*
Label: Death Row
Produced by: Johnny J.
Year: 1996
West coast posturing.

HOW DO YOU SLEEP

Artist: John Lennon
Written by: John Lennon
From the album: *Imagine*
Label: Apple
Produced by: John Lennon
Year: 1971
Post-Beatles post-mortem; giving the bass player some.

HOW DO YOU TALK TO AN ANGEL

Artist: The Heights
Written by: Steve Tyrell, Stephanie Tyrell, Barry Coffing
From the album: *The Heights*
Label: Capitol
Produced by: Steve Tyrell
Year: 1992
From the failed TV series about rock stardom this was a lesson in one-shot rock balladry. Lead singer Jamie Walters would move to a lot across the compound for a recurring role on *Beverly Hills 90120*.

HOW HIGH THE MOON

Artist: Les Paul and Mary Ford
Written by: Nancy Hamilton, Morgan Lewis
Label: Capitol
Produced by: Les Paul
Year: 1951
#1 pop/#5 R&B crossover. Technically and sonically the nature of the electric guitar took a quantum leap toward rock and roll.

HOW LONG

Artist: Ace
Written by: Paul Carrack
From the album: *Five-a-Side*
Label: Anchor
Produced by: John Anthony
Year: 1975
UK balladeer Carrack would return with Squeeze and Mike & the Mechanics.

HOW LONG (BETCHA' GOT A CHICK ON THE SIDE)

Artist: Pointer Sisters
Written by: Anita Pointer, Ruth Pointer, June Pointer, Patricia Pointer
From the album: *Steppin'*
Label: ABC/Blue Thumb
Produced by: Richard Perry
Year: 1975
First #1 R&B/Top 20 crossover for the best sister act since the Andrews Sisters.

HOW MANY MORE TIMES

Artist: Led Zeppelin
Written by: Jimmy Page, John Bonham, John Paul Jones
From the album: *Led Zeppelin*
Label: Atlantic
Produced by: Jimmy Page
Year: 1969
Suggested segue: "How Many More Years" by Howlin' Wolf.

HOW MANY MORE YEARS

Artist: Howlin' Wolf
Written by: Chester Burnette (Howlin' Wolf)
From the album: *Moaning in the Moonlight*
Label: Chess
Produced by: Sam Phillips
Year: 1951
From his first session at Chess, the first entry on the R&B charts for the scarfiying voice of bluesman Chester Burnette.

HOW MUCH I FEEL

Artist: Ambrosia
Written by: David Pack
From the album: *Life Beyond L.A.*
Label: Warner Brothers
Produced by: Freddie Piro, Ambrosia
Year: 1978
Deep in the soft rock pocket.

HOW SOON IS NOW

Artist: The Smiths
Written by: Stephen Morrissey, Johnny Marr
From the album: *Meat Is Murder*
Label: Sire
Produced by: John Porter
Year: 1985
Chilling guitar part by Johnny Marr adds real terror to Morrissey's tale of teenage affliction.

HOW SWEET IT IS (TO BE LOVED BY YOU)

Artist: Marvin Gaye
Written by: Eddie Holland, Lamont Dozier, Brian Holland
From the album: *How Sweet It Is to Be Loved by You*
Label: Tamla
Produced by: Brian Holland, Lamont Dozier
Year: 1964
Motown standard. Covered by Junior Walker (Soul, '66), James Taylor (Warner Brothers, '75).

HOW TO KILL A RADIO CONSULTANT

Artist: Public Enemy
Written by: Carlton Ridenhour, Stuart Robertz, Gary G. Wiz, Cerwin Depper
From the album: *Apocalypse '91 … The Enemy Strikes Black*
Label: Def Jam
Produced by: Stuart Robertz, Cerwin Depper, Gary G. Wiz, the JBL
Year: 1991
Reacting to their lack of rock and roll air play.

HOW TO ROB

Artist: Fifty Cent
Written by: Curtis (50 Cent) Jackson
From the album: *Power of the Dollar*
Label: Columbia
Year: 1999
Gangsta rap, the next generation, a primer, from an album that has yet to be released. Used in the film *In Too Deep* (Columbia, '99). Eminem was listening, contract in hand.

HOW WILL I KNOW

Artist: Whitney Houston
Written by: Gary Merrill, Shannon Rubicam, Narada Michael Walden
From the album: *Whitney Houston*
Label: Arista
Produced by: Narada Michael Walden
Year: 1985
Second of seven straight #1 tunes and her second #1 R&B crossover.

HUCKLEBUCK, THE

Artist: Paul Williams
Written by: Roy Alfred, Andy Gibson
Label: Savoy
Produced by: Teddy Reig
Year: 1949
The honking sax call of the wild introduces a generation to "The Twist" of its era, a #1 R&B (twelve weeks)/Top 10 crossover, covered by Roy Milton (Specialty, '49), Tommy Dorsey (RCA, '49), Frank Sinatra (Columbia, '49), and, of course, Chubby Checker (Parkway, '61).

HUMAN

Artist: Human League
Written by: James Harris III, Terry Lewis
From the album: *Crash*
Label: A&M
Produced by: Jimmy Jam, Terry Lewis
Year: 1986

Miscast collaborators on a hot streak give this anti-soul band a Top 10 R&B/#1 crossover.

HUMAN BEHAVIOUR

Artist: Björk
Written by: Nellee Hooper, Björk Gudmundsdottir
From the album: *Debut*
Label: Elektra
Produced by: Nellee Hooper
Year: 1993
Former lead singer of the Sugarcubes as a decidedly off-kilter Swedish Melanie.

HUMAN BEING

Artist: New York Dolls
Written by: David Johansen, Johnny Thunders
From the album: *In Too Much Too Soon*
Label: Mercury
Produced by: Shadow Morton
Year: 1974
Straddling the line between glam and punk.

HUMAN FLY

Artist: The Cramps
Written by: Kirsty Wallace (Ivy Rorsach), Erick Purkhiser (Lux Interior)
From the album: *Gravest Hits*
Label: IRS
Produced by: Alex Chilton
Year: 1979
Reinventing sci-fi hi-fi with a monster track produced by a minor living legend.

HUMAN NATURE

Artist: Michael Jackson
Written by: John Bettis, Jeffrey Porcaro
From the album: *Thriller*
Label: Epic
Produced by: Quincy Jones, Michael Jackson
Year: 1983
Covered by SWV (RCA, '93).

HUMAN TOUCH

Artist: Bruce Springsteen
Written by: Bruce Springsteen
From the album: *Human Touch*
Label: Columbia
Produced by: Jon Landau, Bruce Springsteen, Chuck Plotkin
Year: 1992
Having achieved love and adulthood at last, the Boss finds it not so scary after all.

HUMANS BEING

Artist: Van Halen
Written by: Eddie Van Halen, Alex Van Halen, Michael Anthony, Sammy Hager
From the album: *Twister Soundtrack*
Label: Warner Sunset
Produced by: Bruce Fairbairn

Year: 1996
White tornado.

HUMBLED IN LOVE

Artist: Leonard Cohen
Written by: Leonard Cohen
From the album: *Recent Songs*
Label: Columbia
Produced by: Leonard Cohen, Henry Lewy
Year: 1979
In his most favorite position.

HUMPIN' AROUND

Artist: Bobby Brown
Written by: Kenny Edmunds (Babyface), Antonio Reid (L.A. Reid), Daryl Simmons
From the album: *Bobby*
Label: MCA
Produced by: Babyface, L. A. Reid
Year: 1992
His sixth and last #1 R&B hit (fifth #1 R&B/Top 10 crossover).

HUMPTY DANCE, THE

Artist: Digital Underground
Written by: Edward Humphries, Greg Jacobs
From the album: *Sex Packets*
Label: Tommy Boy
Produced by: Shock G.
Year: 1990
Novelty rap dance groove.

HUNDRED POUNDS OF CLAY, A

Artist: Gene McDaniels
Written by: Bob Elgin, Kay Rogers, Luther Dixon
From the album: *A Hundred Pounds*
Label: Liberty
Produced by: Snuff Garrett
Year: 1961
Semi biblical novelty rocker.

HUNG ON YOU

Artist: The Righteous Brothers
Written by: Gerry Goffin, Carole King, Phil Spector
From the album: *Back to Back*
Label: Philles
Produced by: Phil Spector
Year: 1965
B-side of "Unchained Melody."

HUNGRY

Artist: Paul Revere and the Raiders
Written by: Barry Mann, Cynthia Weil
From the album: *The Spirit of '67*
Label: Columbia
Produced by: Terry Melcher
Year: 1967
Finally tasting fame after a long apprenticeship.

HUNGRY EYES

Artist: Eric Carmen
Written by: John Nicola, Franke Previte
From the album: *Dirty Dancing Soundtrack*
Label: RCA
Produced by: Jimmy Lenner
Year: 1988
Pop rock ballad from the monster soundtrack of the year.

HUNGRY FREAKS, DADDY

Artist: The Mothers of Invention
Written by: Frank Zappa
From the album: *Freak Out*
Label: Verve
Produced by: Tom Wilson
Year: 1966
Psychedelic doo-wop.

HUNGRY HEART

Artist: Bruce Springsteen
Written by: Bruce Springsteen
From the album: *The River*
Label: Columbia
Produced by: Jon Landau, Bruce Springsteen, Steve Van Zandt
Year: 1980
First hit for the Boss, used prominently in the great Tom Cruise film *Risky Business*.

HUNGRY LIKE THE WOLF

Artist: Duran Duran
Written by: Duran Duran
From the album: *Rio*
Label: Capitol
Produced by: Colin Thurston
Year: 1983
Their first US hit. The international playboy on vacation, taking along a synthesizer.

HUNGRY WOLF

Artist: X
Written by: John Doe, Exene Cervenka
From the album: *Under the Big Black Sun*
Label: Elektra
Produced by: Ray Manzarek
Year: 1982
Capturing the rockabilly edge of punk in L.A.

HUNTER GETS CAPTURED BY THE GAME, THE

Artist: The Marvelettes
Written by: Smokey Robinson
From the album: *The Marvelettes*
Label: Tamla
Produced by: Smokey Robinson
Year: 1967
Marvelettes bag their biggest R&B hit since "Please Mr. Postman."

HURDY GURDY MAN

Artist: Donovan
Written by: Donovan Leitch
From the album: *Hurdy Gurdy Man*
Label: Epic
Produced by: Mickie Most
Year: 1968
The monkey motif, one step removed.

HURRICANE (PART I)

Artist: Bob Dylan
Written by: Bob Dylan, Jacques Levy
From the album: *Desire*
Label: Columbia
Produced by: Don DeVito
Year: 1976
Helping to set Rubin Hurricane Carter free, with a quintessential folk/rock beat.

HURT

Artist: Roy Hamilton
Written by: Jimmie Crane, Al Jacobs
Label: Epic
Year: 1954
Closing out '54 with his fourth Top 10 R&B hit. Cover by Timi Yuro (Liberty, '62) went Top 10 pop.

HURT

Artist: Nine Inch Nails
Written by: Trent Reznor
From the album: *Closer*
Label: TVT
Produced by: Trent Reznor
Year: 1995
Powerful antidrug message is Reznor's favorite song. Covered by Johnny Cash (American, '02).

HURT SO BAD

Artist: Little Anthony and the Imperials
Written by: Teddy Randazzo, Bobby Hart, Bobby Weinstein (Bobby Wilding)
From the album: *Goin' out of My Head*
Label: DCP
Produced by: Teddy Randazzo
Year: 1965
Lounge rock, covered by Linda Ronstadt (Asylum, '80).

HURTING EACH OTHER

Artist: Ruby and the Romantics
Written by: Gary Geld, Peter Udell
Label: Kapp
Produced by: Allen Stanton
Year: 1965
Covered by the Carpenters (A&M, '72).

HURTING KIND (I'VE GOT MY EYES ON YOU)

Artist: Robert Plant
Written by: Phil Johnstone, Robert Plant, Charlie Jones, Chris Blackwell, Doug Boyle
From the album: *Manic Nirvana*
Label: Es Paranza
Produced by: Robert Plant, Phil Johnstone
Year: 1990

HURTS ME TO MY HEART

Artist: Faye Adams
Written by: Charles Singleton, Rose Marie McCoy
Label: Herald
Produced by: Al Silver
Year: 1954
The stellar songwriting team provides Adams with her third straight #1 R&B hit.

HURTS SO GOOD

Artist: Millie Jackson
Written by: Phillip Mitchell
From the album: *It Hurts So Good*
Label: Spring
Year: 1973
Biggest hit for the salty R&B singer is from the blaxploitation classic *Cleopatra Jones*.

HURTS SO GOOD

Artist: John (Cougar) Mellencamp
Written by: John Cougar Mellencamp, George Michael Green
From the album: *American Fool*
Label: Riva
Produced by: John Mellencamp, Don Gehman
Year: 1982
Through the courtesy of MTV, John Cougar's middle-American macho breaks out of the heartland.

HUSH

Artist: Billy Joe Royal
Written by: Joe South
Label: Columbia
Produced by: Joe South
Year: 1967
Beginning a prolific songwriting career. Covered by Deep Purple (Tetragrammaton, '68) on their first album.

HUSHABYE

Artist: The Mystics
Written by: Doc Pomus, Mort Shuman
Label: Laurie
Year: 1959
The Elegants never managed to follow up "Little Star," but the Mystics did, with the aid of a stellar Brill Building team.

HUSTLE, THE

Artist: Van McCoy & the Soul City Symphony
Written by: Van McCoy
From the album: *Disco Baby*
Label: Avco
Produced by: Hugo and Luigi
Year: 1975
Disco hits the mainstream as producer McCoy scores a #1 R&B/#1 crossover with this apt dance step and inadvertent commentary.

HYPNOTIZE

Artist: The Notorious B.I.G.
Written by: Christopher Wallace, Sean Combs, Derek Angelettie, Ronald Lawrence, Andy Armer, Randy Alpert
From the album: *Life after Death*
Label: Arista
Produced by: Sean Combs, Deric Angelettie, Ron Lawrence
Year: 1997
Living large, East coast style.

HYSTERIA

Artist: Def Leppard
Written by: Steve Clark, Joe Elliot, Robert John "Mutt" Lange, Phil Collen, Rick Savage
From the album: *Hysteria*
Label: Mercury
Produced by: Mutt Lange
Year: 1987
Their first Top 10 hit.

I

I.G.Y. (WHAT A BEAUTIFUL WORLD)

Artist: Donald Fagen
Written by: Donald Fagen
From the album: *The Nightfly*
Label: Warner Brothers
Produced by: Gary Katz
Year: 1982
A cool flashback by a Steely Dan cofounder.

I (WHO HAVE NOTHING)

Artist: Ben E. King
Written by: Jerry Leiber, Mike Stoller, Donita Mogol
From the album: *Ben E. King's Greatest Hits*
Label: Atco
Produced by: Jerry Leiber, Mike Stoller
Year: 1963
Benny reaches for the operatic Elvis/Jackie Wilson move.

I ADORE MI AMOR

Artist: Color Me Badd
Written by: Hamza Lee, Color Me Badd
From the album: *C.M.B.*
Label: Giant
Produced by: Hamza Lee, Royal Bayyan
Year: 1991
#1 R&B/#1 crossover blend. Boyz II Men were in the wings.

I AIN'T DONE WRONG

Artist: The Yardbirds
Written by: Keith Relf
From the album: *For Your Love*
Label: Epic
Produced by: Giorgio Gomelsky
Year: 1965

I AIN'T GOIN' OUT LIKE THAT

Artist: Cypress Hill
Written by: Louis Freese (Dr. Freeze), Larry Muggurud, T. Ray
From the album: *Black Sunday*
Label: Ruffhouse
Produced by: T-Ray
Year: 1993
Rugged rap survival sentiments.

I AIN'T GONNA EAT OUT MY HEART ANYMORE

Artist: The Rascals
Written by: Pam Sawyer, Laurie Burton
From the album: *The Young Rascals*
Label: Atlantic
Produced by: Arif Mardin, the Rascals
Year: 1965
Liberated from the discos of 45TH Street, the Young Rascals begin their career with their hungriest rocker.

I AIN'T MARCHIN' ANYMORE

Artist: Phil Ochs
Written by: Phil Ochs
From the album: *I Ain't Marchin' Anymore*
Label: Elektra
Produced by: Paul Rothchild
Year: 1964
First anthem of the freedom marching counterculture of the '60s. To Mississippi and Alabama and Washington, DC, they would march, but not to Vietnam.

I AIN'T SUPERSTITIOUS

Artist: Howlin' Wolf
Written by: Willie Dixon
Label: Chess
Year: 1962
Covered by the Jeff Beck Group (Epic, '68).

I ALMOST HAD A WEAKNESS

Artist: Elvis Costello & the Brodsky Quartet
Written by: Declan McManus (Elvis Costello), Michael Thomas
From the album: *The Juliet Letters*
Label: Warner Brothers
Produced by: Elvis Costello, Kevin Killen
Year: 1993
Completing his journey from the pub to the front parlor, with the world famous classical musicians.

I ALMOST LOST MY MIND

Artist: Ivory Joe Hunter
Written by: Ivory Joe Hunter
Label: MGM
Year: 1950
His second #1 R&B hit.

I ALONE

Artist: Live
Written by: Edward Kowalcyzk, Patrick Dahlheimer, Chad Gracey, Chad Taylor
From the album: *Throwing Copper*
Label: Radioactive/MCA
Produced by: Jerry Harrison
Year: 1994
Overwrought power ballad. Creed was listening.

I AM … I SAID

Artist: Neil Diamond
Written by: Neil Diamond
From the album: *Stones*
Label: Uni
Produced by: Tom Catalano
Year: 1971
Battling his lack of critical esteem, and other mid-life maladies.

I AM A CHILD

Artist: Buffalo Springfield
Written by: Neil Young
From the album: *Last Time Around*
Label: Atco
Produced by: Charles Greene, Brian Stone
Year: 1968
Young and innocent.

I AM A PATRIOT

Artist: Little Steven and the Disciples of Soul
Written by: Steve Van Zandt
From the album: *Voice of America*
Label: EMI-America
Produced by: Little Steven
Year: 1984
Two years after organizing the Sun City Protest Chorus, more impassioned rock from the Boss's former employee.

I AM A ROCK

Artist: Simon and Garfunkel
Written by: Paul Simon
From the album: *Sounds of Silence*
Label: Columbia
Produced by: Bob Johnston
Year: 1966
Folk/rock in denial.

I AM A SCIENTIST

Artist: Guided By Voices
Written by: Robert Pollard
From the album: *Bee Thousand*
Label: Scat/Matador
Produced by: Guided by Voices
Year: 1994
A gift from the prolific mad scientist of low-fi, the sound of the '90s antitechno rebellion.

I AM ONE

Artist: Smashing Pumpkins
Written by: Billy Corgan, James Iha
From the album: *Tristessa*
Label: Sub Pop
Produced by: Butch Vig
Year: 1991
Breaking through on the college circuit.

I AM THE FLY

Artist: Wire
Written by: Colin Newman, Graham Lewis
From the album: *Pink Flag*
Label: Harvest
Produced by: Mike Thorne
Year: 1977
From their landmark album, even terser than the Ramones.

I AM THE WALRUS

Artist: The Beatles
Written by: John Lennon, Paul McCartney
From the album: *Magical Mystery Tour*
Label: Capitol
Produced by: George Martin
Year: 1967
John's most literary affectation and the B-side of "Hello, Goodbye."

I AM WOMAN

Artist: Helen Reddy
Written by: Helen Reddy, Ray Burton
From the album: *I Am Woman*
Label: Capitol
Produced by: Tom Catalano
Year: 1972
Women's lib goes to Las Vegas.

I BEG OF YOU

Artist: Elvis Presley
Written by: Rose Marie McCoy, Kelly Owens
From the album: *Touch of Gold (Vol. I)*
Label: RCA
Produced by: Steve Sholes
Year: 1958
B-side of "Don't."

I BELIEVE

Artist: The Buzzcocks
Written by: Pete Shelley
From the album: *A Different Kind of Tension*
Label: United Artists
Produced by: Martin Rushent
Year: 1979
A mini-rock opera of affirmations.

I BELIEVE I CAN FLY

Artist: R. Kelly
Written by: Robert Kelly
From the album: *Space Jam Soundtrack*
Label: Warner Sunset
Produced by: R. Kelly
Year: 1996
Soaring R&B movie ballad.

I BELIEVE I'LL DUST MY BROOM

Artist: Elmore James
Written by: Robert Johnson
From the album: *Blues after Hours*
Label: Trumpet
Year: 1952
Originated by Robert Johnson (Vocalion, '36). Elmore James's dusty slide guitar style was a major influence on Eric Clapton, Billy Gibbons, and Stevie Ray Vaughan.

I BELIEVE IN YOU (YOU BELIEVE IN ME)

Artist: Johnnie Taylor
Written by: Don Davis
From the album: *Taylored in Silk*
Label: Stax
Produced by: Don Davis
Year: 1973
#1 R&B/Top 20 crossover.

I BELIEVE MY OWN EYES

Artist: Marcia Mitzman and Jonathan Dokuchitz
Written by: Peter Townshend
From the album: *Tommy*
Label: RCA
Produced by: George Martin
Year: 1993
Added to the Townshend rock opera when it reached Broadway, the ultimate end of its twenty-year trail as a musical.

I CAME TO DANCE

Artist: Nils Lofgren
Written by: Nils Lofgren
From the album: *I Came to Dance*
Label: A&M
Produced by: Nilson Lofgren, Andy Newmark
Year: 1977
Ultimate statement of purpose from the itinerant Neil Young and Bruce Springsteen sideman.

I CAN HEAR MUSIC

Artist: The Ronettes
Written by: Jeff Barry, Ellie Greenwich, Phil Spector
Label: Philles
Produced by: Phil Spector
Year: 1966
A Spector low point, the Ronettes's last chart song, spending a week at number 100. Covered by the Beach Boys (Brother, '68).

I CAN HELP

Artist: Billy Swan
Written by: Billy Swan
From the album: *I Can Help*
Label: Monument
Produced by: Billy Swan, Chip Young
Year: 1974
#1 country/#1 crossover for the rockabilly veteran. Covered by Elvis Presley (RCA, '75).

I CAN NEVER GO HOME ANYMORE

Artist: The Shangri-Las
Written by: George Morton, Jerry Grimaldi
From the album: *Past, Present and Future*
Label: Red Bird
Produced by: Shadow Morton
Year: 1965
Their prophetic last hit. Mary and Marge Ganser both died in the '70s.

I CAN SEE CLEARLY NOW

Artist: Johnny Nash
Written by: Johnny Nash
From the album: *I Can See Clearly Now*
Label: Epic
Produced by: Johnny Nash
Year: 1972
First reggae tune to hit #1, backed by some of Bob Marley's Wailers.

I CAN SEE FOR MILES

Artist: The Who
Written by: Townshend, Peter
From the album: *The Who Sell Out*
Label: Decca
Produced by: Kit Lambert
Year: 1967
Their only Top 10 single.

I CAN'T BE SATISFIED

Artist: Muddy Waters
Written by: McKinley Morganfield (Muddy Waters)
Label: Aristocrat
Produced by: Leonard Chess
Year: 1948
Cornerstone in the blues canon.

I CAN'T DANCE

Artist: Genesis
Written by: Phil Collins, Tony Banks, Mike Rutherford
From the album: *We Can't Dance*
Label: Genesis
Produced by: Nick Davis, Genesis
Year: 1991
The theme song of progressive rockers (as well as folkies) everywhere.

I CAN'T DRIVE 55

Artist: Sammy Hagar
Written by: Sammy Hagar
From the album: *VOA*
Label: Geffen
Year: 1984
Rock as social protest on a par with "For What It's Worth"; eventually the speed limits in many states were rolled back to 65.

I CAN'T EXPLAIN

Artist: The Who
Written by: Pete Townshend
From the album: *Meaty, Beaty, Big, and Bouncy*
Label: Decca
Produced by: Kit Lambert
Year: 1965
Townshend's first success at songwriting, the most significant Bottom-10 song of the year; he'd go on to become one of rock's great explainers.

I CAN'T GET NEXT TO YOU

Artist: The Temptations
Written by: Norman Whitfield, Barrett Strong
From the album: *Puzzle People*
Label: Gordy
Produced by: Norman Whitfield
Year: 1969
Their ninth #1 R&B and second #1 R&B/#1 crossover was their biggest hit.

(I CAN'T GET NO) SATISFACTION

Artist: The Rolling Stones
Written by: Mick Jagger, Keith Richards
From the album: *Out of Our Heads*
Label: London
Produced by: Andrew Loog-Oldham
Year: 1965
Fuzz-toned anthem of alienation was their first #1 US/#1 UK crossover and remains their biggest hit. Myth has it the song came from a riff Richards dreamed in his sleep. Covered by the Residents (Ralph, '76), Devo (Warner Bothers, '79).

I CAN'T GO FOR THAT (NO CAN DO)

Artist: Hall & Oates
Written by: Daryl Hall, John Oates, Sara Allen
From the album: *Private Eyes*
Label: RCA
Produced by: Hall & Oates
Year: 1981
On their way toward eclipsing the Everly Brothers as the most successful duo in chart history with their fourth #1 (of six) and only #1 R&B/#1 crossover.

I CAN'T HELP MYSELF (SUGAR PIE, HONEY BUNCH)

Artist: The Four Tops
Written by: Eddie Holland, Lamont Dozier, Brian Holland
From the album: *Four Tops Second Album*
Label: Motown
Produced by: Brian Holland, Lamont Dozier
Year: 1965
Their biggest hit; a #1 R&B/#1 crossover.

I CAN'T HOLD ON

Artist: Karla Bonoff
Written by: Karla Bonoff
From the album: *Karla Bonoff*
Label: Columbia
Produced by: Kenny Edwards
Year: 1977
Linda Ronstadt's favorite singer/songwriter has a lot to say about getting and keeping love.

I CAN'T LIVE WITHOUT MY RADIO

Artist: L.L. Cool J
Written by: James Todd Smith, Rick Rubin
From the album: *Radio*
Label: Def Jam
Produced by: Rick Rubin
Year: 1985
Impressive and propulsive new rap artist expresses timeless rock and roll sentiments. Suggested segue: "Please Don't Take My Air Jordans" by Reg E. Gaines.

I CAN'T QUIT HER

Artist: Blood, Sweat and Tears
Written by: Al Kooper, Irwin Levine
From the album: *Child Is Father to the Man*
Label: Columbia
Produced by: John Simon
Year: 1968
Dylan collaborator and former Royal Teen, Al Kooper reached a blues peak, with the help of future cowriter of "Tie a Yellow Ribbon Round the Old Oak Tree."

I CAN'T STAND IT

Artist: Eric Clapton
Written by: Eric Clapton
From the album: *Another Ticket*
Label: RSO
Produced by: Tom Dowd
Year: 1981
Blues powerless.

I CAN'T STAND THE RAIN

Artist: Ann Peebles
Written by: Donald Bryant, Ann Peebles, Bernard Miller
From the album: *I Can't Stand the Rain*
Label: Hi
Produced by: Willie Mitchell
Year: 1973
Only Top 40 hit for the powerful soul belter.

I CAN'T STOP LOVING YOU

Artist: Don Gibson
Written by: Don Gibson
From the album: *Oh Lonesome Me*
Label: RCA
Produced by: Chet Atkins
Year: 1958
#1 country B-side of "Oh Lonesome Me," which was a #1 country/Top 10 crossover. Reinvented as a gospel soul weeper by Ray Charles (ABC Paramount, '62): #1 R&B/#1 crossover single of the year.

I CAN'T TELL YOU WHY

Artist: Eagles
Written by: Don Henley, Glenn Frey, Timothy Schmit
From the album: *The Long Run*
Label: Asylum
Produced by: Bill Szymczyk
Year: 1979
Tenth and last Top 10 hit, from the movie *Inside Moves*.

I CAN'T TURN YOU LOOSE

Artist: Otis Redding
Written by: Otis Redding, Steve Cropper, McElvoy Robinson
From the album: *Otis Redding Live in Europe*
Label: Volt
Produced by: Otis Redding, Jim Stewart, Steve Cropper
Year: 1965
Originally the B-side of "Just One More Day." Covered by the Chambers Brothers (Columbia, '68).

I CAN'T WAIT

Artist: Nu Shooz
Written by: John Smith
From the album: *Poolside*
Label: Atlantic
Produced by: John Smith, R. Waritz
Year: 1986
One-shot duo from Oregon.

I CAN'T WAIT ANOTHER MINUTE

Artist: Hi-Five
Written by: Eric Foster White
From the album: *Hi-Five*
Label: Jive
Produced by: Eric Foster White
Year: 1991
Teenybop hip hop; #1 R&B/Top 10 crossover.

I COULD HAVE BEEN YOUR BEST OLD FRIEND

Artist: Bonnie Raitt
Written by: Tracy Nelson, Andy McMahon
From the album: *The Glow*
Label: Warner Brothers
Produced by: Bill Payne, George Massenberg
Year: 1976
Helping to put a down payment on Tracy's Tennessee home.

I COULD NEVER LOVE ANOTHER (AFTER LOVING YOU)

Artist: The Temptations
Written by: Norman Whitfield, Barrett Strong, Roger Penzabene
From the album: *Wish It Would Rain*
Label: Gordy
Produced by: Norman Whitfield
Year: 1968
#1 R&B/Top 20 crossover.

I COULD NEVER TAKE THE PLACE OF YOUR MAN

Artist: Prince
Written by: Prince Rogers Nelson
From the album: *Sign 'o' the Times Soundtrack*
Label: Paisley Park
Produced by: Prince
Year: 1988
One of his more perfect singles. From the same album as "If I Was Your Girlfriend" and a natural segue out of "When You Were Mine."

I COULD RULE THE WORLD IF I COULD ONLY GET THE PARTS

Artist: Tin Huey
Written by: Chris Butler
From the album: *Contents Dislodged During Shipment*
Label: Warner Brothers
Produced by: Chris Butler
Year: 1979
Midwestern frat punk band puts the Akron scene on the map. Covered by the Waitresses (Polydor, '82).

I COULDN'T GET HIGH

Artist: The Fugs
Written by: Tuli Kupferberg, Ed Sanders
From the album: *First Album*
Label: ESP
Produced by: Harry Smith
Year: 1965
Pungent satire.

I COUNT THE TEARS

Artist: The Drifters
Written by: Doc Pomus, Mort Shuman
From the album: *Save the Last Dance for Me*
Label: Atlantic
Produced by: Jerry Leiber, Mike Stoller
Year: 1961
Top 10 R&B/Top 20 crossover.

I CRIED A TEAR

Artist: LaVern Baker
Written by: Al Julia, Fred Jay
Label: Atlantic
Produced by: Ahmet Ertegun, Jerry Wexler

Year: 1959
Biggest hit for the influential soul belter; #2 R&B/
Top 10 crossover.

I DIDN'T MEAN TO TURN YOU ON

Artist: Cherrelle
Written by: James Harris III, Terry Lewis
From the album: *Fragile*
Label: Tabu
Produced by: Jimmy Jam, Terry Lewis
Year: 1984
Covered by Robert Palmer (Atlantic, '86).

I DO

Artist: The Marvelows
Written by: Jesse Smith, Johnny Paden, Frank
Paden, Willie Stephenson, Melvin Mason
Label: ABC Paramount
Produced by: Johnny Pate
Year: 1965
Top 10 R&B hit. Covered by the J. Geils Band
(Atlantic, '77).

I DO THE ROCK

Artist: Tim Curry
Written by: Tim Curry, Michael Kamen
From the album: *Fearless*
Label: A&M
Year: 1979
Underground treatise by the star of the cult classic
The Rocky Horror Picture Show.

I DON'T BELIEVE YOU (SHE ACTS LIKE WE NEVER HAVE MET)

Artist: Bob Dylan
Written by: Bob Dylan
From the album: *Another Side of Bob Dylan*
Label: Columbia
Produced by: Tom Wilson
Year: 1964
In the age of the Sexual Revolution, Dylan had as
little clue to the opposite sex as anyone.

I DON'T HAVE THE HEART

Artist: James Ingram
Written by: Allen Rich, Judd Friedman
From the album: *It's Real*
Label: Warner Brothers
Produced by: Thom Bell, James Ingram
Year: 1990
Down the middle of the soul-road.

I DON'T KNOW

Artist: Willie Mabon
Written by: Willie Mabon, Joe Thomas
Label: Chess
Year: 1952
Establishing the Chicago label's blues crossover
potential with a #1 R&B hit.

I DON'T KNOW HOW TO LOVE HIM

Artist: Yvonne Elliman
Written by: Tim Rice, Andrew Lloyd Webber
From the album: *Jesus Christ Superstar*
Label: Decca
Produced by: Tim Rice, Andrew Lloyd Webber
Year: 1971
Love song (of the physical kind) sung by Mary to
Jesus on Broadway via England.

I DON'T KNOW WHAT YOU'VE GOT (BUT IT'S GOT ME)

Artist: Little Richard
Written by: Don Covay, Horace Hall
Label: Vee Jay
Produced by: J. W. Alexander
Year: 1965
The ultimate rocker achieves a soul epiphany.

I DON'T LIKE MONDAYS

Artist: The Boomtown Rats
Written by: Bob Geldof
From the album: *The Fine Art of Surfacing*
Label: Columbia
Produced by: Phil Wainman
Year: 1979
#1 UK/US crossover; post-punk rock journalism
based on the true story of the mass-murderer
Brenda Spencer, who offered the immortal title
phrase to explain why she gunned down eleven
people.

I DON'T LIVE TODAY

Artist: Jimi Hendrix
Written by: Jimi Hendrix
From the album: *Are You Experienced?*
Label: Reprise
Produced by: Chas Chandler.
Year: 1967
The first black artist to become a superstar in the
white genre of psychedelic rock guitar, which was
itself based on second-generation B. B. King, as
processed through Owsley Stanley. Eddie Hazel
was ready to take the baton. Ernie Isley and Vernon
Reid were listening.

I DON'T NEED NO DOCTOR

Artist: Ray Charles
Written by: Nick Ashford, Valerie Simpson
From the album: *A Man and His Soul*
Label: ABC
Produced by: TRC
Year: 1966
Covered by Humble Pie (A&M, '71).

I DON'T THINK SO

Artist: Dinosaur Jr.
Written by: Joseph Mascis
From the album: *Without a Sound*

Label: Sire
Produced by: J. Mascis
Year: 1994
Anti-folk/rock anthem.

I DON'T WANNA GO ON WITH YOU LIKE THAT

Artist: Elton John
Written by: Elton John, Bernie Taupin
From the album: *Reg Strikes Back*
Label: MCA
Year: 1988

I DON'T WANNA GROW UP

Artist: Tom Waits
Written by: Tom Waits
From the album: *Bone Machine*
Label: Island
Produced by: Tom Waits
Year: 1992
Covered by the Ramones (Rykodisc, '95).

I DON'T WANNA LIVE WITHOUT YOUR LOVE

Artist: Chicago
Written by: Diane Warren, Albert Hammond
From the album: *19*
Label: Reprise
Produced by: Ron Nevison
Year: 1988
Their seventeenth Top 10 hit.

I DON'T WANT TO DO WRONG

Artist: Gladys Knight & the Pips
Written by: Johnny Bristol, Catherine Shaffner,
William Guest, Gladys Knight, Merald Knight Jr.,
Walter Jones
From the album: *If I Were Your Woman*
Label: Soul
Produced by: Johnny Bristol
Year: 1971
Concert perennial, establishing their down-home,
common-sense persona.

I DON'T WANT TO GO HOME

Artist: Southside Johnny and the Asbury Jukes
Written by: Steve Van Zandt
From the album: *I Don't Want to Go Home*
Label: Epic
Produced by: Steve Van Zandt
Year: 1976
Their enduring party signature.

(I DON'T WANT TO GO TO) CHELSEA

Artist: Elvis Costello
Written by: Declan McManus (Elvis Costello)
From the album: *Taking Liberties*

Label: Columbia
Produced by: Nick Lowe
Year: 1980
More compulsive nihilism for now people.

I DON'T WANT TO MISS A THING

Artist: Aerosmith
Written by: Diane Warren
From the album: *Armageddon* Soundtrack
Label: Columbia
Year: 1998
Big emotional movie ballad is Aerosmith's only #1.

I DON'T WANT TO SPOIL THE PARTY

Artist: The Beatles
Written by: John Lennon, Paul McCartney
From the album: *Beatles VI*
Label: Capitol
Produced by: George Martin
Year: 1965
To that point, a rare introspective mode. Covered by Rosanne Cash (Columbia, '89).

I DON'T WANT TO TALK ABOUT IT

Artist: Crazy Horse
Written by: Danny Whitten
From the album: *Crazy Horse*
Label: Warner Brothers
Produced by: Jack Nitzsche, Bruce Botnick
Year: 1971
Shining moment for Neil Young's sometime backup band. Covered by Rod Stewart (Warner Brothers, '75).

I DON'T WANT TO WAIT

Artist: Paula Cole
Written by: Paula Cole
From the album: *This Fire*
Label: Warner Brothers
Produced by: Paula Cole, Kevin Killen
Year: 1997
Ballad of female impatience became the theme of the teen soaper *Dawson's Creek*.

I DON'T WANT YOUR LOVE

Artist: Duran Duran
Written by: John Taylor, Nick Rhodes, Simon Lebon
From the album: *Big Thing*
Label: Capitol
Produced by: Duran Duran, J. Elias, D. Abraham
Year: 1988
Recorded as Duranduran.

I DRINK ALONE

Artist: George Thorogood
Written by: George Thorogood

From the album: *Maverick*
Label: EMI-America
Year: 1985
Imbibing the stuff of rock and roll legend. Suggested segues: "One Scotch, One Bourbon, One Beer" by Amos Milburn, "Red Red Wine" by UB40, "What Made Milwaukee Famous (Made a Loser out of Me)" by Jerry Lee Lewis.

I FALL TO PIECES

Artist: Patsy Cline
Written by: Hank Cochran, Harlan Howard
From the album: *Patsy Cline Showcase*
Label: Decca
Produced by: Owen Bradley
Year: 1961
Great country weeper; #1 country/Top 15 crossover.

I FEEL FINE

Artist: The Beatles
Written by: John Lennon, Paul McCartney
From the album: *Beatles '65*
Label: Capitol
Produced by: George Martin
Year: 1964
Their sixth and last #1 of '64. Segue: "Watch Your Step" by Bobby Parker. Lennon claimed this was the earliest use of feedback on record. But the Yardbirds might beg to differ, to say nothing of the Johnny Burnette Trio.

I FEEL FOR YOU

Artist: Prince
Written by: Prince Rogers Nelson
From the album: *Prince*
Label: Warner Brothers
Produced by: Prince
Year: 1979
Cover by Chaka Kahn (Warner Brothers, '84) was the top R&B song of the year, with Stevie Wonder on harmonica.

I FEEL FREE

Artist: Cream
Written by: Jack Bruce, Pete Brown
From the album: *Fresh Cream*
Label: Atco
Produced by: Robert Stigwood
Year: 1967
Clapton's post-Yardbirds/Mayall, pre-Derek and the Dominoes supergroup debut.

I FEEL LIKE A BULLET (IN THE GUN OF ROBERT FORD)

Artist: Elton John
Written by: Elton John, Bernie Taupin
From the album: *Rock of the Westies*
Label: MCA
Produced by: Gus Dudgeon
Year: 1974

Reminiscent of Dylan's "I might look like Robert Ford but I feel just like Jesse James," from "Outlaw Blues."

I FEEL LIKE BREAKING UP SOMEBODY'S HOME TONIGHT

Artist: Ann Peebles
Written by: Timothy Matthews, Al Jackson
From the album: *Straight from the Heart*
Label: Hi
Produced by: Willie Mitchell
Year: 1972
Primal R&B blueprint for Mary J. Blige to emulate.

I FEEL LOVE

Artist: Donna Summer
Written by: Giorgio Morodor, Pete Bellotte, Donna Summer
From the album: *I Remember Yesterday*
Label: Casablanca
Produced by: Pete Bellotte, Giorgio Moroder
Year: 1977
#1 UK smash cements Donna's unrelenting approach to passion.

I FEEL SO BAD

Artist: Chuck Willis
Written by: Chuck Willis
Label: Okeh
Produced by: Zenas "Big Daddy" Sears
Year: 1954
Like a ballgame on a rainy day. Covered by Elvis Presley (RCA, '61).

I FEEL SO GOOD

Artist: Richard Thompson
Written by: Richard Thompson
From the album: *Rumor and Sigh*
Label: Capitol
Produced by: Mitchell Froom
Year: 1991
Ready to rumble, especially on guitar.

I FEEL THE EARTH MOVE

Artist: Carole King
Written by: Carole King
From the album: *Tapestry*
Label: Ode
Produced by: Lou Adler
Year: 1971
Ode to the vicissitudes of California living is the B-side of "It's Too Late."

I FEEL THE SAME

Artist: Bonnie Raitt
Written by: Chris Smither
From the album: *Takin' My Time*
Label: Warner Brothers
Produced by: John Hall
Year: 1973
Torchy blues lament.

I FORGOT TO BE YOUR LOVER

Artist: William Bell
Written by: William Bell, Booker T. Jones
Label: Stax
Produced by: Booker T. Jones
Year: 1968
Top 10 R&B hit. Covered by Billy Idol (Chrysalis, '86).

I FORGOT TO REMEMBER TO FORGET

Artist: Elvis Presley
Written by: Stanley Kesler, Charles Feathers
From the album: *Heartbreak Hotel*
Label: Sun
Produced by: Sam Phillips
Year: 1955
Legendary early Elvis rockabilly classic; #1 country hit, with "Mystery Train" on the B-side.

I FOUGHT THE LAW

Artist: The Crickets
Written by: Sonny Curtis
From the album: *In Style with the Crickets*
Label: Brunswick
Produced by: Norman Petty
Year: 1959
Last blast of rockabilly from the post-Buddy Crickets, featuring the guitar of Sonny Curtis, who would go on to write "The Mary Tyler Moore Show" theme (covered by Husker Du). Covered by the Bobby Fuller Four (Mustang, '66); and the Clash, for whom it was their first US single, backed with "(White Man) In Hammersmith Palais" (Epic, '79).

I FOUND A LOVE

Artist: The Falcons
Written by: Willie Schofield, Robert West, Wilson Pickett
Label: Lupine
Year: 1962
Covered by former group member, Wilson Pickett (Atlantic, '67).

I FOUND THAT ESSENCE RARE

Artist: Gang of Four
Written by: Jon King, Andy Gill, Hugo Burnham, Rob Warr
From the album: *Entertainment*
Label: Warner Brothers
Produced by: Andy Gill
Year: 1980
Formative listening experience for alternative alphabet bands, U2, R.E.M., INXS.

I GET AROUND

Artist: The Beach Boys
Written by: Brian Wilson
From the album: *All Summer Long*
Label: Capitol
Produced by: Brian Wilson
Year: 1964
Their first #1 and biggest all-time hit.

I GET AROUND

Artist: 2Pac
Written by: Tupac Shakur, Shock-G, Roger Troutman, Lester Troutman, S. Murdock
From the album: *Strictly 4 My N.I.G.G.A.Z.*
Label: Interscope
Produced by: D.J. Daryl
Year: 1993
First hit single for the legendary West coast rapper.

I GET WEAK

Artist: Belinda Carlisle
Written by: Diane Warren
From the album: *Heaven on Earth*
Label: MCA
Produced by: Rick Nowels
Year: 1988
Another winner from the undeniable catalogue of Diane Warren, a one-woman West coast Brill Building.

I GO CRAZY

Artist: Flesh for Lulu
Written by: James Mitchell, Kevin Mills, Nick Marsh, Rocco Barker
From the album: *Long Live the New Flesh*
Label: Beggars' Banquet/Capitol
Year: 1987
Gothic glamsters go commercial with this tune from the soundtrack of the film *Some Kind of Wonderful*.

I GO TO EXTREMES

Artist: Billy Joel
Written by: Billy Joel
From the album: *Storm Front*
Label: Columbia
Produced by: Mick Jones, Billy Joel
Year: 1989
Autobiographical self-justification. Follow-up to "You May Be Right."

I GO TO PIECES

Artist: Del Shannon
Written by: Del Shannon
Label: Amy
Produced by: Irving Micahnik, Harry Balk
Year: 1964
Covered by Peter and Gordon (Capitol, '64).

I GOT A FEELING

Artist: Ricky Nelson
Written by: Baker Knight
From the album: *Ricky Sings Again*
Label: Imperial
Produced by: Ricky Nelson, Jimmy Haskell, Ozzie Nelson
Year: 1958
Clean-cut rocker is the B-side of "Lonesome Town." Suggested seque: "Dirty Dirty Feeling" by Elvis Presley.

I GOT A LINE ON YOU

Artist: Spirit
Written by: Randy California
From the album: *The Family That Plays Together*
Label: Ode
Produced by: Lou Adler
Year: 1969
Psychedelic signature.

I GOT A MAN

Artist: Positive K
Written by: Positive K
From the album: *Skills Dat Pay Da Bills*
Label: Island
Produced by: S. Thomas
Year: 1993
The fine art of the pickup, showcased by Mickey and Sylvia in "Love Is Strange," back in '57, is exhibited with high-street style, by K and a determinedly resistant female.

I GOT A NAME

Artist: Jim Croce
Written by: Norman Gimbel, Charles Fox
From the album: *I Got a Name*
Label: ABC
Produced by: Terry Cashman, Tommy West
Year: 1973
Folkie theme from the film *The Last American Hero*.

I GOT A WOMAN (I GOT A SWEETIE)

Artist: Ray Charles
Written by: Ray Charles, Renald Richard
From the album: *Do the Twist*
Label: Atlantic
Produced by: Ahmet Ertegun, Jerry Wexler
Year: 1955
#2 R&B hit, based on an Alex Bradford hymn. Marked the first instance of gospel soul mixing with R&B roots. Covered by Elvis Presley on his first RCA album in '56. Recorded by the Beatles, July '63, but not released until '95, on Capitol.

I GOT LOADED

Artist: Peppermint Harris
Written by: Harrison Nelson
Label: Aladdin
Year: 1951
Crucial #1 R&B ode to the joys of getting plastered. Covered by Los Lobos (Slash, '84), Robert Cray (Hightone, '87).

I GOT LOVE ON MY MIND

Artist: Natalie Cole
Written by: Charles Jackson Jr., Marvin Yancy

From the album: *Unpredictable*
Label: Capitol
Produced by: Chuck Jackson, Marvin Yancey
Year: 1977
#1 R&B/Top 10 crossover is the biggest hit for Nat's daughter, except for her cover of Bruce Springsteen's "Pink Cadillac" in '87.

I GOT NO ANSWERS

Artist: Joan Jett
Written by: Joan Jett, Kenny Laguna
From the album: *Glorious Results of a Misspent Youth*
Label: Boardwalk
Year: 1984
Critically regarded as her ultimate achievement.

I GOT STONED AND I MISSED IT

Artist: Shel Silverstein
Written by: Shel Silverstein
From the album: *Freakin' at the Freaker's Ball*
Label: Columbia
Produced by: Roy Halee
Year: 1973
Covered by Dr. Hook, '75.
A hippie's lament.

I GOT STUNG

Artist: Elvis Presley
Written by: Aaron Schroeder, David Hill
From the album: *50,000,000 Elvis Fans Can't Be Wrong: Elvis' Gold Records (Vol. II)*
Label: RCA
Produced by: Steve Sholes, Chet Atkins
Year: 1958
B-side of the Smiley Lewis classic "One Night."

I GOT THE FEELIN'

Artist: James Brown and the Famous Flames
Written by: James Brown
From the album: *I Got the Feelin'*
Label: King
Produced by: James Brown
Year: 1968
#1 R&B/Top 10 crossover.

I GOT THE HOOK UP

Artist: Master P
Written by: Master P (Percy Miller) and Sons of Funk
From the album: *MP Da Last Don*
Label: No Limit
Year: 1998
Casual sex in the era of *Hoop Dreams* from the movie of the same name, starring the former b-ball bit player turned rap magnate, Percy Miller.

I GOT YOU

Artist: Split Enz
Written by: Neil Finn
From the album: *True Colours*
Label: A&M

Produced by: David Tickle
Year: 1980
Only US hit for the pre-Crowded House Finn brothers from Australia.

I GOT YOU (I FEEL GOOD)

Artist: James Brown and the Famous Flames
Written by: James Brown
From the album: *I Got You (I Feel Good)*
Label: King
Produced by: James Brown
Year: 1965
Defining the electric essence of the moment, James connects with the youth culture for his biggest hit.

I GOT YOU BABE

Artist: Sonny and Cher
Written by: Sonny Bono
From the album: *Look at Us*
Label: Atco
Produced by: Sonny Bono
Year: 1965
In which "He's a Rebel" goes to California in suede and leather and invents folk/rock. Originally the B-side of "It's Gonna Rain." Covered by the Dictators (Epic, '75).

I GOTCHA

Artist: Joe Tex
Written by: Joe Tex
From the album: *I Gotcha*
Label: Dial
Produced by: Buddy Killen
Year: 1972
His biggest all-time hit.

I GOTTA KNOW

Artist: Wanda Jackson
Written by: Thelma Blackman
From the album: *Wanda Jackson*
Produced by: Ken Nelson
Label: Capitol
Year: 1956
Country song with a rock and roll heart.

I GOTTA KNOW

Artist: Elvis Presley
Written by: Paul Evans, Matt Williams
From the album: *Elvis' Golden Records (Vol. III)*
Label: RCA
Produced by: Steve Sholes
Year: 1960
B-side of "Are You Lonesome Tonight."

I GUESS THAT'S WHY THEY CALL IT THE BLUES

Artist: Elton John
Written by: Elton John, Bernie Taupin
From the album: *Too Low for Zero*
Label: Geffen
Produced by: Chris Thomas
Year: 1983

Back in the Top 10 after a four-year layoff. Stevie Wonder on harmonica.

(I GUESS) THE LORD MUST BE IN NEW YORK CITY

Artist: Nilsson
Written by: Harry Nilsson
From the album: *Harry*
Label: RCA
Produced by: Nilsson House Productions
Year: 1969
Nilsson starts letting the quirks out.

I HAD A KING

Artist: Joni Mitchell
Written by: Joni Mitchell
From the album: *Joni Mitchell*
Label: Reprise
Produced by: David Crosby
Year: 1968
The first lady of rock poetry pens her opening memoir.

I HAD TOO MUCH TO DREAM (LAST NIGHT)

Artist: Electric Prunes
Written by: Nancie Mantz, Annette Tucker
From the album: *Electric Prunes*
Label: Reprise
Produced by: Damo Productions
Year: 1967
Prime exponent of the ill-fated pseudo-psychedelic, Boss-town sound.

I HATE MY SCHOOL

Artist: Red Cross
Written by: Steve McDonald, Jeff McDonald
From the album: *Red Cross*
Label: Posh Boy
Produced by: Red Cross
Year: 1980
The Ramones meet Jonathan Richman at Brian Wilson's house.

I HATE MYSELF FOR LOVING YOU

Artist: Joan Jett
Written by: Joan Jett, Desmond Child
From the album: *Up Your Alley*
Label: CBS Associated
Produced by: Kenny Laguna, Desmond Child
Year: 1988
Visiting the noted song doctor for a Top 10 fix.

I HAVE BEEN HERE BEFORE

Artist: Essra Mohawk
Written by: Essra Mohawk
From the album: *Primordial Lovers*
Label: Reprise
Produced by: Frazier Mohawk
Year: 1970

From her critically lauded album, the defining credo for the Secret Diva from Philadelphia.

I HEAR A SYMPHONY

Artist: The Supremes
Written by: Eddie Holland, Lamont Dozier, Brian Holland
From the album: *I Hear a Symphony*
Label: Motown
Produced by: Brian Holland, Lamont Dozier
Year: 1965
6TH straight #1.

I HEAR YOU KNOCKING

Artist: Smiley Lewis
Written by: Dave Bartholomew, Pearl King
From the album: *I Hear You Knocking*
Label: Imperial
Produced by: Dave Bartholemew
Year: 1955
Top 5 R&B hit. Cover by Gale Storm (Dot, '55) went Top 5 pop. Also covered by Dave Edmunds (MAM, '71).

I HEARD A RUMOUR

Artist: Bananarama
Written by: Matt Aitken, Pete Waterman, Mike Stock, Sarah Dallin, Siobhan Fahey, Keren Woodward
From the album: *Wow*
Label: London
Produced by: Mike Stock, Matt Aitken, Pete Waterman
Year: 1987
Winsome UK girl group's last big US hit. Featured in the movie *Disorderlies*.

I HEARD HER CALL MY NAME

Artist: The Velvet Underground
Written by: Lou Reed
From the album: *White Light / White Heat*
Label: Verve
Produced by: Andy Warhol
Year: 1968

I HEARD IT THROUGH THE GRAPEVINE

Artist: Gladys Knight & the Pips
Written by: Norman Whitfield, Barrett Strong
From the album: *Everybody Needs Love*
Label: Soul
Produced by: Norman Whitfield
Year: 1965
One of the most powerful efforts in Motown history, nearly as powerful as the grapevine itself. Marvin Gaye recorded it first but didn't release his version until a year after Gladys Knight & the Pips had a #1 R&B/#2 crossover. Gaye's single was a #1 R&B/#1 crossover (Tamla, '68) and is regarded as one of rock and roll's greatest all-time tracks. Also covered by Creedence Clearwater Revival (Fantasy, '70).

I HONESTLY LOVE YOU

Artist: Olivia Newton-John
Written by: Jeff Barry, Peter Allen
From the album: *If You Love Me (Let Me Know)*
Label: MCA
Produced by: John Farrar
Year: 1974
#1 Grammy winner for the future Boy from Oz, Liza Minnelli's ex-husband Peter Allen, who also wrote "Quiet Please, There's a Lady on Stage" for his then mother-in-law, Judy Garland, "Tenterfield Saddler" about his grandfather in Australia, and "Don't Cry out Loud" for Melissa Manchester.

I JUST CALLED TO SAY I LOVE YOU

Artist: Stevie Wonder
Written by: Stevie Wonder
From the album: *The Woman in Red Soundtrack*
Label: Motown
Produced by: Stevie Wonder
Year: 1984
His big movie ballad is a #1 R&B/#1 crossover. Suggested alternate ring-tone: "Hello" by Lionel Richie.

I JUST CAN'T STOP LOVING YOU

Artist: Michael Jackson with Seidah Garrett
Written by: Michael Jackson
From the album: *Bad*
Label: Epic
Produced by: Quincy Jones
Year: 1987
#1 R&B/#1 crossover.

(I JUST) DIED IN YOUR ARMS

Artist: Cutting Crew
Written by: Nick Eede
From the album: *Broadcast*
Label: Virgin
Produced by: T. Brown, J. Jansen, Cutting Crew
Year: 1987
Synth pop hit peaks at #1.

I JUST WANNA MAKE LOVE TO YOU

Artist: Muddy Waters
Written by: Willie Dixon
Label: Chess
Year: 1954
Initially entitled "Just Make Love to Me," this was Muddy's biggest R&B hit, with a harp solo by Little Walter. Covered by Chuck Berry (Chess, '63), the Rolling Stones (London, '64), the Righteous Brothers (Moonglow, '65), B.B. King (ABC, '77).

I JUST WANNA STOP

Artist: Gino Vannelli
Written by: Ross Vannelli
From the album: *Brother to Brother*
Label: A&M
Produced by: Gino Vannelli, Joe Vannelli
Year: 1978
A rare example of Canadian overstatement.

I JUST WANT TO BE YOUR EVERYTHING

Artist: Andy Gibb
Written by: Barry Gibb
From the album: *Flowing Rivers*
Label: RSO
Produced by: Karl Richardson, Albhy Galuten, Barry Gibb
Year: 1977
In the family tradition, Gibb sibling's debut single hits #1, as would the next two.

I JUST WANT TO CELEBRATE

Artist: Rare Earth
Written by: Dino Fekaris, Nick Zesses
From the album: *One World*
Label: Motown
Produced by: Tom Baird, Rare Earth
Year: 1971
White R&B act from Motown get their first hit that isn't a Temptations cover.

I JUST WASN'T MADE FOR THESE TIMES

Artist: The Beach Boys
Written by: Brian Wilson
From the album: *Pet Sounds*
Label: Capitol
Produced by: Brian Wilson
Year: 1966
Revived as the title of a '95 documentary on Wilson's life.

I KEEP FORGETTIN' (EVERY TIME YOU'RE NEAR)

Artist: Chuck Jackson
Written by: Jerry Leiber, Mike Stoller
From the album: *Any Day Now*
Label: Wand
Year: 1962
Soul ballad remade in '82 by Michael McDonald, who tried to take a writer credit.

I KISSED A GIRL

Artist: Jill Sobule
Written by: Jill Sobule, Robin Eaton
From the album: *Jill Sobule*
Label: Lava
Produced by: Brad Jones, Robin Eaton

Year: 1995
Self-discovery in the nascent Lilith era.

I KNEW I LOVED YOU

Artist: Savage Garden
Written by: Darren Hayes, Daniel Jones
From the album: *Affirmation*
Label: Columbia
Produced by: Darren Hayes, Daniel Jones
Year: 1999
In the sunny tradition of fellow Australians Air Supply.

I KNEW THE BRIDE WHEN SHE USED TO ROCK AND ROLL

Artist: Nick Lowe
Written by: Nick Lowe
From the album: *The Rose of England*
Label: Columbia
Produced by: Huey Lewis and the News
Year: 1985
Midlife crisis, rock and roll style. This remake of earlier track was his last chart hit.

I KNEW YOU WERE WAITING (FOR ME)

Artist: Aretha Franklin and George Michael
Written by: Simon Climie, Dennis Morgan
From the album: *Aretha*
Label: Arista
Produced by: Narada Michael Walden
Year: 1987
This duet was Aretha's biggest international hit.

I KNOW A LITTLE

Artist: Lynyrd Skynyrd
Written by: Steve Gaines
From the album: *Street Survivors*
Label: MCA
Produced by: Lynyrd Skynyrd
Year: 1977
Previewing the two-step.

I KNOW A PLACE

Artist: Petula Clark
Written by: Tony Hatch
From the album: *I Know a Place*
Label: Warner Brothers
Produced by: Tony Hatch
Year: 1965
Following up "Downtown" with further Carnaby Street proselytizing.

(I KNOW I GOT) SKILLZ

Artist: Shaquille O'Neal
Written by: Jeff Fortson, Shaquille O'Neal, Meech Wells
From the album: *Shaq Diesel*
Label: Jive
Produced by: Def Jef, Meech Wells

Year: 1993
No slam dunk in the rap arena.

(I KNOW) I'M LOSING YOU

Artist: The Temptations
Written by: Eddie Holland, Norman Whitfield, Cornelius Grant
From the album: *With a Lot o Soul*
Label: Gordy
Produced by: Norman Whitfield
Year: 1966
Minus Smokey, the Temptations begin to sound more like the Four Tops on this, the last of four straight #1 R&B/Top 10 R&B hits of '66. Covered by Rare Earth (Motown, '70).

I KNOW IT'S GONNA HAPPEN

Artist: Morrissey
Written by: Stephen Morrissey
From the album: *Your Arsenal*
Label: Sire
Produced by: Mick Ronson
Year: 1993

I KNOW IT'S OVER

Artist: The Smiths
Written by: Stephen Morrissey, Johnny Marr
From the album: *The Queen Is Dead*
Label: Sire
Produced by: Stephen Morrissey, Johnny Marr
Year: 1986
Marr's favorite Morrissey performance.

I KNOW WHAT BOYS LIKE

Artist: The Waitresses
Written by: Chris Butler
From the album: *Wasn't Tomorrow Wonderful?*
Label: Polydor
Produced by: Chris Butler
Year: 1982
Living in the post-Blondie material world.

I KNOW (YOU DON'T LOVE ME NO MORE)

Artist: Barbara George
Written by: Barbara George
From the album: *I Know You Don't Love Me No More*
Label: AFO
Produced by: Harold Battiste
Year: 1961
New Orleans soul one-shot.

I KNOW YOU RIDER

Artist: Martin and Neil
Written by: Traditional
From the album: *Tear Down the Walls*
Label: Elektra
Year: 1965

A basic folk/rock repertoire requirement. Covered by the Grateful Dead (Sunflower, '66).

I KNOW YOU'RE OUT THERE SOMEWHERE

Artist: The Moody Blues
Written by: Justin Hayward
From the album: *Sur La Mer*
Label: Polygram
Produced by: Tony Visconti
Year: 1988

I LIE IN THE BED I MADE

Artist: Brother Cane
Written by: Daron Johnson, Marti Frederiksen
From the album: *Wishpool*
Label: Virgin
Year: 1998
End of the century rock position.

I LIKE DREAMING

Artist: Kenny Nolan
Written by: Kenny Nolan Helfman
From the album: *Kenny Nolan*
Label: 20TH Century
Produced by: Kenny Nolan, Charlie Calello
Year: 1977
Nolan's reward for having written "My Eyes Adored You" and "Lady Marmelade," which succeeded each other at #1, while this record stalled at #3. A pretty good year, nonetheless.

I LIKE IT LIKE THAT

Artist: Chris Kenner
Written by: Chris Kenner, Allen Toussaint
Label: Instant
Produced by: Allen Toussaint
Year: 1961
Crescent City soul goes national with this choogling #2 R&B/#2 crossover. Covered by the Dave Clark Five (Epic, '65).

I LIKE THE WAY (THE KISSING GAME)

Artist: Hi-Five
Written by: Teddy Riley, Bernard Belle, David Way
From the album: *Hi-Five*
Label: Jive
Produced by: Teddy Riley
Year: 1990
Teenybop hip hop chart topper.

I LIVE FOR CARS AND GIRLS

Artist: Dictators
Written by: Andy Shernoff
From the album: *The Dictators Go Girl Crazy*
Label: Epic
Produced by: Sandy Pearlman, Murray Krugman
Year: 1975

Pre-glam rocker. Blue Oyster Cult and the Clash were the more significant parts of Pearlman's resume.

I LOVE A RAINY NIGHT

Artist: Eddie Rabbitt
Written by: Eddie Rabbitt, Even Stevens, David Malloy
From the album: *Horizon*
Label: Elektra
Produced by: David Malloy
Year: 1980
#1 country/#1 crossover in the year of the Urban Cowboy.

I LOVE HOW YOU LOVE ME

Artist: The Paris Sisters
Written by: Barry Mann, Larry Koller
Label: Gregmark
Produced by: Phil Spector
Year: 1961
Mesmerizing post-Teddy Bears, pre-Genius, Spectorian balladry.

I LOVE L.A.

Artist: Randy Newman
Written by: Randy Newman
From the album: *Trouble in Paradise*
Label: Warner Brothers
Produced by: Russ Titelman, Lenny Waronker
Year: 1983
Reverse anthem from the movie *Down and out in Beverly Hills*.

I LOVE MUSIC (PART I)

Artist: The O'Jays
Written by: Kenny Gamble, Leon Huff
From the album: *Family Reunion*
Label: Philadelphia International
Produced by: Kenny Gamble
Year: 1975
#1 R&B/Top 10 crossover.

I LOVE ROCK AND ROLL

Artist: Joan Jett
Written by: Jake Hooker, Alan Merrill
From the album: *I Love Rock and Roll*
Label: Boardwalk
Produced by: Ritchie Cordell, Kenny Laguna
Year: 1982
B-side of Jett's cover of "You Don't Own Me" became the year's #1 American bedrock manifesto. Previously a stiff as a UK single for the Arrows, consisting of its expatriate authors.

I LOVE THE NIGHTLIFE (DISCO ROUND)

Artist: Alicia Bridges
Written by: Alicia Bridges, Susan Hutcheson
From the album: *Alicia Bridges*
Label: Polydor

Produced by: Steve Buckingham
Year: 1977
Nasal disco one-shot.

(I LOVE THE SOUND OF) BREAKING GLASS

Artist: Nick Lowe
Written by: Nick Lowe, Andrew Bodnar, Steve Goulding
From the album: *Pure Pop for Now People*
Label: Columbia
Produced by: Nick Lowe
Year: 1978
Biggest UK hit for the multifaceted, many-hatted, retro-kitchy rockologist.

I LOVE THE WAY YOU LOVE

Artist: Marv Johnson
Written by: Berry Gordy Jr., Mikaljohn
From the album: *Marvelous Marv Johnson*
Label: United Artists
Produced by: Berry Gordy
Year: 1959
His biggest hit; Top 5 R&B/Top 10 crossover.

I LOVE YOU

Artist: Climax Blues Band
Written by: Derek Holt
From the album: *Flying the Flag*
Label: Warner Brothers
Year: 1981
Legendary wedding song.

I LOVE YOU ALWAYS FOREVER

Artist: Donna Lewis
Written by: Donna Lewis
From the album: *Now in a Minute*
Label: Atlantic
Year: 1996
Big debut track for the singer from Wales, a one-shot.

I LOVE YOU MORE THAN YOU'LL EVER KNOW

Artist: Blood, Sweat and Tears
Written by: Al Kooper
From the album: *Child Is Father to the Man*
Label: Columbia
Produced by: John Simon
Year: 1968
Future blue-eyed soul classic. Covered by Donnie Hathaway (Atco, '73).

(I LOVE YOU) FOR SENTIMENTAL REASONS

Artist: Nat King Cole Trio
Written by: Deek Watson, William Best

From the album: *Unforgettable*
Year: 1947
#3 R&B hit is his first #1 crossover. Covered by Sam Cooke (Keen, '57), the Cleftones (Gee, '61), James Brown (King, '69), Linda Ronstadt (Asylum, '86).

I LOVE YOU SO

Artist: The Chantels
Written by: Morris Levy, Sonny Norton
From the album: *The Chantels*
Produced by: George Goldner, Richard Barrett
Label: End
Year: 1958
Vocal peak for the great Arlene Smith.

I LOVE YOUR SMILE

Artist: Shanice
Written by: Shanice Wilson, Narada Michael Walden, Sylvester Jackson, Jarvis La Rue Baker
From the album: *Inner Child*
Label: Motown
Produced by: Narada Michael Walden
Year: 1991
#1 R&B/Top 10 crossover.

I MELT WITH YOU

Artist: Modern English
Written by: Modern English
From the album: *After the Snow*
Label: Sire
Year: 1982
Early third invasion technobabble.

I MET HER IN CHURCH

Artist: The Box Tops
Written by: Dan Penn, Spooner Oldham
From the album: *Non Stop*
Label: Mala
Produced by: Dan Penn
Year: 1968
Memphis gospel.

I MET HIM ON A SUNDAY

Artist: The Shirelles
Written by: Mickie Harris, Shirley Owens, Beverly Lee, Doris Kenner
From the album: *Tonight's the Night*
Label: Decca
Produced by: Florence Greenberg
Year: 1958
Their first song, cowritten by the group, a timeless gem of doo-wop love and loss, lasting less than a week. Suggested segue: "Da Doo Ron Ron" by the Crystals (Philles, '63).

I MISS MY HOMIES

Artist: Master P, featuring Pimp C and the Shocker
Written by: Master P, Pimp C, the Shocker
From the album: *Ghetto D*
Label: No Limit
Year: 1997

I MISS YOU

Artist: Klymaxx
Written by: Lynn Malsby
From the album: *Meeting in the Ladies Room*
Label: Constellation
Produced by: Lynn Malsby, Klymaxx
Year: 1985
First and biggest hit for the influential R&B band. TLC and SWV were listening.

I MISUNDERSTOOD

Artist: Richard Thompson
Written by: Richard Thompson
From the album: *Rumor and Sigh*
Label: Capitol
Produced by: Mitchell Froom
Year: 1991
One of his most poignant ballads.

I MUST BE HIGH

Artist: Wilco
Written by: Jeff Tweedy
From the album: *A.M.*
Produced by: Brian Paulson
Label: Sire
Year: 1995
Folk/rock for the new masses.

I NEED A LOVER

Artist: John (Cougar) Mellencamp
Written by: John Mellencamp
From the album: *John Cougar*
Label: Riva
Produced by: Howard Albert, John Albert
Year: 1979
Indiana rocker updates Dylan's "It Ain't Me Babe."

I NEED LOVE

Artist: LL Cool J
Written by: James Todd Smith, Bobby Ervin, Darrell Pierce, Dwayne Simon
From the album: *Bigger and Deffer*
Label: Def Jam
Produced by: LL Cool J, L.A. Posse
Year: 1987
#1 R&B/Top 20 crossover is his chart breakthrough.

I NEED TO KNOW

Artist: Marc Anthony
Written by: Marc Anthony, Corey Rooney
From the album: *Marc Anthony*
Label: Columbia
Year: 1999
Latin all-star goes middle of the road.

I NEED YOU

Artist: The Beatles
Written by: George Harrison
From the album: *Help!*
Label: Capitol
Produced by: George Martin
Year: 1965

I NEED YOUR LOVE TONIGHT

Artist: Elvis Presley
Written by: Sid Wayne, Bix Reichner
From the album: *50,000,000 Elvis Fans Can't Be Wrong: Elvis' Gold Records (Vol. II)*
Label: RCA
Produced by: Steve Sholes, Chet Atkins
Year: 1959
B-side of "(Now and Then There's) a Fool Such as I."

I NEVER CRY

Artist: Alice Cooper
Written by: Vincent Furnier (Alice Cooper), Dick Wagner
From the album: *Alice Cooper Goes to Hell*
Label: Warner Brothers
Produced by: Bob Ezrin
Year: 1976
A million-selling single.

I NEVER LOVED A MAN (THE WAY I LOVE YOU)

Artist: Aretha Franklin
Written by: Ronny Shannon
From the album: *I Never Loved a Man*
Label: Atlantic
Produced by: Jerry Wexler
Year: 1967
Starting off her career on Atlantic, under the wing of Jerry Wexler, with a classic #1 R&B/Top 10 crossover.

(I NEVER PROMISED YOU A) ROSE GARDEN

Artist: Joe South
Written by: Joe South
From the album: *Introspect*
Label: Capitol
Produced by: Joe South
Year: 1969
Cover by Lynn Anderson was a #1 country/Top 5 crossover (Columbia, '71). Also covered by Kon Kan as "I Beg Your Pardon" (Atlantic, '89).

I ONLY HAVE EYES FOR YOU

Artist: The Flamingos
Written by: Harry Warren, Al Dubin
From the album: *Flamingo's Serenade*
Label: End
Produced by: George Goldner
Year: 1959
Achieving the pinnacle of the reverse-cover sound with a tune originated by Dick Powell and Ruby Keeler in the '34 film *Dames.*

I ONLY WANT TO BE WITH YOU

Artist: Dusty Springfield
Written by: Mike Hawker, Ivor Raymonde
From the album: *Stay Awhile/I Only Want to Be with You*
Label: Philips
Produced by: Ivor Raymonde
Year: 1964
Blue-eyed soul from England with a dash of folk was Dusty's first hit. Covered by the Bay City Rollers (Arista, '76).

I ONLY WANT YOU

Artist: The Passions
Written by: Harry Evans
Label: Audicon
Year: 1960
A doo-wop classic that didn't make the charts.

I PITY THE FOOL

Artist: Bobby Bland
Written by: Deadric Malone
From the album: *2 Steps from the Blues*
Label: Duke
Produced by: Joe Scott
Year: 1961
One of his bluesiest refrains, later coopted by Mr. T. #1 R&B/Top 50 crossover. Covered by Ann Peebles (Hi, '71).

I PUT A SPELL ON YOU

Artist: Screaming Jay Hawkins
Written by: Jay Hawkins
From the album: *I Put a Spell on You*
Label: Okeh
Produced by: Leroy Kirkland
Year: 1956
First rock single on Okeh is a stark raver. Covered by Creedence Clearwater Revival (Fantasy, '68), Arthur Brown (Track, '68).

I RAN

Artist: A Flock of Seagulls
Written by: Ali Score, Paul Reynolds, Mike Score, Frank Maudley
From the album: *A Flock of Seagulls*
Label: Jive
Produced by: Mike Howlett
Year: 1982
Perhaps best remembered for Mike Score's hairstyle, parodied by Chandler Bing in a couple of flashback episodes of *Friends.*

I REMEMBER YOU

Artist: Frank Ifield
Written by: Johnny Mercer, Victor Schertzinger
From the album: *Jolly What! The Beatles and Frank Ifield*
Label: VeeJay
Year: 1962

A one-man (yodeling) British invasion, a year too soon. Introduced by Dorothy Lamour in the '42 film *The Fleet's In*. Suggested segue: "Lovesick Blues" by Hank Williams.

I REMEMBER YOU

Artist: Skid Row
Written by: Dave Sabo, Rachel Bolan
From the album: *Skid Row*
Label: Atlantic
Produced by: Michael Wagever
Year: 1990
In the waning days of the surefire arena ballad.

I SAW HER AGAIN LAST NIGHT

Artist: Mamas & the Papas
Written by: John Phillips, Dennis Doherty
From the album: *Mamas & the Papas*
Label: Dunhill
Produced by: Lou Adler
Year: 1966

I SAW HER STANDING THERE

Artist: The Beatles
Written by: John Lennon, Paul McCartney
From the album: *Meet the Beatles*
Label: Capitol
Produced by: George Martin
Year: 1963
The B-side of "I Wanna Hold Your Hand." Covered by Tiffany (MCA, '88).

I SAW THE BEST MINDS OF MY GENERATION ROT

Artist: The Fugs
Written by: Tuli Kupferberg, Ed Sanders
From the album: *Virgin Fugs*
Label: ESP
Year: 1965
Where Allen Ginsberg left off, the Fugs prevailed, merging the poetic with the puerile, the sacred with the profane, "The Swinburne Stomp" with "Group Grope."

I SAW THE LIGHT

Artist: Todd Rundgren
Written by: Todd Rundgren
From the album: *Something/Anything*
Label: Bearsville
Produced by: Todd Rundgren
Year: 1972
Shining moment from the double album by the ubiquitous founder of Runt and the Nazz.

I SECOND THAT EMOTION

Artist: The Miracles
Written by: Smokey Robinson, Al Cleveland
From the album: *Greatest Hits (Vol. II)*
Label: Tamla
Produced by: Smokey Robinson, Al Cleveland
Year: 1967
A #1 R&B/Top 10 crossover inaugurates Smokey's career as the top-billed Miracle.

I SHALL BE RELEASED

Artist: The Band
Written by: Bob Dylan
From the album: *Music from Big Pink*
Label: Capitol
Produced by: John Simon, the Band
Year: 1968
Superior version of one of Dylan's most transcendent ballads, covered by the Box Tops (Mala, '69), Joe Cocker (A&M, '69).

I SHOT THE SHERIFF

Artist: Bob Marley & the Wailers
Written by: Bob Marley
From the album: *Burnin'*
Label: Island
Produced by: Chris Blackwell, the Wailers
Year: 1973
Outlaw reggae. Covered by Eric Clapton (RSO, '74).

I SHOULD BE SO LUCKY

Artist: Kylie Minogue
Written by: Mike Stock, Matt Aiken, Pete Waterman
From the album: *Kylie*
Produced by: Stock, Aitken, Waterman
Label: Geffen
Year: 1988
Soap star makes a seamless dance diva transition with a lead off #1 UK hit.

I SHOULD HAVE KNOWN BETTER

Artist: The Beatles
Written by: John Lennon, Paul McCartney
From the album: *A Hard Day's Night*
Label: United Artists
Produced by: George Martin
Year: 1964
The B-side of "A Hard Day's Night."

I SOLD MY HEART TO THE JUNKMAN

Artist: Etta Jones
Written by: Otis Rene Jr., Leon Rene
Label: RCA
Year: 1947
Originated by Steve Gibson and the Redcaps, with vocals by Damita Jo. Revived by the Starlets in 1962, but mistakenly accredited to the Bluebelles.

I STARTED A JOKE

Artist: The Bee Gees
Written by: Barry Gibb, Robin Gibb, Maurice Gibb
From the album: *Idea*
Label: Atco
Produced by: Robert Stigwood
Year: 1968
Follow-up to "I've Got to Get a Message to You."

I STILL HAVEN'T FOUND WHAT I'M LOOKING FOR

Artist: U2
Written by: Paul Hewson (Bono), Dave Evans (Edge), Adam Clayton, Larry Mullen
From the album: *The Joshua Tree*
Label: Island
Produced by: Brian Eno, Daniel Lanois
Year: 1987
Their second #1.

I SWEAR

Artist: All-4-One
Written by: Frank Myers, Gerry Baker
From the album: *All-4-One*
Label: Blitz
Produced by: David Foster
Year: 1994
John Michael Montgomery had the original, which won a Grammy for Country Song of the Year in 1994. The cover, by the interracial R&B group All-4-One (Atlantic, '94), was a pop number one for eleven weeks and a Top 20 R&B crossover.

I TAKE WHAT I WANT

Artist: Sam and Dave
Written by: Isaac Hayes, David Porter, Mabon Hodges
From the album: *Hold on, I'm Comin'*
Label: Stax
Produced by: Jim Stewart
Year: 1966
Covered by James and Bobby Purify (Bell, '67).

I THANK YOU

Artist: Sam and Dave
Written by: Isaac Hayes, David Porter
From the album: *I Thank You*
Label: Atlantic
Produced by: Isaac Hayes, David Porter
Year: 1968
Their second biggest hit.

I THINK I CAN BEAT MIKE TYSON

Artist: DJ Jazzy Jeff & the Fresh Prince
Written by: Jeff Townes, Will Smith, Pete Q. Harris
From the album: *He's the Deejay, I'm the Rapper*
Label: Jive
Produced by: DJ Jazzy Jeff, the Fresh Prince, Pete Q. Harris, N. Green
Year: 1988
A pugnatious rapper (who would go on to play Muhammed Ali in the movies) launches his big dream.

I THINK I LOVE YOU

Artist: The Partridge Family
Written by: Tony Romeo
From the album: *The Partridge Family Album*
Label: Bell
Produced by: Wes Farrell
Year: 1970
#1 hit from the TV show influenced by the Cowsills, with future teen idol David Cassidy and his real-life stepmother Shirley Jones singing.

I THINK I'M PARANOID

Artist: Garbage
Written by: Duke Erickson, Shirley Manson, Butch Vig, Steve Marker
From the album: *Garbage Version 2.0*
Label: Almo Sounds
Produced by: Butch Vig
Year: 1998
With Shirley Manson deconstructing Debbie Harry.

I THINK IT'S GONNA RAIN TODAY

Artist: Judy Collins
Written by: Randy Newman
From the album: *In My Life*
Label: Elektra
Produced by: Mark Abramson
Year: 1966
Randy Newman reaches the folk intelligentsia with one of his most straightforward and moving ballads. Covered by Newman (Reprise, '68) and Bette Midler in the movie *Beaches* (Atlantic, '83).

I THINK SHE LIKES ME

Artist: Treat Her Right
Written by: Mark Sandman
From the album: *Treat Her Right*
Produced by: Treat Her Right
Label: RCA
Year: 1986
N.Y. bar band blues situation. Sandman would move on to a band called Morphine.

I THINK WE'RE ALONE NOW

Artist: Tommy James and the Shondells
Written by: Ritchie Cordell, Bo Gentry
From the album: *I Think We're Alone Now*
Label: Roulette
Produced by: Bo Gentry, Ritchie Cordell
Year: 1967
In the midst of the pyschedelic revolution, the insidiously catchy sound of bubblegum emerges. Covered by Lene Lovich (Stiff, '79), Tiffany (MCA, '87).

I TOUCH MYSELF

Artist: Divinyls
Written by: Billy Steinberg, Tom Kelly, Christina Amphlett, Mark McEntee

From the album: *Divinyls*
Label: Virgin
Produced by: David Tickle, Divinyls
Year: 1991
Playfully suggestive US Top 10 breakthrough for the Australian punk band. Segues: "She Bop" by Cyndi Lauper, "Turning Japanese" by the Vapors, "Secret" by Madonna.

I TRY

Artist: Macy Gray
Written by: David Wilder, Jinsoo Lim, Jeremy Ruzumna, Natalie McIntyre
From the album: *On How Life Is*
Label: MCA
Year: 1999
Sultry voice in the Billie Holiday to Rickie Lee Jones to Norah Jones continuum.

I TURN TO YOU

Artist: All-4-One
Written by: Diane Warren
From the album: *Space Jam Soundtrack*
Label: Warner Sunset
Year: 1996
Introduced in the film *Space Jam*. Covered by Christina Aguilera (RCA, '99)

I UNDERSTAND JUST HOW YOU FEEL

Artist: The Four Tunes
Written by: Pat Best
From the album: *12 × 4*
Label: Jubilee
Year: 1954
Covered by the G-Clefs (Terrace, '61).

I WALK ON GILDED SPLINTERS

Artist: Dr. John
Written by: Mack Rebennack
From the album: *Gris Gris*
Label: Atlantic
Year: 1968
Psychedelic soul, New Orleans style, from the debut album of the ultimate New Orleans keyboard player and session man, Mack Rebennack, aka Dr. John. Covered in a masterful guitar performance by Duane Allman (Capricorn, '72).

I WALK THE LINE

Artist: Johnny Cash
Written by: Johnny Cash
From the album: *Johnny Cash with His Red and Blue Guitar*
Label: Sun
Produced by: Sam Phillips
Year: 1956
Cash's first #1 country hit is also his first Top 20 crossover.

I WANNA BE ADORED

Artist: Stone Roses
Written by: John Squires, Ian Brown
From the album: *The Stone Roses*
Label: Silvertone
Produced by: John Leckie
Year: 1990
Major rave track.

I WANNA BE A LIFEGUARD

Artist: Blotto
Written by: Bob Rothberg, Sammy Timberg
From the album: *Hello! My Name's Blotto, What's Yours?*
Label: Blotto
Year: 1980
The Ramones go to community college.

I WANNA BE BLACK

Artist: Lou Reed
Written by: Lou Reed
From the album: *Street Hassle*
Label: Arista
Produced by: Lou Reed
Year: 1978
Long-time performance highlight. Suggested segue: "Hail Hail Rock and Roll" by Garland Jeffreys.

I WANNA BE DOWN

Artist: Brandy
Written by: Keith Crouch, Kipper Jones
From the album: *Brandy*
Label: Atlantic
Produced by: Keith Crouch
Year: 1994
#1 R&B/#1 crossover for the girl who played Cinderella in a TV movie.

I WANNA BE RICH

Artist: Calloway
Written by: Reggie Calloway, Vincent Calloway, Melvin Gentry, Belinda Lipscomb
From the album: *All the Way*
Label: Epic
Produced by: Reggie Calloway, Vincent Calloway
Year: 1990
Modern R&B answer to "Money" by Barrett Strong.

I WANNA BE SEDATED

Artist: The Ramones
Written by: Douglas Colvin, John Cummings, Jeff Hyman
From the album: *Road to Ruin*
Label: Sire
Produced by: Ed Stasium
Year: 1978
One of their defining East coast Beach Boys moments. Featured in the '80 movie *Times Square*.

I WANNA BE YOUR BOYFRIEND

Artist: The Ramones
Written by: Douglas Colvin, John Cummings, Jeff Hyman, Thomas Erdelyi
From the album: *The Ramones*
Label: Sire
Produced by: Craig Leon
Year: 1976
Joe Perry of Aerosmith described the adolescent condition as being "a hormone in a sneaker." The Ramones wore this costume on stage and wrote about it better than anyone.

I WANNA BE YOUR DOG

Artist: The Stooges
Written by: James Osterberg (Iggy Pop), Scott Asheton, Ron Asheton, Dave Alexander
From the album: *The Stooges*
Label: Elektra
Produced by: John Cale
Year: 1969
The dog reappears to sum up the nascent punk three-chord revolution. In New York, the Ramones were pricing Kay guitars.

I WANNA BE YOUR JOEY RAMONE

Artist: Sleater-Kinney
Written by: Carrie Brownstein, Corin Tucker
From the album: *Call the Doctor*
Label: Chainsaw
Produced by: Sleater-Kinney
Year: 1996
The legend lives in the hearts of mean girls and riot grrrls alike.

I WANNA BE YOUR LOVER

Artist: Prince
Written by: Prince Rogers Nelson
From the album: *Prince*
Label: Warner Brothers
Produced by: Prince
Year: 1979
Stating his essential and elemental position, with his first #1 R&B/Top 20 crossover.

I WANNA BE YOUR MAN

Artist: The Rolling Stones
Written by: John Lennon, Paul McCartney
Label: London
Produced by: Andrew Loog-Oldham
Year: 1964
B-side of the Stones' first US single, "Not Fade Away." Covered by the Beatles on their first US album (Capitol, '64). For much of the rest of the decade, these two English bands would define American rock and roll.

I WANNA DANCE WITH SOMEBODY (WHO LOVES ME)

Artist: Whitney Houston
Written by: Gary Merrill, Shannon Rubicam
From the album: *Whitney Houston*
Label: Arista
Produced by: Narada Michael Walden
Year: 1987
Her fourth #1.

I WANNA HAVE SOME FUN

Artist: Samantha Fox
Written by: Full Force
From the album: *I Wanna Have Some Fun*
Label: Jive
Produced by: Full Force
Year: 1989
In the absence of a picture disc, her allure wore thin.

I WANNA HOLD YOUR HAND

Artist: The Beatles
Written by: John Lennon, Paul McCartney
From the album: *Meet the Beatles*
Label: Capitol
Produced by: George Martin
Year: 1963
First #1 in the US, fourth #1 in the UK. Coincidentally, the title of Ray Charles' first R&B hit in 1951 was "Baby Let Me Hold Your Hand."

I WANNA KNOW

Artist: Joe
Written by: Joe Thomas, Jolyon Skinner, M. Williams
From the album: *The Wood Soundtrack*
Label: Jive
Produced by: Joe Nicholas, Edwin Nicholas
Year: 2000

I WANNA LOVE HIM SO BAD

Artist: The Jelly Beans
Written by: Jeff Barry, Ellie Greenwich
Label: Red Bird
Produced by: Jeff Barry
Year: 1964
Brill Building studio classic.

I WANNA SEX YOU UP

Artist: Color Me Badd
Written by: Elliot Straite (Dr. Freeze)
From the album: *New Jack City Soundtrack*
Label: Giant
Produced by: Hamza Lee, Royal Bayyan
Year: 1991
#1 R&B/#2 crossover.

(I WANNA) TESTIFY

Artist: Parliament
Written by: George Clinton, Deron Taylor
Label: Revilot
Produced by: George Clinton
Year: 1967
The notorious Funkmaster General Clinton enters the arena with the Parliaments and a Top 10 R&B/Top 20 crossover. Covered by Little Johnny Taylor (Stax, '69).

I WANT A NEW DRUG

Artist: Huey Lewis and the News
Written by: Chris Hayes, Huey Lewis
From the album: *Sports*
Label: Chrysalis
Produced by: Huey Lewis and the News
Year: 1984

I WANT CANDY

Artist: The Strangeloves
Written by: Bob Feldman, Jerry Goldstein, Richard Gottehrer, Bert Berns
From the album: *I Want Candy*
Label: Bang
Produced by: Bob Feldman, Jerry Goldstein, Richard Gottehrer
Year: 1965
Frat house classic from the Brill Building. Covered by Bow Wow Wow (RCA, '82).

I WANT HER

Artist: Keith Sweat
Written by: Keith Sweat, Teddy Riley
From the album: *Make It Last Forever*
Label: Vintertainment
Produced by: Teddy Riley
Year: 1988
#1 R&B/Top 10 crossover introduces new jack swing. R. Kelly was listening.

I WANT IT THAT WAY

Artist: Backstreet Boys
Written by: Max Martin, Andreas Carlsson
From the album: *Millennium*
Label: Jive
Year: 1999
Return of boy band harmony; New Kids on the Block with British accents.

I WANT TO BE WANTED

Artist: Brenda Lee
Written by: Kim Gannon, Pino Spotti, A. Testa
From the album: *This is … Brenda*
Label: Decca
Produced by: Owen Bradley
Year: 1960
A ballad from Italy.

I WANT TO BE YOUR MAN

Artist: Roger
Written by: Larry Troutman

From the album: *Unlimited*
Label: Reprise
Produced by: Roger Troutman
Year: 1987
#1 R&B/Top 10 crossover.

I WANT TO COME OVER

Artist: Melissa Etheridge
Written by: Melissa Etheridge
From the album: *Your Little Secret*
Label: Island
Produced by: Hugh Padgham
Year: 1996

I WANT TO KNOW WHAT LOVE IS

Artist: Foreigner
Written by: Mick Jones
From the album: *Agent Provocateur*
Label: Atlantic
Produced by: Alex Sadkin, Mick Jones
Year: 1984
Their biggest hit, in which they thoroughly renounce their previously sexist ways, with a church choir as witness.

I WANT TO MAKE THE WORLD TURN AROUND

Artist: Steve Miller Band
Written by: Steve Miller
From the album: *Living in the 20th Century*
Label: Capitol
Year: 1986
And return to 1976.

I WANT TO SEE THE BRIGHT LIGHTS TONIGHT

Artist: Richard and Linda Thompson
Written by: Richard Thompson
From the album: *I Want to See the Bright Lights Tonight*
Label: Island
Produced by: Richard Thompson, John Wood
Year: 1974
Introducing the first couple of post-Elizabethan English folk music, star-crossed of course.

I WANT TO TAKE YOU HIGHER

Artist: Sly and the Family Stone
Written by: Sylvester Stewart
From the album: *Stand!*
Label: Epic
Produced by: Sly Stone
Year: 1969
B-side of "Stand" eventually became a Sly staple and personal motto. Covered by Ike and Tina Turner (Liberty, '70).

I WANT TO TELL YOU

Artist: The Beatles
Written by: George Harrison
From the album: *Revolver*
Label: Capitol
Produced by: George Martin
Year: 1966

I WANT TO WALK YOU HOME

Artist: Fats Domino
Written by: Fats Domino
From the album: *Fats Domino Sings Million Record Hits*
Label: Imperial
Produced by: Dave Bartholomew
Year: 1959
His seventh and last #1 R&B, his ninth Top 10.

I WANT YOU

Artist: LL Cool J
Written by: James Todd Smith, Rick Rubin
From the album: *Radio*
Label: Def Jam
Produced by: Rick Rubin
Year: 1985

I WANT YOU

Artist: Bob Dylan
Written by: Bob Dylan
From the album: *Blonde on Blonde*
Label: Columbia
Produced by: Bob Johnston
Year: 1966
Rare instance of Dylan admitting to unrequited lust.

I WANT YOU

Artist: Marvin Gaye
Written by: Leon Ware, Anita Ross
From the album: *I Want You*
Label: Tamla
Produced by: Leon Ware
Year: 1976
#1 R&B/Top 20 crossover. Covered by Madonna and Material Issue (Sire, '95).

I WANT YOU

Artist: Savage Garden
Written by: Darren Hayes, Damon Jones
From the album: *Savage Garden*
Label: Columbia
Year: 1997
Soft rocker.

I WANT YOU BACK

Artist: The Jackson 5
Written by: Freddie Perren, Berry Gordy Jr., Deke Richards, Fonce Mizell
From the album: *Diana Ross Presents the Jackson Five*
Label: Motown

Produced by: Freddie Perren, Berry Gordy Jr., Deke Richards, Fonce Mizell
Year: 1969
With a prepubescent Michael in the lead, this infectious #1 R&B/#1 crossover started off the most impressive debut in history (four straight #1 R&B/#1 crossover hits in ten months).

I WANT YOU BACK

Artist: *NSYNC
Written by: Max Martin, Denniz Pop
From the album: *NSYNC*
Label: RCA
Produced by: Max Martin, Denniz Pop
Year: 1998
From Disneyland via Sweden, a boy band harmony group answers the Jackson 5 thirty years later.

I WANT YOU (SHE'S SO HEAVY)

Artist: The Beatles
Written by: John Lennon, Paul McCartney
From the album: *Abbey Road*
Label: Apple
Produced by: George Martin
Year: 1969
At their heaviest.

I WANT YOU TO BE MY BABY

Artist: Lillian Briggs
Written by: John Hendricks
Label: Epic
Year: 1956
The signature tune of this white, trombone-playing, laundry-truck driver routinely brought the house down at the Apollo Theatre in Harlem. Introduced by Louis Jordan (Decca, '53).

I WANT YOU TO BE MY GIRL

Artist: Frankie Lymon and the Teenagers
Written by: George Goldner, Richard Barrett
From the album: *The Teenagers*
Label: Gee
Produced by: George Goldner
Year: 1956
Second crossover hit for the Harlem wunderkinds, scripted by the twin powers of New York City doo-wop.

I WANT YOU TO WANT ME

Artist: Cheap Trick
Written by: Rick Nielsen
From the album: *In Color*
Label: Epic
Produced by: Cheap Trick
Year: 1977
Touted as the Beatles of the arena age, Cheap Trick updates "I Want to Hold Your Hand."

I WANT YOU, I NEED YOU, I LOVE YOU

Artist: Elvis Presley
Written by: Maurice Mysels, Ira Kosloff
From the album: *Real Elvis*
Label: RCA
Produced by: Steve Sholes
Year: 1956
In the Elvis onslaught of '56, another #1 country/ #1 crossover.

I WANT YOUR SEX

Artist: George Michael
Written by: George Michael
From the album: *Faith*
Label: Columbia
Produced by: George Michael
Year: 1987
George's first solo hit is from the soundtrack of *Beverly Hills Cop*. In the repressive climate of the late '80s, George would quickly disown this song's sexually provocative video.

I WANTED EVERYTHING

Artist: The Ramones
Written by: Douglas Colvin, John Cummings, Jeff Hyman
From the album: *Road to Ruin*
Label: Sire
Year: 1978
Beginning to succumb to their missed opportunities.

I WAS MADE FOR DANCIN'

Artist: Leif Garrett
Written by: Michael Lloyd
From the album: *Feel the Need*
Label: Scotti Brothers
Produced by: Michael Lloyd
Year: 1979
Lone Top 10 hit for the aspiring teen idol who would achieve a more lasting fame as Felix Unger's son Leonard on the TV version of *The Odd Couple*, in which he wasn't that good either, except on the episode when Felix nurses Leonard's frog back to racing health.

I WAS MADE FOR LOVING YOU

Artist: Kiss
Written by: Stanley Eisen (Paul Stanley), Desmond Child, Vini Poncia
From the album: *Dynasty*
Label: Casablanca
Produced by: Vini Poncia
Year: 1979
Third biggest hit.

I WAS MADE TO LOVE HER

Artist: Stevie Wonder
Written by: Stevie Wonder, Henry Cosby, Lula Mae Hardaway
From the album: *I Was Made to Love Her*
Label: Tamla
Produced by: Henry Cosby
Year: 1967
Somewhere between Franklie Lymon and Michael Jackson (and Johnny Puleo); another #1 R&B/Top 10 crossover.

I WAS THE ONE

Artist: Elvis Presley
Written by: Aaron Schroeder, Claude DeMetrius, Hal Blair, Bill Peppers
From the album: *For LP Fans Only*
Label: RCA
Produced by: Steve Sholes
Year: 1956
B-side of "Heartbreak Hotel."

I WASN'T BORN TO FOLLOW

Artist: The Byrds
Written by: Carole King, Gerry Goffin
From the album: *The Notorious Byrd Brothers*
Label: Columbia
Produced by: Gary Usher
Year: 1968
Prodded by the poetry of folk/rock, the Brill Building era's finest chronicler of teen dreams, Gerry Goffin, goes pyschedelic. Included in the film *Easy Rider*. Revived by Carole King in her first band, the City (Ode, '70).

I WILL

Artist: The Beatles
Written by: John Lennon, Paul McCartney
From the album: *The Beatles*
Label: Apple
Produced by: George Martin
Year: 1968

I WILL ALWAYS LOVE YOU

Artist: Dolly Parton
Written by: Dolly Parton
From the album: *Jolene*
Label: RCA
Produced by: Bob Ferguson
Year: 1974
Bluegrass-inflected country yearner with nine lives. Dolly's first recording went #1 country. The revival in the movie version of the musical *The Best Little Whorehouse in Texas* was a #1 country/bottom 40 crossover (MCA, '82). Covered by X's John Doe and Whitney Houston in separate versions in the movie *The Bodyguard*. Whitney's record (Arista, '91) went on to be her fifth #1 R&B/#1 crossover, spending the most weeks at the top of the charts of any single in history.

I WILL DARE

Artist: The Replacements
Written by: Paul Westerberg
From the album: *Let It Be*
Label: Twin/Tone
Produced by: Steve Fjelstad, Paul Westerberg
Year: 1984
Westerberg steps out from his punk beginnings to create the nearest thing to a Minnesota acoustic masterpiece since Bob Zimmerman left Hibbing for Greenwich Village.

I WILL FOLLOW

Artist: U2
Written by: Paul Hewson (Bono), Dave Evans (Edge), Adam Clayton, Larry Mullen
From the album: *Boy*
Label: Island
Produced by: Steve Lillywhite
Year: 1980
First US chart success from their debut album.

I WILL FOLLOW HIM (CHARIOT)

Artist: Little Peggy March
Written by: Jacques Plante, J. W. Stole, Norman Gimble, Arthur Altman
From the album: *I Will Follow Him*
Label: RCA Victor
Produced by: Hugo and Luigi
Year: 1963
A hit in France for Petula Clark. The adapted American lyrics were a natural for Little Peggy (Battavio) from Pennsylvania, given the prevailing dependent girl-group attitudes of '63. The song is more important for the fact that it topped the R&B charts, thus eroding the credibility of that once-peerless indicator of rock and roll hipness to an extent unapproached since Paul Anka's "Diana." An overhaul was in the offing.

I WILL REMEMBER YOU

Artist: Sarah McLachlan
Written by: Seamus Egan, Sarah McLachlan, Dave Merenda
From the album: *The Brothers McMullen Soundtrack*
Label: Arista
Produced by: Sarah McLachlan
Year: 1995
Breakthrough eulogy for the newest folk/rock diva. A live version also charted.

I WILL SURVIVE

Artist: Gloria Gaynor
Written by: Freddie Perren, Dino Fekaris
From the album: *Love Tracks*
Label: Polydor
Produced by: Freddie Perren, Dino Fekaris
Year: 1978
#1 US/UK disco anthem, anticipating the coming plague years ahead, the closing of Studio 54, and the advent of MTV. Covered by Chantay Savage (RCA, '96).

I WISH

Artist: Stevie Wonder
Written by: Stevie Wonder
From the album: *Songs in the Key of Life*
Label: Tamla
Produced by: Stevie Wonder
Year: 1976
#1 R&B/#1 crossover.

I WISH I KNEW (HOW IT WOULD FEEL TO BE FREE)

Artist: Nina Simone
Written by: Billy Taylor, Dick Dallas
From the album: *Silk & Soul*
Label: RCA
Year: 1967
Stirring anthem of black pride. Covered by Solomon Burke (Atlantic, '68).

I WISH IT WOULD RAIN

Artist: The Temptations
Written by: Norman Whitfield, Barrett Strong, Roger Penzabene
From the album: *I Wish It Would Rain*
Label: Gordy
Produced by: Norman Whitfield
Year: 1968
#1 R&B/Top 10 crossover.

I WISH IT WOULD RAIN DOWN

Artist: Phil Collins
Written by: Phil Collins
From the album: *… But Seriously*
Label: Atlantic
Produced by: Hugh Padgham, Phil Collins
Year: 1989
On the way to M.O.R. heaven.

I WISH YOU WOULD

Artist: The Yardbirds
Written by: Billy Boy Arnold
From the album: *For Your Love*
Label: Epic
Produced by: Giorgio Gomelsky
Year: 1964
Prototypical Chicago blues raver was a Marquee Club show-stopper and their first single release, with Allen Toussaint's "A Certain Girl" on the B-side. The Rolling Stones were watching. Covered by the Blasters (Rolling Rock, '80).

I WONDER IF I CARE AS MUCH

Artist: The Everly Brothers
Written by: Don Everly
From the album: *The Everly Brothers*
Label: Cadence
Produced by: Archie Bleyer
Year: 1957
B-side of "Bye Bye Love" marks Don's emergence as a writer.

I WONDER IF I TAKE YOU HOME

Artist: Lisa Lisa and Cult Jam
Written by: Full Force
From the album: *Lisa Lisa and Cult Jam with Full Force*
Label: Columbia
Produced by: Full Force
Year: 1985
Introducing the candy store evangelist Lisa Velez, under the auspices of the uptown production team Full Force.

I WONDER WHAT SHE'S DOING TONIGHT?

Artist: Tommy Boyce and Bobby Hart
Written by: Tommy Boyce, Bobby Hart
From the album: *I Wonder What She's Doing Tonight?*
Label: A&M
Produced by: Tommy Boyce, Bobby Hart
Year: 1967
Post doo-wop flashback for the noted songwriters ("Last Train to Clarksville," "I'm Not Your Stepping Stone").

I WONDER WHY

Artist: Dion and the Belmonts
Written by: Ricardo Weeks, Melvin Anderson
Label: Laurie
Produced by: Gene Schwartz
Year: 1958
Headed by Dion DiMucci, the Elvis of white doo-wop, the Bronx stalwarts spawn a uniquely city-bred sound.

I WON'T BACK DOWN

Artist: Tom Petty
Written by: Tom Petty, Jeff Lynne
From the album: *Full Moon Fever*
Label: MCA
Produced by: Jeff Lynne
Year: 1989
Defending the cause of folk/rock.

I WOULD DIE 4 U

Artist: Prince
Written by: Prince Rogers Nelson
From the album: *Purple Rain Soundtrack*
Label: Warner Brothers
Produced by: Prince
Year: 1984
Following Elvis and the Beatles to the movies, Prince solidifies his bid for iconhood with his fourth hit single from the picture. Along the way, he creates an unfortunate new spelling shorthand that would dominate the '90s.

I WRITE THE SONGS

Artist: Captain and Tennille
Written by: Bruce Johnston
From the album: *Love Will Keep Us Together*
Label: A&M
Year: 1975
Covered by Barry Manilow (Arista, '76), who many people mistakenly assumed wrote the song.

I'D DIE WITHOUT YOU

Artist: P.M. Dawn
Written by: Atrel Cordes
From the album: *Boomerang Soundtrack*
Label: Gee Street
Produced by: P.M. Dawn
Year: 1992
Follow-up to "Set Adrift on Memory Bliss."

I'D DO ANYTHING FOR LOVE (BUT I WON'T DO THAT)

Artist: Meat Loaf
Written by: Jim Steinman
From the album: *Bat out of Hell II: Back into Hell*
Label: MCA
Produced by: Jim Steinman
Year: 1993
Tired of being called Mr. Loaf, both by the *NY Times* and his suburban neighbors, this long-winded comeback track was his biggest hit.

I'D LOVE TO CHANGE THE WORLD

Artist: Ten Years After
Written by: Alvin Lee
From the album: *A Space in Time*
Label: Columbia
Produced by: Ten Years After
Year: 1971
Achieving the Top 40, two years after their big break at Woodstock.

I'D LOVE YOU TO WANT ME

Artist: Lobo
Written by: Kent Lavole
From the album: *Of a Simple Man*
Label: Big Tree
Produced by: Phil Gernhard
Year: 1972

I'D RATHER GO BLIND

Artist: Etta James
Written by: Bill Foster, Ellington Jordan
From the album: *Tell Mama*
Produced by: Rich Hall
Label: Cadet
Year: 1968
Searing blues classic. Covered by Chicken Shack (Epic, '68), and then by Chicken Shack lead singer Christine Perfect (Sire, '69).

I'D REALLY LOVE TO SEE YOU TONIGHT

Artist: England Dan and John Ford Coley
Written by: Parker McGee

From the album: *Nights Are Forever*
Label: Big Tree
Produced by: Kyle Lehning
Year: 1975
Ambling down the middle-of-the-dirt-road.

I'LL ALWAYS LOVE MY MAMA

Artist: The Intruders
Written by: Kenny Gamble, Leon Huff, John Whitehead, Vic Carstarphen
From the album: *Save the Children*
Label: TSOP
Produced by: Kenny Gamble, Leon Huff
Year: 1973
Philly soul greeting card.

I'LL BE

Artist: Edwin McCain
Written by: Edwin McCain
From the album: *Misguided Roses*
Label: Lava
Produced by: Matt Serletic, Kenny Greenberg
Year: 1998
Nu soul ballad.

I'LL BE AROUND

Artist: The Spinners
Written by: Thom Bell, Phil Hurtt
From the album: *The Spinners*
Label: Atlantic
Produced by: Thom Bell
Year: 1972
Defining the dance sound of the early '70s, with a #1 R&B/Top 10 crossover that was originally the B-side of "How Could I Let You Get Away."

I'LL BE DOGGONE

Artist: Marvin Gaye
Written by: Smokey Robinson, Warren Moore, Marv Tarplin
From the album: *Moods of Marvin Gaye*
Label: Tamla
Produced by: Smokey Robinson
Year: 1965
Under the calming influence of Smokey Robinson, a folksy Gaye creates his first #1 R&B/Top 10 crossover.

I'LL BE GOOD TO YOU

Artist: The Brothers Johnson
Written by: Louis Johnson, George Johnson, Senora Sam
From the album: *Look out for #1*
Label: A&M
Produced by: Quincy Jones
Year: 1976
#1 R&B/Top 10 crossover. Cover by Quincy Jones (with Chaka Kahn) was a #1 R&B/Top 20 crossover.

I'LL BE HOME

Artist: The Flamingos
Written by: Ferdinand Washington, Stan Lewis
From the album: *The Flamingos*
Label: Chess
Produced by: Leonard Chess
Year: 1956
The flowering of doo-wop as urban romance. Covered by Pat Boone (Dot, '56).

I'LL BE LOVING YOU (FOREVER)

Artist: New Kids on the Block
Written by: Larry Johnson (Maurice Starr)
From the album: *Hangin' Tough*
Label: Columbia
Produced by: Maurice Starr, Michael Jonzun
Year: 1988
First #1 and biggest R&B crossover (#12) for the Boston-based troupe created by New Edition's Svengali Starr.

I'LL BE MISSING YOU

Artist: Puff Daddy and Faith Evans
Written by: Gordon Sumner (Sting), Todd Gaither, Faith Evans
From the album: *No Way Out*
Label: Arista
Produced by: Sean Combs, Stevie J.
Year: 1997
Using "Every Breath You Take" by the Police to eulogize Christopher Wallace aka the Notorious B.I.G.

I'LL BE SATISFIED

Artist: Jackie Wilson
Written by: Roquel Davis (Tyran Carlo), Berry Gordy, Jr., Gwen Gordy
Label: Brunswick
Produced by: Dick Jacobs, Nat Tarnopol
Year: 1959
In pre-Motown Detroit, the only game in town was Jackie Wilson.

I'LL BE THERE

Artist: The Jackson 5
Written by: Bob West, Berry Gordy Jr., Willie Hutch, Hal Davis
From the album: *Third Album*
Label: Motown
Produced by: Hal Davis
Year: 1970
Their fourth straight #1 R&B/#1 crossover. Covered by Mariah Carey unplugged (Columbia, '92).

I'LL BE THERE FOR YOU

Artist: Bon Jovi
Written by: Jon Bon Jovi, Richie Sambora
From the album: *New Jersey*
Label: Polygram
Produced by: Bruce Fairbairn

Year: 1989
Their fourth #1.

I'LL BE THERE FOR YOU

Artist: The Rembrandts
Written by: David Crane, Martha Kaufman, Allee Willis, Phil Solem, Danny Wilde, Michael Skloff
From the album: *LP*
Label: East/West
Produced by: Gavin MacKillop
Year: 1995
The theme from the sitcom *Friends* was added to the album once the show began to take off in the ratings. Lyric clue: *your love life's d.o.a.*

I'LL BE TRUE

Artist: Faye Adams
Written by: William McLemore
Label: Herald
Produced by: Al Silver
Year: 1954
Her second of three R&B hits.

I'LL BE YOU

Artist: The Replacements
Written by: Paul Westerberg
From the album: *Don't Tell a Soul*
Label: Sire
Produced by: Matt Wallace, the Replacements
Year: 1989
Closest thing to a hit single for the alt-rock standard bearers.

I'LL BE YOUR BABY TONIGHT

Artist: Bob Dylan
Written by: Bob Dylan
From the album: *John Wesley Harding*
Label: Columbia
Produced by: Bob Johnston
Year: 1968
As a pure country throwaway tagged onto the arid Western orientation of the album it was drawn from, this prelude to Bob's full conversion to Nashville was seen by many as the beginning of the end of Dylanology as a legitimate career choice for the downwardly mobile college dropout. For others it was a sign of roots rock to come. Covered by Marianne Faithfull (Immediate, '77).

I'LL BE YOUR EVERYTHING

Artist: Tommy Page
Written by: Jordan Knight, Donnie Wahlberg (Donnie Wood), Tommy Page
From the album: *Paintings in My Mind*
Label: Warner Brothers
Produced by: Jordan Knight, Donnie Wahlberg, Michael Jonzon
Year: 1990
New Kids on the Block protégé rides their coattails.

I'LL BE YOUR MIRROR

Artist: The Velvet Underground
Written by: Lou Reed
From the album: *The Velvet Underground and Nico*
Label: Verve
Produced by: Andy Warhol
Year: 1967
Acid pop, decadent in its simplicity.

I'LL COME RUNNING BACK TO YOU

Artist: Sam Cooke
Written by: Sam Cooke (Charles Cooke)
From the album: *The Man and His Music*
Label: Specialty
Produced by: Art Rupe
Year: 1957
Working from an old existing track, Rupe fashioned this Cooke follow-up to "You Send Me" after he left the label. It was a #1 R&B/Top 20 crossover.

I'LL CRY INSTEAD

Artist: The Beatles
Written by: John Lennon, Paul McCartney
From the album: *A Hard Day's Night*
Label: United Artists
Produced by: George Martin
Year: 1964
On the album, but not in the original movie. Inserted in a later version of the film (1982). Covered by Joe Cocker (Decca, '64) as his first single release in the UK.

I'LL FEEL A WHOLE LOT BETTER

Artist: The Byrds
Written by: Gene Clark
From the album: *Mr. Tambourine Man*
Label: Columbia
Produced by: Terry Melcher
Year: 1965
Jangling toward country/rock.

I'LL FOLLOW THE SUN

Artist: The Beatles
Written by: John Lennon, Paul McCartney
From the album: *Beatles '65*
Label: Capitol
Produced by: George Martin
Year: 1965
Peter-and-Gordonesque folk/rock.

I'LL GET YOU

Artist: The Beatles
Written by: John Lennon, Paul McCartney
From the album: *The Beatles Second Album*
Label: Capitol
Produced by: George Martin
Year: 1963
The B-side of "She Loves You."

I'LL GIVE ALL MY LOVE TO YOU

Artist: Keith Sweat
Written by: Keith Sweat, Bobby Wooten
From the album: *I'll Give All My Love to You*
Label: Elektra
Year: 1990
#1 R&B/Top 10 crossover.

I'LL HAVE TO SAY I LOVE YOU IN A SONG

Artist: Jim Croce
Written by: Jim Croce
From the album: *I Got a Name*
Label: ABC
Produced by: Terry Cashman, Tommy West
Year: 1973
Used as the theme for the TV movie *She Lives*, this became a hit after Croce died in a plane crash.

I'LL KEEP IT WITH MINE

Artist: Bob Dylan
Written by: Bob Dylan
Label: Columbia
Produced by: Tom Wilson
Year: 1966
One of Dylan's legendary early outtakes, a unique love song in which he admits "I can't help it if you might think I'm odd." Nico recorded it on her solo album, *Chelsea Girl* (Verve, '67), which was also produced by Tom Wilson. Covered by Fairport Convention ('67).

I'LL MAKE LOVE TO YOU

Artist: Boyz II Men
Written by: Kenny Edmunds (Babyface)
From the album: *II*
Label: Motown
Produced by: Babyface
Year: 1994
#1 R&B/#1 crossover; a gentlemanly seduction.

I'LL MEET YOU HALFWAY

Artist: The Partridge Family
Written by: Gerry Goffin, Wes Farrell
From the album: *Up to Date*
Label: Bell
Produced by: Wes Farrell
Year: 1971
In the Nelsons/Monkees-TV-family instant hit mold.

I'LL NEVER FIND ANOTHER YOU

Artist: The Seekers
Written by: Tom Springfield
From the album: *Best Of*
Label: Capitol
Produced by: Tom Springfield
Year: 1965
Epitome of folk/rock harmonizing.

I'LL NEVER GET OUT OF THIS WORLD ALIVE

Artist: Hank Williams
Written by: Hank Williams, Fred Rose
Label: MGM
Produced by: Fred Rose
Year: 1952
Prophetic preview of blue-eyed soul, from a country perspective.

I'LL REMEMBER

Artist: Madonna
Written by: Patrick Leonard, Madonna Ciccone, Richard Page
From the album: *With Honors Soundtrack*
Label: Maverick
Produced by: Patrick Leonard, Madonna
Year: 1994
Nailing another big movie ballad.

I'LL REMEMBER (IN THE STILL OF THE NIGHT)

Artist: The Five Satins
Written by: Freddy Parris
From the album: *The Five Satins Sing*
Label: Standord
Produced by: Freddy Parris
Year: 1956
B-side of "The Jones Girl" became one of the most cherished and popular doo-wop classics of all time, though not necessarily the most lucrative.

I'LL RISE

Artist: Ben Harper
Written by: Ben Harper
From the album: *Welcome to the Cruel World*
Label: Virgin
Year: 1993
Gospel-inflected modern folk blues.

I'LL STAND BY YOU

Artist: The Pretenders
Written by: Chrissie Hynde, Billy Steinberg, Tom Kelly
From the album: *Last of the Independents*
Label: Sire
Produced by: Ian Stanley
Year: 1994
Dream assignment for female rock specialists Steinberg and Kelly (Heart, the Bangles) provides the former Pretender Hynde with a heart (as well as a record) of gold.

I'LL STICK AROUND

Artist: Foo Fighters
Written by: Dave Grohl
From the album: *Foo Fighters*
Label: Rosswell/Capitol
Produced by: Barett Jones
Year: 1995
Reassuring legions of Nirvana fans, drummer Dave Grohl forms the Foo Fighters.

I'LL TAKE CARE OF YOU

Artist: Bobby Bland
Written by: Brook Benton
From the album: *Together for the First Time … Live*
Label: Duke
Produced by: Joe Scott
Year: 1960
#2 R&B/Bottom 20 crossover for the great R&B singer.

I'LL TAKE YOU THERE

Artist: The Staple Singers
Written by: Alvertis Isbell
From the album: *Be Altitude: Respect Yourself*
Label: Stax
Produced by: Al Bell
Year: 1972
#1 R&B/#1 crossover follow-up to "Respect Yourself." Covered by Bebe and Cece Winans (Capitol, '91).

I'LL WAIT

Artist: Van Halen
Written by: Eddie Van Halen, Alex Van Halen, Michael Anthony, David Lee Roth, Michael H. McDonald
From the album: *1984*
Label: Warner Brothers
Produced by: Ted Templeman
Year: 1984
Making their commercial move.

I'M A BELIEVER

Artist: The Monkees
Written by: Neil Diamond
From the album: *More of the Monkees*
Label: Colgems
Produced by: Jeff Barry
Year: 1966
Diamond finally sells a perfect pop/rock song to publisher Don Kirshner. Covered by Tin Huey (Warner Brothers, '79), and the Feelies in the '80 movie *Something Wild*.

I'M A BOY

Artist: The Who
Written by: Pete Townshend
From the album: *Meaty Beaty Big and Bouncy*
Label: Decca
Produced by: Kit Lambert
Year: 1971
Suggested segue: "Young Man Blues" by Mose Allison.

I'M A HAPPY MAN

Artist: The Jive Five
Written by: Casey Spencer
Label: United Artists
Year: 1965
Happy to be virtually doo-wop's lone representative on the Top-40 of '65.

I'M A KING BEE

Artist: Slim Harpo
Written by: James Moore (Slim Harpo)
Label: Excello
Produced by: Jay Miller
Year: 1957
Covered by the Rolling Stones (London, '64).

I'M A LOSER

Artist: The Beatles
Written by: John Lennon, Paul McCartney
From the album: *Beatles '65*
Label: Capitol
Produced by: George Martin
Year: 1965
Influenced by Bob Dylan, John Lennon goes back to the couch, foretelling more agonized confessions to come.

I'M A MAN

Artist: Bo Diddley
Written by: Ellas McDaniel (Bo Diddley)
From the album: *Bo Diddley's 16 All-Time Greatest Hits*
Label: Checker
Produced by: Leonard Chess
Year: 1955
Primordial boasting, covered by the Yardbirds (Epic, '65) in a groundbreaking heavy metal rendition.

I'M A MAN

Artist: Fabian
Written by: Doc Pomus, Mort Shuman
From the album: *The Fabulous Fabian*
Label: Chancellor
Produced by: Pete D'Angelis
Year: 1958
Off the Philadelphia assembly line.

I'M A MAN

Artist: Spencer Davis Group
Written by: Steve Winwood, Jimmy Miller
From the album: *I'm a Man*
Label: United Artists
Produced by: Jimmy Miller
Year: 1967
Signature number for the progressive blues supergroup. Winwood would move onto Traffic; Miller would produce the Rolling Stones.

I'M A WOMAN

Artist: Jim Kweskin and the Jug Band featuring Maria Muldaur
Written by: Jerry Leiber, Mike Stoller
From the album: *Jug Band Music*
Label: Vanguard
Year: 1965
Introducing the winsome Maria Muldaur's in-concert seduction number. When she did her own solo version it went Top 20 (Reprise, '75). The definitive pop rendition is by Peggy Lee (Capitol, '63).

(I'M A) ROAD RUNNER

Artist: Jr. Walker and the All-Stars
Written by: Eddie Holland, Lamont Dozier, Brian Holland
From the album: *(I'm a) Road Runner*
Label: Soul
Produced by: Brian Holland, Lamont Dozier
Year: 1965
B-side of "Shotgun" was a Top 5 R&B/Top 20 crossover a year later.

I'M AGAINST IT

Artist: The Ramones
Written by: Douglas Colvin, John Cummings, Jeff Hyman
From the album: *Road to Ruin*
Label: Sire
Produced by: Tommy Erdelyi, Ed Stasium
Year: 1978

I'M ALLOWED

Artist: Buffalo Tom
Written by: Buffalo Tom
From the album: *Big Red Letter Day*
Label: East/West
Produced by: The Robb Brothers, Buffalo Tom
Year: 1994
East coast alt-rock in the Fort Apache mold.

I'M ALRIGHT

Artist: Kenny Loggins
Written by: Kenny Loggins
From the album: *Caddyshack Soundtrack*
Label: Columbia
Produced by: Bruce Botnick, Kenny Loggins
Year: 1980
Taking over Steven Bishop's *Animal House* function.

I'M AN ADULT NOW

Artist: Pursuit of Happiness
Written by: Moe Berg
From the album: *Love Junk*
Label: Chrysalis
Produced by: Todd Rundgren
Year: 1988
The Canadian Jonathan Richman.

I'M BLUE (THE GONG GONG SONG)

Artist: The Ikettes
Written by: Ike Turner
Label: Atco
Year: 1961
Ike's backup singers step out on an Ike original, featuring Tina Turner on lead vocals.

I'M COMING OUT

Artist: Diana Ross
Written by: Nile Rodgers, Bernard Edwards
From the album: *Diana*

Label: Motown
Produced by: Nile Rodgers, Bernard Edwards
Year: 1980
Diana enters the sexual revelation.

I'M EASY

Artist: Keith Carradine
Written by: Keith Carradine
From the album: *Nashville Soundtrack*
Label: ABC
Produced by: Richard Baskin
Year: 1975
Prototypical coffee house ballad from the classic
Altman film won the Oscar for Best Song.

I'M EVERY WOMAN

Artist: Chaka Khan
Written by: Nick Ashford, Valerie Simpson
From the album: *Chaka*
Label: Warner Brothers
Produced by: Arif Mardin
Year: 1978
Her signature declaration; #1 R&B/Top 30 cross-
over. Covered by Whitney Houston in the movie
The Bodyguard (Arista, '92).

I'M FREE

Artist: The Rolling Stones
Written by: Mick Jagger, Keith Richards
From the album: *December's Children (and Every-body's)*
Label: London
Produced by: Andrew Loog-Oldham
Year: 1965
Covered by the Soup Dragons (Big Time, '90).

I'M FREE

Artist: The Who
Written by: Pete Townshend
From the album: *Tommy*
Label: Decca
Produced by: Kit Lambert
Year: 1969
Daltrey's *Tommy* showcase. From here he'd go on
to play Liszt, in the movie *Lisztomania* in 1975.

I'M GOIN' DOWN

Artist: Bruce Springsteen
Written by: Bruce Springsteen
From the album: *Born in the USA*
Label: Columbia
Produced by: Jon Landau, Bruce Springsteen,
Chuck Plotkin
Year: 1984
Battling superstardom to a draw.

I'M GOIN' HOME

Artist: Ten Years After
Written by: Alvin Lee
From the album: *Undead*
Label: Deram
Produced by: Mike Vernon

Year: 1968
Introducing the next great white blues guitar hope
from England, Alvin Lee, with his Woodstock
showpiece.

I'M GONNA BE (500 MILES)

Artist: The Proclaimers
Written by: Craig Reid, Charlie Reid
From the album: *Sunshine on Leith*
Label: Chrysalis
Year: 1989
Best Scottish folk/rock since the Undertones,
revived in the movie *Benny and Joon* (Chrysalis,
'93).

I'M GONNA BE A WHEEL SOMEDAY

Artist: Fats Domino
Written by: Fats Domino, Dave Bartholomew
From the album: *Let's Play Fats Domino*
Label: Imperial
Produced by: Dave Bartholomew
Year: 1959
B-side of "I Want to Walk You Home."

I'M GONNA BE STRONG

Artist: Gene Pitney
Written by: Barry Mann, Cynthia Weil
From the album: *It Hurts to Be in Love*
Label: Musicor
Year: 1964
Pitney's last Top 10 hit in the US; he would have
eight more in England.

I'M GONNA GET MARRIED

Artist: Lloyd Price
Written by: Lloyd Price, Harold Logan
From the album: *Mr. Personality*
Label: ABC Paramount
Year: 1959
#1 R&B/Top 10 crossover.

I'M GONNA LOVE YOU JUST A LITTLE MORE BABE

Artist: Barry White
Written by: Barry White
From the album: *I've Got So Much to Give*
Label: 20TH Century
Produced by: Barry White
Year: 1973
In the deep-toned Isaac Hayes bedside tradition,
heavy Barry's first #1 R&B/Top 10 crossover.

I'M GONNA LOVE YOU TOO

Artist: Buddy Holly
Written by: Joe Mauldin, Norman Petty, Niki
Sullivan
From the album: *Buddy Holly*

Label: Coral
Produced by: Norman Petty
Year: 1958

I'M GONNA MAKE YOU LOVE ME

Artist: Dee Dee Warwick
Written by: Kenny Gamble, Jerry Ross, Jerry A.
Williams
Label: Mercury
Produced by: Jerry Ross
Year: 1967
Compelling soul ballad by Dionne's sister. Covered
by Madeline Bell (Philips, '68), Diana Ross & the
Supremes and the Temptations (Motown, '68).

I'M GONNA PLAY THE HONKY TONKS

Artist: Marie Adams
Written by: Don Robey, Marie Adams
Label: Peacock
Produced by: Don Robey
Year: 1952
Celebrating the timeless urge to play music, even if
you have to travel to the wrong side of the tracks
(unless you already live there) to do it.

I'M GONNA TEAR YOUR PLAYHOUSE DOWN

Artist: Ann Peebles
Written by: Earl Randle
From the album: *Straight from the Heart*
Label: Hi
Produced by: Willie Mitchell
Year: 1972
A rough gem from an underappreciated belter.

I'M HAPPY JUST TO DANCE WITH YOU

Artist: The Beatles
Written by: John Lennon, Paul McCartney
From the album: *A Hard Day's Night*
Label: United Artists
Produced by: George Martin
Year: 1964
The B-side of "I Should Have Known Better."

I'M HENRY VIII, I AM

Artist: Herman's Hermits
Written by: Fred Murray, R.P. Weston
From the album: *Herman's Hermits on Tour*
Label: MGM
Produced by: Mickie Most
Year: 1965
Music Hall standard, introduced in 1911, by
English comedian Harry Champion.

I'M IN LOVE

Artist: Wilson Pickett
Written by: Bobby Womack

From the album: *I'm in Love*
Label: Atlantic
Produced by: Tom Dowd, Tommy Cogbill
Year: 1967
B-side of "Stag-o-Lee." Cover by Aretha Franklin (Atlantic, '74) was a #1 R&B/Top 20 crossover.

I'M IN LOVE AGAIN

Artist: Fats Domino
Written by: Fats Domino, Dave Bartholomew
From the album: *Rock and Rollin' with Fats Domino*
Label: Imperial
Produced by: Dave Bartholomew
Year: 1956
Having opened the commercial door with "Blueberry Hill," Fats took up semipermanent residence on the Top 10, starting with this sashaying original. Covered by Ricky Nelson (Imperial, '58).

I'M IN THE MOOD

Artist: John Lee Hooker
Written by: John Lee Hooker, Bernard Besman
Label: Modern
Produced by: Ralph Bass
Year: 1951
His basic down and dirty boogie that would last a lifetime.

I'M IN YOU

Artist: Peter Frampton
Written by: Peter Frampton
From the album: *I'm in You*
Label: A&M
Produced by: Peter Frampton
Year: 1977
His biggest hit, courtesy of the infernal talk box.

I'M INTO SOMETHING GOOD

Artist: Earl-Jean
Written by: Gerry Goffin, Carole King
Label: Colpix
Produced by: Gerry Goffin, Carole King
Year: 1964
Brill Building castoff gem, covered by Herman's Hermits (MGM, '64).

I'M JUST A SINGER (IN A ROCK AND ROLL BAND)

Artist: The Moody Blues
Written by: John Lodge
From the album: *A Question of Balance*
Label: Threshold
Produced by: Tony Clarke
Year: 1972
The thinking man's version of "Band on the Run."

I'M LEAVING IT UP TO YOU

Artist: Don and Dewey
Written by: Don Harris, Dewey Terry
From the album: *Jungle Hop*
Label: Specialty
Produced by: Sonny Bono
Year: 1957
Important R&B songwriting/performing duo who never hit the charts, but influenced some other legendary duos, like the Righteous Brothers and Sam and Dave, and some others that were not so legendary, like Dale and Grace, who turned this into a #1 hit (Montel, '63). Tune hit #1 the week JFK was assassinated, while Dale and Grace were on tour in Dallas. Covered by the Righteous Brothers (Verve, '66); producer Bono's duo Sonny and Cher (Atco, '66), Linda Ronstadt (Capitol, '70), Donny and Marie Osmond (MGM, '74).

I'M LIVIN' IN SHAME

Artist: The Supremes
Written by: Pam Sawyer, Berry Gordy Jr., Frank Wilson, R. Dean Taylor, Henry Cosby
From the album: *Let the Sunshine In*
Label: Motown
Produced by: The Clan
Year: 1969
Keeping down with the Joneses.

I'M LOOKING FOR SOMEONE TO LOVE

Artist: The Crickets
Written by: Buddy Holly, Norman Petty
From the album: *The Chirpin' Crickets*
Label: Brunswick
Produced by: Norman Petty
Year: 1957
Legendary cut from their first album.

I'M LOOKING THROUGH YOU

Artist: The Beatles
Written by: John Lennon, Paul McCartney
From the album: *Rubber Soul*
Label: Capitol
Produced by: George Martin
Year: 1965
Having passed through the doors of perception, there was no turning back to the days of wide-eyed innocence.

I'M MAD

Artist: Willie Mabon
Written by: Willie Mabon
Label: Chess
Year: 1953
#1 R&B follow-up to the #1 R&B "I Don't Know." Covered by Buddy Johnson (Mercury, '54).

I'M MOVIN' ON

Artist: Hank Snow
Written by: Hank Snow
From the album: *I'm Movin' On*
Label: RCA
Year: 1950
#1 country, with the classic rock and roll attitude and pedigree. Covered by Ray Charles (Atlantic, '59), the Rolling Stones (London, '65), Elvis Presley (RCA, '69), George Thorogood (EMI, '88).

I'M NOT A JUVENILE DELINQUENT

Artist: Frankie Lymon and the Teenagers
Written by: Frankie Lymon
From the album: *Rock and Roll*
Label: Gee
Produced by: George Goldner
Year: 1957
Frankie's plaintive doo-wop quest for acceptance, as showcased in the seminal and much misunderstood Tuesday Weld teen exploitation classic of 1957, *Rock, Rock, Rock*.

I'M NOT FROM HERE

Artist: James McMurtry
Written by: James McMurtry
From the album: *Too Long in the Wasteland*
Label: Columbia
Produced by: John Mellencamp
Year: 1989
The rambling song to end all rambling songs, by the son of author Larry.

I'M NOT IN LOVE

Artist: 10 C.C.
Written by: Graham Gouldman, Eric Stewart
From the album: *The Original Soundtrack*
Label: Mercury
Produced by: 10 c.c.
Year: 1975
Their biggest hit; bigger in England, where some folks think of it as the greatest song of all time.

I'M NOT LIKE EVERYBODY ELSE

Artist: The Kinks
Written by: Ray Davies
Label: Reprise
Produced by: Shel Talmy
Year: 1966
B-side of "Waterloo Sunset" is Ray's defining credo. Michael Jackson would borrow it.

I'M NOT TALKING

Artist: Mose Allison
Written by: Mose Allison
From the album: *The Word from Mose Allison*
Label: Atlantic
Year: 1964
Bluesy tone poem defines his country curmudgeon attitude. Covered by the Yardbirds (Epic, '65). The Who were listening.

(I'M NOT YOUR) STEPPIN' STONE

Artist: Paul Revere and the Raiders
Written by: Tommy Boyce, Bobby Hart
From the album: *Midnight Rider*
Label: Columbia
Produced by: Terry Melcher
Year: 1966
This malleable song of personal protest was covered by the Monkees (Colgems, '66) and the Sex Pistols in the film *The Great Rock 'n' Roll Swindle* (Warner Brothers, '80).

I'M ON FIRE

Artist: Bruce Springsteen
Written by: Bruce Springsteen
From the album: *Born in the USA*
Label: Columbia
Produced by: Jon Landau, Bruce Springsteen, Chuck Plotkin
Year: 1984
As an actor in his videos, Springsteen was better than Dylan and Billy Joel, not as good as Paul Simon or Tom Petty.

I'M READY

Artist: Fats Domino
Written by: Fats Domino, Al Lewis, Sylvester Bradford
From the album: *Fats Domino Sings Million Record Hits*
Label: Imperial
Produced by: Dave Bartholomew
Year: 1959
Fats rocks.

I'M READY

Artist: Muddy Waters
Written by: Willie Dixon
Label: Chess
Year: 1954
From Chicago, the blues get the royal treatment from Muddy, Willie, and little Walter.

I'M READY FOR LOVE

Artist: Martha & the Vandellas
Written by: Eddie Holland, Lamont Dozier, Brian Holland
From the album: *Watchout!*
Label: Gordy
Produced by: Brian Holland, Lamont Dozier
Year: 1966
Top 10 R&B/Top 10 crossover.

I'M SITTIN' ON TOP OF THE WORLD

Artist: Les Paul and Mary Ford
Written by: Sam Lewis, Joe Young, Ray Henderson
Label: Capitol

Produced by: Les Paul
Year: 1953
The great guitar inventor, innovator, inspiration, and influence, Les Paul recorded this standard on one of his signature modified arch-top Gibsons. Covered by Howlin' Wolf (Chess, '66), the Grateful Dead (Warner Brothers, '67). Originated by Al Jolson in '28, and heard in the '46 movie *The Al Jolson Story*.

I'M SO BORED WITH THE USA

Artist: The Clash
Written by: John Mellor (Joe Strummer), Mick Jones
From the album: *The Clash*
Label: Epic
Produced by: Mickey Foote
Year: 1977
Whereas in England the Clash wore T-shirts reading "Passion is a Fashion," "Creative Violence," and "Pure Energy."

I'M SO EXCITED

Artist: Pointer Sisters
Written by: Anita Pointer, Ruth Pointer, June Pointer, Trevor Lawrence
From the album: *So Excited*
Label: Planet
Produced by: Richard Perry
Year: 1982
A bigger hit when it was revived in '84.

I'M SO GLAD

Artist: Cream
Written by: Nehemiah "Skip" James
From the album: *Fresh Cream*
Label: Atco
Produced by: Robert Stigwood
Year: 1967
Making the world safe for Led Zeppelin's blooze metal.

I'M SO INTO YOU

Artist: SWV
Written by: Brian Alexander Morgan
From the album: *It's About Time*
Label: RCA
Produced by: B. A. Morgan
Year: 1993
Mining the antsy-teen girl-group sound of chick hop.

I'M SO LONESOME I COULD CRY

Artist: Hank Williams
Written by: Hank Williams
Label: MGM
Year: 1949
Pining for Audrey. Covered by B. J. Thomas (Scepter, '66).

I'M SO PROUD

Artist: The Impressions
Written by: Curtis Mayfield
From the album: *The Never Ending Impressions*
Label: ABC Paramount
Produced by: Curtis Mayfield
Year: 1964
Revived on the soundtrack to *A Bronx Tale* (Epic Soundtrax, '94).

I'M SO YOUNG

Artist: The Students
Written by: Prez Tyrus
Label: Note
Year: 1958
Revived in '61 on Argo to take advantage of a fleeting doo-wop moment. Covered by the Ronettes (Philles, '64), the Beach Boys (Capitol, '65).

I'M SORRY

Artist: John Denver
Written by: H. J. Deutschendorf Jr. (John Denver)
From the album: *Windsong*
Label: RCA
Produced by: Milt Okun
Year: 1975
Heartfelt #1 country/#1 crossover.

I'M SORRY

Artist: Brenda Lee
Written by: Ronnie Self, Dub Allbritten
From the album: *Brenda Lee*
Label: Decca
Produced by: Owen Bradley
Year: 1960
Original B-side of "That's All You Gotta Do," this weeper became Brenda's biggest hit.

I'M SORRY (BUT SO IS BRENDA LEE)

Artist: Marshall Crenshaw
Written by: Ben Vaughan
From the album: *Downtown*
Label: Warner Brothers
Year: 1985
Smirky but apt. Covered by Ben Vaughan (Fever, '86).

I'M STEPPING OUT

Artist: John Lennon
Written by: John Lennon
From the album: *Milk and Honey*
Label: Polydor
Year: 1984
Outtake from the *Double Fantasy* sessions, released posthumously.

I'M STICKIN' WITH YOU

Artist: Jimmy Bowen
Written by: Jimmy Bowen, Buddy Knox

From the album: *Triple D*
Label: Roulette
Produced by: Norman Petty
Year: 1957
Exploiting the massive clout of rockabilly, the Rhythm Orchids spawned a double A-sided hit for two of its members. The guitarist, Buddy Knox, beat the bass player, Jimmy Bowen, by a country mile, hitting #1 with "Party Doll." Bowen would eventually climb the rungs of the music business ladder to a comparable executive position, a career path shared by many a one-hit wonder.

I'M STILL IN LOVE WITH YOU

Artist: Al Green
Written by: Al Green, Willie Mitchell, Al Jackson
From the album: *I'm Still in Love with You*
Label: Hi
Produced by: Willie Mitchell
Year: 1972
#1 R&B/Top 10 crossover.

I'M STILL STANDING

Artist: Elton John
Written by: Elton John, Bernie Taupin
From the album: *Elton John's Greatest Hits*
Label: Geffen
Produced by: Chris Thomas
Year: 1983
A credo for benchless piano men everywhere. Ben Folds took notice.

I'M STONE IN LOVE WITH YOU

Artist: The Stylistics
Written by: Thom Bell, Linda Creed
From the album: *Round 2: The Stylistics*
Label: Avco
Produced by: Thom Bell
Year: 1972
Their third Top 10 R&B/crossover.

I'M TALKING ABOUT YOU

Artist: Chuck Berry
Written by: Chuck Berry
From the album: *New Jukebox Hits*
Label: Chess
Produced by: Leonard Chess, Phil Chess
Year: 1961
Covered by the Rolling Stones (London, '64).

I'M TELLING YOU NOW

Artist: Freddie and the Dreamers
Written by: Freddy Garrity, Mitch Murray
From the album: *Frantic Freddie*
Label: Tower
Year: 1963
Pop rocker that stiffed in '63, went to #1 in '65.

I'M THAT TYPE OF GUY

Artist: LL Cool J
Written by: James Todd Smith, Dwayne Simon
From the album: *Walking with a Panther*
Label: Def Jam
Produced by: LL Cool J
Year: 1989
His second Top 20 hit.

I'M THE ONLY ONE

Artist: Melissa Etheridge
Written by: Melissa Etheridge
From the album: *Yes I Am*
Label: Island
Produced by: Hugh Padgham, Melissa Etheridge
Year: 1993
Defining the moribund state of female rock in the post-Joan Jett, pre-Liz Phair/PJ Harvey/Courtney Love mini-era.

I'M THE URBAN SPACEMAN

Artist: Bonzo Dog Doo Dah Band
Written by: Neil Innes
From the album: *Urban Spaceman*
Produced by: Paul McCartney
Label: Imperial
Year: 1968
Innes would continue this fanciful mode in Monty Python.

I'M TOO SEXY

Artist: Right Said Fred
Written by: Fred Fairbrass, Richard Fairbrass, Rob Manzoli
From the album: *Right Said Fred*
Label: Charisma
Produced by: Tommy D.
Year: 1992
In a case of life imitating art imitating life, the main claim to fame for one of the members of the band was that he once played the *role* of the guitar player in a Bob Dylan video.

I'M TORE DOWN

Artist: Freddie King
Written by: Sonny Thompson
From the album: *Freddie King Sings the Blues*
Label: Federal
Produced by: Sonny Thompson
Year: 1961
One of six blues sides the guitarist placed on the R&B charts of '61, and the second to be covered by Eric Clapton (Warner Brothers, '94).

I'M TORE UP

Artist: Billy Gayles
Written by: Ike Turner
Label: Federal
Produced by: Ike Turner
Year: 1956
Classic Ike in his R&B session salad days with Ike Turner's Rhythm Rockers.

I'M WAITING FOR THE MAN

Artist: The Velvet Underground
Written by: Lou Reed
From the album: *The Velvet Underground and Nico*
Label: Verve
Produced by: Andy Warhol
Year: 1967
Long Island hippies on the hunt for experience, expensive thrills.

I'M WALKIN'

Artist: Fats Domino
Written by: Fats Domino, Dave Bartholomew
From the album: *Here Stands Fats Domino*
Label: Imperial
Produced by: Dave Bartholomew
Year: 1957
Third straight #1 R&B/Top 10 crossover for Fats, completing an incredible run of five months at #1 on the R&B charts. Covered by Rick Nelson (Imperial, '57).

I'M YOUR BABY TONIGHT

Artist: Whitney Houston
Written by: Kenny Edmunds (Babyface), Antonio Reid (L. A. Reid)
From the album: *I'm Your Baby Tonight*
Label: Arista
Produced by: Babyface, L. A. Reid
Year: 1990
Her third #1 R&B/#1 crossover.

I'M YOUR BOOGIE MAN

Artist: K.C. and the Sunshine Band
Written by: Harry Casey, Richard Finch
From the album: *Part 3*
Label: TK
Produced by: Harry Casey, Richard Finch
Year: 1977
Their fourth #1 and the first not to crossover to #1 R&B (it was #3).

I'M YOUR HOOCHIE COOCHIE MAN

Artist: Muddy Waters
Written by: Willie Dixon
Label: Chess
Year: 1954
The ultimate R&B boast.

I'M YOUR MAN

Artist: Leonard Cohen
Written by: Leonard Cohen
From the album: *I'm Your Man*
Label: Columbia
Produced by: Roscoe Beck, Michel Robidoux, Jean-Michel Reusser
Year: 1988

The first tribute package to the grand old man of rock poetry was entitled *I'm Your Fan*.

I'M YOUR MAN

Artist: Wham!
Written by: George Michael
From the album: *Music from the Edge of Heaven*
Label: Columbia
Produced by: George Michael
Year: 1986
#1 UK/Top 5 US.

I'M YOUR PUPPET

Artist: James & Bobby Purify
Written by: Spooner Oldham, Dan Penn
Label: Bell
Produced by: Papa Don Schroeder
Year: 1966
In the Sam and Dave mold, with access to most of the same material.

I'VE BEEN LONELY TOO LONG

Artist: The Rascals
Written by: Felix Cavaliere, Edward Brigati Jr.
From the album: *Rascals Greatest Hits (Time Peace)*
Label: Atlantic
Produced by: The Rascals, Arif Mardin, Tom Dowd
Year: 1967

I'VE BEEN LOVING YOU TOO LONG

Artist: Otis Redding
Written by: Jerry Butler, Otis Redding
From the album: *The Great Otis Redding Sings Soul Ballads*
Label: Volt
Produced by: Steve Cropper
Year: 1965
This signature ballad was Redding's second biggest R&B/crossover and one of the more transcendent moments of the Monterey Pop Festival, two years later. Covered by Ike and Tina Turner (Blue Thumb, '69).

I'VE BEEN THINKING ABOUT YOU

Artist: Londonbeat
Written by: George Chandler, William Henshall, Jimmy Chambers, Jimmy Helms
From the album: *In the Blood*
Label: Radioactive
Produced by: Martyn Phillips
Year: 1991
Alternative dance track from the UK.

I'VE BEEN WAITING

Artist: Matthew Sweet
Written by: Matthew Sweet
From the album: *Girlfriend*
Label: Zoo
Produced by: Fred Maher, Matthew Sweet
Year: 1991
Pure pop for the '90s.

I'VE BEEN WRONG BEFORE

Artist: H P Lovecraft
Written by: Randy Newman
From the album: *H P Lovecraft*
Label: Phillips 67
Year: 1967
Previewing the work of L.A.'s favorite cynic Randy Newman, in a lazy, hazy setting.

I'VE FOUND SOMEONE OF MY OWN

Artist: Free Movement
Written by: Frank K. Robinson
From the album: *I've Found Someone of My Own*
Label: Decca
Year: 1971

I'VE GOT A ROCK AND ROLL HEART

Artist: Eric Clapton
Written by: Troy Seals, Eddie Setser, Steve Diamond
From the album: *Money and Cigarettes*
Label: Duck
Produced by: Tom Dowd
Year: 1983
Middle-of-the-road soul.

I'VE GOT DREAMS TO REMEMBER

Artist: Otis Redding
Written by: Otis Redding, Velma Redding, Joe Rock
From the album: *Immortal Otis Redding*
Label: Atco
Produced by: Steve Cropper
Year: 1968
Tearful ballad.

I'VE GOT THE MUSIC IN ME

Artist: Kiki Dee
Written by: Bias Boshell
From the album: *I've Got the Music in Me*
Label: Rocket
Produced by: Gus Dudgeon
Year: 1974
Elton John protégé earned her right to sing pop/rock as the first UK act to sign with Motown in '70 ("Love Makes the World Go Round" peaked at #87 in '71).

I'VE GOT TO GET A MESSAGE TO YOU

Artist: Bee Gees
Written by: Barry Gibb, Robin Gibb, Maurice Gibb
From the album: *Idea*
Label: Atco
Produced by: Robert Stigwood
Year: 1968
Dramatic death row ballad is their first US Top 10, second UK #1.

I'VE GOT TO USE MY IMAGINATION

Artist: Gladys Knight & the Pips
Written by: Gerry Goffin, Barry Goldberg
From the album: *Imagination*
Label: Buddah
Produced by: Tony Camillo
Year: 1973
New label, new songwriting partnership, and a #1 R&B/Top 10 crossover from the stellar soul group's best-selling album.

I'VE HAD IT

Artist: The Bell Notes
Written by: Ray Ceroni, Carl Bonura
Label: Time
Produced by: Alan Fredericks
Year: 1958
From the mean streets of Long Island, this song was used to spectacular effect in Martin Scorsese's first film, *Who's That Knocking?* Suggested segue: "Cynical Girl" by Marshall Crenshaw (Warner Brothers, '82).

(I'VE HAD) THE TIME OF MY LIFE

Artist: Bill Medley and Jennifer Warnes
Written by: Franke Previte, John DeNicola, Donald Markowitz
From the album: *Dirty Dancing Soundtrack*
Label: RCA
Produced by: Michael Lloyd
Year: 1987
From the retro movie about perfect love in the Catskills, a knockout ballad.

I'VE JUST SEEN A FACE

Artist: The Beatles
Written by: John Lennon, Paul McCartney
From the album: *Rubber Soul*
Label: Capitol
Produced by: George Martin
Year: 1965
Perfecting their folk/rock chops.

I'VE LOVED HER SO LONG

Artist: Neil Young
Written by: Neil Young
From the album: *Neil Young*
Label: Reprise
Produced by: Jack Nitzsche
Year: 1969
Tortured folk rocker.

I'VE TOLD EVERY LITTLE STAR

Artist: Linda Scott
Written by: Oscar Hammerstein II, Jerome Kern
Label: Canadian-American
Year: 1961
From the '33 film *Music in the Air*.

ICE CREAM CITY

Artist: Shonen Knife
Written by: Michie Nakatori, Naoko Yamano
From the album: *Shonen Knife*
Label: Gastanka
Year: 1990
The girl-group sound in Japanese. Covered by Christmas (Gastanka Rockville, '90).

ICE CREAM FOR CROW

Artist: Captain Beefheart
Written by: Van Don Vliet
From the album: *Ice Cream for Crow*
Label: Virgin
Produced by: Captain Beefheart
Year: 1982
One of his finest efforts, the video of which was shown at the Museum of Modern Art, where being avant-garde still meant something.

ICE ICE BABY

Artist: Vanilla Ice
Written by: Robbie Van Winkle (Vanilla Ice), Earthquake, David Bowie, Queen
From the album: *To the Extreme*
Label: SBK
Year: 1990
Based on Bowie and Queen's "Under Pressure" (Elektra, '77).

IDA RED

Artist: Bob Wills & His Texas Playboys
Written by: Bob Wills, Tiny Moore
Label: Columbia
Year: 1947
Popularized by bluegrass star Gid Tanner (RCA, '37). May have been the inspiration (or at least the original title) for Chuck Berry's "Maybellene."

IDEAL WORLD

Artist: The Christians
Written by: Henry Priestman, Mark Herman
From the album: *The Christians*
Label: Island
Produced by: Laurie Latham
Year: 1988
Mellifluous UK soul with a poignant, pointed message.

IDIOT WIND

Artist: Bob Dylan
Written by: Bob Dylan
From the album: *Blood on the Tracks*
Label: Columbia
Produced by: Phil Ramone, Bob Dylan
Year: 1975
Long-winded, post-domestic diatribe.

IESHA

Artist: Another Bad Creation
Written by: Dallas Austin, Michael Bivens
From the album: *Coolin' at the Playground Ya' Know*
Label: Motown
Produced by: Dallas Austin
Year: 1991
Boy-meets-girl in the new jack swing era.

IF

Artist: Bread
Written by: David Gates
From the album: *Manna*
Label: Elektra
Produced by: David Gates
Year: 1971
Low-carb white bread. Covered by Telly Savalas (MCA, '75).

IF

Artist: Janet Jackson
Written by: James Harris III, Terry Lewis, Janet Jackson
From the album: *janet*
Label: Virgin
Produced by: James Harris III, Terry Lewis, Janet Jackson
Year: 1993
Jackson at her most verbally salacious.

IF HE'S EVER NEAR

Artist: Karla Bonoff
Written by: Karla Bonoff
From the album: *Karla Bonoff*
Label: Columbia
Produced by: Kenny Edwards
Year: 1977
Teary epic from the poet laureate of the singles bar set. Covered by Linda Ronstadt (Asylum, '76).

IF I CAN DREAM

Artist: Elvis Presley
Written by: Earl W. Brown
From the album: *Elvis*
Label: RCA
Produced by: Bones Howe
Year: 1968
Latter-day inspirational showstopper from his '68 comeback TV special that turned into his first live album.

IF I CAN'T HAVE YOU

Artist: Yvonne Elliman
Written by: Barry Gibb, Robin Gibb, Maurice Gibb
From the album: *Love Me*
Label: RSO
Produced by: Freddie Perren
Year: 1977
Soulful rocker from the movie *Saturday Night Fever*.

IF I COULD BUILD MY WHOLE WORLD AROUND YOU

Artist: Marvin Gaye and Tammi Terrell
Written by: Harvey Fuqua, Johnny Bristol, Vernon Bullock
From the album: *United*
Label: Tamla
Produced by: Harvey Fuqua, Johnny Bristol
Year: 1967
Their third R&B Top 10 of '67.

IF I COULD TURN BACK TIME

Artist: Cher
Written by: Diane Warren
From the album: *Heart of Stone*
Label: Geffen
Produced by: Diane Warren, G. Roche
Year: 1989
With the memorably revealing video.

IF I EVER FALL IN LOVE

Artist: Shai
Written by: Carl Martin
From the album: *If I Ever Fall in Love*
Label: Gasoline Alley/MCA
Produced by: Carl Martin
Year: 1992
Shades of doo-wop past. All-4-One and Boyz II Men would eventually dominate their turf.

IF I EVER LOSE MY FAITH IN YOU

Artist: Sting
Written by: Gordon Sumner (Sting)
From the album: *Ten Summoner's Tales*
Label: A&M
Produced by: Hugh Padgham, Sting
Year: 1993
Adult pop for the new age.

IF I FELL

Artist: The Beatles
Written by: John Lennon, Paul McCartney
From the album: *A Hard Day's Night*
Label: United Artists
Produced by: George Martin
Year: 1964
The B-side of "And I Love Her."

IF I HAD A HAMMER

Artist: The Weavers
Written by: Pete Seeger, Lee Hayes
Label: Charter
Produced by: Milt Gabler
Year: 1949

Campfire classic was one of the Weavers' earliest folk hits: from there the Urban Folk Scare became a psychic inevitability. Popularized by Peter, Paul and Mary (Warner Brothers, '62), Trini Lopez (Reprise, '63).

IF I NEEDED SOMEONE

Artist: The Beatles
Written by: George Harrison
From the album: *Yesterday and Today*
Label: Capitol
Produced by: George Martin
Year: 1965
George begins his existential quest.

IF I NEEDED YOU

Artist: Townes Van Zandt
Written by: Townes Van Zandt
From the album: *The Late Great Townes Van Zandt*
Produced by: Jack Clement
Label: Poppy
Year: 1972
Country ballad from the legendary folk poet from Texas.

IF I SHOULD FALL BEHIND

Artist: Bruce Springsteen
Written by: Bruce Springsteen
From the album: *Lucky Town*
Label: Columbia
Produced by: Jon Landau, Bruce Springsteen, Chuck Plotkin
Year: 1992
Graceful romantic ballad.

IF I WAS YOUR GIRLFRIEND

Artist: Prince
Written by: Prince Rogers Nelson
From the album: *Sign o' the Times*
Produced by: Prince
Label: Paisley Park
Year: 1987
One of those trick questions.

IF I WERE A CARPENTER

Artist: Tim Hardin
Written by: Tim Hardin
From the album: *Tim Hardin (Vol. II)*
Label: Verve/Forecast
Produced by: Charles Koppelman, Don Rubin
Year: 1967
Classic folk/rock ballad, covered, if not cloned, by Bobby Darin (Atlantic, '66), the Four Tops (Motown, '68).

IF I WERE YOUR WOMAN

Artist: Gladys Knight & the Pips
Written by: Pam Sawyer, Gloria Jones, Clay McMurray
From the album: *If I Were Your Woman*
Label: Soul

Produced by: Clay McMurray
Year: 1970
#1 R&B/Top 10 crossover.

IF I'D BEEN THE ONE

Artist: 38 Special
Written by: Jeff Carlisi, Don Barnes, Donnie Van Zant, Larry Steele
From the album: *Tour De Force*
Label: A&M
Year: 1983
Modified Lynyrd Skynyrd.

IF IT MAKES YOU HAPPY

Artist: Sheryl Crow
Written by: Sheryl Crow, Jeff Trott
From the album: *Sheryl Crow*
Label: A&M
Year: 1996
Emergent female voice, in a rare mood of acquiescence.

IF LOVING YOU IS WRONG, I DON'T WANT TO BE RIGHT

Artist: Luther Ingram
Written by: Homer Banks, Raymond Jackson, Carl Hampton
From the album: *If Loving You Is Wrong, I Don't Want to Be Right*
Label: Koko
Produced by: Johnny Baylor
Year: 1971
#1 R&B/Top 10 crossover, soul classic.

IF NOT FOR YOU

Artist: Bob Dylan
Written by: Bob Dylan
From the album: *New Morning*
Label: Columbia
Produced by: Bob Johnston
Year: 1970
Country pie in the sky. Covered by George Harrison (Apple, '70), Olivia Newton-John (Uni, '71) for her first UK and US hit.

IF SHE KNEW WHAT SHE WANTS

Artist: Bangles
Written by: Jules Shear
From the album: *Different Light*
Label: Columbia
Produced by: David Kahne
Year: 1986
Wise, witty, and complex rocker stiffed as a single.

IF 6 WAS 9

Artist: Jimi Hendrix
Written by: Jimi Hendrix
From the album: *Axis: Bold as Love*
Label: Reprise

Produced by: Chas Chandler
Year: 1968
Enacting the apocalypse, sexual and instrumental. Featured in the film *Easy Rider*.

IF THAT'S YOUR BOYFRIEND, HE WASN'T LAST NIGHT

Artist: Me'Shell NdegéOcello
Written by: Me'Shell NdegéOcello
From the album: *Plantation Lullabies*
Label: Maverick/Sire
Year: 1993
Madonna discovery's breakthrough R&B-edged single. Later she would team with John Mellencamp on "Wild Night" (Mercury, '94).

IF THERE'S A HEAVEN ABOVE

Artist: Love and Rockets
Written by: David J., Daniel Ash, Kevin Haskins
From the album: *Seventh Dream of Teenage Heaven*
Label: Beggar's Banquet
Produced by: John A. Rivers, Love and Rockets
Year: 1985
An ethereal British dance-hall epiphany.

IF WINTER ENDS

Artist: Bright Eyes
Written by: Conor Oberst
From the album: *Letting off the Happiness*
Label: LBJ
Year: 1998
Out of the heartland, the sobbing squall of a new emotional generation.

IF WISHES CAME TRUE

Artist: Sweet Sensation
Written by: Russell Desalvo, Deena Charles, Bob Steele
From the album: *Love Child*
Label: Atco
Year: 1990
When anonymous one-shot dance tracks ruled the charts and the airwaves.

IF YOU CAN WANT

Artist: The Miracles
Written by: Smokey Robinson
From the album: *Special Occasion*
Label: Tamla
Produced by: Smokey Robinson
Year: 1968
One of Smokey's more visceral laments.

IF YOU CAN'T ROCK ME

Artist: Ricky Nelson
Written by: Willie Jacobs
From the album: *Ricky*
Label: Imperial

Produced by: Ricky Nelson, Jimmy Haskell, Ozzie Nelson
Year: 1957
One of his best nonhits, released in '63 by Imperial long after Rick had left for Decca. It died after a week on the charts as the B-side of the bomb "Old Enough to Love."

IF YOU COULD ONLY SEE

Artist: Tonic
Written by: Emerson Hart
From the album: *Lemon Parade*,
Label: A&M
Year: 1997
Standard issue rock complaint.

IF YOU COULD READ MY MIND

Artist: Gordon Lightfoot
Written by: Gordon Lightfoot
From the album: *Sit down Young Stranger*
Label: Reprise
Produced by: Lenny Waronker, Joe Wissert
Year: 1970
Easy listening folk/rock from Canada.

IF YOU DON'T KNOW ME BY NOW

Artist: Harold Melvin and the Bluenotes
Written by: Kenny Gamble, Leon Huff
From the album: *Harold Melvin & the Bluenotes*
Label: Philadelphia International
Produced by: Kenny Gamble, Leon Huff
Year: 1972
Passionate and poignant Gamble and Huff creation notches a #1 R&B/Top 10 crossover. Suggested Segue: "You Don't Know Me" by Ray Charles.

IF YOU GOTTA GO, GO NOW (OR ELSE YOU GOT TO STAY ALL NIGHT)

Artist: Manfred Mann
Written by: Bob Dylan
Label: HMV
Year: 1965
#2 UK hit. This brilliant folkie seduction number was an early performing highlight for Dylan, but not released by him until '91. In '77 Manfred Mann would introduce Bruce Springsteen's "Blinded by the Light" to the British Top 10.

IF YOU GOTTA MAKE A FOOL OF SOMEBODY

Artist: James Ray
Written by: Rudy Clark
Label: Caprice
Produced by: Neil Galligan
Year: 1962
Top 10 R&B/Top 30 crossover. Covered by Maxine Brown (Wand, '66).

IF YOU HAD MY LOVE

Artist: Jennifer Lopez
Written by: Rodney Jerkins, Corey Rooney, LeShawn Daniels, Fred Jerkins, Jennifer Lopez
From the album: *On the 6*
Label: Work
Year: 1999
Capitalizing on the Latina persona she'd created with her lead in the *Selena* biopic.

IF YOU LEAVE

Artist: Orchestral Manoeuvres in the Dark (OMD)
Written by: OMD
From the album: *Pretty in Pink Soundtrack*
Label: A&M
Produced by: Tom Lord-Alge, OMD
Year: 1986
Breathless ballad from the UK dance masters.

IF YOU LEAVE ME NOW

Artist: Chicago
Written by: Peter Cetera
From the album: *Chicago X*
Label: Columbia
Produced by: James William Guercio
Year: 1976
Chicago's biggest all-time international hit, #1 US/#1 UK

(IF YOU LET ME MAKE LOVE TO YOU) WHY CAN'T I TOUCH YOU

Artist: Ronnie Dyson
Written by: C.C. Courtney, Peter Link
From the album: *Salvation (Musical)*
Label: Columbia
Produced by: Billy Jackson
Year: 1970
From the other first rock musical.

IF YOU LOVE ME (LET ME KNOW)

Artist: Olivia Newton-John
Written by: John Rostill
From the album: *If You Love Me Let Me Know*
Label: MCA
Produced by: John Farrar
Year: 1974
Top 10 country/Top 10 crossover.

IF YOU LOVE SOMEBODY SET THEM FREE

Artist: Sting
Written by: Gordon Sumner (Sting)
From the album: *The Dream of the Blue Turtles*
Label: A&M
Produced by: Pete Smith, Sting
Year: 1985
First and biggest solo hit for the ex-Police man establishes his ultracool, new age meets jazz/rock philosophy.

IF YOU NEED ME

Artist: Wilson Pickett
Written by: Wilson Pickett, Robert Bateman, Sonny Sanders
Label: Double-L
Produced by: Wilson Pickett
Year: 1963
His first R&B/crossover. Covered by Solomon Burke (Atlantic, '63).

IF YOU REALLY LOVE ME

Artist: Stevie Wonder
Written by: Stevie Wonder, Syreeta Wright
From the album: *Where I'm Coming From*
Label: Tamla
Produced by: Stevie Wonder
Year: 1970
Follow up to Stevie's cover of the Beatles' "We Can Work It Out." Like Goffin & King and Barry & Greenwich, the married songwriting team of Syreeta & Stevie was doomed to break up—with only a year's worth of success to show for it before the painful divorce. Suggested segue: Jeff Beck's version of Wonder's tune for Syreeta, "Cause We've Ended as Lovers."

IF YOU TRY

Artist: The Chantels
Written by: Richard Barrett, Nathaniel Nilsen
From the album: *The Chantels*
Produced by: Richard Barrett, George Goldner
Label: End
Year: 1957
Essential ballad for Arlene Smith completists.

IF YOU WANNA BE A BIRD

Artist: The Holy Modal Rounders
Written by: Antonia
From the album: *Moray Eels Eat the Holy Modal Rounders*
Label: Elektra
Produced by: Peter Stampfel
Year: 1965
Jug band revisionaries achieve generational immortality in the '69 film *Easy Rider*.

IF YOU WANNA BE HAPPY

Artist: Jimmy Soul
Written by: Frank Guida Jr., Joseph Royster, Carmela Guida
From the album: *If You Wanna Be Happy*
Label: S.P.Q.R.
Produced by: Frank J. Guida
Year: 1963
Homespun calypso-based advice to the lovelorn; once quoted by Sam Malone on an episode of *Cheers*.

IF YOU WANT ME TO STAY

Artist: Sly and the Family Stone
Written by: Sylvester Stewart
From the album: *Fresh*

Label: Epic
Produced by: Sly Stone
Year: 1973
Sly in a psychedelic funk.

IF YOU WERE A BLUEBIRD

Artist: Joe Ely
Written by: Butch Hancock
From the album: *Joe Ely*
Produced by: Chip Young
Label: MCA
Year: 1977
From Austin, the roots of the coming Americana radio format.

IF YOU'RE READY
(COME GO WITH ME)

Artist: The Staple Singers
Written by: Homer Banks, Ray Jackson, Carl Hampton
From the album: *Be What You are*
Label: Stax
Produced by: Al Bell
Year: 1973
#1 R&B/Top 10 crossover.

I-FEEL-LIKE-I'M-FIXIN'-
TO-DIE RAG

Artist: Country Joe and the Fish
Written by: Joe McDonald
From the album: *I-Feel-Like-I'm-Fixin'-to-Die*
Label: Vanguard
Produced by: Sam Charters
Year: 1967
Anti war anthem from the barricades of Berkeley.

IKO IKO

Artist: The Dixie Cups
Written by: Marylin Jones, Sharon Jones, Joe Jones, Jessie Thomas
From the album: *Chapel of Love*
Label: Red Bird
Produced by: Jerry Leiber, Mike Stoller
Year: 1965
The eternal voice of New Orleans with a voodoo chant from the French Quarter. Featured in the soundtrack for *The Big Easy* (Antilles, '87) and *Rain Man* (Capitol, '89).

IMAGE OF A GIRL

Artist: The Safaris
Written by: Marvin Rosenberg, Richard Clasky
Label: Eldo
Year: 1960
Essential part of the suburban, white doo-wop collection.

IMAGINARY LOVER

Artist: Atlanta Rhythm Section
Written by: Buddy Buie, Dean Daughtry, Robert Nix

From the album: *Champagne Jam*
Label: Polydor
Produced by: Buddy Buie
Year: 1978

IMAGINATION

Artist: The Quotations
Written by: Johnny Burke, Jimmy Van Heusen
Label: Verve
Year: 1961
Doo-wopping the classics, part XXIV. This tune was introduced by Harry Reser (Columbia, '28), but it took the imagination of the Quotations, four guys from Brooklyn, to stretch the title into fifteen syllables.

IMAGINE

Artist: John Lennon
Written by: John Lennon
From the album: *Imagine*
Label: Apple
Produced by: John Lennon, Yoko Ono, Phil Spector
Year: 1971
His belated flower-child anthem.

IMMIGRANT SONG

Artist: Led Zeppelin
Written by: Jimmy Page, Robert Plant
From the album: *Led Zeppelin III*
Label: Atlantic
Produced by: Jimmy Page
Year: 1970
Third Top 20 single for the British blooze band that never released a single in England.

IMPORTANT IN YOUR LIFE

Artist: Modern Lovers
Written by: Jonathan Richman
From the album: *Jonathan Richman and the Modern Lovers*
Label: Beserkley
Produced by: John Cale
Year: 1976
Last of the early, legendary essentials is Jonathan's tribute to doo-wop.

IMPRESSION THAT I GET,
THE

Artist: The Mighty Mighty Bosstones
Written by: Dicky Barrett, Joe Gittleman
From the album: *Let's Face It*
Label: Big Rig
Produced by: Paul Kolderie, Sean Slade
Year: 1997
In the midst of a ska revival.

IMPULSIVE

Artist: Wilson Phillips
Written by: Steve Kipner, Cliff Magness

From the album: *Wilson Phillips*
Label: SBK
Produced by: Glen Ballard
Year: 1990
Third of four #1 singles from the debut album. Ballard would move on to the somewhat more impulsive, if not belligerent, Alanis Morrisette.

IN A BIG COUNTRY

Artist: Big Country
Written by: Big Country
From the album: *The Crossing*
Label: Mercury
Produced by: Steve Lillywhite
Year: 1983
Loping Scottish folk/rock.

IN BETWEEN DAYS
(WITHOUT YOU)

Artist: The Cure
Written by: Robert Smith
From the album: *The Head on the Door*
Label: Elektra
Produced by: Robert Smith, Dave Allen
Year: 1985
Alternative classic on the order of New Order.

IN CROWD, THE

Artist: Dobie Gray
Written by: Billy Page
From the album: *Dobie Gray Sings for the In Crowd*
Label: Charger
Produced by: Fred Darian
Year: 1964
His biggest hit. And for those who didn't make the in crowd, during the same year Bob Dylan was singing, "The losers now will be later to win."

IN DREAMS

Artist: Roy Orbison
Written by: Roy Orbison
From the album: *In Dreams*
Label: Monument
Produced by: Fred Foster
Year: 1963
A recurring Orbisonian theme. Rerecorded for a scene in the film *Blue Velvet*.

IN EVERY DREAM HOME
A HEARTACHE

Artist: Roxy Music
Written by: Bryan Ferry
From the album: *For Your Pleasure*
Label: Warner Brothers
Produced by: Chris Thomas, John Astley, Roxy Music
Year: 1973
The ultimate tortured love song until Stephen Morrissey came along to give new meaning to the genre.

IN GOD'S COUNTRY

Artist: U2
Written by: U2
From the album: *The Joshua Tree*
Produced by: Daniel Lanois, Brian Eno
Label: Island
Year: 1987
Expanding their arena vision.

IN MEMORY OF ELIZABETH REED

Artist: The Allman Brothers
Written by: Dickey Betts
From the album: *Idlewild South*
Label: Atco
Produced by: Adrian Barber
Year: 1970
Epic instrumental helps establish the guitar sound of Southern rock.

IN MY BED

Artist: Dru Hill
Written by: Rafael Brown, Ralph Stacy, Darryl Simmons
From the album: *Dru Hill*
Label: Island
Produced by: Darryl Simmons
Year: 1996
Top 10 R&B/Top 10 crossover.

IN MY DARKEST HOUR

Artist: Megadeth
Written by: Dave Mustaine, Dave Ellefson
From the album: *The Decline and Fall of Western Civilization (Part II): The Metal Years Soundtrack*
Label: Capitol
Year: 1988
Second-generation protest from the former Metallica guitarist: louder, faster, heavier than the bomb.

IN MY HOUSE

Artist: Mary Jane Girls
Written by: Rick James
From the album: *Only Four You*
Label: Gordy
Produced by: Rick James
Year: 1985
Their only Top 10 R&B/Top 10 crossover.

IN MY LIFE

Artist: The Beatles
Written by: John Lennon, Paul McCartney
From the album: *Rubber Soul*
Label: Capitol
Produced by: George Martin
Year: 1965
One of Lennon's best art films. Covered by Judy Collins (Elektra, '67).

IN MY ROOM

Artist: The Beach Boys
Written by: Brian Wilson, Gary Usher
From the album: *Surfer Girl*
Label: Capitol
Produced by: Brian Wilson
Year: 1963
Safe in his lair, with Maureen Love on harp. B-side of "Be True to Your School."

IN QUINTESSENCE

Artist: Squeeze
Written by: Chris Difford, Glenn Tilbrook
From the album: *East Side Story*
Label: A&M
Produced by: Elvis Costello, Roger Bechirian
Year: 1981
Their most quintessential pop concoction.

IN THE AIR TONIGHT

Artist: Phil Collins
Written by: Phil Collins
From the album: *Face Value*
Label: Atlantic
Produced by: Phil Collins
Year: 1981
Atmospheric English rocker gained massive credibility for Collins through its use in the background of the climactic train scene in the Tom Cruise/Rebecca De Mornay film *Risky Business*, and in an early episode of the high-gloss, scene-making TV drama, *Miami Vice*.

IN THE BUSH

Artist: Musique
Written by: Patrick Adams, Sandra Cooper
From the album: *Keep on Jumpin'*
Label: Prelude
Produced by: Patrick Adams
Year: 1978
As only the French could put it. Suggested discotheque segue: "Je T'aime … Moi non plus" by Jane Birkin and Serge Gainsbourg.

IN THE CITY

Artist: The Jam
Written by: Paul Weller
From the album: *In the City*
Label: Polydor
Produced by: Vic Smith, Chris Parry
Year: 1977
Debut release from a second generation Who. Suggested segue: "Holidays in the Sun" by the Sex Pistols.

IN THE CLOSET

Artist: Michael Jackson
Written by: Michael Jackson, Teddy Riley
From the album: *Dangerous*
Label: Epic
Produced by: Michael Jackson, Bill Bottrell
Year: 1991
Attempting to undeify the King of Pop.

IN THE GARDEN

Artist: Van Morrison
Written by: Van Morrison
From the album: *No Guru, No Method, No Teacher*
Label: Polygram
Produced by: Van Morrison
Year: 1986
Overwhelming quasi-religious ballad is one of his most moving moments.

IN THE GHETTO (THE VICIOUS CIRCLE)

Artist: Elvis Presley
Written by: Mac Davis, Billy Strange
From the album: *From Elvis in Memphis*
Label: RCA
Produced by: Chips Moman, Felton Jarvis, Elvis Presley
Year: 1969
In a year of unparalleled interest in all things country, Elvis returned to his Memphis roots. Covered by Dolly Parton (RCA, '69).

IN THE HOUSE OF STONE AND LIGHT

Artist: Martin Page
Written by: Martin Page
From the album: *In the House of Stone and Light*
Label: Mercury
Produced by: Martin Page
Year: 1994
First hit as an artist for the coauthor of "We Built This City."

IN THE JUNGLE

Artist: Kid Creole and the Coconuts
Written by: August Darnell
From the album: *Fresh Fruit in Foreign Places*
Label: Sire/Ze
Produced by: August Darnell
Year: 1981
Dr. Buzzard cofounder's parody of the *Odyssey*, optioned by theatre impressario Joseph Papp.

IN THE MEANTIME

Artist: Spacehog
Written by: Royston Langdon
From the album: *Resident Alient*
Produced by: Bryce Goggin
Label: Elektra
Year: 1995
Royston Langdon's claim to fame aside from marrying Liv Tyler.

IN THE MIDDLE OF A HEARTACHE

Artist: Wanda Jackson
Written by: Laurie Christianson, Pat Franzese, Wanda Jackson
Produced by: Ken Nelson
Label: Capitol

Year: 1961
Her career at a crossroads, the rockabilly queen chooses to follow Patsy Cline into country music territory.

IN THE MIDNIGHT HOUR

Artist: Wilson Pickett
Written by: Wilson Pickett, Steve Cropper
From the album: *In the Midnight Hour*
Label: Atlantic
Produced by: Tom Dowd, Jerry Wexler, Rick Hall, Jim Stewart, Steve Cropper
Year: 1965
Pickett's first #1 R&B hit was produced by a virtual soul Hall of Fame committee.

IN THE NAVY

Artist: The Village People
Written by: Henri Belolo, Jacques Morali, Victor Willis
From the album: *Go West*
Label: Casablanca
Produced by: Jacques Morali
Year: 1979
The one-joke disco band changes costumes.

IN THE RAIN

Artist: The Dramatics
Written by: Tony Hester
From the album: *Whatcha See Is What You Get*
Label: Volt
Produced by: Tony Hester
Year: 1971
Lush and evocative #1 R&B/Top 10 crossover. Missy Elliott would turn it into a hailstorm.

IN THE STREET

Artist: Big Star
Written by: Alex Chilton, Chris Bell
From the album: *#1 Record*
Produced by: John Fry
Label: Ardent
Year: 1972
Ben Vaughan helped turn this slacker anthem into the theme for *That 70s Show*.

IN THE SUMMERTIME

Artist: Mungo Jerry
Written by: Ray Dorset
From the album: *Mungo Jerry*
Label: Janus
Produced by: Barry Murray
Year: 1970
Top UK single of 1970.

IN THE SUN

Artist: Blondie
Written by: Chris Stein
From the album: *Blondie*
Label: Private Stock

Produced by: Richard Gottehrer, Craig Leon
Year: 1977
B-side of "X-Offender" was a postmodern girl-group tribute to the quintessential Disney girl Annette. There wouldn't be another Disney girl to equal her until Britney Spears.

IN THE YEAR 2525 (EXORDIUM AND TERMINUS)

Artist: Zager and Evans
Written by: Rick Evans
From the album: *In the Year 2525 (Exordium and Terminus)*
Label: RCA
Produced by: Denny Zager, Rick Evans
Year: 1969
From Lincoln, Nebraska, into the twenty-sixth century. The #1 one-hit wonder of all time.

IN THEE

Artist: Blue Oyster Cult
Written by: Allen Lanier
From the album: *Mirrors*
Label: Columbia
Produced by: Sandy Pearlman
Year: 1979
A tribute to East Village rock-poet, Patti Smith.

IN TOO DEEP

Artist: Genesis
Written by: Phil Collins, Tony Banks, Mike Rutherford
From the album: *Invisible Touch*
Label: Atlantic
Produced by: Hugh Padgham, Genesis
Year: 1986
Suddenly the Chicago of England.

IN YOUR EYES (THEME FROM *SAY ANYTHING*)

Artist: Peter Gabriel
Written by: Peter Gabriel, Bill Laswell
From the album: *So*
Label: Geffen
Produced by: Peter Gabriel, Daniel Lanois
Year: 1986
Featured in the soundtrack to Cameron Crowe's classic coming-of-age film *Say Anything*.

IN YOUR ROOM

Artist: Bangles
Written by: Billy Steinberg, Tom Kelly, Susannah Hoffs
From the album: *Everything*
Label: Columbia
Produced by: Davitt Sigerson
Year: 1988
As Patty Smyth had before her, another winsome waif (Susannah Hoffs) succumbs to the star-making machine.

IN-A-GADDA-DA-VIDA

Artist: Iron Butterfly
Written by: Doug Ingle
From the album: *In-a-Gadda-Da-Vida*
Label: Atco
Produced by: Jim Hinton
Year: 1968
Epitomizing—or unintentionally parodying—the wretched excess of the FM psychedelic/progressive rock as jazz improvisation era (with half an era left to go). Drum soloist should have listened to Joe Morello. Covered by archetypal death metal band, Slayer, in the wasted youth epic *Less Than Zero* (Def Jam, '87).

INCENSE AND PEPPERMINTS

Artist: Strawberry Alarm Clock
Written by: John Carter, Tim Gilbert
From the album: *Incense and Peppermints*
Label: Uni
Produced by: Frank Slay, Bill Holmes
Year: 1967
Hippiesque.

INCIDENT ON 57TH STREET

Artist: Bruce Springsteen
Written by: Bruce Springsteen
From the album: *The Wild, the Innocent and the E Street Shuffle*
Label: Columbia
Produced by: Jim Cretecos, Mike Appel
Year: 1973
Early Springsteen cityscape. 10:03 live version was released as the B-side of "Fire" in '87.

INCOMPLETE

Artist: Sisqo
Written by: Warren Crawford, Montel Jordan
From the album: *Unleash the Dragon*
Label: Def Soul
Year: 1999
Follow-up to "The Thong Song."

INDEPENDENCE DAY

Artist: Bruce Springsteen
Written by: Bruce Springsteen
From the album: *The River*
Label: Columbia
Produced by: Jon Landau, Bruce Springsteen, Steve Van Zandt
Year: 1980
Squaring things with the old man.

INDEPENDENT WOMAN

Artist: Destiny's Child
Written by: Samuel Barnes, Beyonce Knowles, Jean Claude Olivier, Corey Rooney
From the album: *Charlie's Angels Soundtrack*
Label: Sony
Year: 2000

Capitalizing on their moment for their third #1, before Beyonce took off for solo independence.

INDIAN GIVER

Artist: 1910 Fruitgum Company
Written by: Bobby Bloom, Bo Gentry
From the album: *Indian Giver*
Label: Buddah
Produced by: Jerry Kazenetz, Jeff Katz
Year: 1969
Bloom would shine on "Montego Bay."

INDIAN SUMMER

Artist: Beat Happening
Written by: Beat Happening
From the album: *Jamboree*
Label: K/Sub Pop
Produced by: Mark Lanegan, Gary Lee Connor
Year: 1988
A Jonathan Richman-influenced Velvet Underground-tempered drone.

INDIANA WANTS ME

Artist: R. Dean Taylor
Written by: R. Dean Taylor
From the album: *I Think Therefore I Am*
Label: Rare Earth
Produced by: R. Dean Taylor
Year: 1970
Country-flavored shoot-out from Motown.

INFATUATION

Artist: Rod Stewart
Written by: Rod Stewart, Wayne Hitchings, W. Robinson
From the album: *Camouflage*
Label: Warner Brothers
Produced by: Michael Omartian
Year: 1984
A step down from "Passion," Rod begins his arena-idol period.

INFORMER

Artist: Snow
Written by: Darrin O'Brien (Snow), Shawn Moltke, Edmund Leary
From the album: *12 Inches of Snow*
Label: East West
Produced by: McShan, John Ficariotta
Year: 1993
Snow was in jail when this peaked at #1 (Top 10 R&B crossover).

INNER CITY BLUES (MAKE ME WANNA HOLLER)

Artist: Marvin Gaye
Written by: Marvin Gaye, James Myx Jr.
From the album: *What's Goin' On*
Label: Tamla
Produced by: Marvin Gaye
Year: 1971

A message that would dominate the R&B sensibility by the end of the decade. #1 R&B/Top 10 crossover.

INNER LIGHT, THE

Artist: The Beatles
Written by: George Harrison
From the album: *Rarities*
Label: Capitol
Produced by: George Martin
Year: 1968
George tends to his own garden.

INNOCENT WHEN YOU DREAM (BAR ROOM)

Artist: Tom Waits
Written by: Tom Waits
From the album: *Frank's Wild Years*
Label: Island
Produced by: Tom Waits
Year: 1987
Prominently and poignantly featured in the '95 movie *Smoke*.

INSANE IN THE BRAIN

Artist: Cypress Hill
Written by: Louis Freese (Dr. Freeze), Senen Reyes, Larry Muggurud
From the album: *Black Sunday*
Label: Ruffhouse
Produced by: D. J. Muggs
Year: 1993
A paean to cannabis.

INSIDE OUT

Artist: Eve 6
Written by: Max Collins, James Fagenson, Jonathan Siebels
From the album: *Eve 6*
Label: RCA
Year: 1998
Verbally complex but emotionally distant modernism defines end of the century rock.

INSTANT KARMA (WE ALL SHINE ON)

Artist: John Lennon
Written by: John Lennon
From the album: *Shaved Fish*
Label: Apple
Produced by: Phil Spector
Year: 1970
Primed by Lennon's fabulous neuroticism, Spector pulls out the old Wall of Sound.

INSTITUTIONALIZED

Artist: Suicidal Tendencies
Written by: Mike Muir, Amery Smith, Louis Mayorga
From the album: *Suicidal Tendencies*
Label: Frontier

Year: 1983
Heavy mental.

INTERESTING DRUG

Artist: Morrissey
Written by: Stephen Morrissey, Stephen Street
From the album: *Morrissey*
Label: Sire
Produced by: Stephen Street
Year: 1989
With the lovely Kirsty MacColl in a supporting role.

INTERSTATE LOVE SONG

Artist: Stone Temple Pilots
Written by: Robert DeLeo, Scott Weiland, Dean DeLeo, Eric Kretz
From the album: *Purple*
Label: Atlantic
Produced by: Brendan O'Brien
Year: 1994
Their biggest Top 40 hit.

INTERSTELLAR OVERDRIVE

Artist: Pink Floyd
Written by: Roger Waters, Syd Barrett, Nick Mason, Rick Wright
From the album: *Piper at the Gates of Dawn*
Label: Tower
Produced by: Norman Smith, Joe Boyd
Year: 1967
Psychedelia, high-British style. Covered by Camper Van Beethoven (Pitch-a-Tent, '86).

INTO EACH LIFE SOME RAIN MUST FALL

Artist: The Ink Spots and Ella Fitzgerald
Written by: Allan Robert, Doris Fisher
Label: Decca
Year: 1945
Classic # 1 R&B/#1 crossover helped established two of black music's most treasured legends. Covered by Frankie Avalon (Chancellor, '59), Smokey Robinson (Motown, '80).

INTO THE ARENA

Artist: The Michael Schenker Group
Written by: Michael Schenker
From the album: *The Michael Schenker Group*
Label: Chrysalis
Year: 1980
Glistening guitar rock with a Germanic edge, by the brother of Scorpion founder Rudolf.

INTO THE FIRE

Artist: Sarah McLachlan
Written by: Sarah McLachlan, Pierre Marchand
From the album: *Solace*
Label: Arista
Produced by: Pierre Marchand
Year: 1992
Canadian singer/songwriter begins to heat up.

INTO THE GREAT WIDE OPEN

Artist: Tom Petty and the Heartbreakers
Written by: Tom Petty, Jeff Lynne
From the album: *Into the Great Wide Open*
Label: MCA
Produced by: Jeff Lynne, Tom Petty, Mike Campbell
Year: 1991
A rock and roll parable about "a rebel without a clue," with "a roadie named Bart" in a featured role.

INTO THE GROOVE

Artist: Madonna
Written by: Steve Bray, Madonna Ciccone
From the album: *Desperately Seeking Susan Soundtrack*
Label: Reprise
Produced by: Steve Bray, Madonna
Year: 1986
Like that of Elvis, the Beatles, Jo-Ann Campbell, and Blondie, Madonna's pop success and sex appeal spawned a movie debut, replete with this suggestive dance track, released in England as a single, where it went to #1.

INTO THE HEART

Artist: U2
Written by: Paul Hewson (Bono), Dave Evans (Edge), Adam Clayton, Larry Mullen
From the album: *Boy*
Label: Island
Produced by: Steve Lillywhite
Year: 1980
A new day dawns in Ireland, where, after years of woodshedding, some visionary rockers fashion their reaction to Jimmy Page.

INTO THE MYSTIC

Artist: Van Morrison
Written by: Van Morrison
From the album: *Moondance*
Label: Warner Brothers
Produced by: Van Morrison
Year: 1970
The centerpiece of his classic album and career, Van's ineffable search for the Holy Grail. Covered by Johnny Rivers (Imperial, '70). Featured in the '71 movie *Dusty and Sweets McGee*.

INTO THE NIGHT

Artist: Benny Mardones
Written by: Benny Mardones, Robert Tepper
From the album: *Never Run, Never Hide*
Label: Polydor
Produced by: Barry Mraz
Year: 1980
Dramatic rocker had another chart run in '89.

INTO WHITE

Artist: Cat Stevens
Written by: Cat Stevens
From the album: *Tea for the Tillerman*
Label: A&M
Produced by: Paul Samwell-Smith
Year: 1971
Sensitive singer/songwriter disappears into his teacup.

INTRO

Artist: Bad Brains
Written by: Gary Miller (Dr. Know), Daryl Jenifer
From the album: *I Against I*
Label: SST
Year: 1986
A Van Halenesque speed metal eruption.

INVISIBLE SUN

Artist: The Police
Written by: Gordon Sumner (Sting)
From the album: *Ghost in the Machine*
Label: A&M
Produced by: Hugh Padgham, the Police
Year: 1981
One of the most haunting early-MTV era videos made this song about the troubles in Northern Ireland even more compelling.

INVISIBLE TOUCH

Artist: Genesis
Written by: Phil Collins, Mike Rutherford
From the album: *Invisible Touch*
Label: Atlantic
Produced by: Hugh Padgham, Genesis
Year: 1986
First and only #1 for the former progressive rock icons.

INVITATION TO CRY

Artist: The Magicians
Written by: Alan Gordon, J. Woods
Label: Columbia
Year: 1966
Greenwich Village rock nugget.

IRIS

Artist: Goo Goo Dolls
Written by: John Rzeznik
From the album: *Dizzy up the Girl*
Label: Warner Brothers
Year: 1998
Ballad from the movie *City of Angels*.

IRON MAN

Artist: Black Sabbath
Written by: Tony Iommi, Geezer Butler, Ozzy Osbourne, Bill Ward
From the album: *Paranoid*
Label: Warner Brothers
Produced by: Rodger Bain
Year: 1971
Out of the great primordial sludge of Birmingham, England, a metal monster emerges.

IRONIC

Artist: Alanis Morissette
Written by: Alanis Morissette, Glen Ballard
From the album: *Jagged Little Pill*
Label: Maverick
Produced by: Glen Ballard
Year: 1995
The enormous success of the formerly defunct pop princess from Canada for essentially channeling Tori Amos by way of the overlooked Brenda Khan, was an irony not mentioned in this song.

IS SHE REALLY GOING OUT WITH HIM

Artist: Joe Jackson
Written by: Joe Jackson
From the album: *Look Sharp!*
Label: A&M
Produced by: David Kershenbaum
Year: 1979
Making use of the famous line first uttered by the Shangri-Las in "Leader of the Pack" and then echoed by the Damned in "New Rose," Jackson briefly joins the company of the new English brat pack, along with Graham Parker, Brinsley Schwarz, Nick Lowe, Dave Edmunds, and Elvis Costello.

IS THAT ALL THERE IS

Artist: Peggy Lee
Written by: Jerry Leiber, Mike Stoller
From the album: *Mirrors*
Label: A&M
Produced by: Jerry Leiber, Mike Stoller
Year: 1969
Once she had the fever; now she couldn't care less.

IS THERE SOMETHING I SHOULD KNOW

Artist: Duran Duran
Written by: Duran Duran
From the album: *Arena*
Label: Capitol
Produced by: Duran Duran, Ian Little
Year: 1983
Their first #1 UK.

IS THIS LOVE

Artist: Bob Marley and the Wailers
Written by: Bob Marley
From the album: *Kaya*
Label: Island
Produced by: Bob Marley and the Wailers
Year: 1978
Big UK hit for the reggae pioneer. In the US, he had none.

IS THIS LOVE

Artist: Whitesnake
Written by: David Coverdale, John Sykes
From the album: *Whitesnake*
Label: Geffen

Produced by: Mike Stone, Keith Olsen
Year: 1987
Second of the Coverdale contingent's two Top 10 hits of '87. In every other year combined, they had none.

IS YOU IS OR IS YOU AIN'T MY BABY?

Artist: Louis Jordan and His Tympani Five
Written by: Louis Jordan, Billy Austin
Label: Decca
Produced by: Milt Gabler
Year: 1944
#1 country/#1 R&B/#2 pop crossover from the Marlene Dietrich movie *Follow the Boys*, was the B-side of "G.I. Jive" and launched Jordan as a triple-threat grits-and-boogie man. Covered by Buster Brown (Fire, '60), Joe Jackson (A&M, '81).

ISADORA DUNCAN

Artist: Vic Chesnutt
Written by: Vic Chesnutt
From the album: *Little*
Label: Texas Hotel
Year: 1990
Downcast gem, flavored by a sad harmonica sung by the author of "Lucinda Williams." Suggested segue: "For a Dancer" by Jackson Browne.

ISLAND GIRL

Artist: Elton John
Written by: Elton John, Bernie Taupin
From the album: *Rock of the Westies*
Label: MCA
Produced by: Gus Dudgeon
Year: 1975
His biggest solo hit of the '70s.

ISLANDS IN THE STREAM

Artist: Kenny Rogers and Dolly Parton
Written by: Barry Gibb, Robin Gibb, Maurice Gibb
From the album: *Eyes That See in the Dark*
Label: RCA
Produced by: Barry Gibb, Karl Richardson
Year: 1983
#1 country/#1 crossover. Bee Gees recorded this on a live album (Polydor, '98).

ISN'T IT A PITY

Artist: George Harrison
Written by: George Harrison
From the album: *All Things Must Pass*
Label: Apple
Produced by: Phil Spector
Year: 1970
George in a dour mood, for a change.

ISN'T LIFE STRANGE

Artist: The Moody Blues
Written by: John Lodge
From the album: *Seventh Sojourn*

Label: Threshold
Produced by: Tony Clarke
Year: 1972
From their best-selling album, a summation of their spacey worldview.

ISN'T SHE LOVELY

Artist: Stevie Wonder
Written by: Stevie Wonder
From the album: *Songs in the Key of Life*
Label: Tamla
Produced by: Stevie Wonder
Year: 1976
A birthday song.

ISRAELITES

Artist: Desmond Dekker and the Aces
Written by: Desmond Dekker, Leslie Kong
From the album: *Israelites*
Label: Uni
Produced by: Leslie Kong
Year: 1969
First reggae artist to hit the Top 10 US/#1 UK.

IT AIN'T ME, BABE

Artist: Bob Dylan
Written by: Bob Dylan
From the album: *Another Side of Bob Dylan*
Label: Columbia
Produced by: Tom Wilson
Year: 1964
Unconvinced by girl-group homilies of matrimonial bliss or Smokey Robinson-induced visions of eternal ecstacy, Dylan would lead a new brigade of alienated free thinkers into the depths of the tortured '60s. Covered in a trailblazing surf garage version by the otherwise contented Turtles (White Whale, '65).

IT AIN'T OVER TILL IT'S OVER

Artist: Lennie Kravitz
Written by: Lenny Kravitz
From the album: *Mama Said*
Label: Virgin
Produced by: Lenny Kravitz
Year: 1991
Biggest hit for the Hendrix-influenced rocker.

IT CAME OUT OF THE SKY

Artist: Creedence Clearwater Revival
Written by: John C. Fogerty
From the album: *Willy and the Poor Boys*
Label: Fantasy
Produced by: John C. Fogerty
Year: 1969
A close encounter of the rock and roll kind.

IT DOESN'T MATTER ANY MORE

Artist: Buddy Holly
Written by: Paul Anka

From the album: *The Buddy Holly Story*
Label: Coral
Produced by: Bob Thiele
Year: 1959
Buddy's last hit, released the month he died, went to #1 UK. Covered by Paul Anka (RCA, '63).

IT DON'T COME EASY

Artist: Ringo Starr
Written by: Richard Starkey (Ringo Starr)
From the album: *Blast from Your Past*
Label: Apple
Produced by: George Harrison
Year: 1971
His first hit single as a solo artist.

IT DON'T WORRY ME

Artist: Barbara Harris
Written by: Keith Carradine
From the album: *Nashville Soundtrack*
Label: ABC
Produced by: Richard Baskin
Year: 1975
Ersatz country anthem from the Robert Altman masterwork about the country music mecca.

IT HURT SO BAD

Artist: Susan Tedeschi
Written by: Tom Hambridge
From the album: *Just Won't Burn*
Label: Tone-Cool
Year: 1999
From the Grammy-winning blues debut.

IT HURTS ME TOO

Artist: Junior Wells
Written by: Elmore James
From the album: *Chicago/The Blues Today*
Label: Vanguard
Year: 1966
A Chicago blues guitar/harp standard, with Buddy Guy supplying the fierce guitar to Junior's bittersweet harp. Briefly, a college generation picked up on this sort of Southside blues, among them Mike Bloomfield, Paul Butterfield, Tracy Nelson, and Steve Miller, before Eric Clapton and Cream, Jimi Hendrix and the Experience, and Led Zeppelin arrived from England to bury them under ten thousand amplifiers.

IT HURTS TO BE IN LOVE

Artist: Gene Pitney
Written by: Howard Greenfield, Helen Miller
From the album: *It Hurts to Be in Love*
Label: Musicor
Year: 1964
The East-coast Orbison gets his third-biggest hit.

IT KEEPS RIGHT ON A-HURTIN'

Artist: Johnny Tillotson
Written by: Johnny Tillotsen, Lorene Mann

From the album: *It Keeps Right on a-Hurtin'*
Label: Cadence
Year: 1962
Top 5 country/Top 5 crossover.

IT MIGHT AS WELL RAIN UNTIL SEPTEMBER

Artist: Carole King
Written by: Gerry Goffin, Carole King
Label: Dimension
Produced by: Carole King
Year: 1962
Parlaying a hot '61 and '62, publisher Don Kirshner's prize writer achieves her first chart record (rejected by Bobby Vee), after years of singing demos. That nasal tone would return several years later as the voice of another decade.

IT MIGHT BE YOU

Artist: Stephen Bishop
Written by: Alan Bergman, Marilyn Bergman, Dave Grusin
From the album: *Tootsie Soundtrack*
Label: Warner Brothers
Produced by: Dave Grusin
Year: 1982
Haunting big movie ballad over the final credits of *Tootsie.*

IT MUST HAVE BEEN LOVE

Artist: Roxette
Written by: Per Gessle
From the album: *Pretty Woman Soundtrack*
Label: EMI
Produced by: Clarence Ofwerman
Year: 1990
As perky and inescapable as Julia Roberts in the movie.

IT NEVER RAINS IN SOUTHERN CALIFORNIA

Artist: Albert Hammond
Written by: Albert Hammond, Mike Hazelwood
From the album: *It Never Rains in Southern California*
Label: Mums
Produced by: Don Altfeld, Albert Hammond.
Written in London, where it always rains.

IT ONLY TAKES A MINUTE

Artist: Tavares
Written by: Dennis Lambert, Brian Potter
From the album: *In the City*
Label: Capitol
Produced by: Dennis Lambert, Brian Potter
Year: 1975
Latin-flavored #1 R&B/Top 10 crossover.

IT SHOULD'VE BEEN ME

Artist: Ray Charles

Written by: Memphis Curtis
Label: Atlantic
Produced by: Ahmet Ertegun
Year: 1954
The former Lowell Fulson sideman steps out with his first hit on Atlantic.

IT TAKES A LOT TO LAUGH, IT TAKES A TRAIN TO CRY

Artist: Bob Dylan
Written by: Bob Dylan
From the album: *Highway 61 Revisited*
Label: Columbia
Produced by: Tom Wilson
Year: 1965
A thrilling country blues rock orgasm. When Dylan was booed off the stage at Newport that year, either for the sin of becoming a rock and roller, or for the equal sin of offering only a three-song set, this was one of the three seminal tunes he played, before returning for an acoustic encore. Covered by his guitarist for the night, Mike Bloomfield, in his supersession set with Al Kooper and Steve Stills (Columbia, '68) and the magical Tracy Nelson (Atlantic, '74).

IT TAKES TWO

Artist: Rob Base and DJ E-Z Rock
Written by: Rob Base
From the album: *It Takes Two*
Label: Profile
Produced by: Rob Base, William Hamilton
Year: 1988
Moving hip hop several hops toward its eventual mainstream takeover, this track was named as the #1 single of all time by *Spin* magazine.

IT TAKES TWO

Artist: Marvin Gaye and Kim Weston
Written by: Sylvia Moy, William Stevenson
From the album: *Marvin Gaye and His Girls*
Label: Tamla
Produced by: William Stevenson
Year: 1969
Another promising pair, but she was no Tammi Terrell.

IT TEARS ME UP

Artist: Percy Sledge
Written by: Dan Penn, Spooner Oldham
From the album: *Warm and Tender Soul*
Label: Atlantic
Produced by: Quin Ivy, Marlin Greene
Year: 1966
Top 10 R&B/Top 20 crossover.

IT WAS A GOOD DAY

Artist: Ice Cube
Written by: O'Shea Jackson (Ice Cube)
From the album: *The Predator*
Label: Priority

Produced by: DJ Pooh
Year: 1993

IT WAS I

Artist: Skip and Flip
Written by: Gary Paxton
Label: Brent
Year: 1959
Everlyesque duo also covered Don and Dewey's "Cherry Pie."

IT WASN'T GOD WHO MADE HONKY TONK ANGELS

Artist: Kitty Wells
Written by: J. D. Miller
Label: Decca
Produced by: Owen Bradley
Year: 1952
#1 country hit for the Queen of Country Music; the answer to Hank Thompson's "Wild Side of Life" and Marie Adams' "I'm Gonna Play the Honky Tonks."

IT WILL STAND

Artist: The Showmen
Written by: General Johnson
Label: Minit
Produced by: Allen Toussaint
Year: 1961
One of rock and roll's first anthems.

IT WON'T BE LONG

Artist: The Beatles
Written by: John Lennon, Paul McCartney
From the album: *Meet the Beatles*
Label: Capitol
Produced by: George Martin
Year: 1964

IT WON'T BE WRONG

Artist: The Byrds
Written by: Jim McGuinn (Roger McGuinn), Harvey Gerst
From the album: *Turn! Turn! Turn!*
Label: Columbia
Produced by: Terry Melcher
Year: 1965
Why they were known as "the American Beatles."

IT'S A HEARTACHE

Artist: Bonnie Tyler
Written by: Ronnie Scott, Steve Wolfe
From the album: *It's a Heartache*
Label: RCA
Produced by: David Mackay, Ronnie Scott, Steve Wolfe
Year: 1977
Kim Carnes soundalike with a Top 10 country/Top 10 crossover.

IT'S A LONG WAY TO THE TOP (IF YOU WANT TO ROCK AND ROLL)

Artist: AC/DC
Written by: Bon Scott, Angus Young, Malcom Young
From the album: *High Voltage*
Produced by: Harry Vanda, Malcolm Young
Label: Atlantic
Year: 1976
Early arena anthem was revived at the end of the movie *School of Rock* (2003).

IT'S A MAN'S, MAN'S, MAN'S WORLD (BUT IT WOULDN'T BE NOTHING WITHOUT A WOMAN OR GIRL)

Artist: James Brown and the Famous Flames
Written by: James Brown, Betty Jean Newsome
From the album: *It's a Man's, Man's, Man's World*
Label: King
Produced by: James Brown
Year: 1966
#1 R&B/Top 10 crossover.

IT'S A SHAME

Artist: Spinners
Written by: Stevie Wonder, Lee Garrett, Syreeta Wright
From the album: *2nd Time Around*
Label: V.I.P.
Produced by: Stevie Wonder
Year: 1970
Breakthrough single for the Philly soul combo from Detroit after a decade off the charts.

IT'S A SHAME ABOUT RAY

Artist: The Lemonheads
Written by: Evan Dando, Tom Morgan
From the album: *It's a Shame About Ray*
Label: Atlantic
Produced by: The Robb Brothers, Evan Dando
Year: 1992
College track of the year, from America's greatest college town, Boston.

IT'S A SIN

Artist: Pet Shop Boys
Written by: Neil Tennant, Chris Lowe
From the album: *Actually*
Label: EMI-America
Produced by: J. Mendelsohn
Year: 1987
Second of four #1 hits in England for the alternative dance mavens.

IT'S ALL ABOUT THE BENJAMINS

Artist: Puff Daddy
Written by: Derek Angelettie, Sean Puffy Combs, Stephen Jacobs, Kim Jones, Jason Phillips, David Styles, Christopher Wallace
From the album: *No Way Out*
Label: Bad Boy
Produced by: Sean Combs
Year: 1998
Complaining all the way to the bank.

IT'S ALL DOWN TO GOODNIGHT VIENNA

Artist: Ringo Starr
Written by: John Lennon
From the album: *Goodnight Vienna*
Label: Apple
Produced by: Richard Perry
Year: 1974
Phoning an old friend for a song.

IT'S ALL IN THE GAME

Artist: Tommy Edwards
Written by: Carl Sigman, General Charles Gates Dawes
From the album: *It's All in the Game*
Label: MGM
Produced by: Harry Myerson
Year: 1951
Top 10 R&B/Top 20 crossover. Originally written in 1912. Sigman wrote "Ebb Tide" as well as the Louis Jordan hit, "That Chick's Too Young to Fry." Melody was by former Calvin Coolidge Vice President Dawes. Covered by Nat King Cole (Capitol, '57). Song became a #1 R&B/#1 crossover when Edwards re-recorded it in '58.

IT'S ALL OVER NOW

Artist: The Valentinos
Written by: Bobby Womack, Cecil Womack
Label: Sar
Year: 1964
Essential R&B track spent two weeks in the Bottom 10. Cover by the Rolling Stones (London, '64) went to #1 UK. Also covered by Rod Stewart (Mercury, '70), Bobby Womack (United Artists, '75), Johnny Winter (Blue Sky, '76).

IT'S ALL OVER NOW, BABY BLUE

Artist: Bob Dylan
Written by: Bob Dylan
From the album: *Bringing It All Back Home*
Label: Columbia
Produced by: Tom Wilson
Year: 1965
If love was a four-letter word to Dylan, bad relationships were worth at least four minutes. Covered in a bravura performance by Van Morrison with Them (Parrot, '66).

IT'S ALL RIGHT!

Artist: The Impressions
Written by: Curtis Mayfield
From the album: *The Impressions*
Label: ABC Paramount
Produced by: Curtis Mayfield
Year: 1963
Their first and best-selling single; a #1 R&B/Top 10 crossover.

IT'S ALL TOO MUCH

Artist: The Beatles
Written by: George Harrison
From the album: *Yellow Submarine*
Label: Apple
Produced by: George Martin
Year: 1969
A familiar Harrison theme.

IT'S ALRIGHT, MA (I'M ONLY BLEEDING)

Artist: Bob Dylan
Written by: Bob Dylan
From the album: *Bringing It All Back Home*
Label: Columbia
Produced by: Tom Wilson
Year: 1965
Nothing to live up to, in approximately eight minutes of righteous wrath.

IT'S BEEN A LONG TIME

Artist: Southside Johnny and the Asbury Jukes
Written by: Steve Van Zandt
From the album: *Better Days*
Label: Impact
Produced by: Little Steven
Year: 1991
A sentimental reunion. Suggested segues: "No One to Run With" by the Allman Brothers, "Hanging on to the Good Times" by Little Feat.

IT'S ECSTASY WHEN YOU LAY DOWN NEXT TO ME

Artist: Barry White
Written by: Nelson Pigford, Ekundayo Paris
From the album: *Barry White Sings for Someone You Love*
Label: 20TH Century
Produced by: Barry White
Year: 1977
Triumphal comeback for Ekundayo Paris, with his first hit since "Sooner or Later" by the Grass Roots (Dunhill, '71).

IT'S FOR YOU

Artist: Cilla Black
Written by: John Lennon, Paul McCartney
From the album: *Is It Love*
Label: Capitol
Year: 1964
Big hit in England for the Cavern Club's former hat-check girl, who was discovered by Lennon and McCartney.

IT'S GONNA BE ME

Artist: *NSYNC
Written by: Andreas Carlsson, Max Martin, Rami
From the album: *No Strings Attached*
Label: Jive
Year: 2000
In the waning days of boy band harmony.

IT'S GONNA TAKE A MIRACLE

Artist: The Royalettes
Written by: Teddy Randazzo, Bobby Weinstein, Lou Stallman
From the album: *It's Gonna Take a Miracle*
Label: MGM
Produced by: Teddy Randazzo
Year: 1965
Covered with breathless perfection by Laura Nyro (Columbia, '71).

IT'S GONNA WORK OUT FINE

Artist: Ike and Tina Turner
Written by: Rose Marie McCoy, Sylvia McKinney
Label: Sue
Produced by: Juggy Murray
Year: 1961
Their only Top 20 song aside from "Proud Mary." Rerecorded in '66 under the thumb of Phil Spector, and released on the *River Deep, Mountain High* album (A&M, '69).

IT'S IN THE WAY YOU USE IT

Artist: Eric Clapton
Written by: Eric Clapton, Robbie Robertson
From the album: *August*
Label: Duck
Produced by: Tom Dowd, Phil Collins
Year: 1986
Featured in the '86 film *The Color of Money*.

IT'S JUST A MATTER OF TIME

Artist: Brook Benton
Written by: Clyde Otis, Brook Benton, Belford Hendricks
From the album: *Golden Hits*
Label: Mercury
Produced by: Clyde Otis
Year: 1959
The first hit for cool soul crooner, a #1 R&B/Top 5 crossover.

(IT'S JUST) THE WAY THAT YOU LOVE ME

Artist: Paula Abdul
Written by: Oliver Leiber
From the album: *Forever Your Girl*
Label: Virgin

Produced by: Oliver Leiber
Year: 1988
First dance-hall hit for Janet Jackson's award-winning choreographer. Written and produced by the son of Hall of Fame songwriter Jerry Leiber.

IT'S LATE

Artist: Ricky Nelson
Written by: Dorsey Burnette
From the album: *Ricky Sings Again*
Label: Imperial
Produced by: Ricky Nelson, Jimmy Haskell, Ozzie Nelson
Year: 1959
B-side of "Never Be Anyone Else but You." Ricky's response to "Wake up Little Susie."

IT'S LIKE THAT

Artist: Run-D.M.C.
Written by: Larry Smith, Joseph Simmons, Darryl McDaniels
From the album: *Run-D.M.C.*
Label: Profile
Produced by: Russell Simmons, Larry Smith
Year: 1984
From Hollis, Queens, an ingratiatingly amateurish rap persona immodestly emerges.

IT'S LONELY AT THE TOP

Artist: Randy Newman
Written by: Randy Newman
From the album: *Randy Newman Live*
Label: Reprise
Produced by: Russ Titelman, Lenny Waronker
Year: 1971
Written for Frank Sinatra. Or was it Tom Jones?

IT'S MONEY THAT MATTERS

Artist: Randy Newman
Written by: Randy Newman
From the album: *Land of Dreams*
Label: Reprise
Produced by: Randy Newman
Year: 1988
Like bluesman Robert Johnson, Randy made a deal with the Devil in *Randy Newman's Faust* (Reprise, '95).

IT'S MY LIFE

Artist: The Animals
Written by: Roger Atkins, Carl D'Errico
From the album: Best of the Animals, MGM
Produced by: Mickie Most
Year: 1965
The existential howl of the garage band era. In the '70s, it was a Bruce-Springsteen-in-concert peak, accompanied by an incredible spoken introduction. In the '80s, David Johansen did even more amazing things with it (Blue Sky, '82).

IT'S MY PARTY

Artist: Lesley Gore
Written by: Herb Wiener, John Gluck Jr., Wally Gold
From the album: *I'll Cry If I Want To*
Label: Mercury
Produced by: Quincy Jones
Year: 1963
While all the girls of the era were catering to their guys, they were not necessarily as kind to other girls, a fact Lesley Gore was daring enough to admit, if not wallow in. Turned down by the Shirelles and the Crystals.

IT'S MY TURN

Artist: Diana Ross
Written by: Carole Bayer Sager, Michael Masser
From the album: *To Love Again*
Label: Motown
Year: 1981
Diana's last hit on Motown is a big movie ballad.

IT'S NO CRIME

Artist: Babyface
Written by: Kenny Edmunds (Babyface), Antonio Reid (L. A. Reid), Daryl Simmons
From the album: *Tender Lover*
Label: Solar
Produced by: Babyface, L. A. Reid
Year: 1989
This '80s songwriting and producing giant (with co-partners and fellow members of Deele, Reid, and Simmons) achieved his first Top 10 hit with this ballad.

IT'S NO SECRET

Artist: Jefferson Airplane
Written by: Marty Balin
From the album: *Takes Off*
Label: RCA
Produced by: Matthew Katz, Tony Oliver
Year: 1966
Pre-flyte folk/rock from San Francisco's nascent psychedelic scenemakers.

IT'S NOT OVER ('TIL IT'S OVER)

Artist: Starship
Written by: Robbie Nevil, John Van Torgeron, Phil Galdston
From the album: *No Protection*
Label: Grunt
Produced by: Narada Michael Walden
Year: 1987
Epitomizing the arena-oriented Mickey Thomas era.

IT'S NOT THE SPOTLIGHT

Artist: Gerry Goffin
Written by: Gerry Goffin, Barry Goldberg
From the album: *It Ain't Exactly Entertainment*
Label: Warner Brothers

Produced by: Tom Dowd
Year: 1973
The famed Brill Building lyricist's solo excursion featured material that was not as good as ex-spouse Carole King's, but not that much worse than the stuff by contemporaries like Barry Mann ("The Princess and the Punk") and Jimmy Webb ("P. F. Sloan"). Covered by Rod Stewart (Warner Brothers, '75).

IT'S NOT UNUSUAL

Artist: Tom Jones
Written by: Les Reed, Gordon Mills
From the album: *It's Not Unusual*
Label: Parrot
Year: 1965
Welsh balladeer notches his first #1 in England. From the movie *What's New Pussycat*. Jimmy Page on guitar.

IT'S NOW OR NEVER

Artist: Elvis Presley
Written by: Aaron Schroeder, Wally Gold
From the album: *Elvis' Golden Records (Vol. III)*
Label: RCA
Produced by: Steve Sholes
Year: 1960
Out of the army, Elvis crosses over to the middle-of-the-road for his biggest all-time seller and personal favorite aria. Based on "O Sole Mio."

IT'S ONLY LOVE

Artist: The Beatles
Written by: John Lennon, Paul McCartney
From the album: *Rubber Soul*
Label: Capitol
Produced by: George Martin
Year: 1965
Looking at their favorite subject from a 90-degree angle.

IT'S ONLY MAKE BELIEVE

Artist: Conway Twitty
Written by: Conway Twitty, Jack Nance
From the album: *Conway Twitty Sings*
Label: M-G-M
Produced by: Jim Vinneau
Year: 1958
Future country stalwart Twitty wouldn't have a hit on that chart until he formally renounced rock and roll in the mid-'60s. But the R&B chart welcomed "It's Only Make Believe," when this dramatic, Elvis-inspired #1 crossed over to the Top 20. And Broadway gave Twitty even greater credence (while showing its own ignorance) by naming their prototypical rock and roller Conrad Birdie in the anti-rock musical *Bye Bye Birdie*.

IT'S ONLY ROCK 'N' ROLL (BUT I LIKE IT)

Artist: The Rolling Stones
Written by: Mick Jagger, Keith Richards
From the album: *It's Only Rock 'n' Roll (But I Like It)*
Label: Rolling Stones
Produced by: Glimmer Twins
Year: 1974
Approaching the philosophical maturity of "You Can't Always Get What You Want."

IT'S OVER

Artist: Roy Orbison
Written by: Roy Orbison, Bill Dees
From the album: *More of Roy Orbison's Greatest Hits*
Label: Monument
Produced by: Fred Foster
Year: 1964
Roy in his pained prime.

IT'S PROBABLY ME

Artist: Eric Clapton
Written by: Eric Clapton, Michael Kamen, Sting
From the album: *Demolition Man Soundtrack*
Label: A&M
Produced by: Hugh Padgham
Year: 1992

IT'S RAINING

Artist: Irma Thomas
Written by: Allen Toussaint (Naomi Neville)
Label: Minit
Produced by: Allen Toussaint
Year: 1962
A definitive New Orleans gem.

IT'S RAINING MEN

Artist: The Weather Girls
Written by: Paul Jabara, Paul Shaffer
From the album: *Success*
Label: Columbia
Produced by: Paul Jabara
Year: 1983
Hot dance track on the club circuit introduces the world to the uncredited studio belter Martha Wash.

IT'S REALLY LOVE

Artist: Annette
Written by: Paul Anka
From the album: *Annette Sings Anka*
Label: Buena Vista
Year: 1960
As Judy Collins was to Leonard Cohen, as the Byrds were to Bob Dylan, as Nilsson was to Randy Newman, Annette was to her favorite poet, Paul Anka. This tune would later earn Anka a whole lot more money as the theme to *The Tonight Show with Johnny Carson*.

IT'S SO EASY

Artist: The Crickets
Written by: Buddy Holly, Norman Petty
From the album: *In Style with the Crickets*
Label: Brunswick
Produced by: Norman Petty

Year: 1958
Covered by Linda Ronstadt (Asylum, '77).

IT'S SO HARD TO SAY GOODBYE TO YESTERDAY

Artist: Boyz II Men
Written by: Freddie Perren, Christine Yarian
From the album: *Cooleyhighharmony*
Label: Motown
Produced by: Dallas Austin
Year: 1991
Exemplary vocal harmony, featured in the movie *Lethal Weapon III*.

IT'S STILL ROCK AND ROLL TO ME

Artist: Billy Joel
Written by: Billy Joel
From the album: *Glass Houses*
Label: Columbia
Produced by: Phil Ramone
Year: 1980
The still-angry-but-not-so-young man answers his critics with his first #1.

IT'S THE END OF THE WORLD AS WE KNOW IT (AND I FEEL FINE)

Artist: R.E.M.
Written by: Michael Stipe, Peter Buck, Bill Berry, Mike Mills
From the album: *Document*
Label: IRS
Produced by: Scott Litt, R.E.M.
Year: 1986
Apocalyptic predictions on the order of Bob's "Subterranean Homesick Blues," Chuck's "Too Much Monkey Business," and Billy's "We Didn't Start the Fire." Suggested segue: "Cuyahoga."

IT'S THE SAME OLD SONG

Artist: The Four Tops
Written by: Eddie Holland, Lamont Dozier, Brian Holland
From the album: *Four Tops Second Album*
Label: Motown
Produced by: Brian Holland, Lamont Dozier
Year: 1965
Follow-up to their first hit, "I Can't Help Myself."

IT'S TIME TO CRY

Artist: Paul Anka
Written by: Paul Anka
From the album: *Paul Anka Sings His Big 15 (Vol. II)*.
ABC Paramount
Produced by: Don Costa
Year: 1959
Closing out the decade with his fourth Top 10 hit. After that, he'd start thinking about Vegas.

IT'S TOO LATE

Artist: Carole King
Written by: Toni Stern, Carole King
From the album: *Tapestry*
Label: Ode
Produced by: Lou Adler
Year: 1971
Making it on her own with a new collaborator; her only solo #1.

IT'S TOO LATE

Artist: Chuck Willis
Written by: Chuck Willis
Label: Atlantic
Produced by: Zenas "Big Daddy" Sears
Year: 1956
Country flavored R&B classic. Covered by The Crickets (Coral, '58), Derek & the Dominoes (Atlantic, '70).

IT'S TOO SOON TO KNOW

Artist: The Orioles
Written by: Deborah Chessler
Label: It's a Natural/Jubilee
Year: 1948
Breaking the chains of black music typecasting, Baltimore's Sonny Til & the Orioles create the emotionally charged teen dream of group harmony, otherwise known as doo-wop, with this #1 R&B/Top 20 crossover, the first "race" record to peak that high on the pop charts. Pat Boone didn't get around to covering it for a decade (Dot, '58).

IT'S TRICKY

Artist: Run-D.M.C.
Written by: Darryl McDaniels, Jason Mizell, Rick Rubin, Joe Simmons
From the album: *Raising Hell*
Label: Priority
Produced by: Rick Rubin
Year: 1986

IT'S YOUR THING

Artist: The Isley Brothers
Written by: Ronald Isley, Rudolph Isley, O'Kelly Isley
From the album: *It's Our Thing*
Label: T-Neck
Produced by: Isley Brothers
Year: 1969
Their biggest hit; #1 R&B/#2 crossover.

ITCHIN' FOR A SCRATCH

Artist: The Force M.D.'s
Written by: Robin Halpin, Steve Stein, Doug Wimbish, Keith LeBlanc, the Force M.D.'s
From the album: *Love Letters*
Label: T-Boy
Produced by: Jimmy Jam, Terry Lewis
Year: 1985
Featured in the movie *Rappin'*.

ITCHYCOO PARK

Artist: The Small Faces
Written by: Steve Marriott, Ronnie Lane
From the album: *There Are but Four Small Faces*
Label: Immediate
Produced by: Steve Marriott, Ronnie Lane
Year: 1967
Rod's mod pals answer "Strawberry Fields."

ITSY BITSY TEENIE WEENIE YELLOW POLKADOT BIKINI

Artist: Brian Hyland
Written by: Paul Vance, Lee Pockriss
From the album: *The Bashful Blonde*
Label: Leader
Produced by: Richard Wolfe
Year: 1960
Summertime teen fashion statement. Led to "One Piece Topless Bathing Suit" by the Ripchords and "The Thong Song" by Sisquo.

IVORY TOWER

Artist: Otis Williams and the Charms
Written by: Jack Fulton, Lois Steele
Label: Deluxe
Year: 1956
Top 10 R&B/Top 20 crossover. Covered by Gale Storm (Dot, '56), Cathy Carr (Fraternity, '56).

J

J.A.R. (JASON ANDREW RELVA)

Artist: Green Day
Written by: Mike Dirnt, Green Day
From the album: *Angus Soundtrack*
Label: Reprise
Produced by: Rob Cavallo
Year: 1995

JACK AND DIANE

Artist: John (Cougar) Mellencamp
Written by: John Cougar Mellencamp
From the album: *American Fool*
Label: Riva
Produced by: Don Gehman, John Mellencamp
Year: 1982
His biggest hit; two American kids at #1. Springsteen would follow Mellencamp into this heartland niche in '84, a niche that he himself created in '76 with "Born to Run."

JACK AND JILL

Artist: Raydio
Written by: Ray Parker Jr.
From the album: *Raydio*
Label: Arista
Produced by: Ray Parker Jr.
Year: 1977
First hit for the Ray Parker-led R&B group, a Top 10 R&B/Top 10 crossover.

JACK GETS UP

Artist: Leo Kottke
Written by: Leo Kottke
From the album: *My Father's Face*
Label: Private Music
Produced by: T-Bone Burnette
Year: 1989
A woebegone verbal gem.

JACK YOU'RE DEAD

Artist: Louis Jordan and His Tympani Five
Written by: Richard Miles, Walter Bishop
Label: Decca
Produced by: Milt Gabler
Year: 1947
Hipster treatise on the art of jive. Covered by Joe Jackson (A&M, '81).

JACKIE

Artist: Blue Zone UK
Written by: Billy Steinberg, Tom Kelly
From the album: *Big Thing*
Label: Arista
Year: 1988
Introducing future English R&B chart topper Lisa Stansfield.

JACKIE BLUE

Artist: The Ozark Mountain Daredevils
Written by: Larry Lee, Steve Cash
From the album: *It'll Shine When It Shines*
Label: A&M
Produced by: Glyn Johns, David Anderie
Year: 1975

JACKIE WILSON SAID (I'M IN HEAVEN WHEN YOU SMILE)

Artist: Van Morrison
Written by: Van Morrison
From the album: *St. Dominic's Preview*
Label: Warner Brothers
Produced by: Van Morrison
Year: 1972
Suggested Segue: "When Smokey Sings" by ABC.

JACKSON CANNERY

Artist: Ben Folds Five
Written by: Ben Folds
From the album: *The Ben Folds Five*
Label: Passenger
Produced by: Caleb Southern
Year: 1995
Legendary first single, wherein he inherits his keyboard bashing legacy.

JACOB'S LADDER

Artist: Huey Lewis and the News
Written by: Bruce Hornsby, John Hornsby
From the album: *Fore!*
Label: Chrysalis

Produced by: Huey Lewis and the News
Year: 1986
Benefiting from the burgeoning career of the Southern rock jazzbo, Hornsby, whose "The Way It Is" hit the Top 10 a few months before, this tune became Huey's third #1.

JAILBREAK

Artist: Thin Lizzy
Written by: Phil Lynott
From the album: *Jailbreak*
Label: Mercury
Produced by: John Alcock
Year: 1976
Best guitar moments for Phil Lynott's rebel Irish crew.

JAILHOUSE RAP

Artist: The Fat Boys
Written by: Kurtis Blow, Larry Smith, Mark Morales, Darren Robinson, Damon Wimbley, David Reeve, Sal Abbatiello
From the album: *Fat Boys*
Label: Sutra
Produced by: Kurtis Blow
Year: 1985
Rap answer to Elvis Presley's "Jailhouse Rock" introduces a new force in urban mythology. The Boys would go on to cover "The Twist" and "Wipeout."

JAILHOUSE ROCK

Artist: Elvis Presley
Written by: Jerry Leiber, Mike Stoller
From the album: *Jailhouse Rock*
Label: RCA
Produced by: Steve Sholes, Jerry Leiber, Mike Stoller
Year: 1957
Two years after *Blackboard Jungle*, the image of threatening teens was already fodder for a musical (and not exactly *West Side Story*). Elvis's last #1 R&B/#1 country/#1 crossover. In the film, Mike Stoller is the a piano player in Elvis's band.

JAM ON IT

Artist: Newcleus
Written by: Maurice Cenac
From the album: *Jam on Revenge*
Label: Sunnyview
Produced by: Joe Webb, Frank Fair
Year: 1984
Rap novelty: if the Chipmunks had rhythm.

JAMBALAYA (ON THE BAYOU)

Artist: Hank Williams
Written by: Hank Williams
Label: MGM
Produced by: Fred Rose
Year: 1952
New Orleans tribute, #1 country/Top-30 crossover; covered by Brenda Lee (Decca, '57), Fats Domino (Imperial, '61).

JAMES

Artist: Bangles
Written by: Vicki Peterson
From the album: *All over the Place*
Label: Columbia
Produced by: David Kahne
Year: 1984
Beatlesque harmonies, girl-group attitude, contemporary bite.

JAMES DEAN

Artist: Eagles
Written by: Don Henley, Glenn Frey, Jackson Browne, John David Souther
From the album: *On the Border*
Label: Asylum
Produced by: Bill Szymczyk
Year: 1974
Identifying with the Hollywood antihero. Suggested segue: "James Dean of Indiana" by Phil Ochs, "A Young Man Is Gone" by the Beach Boys.

JAMIE

Artist: Eddie Holland
Written by: William Stevenson, Barrett Strong
From the album: *Eddie Holland*
Label: Motown
Produced by: William Stevenson
Year: 1961
Introducing one-third of Motown's legendary Holland-Dozier-Holland songwriting combine, who first came to Motown's attention as a singer.

JAMIE'S CRYIN'

Artist: Van Halen
Written by: Eddie Van Halen, Alex Van Halen, Michael Anthony, David Lee Roth
From the album: *Van Halen*
Label: Warner Brothers
Produced by: Ted Templeman
Year: 1978
Putting their guitar stamp on a generation.

JAMMIN' ME

Artist: Tom Petty and the Heartbreakers
Written by: Tom Petty, Mike Campbell, Bob Dylan
From the album: *Let Me Up (I've Had Enough)*
Label: MCA
Produced by: Jeff Lynne
Year: 1987
Litany of contemporary woes.

JAMMING

Artist: Bob Marley and the Wailers
Written by: Bob Marley
From the album: *Exodus*
Label: Island
Produced by: Bob Marley and the Wailers
Year: 1977
First UK hit single. Suggested segue: "Master Blaster (Jammin')" by Stevie Wonder.

JANE

Artist: Jefferson Starship
Written by: David Friedberg, Paul Kantner, Jim McPherson, Craig Chaquico
From the album: *Freedom at Point Zero*
Label: Grunt
Produced by: Ron Nevison
Year: 1980
Jefferson now in name only. The rest was Starship.

JANIE'S GOT A GUN

Artist: Aerosmith
Written by: Steven Tyler, Tom Hamilton
From the album: *Pump*
Label: Geffen
Produced by: Bruce Fairbairn
Year: 1989
A tale of revenge, sinuous and sinister, with a 90's twist.

JANIS

Artist: Country Joe and the Fish
Written by: Joe McDonald
From the album: *I-Feel-Like-I'm-Fixin'-to-Die*
Label: Vanguard
Produced by: Sam Charters
Year: 1967
About Joe's San Francisco sweetheart, Janis Joplin, about to go national with Big Brother and the Holding Company.

JAZZ THING, A

Artist: Gang Starr
Written by: Branford Marsalis, Chris Martin, Keith Elam, L.E. Elie
From the album: *Mo' Better Blues Soundtrack*
Label: Columbia
Produced by: Branford Marsalis, DJ Premier
Year: 1990
From the Spike Lee film. Using the form and function of rap to illustrate the history of jazz.

JAZZMAN

Artist: Carole King
Written by: Carole King, Donald Palmer
From the album: *Wrap around Joy*
Label: Ode
Produced by: Lou Adler
Year: 1974
Her second biggest solo hit.

JAZZY BELLE

Artist: OutKast
Written by: Andre Benjamin, Antwan Andre Patton, Organized Noize
From the album: *ATLiens*
Label: LaFace
Produced by: Babyface, L. A. Reid
Year: 1997
Coming up from the Dirty South, a new style of hip hop emerges.

JE T'AIME ... MOI NON PLUS

Artist: Jane Birkin and Serge Gainsbourg
Written by: Serge Gainsbourg
Label: Fontana
Produced by: Jack Beverstock
Year: 1970
Heavy-breathing pre-disco hit that influenced Donna Summer. Introduced by no less an authority than sex icon Brigitte Bardot.

JEALOUS GUY

Artist: John Lennon
Written by: John Lennon
From the album: *Imagine*
Label: Apple
Produced by: John Lennon
Year: 1971
An emotional breakthrough. Covered by Bryan Ferry (Reprise, '89).

JEALOUS KIND

Artist: Joe Cocker
Written by: Robert Guidry (Bobby Charles)
From the album: *Stingray*
Label: A&M
Year: 1976
Covered by Ray Charles (ABC, '76).

JEAN

Artist: Oliver
Written by: Rod McKuen
From the album: *Good Morning Starshine*
Label: Crewe
Produced by: Bob Crewe
Year: 1967
Hummable ballad by the prolific pop poet, from the movie *The Prime of Miss Jean Brodie*.

JEAN GENIE

Artist: David Bowie
Written by: David Bowie
From the album: *Aladdin Sane*
Label: RCA
Produced by: David Bowie
Year: 1972
Title derived from the name of French poet, Jean Genet, and inspired by the American role model for self-destruction, Iggy Pop.

JEAN'S TV

Artist: Commander Venus
Written by: Conor Oberst
From the album: *Uneventful Vacation*
Label: Thick
Year: 1997
Early incarnation of the future wi-fi legend from Nebraska Oberst.

JEFF'S BOOGIE

Artist: The Yardbirds
Written by: Jeff Beck
From the album: *Over Under Sideways Down*
Label: Columbia
Produced by: Paul Samwell-Smith, Simon Napier-Bell
Year: 1966
Beck would mine this vein further in the Jeff Beck Group, with Rod Stewart as his vocalist.

JEMIMA SURRENDER

Artist: The Band
Written by: Levon Helm, Robbie Robertson
From the album: *The Band*
Produced by: John Simon, the Band
Label: Capitol
Year: 1969

JENNY JENNY

Artist: Little Richard
Written by: Richard Penniman (Little Richard), Enotris Johnson
From the album: *Here's Little Richard*
Label: Specialty
Produced by: Art Rupe
Year: 1956

JENNY-LEE

Artist: Jan and Arnie
Written by: Jan Berry, Arnie Ginsburg
From the album: *Jan and Dean's Golden Hits*
Label: Arwin
Produced by: Lou Adler
Year: 1958
California blue-eyed soul, pre-Spector, pre-surf, pre-Arnie's induction into the army, recorded in Jan's garage with Dean sitting in.

JEOPARDY

Artist: The Greg Kihn Band
Written by: Greg Kihn, Steven Wright
From the album: *With the Naked Eye*
Label: Beserkley
Produced by: Matthew King Kaufman
Year: 1983
The answer is: "What is this loopy West coast rocker's biggest hit?"

JEREMY

Artist: Pearl Jam
Written by: Eddie Vedder, Jeff Ament
From the album: *Ten*
Label: Epic
Produced by: Rick Parashar, Pearl Jam
Year: 1991
Prescient portrait of modern-day anomie announces the arrival of the serious grunge alternative (to Nirvana).

JERK OUT

Artist: The Time
Written by: Prince Rogers Nelson, Terry Lewis, James Harris III, Morris Day
From the album: *Pandemonium*
Label: Paisley Park
Year: 1990
The original lineup of Prince's original backing band returns to capture their first #1 R&B/Top 10 crossover.

JERK, THE

Artist: The Larks
Written by: Don Julian
From the album: *The Jerk*
Label: Money
Produced by: A. C. Scott
Year: 1964
New dance gyration written by the former Meadowlark.

JERRY WAS A RACE CAR DRIVER

Artist: Primus
Written by: Les Claypool, Larry LaLonde, Tim Alexander
From the album: *Sailing the Seas of Cheese*
Label: Interscope
Produced by: Primus
Year: 1991
Funked-up fun from San Francisco.

JERRY'S PIGEONS

Artist: Genya Ravan
Written by: Charles Giordano, Joe Rebaudo, Genya Ravan
From the album: *Urban Desire*
Label: 20TH Century
Year: 1978
Out of Goldie & the Gingerbreads and Ten Wheel Drive, and fresh from producing the Dead Boys, a rock and roll survivor named Goldie Yelkowitz continues, a grown-up Shangri-la, if the Shangri-las had lived to grow up.

JERSEY GIRL

Artist: Tom Waits
Written by: Tom Waits
From the album: *Heartattack and Vine*
Label: Asylum
Produced by: Bones Howe
Year: 1980
Tom goes to the carnival and meets Springsteen's Sandy. Covered by Bruce Springsteen (Columbia, '84).

JESSICA

Artist: Allman Brothers
Written by: Dickie Betts
From the album: *Brothers and Sisters*
Label: Capricorn
Produced by: Jerry Sandlin, the Allman Brothers Band
Year: 1973
Betts takes over guitar chores from the deceased Duane, with a laid back Southern preserve.

JESSIE

Artist: Joshua Kadison
Written by: Joshua Kadison
From the album: *Painted Desert Seranade*
Label: SBK
Produced by: Rod Argent, Peter Van Hooke
Year: 1993
Neo-Elton John story song.

JESSIE'S GIRL

Artist: Rick Springfield
Written by: Rick Springfield
From the album: *Working Class Dog*
Label: RCA
Produced by: Keith Olson, Rick Springfield
Year: 1981
Parlaying his soap opera exposure into a soap operatic song attached to a telegenic video and a killer hook for the nascent MTV era. The result went to #1.

JESUS BUILT MY HOTROD

Artist: Ministry
Written by: Ministry
From the album: *Psalm 69*
Label: Sire
Produced by: H. Luxa, H. Pan
Year: 1992
Commercial breakthrough of a sort, with guest vocal by Gibby Haynes of the Butthole Surfers.

JESUS CHRIST SUPERSTAR

Artist: Murray Head
Written by: Tim Rice, Andrew Lloyd Webber
From the album: *Jesus Christ Superstar*
Label: Decca
Produced by: Tim Rice, Andrew Lloyd Webber
Year: 1970
In a karma-conscious, guru-heavy musical period, the future Broadway icons snag a record deal for their Broadway-bound rock opera with this title track.

JESUS CHRIST WAS AN ONLY CHILD

Artist: Modest Mouse
Written by: Modest Mouse
From the album: *The Lonesome Crowded West*
Label: Up
Year: 1997
Rising to the top of the new indie ranks.

JESUS IS JUST ALRIGHT

Artist: The Byrds
Written by: Arthur Reynolds
From the album: *Ballad of Easy Rider*
Label: Warner Brothers
Produced by: Terry Melcher
Year: 1970
Deeper into the Christian life. Covered by the non-denominational Doobie Brothers (Warner Brothers, '73).

JET

Artist: Paul McCartney and Wings
Written by: Paul McCartney, Linda McCartney
From the album: *Band on the Run*
Label: Apple
Produced by: Paul McCartney
Year: 1974
One of his best rockers.

JET AIRLINER

Artist: The Steve Miller Band
Written by: Paul Pena
From the album: *Book of Dreams*
Label: Capitol
Produced by: Steve Miller
Year: 1977
Segue: "Leaving on a Jet Plane" by John Denver.

JET CITY WOMAN

Artist: Queensryche
Written by: Chris DeGarmo, Geoff Tate
From the album: *Empire*
Label: EMI
Produced by: Peter Collins
Year: 1991
Representing thrash in the land of grunge.

JIM DANDY

Artist: LaVern Baker
Written by: Lincoln Chase
Label: Atlantic
Produced by: Ahmet Ertegun, Jerry Wexler
Year: 1957
A likeable, upbeat, heroic kind of rock and roll model, Top 10 R&B/Top 20 crossover.

JIM DANDY GOT MARRIED

Artist: Lavern Baker
Written by: Lincoln Chase, Roquel Davis (Tyrone Carlo), Alonzo Tucker, Al Green
Label: Atlantic
Produced by: Ahmet Ertegun, Jerry Wexler
Year: 1957
The disappointing sequel; three new writers, and a big two weeks on the charts.

JIMMY, JIMMY

Artist: The Undertones
Written by: John O'Neill
From the album: *The Undertones*
Label: Sire
Produced by: the Undertones, Roger Bechirian
Year: 1979
Perfect rock song about a boy gone wrong.

JIMMY MACK

Artist: Martha & the Vandellas
Written by: Eddie Holland, Lamont Dozier, Brian Holland
From the album: *Watchout!*
Label: Gordy
Produced by: Brian Holland, Lamont Dozier

Year: 1967
#1 R&B/Top 10 crossover.

JIVE TALKIN'

Artist: Bee Gees
Written by: Barry Gibb, Robin Gibb, Maurice Gibb
From the album: *Main Course*
Label: RSO
Produced by: Arif Mardin
Year: 1975
Mastering the new language of R&B. Covered by the Blenders (Orchard Lane, '95). A year later, "You Should Be Dancing" would be a Top 10 R&B crossover.

JO JO GUNNE

Artist: Chuck Berry
Written by: Chuck Berry
From the album: *Chuck Berry Is on Top*
Label: Chess
Produced by: Leonard Chess, Phil Chess
Year: 1959
Jay Ferguson named his post-Spirit rock band after this.

JOAN CRAWFORD

Artist: Blue Oyster Cult
Written by: Albert Bouchard, David R. Ruter, John Lennert Rigg
From the album: *Fire of Unknown Origin*
Label: Columbia
Produced by: Martin Birch
Year: 1981
Cult goes Hollywood.

JO-ANN

Artist: The Twintones
Written by: John Cunningham, James Cunningham
Label: RCA
Year: 1957
In the Long Island white doo-wop Hall of Fame; written about their sister. Cover by the Playmates (Roulette, '57), right down to the sax solo, was the hit. Suggested sax segue: "Born Too Late" by the Poni-tails.

JOANNA

Artist: Kool & the Gang
Written by: Robert Bell, Kool & the Gang, James Bonneford
From the album: *In the Heart*
Label: De-Lite
Produced by: Ronald Bell, Kool & the Gang, James Bonneford
Year: 1983
#1 R&B/Top 10 crossover.

JOE STALIN'S CADILLAC

Artist: Camper Van Beethoven
Written by: David Lowery
From the album: *Camper Van Beethoven*

Label: Pitch a Tent
Produced by: Camper Van Beethoven
Year: 1986
Revealing Lowery's winsomely warped post-punk worldview.

JOE'S GARAGE

Artist: Frank Zappa
Written by: Frank Zappa
From the album: *Joe's Garage, Act I*
Label: Zappa
Produced by: Frank Zappa
Year: 1979
Perhaps his most personal and compelling memoir of his funky beginnings.

JOEY

Artist: Bob Dylan
Written by: Bob Dylan, Jacques Levy
From the album: *Desire*
Label: Columbia
Produced by: Don DeVito
Year: 1975
Deifying a mobster (Joey Gallo) way before the advent of *The Sopranos* on TV.

JOHANNESBURG

Artist: Gil Scott-Heron
Written by: Gil Scott-Heron
From the album: *From South Africa to South Carolina*
Label: Arista
Year: 1975
Scott-Heron teams with Brian Jackson to reinvent the genre of funk protest, which he originally invented with "The Revolution Will not Be Televised."

JOHN WESLEY HARDING

Artist: Bob Dylan
Written by: Bob Dylan
From the album: *John Wesley Harding*
Label: Columbia
Produced by: Bob Johnston
Year: 1968
Veering to the western half of country, this brief tune (and album) was reportedly named after blues singer Tim Hardin's great-grandfather.

JOHNNY ANGEL

Artist: Shelley Fabares
Written by: Lyn Duddy, Lee Pockriss
From the album: *Shelley!*
Label: Colpix
Produced by: Stu Phillips
Year: 1962
In the waifish Debbie Reynolds mold, Donna Reed's TV daughter steps forth, bolstered by the Blossoms on backing vocals, featuring Darlene Love.

JOHNNY ARE YOU QUEER

Artist: Josie Cotton

Written by: Bobby Paine, Larson Paine
From the album: *Valley Girl Soundtrack*
Label: Bomp
Produced by: Bobby Paine, Larson Paine
Year: 1981
Disarming Valley Girl punk classic.

JOHNNY B. GOODE

Artist: Chuck Berry
Written by: Chuck Berry
From the album: *One Dozen Berrys*
Label: Chess
Produced by: Leonard Chess, Phil Chess
Year: 1958
The creation of a character and guitar figure that would transcend their time and place, even while defining it in wonderfully choice details in all its innocence and ambition, raw talent and relentless exploitation. Dedicated to Chuck's keyboard player (and possibly an uncredited collaborator) Johnny Johnson. Covered by Jerry Lee Lewis (Mercury, '65), Elvis Presley (RCA, '69), Johnny Winter (Columbia, '69), the Grateful Dead (Warner Brothers, '71), Jimi Hendrix (Reprise, '72), and even Judas Priest (Columbia, '88). Michael J. Fox played it in *Back to the Future*. Bobby Bare tried to satirize it as early as '59 in "The All American Boy."

JOHNNY 99

Artist: Bruce Springsteen
Written by: Bruce Springsteen
From the album: *Nebraska*
Label: Columbia
Produced by: Bruce Springsteen
Year: 1982
Outlaw folk/rock. This downbeat saga of a mass murderer was covered by Johnny Cash (Columbia, '83).

JOHNNY REMEMBER ME

Artist: John Leyton
Written by: Geoffrey Goddárd
Label: Top Rank
Produced by: Joe Meek
Year: 1961
#1 UK hit from the TV show *Harper's West One*. Covered by the Bronski Beat with Marc Almond as part of a medley with "Love to Love You Baby" under the title of "I Feel Love" (MCA, '85).

JOHNNY TOO BAD

Artist: The Slickers
Written by: Roy Beckford, Derrick Crooks, Winston Bailey, John Martyn
From the album: *The Harder They Come Soundtrack*
Label: Island
Produced by: Byron Lee
Year: 1972
Johnny B. Goode goes bad in the outlaw reggae movie *The Harder They Come*.

JOIN TOGETHER

Artist: The Who

Written by: Pete Townshend
From the album: *The Kids Are Alright*
Label: MCA
Produced by: The Who
Year: 1972
Eleventh out of 14 Top 10 hits in England; here they had one. Featured in the '79 film *The Kids Are Alright*.

JOKER, THE

Artist: Steve Miller Band
Written by: Steve Miller, Eddie Curtis
From the album: *The Joker*
Label: Capitol
Produced by: Steve Miller
Year: 1969
First of three #1 hits finds the blues/rocker looking back to earlier efforts like "Enter Maurice" and "Gangster of Love." It is also here where Miller brings the Vernon Green phrase "The pompatus of love" into the rock and roll lexicon.

JOKERMAN

Artist: Bob Dylan
Written by: Bob Dylan
From the album: *Infidels*
Label: Columbia
Produced by: Bob Dylan, Mark Knopfler
Year: 1983
Returning to his biblical influences for a blistering folk/rocker.

JOLLY GREEN GIANT

Artist: The Kingsmen
Written by: Don Harris, Dewey Terry, Lynn Easton
From the album: *The Kingsmen (Vol. III)*
Label: Wand
Year: 1965
Another Don and Dewey classic-turned-Frat-rock-perennial by the Oregon band that made "Louie Louie" famous.

JOURNEY TO THE CENTER OF THE MIND

Artist: Amboy Dukes
Written by: Ted Nugent, Steve Farmer
From the album: *Journey to the Center of the Mind*
Label: Mainstream
Produced by: Bob Shad
Year: 1968
Motor City garage band psychedelia by the avid deer hunter and gonzo guitarist Nugent.

JOY TO THE WORLD

Artist: Three Dog Night
Written by: Hoyt Axton
From the album: *Naturally*
Label: Dunhill
Produced by: Richard Polodor
Year: 1971
Their biggest hit; a modern-day children's song.

JOYRIDE

Artist: Roxette
Written by: Per Gessle
From the album: *Joyride*
Label: EMI
Produced by: Clarence Ofwerman
Year: 1991
Outdoing even their Swedish forebears, Abba, with their fourth #1.

JUDGE NOT

Artist: Bob Marley
Written by: Bob Marley
Label: Beverly's
Produced by: Lesley Kong
Year: 1963
The roots of his reggae and rock.

JUDY IN DISGUISE (WITH GLASSES)

Artist: John Fred and His Playboy Band
Written by: John Fred, Andrew Bernard
From the album: *John Fred and His Playboy Band*
Label: Paula
Produced by: John Fred, Andrew Bernard
Year: 1967
Psychedelic bubblegum chart topper. Suggested segue: "Lucy in the Sky (with Diamonds)" by the Beatles.

JUDY'S TURN TO CRY

Artist: Lesley Gore
Written by: Edna Lewis, Beverly Ross
From the album: *I'll Cry If I Want To*
Label: Mercury
Produced by: Quincy Jones
Year: 1963
Proving herself not above entering a cat fight, Lesley sets out for revenge on the girl who stole her guy in "It's My Party."

JUICY

Artist: The Notorious B.I.G.
Written by: The Notorious B.I.G., Aquil Davidson, Gene Griffin, Teddy Riley, Brandon Mitchell, James Mtume, Markell Riley
From the album: *Ready to Die*
Label: Bad Boy/Arista
Produced by: Sean Combs
Year: 1994
With "Unbelievable" on the B-side.

JUKE

Artist: Little Walter
Written by: Walter Jacobs
Label: Checker
Year: 1952
#1 R&B hit, furthering the evolution of the blues harp. Sonny Terry, Junior Parker, Charlie Musselwhite, John Hammond, John Sebastian, John Lennon, Stevie Wonder were to follow.

JUKE BOX HERO

Artist: Foreigner
Written by: Lou Grammatico (Lou Gramm), Mick Jones
From the album: *4*
Label: Atlantic
Produced by: Mutt Lange
Year: 1981
A cogent look at the sad realities of the rock star's life. But it was no "Lodi."

JULIA

Artist: The Beatles
Written by: John Lennon, Paul McCartney
From the album: *The Beatles*
Label: Apple
Produced by: George Martin
Year: 1968
Lennon's ode to his mother.

JULIE, DO YA LOVE ME

Artist: Bobby Sherman
Written by: Tom Bahler
From the album: *Portrait of Bobby*
Label: Metromedia
Produced by: Jackie Mills
Year: 1970
Teen idle.

JULIE'S IN THE DRUG SQUAD

Artist: The Clash
Written by: John Mellor (Joe Strummer), Mick Jones
From the album: *Give 'Em Enough Rope*
Label: Epic
Produced by: Sandy Pearlman
Year: 1978
A post-hippie vision redefined, cops on acid for Operation Julie.

JUMP

Artist: Kriss Kross
Written by: Jermaine Dupri
From the album: *Totally Krossed Out*
Label: Ruffhouse/Columbia
Produced by: Jermaine Dupri
Year: 1992
Exuberant prepubescent hip hop debut at #1. Suggested segue: "I Want You Back" by the Jackson Five, "Why Do Fools Fall in Love" by Frankie Lymon and the Teenagers.

JUMP

Artist: Van Halen
Written by: Eddie Van Halen, Alex Van Halen, Michael Anthony, David Lee Roth
From the album: *1984*
Label: Warner Brothers
Produced by: Ted Templeman
Year: 1984
Their only #1, with Eddie on synthesizer as well as guitar; to some an accession to the modern rock sound of the '80s, to others a masterful triumph over it.

JUMP AROUND

Artist: House of Pain
Written by: Larry Muggerud, Everlast Schrody
From the album: *House of Pain*
Label: Tommy Boy
Year: 1992
The rap of the Irish.

JUMP (FOR MY LOVE)

Artist: Pointer Sisters
Written by: Marti Sharron, Steve Mitchell, Gary Skardina
From the album: *Break Out*
Label: Planet
Produced by: Richard Perry
Year: 1984
Trading in their retro boogie for a more modern step.

JUMP IN THE FIRE

Artist: Metallica
Written by: James Hetfield, Lars Ulrich, Dave Mustaine
From the album: *Kill 'Em All*
Label: Megaforce
Produced by: Paul Curcio, Mark Whittaker, Metallica
Year: 1983
Out of the California smog, the bastard son of Sabbath emerges.

JUMP TO IT

Artist: Aretha Franklin
Written by: Luther Vandross, Marcus Miller
From the album: *Jump to It*
Label: Arista
Produced by: Luther Vandross
Year: 1982
#1 R&B/Top 25 crossover.

JUMPIN' JUMPIN'

Artist: Destiny's Child
Written by: Missy Elliott, Beyonce Knowles, Falonte Moore
From the album: *The Writing's on the Wall*
Label: Sony
Year: 1999
Saturday night at the club, still the place to be, fifty years on.

JUMPIN' JACK FLASH

Artist: The Rolling Stones
Written by: Mick Jagger, Keith Richards
From the album: *Through the Past Darkly (Big Hits, Vol. II)*
Label: London

Produced by: Jimmy Miller
Year: 1968
#1 UK/Top 10 crossover. Covered by Aretha Franklin (Arista, '86) in the movie of the same name.

JUMPING SOMEONE ELSE'S TRAIN

Artist: The Cure
Written by: Robert Smith, Laurence Tolhurst, Michael Dempsey
From the album: *Boys Don't Cry*
Label: Fiction/PVC
Produced by: Chris Parry
Year: 1979
The early snifflings of mope rock.

JUNGLE BOOGIE

Artist: Kool & the Gang
Written by: Robert Bell, Kool & the Gang
From the album: *Wild and Peaceful*
Label: De-Lite
Produced by: Kool & the Gang
Year: 1973
Funk-and-roll, disco-age standard bearer became their first Top 10 crossover after 10 R&B hits.

JUNGLE FEVER

Artist: Stevie Wonder
Written by: Stevie Wonder
From the album: *Jungle Fever Soundtrack*
Label: Motown
Produced by: Stevie Wonder
Year: 1991
Theme from the Spike Lee movie launches Wonder's 4TH decade on the charts. In 1995 he'd win another Grammy for it.

JUNGLELAND

Artist: Bruce Springsteen
Written by: Bruce Springsteen
From the album: *Born to Run*
Label: Columbia
Produced by: Jon Landau, Mike Appel, Bruce Springsteen
Year: 1975
Almost Coplandesque in its majestic sweep and defining American ambition, within which is embedded a personal history of rock and roll (or at least of New Jersey after dark).

JUNIOR'S BAR

Artist: The Iron City House Rockers
Written by: Joe Grushecky, Gil Snyder, Eddie Britt
From the album: *Have a Good Time (But Get out Alive)*
Label: MCA
Year: 1980
Defining track from the Boss of Pittsburgh.

JUNIOR'S FARM

Artist: Paul McCartney and Wings

Written by: Paul McCartney, Linda McCartney
From the album: *Wings' Greatest*
Label: Apple
Produced by: Paul McCartney
Year: 1974
Suggested segue: "Maggie's Farm" by Bob Dylan.

JUST A DREAM

Artist: Jimmy Clanton
Written by: Jimmy Clanton, Cosimo Matassa
From the album: *Just a Dream*
Label: Ace
Produced by: Johnny Vincent
Year: 1958
Blue-eyed New Orleans soul, influenced by Earl King, leader of the band for which Clanton labelmate Huey Smith played piano.

JUST A FRIEND

Artist: Biz Markie
Written by: Marcel Hall
From the album: *The Biz Never Sleeps*
Label: Cold Chillin'
Produced by: Marcel Hall
Year: 1989
Even rappers get the blues.

JUST A LITTLE

Artist: The Beau Brummels
Written by: Ronald C. Elliott, Robert Durand
From the album: *Introducing the Beau Brummels*
Label: Autumn
Produced by: Sly Stone
Year: 1965
San Francisco in the days when the Grateful Dead were still the Warlocks and Sly was still a DJ.

JUST A SONG BEFORE I GO

Artist: Crosby, Stills & Nash
Written by: Graham Nash
From the album: *CSN*
Label: Atlantic
Produced by: Crosby, Stills & Nash
Year: 1977
Their biggest single.

JUST ABOUT GLAD

Artist: Elvis Costello
Written by: Declan McManus (Elvis Costello)
From the album: *Brutal Youth*
Label: Warner Brothers
Produced by: Mitchell Froom, Elvis Costello
Year: 1994
Segue: "Nearly in Love" by Richard Thompson.

JUST ANOTHER NIGHT

Artist: Mick Jagger
Written by: Mick Jagger
From the album: *She's the Boss*
Label: Columbia
Produced by: Mick Jagger, Bill Laswell
Year: 1985

As a solo artist, Jagger was merely fodder for the aerobics mill.

JUST BECAUSE

Artist: Lloyd Price
Written by: Lloyd Price
From the album: *Exciting Lloyd Price*
Label: ABC Paramount
Year: 1957
First crossover hit for the New Orleans soul man after four Top 10 R&B. Covered by Larry Williams (Specialty, '57).

JUST CAN'T GET ENOUGH

Artist: Depeche Mode
Written by: Vince Clarke
From the album: *Speak and Spell*
Label: Mute
Produced by: Daniel Miller, Depeche Mode
Year: 1981
Modern dance in the age of the synthesizer; their first UK hit.

JUST DROPPED IN (TO SEE WHAT CONDITION MY CONDITION WAS IN)

Artist: Kenny Rogers and the First Edition
Written by: Mickey Newbury
From the album: *The First Edition*
Label: Reprise
Produced by: Mike Post
Year: 1968
First hit for the future middle-of-the-road crooner is in the folkie tradition.

JUST GOT PAID

Artist: Johnny Kemp
Written by: Johnny Kemp, Gene Griffin
From the album: *Secrets of Flying*
Label: Columbia
Produced by: Teddy Riley, Johnny Kemp
Year: 1988
#1 R&B/Top 10 crossover.

JUST KICKIN' IT

Artist: Xscape
Written by: Jermaine Dupri, Manuel Seals
From the album: *Hummin' Comin' at Cha'*
Label: So So Def
Produced by: Jermaine Dupri
Year: 1993
Launching their career from Atlanta with a #1 R&B/#2 crossover.

JUST LIKE A WOMAN

Artist: Bob Dylan
Written by: Bob Dylan
From the album: *Blonde on Blonde*
Label: Columbia
Produced by: Bob Johnston

Year: 1966

Painting his masterpiece. UK Top 10 hit for Manfred Mann (Fontana, '66). Covered by Richie Havens (Verve/Folkways, '66), Joe Cocker (A&M, '69), Rod Stewart (Warner Brothers, '81).

JUST LIKE FIRE WOULD

Artist: The Saints
Written by: Chris Bailey
From the album: *All Fool's Day*
Label: TVT
Produced by: Hugh Jones
Year: 1987

Massive alternative arena hook from Australia. The Hoodoo Gurus would have been proud of it.

JUST LIKE HEAVEN

Artist: The Cure
Written by: Robert Smith, Laurence Tolhurst, Simon Gallup, Purl Thompson, Boris Williams
From the album: *Kiss Me, Kiss Me, Kiss Me*
Label: Elektra
Produced by: Robert Smith, Dave Allen
Year: 1987

JUST LIKE HONEY

Artist: The Jesus and Mary Chain
Written by: James Reid
From the album: *Psychocandy*
Label: Reprise
Produced by: The Jesus and Mary Chain
Year: 1986

College radio track of the year.

JUST LIKE JESSE JAMES

Artist: Cher
Written by: Diane Warren, Desmond Child
From the album: *Heart of Stone*
Label: Geffen
Produced by: Desmond Child
Year: 1989

From the ultimate hired guns of '80s pop-rock songwriting.

(JUST LIKE) ROMEO AND JULIET

Artist: The Reflections
Written by: Bob Hamilton, Freddy Gorman
From the album: *(Just Like) Romeo and Juliet*
Label: Golden World
Produced by: Rob Reeco
Year: 1964

Post doo-wop one-shot. Covered by Sha-Na-Na (Buddah, '74).

(JUST LIKE) STARTING OVER

Artist: John Lennon
Written by: John Lennon
From the album: *Double Fantasy*

Label: Geffen
Produced by: John Lennon, Yoko Ono, Jack Douglas
Year: 1980

His second and last #1 solo single.

JUST LIKE TOM THUMB'S BLUES

Artist: Bob Dylan
Written by: Bob Dylan
From the album: *Highway 61 Revisited*
Label: Columbia
Produced by: Tom Wilson
Year: 1965

Lost in the rain in Juarez. Nina Simone (RCA '69). Covered by Judy Collins (Elektra '71), Linda Ronstadt (Elektra '98).

JUST MY IMAGINATION (RUNNING AWAY WITH ME)

Artist: The Temptations
Written by: Norman Whitfield, Barrett Strong
From the album: *Sky's the Limit*
Label: Gordy
Produced by: Norman Whitfield
Year: 1971

Their biggest hit of the '70s.

JUST ONCE IN MY LIFE

Artist: The Righteous Brothers
Written by: Gerry Goffin, Carole King, Phil Spector
From the album: *Just Once in My Life*
Label: Philles
Produced by: Phil Spector
Year: 1965

Dramatic follow-up to "You've Lost That Lovin' Feelin'."

JUST ONE LOOK

Artist: Doris Troy
Written by: Doris Payne, Gregory Carroll
From the album: *Just One Look*
Label: Atlantic
Produced by: Artie Ripp
Year: 1963

Top 10 R&B/Top 10 crossover. Covered by the Hollies as their first single (Imperial, '64), Linda Ronstadt (Asylum, '78).

JUST ONE SMILE

Artist: Gene Pitney
Written by: Randy Newman
Label: Musicor
Produced by: Gene Pitney
Year: 1966

One of Randy's best early ballads was a UK hit by Gene Pitney in '66, six years after it was written. Covered by Blood, Sweat, & Tears (Columbia, '68).

JUST OUT OF REACH (OF MY TWO OPEN ARMS)

Artist: Solomon Burke
Written by: V. F. Stewart
Label: Atlantic
Produced by: Bert Berns, Jerry Wexler
Year: 1961

Top 10 R&B/Top 30 crossover with a country tune.

JUST PERFECT

Artist: All
Written by: Bill Stephenson
From the album: *Allroy Sez*
Label: Cruz
Year: 1988

Pop punk descendants go to metal beach.

JUST THE MOTION

Artist: Richard and Linda Thompson
Written by: Richard Thompson
From the album: *Shoot out the Lights*
Produced by: Joe Boyd
Label: Hannibal
Year: 1982

From one of folk/rock's defining albums.

JUST THE TWO OF US

Artist: Grover Washington, Jr. and Bill Withers
Written by: Bill Withers, William Salter, Ralph MacDonald
From the album: *Winelight*
Label: Elektra
Produced by: Grover Washington, Ralph MacDonald
Year: 1981

Covered by Will Smith (Columbia, '95).

JUST THE WAY YOU ARE

Artist: Billy Joel
Written by: Billy Joel
From the album: *The Stranger*
Label: Columbia
Produced by: Phil Ramone
Year: 1977

The piano man's crowning lounge ballad. Covered by Frank Sinatra (Reprise, '80).

JUST TO BE CLOSE TO YOU

Artist: Commodores
Written by: Lionel B. Richie Jr.
From the album: *Hot on the Tracks*
Label: Motown
Produced by: James Carmichael, the Commodores
Year: 1976

#1 R&B/Top 10 crossover ballad.

JUST TO BE WITH YOU

Artist: The Passions
Written by: Marv Kalfin
Label: Audicon

Produced by: Paul Swain
Year: 1959
The demo of this future doo-wop standard was performed by the Cousins (aka the Co-sines), the dynamic New York duo of Paul Simon and Carol Klein (aka King).

JUST WALKING IN THE RAIN

Artist: The Prisonaires
Written by: Johnny Bragg, Robert Riley
Label: Sun
Produced by: Sam Phillips
Year: 1953
Jailhouse rock, the real deal. The story of the Prisonaires forms a subplot in the novel *Fortress of Solitude* by Jonathan Lethem. Covered by Johnny Ray (Columbia, '56).

JUST WHAT I NEEDED

Artist: The Cars
Written by: Ric Ocasek
From the album: *The Cars*
Label: Elektra
Produced by: Roy Thomas Baker
Year: 1978
First single for the Boston new wave band.

JUST WHEN I NEEDED YOU MOST

Artist: Randy Van Warmer
Written by: Randy Van Warmer
From the album: *Warmer*
Label: Bearsville
Produced by: Dell Newman
Year: 1979
Folk/rock that crossed over to country.

JUST YOU 'N' ME

Artist: Chicago
Written by: James Pankow
From the album: *Chicago VI*
Label: Columbia
Produced by: James William Guercio
Year: 1973

JUSTIFIED AND ANCIENT

Artist: The KLF
Written by: Jimi Cauty, Bill Drummond
From the album: *The White Room*
Label: Arista
Produced by: KLF
Year: 1991
An inspired marriage of techno and schmaltz, featuring the voice of Country thrush Tammy Wynette.

JUSTIFY MY LOVE

Artist: Madonna
Written by: Lenny Kravitz, Madonna Ciccone
From the album: *The Immaculate Collection*

Label: Sire
Produced by: Lenny Kravitz, Andre Betts
Year: 1990
Looking for new inspiration. Suggested segue: "Security of the First World" by Public Enemy.

JUSTINE

Artist: Don and Dewey
Written by: Don Harris, Dewey Terry
From the album: *Jungle Hop*
Label: Specialty
Produced by: Art Rupe
Year: 1958
One of the classic rock and roll duets. Covered by the Righteous Brothers in the film *A Swingin' Summer*, with Raquel Welch.

K

K. C. LOVIN'

Artist: Little Willie Littlefield
Written by: Jerry Leiber, Mike Stoller
Label: Fury
Produced by: Jerry Leiber, Mike Stoller
Year: 1952
A couple of white wiseguys invade the urban scene. When this was remade as "Kansas City" by Wilbert Harrison (Fury, '59), Leiber and Stoller were already ensconced as the hottest songwriting duo on two coasts. In England, Lennon and McCartney were listening, reading the tiny print under the titles on the singles sleeves and album jackets.

KARMA CHAMELEON

Artist: Culture Club
Written by: Jon Moss, Roy Hay, Michael Craig, George O'Dowd, Phil Pickett
From the album: *Colour by Numbers*
Label: Epic
Produced by: Steve Levene
Year: 1983
Their only #1 single, an irresistible melange, with a hidden tribute to Jamaica.

KARMA POLICE

Artist: Radiohead
Written by: Jonathan Greenwood, Phillip Selway, Edward O'Brien, Thomas Yorke, Colin Greenwood
From the album: *OK Computer*
Label: Capitol
Year: 1997
Key track from the album voted by some fans in England as the best of all time.

KARN EVIL

Artist: Emerson Lake and Palmer (ELP)
Written by: Greg Lake, Keith Emerson, Pete Sinfield
From the album: *Brain Salad Surgery*
Label: Manticore

Produced by: Greg Lake
Year: 1973
Clocking in at just under a 30 minutes for all three parts, more progressive rock than a body, a band, or an entire radio station should be expected to endure at one sitting.

KASHMIR

Artist: Led Zeppelin
Written by: Jimmy Page, Robert Plant, John Bonham
From the album: *Physical Graffiti*
Label: Atlantic
Produced by: Jimmy Page
Year: 1975
Page's magnum Eastern opus was always one of the band's favorites, taking up where even the Yardbirds dared not go. Suggested segue: "East-West" by the Paul Butterfield Blues Band.

KATMANDU

Artist: Cat Stevens
Written by: Cat Stevens
From the album: *Tea for the Tillerman*
Label: A&M
Produced by: Paul Samwell-Smith
Year: 1971
A favorite collegiate summertime hangout in the early '70s. Suggested segues: "Marrakesh Express" by Crosby, Stills & Nash, "Katmandu" by Bob Seger, "Copenhagen" by Johnny Mathis.

KEEP A-KNOCKIN'

Artist: Little Richard
Written by: Richard Penniman (Little Richard)
From the album: *Little Richard*
Label: Specialty
Produced by: Art Rupe, Little Richard
Year: 1957
His most compelling rocker, a Top 5 R&B/Top 10 crossover, featured in the movie *Mr. Rock and Roll*. Covered by the Everly Brothers (Warner Brothers, '65), the Flamin' Groovies (Buddah, '72), Suzi Quatro (Bell, '74), Mott the Hoople (Atlantic, '74), the Blasters (Slash, '82).

(KEEP FEELING) FASCINATION

Artist: Human League
Written by: Phil Oakey, Jo Callis
From the album: *Fascination*
Label: A&M
Produced by: Martin Rushent, Human League
Year: 1983
Definitive synth rock as only the English could construct it.

KEEP IT COMIN', LOVE

Artist: K.C. and the Sunshine Band
Written by: Harry Casey, Richard Finch
From the album: *Part 3*
Label: TK

Produced by: Harry Casey, Richard Finch
Year: 1977
#1 R&B/Top 10 crossover. Their fourth #1 R&B hit. Among predominantly white acts, only Elvis had more, with six.

KEEP IT TOGETHER

Artist: Madonna
Written by: Steve Bray, Madonna Ciccone
From the album: *Like a Prayer*
Label: Sire
Produced by: Steve Bray, Madonna
Year: 1989

KEEP ON DANCING

Artist: The Gentrys
Written by: Willie David Young
From the album: *Keep on Dancing*
Label: MGM
Produced by: Chips Moman
Year: 1965
Anticipating the rise of frat rock.

KEEP ON LOVING YOU

Artist: REO Speedwagon
Written by: Kevin Cronin Jr.
From the album: *Hi Infidelity*
Label: Epic
Produced by: Kevin Cronin Jr., Gary Richrath, Kevin Beamish
Year: 1980
Having gained an inch on the radio, they burst through the door with both shoulders for their first #1 hit. It would take years to get them to leave.

KEEP ON MOVIN'

Artist: Soul II Soul
Written by: Romeo
From the album: *Keep on Movin'*
Label: Virgin
Produced by: Nellee Hooper, Jazzie B.
Year: 1989
#1 R&B/Top 20 crossover.

KEEP ON PUSHING

Artist: The Impressions
Written by: Curtis Mayfield
From the album: *Keep on Pushing*
Label: ABC-Paramount
Produced by: Curtis Mayfield
Year: 1964
Their third and last Top 10 hit. They would have eleven Top 10 R&B hits.

KEEP ON SMILIN'

Artist: Wet Willie
Written by: Jack Hall, Maurice Hirsch, Lewis Ross, John Anthony, James Hall
From the album: *Keep on Smilin'*
Label: Capricorn
Produced by: Tom Dowd
Year: 1974

Only Top 10 hit for the Southern rock contingent from Alabama.

KEEP ON TRUCKIN'

Artist: Eddie Kendricks
Written by: Frank Wilson, Leonard Caston, Anita Poree
From the album: *Eddie Kendricks*
Label: Tamla
Produced by: Frank Wilson, Leonard Caston
Year: 1973
#1 R&B/#1 crossover for the former Temptations frontman.

KEEP SEARCHIN' (WE'LL FOLLOW THE SUN)

Artist: Del Shannon
Written by: Del Shannon
Label: Amy
Produced by: Irving Micahnik, Harry Balk
Year: 1964
Last of his eight UK Top 10s, last of his three here.

KEEP TALKING

Artist: Pink Floyd
Written by: David Gilmour, Polly Samson, Richard Wright
From the album: *The Division Bell*
Label: Columbia
Produced by: David Gilmour, Bob Ezrin
Year: 1994
Featuring the voice of physicist Stephen Hawkings.

KEEP YA HEAD UP

Artist: 2Pac
Written by: Tupac Shakur, Darrell Anderson, Roger Troutman
From the album: *Strictly 4 My N.I.G.G.A.Z.*
Label: Interscope
Produced by: D. J. Daryl
Year: 1993
A pointed and poignant anthem for the urban dispossessed, by the much-publicized actor/rapper/gangsta, who was murdered in '96.

KEEP YOUR HANDS OFF MY BABY

Artist: Little Eva
Written by: Gerry Goffin, Carole King
From the album: *Lllllloco-Motion*
Label: Dimension
Produced by: Gerry Goffin
Year: 1962
In a repressive era for women singers, a positive expression of aggression.

KEEP YOUR HANDS TO YOURSELF

Artist: Georgia Satellites
Written by: Don Baird
From the album: *Georgia Satellites*

Label: Elektra
Year: 1986
Rockabilly in the age of safe sex.

KEEP YOURSELF ALIVE

Artist: Queen
Written by: Brian May
From the album: *Queen*
Label: Elektra
Produced by: Roy Thomas Baker, Queen
Year: 1973
The makings of an arena champion.

KEEPER OF THE CASTLE

Artist: The Four Tops
Written by: Dennis Lambert, Brian Potter
From the album: *Keeper of the Castle*
Label: Dunhill
Produced by: Dennis Lambert, Brian Potter
Year: 1972
Continuing a mini-'70s comeback with a Top 10 hit. Levi Stubbs would later find himself perfectly cast as the voice of the man-eating plant in the movie version of the musical *Little Shop of Horrors*.

KENTUCKY BLUEBIRD

Artist: Lou Johnson
Written by: Burt Bacharach, Hal David
Label: Big Hill
Year: 1964
Covered by Dionne Warwick as "Take a Message to Michael" (Scepter, '66).

KENTUCKY RAIN

Artist: Elvis Presley
Written by: Eddie Rabbitt, Dick Heard
From the album: *Worldwide 50 Gold Award Hits (Vol. I)*
Label: RCA
Produced by: Snuff Garrett, Felton Jarvis, Elvis Presley
Year: 1970
From the classic Memphis sessions that produced "Suspicious Minds."

KENTUCKY WOMAN

Artist: Neil Diamond
Written by: Neil Diamond
From the album: *Neil Diamond's Greatest Hits*
Label: Bang
Produced by: Jeff Barry, Ellie Greenwich
Year: 1967
Covered by Deep Purple (Tetragrammaton, '68).

KEROSENE

Artist: Big Black
Written by: Steve Albini
From the album: *Atomizer*
Label: Touch and Go
Produced by: Steve Albini
Year: 1986
Punk rock redux—louder, faster, angrier—furthering Albini's legendary status in the alt world.

KEY LARGO

Artist: Bertie Higgins
Written by: Sonny Limbo, Bertie Higgins
From the album: *Just Another Day in Paradise*
Label: Kat Family
Produced by: Sonny Limbo, Scott MacLellan
Year: 1982
The best promotion for Key Largo since Bogie.

KICK IN THE EYE

Artist: Bauhaus
Written by: Bauhaus
From the album: *The Mask*
Label: Beggar's Banquet
Year: 1981
First UK alternative hit for the moody progenitors of gothic rock.

KICK OUT THE JAMS

Artist: MC5
Written by: MC5
From the album: *Kick out the Jams*
Label: Elektra
Produced by: Bruce Botnick, Jac Holtzman
Year: 1969
Revolutionary punk noise tract from Detroit. Suggested segue from San Francisco: "Volunteers" by Jefferson Airplane; from New York: "While Light, White Heat" by the Velvet Underground.

KICKS

Artist: Paul Revere and the Raiders
Written by: Barry Mann, Cynthia Weil
From the album: *Midnight Ride*
Label: Columbia
Produced by: Terry Melcher
Year: 1966
Reacting to the reaction, the staff songwriting mainstream strikes back against the counterculture. Revere and the Raiders gain their first and biggest hit.

KID

Artist: The Pretenders
Written by: Chrissie Hynde
From the album: *The Pretenders*
Label: Sire
Produced by: Chris Thomas
Year: 1980
Previewing Hynde's dominant obsession, aside from rock and roll.

KID ABOUT IT

Artist: Elvis Costello
Written by: Declan McManus (Elvis Costello)
From the album: *Imperial Bedroom*
Label: Columbia
Produced by: Geoff Emerich
Year: 1982
Pub rock visits the boite.

KID CHARLEMAGNE

Artist: Steely Dan

Written by: Donald Fagen, Walter Becker
From the album: *The Royal Scam*
Label: ABC
Produced by: Gary Katz
Year: 1976
Caustic ode to the end of the counterculture, with a bravura guitar part by Larry Carlton.

KIDDIO

Artist: Teddy Randazzo
Written by: Brook Benton, Clyde Otis
Label: Vik
Year: 1957
Introduced by Randazzo in the movie *Mr. Rock and Roll*. Cover by Brook Benton (Mercury, '60) was a #1 R&B/Top 10 crossover.

KIDS ARE ALRIGHT, THE

Artist: The Who
Written by: Pete Townshend
From the album: *The Who Sing My Generation*
Label: Decca
Produced by: Kit Lambert
Year: 1966
Pre-arena rock anthem; setting the stage for all other classic rock solidarity statements of the '70s.

KIDS IN AMERICA

Artist: Kim Wilde
Written by: Ricky Wilde, Marty Wilde
From the album: *Kim Wilde*
Label: EMI-America
Produced by: Ricky Wilde
Year: 1982
Cowriter is her father Marty, an Elvis-styled '50s rocker, famed for covering "Endless Sleep" and "A Teenager in Love." Producer is her younger brother.

KILL FOR PEACE

Artist: The Fugs
Written by: Tuli Kupferberg, Ed Sanders
From the album: *The Fugs*
Label: ESP
Produced by: Harry Smith
Year: 1965
Satiric polemic was actually adopted as serious slogan by soldiers in Vietnam. Suggested segue: "Born in the USA" by Bruce Springsteen.

KILL YOUR SONS

Artist: Lou Reed
Written by: Lou Reed
From the album: *Sally Can't Dance*
Label: RCA
Produced by: Steve Katz
Year: 1974
Responding to a dose of shock treatment. Suggested segues: "Gimme Gimme Shock Treatment" by the Ramones, "Knockin' around the Zoo" by James Taylor.

KILLBOY POWERHEAD

Artist: Didjets
Written by: Rick Sims

From the album: *Hornet Pinata*
Label: Touch and Go
Year: 1990
Anarchic power metal rant. Covered by Offspring (Epitaph, '94).

KILLED BY DEATH

Artist: Motorhead
Written by: Ian Kilmeister (Lemmy), Mick Burston
From the album: *No Remorse*
Label: Bronze
Year: 1984
Somewhat redundant as a title, but who's going to say that to Lemmy's face?

KILLER QUEEN

Artist: Queen
Written by: Freddie Mercury
From the album: *Sheer Heart Attack*
Label: Elektra
Produced by: Roy Thomas Baker, Queen
Year: 1974
Probably their most ferocious metal moment.

KILLING AN ARAB

Artist: The Cure
Written by: Robert Smith, Laurence Tolhurst, Michael Dempsey
From the album: *Boys Don't Cry*
Label: Small Wonder/Fiction/PVC
Produced by: Chris Parry
Year: 1979
Led by the ghostly Robert Smith, nerd rock goes to Oxford. In Manchester, Stephen Morrissey decided to name his band the Smiths.

KILLING FLOOR

Artist: Howlin' Wolf
Written by: Chester Burnette (Howling Wolf)
From the album: *Real Folk Blues*
Label: Chess
Produced by: Marshall Chess
Year: 1966
Definitively down and dirty. Covered by the Electric Flag (Columbia, '68).

KILLING IN THE NAME OF

Artist: Rage against the Machine
Written by: Rage against the Machine
From the album: *Rage against the Machine*
Produced by: Garth Richardson, Rage against the Machine
Label: Epic
Year: 1992
Eventually the machine beat them down.

KILLING ME SOFTLY WITH HIS SONG

Artist: Lori Lieberman
Written by: Norman Gimbel, Charles Fox
Label: RCA

Year: 1972
Deifying the folk/rock singer/songwriter Don McLean. Covered by Roberta Flack (Atlantic, '72), the Fugees (Columbia, '96).

KILLING OF GEORGIE (PARTS I AND II)

Artist: Rod Stewart
Written by: Rod Stewart
From the album: *A Night on the Town*
Label: Warner Brothers
Produced by: Tom Dowd
Year: 1977
About the murder of a gay friend.

KIND OF A DRAG

Artist: The Buckinghams
Written by: James Holvay
From the album: *Kind of a Drag*
Label: USA
Produced by: Dan Belloc
Year: 1966
Jazz-inflected pop rock.

KIND OF BOY YOU CAN'T FORGET, THE

Artist: The Raindrops
Written by: Jeff Barry, Ellie Greenwich
From the album: *The Raindrops*
Label: Jubilee
Produced by: Jeff Barry, Ellie Greenwich
Year: 1963
Aka Barry and Greenwich. As good as anything by the Jellybeans, if not the Cookies.

KIND WOMAN

Artist: Buffalo Springfield
Written by: Richie Furay
From the album: *Last Time Around*
Label: Atco
Produced by: Charles Greene, Brian Stone
Year: 1968
Country-oriented folk/rock. Presages the middle-of-the-dirt-road singer/songwriter era of the '70s.

KING HARVEST (HAS SURELY COME)

Artist: The Band
Written by: Robbie Robertson
From the album: *The Band*
Label: Capitol
Produced by: John Simon, the Band
Year: 1968
Suggested segue "Dancing in the Moonlight" by King Harvest.

KING OF PAIN

Artist: The Police
Written by: Gordon Sumner (Sting)
From the album: *Synchronicity*

Label: A&M
Produced by: Hugh Padgham, the Police
Year: 1983
Establishing his permanent persona.

KING OF ROCK

Artist: Run-D.M.C.
Written by: Larry Smith, Joseph Simmons, Darryl McDaniels
From the album: *King of Rock*
Label: Profile
Produced by: Russell Simmons, Larry Smith
Year: 1985
Rappers battle some of rock's ingrained prejudices.

KING OF THE HILL

Artist: Roger McGuinn
Written by: Roger McGuinn, Tom Petty
From the album: *Back from Rio*
Label: Arista
Year: 1990
McGuinn makes a successful comeback (from Florida, not Rio) with a Dylanesque rocker. But soon he'd be supplanted on the folk/rock hill by Wilco.

KING OF THE NEW YORK STREET

Artist: Dion
Written by: Dion DiMucci, Bill Tuohy
From the album: *Yo Frankie*
Label: Arista
Produced by: Dave Edmunds
Year: 1989
Earning his long-overdue solid gold Spauldeen, as presented to him at the Rock and Roll Hall of Fame induction ceremonies by Lou Reed, Billy Joel, and Bruce Springsteen. A major game of stickball ensued.

KING OF THE ROAD

Artist: Roger Miller
Written by: Roger Miller
From the album: *The Return of Roger Miller*
Label: Smash
Produced by: Jerry Kennedy
Year: 1965
#1 country/Top 10 crossover. Won Grammys that year for Best Country Song and Best Rock and Roll Performance.

KING TIM III (PERSONALITY JOCK)

Artist: Fatback
Written by: Bill Curtis, Fred Demery, Earl Skelton
From the album: *Fatback XII*
Label: Spring
Year: 1979
In some literary circles this is considered the first rap song, capturing a sound rising up from the school yards and spray painted streets of Brooklyn.

KING TUT

Artist: Steve Martin and the Toots Uncommons
Written by: Steve Martin
From the album: *A Wild and Crazy Guy*
Label: Warner Brothers
Produced by: Bill McKuen
Year: 1978
Novelty single. But not as funny as "What I Believe" (Warner Brothers, '81). Suggested segue: "Walk Like an Egyptian" by the Bangles.

KINGDOM OF LOVE

Artist: The Soft Boys
Written by: Robyn Hitchcock
From the album: *Underwater Moonlight*
Label: Armageddon
Produced by: Pat Colleer
Year: 1980
Hitchcock would soon go solo.

KISS

Artist: Prince and the Revolution
Written by: Prince Rogers Nelson
From the album: *Parade*
Label: Warner Brothers
Produced by: Prince
Year: 1986
His third #1 R&B/#1 crossover with Wendy of Wendy & Lisa on wah wah. From the movie *Under the Cherry Moon*.

KISS AND SAY GOODBYE

Artist: The Manhattans
Written by: Winfred Lovett
From the album: *The Manhattans*
Label: Columbia
Produced by: the Manhattans, Bobby Martin
Year: 1976
Gerald Alston sings lead on their biggest hit, a #1 R&B/#1 crossover; the second platinum-selling single in history up to that point. "Disco Lady" by Johnny Taylor was the first.

KISS FROM A ROSE

Artist: Seal
Written by: Seal
From the album: *Original Music from the Motion Picture Batman Forever*
Label: ZZT
Year: 1995
Sweet ballad from a not-so-sweet movie.

KISS ME

Artist: Sixpence None the Richer
Written by: Matt Slocum
From the album: *She's All That Soundtrack*
Label: Squint
Produced by: Steve Taylor
Year: 1998

Returning to the days of the Fleetwoods "Come Softly to Me."

KISS ME DEADLY

Artist: Lita Ford
Written by: Mick Smiley
From the album: *Lita*
Label: RCA
Produced by: Mike Chapman
Year: 1988
Former Runaway guitar queen follows in the Chapman-polished footsteps of leatherette goddesses Suzi Quatro and Debbie Harry.

KISS ME ON THE BUS

Artist: The Replacements
Written by: Paul Westerberg
From the album: *Tim*
Label: Sire
Produced by: Tommy Erdelyi
Year: 1985
The eloquent misery of the teenage condition. Their neighbors, Soul Asylum, were paying attention.

KISS ME, SON OF GOD

Artist: They Might Be Giants
Written by: John Flansburgh, John Linnell
From the album: *Lincoln*
Label: Restless
Produced by: Bill Kraus
Year: 1988
A third-world morality tale.

KISS OFF

Artist: Violent Femmes
Written by: Gordon Gano
From the album: *Violent Femmes*
Label: Slash
Produced by: Mark Van Hecke
Year: 1982
Internalizing the Velvet Underground over a junior-high-school squabble.

KISS ON MY LIST

Artist: Hall & Oates
Written by: Daryl Hall, Janna Allen
From the album: *Voices*
Label: RCA
Produced by: Hall & Oates
Year: 1981
Starting off a massive '81 with their second biggest all-time hit. Only the next year's "Maneater" was bigger.

KISS THEM FOR ME

Artist: Siouxsie and the Banshees
Written by: Martin McGarrick
From the album: *Superstition*
Label: Geffen
Produced by: Stephen Hague

Year: 1991
Geisha rock from the girl who sang "Hong Kong Garden."

KISS THIS THING GOODBYE

Artist: Del Amitri
Written by: Justin Currie
From the album: *Waking Hours*
Label: A&M
Produced by: M. Freegard
Year: 1990
Scottish folk/rock.

KISS YOU ALL OVER

Artist: Exile
Written by: Mike Chapman, Nicky Chinn
From the album: *Mixed Emotions*
Label: Warner/Curb
Produced by: Mike Chapman
Year: 1978
After this #1 pop hit, the entire group crossed over to country, where they had many more.

KISSES SWEETER THAN WINE

Artist: The Weavers
Written by: Huddie Ledbetter (Paul Campell), Pete Seeger, Lee Hays, Fred Hellerman, Ronnie Gilbert
Label: Decca
Produced by: Milt Gabler
Year: 1951
The folk verities, life as a kiss; life in a kiss. Covered by Jimmie Rodgers (Roulette, '57).

KISSIN' TIME

Artist: Bobby Rydell
Written by: Leonard Frazier, James Frazier
From the album: *Bobby Sings*
Label: Cameo
Year: 1959
This tune was not only Rydell's chart debut, but it also served a similar purpose for Kiss (Casablanca, '74).

KISSING A FOOL

Artist: George Michael
Written by: George Michael
From the album: *Faith*
Label: Columbia
Produced by: George Michael
Year: 1987
Sixth Top 10 tune from the LP.

KLAN, THE

Artist: Richie Havens
Written by: D. Grey, A. Grey
From the album: *Something Else Again*
Label: Verve/Forecast
Produced by: John Court

Year: 1968
Powerful civil-rights era dirge. Covered by Gil Scott-Heron (Arista, '80).

KNOCK ON WOOD

Artist: Eddie Floyd
Written by: Eddie Floyd, Steve Cropper
From the album: *Knock on Wood*
Label: Stax
Produced by: Jim Stewart
Year: 1966
Cropper repeats his intro to "In the Midnight Hour" backwards; #1 R&B/Top-30 crossover. Covered by Floyd's cohort in the Falcons, Wilson Pickett (Atlantic, '67), King Curtis (Atco, '67), Otis and Carla (Stax '67), Archie Bell and the Drells (Atlantic, '68), Eric Clapton (Duck, '85).

KNOCKIN' AROUND THE ZOO

Artist: James Taylor
Written by: James Taylor
From the album: *James Taylor*
Label: Apple
Produced by: Peter Asher
Year: 1969
About his stay at a high-class sanitarium.

KNOCKIN' BOOTS

Artist: Candyman
Written by: Candyman, Betty Wright, E. Hamilton, A. Hamilton, R. Wylie, W. Clarke
From the album: *Ain't No Shame in My Game*
Label: Epic
Year: 1990
Euphemistic hip hop ditty.

KNOCKIN' DA BOOTS

Artist: H-Town
Written by: Shazam, Dino Conner, Bishop (Stick) Burrell, Roger Troutman
From the album: *Fever for Da Flavor*
Label: Luke
Produced by: Bishop Burrell
Year: 1993
Can't keep a good phrase down; #1 R&B/Top 10 crossover.

KNOCKIN' ON HEAVEN'S DOOR

Artist: Bob Dylan
Written by: Bob Dylan
From the album: *Pat Garrett and Billy the Kid Soundtrack*
Label: Columbia
Produced by: Gordon Carroll
Year: 1973
Written for the film, a pure emotional highlight, and one of his most covered gems: see—Guns N' Roses, Jerry Garcia, Television, Randy Crawford, Danny & Dusty, Roger McGuinn, Wyclef Jean, and Avril Lavigne.

KNOCKING AT YOUR BACK DOOR

Artist: Deep Purple
Written by: Ritchie Blackmore, Ian Gillan, Roger Glover
From the album: *Perfect Stranger*
Label: Mercury
Produced by: Deep Purple, Roger Glover
Year: 1985
Searching for an FM formula in the midst of a folk roots revival and an English synth invasion.

KNOWLEDGE IS KING

Artist: Kool Moe Dee
Written by: P. Q. Harris, Moe Dewese
From the album: *Knowledge Is King*
Label: Jive
Produced by: Pete Q. Harris, Moe Dewese
Year: 1989
One of the heaviest of all rappers challenges his streetwise cronies to raise their level of discourse.

KO KO MO (I LOVE YOU SO)

Artist: Gene and Eunice
Written by: Forrest Wilson, Jake Porter, Eunice Levy
Label: Combo
Year: 1955
Top 10 R&B hit, covered twice in 1955, by Perry Como (RCA) and the Crewcuts (Mercury). RCA gained enough confidence in the teen market through Perry's chart performance to go ahead and sign Elvis Presley. Somewhere Chick Crumpacker was smiling.

KODACHROME

Artist: Paul Simon
Written by: Paul Simon
From the album: *There Goes Rhymin' Simon*
Label: Columbia
Produced by: Paul Samwell-Smith
Year: 1973
Recounting the miserable times of his life.

KOKO JOE

Artist: Don and Dewey
Written by: Sonny Bono
From the album: *Jungle Hop*
Label: Specialty
Produced by: Sonny Bono
Year: 1958
Sonny in his pre-Spector, pre-Cher mode as a staff writer.

KOKOMO

Artist: The Beach Boys
Written by: Mike Love, Terry Melcher, John Phillips, Scott Mackenzie
From the album: *Cocktail Soundtrack*
Label: Elektra
Produced by: Terry Melcher
Year: 1988
Catching one last perfect wave and revisiting #1 for the first time in more than twenty years with another sailing yarn.

KOOKIE LITTLE PARADISE, A

Artist: Jo Ann Campbell
Written by: Bob Hilliard, Lee Pockriss
Label: ABC Paramount
Year: 1960
Hail and farewell to a Blonde Bombshell who fizzled out before her time.

KOOKIE, KOOKIE, LEND ME YOUR COMB

Artist: Edward Byrnes and Connie Stevens
Written by: Irving Taylor
From the album: *Kookie, Kookie, Lend Me Your Comb*
Label: Warner Brothers
Produced by: Karl Engemann
Year: 1959
Fashion advice via the costar of the '59 detective show *77 Sunset Strip*.

KOSMIC BLUES

Artist: Janis Joplin
Written by: Gabriel Mekler, Janis Joplin
From the album: *I Got Dem Ol' Kosmic Blues Again Mama*
Label: Columbia
Produced by: Gabriel Mekler
Year: 1969
Janis's first chart hit after leaving Big Brother and the Holding Company was a rambling, rumbling, existential blues.

KRYPTONITE

Artist: 3 Doors Down
Written by: Brad Arnold, Todd Harrell, Matt Roberts
From the album: *The Better Life*
Produced by: Paul Ebersol
Label: Uptown
Year: 2000

KUNG FU FIGHTING

Artist: Carl Douglas
Written by: Carl Douglas
From the album: *Kung Fu Fighting and Other Great Love Songs*
Label: 20TH Century
Produced by: Biddu
Year: 1974
Topical kick dance number achieved a rare trifecta, hitting #1 R&B/#1 POP/#1 UK. Douglas was the first UK artist to top the US R&B charts.

KYRIE

Artist: Mr. Mister
Written by: Richard Page, Steven George, Robert John "Mutt" Lange
From the album: *Welcome to the Real World*
Label: RCA
Produced by: Mutt Lange
Year: 1985
Utilizing the timeless Gregorian chant for a #1 followup to a #1 ("Broken Wings"). Suggested segue: "Requiem" by the Association, "Sadeness (Part 1)" by Enigma.

L

L.A. BLUES

Artist: The Stooges
Written by: The Stooges
From the album: *Fun House*
Label: Elektra
Produced by: Don Gallucci
Year: 1970
Punk rock rears its ugly rear.

L.A. COUNTY

Artist: Lyle Lovett
Written by: Lyle Lovett
From the album: *Pontiac*
Label: MCA/Curb
Produced by: Tony Brown, Lyle Lovett
Year: 1987
The twisted face of new country.

L.A. FREEWAY

Artist: Jerry Jeff Walker
Written by: Guy Clark
From the album: *A Man Must Carry On*
Label: MCA
Produced by: Free Flow Productions
Year: 1973
One of the all-time great alt/country leaving songs, chiefly about the inability to leave.

L.A. WOMAN

Artist: The Doors
Written by: Jim Morrison, Robbie Krieger, John Densmore, Ray Manzarek
From the album: *L.A. Woman*
Label: Elektra
Produced by: Paul Rothchild
Year: 1971
Trashy older sister of "California Girls."

LA BAMBA

Artist: Ritchie Valens
Written by: William Clauson
From the album: *Richie Valens*
Label: Del-Fi
Produced by: Bob Keane
Year: 1958
B-side of "Oh Donna," a traditional Mexican folk-tune-turned-rock-and-roll classic, was on the

charts when Valens died in the plane crash in Clear Lake, Iowa, along with Buddy Holly and the Big Bopper in '59. The Los Lobos version in the movie of Valens's life, *La Bamba*, went to #1 (Warner Brothers, '87).

LA GRANGE

Artist: ZZ Top
Written by: Billy Gibbons, Dusty Hill, Frank Beard
From the album: *Tres Hombres*
Label: London
Produced by: Bill Ham
Year: 1973
Rockin' boogie celebrates the best little whore-house in Texas. Carol Hall would use the same inspiration for the off-Broadway (and later on Broadway) musical *The Best Little Whorehouse in Texas*, which opened in 1977.

LA ISLA BONITA

Artist: Madonna
Written by: Patrick Leonard, Madonna Ciccone, Bruce Gaitsch
From the album: *True Blue*
Label: Sire
Produced by: Patrick Leonard, Madonna
Year: 1986

LA LA (MEANS I LOVE YOU)

Artist: The Delfonics
Written by: Thom Bell, William Hart
From the album: *La La La (Means I Love You)*
Label: Philly Groove
Produced by: Stan Watson, Thom Bell
Year: 1968
#2 R&B/#4 Philly soul crossover.

LA VILLA STRANGIATA

Artist: Rush
Written by: Gary Lee Weinrib (Geddy Lee), Alex Zivojinovich (Alex Lifeson), Neil Peart
From the album: *Hemispheres*
Label: Mercury
Produced by: Terry Brown, Rush
Year: 1978
Instrumental epic that defines the outsized reach of this virtuosic band.

LADIES FIRST

Artist: Queen Latifah with Monie Love
Written by: Dana Owens (Queen Latifah), Apache, Simone Johnson, Mark James
From the album: *All Hail the Queen*
Label: Tommy Boy
Produced by: D. J. Mark
Year: 1989
Landmark feminist rap.

LADIES NIGHT

Artist: Kool & the Gang

Written by: Robert Bell, Kool & the Gang
From the album: *Ladies Night*
Label: De-Lite
Produced by: Eumir Deodato
Year: 1979
#1 R&B/Top 10 crossover.

LADY

Artist: D'Angelo
Written by: D'Angelo, Rafael Saadiq
From the album: *Brown Sugar*
Label: EMI
Year: 1995
Leading a new, mellow return for R&B.

LADY

Artist: Styx
Written by: Dennis DeYoung
From the album: *Styx II*
Label: Wooden Nickel
Produced by: Styx
Year: 1974
Breakthrough arena ballad deifying the nomenclature that supplanted the '60s endearment "old lady."

LADY D'ARBANVILLE

Artist: Cat Stevens
Written by: Cat Stevens
From the album: *Mona Bone Jakon*
Label: A&M
Produced by: Paul Samwell-Smith
Year: 1970
Written about his girlfriend, Patti. Peter Gabriel on flute.

LADY FRIEND

Artist: The Byrds
Written by: David Crosby
From the album: *The Notorious Byrd Brothers*
Label: Columbia
Produced by: Gary Usher
Year: 1968
Crosby's favorite topic, which would reach its ultimate fruition in "Triad."

LADY IN RED, THE

Artist: Chris Deburgh
Written by: Chris DeBurgh
From the album: *Into the Night*
Label: A&M
Year: 1986
#1 UK/Top 10 US ballad.

LADY JANE

Artist: The Rolling Stones
Written by: Mick Jagger, Keith Richards
From the album: *Aftermath*
Label: London
Produced by: Andrew Loog-Oldham
Year: 1966

B-side of "Mother's Little Helper." Brian Jones on dulcimer, Jack Nitzsche on harpsichord.

LADY MADONNA

Artist: The Beatles
Written by: John Lennon, Paul McCartney
From the album: *Hey Jude*
Label: Capitol
Produced by: George Martin
Year: 1968
Ronnie Scott on sax. The cover by Fats Domino (Reprise, '68) was his first chart single since '64. Sung by Aretha Franklin in 1993 as the theme for the TV show *Grace under Fire*.

LADY MARMELADE

Artist: LaBelle
Written by: Bob Crewe, Kenny Nolan Helfman
From the album: *Nightbirds*
Label: Epic
Produced by: Allen Toussaint
Year: 1974
Philadelphia meets New Orleans on a track previously recorded by its authors as Eleventh Hour (20TH Century, '74). The French chorus means "Will you go to bed with me tonight." LaBelle's biggest hit, a #1 R&B/#1 crossover. Revived by Christina Aguilera, Lil' Kim, Mya, and Pink, in the 2002 movie *Moulin Rouge*.

LADY WILLPOWER

Artist: Gary Puckett and the Union Gap
Written by: Jerry Fuller
From the album: *The Union Gap*
Label: Columbia
Produced by: Jerry Fuller
Year: 1968
Finding the lone holdout to the sexual revolution.

LAID

Artist: James
Written by: Tim Booth, Larry Gott, Saul Davies, Mark Hunter, Jim Glennie, David Bayton-Power
From the album: *Laid*
Label: Mercury
Produced by: Brian Eno
Year: 1994
Invoking the ghost of folk/rock past in the service of a timeless quest. Suggested segue: "Sooner or Later (One of Us Must Know)" by Bob Dylan.

LAKE OF FIRE

Artist: Meat Puppets
Written by: Curt Kirkwood
From the album: *Meat Puppets II*
Label: SST
Produced by: Spot, Meat Puppets
Year: 1982
One of the three tracks on this legendary Arizona punk band's second album covered by the unplugged Nirvana (DGC, '94). The others were "Oh Me" and "Plateau."

LAMB LIES DOWN ON BROADWAY, THE

Artist: Genesis
Written by: Genesis
From the album: *The Lamb Lies down on Broadway*
Label: Atco
Produced by: Brian Eno
Year: 1974
Their progressive rock apex. After this, Peter Gabriel went solo.

(LAMENT OF THE CHEROKEE) INDIAN RESERVATION, THE

Artist: Don Fardon
Written by: John D. Loudermilk
Label: GNP Crescendo
Year: 1968
This was a big hit in England. Covered by Paul Revere and the Raiders (Columbia, '71).

LAND OF A THOUSAND DANCES

Artist: Chris Kenner
Written by: Chris Kenner, Fats Domino
From the album: *Land of a Thousand Dances*
Label: Instant
Produced by: Allen Toussaint
Year: 1963
A New Orleans take on what "The Twist" hath wrought. Covered by Fats Domino (Imperial, '63), Cannibal and the Headhunters (Rampart, '65), Wilson Pickett (Atlantic, '66).

LAND OF CONFUSION

Artist: Genesis
Written by: Phil Collins, Tony Banks, Mike Rutherford
From the album: *Invisible Touch*
Label: Atlantic
Produced by: Hugh Padgham, Genesis
Year: 1986
Kicking off their most successful year.

LAND OF RAPE AND HONEY

Artist: Ministry
Written by: Ministry
From the album: *Land of Rape and Honey*
Label: Sire
Produced by: Alain Jourgensen, Paul Barker
Year: 1988
Fashionably inaccessible, industrial-strength white British rage.

LANDSLIDE

Artist: Fleetwood Mac
Written by: Stephanie Nicks
From the album: *Fleetwood Mac*
Label: Reprise
Produced by: Keith Olson, Fleetwood Mac

Year: 1975
Ethereal Nicks at her most vulnerable in this tale of growing up, written for her father. Covered by Olivia Newton-John (MCA, '81), Smashing Pumpkins (Virgin, '84), the Dixie Chicks (Monument, '00).

LANGUAGE OF VIOLENCE

Artist: Disposable Heroes of Hiphoprisy
Written by: Michael Franti, Mark Pistel
From the album: *Hypocrisy Is the Greatest Luxury*
Label: 4TH and Broadway
Year: 1992
Dead Kennedys survivors keep the (lack of) faith.

LAST CARESS

Artist: The Misfits
Written by: Glenn Danzig
From the album: *Beware the Misfits*
Label: Cherry Red
Year: 1979
The dawning of speedcore metal. Covered by Metallica (Elektra, '87).

LAST CHILD

Artist: Aerosmith
Written by: Steven Tyler, Brad Whitford
From the album: *Rocks*
Label: Columbia
Produced by: Jack Douglas, Aerosmith
Year: 1976

LAST DANCE, THE

Artist: Donna Summer
Written by: Paul Jabara
From the album: *Live and More*
Label: Casablanca
Produced by: Giorgio Moroder
Year: 1978
Oscar winner from the movie *Thank God It's Friday*.

LAST GOODBYE

Artist: Jeff Buckley
Written by: Jeff Buckley
From the album: *Grace*
Label: Columbia
Produced by: Andy Wallace
Year: 1994
Second-generation ethereal soul from the son of the late Tim, who invented the genre.

LAST IN LINE, THE

Artist: Dio
Written by: Ronnie Dio, Vivian Campbell
From the album: *Last in Line*
Label: Warner Brothers
Year: 1984
Dio's metal signature: guitar by Vivian Campbell.

LAST KISS

Artist: Wayne Cochran

Written by: Wayne Cochran
Label: Gala
Year: 1961
Classic car (crash) song—classic car: '54 Chevy Impala. Covered by J. Frank Wilson with the Cavaliers (Josie, '64), Pearl Jam (Epic, '98).

LAST MILE, THE

Artist: Nico
Written by: Jimmy Page, Andrew Loog Oldham
Label: Immediate
Produced by: Jimmy Page
Year: 1965
Before Nico fronted the legendary Velvet Underground, before Page invented the legendary Led Zeppelin.

LAST NIGHT

Artist: Mar-Keys
Written by: Chips Moman, Jerry Lee Smith, Charles Axton
From the album: *Back to Back*
Label: Satellite
Produced by: Chips Moman
Year: 1961
Only hit for the instrumental combo that contained Steve Cropper and Duck Dunn, who would go on to form Booker T. and the MGs, the future house band at Stax.

LAST OF THE FAMOUS INTERNATIONAL PLAYBOYS

Artist: Morrissey
Written by: Stephen Morrissey, Stephen Street
From the album: *Bona Drag*
Label: Warner Brothers
Produced by: Clive Langer, Alan Winstanley
Year: 1990
Purportedly written about the gangster brothers, the Crays.

LAST RESORT

Artist: Papa Roach
Written by: Papa Roach
From the album: *Infest*
Produced by: Jay Baumgardner
Label: Dreamworks
Year: 2000
Suggested segue: "Suicide Solution" by Ozzy Osbourne.

LAST SONG

Artist: Edward Bear
Written by: Lawrence Wayne Evoy
From the album: *Edward Bear*
Label: Capitol
Produced by: Gene Martynec
Year: 1973
More of the Winnie the Pooh influence.

LAST THING ON MY MIND, THE

Artist: Tom Paxton
Written by: Tom Paxton
From the album: *Ramblin' Boy*
Label: Elektra
Year: 1964
Tender folk ballad of male (in)sensitivity, covered by Neil Diamond (MCA, '73).

LAST TIME I SAW RICHARD, THE

Artist: Joni Mitchell
Written by: Joni Mitchell
From the album: *Blue*
Label: Reprise
Produced by: Joni Mitchell
Year: 1971
A bittersweet model for the confessional mode.

LAST TIME, THE

Artist: The Rolling Stones
Written by: Mick Jagger, Keith Richards
From the album: *Out of Our Heads*
Label: London
Produced by: Andrew Loog-Oldham
Year: 1965
Their third #1 UK hit, first they'd written. Suggested segue: "Maybe the Last Time" by the Staple Singers, "Bittersweet Symphony" by the Verve.

LAST TRAIN TO CLARKSVILLE

Artist: The Monkees
Written by: Tommy Boyce, Bobby Hart
From the album: *The Monkees*
Label: Colgems
Produced by: Tommy Boyce, Bobby Hart
Year: 1966
First single for the pre-fab Four. The Clarksville in question was an army base in Tennessee in this veiled protest song.

LAST TRIP TO TULSA

Artist: Neil Young
Written by: Neil Young
From the album: *Neil Young*
Label: Reprise
Produced by: Jack Nitzsche
Year: 1969
Extended metaphorical and guitar explorations. Suggested segue: "The History of Utah" by Camper Van Beethoven.

LATE GREAT JOHNNY ACE, THE

Artist: Paul Simon
Written by: Paul Simon
From the album: *The Concert in Central Park*
Label: Warner Brothers
Produced by: Russ Titelman, Paul Simon
Year: 1982
This tribute to a fallen rock and roll hero was sung in Central Park within earshot of where another rock and roll hero (John Lennon) fell; as seen on the home video, during the tune a misguided admirer rushes the stage.

LATE IN THE EVENING

Artist: Paul Simon
Written by: Paul Simon
From the album: *One Trick Pony Soundtrack*
Label: Warner Brothers
Produced by: Phil Ramone
Year: 1980
Best thing to come from Simon's attempt at filmmaking, inaugurating his fourth decade on the charts.

LATELY

Artist: Stevie Wonder
Written by: Stevie Wonder
From the album: *Hotter Than July*
Label: Tamla
Year: 1980
Cover by Jodeci was a #1 R&B/Top 10 crossover (Uptown, '93).

LATHER

Artist: Jefferson Airplane
Written by: Grace Slick
From the album: *Crown of Creation*
Label: RCA
Produced by: Al Schmitt
Year: 1968
Chronicling the end of the innocence, '60s style. Suggested segues: "Kid Charlemagne" by Steely Dan, "Third Week at the Chelsea" by Jefferson Airplane.

LATIFAH'S HAD IT UP TO HERE

Artist: Queen Latifah
Written by: Dana Owens (Queen Latifah), Vincent Brown, Kier Gist, Anthony Criss
From the album: *Nature of a Sista*
Label: Tommy Boy
Produced by: Queen Latifah, Sha-Kim
Year: 1991
She would soon join the Fresh Prince in Hollywood, with a TV show, followed by a movie career.

LAUGH AT ME

Artist: Sonny
Written by: Sonny Bono
From the album: *The Wondrous World of Sonny and Cher*
Label: Atco
Produced by: Sonny Bono
Year: 1965
Originally released before the advent of Sonny and Cher. Sonny would have the last laugh.

LAUGH, LAUGH

Artist: The Beau Brummels
Written by: Ronald C. Elliot
From the album: *Best of the Beau Brummels*
Label: Autumn
Produced by: Sly Stone
Year: 1964
The San Francisco sound when it was not yet a scene.

LAUGHING

Artist: The Guess Who
Written by: Randall Bachman
From the album: *Canned Wheat Packed by the Guess Who*
Label: RCA
Produced by: Jack Richardson
Year: 1969
Rink rock.

LAUGHTER IN THE RAIN

Artist: Neil Sedaka
Written by: Phil Cody, Neil Sedaka
From the album: *Sedaka's Back*
Label: Rocket
Produced by: Robert Appere, Neil Sedaka
Year: 1974
Completing his long comeback with his first #1.

LAVENDER BLUE (DILLY DILLY)

Artist: Sammy Turner
Written by: Eliot Daniel
From the album: *Moods or Mods*
Label: Big Top
Produced by: Jerry Leiber, Mike Stoller
Year: 1959
Popularized by Dinah Shore in '44 in the movie *So Dear to My Heart*.

LAWDY MISS CLAWDY

Artist: Lloyd Price
Written by: Lloyd Price
From the album: *Exciting Lloyd Price*
Label: Specialty
Produced by: Art Rupe
Year: 1952
At the tender age of 17, Price attempted to take the New Orleans soul chalice from Fats Domino, with Fats' band backing him up and Fats on piano, at Cosimo Matassa's studio in New Orleans, resulting in a #1 R&B hit. Covered by Elvis Presley (RCA, '57), the Beatles in the '70 film *Let It Be*.

LAWYERS, GUNS AND MONEY

Artist: Warren Zevon
Written by: Warren Zevon

From the album: *Excitable Boy*
Label: Asylum
Produced by: Jackson Browne, Waddy Wachtel
Year: 1978
L.A. after the Revolution.

LAWYERS IN LOVE

Artist: Jackson Browne
Written by: Jackson Browne
From the album: *Lawyers in Love*
Label: Asylum
Produced by: Jackson Browne, Greg Ladanyi
Year: 1983
The last word in the troubled history of lawyers and rock. Segue: "Taxman" by the Beatles.

LAY DOWN (CANDLES IN THE RAIN)

Artist: Melanie
Written by: Melanie Safka
From the album: *Candles in the Rain*
Label: Buddah
Produced by: Peter Schekeryk
Year: 1970
A flickering anthem from a wilted flower child at the garden of *Woodstock*.

LAY DOWN SALLY

Artist: Eric Clapton
Written by: Eric Clapton, Marcy Levy, George Terry
From the album: *Slowhand*
Label: RSO
Produced by: Glyn Johns
Year: 1977
So mellow it crossed over to the country charts.

LAY DOWN YOUR WEARY TUNE

Artist: Bob Dylan
Written by: Bob Dylan
Label: Columbia
Produced by: Tom Wilson
Year: 1964
Bucolic early Dylan anthem. Covered by the Byrds (Columbia, '65).

LAY YOUR HANDS ON ME

Artist: Thompson Twins
Written by: Tom Bailey, Alannah Currie, Joe Leeway
From the album: *Here's to Future Days*
Label: Arista
Produced by: Alex Sadkin, Nile Rodgers, Tom Bailey
Year: 1985
Music therapy.

LAY, LADY, LAY

Artist: Bob Dylan
Written by: Bob Dylan

From the album: *Nashville Skyline*
Label: Columbia
Produced by: Bob Johnston
Year: 1969
A simple country love song, rejected by the Everly Brothers as being too risque, this was Dylan's biggest single in three years. Dylanologists and Dylanographers despaired of finding hidden meanings. Covered by Ministry (Warner Brothers, '96).

LAYLA

Artist: Derek and the Dominoes
Written by: Eric Clapton, Jim Gordon, Derek and the Dominos
From the album: *Layla*
Label: Atco
Produced by: Tom Dowd
Year: 1970
Clapton's love song to Patti Harrison is the ultimate guitarists' guitar cut, opening the door for the long-jam style of Southern rock when it charted in '71 (featuring Duane Allman's blistering sidemanship). The Allman Brothers would dominate FM playlists in '72, when "Layla" returned to the charts in the wake of Duane's death, this time peaking in the Top 10. Much later, and beside the point, Clapton would record a completely remodeled "Layla" again (Duck, '94).

LE FREAK

Artist: Chic
Written by: Nile Rodgers, Bernard Edwards
From the album: *C'est Chic*
Label: Atlantic
Produced by: Nile Rodgers, Bernard Edwards
Year: 1978
#1 R&B/#1 crossover; at the time the best-selling single in Atlantic Records' venerable history.

LEAD ME ON

Artist: Maxine Nightingale
Written by: Allee Willis, David Lasley
From the album: *Lead Me On*
Label: Windsong
Produced by: Denny Diante
Year: 1979
Her last dance.

LEADER OF THE BAND

Artist: Dan Fogelberg
Written by: Dan Fogelberg
From the album: *The Innocent Age*
Label: Full Moon
Produced by: Dan Fogelberg, Marty Lewis
Year: 1981
Soapy homage to his dad. Suggested segue: "My Father" by Judy Collins.

LEADER OF THE PACK

Artist: The Shangri-Las
Written by: Jeff Barry, Ellie Greenwich, George Morton

From the album: *The Shangri-Las*
Label: Red Bird
Produced by: Shadow Morton
Year: 1964
Her Ma said he was bad, but she knew he was sad. Their only #1, this "He's a Rebel"-meets-"Teen Angel" also contains the classic opening line: "Is she really going out with him?" Long Island's Billy Joel is on piano.

LEAN ON ME

Artist: Bill Withers
Written by: Bill Withers
From the album: *Still Bill*
Label: Sussex
Produced by: Bill Withers
Year: 1972
Gospel inspired #1 R&B/#1 crossover, covered by Club Nouveau (Tommy Boy, '87).

LEARNING HOW TO LOVE YOU

Artist: John Hiatt
Written by: John Hiatt
From the album: *Bring the Family*
Label: A&M
Produced by: John Chelew
Year: 1987
Emotional highpoint of the Hiatt oeuvre.

LEARNING THE BLUES

Artist: Frank Sinatra
Written by: Dolores Vicki Silvers
From the album: *This Is Sinatra!*
Label: Capitol
Year: 1955
His biggest solo hit (along with "Five Minutes More" from '46). Sinatra had two R&B crossovers in the rock and roll era, "High Hopes" in '59 and "That's Life" in '66.

LEARNING TO FLY

Artist: Tom Petty and the Heartbreakers
Written by: Tom Petty, Jeff Lynne
From the album: *Into the Great Wide Open*
Label: MCA
Produced by: Jeff Lynne, Tom Petty, Mike Campbell
Year: 1991
His essential philosophy: coming down is the hardest thing.

LEATHER AND LACE

Artist: Stevie Nicks and Don Henley
Written by: Stephanie Nicks
From the album: *Bella Donna*
Label: Modern
Produced by: Jimmy Iovine
Year: 1981
Covered by Waylon Jennings and Jessi Colter (RCA, '81) for whom it was originally written.

LEAVE ME ALONE (RUBY RED DRESS)

Artist: Helen Reddy
Written by: Linda Laurie
From the album: *Long Hard Climb*
Label: Capitol
Year: 1973
Linda Laurie is the same girl who sang the haunted "Ambrose Part V."

LEAVE MY KITTEN ALONE

Artist: Little Willie John
Written by: Willie John, Titus Turner, J. McDougal
Label: King
Produced by: Henry Glover
Year: 1959
Influential R&B/crossover. Covered by the Final Gear (Pye, '64). Performed by the Beatles early in their career; released (Capital, '96). But the kitten would never replace the dog (or even the monkey) in the realms of rock and roll euphemism.

LEAVE MY WOMAN ALONE

Artist: Ray Charles
Written by: Ray Charles
From the album: *Yes, Indeed*
Label: Atlantic
Year: 1958
B-side of the R&B hit "Lonely Avenue." Covered by the Everly Brothers (Cadence, '58), Dave Edmunds (RCA, '75).

LEAVING LAS VEGAS

Artist: Sheryl Crow
Written by: Sheryl Crow, Bill Bottrell, David Baerwald, Kevin Gilbert, David Ricketts
From the album: *Tuesday Night Music Club*
Label: A&M
Produced by: Bill Bottrell
Year: 1994
Third single from her debut album, based on the songwriting workshop she used to attend.

LEAVING ON A JET PLANE

Artist: Peter, Paul and Mary
Written by: H. J. Deutschendorf Jr. (John Denver)
From the album: *Album 1700*
Label: Warner Brothers
Produced by: Albert Grossman, Milt Okun
Year: 1967
Folk/rock rambling classic became Peter, Paul and Mary's biggest hit in '69. Covered by John Denver (RCA, '69).

LEFT OF CENTER

Artist: Suzanne Vega and Joe Jackson
Written by: Suzanne Vega, Steve Addabbo
From the album: *Pretty in Pink Soundtrack*
Label: A&M
Year: 1986
Featured in the cult film *Pretty in Pink*.

LEGS

Artist: ZZ Top
Written by: Billy Gibbons, Dusty Hill, Frank Beard
From the album: *Eliminator*
Label: Warner Brothers
Produced by: Bill Ham
Year: 1984
One of their two Top 10 singles. Suggested segue: "Hot Legs" by Rod Stewart.

LEMON SONG, THE

Artist: Led Zeppelin
Written by: Jimmy Page, Robert Plant, John Paul Jones, John Bonham
From the album: *Led Zeppelin II*
Label: Atlantic
Produced by: Jimmy Page
Year: 1969
Establishing Plant's horny blues howl that would plague FM radio for the next two decades. Suggested segues: "Killing Floor" by Howling Wolf, "Traveling Riverside Blues" by Robert Johnson.

LEMON TREE

Artist: Peter, Paul and Mary
Written by: Will Holt
From the album: *Peter, Paul and Mary*
Label: Warner Brothers
Produced by: Albert Grossman, Milt Okun
Year: 1961
Putting Greenwich Village on the folk music map with their first single, Peter, Paul and Mary would soon do the same for a visitor from Minnesota named Zimmerman.

LENINGRAD

Artist: Billy Joel
Written by: Billy Joel
From the album: *Storm Front*
Label: Columbia
Produced by: Mick Jones, Billy Joel
Year: 1989
Suggested segues: "Russians" by Sting, "Nikita" by Elton John.

LENNY BRUCE

Artist: Bob Dylan
Written by: Bob Dylan
From the album: *Shot of Love*
Label: Columbia
Produced by: Chuck Plotkin, Bob Dylan
Year: 1981
Song to a soulmate. Suggested segue: "Lenny's Song" by Tim Hardin.

LEOPARD-SKIN PILL-BOX HAT

Artist: Bob Dylan
Written by: Bob Dylan
From the album: *Blonde on Blonde*
Label: Columbia
Produced by: Bob Johnston

Year: 1966
Apt commentary on fickle fashions. Stiffed as a single.

LESS THAN ZERO

Artist: Elvis Costello
Written by: Declan McManus (Elvis Costello)
From the album: *My Aim Is True*
Label: Columbia
Produced by: Nick Lowe
Year: 1977
His first angry young single inspired the 1985 angry young novel by Brett Easton Ellis.

LET HER CRY

Artist: Hootie and the Blowfish
Written by: Mark Bryan, Dean Felber, Darius Rucker, Jim Sonefeld
From the album: *Cracked Rear View*
Label: Atlantic
Produced by: Don Gehman
Year: 1994
The sensitive side of '90s frat rock.

LET HER GO INTO DARKNESS

Artist: Jonathan Richman
Written by: Jonathan Richman
From the album: *There's Something about Mary Soundtrack*
Label: Capitol
Year: 1998
This '95 tune was used to surprisingly poignant purpose in Jonathan's Greek chorus cameo in the film.

LET HER IN

Artist: John Travolta
Written by: Gary Benson
From the album: *John Travolta*
Label: Midland International
Produced by: Bob Reno
Year: 1976
A quirky stab at teen idolhood from his Vinnie Barbarino period.

LET HIM FLY

Artist: Patti Griffin
Written by: Patti Griffin
From the album: *Living with Ghosts*
Label: A&M
Year: 1996
From her acoustic demo debut; later recut for her move to the electric arena.

LET IT BE

Artist: The Beatles
Written by: John Lennon, Paul McCartney
From the album: *Let It Be*
Label: Apple
Produced by: George Martin

Year: 1970
R.I.P.

LET IT BLEED

Artist: The Rolling Stones
Written by: Mick Jagger, Keith Richards
From the album: *Let It Bleed*
Label: London
Produced by: Jimmy Miller
Year: 1969
Perhaps the most eerily-timed event in rock history, the album *Let It Bleed* hitting the charts on December 6TH, the day the Stones played their fateful free concert in Altamont, CA, captured in the documentary *Gimme Shelter*, during which a gun-wielding man was stabbed to death by Hell's Angels security guards, to the tune of "Under My Thumb" and "Sympathy for the Devil."

LET IT BLURT

Artist: Lester Bangs
Written by: Lester Bangs
Label: Live Wire
Year: 1972
The famed rock critic's ultimate revenge won't harm his written legend much. Richard Meltzer wasn't worried.

LET IT OUT (LET IT ALL HANG OUT)

Artist: Hombres
Written by: B. B. Cunningham, Jerry Lee Masters, Gary Wayne McEwen, Johnny Will Hunter
From the album: *Let It Out (Let It All Hang Out)*
Label: Verve/Forecast
Produced by: Huey Meaux
Year: 1967
Loopy Southern rock one-shot with a nasal twang.

LET IT RAIN

Artist: Eric Clapton
Written by: Richard Martin
From the album: *Eric Clapton*
Label: Atco
Produced by: Delaney Bramlett
Year: 1970

LET IT ROCK

Artist: Chuck Berry
Written by: Chuck Berry
From the album: *Rockin' at the Hops*
Label: Chess
Produced by: Leonard Chess, Phil Chess
Year: 1960
B-side of "Too Pooped to Pop."

LET IT WHIP

Artist: The Dazz Band
Written by: Reggie Andrews, Leon Chancler
From the album: *Keep It Live*
Label: Motown
Produced by: Reggie Andrews

Year: 1982
Disco/jazz concoction is a #1 R&B/Top 10 crossover.

LET ME BE

Artist: The Turtles
Written by: P. F. Sloan
From the album: *It Ain't Me Babe*
Label: White Whale
Produced by: Lee Lasseff, Ted Feigin
Year: 1965
In the disaffected mode of "It Ain't Me Babe," written by L.A.'s most mysterious songwriter (aside from Phil Spector, or maybe Jack Nitzsche or Van Dyke Parks, or possibly Kim Fowley; Brian Wilson was pretty mysterious; Randy Newman was around by then, too, but he wasn't mysterious, just cantankerous).

LET ME BE THERE

Artist: Olivia Newton-John
Written by: John Rostill
From the album: *Let Me Be There*
Label: Mercury
Produced by: John Farrar
Year: 1973
Coy country folk/pop from Australia. Olivia's first single was a Top 10 country/Top 10 crossover. Written by the Shadows former bass player.

(LET ME BE YOUR) TEDDY BEAR

Artist: Elvis Presley
Written by: Bernie Lowe, Kal Mann
From the album: *Loving You*
Label: RCA
Produced by: Steve Sholes
Year: 1957
Philadelphia dance rock songwriters get a leg up on their career with Elvis' second #1 of the year, a #1 country/#1 crossover as well, from the movie *Loving You*.

LET ME DIE IN MY FOOTSTEPS

Artist: Bob Dylan
Written by: Bob Dylan
From the album: *The Freewheelin' Bob Dylan*
Label: Columbia
Produced by: John Hammond
Year: 1963
Anti-bomb-shelter song was contained on early pressings of this album, before being deleted. It can be found, however, on the great bootleg album *The Freewheelin' Bob Dylan Outtakes* (Vigo, '93) which also contains twenty other tunes, including Bob's version of the Big Boy Crudup classic "That's All Right Mama," which has since become celebrated as Elvis's first rock and roll single.

LET ME IN

Artist: The Sensations
Written by: Yvonne Baker

From the album: *Let Me In*
Label: Argo
Produced by: Kae Williams
Year: 1962
A morality tale of winning and losing in the great party era of the early '60s.

LET ME RIDE

Artist: Dr. Dre
Written by: Andre Young (Dr. Dre), Calvin Broadus (Snoop Doggy Dogg)
From the album: *The Chronic*
Label: Death Row
Produced by: Dr. Dre
Year: 1993
Features George Clinton and samples his "Mothership Connection (Star Child)."

LET MY LOVE OPEN THE DOOR

Artist: Pete Townshend
Written by: Pete Townshend
From the album: *Empty Glass*
Label: Atco
Produced by: Chris Thomas
Year: 1980
His first solo album since 1972 finds the lead Who in a mood of rare tranquility.

LET NO MAN STEAL YOUR THYME

Artist: Pentangle
Written by: Terrence Cox, Jacqueline Jackson, Bert Jansch, John Renbourn, Danny Thompson
From the album: *The Pentangle*
Label: Reprise
Year: 1968
Influential acoustic folk lament. Fingerpickers from Paul Simon to Richard Thompson perked up.

LET THE BEAT HIT 'EM

Artist: Lisa Lisa and Cult Jam
Written by: Rob Clivilles, David Cole, Alan Friedman, Duran Ramos
From the album: *Straight outa Hell's Kitchen*
Label: Columbia
Produced by: Rob Clivilles
Year: 1991
The making of a dance-hall diva from Harlem, her second #1 R&B/#1 crossover.

LET THE FOUR WINDS BLOW

Artist: Roy Brown
Written by: Dave Bartholomew, Fats Domino
Label: Imperial
Produced by: Dave Bartholomew
Year: 1957
First and only Top 40 hit by the legendary soul crooner. Covered by Fats Domino, who had an R&B hit with it (Imperial, '61).

LET THE GOOD TIMES ROLL

Artist: Louis Jordan and His Tympani Five
Written by: Louis Jordan, Claude Demetrius
Label: Decca
Produced by: Milt Gabler
Year: 1946
Pioneering jump blues track, covered by Ray Charles (Atlantic, '60). As far back as '46, Jordan had the attitude and the spirit of rock and roll, as well as the wit, the wisdom, the hipster's jive, and the willingness to commercialize. Some thirty years down the line, his material would beat Leiber & Stoller's to the Broadway stage in *Five Guys Named Moe*.

LET THE GOOD TIMES ROLL

Artist: Shirley and Lee
Written by: Lee Leonard
From the album: *Shirley and Lee*
Label: Aladdin
Year: 1956
Ultimate New Orleans party classic; Top 10 R&B/Top 20 crossover.

LET THE LITTLE GIRL DANCE

Artist: Billy Bland
Written by: Henry Glover, Carl Spencer
Label: Old Town
Produced by: Henry Glover
Year: 1960
For wallflowers everywhere.

LET THE MUSIC PLAY

Artist: Shannon
Written by: Chris Barbosa, Ed Chisolm
From the album: *Let the Music Play*
Label: Mirage
Produced by: Loggett, Barbosa
Year: 1984
#1 R&B/Top 10 crossover dance one-shot.

LET THE RIVER RUN

Artist: Carly Simon
Written by: Carly Simon
From the album: *Working Girl Soundtrack*
Label: Arista
Produced by: Carly Simon, Rob Mounsey
Year: 1989
Oscar-winning theme from the Mike Nichols's film *Working Girl*.

LET THEM TALK

Artist: Little Willie John
Written by: Sonny Thompson, Henry Glover
Label: King
Produced by: Henry Glover
Year: 1959
Tortured soul from the original king of pain.

LET THERE BE DRUMS

Artist: Sandy Nelson
Written by: Sandy Nelson, Richard Podolor
From the album: *Let There Be Drums*
Label: Imperial
Year: 1959
Suggested segues: "Topsy, Part Two" by Cozy Cole, "In a Gadda Da Vida" by Iron Butterfly, "The Crunge" by Led Zeppelin, "Badge" by Cream.

LET YOUR HAIR DOWN

Artist: The Temptations
Written by: Norman Whitfield
From the album: *1990*
Label: Gordy
Produced by: Norman Whitfield
Year: 1973
Their twelfth of fourteen #1 R&B hits.

LET 'EM IN

Artist: Paul McCartney and Wings
Written by: Paul McCartney
From the album: *Wings at the Speed of Sound*
Label: Capitol
Produced by: Paul McCartney
Year: 1976
Recovering from the previous "Silly Love Songs."

LET'S DANCE

Artist: David Bowie
Written by: David Bowie
From the album: *Let's Dance*
Label: EMI-America
Produced by: Nile Rodgers, David Bowie
Year: 1983
#1 US/#1 UK smash introduced the world outside of Austin, Texas, to Stevie Ray Vaughan on guitar.

LET'S DANCE

Artist: Chris Montez
Written by: Jim Lee
From the album: *Let's Dance and Have Some Kinda Fun*
Label: Monogram
Produced by: Jimmy Joe Lee
Year: 1962
Frat rock lite.

LET'S DO IT AGAIN

Artist: The Staple Singers
Written by: Curtis Mayfield
From the album: *Let's Do It Again Soundtrack*
Label: Curtom
Produced by: Curtis Mayfield
Year: 1975
A long way from their gospel roots, this titilating title song from the blaxploitation film was a #1 R&B/#1 crossover.

LET'S GET IT ON

Artist: Marvin Gaye
Written by: Marvin Gaye, Edward Townshend
From the album: *Let's Get It On*
Label: Tamla
Produced by: Marvin Gaye, Ed Townshend
Year: 1973
Leaving the barricades and going back to the bedroom, Gaye scores one of his most enduring hits; #1 R&B/#1 crossover.

LET'S GET SERIOUS

Artist: Jermaine Jackson
Written by: Stevie Wonder, Lee Garrett
From the album: *Let's Get Serious*
Label: Motown
Produced by: Stevie Wonder
Year: 1980
Jackson brother's biggest hit; #1 R&B/Top 10 crossover.

LET'S GET TOGETHER

Artist: Hayley Mills
Written by: Richard Sherman, Robert Sherman
From the album: *The Parent Trap Soundtrack*
Label: Buena Vista
Produced by: Tutti Camarata
Year: 1962
From the Maureen O'Hara movie *The Parent Trap*, by the same team that created hits for Annette Funicello.

LET'S GO

Artist: The Cars
Written by: Ric Ocasek
From the album: *Candy-O*
Label: Elektra
Produced by: Roy Thomas Baker
Year: 1979
Rockabilly redux shakes hands with studio tech.

LET'S GO CRAZY

Artist: Prince
Written by: Prince Rogers Nelson
From the album: *Purple Rain Soundtrack*
Label: Warner Brothers
Produced by: Prince
Year: 1984
His second #1 R&B/#1 crossover, from the autobiographical movie.

LET'S GO GET STONED

Artist: Ray Charles
Written by: Nick Ashford, Valerie Simpson, Josie Armstead
From the album: *Let's Go Get Stoned*
Label: ABC
Produced by: Joe Adams
Year: 1966
Ray's seventh and last #1 R&B hit.

LET'S GO, LET'S GO, LET'S GO

Artist: The Midnighters
Written by: Hank Ballard

From the album: *Hank Ballard's Biggest Hits*
Label: King
Year: 1960
Fanning the flames of the dance craze he instigated with "The Twist," Ballard gets his biggest hit, #1 R&B/Top 10 crossover.

LET'S GO TO BED

Artist: The Cure
Written by: Robert Smith, Laurence Tolhurst
From the album: *The Walk*
Label: Sire
Produced by: Robert Smith, Dave Allen
Year: 1983
The notoriously dour and Byronic Smith's idea of a good-time single.

LET'S GO TRIPPING

Artist: Dick Dale
Written by: Dick Dale
From the album: *Surfer's Choice*
Label: Deltone
Produced by: Jim Monsour
Year: 1961
Defining the rippling sound of the surf guitar. Covered by the Beach Boys (Capitol, '63).

LET'S GROOVE

Artist: Earth, Wind & Fire
Written by: Maurice White, Wayne Vaughn, Wanda Vaughn
From the album: *Raise!*
Label: Arc/Columbia
Produced by: Maurice White
Year: 1981
#1 R&B/Top 10 crossover is a world dance groove supreme.

LET'S HANG ON (TO WHAT WE'VE GOT)

Artist: The Four Seasons
Written by: Bob Crewe, Sandy Linzer, Denny Randell
From the album: *Four Seasons Gold Vault of Hits*
Label: Philips
Produced by: Bob Crewe
Year: 1965
Last gasp of Italian soul, as the mass audience drifted toward folk/rock.

LET'S HAVE A PARTY

Artist: Wanda Jackson
Written by: Cliff Friend
From the album: *Wanda Jackson*
Label: Capitol
Produced by: Ken Nelson
Year: 1960
Some say Paul McCartney learned his inspired whoops from Little Richard. I say it was this Wanda Jackson record. Introduced by Elvis Presley in the movie *Loving You* (RCA, '57).

LET'S HAVE A WAR

Artist: Fear
Written by: Lee Ving, Philo Cramer
From the album: *The Record*
Label: Slash
Year: 1982
L.A. punks on the metaphorical edge.

LET'S HEAR IT FOR THE BOY

Artist: Deniece Williams
Written by: Dean Pitchford, Tom Snow
From the album: *Footloose Soundtrack*
Label: Columbia
Produced by: George Duke
Year: 1984
#1 R&B/#1 celluloid crossover. The boy in question was Kevin Bacon.

LET'S LIVE FOR TODAY

Artist: Grass Roots
Written by: Michael Julien, Mogol (Guilio Rapetti), Shel Shapiro, Mike Shepstone
From the album: *Let's Live for Today*
Label: Dunhill
Produced by: Steve Barri
Year: 1967
Based on the Italian hit, "Piangi Con Mi," a Top 10 folk/rocker squarely in tune with the zeitgeist.

LET'S SPEND THE NIGHT TOGETHER

Artist: The Rolling Stones
Written by: Mick Jagger, Keith Richards
From the album: *Between the Buttons*
Label: London
Produced by: Andrew Loog-Oldham
Year: 1967
B-side of "Ruby Tuesday" was censored on *The Ed Sullivan Show*. Jagger sneered the alternate lyric, "Let's spend some time together." Covered by David Bowie (RCA, '73).

LET'S STAY TOGETHER

Artist: Al Green
Written by: Al Green, Willie Mitchell, Al Jackson
From the album: *Let's Stay Together*
Label: Hi
Produced by: Willie Mitchell
Year: 1972
The smoothest of Green's smooth soul sound that owned '72, starting out with this #1 R&B/#1 crossover. Covered by Isaac Hayes (Enterprise, '72), Tina Turner (Capitol, '83).

LET'S STRAIGHTEN IT OUT

Artist: Latimore
Written by: Benny Latimore
From the album: *More More More of Benny Latimore*
Label: Glades
Produced by: Steve Alaimo
Year: 1974

Moody and blues-edged #1 R&B/Top 40 crossover by the T. K. sideman. Robert Cray was listening.

LET'S TALK ABOUT GIRLS

Artist: Chocolate Watchband
Written by: M. Freiser
From the album: *No Way Out*
Label: Tower
Produced by: Ed Cobb
Year: 1966
Garage band nugget produced by a Strawberry Alarm Clock alum.

LET'S TALK ABOUT SEX

Artist: Salt-n-Pepa
Written by: Fingerprints
From the album: *Blacks' Magic*
Label: Next Plateau
Produced by: Herby Luv Bug and the Invincibles
Year: 1991
Ushering in the era of plain talk, on record and daytime TV.

LET'S TWIST AGAIN

Artist: Chubby Checker
Written by: Kal Mann, Dave Appell
From the album: *Let's Twist Again*
Label: Parkway
Produced by: Kal Mann
Year: 1961
Keeping the Twist (and not incidentally, his career) alive.

LET'S WAIT AWHILE

Artist: Janet Jackson
Written by: James Harris III, Terry Lewis, Janet Jackson, Reginald Andrews
From the album: *Control*
Label: A&M
Produced by: Jimmy Jam, Terry Lewis, Janet Jackson
Year: 1986
On her third album, Michael's younger sister breaks into the dance arena on a cautionary note with a #1 R&B/Top 10 crossover.

LET'S WORK TOGETHER (PART I)

Artist: Wilbert Harrison
Written by: Wilbert Harrison
From the album: *Let's Work Together*
Label: Sue
Produced by: Juggy Murray
Year: 1969
A decade after "Kansas City," Harrison returns to the charts. Covered by Canned Heat (Liberty, '70).

LETTER FULL OF TEARS

Artist: Gladys Knight & the Pips
Written by: Don Covay

Label: Fury
Produced by: Marshall Sehorn, Bobby Robinson
Year: 1962
Gladys's first big hit with her cousins, the Pips; Top 10 R&B/Top 20 crossover.

LETTER, THE

Artist: The Box Tops
Written by: Wayne Carson Thompson
From the album: *The Box Tops: "The Letter"/"Neon Rainbow"*
Label: Mala
Produced by: Dan Penn
Year: 1967
One of the more perfect soaring singles of '67. Covered by Joe Cocker (A&M, '70).

LETTER, THE

Artist: Don and Dewey
Written by: Don Harris, Dewey Terry
Label: Specialty
Produced by: Sonny Bono
Year: 1958
Just as Don and Dewey gave Sonny Bono his first big break with "Koko Joe," Sonny returned the favor when Sonny and Cher (aka Caesar and Cleo) covered this as their first single (Vault, '65). Unfortunately, it stiffed.

LETTER, THE

Artist: The Medallions
Written by: Vernon Green
Label: DooTone
Year: 1954
Launching Dootsie Williams' famous L.A. label with a local doo-wop favorite. It is in this tune that the phrase "the pompatus of love," or something along those lines, came into being.

LEVON

Artist: Elton John
Written by: Elton John, Bernie Taupin
From the album: *Madman Across the Water*
Label: Uni
Produced by: Gus Dudgeon
Year: 1971
Listening to a lot of Leon Russell and the Band.

LIAR

Artist: The Rollins Band
Written by: Henry Rollins
From the album: *Weight*
Label: Imago
Produced by: Theo Van Ronk
Year: 1994
Poet Henry gets top billing on this bravura piece of heavy metal as performance art.

LIAR, LIAR

Artist: The Castaways
Written by: James J. Donna
Label: Soma

Year: 1965
Garage gem, covered by Debbie Harry in *Married to the Mob* (Reprise, '88).

LICK IT UP

Artist: Kiss
Written by: Stanley Eisen (Paul Stanley), Vinnie Vincent
From the album: *Lick It Up*
Label: Mercury
Produced by: Gene Simmons, M. Jackson
Year: 1983
Kiss unmasked … as middling middle-aged metal magnates.

LIDO SHUFFLE

Artist: Boz Scaggs
Written by: David Paich, William Scaggs
From the album: *Silk Degrees*
Label: Columbia
Produced by: Joe Wissert
Year: 1976
His defining groove.

LIES (ARE BREAKIN' MY HEART)

Artist: The Knickerbockers
Written by: Buddy Randell, Beau Charles
From the album: *Lies Are Breakin' My Heart*
Label: Challenge
Produced by: Jerry Fuller
Year: 1965
Angst-ridden garage band standard.

LIFE DURING WARTIME

Artist: Talking Heads
Written by: David Byrne
From the album: *Fear of Music*
Label: Sire
Produced by: Brian Eno
Year: 1979
The nervous cousins of the bowery punk scene explain why the disco era is over (in French). Featured in the movie *Times Square*.

LIFE IN A NORTHERN TOWN

Artist: The Dream Academy
Written by: Nick Laird-Clowes, Gilbert Gabriel
From the album: *The Dream Academy*
Label: Warner Brothers
Produced by: Nick Laird-Clowes, David Gilmour, George Nicholson
Year: 1985
Lulling folk/rock pastorale. Suggested segue: "Waterloo Sunset" by the Kinks.

LIFE IN THE FAST LANE

Artist: Eagles
Written by: Don Henley, Glenn Frey, Joe Walsh
From the album: *Hotel California*

Label: Asylum
Produced by: Bill Szymczyk
Year: 1977
Crafty ode to their chosen lifestyle.

LIFE IS A CARNIVAL

Artist: The Band
Written by: Robbie Robertson, Levon Helm, Rick Danko
From the album: *Cahoots*
Label: Capitol
Produced by: The Band
Year: 1971
Prelude to the '80 Jodie Foster movie *Carny*, which Robertson starred in and scored.

LIFE IS A HIGHWAY

Artist: Tom Cochrane
Written by: Tom Cochrane
From the album: *Mad Mad World*
Label: Capitol
Produced by: Joe Hardy, Tom Cochrane
Year: 1992
Watered-down Springsteenian traveling song from the former leader of Red Rider.

LIFE IS A ROCK (BUT THE RADIO ROLLED ME)

Artist: Reunion
Written by: Norman Dolph, Paul DiFranco
Label: RCA
Year: 1974
Twenty years of Top 40 history in two minutes, sung by a man who'd participated in about 19.2% of it, the golden throated Joey Levine (The Voice of Bubblegum). Covered by Tracy Ullman (MCA, '84).

LIFE IS BUT A DREAM

Artist: The Harptones
Written by: Raoul Cita, Hy Weiss
Label: Paradise
Produced by: Raoul Cita
Year: 1954
Sh'boom, sh'boom; the ultimate in doo-wop escapism.

LIFE OF ILLUSION

Artist: Joe Walsh
Written by: Joe Walsh, Kenny Passarelli
From the album: *There Goes the Neighborhood*
Label: Asylum
Produced by: Joe Walsh, George Perry
Year: 1981
The sometime-Eagles guitarist sums it all up for you.

LIFE'LL KILL YA

Artist: Warren Zevon
Written by: Warren Zevon
From the album: *Life'll Kill Ya*

Produced by: Paul Kolderie, Sean Slade
Label: Artemis
Year: 2000
His parting epitaph, three years early.

LIFE'S BEEN GOOD

Artist: Joe Walsh
Written by: Joe Walsh
From the album: *But Seriously, folks*
Label: Asylum
Produced by: Bill Szymczyk
Year: 1978
The best answer to "So You Wanna Be a Rock and Roll Star" by the Byrds.

LIGHT MY FIRE

Artist: The Doors
Written by: Jim Morrison, Robbie Krieger, John Densmore, Ray Manzarek
From the album: *The Doors*
Label: Elektra
Produced by: Paul Rothchild
Year: 1967
Igniting the Summer of Love with Manzarek's B-3 pyrotechnics, Morrison chewing the scenery. Covered by Jose Feliciano (RCA, '68).

LIGHT OF DAY

Artist: The Barbusters
Written by: Bruce Springsteen
From the album: *Light of Day Soundtrack*
Label: Blackheart
Produced by: Jimmy Iovine
Year: 1987
A rock band grows in Cleveland, courtesy of a New Jersey bard, Bruce Springsteen, and a Philadelphia babe, Joan Jett. Michael J. Fox plays the rocker, but he was better in *Back to the Future*.

LIGHTNIN' STRIKES

Artist: Lou Christie
Written by: Twyla Herbert, Lou Sacco (Lou Christie)
From the album: *Lightnin' Strikes*
Label: MGM
Produced by: Charlie Calello
Year: 1966
The male libido as an uncontrollable force of nature. Michael Bolton was listening.

LIGHTNING CRASHES

Artist: Live
Written by: Edward Kowalcyzk, Patrick Dahlheimer, Chad Gracey, Chad Taylor
From the album: *Throwing Copper*
Label: Radioactive/MCA
Produced by: Jerry Harrison
Year: 1994
Hendrixian echoes.

LIGHTS OUT

Artist: Jerry Byrne
Written by: Seth David, Mack Rebennack
Label: Specialty
Produced by: Harold Battiste
Year: 1958
New Orleans rockabilly romp, composed by the once and future Dr. John.

LIGHTS OUT

Artist: UFO
Written by: Michael Schenker, Phil Mogg, Pete Way, Andy Parker
From the album: *Lights Out*
Label: Chrysalis
Produced by: Ron Nevison
Year: 1977
Metal guitar blitz by Schenker.

(LIGHTS WENT OUT IN, THE) MASSACHUSETTS

Artist: Bee Gees
Written by: Barry Gibb, Robin Gibb, Maurice Gibb
From the album: *Horizontal*
Label: Atco
Produced by: Robert Stigwood
Year: 1967
This anguished folkie lament introduced the group with a #1 UK hit.

LIKE A HURRICANE

Artist: Neil Young
Written by: Neil Young
From the album: *American Stars and Bars*
Label: Reprise
Produced by: David Briggs, Tim Mulligan
Year: 1977
Hurricane Neil wipes out Santa Monica.

LIKE A PRAYER

Artist: Madonna
Written by: Patrick Leonard, Madonna Ciccone
From the album: *Like a Prayer*
Label: Sire
Produced by: Patrick Leonard, Madonna Ciccone
Year: 1989
Atoning for previous sins of vanity and taste; her 7TH #1 hit.

LIKE A ROCK

Artist: Bob Seger
Written by: Bob Seger
From the album: *Like a Rock*
Label: Capitol
Produced by: Punch Andrews, Bob Seger, David Cole
Year: 1986
Chevy Metal.

LIKE A ROLLING STONE

Artist: Bob Dylan
Written by: Bob Dylan
From the album: *Highway 61 Revisited*
Label: Columbia
Produced by: Tom Wilson
Year: 1965
Verbose and incandescent, Dylan skewers every frugging go-go girl on *Hullabaloo* and *Shindig*, and with the help of Al Kooper's thrilling organ part, establishes the musical direction home for the remainder of the '60s. Not surprisingly, *Rolling Stone* magazine named it the best song ever. Covered, at long last, by the Rolling Stones (Virgin, '95), but it was a letdown.

LIKE A VIRGIN

Artist: Madonna
Written by: Billy Steinberg, Tom Kelly
From the album: *Like a Virgin*
Label: Sire
Produced by: Nile Rodgers
Year: 1984
First use of the word "virgin" in a rock song since Laura Nyro's "The Confession" earns Madonna her first #1 and only Top 10 R&B/crossover. Steinberg and Kelly would go on to write "Eternal Flame" for Susannah Hoffs of the Bangles. Now there was virgin-like.

LIKE STRANGERS

Artist: The Everly Brothers
Written by: Felice Bryant, Boudleaux Bryant
From the album: *The Fabulous Style of the Everly Brothers*
Label: Cadence
Produced by: Archie Bleyer
Year: 1960
Mining the Cadence catalogue for an appropriate farewell to the Bryants' best clients who'd just signed with Warner Brothers.

LIKE THE WEATHER

Artist: 10,000 Maniacs
Written by: Natalie Merchant
From the album: *In My Tribe*
Label: Elektra
Produced by: Peter Asher
Year: 1987
Breakthrough showcase for Natalie Merchant's eloquently tangled locutions is a modern essay on the old ennui.

LI'L RED RIDING HOOD

Artist: Sam the Sham and the Pharaohs
Written by: Ronald Blackwell
From the album: *Li'l Red Riding Hood*
Label: MGM
Produced by: Stan Kessler
Year: 1966
Scaring all the little girls.

LIMBO ROCK

Artist: The Champs
Written by: Kal Mann (Jon Sheldon), William Strange
Label: Challenge

Year: 1962
Covered by Chubby Checker (Parkway, '62); how low could he go in his battles with Hank Ballard to remain Dance King of the early '60s?

LIMELIGHT

Artist: Rush
Written by: Gary Lee Weinrib (Geddy Lee), Alex Zivojinovich (Alex Lifeson), Neil Peart
From the album: *Moving Pictures*
Label: Mercury
Produced by: Terry Brown, Rush
Year: 1981
The verbose drummer Peart at his most lucid.

LING TING TONG

Artist: The Five Keys
Written by: Mable Godwin
Label: Capitol
Year: 1954
Novelty R&B, covered by the Charms (DeLuxe, '55).

LINGER

Artist: The Cranberries
Written by: Noel Hogan, Dolores O'Riordan
From the album: *Everybody Else Is Doing It, So Why Can't We?*
Label: Island
Produced by: Stephen Street
Year: 1993
In the neo girl-group harmony groove of the '90s, from Ireland.

LIPSTICK ON YOUR COLLAR

Artist: Connie Francis
Written by: Edna Lewis, George Goehring
From the album: *Connie's Greatest Hits*
Label: MGM
Year: 1959
A classic cheating song.

LIPSTICK TRACES (ON A CIGARETTE)

Artist: Bennie Spellman
Written by: Allen Toussaint (Naomi Neville)
Label: Minit
Produced by: Allen Toussaint
Year: 1962
New Orleans soul. Cover by the O'Jays (Imperial, '65) was their first R&B hit.

LIPSTICK VOGUE

Artist: Elvis Costello and the Attractions
Written by: Declan McManus (Elvis Costello)
From the album: *This Year's Model*
Label: Columbia
Produced by: Nick Lowe
Year: 1978
Among the angriest of his early oeuvre.

LISTEN

Artist: Collective Soul
Written by: Ed Roland
From the album: *Disciplined Breakdown*
Label: Atlantic
Year: 1997

LISTEN PEOPLE

Artist: Herman's Hermits
Written by: Graham Gouldman
From the album: *Best of Herman's Hermits (Vol. II)*
Label: MGM
Produced by: Mickie Most
Year: 1966
From the film *When the Boys Meet the Girls*. Gouldman would move on to the Yardbirds and 10 c.c., Herman to hosting oldies nostalgia shows on TV.

LISTEN TO HER HEART

Artist: Tom Petty and the Heartbreakers
Written by: Tom Petty
From the album: *You're Gonna Get It*
Label: Shelter
Produced by: Tom Petty
Year: 1977
Venturing into Crickets territory.

LISTEN TO THE MUSIC

Artist: The Doobie Brothers
Written by: Tom Johnston
From the album: *Talouse Street*
Label: Warner Brothers
Produced by: Ted Templeman
Year: 1972
The advent of Southern folk/rock, by way of San Jose, CA.

LISTEN TO WHAT THE MAN SAID

Artist: Paul McCartney and Wings
Written by: Paul McCartney, Linda McCartney
From the album: *Venus and Mars Rock Show*
Label: Capitol
Produced by: Paul McCartney
Year: 1975
Fourth out of eight #1 hits for Paul's new band. His old band had twenty.

LISTEN TO YOUR HEART

Artist: Roxette
Written by: Per Gessle
From the album: *Look Sharp!*
Label: EMI
Produced by: Clarence Ofwerman
Year: 1989
Second #1 from the album.

LISTENING TO THE LIONS

Artist: Van Morrison
Written by: Van Morrison
From the album: *St. Dominic's Preview*
Label: Warner Brothers
Produced by: Van Morrison
Year: 1972
Confessional rock at its best.

LIT UP

Artist: Buckcherry
Written by: Buckcherry, Joshua Todd
From the album: *Buckcherry*
Label: Dreamworks
Year: 1999

LITHIUM

Artist: Nirvana
Written by: Nirvana
From the album: *Nevermind*
Label: DGC
Produced by: Butch Vig
Year: 1991
Trying to ease the pain of local alt/rock legendhood.

LITTLE BIT ME, A LITTLE BIT YOU, A

Artist: The Monkees
Written by: Neil Diamond
From the album: *Greatest Hits*
Label: Colgems
Produced by: Jeff Barry
Year: 1967
And the littlest bit Monkees, all of whom but Davy Jones boycotted this session.

LITTLE BIT O' SOUL

Artist: The Music Explosion
Written by: John Carter, Ken Lewis Bubble Punk.
From the album: *Little Bit o' Soul*
Label: Laurie
Produced by: Jerry Kazenetz, Jeff Katz
Year: 1965
Prefacing bubble gum with bubble/punk.

LITTLE BIT OF SOAP, A

Artist: The Jarmels
Written by: Bert Berns (Bert Russell)
Label: Laurie
Produced by: Bert Burns
Year: 1961
The essence of early '60s uptown R&B.

LITTLE BITTY PRETTY ONE

Artist: Bobby Day
Written by: Robert Byrd
Label: Class
Year: 1957
First single, before "Rockin' Robin" made him a one-hit wonder. Covered by Thurston Harris (Aladdin, '57).

LITTLE BOXES

Artist: Pete Seeger
Written by: Malvina Reynolds

From the album: *We Shall Overcome*
Label: Columbia
Produced by: John Hammond
Year: 1964
Spiritual father of the folk/rock era, Pete Seeger's only chart appearance of the rock and roll era comes with this one minute Malvina Reynolds anti-suburbia gem. Suggested segues: "Big Yellow Taxi" by Joni Mitchell, "Pink Houses" by John (Cougar) Mellencamp.

LITTLE BY LITTLE

Artist: Robert Plant
Written by: Jezz Woodruffe, Robert Plant
From the album: *Shaken 'N' Stirred*
Label: Es Paranza
Produced by: Tim Palmer
Year: 1985
Chilly echoes of Led Zep past.

LITTLE CHILDREN

Artist: Billy J. Kramer and the Dakotas
Written by: J. Leslie McFarland, Mort Shuman
From the album: *Little Children*
Label: Imperial
Produced by: George Martin
Year: 1964
Their biggest hit; #1 UK/#6 US.

LITTLE DARLIN'

Artist: The Gladiolas
Written by: Maurice Williams
Label: Excello
Year: 1957
Classic early rocker by the author of "Stay." Covered by the Diamonds (Mercury, '57) and Dustin Hoffman and Warren Beatty in the film *Ishtar* (Capitol, '87).

LITTLE DIANE

Artist: Dion
Written by: Dion DiMucci
From the album: *Lovers Who Wander*
Label: Laurie
Produced by: Gene Schwartz
Year: 1962
Noted for its unidentified kazoo solo.

LITTLE EGYPT

Artist: The Coasters
Written by: Jerry Leiber, Mike Stoller
From the album: *Coast Along with the Coasters*
Label: Atco
Produced by: Jerry Leiber, Mike Stoller
Year: 1961
The saga of a fan dancer who goes straight was borrowed from the Coasters by Elvis Presley for use in *Roustabout* (1964), his sixteenth movie, costarring Barbara Stanwyck.

LITTLE GAMES

Artist: The Yardbirds
Written by: Harold Spiro, Phil Wainman
From the album: *Little Games*
Label: Epic
Produced by: Mickie Most
Year: 1967

LITTLE GIRL

Artist: The Syndicate of Sound
Written by: Don Baskin, Bob Gonzalez
From the album: *Little Girl*
Label: Bell
Produced by: Gary Thompson
Year: 1966
Frat house anthem with an edge defines the brief '60s transition from beer to weed. Covered by the Dead Boys (Sire, '77).

LITTLE GIRL OF MINE

Artist: The Cleftones
Written by: George Goldner, Herbert Cox
From the album: *Teenage Party*
Label: Gee
Produced by: George Goldner
Year: 1956
First R&B hit for the great NYC group.

LITTLE GREEN APPLES

Artist: O. C. Smith
Written by: Bobby Russell
From the album: *Hickory Holler Revisited*
Label: Columbia
Produced by: Jerry Fuller
Year: 1968
#2 R&B/#2 crossover was so down-homey it should have hit the country charts as well. Instead, Roger Miller's Top 10 country rendition (Smash, '68) prevented history from being made.

LITTLE GUITARS

Artist: Van Halen
Written by: Eddie Van Halen, Alex Van Halen, Michael Anthony, David Lee Roth
From the album: *Diver Down*
Label: Warner Brothers
Produced by: Ted Templeman
Year: 1982
For chops devotees and instrument manufacturers only.

LITTLE HONDA

Artist: The Hondells
Written by: Brian Wilson
From the album: *Go Little Honda*
Label: Mercury
Year: 1964
Surfing the asphalts—introducing the Honda motorbike.

LITTLE IS ENOUGH, A

Artist: Pete Townshend
Written by: Pete Townshend
From the album: *Empty Glass*
Label: Atco
Produced by: Chris Thomas
Year: 1980
No longer "fearing maturity," Townshend sees even an empty glass as half full.

LITTLE JEANNIE

Artist: Elton John
Written by: Gary Osborne, Elton John
From the album: *21 at 33*
Label: MCA
Produced by: Clive Franks, Elton John
Year: 1980
Elton at midlife crisis.

LITTLE JOHNNY JEWEL

Artist: Television
Written by: Tom Miller (Tom Verlaine), Richard Lloyd
From the album: *Great New York Singles*
Label: ROIR
Produced by: Television
Year: 1974
Tune often cited as influential in starting the Bowery punk scene in New York, along with Patti Smith's "Piss Factory." Covered by Siouxsie and the Banshees (Geffen, '87).

LITTLE LATIN LUPE LU

Artist: The Righteous Brothers
Written by: Bill Medley
From the album: *Right Now*
Label: Moonglow
Produced by: Bill Medley
Year: 1963
First hit for the blue-eyed soul brothers. Covered by an early acolyte, Mitch Ryder and Detroit Wheels (New Voice, '66).

LITTLE LESS CONVERSATION, A

Artist: Elvis Presley
Written by: Mac Davis, Billy Strange
From the album: *Live a Little, Love a Little* Soundtrack
Label: RCA
Year: 1968
Revived in the new millennium for a generation of Elvis fans not even born when he embarrassed himself in this movie.

LITTLE LIES

Artist: Fleetwood Mac
Written by: Christine McVie, Eddy Quintela
From the album: *Tango in the Night*
Label: Warner Brothers
Produced by: Richard Dashut, Lindsay Buckingham
Year: 1987
Ninth and last Top 10 hit.

LITTLE MARIE

Artist: Chuck Berry
Written by: Chuck Berry

From the album: *St. Louis to Liverpool*
Label: Chess
Produced by: Leonard Chess, Phil Chess
Year: 1964
Catching up with the girl from Memphis, Tennessee.

LITTLE MARTHA

Artist: Allman Brothers
Written by: Greg Allman
From the album: *Eat a Peach*
Label: Capricorn
Produced by: Tom Dowd
Year: 1972
Enchanted, acoustic guitar/dobro passing of the torch from the departed Duane to Dicky Betts.

LITTLE MISS CAN'T BE WRONG

Artist: The Spin Doctors
Written by: Chris Barron
From the album: *Pocket Full of Kryptonite*
Label: Epic
Produced by: P. Denenberg, Spin Doctors
Year: 1991
Previewing the return of the hippie guitar band. Blues Traveler and Phish were already jamming.

LITTLE MORE LOVE, A

Artist: Olivia Newton-John
Written by: John Farrar
From the album: *Totally Hot*
Label: MCA
Produced by: John Farrar
Year: 1979
Closing out the decade with her 8TH prissy hit.

LITTLE OLD LADY (FROM PASADENA), THE

Artist: Jan & Dean
Written by: Roger Christian, Don Altfeld
From the album: *The Little Old Lady from Pasadena*
Label: Liberty
Produced by: Jan Berry
Year: 1964
Car classic—classic car line: "only driven once by a little old lady from Pasadena." Go, granny, go!

LITTLE QUEENIE

Artist: Chuck Berry
Written by: Chuck Berry
From the album: *Chuck Berry Is on Top*
Label: Chess
Produced by: Leonard Chess, Phil Chess
Year: 1959
B-side of "Almost Grown" and one of his great live numbers. Covered in '62 concert performance by the Beatles at the Star Club in Germany (Lingasong, '77), the Rolling Stones at Madison Square Garden (London, '70), and Rod Stewart, "Absolutely Live" (Warner Brothers, '82).

LITTLE RED CORVETTE

Artist: Prince
Written by: Prince Rogers Nelson
From the album: *1999*
Label: Warner Brothers
Produced by: Prince
Year: 1982
His first Top 10 R&B/Top 10 crossover, and one of the all-time classic car songs—classic car: the Chevy Corvette—was reportedly written in the back of an Edsel.

LITTLE RED ROOSTER

Artist: Howlin' Wolf
Written by: Willie Dixon
From the album: *Tune Box*
Label: Chess
Year: 1961
The big, bad Wolf earns his place in the rock pantheon along with Dixon. Covered by Sam Cooke (RCA, '63), the Rolling Stones (London, '65).

LITTLE SISTER

Artist: Nico
Written by: Lou Reed, John Cale
From the album: *Chelsea Girl*
Label: Verve
Produced by: Tom Wilson
Year: 1967
Previewing the eerie, dark, and dank Velvet Underground sound.

LITTLE SISTER

Artist: Elvis Presley
Written by: Doc Pomus, Mort Shuman
From the album: *Elvis' Golden Records (Vol. III)*
Label: RCA
Produced by: Steve Sholes
Year: 1961
Great cover by Ry Cooder (Warner Brothers, '79).

LITTLE STAR

Artist: The Elegants
Written by: Vito Picone, Arthur Venosa
Label: Hull/Apt
Year: 1958
When you wish upon a star, be careful what you wish for, it might come true. The Elegants hit number one with their first release, this wishful nursery rhyme disguised as white doo-wop, and never returned to the charts again.

LITTLE THINGS

Artist: Good Charlotte
Written by: Ben Combs, Nik Combs
From the album: *Good Charlotte*
Produced by: Don Gilmore
Label: Columbia
Year: 2000

LITTLE TOWN FLIRT

Artist: Del Shannon
Written by: Del Shannon, Marion McKenzie
From the album: *Little Town Flirt*
Label: Big Top
Produced by: Irving Micahnik, Harry Balk
Year: 1961
Del's 6TH out of eight Top 10 hits in the UK. Suggested segue: "Runaround Sue" by Dion.

LITTLE WALTER

Artist: Tony! Toni! Tone!
Written by: Denzil Foster, Thom McElroy
From the album: *Who*
Label: Wing
Produced by: Denzil Foster, Thom McElroy
Year: 1988
From Oakland, the home of gangsta rap, a crossover hit in the old style, dedicated to the great bluesman.

LITTLE WILD ONE (NO. 5)

Artist: Marshall Crenshaw
Written by: Marshall Crenshaw
From the album: *Downtown*
Label: Warner Brothers
Produced by: T-Bone Burnette
Year: 1985
Return to Beatlesque rockabilly.

LITTLE WILLY

Artist: Sweet
Written by: Mike Day
From the album: *The Sweet*
Label: Bell
Produced by: Mike Chapman, Nicky Chinn
Year: 1973
Became their biggest US hit almost a year after it peaked in England.

LITTLE WING

Artist: Jimi Hendrix
Written by: Jimi Hendrix
From the album: *Axis: Bold as Love*
Label: Reprise
Produced by: Chas Chandler
Year: 1968
In an acoustic mode. Covered by Sting (A&M, '87), Stevie Ray Vaughan (Epic, '91).

LITTLE WOMAN

Artist: Bobby Sherman
Written by: Danny Janssen
From the album: *Bobby Sherman*
Label: Metromedia
Produced by: Jackie Mills
Year: 1969
An unlikely teen idol, separated at birth from Barry Manilow.

LIVE

Artist: Merry-Go-Round
Written by: Emitt Rhodes
From the album: *The Merry-Go-Round*
Label: A&M
Produced by: Larry Marks
Year: 1967
The original folkie sound of the paisley underground. Covered by the Bangles (Columbia, '84).

LIVE AND LEARN

Artist: Joe Public
Written by: Joe Carter, Joseph Sayles, Kev Scott, Dew Wyatt
From the album: *Joe Public*
Label: Columbia
Produced by: Lionel Job, Joe Public
Year: 1992
Hip-hop hit with a down-to-earth message.

LIVE AND LET DIE

Artist: Paul McCartney and Wings
Written by: Paul McCartney, Linda McCartney
From the album: *Wings over America*
Label: Capitol
Produced by: Paul McCartney
Year: 1973
Teaming up with Britain's second most famous artistic creation, James Bond. Covered by Guns N' Roses (Geffen, '91).

LIVE FOREVER

Artist: Oasis
Written by: Noel Gallagher
From the album: *Definitely Maybe*
Label: Epic
Produced by: Noel Gallagher, Mark Coyle, Owen Morris
Year: 1994
Loud rock from England finds favor with guitarist Johnny Marr.

LIVE TO TELL

Artist: Madonna
Written by: Patrick Leonard, Madonna Ciccone
From the album: *True Blue*
Label: Sire
Produced by: Patrick Leonard, Madonna
Year: 1986
Her #1 ballad move, from the movie with her then husband Sean Penn, *At Close Range*.

LIVELY UP YOURSELF

Artist: Bob Marley and the Wailers
Written by: Bob Marley
Label: Green Door
Produced by: Bob Marley and the Wailers
Year: 1972
They updated this old Wailers classic on their album *Natty Dread* (Island, '75).

LIVERPOOL DRIVE

Artist: Chuck Berry
Written by: Chuck Berry
From the album: *Two Great Guitars*
Label: Chess
Produced by: Leonard Chess, Phil Chess
Year: 1964
From his famed guitar duel album with Bo Diddley.

LIVES IN THE BALANCE

Artist: Jackson Browne
Written by: Jackson Browne
From the album: *Lives in the Balance*
Label: Asylum
Produced by: Jackson Browne
Year: 1986
During the era of Iran Contra, this was one of Browne's most powerful global protest tunes.

LIVIN' FOR THE CITY

Artist: Stevie Wonder
Written by: Stevie Wonder
From the album: *Innervisions*
Label: Tamla
Produced by: Stevie Wonder
Year: 1973
From the windows of his mind, Stevie creates an urban anthem; #1 R&B/Top 10 crossover.

LIVIN' FOR YOU

Artist: Al Green
Written by: Al Green, Willie Mitchell
From the album: *Livin' for You*
Label: Hi
Produced by: Willie Mitchell
Year: 1973
#1 R&B/Top 20.

LIVIN' LA VIDA LOCA

Artist: Ricky Martin
Written by: Robi Rosa, Desmond Child
From the album: *Ricky Martin*
Label: Sony
Year: 1999
Exploiting his moment in the salsa spotlight.

LIVIN' ON A PRAYER

Artist: Bon Jovi
Written by: Jon Bon Jovi, Richie Sambora, Desmond Child
From the album: *Slippery When Wet*
Label: Polygram
Produced by: Bruce Fairbairn
Year: 1987
With characters straight from Springsteen's Greasy Lake, the Desmond Child-guided writing team follows up "You Give Love a Bad Name" with an even bigger #1 hit.

LIVIN' ON THE EDGE

Artist: Aerosmith
Written by: Steven Tyler, Joe Perry, Mark Hudson
From the album: *Get a Grip*
Label: Geffen
Produced by: Bruce Fairbairn
Year: 1993
New life for old metal.

LIVIN' THING

Artist: Electric Light Orchestra (ELO)
Written by: Jeff Lynne
From the album: *A New World Record*
Label: United Artists
Produced by: Jeff Lynne
Year: 1976
A modern statement. Queen were listening.

LIVING A LIE

Artist: The dBs
Written by: Chris Stamey, Peter Holsapple
From the album: *Repercussion*
Label: Albion
Produced by: Scott Litt
Year: 1981
From the early pioneers of low-fi, the return of the folkie sensibility in rock drag. R.E.M. was waiting to coopt it; Litt would help them.

LIVING A LITTLE, LAUGHING A LITTLE

Artist: John Hiatt and Elvis Costello
Written by: John Hiatt
From the album: *Warming up to the Ice Age*
Label: Geffen
Produced by: Norbert Putnam
Year: 1985
Blue-eyed soul mates.

LIVING AFTER MIDNIGHT

Artist: Judas Priest
Written by: K. K. Downing, Rob Halford, Glenn Tipton
From the album: *British Steel*
Produced by: Tom Allom
Label: Columbia
Year: 1980
Leading the new age of British heavy metal.

LIVING DOLL

Artist: Cliff Richard
Written by: Lionel Bart
From the album: *Cliff Sings*
Label: ABC Paramount
Year: 1959
The Elvis of England wasn't even Ricky Nelson over here. He'd be back (more than once), but not before the song's composer, Lionel Bart, who beat him to stardom as the composer of the '63 Broadway musical *Oliver*. Cliff's backing band, the Drifters, would evolve into the Shadows and they wouldn't make it over here, either.

LIVING IN AMERICA

Artist: James Brown
Written by: Dan Hartman, Charlie Midnight

From the album: *Gravity*
Label: Scotti Brothers
Produced by: Charlie Midnight
Year: 1986
From the soundtrack of *Rocky IV*.

LIVING IN THE PAST

Artist: Jethro Tull
Written by: Ian Anderson
From the album: *Living in the Past*
Label: Chrysalis
Produced by: Terry Ellis
Year: 1972
Their biggest hit. Twenty-three years later, they'd be rewarded with a Grammy for Best Rock Performance.

LIVING IN THE USA

Artist: Steve Miller Band
Written by: Steve Miller
From the album: *Sailor*
Label: Capitol
Produced by: Steve Miller
Year: 1968
In search of a cheeseburger. Jimmy Buffett had them all.

LIVING IT UP

Artist: Rickie Lee Jones
Written by: Rickie Lee Jones
From the album: *Pirates*
Label: Warner Brothers
Produced by: Russ Titelman, Lenny Waronker
Year: 1982
Female Tom Waits in waiting, paints a frantic urban street scene.

LIVING THROUGH ANOTHER CUBA

Artist: XTC
Written by: Andy Partridge
From the album: *Black Sea*
Label: Virgin
Produced by: Steve Lillywhite
Year: 1980
The pristine popsters in a rare power-protest mode.

LIVING WITHOUT YOU

Artist: Randy Newman
Written by: Randy Newman
From the album: *Randy Newman Creates Something New under the Sun*
Label: Reprise
Produced by: Van Dyke Parks, Lenny Waronker
Year: 1968
Anticipating and lapping the coming singer/songwriter brat pack. Covered by the Nitty Gritty Dirt Band (Liberty, '70), Manfred Mann (Polydor, '72).

LIVING YEARS, THE

Artist: Mike & The Mechanics

Written by: Mike Rutherford, Brian Robertson
From the album: *Living Years*
Label: Atlantic
Produced by: Christopher Neil, Mike Rutherford
Year: 1989
Defining adult-oriented rock.

LOAD OUT, THE

Artist: Jackson Browne
Written by: Jackson Browne, Bryan Garofalo
From the album: *Running on Empty*
Label: Asylum
Produced by: Jackson Browne
Year: 1977
Tales from the road crew.

LOCAL GIRLS

Artist: Graham Parker
Written by: Graham Parker
From the album: *Squeezing out Sparks*
Label: Arista
Year: 1979
Segue: "Factory Girl," The Rolling Stones.

LOCKING UP MY HEART

Artist: The Marvelettes
Written by: Eddie Holland, Brian Holland
From the album: *Marvelous Marvelettes*
Label: Tamla
Produced by: Lamont Dozier
Year: 1963
The advent of the Holland-Dozier-Holland franchise.

LOCO DE AMOR (CRAZY FOR LOVE)

Artist: David Byrne and Celia Cruz
Written by: David Byrne
From the album: *Something Wild Soundtrack*
Label: MCA
Year: 1986
The King of spastic soul teams up with the Queen of salsa.

LOCO-MOTION, THE

Artist: Little Eva
Written by: Gerry Goffin, Carole King
From the album: *Llllloco-Motion*
Label: Dimension
Produced by: Gerry Goffin
Year: 1962
With one of their more mindless ditties, Goffin, King, and their babysitter Eva Boyd create a long-lasting annuity. Carole King sings backup. Hit covers by Grand Funk (Capitol, '74), Kylie Minogue (Geffen, '87).

LODI

Artist: Creedence Clearwater Revival
Written by: John C. Fogerty
From the album: *Green River*

Label: Fantasy
Produced by: John C. Fogerty
Year: 1969
B-side of "Bad Moon Rising." A day in the life of rock and roll has never been better told or sung. Segue: "Rock and Roll (I Gave You the Best Years of My Life) by Kevin Johnson.

LOGICAL SONG, THE

Artist: Supertramp
Written by: Richard Davies, Roger Hodgson
From the album: *Breakfast in America*
Label: A&M
Produced by: Pete Henderson, Supertramp
Year: 1979
Wordy pomp rock from England, where Queen did it better.

LOLA

Artist: The Kinks
Written by: Ray Davies
From the album: *Lola vs. the Powerman and the Moneygoround (Part I)*
Label: Reprise
Produced by: Ray Davies
Year: 1971
Nailing the sexually ambidextrous glitter generation. Covered by the Raincoats (Rough Trade, '79). Blur was listening.

LONDON CALLING

Artist: The Clash
Written by: John Mellor (Joe Strummer), Mick Jones
From the album: *London Calling*
Label: Epic
Produced by: Guy Stevens
Year: 1979
Stevens had produced their early demos.

LONDON'S BURNING

Artist: The Clash
Written by: John Mellor (Joe Strummer), Mick Jones
From the album: *The Clash*
Label: Epic
Produced by: Mickey Foote
Year: 1977
Some of the most incendiary licks of the rock era.

LONELY AT THE BOTTOM

Artist: John Belushi
Written by: Paul Jacobs, John Belushi
From the album: *Lemmings Original Cast Album*
Label: Banana
Produced by: Tony Hendra
Year: 1973
Future *Saturday Night Live* stalwart Belushi perfects his Joe Cocker imitation in the Greenwich Village musical that helped shape the comedy of the classic rock generation.

LONELY AVENUE

Artist: Ray Charles
Written by: Doc Pomus
From the album: *The Ray Charles Story*
Label: Atlantic
Produced by: Ahmet Ertegun, Jerry Wexler
Year: 1956
First R&B hit for two future Rock and Roll Hall of Famers. Early Beatles favorite, covered by the Everly Brothers (Warner Brothers, '65), Los Lobos (Rhino, '95). Suggested segue: "I've Got a New Home," by the Pilgrim Travelers (Specialty, '53).

LONELY BOY

Artist: Paul Anka
Written by: Paul Anka
From the album: *Lonely Boy*
Label: ABC Paramount
Produced by: Don Costa
Year: 1959
Ballad of a teenage dweeb, introduced in the 1959 film *Girls Town*.

LONELY BOY

Artist: Andrew Gold
Written by: Andrew Gold
From the album: *What's Wrong with This Picture?*
Label: Asylum
Produced by: Peter Asher
Year: 1977
Prep rock. Rupert Holmes and Stephen Bishop were studying the changes.

LONELY DAYS

Artist: Bee Gees
Written by: Barry Gibb, Robin Gibb, Maurice Gibb
From the album: *2 Years On*
Label: Atco
Produced by: Robert Stigwood, Bee Gees
Year: 1970
The Beatles are dead; long live the Beatles sound.

LONELY ISLAND

Artist: Sam Cooke
Written by: eden ahbez
Label: Keen
Produced by: Bumps Blackwell
Year: 1957
Recorded by Sam's idol, Nat King Cole, who also recorded "Nature Boy," both written by the quintessential weirdo, ahbez.

LONELY NIGHTS

Artist: The Hearts
Written by: Zell Sanders
Label: Baton
Year: 1955
The essence of tenement soul.

LONELY OL' NIGHT

Artist: John (Cougar) Mellencamp
Written by: John Cougar Mellencamp
From the album: *Scarecrow*
Label: Riva
Produced by: Don Gehman, Little Bastard
Year: 1985
Previewing alt country.

LONELY PEOPLE

Artist: America
Written by: Dan Peek
From the album: *Holiday*
Label: Warner Brothers
Produced by: George Martin, Catherine Peek
Year: 1974
Beatles producer Martin attempts (and fails) to recreate "Eleanor Rigby."

LONELY SURFER, THE

Artist: Jack Nitzsche
Written by: Jack Nitzsche, Marty Cooper
Label: Reprise
Produced by: Jimmy Bowen
Year: 1963
Existential surf music from an L.A. studio legend.

LONELY TEARDROPS

Artist: Jackie Wilson
Written by: Roquel Davis (Tyran Carlo), Berry Gordy Jr., Gwen Gordy
From the album: *Lonely Teardrops*
Label: Brunswick
Produced by: Dick Jacobs, Nat Tarnopol
Year: 1958
First #1 R&B/Top 10 crossover for the magnificently gifted R&B crooner and the song he was singing when a heart attack on stage put him into a coma from which he'd never emerge.

LONELY TEENAGER

Artist: Dion
Written by: Salvatore Pippa, Silvio Faraci, Paolo Di Alfred
From the album: *Dion Sings His Greatest Hits*
Label: Laurie
Produced by: Gene Schwartz
Year: 1960
Describing Dion's condition on his first effort without the Belmonts.

LONELY WEEKENDS

Artist: Charlie Rich
Written by: Charlie Rich
From the album: *Greatest Hits*
Label: Phillips International
Produced by: Sam Phillips
Year: 1960
Echoey rockabilly in the Elvis mode, tough but vulnerable. Suggested segue: "Lonely Saturday Night" by Don French.

LONER, THE

Artist: Neil Young
Written by: Neil Young
From the album: *Neil Young*
Label: Reprise
Produced by: Jack Nitzsche
Year: 1969
Stating Young's theme and credo.

LONESOME TOWN

Artist: Ricky Nelson
Written by: Baker Knight
From the album: *Ricky Sings Again*
Label: Imperial
Produced by: Ricky Nelson, Jimmy Haskell, Ozzie Nelson
Year: 1958
Covered by the Cramps (IRS, '79).

LONG AND WINDING ROAD, THE

Artist: The Beatles
Written by: John Lennon, Paul McCartney
From the album: *Let It Be*
Label: Apple
Produced by: George Martin, Phil Spector
Year: 1970
Phil Spector, who arguably launched the jangly rock alternative '60s with his flashy productions, castanets, and tambourines, winds up with the Beatles' abandoned rooftop tapes and nowhere to go.

LONG AS I CAN SEE THE LIGHT

Artist: Creedence Clearwater Revival
Written by: John C. Fogerty
From the album: *Cosmo's Factory*
Label: Fantasy
Produced by: John C. Fogerty
Year: 1970
B-side of "Looking out My Back Door."

LONG COOL WOMAN (IN A BLACK DRESS)

Artist: The Hollies
Written by: Roger Greenaway, Roger Cook, Harold Clarke
From the album: *Distant Light*
Label: Epic
Produced by: Ron Richards
Year: 1972
Their biggest hit.

LONG DECEMBER, A

Artist: Counting Crows
Written by: Adam Duritz
From the album: *Recovering the Sattelites*
Label: DGC
Produced by: Gil Norton
Year: 1996
Drifting and dreaming, as winter approaches.

LONG DISTANCE RUNAROUND

Artist: Yes
Written by: Jon Anderson
From the album: *Fragile*
Label: Atlantic
Produced by: Eddie Offord, Yes
Year: 1972
Progressive opus from their defining album.

LONG GONE DEAD

Artist: Rank and File
Written by: Chip Kinman, Tony Kinman
From the album: *Long Gone Dead*
Label: Slash
Year: 1984
In the paisley days of a folk/rock renaissance inspired by R.E.M. and the Bangles, a droning tribute to the Flying Burritos.

LONG HONEYMOON, THE

Artist: Elvis Costello
Written by: Declan McManus (Elvis Costello)
From the album: *Imperial Bedroom*
Label: Columbia
Produced by: Geoff Emerich
Year: 1982
One of his finest lyrics.

LONG LIVE OUR LOVE

Artist: The Shangri-Las
Written by: Sidney Barnes, J. J. Jackson
From the album: *Past, Present and Future*
Label: Red Bird
Produced by: Shadow Morton
Year: 1966
Goodbye to the first great girl-group era.

LONG LIVE THE KANE

Artist: Big Daddy Kane
Written by: Antonio Hardy (Big Daddy Kane)
From the album: *Long Live the Kane*
Label: Cold Chillin'
Year: 1988
Self-promotional rap.

LONG LONELY NIGHTS

Artist: Lee Andrews
Written by: Lee Andrews, Tyran Carlo, Douglas Henderson, Mimi Uniman
From the album: *Main Line*
Label: Chess
Year: 1957
Aching post doo-wop ballad from Philadelphia was an early harbinger of Philly soul, to say nothing of Motown.

LONG LONG TIME

Artist: Linda Ronstadt
Written by: Gary White
From the album: *Silk Purse*
Label: Capitol
Produced by: Elliot Mazur
Year: 1970
Folk/rock triumph is her first solo hit after "Different Drum," with the Stone Poneys in '67.

LONG TALL SALLY

Artist: Little Richard
Written by: Enotris Johnson, Richard Penniman, Robert Blackwell
From the album: *Here's Little Richard*
Label: Specialty
Produced by: Bumps Blackwell
Year: 1956
His biggest hit; #1 R&B/Top 10 crossover. Covered by Jerry Lee Lewis (Smash, '64).

LONG TERM PHYSICAL EFFECTS

Artist: Carly Simon
Written by: Carly Simon, Tim Saunders
Label: Decca
Year: 1971
Young Carly sings convincingly about drugs in a cameo appearance in the Milos Foreman cult film *Taking Off*.

LONG TIME

Artist: Boston
Written by: Tom Scholz
From the album: *Boston*
Label: Epic
Produced by: Tom Scholz, John Boylan
Year: 1976
Ushering in the technologically assisted, amplifier-driven sound of arena rock.

LONG TIME GONE

Artist: Crosby, Stills & Nash
Written by: David Crosby
From the album: *Crosby, Stills & Nash*
Label: Atlantic
Year: 1969
In the trippy heyday of their glistening harmonies.

LONG TRAIN RUNNING

Artist: The Doobie Brothers
Written by: Tom Johnston
From the album: *The Captain and Me*
Label: Warner Brothers
Produced by: Ted Templeman
Year: 1973
Crashing the AM top 10 from the other side of the dial (FM).

LONG WHITE CADILLAC

Artist: The Blasters
Written by: Dave Alvin
From the album: *Non Fiction*
Label: Slash
Produced by: The Blasters
Year: 1983
Roots rock tribute to Hank Williams.

LONGER

Artist: Dan Fogelberg
Written by: Dan Fogelberg
From the album: *Phoenix*
Label: Full Moon
Produced by: Dan Fogelberg, Marty Lewis, Norbert Putnam
Year: 1979
Achieving easy-listening nirvana and wedding song eternity.

LONGEST TIME, THE

Artist: Billy Joel
Written by: Billy Joel
From the album: *An Innocent Man*
Label: Columbia
Produced by: Phil Ramone
Year: 1983
Returning to his doo-wop roots.

LONGFELLOW SERENADE

Artist: Neil Diamond
Written by: Neil Diamond
From the album: *Serenade*
Label: Columbia
Produced by: Bob Catalano
Year: 1974
His last big hit of the '70s, aside from "You Don't Bring Me Flowers," a duet with former Brooklyn neighbor Barbra Streisand (Columbia, '78).

LONGVIEW

Artist: Green Day
Written by: Billy Joe Armstrong, Green Day
From the album: *Dookie*
Label: Reprise
Produced by: Rob Cavallo, Green Day
Year: 1994
New neurotic rock for the high school set.

LOOK AT GRANNY RUN RUN

Artist: Howard Tate
Written by: Jerry Ragovoy, Mort Shuman
Label: Verve
Year: 1966
His second biggest R&B hit. Covered by Grand Funk (Capitol, '75), Ry Cooder (Warner Brothers, '79).

LOOK AT LITTLE SISTER

Artist: The Midnighters
Written by: Hank Ballard
From the album: *Mr. Rhythm & Blues (Finger Poppin' Time)*
Label: King
Year: 1960
Hank hails the next generation. Covered in a barn-turner by Stevie Ray Vaughan (Epic, '84).

LOOK AWAY

Artist: Chicago
Written by: Diane Warren
From the album: *19*
Label: Reprise
Produced by: Ron Nevison
Year: 1988
#1 hit of the year from the pen of Brill Building throwback Warren.

LOOK IN MY EYES

Artist: The Chantels
Written by: George Goldner, Richard Barrett
From the album: *There's Our Song Again*
Label: Carlton
Produced by: Richard Barrett
Year: 1961
Spurred by the success of the Shirelles, the original girl group returns with their biggest hit, but without Arlene.

LOOK INTO MY EYES

Artist: Bone Thugs-n-Harmony
Written by: DJ Uneek, Bone Thugs-n-Harmony
From the album: *The Art of War*
Label: Relativity
Year: 1997
Follow up to "Tha Crossroads."

LOOK OF LOVE

Artist: Lesley Gore
Written by: Jeff Barry, Ellie Greenwich
From the album: *Girl Talk*
Label: Mercury
Produced by: Quincy Jones
Year: 1964
An easygoing Gore playing against type.

LOOK OF LOVE (PART ONE), THE

Artist: ABC
Written by: Martin Fry, Mark Lickley, Stephen Singleton, David Palmer
From the album: *The Lexicon of Love*
Label: Mercury
Produced by: Martin Rushent
Year: 1982
Slick, sleek, and Bowiesque synth rock from Britain.

LOOK, THE

Artist: Roxette
Written by: Per Gessle
From the album: *Look Sharp!*
Label: EMI
Produced by: Clarence Ofwerman
Year: 1989
First big hit for the Abbaesque duo. Ace of Base were listening.

LOOK WHAT YOU DONE FOR ME

Artist: Al Green
Written by: Al Green, Willie Mitchell, Al Jackson
From the album: *I'm Still in Love with You*
Label: Hi
Produced by: Willie Mitchell
Year: 1972
Al's second big crossover hit of '72.

LOOKIN' FOR A LOVE

Artist: The Valentinos
Written by: James Alexander, Zelda Samuels
Label: Sar
Year: 1962
Top 10 R&B/Bottom 30 crossover. Covered by the J. Geils Band (Atlantic, '71). Former group member, Bobby Womack, revived it with a #1 R&B/Top 10 hit (United Artists, '74).

LOOKIN' FOR LOVE

Artist: Johnny Lee
Written by: Wanda Mallette, Patti Ryan, Bob Morrison
From the album: *Lookin' for Love*
Label: Asylum
Year: 1980
#1 country/Top 10 crossover, from the movie *Urban Cowboy*.

LOOKIN' OUT MY BACK DOOR

Artist: Creedence Clearwater Revival
Written by: John C. Fogerty
From the album: *Cosmo's Factory*
Label: Fantasy
Produced by: John C. Fogerty
Year: 1970
Their fifth career #2 single without ever having achieved a #1, except in England.

LOOKING FOR A KISS

Artist: New York Dolls
Written by: David Johansen, Johnny Thunders
From the album: *New York Dolls*
Label: Mercury
Produced by: Todd Rundgren
Year: 1973
Signature opus from the ultimate lipstick band. Covered by Jayne County (ESP, '93).

LOOKING FOR A NEW LOVE

Artist: Jody Watley
Written by: Andre Cymone, Jody Watley
From the album: *Jody Watley*
Label: MCA
Produced by: Andre Cymone, David Z.
Year: 1987
Her first #1 R&B/Top 10 crossover.

LOOKING FOR AN ECHO

Artist: The Persuasions
Written by: Richard Reicheg
From the album: *Chirpin'*
Label: Elektra
Produced by: David Darlev
Year: 1977
One of the all-time great acapella commentaries on the doo-wop lifestyle, introduced by Kenny Vance. Featured in the '90 Spike Lee PBS special *Do It Acapell*a (Elektra, '90).

LOOKING FOR THE PERFECT BEAT

Artist: Afrika Bambaataa and Soulsonic Force
Written by: Arthur Baker, John Robie
From the album: *Planetrock—The Album*
Label: Tommy Boy
Produced by: Arthur Baker
Year: 1986
A mastery of sampling art: part computer, part DJ scratching.

LOOKING THROUGH PATIENT EYES

Artist: P.M. Dawn
Written by: Atrel Cordes, George Michael
From the album: *The Bliss Album*
Label: Gee Street
Produced by: P.M. Dawn
Year: 1993
The philosopher kings of new-age rap network with an idol of another era.

LOOKS LIKE WE MADE IT

Artist: Barry Manilow
Written by: Barry Manilow, Bruce Sussman, Jack Feldman
From the album: *This One's for You*
Label: Arista
Produced by: Ron Dante, Barry Manilow
Year: 1976
Poignant love song is his third and last #1.

LOOP DE LOOP

Artist: Johnny Thunder
Written by: Teddy Vann, Joe Dong
From the album: *Loop De Loop*
Label: Diamond
Produced by: Teddy Vann
Year: 1963
Keg rock ditty. Covered by Harry Nilsson (RCA, '74), with Ringo Starr, Keith Moon, and Jim Keltner on drums! Now *that* must have been a party.

LOOSEY'S RAP

Artist: Rick James with Roxanne Shante
Written by: James Johnson Jr.
From the album: *Wonderful*
Label: Reprise
Produced by: Rick James

Year: 1988
His fourth #1 R&B hit, aided by the off-the-top-of-her-head rapping of the former Lolita Gooden of Long Island City, more famous for "Roxanne's Revenge."

LOS ANGELES

Artist: X
Written by: John Doe, Exene Cervenka
From the album: *Los Angeles*
Label: Slash
Produced by: Ray Manzarek
Year: 1980
The slashing and burning of L.A. abetted by a former Door.

LOSER

Artist: Beck
Written by: Beck Hansen, Karl Stephenson
From the album: *Mellow Gold*
Label: Geffen
Produced by: Karl Stephenson, Tom Rothrock
Year: 1993
Literate antifolk, low-fi harangue, defining the slacker essence of a new Beat Generation.

LOSING HAND

Artist: Ray Charles
Written by: Charles Calhoun
From the album: *The Ray Charles Story*
Label: Atlantic
Year: 1954
B-side of "Don't You Know."

LOSING MY RELIGION

Artist: R.E.M.
Written by: Michael Stipe, Peter Buck, Bill Berry, Mike Mills
From the album: *Out of Time*
Label: Warner Brothers
Produced by: Scott Litt, R.E.M.
Year: 1991
Wherein Michael Stipe follows Bono Vox to the Godhead.

LOST IN EMOTION

Artist: Lisa Lisa and Cult Jam
Written by: Full Force
From the album: *Spanish Fly*
Label: Columbia
Produced by: Full Force
Year: 1987
Second straight #1 R&B/#1 crossover, after "Let the Beat Him 'Em."

LOST IN THE FLOOD

Artist: Bruce Springsteen
Written by: Bruce Springsteen
From the album: *Greetings from Asbury Park*
Label: Columbia

Produced by: Jim Cretecos, Mike Appel
Year: 1973
Creating a new urban legend from the walking wounded of the postwar working class. Suggested segue: "Still in Saigon" by the Charlie Daniels Band.

LOST IN THE SUPERMARKET

Artist: The Clash
Written by: John Mellor (Joe Strummer), Mick Jones
From the album: *London Calling*
Label: Epic
Produced by: Guy Stevens
Year: 1979
The Taj Mahal influence.

LOST IN YOUR EYES

Artist: Debbie Gibson
Written by: Debbie Gibson
From the album: *Electric Youth*
Label: Atlantic
Produced by: Debbie Gibson
Year: 1989
Her second straight #1 would be her last Top 10 hit.

LOST JOHNNY

Artist: Hawkwind
Written by: Ian Kilmeister (Lemmy), Mick Farren
From the album: *Hall of the Mountain Grill*
Label: United Artists
Year: 1974
Kilmeister would emerge again in the raging metal monster, Motorhead.

LOST SOMEONE

Artist: James Brown and the Famous Flames
Written by: Bobby Byrd, Eugene Stallworth
From the album: *The Amazing James Brown*
Label: King
Year: 1961
Classic R&B track that Brown revived again in '66. Stiffed on the pop charts both times.

LOST WOMAN SONG

Artist: Ani DiFranco
Written by: Ani DiFranco
From the album: *Little Plastic Castle*
Produced by: Ani DiFranco
Label: Righteous Babe
Year: 1989
Introducing an independent new feminist rock and roll and business model.

LOTTA LOVE

Artist: Neil Young
Written by: Neil Young
From the album: *Comes a Time*
Label: Reprise
Year: 1978

Covered by Nicolette Larson (Warner Brothers, '79).

LOTTA LOVIN'

Artist: Gene Vincent
Written by: Bernice Bedwell
Label: Capitol
Produced by: Ken Nelson
Year: 1957
Second biggest hit for the rockabilly legend.

LOUIE, LOUIE

Artist: Richard Berry
Written by: Richard Berry
Label: Flip
Year: 1956
Introduced by Richard Berry, voice of "Riot in Cell Block #9" by the Robins, and popularized for eternity by the Kingsmen (Wand, '63). For a generation of garage band hopefuls, it would be their three-chord primer. For the FBI, this would conclusively define them for the same generation as latter-day Keystone Kops, as they sought to find obscenities hidden in the mix, an endeavor far more obscene than anything they were able to discern.

LOUIS QUATORZE

Artist: Bow Wow Wow
Written by: Malcolm McLaren, Mathew Ashman, David Della Barbarrosa, Leigh Roy Gorman
From the album: *Your Cassette Pet*
Label: EMI (Import)
Produced by: Malcolm McLaren
Year: 1980
Historical rocker by sexpistols—impressario McLaren's new group more famous for their cover of "I Want Candy" (RCA, '82) and jailbait lead singer Annabella.

LOUISE

Artist: Bonnie Raitt
Written by: Paul Siebel
From the album: *Sweet Forgiveness*
Label: Warner Brothers
Produced by: Paul Rothchild
Year: 1977
Down-and-out character portrait was a staple of Raitt's act for years.

LOUISIANA, 1927

Artist: Randy Newman
Written by: Randy Newman
From the album: *Good Old Boys*
Label: Warner Brothers
Produced by: Russ Titelman, Lenny Waronker
Year: 1974
Atmospheric tune from his New Orleans concept album about the Kingfish, Huey Long. Covered by the Neville Brothers (A&M, '91). Used in the film *Blaze*.

LOUNGIN'

Artist: LL Cool J
Written by: Bernard Wright, James Todd Smith, Rashad Smith, Albert Brown, Kyle West
From the album: *Mr. Smith*
Label: Def Jam
Year: 1996
Coolin' at the studio.

LOVABLE

Artist: Elvis Costello
Written by: Declan McManus (Elvis Costello), Cait O'Riordan
From the album: *King of America*
Label: Columbia
Produced by: T-Bone Burnette, Declan McManus
Year: 1986
But in a curmudgeonly way; written with his then-wife.

LOVE (CAN MAKE YOU HAPPY)

Artist: Mercy
Written by: Jack Sigler
From the album: *The Mercy and Love (Can Make You Happy)*
Label: Sundi
Produced by: Jamie Guyden
Year: 1969

L-O-V-E (LOVE)

Artist: Al Green
Written by: Al Green, Willie Mitchell, Mabon Hodges
From the album: *Al Green Is Love*
Label: Hi
Produced by: Willie Mitchell
Year: 1975
#1 R&B/Top 20 crossover.

LOVE AND AFFECTION

Artist: Joan Armatrading
Written by: Joan Armatrading
From the album: *Joan Armatrading*
Label: A&M
Produced by: Glyn Johns
Year: 1976
Signature moody ballad from the Tracy Chapman of the '70s, only without a fast car.

LOVE AND ANGER

Artist: Kate Bush
Written by: Kate Bush
From the album: *The Sensual World*
Label: Columbia
Produced by: Kate Bush
Year: 1989
The original British techno-babe grows up.

LOVE AND HAPPINESS

Artist: Al Green
Written by: Al Green, Mabon Hodges
From the album: *I'm Still in Love with You*
Label: Hi
Produced by: Willie Mitchell
Year: 1972
One of Green's last chart singles is among his greatest.

LOVE BITES

Artist: Def Leppard
Written by: Steve Clark, Joe Elliott, Robert John "Mutt" Lange, Phil Collen, Rick Savage
From the album: *Hysteria*
Label: Mercury
Produced by: Mutt Lange
Year: 1987
Their only #1 single.

LOVE BIZARRE, A

Artist: Sheila E.
Written by: Prince Rogers Nelson, Sheila Escovedo
From the album: *Romance 1600*
Label: Warner Brothers
Produced by: Sheila E.
Year: 1986
As anyone who's seen the movie *Purple Rain* can tell you.

LOVE BUZZ

Artist: Shocking Blue
Written by: Robbie Van Leeuwen
From the album: *This Is the Shocking Blue*
Label: Colossus
Produced by: Robbie van Leeuwen
Year: 1969
Covered by Nirvana on *Bleach* (Sub Pop, '88) and released as their first single.

LOVE CAME TO ME

Artist: Dion
Written by: Dion DiMucci John Falbo
From the album: *Dion Sings to Sandy (and All His Other Girls)*
Label: Laurie
Produced by: Gene Schwartz
Year: 1962
In Bobby Darin territory.

LOVE CHILD

Artist: The Supremes
Written by: Pam Sawyer, R. Dean Taylor, Frank Wilson, Deke Richards
From the album: *Love Child*
Label: Motown
Produced by: Berry Gordy Jr., Deke Richards, Frank Wilson, Henry Cosby, R. Dean Taylor
Year: 1968
Beginning Diana's faux street period with the Supremes' biggest hit in four years.

LOVE COME DOWN

Artist: Evelyn Champagne King
Written by: Kashif
From the album: *Get Loose*
Label: RCA
Produced by: Kashif
Year: 1982
#1 R&B/Top 20 crossover.

LOVE GROWS (WHERE MY ROSEMARY GOES)

Artist: Edison Lighthouse
Written by: Tony Macaulay, Barry Mason
Label: Bell
Produced by: Tony Macauley
Year: 1970
#1 UK/Top 10 US crossover. Lite-rock perfection.

LOVE GUN

Artist: Kiss
Written by: Stanley Eisen (Paul Stanley)
From the album: *Love Gun*
Label: Casablanca
Produced by: Eddie Kramer, Kiss
Year: 1977
At their euphemistic best.

LOVE HANGOVER

Artist: Diana Ross
Written by: Marilyn McLeod, Pam Sawyer
From the album: *Diana Ross*
Label: Motown
Produced by: Hal Davis
Year: 1976
Diana enters the disco without an escort.

LOVE HAS NO PRIDE

Artist: Bonnie Raitt
Written by: Eric Kaz, Libby Titus
From the album: *Give It Up*
Label: Warner Brothers
Produced by: Michael Cuscuna
Year: 1972
Folk/rock's groveling standard, upon which Eric Kaz based a minor-legendary career and a major league bank account. Covered by Linda Ronstadt (Asylum, '73), Rita Coolidge (A&M, '74), Tracy Nelson (Atlantic, '74), and Kaz's own band, American Flyer (Arista, '76).

LOVE HER MADLY

Artist: The Doors
Written by: Robbie Krieger, Ray Manzarek, John Densmore
From the album: *L.A. Woman*
Label: Elektra
Produced by: Paul Rothchild
Year: 1971
Losing his edge.

LOVE HURTS

Artist: The Everly Brothers
Written by: Boudleaux Bryant
From the album: *A Date with the Everly Brothers*

Label: Warner Brothers
Produced by: Wesley Rose
Year: 1960
Everly album cut is one of Boudleaux Bryant's most enduring classics of the rock era. Covered by Roy Orbison on the B-side of "Running Scared" (Monument, '62), Gram Parsons (Reprise, '74), Nazareth (A&M, '76).

LOVE I LOST, THE

Artist: Harold Melvin and the Bluenotes
Written by: Kenny Gamble, Leon Huff
From the album: *Black and Blue*
Label: Philadelphia International
Produced by: Kenny Gamble, Leon Huff
Year: 1973
#1 R&B/Top 10 crossover from Philadelphia.

LOVE I SAW IN YOU WAS JUST A MIRAGE, THE

Artist: The Miracles
Written by: Smokey Robinson, Marv Tarplin
From the album: *Make It Happen*
Label: Tamla
Produced by: Smokey Robinson
Year: 1967
"Rock's best poet" (B. Dylan) gets metaphor happy.

LOVE IN AN ELEVATOR

Artist: Aerosmith
Written by: Steven Tyler, Joe Perry
From the album: *Pump*
Label: Geffen
Produced by: Bruce Fairbairn
Year: 1989
An anthem for the 60-second man.

LOVE IN VAIN

Artist: The Rolling Stones
Written by: Mick Jagger, Keith Richards
From the album: *Let It Bleed*
Label: London
Produced by: Jimmy Miller
Year: 1969
Drifting with the year's Nashville fever, the Stones go almost country, Delta country that is, with a nod to Robert Johnson.

LOVE IS

Artist: Vanessa Williams and Brian McKnight
Written by: Steve Krikorian (Tonio K.)
From the album: *Beverly Hills 90210 Soundtrack*
Label: Giant
Year: 1993
A remarkably straightforward and uplifting ballad from the pen of the usually twisted and cryptic writer.

LOVE IS A BATTLEFIELD

Artist: Pat Benatar
Written by: Mike Chapman, Holly Knight
From the album: *Live from Earth*

Label: Chrysalis
Produced by: Peter Coleman, Neil Giraldo
Year: 1983
Feisty belter returns to her favorite theme.

LOVE IS A ROSE

Artist: Linda Ronstadt
Written by: Neil Young
From the album: *Prisoner in Disguise*
Label: Asylum
Produced by: Peter Asher
Year: 1975
Covered by Neil Young (Reprise, '77).

LOVE IS A WONDERFUL THING

Artist: Michael Bolton
Written by: Michael Bolton, Andy Goldmark
From the album: *Time, Love and Tenderness*
Label: Columbia
Produced by: Walter Afanasieff, Michael Bolton
Year: 1991
Segue: "Love Is a Wonderful Thing" by the Isley Brothers.

LOVE IS ALIVE

Artist: Gary Wright
Written by: Gary Wright
From the album: *Dream Weaver*
Label: Warner Brothers
Produced by: Gary Wright
Year: 1976
Follow-up to "Dream Weaver."

LOVE IS ALL AROUND

Artist: The Troggs
Written by: Reg Presley
From the album: *Love Is All Around*
Label: Fontana
Produced by: Larry Page
Year: 1967
Repenting from "Wild Thing" with a standout ballad. Covered by Wet Wet Wet in the film *Four Weddings and a Funeral* (Capitol, '94).

LOVE IS EVERYTHING

Artist: Jane Siberry
Written by: Jane Siberry
From the album: *When I Was a Boy*
Label: Reprise
Produced by: Brian Eno, Jane Siberry, Michael Brooks
Year: 1993
Defining moment for the quirky Canadian singer/songwriter.

LOVE IS HERE AND NOW YOU'RE GONE

Artist: The Supremes
Written by: Eddie Holland, Lamont Dozier, Brian Holland

From the album: *The Supremes Sing Holland-Dozier-Holland*
Label: Motown
Produced by: Brian Holland, Lamont Dozier
Year: 1967
Their third straight #1 R&B/crossover is their last hit with Florence Ballard in the group.

LOVE IS IN CONTROL (FINGER ON THE TRIGGER)

Artist: Donna Summer
Written by: Rod Temperton, Quincy Jones, Merria Ross
From the album: *Donna Summer*
Label: Geffen
Produced by: Quincy Jones
Year: 1982

LOVE IS JUST A FOUR-LETTER WORD

Artist: Joan Baez
Written by: Bob Dylan
From the album: *Any Day Now*
Label: Vanguard
Produced by: Maynard Solomon
Year: 1967
Another Dylan anthem of disaffection.

LOVE IS LIKE AN ITCHING IN MY HEART

Artist: The Supremes
Written by: Eddie Holland, Lamont Dozier, Brian Holland
From the album: *Supremes a Go-Go*
Label: Motown
Produced by: Brian Holland, Lamont Dozier
Year: 1966
One of the most uncomfortable metaphors in rock and roll history. Suggested segue: "Poison Ivy" by the Coasters.

LOVE IS LIKE OXYGEN

Artist: Sweet
Written by: Trevor Griffin, Andrew Scott
From the album: *Level Headed*
Label: Capitol
Produced by: Mike Chapman, Nicky Chinn
Year: 1977
Their last Top 10, after which the group expired.

LOVE IS STRANGE

Artist: Mickey and Sylvia
Written by: Elias McDaniel (Ethel Smith), Mickey Baker, Sylvia Robinson
From the album: *New Sounds*
Label: Vik
Produced by: Bob Rolontz
Year: 1957
Stark guitar-driven exchange of vows ("How do you call your lover boy"), with the guitar provided by session ace Mickey Baker. Covered by such loving couples as the Everly Brothers (Warner

Brothers, '65), Sonny and Cher (Reprise, '65), Peaches and Herb (Date, '68), and Paul and Linda McCartney in Wings (Apple, '71). Featured in the movies *Mermaids* and *Dirty Dancing*. Suggested segue, "Billy's Blues" by Billy Stewart (Chess, '56). Sylvia Robinson would go on to found the first rap label, Sugar Hill.

LOVE IS THE DRUG
Artist: Roxy Music
Written by: Roger Lewis
From the album: *Siren*
Label: Atco
Produced by: Chris Thomas
Year: 1976
This cautionary and prophetic disco-age anthem was their first and biggest US hit.

(LOVE IS) THICKER THAN WATER
Artist: Andy Gibb
Written by: Barry Gibb, Andy Gibb
From the album: *Shadow Dancing*
Label: RSO
Produced by: Karl Richardson, Albhy Galuten, Barry Gibb
Year: 1978
Second of three straight #1 number ones.

LOVE LETTERS
Artist: Ketty Lester
Written by: Edward Heyman, Victor Young
Label: Era
Produced by: Ed Cobb
Year: 1962
Soulful version of the title song from the '45 film of the same name was a Top 5 R&B/Top 5 crossover. Covered by Elvis Presley (RCA, '66).

LOVE LIES BLEEDING
Artist: Elton John
Written by: Elton John, Bernie Taupin
From the album: *Goodbye Yellow Brick Road*
Label: MCA
Produced by: Gus Dudgeon
Year: 1973
Part of an 11-minute medley with "Funeral for a Friend," dedicated to John Lennon.

LOVE LIKE BLOOD
Artist: Killing Joke
Written by: Killing Joke
From the album: *Night Time*
Label: EG
Produced by: Chris Kimsey
Year: 1985
Metal mashers at their most accessible; a hit in England.

LOVE, LOVE, LOVE
Artist: The Clovers

Written by: Teddy McRae, Sid Wyche, Sunny David
Label: Atlantic
Produced by: Ahmet Ertegun, Jerry Wexler
Year: 1956
Top 10 R&B/Top 30 crossover. Cover by the Diamonds (Mercury, '56) also hit Top 30.

LOVE MACHINE (PART I)
Artist: The Miracles
Written by: Billy Griffith, Pete Moore
From the album: *City of Angels*
Label: Tamla
Produced by: Freddie Perren
Year: 1975
Post-Smokey, the Miracles go disco, with a Top 10 R&B/#1 crossover.

LOVE MAKES A WOMAN
Artist: Barbara Acklin
Written by: Carl Davis, Eugene Record, William Sanders, George Sims
From the album: *Love Makes a Woman*
Label: Brunswick
Produced by: Barbara Acklin, Eugene Record
Year: 1968
A classy statement of R&B womanhood. Covered by Phoebe Snow (Columbia, '77).

LOVE MAKES THINGS HAPPEN
Artist: Pebbles
Written by: Kenny Edmunds (Babyface), Antonio Reid (L. A. Reid)
From the album: *Always*
Label: MCA
Produced by: L. A. Reid
Year: 1990
The 4TH #1 R&B crossover for one-time Mrs. Reid.

LOVE ME
Artist: Willie & Ruth
Written by: Jerry Leiber, Mike Stoller
Label: Spark
Produced by: Jerry Leiber, Mike Stoller
Year: 1954
Cover by Elvis Presley (RCA, '56) was not released as a single yet made #2 on the charts. Ruth (Brown) would return a few years later with Leiber & Stoller's "Lucky Lips," among many others.

LOVE ME DO
Artist: The Beatles
Written by: John Lennon, Paul McCartney
From the album: *Introducing the Beatles*
Label: Vee Jay
Produced by: George Martin
Year: 1963
Recorded with "(P.S.) I Love You" at their first recording session in '62, this was one of the many undeniable singles rescued in the wake of their

worldwide success in '64. Recycling Brill Building and Motown sounds with a Little-Richardesque vengeance and an Everly-Brothersesque harmony, they went on to display Chuck Berryesque verbal wit and acuity, in a tight Buddy-Holly-and-the-Cricketsesque rock and roll combo setting. A couple of years later John Lennon would become infatuated with Bob Dylan. A couple of years after that, George would lead them to the Mahareeshi. Paul met Linda. John met Yoko. And there you have the '60s.

LOVE ME, I'M A LIBERAL
Artist: Phil Ochs
Written by: Phil Ochs
From the album: *Phil Ochs in Concert*
Label: Elektra
Produced by: Paul Rothchild
Year: 1966
Biting satire of the hands that fed him, book-ending the scathing "Draft Dodger Rag."

LOVE ME LIKE A MAN
Artist: Bonnie Raitt
Written by: Chris Smither
From the album: *Give It Up*
Label: Warner Brothers
Produced by: Michael Cuscuna
Year: 1972
A bluesy standard that defines the early Raitt's accessibly earthy persona.

LOVE ME TENDER
Artist: Elvis Presley
Written by: Vera Watson, Elvis Presley
From the album: *Love Me Tender*
Label: RCA
Produced by: Steve Sholes
Year: 1956
His fifth #1 of '56, from his first motion picture, *Love Me Tender*, with Richard Egan and Debra Paget.

LOVE ME TWO TIMES
Artist: The Doors
Written by: Jim Morrison, Robbie Krieger, John Densmore, Ray Manzarek
From the album: *Strange Days*
Label: Elektra
Produced by: Paul Rothchild
Year: 1967
Frat rock sentiments, Hollywood polish.

LOVE MINUS ZERO/ NO LIMIT
Artist: Bob Dylan
Written by: Bob Dylan
From the album: *Bringing It All Back Home*
Label: Columbia
Produced by: Tom Wilson
Year: 1965
Perhaps his tenderest love song, a portrait of the artist.

LOVE MY WAY

Artist: The Psychedelic Furs
Written by: Richard Butler, Tim Butler, John Ashton, Vincent Ely
From the album: *Mirror Moves*
Label: Columbia
Produced by: Todd Rundgren
Year: 1984
U2 lite.

LOVE OF A LIFETIME

Artist: Firehouse
Written by: Bill Leverty, C. J. Snare
From the album: *Firehouse*
Label: Epic
Produced by: David Prater
Year: 1991

LOVE ON A TWO-WAY STREET

Artist: The Moments
Written by: Sylvia Robinson, Bert Keyes
From the album: *The Moments' Greatest Hits*
Label: Stang
Produced by: Sylvia Robinson
Year: 1970
Previously heard on "Love Is Strange," Sylvia Robinson makes her comeback as writer and producer of this mellow #1 R&B/Top 10 crossover.

LOVE ON THE ROCKS

Artist: Neil Diamond
Written by: Neil Diamond, Gilbert Becaud
From the album: *The Jazz Singer Soundtrack*
Label: Capitol
Produced by: Bob Gaudio
Year: 1981
From his magnificently miscast performance as Sir Laurence Olivier's son, the young Al Jolson.

LOVE ON YOUR SIDE

Artist: Thompson Twins
Written by: Tom Bailey, Alannah Currie, Joe Leeway
From the album: *Side Kicks*
Label: Arista
Produced by: Alex Sadkin
Year: 1983
First UK hit for the synth-rock group from England.

LOVE POTION NUMBER NINE

Artist: The Clovers
Written by: Jerry Leiber, Mike Stoller
From the album: *Love Potion Number Nine*
Label: United Artists
Produced by: Jerry Leiber, Mike Stoller
Year: 1959
Way past their prime, the doo-wop pioneers cash in with their biggest hit. Covered by the Searchers (Kapp, '65).

LOVE RADIATES AROUND

Artist: The Roches
Written by: Mark Johnson
From the album: *Another World*
Label: Warner Brothers
Produced by: Ed Kalehoff, Howard Lindeman
Year: 1985
Folk/rock harmony perfection.

LOVE, REIGN O'ER ME

Artist: The Who
Written by: Pete Townshend
From the album: *Quadrophenia*
Label: Track
Produced by: The Who
Year: 1973
His great sprawling rainy epic.

LOVE ROLLERCOASTER

Artist: Ohio Players
Written by: Leroy Bonner, Ralph Middlebrooks, Marshall Jones, William Beck, Marvin Pierce, Jim Williams, Clarence Satchell
From the album: *Honey*
Label: Mercury
Produced by: Ohio Players
Year: 1975
A disco fan favorite.

LOVE SHACK

Artist: The B-52's
Written by: The B-52's
From the album: *Cosmic Thing*
Label: Reprise
Produced by: Don Was
Year: 1989
A blissful return to the frat house of long ago. Suggested segue: "Sugar Shack" by Jimmy Gilmer & the Fireballs

LOVE SHE CAN COUNT ON, A

Artist: The Miracles
Written by: Smokey Robinson
From the album: *The Fabulous Miracles*
Label: Tamla
Produced by: Smokey Robinson
Year: 1963
Once again, Smokey Robinson transcends his condition with hope, common sense, a wistful grace, and phrases that turn on a dime.

LOVE SO RIGHT

Artist: Bee Gees
Written by: Barry Gibb, Robin Gibb, Maurice Gibb
From the album: *Children of the World*
Label: RSO
Produced by: Robert Stigwood, Bee Gees
Year: 1976
Friday night fever.

LOVE SOMEBODY

Artist: Rick Springfield
Written by: Rick Springfield
From the album: *Hard to Hold Soundtrack*
Label: RCA
Produced by: Bill Drescher, Rick Springfield
Year: 1984
Like Madonna, Debbie Harry, Paul Simon, and Neil Diamond, Rick's movie experience was notable primarily for the hit single it spawned.

LOVE SONG

Artist: The Cure
Written by: Robert Smith, Laurence Tolhurst, Simon Gallup, Purl Thompson, Boris Williams, Roger O'Donnell
From the album: *Disintegration*
Label: Elektra
Produced by: Robert Smith, Dave Allen
Year: 1989
Their only US Top 10; in the UK "Lullaby" also hit Top 10.

LOVE SONG

Artist: The Damned
Written by: Captain Sensible, Rat Scabies, Dave Vanian, Algy Ward
From the album: *Machine Gun Etiquette*
Produced by: Ed Hollis, the Damned
Year: 1979
First chart single for the first punk band.

LOVE SPREADS

Artist: The Stone Roses
Written by: John Squires
From the album: *Second Coming*
Label: Geffen
Produced by: Simon Dawson
Year: 1994
Comeback single.

LOVE STINKS

Artist: The J. Geils Band
Written by: Seth Justman, Peter Wolf
From the album: *Love Stinks*
Label: EMI-America
Produced by: Seth Justman
Year: 1979
An apt career summation at that point in time, before "Centerfold" nearly got them out of debt.

LOVE STRUCK BABY

Artist: Stevie Ray Vaughan
Written by: Stevie Ray Vaughan
From the album: *Texas Flood*
Label: Epic
Produced by: Stevie Ray Vaughan, Double Trouble, Richard Mullen
Year: 1983
A new Hendrixian blues guitar god rises in Austin.

LOVE TAKES TIME

Artist: Mariah Carey
Written by: Ben Margulies, Mariah Carey
From the album: *Mariah Carey*
Label: Columbia
Produced by: David Lawrence
Year: 1990
Second straight #1 R&B/#1 crossover from her debut album.

LOVE THAT BURNS

Artist: Fleetwood Mac
Written by: Peter Green
From the album: *English Rose*
Label: Epic
Produced by: Mike Vernon
Year: 1969
Guitarist Peter Green doing the burning.

LOVE THE ONE YOU'RE WITH

Artist: Stephen Stills
Written by: Stephen Stills
From the album: *Stephen Stills 2*
Label: Atlantic
Produced by: Stephen Sills, Bill Halverson
Year: 1971
Epitomizing the downfall of the sexual revolution, as well as folk/rock.

LOVE TO LOVE YOU BABY

Artist: Donna Summer
Written by: Giorgio Moroder, Pete Bellotte, Donna Summer
From the album: *Love to Love You Baby*
Label: Oasis
Produced by: Pete Bellotte
Year: 1976
The first diva of disco arrives, swooning, from Boston, by way of Germany. A long national simulated orgy would ensue.

LOVE TRAIN

Artist: The O'Jays
Written by: Kenny Gamble, Leon Huff
From the album: *Back Stabbers*
Label: Philadelphia International
Produced by: Kenny Gamble, Leon Huff
Year: 1972
Their biggest hit, a #1 R&B/#1 crossover. Suggested segues: "People Get Ready" by the Impressions, "Peace Train" by Cat Stevens.

LOVE WALKS IN

Artist: Van Halen
Written by: Eddie Van Halen, Alex Van Halen, Michael Anthony, Sammy Hagar
From the album: *5150*
Label: Warner Brothers
Produced by: Van Halen, Don Landee, Mick Jones
Year: 1986
Sammy walks in, Dave walks out.

LOVE WILL FIND A WAY

Artist: Pablo Cruise
Written by: Cory Lerios, David Jenkins
From the album: *World's Away*
Label: A&M
Produced by: Bill Schnee
Year: 1978
Blue-eyed soul, minus the soul.

LOVE WILL KEEP US TOGETHER

Artist: Neil Sedaka
Written by: Howard Greenfield, Neil Sedaka
From the album: *Sedaka's Back*
Label: Rocket
Produced by: Robert Appere, Neil Sedaka
Year: 1974
Last tune written by the storied song-writing team of Sedaka and Greenfield before they broke up in the late '60s, Sedaka moving on to England, Greenfield moving on to Helen Miller, et al. Cover by the Captain & Tenille (A&M, '75) went to #1 and was song of the year, with a shout out to Neil in the outro. The album *Sedaka's Back* compiles three albums he made in England.

LOVE WILL NEVER DO WITHOUT YOU

Artist: Janet Jackson
Written by: James Harris III, Terry Lewis
From the album: *Rhythm Nation 1814*
Label: A&M
Produced by: Jimmy Jam, Terry Lewis
Year: 1989
Fourth #1 from the album.

LOVE WILL TEAR US APART

Artist: Joy Division
Written by: Ian Curtis, Joy Division
From the album: *Substance*
Label: Factory/Qwest
Produced by: Martin Hannett
Year: 1980
Acidic punk metal lament became legendary when Curtis committed suicide just before the band's first American tour. After his death the group reformed as New Order.

LOVE WON'T LET ME WAIT

Artist: Major Harris
Written by: Bobby Eli, Vinnie Barrett
From the album: *My Way*
Produced by: Bobby Eli
Label: Atlantic
Year: 1975
Only #1 R&B/Top 10 crossover for the Philly soul veteran.

LOVE YOU DOWN

Artist: Ready for the World
Written by: Melvin Riley, Gordon Strozier, Gerald Valentine
From the album: *Long Time Coming*
Label: MCA
Produced by: Ready for the World, Gary Spaniola
Year: 1986
#1 R&B/Top 10 crossover.

LOVE YOU INSIDE OUT

Artist: Bee Gees
Written by: Barry Gibb, Robin Gibb, Maurice Gibb
From the album: *Spirits Having Flown*
Label: RSO
Produced by: Albhy Galutin, Karl Richardson, Bee Gees
Year: 1979
Their ninth and last #1.

LOVE YOU SAVE, THE

Artist: The Jackson 5
Written by: Freddie Perren, Berry Gordy Jr., Deke Richards, Fonce Mizell
From the album: *ABC*
Label: Motown
Produced by: Freddie Perren, Berry Gordy Jr., Deke Richards, Fonce Mizell
Year: 1970
Third of four straight #1 R&B/#1 crossovers to launch a legendary career.

LOVE ZONE

Artist: Billy Ocean
Written by: Barry Eastmond, Billy Ocean, Wayne Braithwaite
From the album: *Love Zone*
Label: Jive
Produced by: Mutt Lange
Year: 1986
Third hit from the album; a #1 R&B/Top 10 crossover.

LOVE'S GOT A LINE ON YOU

Artist: Scandal
Written by: Zack Smith, Kathe Green
From the album: *Scandal*
Label: Columbia
Produced by: Vini Poncia
Year: 1983
Perfect power punk from the spunky Patty Smythe. Cyndi Lauper was encouraged.

LOVE'S MADE A FOOL OF YOU

Artist: The Crickets
Written by: Buddy Holly, Bob Montgomery
From the album: *In Style with the Crickets*
Label: Brunswick
Produced by: Norman Petty
Year: 1959

Released by the Crickets as their first post-Buddy single. Covered by Tom Rush (Elektra, '64), the Bobby Fuller Four (Mustang, '66).

LOVE'S THEME

Artist: Love Unlimited
Written by: Barry White
From the album: *Under the Influence Of*
Label: 20TH Century
Produced by: Barry White
Year: 1973
Instrumental interpretation of the Love Man's eternal soul message.

LOVELY RITA

Artist: The Beatles
Written by: John Lennon, Paul McCartney
From the album: *Sgt. Pepper's Lonely Hearts Club Band*
Label: Capitol
Produced by: George Martin
Year: 1967
One of their more obscure characters: Rita the meter maid.

LOVER, PLEASE

Artist: Clyde McPhatter
Written by: Bill Swan
From the album: *Greatest Hits*
Label: Mercury
Year: 1961
Clyde's second biggest hit was written by rockabilly crooner Swan, who would reach the charts with "I Can Help" in '74.

LOVERBOY

Artist: Billy Ocean
Written by: Keith Diamond, Billy Ocean, Robert John "Mutt" Lange, Billy Alessi, Bobby Alessi
From the album: *Suddenly*
Label: Jive
Produced by: Keith Diamond
Year: 1984
Entering the New Jack derby.

LOVERGIRL

Artist: Teena Marie
Written by: Teena Marie Brockert
From the album: *Starchild*
Label: Epic
Produced by: Teena Marie
Year: 1985
Biggest hit for the Rick James discovery, from her sixth album. Often cited as the best white female funk singer.

LOVERS NEVER SAY GOODBYE

Artist: The Flamingos
Written by: Terry Johnson, Paul Wilson
From the album: *Battle of the Groups*
Label: End

Produced by: George Goldner
Year: 1959
Probably their best remembered single. Also known as "Please Wait for Me."

LOVERS WHO WANDER

Artist: Dion
Written by: Dion DiMucci, Ernie Maresca
From the album: *Lovers Who Wander*
Label: Laurie
Produced by: Gene Schwartz
Year: 1962
Trying out for Atlantic City, Dion only made it as far as Palisades Park.

LOVER'S CONCERTO, A

Artist: The Toys
Written by: Sandy Linzer, Denny Randell
From the album: *Toys Sing a Lover's Concerto/and Attack*
Label: Dyno Voice
Produced by: Sandy Linzer, Denny Randell
Year: 1965
Based on a Bach finger exercise.

LOVER'S QUESTION, A

Artist: Clyde McPhatter
Written by: Brook Benton, Jimmy Williams
From the album: *Clyde*
Label: Atlantic
Produced by: Ahmet Ertegun, Jerry Wexler
Year: 1958
Clyde's biggest hit; his only #1 R&B/Top 10 crossover.

LOVES ME LIKE A ROCK

Artist: Paul Simon with the Dixie Humingbirds
Written by: Paul Simon
From the album: *There Goes Rhymin' Simon*
Label: Columbia
Produced by: Phil Ramone, Paul Simon
Year: 1973
One of his biggest hits, presaging further roots rock explorations.

LOVESICK BLUES

Artist: Hank Williams
Written by: Hank Williams
Label: MGM
Produced by: Fred Rose
Year: 1949
Originally released in 1922 by Emmett Miller. Hank's first #1 country/Top 30 crossover spent 42 weeks on the charts. Also crossed over to England, where it was a #1 UK hit for Frank Ifield in '62/Top 50 US (Vee-Jay, '63). Bob Dylan was listening here, the Beatles there.

LOVEY DOVEY

Artist: The Clovers
Written by: Ahmet Ertegun, Memphis Curtis
Label: Atlantic
Produced by: Ahmet Ertegun, Jerry Wexler

Year: 1955
Their 10TH out of 12 Top 5 R&B hits, covered by Clyde McPhatter (Atlantic, '59), Buddy Knox (Liberty, '60), Otis and Carla (Stax, '68).

LOVIN' EVERY MINUTE OF IT

Artist: Loverboy
Written by: Robert John "Mutt" Lange
From the album: *Lovin' Every Minute of It*
Label: Columbia
Produced by: Mutt Lange
Year: 1985
Biggest hit for the arena band from Canada.

LOVIN' YOU

Artist: Minnie Riperton
Written by: Minnie Riperton, Richard Rudolph
From the album: *Perfect Angel*
Label: Epic
Produced by: Stevie Wonder
Year: 1974
Gorgeous falsetto effort from the former lead voice of the artsy Rotary Connection.

LOVING YOU

Artist: Elvis Presley
Written by: Jerry Leiber, Mike Stoller
From the album: *Elvis*
Label: RCA
Produced by: Steve Sholes
Year: 1957
B-side of "Teddy Bear," from the movie *Loving You*.

LOW RIDER

Artist: War
Written by: Sylvester Allen, Lee Oscar Levitin, Morris Dickerson, Leroy "Lonnie" Jordan, Howard Scott, Charles W. Miller, Harold R. Brown
From the album: *Why Can't We Be Friends*
Label: United Artists
Produced by: Jerry Goldstein
Year: 1975
Their only #1 R&B/Top 10 crossover.

LOW SELF OPINION

Artist: The Rollins Band
Written by: Rollins Band
From the album: *The End of Silence*
Label: Imago
Produced by: Andy Wallace
Year: 1991
Suggested segue: "Self Esteem" by Offspring, "Creep" by Radiohead.

LOW SPARK OF HIGH HEELED BOYS, THE

Artist: Traffic
Written by: Steve Winwood, Jim Capaldi
From the album: *The Low Spark of High Heeled Boys*
Label: Island

Year: 1971
Making their Bowie-Reed-Mott the Hoople move.

LOWDOWN

Artist: Boz Scaggs
Written by: David Paich, William Scaggs
From the album: *Silk Degrees*
Label: Columbia
Produced by: Joe Wissert
Year: 1976
His biggest hit.

LUCILLE

Artist: Little Richard
Written by: Richard Penniman (Little Richard),
Albert Collins
From the album: *Little Richard*
Label: Specialty
Produced by: Bumps Blackwell
Year: 1957
His third #1 R&B/Top 20 crossover. Could it be
one bluesman's ode to another's guitar?

LUCILLE

Artist: Kenny Rogers
Written by: Hal Bynum, Roger Bowling
From the album: *Kenny Rogers*
Label: United Artists
Produced by: Larry Butler
Year: 1976
His first solo success is a #1 country/Top 10 cross-
over.

LUCKY LIPS

Artist: Ruth Brown
Written by: Jerry Leiber, Mike Stoller
Label: Atlantic
Year: 1957
After 11 Top 10 R&B tunes, her first crossover hit.
Another reason why Atlantic records was once
known as "The house that Ruth built." Covered by
Cliff Richard (Epic, '63).

LUCKY MAN

Artist: Emerson Lake and Palmer (ELP)
Written by: Greg Lake
From the album: *Emerson Lake and Palmer*
Label: Cotillion
Produced by: Greg Lake
Year: 1971
King Crimson lite.

LUCKY NUMBER

Artist: Lene Lovich
Written by: Lene Lovich, Les Chappell
From the album: *Stateless*
Label: Stiff
Year: 1979
One of the original twisted sisters, along with
Exene Cervenka, Poly Styrene, Ivy Rorschach,
Lydia Lunch, and Nina Hagen.

LUCKY STAR

Artist: Madonna
Written by: Madonna Ciccone
From the album: *Madonna*
Label: Sire
Produced by: Reggie Lucas
Year: 1983
As girlishly innocent as Kathy Young, but with a
devilish master plan.

LUCY IN THE SKY WITH DIAMONDS

Artist: The Beatles
Written by: John Lennon, Paul McCartney
From the album: *Sgt. Pepper's Lonely Hearts Club
Band*
Label: Capitol
Produced by: George Martin
Year: 1967
Considered a thinly veiled celebration of LSD-
inspired imagery by everyone but its writer, John
Lennon, it was never released as a single by the
Beatles. Cover by Elton John (Rocket, '75), went
to #1. Mishearing the lyrics, John Fred wrote
"Judy in Disguise (with Glasses)."

LUKA

Artist: Suzanne Vega
Written by: Suzanne Vega
From the album: *Solitude Standing*
Label: A&M
Produced by: Lenny Kaye, Steve Addabbo
Year: 1987
Top-5 folk/rock fluke on child abuse establishes
Vega as the poet laureate of Greenwich Village,
taking over for Patti Smith. Suggested segue:
"What's the Matter Here" by 10,000 Maniacs.

LULLABY

Artist: The Cure
Written by: Robert Smith, Laurence Tolhurst,
Simon Gallup, Boris Williams, Purl Thompson,
Roger O'Donnell
From the album: *Disintegration*
Label: Elektra
Produced by: Robert Smith, Dave Allen
Year: 1989
Big in the UK.

LULLABY

Artist: Shawn Mullins
Written by: Shawn Mullins
From the album: *Soul's Core*
Label: SMG
Year: 1998
A wise (or is it wise-ass) view of L.A. coffee house
culture, from an Atlanta, Georgia, visitor.

LUST FOR LIFE

Artist: Iggy Pop
Written by: James Osterberg (Iggy Pop)
From the album: *Lust for Life*

Label: RCA
Produced by: David Bowie
Year: 1977
Unrequited.

LYIN' EYES

Artist: Eagles
Written by: Don Henley, Glenn Frey
From the album: *One of These Nights*
Label: Asylum
Produced by: Bill Szymczyk
Year: 1975

M

M.A.R.T.I.N.A.

Artist: Phranc
Written by: Phranc
From the album: *Positively Phranc*
Label: Island
Produced by: Warren Bruleigh
Year: 1991
A frank ode to her lesbian role model Navratilova.

M.T.A., THE

Artist: Will Holt
Written by: Jacqueline Steiner, Bess Hawes
From the album: *The World of Will Holt*
Label: Coral
Year: 1957
Social satire presaging the coming folk scare. Based
on "The Wreck of the Old 97," it was written in
1948 about the Boston political campaign of Walter
F. O' Brien. Covered by the Kingston Trio (Capi-
tol, '59).

MACARENA (BAYSIDE BOYS MIX)

Artist: Los Del Rios
Written by: A. Romero Monge, R. Ruiz
From the album: *Macarena Non Stop*
Label: Ariola
Produced by: Carlos DeYarza, Mike Triay
Year: 1995
Aided and abetted by the all-girl giggling chorus,
this Dance/Chant/Mix became the successor to
"Whoot! (There It Is)" and "The Wave" in the are-
nas, dance halls, soccer stadiums (and probably bull
rings) of the world for a solid year.

MACARTHUR PARK

Artist: Richard Harris
Written by: Jimmy Webb
From the album: *A Tramp Shining*
Label: Dunhill
Produced by: Jimmy Webb
Year: 1968
Webb's lovelorn epiphanies get the standard pop
treatment. Fabled now for the improbable "some-
one left a cake out in the rain" image. Covered for
the disco set by Donna Summer (Casablanca, '78).

MACHINE GUN

Artist: Commodores
Written by: Milan Williams
From the album: *Machine Gun*
Label: Motown
Produced by: James Carmichael, Commodores
Year: 1974
Debuting on the charts with an instrumental.

MACHINE GUN

Artist: Jimi Hendrix
Written by: Jimi Hendrix
From the album: *Band of Gypsies*
Label: Capitol
Year: 1970
One of his more amazing guitar attacks.

MACHO MAN

Artist: The Village People
Written by: Henri Belolo, Jacques Morali, Victor Willis, Peter Whitehead
From the album: *Macho Man*
Label: Casablanca
Produced by: Henri Belolo
Year: 1978
Standard disco pose.

MACK THE KNIFE

Artist: Louis Armstrong
Written by: Berthold Brecht, Kurt Weill and Marc Blitzstein
From the album: *Mack the Knife*
Label: Columbia
Year: 1956
One quintessential musical character introduces another to the risks and delights of the modern world. Three years later, Bobby Darin's version of the updated classic from *The Threepanny Opera* spent nine weeks at #1.

MAD ABOUT YOU

Artist: Belinda Carlisle
Written by: Paula Brown, James Whelan, Mitchell Young Evans
From the album: *Belinda Carlisle*
Label: MCA
Produced by: Rick Nowels
Year: 1986
Post Go-Gos Valley ballad.

MAD MAD ME

Artist: Maria Muldaur
Written by: Wendy Waldman
From the album: *Maria Muldaur*
Label: Warner Brothers
Produced by: Joe Boyd, Lenny Waronker
Year: 1973
Funky rock confessional launches the career of Wendy Waldman, who would have to move to Nashville to achieve further songwriting success.

MAD WORLD

Artist: Tears for Fears
Written by: Roland Orazbel
From the album: *The Hurting*
Label: Mercury
Year: 1982
A year prior to their US takeover, the pioneering UK synth band scores their first #1 UK.

MADAMME GEORGE

Artist: Van Morrison
Written by: Van Morrison
From the album: *Astral Weeks*
Label: Warner Brothers
Produced by: Lee Merenstein
Year: 1969
Brooding, mystical, Joycean character portrait originally recorded as part of the sessions that produced "Brown Eyed Girl," with Bert Berns in New York in '67.

MADONNA OF THE WASPS

Artist: Robyn Hitchcock
Written by: Robyn Hitchcock
From the album: *Queen Elvis*
Label: A&M
Year: 1989
Solo effort from the offbeat British singer/songwriter and former member of the Soft Boys.

MAGGIE MAY

Artist: Rod Stewart
Written by: Rod Stewart, Martin Quittenton
From the album: *Every Picture Tells a Story*
Label: Mercury
Produced by: Rod Stewart
Year: 1971
Rod's ultimate paean to young lust with an older woman was originally the B-side of "Reason to Believe," his first solo single.

MAGGIE'S FARM

Artist: Bob Dylan
Written by: Bob Dylan
From the album: *Bringing It All Back Home*
Label: Columbia
Produced by: Tom Wilson
Year: 1965
Proletariat companion piece to "Subterreanean Homesick Blues." Covered by the Specials (2TONE, '81). Performed with absurdist perfection in the Marlon Brando/Matthew Broderick film, *The Freshman*, by Bert Parks backed by Was (Not Was).

MAGGOT BRAIN

Artist: Funkadelic
Written by: George Clinton, Eddie Hazel
From the album: *Maggot Brain*
Label: Westbound
Produced by: George Clinton

Year: 1971
Channeling Hendrix, Eddie Hazel practices his extended guitar eulogy.

MAGIC

Artist: Olivia Newton-John
Written by: John Farrar
From the album: *Xanadu Soundtrack*
Label: MCA
Produced by: John Farrar
Year: 1980
#1 hit from the film.

MAGIC

Artist: Pilot
Written by: David Payton, William Lyall
From the album: *Pilot*
Label: EMI
Produced by: Alan Parsons
Year: 1975
Coming down from engineering Pink Floyd's *Dark Side of the Moon*, Parsons produces a one-shot.

MAGIC BUS

Artist: The Who
Written by: Pete Townshend
From the album: *Magic Bus*
Label: Decca
Produced by: Kit Lambert
Year: 1968
Supposed drug reference. Suggested segues: "Yellow Submarine" by the Beatles, "Purple Haze" by Jimi Hendrix, "Eight Miles High" by the Byrds, "Along Comes Mary" by the Association, "White Rabbit" by the Jefferson Airplane, "Mellow Yellow" by Donovan, "Puff the Magic Dragon" by Peter, Paul and Mary.

MAGIC CARPET RIDE

Artist: Steppenwolf
Written by: John Kay, Rushton Moreve
From the album: *Steppenwolf the Second*
Label: Dunhill
Produced by: Gabriel Mekler
Year: 1968
Biker ballad follow up to the ultimate biker rocker "Born to Be Wild."

MAGIC MAN

Artist: Heart
Written by: Ann Wilson, Nancy Wilson
From the album: *Dreamboat Annie*
Label: Mushroom
Produced by: Mike Flicker
Year: 1976
Making their case as the female Led Zeppelin.

MAGIC POWER

Artist: Triumph
Written by: Rik Emmett, Gil Moore, Mike Levine
From the album: *Allied Forces*
Label: RCA
Produced by: Dave Thoener, Triumph

Year: 1981
Inspiring Canadian arena showcase for guitarist Emmett.

MAGICAL MYSTERY TOUR

Artist: The Beatles
Written by: John Lennon, Paul McCartney
From the album: *Magical Mystery Tour*
Label: Capitol
Produced by: George Martin
Year: 1967
Skifflesque title tune to the album and TV special.

MAGNET AND STEEL

Artist: Walter Egan
Written by: Walter Egan
From the album: *Not Shy*
Label: Columbia
Produced by: Richard Dashut, Lindsay Buckingham, Walter Egan
Year: 1977
Using the Fleetwood Mac production team as well as Stevie Nicks and Lindsay Buckingham on backing vocal for an L.A. one-shot.

MAINLINE PROSPERITY BLUES

Artist: Richard and Mimi Fariña
Written by: Richard Fariña
From the album: *Reflections in a Crystal Wind*
Label: Vanguard
Year: 1966
Folk/rock depiction of a generation's attraction to drugs.

MAINSTREET

Artist: Bob Seger
Written by: Bob Seger
From the album: *Night Moves*
Label: Capitol
Produced by: Jack Richardson, Bob Seger
Year: 1976
Striving to mythify Michigan the way Springsteen did New Jersey.

MAJOR LEAGUES

Artist: Pavement
Written by: Stephen Malkmus
From the album: *Terror Twilight*
Label: Matador
Year: 1999
Indie darlings crash the show.

MAJOR TOM (COMING HOME)

Artist: Peter Schilling
Written by: Peter Schilling, David Lodge
From the album: *Error in the System*
Label: Elektra
Produced by: Peter Schilling, Armin Sabol
Year: 1983

Answer song to Bowie's "Space Oddity" ten years later. Suggested segues: "Rocket Man" by Elton John, "Ashes to Ashes" by David Bowie.

MAKE A MOVE ON ME

Artist: Olivia Newton-John
Written by: John Farrar, Tom Snow
From the album: *Physical*
Label: MCA
Produced by: John Farrar
Year: 1981
From her ill-advised sex kitten phase.

MAKE EM SAY UHH

Artist: Master P
Written by: Master P, Silkk the Shocker, Fiend, Mia X, Mystikal
From the album: *MP Da Last Don*
Label: No Limit
Year: 1998
Epitomizing rap's entrepreneurial spirit.

MAKE IT EASY ON YOURSELF

Artist: Jerry Butler
Written by: Burt Bacharach, Hal David
From the album: *Jerry Butler's Golden Hits*
Label: Vee Jay
Year: 1962
Brill Building soul, just as Motown was becoming a better option. Covered by the Walker Brothers (Smash, '65), Dionne Warwick (Scepter, '67).

MAKE IT FUNKY (PART I)

Artist: James Brown
Written by: James Brown
From the album: *Revolution of the Mind: Live at the Apollo (Vol. II)*
Label: Polydor
Produced by: James Brown
Year: 1971
Goes without saying.

MAKE IT HOT

Artist: Nicole featuring Missy Elliott and Mocha
Written by: Melissa (Missy) Elliott
From the album: *Make It Hot*
Label: The Gold Mine
Year: 1998
Essential high school posturing, given street cred by powerhouse chaperone Missy.

MAKE IT REAL

Artist: The Jets
Written by: Linda Mallah, Rich Kelly, Dan Powell
From the album: *Magic*
Label: MCA
Produced by: Dan Powell, M. Verdick, Rich Kelly
Year: 1987
Fifth Top 10 dance pop hit from the singing Wolfgramm family from Tonga (by way of Minneapolis).

MAKE IT WITH YOU

Artist: Bread
Written by: David Gates
From the album: *On the Waters*
Label: Elektra
Produced by: David Gates, Robb Royer, James Grafton
Year: 1970
The L.A. session sound of the anti-Randy Newman. Richard Marx would mine this niche.

MAKE ME LOSE CONTROL

Artist: Eric Carmen
Written by: Eric Carmen, Dean Pitchford
From the album: *Best of Eric Carmen*
Label: Arista
Produced by: Jimmy Lenner
Year: 1988
Capitalizing on his movie exposure in the *Dirty Dancing* soundtrack to revitalize his moribund career.

MAKE ME SMILE

Artist: Chicago
Written by: James Pankow
From the album: *Chicago II*
Label: Columbia
Produced by: James William Guercio
Year: 1970
The Big Rock Band sound hits the Top 10 for the first time.

MAKE ME THE WOMAN THAT YOU COME HOME TO

Artist: Gladys Knight & the Pips
Written by: Clay McMurray
From the album: *Standing Ovation*
Label: soul
Produced by: Clay McMurray
Year: 1971
Cozy come-on epitomizes Gladys Knight's position as the soul of monogamy.

MAKE YOU SWEAT

Artist: Keith Sweat
Written by: Keith Sweat, Bobby Wooten, Timothy Gatling
From the album: *I'll Give All My Love to You*
Label: Elektra
Year: 1990
#1 R&B/Top 20 crossover. Suggested segues: "Gonna Make You Sweat (Everybody Dance Now)" by C&C Music Factory (Columbia, '80), "Sweat (La La La La La Long)" by Inner Circle (Big Beat, '93).

MAKIN' IT

Artist: David Naughton
Written by: Freddie Perren, Dino Fekaris
Label: RSO
Year: 1979
Inescapable TV theme by the original "Dr. Pepper guy."

MAKIN' THUNDERBIRDS

Artist: Bob Seger
Written by: Bob Seger
From the album: *The Distance*
Label: Capitol
Produced by: Jimmy Iovine
Year: 1983
Reclaiming his Detroit roots.

MAKING LOVE OUT OF NOTHING AT ALL

Artist: Air Supply
Written by: Jim Steinman
From the album: *Greatest Hits*
Label: Arista
Produced by: Jim Steinman
Year: 1983
Their closest thing to rock: three-day-old Meat Loaf.

MAKING OUR DREAMS COME TRUE

Artist: Cyndi Grecco
Written by: Norman Gimbel, Charles Fox
From the album: *Laverne and Shirley*
Label: Private Stock
Produced by: Charles Fox, James Feliciano
Year: 1976
From the mid-'70s heyday of the TV sitcom theme song.

MAKING PLANS FOR NIGEL

Artist: XTC
Written by: Andy Partridge
From the album: *Drums and Wires*
Label: Virgin
Produced by: Steve Lillywhite
Year: 1982
Art rock goes to Oxford, in Oxford shoes. Covered by Primus (Interscope, '93).

MAMA (CAN I GO OUT TONIGHT)

Artist: Jo-Ann Campbell
Written by: Bo Diddley
From the album: I'm Nobody's Baby
Label: End
Year: 1956
A potential rockabilly queen gets squelched by her parents, society, the record business. Segue: "Party Lights" by Claudine Clark.

MAMA CAN'T BUY YOU LOVE

Artist: Elton John
Written by: Elton John, Bernie Taupin
From the album: *The Thom Bell Sessions*
Label: MCA
Produced by: Thom Bell
Year: 1977

Elton visits a soul guru in Philadelphia for a career makeover.

MAMA DIDN'T LIE

Artist: Jan Bradley
Written by: Curtis Mayfield
Label: Chess
Produced by: Curtis Mayfield
Year: 1963
Low-key soul tribute to the one who really knows best. Suggested segue: "Mama Said" by the Shirelles, "Mama" by Connie Francis, "Shop Around" by the Miracles, "Tell Mama" by Etta James.

MAMA (HE TREATS YOUR DAUGHTER MEAN)

Artist: Ruth Brown
Written by: Johnny Wallace, Herb Lance
From the album: *The Best of LaVern Baker*
Label: Atlantic
Produced by: Ahmet Ertegun, Jerry Wexler, Herb Abrahmson
Year: 1953
Her third #1 R&B hit crossed over to pop, for a week.

MAMA KIN

Artist: Aerosmith
Written by: Steven Tyler
From the album: *Aerosmith*
Label: Columbia
Produced by: Adrian Barber
Year: 1973
Their early arena daze. Covered by Guns N' Roses (Geffen, '86).

MAMA SAID

Artist: The Shirelles
Written by: Luther Dixon, Willie Dennson
From the album: *Greatest Hits*
Label: Scepter
Produced by: Luther Dixon
Year: 1961
Third of four #2 R&B hits.

MAMA SAID KNOCK YOU OUT

Artist: LL Cool J
Written by: James Todd Smith, Marlon Williams
From the album: *Mama Said Knock You Out*
Label: Def Jam
Produced by: Marley Marl
Year: 1991
Defining rap as the new heavyweight arena.

MAMA TOLD ME NOT TO COME

Artist: The Animals
Written by: Randy Newman

From the album: *Eric Is Here*
Label: MGM
Produced by: Mickie Most
Year: 1966
Newman's career-defining, antiparty anthem is more familiarly known as a signature tune by those notorious party animals, Three Dog Night.

MAMA WEER ALL CRAZEE NOW

Artist: Slade
Written by: Noddy Holder, Jim Lea
From the album: *Slayed*
Label: Polydor
Produced by: Chas Chandler
Year: 1972
Signature football anthem in the land where football is played with the foot.

MAMA YOU BEEN ON MY MIND

Artist: Bob Dylan
Written by: Bob Dylan
Label: Columbia
Produced by: Tom Wilson
Year: 1964
Preparing for "She Belongs to Me" and "Just like a Woman." Covered by Joan Baez as "Daddy You Been on My Mind" (Vanguard, '65).

MAMA'S PEARL

Artist: The Jackson 5
Written by: Freddie Perren, Berry Gordy Jr., Deke Richards, Fonce Mizell
From the album: *Third Album*
Label: Motown
Produced by: Freddie Perren, Berry Gordy Jr., Deke Richards, Fonce Mizell
Year: 1970
Revealing the ballad side of 13-year old Michael.

MAMBO BABY

Artist: Ruth Brown
Written by: Charles Singleton, Rose Marie McCoy
Label: Atlantic
Year: 1954
Her fifth #1 R&B hit; the most by a solo female artist, save Aretha, Whitney, Janet, and Mariah.

MAN IN NEED, A

Artist: Richard and Linda Thompson
Written by: Richard Thompson
From the album: *Shoot out the Lights*
Label: Hannibal
Produced by: Joe Boyd
Year: 1982
The ex-husband's lament.

MAN IN THE MIRROR

Michael Jackson
Written by: Siedah Garrett, Greg Ballard
From the album: *Bad*

Label: Epic
Produced by: Quincy Jones
Year: 1987
Contemplating the inner Michael, while the outer Michael was changing every day.

MAN ON THE MOON

Artist: R.E.M.
Written by: Michael Stipe, Peter Buck, Bill Berry, Mike Mills
From the album: *Automatic for the People*
Label: Warner Brothers
Produced by: Scott Litt, R.E.M.
Year: 1993
A tribute to the '70s and '80s, the Law of Gravity, and especially to the wrestling comic from *Taxi*, Andy Kaufman. Suggested segue: "Back in the Day" by Ahmad.

MAN WHO HAS EVERYTHING, THE

Artist: The Morrells
Written by: Ben Vaughan
From the album: *Shake and Push*
Label: Borrowed
Year: 1982
Rootsy rocker. Covered by Ben Vaughan (Enigma, '90).

MAN WHO SHOT LIBERTY VALANCE, THE

Artist: Gene Pitney
Written by: Hal David, Burt Bacharach
From the album: *Only Love Can Break a Heart*
Label: Musicor
Produced by: Burt Bacharach
Year: 1962
Mastering the Country and Eastern style in the big movie tune.

MAN WHO SOLD THE WORLD, THE

Artist: David Bowie
Written by: David Bowie
From the album: *The Man Who Sold the World*
Label: Mercury
Produced by: Tony Visconti
Year: 1970
Protoypically arch early track from the chameleonic superstar who influenced a generation of British rock styles, from glam to 90th, pomp to punk. Covered by Nirvana (DGC, '94).

MAN WITH THE CHILD IN HIS EYES, THE

Artist: Kate Bush
Written by: Kate Bush
From the album: *The Kick Inside*
Label: EMI-America
Produced by: Andrew Powell
Year: 1978

From her startling debut album, the song she sang on her only American TV appearance, on *Saturday Night Live*.

MANDOLIN RAIN

Artist: Bruce Hornsby and the Range
Written by: Bruce Hornsby, John Hornsby
From the album: *The Way It Is*
Label: RCA
Produced by: E. Scheiner, Bruce Hornsby
Year: 1986
Most effective use of the mandolin in Top 10 history.

MANDOLIN WIND

Artist: Rod Stewart
Written by: Rod Stewart
From the album: *Every Picture Tells a Story*
Label: Mercury
Produced by: Tom Dowd
Year: 1971
With Zeppelinesque eclecticism, Rod stretches the boundaries of rock.

MANEATER

Artist: Daryl Hall & John Oates
Written by: Daryl Hall, John Oates, Sara Allen
From the album: H_2O
Label: RCA
Produced by: Hall & Oates
Year: 1982
Returning to their favorite subject for their biggest all-time hit.

MANIAC

Artist: Michael Sembello
Written by: Michael Sembello, Dennis Matkosky
From the album: *Flashdance Soundtrack*
Label: Casablanca
Produced by: Phil Ramone, Michael Sembello
Year: 1983
From the movie that knocked off *Saturday Night Fever*, with a guitar solo that knocked off Eddie Van Halen's in "Beat it."

MANIC DEPRESSION

Artist: Jimi Hendrix
Written by: Jimi Hendrix
From the album: *Are You Experienced?*
Label: Reprise
Produced by: Chas Chandler
Year: 1967
A Seattle native previews the indigenous grunge attitude while singing his guitar solo.

MANIC MONDAY

Artist: Bangles
Written by: Prince Rogers Nelson
From the album: *Different Light*
Label: Columbia
Produced by: David Kahne
Year: 1986

An irresistible rendezvous between the master of salacious funk and the ingénues of paisley innocence, in the backyard of the Mamas & the Papas; a trans-Atlantic #2 US/#2 UK crossover.

MANIMAL

Artist: The Germs
Written by: Paul Beahm (Darby Crash), George Rothenberg
From the album: *The Decline and Fall of Western Civilization*
Label: Slash
Year: 1980
Hard-core legends in their filmic glory.

MANNISH BOY

Artist: Muddy Waters
Written by: Willie Dixon
Label: Chess
Produced by: Leonard Chess
Year: 1955
Muddy's answer to Bo Diddley's "I'm a Man." Tom Cruise's answer to Rebecca De Mornay in the epic train scene in *Risky Business*, segueing out of "In the Air Tonight" by Phil Collins.

MANY RIVERS TO CROSS

Artist: Jimmy Cliff
Written by: Jimmy Cliff
Label: Mango
Produced by: Jimmy Cliff
Year: 1970
The classic never-ending reggae journey, included in the soundtrack to *The Harder They Come* (Mango, '72). Covered by Nilsson (RCA, 74), Linda Ronstadt (Asylum, '75), and UB40 (A&M, '83).

MARCIE

Artist: Joni Mitchell
Written by: Joni Mitchell
From the album: *Joni Mitchell*
Label: Reprise
Produced by: David Crosby
Year: 1968
Influential and quintessential acoustic autobiography of a post-flower child generation.

MARGARITAVILLE

Artist: Jimmy Buffett
Written by: Jimmy Buffett
From the album: *Changes in Latitudes, Changes in Attitudes*
Label: ABC
Produced by: Norbert Putnam
Year: 1977
Buffett's biggest hit and eventual lifestyle.

MARIE MARIE

Artist: The Blasters
Written by: Dave Alvin
From the album: *American Music*
Label: Rolling Rock

Produced by: Ron Weiser
Year: 1980
Chuck Berry, squared.

(MARIE'S THE NAME) HIS LATEST FLAME

Artist: Elvis Presley
Written by: Doc Pomus, Mort Shuman
From the album: *Elvis' Golden Records (Vol. III)*
Label: RCA
Produced by: Steve Sholes
Year: 1961
Double A-side of "Little Sister."

MARILYN

Artist: Dan Bern
Written by: Dan Bern
From the album: *Dan Bern*
Produced by: Chuck Plotkin
Label: Work
Year: 1997
In which the nascent word flinger imagines a different life for Marilyn Monroe if she'd only married risqué novelist Henry Miller instead of serious playwright Arthur Miller.

MARLENE ON THE WALL

Artist: Suzanne Vega
Written by: Suzanne Vega
From the album: *Suzanne Vega*
Label: A&M
Produced by: Lenny Kaye, Steve Addabbo
Year: 1985
Modern folk/rock tribute to Marlene Dietrich was a hit in England and in Greenwich Village. Natalie Merchant was listening.

MARMENDY MILL

Artist: Flo and Eddie
Written by: Howard Kaylan, Mark Volman, Jim Pons, Al Nichol, John Seiter
From the album: *Flo and Eddie*
Label: Reprise
Produced by: Bob Ezrin
Year: 1971
Seven-minute autobiographical opus by the ex-Turtles and part-time Mothers that contains one of the great rock and roll screams.

MARQUEE MOON

Artist: Television
Written by: Tom Miller (Tom Verlaine)
From the album: *Marquee Moon*
Label: Elektra
Produced by: Tom Verlaine, Andy Johns
Year: 1977
The droning apocalyptic New York guitar version of the Butterfield/Bloomfield opus "East West."

MARRAKESH EXPRESS

Artist: Crosby, Stills & Nash
Written by: Graham Nash
From the album: *Crosby, Stills & Nash*

Label: Atlantic
Produced by: Crosby, Stills & Nash
Year: 1969
Anthem for vacationing hippies everywhere.

MARRIED MEN, THE

Artist: The Roches
Written by: Maggie Roche
From the album: *The Roches*
Label: Warner Brothers
Produced by: Robert Fripp
Year: 1979
Greenwich Village liberation tied to Greenwich, Connecticut, guilt. Covered by New Jersey's Phoebe Snow (Columbia, '78), for whom it was a major theme.

MARTHA MY DEAR

Artist: The Beatles
Written by: John Lennon, Paul McCartney
From the album: *The Beatles*
Label: Apple
Produced by: George Martin
Year: 1968
Front parlor pop, written for a sheepdog.

MARY JANE

Artist: Rick James
Written by: Rick James
From the album: *Come and Get It*
Label: Gordy
Year: 1978
A funk master lights it up.

MARY JANE'S LAST DANCE

Artist: Tom Petty
Written by: Tom Petty
From the album: *Greatest Hits*
Label: MCA
Produced by: Rick Rubin, Tom Petty, Mike Campbell
Year: 1993
Petty's biggest hit, after representing the lost cause of folk/rock since 1975, is a mysterious mid-tempo tale of mid-American coming of age.

MARY LOU

Artist: Young Jessie
Written by: Ron Hawkins, Jacqueline Magill
Label: Modern
Year: 1955
Covered by Ronnie Hawkins (Roulette, '59).

MASHED POTATO TIME

Artist: Dee Dee Sharp
Written by: Kal Mann (Jon Sheldon), Harry Land
From the album: *It's Mashed Potato Time*
Label: Cameo
Year: 1962
Her first and her biggest hit, a #1 R&B/Top 10 crossover, coopted from "(Do the) Mashed Potatoes (Part 1)" by Nat Kendrick and the Swans (Dade, '60), and Joey Dee & the Starliters

(Roulette, '61). James Brown, who played organ on the Kendricks tune, later verified the step with his own "Mashed Potatoes, USA." (King, '62). Segue: "Hot Pastrami" by the Dartels.

MASQUERADE

Artist: Gerry Goffin
Written by: Gerry Goffin, Bob Dylan
From the album: *Backroom Blood*
Label: Adelphi
Produced by: Bob Dylan
Year: 1993
The Brill Building lyricist achieves his lifelong folk/rock epiphany.

MASTER AND SERVANT

Artist: Depeche Mode
Written by: Martin Gore
From the album: *Some Great Reward*
Label: Sire
Produced by: Depeche Mode, Daniel Miller, G. Jones
Year: 1985
Dominating the world's dance charts.

MASTER BLASTER (JAMMIN')

Artist: Stevie Wonder
Written by: Stevie Wonder
From the album: *Hotter Than July*
Label: Tamla
Produced by: Stevie Wonder
Year: 1980
#1 R&B/Top 10 crossover.

MASTER DIK

Artist: Sonic Youth
From the album: *Sister*
Label: SST
Produced by: Sonic Youth
Year: 1987
Alternative hero J. Mascis of Dinosaur Jr. guests on guitar.

MASTER OF PUPPETS

Artist: Metallica
Written by: James Hetfield, Lars Ulrich, Cliff Burton, Kirk Hammett
From the album: *Master of Puppets*
Label: Elektra
Produced by: Fleming Rasmussen, Metallica
Year: 1986
Heavier than mere mortal metal.

MASTERPIECE

Artist: The Temptations
Written by: Norman Whitfield
From the album: *Masterpiece*
Label: Gordy
Produced by: Norman Whitfield
Year: 1973
#1 R&B/Top 10 crossover.

MASTERS OF WAR

Artist: Bob Dylan
Written by: Bob Dylan
From the album: *The Freewheelin' Bob Dylan*
Label: Columbia
Produced by: John Hammond
Year: 1963
One of his most cogent antiwar diatribes. Covered by Pearl Jam's Eddie Vedder at the Thirtieth Anniversary Dylan "Bobfest" broadcast in '93.

MATCHBOX

Artist: Carl Perkins
Written by: Blind Lemon Jefferson
From the album: *Dance Album*
Label: Sun
Produced by: Sam Phillips
Year: 1957
Country blues standard by Blind Lemon Jefferson (Paramount, '27). Covered by the Beatles (Capitol, '64).

MATERIAL GIRL

Artist: Madonna
Written by: Peter Brown, Robert Rans
From the album: *Like a Virgin*
Label: Sire
Produced by: Nile Rodgers
Year: 1984
After taking on virginity, Madonna nails capitalism.

MATTER OF TRUST, A

Artist: Billy Joel
Written by: Billy Joel
From the album: *The Bridge*
Label: Columbia
Produced by: Phil Ramone
Year: 1986
Squarely in the pop tradition.

MATTHEW AND SON

Artist: Cat Stevens
Written by: Cat Stevens
From the album: *Matthew and Son*
Label: Deram
Produced by: Mike Hurst
Year: 1967
Donovan, with a beard.

MAXWELL'S SILVER HAMMER

Artist: The Beatles
Written by: John Lennon, Paul McCartney
From the album: *Abbey Road*
Label: Apple
Produced by: George Martin
Year: 1969
The cute Beatle gets cutesy.

MAY THIS BE LOVE

Artist: Jimi Hendrix
Written by: Jimi Hendrix
From the album: *Are You Experienced?*
Label: Reprise
Produced by: Chas Chandler
Year: 1967
Featured in the soundtrack to the Seattle tribute movie *Singles*.

MAYBE

Artist: The Chantels
Written by: Richard Barrett
From the album: *We Are the Chantels*
Label: End
Produced by: George Goldner
Year: 1958
Ethereal Arlene Smith's emotional peak; Top 5 R&B/Top 20 crossover. Covered by the Three Degrees (Roulette, '70).

MAYBE BABY

Artist: The Crickets
Written by: Charles Hardin (Buddy Holly), Norman Petty
From the album: *The Chirpin' Crickets*
Label: Brunswick
Produced by: Norman Petty
Year: 1957
Holly entertains some healthy rockabilly aggression to augment his endearing hillbilly nervousness. In Minnesota, Bob Dylan was listening. In Liverpool, so were the Beatles, who recorded a Holly tune, "That'll Be the Day," as the Quarrymen in '58, and the Hollies, who coopted Buddy's adopted last name.

MAYBE HE'LL KNOW

Artist: Blue Angel
Written by: Cyndi Lauper, John Turi
From the album: *Blue Angel*
Label: Polydor
Produced by: Roy Halee
Year: 1980
A big neo-rockabilly voice comes booming out of Brooklyn. Lauper would go on to have lots of fun.

MAYBE I KNOW

Artist: Lesley Gore
Written by: Jeff Barry, Ellie Greenwich
From the album: *Golden Hits of Lesley Gore*
Label: Mercury
Produced by: Quincy Jones
Year: 1964
One of her more perceptive and reasoned (and rocking) efforts, enabling many of us, for the first time, to actually sympathize with her.

MAYBE I'M AMAZED

Artist: Paul McCartney and Linda McCartney
Written by: Paul McCartney
From the album: *McCartney*
Label: Apple
Produced by: Paul McCartney
Year: 1970
Picking up where the Beatles left off, in the middle-of-the-rock-and-roll-road. Song didn't become a hit single until '77.

MAYBE I'M DOING IT WRONG

Artist: Randy Newman
Written by: Randy Newman
From the album: *Randy Newman Live*
Label: Reprise
Produced by: Russ Titelman, Lenny Waronker
Year: 1971
A Mose Allison meets David Frischberg take on the failure of the sexual revolution.

MAYBE TOMORROW

Artist: Billy Fury
Written by: Ron Wycherly (Billy Fury)
From the album: *The Sound of Fury*
Label: Decca
Year: 1959
First hit for the British rockabilly star who never crossed the pond.

MAYBELLENE

Artist: Chuck Berry
Written by: Chuck Berry
From the album: *Chuck Berry Is on Top*
Label: Chess
Produced by: Leonard Chess, Phil Chess
Year: 1955
Establishing the rock and roll essentials—fast cars and loose women, impeded by the long arm of the Law—and introducing the Louis Jordan of the teen set to the man who took credit for coining the term Rock and Roll, DJ Alan Freed. Epitomizing his country roots, Chuck had originally named the tune after the bluegrass classic "Ida Red," popularized by Gid Tanner and then Bob Wills. Epitomizing his instinctive knowledge of the marketplace, the former hairdresser changed the name to "Maybellene," the best use of product placement until "Smells Like Teen Spirit" by Nirvana nearly 40 years later.

MAYOR OF SIMPLETON

Artist: XTC
Written by: Andy Partridge
From the album: *Oranges and Lemons*
Label: Geffen
Produced by: Paul Fox
Year: 1989
Their biggest US hit.

ME AND A GUN

Artist: Tori Amos
Written by: Tori Amos
From the album: *Little Earthquakes*
Label: Atlantic
Produced by: Ian Stanley

Year: 1992
The singer/songwriter confessional mode reaches remarkable new autobiographical depths in this piano driven tale of rape and recovery.

ME AND ALL THE OTHER MOTHERS

Artist: Loudon Wainwright III
Written by: Loudon Wainwright III
From the album: *Therapy*
Label: Silvertone
Produced by: Loudon Wainwright, Chaim Tannenbaum
Year: 1989
Updating his domestic persona.

ME AND BOBBY MCGEE

Artist: Roger Miller
Written by: Kris Kristofferson, Fred Foster
From the album: *Roger Miller*
Label: Smash
Produced by: Jerry Kennedy
Year: 1967
First appearance of the folk/rock rambling classic went to #12 country. Covered by Kristofferson (Monument, '69). The female version was Janis Joplin's only #1 song (Columbia, '71).

ME AND JULIO DOWN BY THE SCHOOL YARD

Artist: Paul Simon
Written by: Paul Simon
From the album: *Paul Simon*
Label: Columbia
Produced by: Roy Halee, Paul Simon
Year: 1972
Going back to the old neighborhood, where the man at the candy store still called him Paulie, as if to make amends to Julio for ever appearing on *American Bandstand*.

ME AND MRS. JONES

Artist: Billy Paul
Written by: Kenny Gamble, Leon Huff, Cary Gilbert
From the album: *360 Degrees of Billy Paul*
Label: Philadelphia
Produced by: Kenny Gamble, Leon Huff
Year: 1972
Young adultery hits #1 R&B/#1 crossover.

ME AND MY ARROW

Artist: Nilsson
Written by: Harry Nilsson
From the album: *The Point*
Label: RCA
Produced by: Harry Nilsson
Year: 1971
From the animated TV classic, *The Point*, narrated by Ringo Starr.

ME AND THE BOYS

Artist: Bonnie Raitt
Written by: Terry Adams
From the album: *Green Light*
Label: Warner Brothers
Produced by: Rob Fraboni
Year: 1982
Covered by Dave Edmunds (Columbia, '82). Adams's band, the tireless NRBQ, covered it on *God Bless Us All* (Rounder, '87).

ME AND YOU AND A DOG NAMED BOO

Artist: Lobo
Written by: Kent Lavoie
From the album: *Introducing Lobo*
Label: Big Tree
Produced by: Phil Gernhard
Year: 1971
Segue: "Old Shep" by Elvis Presley.

ME, MYSELF AND I

Artist: De La Soul
Written by: Paul Husten, Kevin Mercer, Dave Jolicoeur, Vincent Mason, George Clinton
From the album: *3 Feet High and Rising*
Label: Tommy Boy
Produced by: Paul Husten
Year: 1989
Soulful UK smash, with a sense of history provided by Funkadelic's "(Not Just) Knee Deep."

ME SO HORNY

Artist: 2 Live Crew
Written by: Luther Campbell, David Hobbs, Mark Ross, Chris Wong Won
From the album: *As Nasty as They Wanna Be*
Label: Luke Skywalker
Year: 1989
Raising the bar and lowering the standards on profanity in popular music. Moms Mabley and Redd Foxx were smiling, to say nothing of Millie Jackson.

ME WISE MAGIC

Artist: Van Halen
Written by: Eddie Van Halen, Alex Van Halen, Mark Anthony and David Lee Roth
From the album: *Best of Van Halen, Volume 1*
Label: Warner Brothers
Year: 1996
Recalling their metal-plated golden years.

MEAN MR. MUSTARD

Artist: The Beatles
Written by: John Lennon, Paul McCartney
From the album: *Abbey Road*
Label: Apple
Produced by: George Martin
Year: 1969

The band had been playing too much *Clue* in the studio.

MEAN WOMAN BLUES

Artist: Elvis Presley
Written by: Jerry West, Whispering Smith
From the album: *Loving You*
Label: RCA
Produced by: Steve Sholes
Year: 1957
Covered by Roy Orbison (Monument, '63).

MEET ON THE LEDGE

Artist: Fairport Convention
Written by: Richard Thompson
From the album: *Fairport Convention*
Label: A&M
Produced by: Joe Boyd
Year: 1968
British folk beer-drinking anthem, at the edge of doom, introduces the world to future guitar legend Richard Thompson.

MEET VIRGINIA

Artist: Train
Written by: Charlie Colin, Rob Hotchkiss, Patrick Monahan, Jimmy Stafford, Scott Underwood
From the album: *Train*
Label: Aware
Year: 1999
Where metal, alternative, and Top 40 converge.

MELISSA

Artist: Allman Brothers
Written by: Greg Allman, Stephen Alaimo
From the album: *Eat a Peach*
Label: Capricorn
Produced by: Tom Dowd
Year: 1972
Southern rock classic is a tortured ode to Greg's late brother Duane.

MELLOW YELLOW

Artist: Donovan
Written by: Donovan Leitch
From the album: *Mellow Yellow*
Label: Epic
Produced by: Mickie Most
Year: 1966
Instigated a brief banana-smoking craze.

MEMO FROM TURNER

Artist: Mick Jagger
Written by: Mick Jagger, Keith Richards
From the album: *Metamorphosis*
Label: Abkco
Produced by: Jack Nitzsche
Year: 1970
This is Jagger's most scary, convincing, and lethal performance. From his starring role in the cult film *Performance*.

MEMORIES

Artist: Elvis Presley
Written by: Mac Davis, Billy Strange
From the album: *Elvis*
Label: RCA
Year: 1968
Hallmark of the later (fat Elvis) period.

MEMORIES CAN'T WAIT

Artist: Talking Heads
Written by: David Byrne, Jerry Harrison
From the album: *Fear of Music*
Label: Sire
Produced by: Brian Eno
Year: 1979
Covered by Living Colour (Epic, '88).

MEMORIES OF EL MONTE

Artist: The Penguins
Written by: Frank Zappa, Ray Collins
Label: Original Sound
Year: 1963
Before he took to lovingly satirizing it, Zappa was a doo-wop devotee, as evidenced by the obvious dream-come-true situation of having his first recorded song performed by these L.A. legends.

MEMORY REMAINS, THE

Artist: Metallica
Written by: James Hetfield, Lars Ulrich
From the album: *Reload*
Label: Elektra
Produced by: Bob Rock
Year: 1997
Memories of heavier times.

MEMPHIS

Artist: Chuck Berry
Written by: Chuck Berry
From the album: *Chuck Berry's Greatest Hits*
Label: Chess
Produced by: Leonard Chess, Phil Chess
Year: 1959
B-side of "Back in the USA" introduced the lovelorn 6-year-old Marie to a moist-eyed America, unaccustomed then to the ravages of divorce. Covered by Lonnie Mack (Fraternity, '63).

MEN ARE GETTIN' SCARCE

Artist: Joe Tex
Written by: Joe Tex
Label: Dial
Produced by: Buddy Killen
Year: 1968
Oblique Vietnam war-era implications.

MEN'S ROOM L.A.

Artist: Kinky Friedman
Written by: Kinky Friedman
From the album: *Lasso from El Paso*
Label: Epic
Year: 1976
The dark side of outlaw country. Friedman would extend his kinky ethos in a series of detective novels.

MENDOCINO

Artist: The Sir Douglas Quintet
Written by: Douglas Sahm
From the album: *She's About a Mover*
Label: Smash
Produced by: Amigas de Music
Year: 1969
The Austin sound of alternate Tex-Mex.

MERCEDES BENZ

Artist: Janis Joplin
Written by: Janis Joplin, Bobby Neuwirth, Mike McClure
From the album: *Pearl*
Label: Columbia
Produced by: Paul Rothchild
Year: 1970
The mother of all classic car songs—classic car: the Mercedes Benz, epitomizing consumerism at its most sumptuous level. Eventually used in a Mercedes Benz commercial in '95.

MERCEDES BOY

Artist: Pebbles
Written by: Perri McKissick (Pebbles)
From the album: *Pebbles*
Label: MCA
Produced by: Babyface, L. A. Reid
Year: 1988
Her biggest hit.

MERCURY BLUES

Artist: Steve Miller Band
Written by: K. C. Douglas, Robert Geddins
From the album: *Revolution Soundtrack.*
Label: Capitol
Produced by: Steve Miller
Year: 1969
Classic car song—classic car: the Mercury. Miller's version of the K. C. Douglas original appeared in hippie movie *Revolution*. Covered by David Lindley (Asylum, '81), Alan Jackson (Arista, '93).

MERCY MERCY ME (THE ECOLOGY)

Artist: Marvin Gaye
Written by: Marvin Gaye
From the album: *What's Goin' On*
Label: Tamla
Produced by: Marvin Gaye
Year: 1971
The middle hit in Gaye's social activist period that began with "What's Goin' On" and concluded with "Inner City Blues."

MERCY STREET

Artist: Peter Gabriel
Written by: Peter Gabriel
From the album: *So*
Label: Geffen
Produced by: Peter Gabriel, Daniel Lanois
Year: 1986
Covered by Black Uhuru (Mesa, '93).

MERRY GO ROUND

Artist: The Replacements
Written by: Paul Westerberg
From the album: *All Shook Down*
Label: Sire
Produced by: Scott Litt, Paul Westerberg
Year: 1990
Moving into R.E.M. territory, before the breakup.

MESS O'BLUES, A

Artist: Elvis Presley
Written by: Doc Pomus, Mort Shuman
From the album: *Elvis' Golden Records (Vol. IV)*
Label: RCA
Produced by: Steve Sholes
Year: 1960
Continuing the wildly eclectic nature of his singles, Elvis moves from the opera of "It's Now or Never," to the uptown blues of the B-side.

MESSAGE IN A BOTTLE

Artist: The Police
Written by: Gordon Sumner (Sting)
From the album: *Reggatta de Blanc*
Label: A&M
Produced by: Nigel Grey, the Police
Year: 1979
Their first of five #1 UK hits.

MESSAGE OF LOVE

Artist: The Pretenders
Written by: Chrissie Hynde
From the album: *Pretenders II*
Label: Sire
Produced by: Chris Thomas
Year: 1982

MESSAGE, THE

Artist: Grandmaster Flash and the Furious Five
Written by: Duke Bootee
From the album: *Grandmaster Flash*
Label: Sugarhill
Produced by: Melvin Glover, Sylvia Robinson, Clifton Chase
Year: 1982
Taking off from the Last Poets, this epic poem outlines the precepts of the basic rap worldview of struggle and pain: "Don't push me I'm close to the edge."

MESSAGE TO YOU RUDY

Artist: The Specials
Written by: Lee Scratch Perry, Lee Thompson
From the album: *The Specials*

Produced by: Elvis Costello
Label: Two Tone
Year: 1979
Leaders of the British ska revival cover a reggae classic introduced by Daddy Livingstone.

MESSIAH WILL COME AGAIN, THE

Artist: Roy Buchanon
Written by: Roy Buchanon
From the album: *Roy Buchanon*
Label: Polydor
Year: 1972
Blistering blues guitar epic. Covered by Gary Moore (Virgin, '93).

METAL DRUMS

Artist: Patty Larkin
Written by: Patty Larkin
From the album: *Tango*
Produced by: Will Ackerman, Patty Larkin
Label: High Street
Year: 1991
Post-folk, anticorporate pollution lament.

METHOD OF MODERN LOVE

Artist: Daryl Hall & John Oates
Written by: Daryl Hall, Janna Allen
From the album: *Big Bam Boom*
Label: RCA
Produced by: Hall & Oates, Bob Clearmountain
Year: 1988
Their next to last Top 10 hit was borrowed by the Wu Tang Clan for use in "Method Man."

MEXICAN RADIO

Artist: Wall of Voodoo
Written by: Stan Ridgway, Mark Moreland, Oliver Nanini, Charles Gray
From the album: *Call of the West*
Label: Illegal
Produced by: Richard Mazda
Year: 1982
Early L.A. incessantly catchy roots-rock anthem is of a piece with R.E.M.'s "Radio Free Europe" and a reaction to Elvis Costello's "Radio Radio." Radio wasn't listening to any of them.

MEXICAN, THE

Artist: Babe Ruth
Written by: Ennio Morricone
From the album: *First Base*
Produced by: Alan Shacklock
Label: Harvest
Year: 1972
Bringing the spaghetti western to the urban dancehall.

MEXICO

Artist: Jefferson Airplane

Written by: Grace Slick
From the album: *Early Flight*
Label: Grunt
Year: 1969
B-side of "Have You Seen the Saucers?"

MIAMI 2017 (SEEN THE LIGHTS GO OUT ON BROADWAY)

Artist: Billy Joel
Written by: Billy Joel
From the album: *Turnstiles*
Label: Columbia
Produced by: Phil Ramone
Year: 1976
From the piano bar to the airport lounge.

MIAMI VICE THEME

Artist: Jan Hammer
Written by: Jan Hammer
From the album: *Miami Vice Soundtrack*
Label: MCA
Produced by: Jan Hammer
Year: 1985
As musical director of the stylish TV drama, Hammer was briefly the most important A&R man in showbiz.

MICHAEL THE LOVER

Artist: The Jackson 5
Written by: Larry Brownlee, Charles Matthews
Label: Steel Town
Year: 1967
Unearthed in the 1990s, this rare Jacksons track from their pre-Motown Gary, Indiana, days finds the pre-Gloved-one in "ABC" form.

MICHAEL, ANDREW AND JAMES

Artist: Richard and Mimi Fariña
Written by: Richard Fariña
From the album: *Celebrations for a Grey Day*
Label: Vanguard
Year: 1965
Written about three civil rights workers slain in Mississippi. Suggested segue: "He Was My Brother" by Simon and Garfunkel.

MICHAEL, ROW THE BOAT ASHORE

Artist: The Weavers
Written by: Traditional
From the album: *The Weavers on Tour*
Label: Vanguard
Produced by: Milt Gabler
Year: 1956
Traditional slave song was covered by the Highwaymen (United Artists, '61) as one of the early rash of folk songs to hit the charts in the wake of the Kingston Trio.

MICHELLE

Artist: The Beatles
Written by: John Lennon, Paul McCartney
From the album: *Rubber Soul*
Label: Capitol
Produced by: George Martin
Year: 1965
A McCartney lullabye, with French subtitles.

MICKEY

Artist: Toni Basil
Written by: Mike Chapman, Nicky Chinn
From the album: *Word of Mouth*
Label: Chrysalis
Produced by: Greg Mathieson, Trevor Veitch
Year: 1982
Female football anthem for the choreographer of the pioneering '60s TV rock and roll show *Shindig*. Originated in England as "Kitty" by the group Racey in '79.

MICKEY'S MONKEY

Artist: The Miracles
Written by: Eddie Holland, Lamont Dozier, Brian Holland
From the album: *Miracles Doin' Mickey's Monkey*
Label: Tamla
Produced by: Brian Holland, Lamont Dozier
Year: 1963
Helping to establish rock and roll's favorite primate with a Top 10 R&B/Top 10 crossover.

MIDDLE OF THE ROAD

Artist: The Pretenders
Written by: Chrissie Hynde
From the album: *Learning to Crawl*
Label: Sire
Produced by: Chris Thomas
Year: 1984
Passing the big 3-oh with her warmest snarl.

MIDLIFE CRISIS

Artist: Faith No More
Written by: Faith No More
From the album: *Angel Dust*
Label: Island
Produced by: Matt Wallace, Faith No More
Year: 1992
Too old to mosh, too young to matriculate.

MIDNIGHT AT THE OASIS

Artist: Maria Muldaur
Written by: David Nichtern
From the album: *Maria Muldaur*
Label: Warner Brothers
Produced by: Joe Boyd, Lenny Waronker
Year: 1973
Jim Kweskin jugband front-girl steps forward on a loopy, Bob Willsian lovesong, with a great guitar part by Woodstock's Amos Garrett.

MIDNIGHT BLUE

Artist: Lou Gramm
Written by: Lou Grammatico (Lou Gramm), Bruce Turgon
From the album: *Ready or Not*
Label: Atlantic
Produced by: Pat Moran, Lou Gramm
Year: 1987
Former lead singer utilizes the Foreigner formula.

MIDNIGHT CONFESSIONS

Artist: Grass Roots
Written by: Lou Josie
From the album: *Golden Grass*
Label: Dunhill
Produced by: Steve Barri
Year: 1967
Commercial folk/rock at its peak; the Gin Blossoms were listening, so was Del Amitri.

MIDNIGHT IN A PERFECT WORLD

Artist: DJ Shadow
Written by: Josh Davis, Pokka Pohjoda
From the album: *Endtroducing*
Produced by: DJ Shadow
Label: Mo Wax
Year: 1996
At the high end of the moody techno dance hall art.

MIDNIGHT PLANE TO HOUSTON

Artist: Jim Weatherly
Written by: Jim Weatherly
Label: Amos
Year: 1971
Covered by Cissy Houston as "Midnight Train to Georgia" (Janus, '71). Cover by Gladys Knight & the Pips (Buddah, '73) was a #1 R&B/#1 crossover.

MIDNIGHT RAMBLER

Artist: The Rolling Stones
Written by: Mick Jagger, Keith Richards
From the album: *Let It Bleed*
Label: London
Produced by: Jimmy Miller
Year: 1969
A major move in the Stones' journey from rock and roll to rock.

MIDNIGHT RIDER

Artist: Allman Brothers
Written by: Greg Allman, Kim Payne
From the album: Idlewild South
Label: Capricorn
Produced by: Adrian Barber
Year: 1970
Recorded by both Duane and Greg on early solo albums.

MIDNIGHT SPECIAL

Artist: The Weavers
Written by: Huddie Ledbetter
Label: Decca
Produced by: Milt Gabler
Year: 1952
Polishing another folk perennial from the Leadbelly catalogue. Covered by Paul Evans (Guaranteed, '60), Johnny Rivers (Imperial, '65).

MIGHTY LOVE, A

Artist: Spinners
Written by: Joseph Jefferson, Bruce Hawes, Charles Simmons
From the album: *Mighty Love*
Label: Atlantic
Produced by: Thom Bell
Year: 1973
#1 R&B/Top 20 crossover.

MIGHTY QUINN (QUINN, THE ESKIMO), THE

Artist: Manfred Mann
Written by: Bob Dylan
From the album: *The Mighty Quinn*
Label: Mercury
Produced by: Shel Talmy
Year: 1968
Mann's cover of the best track on Dylan's worst album *(Self Portrait)* went to #1 in the UK and Top 10 in the US. Mann also covered Dylan's "Just Like a Woman," in '66; "Please Mrs. Henry" (from *The Basement Tapes*) in '72; and "Father of Day, Father of Night" (from *New Morning*) in '74, before moving on to Bruce Springsteen covers.

MILES RUNS THE VOODOO DOWN

Artist: Miles Davis
Written by: Miles Davis
From the album: *Bitches Brew*
Label: Columbia
Produced by: Teo Macero
Year: 1970
The mad trumpet genius takes on Jimi Hendrix (with the help of John McLaughlin) and creates fusion.

MILKCOW BLUES BOOGIE

Artist: Elvis Presley
Written by: Kokomo Arnold
From the album: *A Date with Elvis*
Label: Sun
Produced by: Sam Phillips
Year: 1955
Introduced by Kokomo Arnold (RCA, '34). Covered by Ricky Nelson (Imperial, '61).

MILLION DOLLAR BASH

Artist: Bob Dylan
Written by: Bob Dylan
From the album: *The Basement Tapes*
Label: Columbia
Produced by: Bob Dylan, the Band
Year: 1975
Freewheeling fun and games from the post-accident Dylan. The first of many gems released from the vaults.

MILLION MILES AWAY, A

Artist: The Plimsouls
Written by: Peter Case, Joey Alkes, Chris Fradkin
From the album: *Valley Girl Soundtrack*
Label: Bomp
Produced by: Jeff Eyrich
Year: 1981
Legendary West Coast independent single rediscovered by a movie director, the leading A&R men of the decade.

MILLION TO ONE, A

Artist: Jimmy Charles
Written by: Phil Medley
Label: Promo
Year: 1960
Frankie Lymon redux.

MIND GAMES

Artist: John Lennon
Written by: John Lennon
From the album: *Mind Games*
Label: Apple
Produced by: John Lennon
Year: 1973
Problems with his sweetheart and the government.

MINOR THREAT

Artist: Minor Threat
Written by: Ian MacKaye
From the album: *In My Eyes*
Label: Dischord
Produced by: Minor Threat
Year: 1981
Exemplars of the slamming new breed of hard core, the white response to rap.

MINORITY

Artist: Green Day
Written by: Billie Joe Armstrong, Green Day
From the album: *Warning*
Label: Warner Brothers
Produced by: Green Day, Rob Cavallo
Year: 2000
A few years later they'd be severely in the majority.

MINT JULEPS AND NEEDLES

Artist: Brenda Kahn
Written by: Brenda Kahn
From the album: *Epiphany in Brooklyn*
Label: Chaos
Produced by: Brenda Kahn

Year: 1992
Dylanesque portrait of '90s wounded womanhood.

MIRACLES

Artist: Jefferson Starship
Written by: Martyn Buchwald (Marty Balin)
From the album: *Red Octopus*
Label: Grunt
Produced by: Larry Cox, Jefferson Starship
Year: 1975
New name, new era, same psychedelic harmonies.

MISERLOU

Artist: Dick Dale
Written by: N. Roubanis, Milton Leeds, Fred Wise, S. K. Russell
From the album: *Surfer's Choice*
Label: Deltone
Produced by: Jim Monsour
Year: 1961
Bravura surf treatment for the '34 Greek classic.

MISERY

Artist: Soul Asylum
Written by: Dave Pirner
From the album: *Let Your Dim Light Shine*
Produced by: Butch Vig, Soul Asylum
Label: Columbia
Year: 1995
Pirner would move on to the *Chasing Amy* soundtrack.

MISGUIDED ANGEL

Artist: Cowboy Junkies
Written by: Margo Timmons, Peter Moore
From the album: *The Trinity Sessions*
Label: RCA
Produced by: Geoff Emerick
Year: 1988
The defining dirge from the mopey folkies from Toronto.

MISS ANN

Artist: Little Richard
Written by: Richard Penniman (Little Richard), Enotris Johnson
From the album: *Here's Little Richard*
Label: Specialty
Produced by: Art Rupe
Year: 1957
B-side of "Jenny Jenny."

MISS MISERY

Artist: Elliot Smith
Written by: Elliot Smith
From the album: *Good Will Hunting Soundtrack*
Label: Capitol
Year: 1997
Nominated for an Academy Award, where it was performed by the whispery author at the ceremonies with the whole world watching, in a noncareer-defining nonmoment. His tune "Angeles" from the same film should have gotten the nom. Either would have lost to "My Heart Will Go On" anyway.

MISS WORLD

Artist: Hole
Written by: Courtney Love, Kristen Pfaff, Eric Erlandson, Patty Schemel
From the album: *Live through This*
Label: DGC
Produced by: Paul Q. Kolderie, Sean Slade
Year: 1994
Led by Courtney Love, otherwise known as "The Widow," the key track from *Rolling Stone* magazine's Album of the Year for 1994.

MISS YOU

Artist: The Rolling Stones
Written by: Mick Jagger, Keith Richards
From the album: *Some Girls*
Label: Rolling Stones
Produced by: Glimmer Twins
Year: 1978
Their eighth and last US #1.

MISS YOU LIKE CRAZY

Artist: Natalie Cole
Written by: Michael Masser, Gerry Goffin, Preston Glass
From the album: *Good to Be Back*
Label: EMI
Produced by: Michael Masser
Year: 1989
A big ballad return to the Top 10 for Carole King's former collaborator and husband, Gerry Goffin.

MISS YOU MUCH

Artist: Janet Jackson
Written by: James Harris III, Terry Lewis
From the album: *Rhythm Nation 1814*
Label: A&M
Produced by: Jimmy Jam, Terry Lewis
Year: 1989
Her first #1 R&B/#1 crossover.

MISSING

Artist: Everything but the Girl
Written by: Tracy Thorn, Ben Watt
From the album: *The Amplified Heart*
Label: Atlantic
Produced by: Ben Watt, Springheel Jack
Year: 1995
Big dance track.

MISSING SEQUENCES

Artist: Viovod
Written by: Denis Belanger, Denis D'amour, Michel Langevin, Jean Theriault
From the album: *Nothingface*
Label: Mechanic
Year: 1989
Scary metal from Canada.

MISSING YOU

Artist: Diana Ross
Written by: Lionel B. Richie Jr.
From the album: *Swept Away*
Label: RCA
Produced by: Lionel Richie
Year: 1984
A tribute to Marvin Gaye.

MISSING YOU

Artist: John Waite
Written by: John Waite, Chas Sandford, Mark Leonard
From the album: *No Brakes*
Label: EMI-America
Produced by: John Waite, David Thoener, Gary Gersh
Year: 1984
Former Baby's only solo hit.

MISSION IN LIFE, A

Artist: Stan Ridgway
Written by: Stan Ridgway
From the album: *Mosquitos*
Label: Geffen
Produced by: J. Chiconelli, Stan Ridgway
Year: 1989
Former Wall of Voodoo frontman delivers a sleazy Raymond-Chandler-in-Hollywood-through-a-shot-glass epic.

MISSIONARY MAN

Artist: Eurythmics
Written by: Dave Stewart, Annie Lennox
From the album: *Revenge*
Label: MCA
Produced by: Dave Stewart
Year: 1986
Celebrating the traditional position.

MISSISSIPPI

Artist: Sheryl Crow
Written by: Bob Dylan
From the album: *The Globe Sessions*
Label: A&M
Produced by: Sheryl Crow, Rick Rubin
Year: 1998
Crow fulfils her folk/rock promise with one of Dylan's best songs since his heyday. Covered by Dylan on *Love and Theft* (Columbia, '99).

MISSISSIPPI QUEEN

Artist: Mountain
Written by: Leslie West, Corky Laing, Felix Pappalardi, David Rea
From the album: *Mountain Climbing*
Label: Columbia
Produced by: Felix Pappalardi
Year: 1970
East coast answer to Southern rock, powered by Leslie West's guitar.

MISTER CUSTER

Artist: Larry Verne
Written by: Fred Darian, Joseph Van Winkle, Al DeLory
From the album: *Mr. Larry Verne*
Label: Era
Year: 1960
Country novelty that never made the country charts.

MISTRUSTIN' BLUES

Artist: Johnny Otis with Little Esther, Mel Walker, and the Robins
Written by: Johnny Otis
Label: Savoy
Year: 1950
Second straight #1 R&B hit.

MISUNDERSTANDING

Artist: Al B. Sure
Written by: Al B. Sure, D. J. Eddie, F. Nevelle
From the album: *Private Times ... and the Whole 9*
Label: Warner Brothers
Year: 1992
#1 R&B/Top 50 crossover.

MISUNDERSTANDING

Artist: Genesis
Written by: Phil Collins
From the album: *Duke*
Label: Atlantic
Produced by: D. Hentschel, Genesis
Year: 1980

MIXED EMOTIONS

Artist: The Rolling Stones
Written by: Mick Jagger, Keith Richards
From the album: *Steel Wheels*
Label: Rolling Stones
Produced by: Glimmer Twins, Chris Kimsey
Year: 1989
The greatest rock and roll band in the world notches their 23RD and last Top 10 hit.

MIXED UP SHOOK UP GIRL

Artist: Patty and the Emblems
Written by: William Borsey
Label: Herald
Year: 1964
Girl-group classic, covered by Mink DeVille (Capitol, '77).

MMM MMM MMM MMM

Artist: Crash Test Dummies
Written by: Brad Roberts
From the album: *God Shuffled His Feet*
Label: Arista
Produced by: Jerry Harrison, Crash Test Dummies
Year: 1994
Deep-voiced new-age philosophizing hits the top of the charts.

MMMM BOP

Artist: Hanson
Written by: Isaac Hanson, Taylor Hanson, Zac Hanson
From the album: *Middle of Nowhere*
Label: Mercury
Produced by: Dust Brothers
Year: 1997
Song that was roundly rejected by many labels becomes a smash, inaugurating a new generation's guilty pleasure, the boy band sound.

MO MONEY MO PROBLEMS

Artist: The Notorious B.I.G. featuring Puff Daddy, Mase
Written by: Christopher Wallace, Steve Jordan, Mason Betha, Bernard Edwards, Nile Rodgers
From the album: *Life After Death*
Label: Arista
Produced by: Sean Combs
Year: 1997
Cogent street advice.

MOANIN' AT MIDNIGHT

Artist: Howling Wolf
Written by: Chester (Howling Wolf) Burnette, Jules Taub
Produced by: Sam Phillips
Label: Chess
Year: 1950
You'll never forget that wolf man's moan.

MOCKINGBIRD

Artist: Inez and Charlie Foxx
Written by: Inez Foxx, Charlie Foxx
From the album: *Mockingbird*
Label: Symbol
Year: 1963
Updating the children's song. Covered by James Taylor and Carly Simon (Elektra, '74).

MODERN DANCE, THE

Artist: Pere Ubu
Written by: Tom Herman, Scott Krause, Tony Maimone, Allen Ravenstine, Dave Thomas
From the album: *The Modern Dance*
Produced by: Pere Ubu, Kenneth Hamann
Label: Blank
Year: 1976
A disco alternative in Akron, Ohio: shrieking, atonal nihilism.

MODERN LOVE

Artist: David Bowie
Written by: David Bowie
From the album: *Let's Dance*
Label: EMI-America
Produced by: Nile Rodgers, David Bowie
Year: 1983
Bowie at his most danceable.

MODERN WOMAN (FROM *RUTHLESS PEOPLE*)

Artist: Billy Joel
Written by: Billy Joel
From the album: *The Bridge*
Label: Epic
Produced by: Phil Ramone
Year: 1986
From the soundtrack of the hilarious Bette Midler film.

MOHAIR SAM

Artist: Charlie Rich
Written by: Dallas Frazier
Label: Smash
Year: 1965
Funky follow-up to "Lonely Weekends," five years later. Segue: "Amos Moses" by Jerry Reed.

MOLLY (SIXTEEN CANDLES)

Artist: Sponge
Written by: Sponge
From the album: *Rotting Pinata*
Label: Work
Produced by: Sponge, Tim Patalan
Year: 1995
Blistering alternative track turns a revered '50s epic on its ear, with the line "Sixteen candles down the drain."

MOMENTS IN LOVE

Artist: Art of Noise
Written by: Anne Dudley, Trevor Horn, Johnathan Jeczalik, Gary Langan, Paul Morley
From the album: *Into Battle with the Art of Noise*
Label: ZTT
Produced by: Art of Noise
Year: 1984
Gorgeous dance instrumental by the artsy experimentalists, introduced here in its ten-minute version. They have collected and re-recorded and re-mixed this tune probably a dozen times since then.

MOMMY, CAN I GO OUT AND KILL TONIGHT

Artist: The Misfits
Written by: Glenn Danzig
From the album: *Walk Among Us*
Label: Ruby
Year: 1982
Horror metal mayhem. Danzig would be back with "Mother." Suggested segue: "The End" by the Doors.

MOMMY DADDY YOU AND I

Artist: Talking Heads
Written by: David Byrne, Chris Frantz, Tina Weymouth, Jerry Harrison
From the album: *Naked*
Label: Sire

Produced by: Steve Lillywhite, Talking Heads
Year: 1988
Introspective group family portrait.

MONA

Artist: Bo Diddley
Written by: Ellas McDaniel (Bo Diddley)
Label: Checker
Year: 1957
Pastoral and provocative neighborhood girl. Covered by the Rolling Stones (London, '64).

MONA LISA

Artist: Nat King Cole
Written by: Jay Livingston, Ray Evans
From the album: *Unforgettable*
Label: Capitol
Year: 1952
#2 R&B/#1 crossover for the influential crooner, from the movie *Captain Carey, USA*. It would be six years before another black solo artist hit that peak again (Tommy Edwards with "It's all in the Game").

MONDAY, MONDAY

Artist: Mamas & the Papas
Written by: John Phillips
From the album: *If You Can Believe Your Eyes and Ears*
Label: Dunhill
Produced by: Lou Adler
Year: 1966
Their biggest hit, despite the inexplicable lyrics.

MONEY

Artist: Pink Floyd
Written by: Roger Waters
From the album: *Dark Side of the Moon*
Label: Harvest
Produced by: Pink Floyd
Year: 1973
Breakthrough single from legendary band's most legendary album, one that logged about a generation on the charts. Engineered by Alan Parsons.

MONEY CHANGES EVERYTHING

Artist: The Brains
Written by: Tom Gray
From the album: *The Brains*
Label: Mercury
Produced by: Steve Lillywhite
Year: 1980
Remake of their inspired Indie rock single. Covered with decibel-bashing brilliance by Cyndi Lauper (Portrait, '84).

MONEY FOR NOTHING

Artist: Dire Straits
Written by: Mark Knopfler, Gordon Sumner (Sting)
From the album: *Brothers in Arms*
Label: Warner Brothers

Produced by: Neil Dorfsman, Mark Knopfler
Year: 1985
Getting back at MTV for dropping them from the playlist in favor of the prettier "hair" bands of the day.

MONEY HONEY

Artist: The Drifters
Written by: Jesse Stone (Charles Calhoun)
Label: Atlantic
Produced by: Ahmet Ertegun, Jerry Wexler
Year: 1953
A virtual R&B supersession: kingpin producers (Wexler and Ertegun), writer (the prolific Stone, also known as Charles Calhoun), artist (McPhatter, with his new band after leaving the Dominos), and subject matter. The result, the #1 R&B hit of '53. Covered by Ella Mae Morse (Capitol, '54).

MONEY (THAT'S WHAT I WANT)

Artist: Barrett Strong
Written by: Janie Bradford, Berry Gordy Jr.
Label: Anna
Produced by: Berry Gordy Jr.
Year: 1960
An apt signature on the blank check that would soon be Motown; more money for black artists in the '60s. As a songwriter, Barrett Strong, cousin of Nolan Strong, would be one of the bigger beneficiaries.

MONEYTALKS

Artist: AC/DC
Written by: Angus Young, Malcolm Young
From the album: *The Razor's Edge*
Label: Atco
Produced by: Bruce Fairbairn
Year: 1990
If anyone was wondering what AC/DC's biggest hit was; kind of like a belated Grammy for a lifetime Top 40 underachievement.

MONGOLOID

Artist: Devo
Written by: Gerald Casale, Mark Mothersbaugh
From the album: *Are We Not Men? We Are Devo*
Label: Warner Brothers
Produced by: Brian Eno
Year: 1978
Akron assembly-line parodists' post-punk thesis.

MONKBERRY MOON DELIGHT

Artist: Paul McCartney and Linda McCartney
Written by: Paul McCartney, Linda McCartney
From the album: *Ram*
Label: Capitol
Produced by: Paul McCartney
Year: 1971
While Lennon screamed about his mother and his ex-partner, Paul basked in the lush folds of his country home/studio with his lovely wife Linda.

MONKEY

Artist: George Michael
Written by: George Michael
From the album: *Faith*
Label: Columbia
Produced by: George Michael
Year: 1988
Fourth straight #1 tune from *Faith*.

MONKEY GONE TO HEAVEN

Artist: The Pixies
Written by: Charles Francis (Black Francis)
From the album: *Doolittle*
Label: 4AD
Produced by: Gil Norton
Year: 1989
Your basic rock and roll monkey, with strings. Suggested segue: "Verdi Cries" by 10,000 Maniacs.

MONKEY TIME, THE

Artist: Major Lance
Written by: Curtis Mayfield
From the album: *The Monkey Time*
Label: Okeh
Produced by: Curtis Mayfield
Year: 1963
DC/Carolina's beach music classic by a Curtis Mayfield protege; Top 5 R&B/Top 10 crossover. Covered by the Tubes (Capitol, '68).

MONSTER MASH

Artist: Bobby "Boris" Pickett & the Crypt Kickers
Written by: Bobby Pickett, Leona Capizzi
From the album: *The Original Monster Mash*
Label: Garpax
Produced by: Gary Paxton
Year: 1962
This Halloween novelty arose from the dead to hit the Top 10 again in '73.

MONTANA

Artist: The Mothers of Invention
Written by: Frank Zappa
From the album: *Over-nite Sensation*
Label: DiscReet
Produced by: Frank Zappa
Year: 1973
The rise of a dental-floss magnate coincides with Zappa's emergence as a composer of modern music, which he would do from this point on under his own name.

MONTEREY

Artist: The Animals
Written by: Eric Burdon, Victor Briggs, John Weider, Barry Jenkins and Denny McCulloch
From the album: *The Twain Shall Meet*
Label: MGM
Produced by: Tom Wilson
Year: 1967
With Bob Dylan's producer at the helm, Burdon recalls one of the rock generation's seminal high

points, featuring an era-appropriate stirring sitar intro.

MONY MONY

Artist: Tommy James and the Shondells
Written by: Ritchie Cordell, Bo Gentry, Bobby Bloom, Tommy James
From the album: *Crimson and Clover*
Label: Roulette
Produced by: Bo Gentry, Ritchie Cordell
Year: 1968
A bubblegum epiphany, inspired by the insurance company, Mutual of New York. Covered by Billy Idol (Chrysalis, '87).

MOODY BLUE

Artist: Elvis Presley
Written by: Mark James
From the album: *Moody Blue*
Label: RCA
Produced by: Felton Jarvis, Elvis Presley
Year: 1975
Elvis's last #1 country hit, before he left the building, forever.

MOODY RIVER

Artist: Pat Boone
Written by: Gary Bruce
From the album: *Moody River*
Label: Dot
Year: 1961
Pat gets morose, after which he would find religion. Segue: "Last Kiss" by J. Frank Wilson and the Cavaliers.

MOON DAWG

Artist: The Gamblers
Written by: Derry Weaver
Label: World Pacific
Produced by: Nik Venet
Year: 1959
Considered to be the first surf record. Covered by the Beach Boys (Capitol, '62), the Ventures (Dolton, '62), as well as the Surfaris and the Challengers.

MOON IN JUNE

Artist: Soft Machine
Written by: Robert Wyatt
From the album: *Fourth*
Label: Columbia
Produced by: Soft Machine
Year: 1971
Legendary English progressive rock band moves on to fusion.

MOON IS A HARSH MISTRESS, THE

Artist: Judy Collins
Written by: Jimmy Webb.
From the album: *Judith*
Label: Elektra

Produced by: Arif Mardin
Year: 1975
The great lost Webb classic. Covered by Linda Ronstadt (Asylum, '82), who hits a career high note.

MOON RIVER

Artist: Jerry Butler
Written by: Henry Mancini, Johnny Mercer
From the album: *Jerry Butler's Golden Hits*
Year: 1961
Soul version of the classic rambling theme from the Audrey Hepburn movie *Breakfast at Tiffany's*. Won an Oscar for Best Song, Grammys for Record of the Year and Song of the Year. Also a hit for Henry Mancini (RCA, '61).

MOONDANCE

Artist: Van Morrison
Written by: Van Morrison
From the album: *Moondance*
Label: Warner Brothers
Produced by: Van Morrison
Year: 1970
Van's contribution to the world of dance. Later, Michael Jackson would provide the steps.

MOONLIGHT DRIVE

Artist: The Doors
Written by: Jim Morrison, Robbie Krieger, John Densmore
From the album: *Strange Days*
Label: Elektra
Produced by: Paul Rothchild
Year: 1967
B-side of "Love Me Two Times." Loopy lunar guitar by Krieger.

MOONLIGHT FEELS RIGHT

Artist: Starbuck
Written by: Michael Bruce Blackman
From the album: *Moonlight Feels Right*
Label: Private Stock
Produced by: Bruce Blackman, Mike Clark
Year: 1975
Easy/folk listening dance track by an obscure artist who may have provided the inspiration for a coffee house franchise.

MORE LOVE

Artist: The Miracles
Written by: Smokey Robinson
From the album: *Make It Happen*
Label: Tamla
Produced by: Smokey Robinson
Year: 1967
Covered by Kim Carnes (EMI-America, '80).

MORE, MORE, MORE (PART I)

Artist: The Andrea True Connection
Written by: Gregg Diamond

From the album: *More, More, More*
Label: Buddah
Produced by: Greg Diamond
Year: 1976
Former porn star flaunts her persona in the forgiving disco arena.

MORE THAN A FEELING

Artist: Boston
Written by: Tom Scholz
From the album: *Boston*
Label: Epic
Produced by: Tom Scholz, John Boylan
Year: 1976
Landmark of studio heavy metal processing; Scholz went on to found a company to keep him up to his elbows in electronic devices.

MORE THAN I CAN SAY

Artist: The Crickets
Written by: Sonny Curtis, Jerry Allison
From the album: *In Style with the Crickets*
Label: Coral
Produced by: Norman Petty
Year: 1959
The original stiffed as a single. The first cover by Bobby Vee (Liberty, '61) also stiffed. Cover by Leo Sayer (Warner Brothers, '80) reached Top 10.

MORE THAN THIS

Artist: Roxy Music
Written by: Bryan Ferry
From the album: *Avalon*
Label: Warner Brothers
Produced by: Rhett Davies, Roxy Music
Year: 1982
Their weary worldview at its peak. Covered by 10,000 Maniacs (Elektra, '97).

MORE THAN WORDS

Artist: Extreme
Written by: Nuno Bettencourt, Gary Cherone
From the album: *Pornograffiti II*
Label: A&M
Produced by: Michael Wagener
Year: 1990
Unplugged antilove song was their biggest hit.

MORE THAN WORDS CAN SAY

Artist: Alias
Written by: Freddi Curci, Steve DeMarchi
From the album: *Alias*
Label: EMI
Year: 1990

MORE YOU IGNORE ME, THE CLOSER I GET, THE

Artist: Morrissey
Written by: Stephen Morrissey, Boz Boorer
From the album: *Vauxhall and I*

Label: Sire
Produced by: Steve Lillywhite
Year: 1994
Biggest hit from the Proust of rock.

MORNING DEW

Artist: Bonnie Dobson
Written by: Bonnie Dobson, Tim Rose
From the album: *Bonnie Dodson*
Label: RCA
Produced by: Dave Bird, Jack Richardson
Year: 1964
Original folk/rock version of the anti-war, post-bomb standard. Covered by the Grateful Dead (Warner Brothers, '67), Lulu (Epic, '68), the Jeff Beck Group (Epic, '68).

MORNING HAS BROKEN

Artist: Cat Stevens
Written by: Cat Stevens, Eleanor Farjeon
From the album: *Teaser and the Firecat*
Label: A&M
Produced by: Paul Samwell-Smith
Year: 1971
Delicate quasireligious anthem is his biggest hit, foretelling further conversions to come.

MORNING MORNING

Artist: The Fugs
Written by: Tuli Kupferberg
From the album: *The Fugs*
Label: ESP
Produced by: Harry Smith
Year: 1965
The Fugs resident poet at his most simple, poignant, and profound, with not a swear word in sight. Covered by Richie Havens (Verve/Folkways, '66).

MORNING TRAIN

Artist: Sheena Easton
Written by: Florrie Palmer
From the album: *Sheena Easton*
Label: EMI-America
Produced by: Christopher Neil
Year: 1981
Suggested segues: "Uptown" by the Crystals, "9 to 5" by Dolly Parton, "Five O'Clock World" by the Vogues.

MOST BEAUTIFUL GIRL, THE

Artist: Charlie Rich
Written by: Norro Wilson, Billy Sherrill, Rory Bourke
From the album: *Behind Closed Doors*
Label: Epic
Produced by: Billy Sherrill
Year: 1973
#1 country/#1 crossover for the Sun veteran. Norro Wilson's version called "Hey Mister" stiffed (Smash, '68).

MOST BEAUTIFUL GIRL IN THE WORLD

Artist: Prince
Written by: Prince Rogers Nelson
Label: Paisley Park
Produced by: Prince
Year: 1994
Introduced during the evening gown competion of the Miss USA Beauty Pageant, the artist at that point formerly-known-as Prince continues his search for the sacred amidst the profane, and vice-versa.

MOST GIRLS

Artist: Pink
Written by: Kenny Edmunds (Babyface), Damon Thomas
From the album: *Can't Take Me Home*
Produced by: Babyface, L. A. Reid
Label: Arista
Year: 2000
New breakout punk player in a world of pouty pop princesses.

MOST HIGH

Artist: Page and Plant
Written by: Jimmy Page, Robert Plant, Charlie Jones, Michael Lee
From the album: *Walking into Clarksville*
Label: Atlantic
Produced by: Jimmy Page, Robert Plant
Year: 1998

MOST LIKELY YOU GO YOUR WAY (AND I'LL GO MINE)

Artist: Bob Dylan
Written by: Bob Dylan
From the album: *Blonde on Blonde*
Label: Columbia
Produced by: Bob Johnston
Year: 1966
For a while Dylan's concert-opening dialogue/argument with his audience.

MOTEL BLUES

Artist: Loudon Wainwright III
Written by: Loudon Wainwright III
From the album: *Album II*
Label: Atlantic
Year: 1971
His marriage having not panned out, LW takes to the groupie scene, unsuccessfully.

MOTHER

Artist: Danzig
Written by: Glenn Danzig
From the album: *Danzig*
Label: Def American
Produced by: Rick Rubin
Year: 1988

If Jim Morrison had survived, he might have sued the perpetrators of this thundering metal monsterpiece for coopting his act. Revived by Danzig (American, '93).

MOTHER

Artist: John Lennon
Written by: John Lennon
From the album: *John Lennon/Plastic Ono Band*
Label: Apple
Produced by: Phil Spector
Year: 1970
Primal scream therapy. Covered by Barbra Streisand (Columbia, '71).

MOTHER AND CHILD REUNION

Artist: Paul Simon
Written by: Paul Simon
From the album: *Paul Simon*
Label: Columbia
Produced by: Roy Halee, Paul Simon
Year: 1972
Reportedly inspired by a plate of Chinese food, which just goes to show you how much you can trust an author's perception of his own influences.

MOTHER EARTH

Artist: Mother Earth
Written by: Memphis Slim
From the album: *Living with the Animals*
Label: Mercury
Year: 1968
Introducing one of rock's most unmined natural resources, the blistering voice of Tracy Nelson.

MOTHER-IN-LAW

Artist: Ernie K-Doe
Written by: Allen Toussaint
From the album: *Mother-in-Law*
Label: Minit
Produced by: Allen Toussaint
Year: 1961
A #1 R&B/#1 crossover New Orleans classic, establishing Toussaint as the Boss of Bourbon Street, where K-Doe would eventually open up a swinging hot spot.

MOTHER, MOTHER

Artist: Tracy Bonham
Written by: Tracy Bonham
From the album: *The Burdens of Being Upright*
Label: Island
Produced by: Paul Kolderie, Sean Slade
Year: 1996
A parent's worst nightmare, in this case, Led Zeppelin drummer Jon Bonham's.

MOTHER NATURE'S SON

Artist: The Beatles
Written by: John Lennon, Paul McCartney
From the album: *The Beatles*

Label: Apple
Produced by: George Martin
Year: 1968
Tiptoeing through the tulips, high on weed.

MOTHER PLEASE!

Artist: Jo-Ann Campbell
Written by: Jo-Ann Campbell
Label: Cameo
Year: 1963
Still chained to her bedroom, still pleading, a rock-abilly showgirl bows out with nothing to show.

MOTHER POPCORN (YOU GOT TO HAVE A MOTHER FOR ME) (PART I)

Artist: James Brown
Written by: James Brown, Alfred Ellis
From the album: *The Popcorn*
Label: King
Produced by: James Brown
Year: 1969
Fifth of ten single releases in '69 (nine of which crossed over Top 40, three of which were instrumentals), his second #1 R&B/Top 20 crossover, and biggest hit of the year.

MOTHER'S LITTLE HELPER

Artist: The Rolling Stones
Written by: Mick Jagger, Keith Richards
From the album: *December's Children (and Everybody's)*
Label: London
Produced by: Andrew Loog-Oldham
Year: 1965
Invading country music territory for a morality saga of a pill-popping housewife.

MOTHERSHIP CONNECTION (STAR CHILD)

Artist: Parliament
Written by: George Clinton, Bootsy Collins
From the album: *Mothership Connection*
Produced by: George Clinton
Label: Casablanca
Year: 1976
An amazing funk journey takes off.

MOTORCYCLE

Artist: Tico & the Triumphs
Written by: Paul Simon
Label: Madison
Year: 1961
One of Simon's early Brill Building business transactions.

MOTORHEAD

Artist: Motorhead
Written by: Ian Kilmeister (Lemmy), Philthy Taylor, (Fast) Eddie Clarke
From the album: *Motorhead*

Label: Chiswick
Produced by: Speedy Keen
Year: 1977
Remake of an old Hawkwind track launches the connoisseur's mega-metal band.

MOTOWN SONG, THE

Artist: Rod Stewart
Written by: Larry John McNally
From the album: *Vagabond Heart*
Label: Warner Brothers
Produced by: Richard Perry
Year: 1991
Rod revisits the streets of doo-wop.

MOTOWNPHILLY

Artist: Boyz II Men
Written by: Dallas Austin, Michael Bivins, Nathan Morris, Shawn Stockman
From the album: *Cooleyhighharmony*
Label: Motown
Produced by: Dallas Austin
Year: 1991
Tribute to the roots of the '90s harmony hip hop revival.

MOULTY

Artist: The Barbarians
Written by: Doug Morris, Elliot Greenberg, Barbara Baer, Robert Schwartz
Label: Laurie
Produced by: Robert Schwartz
Year: 1966
The ultimate garage punk nugget of a one-armed drummer and his desire to stay in his band. Life would imitate art-imitating-life again, when something similar happened to the drummer in Def Leppard.

MOUNTAIN'S HIGH, THE

Artist: Dick and Deedee
Written by: Dick Gosting
From the album: *The Mountain's High*
Label: Liberty
Produced by: Don Rafkine, Wilder Bros.
Year: 1961
West coast white doo-wop classic in the age of surf.

MOUNTAINS O' THINGS

Artist: Tracy Chapman
Written by: Tracy Chapman
From the album: *Tracy Chapman*
Label: Elektra
Produced by: David Kershenbaum
Year: 1988
Postmodern reaction to "Material Girl" by Madonna.

MOUTH

Artist: Merrill Bainbridge
Written by: Merrill Bainbridge
From the album: *The Garden*

Label: Universal
Year: 1996
Angelic voice, dirty mouth.

MOUTH FOR WAR

Artist: Pantera
Written by: Pantera
From the album: *A Vulgar Display of Power*
Label: Atco
Year: 1992
Metal barrage from the thrash underground.

MOVE IT ON OVER

Artist: Hank Williams
Written by: Hank Williams
Label: MGM
Produced by: Fred Rose
Year: 1947
First single release for country music's lonesomest cowboy and an early blueprint for rockabilly. Here Hank introduces the "big dog" and right away puts him in the dog house. Covered by Hank Williams Jr. (MGM, '65), George Thorogood & the Delaware Destroyers (Rounder, '78).

MOVE OVER

Artist: Janis Joplin
Written by: Janis Joplin
From the album: *Pearl*
Label: Columbia
Produced by: Paul Rothchild
Year: 1970
One of her mellower performances.

MOVE THIS

Artist: Technotronic
Written by: Manuella Kamosi, Thomas De Quincy (Jo Bogaert)
From the album: *Pump up the Jam—the Album*
Label: SBK
Produced by: Jo Bogaert
Year: 1992
In the spirit of Maybellene and Teen Spirit, this was previously a shampoo commercial.

MOVE YOUR BODY (THE HOUSE MUSIC ANTHEM)

Artist: Marshall Jefferson
Written by: Marshall Jefferson
Label: Trax
Year: 1986
A celebrated producer gives props to the underground dance scene of Chicago in the '80s.

MOVIN' 'N GROOVIN'

Artist: Duane Eddy
Written by: Al Casey, Duane Eddy
From the album: *Have Twangy Guitar, Will Travel*
Label: Jamie
Produced by: Lee Hazelwood
Year: 1958

Introducing the "Twangy" guitar, a Gretsch 6120. Suggested segue: "Surfin' USA" by the Beach Boys.

MOVING OUT (ANTHONY'S SONG)

Artist: Billy Joel
Written by: Billy Joel
From the album: *The Stranger*
Label: Columbia
Produced by: Phil Ramone
Year: 1977
Symbolically moving into his own as a singer/songwriter. Later the title of his Broadway collaboration with choreographer Twyla Tharp.

MR. BAD EXAMPLE

Artist: Warren Zevon
Written by: Warren Zevon, Jorge Calderon
From the album: *Mr. Bad Example*
Produced by: Waddy Wachtel
Label: Giant
Year: 1991
His antiheroic credo.

MR. BIG STUFF

Artist: Jean Knight
Written by: Joe Broussard, Ralph Williams, Carrol Washington
From the album: *Mr. Big Stuff*
Label: Stax
Produced by: Wardell Quezerque
Year: 1971
#1 R&B/Top 10 crossover.

MR. BLUE

Artist: The Fleetwoods
Written by: DeWayne Blackwell
From the album: *Mr. Blue*
Label: Dolton
Produced by: Bob Reisdorff
Year: 1959
Their second straight ethereal ditty to peak at #1 closes out '59 on the note that once-feared rock and roll had been vanquished at last. The note would prove to be false.

MR. BOJANGLES

Artist: Jerry Jeff Walker
Written by: Jerry Jeff Walker
From the album: *Jerry Jeff Walker*
Label: Atco
Produced by: Tom Dowd, Dan Elliot
Year: 1968
Greenwich Village underground folk classic, played incessantly on WBAI, with the classic acoustic guitar accompaniment by David Bromberg. Covered by the Nitty Gritty Dirt Band (United Artists, '72).

MR. CROWLEY

Artist: Ozzy Osbourne
Written by: Ozzy Osbourne, Randy Rhoads, Bob Daisley, Lee Kerslake
From the album: *Blizzard of Ozz*
Label: Jet
Produced by: Max Norman
Year: 1981
Helping to establish the heavy metal link to the netherworlds above and below the known with a Randy Rhoads guitar showpiece, dedicated to Alistair Crowley.

MR. DREAM MERCHANT

Artist: Jerry Butler
Written by: Larry Weiss, Jerry Ross
From the album: *Mr. Dream Merchant*
Label: Mercury
Produced by: Jerry Ross
Year: 1967
Cover by New Birth (Buddah, 76) went #1 R&B.

MR. JONES

Artist: Counting Crows
Written by: Adam Duritz, David Bryson, Counting Crows
From the album: *August and Everything After*
Label: DGC
Produced by: T-Bone Burnette
Year: 1993
Updating the same mix of influences that brought Bruce Springsteen to the rock forefront (Van Morrison, Bob Dylan, the Band), including Springsteen himself, this San Francisco mystery figure named after Dylan's "Thin Man" led an alternative rock crusade onto the record charts of '93–'94. Never released as a single, it was nonetheless played (to death) as regularly on hit radio as if it were. In later incarnations, Duritz changed the lyric "I want to be Bob Dylan" to "I want to be Alex Chilton." Geez.

MR. LEE

Artist: The Bobbettes
Written by: Heather Dixon, Helen Gathers, Emma Ruth Pought, Laura Webb, Janine Pought
Label: Atlantic
Year: 1957
The real-life principal of New York's P.S. 109 becomes the stuff of teenage girl-group history. Three years later, the Bobbettes would finish him off in "I Shot Mr. Lee," on Triple X.

MR. LOVERMAN

Artist: Shabba Banks
Written by: Rexton Gordon, Mikey Bennett, H. Lindo
From the album: *Rough & Ready, Vol. 1*
Label: Epic
Year: 1992
Reggae breakthrough track, featured in the film *Deep Cover*.

MR. PITIFUL

Artist: Otis Redding
Written by: Otis Redding, Steve Cropper
From the album: *The Great Otis Redding Sings Soul Ballads*
Label: Volt
Produced by: Steve Cropper
Year: 1965

MR. ROBOTO

Artist: Styx
Written by: Dennis DeYoung
From the album: *Kilroy Was Here*
Label: A&M
Produced by: Styx
Year: 1981
Progressive arena machinations.

MR. SCARY

Artist: Dokken
Written by: George Lynch
From the album: *Back for the Attack*
Label: Elektra
Produced by: Neil Kirwin
Year: 1987
Massive guitar solo from L.A. virtuouso George Lynch.

MR. SOUL

Artist: Buffalo Springfield
Written by: Neil Young
From the album: *Buffalo Springfield Again*
Label: Atco
Produced by: Turk-Pila
Year: 1967
Neil's head was the event of the season and many seasons to come. Suggested segue: "So You Wanna Be a Rock and Roll Star" by the Byrds.

MR. SPACEMAN

Artist: The Byrds
Written by: Jim McGuinn (Roger McGuinn)
From the album: *5D (Fifth Dimension)*
Label: Columbia
Produced by: Allen Stanton
Year: 1966
Suggested segue: "Mr. Bassman" by Johnny Cymbal.

MR. TAMBOURINE MAN

Artist: Bob Dylan
Written by: Bob Dylan
From the album: *Bringing It All Back Home*
Label: Columbia
Produced by: Tom Wilson
Year: 1965
Dylan goes to the Mardi Gras under the influence of Jack Kerouac. With just one of its verses covered by the Byrds (Columbia, '65), this tune launched the '60s jingle-jangle white alternative known as folk/rock, one part Woody Guthrie, one part McGuinn's 12-string Rickenbacker, two parts Creative Writing 101.

MR. TELEPHONE MAN

Artist: New Edition
Written by: Vincent Brantley, Rick Timas
From the album: *New Edition*

Label: MCA
Produced by: Vincent Brantley, Rick Timas
Year: 1984
#1 R&B/Top 20 crossover.

MR. VAIN

Artist: Culture Beat
Written by: Steven Levis, Josie Katzmann, Jay Supreme
From the album: *Serenity*
Label: 550 Music
Year: 1993
Euro-disco refuses to die.

MR. WENDALL

Artist: Arrested Development
Written by: Todd (Speech) Thomas
From the album: *3 years 5 Months and 2 Days in the Life Of*
Label: Chrysalis
Produced by: Speech
Year: 1992
An inspirational neighborhood figure gets the be-bop/hip hop treatment.

MRS. BROWN, YOU'VE GOT A LOVELY DAUGHTER

Artist: Herman's Hermits
Written by: Trevor Peacock
From the album: *Introducing*
Label: MGM
Produced by: Mickie Most
Year: 1965
Skiffle-inspired classic introduced in '63 by Tom Courtenay in a British TV play was their first #1 US and biggest hit.

MRS. GREEN

Artist: The Three O'Clock
Written by: Michael Quercio
From the album: *Arrive Without Traveling*
Produced by: Mike Hedges
Label: IRS
Year: 1985
Mrs. Brown's lovely daughter moves to San Francisco to hang out with neo-hippies.

MRS. ROBINSON

Artist: Simon and Garfunkel
Written by: Paul Simon
From the album: *Bookends*
Label: Columbia
Produced by: Roy Halee, Paul Simon, Art Garfunkel
Year: 1968
Boosted by Joe DiMaggio and *The Graduate*, these East coast quiet revolutionaries achieve a generational epiphany and their second biggest hit. Segue: "Diana" by Paul Anka.

MS. JACKSON

Artist: OutKast

Written by: Andre Benjamin, Antwan Andre Patton, David Sheats
From the album: *Stankonia*
Produced by: OutKast
Label: LaFace
Year: 2000
Pointing to Atlanta as the creative capitol of the Dirty South.

MULE SKINNER BLUES (BLUE YODEL #8)

Artist: The Fendermen
Written by: Jimmie Rodgers, George Vaughan
From the album: *Muleskinner Blues*
Label: Soma
Year: 1960
Introduced by country music pioneer Jimmie Rodgers (Victor, '31).

MULL OF KINTYRE

Artist: Paul McCartney and Wings
Written by: Paul McCartney
From the album: *Wings' Greatest*
Label: Capitol
Produced by: Paul McCartney
Year: 1976
His biggest UK hit, replacing his previous biggest UK hit, a reissue of "She Loves You," at the top of the charts. Not released as a single in the US.

MURDER WAS THE CASE

Artist: Snoop Doggy Dogg
Written by: Calvin Broadus (Snoop Doggy Dogg), Andre Young (Dr. Dre), Delmic Arnaud (Dat Nigga Daz), Warren Griffin (Warren G.)
From the album: *Murder Was the Case*
Label: Death Row
Produced by: Dr. Dre
Year: 1995
Gangsta rap, the movie; answering Michael Jackson's "Thriller" a decade later.

MUSIC

Artist: Madonna
Written by: Mirwais Ahmadzai, Madonna Ciccone
From the album: *Music*
Label: Maverick
Year: 2000

MUSIC IS THE ANSWER

Artist: Colonel Abrams
Written by: Marston Freeman, Colonel Abrams
Label: Warlock
Produced by: Colonel Abrams
Year: 1984
Crucial house music track.

MUST OF GOT LOST

Artist: The J. Geils Band
Written by: Seth Justman, Peter Wolf
From the album: *Nightmares ... and Other Tales from the Vinyl Jungle*

Label: Atlantic
Year: 1974
In their bluesy incarnation, before they found themselves a decade later, strutting in the land of MTV.

MUST TO AVOID, A

Artist: Herman's Hermits
Written by: Steve Barri, P.F. Sloan
From the album: *Hold On*
Label: MGM
Produced by: Mickie Most
Year: 1965
Sampling West coast staff songwriting at its best. Featured in *Hold On*, the Hermits' version of *A Hard Day's Night*.

MUSTA NOTTA GOTTA LOTTA

Artist: Joe Ely
Written by: Joe Ely
From the album: *Musta Notta Gotta Lotta*
Label: SouthCoast
Produced by: Michael Brovsky, Joe Ely
Year: 1981
Hard-hitting autobiographical alt-country standard.

MUSTANG SALLY

Artist: Sir Mack Rice
Written by: Bonnie Rice
Label: Blue Rock
Year: 1965
Car song classic: classic car, the Ford Mustang. Covered by Wilson Pickett (Atlantic, '66), the Young Rascals (Atlantic, '66).

MY BABE

Artist: Little Walter
Written by: Willie Dixon
Label: Chess
Year: 1955
First #1 R&B hit for the legendary Chicago songwriter; second for the legendary blues-harp stylist.

MY BABY

Artist: The Pretenders
Written by: Chrissie Hynde
From the album: *Get Close*
Label: Sire
Produced by: Jimmy Iovine
Year: 1986

MY BABY GIVES IT AWAY

Artist: Pete Townshend and Ronnie Lane
Written by: Pete Townshend
From the album: *Rough Mix*
Label: MCA
Produced by: Glyn Johns
Year: 1977

MY BABY LEFT ME

Artist: Arthur Big Boy Crudup
Written by: Arthur Crudup
Label: RCA
Produced by: Steve Sholes
Year: 1950
Covered by Elvis Presley (RCA, '56), who also covered Crudup's legendary "That's All Right, Mama."

MY BABY MUST BE A MAGICIAN

Artist: The Marvelettes
Written by: Smokey Robinson
From the album: *Sophisticated Soul*
Label: Tamla
Produced by: Smokey Robinson
Year: 1967
Their ninth and last #1 R&B hit.

MY BACK PAGES (I'M YOUNGER THAN THAT NOW)

Artist: Bob Dylan
Written by: Bob Dylan
From the album: *Another Side of Bob Dylan*
Label: Columbia
Produced by: Tom Wilson
Year: 1964
Defining his main enemy as "the mongrel dogs who teach." Covered by the Byrds (Columbia, '65) and revived by Dylan and a backup cast of famous friends at the Bobfest (Columbia, '94).

MY BEAUTIFUL REWARD

Artist: Bruce Springsteen
Written by: Bruce Springsteen
From the album: *Lucky Town*
Label: Columbia
Produced by: Jon Landau, Bruce Springsteen, Chuck Plotkin
Year: 1992
Straightening out his life, but in the process losing a step on the rock and roll muse.

MY BEST FRIEND'S GIRL

Artist: The Cars
Written by: Ric Ocasek
From the album: *The Cars*
Label: Elektra
Produced by: Roy Thomas Baker
Year: 1978
Catchy, punchy, nervy, and nervous new wave smash in England, where the album was recorded.

MY BODY

Artist: LSG
Written by: Darrell Allamby, Lincoln Broder, Antionette Roberson
From the album: *Levert-Sweat-Gill*
Label: East West
Year: 1997
One shot #1 R&B/Top 10 crossover superstar one-off.

MY BOY LOLLIPOP

Artist: Millie Small
Written by: Johnny Roberts, Morris Levy
From the album: *My Boy Lollipop*
Label: Smash
Produced by: Chris Blackwell
Year: 1964
The first hit for Island Records was this Jamaican remake from '56, inspired by the Ska-influenced blue-beat sound.

MY BOYFRIEND

Artist: The Cucumbers
Written by: Jon Fried, Deena Shoskes
From the album: *Fresh Cucumbers*
Label: Fake Doom
Year: 1983
The great girl-group sound returns; but where Deena Shoskes failed to crack the airwaves of '83, Cyndi Lauper, the Bangles, and later Madonna would plow over her tracks by the end of the year. Re-recorded on Profile, '87, by which time the latest girl-group moment would have passed, not to return again until '93–'94.

MY BOYFRIEND'S BACK

Artist: The Angels
Written by: Richard Gottehrer, Robert Feldman, Jerry Goldstein
From the album: *My Boyfriend's Back*
Label: Smash
Produced by: Richard Gottehrer
Year: 1963
The essence of the girl-group ethos, from an era when all such female anthems of acquiescence were written and directed by men.

MY BRAIN IS HANGING UPSIDE DOWN (BONZO GOES TO BITBURG)

Artist: The Ramones
Written by: Douglas Colvin, John Cummings, Jean Beauvoir
From the album: *Animal Boy*
Label: Sire
Produced by: Jean Beauvoir
Year: 1986
Their best protest song since "Do You Remember Rock and Roll Radio," written about the time Ronald Reagan visited a Nazi cemetery.

MY CHERIE AMOUR

Artist: Stevie Wonder
Written by: Stevie Wonder, Henry Cosby, Sylvia Moy
From the album: *My Cherie Amour*
Label: Tamla
Produced by: Henry Cosby
Year: 1969
Going after Smokey Robinson's midtempo crown. Suggested segue: "Michelle" by the Beatles.

MY CITY WAS GONE

Artist: The Pretenders
Written by: Chrissie Hynde
From the album: *Learning to Crawl*
Label: Sire
Produced by: Chris Thomas
Year: 1984
A melancholy trip back to an unrecognizable Ohio. Suggested segues: "Burn on, Big River" by Randy Newman, "Cuyahoga" by R.E.M. A few years later Chrissie would write "Downtown (Akron)." A few years later she would sing "My City Was Gone" at the concert in Cleveland celebrating the opening of the Rock and Roll Hall of Fame.

MY DAD

Artist: Paul Peterson
Written by: Barry Mann, Cynthia Weil
From the album: *My Dad*
Label: Colpix
Produced by: Stu Phillips
Year: 1962
Donna Reed's other singing TV offspring (see: Shelly Fabares) sang this on the show.

MY DEAREST DARLING

Artist: Etta James
Written by: Paul Gayton, Edwin Bocage
From the album: *At Last*
Label: Argo
Year: 1960
Top 5 R&B/Top 40 crossover.

MY DING A LING

Artist: Dave Bartholomew
Written by: Dave Bartholomew, Todd Rhodes
From the album: *In the Alley*
Label: King
Produced by: Dave Bartholomew
Year: 1951
Later became Chuck Berry's biggest hit (Chess, '72).

MY EMPTY ARMS

Artist: Jackie Wilson
Written by: Al Kasha, Hank Hunter
Label: Brunswick
Year: 1961
Less than six months after Elvis had a hit with "O Sole Mio," Jackie responded with this tune, based on "Vesti La Giubba."

MY EVER CHANGING MOODS

Artist: The Style Council
Written by: Paul Weller

From the album: *My Ever Changing Moods*
Label: Geffen
Produced by: Style Council, Peter Wilson
Year: 1984
Only US Top 40 single for a Paul Weller-led group. He had seven Top 10 hits in England with the Style Council after scoring nine Top 10 singles with the Jam.

MY EYES ADORED YOU

Artist: Frankie Valli
Written by: Bob Crewe, Kenny Nolan Helfman
From the album: *Closeup*
Label: Private Stock
Produced by: Bob Crewe
Year: 1974
One of the ultimate rock ballads of unrequited love. His first solo #1.

MY FANTASY

Artist: Guy
Written by: Gene Griffin, William Aquart
From the album: *Do the Right Thing Soundtrack*
Label: Motown
Produced by: Teddy Riley, Gene Griffin
Year: 1988
#1 R&B track from the Spike Lee film.

MY FATHER

Artist: Judy Collins
Written by: Judy Collins
From the album: *Who Knows Where the Time Goes*
Label: Elektra
Produced by: David Anderle
Year: 1968
Folk/rock autobiography, written by one of the era's prime interpreters.

MY FRIENDS

Artist: Red Hot Chili Peppers
Written by: Anthony Keidis, Dave Navarro, Michael (Flea) Balzary, Chad Smith
From the album: *One Hot Minute*
Produced by: Rick Rubin
Label: Warner Brothers
Year: 1995

MY GENERATION

Artist: The Who
Written by: Pete Townshend
From the album: *The Who Sing My Generation*
Label: Decca
Produced by: Kit Lambert
Year: 1965
With two hits under his belt, Pete was ready for a larger statement; inspired by living under the shadow of the bomb, three chords, a stutter, and a big booming sound, he got it.

MY GENERATION, PART TWO

Artist: Todd Snider

Written by: Todd Snider
From the album: *Todd Snider*
Produced by: Tony Brown, Mike Utley
Label: MCA
Year: 1994
Taking up where Townshend left off, the satirical Snider finds nothing to write home about.

MY GIRL

Artist: The Temptations
Written by: Smokey Robinson, Ronald White
From the album: *The Temptations Sing Smokey*
Label: Gordy
Produced by: Smokey Robinson
Year: 1965
Their first #1 R&B/#1 crossover is Smokey's companion to "My Guy," a smiling and refreshing bookend to the usual Motown dramatics.

MY GIRL SLOOPY

Artist: The Vibrations
Written by: Bert Berns (Bert Russell), Wes Farrell
From the album: *Shout*
Label: Atlantic
Year: 1964
Frat rock girlfriend of "Runaround Sue" gets caught in the bad part of town. Covered by the McCoys (Bang, '65) as "Hang on Sloopy" and by the Yardbirds as "My Girl Sloopy" (Epic, '65), featuring Jeff Beck on guitar.

MY GUITAR WANTS TO KILL YOUR MAMA

Artist: The Mothers of Invention
Written by: Frank Zappa
From the album: *Weasels Ripped My Flesh*
Label: Bizarre
Produced by: Frank Zappa
Year: 1970
Moving into his post-verbal stage.

MY GUY

Artist: Mary Wells
Written by: Smokey Robinson
From the album: *Mary Wells Sings My Guy*
Label: Motown
Produced by: Smokey Robinson
Year: 1964
Mary's only #1 hit. Probably would have been a #1 R&B crossover, if there had been an R&B chart in 1964.

MY HAPPINESS

Artist: Connie Francis
Written by: Betty Peterson, Borney Bergantine
From the album: *Connie's Greatest Hits*
Label: MGM
Year: 1959
This '33 tune was popularized by John and Sandra Steele (Damon, '48). Legendary as the first demo Elvis recorded for his mom at Sam Phillips' Sun studios.

MY HEART CAN'T TELL YOU NO

Artist: Rod Stewart
Written by: Simon Climie, Dennis Morgan
From the album: *Out of Order*
Label: Warner Brothers
Produced by: Bernard Edwards
Year: 1988

MY HEART HAS A MIND OF ITS OWN

Artist: Connie Francis
Written by: Howard Greenfield, Jack Keller
From the album: *More Greatest Hits*
Label: MGM
Produced by: Connie Francis
Year: 1960
Same team as "Everybody's Somebody's Fool," same #1 result.

MY HEART IS AN OPEN BOOK

Artist: Carl Dobkins Jr.
Written by: Lee Pockriss, Hal David
From the album: *Carl Dobkins Jr.*
Label: Decca
Year: 1957
The essence of Pat Boone-inspired pop/rock. David Gates may have already been tuned in on his first transistor radio.

MY HOME TOWN

Artist: Bruce Springsteen
Written by: Bruce Springsteen
From the album: *Born in the USA*
Label: Columbia
Produced by: Jon Landau, Bruce Springsteen, Chuck Plotkin
Year: 1984
Narrowing (and mellowing) his view of mythic New Jersey now that he had accomplished his own escape.

MY JUANITA

Artist: The Crests
Written by: Johnny Mastroangelo, Al Browne
Label: Joyce
Year: 1957
Their legendary and highly collectable first release, which went nowhere.

MY LIFE

Artist: Mary J. Blige
Written by: Mary J. Blige, Sean (Puffy) Combs, Delvalle, Chucky Thompson
From the album: *My Life*
Produced by: Sean (Puffy) Combs
Label: MCA
Year: 1994

MY LIFE

Artist: Iris DeMent
Written by: Iris DeMent
From the album: *My Life*
Label: Warner Brothers
Produced by: Jim Rooney
Year: 1994
Confessional folk/rock goes Appalachian.

MY LIFE

Artist: Billy Joel
Written by: Billy Joel
From the album: *52nd Street*
Label: Columbia
Produced by: Phil Ramone
Year: 1978
The irritable young man's answer to "It's My Life" by the Animals.

MY LIFE IS GOOD

Artist: Randy Newman
Written by: Randy Newman
From the album: *Trouble in Paradise*
Label: Warner Brothers
Produced by: Russ Titelman, Lenny Waronker
Year: 1983
His shining moment of unabashed cynicism.

MY LITTLE RED BOOK (ALL I DO IS TALK ABOUT YOU)

Artist: Manfred Mann
Written by: Burt Bacharach, Hal David
From the album: *What's New Pussycat? Soundtrack*
Label: United Artists
Year: 1965
New barstool anthem, introduced in the Woody Allen movie *What's New Pussycat?* Covered by Love (Elektra, '66).

MY LITTLE TOWN

Artist: Paul Simon and Art Garfunkel
Written by: Paul Simon
From the album: *Still Crazy after All These Years*
Label: Columbia
Produced by: Paul Simon, Phil Ramone
Year: 1975
Reuniting with Art Garfunkel after half a decade off, this ripping rocker about escaping from the neighborhood brings them back to the familiar old neighborhood of the Top 10.

MY LOVE

Artist: Paul McCartney and Wings
Written by: Paul McCartney, Linda McCartney
From the album: *Red Rose Speedway*
Label: Apple
Produced by: Paul McCartney
Year: 1973
A straight love song … as opposed to a silly one.

MY LOVIN' (YOU'RE NEVER GONNA GET IT)

Artist: En Vogue
Written by: Thom McElroy, Denzil Foster
From the album: *Funky Divas of soul*
Label: Atco/East West
Produced by: Thomas McElroy, Denzil Foster
Year: 1992
In the world of chick/hop, these were full grown R&B women, and this was their ultimate party girl putdown.

MY MARIA

Artist: B.W. Stevenson
Written by: Daniel Moore, B. W. Stevenson
From the album: *My Maria*
Label: RCA
Produced by: David Kershenbaum
Year: 1973
Texas pop with an inspired falsetto.

MY MOTHER THE WAR

Artist: 10,000 Maniacs
Written by: Natalie Merchant, John Lombardi, Michael Walsh
From the album: *The Wishing Chair*
Label: Elektra
Produced by: Joe Boyd
Year: 1985
Introducing upstate New York's leading candidate in the '80s waif-like thrush sweepstakes, Natalie Merchant, her jazzbo band, and their original signature protest anthem.

MY MY MY

Artist: Johnny Gill
Written by: Kenny Edmunds (Babyface), Daryl Simmons
From the album: *Johnny Gill*
Label: Motown
Produced by: L. A. Reid, Babyface
Year: 1990
#1 R&B/Top 10 crossover for the New Edition graduate.

MY NAME IS

Artist: Eminem
Written by: Claudius Siffre
From the album: *The Slim Shady LP*
Label: Web/Aftermath
Produced by: Dr. Dre
Year: 1999
A new verbal magician emerges from the mean streets of Detroit.

MY NAME IS JONAS

Artist: Weezer
Written by: Steve Cropper, Rivers Cuomo, Patrick Wilson
From the album: *Weezer*
Produced by: Ric Ocasek
Label: Geffen
Year: 1994
Dweeb rock with a goatee.

MY OPENING FAREWELL

Artist: Jackson Browne
Written by: Jackson Browne
From the album: *Saturate Before Using*
Label: Asylum
Produced by: Richard Orshoff
Year: 1972
A major folk/rock artist stakes out his poetic turf, somewhere west of Eric Anderson, east of Tim Buckley. Covered by Bonnie Raitt (Warner Brothers, '77).

MY OWN PRISON

Artist: Creed
Written by: Scott Stapp, Mark Tremonti
From the album: *My Own Prison*
Label: Wind Up
Year: 1997
A Christian message invades the arena for the first time since Stryper reigned.

MY PAL FOOT FOOT

Artist: The Shaggs
Written by: Dorothy Wiggins
From the album: *Philosophy of the World*
Label: Third World
Produced by: Austin Wiggins Jr.
Year: 1969
In the mythology of low-fi, the Shaggs make kindred spirit Jonathan Richman sound like Frank Zappa and Frank Sinatra combined. The album was rereleased in '80. The song was recut on the *Shaggs' Own Thing* (Red Rooster, '82). But it still remained either awesome or awful depending on your tolerance for such things.

MY PERFECT COUSIN

Artist: The Undertones
Written by: Bradley O'Neill, John O'Neill
From the album: *Hypnotized*
Produced by: Roger Bechirian
Label: Sire
Year: 1980
Their only hit, Top 10 UK.

MY PHILOSOPHY

Artist: KRS-One
Written by: Kris Parker (KRS-One)
From the album: *By All Means Necessary*
Label: Jive
Year: 1988
An early rap statement of purpose.

MY PRAYER

Artist: The Platters
Written by: Georges Boulanger, Jimmy Kennedy
Label:
Year: 1956

Borrowing from their mentors in soul harmony, the Ink Spots, the Platters turned their 1939 pop hit into the stuff of anguished teen dramatics in the final thrilling notes, for their second #1.

MY PREROGATIVE

Artist: Bobby Brown
Written by: Gene Griffin, Bobby Brown
From the album: *Don't Be Cruel*
Label: MCA
Produced by: Gene Griffen
Year: 1988
His second straight #1 R&B/#1 crossover.

MY SHARONA

Artist: The Knack
Written by: Berton Averre, Douglas Fieger
From the album: *Get the Knack*
Label: Capitol
Produced by: Mike Chapman
Year: 1979
Power pop one-shot band proved too calculated to sustain their momentum. Revived in the '94 film *Reality Bites* as the slacker anthem it never really was.

MY SISTER

Artist: The Juliana Hatfield Three
Written by: Juliana Hatfield
From the album: *Become What You Are*
Label: Mammoth
Produced by: Scott Litt
Year: 1993
The girl-group sound with a feminist perspective, female sensibility, and alternative cache.

MY SONG

Artist: Johnny Ace
Written by: John Alexander, David Mattis, Johnny Ace
From the album: *Memorial Album For Johnny Ace*
Label: Duke
Year: 1952
Paving the way for soul. Covered by Aretha Franklin on the B-side of "See Saw" (Atlantic, '68)

MY SPECIAL ANGEL

Artist: Bobby Helms
Written by: Jimmy Duncan
From the album: *To My Special Angel*
Label: Decca
Year: 1957
Johnny Ray-influenced rocker was a rare #1 country/Top 10 R&B/Top 10 crossover.

MY STORY

Artist: Chuck Willis
Written by: Chuck Willis
Label: Okeh
Year: 1952

First Top 10 R&B hit for the Johnny Ace-influenced singer/songwriter.

MY SWEET LORD

Artist: George Harrison
Written by: George Harrison, Ronald Mack
From the album: *All Things Must Pass*
Label: Apple
Produced by: Phil Spector
Year: 1970
Unconsciously plagiarizing "He's So Fine" by the Chiffons.

MY THANG

Artist: James Brown
Written by: James Brown
From the album: *Hell*
Label: Polydor
Produced by: James Brown
Year: 1974
#1 R&B/Top 30 crossover.

MY TOOT TOOT

Artist: Jean Knight
Written by: Sidney Simien
From the album: *My Toot Toot*
Label: Mirage
Produced by: I. Bolden
Year: 1985
A Mardi Gras trinket from New Orleans.

MY TOWN

Artist: The Cucumbers
Written by: John Fried, Deena Shoskes
From the album: *The Cucumbers*
Label: Profile
Year: 1987
An ode to Hoboken. Suggested segues: "I'm from New Jersey" by John Gorka, "Jersey Girl" by Tom Waits, "The Eyes of a New York Woman" by Insect Trust.

MY TRUE LOVE

Artist: Jack Scott
Written by: Jack Scott
From the album: *Jack Scott*
Label: Carlton
Produced by: Ed Carlton
Year: 1958
B-side of "Leroy" was Scott's biggest hit; twangy rockabilly from Detroit on the brink of Motown. Robert Gordon was listening in the East, Chris Isaac in the West.

MY TRUE STORY

Artist: The Jive Five
Written by: Eugene Pitt, Oscar Waltzer
From the album: *The Jive Five*
Label: Beltone
Year: 1961

In the waning days of doo-wop, the story of Sue Ann and Earl: a #1 R&B/Top 10 crossover.

MY UNCLE USED TO LOVE ME BUT SHE DIED

Artist: Roger Miller
Written by: Roger Miller
From the album: *Words and Music*
Label: Smash
Produced by: Jerry Kennedy
Year: 1966
Originally a country/crossover novelty that stiffed for Miller on both charts. Covered by folk group Wind in the Willows (Capitol, '68), which featured Debbie Harry as lead blonde.

MY WHOLE WORLD ENDED (THE MOMENT YOU LEFT ME)

Artist: David Ruffin
Written by: Johnny Bristol, Harvey Fuqua, Pam Sawyer, Jimmy Roach
From the album: *My Whole World Ended*
Label: Motown
Produced by: Johnny Bristol, Harvey Fuqua
Year: 1969
His first hit after leaving the Temptations.

MY WISH CAME TRUE

Artist: Elvis Presley
Written by: Ivory Joe Hunter
From the album: *50,000,000 Elvis Fans Can't Be Wrong: Elvis' Gold Records (Vol. II)*
Label: RCA
Produced by: Steve Sholes
Year: 1959
B-side of "A Big Hunk of Love."

MY WORLD IS EMPTY WITHOUT YOU

Artist: The Supremes
Written by: Eddie Holland, Lamont Dozier, Brian Holland
From the album: *I Hear a Symphony*
Label: Motown
Produced by: Brian Holland, Lamont Dozier
Year: 1966

MYRTLE

Artist: Vic Chesnutt
Written by: Vic Chesnutt
From the album: *About to Choke*
Label: Capitol
Year: 1996
Wheelchair-bound Southern songwriter celebrates a Southern belle.

MYSTERIOUS WAYS

Artist: U2
Written by: U2

From the album: *Achtung Baby*
Label: Island
Produced by: Daniel Lanois, Brian Eno
Year: 1991
Describing the way Bono (and the Lord) moves.

MYSTERY ACHIEVEMENT

Artist: The Pretenders
Written by: Chrissie Hynde
From the album: *The Pretenders*
Label: Sire
Produced by: Chris Thomas
Year: 1980

MYSTERY TRAIN

Artist: Junior Parker
Written by: Herman Parker, Sam Phillips
Label: Sun
Produced by: Sam Phillips
Year: 1953
Seminal rocker based on a Carter Family folk song. Covered by Elvis Presley in one of his classic early performances, on the B-side of "I Forgot to Remember to Forget" (Sun, '56), the Paul Butterfield Blues Band (Elektra, '65), the Band (Capitol, '73), Neil Young (Reprise, '83).

MYSTIC EYES

Artist: Them
Written by: Van Morrison
From the album: *Them*
Label: Parrot
Produced by: Bert Berns
Year: 1965

N

NA NA, HEY, HEY, KISS HIM GOODBYE

Artist: Steam
Written by: Gary DeCarlo, Dale Frashuer, Paul Leka
From the album: *Na Na, Hey, Hey, Kiss Him Goodbye*
Label: Fontana
Produced by: Paul Leka
Year: 1969
Ultimate in-the-studio kiss-off, became an in-the-stadium kiss-off anthem.

NADINE (IS IT YOU?)

Artist: Chuck Berry
Written by: Chuck Berry
From the album: *Chuck Berry's Greatest Hits*
Label: Chess
Produced by: Leonard Chess, Phil Chess
Year: 1964
Friend of Maybellene, immortalized while Chuck was in prison.

NAME

Artist: Goo Goo Dolls
Written by: Johnny Rzeznick
From the album: *A Boy Named Goo*
Label: Metal Blade
Produced by: Lou Giordano
Year: 1995
Cautionary ballad helped them make a name for themselves.

NAME GAME, THE

Artist: Shirley Ellis
Written by: Shirley (Ellis) Elliston, Lincoln Chase
From the album: *The Name Game*
Label: Congress
Produced by: Charlie Calello
Year: 1964
Never caught on like *Me-uss-urray*, the mangled language invented by New York City DJ Murray the K.

NASHVILLE CATS

Artist: The Lovin' Spoonful
Written by: John Sebastian
From the album: *Hums of the Lovin' Spoonful*
Label: Kama Sutra
Produced by: Erik Jacobsen
Year: 1966
Tweaking their friends in the country music business. This was their seventh successive Top 10 single out of seven releases. They would never have another one.

NASTY

Artist: Janet Jackson
Written by: James Harris III, Terry Lewis, Janet Jackson
From the album: *Control*
Label: A&M
Produced by: Jimmy Jam, Terry Lewis
Year: 1986
Beginning to show her real musical personality; #1 R&B/Top 10 crossover.

NATIONAL ANTHEM, THE

Artist: Radiohead
Written by: Colin Greenwood, Johnny Greenwood, Ed O'Brien, Phil Selway, Thom Yorke
From the album: *Kid A*
Label: Capitol
Produced by: Nigel Godrich
Year: 2000
The British national anthem that is. Song was originally entitled "Everyone."

NATURAL ONE

Artist: The Folk Implosion
Written by: Lou Barlow, John Davis, Walton Gagel
From the album: *Kids Soundtrack*
Label: London
Produced by: Lou Barlow, Tim O'Heir
Year: 1995
Boston lo-fi spritual leader Barlow returns to Fort Apache to score an indie film. This space-age-marching-band-on-acid number turned into a flukey one-shot hit.

NATURE BOY

Artist: Nat King Cole
Written by: eden ahbez
From the album:
Label: Capitol
Year: 1948
Mystical million-selling tale of Brooklyn boy's spiritual quest for love, as written by the world's first hippie, found favor in many disparate rock and roll camps. Cover by Bobby Darin (Atco, '61) hit the Top 40. Covered by Great Society (Columbia, "65), David Bowie (Hollywood, '02).

NATURE'S WAY

Artist: Spirit
Written by: Randy California
From the album: *Twelve Dreams of Dr. Sardonicus*
Label: Epic
Produced by: Lou Adler
Year: 1970
Loopy ecological lament. Covered by Victoria Williams (Atlantic, '95).

NAUGHTY GIRLS NEED LOVE TOO

Artist: Samantha Fox
Written by: Full Force
From the album: *Samantha Fox*
Label: Jive
Produced by: Full Force
Year: 1988
As a dance-hall chanteuse, Fox was more of a tease than a talent.

NEARLY IN LOVE

Artist: Richard Thompson
Written by: Richard Thompson
From the album: *Daring Adventures*
Label: Polygram
Produced by: Mitchell Froom
Year: 1986
He twists the knife again.

NEAT NEAT NEAT

Artist: The Damned
Written by: Brian James
From the album: *Damned, Damned, Damned*
Label: Stiff
Produced by: Nick Lowe
Year: 1977
Chemically inspired speed merchants of punk.

NEED YOU TONIGHT

Artist: Inxs
Written by: Andrew Farriss, Michael Hutchence
From the album: *Kick*
Label: Atlantic

Produced by: Chris Thomas
Year: 1987
Their only #1.

NEED YOUR LOVE SO BAD

Artist: Little Willie John
Written by: Willie John
From the album: *Little Willie John*
Label: King
Produced by: Henry Glover
Year: 1956
His second Top 10 R&B hit was covered by Irma Thomas, Mother Earth, Fleetwood Mac, the Allman Brothers, John Lee Hooker, Whitesnake, Bonnie Tyler, Eva Cassady, and Sting.

NEEDLE AND THE DAMAGE DONE, THE

Artist: Neil Young
Written by: Neil Young
From the album: *Harvest*
Label: Reprise
Produced by: Elliot Mazur, Neil Young
Year: 1972
The unraveling of a drug-soaked era, written for his late pal Danny Whitten, about whom Nils Lofgren wrote "Beggar's Day."

NEEDLES AND PINS

Artist: Jackie Deshannon
Written by: Sonny Bono, Jack Nitzsche
From the album: *Breaking It up on the Beatles' Tour*
Label: Liberty
Produced by: Jack Nitzsche, Jackie DeShannon
Year: 1963
Anxious epic. Covered by Cher (Imperial, '64), the Searchers (Pye, '65).

NEITHER ONE OF US (WANTS TO BE THE FIRST TO SAY GOODBYE)

Artist: Gladys Knight & the Pips
Written by: Jim Weatherly
From the album: *Neither One of Us*
Label: Soul
Produced by: Joe Porter
Year: 1973
Saying goodbye to Motown (and hello to a Grammy award) with their first peek into the Jim Weatherly catalogue; a #1 R&B/Top 10 crossover. Their next peek was a cover of a song Jim released first on Amos, called "Midnight Plane to Houston." It would be their biggest hit under the title "Midnight Train to Georgia" (Buddah, '73).

NEL BLU DIPINTO DI BLU (VOLARE)

Artist: Domenico Modugno
Written by: Mitchell Parish, Domenico Modugno, Franco Migliacci

From the album: *Nel Blu Dipinto Di Blu (Volare) and Other Italian Favorites*
Label: Decca
Produced by: Mitchell Parish
Year: 1958
#1 Italian pop love song brought into the mainstream by Bobby Rydell (Cameo, '61) and into the alternative rock lexicon by Alex Chilton (Big Time, '87). Winner of the first Grammy Award for Song of the Year.

NEON RAINBOW

Artist: The Box Tops
Written by: Wayne Carson Thompson
From the album: *The Box Tops: "The Letter"/"Neon Rainbow"*
Label: Mala
Produced by: Dan Penn
Year: 1967
Following up "The Letter" with the same team, but less perfect results.

NERVOUS BREAKDOWN

Artist: Eddie Cochran
Written by: Mario Roccuzzo, Eddie Cochran
From the album: *Cherished Memories of Eddie Cochran*
Label: London
Produced by: Eddie Cochran, Jerry Capeheart
Year: 1961

NEVER

Artist: Heart
Written by: Holly Knight, Walter Bloch, Ann Wilson
From the album: *Heart*
Label: Capitol
Produced by: Ron Nevison
Year: 1985
Having paid their arena dues, the Wilson sisters first of six Top 10 lite metal ballads.

NEVER BEEN TO SPAIN

Artist: Three Dog Night
Written by: Hoyt Axton
From the album: *Harmony*
Label: Dunhill
Produced by: Richard Polodor
Year: 1971
Kids' party tune.

NEVER CAN SAY GOODBYE

Artist: The Jackson 5
Written by: Clifton Davis
From the album: *Maybe Tomorrow*
Label: Motown
Produced by: Hal Davis, the Corporation
Year: 1970
After their first four releases, and four #1 R&B/#1 crossovers, they again hit #1 R&B, but peak at #2 on the pop charts. This future disco standard was covered by Isaac Hayes (Enterprise, '71), Gloria Gaynor (MGM, '75).

NEVER DIE YOUNG

Artist: James Taylor
Written by: James Taylor
From the album: *Never Die Young*
Label: Columbia
Produced by: Don Grolnick
Year: 1988
His baby boom statement.

NEVER ENDING SONG OF LOVE

Artist: Delaney and Bonnie
Written by: Delaney Bramlett
From the album: *Motel Shot*
Label: Atco
Produced by: Delaney Bramlett
Year: 1971
A rustic acoustic favorite.

NEVER EVER

Artist: All Saints
Written by: Robert Jazayeri, Shaznay Lewis, Sean Mather
From the album: *All Saints*
Label: London
Year: 1998
Chick/hop, the white division, in the Spice Girls mold, but without the spice.

NEVER GONNA GIVE YOU UP

Artist: Rick Astley
Written by: Mike Stock, Matt Aitken, Pete Waterman
From the album: *Whenever You Need Somebody*
Label: RCA
Produced by: Mike Stock, Matt Aitken, Pete Waterman
Year: 1987
First trans-Atlantic smash for the male dance-hall diva is his biggest, #1 US and UK.

NEVER KNEW LOVE LIKE THIS BEFORE

Artist: Stephanie Mills
Written by: James Mtume, Reggie Lewis
From the album: *Sweet Sensation*
Label: 20TH Century
Produced by: James Mtume
Year: 1980
#1 R&B/Top 10 crossover by the girl who played Dorothy on Broadway in *The Wiz*.

NEVER LIE

Artist: Immature
Written by: Chris Stokes, Claudio Cuen
From the album: *Playtime Is Over*
Label: MCA
Year: 1994
Boyz II Men for the middle school set.

NEVER MAKE A PROMISE

Artist: Dru Hill
Written by: Darryl Simmons
From the album: *Dru Hill*
Label: Island
Year: 1997

NEVER MY LOVE

Artist: The Association
Written by: Don Addrisi, Dick Addrisi
From the album: *Greatest Hits*
Label: Warner Brothers
Produced by: Bones Howe
Year: 1967
Their most enduring ballad, covered by wedding bands everywhere.

NEVER, NEVER GONNA GIVE YA UP

Artist: Barry White
Written by: Barry White
From the album: *Stone Gon'*
Label: 20TH Century
Produced by: Barry White
Year: 1973
Dusky bedroom ballad.

NEVER SURRENDER

Artist: Corey Hart
Written by: Corey Hart
From the album: *Boy in the Box*
Label: EMI-America
Year: 1985
Segue: "No Surrender" by Bruce Springsteen.

NEVER THERE

Artist: Cake
Written by: John McCrea
From the album: *Prolonging the Magic*
Label: Capricorn
Year: 1998
Quirky post-punk rant.

NEW AGE GIRL

Artist: Deadeye Dick
Written by: Caleb Guillotte
From the album: *A Different Story*
Label: Ichaban
Produced by: F. LeBlanc
Year: 1994
"Punk Rock Girl" five years later. Featured in the Jim Carrey movie *Dumb and Dumber*.

NEW AMSTERDAM

Artist: Elvis Costello
Written by: Elvis Costello
From the album: *Get Happy*
Label: Reprise
Produced by: Nick Lowe
Year: 1980
Eloquently malicious.

NEW COAT OF PAINT

Artist: Tom Waits
Written by: Tom Waits
From the album: *Heart of a Saturday Night*
Label: Asylum
Produced by: Bones Howe
Year: 1974

NEW ENGLAND, A

Artist: Billy Bragg
Written by: Billy Bragg
From the album: *Life's a Riot*
Label: Utility/Go Discs
Produced by: Oliver Hatch
Year: 1983
The Woody Guthrie-inspired folk singer's debut UK single established his two major themes: sex and politics, not necessarily in that order. Covered by Kristy MacColl (Stiff, '85).

NEW FORMS

Artist: Roni Size and Reprazent
Written by: Antonia Reed (Bahamadia), Roni Size, Suv
From the album: *New Forms*
Label: Talkin' Loud
Year: 1997
Spacey techno dance track from a new pioneer.

NEW GIRL IN SCHOOL, THE

Artist: Jan and Dean
Written by: Brian Wilson, Jan Berry, Roger Christian, Bob Norman
From the album: *Dead Man's Curve/The New Girl in School*
Label: Liberty
Year: 1964
Covered by Alex Chilton (Arden, '95).

NEW JACK HUSTLER (NINO'S THEME)

Artist: Ice-T
Written by: Tracy Morrow (Ice-T)
From the album: *New Jack City Soundtrack*
Label: Giant
Year: 1991
From the '90s-era blaxploitation film.

NEW KID IN TOWN

Artist: Eagles
Written by: Don Henley, Glenn Frey, John David Souther
From the album: *Hotel California*
Label: Asylum
Produced by: Bill Szymczyk
Year: 1977
Countrypolitan L.A.

NEW LIFE

Artist: Depeche Mode
Written by: Vince Clarke
From the album: *Speak and Spell*
Label: Mute
Produced by: Daniel Miller, Depeche Mode
Year: 1981
Presaging the UK synth invasion of the mid-'80s.

NEW MORNING

Artist: Bob Dylan
Written by: Bob Dylan
From the album: *New Morning*
Label: Columbia
Produced by: Bob Johnson
Year: 1970
On the road from Woodstock to Nashville.

NEW NEW MINGLEWOOD BLUES

Artist: Grateful Dead
Written by: Jerry Garcia, Robert Hunter
From the album: *The Grateful Dead*
Label: Warner Brothers
Produced by: Grateful Dead
Year: 1967
With Gus Cannon and the Jug Stompers' "Minglewood Blues" (RCA '28) in mind, the legendary touring institution and traveling hippie circus and museum first known as Mother Mcree's Uptown Jug Champions, and then as the Warlocks, begin their reign as house band at Ken Kesey's Trips Festivals, led by Captain Trips himself, otherwise known as Jerry Garcia.

NEW NOISE

Artist: Refused
Written by: John Branstrom, Dennis Lyxzen, Kristofer Steen, David Sandstrom
From the album: *Shape of Punk to Come*
Label: Epitaph
Year: 1998
An education, if your ears can stand it.

NEW POLLUTION, THE

Artist: Beck
Written by: Beck Hanson, Michael Simpson, John King
From the album: *Odelay*
Label: DGC
Produced by: Mario Caldato Jr
Year: 1996
An aural collage in the age of too much information.

NEW ROSE

Artist: The Damned
Written by: Brian James
From the album: *The Damned*
Label: Stiff
Produced by: Nick Lowe
Year: 1976
The first single from England's first punk band includes a tribute to the Shangri-Las: "Is she really going out with him." Joe Jackson would later complete the entire song. Covered by Guns N' Roses (Geffen, '89).

NEW SENSATION

Artist: Inxs
Written by: Andrew Farriss, Michael Hutchence
From the album: *Kick*
Label: Atlantic
Produced by: Chris Thomas
Year: 1987
Following up a #2 single with a #3 single.

NEW SPANISH TWO STEP

Artist: Bob Wills & His Texas Playboys
Written by: Bob Wills, Tommy Duncan
Label: Columbia
Year: 1946
Establishing the rhythmic base for country/rock.

NEW WORLD COMING

Artist: Mama Cass
Written by: Barry Mann, Cynthia Well
From the album: *Mama's Big Ones*
Label: Dunhill
Produced by: Steve Barri, Joel Sill
Year: 1970
Solo effort from the Mamas, and the Papas' big Mama fell flat in its lyrical predictions.

NEW WORLD MAN

Artist: Rush
Written by: Gary Lee Weinrib (Geddy Lee), Alex Zivojinovich (Alex Lifeson), Neil Peart
From the album: *Signals*
Label: Mercury
Produced by: Terry Brown, Rush
Year: 1982
Closest thing to a hit for the Ayn Rand-influenced Canadian rock collective.

NEW YEAR'S DAY

Artist: U2
Written by: Paul Hewson (Bono), Dave Evans (Edge), Adam Clayton, Larry Mullen
From the album: *War*
Label: Island
Produced by: Steve Lillywhite, Bill Whelan
Year: 1983
Haunting and powerful dirge offers a symbolic and actual renewal for arena and alternative rock.

NEW YORK CITY (YOU'RE A WOMAN)

Artist: Al Kooper
Written by: Al Kooper
From the album: *New York City (You're a Woman)*
Label: Columbia
Year: 1971
Suggested segue: "American City Suite" by Cashman and West.

NEW YORK GROOVE

Artist: Ace Frehley
Written by: Russ Ballard
From the album: *Ace Frehley*
Label: Casablanca
Produced by: Eddie Kramer, Ace Frehley
Year: 1979
Relatively mellow outing for the legendary Kiss axeman on temporary leave.

NEW YORK MINING DISASTER 1941 (HAVE YOU SEEN MY WIFE MR. JONES)

Artist: Bee Gees
Written by: Barry Gibb, Robin Gibb, Maurice Gibb
From the album: *Bee Gee's First*
Label: Atco
Produced by: Ossie Byrne
Year: 1967
Late entry by way of Australia in the Beatles-influenced British invasion.

NEW YORK, NEW YORK

Artist: Grandmaster Flash and the Furious Five
Written by: Melvin Glover, Sylvia Robinson, Edward Fletcher, Reginald Griffin
Label: Sugarhill
Year: 1983
No fun city.

NEW YORK STATE OF MIND

Artist: Billy Joel
Written by: Billy Joel
From the album: *Turnstiles*
Label: Columbia
Produced by: Phil Ramone
Year: 1976
Homegrown city anthem achieved a Long Island boy epiphany, a cover version by Brooklyn princess Barbra Streisand (Columbia, '77).

NEW YORK STATE OF MIND

Artist: Nas
Written by: Nasir Jones, Chris E. Martin
From the album: *Illmatic*
Label: Columbia
Year: 1994
Powerful street poetry from a rising new force in rap.

NEXT DOOR TO AN ANGEL

Artist: Neil Sedaka
Written by: Howard Greenfield, Neil Sedaka
From the album: *Neil Sedaka Sings His Greatest Hits*
Label: RCA Victor
Produced by: Al Nevins, Don Kirshner
Year: 1962
His sixth and last Top 10 hit of the '60s.

NEXT TIME I FALL, THE

Artist: Peter Cetera with Amy Grant
Written by: Robert Caldwell, Paul Gordon
From the album: *Solitude/Solitaire*
Label: Warner Brothers
Produced by: Michael Omartian
Year: 1986

NIAGARA

Artist: The Wedding Present
Written by: David Gedge
From the album: *Sea Monster*
Label: First Warning
Year: 1991
Alternative angst from England.

NICE & SLOW

Artist: Usher
Written by: Usher Raymond, Harry Casey, Jermaine Dupri, Manuel Seal
From the album: *My Way*
Label: LaFace
Produced by: Jermaine Dupri
Year: 1997
Hip hop on the smooth R&B tip.

NICE TO BE WITH YOU

Artist: Gallery
Written by: Jim Gold
From the album: *Nice to Be with You*
Label: Sussex
Produced by: Dennis Coffey
Year: 1972
Exemplary sunny pop/rock of the post-apocalyptic, everything-is-beautiful singles era of the early '70s.

NICE, NICE, VERY NICE

Artist: Ambrosia
Written by: David Pack, Kurt Vonnegut Jr., Joseph Puerta Jr., Christopher North, Burleigh Drummond
From the album: *Ambrosia*
Label: 20TH Century
Produced by: Freddie Piro
Year: 1975
Lyrics adapted from the Kurt Vonnegut novel, *Cat's Cradle*.

NIGHT

Artist: Jackie Wilson
Written by: Johnny Lehman, Herb Miller
Label: Brunswick
Produced by: MDL
Year: 1960
His biggest hit is another operatic flight, a Top 5 R&B/Top 5 crossover.

NIGHT BEFORE, THE

Artist: The Beatles
Written by: John Lennon, Paul McCartney
From the album: *Help!*
Label: Capitol
Produced by: George Martin
Year: 1965

NIGHT BIRD FLYING

Artist: Jimi Hendrix
Written by: Jimi Hendrix
From the album: *The Cry of Love*
Label: Reprise
Produced by: Jimi Hendrix, Mitch Mitchell, Eddie Kramer
Year: 1971
First of a virtual warehouse full of posthumous noodling.

NIGHT CHICAGO DIED, THE

Artist: Paper Lace
Written by: Peter Callendar, Lionel Stitcher
From the album: *Paper Lace*
Label: Mercury
Produced by: Mitch Murray, Peter Callendar
Year: 1974
The originators of "Billy, Don't Be a Hero" notch another pop-rock novelty; Al Capone as viewed from Nottingham, England.

NIGHT FEVER

Artist: Bee Gees
Written by: Barry Gibb, Robin Gibb, Maurice Gibb
From the album: *Saturday Night Fever*
Label: RSO
Produced by: Albhy Galutin, Karl Richardson, the Bee Gees
Year: 1977
Hitting their career-defining groove with the big movie song from the disco-defining movie.

NIGHT HAS A THOUSAND EYES, THE

Artist: Bobby Vee
Written by: Buddy Bernier, Jerry Brainin
From the album: *The Night Has a Thousand Eyes*
Label: Liberty
Produced by: Snuff Garrett
Year: 1960
Title song from the 1948 movie was covered by Vee in the 1960 movie *Just for Fun*.

NIGHT IN MY VEINS

Artist: The Pretenders
Written by: Chrissie Hynde, Billy Steinberg, Tom Kelly
From the album: *Last of the Independents*
Label: Sire
Produced by: Ian Stanley
Year: 1994
Still on the prowl at forty.

NIGHT IN THE CITY

Artist: Joni Mitchell
Written by: Joni Mitchell
From the album: *Joni Mitchell*
Label: Reprise
Produced by: David Crosby
Year: 1968
Folk/rock 101. Covered by Three Dog Night (Dunhill, '71).

NIGHT MOVES

Artist: Bob Seger
Written by: Bob Seger
From the album: *Night Moves*
Label: Capitol
Produced by: Jack Richardson, Bob Seger
Year: 1976
Invading Mellencamp turf with a poignant reminiscence of a lost Midwestern youth.

NIGHT THE LIGHTS WENT OUT IN GEORGIA, THE

Artist: Vickie Lawrence
Written by: Bobby Russell
From the album: *The Night the Lights Went out in Georgia*
Label: Bell
Produced by: Snuff Garrett
Year: 1973
Faulknerian #1 country/#1 crossover story-song and future TV movie. Suggested TV movie/record segues: "Harper Valley PTA" by Jeannie C. Riley, "Ode to Billie Joe" by Bobbie Gentry, "The Gambler" by Kenny Rogers.

NIGHT THEY DROVE OLD DIXIE DOWN, THE

Artist: The Band
Written by: Robbie Robertson
From the album: *The Band*
Label: Capitol
Produced by: John Simon, the Band
Year: 1968
Country/rock at its rootsiest. Both country covers by Don Rich & the Buckaroos (Capitol, '70) and Alice Creech (Target, '71) stiffed. The (Yankee) version by Joan Baez (Vanguard, '71) was her biggest hit.

(NIGHT TIME IS THE) RIGHT TIME

Artist: Ray Charles
Written by: Lew Herman
From the album: *Ray Charles in Person*
Label: Atlantic
Produced by: Ahmet Ertegun, Jerry Wexler
Year: 1958
Top 5 R&B hit.

NIGHT TRAIN

Artist: Jimmy Forrest
Written by: Oscar Washington, Lewis Simpkins, Jimmy Forrest
Label: United
Year: 1952
Smokin' jazz-flavored sax instrumental. Covered by the Viscounts (Madison, '60), James Brown (King, '62).

NIGHTMARE ON MY STREET, A

Artist: DJ Jazzy Jeff and The Fresh Prince
Written by: Will Smith, Jeff Townes, Pete Q. Harris
From the album: *He's the DJ, I'm the Rapper*
Label: Jive
Produced by: DJ Jazzy Jeff, the Fresh Prince, Pete Q. Harris, N. Green
Year: 1988
Teen Rap on the horror movie tip.

NIGHTS IN WHITE SATIN

Artist: The Moody Blues
Written by: Justin Hayward
From the album: *Days of Future Passed*
Label: Deram
Produced by: Tony Clarke
Year: 1968
Psychedelic Montovani, with a side of Kahlil Gibran. Rereleased in '72.

NIGHTS ON BROADWAY

Artist: Bee Gees
Written by: Barry Gibb, Robin Gibb, Maurice Gibb
From the album: *Main Course*
Label: RSO
Produced by: Arif Mardin
Year: 1975
Moving toward their blue-eyed soul crescendo.

NIGHTSHIFT

Artist: Commodores
Written by: Dennis Lambert, Frannie Golde, Walter Orange
From the album: *Nightshift*
Label: Motown
Produced by: Dennis Lambert
Year: 1985
A moving mid-tempo tribute to Marvin Gaye and Jackie Wilson in R&B heaven.

NIKI HOEKY

P. J. Proby
Written by: Pat Vegas, Lolly Vegas, Jim Ford
From the album: *Enigma*
Label: Liberty
Produced by: Calvin Carter
Year: 1966
Covered by Aretha Franklin (Atlantic, '68). The Vegases would show up in Redbone.

NIKITA

Artist: Elton John
Written by: Elton John, Bernie Taupin
From the album: *Ice on Fire*
Label: Warner Brothers

Produced by: Gus Dudgeon
Year: 1986
Segue: "Leningrad" by Billy Joel.

911 IS A JOKE

Artist: Public Enemy
Written by: Carlton Ridenhour, Hank Shocklee, Keith Shocklee
From the album: *Fear of a Black Planet*
Label: Def Jam
Produced by: Stuart Robertz, Cerwin Depper, Gary G. Wiz, the JBL
Year: 1990
Still keeping an ear to the street.

9 TO 5

Artist: Dolly Parton
Written by: Dolly Parton
From the album: *9 to 5 and Other Odd Jobs*
Label: RCA
Produced by: Mike Post
Year: 1981
Oscar-winning #1 country/#1 crossover.

19

Artist: Paul Hardcastle
Written by: Paul Hardcastle, W. Coutourie, J. McCord
Label: Chrysalis
Produced by: Paul Hardcastle
Year: 1985
Vietnam war commentary.

1952 VINCENT BLACK LIGHTNING

Artist: Richard Thompson
Written by: Richard Thompson
From the album: *Rumor and Sigh*
Label: Capitol
Produced by: Mitchell Froom
Year: 1991
A timeless and compelling modern folk tale, ending in death.

1999

Artist: Prince
Written by: Prince Rogers Nelson
From the album: *1999*
Label: Warner Brothers
Produced by: Prince
Year: 1982
Party anthem for the ultimate party. Revived in time for the Y2K fiasco.

1979

Artist: Smashing Pumpkins
Written by: Billy Corgan
From the album: *Mellon Collie and the Infinite Sadness*
Label: Virgin
Produced by: Alan Moulder, Billy Corgan, Flood
Year: 1995

1977

Artist: The Clash
Written by: John Mellor (Joe Strummer), Mick Jones
From the album: *The Clash*
Label: Epic
Produced by: Mickey Foote
Year: 1977
The B-side of "White Riot" and conclusive proof that the Clash were "No Elvis, No Beatles, No Rolling Stones."

1916

Artist: Motorhead
Written by: Ian Kilmeister (Lemmy)
From the album: *1916*
Label: WTG
Produced by: Peter Solley
Year: 1991
Blitzkrieg ballad.

19TH NERVOUS BREAKDOWN

Artist: The Rolling Stones
Written by: Mick Jagger, Keith Richards
From the album: *Big Hits (High Tide and Green Grass)*
Label: London
Produced by: Andrew Loog-Oldham
Year: 1966
Early attempt at Dylanesque psychodramatics.

98.6

Artist: Keith
Written by: Tony Powers, George Fischoff
From the album: *98.6/Ain't Gonna Lie*
Label: Mercury
Produced by: Jerry Ross
Year: 1966
Basic AM radio reassurance in the midst of the nascent rock revolution.

99 AND A HALF

Artist: Wilson Pickett
Written by: Wilson Pickett, Steve Cropper
From the album: *The Exciting Wilson Pickett*
Label: Atlantic
Produced by: Steve Cropper, Jim Stewart
Year: 1966
One of his greatest performances.

99 LUFTBALONS (99 RED BALLOONS)

Artist: Nena
Written by: Joem Fahrenkrog-Petersen, Karlo Karges, Kevin McAlea
From the album: *99 Luftbalons*
Label: Epic
Year: 1984
The German version was the US hit. Suggested segue: "Shock Den Affen" by Peter Gabriel.

96 TEARS

Artist: ? & the Mysterians
Written by: Rudy Martinez
From the album: *96 Tears*
Label: Cameo
Produced by: Rudy Martinez
Year: 1966
What Max Crook's musitron hath wrought; the Farfisa organ garage band revolution of the mid-'60s epitomized. Covered by Big Maybelle (Rojac, '67), Garland Jeffreys (Epic, '81).

NITE AND DAY

Artist: Al B. Sure
Written by: Al B. Sure, Kyle West
From the album: *In Effect Mode*
Label: Warner Brothers
Produced by: Teddy Riley, Al B. Sure
Year: 1988
Middle-of-the-street crooner breaks in with a #1 R&B/Top 10 crossover.

NITE OWL

Artist: Tony Allen
Written by: Tony Allen
From the album: *Rock and Roll with Tony Allen*
Label: Specialty
Produced by: Bumps Blackwell
Year: 1955
Pioneering doo-wop track that provided "In the Still of the Night" by the Five Satins with its defining "shoo-doot 'n shoo be doos."

NITTY GRITTY, THE

Artist: Shirley Ellis
Written by: Lincoln Chase
Label: Congress
Year: 1963
The phrase has endured longer than the song.

NO CHEMISE, PLEASE!

Artist: Gerry Granahan
Written by: Gerry Granahan, Jodi D'Amour, Arnold Goland
Label: Sunbeam
Year: 1958
Fleeting fashion commentary by the former leader of Dickie Doo and the Don'ts.

NO DIGGITY

Artist: BlackStreet
Written by: Teddy Riley, Chauncey Hannibal, Lynise Walters, Williams Stewart, Dr. Dre
From the album: *Another Level*
Label: BlackStreet
Produced by: Teddy Riley
Year: 1996
One of the best grooves of the decade, where bop hop meets afro bohemia.

NO EASY WAY DOWN

Artist: Dusty Springfield
Written by: Gerry Goffin, Carole King

From the album: *Dusty in Memphis*
Label: Atlantic
Produced by: Tom Dowd, Jerry Wexler, Arif Mardin
Year: 1969
A gem from Goffin and King's "bleak" period highlight's Dusty's Memphis revival. Recorded by Carole King (Ode, '71).

NO EXCUSES

Artist: Alice in Chains
Written by: Jerry Cantrell
From the album: *Jar of Flies*
Label: Columbia
Produced by: Alice in Chains
Year: 1994
Grunge goes metal, the beginning of the end.

NO EXPECTATIONS

Artist: The Rolling Stones
Written by: Mick Jagger, Keith Richards
From the album: *Beggars Banquet*
Label: London
Produced by: Jimmy Miller
Year: 1968
Stones move out of pyschedelia and into blues/rock.

NO FUN

Artist: The Stooges
Written by: Dave Alexander, Ron Asheton, Scott Asheton, James Osterberg (Iggy Pop)
From the album: *The Stooges*
Produced by: John Cale
Label: Elektra
Year: 1969
Cale moves from defining alternative culture with the velvet underground to taking on punk noise. On the other hand, Jonathan Richman was also on his dance card.

NO MATTER WHAT SHAPE (YOUR STOMACH'S IN)

Artist: The T-Bones
Written by: Sascha Burland
From the album: *No Matter What Shape (Your Stomach's In)*
Label: Liberty
Produced by: Joe Saraceno
Year: 1965
Surf music hits the commercial mainstream.

NO MONEY DOWN

Artist: Chuck Berry
Written by: Chuck Berry
From the album: *After School Sessions*
Label: Chess
Produced by: Leonard Chess, Phil Chess
Year: 1957
A look through Chuck's legendary jaundiced eye at life as a used car lot.

NO MONEY DOWN

Artist: Lou Reed
Written by: Lou Reed
From the album: *Mistrial*
Label: RCA
Produced by: Fernando Saunders, Lou Reed
Year: 1986
One of his catchiest tunes, attached to a treatise on trust.

NO MORE LONELY NIGHTS

Artist: Paul McCartney
Written by: Paul McCartney
From the album: *Give My Regards to Broad Street Soundtrack*
Label: Columbia
Produced by: George Martin
Year: 1984
Paul's rock opera—but it was no *Tommy*.

NO MORE MR. NICE GUY

Artist: Alice Cooper
Written by: Vincent Furnier (Alice Cooper), Michael Bruce
From the album: *Billion Dollar Babies*
Label: Warner Brothers
Produced by: Bob Ezrin
Year: 1974
Making the most of a one-joke theme.

NO MORE TEARS (ENOUGH IS ENOUGH)

Artist: Donna Summer and Barbra Streisand
Written by: Paul Jabara, Bruce Roberts
From the album: *On the Radio—Greatest Hits (Vols. I and II)*
Label: Casablanca
Produced by: Giorgio Moroder, Pete Bellotte
Year: 1979
Dueling divas; Donna's fourth and last #1.

NO MYTH

Artist: Michael Penn
Written by: Michael Penn
From the album: *March*
Label: RCA
Produced by: Tony Berg
Year: 1989
Clear-eyed alternative folk/rock by the brother of Sean, husband of Aimee Mann. An "It Ain't Me Babe" for Generation X.

NO NO NO

Artist: Destiny's Child
Written by: Vincent Herbert, Rob Fusari
From the album: *Destiny's Child*
Label: Columbia
Year: 1997
Last great girl-group of the century.

NO NO SONG

Artist: Ringo Starr

Written by: Hoyt Axton, David Jackson Jr.
From the album: *Goodnight Vienna*
Label: Apple
Produced by: Richard Perry
Year: 1974

NO ONE IS TO BLAME

Artist: Howard Jones
Written by: Howard Jones
From the album: *Action Replay*
Label: Elektra
Produced by: Phil Collins
Year: 1986
His biggest hit is a re-record.

NO ONE KNOWS

Artist: Dion and the Belmonts
Written by: Ken Hecht, Emie Maresca
Label: Laurie
Produced by: Gene Schwartz
Year: 1958
A bigger hit than "I Wonder Why," but not as influential; here Dion is more pitiful than cool.

NO ONE LIKE YOU

Artist: Scorpions
Written by: Rudolf Schenker, Klaus Meine
From the album: *Blackout*
Label: Mercury
Produced by: Dieter Dirks
Year: 1982
Signature riff. Segues: "Still Loving You," "Holiday."

NO ORDINARY LOVE

Artist: Sade
Written by: Helen Folesade Adu (Sade), Stuart Matthewman
From the album: *Love Deluxe*
Label: Epic
Produced by: Sade
Year: 1992
Sultry ballad that was crucial in the Robert Redford/Demi Moore movie *Indecent Proposal*.

NO PARTICULAR PLACE TO GO

Artist: Chuck Berry
Written by: Chuck Berry
From the album: *St. Louis to Liverpool*
Label: Chess
Produced by: Leonard Chess, Phil Chess
Year: 1964
By virtue of his rediscovery by the Beatles and the Stones, Chuck Berry returned to the Top 10 after an absence of seven years with this song. Its message, its equanimity, and the humor of the lyrical concept was brilliant, considering the fact that it was written while Chuck was in prison.

NO QUARTER

Artist: Led Zeppelin
Written by: Jimmy Page, Robert Plant, John Paul Jones

From the album: *Houses of the Holy*
Label: Atlantic
Produced by: Jimmy Page
Year: 1973
Revived by Plant and Page on their '94 reunion album, along with "The Battle of Evermore" and "Kashmir."

NO RAIN

Artist: Blind Melon
Written by: Blind Melon
From the album: *Blind Melon*
Label: Capitol
Produced by: Rich Parashar, Blind Melon
Year: 1993
Updated psychedelia-lite.

NO REGRETS

Artist: Tom Rush
Written by: Tom Rush
From the album: *The Circle Game*
Label: Elektra
Produced by: Arthur Gordon
Year: 1968
From the landmark folk/rock album that featured songs by Joni Mitchell, James Taylor and Jackson Browne, an expansive, open D guitar autobiography. Covered in England by the Walker Brothers (GTO, '76), and in America by Emmylou Harris (Reprise, '89).

NO RESERVATIONS

Artist: Hüsker Dü
Written by: Bob Mould
From the album: *Warehouse Songs and Stories*
Label: Warner Brothers
Produced by: Bob Mould, Grant Hart
Year: 1987

NO SCRUBS

Artist: TLC
Written by: Kevin Briggs, Kandi Burruss, Tameka Kottle
From the album: *Fan Mail*
Label: LaFace
Produced by: Kevin "Shekespere" Briggs
Year: 1999
One of the decade's more biting girl group put-downs. It would be answered with "No Pigeons" by Sporty Thievz featuring Mr. Woods, but no one cared.

NO SLEEP TILL BROOKLYN

Artist: The Beastie Boys
Written by: The Beastie Boys, Rick Rubin
From the album: *Licensed to Ill*
Label: Def Jam
Produced by: Rick Rubin
Year: 1986
Establishing Brooklyn as the center of rap America. In L.A., Compton was the left of center.

NO SON OF MINE

Artist: Genesis
Written by: Phil Collins, Tony Banks, Mike Rutherford
From the album: *We Can't Dance*
Label: Atlantic
Produced by: Nick Davis, Genesis
Year: 1991
An attempt at social realism. Collins would exploit this vein further as a solo act. Suggested segue: Mike Rutherford's "The Living Years."

NO TIME

Artist: The Guess Who
Written by: Randall Bachman, Burton Cummings
From the album: *Canned Wheat Packed by the Guess Who*
Label: RCA
Produced by: Jack Richardson
Year: 1969
The answer to Chicago's "Does Anybody Really Know What Time It Is?"

NO TIME

Artist: Lil Kim
Written by: Kipper Jones, Sean Combs, Steve Jordan
From the album: *Hard Core*
Label: Undeas/Big Beat
Year: 1996

NO TIME LIKE THE RIGHT TIME

Artist: The Blues Project
Written by: Al Kooper
From the album: *Blues Project Live at Town Hall*
Label: Verve/Forecast
Produced by: Tom Wilson
Year: 1967
Early Kooper blues/rock rouser powered by the guitar of Danny Kalb.

NO TIME TO CRY

Artist: Iris Dement
Written by: Iris Dement
From the album: *My Life*
Produced by: Jim Rooney
Label: Warner Brothers
Year: 1994
Out past the exurbs of alt country, echoing Appalachia.

NO WOMAN, NO CRY

Artist: Bob Marley & the Wailers
Written by: Bob Marley
From the album: *Natty Dread*
Label: Island
Produced by: Chris Blackwell, the Wailers
Year: 1974
From a government yard in Kingston, one of the all-time reggae love songs.

NOBODY

Artist: Keith Sweat
Written by: Keith Sweat, Fitzgerald Scott
From the album: *Keith Sweat*
Label: Elektra
Year: 1996

NOBODY BUT ME

Artist: The Isley Brothers
Written by: Ronald Isley, Rudolph Isley, O' Kelly Isley
Label: Wand
Year: 1963
Covered by the Human Beinz (Capitol, '68).

NOBODY DOES IT BETTER

Artist: Carly Simon
Written by: Carole Bayer Sager, Marvin Hamlisch
From the album: *Greatest Hits Live*
Label: Elektra
Produced by: Richard Perry
Year: 1977
Title theme for the James Bond film.

NOBODY KNOWS

Artist: Tony Rich Project
Written by: Joseph Rich, Don Dubose
From the album: *Words*
Label: LaFace
Produced by: Tony Rich
Year: 1995
Easy listening R&B.

NOBODY TOLD ME

Artist: John Lennon
Written by: John Lennon
From the album: *Milk and Honey*
Label: Polydor
Year: 1984
His ninth and last Top 10 hit.

NOBODY'S FAULT BUT MY OWN

Artist: Beck
Written by: Beck Hanson
From the album: *Mutations*
Label: DGC
Produced by: Nigel Godrich, Beck Hanson
Year: 1998
Junkyard blues from the Jack Kerovac of the genre.

NONE OF YOUR BUSINESS

Artist: Salt-N-Pepa
Written by: Herb Azor
From the album: *Very Necessary*
Label: Next Plateau
Produced by: S. Azor
Year: 1993
Answering critics of their rough and realistic approach.

NOONWARD RACE, THE

Artist: Mahavishnu Orchestra
Written by: John McLaughlin
From the album: *The Inner Mounting Flame*
Label: Columbia
Year: 1971
Former Miles Davis and Tony Williams Lifetime guitarist McLaughlin moves on to spearhead the fusion movement with this mini rave-up.

NORMAN

Artist: Sue Thompson
Written by: John D. Loudermilk
From the album: *Sue Thompson*
Label: Hickory
Year: 1962
Never made the country charts.

NORTH TO ALASKA

Artist: Johnny Horton
Written by: Mike Phillips
From the album: *Johnny Horton's Greatest Hits*
Label: Columbia
Produced by: Don Law
Year: 1960
Title song from the movie was a #1 country/Top 10 crossover.

NORTHERN SKY

Artist: Nick Drake
Written by: Nick Drake
From the album: *Bryter Layter*
Label: Island
Produced by: Joe Boyd
Year: 1970
The depressive singer/songwriter contemplates the light beyond.

NORWEGIAN WOOD (THIS BIRD HAS FLOWN)

Artist: The Beatles
Written by: John Lennon, Paul McCartney
From the album: *Rubber Soul*
Label: Capitol
Produced by: George Martin
Year: 1965
The sitar joins the autoharp as prime '60s stringed alternatives to the guitar. Segue: "Sonny's Come Home" by Shawn Colvin.

NOT DARK YET

Artist: Bob Dylan
Written by: Bob Dylan
From the album: *Time out of Mind*
Label: Columbia
Produced by: Daniel Lanois
Year: 1997
Fueling another Dylan comeback.

NOT FADE AWAY

Artist: The Crickets

Written by: Buddy Holly, Norman Petty
From the album: *The Chirpin' Crickets*
Label: Brunswick
Produced by: Norman Petty
Year: 1957
B-side of "Oh Boy," covered by the Rolling Stones (London, '64) as their third single and first UK hit. Buddy's "That'll Be the Day" was the Beatles first single (as the Quarrymen).

NOT GON' CRY

Artist: Mary J. Blige
Written by: Kenny (Babyface) Edmunds
From the album: *Waiting to Exhale* Soundtrack
Label: Arista
Produced by: Babyface
Year: 1996
Establishing her take-no-prisoners brand of neo-soul.

(NOT JUST) KNEE DEEP

Artist: Funkadelic
Written by: George Clinton, Philippe Wynn
From the album: *Uncle Jam Wants You*
Label: Warner Brothers
Produced by: George Clinton
Year: 1979
#1 R&B/Bottom 20 crossover.

NOT SLEEPING AROUND

Artist: Ned's Atomic Dustbin
Written by: Ned's Atomic Dustbin
From the album: *Are You Normal*
Label: Chaos
Year: 1992
An alternative hit in the year before alternative hits.

NOT SO SWEET MARTHA LORRAINE

Artist: Country Joe and the Fish
Written by: Joe McDonald
From the album: *Electric Music for the Mind and Body*
Label: Vanguard
Produced by: Sam Charters
Year: 1967
Riding the crest of the San Francisco scene, on the wings of a Farfisa organ. Suggested segue: "Like a Rolling Stone" by Bob Dylan.

NOT TONIGHT

Artist: Lil Kim, Angie Martinez, Left Eye, Da Brat and Missy Elliott
Written by: Kim Jones, Melissa (Missy) Elliott, Lisa Lopes, Shawntae (Da Brat) Harris, Angie Martinez, Ronald Bell, Robert Bell, George Brown, Angie Muhammed, Claydes Smith, James Taylor, Dennis Thomas, Earl Toon
From the album: *Nothing to Lose Soundtrack*
Label: Big Beat
Year: 1997
The reigning queens of hip hop get down and dirty with a Kool and the Gang groove.

NOT TOO SOON

Artist: Throwing Muses
Written by: Tanya Donnelly
From the album: *The Real Ramona*
Label: Sire
Produced by: Dennis Herring
Year: 1992
Young Tanya, before moving up to Belly. Herring earned his underground credentials with Camper Van Beethoven.

NOTHING BUT FLOWERS

Artist: Talking Heads
Written by: David Byrne, Chris Frantz, Tina Weymouth, Jerry Harrison
From the album: *Naked*
Label: Sire
Produced by: Steve Lillywhite
Year: 1988
Their particular neurosis expanded into a postapocalyptic vision. Suggested segues: "Big Yellow Taxi" by Joni Mitchell, "After the Deluge" by Jackson Browne.

NOTHING BUT HEARTACHES

Artist: The Supremes
Written by: Eddie Holland, Lamont Dozier, Brian Holland
From the album: *More Hits by the Supremes*
Label: Motown
Produced by: Brian Holland, Lamont Dozier
Year: 1965
Breaking a string of five #1s in a row.

NOTHING COMPARES 2 U

Artist: The Family
Written by: Prince Rogers Nelson
From the album: *The Family*
Label: Paisley Park
Produced by: Prince
Year: 1985
Career-making cover by Sinead O'Connor (Chrysalis, '90) went to #1.

NOTHING ELSE MATTERS

Artist: Metallica
Written by: James Hetfield, Lars Ulrich
From the album: *Metallica*
Label: Elektra
Produced by: Bob Rock, James Hetfield, Lars Ulrich
Year: 1991
Sludgifying the arena rock ballad.

NOTHING FROM NOTHING

Artist: Billy Preston
Written by: Billy Preston, Bruce Fisher
From the album: *The Kids and Me*
Label: A&M
Produced by: Billy Preston

Year: 1974
Hammond B-3 extravaganza.

NOTHING HAS BEEN PROVED

Artist: Dusty Springfield and the Pet Shop Boys
Written by: Neil Tennant, Chris Lowe
From the album: *Scandal Soundtrack*
Label: Capitol-EMI
Year: 1989
A dance-hall comeback courtesy of a racy English film.

NOTHING WAS DELIVERED

Artist: The Byrds
Written by: Bob Dylan
From the album: *Sweetheart of the Rodeo*
Label: Columbia
Produced by: Gary Usher
Year: 1968
Big Pink anthem of frustration by Dylan and the Band, unreleased by them until *The Basement Tapes* (Columbia, '75).

NOTHING'S GONNA STOP US NOW

Artist: Starship
Written by: Diane Warren, Albert Hammond
From the album: *No Protection*
Label: Grunt
Produced by: Narada Michael Walden
Year: 1987
Their arena high point, from the movie *Mannequin*.

NOTORIOUS

Artist: Duran Duran
Written by: Simon Lebon, Nick Rhodes, John Taylor
From the album: *Greatest*
Label: Capitol
Year: 1986

NOVEMBER RAIN

Artist: Guns N' Roses
Written by: Axl Rose
From the album: *Use Your Illusion I*
Label: Geffen
Produced by: Mike Clink, Guns N' Roses
Year: 1991
Axl shows off his misunderstood, sensitive side with this brooding magnum opus.

NOVEMBER SPAWNED A MONSTER

Artist: Morrissey
Written by: Stephen Morrissey, Clive Langer
From the album: *Bona Drag*
Label: Warner Brothers
Produced by: Clive Langer, Alan Winstanley

Year: 1990
A birthday song.

NOVOCAINE FOR THE SOUL

Artist: Eels
Written by: E. Mark Goldenberg
From the album: *Beautiful Freak*
Label: DreamWorks
Year: 1996

(NOW AND THEN THERE'S) A FOOL SUCH AS I

Artist: Hank Snow
Written by: Bill Trader
Label: RCA
Year: 1952
Top 5 country hit; covered by Jo Stafford (Columbia, '53). Cover by Elvis Presley (RCA, '59) was a Top 10 R&B/Top 20 crossover.

NOW RUN AND TELL THAT

Artist: Denise Lasalle
Written by: Denise O. Jones
From the album: *Trapped by a Thing Called Love*
Label: Westbound
Produced by: Denise LaSalle
Year: 1971
Soul shouter.

NOW THAT I AM DEAD

Artist: French Frith Kaiser Thompson
Written by: Donna Blair, John French
From the album: *Invisible Means*
Label: Windham Hill
Produced by: Henry Kaiser
Year: 1990
From the quintessentially eccentric progressive alternative supergroup, possibly the only real challenger to "Lodi" on the verities of the musician's lifestyle.

NOW THAT WE FOUND LOVE

Artist: The O'Jays
Written by: Kenny Gamble, Leon Huff
From the album: *Ship Ahoy*
Label: Philadelphia International
Produced by: Kenny Gamble, Leon Huff
Year: 1973
Soul classic, covered by Third World (Island, '78), Heavy D & the Boys (Uptown, '91).

NOWADAYS CLANCY CAN'T EVEN SING

Artist: Buffalo Springfield
Written by: Neil Young
From the album: *Buffalo Springfield*
Label: Atco
Produced by: Charles Greene, Brian Stone

Year: 1967
FM staple in the earliest days of FM.

NOWHERE MAN

Artist: The Beatles
Written by: John Lennon, Paul McCartney
From the album: *Yesterday and Today*
Label: Capitol
Produced by: George Martin
Year: 1965
Venturing into Kinksian social satire.

NOWHERE NEAR

Artist: Yo La Tengo
Written by: Ira Kaplan, Georgia Hubley
From the album: *Painful*
Label: Matador
Produced by: Roger Moutenot, Fred Brockman
Year: 1993
Magnificent lo-fi drone, in the Sonic Youth mode.

NOWHERE TO RUN

Artist: Martha & the Vandellas
Written by: Eddie Holland, Lamont Dozier, Brian Holland
From the album: *Dance Party*
Label: Gordy
Produced by: Brian Holland, Lamont Dozier
Year: 1965
Echoing the drastic turmoil of inner city Detroit.

#9 DREAM

Artist: John Lennon
Written by: John Lennon
From the album: *Walls and Bridges*
Label: Apple
Produced by: John Lennon
Year: 1974

#1 CRUSH

Artist: Garbage
Written by: Garbage
From the album: *Romeo and Juliet Soundtrack*
Label: Capitol
Year: 1996

NUMBER OF THE BEAST

Artist: Iron Maiden
Written by: Steve Harris
From the album: *Number of the Beast*
Label: Harvest
Produced by: Martin Birch
Year: 1982
The number, of course, was 666, the devil's 411.

NUTBUSH CITY LIMITS

Artist: Ike and Tina Turner
Written by: Tina Turner
From the album: *Nutbush City Limits*
Label: United Artists

Year: 1973
Covered by Bob Seger (Capitol, '75).

NUTHIN' BUT A "G" THANG

Artist: Dr. Dre
Written by: Calvin Broadus (Snoop Doggy Dogg)
From the album: *The Chronic*
Label: Death Row
Produced by: Dr. Dre
Year: 1993
Updated version of life in the ghetto introduces a major artist and producer in Dr. Dre and a major writer and rapper in Snoop Doggy Dogg (aka Calvin Broadus).

NUTTIN' BUT LOVE

Artist: Heavy D and the Boys
Written by: Dwight Meyers (Heavy D), Kid Capri
From the album: *Nuttin' but Love*
Label: Uptown/MCA
Year: 1994
Breakthrough hit for the New York rapper.

O

O DIO MIO

Artist: Annette
Written by: Al Hoffman, Dick Manning
From the album: *Italianette*
Label: Buena Vista
Year: 1960
An attempt to make the Disney thrush Annette into the West coast Connie Francis, who cut her teeth on "Mama."

O SUPERMAN

Artist: Laurie Anderson
Written by: Laurie Anderson
From the album: *Big Science*
Label: Warner Brothers
Produced by: Roma Baran, Laurie Anderson
Year: 1982
O bohemia! This epic length performance art tone poem was a major smash only in England.

O.K.

Artist: Rock Follies
Written by: Simon Crampton, Emma James, Louis Smith
From the album: *Rock Follies*
Label: Polydor
Year: 1977
Rula Lenska rules! From the PBS rock serial from England: *Upstairs, Downstairs* at the Hard Rock Cafe.

O.P.P. (OTHER PEOPLE'S PROPERTY)

Artist: Naughty by Nature

Written by: Vinnie Brown, Kier Gist, Anthony Criss, the Corporation
From the album: *Naughty by Nature*
Label: Tommy Boy
Year: 1991
Clever new hip hop sloganeering, with samples from the Jackson 5's "ABC."

O'LUCKY MAN

Artist: Alan Price
Written by: Alan Price
From the album: *O'Lucky Man*
Label: Warner Brothers
Year: 1973
Progressive rock staple.

OB-LA-DI, OB-LA-DA

Artist: The Beatles
Written by: John Lennon, Paul McCartney
From the album: *The Beatles*
Label: Apple
Produced by: George Martin
Year: 1968
Their latter-day theme song.

OCEAN, THE

Artist: Led Zeppelin
Written by: Jimmy Page, Robert Plant, John Paul Jones, John Bonham
From the album: *Houses of the Holy*
Label: Atlantic
Produced by: Jimmy Page
Year: 1973

OCTOPUS'S GARDEN

Artist: The Beatles
Written by: Richard Starkey (Ringo Starr)
From the album: *Abbey Road*
Label: Apple
Produced by: George Martin
Year: 1969
One of two songs Ringo wrote for the Beatles. But George helped.

ODE TO BILLIE JOE

Artist: Bobbie Gentry
Written by: Bobbie Gentry
From the album: *Ode to Billy Joe*
Label: Capitol
Produced by: Gordon Kelly, Bobby Paris
Year: 1967
Country narrative landmark went #1 but barely grazed the Country Top 20. It served as the basis for the Robbie Benson movie, thus leading to the commercial inevitability of "The Night the Lights Went out in Georgia."

OFF ON YOUR OWN (GIRL)

Artist: Al B. Sure
Written by: Al B. Sure, Kyle West
From the album: *In Effect Mode*
Label: Warner Brothers
Produced by: Teddy Riley, Al B. Sure

Year: 1988
His second #1 R&B hit.

OFF THE GROUND

Artist: Paul McCartney
Written by: Paul McCartney
From the album: *Off the Ground*
Label: Capitol
Produced by: Paul McCartney
Year: 1993

OFF THE WALL

Artist: Michael Jackson
Written by: Rod Temperton
From the album: *Off the Wall*
Label: Epic
Produced by: Qunicy Jones
Year: 1979
#1 R&B/Top 10 crossover.

OH ATLANTA

Artist: Little Feat
Written by: Billy Payne
From the album: *Feats Don't Fail Me Now*
Label: Warner Brothers
Produced by: Van Dyke Parks, Lowell George
Year: 1974
Country funk tribute to the south when it was only slightly dirty.

OH BABE, WHAT WOULD YOU SAY

Artist: Hurricane Smith
Written by: E. B. Smith
From the album: *Hurricane Smith*
Label: Capitol
Produced by: Norman Smith
Year: 1973
Top 10 US/Top 10 UK crossover for the fifty-year-old deep-voiced record producer.

OH BONDAGE, UP YOURS!

Artist: X-Ray Specs
Written by: Poly Styrene
From the album: *Germ-Free Adolescents*
Label: EMI
Produced by: Fallon Street
Year: 1978
The marvelous shrieking of Marion Elliot (Poly Styrene) highlights the '78 film *Punk Rock Movie*, and the '81 film *DOA: A Rite of Passage*.

OH BOY

Artist: The Crickets
Written by: Sunny West, Bill Tilgham, Norman Petty
From the album: *The Chirpin' Crickets*
Label: Brunswick
Produced by: Norman Petty
Year: 1957
Planting the pop rockabilly root from which every jangling guitar band would draw their nourishment.

OH CAROL

Artist: Neil Sedaka
Written by: Howard Greenfield, Neil Sedaka
From the album: *Neil Sedaka Sings His Greatest Hits*
Label: RCA
Produced by: Al Nevins, Don Kirshner
Year: 1959

Sedaka's first Top 10 hit, allegedly written for Brooklyn neighbor, fan, and pizza parlor love object, Carole Klein (King), who responded with "Oh Neil," on Alpine, which was obviously the wrong name at the right time, because even though it stiffed, it not only caught the attention of another neighborhood Neil—Neil Diamond—but also the ear of Don Kirshner, who signed Carole and her husband Gerry to his publishing company (and the Neils, Sedaka and Diamond, as well), thereby opening the door to several major Brooklyn careers and a jukebox full of classic singles.

OH CATHERINE

Artist: Pere Ubu
Written by: David Thomas, Jim Jones, Eric Drew Feldman, Tony Maimone, Scott Krauss
From the album: *Worlds in Collison*
Label: Fontana
Produced by: Gil Norton
Year: 1991

A love ballad as aching as it is twisted. One of the best definitions of the lifelong rock and roll artist and fan: "There's a place in my heart where the years don't go."

OH! DARLING

Artist: The Beatles
Written by: John Lennon, Paul McCartney
From the album: *Abbey Road*
Label: Apple
Produced by: George Martin
Year: 1969

Psuedo-'50s rock.

OH ENGLAND MY LIONHEART

Artist: Kate Bush
Written by: Kate Bush
From the album: *Lionheart*
Label: EMI-America
Produced by: Andrew Powell
Year: 1980

New English anthem of a cloistered girlhood.

OH GIRL

Artist: The Chi-Lites
Written by: Eugene Record
From the album: *A Lonely Man*
Label: Brunswick
Produced by: Eugene Record
Year: 1972

Smokey soul, in the vulnerable Robinson style, with a sweet, funky harmonica.

OH HAPPY DAY

Artist: Edwin Hawkins Singers
Written by: Edwin Hawkins
From the album: *Let Us Go into the House of the Lord*
Label: Pavilion
Produced by: Lamont Beech
Year: 1969

Hawkins arranged this old gospel favorite, Dorothy Morrison sang lead.

OH JULIE

Artist: The Crescendos
Written by: Ken Moffitt, Noel Ball
From the album: *Oh Julie*
Label: Nasco
Produced by: Noel Ball
Year: 1958

Rockabilly lite. Segue: "Diana."

OH LONESOME ME

Artist: Don Gibson
Written by: Don Gibson
From the album: *Oh Lonesome Me*
Label: RCA
Produced by: Chet Atkins
Year: 1958

#1 country/Top 10 crossover is the biggest hit as a singer for the author of "I Can't Stop Loving You."

OH ME OH MY (I'M A FOOL FOR YOU, BABY)

Artist: Lulu
Written by: Jim Doris
From the album: *Lulu Sings*
Label: Atco
Produced by: Tom Dowd, Jerry Wexler, Arif Mardin
Year: 1970

The producers next offered it to Aretha Franklin (Atlantic, '71), who didn't do as well with it.

OH MY MY

Artist: Ringo Starr
Written by: Richard Starkey (Ringo Starr), Vini Poncia
From the album: *Ringo*
Label: Apple
Produced by: Richard Perry
Year: 1974

OH NO

Artist: Commodores
Written by: Lionel B. Richie Jr.
From the album: *In the Pocket*
Label: Motown
Year: 1981

OH! NO, NOT MY BABY

Artist: Maxine Brown
Written by: Gerry Goffin, Carole King
Label: Wand
Year: 1964

Brill Building soul, written across the street, at 1650 Broadway. Covered by Rod Stewart (Mercury, '73).

OH, PRETTY WOMAN

Artist: Roy Orbison
Written by: Roy Orbison, Bill Dees
From the album: *Oh, Pretty Woman*
Label: Monument
Produced by: Fred Foster
Year: 1964

Roy gets the girl, albeit only for a short time and possibly by accident. Covered by Van Halen (Warner Brothers, '82). Revived in the movie *Pretty Woman,* in which the girl is Julia Roberts who, in a weird Orbisonian twist of irony, was actually gotten in real life by the unlikely, Orbisonesque Lyle Lovett (albeit only for a short time, and possibly by accident).

OH SHEILA

Artist: Ready for the World
Written by: Melvin Riley, Gordon Strozier, Gerald Valentine
From the album: *Ready for the World*
Label: MCA
Produced by: Ready for the World
Year: 1985

#1 R&B/#1 crossover.

OH, SHERRIE

Artist: Steve Perry
Written by: Steve Perry, Randy Goodrum, Bill Cuomo, Craig Krampf
From the album: *Street Talk*
Label: Columbia
Produced by: Steve Perry
Year: 1984

Solo Journeyman's biggest hit.

OH VERY YOUNG

Artist: Cat Stevens
Written by: Cat Stevens
From the album: *Buddha and the Chocolate Box*
Label: A&M
Produced by: Paul Samwell-Smith
Year: 1974

Advice from the Dr. Cat.

OH WELL (PART I)

Artist: Fleetwood Mac
Written by: Peter Green
From the album: *Then Play On*
Label: Reprise
Produced by: Fleetwood Mac
Year: 1969

Fleetwood Mac's only US chart appearance in their bluesy Peter Green incarnation; in the UK they were the #1 band of '69.

OH WHAT A DREAM

Artist: Ruth Brown
Written by: Chuck Wills
Label: Atlantic
Year: 1954
As she did in '53, Brown would spend twenty-six weeks on the R&B charts in '54: sixteen of them with this Chuck Willis original—the tune Alan Freed used to introduce his *Moondog/Rock and Roll Party* radio show to the listeners of 1010 WINS in New York.

OH WHAT A NIGHT

Artist: The Dells
Written by: Marvin Junior, Johnny Funches
From the album: *Love Is Blue*
Label: VeeJay
Produced by: Bobby Miller
Year: 1956
Excellent doo-wop. Their first #1 R&B/Top 10 crossover, re-recorded on Cadet in '69.

OH YOKO

Artist: John Lennon
Written by: John Lennon
From the album: *Imagine*
Label: Apple
Produced by: John Lennon
Year: 1971
An ode to his sweetheart. Suggested segues: "An Innocent Man" by Billy Joel, "Fountain of Sorrow" by Jackson Brown, "My Old Man" by Joni Mitchell, "Be My Yoko Ono" by the Barenaked Ladies.

OHIO

Artist: Crosby, Stills, Nash & Young
Written by: Neil Young
From the album: *So Far*
Label: Atlantic
Produced by: Crosby, Stills, Nash & Young
Year: 1970
Rock as gonzo journalism. Written by Young in response to the murder in Ohio of four students by the National Guard at a protest rally at Kent State in May. Recorded, released, and actually played on the radio a month later.

OL' 55

Artist: Tom Waits
Written by: Tom Waits
From the album: *Closing Time*
Label: Asylum
Produced by: Jerry Yester
Year: 1973
The voice of Beefheart with the soul of Ferlinghetti; the neo-bohemian folk/rock troubadour creates the first car song from Rent-a-Wreck. Covered by the Eagles (Asylum, '74), Sarah McLachlan (Arista, '95).

OL' MAN RIVER

Artist: The Ravens
Written by: Oscar Hammerstein II, Jerome Kern
Label: National
Year: 1947
Majestic ballad from *Showboat*, in which it was introduced by Paul Robeson. Covered by such secular luminaries as Aretha Franklin, Ray Charles, Sam Cooke, the Flamingos, and Duane and Greg in the Allman Joys. Influenced by the Mills Brothers, Baltimore's Ravens do the definitive doo-wop rendition, featuring the bottomless voice of Jimmy Ricks, selling a couple million copies, and opening the black gateway of the rock and roll era to the hallowed halls of Tin Pan Alley.

OLD DAYS

Artist: Chicago
Written by: James Pankow
From the album: *Chicago VIII*
Label: Columbia
Produced by: James William Guercio
Year: 1975
The hits just keep toddling in.

OLD MAN

Artist: Neil Young
Written by: Neil Young
From the album: *Harvest*
Label: Reprise
Produced by: Elliot Mazur, Neil Young
Year: 1972
Suggested segue: "Bookends" by Simon and Garfunkel.

OLD MAN DOWN THE ROAD, THE

Artist: John Fogerty
Written by: John C. Fogerty
From the album: *Centerfield*
Label: Warner Brothers
Produced by: John C. Fogerty
Year: 1985
His biggest solo hit is reputedly about Ronald Reagan. Segue: "Run through the Jungle" by Creedence Clearwater Revival.

OLD TIME ROCK AND ROLL

Artist: Bob Seger
Written by: George Jackson, Harold Jones III
From the album: *Stranger in Town*
Label: Capitol
Produced by: Punch Andrews, Bob Seger
Year: 1977
This durable Seger warhorse achieved legendary status when Tom Cruise played air broom to it in the immortal '83 film *Risky Business*.

OLE MAN TROUBLE

Artist: Otis Redding
Written by: Otis Redding
From the album: *Dock of the Bay*
Label: Volt
Produced by: Steve Cropper
Year: 1968
One of his greatest performances.

OLIVER'S ARMY

Artist: Elvis Costello
Written by: Declan McManus (Elvis Costello)
From the album: *Armed Forces*
Label: Columbia
Produced by: Nick Lowe
Year: 1979
His biggest UK hit is an antiwar tract, with a nice track.

OMAHA

Artist: Moby Grape
Written by: Skip Spence
From the album: *Moby Grape*
Label: Columbia
Produced by: David Rubinson
Year: 1967
The only lasting claim to fame from the great hippie singles band that never was.

ON & ON

Artist: Erykah Badu
Written by: Erykah Badu, Jaborn Jamal
From the album: *Badiszm*
Label: Kedar
Year: 1996
One woman definition of the Afro bohemia genre.

ON AND ON

Artist: Gladys Knight & the Pips
Written by: Curtis Mayfield
From the album: *Claudine*
Label: Buddah
Produced by: Curtis Mayfield
Year: 1974
Their eighth and last Top 10 hit, from the movie *Claudine*.

ON A CAROUSEL

Artist: The Hollies
Written by: Allan Clarke, Graham Nash, Tony Hicks
From the album: *Greatest Hits*
Label: Imperial
Produced by: Ron Richards
Year: 1967
Patented harmonies at their professional peak.

ON BENDED KNEE

Artist: Boyz II Men
Written by: James Harris III, Terry Lewis
From the album: *II*
Label: Motown
Produced by: Babyface
Year: 1994
Doo-wop redux in a politically and sexually correct context.

ON BROADWAY

Artist: The Drifters
Written by: Jerry Leiber, Mike Stoller, Barry Mann, Cynthia Weil

From the album: *Under the Boardwalk*
Label: Atlantic
Produced by: Jerry Leiber, Mike Stoller
Year: 1963
Brill Building Top 10 R&B/Top 10 conference call crossover, with Phil Spector sitting in on guitar. Covered by George Benson (Warner Brothers, '78).

ON MY OWN

Artist: Patti Labelle and Michael McDonald
Written by: Burt Bacharach, Carole Bayer Sager
From the album: *Winner in You*
Label: MCA
Produced by: Burt Bacharach, Carole Sager
Year: 1986
Smash pop ballad went #1 R&B/#1 crossover; true to its title, each artist recorded separately.

ON MY RADIO

Artist: The Selecter
Written by: Neol Davis
From the album: *Too Much Pressure*
Label: Chrysalis
Produced by: Errol Ross
Year: 1979
First and biggest UK hit for the influential Ska band.

ON OUR OWN (FROM *GHOSTBUSTERS II*)

Artist: Bobby Brown
Written by: Kenny Edmunds (Babyface), Antonio Reid (L.A. Reid), Daryl Simmons
From the album: *Ghostbusters II Soundtrack*
Label: Warner Brothers
Produced by: Babyface, L. A. Reid
Year: 1989

ON THE DARK SIDE

Artist: John Cafferty and the Beaver Brown Band
Written by: John Cafferty
From the album: *Eddie and the Cruisers Soundtrack*
Label: Scotti Brothers
Year: 1984
Theme from the nearly credible Springsteen-does-an-Elvis cult film.

ON THE NICKEL

Artist: Tom Waits
Written by: Tom Waits
From the album: *Heartattack and Vine*
Label: Asylum
Produced by: Bones Howe
Year: 1980
Title tune from the great indie movie.

ON THE RADIO

Artist: Donna Summer
Written by: Giorgio Moroder, Donna Summer
From the album: *Greatest Hits (Vols. I and II)*
Label: Casablanca
Produced by: Giorgio Moroder, Pete Bellotte
Year: 1979

ON THE ROAD AGAIN

Artist: Canned Heat
Written by: Al Wilson, Floyd Jones
From the album: *Boogie with Canned Heat*
Label: Liberty
Produced by: Dallas Smith
Year: 1968

ON THE ROAD AGAIN

Artist: Willie Nelson
Written by: Willie Nelson
From the album: *Honeysuckle Rose Soundtrack*
Label: Columbia
Year: 1980
The mainstreaming of outlaw country; a #1 country/Top 20 crossover.

ON THE ROAD TO FAIRFAX COUNTY

Artist: The Roches
Written by: David Massingill
From the album: *Keep on Doing*
Label: Warner Brothers
Produced by: Robert Fripp
Year: 1982
Neo-folkie highlight. In Greenwich Village, Suzanne Vega was listening.

ON THE TURNING AWAY

Artist: Pink Floyd
Written by: David Gilmour, Anthony Moore
From the album: *A Momentary Lapse of Reason*
Label: Columbia
Produced by: Bob Ezrin, David Gilmour
Year: 1987
Gilmour takes over lead guitar chores, a new, mellow era commences.

ON THE WAY HOME

Artist: Buffalo Springfield
Written by: Neil Young
From the album: *Last Time Around*
Label: Atco
Produced by: Charles Greene, Brian Stone
Year: 1968
On to bigger things.

ON THE WINGS OF A NIGHTINGALE

Artist: The Everly Brothers
Written by: Paul McCartney
From the album: *EB84*
Label: Mercury
Produced by: Dave Edmunds
Year: 1984
Never saying never again, the Everly Brothers reunite on the country charts for the first time in 23 years. Produced by one of their biggest British fans,

and written by one of the people in Britain they'd most influenced.

ONCE BITTEN, TWICE SHY

Artist: Ian Hunter
Written by: Ian Hunter
From the album: *Ian Hunter*
Label: Columbia
Produced by: Mick Ronson
Year: 1975
Big arena rocker from the former Hoople. Cover by Great White (Capitol, '89) went to #1.

ONCE I WAS

Artist: Tim Buckley
Written by: Tim Buckley
From the album: *Goodbye and Hello*
Label: Elektra
Produced by: Jerry Yester
Year: 1967
Morose folk/jazz/rock gem from the starcrossed California singer/songwriter who died of a heroin overdose. The B-side of his first single, "Morning Glory," it was featured to bone-chilling effect at the end of the '78 movie *Coming Home*, when the character played by Bruce Dern drowns himself in the Pacific. Eerily, Tim's son Jeff would drown years later.

ONCE IN A LIFETIME

Artist: Talking Heads
Written by: David Byrne, Brian Eno
From the album: *Remain in Light*
Label: Sire
Produced by: Brian Eno
Year: 1981
Byrne legitimizes the video age with this classic treatise on modern anomie and modern dance.

ONCE YOU GET STARTED

Artist: Rufus featuring Chaka Khan
Written by: Gavin Wright
From the album: *Rufusized*
Label: ABC
Produced by: Rufus
Year: 1975
First hit with the incomparable Chaka featured in the credits.

ONE

Artist: Metallica
Written by: James Hetfield, Lars Ulrich
From the album: *... And Justice for All*
Label: Elektra
Produced by: Fleming Rasmussen, Metallica
Year: 1988
Tale adapted from the Dalton Trumbo antiwar novel *Johnny Got His Gun* earns Metallica a Grammy nom.

ONE

Artist: Nilsson
Written by: Harry Nilsson

From the album: *Aeriel Ballet*
Label: RCA
Produced by: Rick Jarrard
Year: 1968
Living in a parallel universe to Randy Newman on the West coast, Harry Nilsson started off as an East coast songwriting wunderkind with quirky pop tunes like this. Covered by Three Dog Night (Dunhill, '69), who took it to the Top 10. A year later they'd bring a Randy Newman cover to #1. Covered by Al Kooper (Columbia, '69).

ONE

Artist: U2
Written by: U2
From the album: *Achtung Baby*
Label: Island
Produced by: Daniel Lanois, Brian Eno
Year: 1991
A heart song for the ages and one of Bono's best lyrics. Suggested segue: "He Ain't Heavy, He's My Brother" by the Hollies.

ONE BAD APPLE (DON'T SPOIL THE WHOLE BUNCH)

Artist: The Osmonds
Written by: George Jackson
From the album: *The Osmonds*
Label: MGM
Produced by: Rick Hall
Year: 1971
The white Jackson family. (Or was that the Wilsons?)

ONE BAD STUD

Artist: The Honeybears
Written by: Jerry Leiber, Mike Stoller
Label: Spark
Produced by: Jerry Leiber, Mike Stoller
Year: 1954
Early classic by the L.A. upstarts Leiber & Stoller. Covered by the Blasters in the 1984 movie *Streets of Fire*.

ONE BIG LOVE

Artist: Patti Griffin
Written by: Patti Griffin, Angelo
From the album: *Flaming Red*
Produced by: Angelo
Label: A&M
Year: 1998
The Classics, "Rain" and "Making Pies" would come later. Covered by Emmylou Harris (Warner Brothers, '98).

ONE FINE DAY

Artist: The Chiffons
Written by: Gerry Goffin, Carole King
From the album: *One Fine Day*
Label: Laurie
Produced by: Mitch Margo, Phil Margo, Hank Medress, Jay Siegel

Year: 1963
Refined hero worship from one of the mellower girl-groups.

ONE GOOD WOMAN

Artist: Peter Cetera
Written by: Peter Cetera, Patrick Leonard
From the album: *One More Story*
Label: Full Moon
Year: 1988

ONE HEADLIGHT

Artist: The Wallflowers
Written by: Jakob Dylan
From the album: *Bringing down the Horse*
Label: Interscope
Produced by: T-Bone Burnette
Year: 1996
A beat-up jalopy carried the first son of folk/rock to his first Grammy.

100%

Artist: Sonic Youth
Written by: Sonic Youth
From the album: *Dirty*
Label: DGC
Produced by: Butch Vig, Edward Douglas
Year: 1992
Endearingly experimental drone band's commercial moment.

100% PURE LOVE

Artist: Crystal Waters
Written by: Crystal Waters, Teddy Douglas, Jay Steinhour, Tommy Davis
From the album: *Storyteller*
Label: Mercury
Produced by: The Basement Boys
Year: 1994
Dance-hall fantasy; Top 10 R&B/Top 10 crossover.

106 BEATS THAT

Artist: Wire
Written by: Colin Newman, Graham Lewis
From the album: *Pink Flag*
Label: Harvest
Produced by: Mike Thorne
Year: 1977
Staccato signals and constant information. Art school punk minimalism from abroad that would reach American rock critics, and some influential bands, here and there, R.E.M., the Cure, and U2 among them.

ONE I LOVE, THE

Artist: R.E.M.
Written by: Michael Stipe, Peter Buck, Bill Berry, Mike Mills
From the album: *Document*
Label: IRS
Produced by: Scott Litt, R.E.M.

Year: 1986
Love in the ruins; their first Top 10 single.

ONE IN A MILLION YOU

Artist: Larry Graham
Written by: Sam Dees
From the album: *One in a Million You*
Label: Warner Brothers
Produced by: Larry Graham, Ron Nadel
Year: 1980
Middle-of-the-R&B-road.

ONE KISS LED TO ANOTHER

Artist: The Coasters
Written by: Jerry Leiber, Mike Stoller
Label: Atco
Produced by: Jerry Leiber, Mike Stoller
Year: 1956
One week on the charts for their first rock and roll crossover.

ONE LOVE

Artist: Bob Marley and the Wailers
Written by: Bob Marley, Bunny Livingston
Label: Island
Produced by: Clement Dodd
Year: 1965
First two-track recording ever made by the Wailers, espousing what Bob Marley would later turn into his personal philosophy. Wailers later performed this with the Impressions' tune "People Get Ready."

ONE MAN'S CEILING IS ANOTHER MAN'S FLOOR

Artist: Paul Simon
Written by: Paul Simon
From the album: *There Goes Rhymin' Simon*
Label: Columbia
Produced by: Paul Simon, the Muscle Shoals Rhythm Section
Year: 1973
One of his finest urban aphorisms.

ONE MILLION BILLIONTH OF A MILLISECOND ON A SUNDAY MORNING

Artist: The Flaming Lips
Written by: Flaming Lips
From the album: *Oh My Gawd! … the Flaming Lips*
Label: Restless
Year: 1987
A new garage era begins in college towns across the land.

ONE MINT JULEP

Artist: The Clovers
Written by: Rudolph Toombs
Label: Atlantic
Produced by: Ahmet Ertegun, Herb Abramson
Year: 1952

Another masterpiece from Toombs. Covered by Ray Charles (ABC Paramount, '61).

ONE MONKEY DON'T STOP NO SHOW

Artist: Big Maybelle
Written by: Charles Singleton, Rose Marie McCoy
From the album: *Big Maybelle Sings Blues ... and Big Maybelle*
Label: Okeh
Produced by: Larry Kirkland
Year: 1954
Choice bit of R&B wisdom from a great songwriting team, with "Whole Lotta Shakin' Goin' On" on the B-side. As a general statement on the power of the monkey, tunes with this title by Joe Tex (Dial, '65) and Honey Cone (Hot Wax, '71) are entirely different songs.

ONE MORE NIGHT

Artist: Phil Collins
Written by: Phil Collins
From the album: *No Jacket Required*
Label: Atlantic
Produced by: Hugh Padgham, Phil Collins
Year: 1985
His second #1.

ONE MORE TRY

Artist: George Michael
Written by: George Michael
From the album: *Faith*
Label: Columbia
Produced by: George Michael
Year: 1987
First #1 R&B/#1 crossover for a white act since K.C. and the Sunshine Band (who did it three times).

ONE MORE TRY

Artist: Timmy T
Written by: Timmy Torres
From the album: *Time after Time*
Label: Quality
Year: 1991

ONE NATION UNDER A GROOVE

Artist: Funkadelic
Written by: George Clinton, Gary Shider, Walter Morrison
From the album: *One Nation under a Groove*
Label: Warner Brothers
Produced by: George Clinton
Year: 1978
Future funk standard was their biggest hit; #1 R&B/Top 30 crossover. Reinterpreted by Ice-T in '94 as "Bop Gun (One Nation)."

ONE NIGHT (OF SIN)

Artist: Smiley Lewis

Written by: Dave Bartholomew, Pearl King
Label: Okeh
Produced by: Dave Bartholemew
Year: 1955
Considered so risqué in '55 that Lewis didn't even make the R&B charts with it. The landscape had changed considerably by the time it was covered by Elvis Presley (RCA, '58). So had the words—from "one night of sin" to "one night with you."

ONE NITE STAN

Artist: Ethel and the Shameless Hussies
Written by: Kacey Jones, Jon Iger
From the album: *Born to Burn*
Label: MCA
Year: 1988
Pithy advice for (and from) the lovelorn. Suggested segues: "The Homecoming Queen's Got a Gun" by Julie Brown, "The Sweater" by Meryn Cadell, "Victims of Their Hair" by Christine Lavin, "Valley Girl" by Moon Zappa, "Ironic" by Alanis Morrisette.

ONE OF A KIND (LOVE AFFAIR)

Artist: Spinners
Written by: Joseph Jefferson
From the album: *The Spinners*
Label: Atlantic
Produced by: Thom Bell
Year: 1972
#1 R&B/Top 20 crossover.

ONE OF THESE NIGHTS

Artist: Eagles
Written by: Don Henley, Glenn Frey
From the album: *One of These Nights*
Label: Asylum
Produced by: Bill Szymczyk
Year: 1975
Second #1 for the country/rock professionals.

ONE OF US

Artist: Joan Osborne
Written by: Eric Bazilian
From the album: *Relish*
Label: Blue Gorilla
Produced by: Rick Chertoff
Year: 1995
Major new folk/rock diva delivers the most unusual lyric to hit the Top 10 all year. Suggested segues: "Dear God" by XTC and "Jesus Is Just Alright with Me" by the Doobie Brothers.

ONE OF US MUST KNOW (SOONER OR LATER)

Artist: Bob Dylan
Written by: Bob Dylan
From the album: *Blonde on Blonde*
Label: Columbia
Produced by: Bob Johnston

Year: 1966
His logical melodic successor to "Like a Rolling Stone," but no anthem.

ONE ON ONE

Artist: Daryl Hall & John Oates
Written by: Daryl Hall
From the album: *H2O*
Label: RCA
Produced by: Hall & Oates
Year: 1983
Their brand of sophisticated blue-eyed soul at its most sensuous: Top 10 R&B/Top 10 crossover.

ONE SCOTCH, ONE BOURBON, ONE BEER

Artist: Amos Milburn
Written by: Rudolph Toombs
From the album: *Rockin' the Boogie*
Label: Aladdin
Year: 1953
Detailing the obsession that would prove to be his downfall Milburn gets his 12TH and last Top 10 R&B hit.

ONE SONG GLORY

Artist: Norbert Leo Butz
Written by: Jonathan Larson
From the album: *Rent Original Cast Album*
Label: Geffen
Year: 1996
Key plot point from the neo-rock opera.

ONE STEP AT A TIME

Artist: Brenda Lee
Written by: Hugh Ashley
Label: Decca
Produced by: Milt Gabler
Year: 1957
Her first country hit; she wouldn't return to this chart for twelve years, during which time she'd account for approximately 50 singles on the pop charts (and a half dozen R&B crossovers). Stevie Nicks and Cyndi Lauper were listening; so was Dolly Parton.

ONE STEP CLOSER

Artist: Linkin Park
Written by: Linkin Park
From the album: *Hybrid Theory*
Produced by: Don Gilmore
Label: Warner Brothers
Year: 2000
New rap/metal merger sparks hope of corporate profit.

ONE STEP UP

Artist: Bruce Springsteen
Written by: Bruce Springsteen
From the album: *Tunnel of Love*
Label: Columbia

Produced by: Jon Landau, Bruce Springsteen, Chuck Plotkin
Year: 1985
His heart still hungry, Springsteen produces his best country song. Eventually covered by astute country star Kenny Chesney (BNA, '02).

ONE SUMMER NIGHT

Artist: The Danleers
Written by: Danny Webb
Label: AMP
Produced by: Danny Webb
Year: 1958
One of the all-time doo-wop summer songs under the moon of love.

ONE SWEET DAY

Artist: Mariah Carey and Boyz II Men
Written by: Mariah Carey, Michael McCary, Nathan Morris, Wayna Morris, Shawn Stockman, Walter Afanasieff
From the album: *Fantasy*
Label: Columbia
Produced by: Walter Afanasieff, Mariah Carey
Year: 1995
Record-setting, multi-Grammy nominated #1 R&B/#1 crossover. But all you had to do was see Mariah's face at the following year's Grammy telecast to know it didn't win any.

ONE THING LEADS TO ANOTHER

Artist: The Fixx
Written by: Cy Curnin, Adam Woods, Jamie West-Oram, Rupert Greenall, Alfred Agius
From the album: *Reach the Beach*
Label: MCA
Produced by: Rupert Hine
Year: 1983
Their biggest hit. Human League, the Eurythmics, Duran Duran, and especially Dexy's Midnight Runners were on the way.

ONE TIME ONE NIGHT

Artist: Los Lobos
Written by: David Hidalgo, Louie Perez
From the album: *By the Light of the Moon*
Label: Slash
Produced by: T-Bone Burnette
Year: 1987
Neo Tex-Mex bar-band classic from East L.A.

ONE TOKE OVER THE LINE

Artist: Brewer & Shipley
Written by: Michael Brewer, Thomas Shipley
From the album: *Tarkio*
Label: Kama Sutra
Produced by: Nick Gravenites
Year: 1971
Requiem for an over-indulgent age.

ONE TOO MANY MORNINGS

Artist: Bob Dylan
Written by: Bob Dylan
From the album: *The Times They Are A-Changin'*
Label: Columbia
Produced by: Tom Wilson
Year: 1964
Ultimate rambler's lament. Covered by Ian and Sylvia (Vanguard, '64), the Beau Brummels (Warner Brothers, '66).

ONE, TWO, THREE (1-2-3)

Artist: Len Barry
Written by: John Madara, David White, Leonard Borisoff
From the album: *1-2-3*
Label: Decca
Produced by: Leon Huff
Year: 1965
Good-time, blue-eyed soul.

1, 2, 3, RED LIGHT

Artist: 1910 Fruitgum Company
Written by: Sal Trimachi, Bobbi Trimachi
From the album: *1, 2, 3 Red Light*
Label: Buddah
Produced by: Jerry Kazenetz, Jeff Katz
Year: 1968
Followup to "Simon Says."

1, 2, 3, 4 (SUMPIN' NEW)

Artist: Coolio
Written by: Artis Ivey Jr. (Coolio), Anthony Sear
From the album: *Gangsta's Paradise*
Label: Tommy Boy
Year: 1995

ONE WAY OR ANOTHER

Artist: Blondie
Written by: Nigel Harrison, Deborah Harry
From the album: *Parallel Lines*
Label: Chrysalis
Produced by: Mike Chapman
Year: 1978
Somewhere the Shangri-las were smiling.

ONE WAY OUT

Artist: Aleck Miller
Written by: Marshall Sehorn, Sonny Boy Williamson (Aleck Miller)
Label: Trumpet
Year: 1951
Essential anthem for the backdoor man. Covered by the Allman Brothers (Capricorn, '72).

ONE WEEK

Artist: Barenaked Ladies
Written by: Ed Robertson

From the album: *Stunt*
Label: Reprise
Produced by: Barenaked Ladies, David Leonard, Susan Rogers
Year: 1998
Packing almost as many words into a breath as the Meat Puppets did in "Sam," the Canadian punsters hit #1.

ONE WHO REALLY LOVES YOU, THE

Artist: Mary Wells
Written by: Smokey Robinson
From the album: *One Who Really Loves You*
Label: Motown
Produced by: Smokey Robinson
Year: 1962
The first lady of Motown gets her first Top 10 R&B/Top 10 crossover.

ONE, THE

Artist: Elton John
Written by: Elton John, Bernie Taupin
From the album: *The One*
Label: MCA
Year: 1992

ONLY A PAWN IN THEIR GAME

Artist: Bob Dylan
Written by: Bob Dylan
From the album: *The Times They Are A-Changin'*
Label: Columbia
Produced by: Tom Wilson
Year: 1964
Memorial to civil rights casualty Medgar Evers, slain in Mississippi in '64.

ONLY FLAME IN TOWN, THE

Artist: Elvis Costello with Daryl Hall
Written by: Declan McManus (Elvis Costello)
From the album: *Goodbye Cruel World*
Label: Columbia
Produced by: Clive Langer, Alan Winstanley
Year: 1984
Blue-eyed soul mates. Segue: "When We Ran" by Elvis Costello and John Hiatt.

ONLY IN AMERICA

Artist: Jay and the Americans
Written by: Jerry Leiber, Mike Stoller, Barry Mann, Cynthia Weil
From the album: *Come a Little Bit Closer*
Label: United Artists
Produced by: Jerry Leiber, Mike Stoller
Year: 1963
Cut by the Drifters but not released (for obvious marketing reasons). Jay and the Americans recorded their version over the Drifters' arrangement.

ONLY IN MY DREAMS

Artist: Debbie Gibson
Written by: Debbie Gibson
From the album: *Out of the Blue*
Label: Atlantic
Produced by: Fred Zarr, Debbie Gibson
Year: 1987
First Top 10 hit for the new teen triple-threat thrush in the Carole King writer/producer/singer mode.

ONLY LOVE CAN BREAK A HEART

Artist: Gene Pitney
Written by: Burt Bacharach, Hal David
From the album: *Only Love Can Break a Heart*
Label: Musicor
Year: 1962
With his biggest hit, Pitney tries out for the Copa with material that was better suited for the writers' other main client, Dionne Warwick, who covered it fifteen years later (Musicor, '77)

ONLY LOVE CAN BREAK YOUR HEART

Artist: Neil Young
Written by: Neil Young
From the album: *After the Goldrush*
Label: Reprise
Produced by: David Briggs, Neil Young, Kendall Pacios
Year: 1970

ONLY LOVED AT NIGHT

Artist: The Raincoats
Written by: Raincoats
From the album: *Odyshape*
Label: Rough Trade
Produced by: Adam Kidron, the Raincoats
Year: 1981
Essential punk sound, influenced Sonic Youth's Kim Gordon and Nirvana's Kurt Cobain.

ONLY ONE

Artist: James Taylor
Written by: James Taylor
From the album: *That's Why I'm Here*
Label: Columbia
Produced by: Frank Filipotti, James Taylor
Year: 1986
One of his best love songs.

ONLY ONE, THE

Artist: Jimmy Page
Written by: Jimmy Page, Robert Plant
From the album: *Outrider*
Label: Geffen
Produced by: Jimmy Page
Year: 1988
Solo effort from Zeppelin founder reunites him with his recalcitrant ex-lead singer. The real reunion wouldn't take place until '94.

ONLY SHALLOW

Artist: My Bloody Valentine
Written by: Belinda Butcher, Kevin Shields
From the album: *Loveless*
Produced by: Kevin Shields, Colm O'Ciosiog
Label: Sire
Year: 1991
Making noise on the new British rave circuit.

ONLY SIXTEEN

Artist: Sam Cooke
Written by: Sam Cooke (Charles Cooke)
Label: Keen
Produced by: Bumps Blackwell
Year: 1959
In one of the year's most soulful pop rockers, Cooke defined a fantasy. Covering it, Dr. Hook (Capitol, '76) just sounded like another dirty old man.

ONLY THE GOOD DIE YOUNG

Artist: Billy Joel
Written by: Billy Joel
From the album: *The Stranger*
Label: Columbia
Produced by: Phil Ramone
Year: 1977
Easily his most heartfelt and profound personal protest song. Banned by the Catholic Church, which immediately established Joel as a rock and roll hero. Segue: "Catholic School Girls Rule" by Red Hot Chili Peppers.

ONLY THE LONELY

Artist: The Motels
Written by: Martha Davis
From the album: *All for One*
Label: Capitol
Produced by: Val Garay
Year: 1982
Stone Poneys wannabes show no respect for an Orbison title.

ONLY THE LONELY (KNOW THE WAY I FEEL)

Artist: Roy Orbison
Written by: Roy Orbison, Joe Melson
From the album: *Roy Orbison's Greatest Hits*
Label: Monument
Produced by: Fred Foster
Year: 1960
His first big hit, setting up a string of tragic operatic pearls.

ONLY THE STRONG SURVIVE

Artist: Jerry Butler
Written by: Kenny Gamble, Leon Huff, Jerry Butler
From the album: *The Ice Man Cometh*
Label: Mercury
Produced by: Kenny Gamble, Leon Huff
Year: 1969
A Philly soul showpiece; #1 R&B/Top 10 crossover is Butler's biggest all-time hit.

ONLY THE YOUNG

Artist: Scandal
Written by: Steve Perry, Neal Schon, Jonathan Cain
From the album: *Warrior*
Label: Columbia
Produced by: Mike Chapman
Year: 1984
Introduced in a feisty rendition by Patty Smyth, in just about her last authentic move. Journey's hit version was featured in the wrestling movie *Vision Quest* (Geffen, '85).

ONLY WOMEN (BLEED)

Artist: Alice Cooper
Written by: Vincent Furnier (Alice Cooper), Dick Wagner
From the album: *Welcome to My Nightmare*
Label: Atlantic
Produced by: Bob Ezrin
Year: 1975
The man with the woman's name walks a mile (or three and a half minutes) in her shoes.

ONLY YOU

Artist: The Platters
Written by: Buck Ram, Ande Rand
From the album: *Encore of Golden Hits*
Label: Mercury
Produced by: Buck Ram
Year: 1955
Their first #1 R&B/Top 10 crossover hit, remade from an earlier failed rendition.

ONLY YOU

Artist: Yazoo
Written by: Vince Clarke
From the album: *Upstairs at Eric's*
Label: Sire
Produced by: Yazoo, Eric Radcliffe
Year: 1982
First trans-Atlantic hit for the dance rock stylist Clarke after leaving Depeche Mode on the way to Erasure.

ONLY YOU KNOW AND I KNOW

Artist: Dave Mason
Written by: Dave Mason
From the album: *Alone Together*
Label: Blue Thumb
Produced by: Tommy LiPuma, Dave Mason
Year: 1970
First solo single from the Traffic cofounder; an FM mini-hit.

OOBY DOOBY

Artist: Roy Orbison
Written by: Wade Moore, Dick Penner
Label: Sun
Produced by: Sam Phillips
Year: 1956
Coaxing the first few rockabilly syllables out of the mouth of the reluctant crooner, Roy.

OOH BABY BABY

Artist: The Miracles
Written by: Smokey Robinson, Warren Moore
From the album: *Going to a Go-Go*
Label: Tamla
Produced by: Smokey Robinson
Year: 1965
Covered by Linda Ronstadt (Asylum, '78).

O-O-H CHILD

Artist: The Five Stairsteps
Written by: Stan Vincent
From the album: *Stairsteps*
Label: Buddah
Produced by: Stan Vincent
Year: 1970
Reassuring family group provide a tonic for the troops, after the scathing '60s. The B-side was their cover of the Beatles' "Dear Prudence."

OOH POO PAH DOO (PART I)

Artist: Jessie Hill
Written by: Jessie Hill
Label: Minit
Produced by: Allen Toussaint
Year: 1960
Prime New Orleansiana. Covered by Ike and Tina Turner (United Artists, '71).

OOO LA LA LA

Artist: Teena Marie
Written by: Teena Marie Brockert, Allen McGrier
From the album: *Naked to the World*
Label: Epic
Produced by: Teena Marie
Year: 1988
The only #1 R&B hit for the great white funk singer hardly crossed over at all.

OOOH! MY SOUL

Artist: Little Richard
Written by: Richard Penniman (Little Richard)
From the album: *Little Richard*
Label: Specialty
Produced by: Art Rupe, Little Richard
Year: 1957

OOP SHOOP

Artist: Shirley Gunter and the Queens
Written by: Joe Josea
From the album: *Black and Blues*
Label: Flair
Year: 1954
First R&B girl-group to hit the charts. The Teen Queens were listening.

OPEN ARMS

Artist: Journey
Written by: Steve Perry, Jonathan Cain
From the album: *Escape*
Label: Columbia
Produced by: Mike Stone, Kevin Elson
Year: 1982
Biggest of six soaring Top 10 hits for the Steve Perry-led arena contingent.

OPEN MY EYES

Artist: The Nazz
Written by: Todd Rundgren
From the album: *Nazz*
Label: SGC
Produced by: Todd Rundgren
Year: 1968
From a Bearsville garage.

OPEN THE DOOR RICHARD

Artist: Dusty Fletcher
Written by: Dusty Fletcher, Jack McVea, Dan Howell, John Mason
Label: Kapp
Year: 1946
Massive modern call-and-response classic of the urban courtyard variety. Covered by the royalty of jump blues and rockabilly: Louis Jordan and Count Basie on the one hand, Billy Lee Riley and Billy Adams on the other.

OPEN YOUR HEART

Artist: Madonna
Written by: Patrick Leonard, Madonna Ciccone Peter Rafelson
From the album: *True Blue*
Label: Sire
Produced by: Patrick Leonard, Madonna
Year: 1986
The album's third #1 song.

OPENED

Artist: The Breeders
Written by: Kim Deal
From the album: *Pod*
Label: 4AD
Produced by: Steve Albini
Year: 1990
The first alterna-femme supergroup of the '90s— with Kim Deal from the Pixies and Tanya Donnelly from Throwing Muses—proves itself with this "History of Utah" for girls.

OPERATION: MINDCRIME

Artist: Queensryche
Written by: Chris DeGarmo, Geoff Tate, Michael Wilton
From the album: *Operation: Mindcrime*
Label: EMI-Manhattan
Produced by: Peter Collins
Year: 1988
Sequestered in Bellevue, Washington, arena mavens attempt to become the American Queen.

OPHELIA

Artist: The Band
Written by: Robbie Robertson
From the album: *Northern Lights/Southern Cross*
Label: Capitol
Produced by: The Band
Year: 1975
Their last waltz.

OPPORTUNITIES (LET'S MAKE LOTS OF MONEY)

Artist: Pet Shop Boys
Written by: Neil Tennant, Chris Lowe
From the album: *Please*
Label: EMI-American
Produced by: J. J. Jeczalik, N. Froome
Year: 1986
Cheeky British techno-duo's clubby anthem.

OPPOSITES ATTRACT

Artist: Paula Abdul
Written by: Oliver Leiber
From the album: *Forever Your Girl*
Label: Virgin
Produced by: Oliver Leiber
Year: 1988
The fourth #1 from the same album, harkening back to a tamer, more malleable era of girl singers and their pop svengalis.

ORANGE CRUSH

Artist: R.E.M.
Written by: Michael Stipe, Peter Buck, Bill Berry, Mike Mills
From the album: *Green*
Label: Warner Brothers
Produced by: Scott Litt, R.E.M.
Year: 1988
Pop diatribe about Agent Orange.

ORDINARY WORLD

Artist: Duran Duran
Written by: Duran Duran
From the album: *Duran Duran*
Label: Capitol
Produced by: Duran Duran, John Jones
Year: 1993
Totally '80s comeback for the first nostalgia act for the MTV generation.

ORGASM ADDICT

Artist: The Buzzcocks
Written by: Pete Shelley, Howard DeVoto
From the album: *Singles Going Steady*
Label: IRS
Produced by: Martin Rushent

Year: 1977
Early influential and inflammatory British single, released after DeVoto left the band; collected in the US (IRS, '79).

ORIGIN OF LOVE

Artist: John Cameron Mitchell
Written by: Stephen Trask
From the album: *Hedwig & the Angry Inch*
Label: Atlantic
Year: 1998
Rock opera meets "Lola" in Germany.

ORINOCO FLOW (SAIL AWAY)

Artist: Enya
Written by: Enya, Roma Ryan
From the album: *Watermark*
Label: Geffen
Year: 1988
With a wash of hypnotic sound, Enya creates Celtic rock.

ORPHAN GIRL

Artist: Emmylou Harris
Written by: Gillian Welch
From the album: *Wrecking Ball*
Label: Asylum
Produced by: Daniel Lanois
Year: 1995
Covered by Gillian Welch (Almo Sounds, '96).

ORPHANS

Artist: Teenage Jesus and the Jerks
Written by: Lydia Lunch
From the album: *Teenage Jesus & the Jerks*
Label: Lust/Unlust
Produced by: Robert Quine
Year: 1979
For punk diehards, produced by Lou Reed's favorite guitarist.

OTHER SIDE OF SUMMER, THE

Artist: Elvis Costello
Written by: Declan McManus (Elvis Costello)
From the album: *Mighty Like a Rose*
Label: Columbia
Produced by: Mitchell Froom, Kevin Killen
Year: 1991
Costello adds to the canon of summer songs his decidedly skewed view.

OTHER SIDE OF THIS LIFE, THE

Artist: The Lovin' Spoonful
Written by: Fred Neil
From the album: *Do You Believe in Magic*
Label: Kama Sutra
Produced by: Erik Jacobsen
Year: 1965

Folk/rock identity crisis. Covered by Jefferson Airplane (RCA, '65), Peter, Paul and Mary (Warner Brothers, '66). Fred Neil's version was on Capitol ('66).

OTHER WOMAN, THE

Artist: Ray Parker Jr.
Written by: Ray Parker Jr.
From the album: *The Other Woman*
Label: Arista
Produced by: Ray Parker Jr.
Year: 1982
Parker steps out from Raydio with a #1 R&B/Top 10 crossover.

OTHERSIDE

Artist: Red Hot Chili Peppers
Written by: Michael (Flea) Balzary, John Frusciante, Anthony Kiedis, Chad Smith
From the album: *Californication*
Produced by: Rick Rubin
Label: Warner Brothers
Year: 2000

OUR DAY WILL COME

Artist: Ruby and the Romantics
Written by: Mort Garson, Bob Hilliard
From the album: *Our Day Will Come*
Label: Kapp
Produced by: Allen Stanton
Year: 1963
#1 R&B/#1 crossover.

OUR FRANK

Artist: Morrissey
Written by: Stephen Morrissey, Mark Nevin
From the album: *Kill Uncle*
Label: Sire
Produced by: Clive Langer, Alan Winstantly
Year: 1991

OUR HOUSE

Artist: Crosby, Stills, Nash & Young
Written by: Graham Nash
From the album: *Deja Vu*
Label: Atlantic
Produced by: Crosby, Stills, Nash & Young
Year: 1970
Contemplating hippie domesticity, in a Laurel Canyon mansion.

OUR HOUSE

Artist: Madness
Written by: Charles Smyth, Christopher Foreman
From the album: *Madness*
Label: Geffen
Produced by: Clive Langer, Alan Winstanley
Year: 1983
Ska with a sense of humor, Monty Pythonesque, of course.

OUR LIPS ARE SEALED

Artist: The Go-Go's
Written by: Jane Weidlin, Terry Hall
From the album: *Beauty and the Beat*
Label: I.R.S.
Produced by: Richard Gottehrer
Year: 1981
Teen beat with angst, from the West-coast Blondie. Covered in a much more ominous version by Fun Boy Three (Chrysalis, '83).

OUT COME THE FREAKS

Artist: Was (Not Was)
Written by: David Weiss (David Was), Donald Fagenson (Don Was)
From the album: *Was (Not Was)*
Label: Ze
Produced by: Don Was, David Was
Year: 1981
Early statement of their soul purpose. Revived on *What up, Dog* (Chrysalis, '88).

OUT IN THE FIELDS

Artist: Garry Moore
Written by: Garry Moore
From the album: *Run for Cover*
Label: Mirage
Produced by: Peter Collins
Year: 1985
Burly beat up British barroom blues guitarist hits the singles charts.

OUT IN THE STREETS

Artist: The Shangri-Las
Written by: Barry Mann, Cynthia Weil
From the album: *Shangri-Las '65*
Label: Red Bird
Produced by: Shadow Morton
Year: 1966
Biker chicks show admirable empathy. Covered by Blondie (Beyond, '99).

OUT OF LIMITS!

Artist: The Marketts
Written by: Michael Z. Gordon
From the album: *Out of Limits!*
Label: Warner Brothers
Produced by: Joe Saraceno
Year: 1963
Surf-drenched instrumental.

OUT OF TEARS

Artist: The Rolling Stones
Written by: Mick Jagger, Keith Richards
From the album: *Voodoo Lounge*
Label: Virgin
Produced by: Don Was, Glimmer Twins
Year: 1994
Like their idols, Muddy and the Wolf, still rocking at 50, if only by the numbers.

OUT OF THE BLUE

Artist: Debbie Gibson
Written by: Debbie Gibson
From the album: *Out of the Blue*
Label: Atlantic
Produced by: Fred Zarr, Debbie Gibson
Year: 1987
Setting up a rivalry with the street-smart mallrat, Tiffany, in the suburban sweetheart sweepstakes of '87.

OUT OF TIME

Artist: Chris Farlowe
Written by: Mick Jagger, Keith Richards
Label: Immediate
Year: 1966
#1 in the UK, a stiff in the States. Stones released it on *Flowers* (London, '67), and put it out as a single themselves in '75, whereupon it stiffed again.

OUT OF TOUCH

Artist: Hall and Oates
Written by: Daryl Hall, John Oates
From the album: *Big Bam Boom*
Label: RCA
Produced by: Hall and Oates, Bob Clearmountain
Year: 1984
Philly-souled out; their sixth and last #1.

OUT OF WORK

Artist: Gary US Bonds
Written by: Bruce Springsteen
From the album: *On the Line*
Label: EMI-America
Produced by: Bruce Springsteen, Steve Van Zandt
Year: 1982
Working class meets middle class with the help of the Boss, who no longer had to worry about this kind of situation.

OUTA-SPACE

Artist: Billy Preston
Written by: Billy Preston, Joe Greene
From the album: *I Wrote a Simple Song*
Label: A&M
Produced by: Billy Preston
Year: 1971
#1 R&B/#2 crossover B3 workout.

OUTSIDE CHANCE

Artist: The Turtles
Written by: Warren Zevon
From the album: *Turtles Golden Hits*
Label: White Whale
Produced by: Joe Wissert
Year: 1967
An excitable boy makes an early career move. He also wrote for Jackie DeShannon.

OUTSIDE OF A SMALL CIRCLE OF FRIENDS

Artist: Phil Ochs
Written by: Phil Ochs
From the album: *Pleasures of the Harbor*
Label: A&M
Year: 1967
Taking off from the killing of Kitty Genovese on a New York city street, while her neighbors watched, to make a larger point about the lack of personal involvement.

OUTSTANDING

Artist: The Gap Band
Written by: Lonnie Simmons, Ray Calhoun.
From the album: *The Gap Band IV*
Label: Total Experience
Produced by: Lonnie Simmons
Year: 1982
#1 R&B track, used by Shaquille O'Neal as part of "I'm Outstanding" (Jive, '93).

OVER MY HEAD

Artist: Fleetwood Mac
Written by: Christine McVie
From the album: *Fleetwood Mac*
Label: Reprise
Produced by: Keith Olson, Fleetwood Mac
Year: 1975
A reminder of the rhythm section's blues heritage.

OVER THE HILLS AND FAR AWAY

Artist: Led Zeppelin
Written by: Jimmy Page, Robert Plant
From the album: *Houses of the Holy*
Label: Atlantic
Produced by: Jimmy Page
Year: 1973
Perfecting the classic acoustic to electric arena rock ballad form.

OVER THE MOUNTAIN, ACROSS THE SEA

Artist: Johnnie and Joe
Written by: Rex Garvin
Label: Chess
Produced by: Zell Sanders
Year: 1957
Essential ode to group harmony.

OVER UNDER SIDEWAYS DOWN

Artist: The Yardbirds
Written by: Keith Relf, James McCarty, Jeff Beck, Paul Samwell-Smith, Chris Dreja
From the album: *Over under Sideways Down*
Label: Epic
Produced by: Paul Samwell-Smith, Simon Napier-Bell
Year: 1966
Their last of five UK Top 10 hits.

OVERCOME

Artist: Tricky
Written by: Adian Thaws (Tricky), Siobhan Fahey, Marcella Detroit
From the album: *Maxinquay*
Label: Virgin
Produced by: Mark Sanders, Tricky
Year: 1995
Surging electronica anthem from the debut album of the Massive Attack alum, with the help of Shakespeare's Sisters.

OVERKILL

Artist: Men At Work
Written by: Colin Hay
From the album: *Cargo*
Label: Columbia
Produced by: Peter Mclan
Year: 1983
Mining Aussie gold with a reggae touch.

OVERKILL

Artist: Motorhead
Written by: Ian Kilmeister (Lemmy), Philthy Taylor, (Fast) Eddie Clarke
From the album: *Overkill*
Label: Bronze
Produced by: Jimmy Miller
Year: 1979
Nothing wrong with the sledgehammer approach.

OVERNIGHT SENSATION (HIT RECORD)

Artist: Raspberries
Written by: Eric Carmen
From the album: *Starting Over*
Label: Capitol
Produced by: Jimmy Ienner
Year: 1974
Having dropped out of frat rock, Eric Carmen describes his encounter with reality. Suggested segues: "So You Wanna Be a Rock and Roll Star" by the Byrds, "Rock and Roll I Gave You the Best Years of My Life" by Kevin Johnson.

OWNER OF A LONELY HEART

Artist: Yes
Written by: Trevor Rabin, Jon Anderson, Chris Squire, Trevor Horn
From the album: *90125*
Label: Atco
Produced by: Trevor Horn
Year: 1983
Watering down their progressive sound for a Top-40 comeback.

OYE COMO VA (LISTEN HOW IT GOES)

Artist: Santana
Written by: Tito Puente

From the album: *Abraxis*
Label: Columbia
Produced by: Fred Catero, Santana
Year: 1971
Eloquent guitar treatment of the Latin standard, introduced by Tito Puente in 1963.

P

P.A.S.S.I.O.N.

Artist: Rythm Syndicate
Written by: Carl Sturken, Evan Rogers
From the album: *Rythm Syndicate*
Label: Impact
Produced by: Carl Sturken, Evan Rodgers
Year: 1991
Neo-disco illiteracy.

P.F. SLOAN

Artist: Jimmy Webb
Written by: Jimmy Webb
From the album: *Words & Music*
Label: Reprise
Produced by: Jim Webb
Year: 1970
A West coast songwriter searches for his hero (P.F. Sloan of Barri & Sloan, authors of "Eve of Destruction," and hits for the Grass Roots and the Turtles, etc.) in a haunting pop rock gem that is equal to Sloan at his best. Covered by the Association (Warner Brothers, '71), re-recorded by Webb (Atlantic, '77). Sloan, meanwhile, turned up with an album entitled *Serenade of the Seven Sisters*, released only in Japan (Pioneer, '94).

(P.S.) I LOVE YOU

Artist: The Beatles
Written by: John Lennon, Paul McCartney
From the album: *Introducing the Beatles*
Label: Vee Jay
Produced by: George Martin
Year: 1963
The B-side of "Love Me Do," recorded at their first session in '62.

P.Y.T. (PRETTY YOUNG THING)

Artist: Michael Jackson
Written by: James Ingram, Quincy Jones
From the album: *Thriller*
Label: Epic
Produced by: Quincy Jones, Michael Jackson
Year: 1983
Takes on new meaning two decades later.

PABLO PICASSO

Artist: Modern Lovers
Written by: Jonathan Richman
From the album: *The Modern Lovers*
Label: Beserkley
Produced by: John Cale

Year: 1970
Could any terminally arrested adolescent have said it better? Lo-fi twenty years ahead of its time.

PACIFIC

Artist: 808 State
Written by: 808 State
From the album: *Quadrastate*
Label: Creed (UK)
Year: 1989
Influenced by Brian Eno, Rick Wakeman, and Kraftwerk, this breakthrough British dance instrumental commentary on the likes of middle-of-the-road sax god Kenny G. created a splinter form known as new age house.

PACK UP YOUR SORROWS

Artist: Richard and Mimi Fariña
Written by: Pauline Marden, Richard Fariña
From the album: *Celebrations for a Grey Day*
Label: Vanguard
Year: 1965
A cultural literary antihero bridges the gap from folk to folk/rock with a particularly adroit use of the dulcimer. Popularized by Fariña's sister-in-law, Joan Baez (Vanguard, '64).

PAID IN FULL

Artist: Eric B & Rakim
Written by: Eric Barrier, and William Griffin
From the album: *Paid in Full*
Label: 4TH and Broadway
Produced by: Eric B & Rakim
Year: 1987
Opening with the classic statement "This is a journey into sound," this single more than fulfills its exciting promise and premise.

PAINT IT BLACK

Artist: The Rolling Stones
Written by: Mick Jagger, Keith Richards
From the album: *Aftermath*
Label: London
Produced by: Andrew Loog-Oldham
Year: 1966
Stones adopt the sitar, briefly.

PAIR OF BROWN EYES, A

Artist: The Pogues
Written by: Paddy McGowan
From the album: *Rum, Sodomy and the Lash*
Label: MCA
Produced by: Elvis Costello
Year: 1985
The Irish-pub sound, as poetic and inebriated as Dylan Thomas or Van Morrison.

PALE BLUE EYES

Artist: The Velvet Underground
Written by: Lou Reed
From the album: *The Velvet Underground*
Label: MGM

Produced by: Andy Warhol, Tom Wilson
Year: 1969
Covered by original Velvets Maureen Tucker (50 Skidillun Watts, '80) and Lou Reed (Arista, '80).

PALISADES PARK

Artist: Freddy Cannon
Written by: Chuck Barris
From the album: *Freddy Cannon at Palisades Park*
Label: Kapp
Year: 1962
It was no Disneyland; it wasn't even Action Park. But Chuck Barris would go on to game show infamy.

PANAMA

Artist: Van Halen
Written by: Eddie Van Halen, Alex Van Halen, Michael Anthony, David Lee Roth
From the album: *1984*
Label: Warner Brothers
Produced by: Ted Templeman
Year: 1984
Taking on the Top 40 with a scorching new attitude.

PANAMA RED

Artist: New Riders of the Purple Sage
Written by: Peter Rowan
From the album: *The Adventures of Panama Red*
Label: Columbia
Produced by: Norbert Putnam
Year: 1973
The stuff of country and folk/rock legend.

PANCHO AND LEFTY

Artist: Townes Van Zandt
Written by: Townes Van Zabdt
From the album: *The Late Great Townes Van Zandt*
Label: Tomato
Produced by: Jack Clement, Kevin Eggers
Year: 1972
The blueprint for outlaw country. Cover by Emmylou Harris (Reprise, '77) went to #1 country. Covered by Willie Nelson and Merle Haggard (Columbia, '83). Guy Clark, Joe Ely, Jerry Jeff Walker, Jimmy Dale Gilmore, Nanci Griffith and John Prine were listening.

PANIC IN DETROIT

Artist: David Bowie
Written by: David Bowie
From the album: *Aladdin Sane*
Label: RCA
Produced by: David Bowie, Ken Scott
Year: 1973

PAPA DON'T PREACH

Artist: Madonna
Written by: Brian Elliott, Madonna Ciccone
From the album: *True Blue*

Label: Sire
Produced by: Steve Bray, Madonna
Year: 1986
Madonna's fourth #1 defined her defiant yet needy attitude. Oddly enough, '40's sex object Betty Hutton sang a song called "Papa Don't Preach to Me" in the 1947 movie *The Perils of Pauline*, written by Frank Loesser (*Guys & Dolls*). Wanda Jackson also covered a Betty Hutton tune: "Hot Dog, That Made Him Mad." (Capitol, '57).

PAPA DON'T TAKE NO MESS

Artist: James Brown
Written by: James Brown, Fred Wesley, John Starks, Charles Bobbit
From the album: *Hell*
Label: Polydor
Produced by: James Brown
Year: 1974
#1 R&B/Top 40 crossover.

PAPA WAS A ROLLIN' STONE

Artist: The Temptations
Written by: Norman Whitfield, Barrett Strong
From the album: *All Directions*
Label: Gordy
Produced by: Norman Whitfield
Year: 1972
Their fourth and last #1. Suggested segue: "Daddy Could Swear, I Declare," by Gladys Knight & the Pips.

PAPA WAS TOO

Artist: Joe Tex
Written by: Joe Tex
From the album: *The Best of Joe Tex*
Label: Dial
Produced by: Buddy Killen
Year: 1966

PAPA'S GOT A BRAND NEW BAG

Artist: James Brown and the Famous Flames
Written by: James Brown
From the album: *Papa's Got a Brand New Bag*
Label: King
Produced by: James Brown
Year: 1965
Defining the rhythmic crossroads of the decade; some would get it and move into soul, others would stay seated, preferring folk/rock.

PAPA-OOM-MOW-MOW

Artist: The Rivingtons
Written by: Al Frazier, Turner Wilson Jr., Carl White, John Harris
From the album: *Doing the Bird*
Label: Liberty
Produced by: Jack Levy, Adam Ross, Al Frazier
Year: 1962

Noted backup band steps forward with West coast surf meets East coast doo-wop classic. Follow-up, "Mama-Oom-Mow-Mow" stiffed.

PAPER BAG

Artist: Fiona Apple
Written by: Fiona Apple
From the album: *When the Pawn...*
Produced by: John Brion
Label: Columbia
Year: 1999
New confessional ingénue goes overboard.

PAPER IN FIRE

Artist: John (Cougar) Mellencamp
Written by: John Mellencamp
From the album: *The Lonesome Jubilee*
Label: Mercury
Produced by: Don Gehman, John Mellencamp
Year: 1987
Moving from rock to roots/rock.

PAPER SUN

Artist: Traffic
Written by: Steve Winwood, James Capaldi
From the album: *Mr. Fantasy*
Label: United Artists
Produced by: Jimmy Miller
Year: 1967
First of four chart singles, none of which broke out of the Bottom 40, for Winwood's post-Spencer Davis, progressive rock supergroup.

PAPERBACK WRITER

Artist: The Beatles
Written by: John Lennon, Paul McCartney
From the album: *Hey Jude*
Label: Capitol
Produced by: George Martin
Year: 1966
Author Mark Shipper borrowed this title for his fictional paperback imagining the world of music if the Beatles had not been successful.

PAPUA, NEW GUINEA

Artist: Future Sound of London
Written by: Garry Cobain, Brian Douglas
From the album: *Accelerator*
Label: Jumpin' & Pumpin'
Produced by: Future Sound of London, Luco, Mental Cube
Year: 1991
Launching the future sound of electronica, with a pumpin' dance track for the ages.

PARADISE

Artist: Sade
Written by: Helen Folesade Adu (Sade), Stewart Matthewman, Andrew Hale, Paul Denman
From the album: *Stronger Than Pride*
Label: Epic
Produced by: Sade

Year: 1988
#1 R&B/Top 20 crossover for the seductively whispery chanteuse.

PARADISE BY THE DASHBOARD LIGHT

Artist: Meat Loaf
Written by: Jim Steinman
From the album: *Bat out of Hell*
Label: Epic
Produced by: Jim Steinman
Year: 1977
Costarring Ellen Foley—later of *Night Court* and a lamentably obscure recording career—and the ineffable Yankee announcer, Phil "The Scooter" Rizzuto, whose words would go on to inspire an entire book of poetry, this backseat psychodrama took your basic teenage lust way past Springsteenian license.

PARADISE CITY

Artist: Guns N' Roses
Written by: Guns N' Roses
From the album: *Appetite for Destruction*
Label: Geffen
Produced by: Mike Clink
Year: 1989
Wearing out their welcome on the Top 10, but not before establishing a new level of bad-boy bravado.

PARALLEL LINES

Artist: Todd Rundgren
Written by: Todd Rundgren
From the album: *Nearly Human*
Label: Warner Brothers
Produced by: Todd Rundgren
Year: 1989
Going beyond mere Beatlemania, Rundgren originally wrote this for a projected Beatles movie musical called *Up Against It*, written by the late Joe Orton. It was finally staged in '89 at the New York Shakespeare Festival, where this tune was sung by Phillip Casanov and Alison Fraser.

PARALYZED

Artist: Elvis Presley
Written by: Otis Blackwell, Elvis Presley
From the album: *Elvis*
Label: RCA
Produced by: Steve Sholes
Year: 1956
Mega-rocking B-side of "Love Me."

PARANOID

Artist: Black Sabbath
Written by: Tony Iommi, Geezer Butler, Ozzy Osbourne, Bill Ward
From the album: *Paranoid*
Label: Warner Brothers
Produced by: Rodger Bain
Year: 1970
Sabbath's first chart single, which defined their lumbering, mouldering attitude.

PARCHMAN FARM

Artist: Mose Allison
Written by: Mose Allison
From the album: *Local Color*
Label: Prestige
Produced by: Bob Weinstock
Year: 1957
The essence of urban cool jazzbo blues. Covered by John Mayall's Bluesbreakers featuring Eric Clapton (Deram, '66), Blue Cheer (Phillips, '68). Segue: "Maggie's Farm" by Bob Dylan.

PARENTS JUST DON'T UNDERSTAND

Artist: D.J. Jazzy Jeff and the Fresh Prince
Written by: Will Smith, Jeff Townes, Pete Q. Harris
From the album: *He's the D.J., I'm the Rapper*
Label: Jive
Produced by: D.J. Jazzy Jeff, the Fresh Prince, Pete Q. Harris, Chuck New
Year: 1989
Sitcom rap, rated PG-13, in which Smith reveals his upper-class roots, if not his Belair destiny, with a line about borrowing his mother's Porsche.

PART OF THE PLAN

Artist: Dan Fogelberg
Written by: Dan Fogelberg
From the album: *Souvenirs*
Label: Full Moon
Produced by: Joe Walsh
Year: 1975
Folkie philosophizing.

PART OF THE UNION

Artist: The Strawbs
Written by: Richard Hudson, John Ford
From the album: *Bursting at the Seams*
Label: A&M
Year: 1973
Biggest UK hit for folk/rock relatives of Fairport Convention that at different times featured Sandy Denny, Rick Wakeman, and Dave Cousins in the band.

PARTICLE MAN

Artist: They Might Be Giants
Written by: John Flansburgh, John Linnell
From the album: *Flood*
Label: Elektra
Produced by: Clive Langer, Alan Winstanley, They Might Be Giants
Year: 1990
Their answer to "1999" by Prince.

PART-TIME LOVE

Artist: Little Johnnie Taylor
Written by: Clay Hammond
From the album: *Raw Blues*
Label: Galaxy
Produced by: Cliff Goldsmith
Year: 1963
#1 R&B/Top 20 crossover; covered by Ann Peebles (Hi, '70).

PART-TIME LOVER

Artist: Stevie Wonder
Written by: Stevie Wonder
From the album: *In Square Circle*
Label: Motown
Produced by: Stevie Wonder
Year: 1985
His 8TH #1 R&B/#1 crossover. Only Michael Jackson has more (if you count his five with the Jackson 5).

PARTY ALL THE TIME

Artist: Eddie Murphy
Written by: Rick James
From the album: *How Could It Be*
Label: Columbia
Produced by: Rick James
Year: 1985
Nearly credible performance, which is more than you can say for most of his movies.

PARTY DOLL

Artist: Buddy Knox
Written by: Jimmy Bowen, Buddy Knox
From the album: *Buddy Knox and Jimmy Bowen*
Label: Roulette
Produced by: Norman Petty
Year: 1957
Norman Petty's pre-Buddy Holly calling card. This double A-sided smash (along with "I'm Stickin' with You" by Jimmy Bowen) gave the Rhythm Orchids all the impetus they needed to break up into two separate solo acts. Proving its rock and roll credibility, this tune crossed over Top-5 R&B but not country (same as Buddy Holly's records). The pop cover by Steve Lawrence (Coral, '57) charted lower than Knox's version. The R&B covers by Wingy Manone (Decca, '57) and Roy Brown (Imperial, '57) were bombs.

PARTY FOR YOUR RIGHT TO FIGHT

Artist: Public Enemy
Written by: Carlton Ridenhour, Hank Shocklee, Eric Sadler
From the album: *It Takes a Nation of Millions to Hold Us Back*
Label: Def Jam
Produced by: Hank Shocklee, Carl Ryder
Year: 1988
Answering the Beastie Boys, who were answering Buffalo Springfield (and the Three Stooges).

PARTY LIGHTS

Artist: Claudine Clark
Written by: Claudine Clark
From the album: *Party Lights*
Label: Chancellor
Produced by: Claudine Clark, Jerry Ragovoy
Year: 1962
True essence of the teenage dilemma in one of the all-time great girl-group era one-shots.

PARTY OUT OF BOUNDS

Artist: The B-52's
Written by: Fred Schneider, Ricky Wilson, Cindy Wilson, Cindy Strickland, Kate Pierson
From the album: *Wild Planet*
Label: Warner Brothers
Produced by: Rhett Davis, the B-52's
Year: 1980
The battle cry for a new decade's new dance generation.

PARTY UP (UP IN HERE)

Artist: DMX
Written by: Kasseem Dean and Earl (DMX) Simmons
From the album: *And Then There Was X*
Label: Def Jam
Year: 1999
A new standard of vocal intimidation.

PARTYMAN

Artist: Prince
Written by: Prince Rogers Nelson
From the album: *Batman Soundtrack*
Label: Warner Brothers
Produced by: Prince
Year: 1989
Party at the Batcave.

PARTYUP

Artist: Prince
Written by: Prince Rogers Nelson
From the album: *Dirty Mind*
Label: Warner Brothers
Produced by: Prince
Year: 1980
Party in Paisley Park.

PASS THE DUTCHIE

Artist: Musical Youth
Written by: Jackie Mitoo, Lloyd Ferguson, Fitzroy Simpson
From the album: *The Youth of Today*
Label: MCA
Produced by: Peter Collins
Year: 1983
The Jackson 5 of reggae sneak a smoke.

PASS THE MIC

Artist: Beastie Boys
Written by: Beastie Boys, Mario Caldato Jr.
From the album: *Check Your Head*
Label: Capitol
Produced by: Mario Caldato Jr.
Year: 1992
From the Improv school of rap.

PASSENGER, THE

Artist: Iggy Pop
Written by: David Bowie, James Osterberg (Iggy Pop)
From the album: *Lust for Life*
Label: RCA
Produced by: David Bowie, Iggy Pop
Year: 1977
Threatening to become the male Nico. Covered by Siouxsie & the Banshees (Geffen, '87).

PASSION

Artist: Rod Stewart
Written by: Rod Stewart, Phil Chen, Jim Cregan, Gary Grainger, Kevin Savigar
From the album: *Foolish Behaviour*
Label: Warner Brothers
Produced by: Rod Stewart Group, Jeremy Andrew Johns, Harry the Hook.
Year: 1980

PASSIONATE KISSES

Artist: Lucinda Williams
Written by: Lucinda Williams
From the album: *Lucinda Williams*
Label: Rough Trade
Year: 1988
New generation folk/rock entitlement at its finest. Covered by Mary Chapin Carpenter (Columbia, '93).

PASTIME PARADISE

Artist: Stevie Wonder
Written by: Stevie Wonder
From the album: *Songs in the Key of Life*
Label: Tamla
Produced by: Stevie Wonder
Year: 1976
This tune had a featured role in the modern R&B classic "Gangsta's Paradise," introduced by Coolio in the film *Dangerous Minds* (MCA, '95).

PASTURES OF PLENTY

Artist: Kingston Trio
Written by: Woody Guthrie
Label: Capitol
Produced by: Voyle Gilmore
Year: 1961
Pioneering folk balladeer's Guthrie's classic American anthem, written in 1941 while he was under the employ of the Bonneville Power Administration. Adapting the ballad "Pretty Polly," Guthrie's celebration of freedom, the land, and the outlaws, outcasts, and outsiders who labored to maintain these precious gifts, influenced a nascent generation of peaceniks, pacificists, and protesters, from Bob Dylan to the Clash. Originally published in the first issue of *Sing Out!* magazine. Covered by Cisco Houston (Vanguard, '60).

PATCHES

Artist: Dickey Lee
Written by: Barry Mann, Larry Kolber

From the album: *The Tale of Patches*
Label: Smash
Year: 1962
Classic country/rock class struggle. Suggested segue: "Poor Side of Town" by Johnny Rivers, "Dawn (Go Away)" by the Four Seasons.

PATCHES (I'M DEPENDING ON YOU)

Artist: The Chairmen of the Board
Written by: General Johnson, Ronald Dunbar
From the album: *Give Me Just a Little More Time*
Label: Invictus
Produced by: Rick Hall
Year: 1970
Covered by Clarence Carter (Atlantic, '70).

PATHS OF VICTORY

Artist: Hamilton Camp
Written by: Bob Dylan
From the album: *Paths of Victory*
Produced by: Jim Dickson
Label: Elektra
Year: 1964
Early optimistic classic Dylan marching song.

PATHS THAT CROSS

Artist: Patti Smith
Written by: Patti Smith, Fred Smith
From the album: *Dream of Life*
Label: Arista
Produced by: Jimmy Iovine, Scott Litt
Year: 1988
Comeback track finds Patti still mystically inclined.

PATIENCE

Artist: Guns N' Roses
Written by: Guns N' Roses
From the album: *G N' R Lies*
Label: Geffen
Produced by: Mike Clink
Year: 1987
Mid-tempo ballad returned to the airwaves after the band's massive breakthrough.

PATTERNS

Artist: Simon and Garfunkel
Written by: Paul Simon
From the album: *Parsley, Sage, Rosemary and Thyme*
Label: Columbia
Produced by: Bob Johnston
Year: 1966
Folk/rock goes into psychoanalysis. Featured in *The Graduate*.

PAUL REVERE

Artist: Beastie Boys
Written by: Adam Horovitz
From the album: *Licensed to Ill*
Label: Def Jam
Produced by: Rick Rubin, Beastie Boys

Year: 1986
Talking up a revolution.

PAY TO CUM

Artist: Bad Brains
Written by: Gary Miller (Dr. Know), Daryl Jenifer, Paul Hudson
Label: X
Produced by: Jimmy Quidd
Year: 1980
Landmark indie fusion of metal, punk, and reggae that launched the career of this jazz-influenced, speedcore band from D.C.

PAY TO PLAY

Artist: Nirvana
Written by: Kurt Cobain
From the album: *Nevermind*
Label: DGC
Produced by: Butch Vig
Year: 1988
Demo version of "Stay Away" celebrates the realities early obscurity in prescene Seattle.

PAYBACK, THE

Artist: James Brown
Written by: James Brown, Fred Wesley, John Starks
From the album: *The Payback*
Label: Polydor
Produced by: James Brown
Year: 1973
From the movie *The Payback*. Covered by Big Black (Homestead, '84).

PAYOFF MIX, THE (MASTERMIX OF G.L.O.B.E. AND WHIZ KID'S "PLAY THAT BEAT MR. DJ)

Artist: Double Dee and Steinski
Written by: Various
From the album: *The Payoff Mix/Lesson Two/Lesson 3*
Label: Tommy Boy
Produced by: Double Dee, Steinski
Year: 1985
An ingenious cult classic of the splice and dice school of DJ multimedia art for the junk culture generation.
Beck was taking notes.

PEACE IN OUR TIME

Artist: Elvis Costello
Written by: Declan McManus (Elvis Costello)
From the album: *Goodbye Cruel World*
Label: Columbia
Produced by: Clive Langer, Alan Winstanley
Year: 1984
Post-nuclear protest.

PEACE LIKE A RIVER

Artist: Paul Simon
Written by: Paul Simon

From the album: *Paul Simon*
Label: Columbia
Produced by: Roy Halee, Paul Simon
Year: 1972
Apart from Garfunkel, a gospel-influenced Simon enters a new era of expression, independence, productivity, and critical respect.

PEACE TRAIN

Artist: Cat Stevens
Written by: Cat Stevens
From the album: *Teaser and the Firecat*
Label: A&M
Produced by: Paul Samwell-Smith
Year: 1971
Answering "People Get Ready" by the Impressions. Covered by 10,000 Maniacs (Elektra, '87).

PEACE WILL COME (ACCORDING TO PLAN)

Artist: Melanie
Written by: Melanie Safka
From the album: *Leftover Wine*
Label: Buddah
Produced by: Peter Schekeryk
Year: 1970
A late-arriving flower child hangs on to the folk/rock sentiments of the '60s.

PEACEFUL

Artist: Kenny Rankin
Written by: Kenny Rankin
From the album: *Like a Seed*
Label: Little David
Year: 1972
Laid-back mellow East coast vocalizing. Covered by Helen Reddy (Capitol, '73).

PEACEFUL EASY FEELING

Artist: Eagles
Written by: Jack Tempchin
From the album: *Eagles*
Label: Asylum
Produced by: Glyn Johns
Year: 1972
First hit for Linda Ronstadt's former backing band is a folk/rock hitchhike classic.

PEACHES EN REGALIA

Artist: Frank Zappa
Written by: Frank Zappa
From the album: *Hot Rats*
Label: Bizarre
Produced by: Frank Zappa
Year: 1969
Classic guitar extravaganza.

PEANUT BUTTER

Artist: The Marathons
Written by: Martin J. Cooper, H. P. Barnum, Clifford Smith, Fred Goldsmith
From the album: *Peanut Butter*

Label: Arvee
Produced by: Fred Smith, Cliff Goldsmith
Year: 1961
One of the great falsetto leads by James Johnson, formerly of the Jayhawks, who were the actual performers of this record, under a nom de plume.

PEANUTS

Artist: Little Joe and the Thrillers
Written by: Joe Cook
Label: Okeh
Produced by: Leroy Kirkland
Year: 1957
Falsetto to die for by Joe Cook.

PEARL OF THE QUARTER

Artist: Steely Dan
Written by: Donald Fagen, Walter Becker
From the album: *Countdown to Ecstasy*
Label: ABC
Produced by: Gary Katz
Year: 1973
Transplanted East coast bohemians visit New Orleans, fall in love.

PEARLE

Artist: Trip Shakespeare
Written by: Matt Wilson
From the album: *Applehead Man*
Label: Gark
Produced by: Mike Hedges
Year: 1988
Wilson went on to semi-bigger things in Semisonic ("Closing Time").

PEEK-A-BOO

Artist: Siouxsie and the Banshees
Written by: Susan Dallion, Steven Bailey, Peter Clarke
From the album: *Peepshow*
Label: Geffen
Year: 1988
This hit US dance track reestablished them as classic weirdos.

PEG

Artist: Steely Dan
Written by: Donald Fagen, Walter Becker
From the album: *Aja*
Label: ABC
Produced by: Gary Katz
Year: 1977
Return to their Top 40 roots results in their biggest hit. Jay Graydon on guitar.

PEGGY SUE

Artist: Buddy Holly
Written by: Buddy Holly, Jerry Allison, Norman Petty
From the album: *The Buddy Holly Story*
Label: Coral
Produced by: Norman Petty

Year: 1957
Buddy's first solo hit, written with and backed by the Crickets, epitomizing not only the self-contained group concept that would flourish with the Beatles in the '60s, but the jangly guitar essence of all alternative rock movements ever since, from Bob Dylan and the Byrds to Joe Ely to Tom Petty and the Heartbreakers to R.E.M. to the Gin Blossoms.

PEGGY SUE GOT MARRIED

Artist: The Crickets
Written by: Buddy Holly
From the album: *The Buddy Holly Story, Volume Two*
Label: Coral
Year: 1959
Years later became the title, if not the basis, for the great Nick Cage/Kathleen Turner retro movie co-starring Marshall Crenshaw. The song was included in the soundtrack (Varese Sarabande, '86).

PENCIL NECK GEEK

Artist: Freddie Blassie
Written by: Martin Margulies, Peter Cicero
From the album: *King of Men*
Label: Rhino
Year: 1977
The rock and wrestling connection comes together on this entirely convincing, threatening oddity/novelty. Wrestler Blassie once appeared on *The Dick Van Dyke Show* doing the Twazzle.

PENETRATION

Artist: The Pyramids
Written by: Steve Leonard
From the album: *The Original Penetration and Other Favorites*
Label: Best
Year: 1964
Early Surf metaphor.

PENGUIN IN BONDAGE

Artist: Frank Zappa
Written by: Frank Zappa
From the album: *Roxy and Elsewhere*
Label: DiscReet
Produced by: Frank Zappa
Year: 1974

PENNY LANE

Artist: The Beatles
Written by: John Lennon, Paul McCartney
From the album: *Magical Mystery Tour*
Label: Capitol
Produced by: George Martin
Year: 1967
An enchanting travelogue, complete with a string of classical trumpets.

PENNYROYAL TEA

Artist: Nirvana
Written by: Nirvana

From the album: *In Utero*
Label: DGC
Produced by: Steve Albini
Year: 1993
The great lost Nirvana single. Kurt's plea for a little herbal relief.

PENSACOLA

Artist: Joan Osborne
Written by: Joan Osborne, Eric Bazilian, Rick Chertoff, Rob Hyman
From the album: *Relish*
Produced by: Rick Chertoff
Label: Blue Gorilla
Year: 1995
Down home in white tornado country.

PEOPLE ARE PEOPLE

Artist: Depeche Mode
Written by: Martin Gore
From the album: *People Are People*
Label: Sire
Produced by: Depeche Mode, Daniel Miller
Year: 1984
Leading the UK synth invasion of the mid-'80s, with a Top 20 hit.

PEOPLE ARE STILL HAVING SEX

Artist: La Tour
Written by: William La Tour
From the album: *La Tour*
Label: Smash
Produced by: La Tour, Mark Picchiotti
Year: 1991
Primal Top-40 reassurance, hip-hop style.

PEOPLE ARE STRANGE

Artist: The Doors
Written by: Jim Morrison, Robbie Krieger, John Densmore, Ray Manzarek
From the album: *Strange Days*
Label: Elektra
Produced by: Paul Rothchild
Year: 1967
Chart-ready alienation.

PEOPLE EVERYDAY

Artist: Arrested Development
Written by: Todd (Speech) Thomas
From the album: *3 years 5 Months and 2 Days in the Life Of*
Label: Chrysalis
Produced by: Speech
Year: 1992
A play on Sly & the Family Stone.

PEOPLE GET READY

Artist: The Impressions
Written by: Curtis Mayfield
From the album: *People Get Ready*
Label: ABC Paramount

Produced by: Johnny Pate
Year: 1965
Their most famous gospel-influenced anthem. Covered by Rod Stewart and Jeff Beck (Epic, '85).

PEOPLE GOT TO BE FREE

Artist: The Rascals
Written by: Felix Cavaliere, Edward Brigati Jr.
From the album: *Freedom Suite*
Label: Atlantic
Produced by: The Rascals
Year: 1968
Blue-skied soul.

PEOPLE HAVE THE POWER

Artist: Patti Smith
Written by: Patti Smith, Fred Smith
From the album: *Dream of Life*
Label: Arista
Produced by: Jimmy Iovine, Scott Litt, Fred Sonic Smith
Year: 1988
The Smiths' version of Lennon and Yoko's "Power to the People." But did they record it in bed?

PEOPLE WHO DIED

Artist: The Jim Carroll Band
Written by: Jim Carroll
From the album: *Catholic Boy*
Label: Atco
Produced by: Bob Clearmountain, Earl McGrath
Year: 1980
Fevered junkie prose/poetry eulogy. Suggested segue: "88 Lines About 44 Women" by the Nails, "Pepper" by the Butthole Surfers.

PEPPER

Artist: Butthole Surfers
Written by: Butthole Surfers
From the album: *Electric Larryland*
Label: Capitol
Produced by: Steve Thompson
Year: 1996
West coast lost youth answer to Jim Carroll's "People Who Died."

PEPPERMINT TWIST

Artist: Joey Dee & the Starlighters
Written by: Henry Glover
From the album: *Doin' the Twist at the Peppermint Lounge*
Label: Roulette
Produced by: Henry Glover
Year: 1961
Having failed to note the historic potential of Hank Ballard's "The Twist," when he first encountered it, on the B-side of his own "Teardrops on Your Letter," Henry Glover redeemed himself by shepherding Joey Dee's celebration of "The Peppermint Twist" to the top of the charts in January of '62, knocking off the second coming of the selfsame "The Twist" in the bargain. In fact, it was the popularity of the Twist at New York's Peppermint

Lounge among the Jet Set glitterati in attendance (Dee led the house band) that pushed the dance into headline news as a Baby Boom phenomenon, making Chubby's historic return to the top inevitable (aided by a key *Ed Sullivan Show* appearance). In the '80's the Peppermint Lounge would briefly reopen, as a music video emporium.

PERCY'S SONG

Artist: Fairport Convention
Written by: Bob Dylan
From the album: *Unhalfbricking*
Label: A&M
Produced by: Joe Boyd, Simon Nicol
Year: 1969
This epic, early-Dylan ramble on injustice was performed by Joan Baez in the '67 documentary *Don't Look Back*.

PERFECT DAY

Artist: Lou Reed
Written by: Lou Reed
From the album: *Transformer*
Produced by: David Bowie
Year: 1972
Idyllic Lou between crises. Featured in the movie *Trainspotting*, 1996.

PERFECT KISS

Artist: New Order
Written by: New Order
From the album: *Low Life*
Label: Qwest
Produced by: New Order
Year: 1985
A synth drum backbeat reflects the nervous energy of a new relationship.

PERFECT SONNET, A

Artist: Bright Eyes
Written by: Conor Oberst
From the album: *Every Day and Every Night*
Label: Saddle Creek
Year: 2000
Anguished emo confessional from the heart and the heartlands.

PERFECT WAY

Artist: Scritti Politti
Written by: Green Strohmeyer-Gartside, David Gamson
From the album: *Cupid and Psyche 85*
Label: Warner Brothers
Produced by: Green Strohmeyer-Gartside, David Gamson
Year: 1985
Only US hit for the alternative politicos.

PERFECT WORLD

Artist: Huey Lewis and the News
Written by: Alex Call

From the album: *Perfect World*
Label: Chrysalis
Produced by: Huey Lewis and the News
Year: 1988

PERFECT WORLD

Artist: Tonio K.
Written by: Glen Burnick, Steve Krikorian (Tonio K.)
From the album: *Romeo Unchained*
Label: What/A&M
Year: 1986
Caustic singer/songwriter at his most chipper. Covered by cowriter Burnick (A&M, '86). Also in the '92 movies *Don't Tell Mom the Babysitter's Dead* and *Son-in-Law*.

PERSONAL JESUS

Artist: Depeche Mode
Written by: Martin Gore
From the album: *Violator*
Label: Sire
Produced by: Depeche Mode, Flood
Year: 1990
Establishing the notion of God as a DJ, starring the lord Jesus Christ himself.

PERSONALITY

Artist: Lloyd Price
Written by: Lloyd Price, Harold Logan
From the album: *Mr. Personality*
Label: ABC-Paramount
Produced by: Don Costa
Year: 1959
His third #1 R&B/Top 10 crossover.

PERSONALITY CRISIS

Artist: New York Dolls
Written by: David Johansen, Johnny Thunders
From the album: *New York Dolls*
Label: Mercury
Produced by: Todd Rundgren
Year: 1973
Their personality crisis: did they want to be art rock or hard rock; the Velvet Underground or Kiss or Mott the Hoople?

PERSONALLY

Artist: Jackie Moore
Written by: Paul Kelly
Label: Columbia
Produced by: William Bell, Paul Mitchell
Year: 1978
Covered by Karla Bonoff (Columbia, '82).

PETER PIPER

Artist: Run-D.M.C.
Written by: Darryl McDaniels, Joe Simmons
From the album: *Raising Hell*
Label: Profile
Produced by: Rick Rubin
Year: 1986

PETS

Artist: Porno for Pyros
Written by: Porno for Pyros
From the album: *Porno for Pyros*
Label: Warner Brothers
Produced by: M. Hyde, Perry Farrell
Year: 1993
Farrell moves on from Jane's Addiction.

PHILADELPHIA

Artist: Neil Young
Written by: Neil Young
From the album: *Philadelphia Soundtrack*
Label: Reprise
Year: 1994
Bookending Springsteen, this was sung over the closing credits, but lost the Oscar to the Boss.

PHILADELPHIA FREEDOM

Artist: Elton John
Written by: Elton John, Bernie Taupin
From the album: *Elton John's Greatest Hits (Vol. II)*
Label: MCA
Produced by: Gus Dudgeon
Year: 1975
Named after Billie Jean King's pro tennis team.

PHOTOGRAPH

Artist: Def Leppard
Written by: Steve Clark, Joe Elliott, Robert John "Mutt" Lange, Pete Willis, Rick Savage
From the album: *Pyromania*
Label: Mercury
Produced by: Mutt Lange
Year: 1983
Leading the British new wave of heavy metal, a sound which would dominate AOR radio for the remainder of the decade.

PHOTOGRAPH

Artist: Ringo Starr
Written by: George Harrison, Richard Starkey (Rings Starr)
From the album: *Ringo*
Label: Apple
Produced by: Richard Perry
Year: 1973
The luckiest Beatle scores his biggest hit. Covered by Camper Van Beethoven (Pitch-a-Tent, '84).

PHYSICAL

Artist: Olivia Newton-John
Written by: Stephen Kipner, Terry Shaddick
From the album: *Physical*
Label: MCA
Produced by: John Farrar
Year: 1981
Olivia stars in her new workout video: for some reason one of the top singles of all time.

PIANO IN THE DARK

Artist: Brenda Russell
Written by: Brenda Russell, Jeff Hull, Scott Cutler
From the album: *Get Here*
Label: A&M
Produced by: Andre Fischer, Brenda Russell, Jeff Hull
Year: 1988

PIANO MAN

Artist: Billy Joel
Written by: Billy Joel
From the album: *Billy Joel*
Label: Columbia
Produced by: Michael Stewart, Phil Ramone
Year: 1971
His autobiographical piano bar claim to fame.

PICK UP THE PIECES

Artist: Average White Band
Written by: Roger Ball, Malcolm Duncan, Alan Garrie, Robbie McIntosh, Owen McIntyre, Jamie Stuart
From the album: *AWB*
Produced by: Arif Mardin
Year: 1975
#1 soul intrumental from Ireland.

PICKIN' UP THE PIECES

Artist: Poco
Written by: Richie Furay
From the album: *Pickin' up the Pieces*
Label: Epic
Year: 1969
Folk/rock supergroup evokes Buffalo Springfield and CSNY, but achieves the success of neither.

PICTURES OF LILY

Artist: The Who
Written by: Pete Townshend
From the album: *Magic Bus/The Who on Tour*
Label: Decca
Produced by: Kit Lambert
Year: 1967
Quintessential adolescent fantasy. Suggested segue: "She Bop" by Cyndi Lauper.

PICTURES OF MATCHSTICK MEN

Artist: Status Quo
Written by: Francis Michael Rossi
From the album: *Messages from the Status Quo*
Label: Concept
Produced by: John Schroeder
Year: 1968
Psychedelic relic was the first of their twenty-one Top 10 UK singles, and their only Top 20 US. Covered by Camper Van Beethoven (Virgin, '89).

PIECE OF CRAP

Artist: Neil Young
Written by: Neil Young
From the album: *Sleeps with Angels*

Label: Reprise
Produced by: David Briggs, Neil Young
Year: 1994
Typically Youngian rant.

PIECE OF MY HEART

Artist: Garnet Mimms & the Enchanters
Written by: Bert Berns (Bert Russell), Jerry
Ragovoy (Norman Meade)
Label: Shout
Produced by: Jerry Ragovoy
Year: 1967
Cover by Erma Franklin (Shout, '67) was a Top 10
R&B/Bottom 40 crossover. Career-defining cover
by Janis Joplin (Columbia, '68) went to #12.

PIED PIPER, THE

Artist: Changin' Times
Written by: Artie Kornfeld, Steve Duboff
Label: Philips
Year: 1965
Covered by Crispian St. Peters (Laurie, '66).

PIGGIES

Artist: The Beatles
Written by: George Harrison
From the album: *The Beatles*
Label: Apple
Produced by: George Martin
Year: 1968
Quintessential moralizing George.

PIGS ON THE WING (PART I)

Artist: Pink Floyd
Written by: Roger Waters
From the album: *Animals*
Label: Columbia
Produced by: Pink Floyd
Year: 1977
A love song.

PILLOW TALK

Artist: Sylvia
Written by: Sylvia Robinson, Michael Burton
From the album: *Pillow Talk*
Label: Vibration
Produced by: Sylvia Robinson, Michael Burton
Year: 1973
Sylvia breaks up with Mickey, goes to the disco and
scores. Rejected by Al Green as being too sexy. But
Donna Summer was paying attention in Germany.

PINBALL WIZARD

Artist: The Who
Written by: Pete Townshend
From the album: *Tommy*
Label: Decca
Produced by: Kit Lambert
Year: 1969
The title tune and first single (Top 20 US/#4 UK)
from the rock opera, leaving unanswered only one
question: Did Townshend ever play pinball?

PINCUSHION

Artist: ZZ Top
Written by: Billy Gibbons, Dusty Hill, Frank Beard
From the album: *Antenna*
Label: RCA
Year: 1994
Latter-day boogie.

PINHEAD

Artist: The Ramones
Written by: Douglas Colvin, John Cummings, Jeff
Hyman, Thomas Erdelyi
From the album: *Leave Home*
Label: Sire
Produced by: Tony Bongiovi, Thomas Erdelyi
Year: 1977
Perhaps a tribute to Foudini's dopey TV pal of the
'50s. Then again, probably not.

PINK

Artist: Aerosmith
Written by: Glen Ballard, Richard Supa, Stephen
Tyler
From the album: *Nine Lives*
Label: Columbia
Produced by: Kevin Shirley
Year: 1997
Back in the pink with all the underage girls and
overage women.

PINK BEDROOM

Artist: John Hiatt
Written by: John Hiatt
From the album: *Slug Line*
Label: MCA
Produced by: Denny Bruce
Year: 1979
Introducing the anti-Mellencamp, the song-writing
voice of maladjusted middle-America. Covered by
Lou Ann Barton, an Austin blues-rock protégé of
Stevie Ray Vaughan's (Spindletop, '86).

PINK CADILLAC

Artist: Bruce Springsteen
Written by: Bruce Springsteen
Label: Columbia
Produced by: Bruce Springsteen, Jon Landau,
Chuck Plotkin, Steve Van Zandt
Year: 1983
Classic car song; classic car, a big, wide Caddy,
only driven once by Aretha Franklin in the "Free-
way of Love" video. B-side of "Dancing in the
Dark." Covered by Natalie Cole (Manhattan, '87).

PINK CASHMERE

Artist: Prince
Written by: Prince Rogers Nelson
From the album: *The Hits/The B Sides*
Label: Paisley Park
Produced by: Prince
Year: 1993
It's official, pink is the new purple. Segue: "Purple
Toupe" by They Might Be Giants.

PINK HOUSES

Artist: John (Cougar) Mellencamp
Written by: John Cougar Mellencamp
From the album: *Uh-Huh*
Label: Riva
Produced by: Don Gehman, Little Bastard
Year: 1983
Updating Malvina Reynolds's "Little Boxes."

PINK MOON

Artist: Nick Drake
Written by: Nick Drake
From the album: *Pink Moon*
Label: Hannibal
Produced by: Joe Boyd
Year: 1972
Ultimate loner's lovelorn lament.

PINK PEGGED SLACKS

Artist: Eddie Cochran
Written by: Eddie Cochran, Hank Cochran, Jerry
Capeheart
From the album: *Singin' to My Baby*
Label: United Artists
Produced by: Snuff Garrett, Eddie Cochran, Jerry
Capeheart
Year: 1956
First single for the stylish rocker.

PINK SHOELACES

Artist: Dodie Stevens
Written by: Mickie Grant
From the album: *Dodie Stevens*
Label: Crystalette
Year: 1958
Top 40 fashion statement by the future author of
the Broadway musical *Don't Bother Me, I Can't Cope.*

PIPELINE

Artist: The Chantays
Written by: Bob Spickard, Brian Carman
From the album: *Pipeline*
Label: Dot
Produced by: Art Wenzel
Year: 1963
Bubbling surf instrumental.

PIRATE LOOKS AT FORTY, A

Artist: Jimmy Buffett
Written by: Jimmy Buffett
From the album: *A1A*
Label: Dunhill
Produced by: Don Gant
Year: 1974
From a Key West good-time vantage point—over a
tall, cool beverage.

PISS FACTORY

Artist: Patti Smith
Written by: Patti Smith, Richard Sohl

Label: M-R-L
Produced by: Lenny Kaye
Year: 1974
Legendary New York single (with "Hey Joe" on the B-side) from the fair rock and roll poet with the great rock and roll voice. Later on *Great N.Y. Singles* (ROIR, '75).

PLACE IN THE SUN, A

Artist: Stevie Wonder
Written by: Ronald Miller, Bryan Wells
From the album: *Down to Earth*
Label: Tamla
Produced by: Clarence Paul
Year: 1966
Inspiring wish fulfillment.

PLANET ROCK

Artist: Afrika Bambaataa and Soulsonic Force
Written by: Arthur Baker, Ellis Williams, John Miller, Bhambatta Aasim, Robert Allen, John Robie
From the album: *Planet Rock—The Album*
Label: Tommy Boy
Produced by: Arthur Baker
Year: 1982
A trailblazing alternative rap meets underground disco synthesis mixed by a future dance music legend, Jellybean Benitez. Soon the mixer would be up there with the producer as the key song-shaper of the '90s.

PLAY THAT FUNKY MUSIC

Artist: Wild Cherry
Written by: Robert Parissi
From the album: *Wild Cherry*
Label: Epic
Produced by: Robert Parissi
Year: 1976
One-shot disco era #1 R&B/#1 crossover.

PLAY WITH FIRE

Artist: The Rolling Stones
Written by: Mick Jagger, Keith Richards, Bill Wyman, Brian Jones, Charlie Watts
From the album: *Out of Our Heads*
Label: London
Produced by: Andrew Loog-Oldham
Year: 1965
For the first and probably only time, the entire group gets a songwriting credit. Phil Spector sits in on acoustic guitar.

PLAYBOY

Artist: The Marvelettes
Written by: Robert Bateman, William Stevenson, Brian Holland
From the album: *Playboy*
Label: Tamla
Produced by: Smokey Robinson, Brianbert

Year: 1962
Their second biggest hit.

PLAYBOYS AND PLAYGIRLS

Artist: Bob Dylan
Written by: Bob Dylan
From the album: *Newport, '63*
Label: Vanguard
Year: 1963
Defying the social order at the hallowed Newport Folk Festival in '63, two years before the deluge.

PLAYGROUND

Artist: Another Bad Creation
Written by: Dallas Austin, Michael Bivens, Kevin Wales
From the album: *Coolin' at the Playground Ya' Know*
Label: Motown
Produced by: Dallas Austin
Year: 1991
Acknowledging that it had been just about 20 years since the advent of the Jackson 5.

PLAYGROUND IN MY MIND

Artist: Clint Holmes
Written by: Paul Vance, Lee Pockriss
From the album: *Playground in My Mind*
Label: Epic
Produced by: Paul Vance
Year: 1973
Sophisticated bubblegum.

PLAYING IN THE BAND

Artist: Bob Weir
Written by: Robert Hunter, Bob Weir, Mickey Hart
From the album: *Ace*
Label: Warner Brothers
Year: 1971
Rhythm guitarist's cheerfully Dead-like anthem.

PLAYMATE

Artist: Pearls Before Swine
Written by: Saxie Dowell
From the album: *One Nation Underground*
Label: ESP
Produced by: Richard Alderson
Year: 1967
Authentic psychedelic underground oddity as sung by the wavery Tom Rapp.

PLEA, THE

Artist: The Chantels
Written by: Arlene Smith
From the album: *We Are the Chantels*
Label: End
Produced by: George Goldner, Richard Barrett
Year: 1957
Why isn't Arlene Smith in the Rock & Roll Hall of Fame?

PLEASANT VALLEY SUNDAY

Artist: The Monkees
Written by: Gerry Goffin, Carole King
From the album: *Pisces, Aquarius, Capricorn and Jones*
Label: Colgems
Produced by: Douglas Farthing Hatelid
Year: 1967
Among the producer's greatest works.

PLEASE COME TO BOSTON

Artist: Dave Loggins
Written by: Dave Loggins
From the album: *Apprentice in a Musical Workshop*
Label: Epic
Produced by: J. Crutchfield
Year: 1974
The first antirambling rock song, qualifying it as a middle-of-the-dirt-road anthem.

PLEASE DON'T GO

Artist: K. C. and the Sunshine Band
Written by: Harry Casey, Richard Finch
From the album: *Do You Wanna Go Party*
Label: TK
Produced by: Harry Casey, Richard Finch
Year: 1979
Their last #1 dance hit is a slow one.

PLEASE DON'T TAKE MY AIR JORDANS

Artist: Reg E. Gaines
Written by: Reg E. Gaines, Philip Damien
From the album: *Please Don't Take My Air Jordans*
Label: Mercury
Produced by: Philip Damien
Year: 1993
Where rap meets poetry on the slamming urban streets of upward mobility.

PLEASE HELP ME I'M FALLING

Artist: Hank Locklin
Written by: Don Robertson, Hal Blair
From the album: *Please Help Me I'm Falling*
Label: RCA
Year: 1960
#1 country/Top 10 crossover.

PLEASE LET ME WONDER

Artist: The Beach Boys
Written by: Brian Wilson, Mike Love
From the album: *Beach Boys Today*
Label: Capitol
Produced by: Brian Wilson
Year: 1965
The B-side of "Help Me, Rhonda."

PLEASE LOVE ME

Artist: B. B. King
Written by: B. B. King, Jules Taub

Label: RPM
Year: 1952
His third #1 R&B hit.

PLEASE LOVE ME FOREVER

Artist: Cathy Jean and the Roommates
Written by: Johnny Malone, Ollie Blanchard
From the album: *At the Hop*
Label: Valmor
Year: 1961
White doo-wop one-shot, girl-group style.

PLEASE MR. PLEASE

Artist: Olivia Newton-John
Written by: John Rostill, Bruce Welch
From the album: *Have You Never Been Mellow?*
Label: MCA
Produced by: John Farrar
Year: 1975
Suggested segue: "Don't Play That Song" by Aretha Franklin.

PLEASE MR. POSTMAN

Artist: The Marvelettes
Written by: Freddie Gorman, William Garrett, Brian Holland, Georgia Dobbins
From the album: *Please Mr. Postman*
Label: Tamla
Produced by: Brian Holland, Robert Bateman
Year: 1961
First and biggest hit for Motown's best girl group, a #1 R&B/#1 crossover. Covered by the Beatles (Capitol, '64). The Carpenters brought it to #1 again (A&M, '75).

PLEASE PLEASE ME

Artist: The Beatles
Written by: John Lennon, Paul McCartney
From the album: *Introducing the Beatles*
Label: Vee Jay
Produced by: George Martin
Year: 1963
Their first hit in England, a year before their ultimate crossover to the US.

PLEASE, PLEASE, PLEASE

Artist: James Brown and the Famous Flames
Written by: James Brown, Johnny Terry
From the album: *Please, Please, Please*
Label: Federal
Produced by: Ralph Bass
Year: 1956
With massive amounts of blood, sweat, soul, and intensity, James Brown begins a thirty-year career on the charts.

PLEASE SAY YOU WANT ME

Artist: The Schoolboys
Written by: Donald Hayes
Label: Okeh
Produced by: Leroy Kirkland
Year: 1957

On every urban streetcorner in the '50s, another Frankie Lymon, yearning for acceptance and assimilation.

PLEASE SEND ME SOMEONE TO LOVE

Artist: Percy Mayfield
Written by: Percy Mayfield
From the album: *Poet of the Blues*
Label: Specialty
Produced by: Art Rupe
Year: 1951
L.A. bluesman's most famous effort. Covered by the Moonglows (Chess, '57), Irma Thomas (Imperial, '64), B.B. King (Bluesway, '68), Solomon Burke (Bell, '69), Esther Phillips (Atlantic, '71), Paul Butterfield's Better Days (Bearsville, '73).

PLEASURE PRINCIPLE, THE

Artist: Janet Jackson
Written by: Monte Moir
From the album: *Control*
Label: A&M
Produced by: Monte Moir
Year: 1986
#1 R&B/Top 10 crossover.

PLEDGING MY LOVE

Artist: Johnny Ace
Written by: Don D.
From the album: *Memorial Album For Johnny Ace*
Produced by: Duke Washington, Ferdinand Robey
Year: 1954
In which the chilling and mournful Ace sings his own epitaph.

PLUSH

Stone Temple Pilots
Written by: Robert DeLeo, Scott Weiland, Dean DeLeo, Eric Kretz
From the album: *Core*
Label: Atlantic
Produced by: Brendan O'Brien
Year: 1993
The hard rock side of alt rock (or was it vice-versa).

PLYNTH (WATER DOWN THE DRAIN)

Artist: The Jeff Beck Group
Written by: Rod Stewart, Nicky Hopkins, Ron Wood
From the album: *Beck-ola*
Label: Epic
Produced by: Mickie Most
Year: 1968
High spot of Beck and Rod's second and last album.

POETRY IN MOTION

Artist: Johnny Tillotson
Written by: Paul Kaufman, Mike Anthony
From the album: *Johnny Tillotson's Best*

Label: Cadence
Produced by: Archie Bleyer
Year: 1960
His biggest hit. Segue: "Backfield in Motion" by Mel and Tim.

POETRY MAN

Artist: Phoebe Snow
Written by: Phoebe Snow Laub
From the album: *Phoebe Snow*
Label: Shelter
Produced by: Dino Airali
Year: 1973
Folkie jazz debut from the coffee houses of New Jersey, where lonely married men are prone to flirt with the hired help. Segue: "The Married Men" by the Roches.

POINT OF NO RETURN

Artist: Expose
Written by: Lewis Martinee
From the album: *Exposure*
Label: Arista
Produced by: Lewis Martinee
Year: 1987
The unstoppable sound of South Beach.

POISON

Artist: Bell Biv Devoe
Written by: Elliot Straite
From the album: *Poison*
Label: MCA
Produced by: Carl Bourelly, Dr. Freeze
Year: 1990
The '50s harmony ethos meets the '90s street.

POISON

Artist: Alice Cooper
Written by: Vincent Furnier (Alice Cooper), Desmond Child, John McCurry
From the album: *Trash*
Label: Epic
Produced by: Desmond Child
Year: 1989

POISON IVY

Artist: The Coasters
Written by: Jerry Leiber, Mike Stoller
From the album: *Yakety Yak*
Label: Atco
Produced by: Jerry Leiber, Mike Stoller
Year: 1959
Their third Top 10 hit of '59 (and fourth #1 R&B overall). Covered by the Kingsmen (Wand, '65), the Rolling Stones (London, '72).

POLICE AND THIEVES

Artist: Junior Murvin
Written by: Junior Murvin
From the album: *Police and Thieves*
Label: Mango
Produced by: Lee Perry

Year: 1976
Subversive reggae classic. Covered by the Clash (Epic, '79).

POLICY OF TRUTH

Artist: Depeche Mode
Written by: Martin Gore
From the album: *Violator*
Label: Sire
Produced by: Depeche Mode, Flood
Year: 1990

POLITICAL SCIENCE

Artist: Randy Newman
Written by: Randy Newman
From the album: *Sail Away*
Label: Warner Brothers
Produced by: Russ Titelman, Lenny Waronker
Year: 1972
Newman's take on *Dr. Strangelove*: "Let's drop the big one and see what happens."

POLITICIAN

Artist: Cream
Written by: Jack Bruce, Pete Brown
From the album: *Wheels of Fire*
Label: Atco
Produced by: Felix Pappalardi
Year: 1968
Segue: "Taxman" by George Harrison.

POLYTHENE PAM

Artist: The Beatles
Written by: John Lennon, Paul McCartney
From the album: *Abbey Road*
Label: Apple
Produced by: George Martin
Year: 1969

PONY

Artist: Ginuine
Written by: Elgin Lumpkin, Tim Mosley, Steve Garrett
From the album: *Ginuine the Bachelor*
Label: 550 Music
Year: 1996
Loping hip hop novelty.

PONY TIME

Artist: Don Covay
Written by: Don Covay, John Berry
Label: Arnold
Produced by: Don Covay
Year: 1961
Six months after "The Twist" and four months after his cover of "The Hucklebuck" merely dented the Top 20, Chubby Checker was back at the top covering a newer dance (Parkway, '62), this one created by Covay's group, the Goodtimers.

POOR LITTLE FOOL

Artist: Ricky Nelson

Written by: Sharon Sheeley
From the album: *Ricky Nelson*
Label: Imperial
Produced by: Ricky Nelson
Year: 1958
His biggest hit of the '50s, also his biggest country/R&B crossover, written by Eddie Cochran's star-crossed girlfriend.

POOR POOR PITIFUL ME

Artist: Warren Zevon
Written by: Warren Zevon
From the album: *Warren Zevon*
Label: Asylum
Produced by: Jackson Browne
Year: 1976
Early ode to self-deprecation. Covered by Linda Ronstadt (Asylum, '77). Suggested segue: "Mr. Pitiful" by Otis Redding.

POOR SIDE OF TOWN

Artist: Johnny Rivers
Written by: Johnny Rivers, Lou Adler
From the album: *Changes*
Label: Imperial
Produced by: Lou Adler
Year: 1966
Segue: "Patches" by Dickie Lee.

POP LIFE

Artist: Prince
Written by: Prince Rogers Nelson
From the album: *Around the World in a Day*
Label: Warner Brothers
Produced by: Prince
Year: 1985

POP MUZIK

Artist: M
Written by: Robin Scott
From the album: *New York-London-Paris-Munich*
Label: Sire
Produced by: Robin Scott
Year: 1979
Trans-Atlantic dance sensation.

POPCORN, THE

Artist: James Brown
Written by: James Brown
From the album: *The Popcorn*
Label: King
Produced by: James Brown
Year: 1969
Instrumental mother of "Mother Popcorn" and all subsequent popcorns, including "Lowdown Popcorn," and "Let a Man Come in and Do the Popcorn (Parts I and II)."

POPSICLES AND ICICLES

Artist: The Murmaids
Written by: David Gates
Label: Chattahoochee

Produced by: Kim Fowley
Year: 1963
The Brill Building sound of L.A. Like trains in the station going in opposite directions, Gates would move to Bread, Fowley to the Runaways.

POPULAR

Artist: Nada Surf
Written by: Matthew Caws, David Lorca
From the album: *High/Low*
Label: Elektra
Produced by: Ric Ocasek
Year: 1996
Brilliant prose poetry on the state of the art of high school bitchery. Segue: "The Sweater" by Meryn Cadell.

PORCELAIN

Artist: Moby
Written by: Richard Melville (Moby) Hall
From the album: *Play*
Label: V2
Produced by: Moby
Year: 1999
Moody techno dance track, heard widely in trendy places like Starbucks, Eddie Bauer, and the Pottery Barn.

PORPOISE SONG, THE

Artist: The Monkees
Written by: Gerry Goffin, Carole King
From the album: *Head!*
Label: Colgems
Produced by: Gerry Goffin
Year: 1968
Theme from the roundly misunderstood cult classic *Head!*, which marked the official demise of the Monkees. Soon Peter Tork would be living in a rented room in the mansion he once owned.

POSITIVELY 4TH STREET

Artist: Bob Dylan
Written by: Bob Dylan
From the album: *Bob Dylan's Greatest Hits*
Label: Columbia
Produced by: Bob Johnston
Year: 1965
A new-fashioned tongue lashing directed at his cronies from the old neighborhood. Covered by Victoria Williams (Razor & Tie, '93), the Beat Farmers (Sector 2, '95). Would become the title of David Hajdu's provocative book on Dylan, Baez and the sixties.

POSSESSION

Artist: Sarah McLachlan
Written by: Sarah McLachlan
From the album: *Fumbling Towards Ecstacy*
Produced by: Pierre Marchand
Label: Arista
Year: 1994
Finding her voice, midway between folk/rock and pop.

POUR SOME SUGAR ON ME

Artist: Def Leppard
Written by: Steve Clark, Joe Elliott, Robert John "Mutt" Lange, Phil Collen, Rick Savage
From the album: *Hysteria*
Label: Mercury
Produced by: Mutt Lange
Year: 1988
Sweet taste of success; second Top 10 hit from the album.

POURING IT ALL OUT

Artist: Graham Parker
Written by: Graham Parker
From the album: *Heat Treatment*
Label: Mercury
Produced by: Mutt Lange
Year: 1976
His soulful rage finds momentary release.

POWDERFINGER

Artist: Neil Young
Written by: Neil Young
From the album: *Rust Never Sleeps*
Label: Reprise
Produced by: Neil Young, Tim Mulligan, David Briggs
Year: 1979
Covered by the Cowboy Junkies (RCA, '90).

POWER

Artist: The Doobie Brothers, John Hall and James Taylor
Written by: John J. Hall, Johanna Hall
From the album: *No Nukes*
Label: Asylum
Produced by: John Hall, Jackson Browne, Bonnie Raitt, Graham Nash
Year: 1979
Antinuke folk/rock all-star harmonizing. The Halls would write "Still the One" for John's group, Orleans.

POWER AND THE GLORY, THE

Artist: Phil Ochs
Written by: Phil Ochs
From the album: *All the News That's Fit to Sing*
Label: Elektra
Produced by: Paul Rothchild, Jac Holzman
Year: 1963
Patriotic protest by the Ohio song journalist, covered in an irony Ochs himself was the first to appreciate, by his natural political archrival, Anita Bryant (Columbia, '67).

POWER OF GOODBYE, THE

Artist: Madonna
Written by: Madonna Cicconne, Rich Nowels
From the album: *Ray of Light*
Label: Maverick
Year: 1998
She delivers a big movie ballad.

POWER OF LOVE, THE

Artist: Huey Lewis and the News
Written by: Chris Hayes, Huey Lewis, Johnny Colla
From the album: *Back to the Future Soundtrack*
Label: Chrysalis
Produced by: Huey Lewis and the News
Year: 1985
Their first #1, from the classic film *Back to the Future*.

POWER OF TWO

Artist: The Indigo Girls
Written by: Emily Saliers
From the album: *Swamp Ophelia*
Label: Epic
Produced by: Peter Collins
Year: 1994
The Simon and Garfunkel of the '90s, transmogrified, with a great song about togetherness.

POWER, THE

Artist: Snap
Written by: Benito Benites, John Garrett III, Deron Butler, Toni C.
From the album: *World Power*
Label: Arista
Produced by: Snap
Year: 1990
Monster club crossover.

POWER TO THE PEOPLE

Artist: John Lennon
Written by: John Lennon
From the album: *Shaved Fish*
Label: Apple
Produced by: Phil Spector
Year: 1970
A classic marching song, nearing the end of the era of marches.

PRAISE YOU

Artist: Fatboy Slim
Written by: Quentin Leo Cook, Camille Yarborough
From the album: *You've Come a Long Way Baby*
Label: Skint/Astralwerks
Produced by: Norman Cook
Year: 1999
Dance-hall maverick scores big at the dance-hall nevertheless.

PRAY

Artist: M. C. Hammer
Written by: Prince Rogers Nelson, M. C. Hammer (Stanley Burrell)
From the album: *Please Hammer Don't Hurt 'Em*
Label: Capitol
Produced by: Hammer
Year: 1990

PRAYER FOR THE DYING

Artist: Seal
Written by: Sealhenry Samuel, Isidore
From the album: *Seal*
Label: ZTT/Sire
Produced by: Trevor Horn
Year: 1994
Poignant antigangsta rap warning.

PRAYING FOR TIME

Artist: George Michael
Written by: George Michael
From the album: *Listen Without Prejudice (Vol. I)*
Label: Columbia
Produced by: George Michael
Year: 1990
Having paid the price of fame with critical disdain, George settles for another #1.

PRECIOUS AND FEW

Artist: Climax
Written by: Walter Nims
From the album: *Climax*
Label: Carousel
Produced by: Larry Cox
Year: 1972
Featuring the voice of Sonny Geraci, last heard on "Time Won't Let Me" by the Outsiders.

PRECIOUS DECLARATION

Artist: Collective Soul
Written by: Ed Roland
From the album: *Disciplined Breakdown*
Label: Atlantic
Produced by: Ed Roland, Matt Serletic
Year: 1997

PRESENCE OF THE LORD

Artist: Blind Faith
Written by: Eric Clapton
From the album: *Blind Faith*
Label: Atco
Produced by: Jimmy Miller
Year: 1969
Cream meets Traffic at the crossroads of progressive rock and gospel.

PRESSURE DROP

Artist: Toots and the Maytals
Written by: Frederick Toots Hibbert
Label: Trojan
Produced by: Leslie Kong
Year: 1970
Reggae classic included on the *The Harder They Come* Soundtrack. Covered by Robert Palmer (Island, '75), the Clash (Epic, '80), Izzy Stradlin (Geffen, '92).

PRETENDER, THE

Artist: Jackson Browne
Written by: Jackson Browne
From the album: *The Pretender*
Label: Asylum
Produced by: Jon Landau
Year: 1976
Epic statement falls short.

PRETTY BALLERINA

Artist: The Left Banke
Written by: Michael Brown
From the album: *Walk Away Renee/Pretty Ballerina*
Label: Smash
Produced by: Harry Lookofsky, Bill Jerome, Steve Jerome
Year: 1967
Art-pop swan song, the result of too much hanging out at the ASCAP building, right across the street from Lincoln Center.

PRETTY BOY FLOYD

Artist: Rambling Jack Elliot
Written by: Woody Guthrie
From the album: *Jack Elliott Sings the Songs of Woody Guthrie*
Label: Prestige
Year: 1957
Written in 1942, this song advances the radical notion of the noble outlaw as common man and the system as villain, from which the cause of rock and roll, punk rock, outlaw country and rap will prove inextricable. Covered by Joan Baez (Vanguard, '62), the Byrds (Columbia, '68), Melanie (Neighborhood, '73), Bob Dylan (Columbia, '88).

PRETTY FLAMINGO

Artist: Manfred Mann
Written by: Mark Barkan
From the album: *Pretty Flamingo*
Label: United Artists
Produced by: John Burgess
Year: 1966
Covered by Tommy Roe (ABC/Paramount, '66), Rod Stewart (Warner Brothers, '76).

PRETTY FLY FOR A WHITE GUY

Artist: Offspring
Written by: Offspring
From the album: *Americana*
Label: Epic
Year: 1998
Attempting to cope with the rap takeover, with typical hipster mock self-awareness.

PRETTY GIRLS EVERYWHERE

Artist: Eugene Church
Written by: Eugene Church, Thomas Williams
Label: Class

Year: 1959
Top 10 R&B/Top 40 beach music crossover.

PRETTY IN PINK

Artist: The Psychedelic Furs
Written by: Richard Butler, Tim Butler, John Ashton, Vincent Ely, Roger Morris
From the album: *Talk Talk Talk*
Label: Columbia
Produced by: Steve Lillywhite
Year: 1981
Updated folk/rocker, with a touch of Velvet. Inspired the '86 movie *Pretty in Pink*, and served as its title track.

PRETTY LITTLE ANGEL EYES

Artist: Curtis Lee
Written by: Tommy Boyce, Curtis Lee
Label: Dunes
Produced by: Phil Spector
Year: 1961
Brill Building soul reaches Spectorian perfection.

PRETTY ON THE INSIDE

Artist: Hole
Written by: Hole
From the album: *Pretty on the Inside*
Label: Caroline
Produced by: Kim Gordon, Don Fleming
Year: 1991
Hoisting a glass to the punk poet Patty Smith.

PRETTY THING

Artist: Bo Diddley
Written by: Willie Dixon
From the album: *Bo Diddley*
Label: Checker
Produced by: Willie Dixon
Year: 1958

PRETTY VACANT

Artist: The Sex Pistols
Written by: Steve Jones, Paul Cook, Glen Matlock, John Lydon (Johnny Rotten)
From the album: *Never Mind the Bollocks, Here's the Sex Pistols*
Label: Warner Brothers
Produced by: Chris Thomas, Bill Price
Year: 1977
A worldview and a legacy.

PRICE OF LOVE

Artist: The Everly Brothers
Written by: Don Everly, Phil Everly
From the album: *In Our Image*
Label: Warner Brothers
Year: 1965
One of their favorite concert openers, this was a #2 hit in England, where it was heard and eventually covered by Bryan Ferry (Polydor, '77).

PRIDE (IN THE NAME OF LOVE)

Artist: U2
Written by: Paul Hewson (Bono), Dave Evans (Edge), Adam Clayton, Larry Mullen
From the album: *The Unforgettable Fire*
Label: Island
Produced by: Brian Eno, Daniel Lanois
Year: 1984
Cracking the American Top 40 with a stirring tribute to Martin Luther King Jr.

PRIDE AND JOY

Artist: David Coverdale and Jimmy Page
Written by: Jimmy Page, David Coverdale
From the album: *Coverdale/Page*
Label: Geffen
Year: 1993
Metal throwdown.

PRIDE AND JOY

Artist: Marvin Gaye
Written by: Marvin Gaye, Norman Whitfield, William Stevenson
From the album: *Marvin Gaye/Greatest Hits*
Label: Tamla
Produced by: William Stevenson
Year: 1963
His first big hit; #2 R&B/Top 10 crossover.

PRIDE AND JOY

Artist: Stevie Ray Vaughan
Written by: Stevie Ray Vaughan
From the album: *Texas Flood*
Label: Epic
Produced by: Stevie Ray Vaughan, Double Trouble, Richard Mullen
Year: 1983
An early defining blues guitar classic.

PRIDE OF MAN

Artist: Quicksilver Messenger Service
Written by: Hamilton Camp
From the album: *Quicksilver Messenger Service*
Label: Capitol
Produced by: Nick Gravenites, Harvey Brooks
Year: 1968
Biblical folk/rocker, introduced by Bob (Hamilton) Camp, became a psychedelic staple. Covered by the Washington Squares (Gold Castle, '89).

PRINCE, THE

Artist: Diamond Head
Written by: Sean Harris, Brian Tatler
From the album: *Lightning to the Nations*
Produced by: Sean Harris, Brian Tatler
Label: Earmark
Year: 1982
Metallica was listening, as well as wearing the band's t-shirts.

PRISONER OF LIFE

Artist: Johnny Adams
Written by: Doc Pomus, Mack Rebennack
From the album: *Johnny Adams Sings Doc Pomus*
Label: Rounder
Year: 1991
This inspired collaboration between two revered rock and roll doctors (Pomus and John) found its way into the Robert Altman movie *Short Cuts*, performed by the legendary swinger, Annie Ross.

PRISONER OF LOVE

Artist: James Brown and the Famous Flames
Written by: Leo Robin, Russ Columbo, Clarence Gaskill
From the album: *Prisoner of Love*
Label: King
Produced by: James Brown
Year: 1963
Brown's eighteenth R&B hit was his first Top-20 crossover. Originated by Russ Columbo in '31.

PRIVATE EYES

Artist: Daryl Hall & John Oates
Written by: Daryl Hall, Janna Allen, Sara Allen, Warren Pash
From the album: *Private Eyes*
Label: RCA
Produced by: Hall and Oates
Year: 1981
Their second #1 of '81.

PRIVATE IDAHO

Artist: The B-52's
Written by: Fred Schneider, Ricky Wilson, Cindy Wilson, Keith Strickland, Kate Pierson
From the album: *Wild Planet*
Label: Warner Brothers
Produced by: Rhett Davies, the B-52's
Year: 1980
Advancing their kitschy disco vision with an all-purpose metaphor.
Ten years later, the movie *My Own Private Idaho* would take it to extremes

PROBLEMS

Artist: The Everly Brothers
Written by: Boudleaux Bryant, Felice Bryant
From the album: *The Everly Brothers Best*
Label: Cadence
Produced by: Archie Bleyer
Year: 1958
Suggested segue: "Help" by the Beatles, "19TH Nervous Breakdown" by the Rolling Stones, "At Seventeen" by Janis Ian.

PROMISE OF A NEW DAY

Artist: Paula Abdul
Written by: Peter Lord, Sondra St. Victor, V. Jeffrey Smith, Paula Abdul
From the album: *Spellbound*
Label: Virgin
Produced by: Peter Lord
Year: 1991
A good voice and a good era for pop/rock teen love ballads.

PROMISE, THE

Artist: Bruce Springsteen
Written by: Bruce Springsteen
From the album: *Tracks*
Label: Columbia
Year: 1999
Rekindling his proleteriat passions.

PROMISED LAND

Artist: Chuck Berry
Written by: Chuck Berry
From the album: *St. Louis to Liverpool*
Label: Chess
Produced by: Leonard Chess, Phil Chess
Year: 1964
Closing out his '64 comeback with his fifth chart record of the year.

PROMISES

Artist: Eric Clapton
Written by: Richard Feldman, Roger Linn
From the album: *Backless*
Label: RSO
Produced by: Glyn Johns
Year: 1978
Top 10 tune done in Tulsa time.

PROUD MARY

Artist: Creedence Clearwater Revival
Written by: John C. Fogerty
From the album: *Bayou Country*
Label: Fantasy
Produced by: John C. Fogerty
Year: 1969
First of three amazing singles to peak at #2 in '69. Country cover by Anthony Armstrong Jones (Chart, '69), top 5 R&B/Top 5 crossover by Ike and Tina Turner (Liberty, '71).

PROUD TO FALL

Artist: Ian McCullough
Written by: Ian McCullough
From the album: *Candleland*
Label: Sire
Year: 1989
Solo hit for the Echo & the Bunnymen lead singer.

PROVE IT ALL NIGHT

Artist: Bruce Springsteen
Written by: Bruce Springsteen
From the album: *Darkness on the Edge of Town*
Label: Columbia
Produced by: Jon Landau, Bruce Springsteen
Year: 1978
His version of "Sixty Minute Man" was an apt appraisal of his legendary performing prowess.

PSYCHEDELIC SHACK

Artist: The Temptations
Written by: Norman Whitfield, Barrett Strong
From the album: *Psychedelic Shack*
Label: Gordy
Produced by: Norman Whitfield
Year: 1969
Motown visits San Francisco; San Francisco wins.

PSYCHO CIRCUS

Artist: Kiss
Written by: Paul Stanley, Chris Cuomo
From the album: *Psycho Circus*
Label: Mercury
Produced by: Bruce Fairbairn
Year: 1998
Kiss fans are still fanatic.

PSYCHO KILLER

Artist: Talking Heads
Written by: David Byrne, Tina Weymouth, Chris Frantz
From the album: *Talking Heads '77*
Label: Sire
Produced by: Tony Bongiovi, Lance Quinn, Talking Heads
Year: 1977
The auspicious debut of the artsy, proto-nerd band from the Rhode Island School of Design, a tribute to New York-based serial killer David Berkowitz, with some of the lyrics in French.

PSYCHOTIC REACTION

Artist: The Count Five
Written by: Ken Ellner, Roy Chaney, Craig Atkinson, John Byrne, John Michalski
From the album: *Psychotic Reaction*
Label: Double Shot
Produced by: Joe Hooven, Hal Wynn
Year: 1966
Garage band psychedelia from San Jose.

PUBLIC EXECUTION, A

Artist: Mouse
Written by: Knox Henderson, Ronny Weiss
Label: Fratemity
Year: 1966
Only in the '60s.

PUFF (THE MAGIC DRAGON)

Artist: Peter, Paul & Mary
Written by: Peter Yarrow, Leonard Lipton
From the album: *Moving*
Label: Warner Brothers
Produced by: Albert Grossman, Milt Okun
Year: 1963
The first drug song for children, if you believed the urban legends, or the censors.

PULL UP TO THE BUMPER

Artist: Grace Jones
Written by: Sly Dunbar, Robbie Shakespeare, Dan Manno
From the album: *Nightclubbing*
Label: Island
Produced by: Sly Dunbar, Robbie Shakespeare
Year: 1981
Mondo-bizarro model turned disco singer delivers her ultimate manifesto, propelled by the reggae rhythm section turned funk superstars.

PULLING MUSSELS (FROM A SHELL)

Artist: Squeeze
Written by: Chris Difford, Glenn Tilbrook
From the album: *Argybargy*
Label: A&M
Produced by: Squeeze, John Wood
Year: 1980
Defining their parlor-room soul.

PUMP IT UP

Artist: Elvis Costello
Written by: Declan McManus (Elvis Costello)
From the album: *This Year's Model*
Label: Columbia
Produced by: Nick Lowe
Year: 1978
One of his most enduring verbal flights. Suggested segue: "Subterranean Homesick Blues" by Bob Dylan.

PUMP UP THE JAM

Artist: Technotronic featuring Felly
Written by: Manuella Kamosi, Thomas De Quincey (Jo Bogaert)
From the album: *Pump up the Jam—the Album*
Label: Arista
Produced by: Jo Bogaert
Year: 1989
Undeniable dance-hall smash.

PUMP UP THE VOLUME

Artist: M.A.R.R.S.
Written by: Steve Young, Andrew Biggs
Label: 4TH and Broadway
Produced by: Martyn Young
Year: 1988
Enormous dance hit in the U.S. and London.

PUNK ROCK GIRL

Artist: Dead Milkmen
Written by: Dead Milkmen
From the album: *Beezlebubba*
Label: Enigma
Produced by: Brian Beattie, Mike Stewart
Year: 1989
Leaders of the suburban punk garage movement of the '80s finally achieve a semiclassic.

PUPPET ON A STRING

Artist: Sandie Shaw
Written by: Phil Coulter, Bill Martin
Label: Pye
Year: 1967
Big international contest winner is the third #1 UK for the English thrush who never had much success over here.

PUPPY LOVE

Artist: Paul Anka
Written by: Paul Anka
From the album: *Paul Anka Sings His Big 15*
Label: ABC–Paramount
Produced by: Don Costa
Year: 1960
Trying out for Vegas, even though he wasn't old enough to drink, Anka's sedate take on his teen romance with Annette is as cute and cuddly as a baby schnauzer. The only thing to fear was the cover, by the similarly eager Donny Osmond, a mere twelve years later (MGM, '72).

PURE AND EASY

Artist: Pete Townshend
Written by: Pete Townshend
From the album: *Who Came First*
Label: Track
Produced by: Glyn Johns
Year: 1972
Reflecting a newfound but short-lived contentment.

PURPLE HAZE

Artist: Jimi Hendrix
Written by: Jimi Hendrix
From the album: *Are You Experienced?*
Label: Reprise
Produced by: Chas Chandler
Year: 1967
The aural equivalent of the acid experience on electric guitar: life-changing, life-threatening, and revealingly unreal. Made the Top 10 in England, Bottom 40 here.

PURPLE PEOPLE EATER, THE

Artist: Sheb Wooley
Written by: Sheb Wooley
From the album: *Sheb Wooley*
Label: M-G-M
Produced by: Neeley Plumb
Year: 1958
Novelty hit.

PURPLE RAIN

Artist: Prince
Written by: Prince Rogers Nelson
From the album: *Purple Rain Soundtrack*
Label: Warner Brothers
Produced by: Prince

Year: 1984
Third hit from the biopic.

PURPLE TOUPEE

Artist: They Might Be Giants
Written by: John Flansburgh, John Linnell
From the album: *Lincoln*
Label: Restless
Produced by: Bill Kraus
Year: 1988
Wordy Brooklynites perform their tribute to Prince and the '60s.

PUSH

Artist: Matchbox Twenty
Written by: Matt Serletic, Rob Thomas
From the album: *Yourself or Someone Like You*
Label: Lava
Produced by: Matt Serletic
Year: 1997
Not really mysogynistic, just aggravated.

PUSH IT

Artist: Salt-n-Pepa
Written by: Herb Azor
From the album: *Hot, Cool, and Vicious*
Label: Next Plateau
Produced by: Herby Luv Bug
Year: 1988
First hit for the aggressive female hip-hop trio covers all the bases from the Kinks to Van Halen to Devo.

PUSH TH' LITTLE DAISIES

Artist: Ween
Written by: Aaron Freeman, Michael Melchiardo
From the album: *Pure Guava*
Label: Elektra
Year: 1993
Nerd/rock with a clip-on penknife.

PUSHER, THE

Artist: Steppenwolf
Written by: Hoyt Axton
From the album: *Steppenwolf*
Label: Ode
Produced by: Gabriel Mekler
Year: 1968
Antidrug lament, featured in *Easy Rider*. Suggested segues: "The Needle and the Damage Done" by Neil Young, "That Smell" by Lynyrd Skynyrd.

PUSHERMAN

Artist: Curtis Mayfield
Written by: Curtis Mayfield
From the album: *Superfly Soundtrack*
Label: Curtom
Produced by: Curtis Mayfield
Year: 1972

Gangsta rap, without the rap. Suggested segue: "Home Is Where the Hatred Is" by Gil Scott-Heron.

PUSHIN' TOO HARD

Artist: The Seeds
Written by: Sky Saxon
From the album: *Pushin' Too Hard*
Label: GNP-Crescendo
Produced by: Marcus Tybalt
Year: 1967
The ultimate garage anthem, whose place in history was sealed by its inclusion in the Jack Nicholson pre-*Easy Rider* classic *Psyche Out*.

PUSHOVER

Artist: Etta James
Written by: Roquel Davis (Tyran Carlo), Tony Clarke
From the album: *Etta James' Top Ten*
Label: Argo
Year: 1963
Top 10 R&B/Top 30 crossover.

PUT A LITTLE LOVE IN YOUR HEART

Artist: Jackie Deshannon
Written by: Jimmy Holiday, Randy Myers, Jackie DeShannon
From the album: *Put a Little Love in Your Heart*
Label: Imperial
Produced by: VME
Year: 1969
Her biggest hit. Covered by the Circle Jerks (Faulty Products, '82), Annie Lennox and Al Green in the '88 movie *Scrooged*.

PUT ME ON TOP

Artist: Aimee Mann
Written by: Aimee Mann
From the album: *Whatever*
Produced by: Jon Brion
Label: Geffen
Year: 1993
Out of 'Til Tuesday, Aimee Mann makes her case, sexually and professionally.

PUT YOUR HAND IN THE HAND

Artist: Anne Murray
Written by: Gene Maclellan
From the album: *Snowbird*
Label: Capitol
Produced by: Brian Ahern
Year: 1970
Top 40 pop-gospelizing was nearly the follow-up single to "Snowbird." Instead, another Canadian act, Ocean (Kama Sutra, '71) had a Top 10 hit with it.

PUT YOUR HANDS WHERE MY EYES COULD SEE

Artist: Busta Rhymes
Written by: Trevor Smith, Darrol Durant, R. Munroe, Jimmy Seals
From the album: *When Disaster Strikes*
Label: Elektra
Produced by: Shamello, Buddah
Year: 1997
Big rap track.

PUT YOUR HEAD ON MY SHOULDER

Artist: Paul Anka
Written by: Paul Anka
From the album: *Paul Anka Sings His Big 15*
Label: ABC-Paramount
Produced by: Don Costa
Year: 1959

PUTTIN' ON THE RITZ

Artist: Taco
Written by: Irving Berlin
From the album: *After Eight*
Label: RCA
Produced by: David Parker
Year: 1983
Eternal disco novelty, complete with megaphone. Introduced by Harry Richman (Brunswick, '30). Suggested segue: "Winchester Cathedral" by the New Vaudeville Band.

PUTTY IN YOUR HANDS

Artist: The Shirelles
Written by: John Patton, Edward Snyder
From the album: *Baby, It's You*
Label: Scepter
Produced by: Luther Dixon
Year: 1962
Covered by the Yardbirds (Epic, '65).

Q

QUARTER TO THREE

Artist: Gary US Bonds
Written by: Frank J. Guida, Gene Barge, Joe Royster, Gary Anderson (US Bonds)
From the album: *Dance 'Til Quarter to Three*
Label: LeGrand
Produced by: Frank J. Guida
Year: 1961
Stoking the relentless dance groove of '61. Gene Barge on sax became better known as Daddy Gee; the rhythm track, entitled "A Night with Daddy Gee," rewritten by Bonds, was provided by the very Church Street Five mentioned in the lyrics.

QUEEN IS DEAD, THE

Artist: The Smiths
Written by: Stephen Morrissey, Johnny Marr

From the album: *The Queen Is Dead*
Label: Sire
Produced by: Stephen Morrissey, Johnny Marr
Year: 1986
Answering "Anarchy in the UK," by the Sex Pistols.

QUEEN JANE APPROXIMATELY

Artist: Bob Dylan
Written by: Bob Dylan
From the album: *Highway 61 Revisited*
Label: Columbia
Produced by: Tom Wilson
Year: 1965
Reverential reference to his one-time benefactress Baez.

QUEEN OF HEARTS

Artist: Dave Edmunds
Written by: Hank DeVito
From the album: *Repeat When Necessary*
Label: Swan Song
Year: 1979
Cover by Juice Newton (Capitol, '81) was #1 country/Top 10 crossover, produced by Edmunds.

QUEEN OF THE HOP

Artist: Bobby Darin
Written by: Woody Harris, Bobby Darin
From the album: *The Bobby Darin Story*
Label: Atco
Produced by: Ahmet Ertegun
Year: 1958
Follow-up to "Splish Splash." Segue: "Queen of the Beach" by Carole King.

QUESTION

Artist: The Moody Blues
Written by: Justin Hayward
From the album: *A Question of Balance*
Label: Threshold
Produced by: Tony Clarke
Year: 1970
This first instance of new-age arena rock is their biggest UK hit.

QUICK ONE WHILE HE'S AWAY, A

Artist: The Who
Written by: Pete Townshend
From the album: *Happy Jack*
Label: Decca
Produced by: Kit Lambert
Year: 1967
Practicing for *Tommy* with a ten-minute mini rock-opera. Segue: *SF Sorrow* by the Pretty Things,

QUICKSAND

Artist: Martha & the Vandellas
Written by: Eddie Holland, Lamont Dozier, Brian Holland

From the album: *Greatest Hits*
Label: Gordy
Produced by: Brian Holland, Lamont Dozier
Year: 1963
Follow-up to "Heat Wave."

QUIET STORM

Artist: Smokey Robinson
Written by: Smokey Robinson, Rose Ella Jones
From the album: *Quiet Storm*
Label: Tamla
Produced by: Smokey Robinson
Year: 1976
Minor impact on the charts, major impact on the course of R&B radio.

QUIT PLAYING GAMES (WITH MY HEART)

Artist: Backstreet Boys
Written by: Max Martin, Herbert Crichlow
From the album: *Backstreet Boys*
Label: Jive
Year: 1997
The new kids on the boy band harmony block.

QUITS

Artist: Gary Stewart
Written by: Danny O'Keefe
Label: RCA
Year: 1975
Early classic of outlaw country. O'Keefe's compositions include "Good Time Charlie's Got the Blues" and "The Road."

R

RACE WITH THE DEVIL

Artist: Gene Vincent
Written by: Gene Vincent, Sheriff Tex Davis
Label: Capitol
Produced by: Ken Nelson
Year: 1956
Covered by Stray Cats (EMI, '86).

RADAR LOVE

Artist: Golden Earring
Written by: Barry Hays, George Kooymans
From the album: *Moontan*
Label: Track
Produced by: Shell Schellekens
Year: 1974
Eurometal CB radio classic. Covered by White Lion (Atlantic, '89). Segue: "I Can't Drive 55" by Sammy Hagar.

RADIATION VIBE

Artist: Fountains of Wayne
Written by: Chris Collingwood, Adam Schlesinger
From the album: *Fountains of Wayne*

Label: Tag
Produced by: Adam Schlesinger
Year: 1996
In the pure American pop tradition of Marshall Crenshaw.

RADIO FREE EUROPE

Artist: R.E.M.
Written by: Michael Stipe, Peter Buck, Bill Berry, Mike Mills
From the album: *Chronic Town*
Label: Hibtone
Produced by: Mitch Easter, Don Dixon
Year: 1980
Like its historical counterpart, this plucky little tune came whistling out of the static of Reagan-era America, carrying with it the ineffable sound of freedom to a downtrodden generation of starving Top-40 diehards. Taking wing like the Byrds out of ancient Athens, the dreamsound of R.E.M. was borne on the wings of an aching emptiness only a rootsy, poetic, three-chord band could counter. Suggested segues: "Mexican Radio" by Wall of Voodoo, "Mohammed's Radio" by Warren Zevon, "Radio Radio" by Elvis Costello, "I Can't Live without My Radio" by L L Cool J, "Video Killed the Radio Star" by the Buggles.

RADIO RADIO

Artist: Elvis Costello
Written by: Declan McManus (Elvis Costello)
From the album: *This Year's Model*
Label: Columbia
Produced by: Nick Lowe
Year: 1978
An anthem for anyone who's ever bitten the hand that feeds them. Costello sang this antimedia/anti-audience song, orginally called "Radio Soul," during his first appearance on *Saturday Night Live* in defiance of the producer, and was banned from further shows forthwith. Later he would redeem himself with a winning self-parody on *The Larry Sanders Show*

RADIO WAVES

Artist: Roger Waters
Written by: Roger Waters
From the album: *K.A.O.S.*
Label: Columbia
Year: 1987

RAG DOLL

Artist: Aerosmith
Written by: Steven Tyler, Joe Perry, Jim Valliance, Holly Knight
From the album: *Permanent Vacation*
Label: Geffen
Produced by: Bruce Fairbairn
Year: 1987

RAG DOLL

Artist: Four Seasons
Written by: Bob Gaudio, Bob Crewe

From the album: *Rag Doll*
Label: Philips
Produced by: Bob Crewe
Year: 1964
Defining their quintessential New Jersey attraction for the underdog.

RAG, MAMA, RAG

Artist: The Band
Written by: Robbie Robertson
From the album: *The Band*
Label: Capitol
Produced by: John Simon, the Band
Year: 1968
Cajun jug-band music.

RAIN

Artist: The Beatles
Written by: John Lennon, Paul McCartney
From the album: *Hey Jude*
Label: Capitol
Produced by: George Martin
Year: 1966
B-side of "Paperback Writer."

RAIN, THE

Artist: Oran "Juice" Jones
Written by: Vince Bell
From the album: *Juice*
Label: Columbia
Produced by: Vincent Ball, Russell Simmons
Year: 1986

RAIN, THE (SUPA DUPA FLY)

Artist: Missy Elliott
Written by: Missy Elliot, Tim Mosley, Donald Bryant, Ann Peebles, Kenneth Miller
From the album: *Supa Dupa Fly*
Label: East West
Year: 1997
With thunderous authenticity, the new goddess of rap reinvents the Dramatics' "In the Rain."

RAIN, THE PARK AND OTHER THINGS, THE

Artist: The Cowsills
Written by: Artie Kornfeld, Steve Duboff
From the album: *The Cowsills*
Label: MGM
Produced by: Bill Cowsill, Bob Cowsill
Year: 1967
Their first and biggest hit; in Hollywood, the Partridge Family was being created in their image.

RAINBOW IN THE DARK

Artist: Dio
Written by: Ronnie Dio, Vivian Campbell
From the album: *Holy Diver*
Label: Warner Brothers
Year: 1983

Former Elf celebrates his Solohood, courtesy of Viv Campbell's guitar heroics.

RAINDROPS

Artist: Dee Clark
Written by: Dee Clark
Label: Vee Jay
Year: 1961
Clyde McPhatter, without the edge of anguish.

RAINDROPS KEEP FALLIN' ON MY HEAD

Artist: B. J. Thomas
Written by: Burt Bacharach, Hal David
From the album: *Raindrops Keep Fallin' on My Head*
Label: Scepter
Produced by: Burt Bacharach, Hal David
Year: 1970
Lilting theme to *Butch Cassidy and the Sundance Kid* brings B. J. instant, if brief, hip credibility and a #1 song. Bacharach and David get an Oscar.

RAINING DOWN ON BLEECKER STREET

Artist: Devonsquare
Written by: Tom Dean, Alana MacDonald, Herb Ludwig
From the album: *If You Could See Me Now*
Label: Atlantic
Produced by: Shane Reisher
Year: 1992
Retro folk/rock tale laments the end of the bohemian dream. Suggested segue: "Hey, Jack Kerouac" by 10,000 Maniacs, "Cassady" by Bob Weir.

RAINING IN MY HEART

Artist: Buddy Holly
Written by: Buddy Holly
From the album: *The Buddy Holly Story*
Label: Coral
Produced by: Norman Petty
Year: 1959
B-side of his last hit, "It Doesn't Matter Anymore." Covered by Bobby Vee (Liberty, '62).

RAINY DAY MAN

Artist: James Taylor
Written by: James Taylor, Zack Weisner
From the album: *James Taylor*
Label: Columbia
Produced by: Peter Asher
Year: 1969
The laid-back mellow singer/songwriter era of the '70's starts early. Covered by Bonnie Raitt (Warner Brothers, '74).

RAINY DAY WOMEN #12 AND 35

Artist: Bob Dylan
Written by: Bob Dylan
From the album: *Blonde on Blonde*
Label: Columbia
Produced by: Bob Johnston
Year: 1966
Treatise on the various meanings of getting stoned (including by the audience, on tour).

RAINY DAYS AND MONDAYS

Artist: The Carpenters
Written by: Paul Williams, Roger Nichols
From the album: *The Carpenters*
Label: A&M
Produced by: Jack Daugherty
. Year: 1971
Melodious and melancholy showpiece for the blue angel, Karen Carpenter.

RAINY NIGHT IN GEORGIA, A

Artist: Brook Benton
Written by: Tony Joe White
From the album: *Brook Benton Today*
Label: Cotillion
Produced by: Arif Mardin
Year: 1970
A #1 R&B/Top 10 crossover. A year later Dee Dee Warwick put out "Cold Night in Georgia" (Cotillion, '71), but it stiffed.

RAISED ON PROMISES

Artist: Sam Phillips
Written by: Sam Phillips
From the album: *Cruel Inventions*
Label: Virgin
Produced by: T-Bone Burnette
Year: 1991
Female rocker with a name taken from Elvis's first mentor, a title taken from the opening line of Tom Petty's "American Girl," and a voice taken from Wanda Jackson.

RAISED ON ROBBERY

Artist: Joni Mitchell
Written by: Joni Mitchell
From the album: *Court and Spark*
Label: Asylum
Produced by: Joni Mitchell
Year: 1974
A three-minute lifetime of complicated relationships.

RAMA LAMA DING DONG (LAMA RAMA DING DONG)

Artist: The Edsels
Written by: George Jones Jr.
Label: Dub/Twin
Year: 1958
Essential doo-wop hit originally listed as "Lama Rama Ding Dong." Re-released in '61 with a corrected title.

RAMBLIN' GAMBLIN' MAN

Artist: Bob Seger
Written by: Bob Seger
From the album: *Ramblin' Gamblin' Man*
Label: Capitol
Produced by: Hideout Product
Year: 1969
First single for the soulful hard rock journeyman and his band, the System, hits Top 20. It would be eight years and many more miles before he would better it.

RAMBLIN' MAN

Artist: Allman Brothers
Written by: Dickie Betts
From the album: *Brothers and Sisters*
Label: Capricorn
Produced by: Jerry Sandlin, the Allman Brothers Band
Year: 1973
Glorifying the drifting, grifting way of life, much like Harry McClintock did in "The Big Rock Candy Mountain," thirty or forty years earlier, but with lots of beautiful layered guitars. The Eagles were taking notes and making charts for "Hotel California."

RAMBLING BOY

Artist: Judy Collins
Written by: Tom Paxton
From the album: *5th*
Label: Elektra
Produced by: Mark Abramson, Jac Holzman
Year: 1965
Fireside folk favorite of the rambling school.

RAPE ME

Artist: Nirvana
Written by: Kurt Cobain
From the album: *In Utero*
Label: DGC
Produced by: Nirvana
Year: 1993
A plea to his devouring fans, unheeded.

RAPPER, THE

Artist: The Jaggerz
Written by: Donnie Iris
From the album: *We Went to Different Schools Together*
Label: Kama Sutra
Produced by: Sixuvus Productions
Year: 1970
When rapping was only the inevitable result of too much coffee instead of an urban lifestyle commentary.

RAPPER'S DELIGHT

Artist: The Sugar Hill Gang
Written by: Nile Rodgers, Bernard Edwards, Sylvia Robinson, Big Bank Hank Jackson, Wonder Mike Wright, Master Gee O'Brien

Label: Sugar Hill
Produced by: Sylvia Robinson
Year: 1979
Credited as the first rap record, based on Chic's disco classic "Good Times," this establishes the innocent rhythm and simple rhyme of the streetwise urban boasting genre. That would soon change.

RAPTURE

Artist: Blondie
Written by: Deborah Harry, Chris Stein
From the album: *Autoamerican*
Label: Chrysalis
Produced by: Mike Chapman
Year: 1981
One of the first white girls to make the disco/rap connection and the first #1 song to feature a prominent rap. As a rapper, however, Debby made a great waitress.

RASPBERRIES, LILACS AND LIME

Artist: Bette Midler
Written by: Jerry Blatt
Year: 1972
Closing song from the Holly Woodlawn movie *A Scarecrow in a Garden of Cucumbers*, this incredible lullaby just predates Midler's emergence from the bathhouse to greater glory and is still one of the best things she's ever done.

RASPBERRY BERET

Artist: Prince
Written by: Prince Rogers Nelson
From the album: *Around the World in a Day*
Label: Warner Brothers
Produced by: Prince
Year: 1985
Another shade of purple.

RATTLESNAKE SHAKE

Artist: Fleetwood Mac
Written by: Peter Green
From the album: *Then Play On*
Label: Reprise
Produced by: Mike Verson
Year: 1969
A Fleetwood fixture until Green followed Syd Barrett into the rock and roll void.

RAUNCHY

Artist: Bill Justis
Written by: Bill Justis Jr., Sidney Manker
From the album: *Cloud Nine*
Label: Phillips-International
Produced by: Sam Phillips
Year: 1957
Perfectly named instrumental: Justis on sax, Sid Manker on guitar; Duane Eddy, Link Wray, Dick Dale waiting in the wings to explode.

RAVE ON

Artist: Buddy Holly
Written by: Sunny West, Norman Petty, Bill Tilghman
From the album: *Buddy Holly*
Label: Coral
Produced by: Norman Petty, Bob Thiele
Year: 1958
For those who think a kid in glasses couldn't rock. Covered by Marshall Crenshaw (Warner Brothers, '84). Elvis Costello, four years old, no longer saw the need for contact lenses.

RAW POWER

Artist: The Stooges
Written by: James Osterberg (Iggy Pop), James Williamson
From the album: *Raw Power*
Label: Columbia
Produced by: David Bowie
Year: 1973
Raw, anyway.

RAWHIDE

Artist: Link Wray
Written by: Milt Grant, Link Wray
Label: Epic
Produced by: Milt Grant
Year: 1959
Instrumentally tackling the roots of the gangsta ethos, Dodge City.

RAY OF LIGHT

Artist: Madonna
Written by: Madonna Ciccone, William Orbit, Dave Curtis, Clive Muldoon, Christine Leach
From the album: *Ray of Light*
Label: Maverick
Produced by: William Orbit
Year: 1998
Madonna is a mom.

REACH OUT AND TOUCH (SOMEBODY'S HAND)

Artist: Diana Ross
Written by: Nick Ashford, Valerie Simpson
From the album: *Diana Ross*
Label: Motown
Produced by: Nick Ashford, Valerie Simpson
Year: 1970
Recycling the era's prevailing communal feeling on her first solo single, Ross comes up with a future phone company commercial.

REACH OUT, I'LL BE THERE

Artist: The Four Tops
Written by: Eddie Holland, Lamont Dozier, Brian Holland
From the album: *Reach Out*
Label: Motown
Produced by: Brian Holland, Lamont Dozier

Year: 1965
Their second #1 R&B/#1 crossover.

REACH OUT OF THE DARKNESS

Artist: Friend and Lover
Written by: Jim Post
Label: Verve/Forecast
Produced by: Joe South, Bill Lowery
Year: 1968
Revealingly needy folk/rock one-shot.

READY OR NOT

Artist: After 7
Written by: Kenny (Babyface) Edmunds, Antonio (L. A.) Reid
From the album: *After 7*
Label: Virgin
Produced by: Babyface, L. A. Reid
Year: 1989
Babyface and brothers gonna work it out.

READY OR NOT

Artist: Jackson Browne
Written by: Jackson Browne
From the album: *For Everyman*
Label: Asylum
Produced by: Jackson Browne
Year: 1973
She's havin' his baby. Browne's coming-of-age saga.

READY TEDDY

Artist: Little Richard
Written by: John Marascalco, Robert Blackwell
From the album: *Here's Little Richard*
Label: Specialty
Produced by: Bumps Blackwell
Year: 1956
B-side of "Rip It Up." Heard in the movie *La Dolce Vita* as sung by a Little Richard impersonator. Covered by Elvis Presley (RCA, '56), John Lennon (Apple, '75).

REAL GOOD FOR FREE

Artist: Joni Mitchell
Written by: Joni Mitchell
From the album: *Miles of Aisles*
Label: Asylum
Produced by: Joni Mitchell
Year: 1974
A street musician observed.

REAL LOVE

Artist: Mary J. Blige
Written by: Mark Rooney, Mark Morales
From the album: *What's the 411?*
Label: Uptown
Produced by: Dave Hall
Year: 1992
New soul temptress bares all.

REAL LOVE

Artist: The Doobie Brothers
Written by: Michael McDonald, Patrick Henderson
From the album: *One Step Closer*
Label: Warner Brothers
Produced by: Ted Templeman
Year: 1980

REAL LOVE

Artist: John Lennon
Written by: John Lennon
From the album: *Imagine Soundtrack*
Label: Apple
Year: 1988
The work tape of a "new" Lennon song, used in the biopic *Imagine*. It would resurface in '95, with the voices of Paul, George and Ringo added, along with "Free as a Bird," another track from the same era, as the first two new Beatles songs since '70.

REAL LOVE

Artist: Jody Watley
Written by: Andre Cymone, Jody Watley
From the album: *Larger Than Life*
Label: MCA
Produced by: Andre Cymone
Year: 1989
#1 R&B/Top 10 crossover.

REAL ME, THE

Artist: The Who
Written by: Pete Townshend
From the album: *Quadrophenia*
Label: Track
Produced by: The Who
Year: 1973
Returning to his roots among the Mods, Townshend writes his most revealing rocker.

REAL REAL REAL

Artist: Jesus Jones
Written by: Jesus Jones
From the album: *Doubt*
Label: SBK
Produced by: Jesus Jones
Year: 1991
Follow-up to the historic "Right Here, Right Now."

REAL WILD CHILD

Artist: Ivan (Jerry Allison)
Written by: John O' Keefe, John Greenan, David Owens
Label: Coral
Year: 1958
Rockabilly one-off by the Crickets' drummer. Covered by Jerry Lee Lewis (Sun, '58), Iggy Pop (A&M, '87).

REAL WORLD

Artist: Matchbox Twenty
Written by: Rob Thomas

From the album: *Yourself or Someone Like You*
Label: Lava
Produced by: Matt Serletic
Year: 1997
His response to Bob Dylan's "It Ain't Me Babe."

REALLY ROSIE

Artist: Carole King
Written by: Maurice Sendak, Carole King
From the album: *Really Rosie*
Label: Ode
Produced by: Lou Adler
Year: 1975
Plucky title tune from the musical special she wrote with the renowned children's book author.

RE-ARRANGED

Artist: Limp Bizkit
Written by: William Durst, Samuel Rivers, Wesley Borland, John Otto, Eric Barrier, Charles Bobbit, James Brown, Bobby Byrd, Leo Dimant, William Griffin
From the album: *Significant Other*
Label: Flip
Year: 1999
Rap/metal hybrid defines the new uneasy end of century ethos.

REASON TO BELIEVE

Artist: Tim Hardin
Written by: Tim Hardin
From the album: *Tim Hardin*
Label: Verve/Forecast
Produced by: Erik Jacobsen
Year: 1966
Cagey love ballad is one of his most enduring and fragile folk/blues rockers. Covered by Bobby Darin (Atlantic, '67), Rod Stewart (Warner Brothers, '94).

REASONS

Artist: Earth, Wind & Fire
Written by: Maurice White, Philip Bailey, Verdine White
From the album: *That's the Way of the World*
Label: Columbia
Produced by: Maurice White
Year: 1975
Early classic ballad.

REBEL REBEL

Artist: David Bowie
Written by: David Bowie
From the album: *Diamond Dogs*
Label: RCA
Produced by: David Bowie
Year: 1974
Glam rock rallying cry. Segue: "All the Young Dudes," by Mott the Hoople.

REBEL ROUSER

Artist: Duane Eddy
Written by: Duane Eddy, Lee Hazelwood

From the album: *Have Twangy Guitar Will Travel*
Label: Jamie
Produced by: Lee Hazelwood, Lester Sill
Year: 1958
B-side of "Stalkin" was Eddy's first smash, establishing the solo guitar hero as a genuine rock and roll love object.

REBEL YELL

Artist: Billy Idol
Written by: William Broad (Billy Idol), Steve Stevens
From the album: *Rebel Yell*
Label: Chrysalis
Produced by: Keith Forsey
Year: 1984
Jim Morrison as Eddie Cochran.

REBIRTH OF SLICK (COOL LIKE DAT)

Artist: Digable Planets
Written by: Digable Planets
From the album: *Reachin' (New Refutation of Time and Space)*
Label: Pendulum
Produced by: Butterfly
Year: 1993
Establishing the new jazz/rap fusion of bop hop.

RECONSIDER BABY

Artist: Lowell Fulson
Written by: Lowell Fulson
Label: Checker
Year: 1954
Covered by Elvis Presley (RCA, '60), B. B. King (ABC, '75).

RED CADILLAC AND A BLACK MOUSTACHE, A

Artist: Warren Smith
Written by: Lilly May, Hayden Thompson
Produced by: Sam Phillips, Jack Clement
Label: Sun
Year: 1956
Long-buried rockabilly classic, not released until '73.

RED GUITAR

Artist: Loudon Wainwright III
Written by: Loudon Wainwright III
From the album: *Album III*
Label: Columbia
Produced by: Thomas Jefferson Kaye
Year: 1972
A classic modern folk morality tale.

RED HOT

Artist: The Five Scamps
Written by: Earl Robinson, James Whitcomb
Label: Okeh
Year: 1949

Seminal R&B rocker. Covered by Billy Lee Riley (Sun, '57), Sam the Sham and the Pharoahs (MGM, '65), Robert Gordon with Link Wray (RCA, '77).

RED HOUSE

Artist: Jimi Hendrix
Written by: Jimi Hendrix
From the album: *Smash Hits*
Label: Reprise
Produced by: Jimi Hendrix
Year: 1969
Out of T-Bone Walker by way of Pharoah Sanders, a quintessential blues guitar extravaganza from the vault.

RED RAIN

Artist: Peter Gabriel
Written by: Peter Gabriel
From the album: *So*
Label: Geffen
Produced by: Peter Gabriel, Daniel Lanois
Year: 1986
Intense ecological rocker kicks off his most celebrated album.

RED RED WINE

Artist: Neil Diamond
Written by: Neil Diamond
From the album: *Just for You*
Label: Bang
Produced by: Jeff Barry, Ellie Greenwich
Year: 1967
Originally a Top 40 stiff. Cover by UB40 (A&M, '84) was #1 UK/#1 U.S. when re-released in '88.

RED RIVER ROCK

Artist: Johnny & the Hurricanes
Written by: Tom King, Ira Mack, Fred Mendelsohn
Label: Warwick
Year: 1959
Big winner in the post Duane Eddy twangy guitar goldrush of '59.

RED RUBBER BALL

Artist: The Cyrcle
Written by: Paul Simon, Bruce Woodley
From the album: *Red Rubber Ball*
Label: Columbia
Produced by: John Simon
Year: 1966
A Spaldeen, of course.

RED SHOES, THE

Artist: Kate Bush
Written by: Kate Bush
From the album: *The Red Shoes*
Label: Columbia
Produced by: Kate Bush
Year: 1993
Spinning her own mystical take on the famous ballet film.

REDEMPTION SONG

Artist: Bob Marley & the Wailers
Written by: Bob Marley & the Wailers, Chris Blackwell
From the album: *Uprising*
Label: Island
Produced by: Bob Marley & the Wailers
Year: 1980
Last song Marley recorded (and performed) before his death; an apt summation.

REDNECK FRIEND

Artist: Jackson Browne
Written by: Jackson Browne
From the album: *For Everyman*
Label: Asylum
Produced by: Jackson Browne
Year: 1973
One of Browne's best and earthiest metaphors.

REDSOX ARE WINNING, THE

Artist: Earth Opera
Written by: Peter Rowan
From the album: *Earth Opera*
Label: Elektra
Produced by: Peter K. Siegel
Year: 1969
Early psychedelic bluegrass homage to a Boston obsession. Seigel was once a member of the Even Dozen Jugband. The members of Camper Van Beethoven would have been listening if anyone had played Earth Opera on the West coast.

REELIN' AND ROCKIN'

Artist: Chuck Berry
Written by: Chuck Berry
From the album: *One Dozen Berrys*
Label: Chess
Produced by: Leonard Chess, Phil Chess
Year: 1958
Chuck's version of "Rock around the Clock" was re-released in '73 as his last chart single.

REELING IN THE YEARS

Artist: Steely Dan
Written by: Donald Fagen, Walter Becker
From the album: *Can't Buy a Thrill*
Label: ABC
Produced by: Gary Katz
Year: 1972
1973, when this was released as a single, was one of the great years for wiseguys. Suggested segues: "Kodachrome" by Paul Simon, "You're So Vain" by Carly Simon, "The Cover of Rolling Stone" by Dr. Hook, "Dead Skunk" by Loudon Wainwright III.

REET PETITE

Artist: Jackie Wilson
Written by: Roquel Davis (Tyran Carlo), Berry Gordy Jr.
From the album: *He's So Fine*

Label: Brunswick
Produced by: Dick Jacobs
Year: 1957
With a title borrowed from a Louis Jordan movie, the careers of two former Detroit boxers move from Golden Gloves that much closer to gold records.

REFLECTIONS

Artist: The Supremes
Written by: Eddie Holland, Lamont Dozier, Brian Holland
From the album: *Reflections*
Label: Motown
Produced by: Brian Holland, Lamont Dozier
Year: 1967
Their first release in sixteen months that didn't hit #1 (encompassing four singles).

REFLEX, THE

Artist: Duran Duran
Written by: Duran Duran
From the album: *Seven and the Ragged Tiger*
Label: Capitol
Produced by: Duran Duran, Alex Sadkin, Ian Little
Year: 1983
At their commercial peak; #1 U.S./U.K.

REFUGEE

Artist: Tom Petty and the Heartbreakers
Written by: Tom Petty, Mike Campbell
From the album: *Damn the Torpedoes*
Label: Backstreet
Produced by: Jimmy Lovine, Tom Petty
Year: 1979
A gem of coiled tension and release, thanks to Mike Cambell's restrained guitar.

REGRET

Artist: New Order
Written by: Bernard Summer, Stephen Morris, Peter Hook, Gillian Gilbert, Stephen Hague
From the album: *Republic*
Label: Qwest
Produced by: Stephen Hague
Year: 1993

REGULATE

Artist: Warren G. with Nate Dogg
Written by: Warren Griffin, Nate Dogg
From the album: *Above the Rim Soundtrack*
Label: Death
Produced by: Warren Griffin
Year: 1994
Jazzy rap with an urban edge.

RELAX

Artist: Frankie Goes to Hollywood
Written by: Peter Gill, William Johnson, Mark O'Toole
From the album: *Welcome to the Pleasure Dome*
Label: Island

Produced by: Trevor Horn
Year: 1984
Sexually subversive #1 U.K./Bottom 40 U.S. crossover.

RELEASE ME

Artist: Wilson Phillips
Written by: Wilson Phillips
From the album: *Wilson Phillips*
Label: SBK
Produced by: Glen Ballard
Year: 1990
Second #1 from the album.

RELEASE ME!

Artist: Esther Phillips
Written by: Eddie Miller, W. S. Stevenson
From the album: *Release Me!*
Label: Lenox
Year: 1965
#1 R&B/Top 10 crossover was originally a country hit for Jimmy Heaps (Capitol, '54) and Ray Price (Columbia, '54).

REMEDY

Artist: The Black Crowes
Written by: Chris Robinson, Rich Robinson
From the album: *The Southern Harmony and Musical Companion*
Produced by: George Krakoulias
Label: Def American
Year: 1992
Blues rock on a southern roll with jam.

REMEMBER THE TIME

Artist: Michael Jackson
Written by: Michael Jackson, Teddy Riley, Bernard Belle
From the album: *Dangerous*
Label: Epic
Produced by: Michael Jackson, Bill Bottrell
Year: 1991
#1 R&B/Top 10 crossover.

REMEMBER THEN

Artist: The Earls
Written by: Stan Vincent, Tony Powers, Beverly Ross
From the album: *Remember Me, Baby*
Label: Old Town
Year: 1962
End of the doo-wop era on radio. After that, you'd only see it on PBS specials.

REMEMBER (WALKING IN THE SAND)

Artist: The Shangri-Las
Written by: George Morton
From the album: *The Shangri-Las*
Label: Red Bird

Produced by: Jeff Barry, Ellie Greenwich, Artie Ripp
Year: 1964
The girl-group sound and attitude brought up a dramatic notch to the level of soap opera. First hit for the rebel sisters act (Betty and Mary Weiss, Marge and Mary Ann Ganser) from Queens, New York, was covered by Goffin and King's daughter, Louise, in a sentimental Brill Building tribute (Asylum, '79), and Aerosmith, in an obvious New York Dolls move (Columbia, '80).

REMINISCING

Artist: Little River Band
Written by: Graham Goble
From the album: *Sleeper Catcher*
Label: Harvest
Produced by: John Boylan, Little River Band
Year: 1978
Middle-of-the-Aussie-Road.

RENE AND GEORGETTE MAGRITTE WITH THEIR DOG AFTER THE WAR

Artist: Paul Simon
Written by: Paul Simon
From the album: *Hearts and Bones*
Label: Warner Brothers
Produced by: Roy Halee, Paul Simon, Russ Titelman
Year: 1983
A Sunday afternoon in the recording studio with Paul, this is Simon's tribute to doo-wop. Segue: "An Innocent Man" by Billy Joel.

RENEGADE

Artist: Warren Zevon
Written by: Warren Zevon
From the album: *Mr. Bad Example*
Label: Giant
Produced by: Waddy Wachtel
Year: 1991
One of his folk/rock peaks, metaphorically comparing an alternate-culture reprobate to a surviving Civil War soldier.

RENO, NEVADA

Artist: Dick and Mimi Fariña
Written by: Richard Fariña
From the album: *Celebrations for a Grey Day*
Label: Vanguard
Year: 1965
The only single for the influential folk/rock duo didn't make the charts.

REPETITION

Artist: The Fall
Written by: Mark E. Smith
From the album: *Early Years, '77–'79*
Label: Faulty Productions
Year: 1977
Experimentalist noise; influenced Public Image.

REPTILE

Artist: The Church
Written by: Steve Kilbey, the Church
From the album: *Starfish*
Label: Arista
Produced by: Greg Ladanyi, Waddy Wachtel, the Church
Year: 1988
Slithery rave rock before the advent of ecstasy.

RESCUE ME

Artist: Fontella Bass
Written by: Carl William Smith, Raymond Miner
From the album: *The 'New' Look*
Label: Checker
Produced by: Billy Davis, Carl Smith, Reynard Miner
Year: 1965
#1 R&B/Top 10 crossover.

RESCUE ME

Artist: Madonna
Written by: Shep Pettibone, Madonna Ciccone
From the album: *The Immaculate Collection*
Label: Sire
Produced by: Shep Pettibone, Madonna
Year: 1990

RESPECT

Artist: Otis Redding
Written by: Otis Redding
From the album: *Otis Blue/Otis Redding Sings Soul*
Label: Volt
Produced by: Steve Cropper
Year: 1965
An anthem for the downtrodden everywhere. Top 5 R&B/Top 40 crossover. Cover by Aretha Franklin (Atlantic, '67) was a #1 R&B/#1 crossover, springing Otis as well as Aretha nationwide.

RESPECT YOURSELF

Artist: The Staple Singers
Written by: Mack Rice, Luther Ingram
From the album: *Be Altitude: Respect Yourself*
Label: Stax
Produced by: Al Bell
Year: 1971
#2 R&B/Top 15 crossover is a prescription for curing contemporary ills.

REST IN PEACE

Artist: Extreme
Written by: Gary Cherone, Nuno Bettencourt
From the album: *III Sides to Every Story*
Label: A&M
Produced by: Nuno Bettencourt, Bob St. John
Year: 1992
Cherone would pop up in Van Halen in '98, fired in '99.

RESTLESS KID

Artist: Ricky Nelson
Written by: Johnny Cash
From the album: *Ricky Sings Again*
Label: Imperial
Produced by: Ricky Nelson, Jimmy Haskell, Ozzie Nelson
Year: 1958
Title song for the John Wayne movie in which Ricky had his film debut. But he was no Elvis.

RETURN OF THE GRIEVOUS ANGEL

Artist: Gram Parsons
Written by: Gram Parsons
From the album: *Grievous Angel*
Label: Reprise
Produced by: Gram Parsons
Year: 1974
Latter-day signature for the legendary progenitor of country/rock and alt/country.

RETURN OF THE MACK

Artist: Mark Morrison
Written by: Mark Morrison
From the album: *Return of the Mack*
Label: Atlantic
Year: 1997

RETURN TO INNOCENCE

Artist: Enigma
Written by: Michael Cretu
From the album: *Cross of Changes*
Label: Charisma
Year: 1994
Greek songwriter samples Native-American flavors.

RETURN TO SENDER

Artist: Elvis Presley
Written by: Otis Blackwell, Winfield Scott
From the album: *Girls! Girls! Girls!*
Label: RCA
Produced by: Steve Sholes
Year: 1962
As further psychic, as well as statistical evidence, that a changing of the guard was afoot in '62, this tune spent five weeks at #2 on the charts, kept out of #1 by "He's a Rebel" and then "Big Girls Don't Cry." Not only did it fail to make what would have seemed the obligatory if not honorary final step to #1 (as did "Can't Help Falling in Love" earlier in the year), but it would represent Elvis' highest charting item for virtually the remainder of the decade (until "Suspicious Minds" became his last #1 late in '69).

REUNITED

Artist: Peaches and Herb
Written by: Freddie Perren, Dino Fekaris
From the album: *2 Hot!*
Label: Polydor
Produced by: Freddie Perren
Year: 1978
#1 R&B/#1 crossover and slow dance anthem.

REUTERS

Artist: Wire
Written by: Colin Newman, Graham Lewis
From the album: *Pink Flag*
Label: Harvest
Produced by: Mike Thorne
Year: 1977
More of their dit-dot-dash approach to rock.

REVEREND MR. BLACK, THE

Artist: The Kingston Trio
Written by: Billy Edd Wheeler, Jed Peters
From the album: *Kingston Trio #16*
Label: Capitol
Produced by: Voile Gillmore
Year: 1963
Based on an old Carter Family folk tune.

REVOLUTION

Artist: Arrested Development
Written by: Todd (Speech) Thomas
From the album: *Malcolm X Soundtrack*
Label: Chrysalis
Produced by: Speech
Year: 1992
Title song from the Spike Lee epic on the life of Malcolm X. After this, Arrested Development couldn't get arrested.

REVOLUTION

Artist: The Beatles
Written by: John Lennon, Paul McCartney
From the album: *The Beatles*
Label: Apple
Produced by: George Martin
Year: 1968
The B-side of "Hey Jude." Overtly detaching themselves from the counterculture they had set in motion, as said counterculture hurtled toward its Armageddon on the streets of Chicago.

REVOLUTION 9

Artist: The Beatles
Written by: John Lennon, Paul McCartney
From the album: *The Beatles*
Label: Apple
Produced by: George Martin
Year: 1968
An experimental jag that ran about eight minutes too long.

REVOLUTION WILL NOT BE TELEVISED, THE

Artist: The Last Poets
Written by: Gil Scott-Heron
From the album: *The Revolution Will Not Be Televised*
Label: Douglas
Produced by: Bob Thiele
Year: 1971
Early example of rap or late example of beat jazz poetry set to rock, this lyrically explicit rant moved with a powerful rhythmic force through the entire black community. Covered by LaBelle (Epic, '73), Gil Scott-Heron & the Flying Dutchman (Arista, '74).

RHIANNON (WILL YOU EVER WIN)

Artist: Fleetwood Mac
Written by: Stephanie Nicks
From the album: *Fleetwood Mac*
Label: Reprise
Produced by: Keith Olson, Fleetwood Mac
Year: 1975
Stevie Nicks invents herself as the original "Witchy Woman."

RHYTHM IS A DANCER

Artist: Snap
Written by: Benito Benites, John Garrett III
From the album: *The Madman's Return*
Label: Arista
Produced by: Snap
Year: 1992
World wide Euro disco smash.

RHYTHM IS GONNA GET YOU

Artist: Miami Sound Machine
Written by: Gloria Estefan, Enrique Garcia
From the album: *Let It Loose*
Label: Epic
Produced by: Emilio Estefan
Year: 1987
Gloria Estefan takes over the band and the sound, and takes it down 95 to the Fontainbleu.

RHYTHM NATION

Artist: Janet Jackson
Written by: James Harris III, Terry Lewis, Janet Jackson
From the album: *Rhythm Nation 1814*
Label: A&M
Produced by: Jimmy Jam, Terry Lewis
Year: 1989
#1 R&B/Top 10 crossover. Janet gets her groove on that would own the 90's.

RHYTHM OF MY HEART

Artist: Rod Stewart
Written by: Marc Jordan, John Capek
From the album: *Vagabond Heart*
Label: Warner Brothers
Year: 1991
Rod does M.O.R. A decade away from doing standards.

RHYTHM OF THE NIGHT

Artist: Debarge
Written by: Diane Warren
From the album: *Rhythm of the Night*
Label: Motown
Produced by: Richard Perry
Year: 1985
From the movie *The Last Dragon*.

RHYTHM OF THE RAIN

Artist: The Cascades
Written by: John Gummoe
From the album: *Rhythm of the Rain*
Label: Valiant
Year: 1963
One-shot thunderbolt.

RICH GIRL

Artist: Daryl Hall & John Oates
Written by: Daryl Hall
From the album: *Bigger Than the Both of Us*
Label: RCA
Produced by: Chris Bond
Year: 1976
Finding their true subject matter—the suburban princess—and achieving their first #1.

RICO SUAVE

Artist: Gerardo
Written by: Gerardo Mejia, Christian Carlos Warren
From the album: *Mo' Ritmo*
Label: Interscope
Produced by: Michael Sembello
Year: 1991
Latino posturing that defines the '90s urban cultural mix.

RID OF ME

Artist: P.J. Harvey
Written by: Polly Jean Harvey
From the album: *Rid of Me*
Produced by: Steve Albini
Label: Island
Year: 1993

RIDE

Artist: Dee Dee Sharp
Written by: Kal Mann (Jon Sheldon), Dave Leon
Label: Cameo
Year: 1963
Her third Top 10 hit of 1962

RIDE A WHITE SWAN

Artist: T. Rex
Written by: Marc Feld (Marc Bolan)
From the album: *T-Rex*
Label: Reprise
Produced by: Tony Visconti
Year: 1971
First big UK hit for the metal Donovan, rode the Bottom 40 here.

RIDE CAPTAIN RIDE

Artist: Blues Image
Written by: Frank Konte, Carlos Pinera
From the album: *Open*
Label: Atco
Produced by: Richard Polodor
Year: 1970
The beginning of classic rock; the beginning of the end of FM radio.

RIDE LIKE THE WIND

Artist: Christopher Cross
Written by: Christopher Geppert
From the album: *Christopher Cross*
Label: Warner Brothers
Produced by: Michael Omartian
Year: 1980
Launching his multi-Grammy-winning career

RIDE MY SEE SAW

Artist: The Moody Blues
Written by: John Lodge
From the album: *In Search of the Lost Chord*
Label: Deram
Produced by: Tony Clarke
Year: 1968
Balanced between New Age and M.O.R.

RIDE ON TIME

Artist: Black Box
Written by: Mirko Limoni, Daniele Davoli, Valerio Semplici, Dan Hartman
From the album: *Dreamland*
Label: RCA
Produced by: Groove Groove Melody
Year: 1989
#1 UK debut with vocals sampled from Loleatta Holloway's "Love Sensation." Segue: "Good Vibrations" by Marky Mark and the Funky Bunch.

RIDE THE WILD SURF

Artist: Jan & Dean
Written by: Brian Wilson, Jan Berry, Roger Christian
From the album: *Ride the Wild Surf Soundtrack*
Label: Liberty
Produced by: Jan Berry
Year: 1964
Theme from the classic beach movie.

RIDE YOUR PONY

Artist: Lee Dorsey
Written by: Allen Toussaint (Naomi Neville)
From the album: *The New Lee Dorsey*
Label: Amy
Produced by: Allen Toussaint
Year: 1965
New Orleans soul.

RIDERS ON THE STORM

Artist: The Doors
Written by: Jim Morrison, Robbie Krieger, John Densmore, Ray Manzarek
From the album: *L.A. Woman*
Label: Elektra
Produced by: Paul Rothchild
Year: 1971
Riding the storm to the end. Song peaked on the charts a month after Morrison's death in Paris.

RIDING WITH MARY

Artist: X
Written by: John Doe, Exene Cervenka
From the album: *Under the Big Black Sun*
Label: Elektra
Produced by: Ray Manzarek
Year: 1982
One of their most powerful efforts.

RIDING WITH THE KING

Artist: John Hiatt
Written by: John Hiatt
From the album: *Riding with the King*
Label: Geffen
Produced by: Nick Lowe
Year: 1983
Fixating on his/our Elvis fixation.

RIGHT BACK WHERE WE STARTED FROM

Artist: Maxine Nightingale
Written by: Pierre Tubbs, Vincent Edwards
From the album: *Right Back Where We Started From*
Label: United Artists
Produced by: Pierre Tubbs
Year: 1976
UK disco/Top 10 crossover.

RIGHT HERE

Artist: SWV
Written by: Brian Alexander Morgan
From the album: *It's About Time*
Label: RCA
Produced by: B. A. Morgan, Genard Parker
Year: 1992
Remix of their first hit was a #1 R&B/Top 10 crossover, aided by a touch of Michael Jackson's "Human Nature." The B-side "Downtown" scored as well.

RIGHT HERE, RIGHT NOW

Artist: Jesus Jones
Written by: Mike Edwards
From the album: *Doubt*
Label: SBK
Produced by: Jesus Jones
Year: 1991
International smash written about the razing of the Berlin Wall. Suggested segue: "Winds of Change" by the Scorpions.

RIGHT HERE WAITING

Artist: Richard Marx
Written by: Richard Marx, David Cole
From the album: *Repeat Offender*

Label: EMI
Produced by: David Cole, Richard Marx
Year: 1989
His third straight and biggest #1 single.

RIGHT IN TIME

Artist: Lucinda Williams
Written by: Lucinda Williams
From the album: *Car Wheels on a Gravel Road*
Label: Mercury
Produced by: Lucinda Williams, Roy Bittan
Year: 1998
Finding her rhythmic soulmate.

RIGHT NOW

Artist: Al B. Sure
Written by: Al B. Sure, Kyle West
From the album: *Sexy Versus*
Label: Warner Brothers
Produced by: Kyle West, Al B. Sure
Year: 1992
#1 R&B/Top 50 crossover.

RIGHT NOW

Artist: Van Halen
Written by: Eddie Van Halen, Alex Van Halen, Michael Anthony, Sammy Hagar
From the album: *For Unlawful Carnal Knowledge*
Label: Warner Brothers
Produced by: Ted Templeman, Andy Johns, Van Halen
Year: 1991
Obvious album title, obvious sound.

RIGHT ON TRACK

Artist: The Breakfast Club
Written by: Steve Bray, Steve Gilroy
From the album: *The Breakfast Club*
Label: MCA
Produced by: Jimmy Iovine
Year: 1987
One-shot hit for Madonna's old band.

RIGHT OR WRONG (I'LL BE WITH YOU)

Artist: Wanda Jackson
Written by: Wanda Jackson
From the album: *Right or Wrong*
Produced by: Paul Cohen, Tom Thack, Ken Nelson
Label: Capitol
Year: 1961
Displaying her country side. One can only imagine what side "Funnel of Love" on the B-side displayed.

RIGHT PLACE WRONG TIME

Artist: Dr. John
Written by: Mac Rebennack
From the album: *In the Right Place*
Label: Atco

Produced by: Allen Toussaint
Year: 1973
Former Bourbon Street straw boss fronts the classic New Orleans house band, the Meters.

RIGHT SIDE OF MY BRAIN

Artist: Angry Samoans
Written by: Todd Homer
From the album: *Inside My Brain*
Label: Bad Trip
Year: 1980
Quintessential L.A. punk.

RIKKI DON'T LOSE THAT NUMBER

Artist: Steely Dan
Written by: Donald Fagen, Walter Becker
From the album: *Pretzel Logic*
Label: ABC
Produced by: Gary Katz
Year: 1974
Their biggest single: intricate, swinging, twisted. Suggested segue: "Song for My Father" by Horace Silver.

RING MY BELL

Artist: Anita Ward
Written by: Frederick Knight
From the album: *Songs of Love*
Label: Juana
Produced by: Frederick Knight
Year: 1979
#1 R&B/#1 disco crossover.

RING OF FIRE

Artist: Johnny Cash
Written by: Merle Kilgore, June Carter
From the album: *Ring of Fire: The Best of Johnny Cash*
Label: Columbia
Produced by: Don Law, Frank Jones
Year: 1963
#1 country/Top 20 crossover. Rock and roll attitude, country retribution.

RINGO, I LOVE YOU

Artist: Bonnie Jo Mason
Written by: Peter Anders, Vini Poncia
Label: Annette
Produced by: Phil Spector
Year: 1964
Cher, in an earlier, more starstruck period.

RIO

Artist: Duran Duran
Written by: Duran Duran
From the album: *Rio*
Label: Capitol
Produced by: Colin Thurston
Year: 1983
Bringing the Indiana Jones ethos to the rock video genre.

RIO GRANDE

Artist: Brian Wilson
Written by: Brian Wilson, Andy Paley
From the album: *Brian Wilson*
Label: Reprise
Produced by: Brian Wilson, Lenny Waronker, Andy Paley
Year: 1988
Getting back to work on "Surf's Up." In another seven years there would be *Orange Crate Art*, with Van Dyke Parks.

RIOT IN CELL BLOCK #9

Artist: The Robins
Written by: Jerry Leiber, Mike Stoller
Label: Spark
Produced by: Jerry Leiber, Mike Stoller
Year: 1954
Landmark of L.A. rock and roll, sung by the ubiquitous Richard Berry, author of "Louie Louie." But if you want to hear the definitive female jailbird version, you have to turn to Wanda Jackson (Capitol, '60). Also covered by Dr. Feelgood (Columbia, '76). Segue: "Tenth and Greenwich" from *Ain't Supposed to Die a Natural Death*.

RIP IT UP

Artist: Little Richard
Written by: John Marascalco, Robert Blackwell
From the album: *Here's Little Richard*
Label: Specialty
Produced by: Bumps Blackwell
Year: 1956
His biggest R&B hit: #1 R&B/Top 20 crossover. Covered by Bill Haley and His Comets (Decca, '56), Elvis Presley (RCA, '57), the Everly Brothers (Cadence, '60).

RIP OFF, THE

Artist: Laura Lee
Written by: Angelo Bond, William Weatherspoon
From the album: *Laura Lee*
Label: Hot Wax
Produced by: William Weatherspoon
Year: 1972
Taking up where even the strident "Women's Love Rights" feared to tread. Segue: "I Am Woman" by Helen Reddy.

RIPPLE

Artist: The Grateful Dead
Written by: Jerry Garcia, Robert Hunter
From the album: *American Beauty*
Label: Warner Brothers
Produced by: The Grateful Dead
Year: 1970
Traveling through the mystic waters of life, aided by Jerry's guitar and David Grisman's mandolin.

RISE ABOVE

Artist: Black Flag
Written by: Greg Ginn

From the album: *Damaged*
Label: SST
Produced by: Spot, Black Flag
Year: 1981
Hardcore's first poet manqué, Henry Rollins, debuted as a singer with this punk rock classic.

RIVER

Artist: Joni Mitchell
Written by: Joni Mitchell
From the album: *Blue*
Label: Reprise
Produced by: Joni Mitchell
Year: 1971
Celebrating Christmas in the land without snow—or good will toward men—and dreaming of Canada. Covered by fellow Canadian, Sarah McLachlan (Epic, '95).

RIVER DEEP, MOUNTAIN HIGH

Artist: Ike and Tina Turner
Written by: Jeff Barry, Ellie Greenwich, Phil Spector
From the album: *River Deep, Mountain High*
Label: Philles
Produced by: Phil Spector
Year: 1966
Their fifteenth biggest hit (Bottom 10) was Phil Spector's greatest professional disappointment. Covered by Deep Purple (Tetragrammaton,'69); the Supremes and Four Tops (Motown, '71) had the biggest hit.

RIVER OF DREAMS

Artist: Billy Joel
Written by: Billy Joel
From the album: *River of Dreams*
Label: Columbia
Produced by: Mick Jones, Billy Joel
Year: 1993
Constantly played on the jukebox at Italian restaurants everywhere.

RIVER, THE

Artist: Bruce Springsteen
Written by: Bruce Springsteen
From the album: *The River*
Label: Columbia
Produced by: Jon Landau, Bruce Springsteen, Steve Van Zandt
Year: 1980
He gets Mary from "Thunder Road" pregnant and that was all she wrote.

RIVERS OF BABYLON

Artist: The Melodians
Written by: Fred Farian, G. Reyam, B. Dowe, F. McNaughton
Label: Mango
Produced by: Leslie Kong
Year: 1970

Traditional African slave tune featured on the soundtrack of the reggae coming-of-age movie classic *The Harder They Come* (Mango, '75). Covered by Linda Ronstadt (Asylum, '76). UK song of the year by Boney M. (Sire, '78).

ROAD RUNNER

Artist: Modern Lovers
Written by: Jonathan Richman
From the album: *Beserkely Chartbusters*
Label: Beserkely
Produced by: John Cale
Year: 1971
Answering James Taylor's New England ode to collegiate rambling, "Sweet Baby James," in the voice of the beknighted high-school bag boy at the Stop & Shop with a taste for Tastee Freeze and modern music. A hit in England in '77. Covered by Joan Jett (CBS/Associated, '86).

ROAD TO CAIRO

Artist: David Ackles
Written by: David Ackles
From the album: *David Ackles*
Label: Elektra
Produced by: David Anderle, Russ Miller
Year: 1968
A deadbeat dad and his thwarted attempts at reconciliation make a thrilling ride for mordant music fans. Covered by Brian Auger and the Trinity with Julie Driscoll (Polydor, '70), Howard Jones (Elektra, '90).

ROAD TO NOWHERE

Artist: Talking Heads
Written by: David Byrne, Chris Frantz, Tina Weymouth, Jerry Harrison
From the album: *Little Creatures*
Label: Sire
Produced by: Talking Heads
Year: 1985
The Heads turn ebullient and garner their only Top 10 UK hit.

ROAD, THE

Artist: Danny O'Keefe
Written by: Danny O'Keefe
From the album: *O'Keefe*
Label: Signpost
Produced by: Arif Mardin
Year: 1972
Superbly detailed and bitter picture of the rock and roll life. Covered by Jackson Browne (Asylum, '78).

ROADHOUSE BLUES

Artist: The Doors
Written by: Jim Morrison, Robbie Krieger, John Densmore, Ray Manzarek
From the album: *Morrison Hotel/Hard Rock Cafe*
Label: Elektra
Produced by: Paul Rothchild
Year: 1970

From whence emerged the prophetic: *No one here gets out alive.*

ROAM

Artist: The B-52's
Written by: The B-52's, Robert Waldrop
From the album: *Cosmic Thing*
Label: Reprise
Produced by: Nile Rodgers
Year: 1989
The B-52's cling to their manic groove despite the AIDS-related death of their founding guitarist, Ricky Wilson.

ROCK A-BEATING BOOGIE

Artist: Bill Haley and His Comets
Written by: Bill Haley
From the album: *Rock Around the Clock*
Label: Essex
Produced by: Milt Gabler
Year: 1952
Introducing the first country/rock dance band, trying to exploit the rhythms of "The Hucklebuck" for a new generation. Song was previously released by Haley guitarist Danny Cedrone's first group, the Esquire Boys.

ROCK AND A HARD PLACE

Artist: The Rolling Stones
Written by: Mick Jagger, Keith Richards
From the album: *Steel Wheels*
Label: Rolling Stones Records
Produced by: Glimmer Twins, Chris Kimsey
Year: 1989
Where they never wanted to be at 50.

ROCK AND ROLL

Artist: Led Zeppelin
Written by: Jimmy Page, Robert Plant, John Paul Jones, John Bonham
From the album: *Led Zeppelin IV (Untitled)*
Label: Atlantic
Produced by: Jimmy Page
Year: 1971
One of the classic heavy metal riffs, found embedded in the far wall at Detroit's Cobo arena. Or else something they played once at a sound-check somewhere.

ROCK AND ROLL

Artist: Wild Bill Moore
Written by: Willliam Moore, Jules Taub
Label: Savoy
Year: 1949
Honking sax man gets the message and the groove.

ROCK AND ROLL

Artist: The Velvet Underground
Written by: Lou Reed
From the album: *Loaded*
Label: Cotillion
Produced by: The Velvet Underground

Year: 1970
Their lives were saved by rock and roll; they saved rock and roll in the process. Covered by a solo Lou Reed (RCA, '74).

ROCK AND ROLL (PART II)

Artist: Gary Glitter
Written by: Gary Glitter, Mike Leander
From the album: *Glitter*
Label: Bell
Produced by: Mike Leander
Year: 1972
Goal!!!!

ROCK AND ROLL ALL NIGHT

Artist: Kiss
Written by: Stanley Eisen (Paul Stanley), Gene Simmons
From the album: *Dressed to Kill*
Label: Casablanca
Produced by: Neil Bogart, Kiss
Year: 1975
Following up "Kissing Time" with a more appropriately suggestive rocker.

ROCK AND ROLL DREAMS COME THROUGH

Artist: Jim Steinman
Written by: Jim Steinman
From the album: *Bad for Good*
Label: Cleveland
Produced by: Jim Steinman
Year: 1981
Covered by Meat Loaf (Epic, '93).

ROCK AND ROLL GIRLS

Artist: John Fogerty
Written by: John C. Fogerty
From the album: *Centerfield*
Label: Warner Brothers
Produced by: John C. Fogerty
Year: 1985
The Northern California answer to Brian Wilson's L.A.-oriented "California Girls."

ROCK AND ROLL HOOCHIE KOO

Artist: Johnny Winter
Written by: Rick Derringer
From the album: *Johnny Winter And*
Label: Columbia
Produced by: Rick Derringer
Year: 1974
Bar band party anthem. Derringer released his own version (Blue Sky, '74).

ROCK AND ROLL IS HERE TO STAY

Artist: Danny and the Juniors

Written by: Dave White
Label: ABC
Produced by: Arthur Singer
Year: 1958
Suggested segues: "It Will Stand" by the Showmen, "Roll Over Beethoven" by Chuck Berry.

ROCK AND ROLL MUSIC

Artist: Chuck Berry
Written by: Chuck Berry
From the album: *One Dozen Berrys*
Label: Chess
Produced by: Leonard Chess, Phil Chess
Year: 1957
His first of many anthems dedicated to the music. Covered by the Beatles (Capitol, '65), the Archies (Calendar, '69).

ROCK AND ROLL NEVER FORGETS

Artist: Bob Seger
Written by: Bob Seger
From the album: *Night Moves*
Label: Capitol
Produced by: Jack Richardson, Bob Seger
Year: 1976
As success beckons, Seger looks back on what brought him here, with his best bar-room rocker.

ROCK AND ROLL WOMAN

Artist: Buffalo Springfield
Written by: Stephen Stills
From the album: *Buffalo Springfield Again*
Label: Atco
Produced by: Stephen Stills, Neil Young
Year: 1967
Stills would move on to Judy Collins, a folk music woman.

ROCK AROUND WITH OLLIE VEE

Artist: Buddy Holly
Written by: Sonny Curtis
From the album: *The Nashville Sessions*
Label: Coral
Produced by: Owen Bradley
Year: 1956
Buddy's first solo single, written by a future Cricket, who also wrote the theme for *The Mary Tyler Moore Show*.

ROCK BOX

Artist: Run-D.M.C.
Written by: Larry Smith, Joseph Simmons, Darryl McDaniels
From the album: *Run-D.M.C.*
Label: Profile
Produced by: Russell Simmons, Larry Smith
Year: 1984

Boom box classic, presaging their hard rock union with Aerosmith on "Walk This Way" a couple of years up the block.

R-O-C-K IN THE USA. (A SALUTE TO '60S ROCK)

Artist: John (Cougar) Mellencamp
Written by: John Cougar Mellencamp
From the album: *Scarecrow*
Label: Riva
Produced by: Don Gehman, Little Bastard
Year: 1985
Homage to Mitch Ryder and James Brown.

ROCK ISLAND LINE

Artist: The Weavers
Written by: Huddie Ledbetter (Leadbelly)
Label: Charter
Produced by: Milt Gabler
Year: 1949
Introduced by Leadbelly in 1937. Hit by British folkie Lonnie Donnegan (Dot '56).

ROCK LOBSTER

Artist: The B-52's
Written by: Fred Schneider, Ricky Wilson
From the album: *The B-52's*
Label: Warner Brothers
Produced by: Chris Blackwell
Year: 1979
Punk goes disco, with a cheeky attitude. Featured in Paul Simon's movie, *One Trick Pony* (Warner Brothers, '80).

ROCK ME

Artist: Muddy Waters
Written by: McKinley Morganfield (Muddy Waters)
From the album: *Trouble No More*
Label: Chess
Year: 1956
Like my back ain't got no bone. Basis of a dozen songs by the Rolling Stones, two dozen by Led Zeppelin, everything by AC/DC.

ROCK ME ALL NIGHT LONG

Artist: The Ravens
Written by: Jimmy Ricks, Bill Sanford
Label: Mercury
Year: 1952
Their biggest R&B hit. Covered by Ella Mae Morse (Capitol, '54).

ROCK ME AMADEUS

Artist: Falco
Written by: Rob Bolland, Ferdi Bolland, Hans Hoelzl (Falco)
From the album: *Falco 3*
Label: A&M
Produced by: Rob Bolland, Ferdi Bolland

Year: 1986
German novelty song about the classical composer Mozart.

ROCK ME BABY

Artist: B. B. King
Written by: B. B. King, Jules Bihari
Label: Kent
Produced by: Jules Bihari
Year: 1964
Grandfathering the age of blues/rock.

ROCK ME GENTLY

Artist: Andy Kim
Written by: Andy Youachim (Andy Kim)
From the album: *Andy Kim*
Label: Capitol
Produced by: Michael Omartian
Year: 1974

ROCK ME ON THE WATER

Artist: Jackson Browne
Written by: Jackson Browne
From the album: *Saturate Before Using*
Label: Asylum
Produced by: Richard Orshoff
Year: 1972
The second single from the folk/rock album of the year.

ROCK ME TONITE

Artist: Billy Squier
Written by: Billy Squier
From the album: *Signs of Life*
Label: Capitol
Produced by: Jim Steinman
Year: 1984
Possibly the worst video of all time erases his career.

ROCK MY PLIMSOUL

Artist: The Jeff Beck Group
Written by: Jeff Beck
From the album: *Truth*
Label: Epic
Produced by: Mickie Most
Year: 1968
Introducing rock's British odd couple—the reclusive guitar star, Jeff Beck, and the effusive front man, Rod "the Mod" Stewart.

ROCK N ROLL

Artist: Mos' Def
Written by: Dante Smith & Fernandez
From the album: *Black on Both Sides*
Label: Rawkus
Year: 1999
A ferocious version of an old argument, stated more elegantly by Garland Jeffreys in "Hail Hail Rock and Roll."

ROCK 'N' ROLL FANTASY

Artist: Bad Company
Written by: Paul Rodgers
From the album: *Desolation Angels*
Label: Swan Song
Produced by: Bad Company
Year: 1979
Writing about what they know. Segue: "Jukebox Hero" by Foreigner.

ROCK 'N' ROLL FANTASY, A

Artist: The Kinks
Written by: Ray Davies
From the album: *Misfits*
Label: Arista
Produced by: Ray Davies
Year: 1977
Back in a dance hall daze.

ROCK 'N' ROLL HEAVEN

Artist: The Righteous Brothers
Written by: John Stevenson, Alan O'Day
From the album: *Give It to the People*
Label: Haven
Produced by: Dennis Lambert, Brian Potter
Year: 1973
Their third biggest hit.

(ROCK 'N' ROLL I GAVE YOU) THE BEST YEARS OF MY LIFE

Artist: Kevin Johnson
Written by: Kevin Johnson
Label: Mainstream
Year: 1973
Dismal autobiography of the eternal rock and roll dreamer. Ironically, Mac Davis's watered-down cover (Columbia, '75) was nearly a hit.

ROCK 'N' ROLL IS KING

Artist: Electric Light Orchestra (ELO)
Written by: Jeff Lynne
From the album: *Secret Messages*
Label: A&M
Produced by: Jeff Lynne
Year: 1983
Suggested segues: "Sweet Little Rock and Roll" and "Roll Over Beethoven" by Chuck Berry.

ROCK N' ME

Artist: Steve Miller Band
Written by: Steve Miller
From the album: *Fly Like an Eagle*
Label: Capitol
Produced by: Steve Miller
Year: 1976
A business relationship.

ROCK OF AGES

Artist: Def Leppard

Written by: Steve Clark, Joe Elliott, Robert John "Mutt" Lange
From the album: *Pyromania*
Label: Mercury
Produced by: Mutt Lange
Year: 1983
Out of the hockey rinks and into the football stadiums.

ROCK ON

Artist: David Essex
Written by: David Essex
From the album: *rock On*
Label: Columbia
Produced by: Jeff Wayne
Year: 1973
Leather rocker from the angry young British film *That'll Be the Day*.

ROCK STEADY

Artist: Aretha Franklin
Written by: Aretha Franklin
From the album: *To Be Young, Gifted and Black*
Label: Atlantic
Produced by: Tom Dowd, Jerry Wexler, Arif Mardin
Year: 1971
Top 10 R&B/Top 10 crossover.

ROCK STEADY

Artist: The Whispers
Written by: Kenny Edmunds (Babyface), D. Ladd, Boaz Watson
From the album: *Just Gets Better with Time*
Label: Solar
Produced by: Babyface, L. A. Reid
Year: 1987
Biggest hit for the twenty-five year old group; #1 R&B/Top 10 crossover.

ROCK THE BELLS

Label: L L Cool J
Written by: James (L L Cool J) Smith, Rick Rubin
From the album: *Radio*
Produced by: Rick Rubin
Label: Def Jam
Year: 1985
Answering the bell for round one of a knockout career.

ROCK THE BOAT

Artist: The Hues Corporation
Written by: Waldo Holmes
From the album: *Freedom for the Stallion*
Label: RCA
Produced by: John Florez
Year: 1974
Disco floats.

ROCK THE CASBAH

Artist: The Clash
Written by: John Mellor (Joe Strummer), Mick Jones, Paul Simonon, Topper Headon

From the album: *Combat Rock*
Label: Epic
Produced by: Glyn Johns
Year: 1982
Their only U.K. Top 10/U.S. Top-40 hit turned out to be more timeless than anyone could have predicted.

ROCK THERAPY

Artist: Johnny Burnette and the Rock and Roll Trio
Written by: Len Moore, Alice Bayer, Mort Subotsky
From the album: *Johnny Burnette and the Rock and Roll Trio*
Label: Coral
Produced by: Owen Bradley
Year: 1956
Covered by the Stray Cats (EMI, '86).

ROCK THIS TOWN

Artist: Stray Cats
Written by: Brian Setzer
From the album: *Built for Speed*
Label: EMI-America
Produced by: Dave Edmunds
Year: 1982
Slickest single from the roots/rock revivalists.

ROCK WIT'CHA

Artist: Bobby Brown
Written by: Babyface (Kenny Edmunds), Daryl Simmons
From the album: *Don't Be Cruel*
Label: MCA
Produced by: Babyface, L. A. Reid
Year: 1988

ROCK WITH IT

Artist: Johnny Moore and the Three Blazers
Written by: Billy Valentine, B. Goldberg
Label: RCA
Year: 1950
Seminal pre-rock trio's signature rocker, featuring Moore on guitar, Charles Brown on vocals.

ROCK WITH YOU

Artist: Michael Jackson
Written by: Rod Temperton
From the album: *Off the Wall*
Label: Epic
Produced by: Quincy Jones
Year: 1979
#1 R&B/#1 crossover.

ROCK YOU LIKE A HURRICANE

Artist: Scorpions
Written by: Rudolf Schenker, Klaus Meine
From the album: *Love at First Sting*
Label: Mercury
Produced by: Dieter Dirks

Year: 1984
A good year for their signature riff. Segue: "No One Like You" by the Scorpions.

ROCK YOUR BABY

Artist: George McCrae
Written by: Harry Casey, Richard Finch
From the album: *Rock Your Baby*
Label: T.K.
Produced by: Harry Casey
Year: 1974
Sunshine state groove mavens Casey and Finch pave the way for disco's dominance, with a #1 R&B/#1 crossover for their label mate.

ROCKABILLY BOOGIE

Artist: Johnny Burnette and the Rock and Roll Trio
Written by: Johnny Burnette, Dorsey Burnette, Henry Jerome, G. Hawkins
From the album: *Johnny Burnette and the Rock and Roll Trio*
Label: Coral
Produced by: Owen Bradley
Year: 1956
Establishing Memphis as the first Rock and Roll underground scene, with the Elvis Presley Band (Scotty Moore, Bill Black, D. J. Fontana), and the Rockabilly Trio (Johnny and Dorsey Burnette, and Paul Burlison). Johnny and Elvis both went to Humes High (as did Thomas Wayne, whose records were produced by Scotty Moore) and worked for the same electric company. The comparisons end after that.

ROCKAFELLA SKANK, THE

Artist: Fatboy Slim
Written by: Norman (Fatboy Slim) Cook, John Barry, Terry Winford
From the album: *You've Come a Long Way Baby*
Label: Astralwerks
Produced by: Norman Cook
Year: 1998
Infectious dance track introduces a new "funk soul brother."

ROCKAWAY BEACH

Artist: The Ramones
Written by: Douglas Colvin, John Cummings, Jeff Hyman, Thomas Erdelyi
From the album: *Leave Home*
Label: Sire
Produced by: Tony Bongiovi, Thomas Erdelyi
Year: 1977
Punk rock classic shoulda been a national contender, but failed to make it out of Queens, New York.

ROCKET 88

Artist: Jackie Brenston and His Delta Cats
Written by: Jackie Brenston
Label: Chess

Produced by: Sam Phillips
Year: 1951
Elvis Presley's mentor, Sam Phillips, gets the rock and roll bug. With Ike Turner on keyboards predating Jerry Lee Lewis, and Jackie Brenston on sax and vocals, this presages a sound still four years from taking over the planet. Immediately covered by Bill Haley and His Saddlemen (Holiday, '51). The first classic car song of the rock and roll era—classic car: the Olds 88. Suggested segue: "Cadillac Boogie" by Jimmy Liggins (Specialty, '47).

ROCKET IN MY POCKET

Artist: Little Feat
Written by: Lowell George
From the album: *Time Loves a Hero*
Label: Warner Brothers
Produced by: Ted Templeman
Year: 1977
George's choogling funk signature.

ROCKET MAN (I THINK IT'S GONNA BE A LONG LONG TIME)

Artist: Elton John
Written by: Elton John, Bernie Taupin
From the album: *Honky Chateau*
Label: Uni
Produced by: Gus Dudgeon
Year: 1972
Sci-fi hi-fi speculation about Mars as a place to raise your kids. Covered by Kate Bush (MCA, '93). Suggested segues: "Starman" by David Bowie, "Major Tom" by Peter Schilling.

ROCKIN'

Artist: The Robins
Written by: Bobby Nunn, Jules Taub (Jules Bihari)
Label: Modern
Year: 1951
Supposedly cowritten by the owner of pioneering L.A. indie, Modern records.

ROCKIN' ALL OVER THE WORLD

Artist: John Fogerty
Written by: John C. Fogerty
From the album: *John Fogerty*
Label: Asylum
Produced by: John C. Fogerty
Year: 1975
Suggested segue: "Rockin' in the Free World" by Neil Young, "Back in the USA" by Chuck Berry.

ROCKIN' AT MIDNIGHT

Artist: Roy Brown
Written by: Roy Brown
Label: De Luxe
Year: 1949
Classic blues crooning. Covered by the Honeydrippers (Es Paranza, '84).

ROCKIN' CHAIR

Artist: Gwen McCrae
Written by: Clarence Read, Walter Clark
From the album: *Rockin' Chair*
Label: Cat
Produced by: Steve Alaimo, Walter Clark, Clarence Read
Year: 1975
Fierce #1 R&B/Top 10 crossover, with former duet partner, husband George, on backups.

ROCKIN' IN THE FREE WORLD

Artist: Neil Young
Written by: Neil Young
From the album: *Freedom*
Label: Reprise
Produced by: Nico Bolas, Neil Young
Year: 1989
The '80s are over. A flannel anthem for the new world from the forever-inflammable Young.

ROCKIN' IS OUR BUSINESS

Artist: The Treniers
Written by: Claude Trenier, Clifton Trenier
Label: Okeh
Year: 1952
The uptempo R&B novelty act performed this crucial number on the Dean Martin and Jerry Lewis *Colgate Comedy Hour,* one of Elvis's favorite TV shows.

ROCKIN' PNEUMONIA AND THE BOOGIE WOOGIE FLU

Artist: Huey Smith
Written by: Huey Smith
From the album: *Havin' a Good Time*
Label: Ace
Produced by: Johnny Vincent
Year: 1957
First hit for the New Orleans label.

ROCKIN' ROBIN

Artist: Bobby Day
Written by: Leon Rene (Jimmie Thomas)
From the album: *Rockin' with Robin*
Label: Class
Produced by: Leon Rene
Year: 1958
Written under a pseudonym by the author of "When the Swallows Come Back to Capistrano." Covered by Michael Jackson (Epic, 70).

ROCKIN' ROLL BABY

Artist: The Stylistics
Written by: Thom Bell, Linda Creed
From the album: *Rockin' Roll Baby*
Label: Avco
Produced by: Thom Bell
Year: 1973
Highlight of their third album; a hit in England, a Top 10 R&B/Top-20 crossover here.

ROCKIN' THE HOUSE

Artist: Memphis Slim
Written by: Peter (Memphis Slim) Chatman
Label: King
Year: 1948
Legendary blues man was better known for "Everyday I Have the Blues."

ROCKING GOOD WAY (TO MESS AROUND AND FALL IN LOVE), A

Artist: The Spaniels
Written by: Brook Benton, Jesus De Luchi, Clyde Otis
Label: Vee-Jay
Year: 1958
#1 R&B/Top 10 crossover for Dinah Washington and Brook Benton (Mercury, '60). Marvin and Tammy were listening.

ROCKIT

Artist: Herbie Hancock
Written by: Herbie Hancock, Bill Laswell, Michael Beinhorn
From the album: *Future Shock*
Label: Columbia
Produced by: Herbie Hancock, Material
Year: 1983
Pop funk novelty breakthrough for the veteran jazz keyboardist is a definition of the term "turntable hit."

ROCKS OFF

Artist: The Rolling Stones
Written by: Mick Jagger, Keith Richards
From the album: *Exile on Main Street*
Produced by: Jimmy Miller
Label: Rolling Stones
Year: 1972

ROCKY MOUNTAIN HIGH

Artist: John Denver
Written by: H. J. Deutschendorf Jr. (John Denver), Michael Taylor
From the album: *Rocky Mountain High*
Label: RCA
Produced by: Milt Okun
Year: 1973
Southwestern take on "I Am, I Said" by Brooklyn's Neil Diamond.

ROCKY MOUNTAIN WAY

Artist: Joe Walsh
Written by: Joe Walsh, Kenny Passarelli, Joey Vitale, Roche Grace
From the album: *The Smoker You Drink, the Player You Get*
Label: Dunhill
Produced by: Bill Szymczyk, Joe Walsh
Year: 1973
His post-James Gang rock guitar classic. The Eagles were listening.

ROCKY RACOON

Artist: The Beatles
Written by: John Lennon, Paul McCartney
From the album: *The Beatles*
Label: Apple
Produced by: George Martin
Year: 1968
Pitching their latest kiddie cartoon concept, Paul offers his apologies to Bob Dylan. Covered by Richie Havens (Stormy Forest, '72).

ROLL AWAY THE STONE

Artist: Leon Russell
Written by: Leon Russell, Greg Dempsey
From the album: *Leon Russell*
Label: Shelter
Produced by: Denny Cordell
Year: 1970
FM hit that established the former Phil Spector session ace as a soulful rocker.

ROLL OVER BEETHOVEN

Artist: Chuck Berry
Written by: Chuck Berry
From the album: *Chuck Berry Is on Top*
Label: Chess
Produced by: Leonard Chess, Phil Chess
Year: 1959
Advocating his favorite cause. Cover by the Beatles (Capitol, '64) effectively returned Berry to the spotlight. Also covered by Electric Light Orchestra (United Artists, '73).

ROLL THE BONES

Artist: Rush
Written by: Gary Lee Weinrib (Geddy Lee), Alex Zivojinovich (Alex Lifeson), Neil Peart
From the album: *Roll the Bones*
Label: Atlantic
Produced by: Rupert Hine, Rush
Year: 1991
Uptight trio gets loose.

ROLL WITH IT

Artist: Steve Winwood
Written by: Steve Winwood, Will Jennings
From the album: *Roll with It*
Label: Virgin
Produced by: Steve Winwood, Tom Lord-Alge
Year: 1988
His biggest single.

ROLLIN' STONE

Artist: Muddy Waters
Written by: McKinley Morganfield (Muddy Waters)
From the album: *Best of Muddy Waters*
Label: Chess
Year: 1950
An essential Chicago blues drawing board for rock and roll that also served as the basis of a legendary

group, a monumental Dylan title, and a ground-breaking magazine of the counterculture. Beyond all that, it launched the Chess label from the plucky Aristocrat in 1950.

ROMANTIC

Artist: Karyn White
Written by: James Harris III, Terry Lewis, Karyn White
From the album: *Ritual of Love*
Label: Warner Brothers
Produced by: Jimmy Jam, Terry Lewis
Year: 1991
#1 R&B/#1 crossover.

ROMEO AND JULIET

Artist: Dire Straits
Written by: Mark Knopfler
From the album: *Making Movies*
Label: Warner Brothers
Produced by: Mark Knopfler, Jimmy Lovine
Year: 1980
Tortured love song, great guitar part. Covered by the Indigo Girls (Epic, '93).

ROMEO IS BLEEDING

Artist: Tom Waits
Written by: Tom Waits
From the album: *Blue Valentine*
Label: Elektra
Produced by: Bones Howe
Year: 1978
One of the essential L.A. street songs. Segue: "Born and Raised in Compton" by NWA.

ROMEO'S TUNE

Artist: Steve Forbert
Written by: Steve Forbert
From the album: *Jackrabbit Slim*
Label: Nemperor
Produced by: John Simon
Year: 1979
A fresh new folk/rock voice. Segues: "Luka" by Suzanne Vega, "Fast Car" by Tracy Chapman, "Lullaby" by Shawn Mullins.

ROMPING THROUGH THE SWAMP

Artist: Dave Van Ronk and the Hudson Dusters
Written by: Peter Stampfel
From the album: *Dave Van Ronk & the Hudson Dusters*
Label: Verve
Year: 1968
With completely bizarre material like this, it's no wonder Van Ronk's attempt to cross over from folk to folk/rock cost him his entire bank account. Covered by Stamfel with the Holy Modal Rounders (Rounder, '77).

RONI

Artist: Bobby Brown
Written by: Kenny Edmunds (Babyface)

From the album: *Don't Be Cruel*
Label: MCA
Produced by: Babyface, L. A. Reid
Year: 1989

ROOM FULL OF MIRRORS

Artist: Jimi Hendrix
Written by: Jimi Hendrix
From the album: *Rainbow Bridge*
Label: Reprise
Year: 1971
Saves the epic hippie movie *Rainbow Bridge*. Covered by the Pretenders (Sire, '86).

ROOM TO MOVE

Artist: John Mayall's Bluesbreakers with Jon Mark and Johnny Almond
Written by: John Mayall
From the album: *The Turning Point*
Label: Polydor
Year: 1969
A new era for the bluesmeister Mayall.

ROOSTER

Artist: Alice in Chains
Written by: Jerry Cantrell
From the album: *Dirt*
Produced by: Dave Jerden
Label: Columbia
Year: 1992
Grunge epic dedicated to Cantrell's father, who served in Vietnam.

ROOTS, ROCK, REGGAE

Artist: Bob Marley & the Wailers
Written by: Vincent Ford
From the album: *Rastaman Vibrations*
Label: Island
Produced by: Bob Marley & the Wailers
Year: 1976
Their only American chart appearance. They had six Top 10 hits in England.

ROSALITA (COME OUT TONIGHT)

Artist: Bruce Springsteen
Written by: Bruce Springsteen
From the album: *The Wild, the Innocent and the E Street Shuffle*
Label: Columbia
Produced by: Jim Cretecos, Mike Appel
Year: 1973
One of his legendary all-stops-out rollicking rockers. Success as the best revenge on all the girls who snubbed him in high school.

ROSALYN

Artist: Pretty Things
Written by: Jimmy Duncan, Bill Farley
From the album: *The Pretty Things*
Label: Fontana
Year: 1964

First UK single for the latter-day Stones clones. Covered by David Bowie (RCA, '73). The New York Dolls were listening.

ROSANNA

Artist: Toto
Written by: David Paich
From the album: *Toto*
Label: Columbia
Produced by: Toto
Year: 1982
Studio pros pine for actress Rosanna Arquette.

ROSE AND A BABY RUTH, A

Artist: George Hamilton IV
Written by: John D. Loudermilk
From the album: *George Hamilton IV on Campus*
Label: ABC Paramount
Year: 1956
Story of a cheap date. Both artist and writer would find future success in country music.

ROSE IS STILL A ROSE, A

Artist: Aretha Franklin
Written by: Lauryn Hill, Edie Brickell, Kenny Withrow
From the album: *A Rose Is Still a Rose*
Label: Arista
Produced by: Lauryn Hill
Year: 1998
A mentor meets a superstar in an invigorating passing of the R&B torch. Why they needed to sample "What I Am" by Edie Brickell & the New Bohemians remains a creative mystery.

ROSE, THE

Artist: Bette Midler
Written by: Amanda McBroom
From the album: *The Rose Soundtrack*
Label: Atlantic
Produced by: Paul Rothchild
Year: 1979
The best thing to emerge from the Janis Joplin biopic, a #1 hit for the quirky McBroom. Rothchild also produced the Joplin album *Pearl*.

ROSES ARE RED (MY LOVE)

Artist: Bobby Vinton
Written by: Al Byron, Paul Evans
From the album: *Roses Are Red*
Label: Epic
Produced by: Bob Morgan
Year: 1961
Cowriter Evans finally squares his tab at the Turf Cafe with the year's biggest graduation/wedding ballad.

ROUGH BOYS

Artist: Pete Townshend
Written by: Pete Townshend
From the album: *Empty Glass*
Label: Atco

Produced by: Chris Thomas
Year: 1980
Contemplating his lost Mod youth.

ROUND HERE

Artist: Counting Crows
Written by: Adam Duritz
From the album: *August and Everything After*
Label: DGC
Produced by: T-Bone Burnette, Counting Crows
Year: 1993
Earnest frat rock of the '90s.

ROUNDABOUT

Artist: Yes
Written by: Jon Anderson, Steve Howe
From the album: *Fragile*
Label: Atlantic
Produced by: Eddie Offord, Yes
Year: 1972
Their signature opus and biggest hit of the '70s.

ROWBOAT

Artist: Beck
Written by: Beck Hanson
From the album: *Stereopathic Soul Manure*
Label: Flipside
Produced by: Rick Rubin
Year: 1994
Covered by Johnny Cash (American, '96)

ROXANNE

Artist: The Police
Written by: Gordon Sumner (Sting)
From the album: *Outlandos d'Amour*
Label: A&M
Produced by: The Police
Year: 1978
Their first US hit. Joining an exclusive sorority that includes "Suzanne" by Leonard Cohen, "Ruby Tuesday" by the Rolling Stones, "Nadine" by Chuck Berry, "Gloria" by Them, "Runaround Sue" by Dion, "Queen Jane Approximately" by Bob Dylan, "Rosalita" by Bruce Springsteen, and, of course, "Roxanne, Roxanne" by UTFO. Sting does an outstanding acoustic solo version of this on a *Secret Policeman's Other Ball* album (Island, '82).

ROXANNE, ROXANNE

Artist: UTFO
Written by: Curtis Bedeau, Frederick Reeves, Lucien George, Hugh Clark, Jeffrey Campbell, Gerard Charles, Shaun Fequire, Brian George, Paul George
From the album: *UTFO*
Label: Select
Produced by: Full Force
Year: 1985
The Gloria of Rap, if not the Annie, "Roxanne" would spawn a year's worth of rebuttals and revisions, including "Roxanne's Revenge" by Roxanne Shante (Pop Art, '85). Originally the A-side was

"The Real Roxanne." But there was also "Roxanne's Doctor—The Real Man," "Queen of Rox (Shante Rox-On)," "Sparky's Turn (Roxanne You're Thru)," and "Roxanne's a Man (The Untold Story)."

RUB YOU THE RIGHT WAY

Artist: Johnny Gill
Written by: James Harris III, Terry Lewis
From the album: *Johnny Gill*
Label: Motown
Produced by: Jimmy Jam, Terry Lewis
Year: 1990
His biggest hit.

RUBBER BALL

Artist: Bobby Vee
Written by: Aaron Schroeder, Anne Orlowski
From the album: *Bobby Vee*
Label: Liberty
Produced by: Snuff Garrett
Year: 1960
Another cameo for the legendary Spauldeen.

RUBBER BISCUIT

Artist: The Chips
Written by: Charles Johnson
Label: Josie
Year: 1956
Novelty R&B with profound implications, subverted by the Blues Brothers (Atlantic, '79).

RUBBER BULLETS

Artist: 10 C. C.
Written by: Lawrence Creme, Kevin Godley, Graham Gouldman
From the album: *Rubber Bullets*
Label: UK
Produced by: Strawberry Productions
Year: 1973
First big hit, #1 UK, establishes their brand of satiric art rock.

RUBBERBAND GIRL

Artist: Kate Bush
Written by: Kate Bush
From the album: *The Red Shoes*
Label: Columbia
Produced by: Kate Bush
Year: 1993
Reestablishing herself as the reigning queen of progressive confessional alt/rock.

RUBBERBAND MAN, THE

Artist: Spinners
Written by: Thom Bell, Linda Creed
From the album: *Happiness Is Being with the Detroit Spinners*
Label: Atlantic
Produced by: Thom Bell
Year: 1976

Their last #1 R&B/Top 10 crossover is their biggest hit (aside from their duet with Dionne Warwick on "Then Came You"), and Phillippe Wynne's defining moment.

RUBBERNECKIN'

Artist: Elvis Presley
Written by: Dory Jones, Bunny Warren
From the album: *Change of Habit Soundtrack*
Label: RCA
Year: 1968
Rediscovered in the 21ST Century.

RUBY BABY

Artist: The Drifters
Written by: Jerry Leiber, Mike Stoller
From the album: *Rockin' and Driftin'*
Label: Atlantic
Produced by: Neshui Ertegun
Year: 1956
Covered by Dion (Columbia, '63).

RUBY TUESDAY

Artist: The Rolling Stones
Written by: Mick Jagger, Keith Richards
From the album: *Between the Buttons*
Label: London
Produced by: Andrew Loog-Oldham
Year: 1967
Out of the pages of Carnaby Street's trendiest fashion magazine; if Keith had been writing this the next morning it would have been called "Ruby Wednesday." Brian Jones on flute.

RUDE BOY

Artist: The Wailers
Written by: Bob Marley
Produced by: Clement Coxsone
Label: Coxsone
Year: 1966
The Wailers launch a career with this rebellious portrait.

RUFFNECK

Artist: MC Lyte
Written by: MC Lyte
From the album: *Ain't No Other*
Label: First Priority
Year: 1993
Smoking in the girl's room.

RUMBLE

Artist: Link Wray
Written by: Link Wray
Label: Cadence
Produced by: Milt Grant
Year: 1958
Instrumental version of teen gang warfare, á la *West Side Story* and Wray's trusty Danelectro Longhorn. So effective it was banned on New York radio.

RUMORS

Artist: Timex Social Club
Written by: Marcus Thompson, Michael Marshall, Alex Hill
From the album: *Vicious Rumors*
Label: Danya
Produced by: Denzil Foster, Jay King
Year: 1986
#1 R&B/Top 10 crossover.

RUMP SHAKER

Artist: Wreckx-N-Effect
Written by: Aquil Davidson, David Wynn, Markell Riley, Teddy Riley, Anton Hollins
From the album: *Hard or Smooth*
Label: MCA
Produced by: Teddy Riley
Year: 1992
The anatomy of a hip hop hit.

RUN AROUND

Artist: Blues Traveler
Written by: John Popper
From the album: *Four*
Label: A&M
Produced by: S. Thompson, M. Barbiero
Year: 1994
The return of the rock harmonica, in an advanced Springsteenian boogie setting that would have made Rosalita as well as Paul Butterfield smile.

RUN AWAY

Artist: Real McCoy
Written by: Olaf Jeglitza, Quickmix, J. Wind
From the album: *Another Night*
Label: Arista
Produced by: J. Wind, Quickmix, O-Jay
Year: 1995
Euro-groove.

RUN FOR THE ROSES

Artist: Dan Fogelberg
Written by: Dan Fogelberg
From the album: *The Innocent Age*
Label: Full Moon
Produced by: Dan Fogelberg, Marty Lewis
Year: 1982
Should be the new national anthem of Kentucky.

RUN FOR YOUR LIFE

Artist: The Beatles
Written by: John Lennon, Paul McCartney
From the album: *Rubber Soul*
Label: Capitol
Produced by: George Martin
Year: 1965
The natural follow-up to "Help!"

RUN LIKE A THIEF

Artist: J. D. Souther
Written by: John David Souther

From the album: *John David Souther*
Label: Elektra
Year: 1972
The essential folk/rock yin and yang, succumbing first to unstoppable lust and then to unendurable guilt. Covered by Bonnie Raitt (Warner Brothers, '75).

RUN LIKE HELL

Artist: Pink Floyd
Written by: Roger Waters, David Gilmour
From the album: *The Wall*
Label: Columbia
Produced by: Roger Waters, David Gilmour, Bob Ezrin
Year: 1979

RUN THROUGH THE JUNGLE

Artist: Creedence Clearwater Revival
Written by: John C. Fogerty
From the album: *Cosmo's Factory*
Label: Fantasy
Produced by: John C. Fogerty
Year: 1970
Back to their swampy roots.

RUN TO HIM

Artist: Bobby Vee
Written by: Gerry Goffin, Jack Keller
From the album: *Take Good Care of My Baby*
Label: Liberty
Produced by: Snuff Garrett
Year: 1961
Follow-up to his only #1, "Take Good Care of My Baby," peaks at #2. The oldies circuit beckoned.

RUN TO THE HILLS

Artist: Iron Maiden
Written by: Steve Harris
From the album: *Number of the Beast*
Label: Harvest
Produced by: Martin Birch
Year: 1982
British metal classic was their first UK Top 10.

RUN TO YOU

Artist: Bryan Adams
Written by: Bryan Adams, Jim Vallance
From the album: *Reckless*
Label: A&M
Produced by: Bryan Adams Bob Clearmountain
Year: 1984
Working on his rock credentials.

RUNAROUND SUE

Artist: Dion
Written by: Dion DiMucci, Emie Maresca
From the album: *Runaround Sue*
Label: Laurie
Produced by: Gene Schwartz
Year: 1961

His biggest, and one of his best. He would follow it up with his own answer song, "The Wanderer."

RUNAWAY

Artist: Bon Jovi
Written by: Jon Bon Jovi, George Karak
From the album: *Bon Jovi*
Label: Mercury
Produced by: Tony Bongiovi, Lance Quinn
Year: 1984
Streetwise arena rock is their first and still one of their most believable hits.

RUNAWAY

Artist: Del Shannon
Written by: Del Shannon, Max Crook
From the album: *Little Town Flirt*
Label: Big Top
Produced by: Irving Micahnik, Harry Balk
Year: 1961
Shannon's first and biggest hit (#1 US/UK), sported a trademark Farfisa organ sound that would launch a million '60s garage bands—even though it was actually Max Crook's Musitron.

RUNAWAY BOYS

Artist: Stray Cats
Written by: Brian Setzer
From the album: *Stray Cats*
Label: Arista
Produced by: Dave Edmunds
Year: 1981
Rockabilly redux by a Long Island band that ran away to England.

RUNAWAY CHILD, RUNNING WILD

Artist: The Temptations
Written by: Norman Whitfield, Barrett Strong
From the album: *Cloud Nine*
Label: Gordy
Produced by: Norman Whitfield
Year: 1969
Their fifth #1 R&B/Top 10 crossover. Suggested segues: "She's Leaving Home" by the Beatles, "Love Child" by the Supremes, "Runaway" by Bon Jovi.

RUNAWAY TRAIN

Artist: Soul Asylum
Written by: Dave Pirner
From the album: *Grave Dancers Union*
Label: Columbia
Produced by: Michael Beinhorn
Year: 1992
Grammy for Rock Song of the Year.

RUNNIN' AWAY

Artist: Sly & the Family Stone
Written by: Sylvester Stewart
From the album: *There's a Riot Goin' On*
Label: Epic
Produced by: Sly Stone

Year: 1971
Chronicling the despair of the ghetto.

RUNNIN' DOWN A DREAM

Artist: Tom Petty and the Heartbreakers
Written by: Tom Petty, Jeff Lynne, Mike Campbell
From the album: *Full Moon Fever*
Label: MCA
Produced by: Jeff Lynne
Year: 1989
His essential folk/rock groove. Segue: "Runaway" by Del Shannon.

RUNNIN' WITH THE DEVIL

Artist: Van Halen
Written by: Eddie Van Halen, Alex Van Halen, Michael Anthony, David Lee Roth
From the album: *Van Halen*
Label: Warner Brothers
Produced by: Ted Templeman
Year: 1978
First track off their first album followed up "You Really Got Me" as a single, but stiffed on the charts.

RUNNING BEAR

Artist: Johnny Preston
Written by: J. P. Richardson
From the album: *Running Bear*
Label: Mercury
Produced by: J. P. Richardson
Year: 1959
Teenage horse opera/soap opera, with the recently departed Richardson (The Big Bopper) on accompanying war-whoops, adding another tragic dimension.

RUNNING ON EMPTY

Artist: Jackson Browne
Written by: Jackson Browne
From the album: *Running on Empty*
Label: Asylum
Produced by: Jackson Browne
Year: 1977
A virtual autobiography.

RUNNING SCARED

Artist: Roy Orbison
Written by: Roy Orbison, Joe Melson
From the album: *Crying*
Label: Monument
Produced by: Fred Foster
Year: 1961
His first #1.

RUNNING TO STAND STILL

Artist: U2
Written by: U2
From the album: *The Joshua Tree*
Label: Island
Produced by: Daniel Lanois, Brian Eno
Year: 1987
Addict's lament.

RUNNING UP THAT HILL

Artist: Kate Bush
Written by: Kate Bush
From the album: *Hounds of Love*
Label: EMI-America
Produced by: Kate Bush
Year: 1985
A personal and artistic peak; her only US Top 40.

RUSH

Artist: Big Audio Dynamite
Written by: Mick Jones
From the album: *The Globe*
Label: Columbia
Produced by: Mick Jones, Climax, D. J. Shappe
Year: 1991
An outgrowth of the Clash.

RUSH, RUSH

Artist: Paula Abdul
Written by: Peter Lord
From the album: *Spellbound*
Label: Virgin
Produced by: Peter Lord
Year: 1991
Shortly after this, her sixth #1, Abdul's career was derailed by charges that she didn't really sing on all, some, or at least one of her records. She was eventually exonerated and bequeathed a position of eminence on the TV franchise *American Idol*, where she was again derailed by charges that... .

RUST NEVER SLEEPS (HEY HEY MY MY INTO THE BLACK)

Artist: Neil Young
Written by: Neil Young
From the album: *Rust Never Sleeps*
Label: Reprise
Produced by: Neil Young, David Briggs, Tim Mulligan
Year: 1979
From whence came the maxim: "It's better to burn out than to fade away."

RUSTY CAGE

Artist: Soundgarden
Written by: Chris Cornell
From the album: *Badmotorfinger*
Produced by: Terry Date, Soundgarden
Label: A&M
Year: 1991
Covered by Johnny Cash (American, '96).

S

S.F. SORROW IS BORN

Artist: Pretty Things
Written by: John Alder, Phil May, Jonathan Povey, Richard Taylor, Alan Waller
From the album: *S.F. Sorrow*

Label: Rare Earth
Year: 1969
May have been the world's first rock opera, but it was no *Tommy*.

SABRE DANCE

Artist: Love Sculpture
Written by: Aram Khachaturian
From the album: *Form and Feeling*
Label: Parlaphone
Produced by: Dave Edmunds
Year: 1968
Dave Edmunds begins his archetypically loopy career with a UK hit cover of the classical evergreen.

SAD EYES

Artist: Robert John
Written by: Robert John
From the album: *Robert John*
Label: EMI-America
Produced by: George Tobin
Year: 1979
Frankie Valliesque falsetto.

SAD MOVIES ALWAYS MAKE ME CRY

Artist: Sue Thompson
Written by: John D. Loudermilk
From the album: *Sue Thompson*
Label: Hickory
Year: 1961

SAD SONGS (SAY SO MUCH)

Artist: Elton John
Written by: Elton John, Bernie Taupin
From the album: *Breaking Hearts*
Label: Geffen
Produced by: Chris Thomas
Year: 1984
Sequel to "I Guess That's Why They Call It the Blues."

SADENESS (PART I)

Artist: Enigma
Written by: M. C. Curly, F. Gregorian, David Fairstein
From the album: *MCMXC A.D.*
Label: Charisma
Year: 1991
Nailing the Gregorian mood of the early '90s.

SAD-EYED LADY OF THE LOWLANDS

Artist: Bob Dylan
Written by: Bob Dylan
From the album: *Blonde on Blonde*
Label: Columbia
Produced by: Bob Johnston
Year: 1966
All of side IV, dedicated to his then-wife, Sara.

SAFE EUROPEAN HOME

Artist: The Clash
Written by: John Mellor (Joe Strummer), Mick Jones
From the album: *Give 'Em Enough Rope*
Label: Epic
Produced by: Sandy Pearlman
Year: 1978
Written in the Pegasus Hotel, Kingston, Jamaica.

SAFETY DANCE

Artist: Men without Hats
Written by: Ivan Doroschuk
From the album: *Rhythm of Youth*
Label: Backstreet
Produced by: Z. B. Held, Men Without Hats
Year: 1983
British synth invasion one-shot.

SAIGON BRIDE

Artist: Joan Baez
Written by: Joan Baez, Nina Dusheck
From the album: *Children of Darkness*
Label: Vanguard
Year: 1967
Potent protest.

SAIL AWAY

Artist: Randy Newman
Written by: Randy Newman
From the album: *Sail Away*
Label: Warner Brothers
Produced by: Russ Titelman, Lenny Waronker
Year: 1972
Newman's own favorite, a treatise on racism.

SAIL ON

Artist: Commodores
Written by: Lionel B. Richie Jr.
From the album: *Midnight Magic*
Label: Motown
Produced by: James Carmichael, the Commodores
Year: 1979
Charley Pride would have been proud of this.

SAIL ON SAILOR

Artist: The Beach Boys
Written by: Jack Rieley, Ray Kennedy, Brian Wilson, Tandyn Almer
From the album: *Holland*
Label: Brother
Produced by: Brian Wilson
Year: 1973
Off the surfboard and onto the yacht.

SAILING

Artist: Christopher Cross
Written by: Christopher Geppert
From the album: *Christopher Cross*
Label: Warner Brothers
Produced by: Michael Omartian
Year: 1980
Cross won five Grammies in '81, including Best New Artist and Album of the Year; "Sailing" won Song of the Year and Record of the Year and peaked at #1.

SAILING

Artist: Sutherland Brothers and Quiver
Written by: Gavin Sutherland
From the album: *Lifeboat*
Label: Island
Year: 1973
Covered by Rod Stewart (Warner Brothers, '75).

SAILING TO PHILADELPHIA

Artist: Mark Knopfler and James Taylor
Written by: Mark Knoplfer, James Taylor
From the album: *Sailing to Philadelphia*
Produced by: Mark Knopfler, Chuck Ainley
Label: Warner Brothers
Year: 2000
Folk/rock lives in this enchanting tale of explorers Mason and Dixon.

SAILOR (YOUR HOME IS THE SEA)

Artist: Lolita
Written by: Alan Holt, Fini Busch, Werner Schaffenberger
Label: Kapp
Year: 1960
Representing Austria on the charts. Suggested segues: "Schock den Affen" by Peter Gabriel, "99 Luftballons" by Nena, "Lucky Number" by Lene Lovich.

SAILS OF CHARON, THE

Artist: Scorpions
Written by: Uli Roth
From the album: *Taken by Force*
Label: RCA
Produced by: Dieter Dirks
Year: 1977
Mystically inclined guitar legend Uli Roth's showpiece that laid the groundwork for the heavy metal excursions of the '80s. Every fleet-fingered aspiring virtuoso, from Randy Rhoads (Ozzy Osbourne) to Yngwie Malmsteen to Jason Becker (David Lee Roth) was listening.

SAINTS

Artist: The Breeders
Written by: Kim Deal
From the album: *Last Splash*
Label: 4AD
Produced by: Kim Deal
Year: 1993

SALLY

Artist: Sade
Written by: Helen Folesade Adu (Sade), Stuart Matthewman
From the album: *Diamond Life*
Label: Epic
Produced by: R. Millar
Year: 1985
Moody decadence, with a mellow international character. Suggested segues: "Seems So Long Ago, Nancy" by Leonard Cohen, "Chelsea Girls" by Nico.

SALLY CAN'T DANCE

Artist: Lou Reed
Written by: Lou Reed
From the album: *Sally Can't Dance*
Label: RCA
Produced by: Steve Katz
Year: 1974
Covered by the Andrea True Connection (Buddah, '77).

SALLY GO'ROUND THE ROSES

Artist: The Jaynettes
Written by: Zell Sanders, Lona Stevens
From the album: *Sally Go 'Round the Roses*
Label: Tuff
Produced by: Abner Spector
Year: 1963
An eerie, foreboding tale that seemed to forecast the end of the girl-group era. Segue: "Party Lights" by Claudine Clark.

SALT OF THE EARTH, THE

Artist: The Rolling Stones
Written by: Mick Jagger, Keith Richards
From the album: *Beggars Banquet*
Label: London
Produced by: Jimmy Miller
Year: 1968
Down to earth rocker.

SALTY DOG, A

Artist: Procol Harum
Written by: Gary Brooker, Keith Reid
From the album: *Too Much Between Us*
Label: A&M
Year: 1967
Progressive rockers borrow a blues metaphor.

SALVATION

Artist: The Cranberries
Written by: Noel Hogan, Dolores O'Riordan
From the album: *To the Faithful Departed*
Label: Island
Produced by: Bruce Fairbairn
Year: 1996
Celtic harmon on the U2 tip.

SAM

Artist: Meat Puppets
Written by: Curt Kirkwood

From the album: *Forbidden Places*
Label: London
Produced by: Pete Anderson
Year: 1991
Wordiest song to gain radio airplay since Meat Loaf.

SAM STONE

Artist: John Prine
Written by: John Prine
From the album: *John Prine*
Label: Atlantic
Produced by: Arif Mardin
Year: 1971
Nobody's war hero.

SAME OLD LANG SYNE

Artist: Dan Fogelberg
Written by: Dan Fogelberg
From the album: *The Innocent Age*
Label: Full Moon
Produced by: Dan Fogelberg, Marty Lewis
Year: 1980
Harry Chapinesque champagne commercial.

SAN DIEGO SERENADE

Artist: Tom Waits
Written by: Tom Waits
From the album: *The Heart of Saturday Night*
Label: Asylum
Produced by: Bones Howe
Year: 1974
Bleary beatnik tribute to the morning after. Covered by Juice Newton (Capitol, '80), Dion (Arista, '89), Nanci Griffith (MCA, '91).

SAN FRANCISCAN NIGHTS

Artist: The Animals
Written by: Eric Burdon. Victor Briggs, Barry Jenkins, Denny McCulloch
From the album: *Winds of Change*
Label: MGM
Produced by: Mickie Most
Year: 1967
While he was still in the neighborhood (see "Monterey") Eric Burdon was briefly taken in by hippies during the Summer of Love.

SAN FRANCISCO (BE SURE TO WEAR SOME FLOWERS IN YOUR HAIR)

Artist: Scott McKenzie
Written by: John Phillips
From the album: *The Voice of Scott McKenzie*
Label: Ode
Produced by: John Phillips
Year: 1967
Reducing the Summer of Love to a hippie theme park in San Francisco, written by the man who did the same for Monterey.

SAN FRANCISCO (YOU'VE GOT ME)

Artist: The Village People
Written by: Henri Belolo, Jacques Morali, Phil Hurtt, Peter Whitehead
From the album: *Village People*
Label: Casablanca
Produced by: Henri Belolo
Year: 1977
Long-lasting dance anthem of the chic disco set, from Sausalito to Fire Island.

SAN FRANCISCO BAY BLUES

Artist: Jesse Fuller
Written by: Jesse Fuller
Label: World Song
Year: 1954
One man jug band classic of the coming folk scare, chronicling the appeal of the incipient bohemian nexus, San Francisco, where Jerry Garcia was only a few years away from forming Mother Macree's Uptown Jug Champions. Covered by Peter, Paul, and Mary (Warner Brothers, '65), Richie Havens (Verve, '66), Rambling Jack Elliot. Fuller recorded this again on Good Time Jazz in '58, Folk Lyric in '62, Folk Lore in '63, Vanguard in '64, and Fontana in '65. (Topic, '58).

SAN FRANCISCO GIRLS (THE RETURN OF THE NATIVE)

Artist: Fever Tree
Written by: Scott Holtzman, Vivian Holtzman, Michael Knust
From the album: *Fever Tree*
Label: Uni
Produced by: Scott Holtzman, Vivian Holtzman
Year: 1968
Atmospheric nostalgia for the waning days of hippie splendor and grass.

SANCTIFIED LADY

Artist: Marvin Gaye
Written by: Marvin Gaye, Gordon Banko
From the album: *Dream of a Lifetime*
Label: Columbia
Produced by: Brian Holland, Lamont Dozier
Year: 1985
Funk from over the edge, posthumously released after Gaye was shot to death by his father in '84.

SANTA MONICA (WATCH THE WORLD DROWN)

Artist: Everclear
Written by: Art Alexakis, Greg Ecklund, Craig Montoya
From the album: *Sparkle and Fade*
Label: Tim Kerr
Produced by: Art Alexakis

Year: 1996
Art Alexakis comes home to recover.

SANTERIA

Artist: Sublime
Written by: Sublime
From the album: *Sublime*
Label: MCA
Year: 1997
Voodoo reggae with a punk edge.

SARA

Artist: Bob Dylan
Written by: Bob Dylan
From the album: *Desire*
Label: Columbia
Produced by: Don DeVito
Year: 1976
A mere song for his wife where once he wrote an entire side of an album for her. Soon they would be divorced.

SARA

Artist: Fleetwood Mac
Written by: Stephanie Nicks
From the album: *Tusk*
Label: Warner Brothers
Produced by: Fleetwood Mac
Year: 1979
Stevie's trademark folk swirl.

SARA

Artist: Starship
Written by: Peter Wolf, Ina Wolf
From the album: *Knee Deep in the Hoopla*
Label: Grunt
Produced by: Dennis Lambert
Year: 1985
The Jefferson Airplane/Jefferson Starship, stripped of everything but their adopted name, get their second straight #1.

SARA SMILE

Artist: Daryl Hall & John Oates
Written by: Daryl Hall, John Oates
From the album: *Daryl Hall & John Oates*
Label: RCA
Produced by: Chris Bond
Year: 1975
Their first big hit, dedicated to future collaborator Sara Allen.

SARAN WRAP

Artist: The Fugs
Written by: Tuli Kupferberg, Ed Sanders
From the album: *Virgin Fugs*
Label: ESP
Produced by: Harry Smith
Year: 1965
Safe sex in the era of free love.

SAT IN YOUR LAP

Artist: Kate Bush
Written by: Kate Bush
From the album: *The Dreaming*
Label: EMI-America
Produced by: Kate Bush
Year: 1982
In quest of the unknowable. Suggested segue: "I Am the Walrus" by the Beatles.

SATELLITE OF LOVE

Artist: Lou Reed
Written by: Lou Reed
From the album: *Transformer*
Label: RCA
Produced by: David Bowie
Year: 1972
Lou's answer to "Under the Moon of Love" by the Crests. Covered by U2 (Island, '92).

SATISFIED

Artist: Richard Marx
Written by: Richard Marx, David Cole
From the album: *Repeat Offender*
Label: EMI
Produced by: David Cole, Richard Marx
Year: 1989
#1 follow up to the #1 "Hold onto the Nights."

SATURDAY IN THE PARK

Artist: Chicago
Written by: Robert Lamm
From the album: *Chicago V*
Label: Columbia
Produced by: James William Guercio
Year: 1972
Mainstream jazz-flavored pop is Lamm's last big hit.

SATURDAY NIGHT

Artist: The Bay City Rollers
Written by: Phil Coulter, William MacPherson
From the album: *Rock and Roll Love Letter*
Label: Arista
Produced by: Phil Coulter, William MacPherson
Year: 1975
This '73 UK flop went straight to #1 in the US after auspiciously kicking off Howard Cosell's *Saturday Night* TV variety show, which subsequently went straight into the dumper. Revived in Mike Myers' heavily Scots-flavored soundtrack to *So I Married an Axe Murderer* (Chaos, '93).

SATURDAY NIGHT FISH FRY

Artist: Louis Jordan and His Tympani Five
Written by: Louis Jordan, Ellis Walsh
Label: Decca
Produced by: Milt Gabler
Year: 1949

Wine, women, song, plus a visit from the police, a perfect #1 R&B/Top 30 recipe for the upcoming rock and roll rebellion.

SATURDAY NIGHT SPECIAL

Artist: Lynyrd Skynyrd
Written by: Ronnie Van Zant, Edward King
From the album: *Nuthin' Fancy*
Label: MCA
Produced by: Tom Dowd
Year: 1975
Smokin' groove.

SATURDAY NIGHT'S ALRIGHT (FOR FIGHTING)

Artist: Elton John
Written by: Elton John, Bernie Taupin
From the album: *Don't Shoot Me, I'm Only the Piano Player*
Label: MCA
Produced by: Gus Dudgeon
Year: 1972
Trying out his Jerry Lee Lewis groove.

SAVE IT FOR LATER

Artist: The English Beat
Written by: The English Beat
From the album: *Special Beat Service*
Label: I.R.S.
Produced by: Bob Sergeant
Year: 1982

SAVE IT FOR ME

Artist: The Four Seasons
Written by: Bob Gaudio, Bob Crewe
From the album: *Rag Doll*
Label: Philips
Produced by: Bob Crewe
Year: 1964
Traditional arrangement.

SAVE ME

Artist: Aimee Mann
Written by: Aimee Mann
From the album: *Magnolia Soundtrack*
Year: 1999
Nominated for an Academy Award.

SAVE THE BEST FOR LAST

Artist: Vanessa Williams
Written by: Wendy Waldman, Phil Galdston, Jon Lind
From the album: *The Comfort Zone*
Label: Wing
Produced by: Keith Thomas
Year: 1992
Answering the question whatever happened to Wendy Waldman, this #1 R&B/#1 crossover moved the one-time quirky and soulful singer/songwriter one small step closer to Diane Warren territory.

SAVE THE COUNTRY

Artist: Laura Nyro
Written by: Laura Nyro
From the album: *New York Tendaberry*
Label: Columbia
Produced by: Roy Halee, Laura Nyro
Year: 1969
Having conquered the Top 40, Nyro turns to stoopside politics. Covered by the Fifth Dimension (Bell, '70), Thelma Houston (Dunhill, '70).

SAVE THE LAST DANCE FOR ME

Artist: The Drifters
Written by: Doc Pomus, Mort Shuman
From the album: *Up on the Roof, the Best of the Drifters*
Label: Atlantic
Produced by: Jerry Leiber, Mike Stoller
Year: 1960
The Drifters partake of the second great dance era with their only #1 R&B/#1 crossover.

SAVE TONIGHT

Artist: Eagle Eye Cherry
Written by: Eagle Eye Cherry
From the album: *Desireless*
Label: Work
Year: 1998
Son of trumpeter Don, brother of rocker Neneh, is leaving on a moped.

SAVE YOUR HEART FOR ME

Artist: Brian Hyland
Written by: Gary Geld, Peter Udell
Label: ABC-Paramount
Produced by: Snuff Garrett
Year: 1963
Covered by Gary Lewis and the Playboys (Imperial, '65).

SAVED

Artist: Laverne Baker
Written by: Jerry Leiber, Mike Stoller
From the album: *Saved*
Label: Atlantic
Produced by: Jerry Leiber, Mike Stoller
Year: 1961
Gospel shouter that translated well to Broadway. Covered by Elvis Presley (RCA, '68).

SAVING ALL MY LOVE FOR YOU

Artist: Marilyn McCoo and Billy Davis Jr.
Written by: Michael Masser, Gerry Goffin
From the album: *Marilyn and Billy*
Label: Columbia
Year: 1985
The Clive Davis magic touch. When his newest and greatest diva Whitney Houston covered this tune it became the first of her six #1 R&B/#1 crossovers

(Arista, '85) and a nifty feather in the cap of former Carole King husband and lyricist Gerry Goffin.

SAVING FOREVER FOR YOU

Artist: Shanice
Written by: Diane Warren
From the album: *Beverly Hills 90210 Soundtrack*
Label: Giant
Produced by: David Foster
Year: 1992
From the growing Diane Warren hit factory.

SAVOY TRUFFLE

Artist: The Beatles
Written by: George Harrison
From the album: *The Beatles*
Label: Apple
Produced by: George Martin
Year: 1968
A George trifle.

SAY GOODBYE TO HOLLYWOOD

Artist: Billy Joel
Written by: Billy Joel
From the album: *Turnstiles*
Label: Columbia
Produced by: Phil Ramone
Year: 1976
Suggested segue: "I Love L.A." by Randy Newman. Covered by Ronnie Spector & the E Street Band (Cleveland International, '77).

SAY, HAS ANYBODY SEEN MY SWEET GYPSY ROSE

Artist: Tom Orlando & Dawn
Written by: Irwin Levine, L. Russell Brown
From the album: *Dawn's New Ragtime Follies*
Label: Bell
Produced by: Hank Medress, Dave Appel
Year: 1973
Ragtime folly.

SAY IT ISN'T SO

Artist: Daryl Hall & John Oates
Written by: Daryl Hall
From the album: *Rock 'N Soul (Part I)*
Label: RCA
Produced by: Hall and Oates
Year: 1984

SAY IT LOUD—I'M BLACK AND I'M PROUD

Artist: James Brown and the Famous Flames
Written by: James Brown, Alfred Ellis
From the album: *Say It Loud—I'm Black and I'm Proud*
Label: King
Produced by: James Brown
Year: 1968

#1 R&B/Top 10 crossover, released five months after the assassination of Martin Luther King Jr.

SAY MAN

Artist: Bo Diddley
Written by: Ellas McDaniel (Bo Diddley), Jerome Green
From the album: *Have Guitar Will Travel*
Label: Checker
Produced by: Leonard Chess
Year: 1959
Off-the-cuff studio version of the dozens gave Bo his biggest chart success. Three months later "Say Man Back Again" was a bomb.

SAY MY NAME

Artist: Destiny's Child
Written by: LaShawn Daniels, Fred Jerkins, Rodney Jerkins, Letoya Luckett, Beyonce Knowles, Kelendria Rowland, Latania Roberson
From the album: *The Writing's on the Wall*
Label: Columbia
Year: 1999
Winner of two R&B Grammys.

SAY SAY SAY

Artist: Paul McCartney and Michael Jackson
Written by: Paul McCartney, Michael Jackson
From the album: *Pipes of Peace*
Label: Columbia
Produced by: George Martin
Year: 1983
A mega-merger between the artist and his publisher gives McCartney his twenty-eight and final #1.

SAY YOU LOVE ME

Artist: Fleetwood Mac
Written by: Christine McVie
From the album: *Fleetwood Mac*
Label: Reprise
Produced by: Keith Olson, Fleetwood Mac
Year: 1975

SAY YOU, SAY ME

Artist: Lionel Richie
Written by: Lionel B. Richie
From the album: *Dancing on the Ceiling*
Label: Motown
Produced by: Lionel Richie, James Anthony Carmichael
Year: 1985
#1 R&B/#1 crossover Oscar winner from the movie *White Nights*.

SAY YOU'LL BE THERE

Artist: Spice Girls
Written by: Melanie Brown, Geraldine Halliwell, Victoria Adams, Melanie Chisholm, Emma Lee Burton, Elliot Kennedy
From the album: *Spice*
Label: Virgin

Year: 1997
Girl power arrives.

SCAR TISSUE

Artist: Red Hot Chili Peppers
Written by: Anthony Keidis, Michael (Flea) Balzary, John Frusciante, Chad Smith
From the album: *Californication*
Label: Warner Brothers
Produced by: Rick Rubin
Year: 1999
Grammy winning modern rock staple.

SCARBOROUGH FAIR (CANTICLE)

Artist: Simon and Garfunkel
Written by: Paul Simon, Art Garfunkel
From the album: *Parsley, Sage, Rosemary and Thyme*
Label: Columbia
Produced by: Bob Johnston
Year: 1966
In the Dylan new tradition: updating an old Elizabethan air.

SCENARIO

Artist: A Tribe Called Quest
Written by: Ali Shaheed Muhammed, Phife Dawg, Bryan Higgins, P.J. Jackson, T. Smith
From the album: *The Low End Theory*
Label: Jive
Produced by: Skeff Anselm, A Tribe Called Quest
Year: 1992
First chart hit.

SCENES FROM AN ITALIAN RESTAURANT

Artist: Billy Joel
Written by: Billy Joel
From the album: *The Stranger*
Label: Columbia
Produced by: Phil Ramone
Year: 1977
The Syosset, Long Island, yuppie version of "The Way We Were" by Barbra Streisand.

SCHOOL DAY

Artist: Chuck Berry
Written by: Chuck Berry
From the album: *After School Sessions*
Label: Chess
Produced by: Leonard Chess, Phil Chess
Year: 1957
A teenage day-in-the-life.

SCHOOL DAYS

Artist: Loudon Wainwright
Written by: Loudon Wainwright
From the album: *Loudon Wainwright III*
Label: Atlantic
Produced by: Milton Kramer

Year: 1970
The folk tragicomic recalls his early days.

SCHOOL IS OUT

Artist: Gary US Bonds
Written by: Gary Anderson (US Bonds), Gene Barge
From the album: *Dance Til Quarter to Three*
Label: LeGrand
Produced by: Frank J. Guida
Year: 1961
Summertime anthem. Suggested segue: "School's Out" by Alice Cooper.

SCHOOL'S OUT

Artist: Alice Cooper
Written by: Vincent Furnier (Alice Cooper), Michael Bruce
From the album: *School's Out*
Label: Warner Brothers
Produced by: Bob Ezrin
Year: 1972
The "Summertime Blues" of the '70s. But not the "Summertime Summertime."

SCIENCE FICTION DOUBLE FEATURE

Artist: Jamie Donnelly
Written by: Richard O'Brien
From the album: *The Rocky Horror Picture Show Cast Album*
Label: Ode
Year: 1974
From the cult musical that became a midnight cult film. Over the film's opening credits.

SEA CRUISE

Artist: Frankie Ford
Written by: Huey Smith
From the album: *Let's Take a Sea Cruise*
Label: Ace
Produced by: Johnny Vincent
Year: 1959
His first and biggest hit, with Huey Piano Smith providing the song, and his band, the Clowns, the backing tracks.

SEA OF LOVE

Artist: Phil Phillips
Written by: George Khoury, Phil Battiste
Label: Mercury
Produced by: Eddie Shuler
Year: 1959
#1 R&B/Top 10 crossover, influenced by the timeless depths of the Mississippi. Covered by the Honeydrippers (Esperanza, '84). Suggested segue: "Black Water" by the Doobie Brothers.

SEALED WITH A KISS

Artist: Brian Hyland
Written by: Peter Udell, Gary Geld
From the album: *Sealed with a Kiss*

Label: ABC Paramount
Produced by: Snuff Garrett
Year: 1962
Segue: See you in September by the Tempos.

SEARCH AND DESTROY

Artist: The Stooges
Written by: James Osterberg (Iggy Pop), James Williamson
From the album: *Raw Power*
Label: Columbia
Produced by: David Bowie
Year: 1973
Outlining the punk philosophy.

SEARCH IS OVER, THE

Artist: Survivor
Written by: Frankie Sullivan, Jim Peterik
From the album: *Vital Signs*
Label: Epic
Produced by: Ron Nevison
Year: 1984
Searching for the lost power chord, a corporate rock peak worthy of Asia, or even Toto.

SEARCHIN'

Artist: The Coasters
Written by: Jerry Leiber, Mike Stoller
From the album: *The Coasters*
Label: Atco
Produced by: Jerry Leiber, Mike Stoller
Year: 1957
Calling on a lineup of detective superheroes, in one of their more perfect novelty conceits. #1 R&B/Top 10.

SEARCHING FOR A HEART

Artist: Warren Zevon
Written by: Warren Zevon
From the album: *Love at Large Soundtrack*
Label: Movie Music
Year: 1990
Used even more powerfully a couple of years later in the Lawrence Kasdan epic of baby-boom generational malaise *Grand Canyon* (Milan, '92).

SEASON OF THE WITCH

Artist: Donovan
Written by: Donovan Leitch
From the album: *Catch the Wind*
Label: Hickory
Produced by: Steve Hoffman
Year: 1965
The rockin' side of Donovan. Covered by Al Kooper (Columbia, '68), Vanilla Fudge (Atco, '68).

SEASONS CHANGE

Artist: Expose
Written by: Lewis Martinee
From the album: *Exposure*
Label: Arista
Produced by: Lewis Martinee

Year: 1987
Their first #1 slow dance and fourth Top 10 from the same album.

SEASONS IN THE SUN

Artist: The Kingston Trio
Written by: Rod McKuen, Jacques Brel
From the album: *Time to Think*
Label: Capitol
Produced by: Voile Gillmore
Year: 1963
Folky adaptation of the Brel classic by rock poet manqué Rod McKuen. Only the French could write such jaunty pop songs about death. Covered by Terry Jacks (Bell, '74).

SEASONS OF LOVE

Artist: Cast of *Rent*
Written by: Jonathan Larson
From the album: *Rent Original Cast Album*
Label: Geffen
Year: 1996
Single from the rock opera was performed on the album by Stevie Wonder.

SEASONS OF WITHER

Artist: Aerosmith
Written by: Steven Tyler
From the album: *Get Your Wings*
Label: Columbia
Produced by: Jack Douglas, Ray Colcord
Year: 1974
Plodding toward the holy grail of sludge.

SECOND HAND LOVE

Artist: Connie Francis
Written by: Hank Hunter, Phil Spector
From the album: *Connie Francis Sings*
Label: MGM
Produced by: Phil Spector
Year: 1962
Rare Spector collaboration and production.

SECOND TIME AROUND, THE

Artist: Shalamar
Written by: William Shelby, Leon Sylvers
From the album: *Big Fun*
Label: Solar
Produced by: Leon Sylvers
Year: 1979
#1 R&B/Top 10 crossover.

SECRET

Artist: Madonna
Written by: Dallas Austin, Madonna Ciccone
From the album: *Bedtime Stories*
Label: Maverick
Produced by: Dallas Austin, Madonna
Year: 1994
Channeling Oprah and Dr. Ruth. Suggested segue: "I Touch Myself" by the Divinyls.

SECRET AGENT MAN

Artist: Johnny Rivers
Written by: Steve Barri, P. F. Sloan
From the album: *... and I Know You Wanna Dance*
Label: Imperial
Produced by: Lou Adler
Year: 1966
TV theme song.

SECRET GARDEN

Artist: Bruce Springsteen
Written by: Bruce Springsteen
From the album: *Greatest Hits*
Label: Columbia
Year: 1995
Little big ballad from *Jerry McGuire*. Show him the Oscar!

SECRET LOVERS

Artist: Atlantic Starr
Written by: David Lewis, Wayne Lewis
From the album: *As the Band Turns*
Label: A&M
Produced by: David Lewis, Wayne Lewis
Year: 1986
The first Top 10 hit.

SECRET SHARER

Artist: Half Japanese
Written by: Jad Fair
From the album: *Sing No Evil*
Label: Iridescence
Year: 1984
Jonathan Richman innocence, squared.

SECURITY

Artist: Otis Redding
Written by: Otis Redding
From the album: *Pain in My Heart*
Label: Atco
Produced by: Jim Stewart
Year: 1964
Covered by Etta James (Cadet, '68).

SECURITY OF THE 1ST WORLD

Artist: Public Enemy
Written by: Carlton Ridenhour, James Boxley, Eric Sadler
From the album: *It Takes a Nation of Millions to Hold Us Back*
Label: Def Jam
Produced by: Hank Shocklee, Carl Ryder
Year: 1988
Suggested segue: "Justify My Love" by Madonna.

SEE A LITTLE LIGHT

Artist: Bob Mould
Written by: Bob Mould
From the album: *Workbook*
Label: Virgin
Produced by: Bob Mould
Year: 1989
Richard Thompson-influenced former guitarist of Hüsker Dü writes a song with a Top 40 hook. Later he would form Sugar and go for the rock mainstream.

SEE EMILY PLAY

Artist: Pink Floyd
Written by: Roger Waters
From the album: *Pink Floyd*
Label: Harvest
Produced by: Norman Smith
Year: 1968
Early psychedelic mood piece for a Tuesday afternoon was their first UK smash, originally entitled "Games for May."

SEE ME, FEEL ME

Artist: The Who
Written by: Pete Townshend
From the album: *Tommy*
Label: Decca
Produced by: Kit Lambert
Year: 1969
The biggest *Tommy* single, peaking in the US at #12.

SEE MY FRIENDS

Artist: The Kinks
Written by: Ray Davies
From the album: *Kinks Kinkdom*
Label: Reprise
Produced by: Shel Talmy
Year: 1966
Positively Carnaby Street.

SEE YOU IN SEPTEMBER

Artist: The Tempos
Written by: Sid Wayne, Sherman Edwards
From the album: *Speaking of the Tempos*
Label: Climax
Year: 1959
Covered by the Happenings (B. T. Puppy, '66).

SEE YOU LATER, ALLIGATOR

Artist: Bobby Charles
Written by: Robert Guidry
Label: Chess
Year: 1955
A Louisiana farewell. Covered by Bill Haley and His Comets (Decca, '56).

SEEDS

Artist: Bruce Springsteen
Written by: Bruce Springsteen
From the album: *Bruce Springsteen and the E Street Band Live, 1975–1985*
Label: Columbia
Produced by: Bruce Springsteen, Jon Landau, Chuck Plotkin
Year: 1985
Entering his Guthriesque folk troubadour phase.

SEEKER, THE

Artist: The Who
Written by: Pete Townshend
From the album: *Meaty Beaty Big and Bouncy*
Label: Decca
Produced by: Kit Lambert
Year: 1971
Meier Baba was listening.

SEEMS SO LONG AGO, NANCY

Artist: Leonard Cohen
Written by: Leonard Cohen
From the album: *Songs from a Room*
Label: Columbia
Produced by: Bob Johnston
Year: 1969
Sad tale of a party girl in the era of sad parties.

SEESAW

Artist: Don Covay
Written by: Don Covay, Steve Cropper
Label: Atlantic
Produced by: Don Covay
Year: 1965
Top 10 R&B/Top 50 crossover. Covered by Aretha Franklin (Atlantic, '68).

SEETHER

Artist: Veruca Salt
Written by: Nina Gordon
From the album: *American Thighs*
Label: Minty Fresh
Produced by: Brad Wood
Year: 1994
Edgy alt girl-group sound of the '90s. Wood had more success with Liz Phair.

SELF CONTROL

Artist: Laura Branigan
Written by: Steve Piccolo, Giancarlo Bigazzi, Raffaele Riefolo
From the album: *Self Control*
Label: Atlantic
Produced by: Jack White, Robbie Buchanon
Year: 1984

SELF DESTRUCTION

Artist: Stop the Violence
Written by: Dwight Myers, Doug E. Fresh, MC Lyte, Moe DeWese, Carlton Ridenhour, William Drayton
From the album: *Self Destruction*
Label: Jive
Produced by: KRS-One, D-Nice
Year: 1989
A gaggle of all-stars address rap's bad rep.

SELF ESTEEM

Artist: Offspring
Written by: Dexter Holland, Greg K., Noodles, Ron Welty
From the album: *Smash*
Label: Epitaph
Produced by: Thom Wilson
Year: 1994
Dealing with a perennial adolescent trauma.

SELLING THE DRAMA

Artist: Live
Written by: Edward Kowalcyzk, Patrick Dahlheimer, Chad Gracey, Chad Taylor
From the album: *Throwing Copper*
Label: Radioactive
Produced by: Jerry Harrison
Year: 1994
Overdramatic arena theatrics.

SEMI-CHARMED LIFE

Artist: Third Eye Blind
Written by: Stephan Jenkins
From the album: *Third Eye Blind*
Label: Elektra
Year: 1997
New generation San Francisco rockers in a post-Fillmore post-acid world of crystal meth.

SEND ME ON MY WAY

Artist: Rusted Root
Written by: Mike Gladicki, Rusted Root
From the album: *When I Woke*
Label: Polygram
Produced by: Bill Bottrell
Year: 1995
World beat from Pittsburgh.

SEND ME SOME LOVIN'

Artist: Little Richard
Written by: John Marascalco, Leo Price
From the album: *Little Richard*
Label: Specialty
Produced by: Art Rupe
Year: 1957
B-side of "Lucille."

SEND ONE YOUR LOVE

Artist: Stevie Wonder
Written by: Stevie Wonder
From the album: *Journey Through the Secret Life of Plants*
Label: Tamla
Produced by: Stevie Wonder
Year: 1979

SENDING ALL MY LOVE

Artist: Linear
Written by: Tolga Katas, Charlie Pennachio
From the album: *Linear*
Label: Atlantic
Produced by: Tolga Katas
Year: 1990
Miami dance mix.

SENSE OF PURPOSE

Artist: The Pretenders
Written by: Chrissie Hynde
From the album: *Packed*
Label: Sire
Produced by: Chriss Hynde
Year: 1990
Revived on her acoustic *Isle of View* (Warner Brothers, '95).

SENSES WORKING OVERTIME

Artist: XTC
Written by: Andy Partridge
From the album: *English Settlement*
Label: Epic
Produced by: Hugh Padgham, XTC
Year: 1982
A creative frenzy elsewhere described by Partridge as "Billy Bolts."

SENSITIVE NEW AGE GUYS

Artist: Christine Lavin
Written by: Christine Lavin, John Gorka
From the album: *Attainable Love*
Label: Philo
Year: 1990
A folkie anthem lampooning the metrosexual male.

SENSITIVITY

Artist: Ralph Tresvant
Written by: James Harris III, Terry Lewis
From the album: *Ralph Tresvant*
Label: MCA
Produced by: Daryl Simmons, Kayo
Year: 1991
#1 R&B/Top 10 crossover.

SENTIMENTAL LADY

Artist: Fleetwood Mac
Written by: Bob Welch
From the album: *Bare Trees*
Label: Warner Brothers
Produced by: Fleetwood Mac
Year: 1972
Covered by Bob Welch (Capitol, '77).

SEPARATE LIVES (LOVE THEME FROM WHITE NIGHTS)

Artist: Phil Collins and Marilyn Michaels
Written by: Stephen Bishop
From the album: *White Nights Soundtrack*
Label: Atlantic
Produced by: Arif Mardin, Phil Collins, Hugh Padgham

Year: 1985
#1 theme from the movie.

SEPARATE WAYS

Artist: Elvis Presley
Written by: Bobby West, Richard Mainegra
From the album: *Separate Ways*
Label: RCA
Year: 1970
Staple of his Las Vegas period.

SEPARATE WAYS (WORLDS APART)

Artist: Journey
Written by: Steve Perry, Jonathan Cain
From the album: *Frontiers*
Label: Columbia
Produced by: Mike Stone, Kevin Elson
Year: 1983
Tear-jerking arena ballad soars on Steve Perry's indestructible pipes.

SEPTEMBER

Artist: Earth, Wind & Fire
Written by: Maurice White, Allee Willis, Albert McKay
From the album: *Best of Earth, Wind & Fire (Vol. I)*
Label: Arc
Produced by: Maurice White
Year: 1979
Remembering his doo-wop roots for #1 R&B/Top 10 crossover.

SEPTEMBER GURLS

Artist: Big Star
Written by: Alex Chilton
From the album: *Radio City*
Label: Ardent
Produced by: John Fry
Year: 1974
Chilton's most accessibly haunting post-Box Tops tune. Covered by the Searchers (Sire, '81), the Bangles (Columbia, '86).

SERIES OF DREAMS

Artist: Bob Dylan
Written by: Bob Dylan
From the album: *The Bootleg Series*
Label: Columbia
Produced by: Daniel Lanois
Year: 1991

SERPENTINE FIRE

Artist: Earth, Wind & Fire
Written by: Maurice White, Reginald Burke, Verdine White
From the album: *All 'N' All*
Label: Columbia
Produced by: Maurice White
Year: 1977
Tribute to yoga is a #1 R&B/Top 20 crossover.

SET ADRIFT ON MEMORY BLISS

Artist: P.M. Dawn
Written by: Atrel Cordes, Gary Kemp
From the album: *Of the Heart, of the Soul, and of the Cross*
Label: Gee Street
Produced by: P.M. Dawn
Year: 1991
Hip hop meets soul at the corner of doo-wop and Ashbury.

SET ME FREE

Artist: Utopia
Written by: Todd Rundgren, Roger Powell, Kasim Sultan, John Wilcox
From the album: *Adventures in Utopia*
Label: Bearsville
Produced by: Todd Rundgren
Year: 1980
Todd's house band in Woodstock play their version of (Catskill) Mountain Music.

SET ME FREE (PRIVILEGE)

Artist: Paul Jones
Written by: Mike Leander, Mark London
From the album: *Privilege Soundtrack*
Label: Uni
Year: 1967
From the influential rock movie *Privilege*, by the lead singer of Manfred Mann. Covered by the Patti Smith Group (Arista, '78).

SET THE CONTROLS FOR THE HEART OF THE SUN

Artist: Pink Floyd
Written by: Roger Waters
From the album: *Saucerful of Secrets*
Label: Tower
Produced by: Norman Smith
Year: 1968
Moving from rave up to freak out.

SET THIS HOUSE ABLAZE

Artist: Paul Weller
Written by: Paul Weller
From the album: *Sound Affects*
Label: Polydor
Year: 1981
Former leader of the Jam has his biggest solo hit.

SET YOU FREE THIS TIME

Artist: The Byrds
Written by: Jim McGuinn (Roger McGuinn)
From the album: *Turn! Turn! Turn!*
Label: Columbia
Produced by: Terry Melcher
Year: 1965
B-side of "I'll Feel a Whole Lot Better."

SETTING SUN

Artist: Chemical Brothers
Written by: Tom Rowlands, Ed Simmons, Noel Gallagher
From the album: *Dig Your Own Hole*
Label: Astralwerks
Produced by: Chemical Brothers
Year: 1996
Leading edge electronica.

7

Artist: Prince
Written by: Prince Rogers Nelson
Label: Paisley Park
Produced by: Prince
Year: 1993
By then known by a symbol, Prince writes a mysterious tale about a number.

7 AND 7 IS

Artist: Love
Written by: Arthur Lee
From the album: *Da Capo*
Label: Elektra
Produced by: Jac Holtzman
Year: 1966
Biggest hit for the psychedelic soul band.

SEVEN BRIDGES ROAD

Artist: Tracy Nelson
Written by: Steve Young
From the album: *Bring Me Home*
Label: Reprise
Year: 1971
Rock's forgotten diva unearths a country/rock classic. Covered by Steve Young (Blues Classics, '75), Eagles (Asylum, '80).

SEVEN DAYS

Artist: Clyde McPhatter
Written by: Willis Carroll, Carmen Taylor
From the album: *Clyde McPhatter and the Drifters*
Label: Atlantic
Produced by: Ahmet Ertegun, Jerry Wexler
Year: 1956
Honey-voiced lead singer of the Drifters goes solo with a Top 10 R&B/Top 50 classic.

7 DEADLY SINS

Artist: Traveling Wilburys
Written by: The Traveling Wilburys
From the album: *Traveling Wilburys (Vol. III)*
Label: Wilbury
Produced by: Spike Wilbury, Clayton Wilbury
Year: 1990
Extended joke takeoff on "The Ten Commandments of Love."

SEVEN LITTLE GIRLS (SITTING IN THE BACK SEAT)

Artist: Paul Evans
Written by: Bob Hilliard, Lee Pockriss
From the album: *Fabulous Teens*
Label: Guaranteed
Year: 1959
Novelty from the coauthor of Bobby Vinton's "Roses Are Red" and "When" by the Kalin Twins.

7:00 NEWS/SILENT NIGHT

Artist: Simon and Garfunkel
Written by: Paul Simon
From the album: *Parsley, Sage, Rosemary and Thyme*
Label: Columbia
Produced by: Bob Johnston
Year: 1966
Antiwar aural collage.

SEVEN ROOMS OF GLOOM

Artist: The Four Tops
Written by: Eddie Holland, Lamont Dozier, Brian Holland
From the album: *Reach Out*
Label: Motown
Produced by: Brian Holland, Lamont Dozier
Year: 1967

SEVEN YEAR ACHE

Artist: Rosanne Cash
Written by: Rosanne Cash
From the album: *Seven Year Ache*
Label: Columbia
Produced by: Rodney Crowell
Year: 1981
First #1 country hit for Johnny's daughter and her only crossover.

SEVENTEEN

Artist: Boyd Bennett
Written by: John Young Jr., Chuck Gorman, Boyd Bennett
From the album: *Boyd Bennett*
Label: King
Produced by: Henry Glover
Year: 1955
A rockabilly crossover.

SEVENTH SON

Artist: Mose Allison
Written by: Willie Dixon
From the album: *Creek Bank*
Label: Prestige
Produced by: Bob Weinstock
Year: 1958
Definitive version of the blues-boasting classic from an album most likely coveted in England. Among its covers were Allison's version of Charlie Parker's "Yardbird Suite" and Ray Charles' "Baby Let Me Hold Your Hand." Covered by John Hammnd Jr. (Vanguard, '64), Tim Hardin (Verve Forecast, '64), Johnny Rivers (Imperial, '65).

SEX (I'M A)

Artist: Berlin
Written by: John Crawford, David Diamond, Terri Nunn

From the album: *Pleasure Victim*
Label: Warner Brothers
Produced by: Daniel Van Patten, Maomen
Year: 1983
A Debbie Harry pretender creates a one-shot photo opportunity.

SEX AND CANDY

Artist: Marcy Playground
Written by: John Wozniak
From the album: *Marcy Playground*
Label: Mammoth
Year: 1997
Taking the "Good Morning, Little Schoolgirl" ethos a bit too far.

SEX AND DRUGS AND ROCK 'N' ROLL

Artist: Ian Dury and the Blockheads
Written by: Ian Dury, Chaz Jankel
From the album: *New Boots and Panties*
Label: Stiff
Produced by: Laurie Latham, Peter Jenner, Rick Walton
Year: 1978
Pub rock anthem for the antidisco crowd.

SEX BOMB

Artist: Flipper
Written by: Will Shatter
From the album: *Generic Flipper Album*
Label: Def American
Produced by: Flipper, Chris
Year: 1980
San Francisco punk anthem.

SEX JUNKIE

Artist: The Plasmatics
Written by: Rod Swenson, Richie Stotts
From the album: *Metal Priestess*
Label: Stiff America
Produced by: Dan Hartman, Rod Swenson
Year: 1981
This former porno queen's personal philosophy is recommended only for true connoisseurs of bad taste. Suggested segue: "More More More" by the Andrea True Connection.

SEXUAL HEALING

Artist: Marvin Gaye
Written by: Marvin Gaye, Odell Brown, David Ritz
From the album: *Midnight Love*
Label: Columbia
Produced by: Marvin Gaye
Year: 1982
Perhaps his crowning achievement, the bedroom ballad as lifesaving philosophy: #1 R&B/#1 crossover.

SEXUALITY

Artist: Billy Bragg

Written by: Billy Bragg, Johnny Marr
From the album: *Don't Try This at Home*
Label: Elektra
Produced by: Johnny Marr
Year: 1991
Refining his sexual politics for his US folk/rock breakthrough.

SEXY EYES

Artist: Dr. Hook
Written by: Christopher Dunn, Robert Mather, Keith Steagal
From the album: *Sometimes You Win*
Label: Capitol
Produced by: Ron Haffkine
Year: 1978

SEXY SADIE

Artist: The Beatles
Written by: John Lennon, Paul McCartney
From the album: *The Beatles*
Label: Apple
Produced by: George Martin
Year: 1968
Bashing the Mahareeshi.

SEXY WAYS

Artist: The Midnighters
Written by: Hank Ballard
From the album: *The Midnighters*
Label: Federal
Produced by: Henry Glover
Year: 1954
Continuing the R&B tradition for stretching the boundaries of raunch.

SEYMOUR STEIN

Artist: Belle & Sebastian
Written by: Steve Jackson
From the album: *The Boy with the Arab Strap*
Label: Matador
Year: 1998
Celebrating the founder of pioneering indie label Sire Records.

SGT. PEPPER'S LONELY HEARTS CLUB BAND

Artist: The Beatles
Written by: John Lennon, Paul McCartney
From the album: *Sgt. Pepper's Lonely Hearts Club Band*
Label: Capitol
Produced by: George Martin
Year: 1967
The title tune from their legendary concept album, reportedly inspired by the Who's mini opera, "A Quick One." No singles were released from this album.

SHADOW DANCING

Artist: Andy Gibb
Written by: Barry Gibb, Robin Gibb, Maurice Gibb, Andy Gibb

From the album: *Shadow Dancing*
Label: RSO
Produced by: Karl Richardson, Albhy Galuten, Barry Gibb
Year: 1978
A family affair; #1 single of the year.

SHAH SLEEPS IN LEE HARVEY OSWALD'S GRAVE, THE

Artist: Butthole Surfers
Written by: Gibby Hayes
From the album: *Butthole Surfers*
Label: Alternative Tentacles
Year: 1983
Scathing post-hippie diatribe.

SHAKE

Artist: Sam Cooke
Written by: Sam Cooke
From the album: *Shake*
Label: RCA
Produced by: Sam Cooke
Year: 1965
Cooke's fifth and last Top 10 hit. Covered by Otis Redding (Volt, '65).

SHAKE A HAND

Artist: Faye Adams
Written by: Joe Morris
Label: Herald
Produced by: Al Silver
Year: 1953
This influential #1 R&B shouter launched the careers of Adams and NY record magnate Silver. Has found its way into the repertoires of LaVern Baker, Ruth Brown, and the one-off pairing of Jackie Wilson and Linda Hopkins.

SHAKE IT UP

Artist: The Cars
Written by: Ric Ocasek
From the album: *Shake It Up*
Label: Elektra
Produced by: Ray Thomas Baker
Year: 1982
Punk-lite.

SHAKE ME, WAKE ME (WHEN IT'S OVER)

Artist: The Four Tops
Written by: Eddie Holland, Lamont Dozier, Brian Holland
From the album: *On Top*
Label: Motown
Produced by: Brian Holland, Lamont Dozier
Year: 1966

SHAKE, RATTLE AND ROLL

Artist: Joe Turner
Written by: Jesse Stone (Charles Calhoun)

From the album: *Joe Turner*
Label: Atlantic
Produced by: Ahmet Ertegun, Jerry Wexler
Year: 1954
For adults only (see: "I'm like a one-eyed cat, peeping in a seafood store"). A cleaned-up version by Bill Haley and His Comets (Decca, '55) was deemed more suitable for the new teen audience.

(SHAKE, SHAKE, SHAKE) SHAKE YOUR BOOTY

Artist: K. C. and the Sunshine Band
Written by: Harry Casey, Richard Finch
From the album: *Part 3*
Label: TK
Produced by: Harry Casey, Richard Finch
Year: 1976
When you add their five #1 hits to the fact that Casey and Finch also produced "Rock Your Baby" by George McCrae, you can see why they, and not John Travolta or the Bee Gees, should be known as the undisputed kings of disco, though they preferred to think of it as rhythm and blues.

SHAKE SOME ACTION

Artist: Flamin' Groovies
Written by: Chris Wilson, Cyril Jordan
From the album: *Shake Some Action*
Label: Sire
Produced by: Dave Edmunds
Year: 1976
Belated retro rocker.

SHAKE YOU DOWN

Artist: Gregory Abbott
Written by: Gregory Abbott
From the album: *Shake You Down*
Label: Columbia
Produced by: Gregory Abbott
Year: 1986
Massive #1 R&B/#1 crossover one-shot from the husband of Freda Payne.

SHAKE YOUR BODY (DOWN TO THE GROUND)

Artist: The Jacksons
Written by: Stephen Jackson, Michael Jackson
From the album: *Destiny*
Label: Epic
Produced by: The Jacksons
Year: 1978

SHAKE YOUR GROOVE THING

Artist: Peaches and Herb
Written by: Freddie Perren, Dino Fekaris
From the album: *2 Hot!*
Label: Polydor
Produced by: Freddie Perren
Year: 1978
Disco move.

SHAKE YOUR LOVE

Artist: Debbie Gibson
Written by: Debbie Gibson
From the album: *Out of the Blue*
Label: Atlantic
Produced by: Fred Zarr, Debbie Gibson
Year: 1987
Debbie does rock, before moving on to Broadway.

SHAKE YOUR MONEY MAKER

Artist: The Paul Butterfield Blues Band
Written by: Elmore James
From the album: *The Paul Butterfield Blues Band*
Label: Elektra
Produced by: Paul Rothchild
Year: 1965
Paying tribute to Elmore James, a master blues guitar influence on Michael Bloomfield as well as many other members of rock's guitaristocracy.

SHAKE YOUR RUMP

Artist: Beastie Boys
Written by: Darryl McDaniels, Rick Rubin, Joseph Simmons
From the album: *Paul's Boutique*
Produced by: Beastie Boys, Dust Brothers
Label: Def Jam
Year: 1989
Early-defining groove.

SHAKEDOWN

Artist: Bob Seger
Written by: Harold Faltermeyer, Keith Forsey, Bob Seger
From the album: *Beverly Hills Cop II Soundtrack*
Label: MCA
Produced by: Harold Faltermeyer, Keith Forsey
Year: 1987
Seger's new Hollywood connections pay off with a #1 single.

SHAKIN' ALL OVER

Artist: Johnny Kidd and the Pirates
Written by: Fred Heath (Johnny Kidd)
Label: HMV
Year: 1960
Presleyesque rocker. Covered by The Guess Who (Scepter, '65).

SHA-LA-LA

Artist: The Shirelles
Written by: Robert Mosley, Robert Taylor
Label: Scepter
Produced by: Luther Dixon
Year: 1964
Covered by Manfred Mann (Ascot, '64).

SHA-LA-LA (MAKE ME HAPPY)

Artist: Al Green

Written by: Al Green
From the album: *Al Green Explores Your Mind*
Label: Hi
Produced by: Willie Mitchell
Year: 1974

SHAMBALA

Artist: B.W. Stevenson
Written by: Daniel Moore
From the album: *My Maria*
Label: RCA
Produced by: David Kershenbaum
Year: 1973
Good-time folk/rock. Covered by Three Dog Night (Dunhill, '73).

SHAME

Artist: Evelyn Champagne King
Written by: John Fitch, Reuben Cross
From the album: *Smooth Talk*
Label: RCA
Produced by: T. Life
Year: 1978
Her biggest disco hit.

SHAME ON THE MOON

Artist: Bob Seger
Written by: Rodney Crowell
From the album: *The Distance*
Label: Capitol
Produced by: Jimmy Iovine
Year: 1982
With a country songwriter, Seger gains his second biggest hit single and his only country crossover.

SHAME, SHAME, SHAME

Artist: Shirley and Company
Written by: Sylvia Robinson
From the album: *Shame, Shame, Shame*
Label: Vibration
Produced by: Sylvia Robinson
Year: 1974
#1 R&B/Top 20 crossover for Shirley of Shirley and Lee.

SHANGHAI NOODLE FACTORY

Artist: Traffic
Written by: Steve Winwood, James Capaldi, Chris Wood
From the album: *Last Exit*
Label: United Artists
Produced by: Jimmy Miller
Year: 1969
Where progressive psychedelia was born.

SHANNON

Artist: Henry Gross
Written by: Henry Gross
From the album: *Release*
Label: Lifesong
Produced by: Terry Cashman, Tommy West

Year: 1976
Brooklyn-born Henry's falsetto answer to "Old Shep."

SHAPE I'M IN, THE

Artist: The Band
Written by: Robbie Robertson
From the album: *Stage Fright*
Label: Capitol
Produced by: The Band
Year: 1970
A recovery from their Woodstock nonappearance.

SHAPE OF MY HEART

Artist: Backstreet Boys
Written by: Max Martin, Lisa Miskovsky, Rami
From the album: *Black & Blue*
Label: Jive
Year: 2000
Blissful harmonizing.

SHAPES OF THINGS

Artist: The Yardbirds
Written by: Keith Relf, James McCarty, Paul Samwell-Smith
From the album: *Yardbirds' Greatest Hits*
Label: Epic
Produced by: Giorgio Gomelsky
Year: 1966
Their answer to "My Generation" by the Who.

SHARE THE LAND

Artist: The Guess Who
Written by: Burton Cummings
From the album: *Share the Land*
Label: RCA
Produced by: Jack Richardson
Year: 1970
Ecological anthem.

SHARE YOUR LOVE WITH ME

Artist: Bobby Bland
Written by: Deadric Malone, Al Braggs
From the album: *Call on Me/That's The Way Love Is*
Label: Duke
Year: 1963
Cover by Aretha Franklin was #1 R&B/Top 20 crossover (Atlantic, '69).

SHARKEY'S DAY

Artist: Laurie Anderson
Written by: Laurie Anderson
From the album: *Mister Heartbreak*
Label: Warner Brothers
Produced by: Laurie Anderson, Bill Laswell
Year: 1984
A beat generation multimedia day-in-the-life; Joni Mitchell meets Gertrude Stein, with dour narrative

by William Burroughs, and squealing guitar by Adrian Belew.

SHARP DRESSED MAN

Artist: ZZ Top
Written by: Billy Gibbons, Dusty Hill, Frank Beard
From the album: *Eliminator*
Label: Warner Brothers
Produced by: Bill Ham
Year: 1983
Cleaning up good for MTV.

SHATTERED

Artist: The Rolling Stones
Written by: Mick Jagger, Keith Richards
From the album: *Some Girls*
Label: Rolling Stones
Produced by: Glimmer Twins
Year: 1978
Not as dramatic as it sounds.

SHATTERED DREAMS

Artist: Johnny Hates Jazz
Written by: Clark Datchler
From the album: *Turn Back the Clock*
Label: Virgin
Produced by: Calvin Hayes, Mike Nocito
Year: 1988
Top 10 US a year after it was Top 10 UK.

SH-BOOM (LIFE COULD BE A DREAM)

Artist: The Chords
Written by: James Keyes, Claude Feaster, Carl Feaster, Floyd F. McRae, James Edwards
Label: Cat
Produced by: Ahmet Ertegun, Jerry Wexler
Year: 1954
Dreamy doo-wop B-side of "Cross over the Bridge" was a Top 5 R&B/Top 10 crossover and is regarded as one of the essential bridges from R&B to rock, produced by a couple of future Hall or Famers. Crewcuts cover went to #1 (Mercury, '54).

SHE

Artist: Gram Parsons
Written by: Gram Parsons, Chris Ethridge
From the album: *GP*
Label: A&M
Produced by: Gram Parsons, Rik Grech
Year: 1971
Prime country song from the genre's holiest rock and roller. Covered by Emmylou Harris (Reprise, '76).

SHE AIN'T WORTH IT

Artist: Glenn Medeiros featuring Bobby Brown
Written by: Bobby Brown, Antonia Armato, Ian Prince
From the album: *Glenn Medeiros*

Label: MCA
Produced by: Ian Prince, Denny Diante
Year: 1990
#1 tune, but the presence of Bobby Brown only got him a Top 50 R&B crossover.

SHE BANGS THE DRUM

Artist: The Stone Roses
Written by: John Squire, Ian Brown
From the album: *The Stone Roses*
Label: Silvertone
Produced by: John Leckie
Year: 1989
First UK chart single for the new English rave guitar band.

SHE BELONGS TO ME

Artist: Bob Dylan
Written by: Bob Dylan
From the album: *Bringing It All Back Home*
Label: Columbia
Produced by: Tom Wilson
Year: 1965
Portrait of the artist as a young punk. Produced the title of his defining documentary *Don't Look Back*. B-side of "Subterranean Homesick Blues." Covered by Rick Nelson (Decca, '69).

SHE BLINDED ME WITH SCIENCE

Artist: Thomas Dolby
Written by: Thomas Dolby, Joe Kerr
From the album: *Blinded by Science*
Label: Capitol
Produced by: Thomas Dolby, Tim Greene
Year: 1983
Synthesized rock with a pen-holder, defining the year's British invasion.

SHE BOP

Artist: Cyndi Lauper
Written by: Cyndi Lauper, Stephen Lunt, Gary Corbett, Rick Chertoff
From the album: *She's So Unusual*
Label: Portrait
Produced by: Rick Chertoff
Year: 1984
Brenda Lee grows up. Suggested segues: "I Touch Myself" by the Divinyls, "Secret" by Madonna.

SHE CAME IN THROUGH THE BATHROOM WINDOW

Artist: The Beatles
Written by: John Lennon, Paul McCartney
From the album: *Abbey Road*
Label: Apple
Produced by: George Martin
Year: 1969
McCartney at his most Lennonesque (or was it vice-versa?). Covered by Joe Cocker (A&M, '70).

SHE COMES IN COLORS

Artist: Love
Written by: Arthur Lee
From the album: *Da Capo*
Label: Elektra
Produced by: Jac Holzman
Year: 1968
Acid flashback.

SHE CRACKED

Artist: Modern Lovers
Written by: Jonathan Richman
From the album: *The Modern Lovers*
Label: Beserkley
Produced by: John Cale
Year: 1971
Pristine, elemental, rock and roll purity. The Ramones were listening. The Talking Heads were preparing their intellectualized response.

SHE CRIED

Artist: Jay and the Americans
Written by: Ted Daryll, Greg Richards
From the album: *She Cried*
Label: United Artists
Produced by: Jerry Leiber, Mike Stoller
Year: 1962
Covered by the Shangri-Las in the equal opportunity "He Cried" (Red Bird, '66).

SHE DON'T USE JELLY

Artist: The Flaming Lips
Written by: Flaming Lips
From the album: *Transmissions from the Satellite Heart*
Label: Warner Brothers
Produced by: Flaming Lips, Keith Cleversley
Year: 1995
Long-time indie subversives make their droll chart breakthrough.

SHE DRIVES ME CRAZY

Artist: Fine Young Cannibals
Written by: David Steele, Roland Gift
From the album: *The Raw and the Cooked*
Label: IRS
Produced by: David Z., Fine Young Cannibals, Andy Cox
Year: 1989
Their first and biggest hit.

SHE EVEN WOKE ME UP TO SAY GOODBYE

Artist: Jerry Lee Lewis
Written by: Mickey Newbury, Douglas Gilmore
From the album: *She Even Woke Me up to Say Goodbye*
Label: Smash
Produced by: Jerry Kennedy
Year: 1970
Defining the outlaw country sensibility a few years early.

SHE HATES TO GO HOME

Artist: Marshall Crenshaw
Written by: Marshall Crenshaw, Leroy Preston
From the album: *Good Evening*
Label: Warner Brothers
Year: 1989

SHE LOVES THE JERK

Artist: John Hiatt
Written by: John Hiatt
From the album: *Riding with the King*
Label: Geffen
Produced by: Ron Nagle, Scott Matthews
Year: 1983
Prototypical Hiatt loser suffering fools with everyday Midwestern stoicism.

SHE LOVES YOU

Artist: The Beatles
Written by: John Lennon, Paul McCartney
From the album: *The Beatles Second Album*
Label: Swan
Produced by: George Martin
Year: 1963
The third of their four #1 UK singles in '63 and #1 in the US in '64.

SHE SAID

Artist: Hasil Adkins
Written by: Hasil Adkins
From the album: *Chicken Walk*
Label: Norton
Year: 1956
Crazed rockabilly track from the original West Virginia wildman. Covered by the Cramps.

SHE SAID THE SAME THINGS TO ME

Artist: John Hiatt
Written by: John Hiatt
From the album: *Warming up to the Ice Age*
Label: A&M
Produced by: Norbert Putnam
Year: 1985
Hiatt's epic struggle to comprehend the opposing sex.

SHE SAID YEAH

Artist: Larry Williams
Written by: Sonny Bono, George Jackson
Label: Specialty
Produced by: Sonny Bono
Year: 1958
Sonny Bono gets a leg up in the business. Covered by the Rolling Stones (London, '64).

SHE SELLS SANCTUARY

Artist: The Cult
Written by: Ian Astbury, Billy Duffy
From the album: *Love*
Label: Sire

Year: 1985
Alternative smash for an otherwise typical Generation X hard rock band.

SHE TALKS TO ANGELS

Artist: The Black Crowes
Written by: Rich Robinson, Chris Robinson
From the album: *Shake Your Moneymaker*
Label: Def American
Produced by: Rick Rubin, George Drakoulias
Year: 1990
Smoldering neo-blues rock.

SHE TWISTS THE KNIFE AGAIN

Artist: Richard Thompson
Written by: Richard Thompson
From the album: *Across a Crowded Room*
Label: Polygram
Produced by: Joe Boyd
Year: 1985
Showing no mercy, especially on guitar.

SHE WAS HOT

Artist: The Rolling Stones
Written by: Mick Jagger, Keith Richards
From the album: *Undercover*
Label: Rolling Stones
Produced by: Glimmer Twins, Chris Kimsey
Year: 1983
Restating their enduring message.

SHE WORKS HARD FOR THE MONEY

Artist: Donna Summer
Written by: Michael Omartian, Donna Summer
From the album: *She Works Hard for the Money*
Label: Mercury
Produced by: Michael Omartian
Year: 1983
Returning to her disco roots, with a #1 R&B/Top 10 crossover.

SHE'D RATHER BE WITH ME

Artist: The Turtles
Written by: Garry Bonner, Alan Gordon
From the album: *Turtles Golden Hits*
Label: White Whale
Produced by: Joe Wissert
Year: 1967
A big year for Bonner and Gordon.

SHEELA-NA-GIG

Artist: PJ Harvey
Written by: Polly Jean Harvey
From the album: *Dry*
Produced by: P. J. Harvey
Year: 1992

With a nod to Sinead O'Connor and Patti Smith, when Polly Jean Harvey sings "I'm gonna wash that man right out of my hair," you know it's not with shampoo … more like (with a nod to the Flaming Lips) gasoline.

SHEENA IS A PUNK ROCKER

Artist: The Ramones
Written by: Douglas Colvin, John Cummings, Jeff Hyman, Thomas Erdelyi
From the album: *Leave Home*
Label: Sire
Produced by: Tony Bongiovi, Thomas Erdelyi
Year: 1977
Their first bid for Top 40 immortality, which failed miserably. They'd become immortal nevertheless.

SHEER HEART ATTACK

Artist: Queen
Written by: Roger Taylor
From the album: *News of the World*
Label: Elektra
Produced by: Queen
Year: 1977
When they were still arena rockers, rather than arena icons.

SHEILA

Artist: Tommy Roe
Written by: Tommy Roe
From the album: *Sheila*
Label: ABC
Produced by: Felton Jarvis
Year: 1962
His debut single, priming the populace for a true Buddy Holly/Crickets revival, still a year or so in the offing.

SHELTER FROM THE STORM

Artist: Bob Dylan
Written by: Bob Dylan
From the album: *Blood on the Tracks*
Label: Columbia
Produced by: Phil Ramone, Bob Dylan
Year: 1975
A ripping yarn from his mid-70s comeback period.

SHERRY

Artist: The Four Seasons
Written by: Bob Gaudio
From the album: *Sherry and 11 Others*
Label: Vee Jay
Produced by: Bob Crewe
Year: 1962
#1 R&B/#1 crossover, recorded at the same session that produced "Big Girls Don't Cry." Italian soul at its commercial peak, in the anguished falsetto of New Jersey's Frankie Valli.

SHE'S A BAD MAMA JAMA

Artist: Carl Carlton
Written by: Leon Haywood
From the album: *Carl Carlton*
Label: 20TH Century Fox
Produced by: Leon Haywood
Year: 1981

SHE'S A BEAUTY

Artist: The Tubes
Written by: Steve Lukather, David Foster, Fee Waybill
From the album: *Outside Inside*
Label: Capitol
Produced by: David Foster
Year: 1983
Wacky performance troupe cashes in. The Residents weren't listening.

SHE'S A FOOL

Artist: Lesley Gore
Written by: Ben Raleigh, Mark Barkan
From the album: *Lesley Gore Sings of Mixed up Hearts*
Label: Mercury
Produced by: Quincy Jones
Year: 1963
Finishing the "It's My Party" trilogy.

SHE'S A JAR

Artist: Wilco
Written by: Wilco
From the album: *Summer Teeth*
Produced by: Wilco
Label: Warner Brothers
Year: 1999
Alt/country folk/rock standard bearer.

SHE'S A LADY

Artist: John Sebastian
Written by: John B. Sebastian
From the album: *John B. Sebastian*
Label: Kama Sutra
Produced by: Paul Rothchild
Year: 1969
Written for the Dustin Hoffman musical, *Jimmy Shine*. Released as a single just after John left the Lovin' Spoonful.

SHE'S A RAINBOW

Artist: The Rolling Stones
Written by: Mick Jagger, Keith Richards
From the album: *Their Satanic Majesties Request*
Label: London
Produced by: Andrew Loog-Oldham
Year: 1967
Another ill-fated attempt to merge with the flower child zeitgeist.

SHE'S A WOMAN

Artist: The Beatles
Written by: John Lennon, Paul McCartney

From the album: *Beatles '65*
Label: Capitol
Produced by: George Martin
Year: 1964
B-side of "I Feel Fine" was their nod to the girl-group mentality of the early '60s.

SHE'S ABOUT A MOVER

Artist: The Sir Douglas Quintet
Written by: Douglas Sahm
From the album: *She's About a Mover*
Label: Tribe
Produced by: Huey Meaux
Year: 1965
A Tex-Mex/Creole gumbo.

SHE'S ALL I EVER HAD

Artist: Ricky Martin
Written by: Robi Rosa, Jorge Noriega, Jon Secada
From the album: *Ricky Martin*
Label: Sony
Produced by: Robi Rosa, Jon Secada
Year: 1999
Exploiting his window of salsa opportunity.

SHE'S ALWAYS A WOMAN

Artist: Billy Joel
Written by: Billy Joel
From the album: *The Stranger*
Label: Columbia
Produced by: Phil Ramone
Year: 1977
The Long Island hippie version of "She Belongs to Me" by Bob Dylan.

SHE'S AS BEAUTIFUL AS A FOOT

Artist: Blue Oyster Cult
Written by: Richard Meltzer, Jack Bouchard, Allen Lanier
From the album: *Blue Oyster Cult*
Label: Columbia
Produced by: Sandy Pearlman
Year: 1972
The rock critic's revenge; the noted author, Meltzer, earns more in royalties writing for these addled metalheads than he could ever expect from epic tomes like *The Aesthetics of Rock*. John ("I have seen the future of rock and roll") Landau was listening and learning.

SHE'S GONE

Artist: Daryl Hall & John Oates
Written by: Daryl Hall, John Oates
From the album: *Abandoned Luncheonette*
Label: Atlantic
Produced by: Arif Mardin
Year: 1974
Philly soul with a New York accent. Cover by Tavares (Capitol, '73) went #1 R&B. Hall and Oates' version hit Top 10 when re-released in '76.

SHE'S GOT YOU

Artist: Patsy Cline
Written by: Hank Cochran
From the album: *The Patsy Cline Story*
Label: Decca
Produced by: Owen Bradley
Year: 1962
Mournful #1 country/Top 20 crossover.

SHE'S IN LOVE

Artist: Brenda Kahn
Written by: Brenda Kahn
From the album: *Epiphany in Brooklyn*
Label: Chaos
Produced by: David Kahne
Year: 1992
Post-Bangles waif toughs it out on the streets of anti-folk rock.

SHE'S JUST MY STYLE

Artist: Gary Lewis and the Playboys
Written by: Leon Russell, Gary Lewis, Thomas Lesslie, Al Capps
From the album: *She's Just My Style*
Label: Liberty
Produced by: Snuff Garrett
Year: 1965
Post-surf L.A. studio pop/rock.

SHE'S LEAVING HOME

Artist: The Beatles
Written by: John Lennon, Paul McCartney
From the album: *Sgt. Pepper's Lonely Hearts Club Band*
Label: Capitol
Produced by: George Martin
Year: 1967
"Sweet Little Sixteen" meets the '60s.

SHE'S LIKE THE WIND

Artist: Patrick Swayze with Wendy Fraser
Written by: Patrick Swayze, Stacey Widelitz
From the album: *Dirty Dancing Soundtrack*
Label: RCA
Produced by: Michael Lloyd
Year: 1987
Hunk rock.

SHE'S NO LADY

Artist: Lyle Lovett
Written by: Lyle Lovett
From the album: *Pontiac*
Label: Curb
Produced by: Tony Brown, Lyle Lovett
Year: 1987
Alt/country diatribe could have been about his former wife, Julia Roberts.

SHE'S NOT THERE

Artist: The Zombies
Written by: Rod Argent
From the album: *The Zombies*
Label: Parrot
Produced by: Ken Jones
Year: 1964
In the same moody mold as the Jaynetts' "Sally Go round the Roses." Buddy Miles on drums. Covered by Santana (Columbia, '77).

SHE'S NOT YOU

Artist: Elvis Presley
Written by: Jerry Leiber, Mike Stoller, Doc Pomus
From the album: *Elvis' Golden Records (Vol. III)*
Label: RCA
Produced by: Steve Sholes
Year: 1962
The Brill Building brain-trust give Elvis his twelfth #1.

SHE'S ON IT

Artist: Beastie Boys
Written by: Adam Horowitz, Rick Rubin
From the album: *Krush Groove Soundtrack*
Label: Warner Brothers
Produced by: Rick Rubin
Year: 1985
What if the Beatles first got together in the 80's?

SHE'S OUT OF MY LIFE

Artist: Michael Jackson
Written by: Tom Bahler
From the album: *Off the Wall*
Label: Epic
Produced by: Quincy Jones
Year: 1979
His most convincing high note, ending on a tear.

SHE'S PLAYING HARD TO GET

Artist: Hi-Five
Written by: Timmy Allen, William Walton
From the album: *Keep It Goin' On*
Label: Jive
Produced by: Timmy Allen
Year: 1992
And then their voices changed.

(SHE'S) SEXY AND 17

Artist: Stray Cats
Written by: Brian Setzer
From the album: *Rant n' Rave with the Stray Cats*
Label: EMI-America
Produced by: Dave Edmunds
Year: 1983
Their biggest hit. Segue: "You're Sixteen" by Johnny Barnette, "I Saw Her Standing There" by The Beatles, "Hey Nineteen" by Steely Dan.

(SHE'S) SOME KIND OF WONDERFUL

Artist: Soul Brothers Six
Written by: Ralph Ellison

Label: Atlantic
Year: 1967
Covered by Grand Funk (Capitol, '75), Buddy Guy (Silvertone, '93).

SHIMMER

Artist: Fuel
Written by: Carl Bell
From the album: *Sunburn*
Label: 550
Year: 1998
Biggest modern rock song of the year.

SHIMMY, SHIMMY KO-KO BOP

Artist: Little Anthony and the Imperials
Written by: Bob Smith
From the album: *We Are Little Anthony and the Imperials*
Label: End
Produced by: George Goldner
Year: 1959
Alan Freed's farewell song over 1010 WINS in New York City. Soon Anthony would be leaving as well, for Las Vegas.

SHINE

Artist: Collective Soul
Written by: Ed Roland
From the album: *Hints, Allegations and Things Left Unsaid*
Label: Atlantic
Produced by: Ed Roland
Year: 1994
Uplifting modified Southern rocker.

SHINE A LITTLE LOVE

Artist: Electric Light Orchestra (ELO)
Written by: Jeff Lynne
From the album: *Discovery*
Label: Jet
Produced by: Jeff Lynne
Year: 1979

SHINE ON BRIGHTLY

Artist: Procol Harum
Written by: Keith Reid, Gary Brooker
From the album: *Shine on Brightly*
Label: A&M
Year: 1968
Progressive bluster.

SHINE ON, YOU CRAZY DIAMOND

Artist: Pink Floyd
Written by: Roger Waters
From the album: *Wish You Were Here*
Label: Columbia
Produced by: Pink Floyd
Year: 1975

A tribute to the lamented, lost Syd Barrett, who reportedly wandered unnoticed into the sessions for the tune.

SHINING STAR

Artist: Earth, Wind & Fire
Written by: Maurice White, Philip Bailey, Larry Dunn
From the album: *That's the Way of the World*
Label: Columbia
Produced by: Maurice White, Charles Stepney
Year: 1975
Movie misstep nevertheless results in their shining moment; #1 R&B/#1 crossover.

SHINING STAR

Artist: The Manhattans
Written by: Leo Graham Jr., Paul Richmond
From the album: *After Midnight*
Label: Columbia
Produced by: Leo Graham
Year: 1980

SHINY HAPPY PEOPLE

Artist: R.E.M.
Written by: Michael Stipe, Peter Buck, Bill Berry, Mike Mills
From the album: *Out of Time*
Label: Warner Brothers
Produced by: Scott Litt, R.E.M.
Year: 1991
A satirical statement. Or was it?

SHIP ON A STORMY SEA

Artist: Jimmy Clanton
Written by: Jimmy Clanton, Cosima Matassa, Seth David, Mack Rebennack
Label: Ace
Produced by: Johnny Vincent
Year: 1959
The cream of New Orleans musical society gave Clanton this obscure companion to "Sea of Love."

SHIPBUILDING

Artist: Elvis Costello
Written by: Declan McManus (Elvis Costello), Clive Langer
From the album: *Punch the Clock*
Label: Columbia
Produced by: Clive Langer, Alan Winstanley
Year: 1983
Evocative antiwar scenario. Chet Baker on sax.

SHIPS

Artist: Ian Hunter
Written by: Ian Hunter
From the album: *You're Never Alone with a Schizophrenic*
Label: Chrysalis
Produced by: Mick Ronson, Ian Hunter
Year: 1979
Covered by Barry Manilow (Arista, '79).

SHOCK THE MONKEY

Artist: Peter Gabriel
Written by: Peter Gabriel
From the album: *Peter Gabriel (Security)*
Label: Geffen
Produced by: David Lord, Peter Gabriel
Year: 1982
Even better in its original German version, entitled "Schock den Affen" (Warner Brothers, '83). Suggested segue: "Morgen" by Ivo Robic.

SHOCKER IN GLOOMTOWN

Artist: Guided by Voices
Written by: Dave Pollard
From the album: *The Grand Hour*
Label: Scat
Year: 1992
Indie amateurs go pro. Covered by the Breeders (4AD, '92).

SHOESHINE BOY

Artist: Eddie Kendricks
Written by: Harry Booker, Linda Allen
From the album: *For You*
Label: Tamla
Produced by: Leonard Caston, Frank Wilson
Year: 1975
#1 R&B/Top 20 crossover.

SHOO-BE-DOO-BE-DOO-DAY

Artist: Stevie Wonder
Written by: Stevie Wonder, Henry Cosby, Sylvia Moy
From the album: *For Once in My Life*
Label: Tamla
Produced by: Henry Cosby
Year: 1968
#1 R&B/Top 10 crossover.

SHOOP

Artist: Salt-n-Pepa
Written by: Mark Sparks, Cheryl James, Sandy Denton, Otwane Roberts, Nate Turner
From the album: *Very Necessary*
Label: Next Plateau
Produced by: Mark Sparks, Cheryl James
Year: 1993
Their biggest hit sports a euphemistic hook.

SHOOP, SHOOP SONG (IT'S IN HIS KISS), THE

Artist: Betty Everett
Written by: Rudy Clark
From the album: *It's in His Kiss*
Label: Vee Jay
Produced by: Calvin Carter
Year: 1964
Winsome pop/soul philosophy. Covered by Cher in the film *Mermaids* (Geffen, '91).

SHOOT OUT THE LIGHTS

Artist: Richard and Linda Thompson
Written by: Richard Thompson
From the album: *Shoot out the Lights*
Label: Hannibal
Produced by: Joe Boyd
Year: 1982
The Thompsons part ways, and as a parting shot Richard delivers one of the great guitar parts of the decade.

SHOP AROUND

Artist: The Miracles
Written by: Smokey Robinson, Berry Gordy Jr.
From the album: *Greatest Hits from the Beginning*
Label: Tamla
Produced by: Berry Gordy Jr.
Year: 1961
Launching the philosophical soul of Smokey Robinson with Motown's first #1 R&B/Top 10 crossover. Covered by the Captain & Tennille (A&M, '76).

SHOPLIFTERS OF THE WORLD UNITE

Artist: The Smiths
Written by: Stephen Morrissey, Johnny Marr
From the album: *Louder Than Bombs*
Label: Sire
Produced by: Stephen Morrissey, Johnny Marr
Year: 1987
Deifying deviance.

SHOPPING FOR CLOTHES

Artist: The Coasters
Written by: Jerry Leiber, Mike Stoller
Label: Atco
Produced by: Jerry Leiber, Mike Stoller
Year: 1960
Coasters confront the limits of rock and roll success.

SHORT DICK MAN (SHORT SHORT MAN)

Artist: Twenty Fingers
Written by: Manfred Mohr, Charles Babie
Label: Zoo
Produced by: Charles Babie
Year: 1994
The less said the better.

SHORT FAT FANNIE

Artist: Larry Williams
Written by: Larry Williams
Label: Specialty
Produced by: Bumps Blackwell
Year: 1957
First hit for Lloyd Price's former chauffeur; a Top 5 R&B/Top 10 crossover, in the Little Richard mode.

SHORT MAN'S ROOM

Artist: Joe Henry
Written by: Joe Henry
From the album: *Short Man's Room*
Label: Mammoth
Year: 1992
Quirky alt/country gem.

SHORT PEOPLE

Artist: Randy Newman
Written by: Randy Newman
From the album: *Little Criminals*
Label: Warner Brothers
Produced by: Russ Titelman, Lenny Waronker
Year: 1977
Is to Newman's oeuvre what "Dead Skunk" is to Loudon Wainwright's and "Brand New Key" is to Melanie's; a hit single that defines him to the masses while not only failing to illuminate the dimension of the artist's ongoing talent but obliterating it in a hail of misguided criticism.

SHORT SHORTS

Artist: Royal Teens
Written by: Bob Gaudio, Tom Austin, Bill Dalton, Bill Crandall
Label: ABC Paramount
Year: 1957
The white streetcorner sound of the '50s, one part doo-wop, three parts voyeurism.

SHOT BY BOTH SIDES

Artist: Magazine
Written by: Howard DeVoto
From the album: *Real Life*
Label: Virgin
Produced by: Toni Bongiovi, Magazine
Year: 1979
DeVoto's post-Buzzcocks one-shot.

SHOT IN THE DARK

Artist: Ozzy Osbourne
Written by: Ozzy Osbourne, Phil Soussan
From the album: *The Ultimate Sin*
Label: CBS-Associated
Produced by: Ron Nevison
Year: 1986
Best of the post-Randy Rhoads era, featuring Jake E. Lee on lead guitar.

SHOT OF RHYTHM AND BLUES, A

Artist: Arthur Alexander
Written by: Terry Thompson
From the album: *You Better Move On*
Label: Dot
Year: 1962
The B-side of "You Better Move On," covered by the Beatles.

SHOTGUN

Artist: Jr. Walker and the All-Stars

Written by: Autry DeWalt
From the album: *Shotgun*
Label: Soul
Produced by: Berry Gordy
Year: 1965
Uptown soul with horns. A #1 R&B/Top 10 crossover.

SHOULD I STAY OR SHOULD I GO

Artist: The Clash
Written by: John Mellor (Joe Strummer), Mick Jones
From the album: *Combat Rock*
Label: Epic
Produced by: Glyn Johns
Year: 1982
Their last chart single, coopted by Levi's in 1991.

SHOULD WE TELL HIM

Artist: The Everly Brothers
Written by: Don Everly, Phil Everly
From the album: *The Everly Brothers*
Label: Cadence
Produced by: Archie Bleyer
Year: 1958
The B-side of "This Little Girl of Mine" was their first collaborative hit.

SHOULD'VE KNOWN BETTER

Artist: Richard Marx
Written by: Richard Marx
From the album: *Richard Marx*
Label: EMI-Manhattan
Produced by: H. Gatica
Year: 1987
White Bread still tops the charts.

SHOULD'VE NEVER LET YOU GO

Artist: Neil and Dara Sedaka
Written by: Phil Cody, Neil Sedaka
From the album: *In the Pocket*
Label: Elektra
Produced by: Robert Appere, Neil Sedaka
Year: 1980
With his daughter, Sedaka makes another comeback.

SHOULDN'T HAVE TOOK MORE THAN YOU GAVE

Artist: Dave Mason
Written by: Dave Mason
From the album: *Alone Together*
Label: Blue Thumb
Produced by: Tommy LiPuma, Dave Mason
Year: 1970
Former Traffic founder perfects his anxious folk/rock.

SHOUT

Artist: Tears for Fears
Written by: Roland Orzabal, Ian Stanley
From the album: *Songs from the Big Chair*
Label: Mercury
Produced by: Chris Hughes
Year: 1985
Released in England before "Everybody Wants to Rule the World," this became the second straight US #1 for the duo; Wham! for closeted intellectuals.

SHOUT (PARTS I AND II)

Artist: The Isley Brothers
Written by: Ronald Isley, Rudolph Isley, O'Kelly Isley
From the album: *Shout*
Label: RCA
Produced by: Hugo and Luigi
Year: 1959
Deep into rock and roll's softest year, a cry in the wilderness, "A little bit louder now!" Prelude to the original party rave-up of "Part II," their first of many.

SHOUT! SHOUT! KNOCK YOURSELF OUT!

Artist: Ernie Maresca
Written by: Ernie Maresca, Thomas Bogdany
From the album: *Shout! Shout! Knock Yourself Out*
Label: Seville
Year: 1962
Dion's producer jumps into the dance fray.

SHOW AND TELL

Artist: Al Wilson
Written by: Jerry Fuller
From the album: *Show and Tell*
Label: Rocky Road
Produced by: Jerry Fuller
Year: 1973
His biggest hit and only #1 was originally the B-side of "Queen of the Ghetto."

SHOW BIZ KIDS

Artist: Steely Dan
Written by: Donald Fagen, Walter Becker
From the album: *Countdown to Ecstasy*
Label: ABC
Produced by: Gary Katz
Year: 1973
Venting their spleen on their adopted L.A.

SHOW ME

Artist: The Pretenders
Written by: Chrissie Hynde
From the album: *Learning to Crawl*
Label: Sire
Produced by: Chris Thomas
Year: 1984
Trying to present a brave front for the next generation.

SHOW ME LOVE

Artist: Robin S.
Written by: Allen George, Fred McFarlane
From the album: *Show Me Love*
Label: Big Beat
Produced by: Allen George, Fred McFarlane
Year: 1993
Top 10 R&B/Top 10 crossover.

SHOW ME THE MEANING

Artist: Backstreet Boys
Written by: Herbert Crichlow, Max Martin
From the album: *Millennium*
Label: Jive
Year: 2000
Boy band ballad.

SHOW ME THE WAY

Artist: Peter Frampton
Written by: Peter Frampton
From the album: *Frampton Comes Alive*
Label: A&M
Produced by: Peter Frampton
Year: 1975
Featuring his trademark Wah Wah sound.

SHOW ME THE WAY

Artist: Styx
Written by: Dennis DeYoung
From the album: *Edge of the Century*
Label: A&M
Produced by: Styx
Year: 1991
Adopted by our boys in the first Gulf War.

SHOW, THE

Artist: Doug E. Fresh and the Get Fresh Crew
Written by: Douglas David, Ricky Walters
From the album: *Rap's Greatest Hits*
Label: Reality/Danga
Year: 1985
Early rap poetics.

SHOWER ME WITH YOUR LOVE

Artist: Surface
Written by: Bernard Jackson
From the album: *Second Wave*
Label: Columbia
Produced by: Bernard Jackson, David Townshend, David Conley
Year: 1988
Their first #1 R&B/Top 10 crossover.

SHOWER THE PEOPLE

Artist: James Taylor
Written by: James Taylor
From the album: *In the Pocket*
Label: Warner Brothers
Produced by: Russ Titelman, Lenny Waronker
Year: 1976
Apple flashback.

SHREDDING THE DOCUMENT

Artist: John Hiatt
Written by: John Hiatt
From the album: *Walk On*
Label: MCA
Produced by: Don Smith
Year: 1995
Hiatt puts his most frenzied neuroticism together with his most danceable track, to produce one of year's greatest songs.

SHUT DOWN

Artist: The Beach Boys
Written by: Brian Wilson, Roger Christian
From the album: *Shut Down*
Label: Capitol
Produced by: Brian Wilson
Year: 1963
Growing up under the hood, part two.

SHUT 'EM DOWN

Artist: Public Enemy
Written by: Charles Ridenhour
From the album: *Apocalypse '91 … The Enemy Strikes Black*
Label: Def Jam
Produced by: Stuart Robertz, Cerwin Depper, Gary G. Wiz, the JBL
Year: 1990

SICK AND TIRED

Artist: Chris Kenner
Written by: Dave Bartholomew, Chris Kenner
Label: Imperial
Produced by: Dave Bartholemew
Year: 1957
Early work from the itinerant New Orleans wunderkind Kenner. Covered by Fats Domino (Imperial, '58).

SIDESHOW

Artist: Blue Magic
Written by: Vinnie Barrett, Bobby Eli
From the album: *Blue Magic*
Label: Atco
Produced by: Norman Harris
Year: 1974
#1 R&B/Top 10 crossover.

SIDEWALK TALK

Artist: Jellybean
Written by: Madonna Ciccone
Label: EMI-America
Produced by: Jellybean Benitez
Year: 1985
Dance hit produced by a former Madonna protege.

SIGN 'O' THE TIMES

Artist: Prince
Written by: Prince Rogers Nelson
From the album: *Sign 'o' the Times Soundtrack*
Label: Paisley Park
Produced by: Prince
Year: 1987
#1 R&B/Top 10 crossover from his new movie. But it was no *Purple Rain*.

SIGN ON THE WINDOW

Artist: Bob Dylan
Written by: Bob Dylan
From the album: *New Morning*
Label: Columbia
Produced by: Bob Johnston
Year: 1970
Thoroughly domesticated Bob, surrounded by wife and kids, holed up in a remote cabin in Utah; what's that all about?

SIGN, THE

Artist: Ace of Base
Written by: Jonas (Joker) Berggren
From the album: *The Sign*
Label: Arista
Produced by: Joker, Denniz PoP, Carr
Year: 1993
Harmonious dance track, notable for its marathon chart run.

SIGN YOUR NAME

Artist: Terence Trent D'Arby
Written by: Terence Trent D'Arby
From the album: *The Hardline According to Terence Trent D'Arby*
Label: Columbia
Produced by: Martyn Ware
Year: 1987

SIGNED, SEALED, DELIVERED, I'M YOURS

Artist: Stevie Wonder
Written by: Stevie Wonder, Lee Garrett, Lula Mae Hardaway, Syreeta Wright
From the album: *Signed, Sealed, Delivered*
Label: Tamla
Produced by: Stevie Wonder
Year: 1970
The entire Hardaway family celebrates Stevie's new contract with a #1 R&B/Top 10 crossover.

SIGNS

Artist: Five Man Electrical Band
Written by: Arthur Thomas
From the album: *Goodbyes and Butterflys*
Label: Lionel
Produced by: Dallas Smith
Year: 1971
Muted protest. Covered by Tesla (Geffen, '90).

SILENCE IS GOLDEN

Artist: The Four Seasons
Written by: Bob Gaudio, Bob Crewe
From the album: *Born to Wander*
Label: Philips
Produced by: Bob Crewe
Year: 1964
B-side of "Rag Doll" was made into a big hit by the Tremelos (Epic, '67).

SILENT ALL THESE YEARS

Artist: Tori Amos
Written by: Tori Amos
From the album: *Little Earthquakes*
Label: Atlantic
Produced by: Davitt Sigerson
Year: 1992
Breaking the bonds of girl-group suppression, this is a powerful tale of finding one's voice as a female in the '90s.

SILENT LUCIDITY

Artist: Queensryche
Written by: Chris DeGarmo
From the album: *Empire*
Label: EMI
Produced by: Peter Collins
Year: 1991
Venturing onto Pink Floydian terrain for their biggest hit.

SILHOUETTES

Artist: The Rays
Written by: Frank Slay Jr., Bob Crewe
Label: Cameo
Produced by: Bob Crewe
Year: 1957
Teen doo-wop mistaken identity classic with the Philadelphia sound. Segue: "Fool in the Rain" by Led Zeppelin.

SILLY LOVE SONGS

Artist: Paul McCartney and Wings
Written by: Paul McCartney
From the album: *Wings at the Speed of Sound*
Label: Capitol
Produced by: Paul McCartney
Year: 1976
His ultimate latter-day statement of purpose is his first solo songwriting hit.

SILVER MACHINE

Artist: Hawkwind
Written by: Dave Brock, Robert Calvert
Label: United Artists
Year: 1972
English relic of the psychedelic era was their biggest UK hit—charting again in '78 and '83. This is the band from whence sprang Lemmy Kilmeister (aka Motorhead).

SILVER ROCKET

Artist: Sonic Youth
Written by: Sonic Youth
From the album: *Daydream Nation*
Label: Blast First
Produced by: Nicholas Sansone, Sonic Youth
Year: 1988
Their trademark droning sound is now almost arenaesque.

SILVER SPRINGS

Artist: Fleetwood Mac
Written by: Stevie Nicks
From the album: *The Dance*
Label: Reprise
Produced by: Elliot Scheiner
Year: 1977
Nonalbum B-side of "Go Your Own Way." Revived in 1997.

SILVIO

Artist: Bob Dylan
Written by: Bob Dylan, Robert Hunter
From the album: *Down in the Groove*
Label: Columbia
Produced by: Bob Dylan
Year: 1988
Artistically challenging collaboration with the Dead's head writer. Dylanologists might have had a field day with it, had there been any left in the field.

SIMMER DOWN

Artist: The Wailers
Written by: Bob Marley
Produced by: Clement Dodd
Label: Coxsong
Year: 1964
Legendary first single for the pioneering reggae champions.

SIMON SAYS

Artist: 1910 Fruitgum Company
Written by: Elliot Chiprut
From the album: *Simon Says*
Label: Buddah
Produced by: Jerry Kazenetz, Jeff Katz
Year: 1968
Kazenetz and Katz invent the bubble formula.

SIMON SMITH AND THE AMAZING DANCING BEAR

Artist: Harper's Bizarre
Written by: Randy Newman
From the album: *Feelin' Groovy*
Label: Warner Brothers
Produced by: Lenny Waronker
Year: 1966
Quirky Warner Brothers' house songwriter begins to get weird. Covered in England by Alan Price

(Decca, '67). Newman recorded his own version (Reprise, '72).

SIMPLE TWIST OF FATE

Artist: Bob Dylan
Written by: Bob Dylan
From the album: *Blood on the Tracks*
Label: Columbia
Produced by: Phil Ramone, Bob Dylan
Year: 1975
Twisted story song.

SIMPLY IRRESISTIBLE

Artist: Robert Palmer
Written by: Robert Palmer
From the album: *Irresistible*
Label: Island
Produced by: Robert Palmer
Year: 1988
Aided by a compulsively viewable video featuring several stunning models as his backup band.

SIN CITY

Artist: The Flying Burrito Brothers
Written by: Gram Parsons
From the album: *The Gilded Palace of Sin*
Label: A&M
Produced by: Flying Burrito Brothers, Larry Marks, Henry Levy
Year: 1969
From one of the most influential country/rock albums of the '60s. Covered by Parsons' soulmate, Emmylou Harris (Reprise, '76).

SINCE I DON'T HAVE YOU

Artist: The Skyliners
Written by: James Beaumont, Janet Vogel, Joseph Verscharen, Wally Lester, John Taylor
From the album: *The Skyliners*
Label: Calico
Produced by: Joe Rock
Year: 1959
First and biggest hit, with the high note of alltime. Was that Janet Vogel or a Stradivarius?

SINCE I FELL FOR YOU

Artist: Annie Laurie
Written by: Buddy Johnson
Label: De Luxe
Year: 1947
Top 5 R&B/Top 20 crossover ballad, with Paul Gayton's band. Johnson wrote the R&B classic "Did You See Jackie Robinson Hit That Ball." Covered by Lenny Welch (Cadence, '63).

SINCE I MET YOU BABY

Artist: Ivory Joe Hunter
Written by: Ivory Joe Hunter
From the album: *16 of His Greatest Hits*
Label: Atlantic
Produced by: Ahmet Ertegun, Jerry Wexler

Year: 1956
Smooth blues.

SINCE YOU'RE GONE

Artist: The Cars
Written by: Ric Ocasek
From the album: *Shake It Up*
Label: Elektra
Produced by: Ray Thomas Baker
Year: 1982
The Cars turn to video to make their mark, where they quickly stack up with Nesmith and Rundgren.

SINCERELY

Artist: The Moonglows
Written by: Harvey Fuqua, Alan Freed
Label: Chess
Year: 1955
First collaboration between two future powers of the rock and roll era, a Top 10 R&B/Top 20 cross-over. Freed would go on to become a martyred DJ; Fuqua a legendary writer and producer. The tune, meanwhile, merely went on to become a standard, doo-wop and otherwise. The pop cover by the McGuire Sisters (Coral, '55) went to #1.

SING A SONG

Artist: Earth, Wind & Fire
Written by: Maurice White, Albert McKay
From the album: *Gratitude*
Label: Columbia
Produced by: Maurice White, Charles Stepney
Year: 1975
Their first #1 R&B/Top 10 crossover. The world beat Beatles to George Clinton's Rolling Stones.

SING ME BACK HOME

Artist: The Everly Brothers
Written by: Gram Parsons
From the album: *Roots*
Label: Warner Brothers
Year: 1968
#1 country hit by Merle Haggard (Capitol, '67). Covered by the Flying Burrito Brothers (A&M, '72).

SINGING THE BLUES

Artist: Marty Robbins
Written by: Melvin Endsley
Label: Columbia
Produced by: Don Law
Year: 1955
#1 country/Top 20 crossover, covered by Guy Mitchell (Columbia, '55).

SINGLE LIFE, THE

Artist: Cameo
Written by: Larry Blackmon, Tomi Jenkins
From the album: *Single Life*
Label: Atlanta Artists
Produced by: Larry Blackmon

Year: 1985
One of Blackmon's best party records.

SINK THE BISMARCK

Artist: Johnny Horton
Written by: Tillman Franks, Johnny Horton
From the album: *Johnny Horton's Greatest Hits*
Label: Columbia
Year: 1960
Based on but not in the movie.

SINNER'S PRAYER

Artist: Ray Charles
Written by: Lowell Fulson
Label: Atlantic
Year: 1952
B-side of his first Atlantic single "It Should've Been Me."

SIR DUKE

Artist: Stevie Wonder
Written by: Stevie Wonder
From the album: *Songs in the Key of Life*
Label: Tamla
Produced by: Stevie Wonder
Year: 1976
#1 R&B/#1 crossover is his biggest hit, a tribute to Duke Ellington.

SISTER CHRISTIAN

Artist: Night Ranger
Written by: Kelly Keagy
From the album: *Midnight Madness*
Label: Camel
Produced by: Pat Glasser, Paul Glasser
Year: 1984
Perhaps the guiltiest of all the 80's hair band guilty pleasures. Prominently used in the movie *Boogie Nights*.

SISTER GOLDEN HAIR

Artist: America
Written by: Gerry Beckley
From the album: *Hearts*
Label: Warner Brothers
Produced by: George Martin
Year: 1975
Professional folk/rock.

SISTER HAVANA

Artist: Urge Overkill
Written by: Urge Overkill
From the album: *Saturation*
Label: Geffen
Produced by: Butcher Brothers
Year: 1993
Early alternative statement from Chicago, Illinois, dressed up in Styx clothing.

SISTER MORPHINE

Artist: The Rolling Stones

Written by: Mick Jagger, Keith Richards
From the album: *Sticky Fingers*
Label: Rolling Stones
Produced by: Jimmy Miller
Year: 1971
Druggy dirge, covered by Marianne Faithfull, for whom it was written (Island, '90).

SISTER RAY

Artist: The Velvet Underground
Written by: Lou Reed
From the album: *White Light/White Heat*
Label: Verve
Produced by: Andy Warhol
Year: 1968
Ending the good-vibrations era of "acid, incense, and balloons" with the ultimate, 17-minute (bad) trip. Covered by Joy Division (Factory, '81).

SISTERS ARE DOIN' IT FOR THEMSELVES

Artist: Eurythmics and Aretha Franklin
Written by: Annie Lennox, Dave Stewart
From the album: *Be Yourself Tonight*
Label: RCA
Produced by: Dave Stewart
Year: 1985
Twin divas Lennox and Franklin have an uplifting contemporary message. Suggested segue: Streisand and Summer's "No More Tears."

SISTERS OF MERCY

Artist: Judy Collins
Written by: Leonard Cohen
From the album: *Wildflowers*
Label: Elektra
Produced by: Mark Abrahmson
Year: 1968
On Cohen's first album (Columbia, '68) and featured in *McCabe & Mrs. Miller*. Covered by Sting (A&M, '95).

SIT DOWN I THINK I LOVE YOU

Artist: The Mojo Men
Written by: Stephen Stills
Label: Reprise
Year: 1966
Essential garage band folk/rock. Covered by Stills' band, Buffalo Springfield (Atco, '67).

SITTIN' IN THE BALCONY

Artist: Eddie Cochran
Written by: John Loudermilk
From the album: *Singin' to My Baby*
Label: Liberty
Produced by: Snuff Garrett, Eddie Cochran, Jerry Capehart
Year: 1957
An L.A. leather rocker tosses spitballs at the establishment. Introduced by the pseudonymous author, Johnny Dee (Colonial, '57).

(SITTIN' ON) THE DOCK OF THE BAY

Artist: Otis Redding
Written by: Otis Redding, Steve Cropper
From the album: *Dock of the Bay*
Label: Volt
Produced by: Steve Cropper
Year: 1968
His poignant rambling farewell, folkish and elegiac, is his first and only #1 R&B/#1 crossover, posthumously.

SITTIN' UP IN MY ROOM

Artist: Brandy
Written by: Kenny Edmonds (Babyface)
From the album: *Waiting to Exhale Soundtrack*
Label: Arista
Year: 1995
Subteen hip hop sweetheart waits for you to call.

SITTING IN LIMBO

Artist: Jimmy Cliff
Written by: Jimmy Cliff, Gilly Bright-Plummer
Label: Mango
Produced by: Jimmy Cliff
Year: 1972
Reggae classic included in the '75 film *The Harder They Come*. Covered by Three Dog Night (Dunhill, '73).

SIX DAYS ON THE ROAD

Artist: Dave Dudley
Written by: Earl Green, Carl Montgomery
Label: Golden Wing
Year: 1963
#2 country/Top 40 crossover establishes the trucker school of alternative country/rock.

6' 1"

Artist: Liz Phair
Written by: Liz Phair
From the album: *Exile in Guyville*
Label: Matador
Produced by: Liz Phair, Brad Wood
Year: 1993
Janis Ian turns 18, grows several inches over the summer. A new empowering anthem for females of all sizes.

SIX NIGHTS A WEEK

Artist: The Crests
Written by: Billy Dawn Smith
From the album: *The Angels Listened In*
Label: Coed
Year: 1959
Attempting to follow up "16 Candles."

634-5789

Artist: Wilson Pickett
Written by: Steve Cropper, Eddie Floyd
From the album: *Exciting Wilson Pickett*
Label: Atlantic
Produced by: Steve Cropper, Jim Stewart
Year: 1966
His biggest R&B hit; #1 R&B/Top 20. The Marvelettes were on the party line at "Beechwood 4-5789" (Tamla, '62).

SIXTEEN BLUE

Artist: The Replacements
Written by: Paul Westerberg
From the album: *Let It Be*
Produced by: Peter Jasperson, Steven Fjelstad
Label: Twin Tone
Year: 1984

16 CANDLES

Artist: The Crests
Written by: Luther Dixon, Allyson Khent
From the album: *The Crests Sing All the Biggies*
Label: Coed
Produced by: Luther Dixon
Year: 1959
Originally titled "21 Candles," and the B-side of "Beside You," this tune encapsulates the essence of city soul and marks the ascent of Johnny Maestro and the arrival of Luther Dixon. Against a backdrop of the Buddy Holly crash the week the song peaked on the radio, they were memorial candles too. Suggested segue: "Molly" by Sponge (Work, '95), which contains the haunting chorus: "16 candles down the drain."

SIXTEEN REASONS (WHY I LOVE YOU)

Artist: Connie Stevens
Written by: Bill Post, Doree Post
Label: Warner Brothers
Year: 1960
Hollywood pop rock answer to "The Ten Commandments of Love."

6TH AVENUE HEARTBREAK

Artist: The Wallflowers
Written by: Jacob Dylan
From the album: *Bringing down the Horse*
Label: Interscope
Produced by: T-Bone Burnette
Year: 1996
Positively Avenue of the Americas: the son invades the father's old neighborhood for his first folk/rock hit.

SIXTY MINUTE MAN

Artist: The Dominoes
Written by: Billy Ward, Rose Marks
Label: Federal
Produced by: Ralph Bass
Year: 1951
The advent of Lovin' Dan, the black backdoor man who spent a full sixty minutes in the bedrooms of the middle class, thereby changing the sexual rhythms of popular music forever.

SKELETONS

Artist: Stevie Wonder
Written by: Stevie Wonder
From the album: *Characters*
Label: Motown
Produced by: Stevie Wonder
Year: 1987
#1 R&B/Top 20 crossover.

SKINNY LEGS AND ALL

Artist: Joe Tex
Written by: Joe Tex
From the album: *Live and Lively*
Label: Dial
Produced by: Buddy Killen
Year: 1967
Inverse fashion statement was his second biggest hit.

SKINNY MINNIE

Artist: Bill Haley and His Comets
Written by: Bill Haley, Arrett "Rusty" Keefer, Catherine Cafra, Milt Gabler
Label: Decca
Produced by: Milt Gabler
Year: 1958
Plainly out of steam by now, Bill and the gang were determined to go down swinging. They followed this up with "Lean Jean," which was an even bigger bomb.

SKY HIGH

Artist: Jigsaw
Written by: Des Dyer, Clive Scott
From the album: *Sky High*
Label: Chelsea
Produced by: Chas Peate
Year: 1975
From the movie *The Dragon Flies*.

SKY IS CRYING, THE

Artist: Elmore James
Written by: Elmore James
Label: Fire
Produced by: Bobby Robinson
Year: 1960
In the days when a hair-raising blues tune could still make the R&B charts. Covered by Stevie Ray Vaughan (Epic, '90).

SKY PILOT

Artist: Animals
Written by: Eric Burdon, Victor Briggs, John Weider, Barry Jenkins, Denny McCulloch
From the album: *The Twain Shall Meet*
Label: MGM
Produced by: Tom Wilson
Year: 1968
Having tackled a couple of California countercultural peaks, this time the boys take on a Vietnam War story.

SLAM

Artist: Onyx
Written by: Chylow Parker, Jason Mizell, T. Taylor, K. Jones, F. Scruggs
From the album: *Bacdafucup*
Label: JMJ
Produced by: Chyskillz, Jam Master Jay
Year: 1993
The anger of Public Enemy without the redeeming social significance.

SLAVE TO LOVE

Artist: Bryan Ferry
Written by: Bryan Ferry
From the album: *Boys and Girls*
Label: Warner Brothers
Produced by: Bryan Ferry, Rhett Davies
Year: 1985
Reinventing Frank Sinatra-style romantic pop in England in the '80s just as the Beatles reinvented rock and roll in England in the '60s.

SLEDGEHAMMER

Artist: Peter Gabriel
Written by: Peter Gabriel
From the album: *So*
Label: Geffen
Produced by: Peter Gabriel, Daniel Lanois
Year: 1986
His biggest hit.

SLEEP

Artist: Little Willie John
Written by: Eric Burtnett, Adam Giebel
Label: King
Produced by: Henry Glover
Year: 1960
Haunting Top 10 R&B/Top 15 crossover.

SLEEP WALK

Artist: Santo and Johnny
Written by: Ann Farina, John Farina, Santo Farina
From the album: *Santo and Johnny*
Label: Canadian-American
Year: 1959
First #1 appearance for the steel guitar.

SLEEPING BAG

Artist: ZZ Top
Written by: Billy Gibbons, Dusty Hill, Frank Beard
From the album: *Afterburner*
Label: Warner Brothers
Produced by: Bill Ham
Year: 1985
Their second Top 10 single; the other one was "Legs."

SLEEPS WITH ANGELS

Artist: Neil Young
Written by: Neil Young
From the album: *Sleeps with Angels*
Label: Reprise
Produced by: David Briggs, Neil Young
Year: 1994
Tribute to Kurt Cobain.

SLIDE

Artist: Goo Goo Dolls
Written by: John Rzeznick
From the album: *Dizzy up the Girl*
Label: Reprise
Year: 1998
Marriage proposal brought on by an unexpected pregnancy.

SLIP AWAY

Artist: Clarence Carter
Written by: William Armstrong, Wilbur Terrell, Marcus Daniel
From the album: *This Is Clarence Carter*
Label: Atlantic
Produced by: Rick Hall
Year: 1967
A classic cheating song, Muscle-Shoals style.

SLIP KID

Artist: The Who
Written by: Pete Townshend
From the album: *The Who by Numbers*
Label: MCA
Produced by: Glyn Johns
Year: 1975
Powerful Townshend; from whence came: "No easy way to be free."

SLIP SLIDIN' AWAY

Artist: Paul Simon
Written by: Paul Simon
From the album: *Greatest Hits, Etc.*
Label: Columbia
Produced by: Phil Ramone, Paul Simon
Year: 1977
Segue: "Road to Cairo" by David Ackles.

SLIPPERY WHEN WET

Artist: Commodores
Written by: Lionel B. Richie Jr., Ronald La Pread, Thomas McClary, Walter Orange, William King Jr., Milan Williams
From the album: *Caught in the Act*
Label: Motown
Produced by: James Carmichael, Commodores
Year: 1975
#1 R&B/Top 20 funk crossover.

SLIPPIN' AND SLIDIN'

Artist: Little Richard
Written by: Richard Penniman (Little Richard), Albert Collins, Edwin Bocage, James Smith
From the album: *Here's Little Richard*
Label: Specialty
Produced by: Bumps Blackwell
Year: 1956
B-side of "Long Tall Sally."

SLOTH

Artist: Fairport Convention
Written by: Dave Mattacks, Simon Nicol, Dave Pegg, Dave Swarbrick, Richard Thompson
From the album: *Full House*
Label: A&M
Produced by: Joe Boyd
Year: 1970
An epic folk/rock call to arms.

SLOW DANCE (HEY MR. DJ)

Artist: R. Kelly
Written by: Robert Kelly
From the album: *Born into the '90s*
Label: Jive
Produced by: Robert Kelly
Year: 1992

SLOW DANCING

Artist: The Funky Kings
Written by: Jack Tempchin
Label: Arista
Produced by: Paul Rothschild
Year: 1975
Belated prom classic when it was covered by Johnny Rivers (Big Tree, '75) as "Swayin' to the Music."

SLOW DEATH

Artist: Flamin' Groovies
Written by: Roy A. Loney, Cyrill Jordan
From the album: *Slow Death*
Label: United Artists
Produced by: Dave Edmunds
Year: 1972
Quintessential punk rockabilly track, released in the UK as a single. Covered by the Dictators (Epic, '78).

SLOW DOWN

Artist: Larry Williams
Written by: Larry Williams
Label: Specialty
Produced by: Art Rupe
Year: 1957
B-side of "Dizzy Miss Lizzy." Covered by the Beatles (Capitol, '64).

SLOW HAND

Artist: Pointer Sisters
Written by: John Bettis, Mike Clark
From the album: *Black and White*
Label: Planet
Produced by: Richard Perry
Year: 1981
Smoldering bedroom ballad and philosophy. Not about Eric Clapton.

SLOW RIDE

Artist: Foghat
Written by: Dave Peverett
From the album: *Fool for the City*
Label: Bearsville
Produced by: Nick Jameson
Year: 1976
Indomitable boogie.

SLOW TWISTIN'

Artist: Chubby Checker and Dee Dee Sharp
Written by: John Sheldon (Kal Mann)
From the album: *For Teen Twisters Only*
Label: Parkway
Produced by: Kal Mann
Year: 1961
Seemingly impossible variation on the after shower dance.

SLUM GODDESS

Artist: The Fugs
Written by: Tuli Kupferberg, Ed Sanders
From the album: *First Album*
Label: ESP
Produced by: Harry Smith
Year: 1965
When the Fugs sang to the various slum goddesses in attendance at the Dom on St. Marks Place on the Lower East Side of New York, among those taking notice was the artist Andy Warhol. Soon an alternative to folk/rock would arise, in the repertoire of the Velvet Underground, Andy's house band at the Dom when it reopened as the Electric Circus.

SMALL TOWN

Artist: John (Cougar) Mellencamp
Written by: John Cougar Mellencamp
From the album: *Scarecrow*
Label: Riva
Produced by: Don Gehman, Little Bastard
Year: 1985
Jack and Diane reminisce. Segue: "Glory Days" by Bruce Springsteen.

SMALL TOWN BOY

Artist: Bronski Beat
Written by: Jimmy Somerville, Larry Steinbachek, Steve Bronski
From the album: *The Age of Consent*
Label: MCA
Produced by: Mike Thorne
Year: 1985
Alternative dance-hall falsetto.

SMALL TOWN TALK

Artist: Paul Butterfield's Better Days
Written by: Robert Guidry (Bobby Charles)
From the album: *It All Comes Back*
Label: Bearsville
Produced by: Nick Jameson, Geoff Muldaur, Paul Butterfield
Year: 1973
Woodstock Valley PTA, as sung by Maria Muldaur's ex, Geoff. Covered by Rick Danko (Capitol, '77).

SMELLS LIKE TEEN SPIRIT

Artist: Nirvana
Written by: Kurt Cobain, Krist Novaselic, Dave Grohl
From the album: *Nevermind*
Label: DGC
Produced by: Butch Vig
Year: 1991
The "Like a Rolling Stone" of its era, a curious little buzzsaw track as unassuming as Dylan's was grandiose, that launched a thousand alternative bands, most of them from or en route to Seattle, along with half the record business of the '90s. Opened the door for guitar bands again, lyrics that cut cryptically to the nub, lead singers who wore flannel instead of spandex and flailed around the stage looking for a place to hide or throw up or both. The Replacements had a replacement at last.

SMILING FACES SOMETIMES

Artist: Undisputed Truth
Written by: Norman Whitfield, Barrett Strong
From the album: *The Undisputed Truth*
Label: Gordy
Produced by: Norman Whitfield
Year: 1971
Capturing the early '70s penchant for cautionary R&B. Ten years later, all such caution would be thrown to the wind, lyrically at least.

SMOKE FROM A DISTANT FIRE

Artist: Sanford Townshend Band
Written by: Ed Sanford, John Townshend, Steven Stewart
From the album: *Sanford Townshend Band*
Label: Warner Brothers
Produced by: Barry Beckett, Jerry Wexler
Year: 1976
L.A. meets Memphis; L.A. wins.

SMOKE GETS IN YOUR EYES

Artist: The Platters
Written by: Otto Harbach, Jerome Kern
From the album: *Remember When*
Label: Mercury
Produced by: Buck Ram
Year: 1958
Introduced in the '33 musical *Roberta*; their fourth and last #1 hit.

SMOKE ON THE WATER

Artist: Deep Purple
Written by: Ritchie Blackmore, Ian Gillan, Roger Glover, Jon Lord, Ian Paice
From the album: *Machine Head*
Label: Warner Brothers
Produced by: Deep Purple
Year: 1972
Celebrating a hot night in Montreaux, opening for Frank Zappa.

SMOKESTACK LIGHTNING

Artist: Howlin' Wolf
Written by: Chester Burnette (Howling Wolf)
From the album: *Moaning in the Moonlight*
Label: Chess
Year: 1956
His second big R&B hit.

SMOKEY JOE'S CAFÉ

Artist: The Robins
Written by: Jerry Leiber, Mike Stoller
From the album: *Yakety Yak*
Label: Spark
Produced by: Jerry Leiber, Mike Stoller
Year: 1955
Epic L.A. story-song was the group's only R&B/crossover. Would be moved, forty years later, lock, stock, and bass notes, to Broadway, as the venue for a Leiber and Stoller career review/revue. Covered by Loudon Wainwright (Columbia, '73).

SMOKEY PLACES

Artist: The Corsairs
Written by: Abner Spector
Label: Tuff
Year: 1961
In the moody, misty mold of the Impressions' "Gypsy Woman."

SMOKIE (PART II)

Artist: Bill Black's Combo
Written by: Bill Black
Label: Hi
Year: 1959
#1 R&B/Top 20 crossover instrumental by Elvis's bassman, in a rock-n-soul combo setting (see Booker T. and the MGs) that would result in four more Top 20 hits for him in the next year.

SMOKIN' IN THE BOYS ROOM

Artist: Brownsville Station
Written by: Cub Koda, Michael Lutz
From the album: *Yeah!*
Label: Big Tree
Year: 1973
Teen metal anthem. Covered by Motley Crue (Elektra, '85).

SMOKING GUN

Artist: Robert Cray
Written by: Bruce Bromberg (D. Amy), Robert Cray, Richard Cousins
From the album: *Strong Persuader*

Label: Mercury
Produced by: Bruce Bromberg, Dennis Walker
Year: 1987
The bluesiest cut to hit Top 30 since B. B. King.

SMOOTH

Artist: Santana and Rob Thomas
Written by: Itaal Shur, Rob Thomas
From the album: *Supernatural*
Label: Arista
Produced by: Matt Serletic
Year: 1999
Jazzy Latin flavored #1 hit from the massive comeback album by the influential rock guitarist, matched with the leader of Matchbox Twenty. Won Grammies for Record and Song of the Year.

SMOOTH CRIMINAL

Artist: Michael Jackson
Written by: Michael Jackson
From the album: *Bad*
Label: Epic
Produced by: Quincy Jones
Year: 1987

SMOOTH OPERATOR

Artist: Sade
Written by: Helen Folesade Adu (Sade), Raymond St. John
From the album: *Diamond Life*
Label: Epic
Produced by: R. Millar
Year: 1985
Languidly continental.

SMUGGLER'S BLUES

Artist: Glenn Frey
Written by: Glenn Frey, Jack Tempchin
From the album: *The Allnighter*
Label: MCA
Produced by: Glenn Frey, Allen Blazek
Year: 1985
From an episode of *Miami Vice*, in which he had a major supporting role.

SNAP YOUR FINGERS

Artist: Joe Henderson
Written by: Grady Martin, Alex Zanetis
From the album: *Snap Your Fingers*
Label: Todd
Produced by: Jerry Ross
Year: 1962
Jazzy Top 10 R&B/Top 10 crossover.

SNATCHING IT BACK

Artist: Clarence Carter
Written by: George Jackson, Clarence Carter
From the album: *Testifying*
Label: Atlantic
Produced by: Rick Hall

Year: 1969
Top 5 R&B hit is a soul classic.

SNOOPY VERSUS THE RED BARON

Artist: The Royal Guardsmen
Written by: Phil Gernhard, Richard L. Holler
From the album: *Snoopy vs. the Red Baron*
Label: Laurie
Produced by: Phil Gernhard
Year: 1966
Novelty hit represents the underexplored Peanuts influence on rock and roll, which is 99% connected to the output of the Royal Guardsmen, who followed up this tune with "Return of the Red Baron" in '67 and "Snoopy for President" in '68, with diminishing returns. ("Charlie Brown" by the Coasters is not believed to have anything to do with the noted comic strip). Of course, there's the musical *You're a Good Man, Charlie Brown*, which opened in 1967 and contained a song called "Red Baron." And "Linus and Lucy" from Vince Guaraldi's *It's a Charlie Brown Christmas* (Fantasy, '87) remains a perennial holiday favorite.

SNOW QUEEN

Artist: The City
Written by: Gerry Goffin, Carole King
From the album: *Now That Everything's Been Said*
Label: Ode
Produced by: Lou Adler
Year: 1968
Elaborate writer's demo from Carole King's presolo days, with Danny Kortchmar on guitar. Covered by the Association (Columbia, '72).

SNOWBIRD

Artist: Anne Murray
Written by: Gene Maclellan
From the album: *Snowbird*
Label: Capitol
Produced by: Brian Ahern
Year: 1970
Top 10 Country/Top 10 crossover introduces a new thrush from Canada.

SO ALIVE

Artist: Love and Rockets
Written by: Daniel Ash, Love and Rockets
From the album: *Love and Rockets*
Label: Beggar's Banquet
Produced by: Jon Fryer, Love and Rockets
Year: 1989
Bauhaus grads move into T-Rex territory for their first and only hit.

SO FAR AWAY

Artist: Carole King
Written by: Carole King
From the album: *Tapestry*
Label: Ode
Produced by: Lou Adler

Year: 1971
Cross-country break up ballad, scripted solo by Carole after years of writing with Gerry Goffin.

SO FINE

Artist: The Fiestas
Written by: John Veliotis (Johnny Otis)
Label: Old Town
Produced by: Henry Glover
Year: 1959
Evocative post-doo-wop standard. Sounds like it was recorded in a men's room.

SO IN TO YOU

Artist: Atlanta Rhythm Section
Written by: Buddy Buie, Dean Daughtry, Robert Nix
From the album: *A Rock and Roll Alternatives*
Label: Polydor
Produced by: Buddy Buie
Year: 1976
Southern pop/rock.

SO IT GOES

Artist: Nick Lowe
Written by: Nick Lowe
From the album: *Pure Pop for Now People*
Label: Columbia
Produced by: Nick Lowe
Year: 1978
First single release for the notorious English label Stiff, future home of Elvis Costello.

SO LONELY

Artist: The Police
Written by: Gordon Sumner (Sting)
From the album: *Outlandos d'Amour*
Label: A&M
Produced by: The Police
Year: 1978
Big hit in England when it was reissued in '80, after the first wave of their success.

SO LONG DAD

Artist: Randy Newman
Written by: Randy Newman
From the album: *Randy Newman Creates Something New under the Sun*
Label: Reprise
Produced by: Van Dyke Parks, Lenny Waronker
Year: 1968
Brief, pointed, droll, and unforgettable reaction to the prolix effusions of the '60s.

SO LONG I'M GONE

Artist: Warren Smith
Written by: Roy Orbison, Sam Phillips
From the album: *First Country Collection*
Label: Sun
Produced by: Sam Phillips
Year: 1957

Early Roy Orbison rockabilly effort was country star Smith's only Top 100 appearance.

SO LONG IT'S BEEN GOOD TO KNOW YOU (DUSTY OLD DUST)

Artist: The Weavers
Written by: Woody Guthrie
Label: Decca
Produced by: Milt Gabler
Year: 1951
One of Woody Guthrie's earliest tunes, this dust bowl ballad was written circa 1935.

SO LONG, MARIANNE

Artist: Leonard Cohen
Written by: Leonard Cohen
From the album: *Songs of Leonard Cohen*
Label: Columbia
Produced by: John Simon
Year: 1968
One of the less complicated breakup tunes from the author of the novel *Beautiful Losers*. Covered by the group James (Atlantic, '91).

SO MUCH IN LOVE

Artist: The Tymes
Written by: William Jackson, Roy Straigis, George Williams
From the album: *So Much in Love*
Label: Parkway
Produced by: Billy Jackson
Year: 1963
Their first and biggest hit is a beach music classic: Top 5 R&B/#1 crossover. Covered by All-4-One (Atlantic, '94).

SO MUCH TO SAY

Artist: Dave Matthews Band
Written by: Dave Matthews, Boyd Tinsley, Peter Grieser
From the album: *Crash*
Label: RCA
Produced by: Steve Lillywhite
Year: 1996
But they'd rather play.

SO SAD (TO WATCH GOOD LOVE GO BAD)

Artist: The Everly Brothers
Written by: Don Everly
From the album: *It's Everly Time*
Label: Warner Brothers
Produced by: Wesley Rose
Year: 1960
Could Don have been writing about their brotherly relationship, which would come to parting of the ways in 1973?

SO VERY HARD TO GO

Artist: Tower of Power

Written by: Emilio Castillo, Stephen Kupka
From the album: *Tower of Power*
Label: Warner Brothers
Produced by: Tower of Power
Year: 1973
San Francisco big-band funk.

SO WHAT

Artist: Miles Davis
Written by: Miles Davis
From the album: *Kind of Blue*
Label: Columbia
Produced by: Irving Townsend
Year: 1959
With a trumpet solo by Davis that launched a generation's interest in jazz.

SO WHAT'CHA WANT

Artist: Beastie Boys
Written by: Beastie Boys
From the album: *Check Your Head*
Label: Capitol
Produced by: Mario Caldato Jr.
Year: 1992

SO YOU THINK YOU'RE IN LOVE

Artist: Robyn Hitchcock and the Egyptians
From the album: *Perplex Island*
Label: A&M
Year: 1991
English alt/rock legend achieves his only #1 alt/rock hit.

SO YOU WANNA BE A ROCK AND ROLL STAR

Artist: The Byrds
Written by: Roger McGuinn, Chris Hillman
From the album: *Younger Than Yesterday*
Label: Columbia
Produced by: Gary Usher
Year: 1967
A cautionary tale, inspired by their run-ins with the FBI. Suggested segue: "Johnny B. Goode" by Chuck Berry.

SOCIETY'S CHILD (BABY, I'VE BEEN THINKING)

Artist: Janis Ian
Written by: Janis Fink (Janis Ian)
From the album: *Janis Ian*
Label: Verve Forecast
Produced by: Shadow Morton
Year: 1967
Travails of an interracial teen relationship; outspoken for its time. Covered by Spooky Tooth (A&M, '71). Suggested segues: "Brother Louie" by Stories, "I Believe" by Soul for Real.

SOCK IT TO ME, BABY

Artist: Mitch Ryder and the Detroit Wheels
Written by: Bob Crewe, L. Russell Brown
From the album: *Sock It to Me*
Label: New Voice
Produced by: Bob Crewe
Year: 1967
Blue-eyed, Motor-city soul. L. Russell Brown would be back with Tony Orlando & Dawn.

SOCK IT 2 ME

Artist: Missy Elliott
Written by: Melissa (Missy) Elliott
From the album: *Supa Dupa Fly*
Label: East West
Year: 1997
An authentic new voice in hip-hop revives a fabled TV catch phrase.

SOFT AND WET

Artist: Prince
Written by: Prince Rogers Nelson, Christopher Moon
From the album: *Prince—For You*
Label: Warner Brothers
Produced by: Prince
Year: 1976
The anti-Michael Jackson emerges from Minneapolis.

SOLD AMERICAN

Artist: Kinky Friedman
Written by: Kinky Friedman
From the album: *Sold American*
Label: Vanguard
Produced by: Chuck Glaser
Year: 1973
Blistering outlaw country lament.

SOLD ME DOWN THE RIVER

Artist: The Alarm
Written by: Eddie Macdonald, Mike Peters
From the album: *Change*
Label: IRS
Produced by: Tony Visconti
Year: 1989
The rebel intensity of a U2 track.

SOLDIER BOY

Artist: The Shirelles
Written by: Florence Greenburg (Florence Green), Luther Dixon
From the album: *Baby, It's You*
Label: Scepter
Produced by: Luther Dixon
Year: 1961
Their biggest hit; a #2 R&B/#1 crossover.

SOLDIER OF LOVE

Artist: Donny Osmond
Written by: Cal Sturken, Evan Rogers
From the album: *Donny Osmond*

Label: Capitol
Produced by: Carl Sturken, Evan Rogers
Year: 1989

SOLDIERS OF LOVE

Artist: Arthur Alexander
Written by: Buzz Cason, Tony Moon
From the album: *You Better Move On*
Label: Dot
Year: 1962
Early Beatles performing favorite, covered by Marshall Crenshaw, who played John Lennon in *Beatlemania*.

SOLID

Artist: Ashford and Simpson
Written by: Nick Ashford, Valerie Simpson
From the album: *Solid*
Label: Capitol
Produced by: Nick Ashford, Valerie Simpson
Year: 1984
#1 R&B/Top 20 crossover is the biggest hit for the solid songwriting team.

SOLITARY MAN

Artist: Neil Diamond
Written by: Neil Diamond
From the album: *The Feel of Neil Diamond*
Label: Bang
Produced by: Jeff Barry, Ellie Greenwich
Year: 1966
Brooding loner's lament by the last of the Brill Building rock generation. Covered by Chris Isaak (Warner Brothers, '92).

SOLO

Artist: Sandy Denny
Written by: Sandy Denny
From the album: *Like an Old Fashioned Waltz*
Label: Island
Produced by: Trevor Lucas
Year: 1974
The legendary folk voice from Fairport Convention; her poignant opening farewell.

SOLO FLIGHT

Artist: Charlie Christian
Written by: Charlie Christian, Benny Goodman, Jimmy Mundy
From the album: *Genius of the Electric Guitar*
Label: Columbia
Produced by: Jimmy Mundy
Year: 1944
Posthumous hit for Benny Goodman's legendary guitarist, recorded in 1941, was a #1 R&B/Top 20 crossover, influencing a generation of electric guitar players.

SOLSBURY HILL

Artist: Peter Gabriel
Written by: Peter Gabriel
From the album: *Peter Gabriel*

Label: Atco
Produced by: Bob Ezrin
Year: 1977
Artistic voice of Genesis goes solo with this melancholy rocker about leaving Genesis.

SOME GUYS HAVE ALL THE LUCK

Artist: The Persuaders
Written by: Jeff Fortgang
Label: Atco
Year: 1971
Covered by Robert Palmer (Island, 82), Rod Stewart (Warner Brothers, '84).

SOME KIND A WONDERFUL

Artist: The Drifters
Written by: Jerry Leiber, Mike Stoller
From the album: *Save the Last Dance for Me*
Label: Atlantic
Produced by: Jerry Leiber, Mike Stoller
Year: 1961
Top 10 R&B/Top 40 crossover.

SOME LIKE IT HOT

Artist: The Power Station
Written by: Robert Palmer, Andy Taylor, John Taylor
From the album: *The Power Station*
Label: Capitol
Produced by: Bernard Edwards
Year: 1985
All-star double date between Duran Duran and Robert Palmer results in a one-off one-shot.

SOMEBODY LOAN ME A DIME

Artist: Fenton Robinson
Written by: Fenton Robinson
Label: Palos
Year: 1967
Covered by Boz Scaggs (with Duane Allman on guitar) as "Loan Me a Dime" (Atlantic, '69).

SOMEBODY TO LOVE

Artist: Queen
Written by: Freddie Mercury
From the album: *A Day at the Races*
Label: Elektra
Produced by: Queen
Year: 1976
Arena operatics.

SOMEBODY TO SHOVE

Artist: Soul Asylum
Written by: Dave Pirner
From the album: *Grave Dancers Union*
Label: Columbia
Produced by: Michael Beinhorn
Year: 1992

SOMEBODY'S WATCHING ME

Artist: Rockwell
Written by: Rockwell
From the album: *Somebody's Watching Me*
Label: Motown
Produced by: Curtis Anthony Nolen, Rockwell
Year: 1984
Year-appropriate track about paranoia was a Motown inside job, written and sung by Kennedy Gordy, son of Motown founder Berry (with Michael Jackson providing backup singing). It was a #1 R&B/#2 crossover. Suggested segues: "Who Can It Be Now" by Men at Work, "Paranoia" by the Kinks.

SOMEDAY NEVER COMES

Artist: Creedence Clearwater Revival
Written by: John C. Fogerty
From the album: *Mardi Gras*
Label: Fantasy
Produced by: John C. Fogerty
Year: 1972
Going out on a down note.

SOMEDAY, SOMEWAY

Artist: Robert Gordon
Written by: Marshall Crenshaw
From the album: *Are You Gonna Be the One*
Label: RCA
Produced by: Robert Gordon, Lance Quinn, Scott Litt
Year: 1981
Quintessential neo-rockabilly charmer. Covered by Marshall Crenshaw (Warner Brothers, '82).

SOMEDAY SOON

Artist: Ian and Sylvia
Written by: Ian Tyson
From the album: *Northern Journey*
Label: Vanguard
Year: 1964
Rodeo rider meets the parents. Covered by Judy Collins (Elektra, '68).

SOMEDAY WE'LL ALL BE FREE

Artist: Donnie Hathaway
Written by: Donnie Hathaway
From the album: *Extension of a Man*
Label: Atco
Year: 1973
Career song for the R&B crooner. Covered by Aretha Franklin in the movie *Malcolm X* (Qwest '92).

SOMEDAY WE'LL BE TOGETHER

Artist: Johnnie and Jackey
Written by: Johnnie Bristol, Jackey Beavers, Harvey Fuqua

Label: Tri-Phi

Year: 1961

What became the Supremes' farewell single was neither especially written for the occasion nor actually sung by the Supremes. Diana and a pair of stand-in Supremes sang this nine-year-old tune, first immortalized by Bristol in a duet with Jackey Beavers that went nowhere on the charts. It was the Supremes' fifth #1 R&B/#1 crossover.

SOMEONE SAVED MY LIFE TONIGHT

Artist: Elton John

Written by: Elton John, Bernie Taupin

From the album: *Captain Fantastic and the Red Dirt Cowboy*

Label: MCA

Produced by: Gus Dudgeon

Year: 1975

SOMEONE TO LAY DOWN BESIDE ME

Artist: Linda Ronstadt

Written by: Karla Bonoff

From the album: *Hasten down the Wind*

Label: Capitol

Produced by: Peter Asher

Year: 1976

Theme song of the L.A. singles scene. Covered by Karla Bonoff (Columbia, '77).

SOMEONE TO LOVE

Artist: The Great Society

Written by: Darby Slick.

From the album: *Conspicuous Only in its Absence*

Label: Columbia

Year: 1965

Local anthem was covered by Grace Slick's new band, Jefferson Airplane, as "Somebody to Love" (RCA, '67), which became the first national hit from psychedelic San Francisco. The Great Society album, meanwhile, would sit in the can until 1968.

SOMEPLACE WHERE LOVE CAN'T FIND ME

Artist: Marshall Crenshaw

Written by: John Hiatt

From the album: *Good Evening*

Label: Warner Brothers

Produced by: David Kershenbaum, Paul McKenna

Year: 1989

A meeting of the quirky minds.

SOMETHIN' ELSE

Artist: Eddie Cochran

Written by: Sharon Sheeley, Eddie Cochran

From the album: *Eddie Cochran*

Label: Liberty

Year: 1959

Cochran's second most enduring rocker. Covered in an appropriately stomping rendition by the duo of Tanya Tucker and Little Richard (MCA, '94).

SOMETHING

Artist: The Beatles

Written by: George Harrison

From the album: *Abbey Road*

Label: Apple

Produced by: George Martin

Year: 1969

George's shining ballad moment was first on the B-side of "Come Together." Covered by Frank Sinatra (Reprise, '72).

SOMETHING ABOUT THE WAY YOU LOOK TONIGHT

Artist: Elton John

Written by: Elton John, Bernie Taupin

From the album: *Big Picture*

Produced by: Chris Thomas

Label: Rocket

Year: 1997

SOMETHING GOOD

Artist: The Utah Saints

Written by: Jez Willis, Kate Bush

From the album: *Something Good*

Label: PLG

Produced by: The Utah Saints

Year: 1992

Hypnotic British raver updates Bush's classic "Cloudbusting" (EMI-America, '83).

SOMETHING HAPPENED ON THE WAY TO HEAVEN

Artist: Phil Collins

Written by: Phil Collins

From the album: *… But Seriously folks*

Label: Atlantic

Produced by: Hugh Padgham, Phil Collins

Year: 1989

Collins at his commercial peak.

SOMETHING HAPPENED TO ME YESTERDAY

Artist: The Rolling Stones

Written by: Mick Jagger, Keith Richards

From the album: *Between the Buttons*

Label: London

Produced by: Andrew Loog-Oldham

Year: 1967

The Stones' attempt at McCartneyesque cuteness.

SOMETHING HE CAN FEEL

Artist: Aretha Franklin

Written by: Curtis Mayfield

From the album: *Sparkle*

Label: Atlantic

Produced by: Curtis Mayfield

Year: 1976

#1 R&B/Top 30 crossover, introduced by Irene Cara and Lonette McKee in the film *Sparkle*. Covered by En Vogue (Atlantic, '92).

SOMETHING IN THE AIR

Artist: Thunderclap Newman

Written by: Speedy Keen

From the album: *Hollywood Dream*

Label: Track

Produced by: Pete Townshend

Year: 1969

High on Woodstock dreams Thunderclap Newman celebrates the Revolution as if it were a fait accompli, much as Phil Ochs, a few years earlier, declared the Vietnam War over (but that didn't end until 1972, in the middle of a Neil Young concert, at around the same time as the Revolution). #1 UK hit was featured in the movie *The Strawberry Statement* (MGM, '70). Covered by Tom Petty (MCA, '95).

SOMETHING IN THE WAY SHE MOVES

Artist: Tom Rush

Written by: James Taylor

From the album: *The Circle Game*

Label: Elektra

Produced by: Arthur Gordon

Year: 1968

Bostonian folk/blues stylist gives credibility to the future laid-back mainstay James Taylor.

SOMETHING NEW

Artist: The Smithereens

Written by: Pat DiNizio

From the album: *Green Thoughts*

Label: Enigma

Produced by: Don Dixon

Year: 1988

Hoboken band pays tribute to the circa-1965 Beatles.

SOMETHING SO RIGHT

Artist: Paul Simon

Written by: Paul Simon

From the album: *There Goes Rhymin' Simon*

Label: Columbia

Produced by: Phil Ramone, Paul Simon

Year: 1973

Simon at his most Sondheimesque. (Or is it Woody Allenesque?)

SOMETHING SO STRONG

Artist: Crowded House

Written by: Neil Finn, Mitchell Froom

From the album: *Crowded House*

Label: Capitol

Produced by: Mitchell Froom

Year: 1987

Their initial single, which became their second Top 10 hit when it was re-released after the success of the first, "Don't Dream It's Over."

SOMETHING TO BELIEVE IN

Artist: Poison

Written by: Bobby Dall, C. C. Deville, Brett Michaels, Rikki Rockett

From the album: *Flesh and Blood*
Label: Enigma
Year: 1990

SOMETHING TO TALK ABOUT

Artist: Bonnie Raitt
Written by: Shirley Eikhard
From the album: *Luck of the Draw*
Label: Capitol
Produced by: Don Was, Bonnie Raitt
Year: 1991
Establishing former blues/rocker Bonnie Raitt as the middle-of-the-dirt-road Queen of the Baby Boom Hop at last.

SOMETHING YOU GOT

Artist: Alvin Robinson
Written by: Chris Kenner
Label: Tiger
Produced by: Joe Jones
Year: 1964
New Orleans classic. Covered by Chuck Jackson and Maxine Brown (Wand, '65).

SOMETHING'S GOT A HOLD ON ME

Artist: Etta James
Written by: Pearl Woods, Leroy Kirkland, Etta James
From the album: *Etta James' Top Ten*
Label: Argo
Year: 1962
Top 10 R&B/Top-40 crossover.

SOMETIMES (WHEN I'M ALL ALONE)

Artist: Danny and the Juniors
Written by: Dave White
Label: ABC Paramount
Year: 1957
Wasted on the B-side of "At the Hop," the great lost Italian soul classic that should have been covered by the Royal Teens or Randy & the Rainbows.

SOMETIMES LOVE JUST AIN'T ENOUGH

Artist: Patty Smyth
Written by: Patty Smyth, Glen Burtnik
From the album: *Patty Smyth*
Label: MCA
Produced by: Roy Bittan
Year: 1992
Leaving the lower east side candy store and stoop behind the formerly funky Scandal vamp (and ex-wife of punk icon Richard Hell) begins her life as a Hollywood belter.

SOMETIMES WHEN WE TOUCH

Artist: Dan Hill
Written by: Barry Mann, Dan Hill
From the album: *Longer Fuse*
Label: 20TH Century
Produced by: Matthew McCauley, Fred Mollin
Year: 1977
An arena ballad for the coffee house.

SOMEWHERE DOWN THE CRAZY RIVER

Artist: Robbie Robertson
Written by: Robbie Robertson
From the album: *Robbie Robertson*
Label: Geffen
Produced by: Robbie Robertson, Daniel Lanois
Year: 1987
With the help of U2's Edge and Bono the Band and Dylan guitarist lays down an Everglades tribute.

SOMEWHERE THERE'S A FEATHER

Artist: Nico
Written by: Jackson Browne
From the album: *Chelsea Girl*
Label: Verve
Produced by: Tom Wilson
Year: 1967
From Browne's early, Greenwich Village period, which roughly coincided with Joni Mitchell's early, Greenwich Village period; then they both moved out West to start the laid-back/mellow/L.A./singer-songwriter period that would define the '70s.

SON OF A PREACHER MAN

Artist: Dusty Springfield
Written by: John Hurley, Ronnie Wilkins
From the album: *Dusty in Memphis*
Label: Atlantic
Produced by: Tom Dowd, Jerry Wexler, Arif Mardin
Year: 1969
Dusty third Top 10 (and last for nearly 20 years). The R&B version by Aretha Franklin (Atlantic, '70) was the B-side of "Call Me." Revived in the '94 movie *Pulp Fiction*.

SON OF SUZY CREAMCHEESE

Artist: The Mothers of Invention
Written by: Frank Zappa
From the album: *Absolutely Free*
Label: Verve
Produced by: Tom Wilson
Year: 1967
Zappa's most beloved character, aside from Uncle Meat, was an L.A. dress designer named Suzy Creamcheese.

SONG FOR A FUTURE GENERATION

Artist: The B-52's
Written by: Fred Schneider, Ricky Wilson, Cindy Wilson, Julie Strickland, Kate Pierson
From the album: *Whammy*
Label: Warner Brothers
Produced by: Steven Starley
Year: 1983

SONG FOR ADAM

Artist: Jackson Browne
Written by: Jackson Browne
From the album: *Saturate Before Using*
Label: Asylum
Produced by: Richard Orshoff
Year: 1972
Quintessential '60s character portrait of a wasted mystical rambler. Suggested segue: "Stoney" by Jerry Jeff Walker.

SONG FOR THE DREAMERS

Artist: Danny and Dusty
Written by: Steve Wynn, Dan Stuart
From the album: *The Lost Weekend*
Label: A&M
Produced by: Paul Cutter
Year: 1985
A raucous paisley underground all-star drinking song introduces the genre known as cow punk. Dedicated to dreamers everywhere, but especially baseball's fabulous Rynes, Duren, and Sandberg.

SONG FOR YOU

Artist: Leon Russell
Written by: Leon Russell
From the album: *Leon Russell*
Label: Shelter
Produced by: Denny Cordell
Year: 1970
One of his most enduring ballads.

SONG IS OVER, THE

Artist: The Who
Written by: Pete Townshend
From the album: *Who's Next*
Label: Decca
Produced by: The Who
Year: 1971
Ballad from their first studio album after *Tommy*.

SONG REMAINS THE SAME, THE

Artist: Led Zeppelin
Written by: Jimmy Page, Robert Plant
From the album: *Houses of the Holy*
Label: Atlantic
Produced by: Jimmy Page
Year: 1973
Reappears as the title song of their '76 rockumentary.

SONG TO WOODY

Artist: Bob Dylan
Written by: Bob Dylan

From the album: *Bob Dylan*
Label: Columbia
Produced by: John Hammond
Year: 1962
The very first thing Bob Dylan wanted to do was to acknowledge his debt to Woody Guthrie and simultaneously break away.

SONG 2

Artist: Blur
Written by: Damon Albarn, Graham Coxon, Steven James, David Rowntree
From the album: *Blur*
Label: Virgin
Year: 1997
A tribute to grunge, played at soccer stadiums worldwide.

SONGS SUNG BLUE

Artist: Neil Diamond
Written by: Neil Diamond
From the album: *Moods*
Label: Uni
Produced by: Tom Catalano
Year: 1972
His second of three #1 tunes.

SONGS TO AGING CHILDREN COME

Artist: Joni Mitchell
Written by: Joni Mitchell
From the album: *Clouds*
Label: Reprise
Produced by: Joni Mitchell
Year: 1969
Featured in the cult classic film *Alice's Restaurant*, where it had much more of a generationally appropriately elegiac flavor than *Woodstock*.

SONIC REDUCER

Artist: The Dead Boys
Written by: Stiv Bators, Cheetah Chrome, David Thomas, Johnny Blitz, Jeff Magnum, Jimmy Zero
From the album: *Young Loud and Snotty*
Label: Sire
Produced by: Genya Raven
Year: 1977
Punk anthem of ear-challenging intensity.

SOON

Artist: My Bloody Valentine
Written by: Kevin Shields
From the album: *Loveless*
Produced by: Kevin Shields, Colm O'Ciosoig
Label: Sire
Year: 1991
A noisy symphony for schizoid shoegazers.

SOONER OR LATER

Artist: Grass Roots

Written by: Gary Zekley, Mitch Bottler, Adeneyi Paris, Ted McNamara, Ekundayo Paris
From the album: *Their 16 Greatest*
Label: Dunhill
Produced by: Steve Barri
Year: 1971
Of their sixteen greatest, this ranks number three.

SOONER OR LATER (I ALWAYS GET MY MAN)

Artist: Madonna
Written by: Stephen Sondheim
From the album: *I'm Breathless*
Label: Sire
Produced by: Madonna, Patrick Leonard
Year: 1990
Featured in the movie *Dick Tracy*, and the most successful of Madonna's three collaborations with the noted theater songwriter Sondheim ("More" and "What Can You Lose" were the other two), this single won the Oscar for Best Song. But Madonna on Broadway in *Speed the Plow* was a "fiasco at the Belasco."

SOPHISTICATED CISSY

Artist: The Meters
Written by: Arthur Neville, Leo Nocentelli, George Porter, Joseph Modeliste
From the album: *The Meters*
Label: Josie
Produced by: Allen Toussaint, Marshall Sehorn
Year: 1969
Local legends introduce their psychedelicized New Orleans funk to the charts; Top 10 R&B/Top 30 crossover.

SORRY, I RAN ALL THE WAY HOME

Artist: The Impalas
Written by: Harry Giosasi, Artie Zwirn
From the album: *Sorry, I Ran All the Way Home*
Label: Cub
Produced by: Leroy Holmes
Year: 1959
Late Italian soul era lament. Revived by Marshall Crenshaw in the '86 movie *Peggy Sue Got Married*.

SORRY SEEMS TO BE THE HARDEST WORD

Artist: Elton John
Written by: Elton John, Bernie Taupin
From the album: *Blue Moves*
Label: Rocket
Produced by: Gus Dudgeon
Year: 1976
Nearly getting down to self-examination. Suggested segue: "I'm Sorry" by John Denver.

SORRY SOMEHOW

Artist: Hüsker Dü
Written by: Grant Hart

From the album: *Candy Apple Grey*
Label: Warner Brothers
Produced by: Bob Mould, Grant Hart
Year: 1986
Grant Hart explains his divorce, in the underground icons' first overground release.

SOUL DEEP

Artist: The Box Tops
Written by: Wayne Carson Thompson
From the album: *Soul Deep*
Label: Mala
Produced by: Chips Moman, Tommy Cogbill
Year: 1969

SOUL MAN

Artist: Sam and Dave
Written by: Isaac Hayes, David Porter
From the album: *Soul Men*
Label: Stax
Produced by: Isaac Hayes, David Porter
Year: 1967
#1 R&B/Top 10 crossover, in which the legendary exhortation "Play it, Steve!" (Cropper) entered the lexicon of rock and roll.

SOUL MEETING

Artist: Solomon Burke (The Soul Clan)
Written by: Don Covay
From the album: *The Very Best of Solomon Burke*
Label: Atco
Produced by: Don Covay
Year: 1968
Legendary all-star one-off featuring Burke and Covay.

SOUL ON FIRE

Artist: Lavern Baker
Written by: Ahmet Ertegun, Jerry Wexler, LaVern Baker
Label: Atlantic
Produced by: Ahmet Ertegun, Jerry Wexler
Year: 1953
The incomparable production team of Wexler and Ertegun enter the rock and roll era with the former Little Miss Sharecropper's first recording for the new Atlantic label.

SOUL SACRIFICE

Artist: Santana
Written by: Carlos Santana
From the album: *Santana*
Label: Columbia
Produced by: Brent Dangerfield, Santana
Year: 1969
Latin-flavored percussion extravaganza, led by Carlos but dominated by drummer Michael Shrieve.

SOUL SISTER, BROWN SUGAR

Artist: Sam and Dave
Written by: Isaac Hayes, David Porter

Label: Atlantic
Produced by: Isaac Hayes, David Porter
Year: 1968

SOUL TO SQUEEZE

Artist: Red Hot Chili Peppers
Written by: Anthony Kiedis, Michael Balzary
(Flea), John Frusciante, Chad Smith
From the album: *The Coneheads Soundtrack*
Label: Sire
Produced by: Rick Rubin
Year: 1993

SOUL TWIST

Artist: King Curtis
Written by: Curtis Ousley (King Curtis)
From the album: *Soul Serenade*
Label: Enjoy
Produced by: Bobby Robinson
Year: 1962
#1 R&B/Top 20 crossover for the sax giant.

SOUNDS OF SILENCE, THE

Artist: Simon and Garfunkel
Written by: Paul Simon
From the album: *Wednesday Morning 3 A.M.*
Label: Columbia
Produced by: Tom Wilson
Year: 1964
This obscure acoustic album cut of '64 became an
AM radio fave in '65 and the #1 folk/rock classic
of '66, through the magic of the marketplace (and
an additional electric backing track).

SOUR TIMES

Artist: Portishead
Written by: Geoffrey Barrow, Betty Gibbons,
Adrian Utley, Lalo Schifrin, Henry Brooks, Otis
Turner
From the album: *Dummy*
Label: London
Produced by: Adrian Utley, Portishead
Year: 1994
The post-waif voice of Beth Gibbons is so sweet as
it wafts over a moody industrial cityscape.

SOUTH CENTRAL RAIN

Artist: R.E.M.
Written by: Michael Stipe, Peter Buck, Bill Berry,
Mike Mills
From the album: *Reckoning*
Label: IRS
Produced by: Don Dixon, Mitch Easter
Year: 1983
In the heyday of MTV, with most of the under-
ground still too numb to react against the corpora-
tizing of the aural landscape, the weary beats of
R.E.M. provided dreary solace, an instant classic
ensuring the enduring jangly essence of the surviv-
ing counter culture, chirping in the dead grass like
beetles … or crickets.

SOUTH SIDE

Artist: Moby
Written by: Moby
From the album: *Play*
Label: V2
Produced by: Moby
Year: 2000
With a radio-friendly voice provided by Gwen
Stefani of No Doubt, the ubiquitous electronica
maven gets a hit single.

SOUTH STREET

Artist: The Orlons
Written by: Kal Mann, Dave Appell
From the album: *South Street*
Label: Cameo
Year: 1963
In Philadelphia, where "all the hippies meet," the
hippies in question walked in pointy-toed Italian
dancing shoes, years before a whole different sort
of hippie donned moccasins in San Francisco.

SOUTHERN CROSS

Artist: Crosby, Stills & Nash
Written by: Stephen Stills, Richard Curtis, Michael
Curtis
From the album: *Daylight Again*
Label: Atlantic
Produced by: Crosby, Stills & Nash, Stanley
Johnson, Steve Gursky
Year: 1982
Life in semiretirement; Stills's version of a sailing
song.

SOUTHERN MAN

Artist: Neil Young
Written by: Neil Young
From the album: *After the Goldrush*
Label: Reprise
Produced by: David Briggs, Neil Young, Kendall
Pacios
Year: 1970
Young relocates his political rage from Ohio to Ala-
bama.

SOUTHERN NIGHTS

Artist: Allen Toussaint
Written by: Allen Toussaint
From the album: *Southern Nights*
Label: Reprise
Produced by: Allen Toussaint
Year: 1975
What doesn't become a legendary producer most?
Singing his own material. Cover by Glen Campbell
was a rare #1 country/#1 crossover (Capitol,
'77).

SOWING THE SEEDS OF LOVE

Artist: Tears for Fears
Written by: Roland Orzabel, Curt Smith

From the album: *The Seeds of Love*
Label: Fontana
Produced by: Tears for Fears
Year: 1989
Their fourth and last Top 10 hit benefited from a
great video.

SPACE COWBOY

Artist: Steve Miller Band
Written by: Steve Miller
From the album: *Brave New World*
Label: Capitol
Produced by: Steve Miller
Year: 1969
Defining his early psychedelic blues period. Tracy
Nelson was listening, disapprovingly.

SPACE ODDITY

Artist: David Bowie
Written by: David Bowie
From the album: *Man of Words—Man of Music*
Label: Mercury
Produced by: Mike Vernon
Year: 1968
An English music-hall original, formerly known as
Davy Jones, reinvents himself for the space age
with a tune inspired by Stanley Kubrick's *2001: A
Space Odyssey*. Written for the film *Love You till Tues-
day*, it was a hit in England in '69; re-released, it
was a hit in the US (RCA, '73). Suggested segue:
"Major Tom (Coming Home)" by Peter Schilling.

SPACE RACE

Artist: Billy Preston
Written by: Billy Preston
From the album: *Everybody Likes Some Kind of Music*
Label: A&M
Produced by: Billy Preston
Year: 1973
Adhering to the year's soul flavor, this instrumental
groove was a #1 R&B/Top 10 crossover.

SPACE TRUCKIN'

Artist: Deep Purple
Written by: Ritchie Blackmore, Ian Gillan, Roger
Glover, Jon Lord, Ian Paice
From the album: *Machine Head*
Label: Warner Brothers
Produced by: Deep Purple
Year: 1972
A Ritchie Blackmore guitar showpiece.

SPANISH HARLEM

Artist: Ben E. King
Written by: Jerry Leiber, Phil Spector
From the album: *Spanish Harlem*
Label: Atco
Produced by: Jerry Leiber, Mike Stoller
Year: 1961
The Brill Building sound of the city, captured for
eternity, like some gorgeous graffiti signature on

the side of an abandoned tenement. Covered by Aretha Franklin (Atlantic, '71).

SPANISH HARLEM INCIDENT

Artist: Bob Dylan
Written by: Bob Dylan
From the album: *Another Side of Bob Dylan*
Label: Columbia
Produced by: Tom Wilson
Year: 1964
Dylan's raggedly rhapsodic answer to city living and "Spanish Harlem." Covered by the Byrds (Columbia, '65).

SPARE CHAYNGE

Artist: Jefferson Airplane
Written by: Jack Casady, Stewart Dryden, Jorma Kaukonen
From the album: *After Bathing at Baxters*
Produced by: Rick Jarrard
Label: RCA
Year: 1967 .
When psychedelia reigned.

SPECIAL

Artist: Garbage
Written by: Duke Erickson, Shirley Manson, Steve Marker, Butch Vig
From the album: *Version 2.0*
Label: Almo Sounds
Produced by: Butch Vig
Year: 1998

SPECIAL LADY

Artist: Ray, Goodman and Brown
Written by: Harold Ray, Al Goodman, L. Walter
From the album: *Ray, Goodman and Brown*
Label: Polydor
Produced by: Vince Castellano
Year: 1979
#1 R&B/Top 10 crossover.

SPEEDOO

Artist: The Cadillacs
Written by: Esther Navarro
From the album: *The Fabulous Cadillacs*
Label: Josie
Year: 1955
Introducing Mr. Earl, as in Earl Carroll, lead singer of the Cadillacs.

SPIDERS AND SNAKES

Artist: Jim Stafford
Written by: Jim Stafford, David Bellamy
From the album: *Jim Stafford*
Label: MGM
Produced by: Lobo
Year: 1973
Country/rock novelty.

SPIDERWEBS

Artist: No Doubt
Written by: Eric Stefani, Tony Kenal
From the album: *Tragic Kingdom*
Label: Trauma
Produced by: Matthew Wilder
Year: 1995
A new city girl emerges in the person of Gwen Stefani, sauntering up the avenue in green and gold like a member of the Shangri-Las who'd just gotten back from vacationing in Jamaica.

SPIES LIKE US

Artist: Paul McCartney
Written by: Paul McCartney
From the album: *Spies Like Us Soundtrack*
Label: Capitol
Produced by: Paul McCartney
Year: 1986
Paul follows up his previous Bond pairing, "Live and Let Die."

SPILL THE WINE

Artist: Eric Burden and War
Written by: Sylvester Allen, Lee Oscar Levitin, Morris Dickerson, Leroy "Lonnie" Jordan, Howard Scott, Charles W. Miller, Harold R. Brown
From the album: *Eric Burdon Declares War*
Label: MGM
Produced by: Jerry Goldstein
Year: 1970
The former Animal's last big blue-eyed soul hit comes with a black backing band that would go on to a significant funk career of their own.

SPIN THE BLACK CIRCLE

Artist: Pearl Jam
Written by: Eddie Vedder, Stone Gossard, Jeff Ament, Mike McCready, Dave Abbruzzese
From the album: *Vitology*
Label: Epic
Produced by: Brendan O'Brien, Pearl Jam
Year: 1994
A tribute to vinyl.

SPINNING WHEEL

Artist: Blood, Sweat, & Tears
Written by: David Clayon Thomas
From the album: *Blood, Sweat & Tears*
Label: Columbia
Produced by: James William Guercio
Year: 1969
The second, more successful and less-interesting incarnation of Blood, Sweat & Tears finds producer Guercio practicing for Chicago.

SPIRIT IN THE DARK

Artist: Aretha Franklin
Written by: Aretha Franklin
From the album: *Spirit in the Dark*
Label: Atlantic

Produced by: Jerry Wexler, Tom Dowd, Arif Mardin
Year: 1970

SPIRIT IN THE NIGHT

Artist: Bruce Springsteen
Written by: Bruce Springsteen
From the album: *Greetings from Asbury Park*
Label: Columbia
Produced by: Jim Cretecos, Mike Appel
Year: 1973
Indelible early guided tour through Mr. Springsteen's mythic folk/rock meets Jersey soul under the boardwalk neighborhood. Covered by Manfred Mann (Warner Brothers, '75).

SPIRIT IN THE SKY

Artist: Norman Greenbaum
Written by: Norman Greenbaum
From the album: *Spirit in the Sky*
Label: Reprise
Produced by: Erik Jacobsen
Year: 1970
Echoing the era's pop spiritual sound ("Instant Karma," "Put Your Hand in the Hand," "Oh Happy Day") the writer of "The Eggplant That Ate Chicago" had a true religious experience when Dorothy Morrison's cover of this tune (Buddah, '70) won a Grammy for best gospel performance.

SPIRIT OF RADIO, THE

Artist: Rush
Written by: Gary Lee Weinrib (Geddy Lee), Alex Zivojinovich (Alex Lifeson), Neil Peart
From the album: *Permanent Waves*
Label: Mercury
Produced by: Terry Brown, Rush
Year: 1980
Radio breakthrough for the severe Canadian metal trio.

SPIRIT OF THE BOOGIE

Artist: Kool & the Gang
Written by: Robert Bell, Kool & the Gang
From the album: *Spirit of the Boogie*
Label: De-Lite
Produced by: Ronald Bell
Year: 1975
#1 R&B/Top 40 crossover.

SPIRITS IN THE MATERIAL WORLD

Artist: The Police
Written by: Gordon Sumner (Sting)
From the album: *Ghost in the Machine*
Label: A&M
Produced by: Hugh Padgham, the Police
Year: 1982
A polished nod to George Harrison's "All Things Must Pass." Answered persuasively by Madonna

with "Material Girl" in '84. Segue: "Dust in the Wind" by Kansas.

SPIRITUAL HIGH (STATE OF INDEPENDENCE)

Artist: Moodswings
Written by: Vangelis, Jon Anderson, J. T. F. Hood, Grant Showbiz
From the album: *Moodfood*
Label: Arista
Year: 1992
Modern English dancehall rush, featuring the voice of Pretender Chrissie Hynde, and heard in the movie *Single White Female*.

SPLENDOR IN THE GRASS

Artist: Jackie DeShannon
Written by: Jackie DeShannon
Label: Imperial
Year: 1965
Immortalizing the Natalie Wood/Warren Beatty movie, DeShannon writes a lost youth epic. Covered by the Boys (Buddah, '65).

SPLISH SPLASH

Artist: Bobby Darin
Written by: Bobby Darin, Murray Kaufman (Jean Murray)
From the album: *The Bobby Darin Story*
Label: Atco
Produced by: Ahmet Ertegun
Year: 1958
Darin's Top 10 breakthrough is an embarrassing teenybop ditty about being embarrassed while taking a bath (considering Darin's Bronx roots, presumably in the kitchen). Title was actually provided by the New York DJ mother Jean.

SPOOKY

Artist: The Classics IV and Dennis Yost
Written by: Harvey Middlebrooks, Mike Shapiro
From the album: *Spooky*
Label: Imperial
Produced by: Buddy Buie
Year: 1968
Consummate easy pop listening. Covered by the Atlanta Rhythm Section (Polydor, '79).

SPOONFUL

Artist: Howlin' Wolf
Written by: Willie Dixon
Label: Chess
Year: 1961
Remake of the Charlie Patton 1929 original gave the good time rock and roll jug band the Lovin' Spoonful a name. Covered by the Allman Joys (Deal, '67).

SPOONMAN

Artist: Soundgarden
Written by: Chris Cornell
From the album: *Superunknown*

Label: A&M
Produced by: Michael Beinhorn, Soundgarden
Year: 1994
Local character.

SPRAWL, THE

Artist: Sonic Youth
Written by: Sonic Youth
From the album: *Daydream Nation*
Label: Enigma/Blast First
Produced by: Nicholas Sansone, Sonic Youth
Year: 1988
Wherein bassist Kim Gordon inspires a generation of angry young women.

SPY IN THE HOUSE OF LOVE

Artist: Was (Not Was)
Written by: David Weiss (David Was), Donald Fagenson (Don Was)
From the album: *What up, Dog*
Label: Chrysalis
Produced by: Paul Stavely O'Duffy
Year: 1988
Twisted blue-eyed soul in the Steely Dan mode.

SQUARE PEGS

Artist: The Waitresses
Written by: Chris Butler, Daniel Klayman, Marc Williams, Tracy Wormworth, Patty Donahue, William Ficca
From the album: *I Could Rule the World If I Could Only Get the Parts*
Label: Polydor
Produced by: Christopher Butler
Year: 1983
Landing the American dream of a TV theme song in which everyone splits the credits. But the show, starring Sarah Jessica Parkes, didn't last the season.

SQUEEZE BOX

Artist: The Who
Written by: Pete Townshend
From the album: *The Who by Numbers*
Label: MCA
Produced by: Glyn Johns
Year: 1975
Returning to the dancehall whimsey of "Happy Jack."

ST. ELMO'S FIRE (MAN IN MOTION)

Artist: John Parr
Written by: David Foster, John Parr
From the album: *St. Elmo's Fire Soundtrack*
Label: Atlantic
Produced by: David Foster
Year: 1985
Emotionally-charged movie ballad.

ST. STEPHEN

Artist: The Grateful Dead

Written by: Jerry Garcia, Bob Hunter, Phil Lesh
From the album: *Aoxomoxoa*
Label: Warner Bros.
Produced by: Bob Matthew, Betty Cantor
Year: 1969
A concert favorite, collected on upwards of 50 million bootleg tapes.

ST. THERESA

Artist: Joan Osborne
Written by: Joan Osborne, Rick Chertoff, Rob Hyman, Eric Bazilian
From the album: *Relish*
Produced by: Rick Chertoff
Label: Mercury
Year: 1995
Following up "One of Us" with a song about a different sort of religious figure.

STAGE FRIGHT

Artist: The Band
Written by: Robbie Robertson
From the album: *Stage Fright*
Label: Capitol
Produced by: *The Band*
Year: 1970
Expounding upon the possible reason for it.

STAGGER LEE

Artist: Lloyd Price
Written by: Lloyd Price, Harold Logan
From the album: *Exciting Lloyd Price*
Label: ABC Paramount
Produced by: Don Costa
Year: 1958
New Orleans mythology, updated for a #1 R&B/#1 crossover. Viewed as setting the stage for both outlaw country and gangsta rap. See "Stack O Lee Blues," '28. Covered by Fred Waring's Pennsylvanians (Victor, '24), Mississippi John Hurt (Okeh, '28).

STAIRWAY TO GILLIGAN'S ISLAND

Artist: Little Roger & the Goosebumps
Written by: Robert Plant, Jimmy Page, S. Schwartz, G. Wyle
From the album: *Earth Quake*
Label: Splash
Produced by: Kenny Laguna, Matthew King Kaufman, Glen Kolotkin
Year: 1978
Inspired cross-cultural melange uniting the Led Zeppelin classic to the classic TV show. Much fun, except for all the lawsuits. Covered, ironically, by Led Zeppelin live at Knebworth (Atlantic, '79). Big Daddy was listening. Dr. Demento was compiling.

STAIRWAY TO HEAVEN

Artist: Led Zeppelin
Written by: Jimmy Page, Robert Plant

From the album: *Led Zeppelin IV (Untitled)*
Label: Atlantic
Produced by: Jimmy Page
Year: 1971
Plant and Page write their wedding song: the marriage of Elizabethan imagery and heavy metal alchemy, ceremoniously replayed over FM radio every hour on the hour ever since. The #1 rock track until otherwise advised.

STAIRWAY TO HEAVEN

Artist: Neil Sedaka
Written by: Howard Greenfield, Neil Sedaka
From the album: *Neil Sedaka Sings His Greatest Hits*
Label: RCA Victor
Produced by: Al Nevins, Don Kirshner
Year: 1960
Jimmy Page wasn't listening.

STAN

Artist: Eminem
Written by: Marshall Mathers, Dido Armstrong, Paul Herman
From the album: *The Marshall Mathers LP*
Label: Interscope
Produced by: Mel-Man
Year: 2000
White rap's most authentic new voice takes on his own worst enemy, himself, in this penetrating study of the performer/fan relationship.

STAND!

Artist: Sly & the Family Stone
Written by: Sylvester Stewart
From the album: *Stand!*
Label: Epic
Produced by: Sly Stone
Year: 1969
Funk polemic.

STAND

Artist: R.E.M.
Written by: Michael Stipe, Peter Buck, Bill Berry, Mike Mills
From the album: *Green*
Label: Warner Brothers
Produced by: Scott Litt, R.E.M.
Year: 1988
Pop polemic.

STAND BACK

Artist: Stevie Nicks
Written by: Stephanie Nicks, Prince Rogers Nelson
From the album: *The Wild Heart*
Label: Modern
Produced by: Jimmy Iovine
Year: 1983
Stevie's best rocker was inspired by Prince's "Little Red Corvette."

STAND BY ME

Artist: Ben E. King

Written by: Jerry Leiber, Mike Stoller, Ben E. King
From the album: *Ben E. King's Greatest Hits*
Label: Atco
Produced by: Jerry Leiber, Mike Stoller
Year: 1961
#1 R&B/Top 10 crossover, based on the spiritual "Lord, Stand by Me." Revived in the '86 movie *Stand by Me.*

STAND BY YOUR MAN

Artist: Tammy Wynette
Written by: Tammy Wynette, Billy Sherrill
From the album: *Stand by Your Man*
Label: Epic
Produced by: Billy Sherrill
Year: 1968
Mainstream sentiments in the face of the counterculture give Wynette a #1 country/#1 UK/Top 20 crossover.

STAND OR FALL

Artist: The Fixx
Written by: Cy Curnin, Adam Woods, Jamie West-Oram, Peter Greenall, Charles Barrett
From the album: *Shuttered Rooms*
Label: MCA
Produced by: Rupert Hine
Year: 1982
Video-age anxiety presages a new British invasion. Thomas Dolby was in synch.

STAND TALL

Artist: Burton Cummings
Written by: Burton Cummings
From the album: *Burton Cummings*
Label: Portrait
Produced by: Richard Perry
Year: 1976
Suggested segue: "Hold Your Head Up" by Argent.

STAND UP

Artist: Ferron
Written by: Ferron
From the album: *Phantom Center*
Label: Chameleon
Year: 1990
Feminist folkie anthem that influenced the Indigo Girls.

STANDING IN THE SHADOWS OF LOVE

Artist: The Four Tops
Written by: Eddie Holland, Lamont Dozier, Brian Holland
From the album: *Reach Out*
Label: Motown
Produced by: Brian Holland, Lamont Dozier
Year: 1966

STANDING OUTSIDE OF A BROKEN PHONE BOOTH WITH MONEY IN MY HAND

Artist: Primitive Radio Gods
Written by: Chris O'Connor
From the album: *The Cable Guy Soundtrack*
Label: Work
Year: 1996
Homemade track gained Top 40 access when it appeared in the Jim Carrey film. Samples B. B. King.

STAR STAR

Artist: The Rolling Stones
Written by: Mick Jagger, Keith Richards
From the album: *Goat's Head Soup*
Label: Rolling Stones
Produced by: Jimmy Miller
Year: 1972
A slice of performing life a la "Stray Cat Blues." Previously known as "Star Fucker." Suggested segues: "Sweet Little Sixteen" by Chuck Berry, "Hot Blooded" by Foreigner, "Sexy and Seventeen" by the Stray Cats. The Plaster Casters were waiting.

STAR WARS THEME

Artist: Meco
Written by: John Williams
From the album: *Star Wars and Other Galactic Funk*
Label: Millenium
Produced by: M. Monardo, H. Wheeler, Tony Bongiovi
Year: 1977
Space age disco.

STARING AT THE SUN

Artist: U2
Written by: Paul (Bono) Hewson, Dave (The Edge) Evans)
From the album: *Pop*
Label: Island
Produced by: Butch Vig
Year: 1997

STARS

Artist: Hear 'N' Aid
Written by: Ronnie Dio, Vivian Campbell, Jimmy Bain
From the album: *Hear 'n' Aid*
Label: Mercury
Produced by: Ronnie James Dio
Year: 1986
Heavy metal charity rocker, with a slew of featured solos.

STARS OF TRACK AND FIELD

Artist: Belle & Sebastian
From the album: *If You're Feeling Sinister*
Label: Sire

Produced by: Tony Dougan
Year: 1996
Neo folk/rock harmonizing.

START ME UP

Artist: The Rolling Stones
Written by: Mick Jagger, Keith Richards
From the album: *Tattoo You*
Label: Rolling Stones
Produced by: Glimmer Twins
Year: 1981
Another classic riff, this one rented by Microsoft Windows.

START MOVIN'

Artist: Sal Mineo
Written by: David Hill, Bobby Stevenson
From the album: *Sal Mineo*
Label: Epic
Year: 1957
Rebel without a hook.

START TOGETHER

Artist: Sleater-Kinney
Written by: Carrie Brownstein
From the album: *The Hot Rock*
Label: Kill Rock Stars
Year: 1999
The latest and greatest white female rock and roll hopes.

STATE OF LOVE AND TRUST

Artist: Pearl Jam
Written by: Jeff Ament, Mike McCready, Eddie Vedder
From the album: *Singles Soundtrack*
Produced by: Rick Parashar
Label: Epic
Year: 1992
Seattle superstars immortalize their town just before it became a scene.

STATE OF SHOCK

Artist: The Jacksons
Written by: Michael Jackson, Randy Hansen
From the album: *Victory*
Label: Epic
Year: 1984
Mike meets Mick Jagger in a danceoff reminiscent of the great Gene Kelly—Fred Astaire battles of old.

STATUS BACK BABY

Artist: The Mothers of Invention
Written by: Frank Zappa
From the album: *Absolutely Free*
Label: Verve
Produced by: Tom Wilson
Year: 1967
No life after high school.

STAY (I MISSED YOU)

Artist: Lisa Loeb and Nine Stories
Written by: Lisa Loeb
From the album: *Reality Bites Soundtrack*
Label: RCA
Produced by: J. Patino
Year: 1994
Nerd rock's finest hour occured at the very end of the Generation Xcult movie. If you left early you missed it. If you didn't listen to the radio for the next year and a half, you might have missed it too. Janis Ian was proud, to say nothing of Gilbert O'Sullivan.

STAY

Artist: Shakespeare's Sister
Written by: Siobhan Fahey, Marcella Levy (Marcella Detroit), Dave Stewart
From the album: *Hormonally Yours*
Label: London
Year: 1992
Bananarama redux.

STAY

Artist: Maurice Williams and the Zodiacs
Written by: Maurice Williams
From the album: *Stay*
Label: Herald
Produced by: Phil Gernhard, Johnny McCullough
Year: 1960
The author of "Little Darlin' " breaks through with a Top 5 R&B/#1 crossover. Covered by the Four Seasons (Vee-Jay, '64), Jackson Browne (Asylum, '77).

STAY AWHILE

Artist: The Bells
Written by: Ken Tobias
From the album: *Fly Little White Dove Fly*
Label: Polydor
Produced by: Cliff Edwards
Year: 1971
Big-time border crossover: Top 10 in the US and #1 in Canada.

STAY FREE

Artist: The Clash
Written by: John Mellor (Joe Strummer), Mick Jones
From the album: *Give 'Em Enough Rope*
Label: Epic
Produced by: Sandy Pearlman
Year: 1978
Ballad about a real-life rude boy.

STAY IN MY CORNER

Artist: The Dells
Written by: Wade Flemons, Bobby Miller, Barrett Strong
From the album: *There Is*
Label: Vee-Jay/Cadet
Produced by: Bobby Miller

Year: 1965
Rerecorded version of the doo-wop classic was a #1 R&B/Top 10 crossover (Cadet, '68) and is included on the album.

STAY UP LATE

Artist: Talking Heads
Written by: David Byrne, Chris Frantz, Tina Weymouth, Jerry Harrison
From the album: *Little Creatures*
Label: Sire
Produced by: Talking Heads
Year: 1985
Nerd rockers at home.

STAY WITH ME

Artist: Lorraine Ellison
Written by: Jerry Ragovoy, George David Weiss
Label: Warner Brothers
Produced by: Jerry Ragovoy
Year: 1966
Essential soul thriller. Covered by Bette Midler's Janis Joplin in *The Rose* in '79.

STAY WITH ME

Artist: The Faces
Written by: Rod Stewart, Ron Wood
From the album: *A Nod Is as Good as a Wink to a Blind Horse*
Label: Warner Brothers
Produced by: Glyn Johns, Faces
Year: 1972
One of Rod's early seduction anthems. Revived by Stewart and his erstwhile guitarmate Wood during Rod's later, acoustically sedate period (Warner Brothers, '94).

STAYIN' ALIVE

Artist: The Bee Gees
Written by: Barry Gibb, Robin Gibb, Maurice Gibb
From the album: *Saturday Night Fever*
Label: RSO
Produced by: Albhy Galutin, Karl Richardson, the Bee Gees
Year: 1977
Theme from the disco movie.

STEAL AWAY

Artist: Jimmy Hughes
Written by: Jimmy Hughes
From the album: *Steal Away*
Label: Fame
Year: 1964
Soul chestnut covered by Johnnie Taylor (Stax, '70).

STEAM

Artist: Peter Gabriel
Written by: Peter Gabriel
From the album: *US*

Label: Geffen
Produced by: Peter Gabriel, Daniel Lanois
Year: 1992
Great video.

STEAMROLLER BLUES

Artist: James Taylor
Written by: James Taylor
From the album: *Sweet Baby James*
Label: Warner Brothers
Produced by: Peter Asher
Year: 1970
Covered by Elvis Presley on the triumphant *Aloha from Hawaii via Satellite* TV special (RCA, '73).

STELLAR

Artist: Incubus
Written by: Brandon Boyd, Mike Einziger, Alex Katunich, Chris Kilmore, Jose Antonio Pasillas
From the album: *Make Yourself*
Label: Sony
Year: 1999
Big modern rock track from their breakthrough album.

STEP BY STEP

Artist: The Crests
Written by: Billy Dawn Smith, Ollie Jones
From the album: *The Best of the Crests*
Label: Coed
Year: 1960
Their second biggest hit.

STEP BY STEP

Artist: New Kids on the Block
Written by: Larry Johnson (Maurice Starr)
From the album: *Step by Step*
Label: Columbia
Produced by: Maurice Starr
Year: 1989
The year's only male competition for Tiffany and Debbie Gibson.

STEP BY STEP

Artist: Eddie Rabbitt
Written by: Eddie Rabbitt, Even Stevens, David Malloy
From the album: *Step by Step*
Label: Elektra
Produced by: David Malloy
Year: 1981
#1 country/Top 10 middle-of-the-country-road crossover.

STEP RIGHT UP

Artist: Tom Waits
Written by: Tom Waits
From the album: *Small Change*
Label: Asylum
Produced by: Bones Howe

Year: 1976
Waits brings new meaning to the term *barker*. Beatnik poetry meets product placement.

STEPPIN' OUT

Artist: Joe Jackson
Written by: Joe Jackson
From the album: *Night and Day*
Label: A&M
Produced by: David Kershenbaum, Joe Jackson
Year: 1982
Jackson steps out of the pub/rock pack, moves back into the shadows of '40s jump blues.

STEPPIN' OUT

Artist: John Mayall's Bluesbreakers
Written by: James Bracken
From the album: *John Mayall's Bluesbreakers*
Label: London
Produced by: Mike Vernon
Year: 1967
Early Clapton guitar highlight.

STICK UP

Artist: Honey Cone
Written by: General Johnson, Greg S. Perry, Angelo Bond
From the album: *Soulful Tapestry*
Label: Hot Wax
Produced by: Greg S. Perry
Year: 1971
#1 R&B/#11 crossover, follows the #1 R&B/#1 crossover "Want Ads."

STILL

Artist: Commodores
Written by: Lionel B. Richie Jr.
From the album: *Midnight Magic*
Label: Motown
Produced by: James Carmichael, Commodores
Year: 1979
Their second #1 R&B/#1 crossover, following "Three Times a Lady."

STILL A "G" THANG

Artist: Snoop Doggy Dogg
Written by: Calvin Broadus, Cecil Womack
From the album: *Da Game Is to Be Sold, Not to Be Told*
Label: No Limit
Produced by: Dr. Dre
Year: 1998

STILL ALIVE AND WELL

Artist: Hoodoo Rhythm Devils
Written by: Rick Derringer
Label: Capitol
Year: 1972
Cover by Johnny Winter remains his classic blues/rock signature (Columbia, '73).

STILL CRAZY AFTER ALL THESE YEARS

Artist: Paul Simon
Written by: Paul Simon
From the album: *Still Crazy After All These Years*
Label: Columbia
Produced by: Phil Ramone, Paul Simon
Year: 1975
East coast nostalgic answer to Dan Fogelberg's "Same Old Lang Syne."

STILL I'M SAD

Artist: The Yardbirds
Written by: James McCarty, Paul Samwell-Smith
From the album: *Having a Rave up with the Yardbirds*
Label: Epic
Produced by: Paul Samwell-Smith
Year: 1965
B-side of "Evil Hearted You" continues their Indian-music-inspired psychedelic experimentations.

STILL IN SAIGON

Artist: Charlie Daniels
Written by: Dan Daley
From the album: *Windows*
Label: Epic
Produced by: John Boylan
Year: 1982
Country/rock tale of a returning Vietnam vet is one of the best postwar, antiwar songs ever.

STILL LOVING YOU

Artist: Scorpions
Written by: Rudolf Schenker, Klaus Meine
From the album: *Love at First Sting*
Label: Mercury
Produced by: Dieter Dirks
Year: 1984
For fans of the Scorpions signature riff.

STILL NOT A PLAYER

Artist: Big Punisher featuring Joe
Written by: Brenda Russell, Jerome Foster, Michelle Williams, Rodney Jerkins, Japhe Tejeda, Joe Thomas, Jolyon Skinner
From the album: *Capital Punishment*
Label: Loud
Produced by: Knobody, Dahoud, Nomad
Year: 1998
East coast rapper cements a legend; the crooner Joe would move to more of an R&B flava.

STILL OF THE NIGHT

Artist: Whitesnake
Written by: David Coverdale, John Sykes
From the album: *Whitesnake*
Label: Geffen
Produced by: Keith Olsen

Year: 1987
Former Deep Purple frontman comes up with a standard issue Led Zeppelin tune, leading the wave of '80s hair bands to a '90s cul-de-sac.

STILL THE ONE

Artist: Orleans
Written by: John Hall, Johanna Hall
From the album: *Waking and Dreaming*
Label: Asylum
Produced by: Chuck Plotkin
Year: 1976
Wedding and anniversary song of enduring marital bliss. Nothing to do with Shania Twain.

STILL THE SAME

Artist: Bob Seger
Written by: Bob Seger
From the album: *Stranger in Town*
Label: Capitol
Produced by: Punch Andrews, Bob Seger
Year: 1977
Following his breakthrough of "Night Moves" with a reassuring rocker.

STILL … YOU TURN ME ON

Artist: Emerson Lake and Palmer (ELP)
Written by: Greg Lake
From the album: *Brain Salad Surgery*
Label: Manticore
Produced by: Greg Lake
Year: 1973

STINKFIST

Artist: Tool
Written by: Tool
From the album: *Tool*
Label: Volcano
Year: 1996
Sexually disturbing metal mayhem.

STIR IT UP

Artist: Bob Marley & the Wailers
Written by: Bob Marley
Label: Trojan
Produced by: Bob Marley & the Wailers, Chris Blackwell
Year: 1968
Covered by Johnny Nash, who had a hit in England with it (CBS, '71) and in the US (Epic, '72). Re-recorded by Marley & the Wailers (Island, '75).

STOLEN CAR

Artist: Beth Orton
Written by: Beth Orton, Ted Barnes, William Blanchard, Sean Read
From the album: *Central Reservation*
Label: DeConstruction
Produced by: Victor Van Vught
Year: 1999

Following in the British folk/rock tradition of Sandy Denny and Christine Perfect.

STOLEN CAR

Artist: Bruce Springsteen
Written by: Bruce Springsteen
From the album: *The River*
Label: Columbia
Produced by: Jon Landau, Bruce Springsteen, Steve Van Zandt
Year: 1980
On the way to *Nebraska*, Bruce considers junking the hot rod metaphors that had sustained his life and career to that point.

STOMP

Artist: The Brothers Johnson
Written by: Louis Johnson, George Johnson, Rod Temperton, Valerie Johnson
From the album: *Light up the Night*
Label: A&M
Produced by: Quincy Jones
Year: 1979
#1 R&B/Top 10 crossover.

STONE COLD

Artist: Rainbow
Written by: Ritchie Blackmore, Roger Glover, Joe Lynn Turner
From the album: *Straight Between the Eyes*
Label: Mercury
Produced by: Roger Glover
Year: 1983
Taking the arena formula straight to the bank. But the bank was closed.

STONE COLD CRAZY

Artist: Queen
Written by: Freddie Mercury, Brian May, Roger Taylor, John Deacon
From the album: *Sheer Heart Attack*
Label: Elektra
Produced by: Roy Thomas Baker, Queen
Year: 1974
Signature early rocker.

STONE COLD DEAD IN THE MARKET (HE HAD IT COMING)

Artist: Ella Fitzgerald with Louis Jordan & His Tympani Five
Written by: Wilmoth Houdini
Label: Decca
Produced by: Milt Gabler
Year: 1946
Titanic meeting of the First Lady of Scat and the Sultan of Cool produces a #1 R&B/Top 10 crossover.

STONE COLD FEVER

Artist: Humble Pie

Written by: Peter Frampton, Steve Marriott, Greg Ridley, Jerry Shirley
From the album: *Rock On*
Produced by: Humble Pie, Glynn Johns
Label: A&M
Year: 1971
Their arena closer.

STONE FREE

Artist: Jimi Hendrix
Written by: Jimi Hendrix
From the album: *Smash Hits*
Label: Reprise
Produced by: Jimi Hendrix
Year: 1968

STONED LOVE

Artist: The Supremes
Written by: Frank Wilson, Yennik Samoht
From the album: *New Ways But Love Stays*
Label: Motown
Produced by: Frank Wilson
Year: 1970
#1 R&B/Top 10 crossover. But whatever happened to Thomas Kinney?

STONED SOUL PICNIC

Artist: Laura Nyro
Written by: Laura Nyro
From the album: *Eli and the Thirteenth Confession*
Label: Columbia
Produced by: Laura Nyro, Charlie Calello
Year: 1968
Laura at Monterey in '67—critically stoned, no picnic. The Fifth Dimension's cover (Soul City, '68), a Top 10 R&B/Top 5 crossover was a measure of retribution.

STONES IN THE ROAD

Artist: Joan Baez
Written by: Mary Chapin-Carpenter
From the album: *Play Me Backwards*
Label: Virgin
Produced by: Wally Wilson, Kenny Greenberg
Year: 1992
Previewing a folk/rock classic written and later performed by Carpenter, a Princeton-graduate-turned-new country superstar (Columbia, '94).

STONEY END

Artist: Laura Nyro
Written by: Laura Nyro
From the album: *More Than a New discovery*
Label: Verve Forecast
Produced by: Milt Okun
Year: 1967
Essential folk rock existentialism. Kate Bush and Tori Amos took notes. Covered by the Fifth Dimension (Bell, '71), Barbra Streisand (Columbia, '71).

STOOD UP

Artist: Ricky Nelson
Written by: Dub Dickerson, Erma Herrold
From the album: *Ricky*
Label: Imperial
Produced by: Ricky Nelson, Jimmy Haskell, Ozzie Nelson
Year: 1957
Aided no doubt by his clean-cut TV persona, Nelson emulated his idol Elvis's cross-cultural clout by having a Top 10 R&B/Top 10 country/Top 10 crossover with this ditty.

STOP DRAGGIN' MY HEART AROUND

Artist: Stevie Nicks and Tom Petty
Written by: Tom Petty, Mike Campbell
From the album: *Bella Donna*
Label: Modern
Produced by: Jimmy Iovine, Tom Petty
Year: 1981
Dylanesque rocker.

STOP THAT TRAIN

Artist: Bob Marley and the Wailers
Written by: Bob Marley
Label: Summit
Year: 1971

STOP THE VIOLENCE

Artist: Boogie Down Productions
Written by: Lawrence Parker
From the album: *By All Means Necessary*
Label: Jive
Produced by: KRS-One
Year: 1988
Cautionary rap classic by a major artist in the genre of heavy street poetics, written about the death of his former collaborator, Scott La Rock.

STOP YOUR SOBBING

Artist: The Kinks
Written by: Ray Davies
From the album: *You Really Got Me*
Label: Reprise
Produced by: Shel Talmy
Year: 1964
Covered by the Pretenders (Sire, '80).

STOP! IN THE NAME OF LOVE

Artist: The Supremes
Written by: Eddie Holland, Lamont Dozier, Brian Holland
From the album: *More Hits by the Supremes*
Label: Motown
Produced by: Brian Holland, Lamont Dozier
Year: 1965
Fourth of six straight #1 hits.

STORIES WE COULD TELL, THE

Artist: The Everly Brothers
Written by: John Sebastian
From the album: *The Stories We Could Tell*
Label: RCA
Produced by: Paul Rothchild
Year: 1972
There would be no more stories until their '84 comeback. Revived by John Sebastian (Shanachie, '93).

STORMY

Artist: The Classics IV and Dennis Yost
Written by: Buddy Buie, James B. Cobb
From the album: *Mamas and Papas/Soul Train*
Label: Imperial
Produced by: Buddy Buie
Year: 1968

STORMY LOVE

Artist: Laura Nyro
Written by: Laura Nyro
From the album: *Smile*
Label: Columbia
Produced by: Laura Nyro, Charlie Calello
Year: 1976
Revealing the ghosts that haunted her five-year silence.

STORY OF ROCK AND ROLL, THE

Artist: The Turtles
Written by: Harry Nilsson
From the album: *The Turtles, More Golden Hits*
Label: White Whale
Produced by: Chip Douglas
Year: 1968
Rare early Nilsson saga. Suggested segue: "The Story of Bo Diddley" by the Animals (MGM, '65).

STORY UNTOLD

Artist: The Nutmegs
Written by: Leroy Griffin, Marty Wilson
Label: Herald
Produced by: Al Silver
Year: 1955
An essential doo-wop teen romance.

STRAIGHT ON

Artist: Heart
Written by: Ann Wilson, Nancy Wilson
From the album: *Dog and Butterfly*
Label: Portrait
Produced by: Mike Flicker
Year: 1978
Straight-ahead rocker.

STRAIGHT OUTTA COMPTON

Artist: NWA
Written by: Eric Wright (Easy E), O'Shea Jackson (Ice Cube), Lorenzo Patterson (MC Ren)
From the album: *Straight Outta Compton*
Label: Ruthless
Produced by: Dr. Dre
Year: 1988
Almost as much sex, violence and profanity as a typical R-rated movie.

STRAIGHT UP

Artist: Paula Abdul
Written by: Elliot Wolff
From the album: *Forever Your Girl*
Label: Virgin
Produced by: Elliot Wolff
Year: 1988
Janet Jackson's former choreographer inaugurates the latest dance era on the charts, with a #1 smash.

STRAIGHTEN UP AND FLY RIGHT

Artist: Nat King Cole
Written by: Nat Cole, Irving Mills
Label: Capitol
Year: 1944
Written in 1937, this landmark #1 country/#1 R&B/#2 crossover was reportedly sold to Irving Mills for $50. It launched the King Cole Trio as a big influence on Johnny Moore's Three Blazers, with Charles Brown, Ray Charles, Sam Cooke, and many others listening. Covered by Linda Ronstadt (Asylum, '86).

STRANDED IN THE JUNGLE

Artist: The Cadets
Written by: Ernestine Smith, James Johnson
From the album: *Rockin' 'n' Reelin'*
Label: Modern
Year: 1956
The Leiber and Stoller storyline goes doo-wop. Introduced by another L.A. R&B group, the Jayhawks (Flash, '56). Meanwhile, back in the states, the Coasters were getting ready to go nationwide.

STRANGE

Artist: Wire
Written by: Colin Newman, Graham Lewis, Bruce Gilbert, Robert Gotobed
From the album: *Pink Flag*
Label: Harvest
Produced by: Mike Thorne
Year: 1977
Covered by R.E.M. (IRS, '87).

STRANGE BREW

Artist: Cream
Written by: Eric Clapton, Felix Pappalardi, Gail Collins
From the album: *Disraeli Gears*
Label: Atco
Produced by: Felix Pappalardi

Year: 1967
Fermented psychedelia with a blues chaser.

STRANGE FEELING

Artist: Tim Buckley
Written by: Tim Buckley
From the album: *Happy/Sad*
Label: Elektra
Produced by: Jerry Yester
Year: 1969
Folk/jazz epic from the tormented singer/song-writer.

STRANGE I KNOW

Artist: The Marvelettes
Written by: Freddie Gorman, Lamont Dozier, Brian Holland
From the album: *Marvelous Marvelettes*
Label: Tamla
Produced by: Brian Holland, Robert Bateman
Year: 1962
Top 10 R&B hit. With the addition of Lamont Dozier, two-thirds of Motown's most famous songwriting aggregate was now in place.

STRANGE MAGIC

Artist: Electric Light Orchestra (ELO)
Written by: Jeff Lynne
From the album: *Face the Music*
Label: United Artists
Produced by: Jeff Lynne
Year: 1975
Perfecting their Beatlesque studio rock craft.

STRANGE WEATHER

Artist: Marianne Faithfull
Written by: Tom Waits, Kathleen Brennan
From the album: *Strange Weather*
Label: Island
Produced by: Mark Miller Mundy
Year: 1987
Tom Waits finds his female voice. Covered by Waits in *Big Time* (Island, '88).

STRANGER IN THE HOUSE

Artist: Rachel Sweet
Written by: Elvis Costello
From the album: *Fool Around*
Label: Stiff
Produced by: Liam Sternberg
Year: 1979
A Brenda Lee-influenced rocker. Covered by Elvis Costello (Columbia, '80). Liam Sternberg would move on to the Beatles-influenced Bangles.

STRANGER IN TOWN

Artist: Del Shannon
Written by: Del Shannon
Label: Amy

Produced by: Irving Micahnik, Harry Balk
Year: 1965
More of a solitary man than Neil Diamond, more of a loner than Neil Young, Del Shannon rides into the sunset after three Top 10 hits in the US, eight in the UK.

STRANGER SONG

Artist: Leonard Cohen
Written by: Leonard Cohen
From the album: *Songs of Leonard Cohen*
Label: Columbia
Produced by: John Simon
Year: 1968
Literary and morose folk/rock tale that was perfectly placed by Robert Altman in his movie *McCabe and Mrs. Miller*.

STRANGLEHOLD

Artist: Ted Nugent
Written by: Ted Nugent
From the album: *Ted Nugent*
Label: Epic
Year: 1975
Motor City guitar madman stalks the wild chord.

STRAWBERRY FIELDS FOREVER

Artist: The Beatles
Written by: John Lennon, Paul McCartney
From the album: *Magical Mystery Tour*
Label: Capitol
Produced by: George Martin
Year: 1967
The B-side of "Penny Lane." Lennon's enduring epitaph. The real Strawberry Field, however, the children's home for the poor on whose sumptuous grounds Lennon and his friends used to play, was shuttered in 2005.

STRAWBERRY LETTER 23

Artist: Shuggie Otis
Written by: Shuggie Otis
From the album: *Freedom Flight*
Label: Epic
Produced by: Johnny Otis
Year: 1971
Great track by the fifteen-year-old guitar hero son of legendary producer Johnny. Cover by the Brothers Johnson (A&M, '77) was a #1 R&B/Top 10 crossover produced by Quincy Jones and featured in the blaxploitation tribute film *Jackie Brown* (Warner Brothers, '97). Also covered by Tevin Campbell (Qwest, '91).

STRAY CAT BLUES

Artist: The Rolling Stones
Written by: Mick Jagger, Keith Richards
From the album: *Beggars Banquet*
Label: London
Produced by: Jimmy Miller

Year: 1968
Mick rewrites "Sweet Little Sixteen" according to his own experience.

STRAY CAT STRUT

Artist: Stray Cats
Written by: Brian Setzer
From the album: *Built for Speed*
Label: EMI-America
Produced by: Dave Edmunds
Year: 1982
Their biggest retro-rockabilly hit.

STREAK, THE

Artist: Ray Stevens
Written by: Ray Stevens
From the album: *Boogity Boogity*
Label: Barnaby
Produced by: Ray Stevens
Year: 1974
Observant Top 10 country/#1 crossover, observed most closely that year by David Niven at the Oscar ceremonies.

STREET FIGHTING MAN

Artist: The Rolling Stones
Written by: Mick Jagger, Keith Richards
From the album: *Beggars Banquet*
Label: London
Produced by: Jimmy Miller
Year: 1968
Answering "All You Need Is Love" and "Why Don't We Do It in the Road" with a remake of "Dancing in the Street," which, in one of the lower moments of rock and roll history, Jagger would cover with David Bowie (EMI-America, '85).

STREET IN THE CITY

Artist: Pete Townshend and Ronnie Lane
Written by: Pete Townshend
From the album: *Rough Mix*
Label: MCA
Produced by: Glyn Johns
Year: 1977
One of his finest songs.

STREET ROCK

Artist: Kurtis Blow with Bob Dylan
Written by: Kurtis Blow, Bill Black, Tashim
From the album: *Kingdom Blow*
Label: Polygram
Year: 1986
Dylan's first rap since "Talking World War III."

STREET SPIRIT

Artist: Radiohead
From the album: *The Bends*
Label: Capitol
Produced by: John Leckie
Year: 1995
Closing track on the album that introduced Radiohead to the wonders of the recording studio.

STREETS OF LONDON

Artist: Ralph McTell
Written by: Ralph McTell
From the album: *You Well Meaning Brought Me Here*
Label: Paramount
Produced by: Gus Dudgeon
Year: 1971
Traditional-sounding folk elegy that found its way into the hands of Elton John's hot producer and then onto FM play lists. Suggested segue: "Dirty Old Town" by Rod Stewart.

STREETS OF PHILADELPHIA

Artist: Bruce Springsteen
Written by: Bruce Springsteen
From the album: *Philadelphia Soundtrack*
Label: Epic Soundtrack
Produced by: Chuck Plotkin, Bruce Springsteen
Year: 1993
Entering his downbeat soundtrack phase, with five Grammys, a Golden Globe, and an Oscar. Next would be "Dead Man Walking."

STRIKE IT UP

Artist: Black Box
Written by: Mirko Limoni, Daniele Davoli, Valerio Semplici
From the album: *Dreamland*
Label: RCA
Produced by: Groove Groove Melody
Year: 1990
Big dance hit that established uncredited studio vocalist Martha Wash as the Darlene Love of the '90s.

STROKE, THE

Artist: Billy Squier
Written by: Billy Squier
From the album: *Don't Say No*
Label: Capitol
Produced by: Mack, Billy Squier
Year: 1981
Led Zeppelin-inspired rocker, with Kiss-inspired euphemism.

STROKE YOU UP

Artist: Changing Faces
Written by: Robert Kelly
From the album: *Changing Faces*
Label: Big Beat
Produced by: Robert Kelly
Year: 1994
An R&B homage to foreplay in the post-erotic era.

STROLL ON

Artist: The Yardbirds
Written by: Keith Relf, James McCarty, Jeff Beck, Chris Dreja
From the album: *Blow Up Soundtrack*
Label: MGM
Produced by: Peter Spargo
Year: 1967
As seen in the fashionable film *Blow Up*, while they bashed their guitars à la Townshend.

STROLL, THE

Artist: The Diamonds
Written by: Clyde Otis, Nancy Lee
From the album: *Collection of Golden Hits*
Label: Mercury
Produced by: David Carroll
Year: 1957
The infamous Canadian Cover Kings sing a Clyde Otis tune. But it was Chuck Willis who was the "King of the Stroll."

STRONG ENOUGH

Artist: Sheryl Crow
Written by: Sheryl Crow, Bill Bottrell, David Baerwald, Kevin Gilbert, David Ricketts, Brian Macleod
From the album: *Tuesday Night Music Club*
Label: A&M
Produced by: Bill Bottrell
Year: 1995
Trying out her material on a wider audience.

STRONGER THAN THE WIND

Artist: Tina Turner
Written by: Essra Mohawk, Tony Sciuto
Label: Capitol
Produced by: Terry Britten
Year: 1989
European B-side is another milestone in Mohawk's legendary underground career.

STRUTTER

Artist: Kiss
Written by: Gene Simmons
From the album: *Kiss*
Label: Casablanca
Produced by: Kenny Kerner, Richie Wise
Year: 1974
Glittery arena anthem for the masked band; re-recorded in '78.

STRYCHNINE

Artist: The Sonics
Written by: Gerald Roglie
From the album: *Here Are the Sonics'*
Label: Etiquette
Produced by: Etiquette
Year: 1965
A garage band grenade from the state of Washington.

STUBBORN KIND OF FELLOW

Artist: Marvin Gaye
Written by: William Stevenson, George Gordy, Marvin Gaye
From the album: *Marvin Gaye / Greatest Hits*
Label: Tamla
Produced by: William Stevenson
Year: 1962
Introducing Motown session drummer Marvin Gaye, in his early backwoods incarnation.

STUCK IN THE MIDDLE WITH YOU

Artist: Stealer's Wheel
Written by: Joe Egan, Gerry Rafferty
From the album: *Stealer's Wheel*
Label: A&M
Produced by: Jerry Leiber, Mike Stoller
Year: 1973
Bargain-basement Steely Dan. Rafferty would move on to "Baker Street."

STUCK INSIDE OF MOBILE WITH THE MEMPHIS BLUES AGAIN

Artist: Bob Dylan
Written by: Bob Dylan
From the album: *Blonde on Blonde*
Label: Columbia
Produced by: Bob Johnston
Year: 1966
One of his greatest verbal challenges, baffling Dylanographers and Dylanologists to this day.

STUCK ON YOU

Artist: Elvis Presley
Written by: Aaron Schroeder
From the album: *Elvis' Golden Records (Vol. IV)*
Label: RCA
Produced by: Steve Sholes
Year: 1960
His first post-army release and his thirteenth #1.

STUCK WITH YOU

Artist: Huey Lewis and the News
Written by: Chris Hayes, Huey Lewis
From the album: *Fore!*
Label: Chrysalis
Produced by: Huey Lewis and the News
Year: 1986
Evoking the classic hooks of Top 40's heyday.

STUMBLIN' IN

Artist: Suzi Quatro
Written by: Mike Chapman, Nicky Chinn
From the album: *If You Knew Suzi*
Label: RSO
Produced by: Mike Chapman
Year: 1978
US expatriate Quatro's nearly country/rock duet with Chris Norman was her only US hit; she had five in the UK (this one not among them). By this time she had fallen into tepid self-parody as Leather Tuscadero on TV's *Happy Days*.

STUPID CUPID

Artist: Connie Francis
Written by: Howard Greenfield, Neil Sedaka
From the album: *Connie's Greatest Hits*
Label: MGM
Year: 1958

Kicking Don Kirshner and Al Nevins's Broadway publishing empire into high gear, the Brighton Beach duo of Sedaka and Greenfield contributed this Top 20 pop rock ditty to New Jersey's aspiring diva, Connie Francis, just coming off "Who's Sorry Now." Soon thereafter, Connie would be on her way to Atlantic City and Sedaka and Greenfield would sign a songwriting deal for $50 a week.

STUPID GIRL

Artist: Garbage
Written by: Joe Strummer, Mick Jones, Duke Erickson, Shirley Manson, Steve Marker, Butch Vig
From the album: *Garbage*
Label: Almo Sounds
Produced by: Butch Vig
Year: 1995
Samples "Train in Vain (Stand by Me)" by the Clash.

SUAVECITO

Artist: Malo
Written by: Richard Bean, Abel Zarate, Pablo Tellez
From the album: *Malo*
Label: Warner Brothers
Produced by: David Rubinson
Year: 1972
Compellingly Santanaesque.

SUBSTITUTE

Artist: The Who
Written by: Pete Townshend
Label: Decca
Produced by: The Who
Year: 1966
Keith Moon at his best. Not available on an album until it appeared on *Live at Leeds* in 1970.

SUBTERRANEAN HOMESICK BLUES

Artist: Bob Dylan
Written by: Bob Dylan
From the album: *Bringing It All Back Home*
Label: Columbia
Produced by: Tom Wilson
Year: 1965
Dylan's first music video, costarring Allen Ginsberg, opened the classic documentary *Don't Look Back*. From whence came the radical slogan: "You don't need a weatherman to know which way the wind blows." Covered by Harry Nilsson (RCA, '74). Suggested segues: "Too Much Monkey Business," by Chuck Berry, "It's the End of the World as We Know It (and I Feel Fine)" by R.E.M., "We Didn't Start the Fire" by Billy Joel, "Pump It Up" by Elvis Costello.

SUCH A NIGHT

Artist: The Drifters
Written by: Lincoln Chase
Label: Atlantic

Produced by: Ahmet Ertegun, Jerry Wexler
Year: 1954
Racy R&B classic was the Drifters second hit. Covered by Johnny Ray (Columbia, '54), Elvis Presley (RCA, '60).

(SUCH AN) EASY QUESTION

Artist: Elvis Presley
Written by: Otis Blackwell, Winfield Scott
From the album: *Pot Luck*
Label: RCA
Year: 1965
A landmark (or possibly headstone) in Presley's career, his first appearance at #1 on the adult contemporary chart.

SUCKER MC'S (KRUSH GROOVE)

Artist: Run-D.M.C.
Written by: Larry Smith, Joseph Simmons, Darryl McDaniels
From the album: *Run-D.M.C.*
Label: Profile
Produced by: Russell Simmons
Year: 1984
B-side of "It's Like That."

SUDDENLY

Artist: Billy Ocean
Written by: Keith Diamond, Billy Ocean
From the album: *Suddenly*
Label: Jive
Produced by: Keith Diamond
Year: 1984

SUDDENLY LAST SUMMER

Artist: The Motels
Written by: Martha Davis
From the album: *Little Robbers*
Label: Capitol
Year: 1983
Recalling the turgid movie it was named after.

SUDDENLY SEYMOUR

Artist: Ellen Greene and Lee Wilkoff
Written by: Howard Ashman, Alan Menken
From the album: *Little Shop of Horrors*
Label: Warner Brothers
Produced by: Phil Ramone
Year: 1982
Key retro doo-wop ballad from the hip musical by the future Disney ("Under the Sea," "Kiss the Girl") songwriting stalwarts. Reprised by Greene and Rick Moranis in the movie (Geffen, '86).

SUEDEHEAD

Artist: Morrissey
Written by: Stephen Morrissey, Stephen Street
From the album: *Viva Hate*
Label: Sire
Produced by: Stephen Street

Year: 1988
First UK solo single hit for the former head case from the Smiths, an anti-Sinatra to do Bryan Ferry proud.

SUFFRAGETTE CITY

Artist: David Bowie
Written by: David Bowie
From the album: *The Rise and Fall of Ziggy Stardust and the Spiders from Mars*
Label: RCA
Produced by: Ken Scott, David Bowie
Year: 1972
One of his best rockers.

SUGAR DADDY

Artist: The Jackson 5
Written by: Freddie Perren, Berry Gordy Jr., Deke Richards, Fonce Mizell
From the album: *Jackson 5 Greatest Hits*
Label: Motown
Produced by: Freddie Perren, Berry Gordy Jr., Deke Richards, Fonce Mizell
Year: 1971

SUGAR MAGNOLIA

Artist: Grateful Dead
Written by: Bob Weir, Robert Hunter
From the album: *American Beauty*
Label: Warner Brothers
Produced by: Grateful Dead
Year: 1970
Moving with all deliberate speed into country/rock jamming.

SUGAR MAMA

Artist: Bonnie Raitt
Written by: Delbert McClinton, Glen Clark
From the album: *Home Plate*
Label: Warner Brothers
Produced by: Paul Rothchild
Year: 1975
Burnishing her legend as a country/blues interpreter.

SUGAR MOUNTAIN

Artist: Neil Young
Written by: Neil Young
From the album: *Decade*
Label: Reprise
Year: 1969
Neil's epic farewell to childhood and favorite B-side, written in Ann Arbor in 1968. B-side of his first solo single "The Loner," as well as "Cinnamon Girl," "When You Dance" and "Heart of Gold." Used in Young's film *Rust Never Sleeps*. Joni Mitchell heard it and wrote "The Circle Game."

SUGAR SHACK

Artist: Jimmy Gilmer and the Fireballs
Written by: Keith McCormack, Faye Voss

From the album: *Sugar Shack*
Label: Dot
Produced by: Norman Petty
Year: 1963
White post-rockabilly #1 R&B/#1 crossover was the top song of 1963. Norman Petty had produced fellow Texans, Buddy Holly and the Crickets.

SUGAR SUGAR

Artist: The Archies
Written by: Jeff Barry, Andy Kim
From the album: *Everything's Archie*
Label: Calandar
Produced by: Jeff Barry
Year: 1969
Ultimate pop confection from the same factory that created the Monkees' hits, sung by ubiquitous studio hand Ron Dante. Covered by Wilson Pickett a year later in the sugar-free version (Atlantic, '70).

SUGAR WALLS

Artist: Sheena Easton
Written by: Alexander Nevermind (Prince)
From the album: *A Private Heaven*
Label: EMI-America
Produced by: Greg Mathieson
Year: 1984
Sexual innuendo hit of the year. Top 10 R&B/Top 10 crossover. Easton would soon show up on *Miami Vice* as Don Johnson's doomed love interest.

SUGAREE

Artist: Jerry Garcia
Written by: Jerry Garcia, Robert Hunter
From the album: *Garcia*
Label: Warner Brothers
Produced by: Bob Matthews, Betty Cantor, Ramrod
Year: 1972
The bluegrass side of Captain Trips resurfaces, epitomizing the country/folk rock sound of '72. Recorded live by the full band (Warner Brothers, '76).

SUICIDE BLONDE

Artist: Inxs
Written by: Andrew Farriss, Michael Hutchence
From the album: *X*
Label: Atlantic
Year: 1990
Hutchence would commit suicide in 1997.

SUICIDE SOLUTION

Artist: Ozzy Osbourne
Written by: Ozzy Osbourne, Randy Rhoads, Bob Daisley, Lee Kerslake
From the album: *Blizzard of Ozz*
Label: Jet
Produced by: Max Norman
Year: 1981
Widely misunderstood antidrug lament.

SUIT, THE

Artist: Public Image Ltd. (P.I.L.)
Written by: Public Image Ltd.
From the album: *Second Edition*
Label: Warner Brothers
Produced by: Public Image Ltd.
Year: 1979
Almost likeable, in a trancelike way.

SUITE: JUDY BLUE EYES

Artist: Crosby, Stills & Nash
Written by: Stephen Stills
From the album: *Crosby, Stills & Nash*
Label: Atlantic
Produced by: Crosby, Stills & Nash
Year: 1969
Tribute to Judy Collins.

SUKIYAKI (MY FIRST LONELY NIGHT)

Artist: Kyu Sakamoto
Written by: Tom Leslie, Buzz Cason, Hachidai Nakamura, Rokusuke Ei
From the album: *Sukiyaki and Other Japanese Hits*
Label: Capitol
Produced by: Koji Kusano
Year: 1963
Haunting rocker from Japan, where heavy metal guitarists go after they die (in the US market). Covered by A Taste of Honey (Capitol, '80), 4 P.M. (Next Plateau/London, '94).

SULTANS OF SWING

Artist: Dire Straits
Written by: Mark Knopfler
From the album: *Dire Straits*
Label: Warner Brothers
Produced by: Muff Winwood
Year: 1979
Guitar-powered return to the days of Hank Marvin and the Shadows.

SUMMER

Artist: War
Written by: Sylvester Allen, Lee Oscar Levitin, Morris Dickerson, Leroy "Lonnie" Jordan, Howard Scott, Charles W. Miller, Harold R. Brown, Gerald Goldstein
From the album: *Greatest Hits*
Label: United Artists
Produced by: Jerry Goldstein
Year: 1976
Their sixth Top 10 R&B/Top 10 crossover.

SUMMER BABE

Artist: Pavement
Written by: Stephen Malkmus
From the album: *Slanted and Enchanted*
Label: Matador
Produced by: Pavement
Year: 1992
Still the best of their singles.

SUMMER BREEZE

Artist: Seals and Crofts
Written by: James Seals, Darrell Crofts
From the album: *Summer Breeze*
Label: Warner Brothers
Produced by: Louie Shelton
Year: 1971
Lilting folk/rock air. In a statistical quirk that would be more appropriate for a heavy metal band, all three of Seals and Crofts' Top 10 hits peaked at #6, undoubtedly prompting their conversion to the Bahai religion.

SUMMER GIRLS

Artist: LFO
Written by: Rich Cronin, Brad Young, Dow Brain
From the album: *LFO*
Label: Logic
Produced by: Rich Conin, Brad Young, Dow Brain
Year: 1999
An advertisment for preppy clothiers Abercrombie & Fitch.

SUMMER IN THE CITY

Artist: The Lovin' Spoonful
Written by: John Sebastian, Mark Sebastian, Steve Boone
From the album: *Hums of the Lovin' Spoonful*
Label: Kama Sutra
Produced by: Erik Jacobsen
Year: 1966
Reinventing "Up on the Roof" for their only #1, complete with jackhammer.

SUMMER NIGHTS

Artist: Carole Demas and Barry Bostwick
Written by: Jim Jacobs, Warren Casey
From the album: *Grease Original Cast Album*
Label: MGM
Year: 1972
A convincingly dumb and innocent summer song, from the musical that brought back the *sturm* of the '50s, stripped of all its redeeming *drang*. Covered in the movie version, which stripped even the relatively meager *sturm* from the questionable concept, by John Travolta and Olivia Newton-John (RSO, '78).

SUMMER OF DRUGS

Artist: Victoria Williams
Written by: Victoria Williams
From the album: *Swing the Statue*
Label: Rough Trade
Year: 1990
Harrowing response to the "Summer of Love," 25 years later. Covered by Soul Asylum (Thirsty Ear/Chaos, '93).

SUMMER OF '69

Artist: Bryan Adams
Written by: Bryan Adams, Jim Vallance
From the album: *Reckless'*

Label: A&M
Produced by: Bryan Adams, Bob Clearmountain
Year: 1984
Invading Bruce Springsteen's emotional space, as well as his girlfriend's front porch, Adams blurs his identity enough to produce his most recurrent anthem. Later he denied the obvious autobiographical fallacies to claim the song was really about sex.

SUMMER RAIN

Artist: Johnny Rivers
Written by: James Hendricks
From the album: *Realizations*
Label: Imperial
Produced by: Lou Adler
Year: 1968
A personal autobiographical peak.

SUMMER SONG, A

Artist: Chad and Jeremy
Written by: Clive Metcalfe, Keith Noble, David Stuart
From the album: *Best of Chad and Jeremy*
Label: World
Produced by: Shel Talmy
Year: 1966
Breezy folk/rock. Seals and Crofts were listening.

SUMMER'S CAULDRON

Artist: XTC
Written by: Andy Partridge
From the album: *Skylarking*
Label: Geffen
Produced by: Todd Rundgren
Year: 1987
"One Summer Night" in England.

SUMMERTIME

Artist: D. J. Jazzy Jeff and the Fresh Prince
Written by: Kool & the Gang, Will Smith, Fingers, Hula
From the album: *Homebase*
Label: Jive
Produced by: Hula, Fingers
Year: 1991
#1 R&B/Top 10 crossover rap concoction with a Kool groove sampled from "Summer Madness."

SUMMERTIME

Artist: Billy Stewart
Written by: DuBose Heyward, George Gershwin
From the album: *Unbelievable*
Label: Chess
Produced by: Billy Davis
Year: 1966
Jumping remake of the '36 classic from *Porgy and Bess*. Covered by Janis Joplin (Columbia, '67) as a gorgeous ballad.

SUMMERTIME BLUES

Artist: Eddie Cochran

Written by: Eddie Cochran, Jerry Capeheart
From the album: *Summertime Blues*
Label: Liberty
Produced by: Eddie Cochran, Jerry Capeheart
Year: 1958
Timeless essay on the teenage condition exacerbated by the season itself—oppressive idleness, endless, sunbaked alienation. As a black-leather James Dean biker type in a L.A. on the edge of the Beach Boys, no one could have been more out of place or out of time than Cochran, whose time would soon run out. Covered by Blue Cheer (Phillips, '68), the Who (Decca, '70).

SUMMERTIME, SUMMERTIME

Artist: The Jamies
Written by: Tom Jameson, Sherm Feller
Label: Epic
Year: 1958
The ultimate song of summer freedom, played every June on the last day of school. Suggested segues: "One Summer Night" by the Danleers, for the ultimate summer fantasy expectation and "Summertime Blues" by Eddie Cochran, for the more probable painful reality. Featured in the '78 Harvey Keitel cult movie *Fingers*.

SUN AIN'T GONNA SHINE ANYMORE, THE

Artist: Frankie Valli
Written by: Bob Gaudio, Bob Crewe
From the album: *Solo*
Label: Phillips
Produced by: Bob Crewe
Year: 1965
Cover by the Walker Brothers (Smash, '66) was a US/UK hit.

SUN CITY

Artist: Artists United Against Apartheid
Written by: Steven Van Zandt
From the album: *Sun City*
Label: Manhattan
Produced by: Steven Van Zandt, Arthur Baker
Year: 1985
The superstar concept of "We Are the World" as applied to artists protesting apartheid in South Africa, spearheaded by a New Jersey guitar hero/activist, former Springsteen sideman and future Tony Soprano henchman and Satellite Radio DJ.

SUNDAY, BLOODY SUNDAY

Artist: U2
Written by: Paul Hewson (Bono), Dave Evans (Edge), Adam Clayton, Larry Mullen
From the album: *War*
Label: Island
Produced by: Steve Lillywhite, Bill Whelan
Year: 1983
Bringing their surging Celtic drone to a higher emotional level.

SUNDAY GIRL

Artist: Blondie
Written by: Chris Stein
From the album: *Parallel Lines*
Label: Chrysalis
Produced by: Mike Chapman
Year: 1979
#1 in the UK. Harriet Gavurin, to say nothing of Hope Sandoval, was listening.

SUNDAY KIND OF LOVE, A

Artist: The Harptones
Written by: Barbara Belle, Anita Leonard, Stan Rhodes, Louis Prima
Label: Bruce
Produced by: George Goldner
Year: 1953
The ultimate doo-wop version of this classic ballad, which failed to score on either the pop or the R&B chart. Introduced in 1947 by Jo Stafford.

SUNDAY MORNIN' COMING DOWN

Artist: Kris Kristofferson
Written by: Kris Kristofferson
From the album: *Kris Kristofferson*
Label: Monument
Produced by: Fred Foster
Year: 1969
Down and out on the streets of Nashville, but at least he had "Me and Bobby McGee" in the bank. A #1 country/Top 50 crossover by Johnny Cash (Columbia, '70).

SUNDAY MORNING

Artist: The Velvet Underground
Written by: Lou Reed
From the album: *The Velvet Underground and Nico*
Label: Verve
Produced by: Tom Wilson
Year: 1967
Iron-fisted decadence in a velvet glove.

SUNDAY WILL NEVER BE THE SAME

Artist: Spanky and Our Gang
Written by: Terry Cashman, Gene Pistilli
From the album: *Spanky and Our Gang*
Label: Mercury
Produced by: Jerry Ross
Year: 1967
Harmony-oriented folk/rock throwback to 1965.

SUNDOWN

Artist: Gordon Lightfoot
Written by: Gordon Lightfoot
From the album: *Sundown*
Label: Reprise
Produced by: Lenny Waronker
Year: 1974
Mellow folk/rocker is his biggest hit.

SUNNY AFTERNOON

Artist: The Kinks
Written by: Ray Davies
From the album: *Face to Face*
Label: Reprise
Produced by: Shel Talmy
Year: 1966
Happy-go-lucky Ray, on the edge of doom. Suggested segue: "Taxman" by the Beatles.

SUNNY CAME HOME

Artist: Shawn Colvin
Written by: Shawn Colvin, John Leventhal
From the album: *A Few Small Repairs*
Label: Columbia
Produced by: John Leventhal
Year: 1997
Folk/rock singer breaks through with a haunting tale of a homecoming gone awry. Won Record and Song of the Year Grammys. Segue: "Burning down the House" by Talking Heads.

SUNNY GOODGE STREET

Artist: Donovan
Written by: Donovan Leitch
From the album: *Fairy Tales*
Label: Hickory
Produced by: Geoff Stevens, Terry Kennedy, Peter Eden
Year: 1965
Fey travelogue. Covered by Judy Collins (Elektra, '67).

SUNSHINE

Artist: Jonathan Edwards
Written by: Andy Yoakim (Andy Kim)
From the album: *Jonathan Edwards*
Label: Capricorn
Produced by: Peter Casperson
Year: 1972
Exploiting the year's predominating metaphor, as the alternate culture packed up and moved back home.

SUNSHINE OF YOUR LOVE

Artist: Cream
Written by: Eric Clapton, Jack Bruce, Peter Brown
From the album: *Disraeli Gears*
Label: Atco
Produced by: Felix Pappalardi
Year: 1968
Their best-selling single, a Top 10 US/Top 30 UK high-powered blues blast, covered by every nascent bar band on two continents.

SUNSHINE ON MY SHOULDERS

Artist: John Denver
Written by: H. J. Deutschendorf Jr. (John Denver), Michael Taylor, Richard Kniss
From the album: *Poems, Prayers and Promises*
Label: RCA
Produced by: Milt Okun
Year: 1974
His first #1. Defining the era's sundrenched, rose-colored folk/rock motif.

SUNSHINE SUPERMAN

Artist: Donovan
Written by: Donovan Leitch
From the album: *Sunshine Superman*
Label: Epic
Produced by: Mickie Most
Year: 1966
The only #1 for the folk/rock flower child.

SUNSHINE, LOLLIPOPS AND RAINBOWS

Artist: Lesley Gore
Written by: Howard Liebling, Marvin Hamlisch
From the album: *Golden Hits of Lesley Gore*
Label: Mercury
Produced by: Quincy Jones
Year: 1965
Gore at her most uncharacteristically winsome. Hamlisch would move on from her another suburban princess, Carole Bayer Sager.

SUNSHINE, SUNSHINE

Artist: James Taylor
Written by: James Taylor
From the album: *James Taylor*
Label: Apple
Produced by: Peter Asher
Year: 1969
Actually, an anti-sunshine song. Introduced by Tom Rush (Elektra, '68).

SUPER BAD

Artist: James Brown
Written by: James Brown
From the album: *Super Bad*
Label: King
Produced by: James Brown
Year: 1970
Michael Jackson was taking notes.

SUPER FREAK

Artist: Rick James
Written by: James Johnson Jr.
From the album: *Street Songs*
Label: Gordy
Produced by: Rick James
Year: 1981
His defining groove.

SUPER NOVA

Artist: Liz Phair
Written by: Liz Phair
From the album: *Whip Smart*
Label: Matador
Produced by: Liz Phair
Year: 1994
Sophomore blues.

SUPERFLY

Artist: Curtis Mayfield
Written by: Curtis Mayfield
From the album: *Superfly Soundtrack*
Label: Curtom
Produced by: Curtis Mayfield
Year: 1972
Its legend is exceeded only by its enduring fashion statement.

SUPERGIRL

Artist: The Fugs
Written by: Tuli Kupferberg, Ed Sanders
From the album: *First Album*
Label: ESP
Produced by: Harry Smith
Year: 1965
Rampant sexism, hippie-style.

SUPERMAN

Artist: The Clique
Written by: Gary Zekely, Mitch Bottler
From the album: *The Clique*
Label: White Whale
Year: 1968
Legendary B-side of bubblegum hit, "Sugar on Sunday." Unearthed by R.E.M. (IRS, '86). Gary Zekely briefly considered a comeback.

SUPERNATURAL THING (PART I)

Artist: Ben E. King
Written by: Gwen Guthrie, Patrick Grant
From the album: *Supernatural*
Label: Atlantic
Produced by: Tony Silvester, Bert Coteaux
Year: 1975
A #1 R&B/Top 10 disco-era comeback.

SUPERSONIC

Artist: Oasis
Written by: Noel Gallagher
From the album: *Definitely Maybe*
Label: Epic
Produced by: Noel Gallagher, Mark Coyle, Owen Morris
Year: 1994
New generation takes over the studio.

SUPERSTAR

Artist: Carpenters
Written by: Leon Russell, Bonnie Bramlett
From the album: *Now and Then*
Label: A&M
Produced by: Jack Daugherty
Year: 1971
"Sweet Little Sixteen" from the girl's point of view.

SUPERSTAR, REMEMBER HOW YOU GOT WHERE YOU ARE

Artist: The Temptations
Written by: Norman Whitfield, Barrett Strong
From the album: *Solid Rock*
Label: Gordy
Produced by: Norman Whitfield
Year: 1971
R&B moralizing.

SUPERSTITION

Artist: Stevie Wonder
Written by: Stevie Wonder
From the album: *Talking Book*
Label: Tamla
Produced by: Stevie Wonder
Year: 1972
Taking over his own writing and production reigns, Stevie finds a new soulful voice, adult perspective, rocking attitude, and his first #1 R&B/#1 crossover in nearly a decade, with a song he wrote for Jeff Beck. Beck's version came out a year later (Epic '73).

SUPERWOMAN

Artist: Karyn White
Written by: Kenny Edmunds (Babyface), Antonio Reed (L. A. Reid), Daryl Simmons
From the album: *Karyn White*
Label: Warner Brothers
Produced by: Babyface, L. A. Reid
Year: 1988
#1 R&B/Top 10 crossover and the top R&B song of 1988.

SUPERWOMAN (WHERE WERE YOU WHEN I NEEDED YOU)

Artist: Stevie Wonder
Written by: Stevie Wonder
From the album: *Music of My Mind*
Label: Tamla
Produced by: Stevie Wonder
Year: 1972
Bye-bye Syreeta.

SUPPER'S READY

Artist: Genesis
Written by: Peter Gabriel, Tony Banks
From the album: *Foxtrot*
Label: Charisma
Produced by: Dave Hitchcock
Year: 1972
Genesis in the beginning, with Peter Gabriel's fabled classical rock operetta.

SURE AS I'M SITTIN' HERE

Artist: Three Dog Night

Written by: John Hiatt
From the album: *Hard Labor*
Label: Dunhill
Produced by: Richard Podolor
Year: 1974
Three Dog Night goes out as they came in, introducing another fine songwriter to the industry, with a Top 20 hit. Hiatt would write Bonnie Raitt's "Thing Called Love" among many others.

SURF CITY

Artist: Jan & Dean
Written by: Brian Wilson, Jan Berry
From the album: *Surf City and Other Swingin' Cities*
Label: Liberty
Produced by: Jan Berry
Year: 1963
Their biggest hit, a generation's biggest fantasy: two girls for every boy.

SURFER GIRL

Artist: The Beach Boys
Written by: Brian Wilson
From the album: *Surfer Girl*
Label: Capitol
Produced by: Brian Wilson
Year: 1963
Doo-wop meets Disney at Muscle Beach. The first song Brian ever wrote.

SURFER JOE

Artist: The Surfaris
Written by: Ron Wilson
From the album: *Wipe Out*
Label: Dot
Produced by: Dale Smallin
Year: 1963
Where have you gone Murf the Surf? Don't believe Ron and Brian were related, except by obsession.

SURFER'S HOLIDAY

Artist: Dick Dale
Written by: Brian Wilson
From the album: *Surfer's Holiday Soundtrack*
Label: AIP
Year: 1964
Before new wave there was only one kind of wave.

SURFER'S STOMP

Artist: The Marketts
Written by: Joe Saraceno, Michael Daughtry
Label: Liberty
Produced by: Joe Saraceno
Year: 1962
Often thought of as the first surf music hit, beating the Beach Boys to the Top 40. But Dick Dale had broken the ground a few months before this, with "Let's Go Trippin'," which peaked late in '61. But tell that to the Gamblers, whose "Moon Dawg" came out in '59.

SURFIN'

Artist: The Beach Boys
Written by: Brian Wilson
From the album: *Surfin' Safari*
Label: X/Candix
Produced by: Hite Morgan
Year: 1961
Mixing the urban soul of white doo-wop and the white-bucked suburban pop of the Four Freshmen with the sound of the surf, the Beach Boys officially opened the gates to rock's new frontier—the teen dream of California in the '60s.

SURFIN' BIRD

Artist: The Trashmen
Written by: Al Frazier, John Earl Harris, Carl White, Turner Wilson
From the album: *Surfin' Bird*
Label: Garrett
Year: 1963
Inspired by—and indeed credited to—the Rivingtons, who both sang and wrote the immortal surf nightmare "The Bird's the Word." Covered by neo-surf punk rockers the Cramps (IRS, '79). Note the presence of another Wilson in the writing credits. Coincidence? Beats me.

SURFIN' SAFARI

Artist: The Beach Boys
Written by: Brian Wilson, Mike Love
From the album: *Surfin' Safari*
Label: Capitol
Produced by: Nik Venet
Year: 1962
Offering a West Coast Brill Building pop alternative: dancing on the waves.

SURFIN' USA

Artist: The Beach Boys
Written by: Brian Wilson, Chuck Berry
From the album: *Surfin' USA*
Label: Capitol
Produced by: Nik Venet
Year: 1963
Revisiting the original icon—"Sweet Little Sixteen."

SURRENDER

Artist: Cheap Trick
Written by: Rick Nielsen
From the album: *Heaven Tonight*
Label: Epic
Produced by: Tom Werman
Year: 1976
Good-time arena rock.

SURRENDER

Artist: Elvis Presley
Written by: Doc Pomus, Mort Shuman, E. De Curtis, G. B. De Curtis
From the album: *Elvis' Golden Records (Vol. III)*
Label: RCA

Produced by: Steve Sholes
Year: 1961
Based on the aria "Torna a Sorrento (Come Back to Sorrento)," the King's only #1 of '61.

SUSIE DARLIN'

Artist: Robin Luke
Written by: Robin Luke
Label: Dot
Year: 1958
The first and last word in Hawaiian rockabilly.

SUSPENDED IN GAFFA

Artist: Kate Bush
Written by: Kate Bush
From the album: *The Dreaming*
Label: EMI-America
Produced by: Kate Bush
Year: 1982
English warbler begins to get strange.

SUSPICION

Artist: Elvis Presley
Written by: Doc Pomus, Mort Shuman
From the album: *Pot Luck*
Label: RCA
Year: 1962
Elvis's version was a hit in England. Covered by Terry Stafford (Crusader, '64).

SUSPICIOUS MINDS

Artist: Elvis Presley
Written by: Mark James
From the album: *From Memphis to Vegas*
Label: RCA
Produced by: Chips Moman, Felton Jarvis, Elvis Presley
Year: 1969
Cut in Memphis and introduced at his first live performance since '61, at the Las Vegas Hilton, this was his first #1 since "Good Luck Charm" in '62, eighteenth overall, and last of the century. Covered for the country market by Waylon Jennings and Jessi Colter (RCA, '70).

SUSSUDIO

Artist: Phil Collins
Written by: Phil Collins
From the album: *No Jacket Required*
Label: Atlantic
Produced by: Hugh Padgham, Phil Collins
Year: 1985
Third #1. Segue: "1999" by Prince.

SUZANNE

Artist: Judy Collins
Written by: Leonard Cohen
From the album: *In My Life*
Label: Elektra
Produced by: Mark Abramson
Year: 1966

One of the most indelible character portraits of the decade, by Canada's past master of melancholy, gets the Collins seal of approval. Released by Leonard Cohen on his first album (Columbia, '68). A single by Noel Harrison stiffed (Reprise, '67).

SUZIE Q

Artist: Dale Hawkins
Written by: Dale Hawkins, Stanley Lewis, Eleanor Broadwater
From the album: *Suzie Q*
Label: Checker
Year: 1957
Blistering rockabilly classic. Covered by Creedence Clearwater Revival (Fantasy, '68).

SWALLOW MY PRIDE

Artist: Green River
Written by: Mark Arm, Steve Turner
From the album: *Come on Down*
Label: Homestead
Produced by: Jack Endino
Year: 1985
Setting the outlines of grunge in Seattle.

SWALLOW THAT

Artist: Superchunk
Written by: Jonathan Wurster, James Wilbur, Ralph McLaughan, Laura Ballance
From the album: *On the Mouth*
Label: Matador
Year: 1992
Big on the college circuit.

SWAN DIVE

Artist: Ani Difranco
Written by: Ani Difranco
From the album: *Little Plastic Castle*
Label: Righteous Babe
Produced by: Ani DiFranco
Year: 1998
The anti-Lilith.

SWEATER, THE

Artist: Meryn Cadell
Written by: Meryn Cadell
From the album: *Angel Food for Thought*
Label: Reprise
Produced by: John Tucker, Meryn Cadell
Year: 1992
Plundering the depths of the preteen female psyche in the guise of a suburban tone poem.

SWEET AND INNOCENT

Artist: Roy Orbison
Written by: Joe South
Label: RCA
Produced by: Chet Atkins
Year: 1958
Minor Roy trifle introduces a major writer. Covered by the Osmonds (MGM, '71).

SWEET BABY JAMES

Artist: James Taylor
Written by: James Taylor
From the album: *Sweet Baby James*
Label: Warner Brothers
Produced by: Peter Asher
Year: 1970
New England cowboy lullaby.

SWEET BLINDNESS

Artist: Laura Nyro
Written by: Laura Nyro
From the album: *Eli and the Thirteenth Confession*
Label: Columbia
Produced by: Laura Nyro, Charlie Calello
Year: 1968
Celebrating the evil grape. Covered by her favorite clients, the Fifth Dimension (Soul City, '68).

SWEET CAROLINE

Artist: Neil Diamond
Written by: Neil Diamond
From the album: *Gold*
Label: Uni
Produced by: Tom Catalano
Year: 1969
His biggest hit of the '60s.

SWEET CHILD O' MINE

Artist: Guns N' Roses
Written by: Guns N' Roses
From the album: *Appetite for Destruction*
Label: Geffen
Produced by: Mike Clink
Year: 1988
Their first and biggest hit; #1 ballad from the L.A. bad boys.

SWEET DREAMS (ARE MADE OF THIS)

Artist: Eurythmics
Written by: Annie Lennox, Dave Stewart
From the album: *Sweet Dreams (Are Made of This)*
Label: RCA
Produced by: Dave Stewart
Year: 1983
#1 US/#2 UK crossover established their synth-laden new wave/new age existential harmony.

SWEET DREAMS

Artist: Don Gibson
Written by: Don Gibson
From the album: *Sweet Dreams*
Label: RCA
Produced by: Chet Atkins
Year: 1960
Covered by Patsy Cline (Decca, '63).

SWEET EMOTION

Artist: Aerosmith
Written by: Steven Tyler, Tom Hamilton

From the album: *Toys in the Attic*
Label: Columbia
Produced by: Jack Douglas
Year: 1975
Arena favorite. Sung over the opening credits to the movie *Dazed and Confused* (Medicine, '93).

SWEET GENE VINCENT

Artist: Ian Dury and the Blockheads
Written by: Ian Dury, Chaz Jankel
From the album: *New Boots and Panties*
Label: Stiff
Produced by: Laurie Latham, Peter Jenner, Rick Walton
Year: 1977
Poignant ballad, about a man after Dury's own gimpy heart.

SWEET HARMONY

Artist: Smokey Robinson
Written by: Smokey Robinson
From the album: *Smokey*
Label: Tamla
Produced by: Smokey Robinson
Year: 1973
Smokey's first solo hit typifies his life's philosophy.

SWEET HITCH-HIKER

Artist: Creedence Clearwater Revival
Written by: John C. Fogerty
From the album: *Mardi Gras*
Label: Fantasy
Produced by: John C. Fogerty
Year: 1971
Their ninth and last Top 10 single.

SWEET HOME ALABAMA

Artist: Lynyrd Skynyrd
Written by: Ronnie Van Zant, Edward King, Gary Rossington
From the album: *Second Helping*
Label: MCA
Produced by: Al Kooper
Year: 1973
In answer to and challenging Neil Young's "Southern Man."

SWEET JANE

Artist: The Velvet Underground
Written by: Lou Reed
From the album: *Loaded*
Label: Cotillion
Produced by: The Velvet Underground
Year: 1970
Lou takes on the protest kids with a gleeful snarl (especially on the word *clerk*). Classic guitar part by Steve Hunter. Covered by Mott the Hoople (Columbia, '70), Lou Reed (RCA, '74), and Cowboy Junkies (RCA, '88), whose cowboys-on-Librium version was used in the '94 film *Natural Born Killers*.

SWEET LITTLE ROCK AND ROLLER

Artist: Chuck Berry
Written by: Chuck Berry
From the album: *Chuck Berry Is on Top*
Label: Chess
Produced by: Leonard Chess, Phil Chess
Year: 1959
One of his more moving tributes. Covered by Rod Stewart (Mercury, '74).

SWEET LITTLE SIXTEEN

Artist: Chuck Berry
Written by: Chuck Berry
From the album: *One Dozen Berrys*
Label: Chess
Produced by: Leonard Chess, Phil Chess
Year: 1958
In a genre rapidly becoming self-obsessed, this was the most astute song yet, promoting not only the inevitability of rock and roll, but the mundane actuality thereof.

SWEET LOVE

Artist: Anita Baker
Written by: Anita Baker, Louis Johnson, Gary Bias
From the album: *Rapture*
Label: Elektra
Produced by: Michael Powell
Year: 1986
Ballad breakthrough for the Sarah Vaughan-influenced singer.

SWEET LOVE

Artist: Commodores
Written by: Lionel B. Richie Jr., Ronald La Pread, Thomas McClary, Walter Orange, William King Jr., Milan Williams
From the album: *Movin' On*
Label: Motown
Produced by: James Carmichael, Commodores
Year: 1975
Lionel Richie displays an early ear for the Top 10.

SWEET LULLABY

Artist: Deep Forest
Written by: Eric Mouquet, Miguel Sanchez
From the album: *Deep Forever*
Label: 550 Music
Produced by: Dan Laxman
Year: 1994
Defining new age world music; a pygmy ballet from Australia.

SWEET NOTHIN'S

Artist: Brenda Lee
Written by: Ronnie Self
From the album: *Brenda Lee*
Label: Decca
Produced by: Owen Bradley
Year: 1960

The first Top 10 hit for the country belter had a little bit of rockabilly flavor.

SWEET OLD WORLD

Artist: Lucinda Williams
Written by: Lucinda Williams
From the album: *Sweet Old World*
Label: Chameleon
Produced by: Lucinda Williams, Gurf Morlix
Year: 1993
Eulogy for a friend. Covered by Emmylou Harris (Reprise, '95). Suggested segue: "What's Good" by Lou Reed.

SWEET PEA

Artist: Tommy Roe
Written by: Tommy Roe
From the album: *Sweet Pea*
Label: ABC
Produced by: Felton Jarvis
Year: 1966
Paving the way for bubblegum. Kazenetz and Katz were listening.

SWEET SEASONS

Artist: Carole King
Written by: Carole King, Toni Stern
From the album: *Carol King: Music*
Label: Ode
Produced by: Lou Adler
Year: 1971
Rehearsing for immortality, one album later.

SWEET SIXTEEN

Artist: B. B. King
Written by: B. B. King, Joe Josea
From the album: *Live in Cook County Jail*
Label: Kent
Year: 1961
His biggest R&B hit of the '60s was recorded in a location appropriate for its subject matter.

SWEET SIXTEEN BARS

Artist: Ray Charles
Written by: Ray Charles
From the album: *Great Ray Charles*
Label: Atlantic
Produced by: Ahmet Ertegun, Jerry Wexler
Year: 1958
In the tradition of Amos Milburn's "One Scotch, One Bourbon, One Beer."

SWEET SOUL MUSIC

Artist: Arthur Conley
Written by: Otis Redding, Arthur Conley
From the album: *Sweet Soul Music*
Label: Atco
Produced by: Otis Redding
Year: 1967
In the heyday of soul, this R&B/crossover classic just missed the top on both charts. Suggested segue: "Yeah Man" by Sam Cooke (RCA, '65).

SWEET SURRENDER

Artist: Sarah McLachlan
Written by: Sarah McLachlan, Pierre Marchand
From the album: *Surfacing*
Label: Arista
Producer: Pierre Marchand
Year: 1997
Establishing a new singer/songwriter icon.

(SWEET, SWEET BABY) SINCE YOU'VE BEEN GONE

Artist: Aretha Franklin
Written by: Aretha Franklin, Ted White
From the album: *Lady Soul*
Label: Atlantic
Produced by: Jerry Wexler
Year: 1967
Her fourth #1 R&B/Top 10 crossover, from her breakthrough soul album.

SWEET TALKIN' WOMAN

Artist: Electric Light Orchestra (ELO)
Written by: Jeff Lynne
From the album: *Out of the Blue*
Label: Jet
Produced by: Jeff Lynne
Year: 1977

SWEET THING

Artist: Rufus featuring Chaka Khan
Written by: Tony Maiden, Chaka Khan
From the album: *Rufusized*
Label: ABC
Produced by: Rufus
Year: 1975
#1 R&B/Top 10 crossover is Chaka's biggest hit with the band before going solo.

SWEETEST DROP, THE

Artist: Peter Murphy
Written by: Peter Murphy, Paul Statham
From the album: *Holy Smoke*
Label: Beggar's Banquet
Produced by: Mike Thorne, Peter Murphy
Year: 1992
Bauhaus founder at his most portentous.

SWEETEST TABU

Artist: Sade
Written by: Helen Folesade Adu (Sade), Martin Ditcham
From the album: *Promise*
Label: Epic
Produced by: Sade, Robin Miller
Year: 1986
Is Sade seductive voice.

SWEETEST THING I'VE EVER KNOWN, THE

Artist: Juice Newton

Written by: Otha Young
Label: RCA
Year: 1975
Pretty country/rock ballad. Re-release (Capitol, '81) was a #1 country/Top 10 crossover.

SWEETS FOR MY SWEET

Artist: The Drifters
Written by: Doc Pomus, Mort Shuman
From the album: *Up on the Roof, the Best of the Drifters*
Label: Atlantic
Produced by: Jerry Leiber, Mike Stoller
Year: 1961
Their third straight Top 10 R&B/Top 20 crossover.

SWIMMING SONG, THE

Artist: Loudon Wainwright III
Written by: Loudon Wainwright III
From the album: *Attempted Moustache*
Label: Columbia
Year: 1973
Investigating his suburban roots in Cheeverland.

SWINGIN' PARTY

Artist: The Replacements
Written by: Paul Westerberg
From the album: *Tim*
Label: Sire
Produced by: Tommy Erdelyi
Year: 1985
An alternative summit, as a Ramone produces the Replacements.

SWINGIN' SCHOOL

Artist: Bobby Rydell
Written by: Kal Mann, Bernie Lowe, Dave Appell
From the album: *Bobby's Biggest Hits*
Label: Cameo
Year: 1960
From the Tuesday Weld movie *Because They're Young*.

SWINGIN' THE BOOGIE

Artist: Hadda Brooks
Written by: Hadda Brooks
Label: Modern
Year: 1945
Swingin' instrumental.

SYLVIA'S MOTHER

Artist: Dr. Hook
Written by: Shel Silverstein
From the album: *Dr. Hook and the Medicine Show*
Label: Columbia
Produced by: Ron Haffkine
Year: 1972
Playboy magazine's best songwriting cartoonist finds a pop/rock group with similar sensibilities. Their biggest hit is among their straighter efforts. Segue:

"Mrs. Brown, You've Got a Lovely Daughter" by Herman's Hermits.

SYMPATHY FOR THE DEVIL

Artist: The Rolling Stones
Written by: Mick Jagger, Keith Richards
From the album: *Beggars Banquet*
Label: London
Produced by: Jimmy Miller
Year: 1968
At their most intense and focused; recorded the day after Bobby Kennedy was shot in L.A., it features Jagger extemporaneously shouting out who killed the Kennedys. A: It was you and me. Covered by Guns n' Roses in the film *Interview with the Vampire* (Geffen, '95).

SYMPHONY OF DESTRUCTION

Artist: Megadeth
Written by: Dave Mustaine
From the album: *Countdown to Extinction*
Label: Capitol
Year: 1992
Their signature sound and message.

T

TAINTED LOVE

Artist: Gloria Jones
Written by: Ed Cobb
Label: Champion
Year: 1964
Moody R&B gem, covered by Soft Cell (Sire, '81).

TAKE A BOW

Artist: Madonna
Written by: Kenny Edmunds (Babyface), Madonna Ciccone
From the album: *Bedtime Stories*
Label: Maverick
Produced by: Madonna, Babyface
Year: 1994
Her biggest hit.

TAKE A CHANCE ON ME

Artist: Abba
Written by: Benny Andersson
From the album: *The Album*
Label: Atlantic
Produced by: Benny Andersson, Bjorn Ulvaeus
Year: 1977
Broadway producers took a chance, and a hit show resulted.

TAKE A LETTER, MARIA

Artist: R. B. Greaves
Written by: Ronald Bertram Greaves (Sonny Childe)
From the album: *R. B. Greaves*
Label: Atco

Produced by: Ahmet Ertegun
Year: 1969
Top 10 R&B/#2 crossover for a cousin of Sam Cooke. Covered by Anthony Armstrong Jones on the country chart (Chart, '70).

TAKE A MESSAGE TO MARY

Artist: The Everly Brothers
Written by: Boudleaux Bryant, Felice Bryant
From the album: *The Fabulous Style of the Everly Brothers*
Label: Cadence
Produced by: Archie Bleyer
Year: 1959
Covered by Bob Dylan (Columbia, '69).

TAKE A PICTURE

Artist: Filter
Written by: Richard Patrick
From the album: *Title of Record*
Label: Warner Brothers
Year: 1999

TAKE GOOD CARE OF MY BABY

Artist: Dion
Written by: Gerry Goffin, Carole King
From the album: *Runaround Sue*
Label: Laurie
Produced by: Gene Schwartz
Year: 1961
Cover by the Hollyesque Bobby Vee (Liberty, '61) became his biggest hit.

TAKE IT AWAY

Artist: Paul McCartney
Written by: Paul McCartney
From the album: *Tug of War*
Label: Columbia
Produced by: George Martin
Year: 1982
Reuniting with the former Beatle producer Martin for another visit to the Top 10.

TAKE IT EASY

Artist: Eagles
Written by: Jackson Browne, Glenn Frey
From the album: *The Eagles*
Label: Asylum
Produced by: Glyn Johns
Year: 1972
Defining the sunbaked country folk soul of Winslow, Arizona, Jackson Browne makes it big in L.A.

TAKE IT ON THE RUN

Artist: Reo Speedwagon
Written by: Gary Richrath
From the album: *Hi Infidelity*
Label: Epic

Produced by: Kevin Cronin Jr., Gary Richrath, Kevin Beamish
Year: 1980
Follow-up to the #1 "Keep on Loving You."

TAKE IT SO HARD

Artist: Keith Richards
Written by: Keith Richards, Steve Jordan
From the album: *Talk Is Cheap*
Label: Virgin
Produced by: Steve Jordan, Keith Richards
Year: 1988
Rare solo effort by the Rolling Stones' lead guitarist/songwriter. Luckily, he never gave up his night job.

TAKE IT TO THE LIMIT

Artist: Eagles
Written by: Don Henley, Randy Meisner
From the album: *One of These Nights*
Label: Asylum
Produced by: Bill Szymczyk
Year: 1976
Hollywood goes country and vice-versa.

TAKE ME (JUST AS I AM)

Artist: Solomon Burke
Written by: Dan Penn, Spooner Oldham
From the album: *Best of Solomon Burke*
Label: Atlantic
Produced by: Chips Moman, Dan Penn
Year: 1966
Early classic from the Memphis songwriting team.

TAKE ME HOME, COUNTRY ROAD

Artist: John Denver
Written by: H. J. Deutschendorf Jr. (John Denver), Taffy Nivert, Bill Danoff
From the album: *Poems, Prayers and Promises*
Label: RCA
Produced by: Milt Okun
Year: 1971
Chad Mitchell trio leader graduates from folk to folk/rock with a rambling classic. Covered by Olivia Newton-John (MCA, '73), Toots and the Maytals (Island, '75).

TAKE ME HOME TONIGHT

Artist: Eddie Money
Written by: Mike Leeson, Peter Vale, Jeff Barry, Ellie Greenwich, Phil Spector
From the album: *Can't Hold Back*
Label: Columbia
Produced by: Ritchie Zito, Eddie Money
Year: 1986
For reviving the ineffable voice of Ronnie Spector in "Be My Baby" and not on a sample, either, Money is rewarded with his biggest hit.

TAKE ME IN YOUR ARMS (ROCK ME A LITTLE WHILE)

Artist: Kim Weston
Written by: Eddie Holland, Lamont Dozier, Brian Holland
Label: Gordy
Produced by: Brian Holland, Lamont Dozier
Year: 1965
Simmering soul ballad was a Top 10 R&B/Top 50 crossover.

TAKE ME TO THE PILOT

Artist: Elton John
Written by: Elton John, Bernie Taupin
From the album: *Elton John*
Label: MCA
Produced by: Gus Dudgeon
Year: 1970
Prelude to "Rocket Man."

TAKE ME TO THE RIVER

Artist: Al Green
Written by: Al Green, Mabon Hodges
From the album: *Al Green Explores Your Mind*
Label: Hi
Produced by: Willie Mitchell
Year: 1973
His gospel imagery attracts the rock crowd with a cover by Talking Heads (Sire, '78), Annie Lennox (Arista, '00).

TAKE MY BREATH AWAY (LOVE THEME FROM TOP GUN)

Artist: Berlin
Written by: Giorgio Moroder, Tom Whitlock.
From the album: *Count Three and Pray*
Label: Columbia
Produced by: Giorgio Moroder
Year: 1986
Big movie ballad from *Top Gun*.

TAKE OFF

Artist: Bob and Doug McKenzie
Written by: Kerry Crawford, Jonathan Goldsmith, Mark Giacommelli, Rick Moranis, Dave Thomas
From the album: *Great White North*
Label: Mercury
Produced by: Marc Giacommelli
Year: 1982
Canadian novelty by the *SCTV* geeks Moranis and Thomas. Twenty years later they'd still be doing this schtik.

TAKE ON ME

Artist: Aha
Written by: Pal Weaktaar, Mags Furuholem, Marten Harket
From the album: *Hunting High and Low*

Label: Warner Brothers
Produced by: Alan Tarney
Year: 1985
In this case, the video production and exposure of the song was at least as important to its success as the lyrics and (soaring) melody.

TAKE THE LONG WAY HOME

Artist: Supertramp
Written by: Richard Davies, Roger Hodgson
From the album: *Breakfast in America*
Label: A&M
Produced by: Pete Henderson, Supertramp
Year: 1979

TAKE THE MONEY AND RUN

Artist: Steve Miller Band
Written by: Steve Miller
From the album: *Fly Like an Eagle*
Label: Capitol
Produced by: Steve Miller
Year: 1976

TAKE THE SKINHEADS BOWLING

Artist: Camper Van Beethoven
Written by: Camper Van Beethoven
From the album: *Telephone Free Landslide Victory*
Label: Independent Project
Produced by: Camper Van Beethoven
Year: 1985
Cow punk attitude with a Middle Eastern flavor meets an American obsession.

TAKE THESE CHAINS FROM MY HEART

Artist: Hank Williams
Written by: Fred Rose, Hy Heath
Label: MGM
Produced by: Fred Rose
Year: 1953
Hank's seventh and last #1 country hit. Covered by Ray Charles (ABC Paramount, '63).

TAKE THIS LONGING

Artist: Leonard Cohen
Written by: Leonard Cohen
From the album: *New Skin for an Old Ceremony*
Label: Columbia
Produced by: Leonard Cohen, John Lissauer
Year: 1974
Deep in the maw of desire/depression.

TAKE TIME TO KNOW HER

Artist: Percy Sledge
Written by: Steve Davis
From the album: *Take Time to Know Her*
Label: Atlantic
Produced by: Quin Ivy, Marlin Greene
Year: 1968
Sledge in Otis Redding territory.

TAKE YOUR TIME (DO IT RIGHT) PART I

Artist: S.O.S. Band
Written by: Harold Clayton, Sigidi
From the album: *S.O.S.*
Label: Tabu
Produced by: Jimmy Jam, Terry Lewis
Year: 1980
Top 5 R&B/Top 5 crossover is their first and biggest hit.

TAKIN' CARE OF BUSINESS

Artist: Bachman Turner Overdrive
Written by: Randy Bachman
From the album: *Bachman Turner Overdrive II*
Label: Mercury
Produced by: Randy Bachman
Year: 1973
Roadhouse metal by a Guess Who graduate.

TAKIN' IT TO THE STREETS

Artist: The Doobie Brothers
Written by: Michael McDonald
From the album: *Takin' It to the Streets*
Label: Warner Brothers
Produced by: Ted Templeman
Year: 1976
Suggested segue: "Street Fighting Man" by the Rolling Stones.

TALENT SHOW

Artist: The Replacements
Written by: Paul Westerberg
From the album: *Don't Tell a Soul*
Label: Sire
Produced by: Matt Wallace, the Replacements
Year: 1989
Muted anthem for local bands everywhere.

TALES OF BRAVE ULYSSES

Artist: Cream
Written by: Eric Clapton
From the album: *Disraeli Gears*
Label: Atco
Produced by: Felix Pappalardi
Year: 1968
James Joycean psychedelia.

TALK DIRTY TO ME

Artist: Poison
Written by: Bobby Dall, C. C. Deville, Brett Michaels, Rikki Rockett
From the album: *Look What the Cat Dragged In*
Label: Enigma
Produced by: R. Browde
Year: 1987
Blow-dried hair band antics.

TALK OF THE TOWN

Artist: The Pretenders
Written by: Chrissie Hynde
From the album: *Pretenders II*
Label: Sire
Produced by: Chris Thomas
Year: 1982
One of their earliest and best singles.

TALK, TALK

Artist: The Music Machine
Written by: Thomas Sear Bonniwell
From the album: *(Turn on) The Music Machine*
Label: Original Sound
Produced by: Maurice Bercov
Year: 1966
L.A. Garage.

TALK TO ME

Artist: Stevie Nicks
Written by: Chas Sandford
From the album: *Rock a Little*
Label: Modern
Produced by: Jimmy Iovine, Rick Nowels
Year: 1986
Stevie's biggest solo hit. Nowels would move on to ex-Go-Go Belinda Carlisle.

(TALK TO ME OF) MENDOCINO

Artist: Kate and Anna McGarrigle
Written by: Kate McGarrigle
From the album: *Kate and Anna McGarrigle*
Label: Warner Brothers
Produced by: Joe Boyd, Greg Prestopino
Year: 1975
One of the rare female rambling classics. Covered by Linda Ronstadt (Asylum, '82).

TALK TO ME, TALK TO ME

Artist: Little Willie John
Written by: Joe Seneca
From the album: *There Is Someone in This World for Me*
Label: King
Produced by: Henry Glover
Year: 1958
His biggest hit of the '50s; Top 10 R&B/Top-20 crossover. Covered by Sunny & the Sunglows (Tear Drop, '63).

TALKING IN THE DARK

Artist: Elvis Costello
Written by: Declan McManus (Elvis Costello)
From the album: *Taking Liberties*
Label: Columbia
Produced by: Nick Lowe
Year: 1980
Covered by Linda Ronstadt (Asylum, '80).

TALKING IN YOUR SLEEP

Artist: The Romantics
Written by: Jimmy Marinos, Wally Palmar, Mike Skill, Coz Canler, Pete Solley
From the album: *In Heat*
Label: Nemperor
Produced by: Pete Solley
Year: 1983
Biggest hit for the skinny-tie '80s band. But it was no "What I Like About You."

TALKING LOUD AND SAYIN' NOTHING (PART II)

Artist: James Brown
Written by: James Brown, Bobby Byrd
From the album: *There It Is*
Label: Polydor
Produced by: James Brown
Year: 1972
#1 R&B/Top 30 crossover.

TALL COOL ONE

Artist: Robert Plant
Written by: Phil Johnstone, Robert Plant
From the album: *Now and Zen*
Label: Es Paranza
Produced by: T. Palmer, Robert Plant, Phil Johnstone
Year: 1988
With a guitar solo by former Zep-mate Jimmy Page.

TALL COOL ONE

Artist: Wailers
Written by: Kent Morrill, John Greek, Rich Dangel
From the album: *The Fabulous Wailers*
Label: Golden Crest
Year: 1959
Grandfathering grunge: out of Olympia, Washington, a "Harlem Nocturne" of the Northwest. Hendrix was listening. The Sonics were listening. Queensryche, maybe not. Covered by the Kingsmen (Wand, '65).

TALL PAUL

Artist: Annette
Written by: Bob Roberts, Bob Sherman, Dick Sherman
From the album: *Annette: The Story of My Teens*, Disneyland
Produced by: Tutti Camarata
Year: 1959
As a measure of pop music's cyclical nature, the rock and roll generation's first sex symbol, like the late 90's crop, was manufactured by Walt Disney. This ode to Annette's purported boyfriend, the short Paul Anka, was appropriately scripted by Disney's house writers, the Sherman Brothers. Oddly, it was originally written for Annette's sister Mouseketeer, Judy Harriet, but Annette ultimately got the song and all those beach movies with medium-sized Frankie (Avalon).

TALLAHASSEE LASSIE

Artist: Freddy Cannon
Written by: Frank Slay, Bob Crewe, Frederick A. Picariello (Freddy Cannon)
From the album: *The Explosive Freddy Cannon*
Label: Swan
Year: 1959
The Philly sound in its rock and roll incarnation.

TAMMY

Artist: Debbie Reynolds
Written by: Jay Livingston, Ray Evans
From the album: *Tammy and the Bachelor Soundtrack*
Label: Coral
Year: 1957
The ultimate wispy, ethereal girl singer and song: Olivia Newton-John, nine years old, saw her future. Natalie Merchant and Harriet Wheeler, not even born yet, would carry it on. Paul Simon, sixteen-years-old, would marry Debbie's daughter, Carrie, briefly.

TANGERINE

Artist: Led Zeppelin
Written by: Jimmy Page
From the album: *Led Zeppelin III*
Label: Atlantic
Produced by: Jimmy Page
Year: 1970
Page on steel guitar, mapping out the master plan for "Stairway to Heaven."

TANGLED UP IN BLUE

Artist: Bob Dylan
Written by: Bob Dylan
From the album: *Blood on the Tracks*
Label: Columbia
Produced by: Phil Ramone, Bob Dylan
Year: 1975
Another convoluted gem from the comeback album, with assistance from Dylan's brother David. But he would never come all the way back, and neither would the sound, the fury, or the dreams he inspired. Segue: "Only Want to Be With You" by Hootie and the Blowfish.

TAPESTRY

Artist: Carole King
Written by: Carole King
From the album: *Tapestry*
Label: Ode
Produced by: Lou Adler
Year: 1971
Title tune from her landmark album of homemade Brooklyn soul, recorded in L.A.

TARZAN BOY

Artist: Baltimora
Written by: Naimy Hackett, Maurizio Bassi
From the album: *Living in the Background*
Label: Capitol
Produced by: Maurizio Bassi

Year: 1986
Italian novelty.

TASTE OF HONEY, A

Artist: Bobby Scott
Written by: Ric Marlow, Bobby Scott
From the album: *A Taste of Honey*
Year: 1960
Classic jazz/rock instrumental first performed in the play *A Taste of Honey*. Covered by Martin Denny (Liberty, '62), the Beatles (Capitol, '64), Herb Alpert & the Tijuana Brass (A&M, '65). Used in film version of the play, starring Rita Tushingham. Segue: "Brandy (You're a Fine Girl)" by Looking Glass.

TAXI

Artist: Harry Chapin
Written by: Harry Chapin
From the album: *Heads and Tails*
Label: Elektra
Produced by: Paul Leka
Year: 1972
Former filmmaker spins an epic length saga, redeemed by the cello solo.

TAXI BLUES

Artist: Little Richard
Written by: Leonard Feather
Label: Camden
Year: 1951
His first R&B effort, before he caught the rock and roll bug, written by a noted jazz commentator.

TAXMAN

Artist: The Beatles
Written by: George Harrison
From the album: *Revolver*
Label: Capitol
Produced by: George Martin
Year: 1966
George at his most believable. Segue: "Batman" by Neil Hefti.

TEACH YOUR CHILDREN

Artist: Crosby, Stills, Nash & Young
Written by: Graham Nash
From the album: *Deja Vu*
Label: Atlantic
Produced by: Crosby, Stills, Nash & Young
Year: 1970
Jerry Garcia on pedal steel. Has since become a theme song for various educational and social public service organizations.

TEACHER, TEACHER

Artist: Rockpile
Written by: Eddie Phillips, Ken Pickett
From the album: *Seconds of Pleasure*
Label: Columbia
Produced by: Rockpile
Year: 1980

Only semihit from the only album by the Dave Edmunds/Nick Lowe UK one-off super/backing group.

TEAR DROPS

Artist: Lee Andrews and the Hearts
Written by: Roy Calhoun, Edwin Charles, Helen Stanley
From the album: *Main Line*
Label: Chess
Year: 1957
Doo-wop, Philadelphia style.

TEAR IT UP

Artist: Johnny Burnette and the Rock and Roll Trio
Written by: Johnny Burnette, Dorsey Burnette, Paul Burlison
From the album: *Johnny Burnette and the Rock and Roll Trio*
Label: Coral
Produced by: Owen Bradley
Year: 1956
The first release by the first underground rock and roll band. Covered by the Cramps (IRS, '80), Rod Stewart (Warner Brothers, '81).

TEAR STAINED LETTER

Artist: Richard Thompson
Written by: Richard Thompson
From the album: *Hand of Kindness*
Label: Hannibal
Produced by: Joe Boyd
Year: 1983
A bitter, beer-hall jig. Covered by Patty Loveless (Epic, '96).

TEAR THE ROOF OFF THE SUCKER (GIVE UP THE FUNK)

Artist: Parliament
Written by: George Clinton, William "Bootsie" Collins, Jerome Brailey
From the album: *Mothership Connection*
Label: Casablanca
Produced by: George Clinton
Year: 1976
Clinton's biggest hit from all his various incarnations.

TEARDROPS FROM MY EYES

Artist: Ruth Brown and Her Rhythm Makers
Written by: Rudolph Toombs
Label: Atlantic
Year: 1950
#1 R&B smash by former Lucky Millinder front woman, from the pen of one of the genre's finest writers.

TEARDROPS ON YOUR LETTER

Artist: The Midnighters
Written by: Henry Glover
From the album: *Hank Ballard's Biggest Hits*
Label: King
Produced by: Henry Glover
Year: 1959
Inspired no covers, ignited no crazes, and lapsed in the Bottom 20, unlike its legendary B-side, "The Twist."

TEARDROPS WILL FALL

Artist: Dickey Doo and the Don'ts
Written by: Marion Smith, Dickey Doo
Label: Swan
Year: 1959
Rescued from cruel obscurity by Ry Cooder (Reprise, '72).

TEARS IN HEAVEN

Artist: Eric Clapton
Written by: Eric Clapton, Will Jennings
From the album: *Rush Soundtrack*
Label: Reprise
Produced by: Russ Titelman
Year: 1991
This exquisite soundtrack ballad from a film about drug addicts enabled Clapton to express his grief over losing his young son in a tragic fall. Winner of three Grammys.

TEARS OF A CLOWN, THE

Artist: The Miracles
Written by: Smokey Robinson, Henry Cosby, Stevie Wonder
From the album: *Make It Happen*
Label: Tamla
Produced by: Smokey Robinson, Henry Cosby
Year: 1967
Biggest hit for Smokey Robinson and the Miracles, a #1 R&B/#1 crossover, was first released in the UK, where it also hit #1. The fruition of Smokey's literary soul aspirations, it was already three years old at the time. Covered by the English Beat (2-Tone, '79).

TEARS OF RAGE

Artist: The Band
Written by: Bob Dylan, Richard Manuel
From the album: *Music from Big Pink*
Label: Capitol
Produced by: John Simon, The Band
Year: 1968
A recovery ballad, cowritten by one who did (Dylan), and one who didn't (Manuel).

TEARS ON MY PILLOW

Artist: Little Anthony and the Imperials
Written by: Sylvester Bradford, Al Lewis
From the album: *We Are Little Anthony and the Imperials*
Label: End
Produced by: George Goldner
Year: 1958
Echoes of a golden age (echoes of "Earth Angel") and, according to Bob Dylan, the last song of the rock and roll era. Covered by Kylie Minogue (Geffen, '90).

TEARS TO FORGET

Artist: Soundgarden
Written by: Chris Cornell, Kim Thayil, Hino Yamagoto
From the album: *Deep Six*
Label: C/Z
Year: 1985
Laying their claim as the first grunge group. Song would later appear on their first EP.

TEE'S HAPPY

Artist: Northend
Written by: Arthur Baker, A. Carbone, Presto
Label: Deep Beats
Year: 1983
House anthem dedicated to pioneering deejay Tee Scott. Segue: "Holiday" by Madonna.

TEEN AGE CRUSH

Artist: Tommy Sands
Written by: Audrey Allison, Joe Allison
From the album: *Steady Date with Tommy Sands*
Label: Capitol
Year: 1957
Introduced on the TV drama *The Singing Idol*. Teen idol Sands would never recover from being verbally ripped to shreds by Bob Dylan on *The Les Crane Show* a few years later.

TEEN ANGEL

Artist: Mark Dinning
Written by: Jean Dinning Surrey
From the album: *Teen Angel*
Label: MGM
Produced by: Jim Vinneau
Year: 1959
Chart-topping weeper, exploiting the somber mood of a generation still mourning their first rock and roll casualties, Richie Valens and Buddy Holly.

TEEN ANGST (WHAT THE WORLD NEEDS NOW)

Artist: Cracker
Written by: David Lowery
From the album: *Kerosene Hat*
Label: Virgin
Produced by: Don Smith
Year: 1991
Lowery leavens his acid punk vision of Camper Van Beethoven with a solid belt of alt/rock.

TEEN BEAT

Artist: Sandy Nelson
Written by: Sandy Nelson, Arthur Egnoian
Label: Original Sound
Year: 1959
Drum solo.

TEEN TOWN

Artist: Weather Report
Written by: Jaco Pastorius
From the album: *Heavy Weather*
Label: Columbia
Produced by: Joe Zawinul, Jaco Pastorius
Year: 1977
Bass workout from a master, Jaco Pastorius.

TEENAGE HEAD

Artist: Flamin' Groovies
Written by: Roy A. Loney, Cyril Jordan
From the album: *Teenage Head*
Label: Buddah
Produced by: Richard Robinson
Year: 1971
The anti-Beach Boys return to the East Coast. Covered by Ducks Deluxe (RCA, '75).

TEENAGE HEAVEN

Artist: Eddie Cochran
Written by: Eddie Cochran, Jerry Capeheart
Label: Liberty
Year: 1959
Pre-posthumous tribute/prophecy was his last chart single.

TEENAGE IDOL

Artist: Rick Nelson
Written by: Jack Lewis
From the album: *It's up to You*
Label: Imperial
Produced by: Ozzie Nelson, Jimmy Haskell
Year: 1962
Written for a Bobby Vee movie. Suggested segue: "Jukebox Hero" by Foreigner.

TEENAGE KICKS

Artist: The Undertones
Written by: John O'Neill
From the album: *Teenage Kicks*
Label: Good Vibrations
Produced by: the Undertones
Year: 1978
Irish answer to the Buzzcocks. Influential British DJ John Peel's all-time favorite single.

TEENAGE LOBOTOMY

Artist: The Ramones
Written by: Douglas Colvin, John Cummings, Jeff Hyman, Thomas Erdelyi
From the album: *The Ramones*
Label: Sire
Produced by: Craig Leon
Year: 1976
A one-joke band, repeating endlessly, endlessly repeatable.

TEEN-AGE RIOT

Artist: Sonic Youth
Written by: Sonic Youth
From the album: *Daydream Nation*
Label: Blast First
Produced by: Nicholas Sansone, Sonic Youth
Year: 1988
Achieving their longed-for guitar drone epiphany. Suggested segue: "Marquee Moon" by Television, from the same neighborhood a decade earlier.

TEENAGE SUICIDE (DON'T DO IT)

Artist: Big Fun
Written by: Don Dixon
From the album: *Heathers Soundtrack*
Year: 1989
The big song from the teen cult movie *Heathers*, sung by the Athens Mafia—Mitch Easter, Don Dixon, Marti Jones and Angie Carlson.

TEENAGER IN LOVE, A

Artist: Dion and the Belmonts
Written by: Doc Pomus, Mort Shuman
From the album: *A Teenager in Love*
Label: Laurie
Produced by: Gene Schwartz
Year: 1959
This mournful, coming of puberty epic is Dion and the Belmonts' biggest hit, aside from their cover of "Where or When."

TEENAGER'S ROMANCE

Artist: Ricky Nelson
Written by: Dave Gillam
From the album: *Teen Time*
Label: Verve
Produced by: Ricky Nelson, Jimmy Haskell
Year: 1957
B-side of his first single, which actually did better than the A-side, "I'm Walking," a cover of the Fats Domino tune.

TELEGRAM SAM

Artist: T. Rex
Written by: Marc Feld (Marc Bolan)
From the album: *The Slider*
Label: Reprise
Produced by: Tony Visconti
Year: 1972
#1 UK. Covered by Bauhaus (4AD, '81). Bolan's biggest US hit, aside from "Bang a Gong," clocking in at #67.

TELEPHONE LINE

Artist: Electric Light Orchestra (ELO)
Written by: Jeff Lynne
From the album: *A New World Record*
Label: United Artists/Jet
Produced by: Jeff Lynne
Year: 1976

TELEPHONE ROAD

Artist: Steve Earle
Written by: Steve Earle
From the album: *El Corazon*
Label: Warner Brothers
Produced by: Twangtrust
Year: 1997
A rural slice of alt/country life.

TELL HER ABOUT IT

Artist: Billy Joel
Written by: Billy Joel
From the album: *An Innocent Man*
Label: Columbia
Produced by: Phil Ramone
Year: 1983
Revisiting Motown by way of the Brill Building, out of his Long Island home studio.

TELL HER NO

Artist: The Zombies
Written by: Rod Argent
From the album: *The Zombies*
Label: Parrot
Produced by: Ken Jones
Year: 1964
Rod Argent would move on to Argent.

TELL HIM

Artist: The Exciters
Written by: Bert Burns (Bert Russell)
From the album: *Tell Him*
Label: United Artists
Produced by: Jerry Leiber, Mike Stoller
Year: 1963
Aggressive girl-group advice in the Brill Building/R&B mode.

TELL HIM NO

Artist: Travis and Bob
Written by: Travis Pritchett
Label: Sandy
Year: 1959
They were no Skip and Flip.

TELL IT LIKE IT IS

Artist: Aaron Neville
Written by: Lee Diamond, George Davis
From the album: *Tell It Like It Is*
Label: Par Lo
Produced by: George David
Year: 1966
Essential #1 R&B/Top 10 crossover for the New Orleans soul man, Neville.

TELL LAURA I LOVE HER

Artist: Ray Peterson
Written by: Jeff Barry, Ben Raleigh
From the album: *Tell Laura I Love Her*
Label: RCA
Produced by: Dick Pierce
Year: 1960
The essential teen car wreck epic.

TELL MAMA

Artist: Etta James
Written by: Clarence Carter, Marcus Daniel, Wilbur Terrell
From the album: *Tell Mama*
Label: Cadet
Produced by: Rick Hall
Year: 1967
Biggest crossover hit for the famed soul belter.

TELL ME (YOU'RE COMING BACK)

Artist: The Rolling Stones
Written by: Mick Jagger, Keith Richards
From the album: *The Rolling Stones*
Label: London
Produced by: Andrew Loog-Oldham
Year: 1964
Introducing the formidable blues/rock songwriting team of Jagger and Richards to each other and the American public. Stones' first Top 40 hit also introduces Harvey Keitel in the rock and roll-obsessed '73 Martin Scorsese film classic *Mean Streets*.

TELL ME SO

Artist: The Orioles
Written by: Deborah Chessler
Label: Jubilee
Year: 1949
#1 R&B classic in the dawning days of doo-wop.

TELL ME SOMETHING GOOD

Artist: Rufus
Written by: Stevie Wonder
From the album: *Rags to Rufus*
Label: ABC
Produced by: Rufus, Bob Monaco
Year: 1974
Their breakthrough hit, a Top 5 R&B/Top 5 crossover, after which lead singer Chaka Khan began to get equal billing.

TELL ME WHY

Artist: The Beatles
Written by: John Lennon, Paul McCartney
From the album: *A Hard Day's Night*
Label: United Artists
Produced by: George Martin
Year: 1964

TELL ME WHY

Artist: Norman Fox and the Rob Roys
Written by: Marshall Helfand, Don Carter
Label: Back Beat
Year: 1957
Doo-wop gem, covered by the Dion-less Belmonts (Sabrina, '61).

TELL THAT GIRL TO SHUT UP

Artist: Holly and the Italians

Written by: Holly Vincent
From the album: *The Right to Be Italian*
Label: Virgin
Produced by: Chris Butler
Year: 1981
The voice of the beehive, from the hairdresser's mouth, produced by an Ohio auteur.

TELL THE TRUTH

Artist: The 5 Royales
Written by: Lowman Pauling
Label: King
Year: 1957
Covered by Ray Charles (Atlantic, '60), Ike and Tina Turner (Warner Brothers, '65).

TELLING ME LIES

Artist: Linda Thompson
Written by: Linda Thompson, Betsy Cook
From the album: *One Clear Moment*
Label: Warner Brothers
Produced by: Hugh Murphey
Year: 1985
The more dispassionate half of Richard and Linda Thompson, showcases her anger, in a pleasant Fleetwood Macian setting. Covered by Dolly Parton, Linda Ronstadt, and Emmylou Harris as the Trio (Warner Brothers, '86).

TELSTAR

Artist: The Tornadoes
Written by: Joe Meek
From the album: *The Original Telstar*
Label: London
Produced by: Joe Meek
Year: 1962
Soaring instrumental is the first British single to top the American Top 40 and the top UK single of 1962, powered by Joe Meek's clavioline. An invasion was imminent.

TEMPTATION

Artist: Heaven 17
Written by: Glenn Gregory, Ian Craig Marsh, Martyn Ware
From the album: *The Luxury Gap*
Label: Sire
Produced by: Greg Walsh, B.E.F.
Year: 1982
Terrific synthesizer workout.

TEMPTATION

Artist: New Order
Written by: New Order
From the album: *1981–1982*
Label: Factory
Produced by: New Order
Year: 1982
Out of the ashes of Joy Division, a new British techno-dance combo emerges.

TEMPTED

Artist: Squeeze

Written by: Chris Difford, Glenn Tilbrook
From the album: *East Side Story*
Label: A&M
Produced by: Elvis Costello, Roger Bechirian
Year: 1981
Paul Carrack's best vocal with the band was their first American hit.

TEN COMMANDMENTS OF LOVE, THE

Artist: The Moonglows
Written by: Marshall Paul
Label: Chess
Year: 1958
This Top 10 R&B/Top 30 crossover is a cornerstone doo-wop philosophical statement, even though it's a commandment short.

10,000 THINGS

Artist: Green River
Written by: Jeff Ament, Mark Arm, Stone Gossard, Alex Vincent, Bruce Fairweather
From the album: *Deep Six*
Label: C/Z
Year: 1985
Landmark early grunge classic. Ament and Gossard would move on to Pearl Jam.

TENDER LOVE

Artist: Force MD'S
Written by: James Harris III, Terry Lewis
From the album: *Chillin'*
Label: Warner Brothers
Produced by: Jimmy Jam, Terry Lewis
Year: 1985
Evoking the great doo-wop ballads of old; from the film *Krush Groove*.

TENDER LOVER

Artist: Babyface
Written by: Kenny Edmunds (Babyface), Antonio Reid (L. A. Reid), Pete Q. Smith
From the album: *Tender Lover*
Label: Solar
Produced by: Babyface, L. A. Reid
Year: 1989

TENNESSEE

Artist: Arrested Development
Written by: Todd (Speech) Thomas
From the album: *3 Years 5 Months and 2 Days in the Life Of*
Label: Chrysalis
Produced by: Speech
Year: 1992
Masquerading as a painful history lesson, this is the roots-meets-rap breakthrough single, written after Thomas lost two close relatives in quick succession, briefly united the warring camps of hip hop and alternative music under the world-beat banner, giving rise to the jazz/rock/rap fusions of

US3, Digable Planets, Rusted Root and Zap Mama.

TENNESSEE FLAT-TOP BOX

Artist: Johnny Cash
Written by: Johnny Cash
From the album: *Ring of Fire: The Best of Johnny Cash*
Label: Columbia
Produced by: Don Law, Frank Jones
Year: 1961
Covered by daughter Rosanne Cash (Columbia, '87).

TENTH AND GREENWICH

Artist: Beatrice Winde
Written by: Melvin Van Peebles
From the album: *Ain't Supposed to Die a Natural Death Original Cast Album*
Label: A&M
Year: 1971
Haunting ode to the Women's House of Detention, introduced in Van Peebles' classic musical prelude to the blaxploitation heyday of '70s soul.

TENTH AVENUE FREEZE OUT

Artist: Bruce Springsteen
Written by: Bruce Springsteen
From the album: *Born to Run*
Label: Columbia
Produced by: Jon Landau, Mike Appel, Bruce Springsteen
Year: 1975
Being the Belmar, New Jersey biography of the E Street Band.

TEQUILA

Artist: The Champs
Written by: Chuck Rio
From the album: *Go Champs Go*
Label: Challenge
Produced by: Joe Johnson
Year: 1958
Intoxicating instrumental, originally the B-side of "Train to Nowhere."

TEQUILA SUNRISE

Artist: Eagles
Written by: Don Henley, Glenn Frey
From the album: *Desperado*
Label: Asylum
Produced by: Glyn Johns
Year: 1973
A parched anthem for the fern-bar crowd.

TERRAPIN

Artist: Syd Barrett
Written by: Syd Barrett
From the album: *The Madcap Laughs/Syd Barrett*

Label: Harvest
Produced by: Malcolm Jones
Year: 1974
Pink Floyd cofounder-cum-acid-casualty becomes the psychedelic metal answer to Jonathan Richman.

TERRIFYING LOVE

Artist: Marshall Crenshaw
Written by: Marshall Crenshaw
From the album: *Downtown*
Label: Warner Brothers
Produced by: T-Bone Burnette
Year: 1985
Buddy Holly graduates, moves in with Peggy Sue, but it turns out to be a nightmare.

TEST FOR ECHO

Artist: Rush
Written by: Geddy Lee, Alex Lifeson, Neil Peart, Pye Dubois
From the album: *Test for Echo*
Label: Atlantic
Year: 1996

TEXAS CHAINSAW MASSACRE BOOGIE

Artist: The Tyla Gang
Written by: Sean Tyla
From the album: *Hits Greatest Stiffs*
Label: Stiff
Year: 1976
Tyla would move on to Ducks Deluxe.

TEXAS FLOOD

Artist: Stevie Ray Vaughan & Double Trouble
Written by: Larry Davis, Joseph Wade Scott
From the album: *Texas Flood*
Label: Columbia
Produced by: Stevie Ray Vaughan, Double Trouble, Richard Mullen
Year: 1983
Original by Larry Davis in 1958; turned into a guitar extravaganza by the Austin legend.

THANK GOD I FOUND YOU

Artist: Mariah Carey with Joe and 98 Degrees
Written by: James Harris III (Jimmy Jam), Terry Lewis, Mariah Carey
From the album: *Rainbow*
Label: Columbia
Year: 1998

THANK GOD I'M A COUNTRY BOY

Artist: John Denver
Written by: John Sommers
From the album: *Back Home Again*
Label: RCA
Produced by: Milt Okun
Year: 1974
#1 country/#1 crossover.

THANK GOD IT'S FRIDAY

Artist: Love and Kisses
Written by: Robert Costandinos
From the album: *Thank God It's Friday Soundtrack*
Label: Casablanca
Produced by: Robert Costandinos
Year: 1978
Disco self-promotion from the film. But it was no *Saturday Night Fever*.

THANK YOU

Artist: Dido
Written by: Dido Armstrong, Paul Herman
From the album: *No Angel*
Label: Arista
Produced by: Dido, Rollo
Year: 1999
Finding comfort in the everyday nuances of a relationship, Dido moves into her own as a soloist. Used behind the credits in the Gwyneth Paltrow film *Sliding Doors* and, even more prominently, by Eminem in "Stan," where Dido joined him in the video.

THANK YOU (FALETTINGME BE MICE ELF AGIN)

Artist: Sly & the Family Stone
Written by: Sylvester Stewart
From the album: *Greatest Hits*
Label: Epic
Produced by: Sly Stone
Year: 1970
Their second #1 R&B/#1 crossover: a funk landmark, fashionable, irresistible, irreverent, and bouncy.

THANK YOU FOR BEING A FRIEND

Artist: Andrew Gold
Written by: Andrew Gold
From the album: *All This and Heaven Too*
Label: Asylum
Produced by: Andrew Gold, Brock Walsh
Year: 1978
Resurfaced as the theme song for the TV show *The Golden Girls*.

THANK YOU GIRL

Artist: The Beatles
Written by: John Lennon, Paul McCartney
From the album: *Jolly What! the Beatles and Frank Ifield*
Label: Vee Jay
Produced by: George Martin
Year: 1963
The B-side of the original release of "From Me to You."

THANK YOU JOHN

Artist: Alex Chilton
Written by: Willie Turbington
From the album: *Feudalist Tarts*

Label: Big Time
Produced by: Alex Chilton
Year: 1985
A critical cult hero returns to the fold with a great song, not his own.

THANK YOU, PRETTY BABY

Artist: Brook Benton
Written by: Clyde Otis, Brook Benton
Label: Mercury
Produced by: Clyde Otis
Year: 1959
#1 R&B/Top 20 crossover.

THANKS FOR MY CHILD

Artist: Cheryl Pepsii Riley
Written by: Full Force
From the album: *Me, Myself and I*
Label: Columbia
Produced by: Full Force
Year: 1988
#1 R&B/Top 40 crossover was a rallying cry for single mothers.

THAT GIRL

Artist: Stevie Wonder
Written by: Stevie Wonder
From the album: *Stevie Wonder's Original Musiquarium*
Label: Tamla
Produced by: Stevie Wonder
Year: 1982
#1 R&B/Top 10 crossover.

THAT GIRL BELONGS TO YESTERDAY

Artist: Gene Pitney
Written by: Mick Jagger, Keith Richards
From the album: *It Hurts to Be in Love*
Label: Musicor
Year: 1964
Big hit in England with a custom-penned early Jagger/Richards gem.

THAT IS ROCK AND ROLL

Artist: The Coasters
Written by: Jerry Leiber, Mike Stoller
Label: Atco
Produced by: Jerry Leiber, Mike Stoller
Year: 1959
Critically revered B-side of "Along Came Jones." Covered by Sylvester and the Hot Band (Blue Thumb, '73).

THAT LADY

Artist: The Isley Brothers
Written by: Ernie Isley, Marvin Isley, Chris Jasper
From the album: *3 + 3*
Label: T-Neck
Produced by: The Isley Brothers
Year: 1973
Funk rock classic began life as "Who's That Lady" (United Artists, '64); updated by the younger generation (with cousin Chris) for their last Top 10 hit, courtesy of Ernie's ineffable wah wah tribute to former band member, Jimi Hendrix.

THAT OLD SWEET ROLL

Artist: The City
Written by: Carole King, Gerry Goffin
From the album: *Now That Everything's Been Said*
Label: Ode
Produced by: Lou Adler
Year: 1968
Transplanted Broadway jazz. Covered by Blood, Sweat and Tears (Columbia, '71) as "Hi De Ho."

THAT SMELL

Artist: Lynyrd Skynyrd
Written by: Ronnie Van Zant, Allen Collins
From the album: *Street Survivors*
Label: MCA
Produced by: Lynyrd Skynyrd
Year: 1977
The smell of death would follow Skynyrd after the release of this album, when three band members went down in a plane crash.

THAT SONG ABOUT THE MIDWAY

Artist: Joni Mitchell
Written by: Joni Mitchell
From the album: *Clouds*
Label: Reprise
Produced by: Joni Mitchell
Year: 1969
Too long at the affair. Covered by Bonnie Raitt (Warner Brothers, '74).

THAT SUMMER FEELING

Artist: Modern Lovers
Written by: Jonathan Richman
From the album: *Jonathan Richman Sings*
Label: Sire
Produced by: Peter Bernstein
Year: 1983
A stab at solo greatness finds the inner child still beaming.

THAT'LL BE THE DAY

Artist: The Crickets
Written by: Buddy Holly, Norman Petty, Jerry Allison
From the album: *The Chirpin' Crickets*
Label: Brunswick
Produced by: Norman Petty
Year: 1957
Inspired by Norman Petty's production of "Party Doll" by fellow Texan and fellow Buddy, Knox, Holly brought his band to Clovis, New Mexico, to recut this flop on Decca. Like the Rockabilly Trio (already defunct) and the Blue Caps (peaked), the Crickets were a band: unlike the others, and more like the Beatles, they had Buddy Holly, the first great rock and roll singer/songwriter, who had a catalogue of future standards in his head, just waiting to be unloaded. The title was derived from the John Wayne movie, *The Searchers*. The first song John Lennon learned on guitar was covered by the Quarrymen (the future Beatles) in '58.

THAT'S ALL

Artist: Genesis
Written by: Phil Collins, Tony Banks, Mike Rutherford
From the album: *Genesis*
Label: Atlantic
Produced by: Hugh Padgham, Genesis
Year: 1983
Their first US Top 10.

THAT'S ALL RIGHT, MAMA

Artist: Arthur Big Boy Crudup
Written by: Arthur Crudup
From the album: *That's All Right, Mama*
Label: RCA
Produced by: Lester Melrose
Year: 1947
Essential Mississippi bar band blues. Covered by Elvis Presley in his legendary first Sun session in Memphis, July 7, 1954, and released two weeks later, in a recording later deemed the single most momentous turning point in the history of rock and roll. Covered by Bob Dylan but not used on the *Freewheelin'* album (Columbia, '63).

THAT'S ALL YOU GOTTA DO

Artist: Brenda Lee
Written by: Jerry Reed
From the album: *Brenda Lee*
Label: Decca
Produced by: Owen Bradley
Year: 1960
A-side of "I'm Sorry" enabled country wild man Jerry Reed to eventually get hot himself.

THAT'S AMORE

Artist: Dean Martin
Written by: Jack Brooks, Harry Warren
Label: Capitol
Produced by: Lee Gillette
Year: 1953
There's no discounting Dino's influence on the early—as well as the later—Elvis Presley.

THAT'S HOW STRONG MY LOVE IS

Artist: Otis Redding
Written by: O.V. Wright, Roosevelt Jamison
From the album: *The Great Otis Redding Sings Soul Ballads*
Label: Volt

Produced by: Steve Cropper
Year: 1965
Wright cut the song, too, on a small local label.

THAT'S JUST WHAT YOU ARE

Artist: Aimee Mann
Written by: Aimee Mann, Jon Bryon
From the album: *I'm with Stupid*
Label: Geffen
Produced by: Jon Brion
Year: 1994
Much cooler than her tempestuous sisters.

THAT'S OLD FASHIONED

Artist: The Everly Brothers
Written by: Bill Giant, Bernie Baum, Florence Kaye
From the album: *The Golden Hits of the Everly Brothers*
Label: Warner Brothers
Produced by: Wesley Rose
Year: 1962
Their 14TH and last appearance on the Top 10.

THAT'S ROCK 'N' ROLL

Artist: Shaun Cassidy
Written by: Eric Carmen
From the album: *Shaun Cassidy*
Label: Warner Brothers
Produced by: Michael Lloyd
Year: 1977
Teenybop pop by David's brother.

THAT'S THE JOINT

Artist: Funky Four Plus Two
Written by: Keith Caesar, Jeff Myree, Rodney Stone, Sharon Green, Kevin Smith, Sylvia Robinson, Jiggs Chase
Produced by: Sylvia Inc., Jigsaw Inc.
Label: Sugar Hill
Year: 1981
Legendary early rap track.

THAT'S THE WAY (I LIKE IT)

Artist: K. C. and the Sunshine Band
Written by: Harry Casey, Richard Finch
From the album: *K. C. and the Sunshine Band*
Label: TK
Produced by: Harry Casey, Richard Finch
Year: 1975
Their second straight #1 R&B/#1 crossover, the only time a white-led act has accomplished this feat in the post-Elvis era.

THAT'S THE WAY I'VE ALWAYS HEARD IT SHOULD BE

Artist: Carly Simon
Written by: Carly Simon, Jacob Brackman
From the album: *Carly Simon*
Label: Elektra
Produced by: Eddie Kramer
Year: 1971
Performed in an early rock video by Carly at her Upper West Side New York apartment, in a floor-length pink gown, as broadcast on PBS's lost classic TV series *The Great American Dream Machine*.

THAT'S THE WAY LOVE GOES

Artist: Janet Jackson
Written by: James Harris III, Terry Lewis, Janet Jackson
From the album: *janet*
Label: Virgin
Produced by: Jimmy Jam, Terry Lewis, Janet Jackson
Year: 1993
A #1 R&B/#1 crossover.

THAT'S THE WAY LOVE IS

Artist: Bobby Bland
Written by: Deadric Malone
Label: Duke
Year: 1963
#1 R&B/Top 40 crossover.

THAT'S THE WAY LOVE IS

Artist: Marvin Gaye
Written by: Norman Whitfield, Barrett Strong
From the album: *M.P.G.*
Label: Tamla
Produced by: Norman Whitfield
Year: 1969

THAT'S THE WAY OF THE WORLD

Artist: Earth, Wind & Fire
Written by: Maurice White, Philip Bailey, Larry Dunn
From the album: *That's the Way of the World*
Label: Columbia
Produced by: Maurice White, Charles Stepney
Year: 1975
Title tune from their movie debut.

THAT'S WHAT FRIENDS ARE FOR

Artist: Rod Stewart
Written by: Burt Bacharach, Carole Bayer Sager
From the album: *Nightshift Soundtrack*
Label: Warner Brothers
Year: 1982
Introduced by Rod in the film *Nightshift*. Cover by Dionne Warwick and Friends—Elton John, Gladys Knight and Stevie Wonder (Arista, '85)—was a #1 R&B/#1 crossover and Song of the Year Grammy winner, with the proceeds for that recording going to the American Foundation for AIDS Research.

THAT'S WHEN I REACH FOR MY REVOLVER

Artist: Mission of Burma
Written by: Clint Conley
From the album: *Signals, Calls and Marches*
Label: Ace of Hearts
Produced by: Richard W. Harte
Year: 1981
Classic track from the critically acclaimed political protest band.

THAT'S WHY

Artist: Jackie Wilson
Written by: Roquel Davis (Tyran Carlo), Berry Gordy, Jr., Gwen Gordy
Label: Brunswick
Produced by: Dick Jacobs, Nat Tarnopol
Year: 1959
Padding the coffers for Detroit's musical legacy in the making, Gordy's Motown edifice. But Jackie Wilson, its spiritual heir, would never be part of it.

THEM CHANGES

Artist: Buddy Miles
Written by: Buddy Miles
From the album: *Them Changes*
Label: Mercury
Produced by: Robin McBride
Year: 1970
Giving the drummer some.

THEM HEAVY PEOPLE

Artist: Kate Bush
Written by: Kate Bush
From the album: *The Kick Inside*
Label: EMI-America
Produced by: Andrew Powell
Year: 1978
Future queen of the Fairlight synthesizer exercises her extraordinary vocal and instrumental chops.

THEME FOR *AN IMAGINARY WESTERN*

Artist: Mountain
Written by: Jack Bruce, Pete Brown
From the album: *Mountain Climbing*
Label: Windfall
Produced by: Felix Pappalardi
Year: 1970
Leslie West's guitar epiphany.

THEME FROM *ENDLESS SUMMER*

Artist: The Sandals
Written by: Gaston Georis, John Blakely
From the album: *The Endless Summer Soundtrack*
Label: World Pacific
Produced by: Richard Bock
Year: 1964
Signing their guitar signature on a celluloid celebration of the surf.

THEME FROM *S.W.A.T.*

Artist: Rhythm Heritage
Written by: Barry DeVorzon
From the album: *Disco-Fied*
Label: ABC
Produced by: Steve Barri, Michael Omartian
Year: 1975
Popular ersatz disco jazz/R&B/funk fusion that would dominate detective show TV soundtracks and especially NBA broadcasts of the Dr. J era.

THEME FROM *SHAFT* (WHO SHAFT WHERE)

Artist: Isaac Hayes
Written by: Isaac Hayes
From the album: *Shaft*
Label: Enterprise
Produced by: Isaac Hayes
Year: 1971
The seductive sound of blaxploitation, one part disco, one part the Bar-Kays, and two parts R&B.

THEME FROM *TROUBLE MAN*

Artist: Marvin Gaye
Written by: Marvin Gaye
From the album: *Trouble Man*
Label: Tamla
Produced by: Marvin Gaye
Year: 1972
Outlaw R&B, a few years before rap.

THEMES FOR GREAT CITIES

Artist: Simple Minds
Written by: Simple Minds
From the album: *Sons and Fascination/Sister Feelings Call*
Label: Virgin
Produced by: Steve Hillage
Year: 1981
Exhilaratingly chaotic mood music for after the apocalypse.

THEN CAME THE CHILDREN

Artist: Paul Siebel
Written by: Paul Siebel
From the album: *Philadelphia Folk Festival*
Label: Flying Fish
Year: 1978
Achieving a flower child folk epiphany about ten years too late.

THEN CAME YOU

Artist: Dionne Warwick with the Spinners
Written by: Sherman Marshall, Phillip Pugh
From the album: *Then Came You*
Label: Atlantic
Produced by: Thom Bell
Year: 1974
Her biggest hit, a #1 R&B/#1 crossover.

THEN HE KISSED ME

Artist: The Crystals
Written by: Jeff Barry, Ellie Greenwich, Phil Spector
From the album: *Uptown Twist*
Label: Philles
Produced by: Phil Spector
Year: 1963
Sheer Brill brilliance, featuring the uncredited voice of Darlene Love.

THEN YOU CAN TELL ME GOODBYE

Artist: The Casinos
Written by: John D. Loudermilk
From the album: *Then You Can Tell Me Goodbye*
Label: Fraternity
Produced by: Gene Hughes
Year: 1967
The country reaction to a year of R&B cheating songs: a fidelity song. The Casinos version went Top 10 in '67. Cover by Eddy Arnold went #1 country (RCA, '68).

THERE BUT FOR FORTUNE

Artist: Phil Ochs
Written by: Phil Ochs
From the album: *I Ain't Marchin' Anymore*
Label: Elektra
Produced by: Paul Rothchild
Year: 1964
Folk anthem with a relatively moderate message for Ochs. Covered by Joan Baez (Vanguard, '65) for her first folk/rock hit.

THERE GOES MY BABY

Artist: The Drifters
Written by: Benjamin Nelson, Lover Patterson, George Treadwell
From the album: *Drifters' Greatest Hits*
Label: Atlantic
Produced by: Jerry Leiber, Mike Stoller
Year: 1959
Drifting along with the year's prevailing softening of rock and roll, the new Drifters add strings to their patented sound and for their efforts gain a #1 R&B/#2 crossover.

THERE IS A LIGHT THAT NEVER GOES OUT

Artist: The Smiths
Written by: Stephen Morrissey, Johnny Marr
From the album: *The Queen Is Dead*
Produced by: Stephen Morrissey, Johnny Marr
Label: Sire
Year: 1986

THERE IS A MOUNTAIN

Artist: Donovan
Written by: Donovan Leitch
From the album: *Donovan in Concert*
Label: Epic
Produced by: Mickie Most
Year: 1967
At the peak of his pop mysticism.

THERE IS SOMEONE IN THIS WORLD FOR ME

Artist: Little Willie John
Written by: Darlynn Bonner
From the album: *There Is Someone in This World for Me*
Label: King
Produced by: Henry Glover
Year: 1958
One of his best performances.

THERE IS SOMETHING ON YOUR MIND

Artist: Big Jay McNeely
Written by: Big Jay McNeely
Label: Swingin'
Year: 1957
McNeely on sax, vocals by Little Sonny. Covered by New Orleans cross dressing crossover soul man Bobby Marchan (Fire, '60) on which he inserted the classic spoken part, detailing how, in "Hey Joe" terms, he shot his woman down. Suggested segue: "Here Comes the Judge" by Shorty Long.

THERE SHE GOES

Artist: The L.A.'s
Written by: Lee Mavers
From the album: *The L.A.'s*
Label: London
Produced by: Steve Lillywhite
Year: 1991
Ineffable British trifle, originally released in 1988, writ large in the Mike Myers movie *So I Married an Axe Murderer*, as is a version by the Boo Radleys (Chaos, '93).

THERE YOU GO

Artist: Pink
Written by: Kevin (Shekspere) Briggs, Kandi Burruss, Alecia (Pink) Moore
From the album: *Can't Take Me Home*
Produced by: Kevin Briggs
Label: La Face
Year: 2000
In the pop poster girl wars of the early millennium, Pink was originally the scruffy counterpart to the more virginal Christina and Britney. Later, Christina and Britney would become less virginal, and Pink would become punk, wherein she competed against Avril, who actually seemed more virginal than Christina and Britney.

THERE'LL BE SAD SONGS (TO MAKE YOU CRY)

Artist: Billy Ocean
Written by: Barry Eastmond, Billy Ocean, Wayne Braithwaite

From the album: *Love Zone*
Label: Jive
Produced by: Mutt Lange
Year: 1986
Sultry ballad is his second #1 R&B/#1 crossover.

THERE'S A GUY WORKS DOWN THE CHIP SHOP SWEARS HE'S ELVIS

Artist: Kirsty MacColl
Written by: Kirsty MacColl, Philip Rambow
From the album: *Desperate Character*
Label: Polydor
Produced by: Bazza
Year: 1981
Local color, British style.

THERE'S A KIND OF A HUSH (ALL OVER THE WORLD)

Artist: Herman's Hermits
Written by: Les Reed, Geoff Stevens
From the album: *There's a Kind of a Hush*
Label: MGM
Year: 1967
Their eleventh and last Top 10 hit.

THERE'S A MOON OUT TONIGHT

Artist: The Capris
Written by: Al Striano, Al Gentile
From the album: *There's a Moon out Tonight*
Label: Old Town
Year: 1961
Essence of Italian soul.

THERE'S A PLACE

Artist: The Beatles
Written by: John Lennon, Paul McCartney
From the album: *Introducing the Beatles*
Label: Vee Jay
Produced by: George Martin
Year: 1963
Pristine ballad from the '63 LP that also contains "Twist and Shout."

(THERE'S) ALWAYS SOMETHING THERE TO REMIND ME

Artist: Lou Johnson
Written by: Burt Bacharach, Hal David
Label: Big Hill
Year: 1964
Covered by Naked Eyes (EMI-America, '83).

THERE'S NO OTHER

Artist: The Crystals
Written by: Phil Spector, Leroy Bates

From the album: *He's a Rebel*
Label: Philles
Produced by: Phil Spector
Year: 1961
B-side of their first release, "Oh Boy Maybe Baby"; preview of Spectorian girl-group greatness to come.

THESE ARE DAYS

Artist: 10,000 Maniacs
Written by: Natalie Merchant, Peter Buck
From the album: *Our Time in Eden*
Label: Elektra
Produced by: Paul Fox
Year: 1992

THESE ARMS OF MINE

Artist: Otis Redding
Written by: Otis Redding
From the album: *The History of Otis Redding*
Label: Volt
Produced by: Jim Stewart
Year: 1963
First R&B/crossover for the John Henry of soul music, hoisting the scene onto his back like a nine-pound hammer.

THESE BOOTS ARE MADE FOR WALKING

Artist: Nancy Sinatra
Written by: Lee Hazelwood
From the album: *Boots*
Label: Reprise
Produced by: Lee Hazelwood
Year: 1966
The liberated housewife moves to Las Vegas. Covered by Sam Philips in the film *Ready to Wear* (Columbia, '94) and used in the prostitute scene in *Full Metal Jacket*.

THESE DAYS

Artist: Nico
Written by: Jackson Browne
From the album: *Chelsea Girl*
Label: Verve
Produced by: Tom Wilson
Year: 1967
A standard of the Greenwich Village introspective folk repertoire. Covered by Tom Rush (Elektra, '68), Jackson Browne (Asylum, '72), Gregg Allman (Capricorn, '73), 10,000 Maniacs (Elektra, '88).

THESE DREAMS

Artist: Heart
Written by: Bernie Taupin, Martin Page
From the album: *Heart*
Label: Capitol
Produced by: Ron Nevison
Year: 1986

With Elton's word man, Bernie, Heart achieves their first #1 thanks to Nancy Wilson's nasal congestion and Stevie Nicks' bad judgment.

THESE EYES

Artist: The Guess Who
Written by: Randall Bachman, Burton Cummings
From the album: *Wheatfield Soul*
Label: RCA
Produced by: Jack Richardson
Year: 1969
First big hit for the Canadian arena rockers topped the charts in Canada and led to their US label deal.

THESE 23 DAYS IN SEPTEMBER

Artist: David Blue
Written by: David Blue
From the album: *These 23 Days in September*
Label: Asylum
Produced by: Gabriel Mekler
Year: 1968
Greenwich Village post-folkie advances from Dylanology to Jackson-Brownean singer/songwriterism with a moody tone poem.

THEY DANCE ALONE

Artist: Sting
Written by: Gordon Sumner (Sting)
From the album: *Nothing Like the Sun*
Label: A&M
Produced by: Hugh Padgham, Sting
Year: 1987
One of his most haunting songs; "Invisible Sun" for the rebels of South America and the women they left behind. Branford Marsalis on sax.

THEY DON'T KNOW

Artist: Kirsty MacColl
Written by: Kirsty MacColl
Label: Stiff
Year: 1979
Her debut stiff on Stiff. Covered by Tracy Ullman (MCA, '84).

(THEY LONG TO BE) CLOSE TO YOU

Artist: Dionne Warwick
Written by: Burt Bacharach, Hal David
From the album: *Make Way for Dionne Warwick*
Label: Scepter
Produced by: Burt Bacharach, Hal David
Year: 1963
Gossamer pop/rock ballad, covered by Dusty Springfield (Atlantic, '67), the Carpenters (A&M, '70).

THEY WANT MONEY

Artist: Kool Moe Dee
Written by: Mo Dewese, Teddy Riley
From the album: *Knowledge Is King*

Label: Jive
Year: 1989
Powerful rap statement.

THEY'RE COMING TO TAKE ME AWAY, HA-HAAA!

Artist: Napoleon XIV
Written by: Rosemary Djivre
From the album: *They're Coming to Take Me Away, Ha-Haaa!*
Label: Warner Brothers
Produced by: Jepalana Productions
Year: 1966
A perverse novelty, written about a lost dog, that was banned on some stations, featured on others. Definitely up there with "Ambrose Part V" by Linda Laurie, and the immortal "I Put a Spell on You" by Screaming Jay Hawkins. Suggested segues: "Shannon" by Henry Gross, "Old Shep" by Elvis Presley, "Puppy Love" by Jerry Samuel.

THICK AS A BRICK

Artist: Jethro Tull
Written by: Ian Anderson
From the album: *Thick as a Brick*
Label: Chrysalis
Produced by: Ian Anderson, Terry Ellis
Year: 1972
Album version takes up the entire album. Single version used in a commercial for Hundai in 2001.

THIEVES IN THE TEMPLE

Artist: Prince
Written by: Prince Rogers Nelson
From the album: *Graffiti Bridge Soundtrack*
Label: Paisley Park
Produced by: Prince
Year: 1990
#1 R&B/Top 10 crossover from the movie.

THIN LINE BETWEEN LOVE AND HATE

Artist: The Persuaders
Written by: Richard Poindexter, Robert Poindexter, Jackie Members
From the album: *Thin Line between Love and Hate*
Label: Atco
Produced by: Richard Poindexter, Robert Poindexter
Year: 1971
#1 R&B/Top 20 crossover. Covered by the Pretenders (Sire, '84). Covered by H-town (JAC/MAC, '96) as the title song for the movie.

THING CALLED LOVE

Artist: John Hiatt
Written by: John Hiatt
From the album: *Bring the Family*
Label: A&M
Produced by: John Chelew
Year: 1987
Middle-of-the-dirt-road cover by Bonnie Raitt (Capitol, '89) helped to transform her career, to say nothing of Hiatt's.

THINGS

Artist: Bobby Darin
Written by: Bobby Darin
From the album: *Things and Other Things*
Label: Atco
Year: 1962
Breezy pop rocker.

THINGS CAN ONLY GET BETTER

Artist: Howard Jones
Written by: Howard Jones
From the album: *Things Can Only Get Better*
Label: Elektra
Produced by: Phil Collins, Hugh Padgham
Year: 1985

THINGS COULD TURN AROUND

Artist: fIREHOSE
Written by: Kira Roessler, Mike Watt
From the album: *Ragin', Full On*
Label: SST
Produced by: Ethan James, Mike Watt
Year: 1986
From the ashes of the Minutemen, Mike Watt reemerges with a hopeful song.

THINGS HAVE CHANGED

Artist: Bob Dylan
Written by: Bob Dylan
From the album: *Things Have Changed*
Produced by: Bob Dylan, Don DeVito
Label: Columbia
Year: 2000
Strong statement of disaffection, from *The Wonder Boys* soundtrack.

THINGS THAT I USED TO DO

Artist: Eddie "Guitar Slim" Jones
Written by: Eddie "Guitar Slim" Jones
Label: Specialty
Produced by: Ray Charles
Year: 1954
Classic #1 R&B blues track, covered by James Brown (Kent, '64), Chuck Berry (Chess, '64), Jimi Hendrix (Reprise, '69), Stevie Ray Vaughan (Epic, '84).

THINGS THAT MAKE YOU GO HMMMM

Artist: C&C Music Factory
Written by: Rob Clivilles, Freedom Williams
From the album: *Gonna Make You Sweat*
Label: Columbia
Produced by: Rob Clivilles, David Cole
Year: 1991
Leading another new generation to the disco.

THINGS WE DO FOR LOVE, THE

Artist: 10 C.C.
Written by: Graham Gouldman, Eric Stewart
From the album: *Deceptive Bends*
Label: Mercury
Produced by: 10 c.c.
Year: 1977
One of their eleventh Top 10 hits in the UK.

THINGS WE SAID TODAY

Artist: The Beatles
Written by: John Lennon, Paul McCartney
From the album: *Something New*
Label: Capitol
Produced by: George Martin
Year: 1964
One of their finest melodies, attached to one of their finest album cuts. Written by Paul for Jane Asher, while cruising in the Caribbean on a yacht.

THINK

Artist: The 5 Royales
Written by: Lowman Pauling
Label: King
Year: 1957
Covered by James Brown (Federal, '60).

THINK

Artist: Aretha Franklin
Written by: Aretha Franklin, Ted White
From the album: *Aretha Now*
Label: Atlantic
Produced by: Jerry Wexler
Year: 1968
Continuing a streak of six out of seven #1 R&B/Top 10 crossover singles.

THINK FOR YOURSELF

Artist: The Beatles
Written by: George Harrison
From the album: *Rubber Soul*
Label: Capitol
Produced by: George Martin
Year: 1965
Early Harrison at the podium giving himself a pep talk.

THINK IT OVER

Artist: The Crickets
Written by: Buddy Holly, Norman Petty, Jerry Allison
From the album: *The Buddy Holly Story*
Label: Brunswick
Produced by: Norman Petty
Year: 1958

THIRD WEEK AT THE CHELSEA

Artist: Jefferson Airplane
Written by: Jorma Kaukonen
From the album: *Bark*
Label: Grunt
Produced by: Jefferson Airplane
Year: 1971
Jorma's eminently hummable folk rock-cum-psy-chedelic-bluegrass farewell to the Sunshine era. Hot Tuna was in the wings.

THIRSTY BOOTS

Artist: Judy Collins
Written by: Eric Andersen
From the album: *5th*
Label: Elektra
Produced by: Mark Abramson, Jac Holzman
Year: 1965
Classic peace marching song.

13 QUESTION METHOD

Artist: Chuck Berry
Written by: Chuck Berry
From the album: *New Jukebox Hits*
Label: Chess
Produced by: Leonard Chess, Phil Chess
Year: 1961

THIRTEEN STEPS LEAD DOWN

Artist: Elvis Costello
Written by: Declan McManus (Elvis Costello)
From the album: *Brutal Youth*
Label: Warner Brothers
Produced by: Mitchell Froom, Elvis Costello
Year: 1994
When seen on American TV for the first time since being banned from *Saturday Night Live* he was singing this tune on *The Larry Sanders Show* and trashing his dressing room in a thoroughly satisfying comic performance. He would further burnish his image as a curmudeon with an appearance on the TV show *Two and a Half Men*.

THIRTY DAYS

Artist: Chuck Berry
Written by: Chuck Berry
From the album: *Greatest Hits*
Label: Chess
Produced by: Leonard Chess, Marshall Chess
Year: 1955
Berry's second single presages future run-ins with the law. A line in the song presages the Rolling Stones' "Satisfaction."

30 SECONDS OVER TOKYO

Artist: Pere UBU
Written by: Peter Laughner
From the album: *Datapanik in the Year Zero*
Label: Radar
Year: 1978
Early exponent of the Akron-based American punk scene is an atonal aural explosion. Collected on Peter Laughner's posthumous album (Coolie, '82).

32 FLAVORS

Artist: Ani DiFranco
Written by: Ani DiFranco
From the album: *Not a Pretty Girl*
Label: Righteous Babe
Produced by: Ani DiFranco
Year: 1994
Ode to multiplicity. Covered by Alana Davis (Capitol, '96). Segue: "Bitch" by Meredith Brooks.

THIS BITTER EARTH

Artist: Dinah Washington
Written by: Clyde Otis
From the album: *Unforgettable*
Label: Mercury
Year: 1960
#1 R&B/Top 30 crossover.

THIS BOY (RINGO'S THEME)

Artist: The Beatles
Written by: John Lennon, Paul McCartney
From the album: *A Hard Day's Night*
Label: United Artists
Produced by: George Martin
Year: 1964
The B-side of "All My Lovin," included in *A Hard Day's Night* during the Ringo showcase sequence, from which all of his subsequent commercial endorsement sprang.

THIS CHARMING MAN

Artist: The Smiths
Written by: Stephen Morrissey, Johnny Marr
From the album: *The Smiths*
Label: Sire
Produced by: John Porter
Year: 1984
Added to the US release of the album.

THIS CORROSION

Artist: Sisters of Mercy
Written by: Andrew Eldritch
From the album: *Floodland*
Label: Elektra
Produced by: Jim Steinman
Year: 1988
Biggest of six UK hits for the gothic metal answer to Meat Loaf.

THIS D.J.

Artist: Warren G.
Written by: Warren Griffin
From the album: *Regulate ... the G Funk Era*
Label: Violator/Ral
Produced by: Warren Griffin
Year: 1994

THIS DIAMOND RING

Artist: Gary Lewis and the Playboys
Written by: Irwin Levine, Al Kooper, Bob Brass
From the album: *This Diamond Ring*
Label: Liberty
Produced by: Snuff Garrett
Year: 1964
Rejected by Bobby Vee. Performed briefly by Gary in his father Jerry's '65 film *The Family Jewels*. Covered by Al Kooper (United Artists, '77). Segue: "Band of Gold" by Freda Payne, "Wedding Bell Blues" by the 5th Dimension.

THIS GIRL IS A WOMAN NOW

Artist: Gary Puckett and the Union Gap
Written by: Victor Millrose, Abe Bernstein
From the album: *The New Gary Puckett & the Union Gap*
Label: Columbia
Produced by: Dick Glasser
Year: 1969
Their fifth Top 10 performance is basically the same old song, just with a new producer.

THIS HOUSE

Artist: Tracie Spencer
Written by: Matt Sherrod, Paul Sherrod, Sir Spence
From the album: *Make the Difference*
Label: Capitol
Produced by: Robert Sherrod, Paul Sherrod
Year: 1991
Subteen thrush, straight outta *Star Search*.

THIS I PROMISE YOU

Artist: *NSYNC
Written by: Richard Marx
From the album: *No Strings Attached*
Produced by: Richard Marx
Label: Jive
Year: 2000
Perfect match of ballad writer and balladeers.

THIS I SWEAR

Artist: The Skyliners
Written by: Jimmy Beaumont, Janet Vogel, Joe Verscharen, Wally Lester, Lennie Martin, Joe Rock, Jack Taylor
From the album: *The Skyliners*
Label: Calico
Produced by: Joe Rock
Year: 1959
No unbelievable high notes, but this is Phil Spector's all-time favorite song.

THIS IS A CALL

Artist: Foo Fighters
Written by: Dave Grohl
From the album: *Foo Fighters*
Label: Rosswell
Year: 1995

THIS IS HOW WE DO IT

Artist: Montel Jordan
Written by: Montell Jordan, Oji Pierce, R. Walters
From the album: *This Is How We Do It*
Label: PMP
Produced by: Montel Jordan, Oji Pierce
Year: 1995

THIS IS MY COUNTRY

Artist: The Impressions
Written by: Curtis Mayfield
From the album: *This Is My Country*
Label: Curtom
Produced by: Curtis Mayfield
Year: 1968
Curtis paves the way for Marvin Gaye's chart-topping social commentaries, with this Top 10 R&B/ Top 25 crossover.

THIS IS NOT A LOVE SONG

Artist: Public Image Ltd. (P.I.L.)
Written by: Johnny Lydon, Keith Levine, Martin Atkins
From the album: *PiL*
Label: Virgin
Produced by: John Lydon, Martin Atkins
Year: 1983
Biggest UK hit for Johnny Rotten's post-Sex Pistols outfit.

THIS IS POP

Artist: XTC
Written by: Andy Partridge
From the album: *White Music*
Label: Virgin
Produced by: Mutt Lange
Year: 1979
Archetypal English art band's impure indulgence for pop people.

THIS IS THE TIME

Artist: Billy Joel
Written by: Billy Joel
From the album: *The Bridge*
Label: Columbia
Produced by: Phil Ramone
Year: 1986
Joel's enduring wedding/sweet-sixteen/bar-mitzvah standard.

THIS LAND IS YOUR LAND

Artist: The Weavers
Written by: Woody Guthrie
From the album: *The Weavers at Home*
Label: Vanguard
Produced by: Milt Gabler
Year: 1956
Originally written as a working class reaction to Irving Berlin's "America the Beautiful," this Guthrie classic, released in 1951, would soon be adopted as a national anthem by a new generation

at the edge of a New Frontier. Covered by the New Christy Minstrels (Columbia, '63), Bobb B. Soxx & the Blue Jeans (Philles, '64).

THIS LITTLE BIRD

Artist: Marianne Faithfull
Written by: John D. Loudermilk
From the album: *Marianne Faithfull*
Label: London
Produced by: Tony Calder
Year: 1965
Also recorded by Loudermilk (Decca, '65).

THIS LITTLE GIRL

Artist: Gary US Bonds
Written by: Bruce Springsteen
From the album: *Dedication*
Label: EMI-America
Produced by: Bruce Springsteen, Steve Van Zandt
Year: 1981
Comeback hit for the noted East coast rocker.

THIS LITTLE GIRL OF MINE

Artist: Ray Charles
Written by: Ray Charles
From the album: *Ray Charles*
Label: Atlantic
Produced by: Ahmet Ertegun, Jerry Wexler
Year: 1955
Based on the gospel classic "This Little Light of Mine." Covered by the Everly Brothers (Cadence, '58).

THIS LITTLE GIRL'S GONE ROCKIN'

Artist: Ruth Brown
Written by: Bobby Darin, Mann Curtis
Label: Atlantic
Year: 1958
After five #1 R&B hits, her biggest crossover, nudging into the Top 25.

THIS MAGIC MOMENT

Artist: The Drifters
Written by: Doc Pomus, Mort Shuman
From the album: *Up on the Roof, the Best of the Drifters*
Label: Atlantic
Produced by: Jerry Leiber, Mike Stoller
Year: 1960
Has a Latin flavor to it.

THIS MASQUERADE

Artist: Leon Russell
Written by: Leon Russell
From the album: *Carny*
Label: Shelter
Produced by: Denny Cordell, Leon Russell
Year: 1972
The mellow laid-back sound of L.A. in the '70s. Covered by George Benson (Warner Brothers, '76).

THIS NOTE'S FOR YOU

Artist: Neil Young and the Bluenotes
Written by: Neil Young
From the album: *This Note's for You*
Label: Reprise
Produced by: Neil Young, Nico Bolas
Year: 1988
Anti-commerce diatribe is Young's answer to "Money for Nothing" by Dire Straits. It wound up winning a video award on MTV.

THIS OLD HEART OF MINE (IS WEAK FOR YOU)

Artist: The Isley Brothers
Written by: Eddie Holland, Lamont Dozier, Brian Holland, Sylvia Moy
From the album: *This Old Heart of Mine*
Label: Tamla
Produced by: Brian Holland, Lamont Dozier
Year: 1966
Isley Brothers Motown debut was their first hit in England. Covered by Rod Stewart (Warner Brothers, '75).

THIS SONG

Artist: George Harrison
Written by: George Harrison
From the album: *Thirty-Three and 1/3*
Label: Dark Horse
Produced by: George Harrison
Year: 1976
Responding with notable, if not previously noticeable, humor to the "My Sweet Lord" plagiarism fiasco.

THIS TIME

Artist: Troy Shondell
Written by: Chips Moman
Label: Gold Crest/Liberty
Produced by: Troy Shondell
Year: 1961
In the Don French/Rod Bernard Elvis wannabe mold.

THIS TOWN AIN'T BIG ENOUGH FOR THE BOTH OF US

Artist: Sparks
Written by: Ron Mael
From the album: *Kimono My House*
Label: Island
Produced by: Muff Winwood
Year: 1974
Off-kilter duo scores their biggest UK hit.

THIS USED TO BE MY PLAYGROUND

Artist: Madonna
Written by: Shep Pettibone, Madonna Ciccone
From the album: *Barcelona Gold*
Label: Warner Brothers

Produced by: Shep Pettibone, Madonna
Year: 1992
Oscar-caliber ballad, from the movie *A League of Their Own* moves Madonna up to a new, rarified level of schmaltz.

THIS WHEEL'S ON FIRE

Artist: The Band
Written by: Bob Dylan
From the album: *Music from Big Pink*
Label: Capitol
Produced by: John Simon, the Band
Year: 1968
An epic of coiled frustration, written during Dylan's post-*Blonde-on-Blonde* creative ferment at Big Pink, and performed by the house band there in an album that could have been titled (or subtitled) *The Basement Tapes, Volume II* (or *I*, as the case may be). Covered by the Byrds (Columbia, '69).

THIS WILL BE
(AN EVERLASTING LOVE)

Artist: Natalie Cole
Written by: Charles Jackson Jr., Marvin Yancy
From the album: *Inseparable*
Label: Capitol
Produced by: Chuck Jackson, Marvin Yancey
Year: 1975
#1 R&B/Top 10 crossover; after briefly vying for Aretha's Queen of Soul crown, Natalie settled for Roberta Flack's stylish pop chapeau.

THIS WOMAN'S WORK

Artist: Kate Bush
Written by: Kate Bush
From the album: *The Sensual World*
Label: Columbia
Produced by: Kate Bush
Year: 1988
Used in the waiting-room scene in the movie *She's Having a Baby*, one of Bush's most magnificent performances. Cloned by Maxwell (Columbia, '97).

THONG SONG

Artist: Sisqo
Written by: Rob Robinson, Robi Rosa, Mark Andrews, Desmond Child, Tim Kelley
From the album: *Unleash the Dragon*
Label: Def Soul
Year: 1999
Commenting on the year's raciest fashion statement. Segue: "Short Shorts" by the Royal Teens, "Itsy Bitsy Teeny Weeny Yellow Polka Dot Bikini" by Brian Hyland.

THORN IN MY PRIDE

Artist: The Black Crowes
Written by: Chris Robinson, Rich Robinson
From the album: *The Southern Harmony and Musical Companion*
Produced by: George Drakoulias

Label: Def American
Year: 1980
A good old-fashioned Southern style jam.

THOSE OLDIES BUT GOODIES (REMIND ME OF YOU)

Artist: Little Caesar and the Romans
Written by: Paul Politti, Nick Curinga
From the album: *Memories of Those Oldies but Goodies*
Label: Del-Fi
Year: 1961
Celebrating and mourning the end of the doo-wop era. Segue: "Looking for an Echo" by the Persuasions.

THOSE WERE THE DAYS

Artist: The Limeliters
Written by: Gene Raskin
From the album: *Folk Matinee*
Label: RCA
Year: 1962
Updated Russian folk tune. Covered by Mary Hopkin (Apple, '68) and produced by Paul McCartney. It was Apple's second release and kept out of #1 only by Apple's first release, "Hey Jude."

THOU SHALT NOT STEAL

Artist: Kitty Wells
Written by: John D. Loudermilk
Label: Decca
Year: 1954
Country classic, covered by John D. Loudermilk (RCA, '62), Dick and DeeDee (Warner Brothers, '65).

THOUSAND MILES AWAY, A

Artist: The Heartbeats
Written by: James Sheppard, William H. Miller
From the album: *A Thousand Miles Away*
Label: Hull/Rama
Produced by: Bea Casalin, George Goldner
Year: 1956
B-side of "Oh Baby Don't." Doo wop standard written by Queens, New York native James Shepherd ("Daddy's Home") about his girlfriend who'd moved to Texas.

THOUSAND STARS, A

Artist: The Rivilers
Written by: Eugene Pearson
Label: Flyright
Year: 1956
Covered by Kathy Young with the Innocents (Indigo, '60) and Billy Fury in the '74 film *Stardust*.

3 A.M.

Artist: Matchbox Twenty
Written by: Matt Serletic, Rob Thomas
From the album: *Yourself or Someone Like You*
Label: Lava

Produced by: Matt Serletic
Year: 1997

3 A.M. ETERNAL

Artist: The KLF
Written by: Jimi Cauty, Bill Drummond, T. Thorpe
From the album: *The White Room*
Label: Arista
Produced by: The KLF
Year: 1991
Spacey UK dance track by the Scottish merry prankster, Drummond, and his group, formerly known as the Justified Ancients of Mu Mu. Group named their indie label Kopyright Liberation Front. Went Top 10 in the US.

THREE BELLS, THE

Artist: The Browns
Written by: Bert Reisfeld, Jean Villard
From the album: *Sweet Sounds by the Browns*
Label: RCA
Produced by: Chet Atkins
Year: 1959
Country and western mortality tale from 1946, popularized by Edith Piaf.

THREE DAYS

Artist: Jane's Addiction
Written by: Jane's Addiction
From the album: *Ritual de lo Habitual*
Produced by: Dave Jerden, Perry Farrell
Label: Warner Brothers
Year: 1990
Defining rocker.

THREE FLIGHTS UP

Artist: Frank Christian
Written by: Frank Christian
From the album: *Fast Folk Sixth Anniversary Issue*
Label: Fast Folk
Year: 1988
Evocative urban folk tale of bohemian living. Covered by Nanci Griffith (Elektra, '92) with Christian reprising his wonderful guitar part.

THREE LITTLE BIRDS

Artist: Bob Marley and the Wailers
Written by: Bob Marley
From the album: *Exodus*
Produced by: Bob Marley and the Wailers
Label: Island
Year: 1977
Reggae gets back to nature.

THREE MARLENAS

Artist: The Wallflowers
Written by: Jakob Dylan
From the album: *Bringing down the Horse*
Label: Interscope
Produced by: T-Bone Burnette
Year: 1996

Stealing the piping organ from Al Kooper's part in the elder Dylan's "Like a Rolling Stone."

3 O'CLOCK BLUES

Artist: Lowell Fulson
Written by: Lowell Fulson
Label: Down Town
Produced by: Bob Geddins
Year: 1948
Cover by B. B. King (RPM, '51) was the legendary bluesman's first #1 R&B hit. Also covered by Ike and Tina Turner (Blue Thumb, '69).

THREE STARS

Artist: Eddie Cochran
Written by: Tommy Dee
Label: Liberty
Year: 1959
Fixated by the deaths of three contemporaries, Cochran introduces this memorial. Covered by Dee, with Carol Kay (Crest, '59).

THREE STEPS TO HEAVEN

Artist: Eddie Cochran
Written by: Eddie Cochran, Bob Cochran
From the album: *Eddie Cochran*
Label: Liberty
Produced by: Eddie Cochran, Jerry Capeheart
Year: 1960
His biggest UK hit, stiffed in the US.

THREE TIMES A LADY

Artist: Commodores
Written by: Lionel B. Richie Jr.
From the album: *Natural High*
Label: Motown
Produced by: James Carmichael, Commodores
Year: 1978
#1 R&B/#1 crossover.

THREE TIMES IN LOVE

Artist: Tommy James and the Shondells
Written by: Tommy James, Rick Serota
From the album: *Three Times in Love*
Label: Millennium
Produced by: Tommy James
Year: 1980
Still blowing bubbles after all these years.

THRILL IS GONE, THE

Artist: B. B. King
Written by: Lew Brown, Ray Henderson
From the album: *Completely Well*
Label: Bluesway
Produced by: Bill Szymczyk
Year: 1969
A belated reward for his Hall of Fame career; a Top 10 R&B/Top 20 crossover with this '31 evergreen.

THRILL OF IT ALL

Artist: Roxy Music

Written by: Bryan Ferry
From the album: *Country Life*
Label: Atco
Year: 1974

THRILLER

Artist: Michael Jackson
Written by: Rod Temperton
From the album: *Thriller*
Label: Epic
Produced by: Quincy Jones, Michael Jackson
Year: 1983
The seventh Top 10 hit from the album: Michael meets the freaks in a 20-minute video, wherein he confides the immortal line "I'm not like the other boys."

THROUGH BEING COOL

Artist: Devo
Written by: Mark Mothersbaugh, Bob Mothersbaugh, Gerald Casale
From the album: *New Traditionalists*
Label: Warner Brothers
Produced by: Devo
Year: 1981
Revenge of the nerds.

THROUGH THE STORM

Artist: Aretha Franklin and Elton John
Written by: Diane Warren, Albert Hammond
From the album: *Through the Storm*
Label: Arista
Produced by: Narada Michael Walden
Year: 1989
Queen of Soul meets Sir Elton.

THROUGH YOUR HANDS

Artist: John Hiatt
Written by: John Hiatt
From the album: *Stolen Moments*
Label: A&M
Produced by: Glyn Johns
Year: 1990
One of his more pointed, poignant messages. Covered by David Crosby (Atlantic, '92).

THROWING IT ALL AWAY

Artist: Genesis
Written by: Phil Collins, Tony Banks, Mike Rutherford
From the album: *Invisible Touch*
Label: Atlantic
Produced by: Hugh Padgham, Genesis
Year: 1986
For a chance to be the progressive Chicago.

THUNDER ISLAND

Artist: Jay Ferguson
Written by: Jay Ferguson
From the album: *Thunder Island*
Label: Asylum

Produced by: Bill Szymczyk
Year: 1977
One-shot single for the former coleader of Spirit.

THUNDER KISS

Artist: White Zombie
Written by: Rob Straker (Rob Zombie), White Zombie
From the album: *La Sexorcisto: Devil Music, Vol. 1*
Label: Geffen
Produced by: Rob Date, White Zombie
Year: 1994
Musical equivalent of a monster truck rally.

THUNDER ROAD

Artist: Bruce Springsteen
Written by: Bruce Springsteen
From the album: *Born to Run*
Label: Columbia
Produced by: Jon Landau, Mike Appel, Bruce Springsteen
Year: 1975
Orbisonian tragedy, Spectorian romance: a quintessential Springsteenian tale of growing up, in which we meet Mary for the first time. She'd reappear in "The River."

THUNDERCRACK

Artist: Bruce Springsteen
Written by: Bruce Springsteen
From the album: *Tracks*
Label: Columbia
Year: 1973
Before "Rosalita," this girl with the "heart of a ballerina" was Springsteen's favorite crowd pleaser.

TICKET TO RIDE

Artist: The Beatles
Written by: John Lennon, Paul McCartney
From the album: *Help!*
Label: Capitol
Produced by: George Martin
Year: 1965
Or, as latter-day Beatlesologists suggest, did the title refer to the English red-light town of Ryde? Or perhaps to Hamburg prostitutes. Paul on guitar. The cover by the Carpenters (A&M, '70) was their debut single.

TIDE IS HIGH, THE

Artist: Paragons
Written by: John Holt
Label: Trojan
Year: 1963
From the reggae repertoire of John Holt, Jamaica's top progenitor of Lover's Rock, a tune cherished by the reggae-influenced punk bands in England of the mid-'70s and covered by the girl-group-influenced punk band in New York City, Blondie (Chrysalis, '80). It went on to replace John Lennon's "Just Like Starting Over" at the top of the charts.

TIE A YELLOW RIBBON ROUND THE OLD OAK TREE

Artist: Tony Orlando & Dawn
Written by: Irwin Levine, L. Russell Brown
From the album: *Tuneweaving*
Label: Bell
Produced by: Irwin Levine, L. Russell Brown
Year: 1973
Based on a true story, this semicontagious slice of life imitated reality when the tune was used to welcome back the hostages from Tehran.

TIGER

Artist: Fabian
Written by: Ollie Jones
From the album: *Hold That Tiger*
Label: Chancellor
Produced by: Pete D'Angelis
Year: 1959
Biggest hit for the Philadelphia poster boy.

TIGER WOODS

Artist: Dan Bern
Written by: Dan Bern
From the album: *50 Eggs*
Produced by: Ani Difranco
Label: Work
Year: 1998
Folk/rock tribute to the golfer, among other things.

TIGHT CONNECTION TO MY HEART (HAS ANYBODY SEEN MY LOVE)

Artist: Bob Dylan
Written by: Bob Dylan
From the album: *Empire Burlesque*
Label: Columbia
Year: 1985

TIGHT ROPE

Artist: Leon Russell
Written by: Leon Russell
From the album: *Carney*
Label: Shelter
Produced by: Denny Cordell, Leon Russell
Year: 1972
His best-selling single.

TIGHTEN UP

Artist: Archie Bell & the Drells
Written by: Billy Buttier, Archie Bell
From the album: *Tighten Up*
Label: Atlantic
Produced by: Skipper Lee Frazier
Year: 1968
#1 R&B/#1 crossover beach-music classic.

TIL I HEAR IT FROM YOU

Artist: Gin Blossoms
Written by: Jessie Valenzuela, Rob Wilson, Marshall Crenshaw
From the album: *Empire Records Soundtrack*
Label: A&M
Year: 1995
Latter-day folk/rock brilliance.

TIL I KISSED YOU

Artist: The Everly Brothers
Written by: Don Everly
From the album: *The Fabulous Style of the Everly Brothers*
Label: Cadence
Produced by: Archie Bleyer
Year: 1959
Adding a drumbeat by Cricket Jerry Allison, the Everlys produce their last Top 5 hit for Cadence (accompanied by the rest of the Crickets).

TIME

Artist: Pink Floyd
Written by: Roger Waters, David Gilmour, Nick Mason, Rick Wright
From the album: *Dark Side of the Moon*
Label: Harvest
Produced by: Pink Floyd
Year: 1973
Reflecting on Thoreau's lives of quiet desperation, powered by a David Gilmour guitar solo. Suggested segue: *The Wizard of Oz* or *Dark Side of the Rainbow*.

TIME (CLOCK OF THE HEART)

Artist: Culture Club
Written by: Roy Hay, Jon Moss, Michael Craig
From the album: *Kissing to Be Clever*
Label: Epic
Produced by: Steve Levene
Year: 1983

TIME AFTER TIME

Artist: Cyndi Lauper
Written by: Cyndi Lauper, Rob Hyman
From the album: *She's So Unusual*
Label: Portrait
Produced by: Rick Chertoff
Year: 1984
This three-hankie ballad was her first #1. Covered by Miles Davis (Columbia, '85)

TIME AND LOVE

Artist: Laura Nyro
Written by: Laura Nyro
From the album: *New York Tendaberry*
Label: Columbia
Produced by: Roy Halee, Laura Nyro
Year: 1969
Covered by her Brooklyn reverse mirror image, Barbra Streisand (Columbia, '71).

TIME FOR ME TO FLY

Artist: Reo Speedwagon
Written by: Kevin Cronin Jr.
From the album: *You Can Tune a Piano But You Can't Tuna Fish*
Label: Epic
Produced by: Kevin Cronin
Year: 1978
Commercial breakthrough for the Midwestern warhorse road band.

TIME HAS COME TODAY

Artist: The Chambers Brothers
Written by: Joseph Chambers, Willie Chambers
From the album: *The Time Has Come*
Label: Columbia
Produced by: David Robinson
Year: 1967
One of the most enduring '60s chants, primarily by virtue of its inclusion in several period films, including *Coming Home* ('78) and *The Doors* ('91).

TIME IN A BOTTLE

Artist: Jim Croce
Written by: Jim Croce, Tommy West
From the album: *You Don't Mess Around with Jim*
Label: ABC
Produced by: Terry Cashman
Year: 1972
Featured in the 1973 TV movie *She Lives*, this poignant easy listening folk/rocker soared to #1 after Croce was killed in a plane crash two weeks after the movie aired.

TIME IS ON MY SIDE

Artist: Irma Thomas
Written by: Jerry Ragovoy
From the album: *Wish Someone Would Care*
Label: Imperial
Year: 1964
B-side of "Anyone Who Knows What Love Is (Will Understand)." Covered by the Rolling Stones (London, '64).

TIME IS TIGHT

Artist: Booker T. and the MG's
Written by: Steve Cropper, Booker T. Jones, Al Jackson Jr., Donald V. Dunn
From the album: *Uptight*
Label: Stax
Produced by: Booker T. Jones
Year: 1969

TIME OF THE SEASON

Artist: The Zombies
Written by: Rod Argent
From the album: *Odyssey and Oracle*
Label: Date
Produced by: Rod Argent, Chris White
Year: 1967
Jazz-flavored mystic rocker.

TIME OUT OF MIND

Artist: Steely Dan
Written by: Donald Fagen, Walter Becker
From the album: *Gaucho*
Label: MCA
Produced by: Gary Katz
Year: 1980
Their last hit for twenty years.

TIME PASSAGES

Artist: Al Stewart
Written by: Al Stewart, Peter White
From the album: *Time Passages*
Label: Arista
Produced by: Alan Parsons
Year: 1978
Biggest hit for the Scottish folkie.

TIME PASSES SLOWLY

Artist: Bob Dylan
Written by: Bob Dylan
From the album: *New Morning*
Label: Columbia
Produced by: Bob Johnston
Year: 1970
Bob returns to his country and northern roots.

TIME THE AVENGER

Artist: The Pretenders
Written by: Chrissie Hynde
From the album: *Learning to Crawl*
Label: Sire
Produced by: Chris Thomas
Year: 1984
Another midlife crisis ode.

TIME WARP

Artist: Cast of *Rocky Horror Picture Show*
Written by: Richard O'Brien
From the album: *The Rocky Horror Picture Show*
Label: Ode
Year: 1974
Cheerfully flaky cross-dressing anthem.

TIME WON'T LET ME

Artist: The Outsiders
Written by: Chet Kelley, Tom King
From the album: *Time Won't Let Me*
Label: Capitol
Produced by: Tom King
Year: 1966
Existential folk/rock.

TIMELESS

Artist: Goldie
Written by: Diane Charlemagne, Rob Playford,
Clifford Price (Goldie)
From the album: *Timeless*
Label: ffrr
Year: 1994

Introducing the jungle beat of drum n bass to popular dance society.

TIMES THEY ARE A-CHANGIN', THE

Artist: Bob Dylan
Written by: Bob Dylan
From the album: *The Times They Are A-Changin'*
Label: Columbia
Produced by: Tom Wilson
Year: 1964
Putting the post-Kennedy generational malaise into countercultural perspective. #7 in the UK.

TIMOTHY

Artist: The Buoys
Written by: Rupert Holmes
From the album: *Timothy*
Label: Scepter
Year: 1971
The dark side of bubblegum. Segue: "Big Bad John."

TIN CAN ALLEY

Artist: Eric Andersen
Written by: Eric Andersen
From the album: *More Hits from Tin Can Alley*
Label: Vanguard
Produced by: Al Gorgoni
Year: 1968
When folk turned to folk/rock, in the mid-60s, few of the Greenwich Village elite were able to make the cut. This Dylanesque, all-inclusive, anti-urban diatribe from the recovered romantic balladeer was his last best shot.

TIN MAN

Artist: America
Written by: Lee Bunnell
From the album: *Holiday*
Label: Warner Brothers
Produced by: George Martin
Year: 1974
George Martin carries his ecumenical post-Beatles fantasies of continued generational relevance into the Land of Oz, perhaps inadvertently awakening the sensibilities of Australia's Little River Band, to say nothing of Rick Springfield and even less about Air Supply.

TIN PAN ALLEY

Artist: Stevie Ray Vaughan
Written by: Les Reed
From the album: *Couldn't Stand the Weather*
Label: Epic
Year: 1984
Stevie's extended blues blast.

TING-A-LING

Artist: The Clovers
Written by: Ahmet Ertegun
Label: Atlantic

Produced by: Ahmet Ertegun, Herb Abramson
Year: 1952
#1 R&B, up-tempo.

TIP TOE THROUGH THE TULIPS

Artist: Tiny Tim
Written by: Al Dubin, Joe Burke
From the album: *God Bless Tiny Tim*
Label: Reprise
Produced by: Richard Perry
Year: 1968
Warbling ukulele remake of the 1929 standard. Paved the way for Taco, the New Vaudeville Band, and Pee Wee Herman, to say nothing of Tiny's wedding to Miss Vicki on *The Tonight Show* in 1969.

TIPITINA

Artist: Professor Longhair
Written by: Henry Roeland Byrd (Roy Byrd)
Label: Mercury
Year: 1954
Ode to the famed New Orleans nightspot was this influential keyboard man's signature tune.

TIRED OF BEING ALONE

Artist: Al Green
Written by: Al Green
From the album: *Al Green Gets Next to You*
Label: Hi
Produced by: Willie Mitchell
Year: 1971
Green goes gold; his only #1 single.

TIRED OF TOEIN' THE LINE

Artist: Rocky Burnette
Written by: Rocky Burnette, Ron Coleman
From the album: *The Son of Rock and Roll*
Label: EMI-America
Produced by: Jim Seiter, Bill House
Year: 1980
The son of Johnny, with a neo-rockabilly one-shot.

TIRED OF WAITING FOR YOU

Artist: The Kinks
Written by: Ray Davies
From the album: *Kinks Size*
Label: Reprise
Produced by: Shel Talmy
Year: 1965
Their biggest hit in the US, third biggest in the UK.

TO BE LOVED

Artist: Jackie Wilson
Written by: Berry Gordy Jr.
From the album: *He's So Fine*
Label: Brunswick
Produced by: Milton DeLugg
Year: 1958

One of the great voices of the R&B/doo-wop age breaks out of Detroit with his first big soulful, operatic R&B/crossover, written by future Motown founder, Berry Gordy.

TO BE WITH YOU

Artist: Mr. Big
Written by: Eric Martin, David Grahame
From the album: *Lean into It*
Label: Atlantic
Produced by: Kevin Elson
Year: 1992
The dread rock ballad produces the dread hit single, anathema for a metal band that wants to sustain arena credibility with heavy, axe-wielding tunes like "Addicted to That Rush."

TO BE YOUNG

Artist: Lonesome Val
Written by: Val Haymes
From the album: *Lonesome Val*
Label: Restless/Bar None
Year: 1990
Reinventing Katrina and the Waves as a New York power punk band.

TO BE YOUNG, GIFTED AND BLACK

Artist: Nina Simone
Written by: Nina Simone, Weldon Irvine Jr.
From the album: *Silk and Soul*
Label: RCA
Produced by: Stroud Productions
Year: 1969
Jazz singer Simone pens a classic positive anthem and gets her only Top 10 on the R&B charts. Covered by Aretha Franklin (Atlantic, '71).

TO HELL WITH POVERTY

Artist: Gang of Four
Written by: Andy Gill, Hugo Burnham, Jon King
From the album: *Another Day/Another Dollar*
Label: Warner Brothers
Year: 1982
Their classic single.

TO KINGDOM COME

Artist: The Band
Written by: Robbie Robertson
From the album: *Music from Big Pink*
Label: Capitol
Produced by: John Simon, the Band
Year: 1968
Unaved the way for a back-to-the-soil revolution of the late '60s.

TO KNOW HIM IS TO LOVE HIM

Artist: The Teddy Bears
Written by: Phil Spector
From the album: *The Teddy Bears Sing*
Label: Dore
Produced by: Phil Spector
Year: 1958
The neo-girl-group, pre-Fleetwoods, soft rock sound of the Teddy Bears shows little of Phil Spector's dramatic production flair, except for its incipient megalomania. The #1 record, originally the B-side of "Don't You Worry My Little Pet," would be all the resume he would need to launch a monster career. Group member Annette Kleinbard became a successful songwriter as well, under the name of Carol Connors. Drummer Sandy Nelson went on to "Teen Beat."

TO LIVE IS TO FLY

Artist: Townes Van Zandt
Written by: Townes Van Zandt
From the album: *High, Low and in Between*
Produced by: Kevin Eggers
Label: Poppy
Year: 1972
Mournful epic epitomizes the dour Van Zandt worldview.

TO LOVE SOMEBODY

Artist: Bee Gees
Written by: Barry Gibb, Robin Gibb, Maurice Gibb
From the album: *Horizontal*
Label: Atco
Produced by: Robert Stigwood
Year: 1967
Torchy pop/rock, Covered by Janis Joplin (Columbia, '69).

TO MAKE YOU FEEL MY LOVE

Artist: Bob Dylan
Written by: Bob Dylan
From the album: *Time out of Mind*
Label: Columbia
Produced by: Daniel Lanois
Year: 1997
Unusually accessible Dylan ballad. Covered by Billy Joel (Columbia '97) and Garth Brooks and Trisha Yearwood in the film *Hope Floats* (Capitol, '98), where it was nominated for a Grammy for Best Country Song.

TO SING FOR YOU

Artist: Donovan
Written by: Donovan Leitch
From the album: *Catch the Wind*
Label: Hickory
Produced by: Steve Hoffman
Year: 1965
Introducing "the English Dylan" to Bob, his audience and entourage, in the classic documentary *Don't Look Back*; with this song, Donovan joins Tommy Sands on *The Les Crane Show* and the reporter from *Time*, in the movie, as another Dylan media victim.

TO SIR, WITH LOVE

Artist: Lulu
Written by: Don Black, Marc London
From the album: *Lulu Sings*
Label: Epic
Produced by: Mickie Most
Year: 1967
Title song from the film in which Lulu costarred with Sidney Poitier was the top rock ballad of the year. Originally the B-side of "Let's Pretend." Covered by Natalie Merchant and Michael Stipe (Elektra, '94).

TO THE AISLE

Artist: The Five Satins
Written by: Billy Dawn Smith, Stuart Wiener
From the album: *The Five Satins Sing*
Label: Ember
Year: 1957
Classic doo-wop ballad, espousing harmony and monogamy.

TO ZION

Artist: Lauryn Hill
Written by: Lauryn Hill, Norman Gimble, Charles Fox
From the album: *The Miseducation of Lauryn Hill*
Label: Ruffhouse
Produced by: Lauryn Hill
Year: 1998
Dedicated to Hill's son. Samples the Gimble & Fox tune "Killing Me Softly with His Song," revived in 1996 by Hill's original group, the Fugees.

TOAD

Artist: Cream
Written by: Ginger Baker
From the album: *Fresh Cream*
Label: Atco
Produced by: Robert Stigwood
Year: 1967
Drum showpiece for Baker.

TOBACCO ROAD

Artist: The Nashville Teens
Written by: John D. Loudermilk
From the album: *Possibly*
Label: London
Produced by: Mickie Most
Year: 1964
English band and producer, Nashville songwriter; UK/US crossover smash.

TODAY

Artist: Jefferson Airplane
Written by: Martyn Buchwald (Marty Balin), Paul Kantner
From the album: *Embryonic Journey*
Produced by: Rick Jarrard
Label: RCA
Year: 1967
Marty Balin steps forward on a folkie ballad.

TODAY

Artist: Smashing Pumpkins
Written by: Billy Corgan
From the album: *Siamese Dream*
Label: Virgin
Produced by: Butch Vig
Year: 1993
Anguished rocker defines Chicago band's polished sound. They'd follow it up in '95 with "Tonight Tonight."

TODAY I MET THE BOY I'M GONNA MARRY

Artist: Darlene Love
Written by: Tony Powers, Ellie Greenwich, Phil Spector
Label: Philles
Produced by: Phil Spector
Year: 1963
Last gasp of Brill-styled R&B romanticized relationships. Covered by a midlife crisis Ellie Greenwich (Verve, '73).

TOGETHER AGAIN

Artist: Janet Jackson
Written by: James Harris, Terry Lewis, Janet Jackson, Rene Elizondo
From the album: *Velvet Rope*
Label: Virgin
Year: 1997
Her 7TH and last #1 song.

TOGETHER FOREVER

Artist: Rick Astley
Written by: Mike Stock, Matt Aitken, Pete Waterman
From the album: *Whenever You Need Somebody*
Label: RCA
Produced by: Mike Stock, Matt Aitken, Pete Waterman
Year: 1988
Teenybop dance groove redux; his second straight #1.

TOGETHER OR ALONE

Artist: Sebadoh
Written by: Lou Barlow
From the album: *Bakesale*
Label: Sub Pop
Year: 1994
Critical fave.

TOM DOOLEY

Artist: The Kingston Trio
Written by: Dave Guard (Arranged)
From the album: *The Kingston Trio*
Label: Capitol
Produced by: Voile Gillmore
Year: 1958
This altered traditional Blue Ridge Mountain folk ballad is credited with launching not only the career of Capitol's largest-selling act until the Beatles, but the folk boom of the '60s as well. Actually, what the Kingston Trio launched was the upscale collegiate answer to doo-wop. It was the reaction to this sound that produced the folk scare of the early '60s, led by Bob Dylan and Phil Ochs.

TOM SAWYER

Artist: Rush
Written by: Gary Lee Weinrib (Geddy Lee), Alex Zivojinovich (Alex Lifeson), Neil Peart
From the album: *Moving Pictures*
Label: Mercury
Produced by: Terry Brown, Rush
Year: 1981
The most novelistic of all metal bands mines the classics.

TOM TRAUBERT'S BLUES

Artist: Tom Waits
Written by: Tom Waits
From the album: *Small Change*
Label: Asylum
Produced by: Bones Howe
Year: 1976
Covered by Rod Stewart (Warner Brothers, '94).

TOM'S DINER

Artist: Suzanne Vega
Written by: Suzanne Vega
From the album: *Solitude Standing*
Label: A&M
Produced by: Lenny Kaye, Steve Addabbo
Year: 1987
Spoken cityscape reverie; Vega as a rock and roll Sylvia Plath. Revived in a souped-up dance-hall version by the DNA production team (A&M, '90).

TOMMY GUN

Artist: The Clash
Written by: John Mellor (Joe Strummer), Mick Jones
From the album: *Give 'Em Enough Rope*
Label: Epic
Produced by: Sandy Pearlman
Year: 1978
Their first hit single.

TOMORROW

Artist: Morrissey
Written by: Stephen Morrissey, Alain Gordon White
From the album: *Your Arsenal*
Label: Sire
Produced by: Stephen Street, Mick Ronson
Year: 1992
His biggest rock hit.

TOMORROW

Artist: Silverchair
Written by: Ben Gillies, Darrel Johns
From the album: *Frogstomp*
Produced by: Kevin Shirley
Label: Epic
Year: 1995

TOMORROW IS A LONG TIME

Artist: Bob Dylan
Written by: Bob Dylan
From the album: *The Freewheelin' Bob Dylan*
Label: Columbia
Produced by: John Hammond
Year: 1962
A quintessential rambling song. Covered by Elvis Presley in the movie *Spinout* ('66); his only other cover of a Dylan song was "Don't Think Twice" (RCA, '73). Also covered by Sandy Denny (A&M, '72).

TOMORROW NEVER KNOWS

Artist: The Beatles
Written by: John Lennon, Paul McCartney
From the album: *Revolver*
Label: Capitol
Produced by: George Martin
Year: 1966
First song recorded for *Revolver* features John Lennon on acid interpreting the *Tibetan Book of the Dead*. Now that's a long way from "That'll Be the Day."

TOMORROW NIGHT

Artist: Lonnie Johnson
Written by: Sam Coslow, Will Grosz
Label: King
Year: 1948
#1 R&B/Top 20 crossover. This swing standard introduced by Horace Heidt (Columbia, '39) became, in the hands of Johnson, an electric guitar classic. Covered by LaVern Baker, Charles Brown, Big Joe Turner, Etta Jones, Elvis Presley.

TOMORROW NIGHT

Artist: The Shoes
Written by: Jeff Murphy, Gary Klebe
From the album: *Present Tense*
Label: Elektra
Year: 1979
Low-fi superheroes of the Midwest. This is a re-recording of their Bomp single of '78.

TONIGHT I THINK I'M GONNA GO DOWNTOWN

Artist: Jimmie Dale Gilmore and the Flatlanders
Written by: Jimmie Dale Gilmore, John Reed
From the album: *One More Road*
Label: Charly
Produced by: Royce Clark
Year: 1972
Legendary alt/country track, introduced by Gilmore's short-lived but long-remembered band with Joe Ely and Butch Hancock, the Flatlanders,

whose only album was released on cassette (like most of Hancock's other product) by a small Nashville label run by Shelby Singleton. Release on vinyl didn't come until 1980. Rereleased by Rounder in 1990. Covered by Joe Ely (MCA, '78), Nanci Griffith (Philo, '85), Jimmie Dale Gilmore (Nonesuch, '91).

TONIGHT I'LL BE STAYING HERE WITH YOU

Artist: Bob Dylan
Written by: Bob Dylan
From the album: *Nashville Skyline*
Label: Columbia
Produced by: Bob Johnston
Year: 1969
Thoroughly Nashville Bob.

TONIGHT SHE COMES

Artist: The Cars
Written by: Ric Ocasek
From the album: *Greatest Hits*
Label: Elektra
Produced by: M. Shipley, the Cars
Year: 1985
Pure pop anticlimax.

TONIGHT, TONIGHT

Artist: Smashing Pumpkins
Written by: Billy Corgan,
From the album: *Mellon Collie and the Infinite Sadness*
Label: Virgin
Produced by: Flood, Alan Moulder, Billy Corgan
Year: 1995
With a 30-piece string section and an award winning video.

TONIGHT, TONIGHT, TONIGHT

Artist: Genesis
Written by: Phil Collins, Tony Banks, Mike Rutherford
From the album: *Invisible Touch*
Label: Atlantic
Produced by: Hugh Padgham, Genesis
Year: 1987

TONIGHT WE MURDER

Artist: Ministry
Written by: Alain Jourgenson, Paul Barker, Nardiello
Label: Sire
Produced by: Alain Jourgenson, Paul Barker, Nardiello
Year: 1988
Hard-to-find non-album B-side.

TONIGHT YOU BELONG TO ME

Artist: Patience and Prudence

Written by: Billy Rose, Billy David
Label: Liberty
Year: 1956
Pre-girl-group, preteen standard, introduced by Gene Austin in '27.

TONIGHT'S THE NIGHT

Artist: Solomon Burke
Written by: Solomon Burke, Don Covay
From the album: *Best of Solomon Burke*
Label: Atlantic
Year: 1965
#2 R&B/Top 30 crossover.

TONIGHT'S THE NIGHT

Artist: The Shirelles
Written by: Luther Dixon, Shirley Owens
From the album: *Tonight's the Night*
Label: Scepter
Produced by: Luther Dixon
Year: 1960
Introducing Luther Dixon to the Shirelles; introducing the Shirelles to the national market.

TONIGHT'S THE NIGHT (GONNA BE ALL RIGHT)

Artist: Rod Stewart
Written by: Rod Stewart
From the album: *A Night on the Town*
Label: Warner Brothers
Produced by: Tom Dowd
Year: 1976
Over-the-top seduction song was his biggest hit, banned in the UK.

TONITE TONITE

Artist: The Mellow Kings
Written by: Billy Myles
Label: Herald
Produced by: Al Silver
Year: 1957
Doo-wop enters the white neighborhood, where, for a long while, it passed for black, even though it never made the R&B chart.

TOO BUSY THINKING ABOUT MY BABY

Artist: Marvin Gaye
Written by: Norman Whitfield, Barrett Strong, Janie Bradford
From the album: *M.P.G.*
Label: Tamla
Produced by: Norman Whitfield
Year: 1969
His fourth #1 R&B/Top 10 crossover, second in a row, following up his version of "I Heard It through the Grapevine."

TOO CLOSE

Artist: Next

Written by: Keir Gist, Darren Lighty, Robert Huggar, Raphael Brown, Robert Ford, Denzil Miller, James Moore, Kurt Walker
From the album: *Rated Next*
Label: Arista
Produced by: Kaygee, Darren Lighty
Year: 1997

TOO FUNKY

Artist: George Michael
Written by: George Michael
From the album: *Red Hot and Dance*
Label: Columbia
Produced by: George Michael
Year: 1992
Returning to his long suit as a male model, with his sexiest video yet.

TOO HOT

Artist: Kool & the Gang
Written by: George Brown
From the album: *Ladies Night*
Label: De-Lite
Produced by: Eumir Deodato
Year: 1979

TOO LATE FOR GOODBYES

Artist: Julian Lennon
Written by: Julian Lennon
From the album: *Valotte*
Label: Atlantic
Produced by: Phil Ramone
Year: 1985
Tribute to his father. Suggested segues: "All Those Years Ago" by George Harrison, "Here Today" by Paul McCartney, "Early 1970" by Ringo Starr.

TOO LATE TO TURN BACK NOW

Artist: The Cornelius Brothers and Sister Rose
Written by: Eddie Cornelius
From the album: *The Cornelius Brothers and Sister Rose*
Label: United Artists
Produced by: Bob Archibald
Year: 1972

TOO MANY CREEPS

Artist: Bush Tetras
Written by: Bush Tetras
From the album: *Too Many Creeps*
Label: 99
Year: 1981
Defining No Wave anthem from the streets of New York.

TOO MUCH

Artist: Dave Matthews Band
Written by: Dave Matthews
From the album: *Crash*
Label: RCA

Produced by: Steve Lillywhite
Year: 1996

TOO MUCH

Artist: Elvis Presley
Written by: Bernard Weinman, Lee Rosenberg
From the album: *Elvis' Golden Records*
Label: RCA
Produced by: Steve Sholes
Year: 1957
Abetted by an appearance on *The Ed Sullivan Show*, this became Elvis' first of four straight #1s of '57. Originated by Bernard Hardison in '54.

TOO MUCH HEAVEN

Artist: Bee Gees
Written by: Barry Gibb, Robin Gibb, Maurice Gibb
From the album: *Spirits Having Flown*
Label: RSO
Produced by: Albhy Galutin, Karl Richardson, Bee Gees
Year: 1978
Luxuriating in their Miami period.

TOO MUCH MONKEY BUSINESS

Artist: Chuck Berry
Written by: Chuck Berry
From the album: *After School Sessions*
Label: Chess
Produced by: Leonard Chess, Phil Chess
Year: 1957
Chronicling the life and times of his neighborhood like a duck-walking Nelson Algren. Covered by Tom Rush (Elektra, '65), the Kinks (Capitol, '65), Elvis Presley (RCA Camden, '69).

TOO MUCH OF NOTHING

Artist: Peter, Paul and Mary
Written by: Bob Dylan
From the album: *Late Again*
Label: Warner Brothers
Produced by: Albert Grossman, Milt Okun
Year: 1967
Another product of Dylan's prolific recuperation period with the Band at Big Pink, which would finally surface on *The Basement Tapes* (Columbia, '75). This version hit the Top 40 late in '67, apparently detailing the progress of Dylan's convalescent, and yet creatively abundant, state.

TOO MUCH TIME ON MY HANDS

Artist: Styx
Written by: Tommy Shaw
From the album: *Paradise Theater*
Label: A&M
Produced by: Styx
Year: 1981
Shaw would move on to Damn Yankees in the '90s.

TOO MUCH TOO YOUNG

Artist: The Specials
Written by: Jerry Dammers
From the album: *The Specials*
Label: 2-Tone
Produced by: Elvis Costello
Year: 1979
Their first #1 UK hit.

TOO OLD TO ROCK 'N' ROLL: TOO YOUNG TO DIE

Artist: Jethro Tull
Written by: Ian Anderson
From the album: *Too Old to Rock 'N' Roll: Too Young to Die*
Label: Chrysalis
Produced by: Ian Anderson
Year: 1976
Their defining credo; in '89 these progressive folkies won a Hard Rock Grammy.

TOO POOPED TO POP

Artist: Chuck Berry
Written by: Chuck Berry
From the album: *Rockin' at the Hops*
Label: Chess
Produced by: Leonard Chess, Phil Chess
Year: 1960
Too pooped to partake in the dance crazes of the early '60s, and in the pen by '62, this was Chuck's only chart record until the Beatles and the Stones restored him to his place of esteem in '64.

TOO SHY

Artist: Kajagoogoo
Written by: Chris Hamill (Limahl), Nick Beggs
From the album: *White Feathers*
Label: Capitol
Produced by: Nick Rhodes
Year: 1983
Synth-wave surfers.

TOO WEAK TO FIGHT

Artist: Clarence Carter
Written by: John Keyes, Clarence Carter, Rick Hall, George Jackson
From the album: *Dynamic Clarence Carter*
Label: Atlantic
Produced by: Rick Hall
Year: 1969

TOP FORTY OF THE LORD, THE

Artist: Sha-Na-Na
Written by: Scott Simon
From the album: *Sha-Na-Na*
Label: Buddah
Produced by: Erwin Kramer
Year: 1971
Ingenious Top 40 show band and TV concept tries its hand at a semiserious spoof.

TOP OF THE WORLD

Artist: Carpenters
Written by: John Bettis, Richard Carpenter
From the album: *A Song for You*
Label: A&M
Produced by: Jack Daugherty, Richard Carpenter, Karen Carpenter
Year: 1973
Their biggest hit since their cover of "Close to You," in 1970.

TOP OF THE WORLD

Artist: Van Halen
Written by: Eddie Van Halen, Alex Van Halen, Michael Anthony, Sammy Hagar
From the album: *For Unlawful Carnal Knowledge*
Label: Warner Brothers
Produced by: Ted Templeman, Andy Johns, Van Halen
Year: 1991
Riding an aging arena warhorse into the new alternative age.

TOPSY (PART II)

Artist: Cozy Cole
Written by: Edgar Battle, Edward Durham
Label: Love
Year: 1958
The original "Topsy" was released by Benny Goodman (Victor, '38).

TORN

Artist: Ednaswap
Written by: Scott Cutler, Anne Preven, Phil Thornally
From the album: *Chicken*
Label: Island
Year: 1996
Stiffed when introduced by the Cutler and Preven group. But became a hit a couple of years later when the pert Aussie model Natalie Imbruglia (RCA, '98) caught the tail end of the waiflike thrush invasion, clinging to the heels of fellow Australian Merrill Bainbridge. Meanwhile, Kasey Chambers languished. And Ednaswap was dropped.

TORN BETWEEN TWO LOVERS

Artist: Mary MacGreggor
Written by: Phil Jarrell, Peter Yarrow
From the album: *Tom between Two Lovers*
Label: Ariola
Produced by: Barry Beckett, Peter Yarrow
Year: 1977
In the delicate folk pop tradition of "We'll Sing in the Sunshine," a truly unsettling proposition. Segue: "Triad" by Jefferson Airplane.

TOSSIN' AND TURNIN'

Artist: Bobby Lewis
Written by: Malou Rene, Ritchie Adams

From the album: *Tossin' and Turnin'*
Label: Beltone
Produced by: Joe Rene
Year: 1961
#1 R&B/#1 crossover; the biggest hit of the year.

TOTAL ECLIPSE OF THE HEART

Artist: Bonnie Tyler
Written by: Jim Steinman
From the album: *Faster Than the Speed of Night*
Label: Columbia
Produced by: Jim Steinman
Year: 1983
A #1 single in the US and the UK, on the grandeur scale halfway between Reparata and the Delrons and Meat Loaf. Features Roy Bittan on keyboards, Max Weinberg on drums and Rick Derringer on guitar.

TOUCH ME

Artist: The Doors
Written by: Jim Morrison, Robbie Krieger, John Densmore, Ray Manzarek
From the album: *The Soft Parade*
Label: Elektra
Produced by: Paul Rothchild
Year: 1969
Their last visit to the Top 10. Segue: "I Touch Myself" by the Divinyls.

TOUCH ME (ALL NIGHT LONG)

Artist: Wish (Featuring Fonda Rae)
Written by: Delyle Carmichael, Patrick Adams
Label: Personal
Year: 1985
Big in the clubs. Covered by Cathy Dennis (Polydor, '90).

TOUCH ME (I WANT YOUR BODY)

Artist: Samantha Fox
Written by: Michael Shreeve, J. Astrop, Pete Q. Harris
From the album: *Touch Me*
Label: Jive
Produced by: J. Astrop, Pete Q. Harris
Year: 1987
As a trailblazing icon for horny young boys, Samantha took off her top in the newspapers several years before Madonna took it all off in a book.

TOUCH ME I'M SICK

Artist: Mudhoney
Written by: Steve Turner, Mark Arm
From the album: *Superfuzz Bigmuff*
Label: Sub Pop
Produced by: Jack Endino

Year: 1988
Key single from the legendary Seattle scenesters.

TOUCH OF GREY

Artist: Grateful Dead
Written by: Jerry Garcia, Robert Hunter
From the album: *In the Dark*
Label: Arista
Produced by: Jerry Garcia, J. Cutler
Year: 1987
After twenty years, a Top 10 single.

TOUCH THE HEM OF HIS GARMENT

Artist: The Soul Stirrers
Written by: Sam Cooke
Label: Specialty
Produced by: Art Rupe
Year: 1956
Tapping the gospel roots of one of rock's most soulful crooners.

TOUCH, PEEL AND STAND

Artist: Days of the New
Written by: Travis Meeks
From the album: *Days of the New*
Label: Geffen
Year: 1997
Nu metal breakthrough.

TOUCHA-TOUCHA-TOUCH ME

Artist: Susan Sarandon
Written by: Richard O'Brien
From the album: *The Rocky Horror Picture Show Cast Album*
Label: Ode
Year: 1974
A cameo cutie from the classic cult musical.

TOURNIQUET

Artist: Marilyn Manson
Written by: Brian (Marilyn Manson) Warner, Daisy Berkowitz, Twiggy Ramirez
From the album: *Antichrist Superstar*
Produced by: Trent Reznor, Dave Ogilve
Label: Nothing
Year: 1996
His reverse Frankenstein fantasies date back to high school poetry.

TOWER OF SONG

Artist: Leonard Cohen
Written by: Leonard Cohen
From the album: *I'm Your Man*
Label: Columbia
Year: 1988
Covered by Nick Cave and the Bad Seeds (Atlantic, '91).

TOWER OF STRENGTH

Artist: Gene McDaniels
Written by: Burt Bacharach, Bob Hilliard
From the album: *Tower of Strength*
Label: Liberty
Produced by: Snuff Garrett
Year: 1961

TOWN WITHOUT PITY

Artist: Gene Pitney
Written by: Ned Washington, Dimitri Tiomkin
From the album: *World-Wide Winners*
Label: Musicor
Year: 1961
Title song from the western movie, nominated for an Oscar.

TOY SOLDIERS

Artist: Martika
Written by: Martika Marrero, Michael Jay
From the album: *Martika*
Label: Columbia
Produced by: Michael Jay
Year: 1989
Hidden in the bubble wrapping was a protest song not unlike "Which Way You Goin' Billy."

TRACES

Artist: The Classics IV and Dennis Yost
Written by: Buddy Buie, James B. Cobb Jr., Emory Gordy Jr.
From the album: *Traces*
Label: Imperial
Produced by: Buddy Buie
Year: 1969

TRACKS OF MY TEARS, THE

Artist: The Miracles
Written by: Smokey Robinson, Pete Moore, Marv Tarplin
From the album: *Going to a Go-Go*
Label: Tamla
Produced by: Smokey Robinson
Year: 1965
Their remaining hits would be recorded as Smokey Robinson and the Miracles. Covered by Aretha Franklin (Atlantic, '69), Linda Ronstadt (Asylum, '75).

TRACY

Artist: The Cuff Links
Written by: Paul Vance, Lee Pockriss
From the album: *Tracy*
Label: Decca
Produced by: Paul Vance
Year: 1969
Another day's work for studio singer Ron Dante.

TRAGEDY

Artist: Bee Gees
Written by: Barry Gibb, Robin Gibb, Maurice Gibb

From the album: *Spirits Having Flown*
Label: RSO
Produced by: Albhy Galutin, Karl Richardson, Bee Gees
Year: 1978
Reviving the spirit of "Massachusetts."

TRAGEDY

Artist: Thomas Wayne
Written by: Gerald Nelson, Fred Burch
Label: Fernwood
Produced by: Scotty Moore
Year: 1959
Prescient gloom-and-doom sentiments from an Elvis classmate, protege of Scotty Moore. Released a week or so before "The Day the Music Died."

TRAIN IN VAIN (STAND BY ME)

Artist: The Clash
Written by: John Mellor (Joe Strummer), Mick Jones
From the album: *London Calling*
Label: Epic
Produced by: Guy Stevens
Year: 1979
Punk rock's last best hope marked the end of a decade of recession and repression in England with their first hit in the US.

TRAIN KEPT A-ROLLIN', THE

Artist: Johnny Burnette and the Rock and Roll Trio
Written by: Tiny Bradshaw, Syd Nathan (Lois Mann), Howie Kay
From the album: *Johnny Burnette and the Rock and Roll Trio*
Label: Coral
Produced by: Owen Bradley
Year: 1956
A Tiny Bradshaw R&B tune, transformed by Paul Burlison's accidental fuzztone experiments into the first guitar classic of the rock and roll era. Covered by actor Jim Dale in the '57 movie *The 6.5 Special*, the Yardbirds (Epic, '69), Aerosmith (Columbia, '74), Jeff Beck in the '89 movie, *Twins*.

TRAMP

Artist: Lowell Fulson
Written by: Lowell Fulson, Jimmy McCracklin
From the album: *The Tramp*
Label: Kent
Produced by: Lowell Fulson
Year: 1967
Covered by Otis and Carla (Stax, '67).

TRAMPLED UNDER FOOT

Artist: Led Zeppelin
Written by: Jimmy Page, Robert Plant, John Paul Jones
From the album: *Physical Graffiti*

Label: Swan Song
Produced by: Jimmy Page
Year: 1975

TRANCE ON SEDGWICK STREET

Artist: Terry Callier
Written by: Terry Callier
From the album: *Occasional Rain*
Label: Cadet
Year: 1972
Early psychedelic soul man from Chicago offers a haunting street scene worthy of a Romare Beardon painting.

TRANS EUROPE EXPRESS

Artist: Kraftwerk
Written by: Ralf Hutter, Florian Schneider
From the album: *Trans Europe Express*
Label: Capitol
Produced by: Ralf Hutter, Florian Schneider
Year: 1977
The new romantics in England—the Jesus and Mary Chain, My Bloody Valentine, the Cocteau Twins—were listening; so were the hip hop DJs of America.

TRANSFUSION

Artist: Nervous Norvus
Written by: Jimmy Drake (Nervous Norvus)
Label: Dot
Year: 1956
Rockabilly novelty, introducing to the teen market the plentious wreck on the highway (or on the railroad tracks) subgenre.

TRAPPED BY A THING CALLED LOVE

Artist: Denise Lasalle
Written by: Denise O. Jones
From the album: *Trapped by a Thing Called Love*
Label: Westbound
Produced by: Denise LaSalle
Year: 1971
#1 R&B/Top 20 crossover.

TRASH

Artist: New York Dolls
Written by: David Johansen, Syl Sylvain
From the album: *New York Dolls*
Label: Mercury
Produced by: Todd Rundgren
Year: 1973
Operating out of Andy Warhol's Max's Kansas City, they come up with their defining metaphor. Includes an homage to Mickey and Sylvia: "How do you call your lover boy?"

TRAVELIN' BAND

Artist: Creedence Clearwater Revival

Written by: John C. Fogerty
From the album: *Cosmo's Factory*
Label: Fantasy
Produced by: John C. Fogerty
Year: 1970
Suggested segues: "Band on the Run" by Wings, "Homeward Bound" by Simon and Garfunkel, "Jukebox Hero" by Foreigner, "You're Probably Wondering Why I'm Here" by the Mothers of Invention.

TRAVELIN' MAN

Artist: Ricky Nelson
Written by: Jerry Fuller
From the album: *Rick Is 21*
Label: Imperial
Produced by: Rick Nelson
Year: 1961
The fulfillment of his signature country pop/rock was his biggest all-time hit. Suggested segue: "The Wanderer" by Dion.

TRAVELING RIVERSIDE BLUES

Artist: Led Zeppelin
Written by: Jimmy Page, Robert Plant, Robert Johnson
Label: Atlantic
Produced by: John Walters
Year: 1969
Written and recorded in '36 by Robert Johnson. This classic performance first heard over BBC radio.

TREASURE OF LOVE

Artist: Clyde McPhatter
Written by: Joe Shapiro, Lou Stallman
From the album: *Clyde McPhatter and the Drifters*
Label: Atlantic
Produced by: Ahmet Ertegun, Jerry Wexler
Year: 1956
Second top 10 R&B/Top 20 crossover for the former Dominoes lead singer.

TREAT HER LIKE A LADY

Artist: The Cornelius Brothers and Sister Rose
Written by: Eddie Cornelius
From the album: *The Cornelius Brothers and Sister Rose*
Label: United Artists
Produced by: Bob Archibald
Year: 1971

TREAT HER RIGHT

Artist: Roy Head
Written by: Roy Head
From the album: *Treat Me Right*
Label: Back Beat
Year: 1965
His first and biggest hit.

TREAT ME NICE

Artist: Elvis Presley
Written by: Jerry Leiber, Mike Stoller
From the album: *Elvis' Golden Records*
Label: RCA
Produced by: Steve Sholes, Jerry Leiber, Mike Stoller
Year: 1957
B-side of "Jailhouse Rock."

TRENCHTOWN ROCK

Artist: Bob Marley & the Wailers
Written by: Bob Marley
Label: Island
Produced by: Lee Perry
Year: 1971
Eloquent and authentic survival anthem about a hurricane-ravaged part of Jamaica. Covered by Sublime (Gasoline Alley, '97).

TRIAD

Artist: The Byrds
Written by: David Crosby
Label: Columbia
Produced by: Gary Usher
Year: 1967
Crosby's attempt at making trouble, with his band, and with the opposite sex. Covered in the female version by Grace Slick with Jefferson Airplane (RCA, '68). Segue: "Torn between Two Lovers" by Mary MacGreggor.

TRIBUTE TO A KING, A

Artist: William Bell
Written by: William Bell, Booker T. Jones
Label: Stax
Produced by: Booker T. Jones
Year: 1968
Tribute to Otis Redding.

TRICKLE TRICKLE

Artist: The Videos
Written by: Clarence Bassett Jr.
Label: Casino
Year: 1958
Where doo-wop merges with scat. Covered by Manhattan Transfer (Atlantic, '80). Segue: "Rain on the Roof" by the Lovin' Spoonful.

TRIPPIN' ON A HOLE IN A PAPER HEART

Artist: Stone Temple Pilots
Written by: Dean DeLeo, Robert DeLeo, Scott Weiland, Eric Kretz
From the album: *Tiny Music … Songs from the Vatican Gift Shop*
Label: Atlantic
Produced by: Brendan O'Brien
Year: 1996

TRIPPING BILLIES

Artist: Dave Matthews Band
Written by: Dave Matthews
From the album: *Remember Two Things*
Label: Bama Rags
Produced by: John Alagia
Year: 1993
Early performance favorite.

TROOPER, THE

Artist: Iron Maiden
Written by: Steve Harris
From the album: *Piece of Mind*
Label: Harvest
Produced by: Martin Birch
Year: 1983
A blast from Harris' monster bass.

TROUBLE BLUES

Artist: Charles Brown
Written by: Roy Brown
Label: Deluxe
Year: 1949
Bluesy #1 R&B ballad was covered by Sam Cooke (RCA, '63).

TROUBLE COMIN' EVERY DAY

Artist: The Mothers of Invention
Written by: Frank Zappa
From the album: *Freak Out*
Label: Verve
Produced by: Tom Wilson
Year: 1966
Prefiguring the kids versus cops confrontations of L.A. high society. Suggested Segue: "For What It's Worth" by Buffalo Springfield.

TROUBLE ME

Artist: 10,000 Maniacs
Written by: Natalie Merchant, Dennis Drew
From the album: *Blind Man's Zoo*
Label: Elektra
Produced by: Peter Asher
Year: 1989

TROUBLED TIMES

Artist: Fountains of Wayne
Written by: Chris Collingwood, Adam Schlesinger
From the album: *Utopia Parkway*
Label: Atlantic
Produced by: Adam Schleshinger, Chris Collingwood
Year: 1999

TROUBLES, THE

Artist: The Roches
Written by: Maggie Roche, Suzzy Roche, Terre Roche
From the album: *The Roches*
Label: Warner Brothers

Produced by: Robert Fripp
Year: 1979
Commenting on Northern Ireland. Segue: "Zombie" by the Cranberries.

TROY

Artist: Sinead O'Connor
Written by: Sinead O'Connor
From the album: *The Lion and the Cobra*
Label: Chrysalis
Produced by: Kevin Maloney, Sinead O'Connor
Year: 1988
Joycean epic jumpstarts the controversial career of this striking Irish rebel girl.

TRUCKIN'

Artist: Grateful Dead
Written by: Robert Hunter, Jerry Garcia, Philip Lesh, Bob Weir, Billy Kreutzmann
From the album: *American Beauty*
Label: Warner Brothers
Produced by: Grateful Dead
Year: 1970
Detailing a long, strange trip that would only get longer and stranger, eventually logging more miles and reels of tape than any rock band before or since.

TRUE

Artist: Spandau Ballet
Written by: Gary Kemp
From the album: *True*
Label: Chrysalis
Produced by: Tony Swain, Steve Jolley
Year: 1983
First of the new British romantics acts, with their only UK #1 out of ten Top 10 hits, and their only US Top 10 crossover.

TRUE BLUE

Artist: Madonna
Written by: Steve Bray, Madonna Ciccone
From the album: *True Blue*
Label: Sire
Produced by: Steve Bray, Madonna
Year: 1986
Bigger in England, where it was her third #1.

TRUE COLORS

Artist: Cyndi Lauper
Written by: Billy Steinberg, Tom Kelly
From the album: *True Colors*
Label: Portrait
Produced by: Lenny Petze, Cyndi Lauper
Year: 1986
Suggested segues: "Kodachrome" by Paul Simon and "The Times of Your Life" by Paul Anka.

TRUE FINE MAMA

Artist: Little Richard
Written by: Richard Penniman (Little Richard)
From the album: *Here's Little Richard*

Label: Specialty
Produced by: Art Rupe
Year: 1955
Emerging from the limits of R&B as a rocker unrestrained.

TRUE LOVE WAYS

Artist: Buddy Holly
Written by: Buddy Holly, Norman Petty
From the album: *The Buddy Holly Story*
Label: Coral
Produced by: Bob Thiele
Year: 1958
Covered by Peter and Gordon (Capitol, '65), and performed by Trent Reznor in the '87 Michael J. Fox/Joan Jett film *Light of Day*.

TRULY MADLY DEEPLY

Artist: Savage Garden
Written by: Darren Hayes, Daniel Jones
From the album: *Savage Garden*
Produced by: Darren Hayes, Daniel Jones, Charles Fisher
Label: Columbia
Year: 1997
Out of the Air Supply warehouse.

TRY (JUST A LITTLE BIT HARDER)

Artist: Garnet Mimms & the Enchanters
Written by: Jerry Ragovoy (Norman Meade), Chip Taylor
Label: United Artists
Produced by: Jerry Ragovoy
Year: 1963
As a Ragovoy pipeline to soul glory, Mimms was again the perfect foil. Covered by Janis Joplin (Columbia, '69).

TRY A LITTLE TENDERNESS

Artist: Otis Redding
Written by: Harry Woods, Jimmy Campbell, Reg Connerly
From the album: *Dictionary of Soul*
Label: Volt
Produced by: Otis Redding, Jim Stewart, Steve Cropper
Year: 1966
Popularized by Ruth Etting in '32, reluctantly renovated and rehabilitated by Otis a generation later.

TRY ME

Artist: James Brown and the Famous Flames
Written by: James Brown
From the album: *Try Me*
Label: Federal
Produced by: Andy Gibson
Year: 1958
His first #1 R&B hit.

TRYIN' TO LOVE TWO

Artist: William Bell
Written by: William Bell, Paul Mitchell
From the album: *Coming back for More*
Label: Mercury
Produced by: Paul Mitchell
Year: 1977
His only Top 10 hit.

TRYING TO GET TO YOU

Artist: Elvis Presley
Written by: Charles Singleton, Rose Marie McCoy
From the album: *Elvis Presley*
Produced by: Sam Phillips
Year: 1955
By a top songwriting team of the era, one of El's favorites and a future rockabilly standard. Among the five previously unreleased Sun Records originals on his first RCA album. Covered by Roy Orbison, Ricky Nelson, Jimmie Dale Gilmore, the Stray Cats, and Motorhead's frontman, Lemmy Kilmeister.

TRYING TO HOLD ON TO MY WOMAN

Artist: Lamont Dozier
Written by: McKinley Jackson, James Reddick
From the album: *Out Here on My Own*
Label: ABC
Year: 1974
Sprung from the Motown confines of the Holland Brothers, Dozier returns to his singing roots.

TRYING TO LIVE MY LIFE WITHOUT YOU

Artist: Otis Clay
Written by: Eugene Williams
Label: Hi
Produced by: Willie Mitchell
Year: 1972
Revered R&B cut. Covered by Bob Seger (Capitol, '81). Suggested segue: "The Long Run" by the Eagles.

TSOP (THE SOUND OF PHILADELPHIA)

Artist: MFSB
Written by: Kenny Gamble, Leon Huff
From the album: *Love Is the Message*
Label: Philadelphia International
Produced by: Kenny Gamble, Leon Huff
Year: 1973
Theme for *Soul Train*, TV's landmark black bandstand show, was a #1 R&B/#1 crossover, certifying Philadelphia as the teen dance capitol of black America, as it had been a decade and a half ago for white America.

TUBTHUMPING

Artist: Chumbawamba
Written by: Chumbawamba

From the album: *Tubthumper*
Label: Republic
Year: 1997
Rousing political, football and beerhall anthem was their only US hit.

TUBULAR BELLS

Artist: Mike Oldfield
Written by: Mike Oldfield
From the album: *Tubular Bells*
Label: Virgin
Produced by: Mike Oldfield
Year: 1974
Virgin Records is launched with the theme from the movie *The Exorcist*. Narrated by Viv Stanshall.

TUCUMSEH VALLEY

Artist: Townes Van Zandt
Written by: Townes Van Zandt
From the album: *For the Sake of the Song*
Produced by: Jack Clement, Jim Malloy
Label: Poppy
Year: 1968
Tale of distraught waitress typifies Van Zandt's rustic poetry that influenced several generations of alt/country artists.

TUESDAY AFTERNOON (FOREVER AFTERNOON)

Artist: The Moody Blues
Written by: Justin Hayward
From the album: *Days of Future Passed*
Label: Deram
Produced by: Tony Clarke
Year: 1968
Medley with "Nights in White Satin" could kill an entire day.

TUFF

Artist: Ace Cannon
Written by: Ace Cannon
From the album: *Tuff-Sax*
Label: Hi
Year: 1961
Sax instrumental.

TUFF ENUFF

Artist: The Fabulous Thunderbirds
Written by: Kim Wilson
From the album: *Tuff Enuff*
Label: Epic
Produced by: Dave Edmunds
Year: 1986
Rockabilly redux from Texas, with horns, breaks into the Top 10.

TULANE

Artist: Chuck Berry
Written by: Chuck Berry
From the album: *Back Home*
Label: Chess
Produced by: Leonard Chess, Phil Chess

Year: 1970
Berry's look back at the '60s.

TULSA TIME

Artist: Eric Clapton
Written by: Danny Flowers
From the album: *Backless*
Label: RSO
Produced by: Jon Astley
Year: 1978
Recorded live at Budokan, Japan. Originated on the country charts by Don Williams.

TUMBLING DICE

Artist: The Rolling Stones
Written by: Mick Jagger, Keith Richards
From the album: *Exile on Main Street*
Label: Rolling Stones
Produced by: Jimmy Miller
Year: 1972
Covered by Linda Ronstadt (Asylum, '77).

TUMBLING DOWN

Artist: Ziggy Marley
Written by: Ziggy Marley, Tyrone Downe
From the album: *Conscious Party*
Label: Virgin
Produced by: Jerry Harrison, Chris Frantz
Year: 1988
Second generation #1 R&B/reggae crossover.

TUNNEL OF LOVE

Artist: Dire Straits
Written by: Mark Knopfler
From the album: *Making Movies*
Label: Warner Brothers
Produced by: Mark Knopfler, Jimmy Iovine
Year: 1980
Some of Knopfler's finest guitar moments.

TUNNEL OF LOVE

Artist: Bruce Springsteen
Written by: Bruce Springsteen
From the album: *Tunnel of Love*
Label: Columbia
Produced by: Jon Landau, Bruce Springsteen, Chuck Plotkin
Year: 1985
Harrowing vision of love as a scary hall of mirrors.

TUPELO HONEY

Artist: Van Morrison
Written by: Van Morrison
From the album: *Tupelo Honey*
Label: Warner Brothers
Produced by: Van Morrison, Ted Templeman
Year: 1971
Walking in Memphis years before Marc Cohn.

TURN BACK THE HANDS OF TIME

Artist: Tyrone Davis
Written by: Jack Daniels, Bonnie Thompson
From the album: *Turn Back the Hands of Time*
Label: Dakar
Produced by: Willie Henderson
Year: 1970
The mid-tempo groove of the year gives him his second #1 R&B/Top 10 crossover.

TURN ON THE NEWS

Artist: Hüsker Dü
Written by: Grant Hart
From the album: *Zen Arcade*
Label: SST
Produced by: Spot, Hüsker Dü
Year: 1984
Essential speedcore anthem from the Minneapolis anti-Prince rockers, cohorts of the Replacements and Soul Asylum.

TURN ON YOUR LOVE LIGHT

Artist: Bobby Bland
Written by: Deadric Malone, Joseph Scott
From the album: *Here's the Man*
Label: Duke
Produced by: Joe Scott
Year: 1961
His most revered rockin' soul and a Top 10 R&B/Top 30 crossover.

TURN THE BEAT AROUND (LOVE TO HEAR PERCUSSION)

Artist: Vickie Sue Robinson
Written by: Peter Jackson, Gerald Jackson
From the album: *Never Gonna Let You Go*
Label: RCA
Produced by: Warren Schatz
Year: 1976
Classic of the disco age. Covered by Gloria Estefan (Epic, '95).

TURN THE PAGE

Artist: Bob Seger
Written by: Bob Seger
From the album: *Back in '72*
Produced by: Punch Andrews
Label: Palladium
Year: 1972
When it seemed the touring life would never end. Segue: "Lodi" by Creedence Clearwater Revival. Covered by Metallica (Elektra, '98).

TURN! TURN! TURN! (TO EVERYTHING THERE IS A SEASON)

Artist: Pete Seeger
Written by: Pete Seeger
From the album: *The Bitter & the Sweet*
Label: Columbia
Produced by: John Hammond
Year: 1962
From the Bible by way of the prophet Pete Seeger. Covered by the Limeliters (RCA, '62). The Byrds (Columbia, '65) brought it to #1, helping usher in folk/rock.

TURNED UP TOO LATE

Artist: Graham Parker
Written by: Graham Parker
From the album: *Heat Treatment*
Label: Mercury
Produced by: Mutt Lange
Year: 1976
His revenge fantasy toward a fickle public would never be fulfilled.

TURNING JAPANESE

Artist: The Vapors
Written by: David Fenton
From the album: *New Clear Days*
Label: United Artists
Produced by: Vic Coppersmith Heaven
Year: 1981
Has come to be thought of as an ode to masturbation. Covered by Liz Phair (Matador, '95).

TURQUOISE

Artist: Donovan
Written by: Donovan Leitch
From the album: *Real Donovan*
Label: Hickory
Produced by: Mickie Most
Year: 1966
Donovan gets the blues. Suggested segue: "Mama You Been on My Mind" by Bob Dylan. Covered by Joan Baez (Vanguard, '67).

TUSH

Artist: ZZ Top
Written by: Billy Gibbons, Dusty Hill, Frank Beard
From the album: *Fandango*
Label: London
Produced by: Bill Ham
Year: 1975
Their first and biggest hit of the '70s. Featured in the '82 film *An Officer and a Gentleman*.

TUSK

Artist: Fleetwood Mac
Written by: Lindsay Buckingham
From the album: *Tusk*
Label: Warner Brothers
Produced by: Fleetwood Mac
Year: 1979
White elephant.

TUTTI FRUTTI

Artist: Little Richard
Written by: Richard Penniman (Little Richard), Robert Blackwell, Dorothy LaBostrie
From the album: *Here's Little Richard*
Label: Specialty

Produced by: Bumps Blackwell
Year: 1955
Arguably the first pure rock and roll performance on record, a New Orleans collaboration, some say whitewash, introducing the future self-proclaimed "Queen of Rock and Roll." Covered by Elvis Presley (RCA, '56), Pat Boone (Dot, '56).

TV EYE

Artist: The Stooges
Written by: Dave Alexander, Ron Asheton, Scott Asheton, James Osterberg (Iggy Pop)
From the album: *Fun House*
Produced by: Don Galluci
Label: Elektra
Year: 1970
One of the great rock and roll screams, up there with Frank Zappa near the end of "You're Probably Wondering Why I'm Here."

TV PARTY

Artist: Black Flag
Written by: Greg Ginn
From the album: *Damaged*
Label: SST
Produced by: Spot, Black Flag
Year: 1981
What might have happened if the Sex Pistols had come from the vast wasteland of suburban L.A.

TV SET

Artist: The Cramps
Written by: Ivy Rorschach, Lux Interior
From the album: *Songs the Lord Taught Us*
Produced by: Alex Chilton
Label: IRS
Year: 1980
Citing their biggest influence, other than horror movies.

TVC 15

Artist: David Bowie
Written by: David Bowie
From the album: *Station to Station*
Label: RCA
Produced by: Harry Maslin, David Bowie
Year: 1976
Disco-age experimentalism.

TWEEDLEE DEE

Artist: LaVern Baker
Written by: Winfield Scott
Label: Atlantic
Produced by: Ahmet Ertegun, Jerry Wexler
Year: 1954
Top 10 R&B/Top 20 crossover. The pop cover by Georgia Gibbs went to #2 (Mercury, '54).

TWELVE-THIRTY (YOUNG GIRLS ARE COMING TO THE CANYON)

Artist: Mamas & the Papas

Written by: John Phillips
From the album: *Farewell to the First Golden Era*
Label: Dunhill
Produced by: Lou Adler
Year: 1967
The prologue to "Life in the Fast Lane" by the Eagles.

TWENTY FLIGHT ROCK

Artist: Eddie Cochran
Written by: Eddie Cochran, Ned Fairchild
From the album: *Singin' to My Baby*
Label: Liberty
Produced by: Snuff Garrett, Eddie Cochran, Jerry Capeheart
Year: 1956
Introduced in a scintillating cameo in the movie *The Girl Can't Help It*. Early indication of the power of the music video.

20TH CENTURY FOX

Artist: The Doors
Written by: Jim Morrison, Ray Manzarek
From the album: *The Doors*
Label: Elektra
Produced by: Paul Rothchild
Year: 1967
Film students, more than a decade before MTV, move over to the then more relevant generational art form—the rock album cut.

21ST CENTURY DIGITAL BOY

Artist: Bad Religion
Written by: Brett Gurewitz
From the album: *Stranger Than Fiction*
Label: Atlantic
Produced by: Andy Wallace
Year: 1994
Breakthrough anthem for this veteran hardcore band.

21ST CENTURY SCHIZOID MAN

Artist: King Crimson
Written by: Robert Fripp, Ian MacDonald, Greg Lake, Mike Giles, Pete Sinfield
From the album: *In the Court of the Crimson King*
Label: Atlantic
Produced by: King Crimson
Year: 1969
Progressive supergroup at its most paranormal.

25 OR 6 TO 4

Artist: Chicago
Written by: Robert Lamm
From the album: *Chicago II*
Label: Columbia
Produced by: James William Guercio
Year: 1970
Lamm establishes Chicago's early voice as the first Big Rock Band of the Big Rock Band era.

2112

Artist: Rush
Written by: Geddy Lee, Alex Lifeson, Neil Peart
From the album: *La Villa Strangiato*
Label: Seagull
Produced by: Rush, Terry Brown
Year: 1976

TWIGGS APPROVED

Artist: The Dixie Dregs
Written by: Steve Morse
From the album: *Dregs of the Earth*
Label: Arista
Produced by: Steve Morse
Year: 1980
Progressive Southern rock guitar classic.

TWILIGHT TIME

Artist: The Platters
Written by: Buck Ram, Morty Nevins, Al Nevins, Artie Dunn
From the album: *Encore of Golden Hits*
Label: Mercury
Produced by: Buck Ram
Year: 1958
Their third #1 R&B/#1 crossover. Written and introduced by the Three Suns (Victor, '50).

TWILIGHT ZONE

Artist: Golden Earring
Written by: George Kooymans
From the album: *Cut*
Label: 21 Records
Produced by: Fred Hadyen, Golden Earring
Year: 1983
The only US Top 10 hit for the influential Dutch metal band.

TWIST AND CRAWL

Artist: The English Beat
Written by: English Beat
From the album: *I Just Can't Stop It*
Label: Sire
Produced by: Bob Sergeant
Year: 1980
Speaking for a new generation of English punky reggae bands, here is where they uttered the immortal line: "Feel like a Beatle on its back."

TWIST AND SHOUT

Artist: The Isley Brothers
Written by: Bert Berns (Bert Russell), Phil Medley
From the album: *Twist and Shout*
Label: Wand
Year: 1962
Out of the '57 Twist varieties, the one true enduring classic, copped from Phil Spector's failed production with the Top Notes a year before. Covered by the Beatles (Tollie/Capitol, '64).

TWIST OF FATE

Artist: Olivia Newton-John
Written by: Stephen Kipner, Peter Beckett

From the album: *Two of a Kind Soundtrack*
Label: MCA
Produced by: John Parrar
Year: 1983
Her fourteeth and last Top 10 hit.

TWIST, THE

Artist: The Midnighters
Written by: Hank Ballard
From the album: *Hank Ballard's Biggest Hits*
Label: King
Produced by: Henry Glover
Year: 1959
B-side of "Teardrops on Your Letter." Covered by Dick Clark discovery Chubby Checker (Parkway, '60) in a note for note copy of Hank's version, "The Twist" ushered in the Baby Boom's first dance era; the record made music history as well, returning to #1 sixteen months after leaving that slot, when the Jet Set adopted the dance. Ballard's version was a hit twice as well. Suggested segue: "What'cha Gonna Do" by the Drifters.

TWISTED

Artist: Annie Ross
Written by: Annie Ross, Wardell Gray
Label: Prestige
Year: 1953
Famous jazz-based tone poem tribute to an analyst was an early classic of vocalese. When Ross formed the legendary Lambert, Hendricks & Ross, it was included on their album *Everybody's Boppin'* (Columbia, '59). Covered by Joni Mitchell, who had revered Lambert, Hendricks & Ross since childhood, once referring to them as her Beatles (Asylum, '74).

TWISTIN' THE NIGHT AWAY

Artist: Sam Cooke
Written by: Sam Cooke
From the album: *Twistin' the Night Away*
Label: RCA Victor
Produced by: Hugo and Luigi
Year: 1962
#1 R&B/Top 10 crossover with a little twist of soul.

2 BECOME 1

Artist: Spice Girls
Written by: Melanie Brown, Geraldine Halliwell, Victoria Adams, Melanie Chisholm, Emma Lee Burton, Richard Stannard, Matt Rowe
From the album: *Spice*
Label: Virgin
Year: 1997
Or, in this case, the third single becomes indistinguishable from the first two.

TWO FACES HAVE I

Artist: Lou Christie

Written by: Twyla Herbert, Lou Sacco (Lou Christie)
From the album: *Lou Christie*
Label: Roulette
Produced by: Nick Cenci
Year: 1963
Two faces, four voices, and a pseudonym; Lou Sacco comes clean.

2-4-6-8 MOTORWAY

Artist: Tom Robinson
Written by: Tom Robinson
From the album: *Power in the Darkness*
Label: Harvest
Produced by: Vic Maile
Year: 1978
Rousing rocker was a big hit in the UK.

TWO HEARTS

Artist: Phil Collins
Written by: Phil Collins, Lamont Dozier
From the album: *Buster Soundtrack*
Label: Atlantic
Produced by: Phil Collins
Year: 1988
Written with the great Motown collaborator, who gained his first Grammy nomination.

TWO HEARTS BEAT AS ONE

Artist: U2
Written by: Paul Hewson (Bono), Dave Evans (Edge), Adam Clayton, Larry Mullen
From the album: *War*
Label: Island
Produced by: Steve Lillywhite, Bill Whelan
Year: 1983
Second single from the album.

2 LEGIT TO QUIT

Artist: M. C. Hammer
Written by: Felton Pilate, M. C. Hammer (Stanley Burrell), James Earley, Michael Kelly, Louis Burrell
From the album: *2 Legit to Quit*
Label: Capitol
Produced by: Hammer, Felton Pilate
Year: 1991
Amid rumors that he wasn't so legit after all, a defensive posture.

TWO LOVERS

Artist: Mary Wells
Written by: Smokey Robinson
From the album: *Two Lovers*
Label: Motown
Produced by: Smokey Robinson
Year: 1962
Essential Mary; quintessential Smokey; a #1 R&B/Top 10 crossover.

TWO OCCASIONS

Artist: The Deele

Written by: Kenny Edmunds (Babyface), Antonio Reid (L. A. Reid), Darnell Johnson
From the album: *Eyes of a Stranger*
Label: Solar
Produced by: Babyface, L. A. Reid
Year: 1987
#1 R&B/Top 10 crossover for the superstar writing/production team of the '90s and their first band.

TWO OF HEARTS

Artist: Stacey Q
Written by: John Mitchell, Sue Gatlin, Tim Greene
From the album: *Better Than Heaven*
Label: Atlantic
Produced by: J. St. James
Year: 1986
Dance floor crossover.

TWO OF US, THE

Artist: The Beatles
Written by: John Lennon, Paul McCartney
From the album: *Let It Be*
Label: Apple
Produced by: George Martin
Year: 1970
Rare John and Paul duet on a song that could have been about John and Paul but was probably about Paul and Linda. Covered in 1991 by another hip couple, Aimee Mann and Michael Penn in the movie *I Am Sam*.

TWO OUT OF THREE AIN'T BAD

Artist: Meat Loaf
Written by: Jim Steinman
From the album: *Bat out of Hell*
Label: Cleveland International
Produced by: Jim Steinman
Year: 1977
Verbose rocker sets the stage for future epics.

TWO PRINCES

Artist: The Spin Doctors
Written by: The Spin Doctors
From the album: *Pocket Full of Kryptonite*
Label: Epic Associated
Produced by: F. Aversa, The Spin Doctors
Year: 1992
Post Love Generation parable was their biggest hit.

TWO TICKETS TO PARADISE

Artist: Eddie Money
Written by: Edward Mahoney (Eddie Money)
From the album: *Eddie Money*
Label: Columbia
Produced by: Bruce Botnick
Year: 1977
Working-class rock from San Francisco.

2,000 LIGHT YEARS FROM HOME

Artist: The Rolling Stones
Written by: Mick Jagger, Keith Richards
From the album: *Their Satanic Majesties Request*
Label: London
Produced by: Andrew Loog-Oldham
Year: 1967
A brief and messy fling with psychedelia.

2000 MILES

Artist: The Pretenders
Written by: Chrissie Hynde
From the album: *Learning to Crawl*
Label: Sire
Produced by: Chris Thomas
Year: 1984
B-side of "Back on the Chain Gang" is a moving and memorable ode to Ray Davies, at Christmas time.

TWO TO MAKE IT RIGHT

Artist: Seduction
Written by: David Cole
From the album: *Nothing Matters without Love*
Label: Vendetta
Produced by: Rob Clivilles
Year: 1989
Big track from one of the hottest writing/producing combos of the '90s dance hall.

TWO TRIBES

Artist: Frankie Goes to Hollywood
Written by: Peter Gill, William Johnson, Mark O'Toole
From the album: *Welcome to the Pleasure Dome*
Label: Island
Produced by: Trevor Horn
Year: 1984
Second of three straight #1 UK hits. Only "Relax" hit the Top 10 in the US.

TWO TUB MAN

Artist: Dictators
Written by: Andy Shernoff
From the album: *The Dictators Go Girl Crazy*
Label: Epic
Produced by: Sandy Pearlman, Murray Krugman
Year: 1975
Trying to extend the Blue Oyster Cult franchise.

TYPICAL GIRLS

Artist: The Slits
Written by: Viv Albertine, Ariane Forster, Paloma McLardy, Teresa Pollitt
From the album: *Cut*
Label: Antilles
Produced by: Dennis Bovell
Year: 1979
The Shaggs a decade later, moved to England and gone on the dole.

TYPICAL MALE

Artist: Tina Turner
Written by: Terry Britten, Graham Lyle
From the album: *Break Every Rule*
Label: Capitol
Year: 1986
Her second-biggest solo hit.

U

U CAN'T TOUCH THIS

Artist: M. C. Hammer
Written by: Rick James, M. C. Hammer (Stanley Burrell), James Miller
From the album: *Please Hammer Don't Hurt 'Em*
Label: Capitol
Produced by: Hammer
Year: 1990
James's "Super Freak" sparks Hammer's rise to stardom.

U GOT THE LOOK

Artist: Prince with Sheena Easton
Written by: Prince Rogers Nelson
From the album: *Sign 'o' the Times Soundtrack*
Label: Paisley Park
Produced by: Prince
Year: 1987
Easton had hit the Top 10 with Prince's "Sugar Walls" two years earlier.

U.N.I.T.Y.

Artist: Queen Latifah
Written by: Dana Owens (Queen Latifah), Joe Sample
From the album: *Black Reign*
Label: Motown
Produced by: Kaygee, Mufi
Year: 1993
Communal rap anthem.

US BLUES

Artist: Grateful Dead
Written by: Jerry Garcia, Robert Hunter
From the album: *From the Mars Hotel*
Label: Grateful Dead
Year: 1974

US MALE

Artist: Jerry Reed
Written by: Jerry Reed
From the album: *The Unbelievable Guitar and Voice of Jerry Reed*
Label: RCA
Produced by: Chet Atkins
Year: 1967
Covered by Elvis Presley (RCA, '68).

UBANGI STOMP

Artist: Warren Smith
Written by: Charles Underwood

Produced by: Sam Phillips, Jack Clement
Label: Sun
Year: 1956
Important rockabilly track.

UM UM UM UM UM UM

Artist: Major Lance
Written by: Curtis Mayfield
From the album: *Um, Um, Um, Um, Um, Um/The Best of Major Lance*
Label: Okeh
Produced by: Carl Davis
Year: 1963
His biggest hit.

UNBELIEVABLE

Artist: EMF
Written by: James Atkin, Ian Dench, Zak Foley, Mark Decloedt, Derry Brownson
From the album: *Schubert Dip*
Label: EMI
Produced by: EMF, Ralph Jezzard
Year: 1991
#1 US/UK breakthrough for the British post psychedelic rave sound.

UNCHAIN MY HEART

Artist: Ray Charles
Written by: Agnes Jones, Freddy James
From the album: *Ray Charles' Greatest Hits*
Label: ABC-Paramount
Produced by: Sid Feller
Year: 1961
Ray's second straight #1 R&B/Top 10 crossover of '61.

UNCHAINED MELODY

Artist: Roy Hamilton
Written by: Alex North, Hy Zaret
Label: Epic
Year: 1955
This intense ballad from the movie *Unchained* gives Hamilton his biggest hit, a #1 R&B/Top 10 crossover. Covered by Al Hibbier (Decca, '55), the Righteous Brothers (Philles, '65).

UNCLE ALBERT/ADMIRAL HALSEY

Artist: Paul McCartney and Linda McCartney
Written by: Paul McCartney, Linda McCartney
From the album: *Ram*
Label: Apple
Produced by: Paul McCartney, Linda McCartney
Year: 1971
Extolling the simple pleasures of post-Beatlemania, with his wife in the John Lennon (or is it Ringo Starr?) role, Paul gains his first semisolo #1.

UNCLE JOHN'S BAND

Artist: Grateful Dead
Written by: Robert Hunter, Jerry Garcia

From the album: *Workingman's Dead*
Label: Warner Brothers
Produced by: Bob Matthews, Betty Cantor, Grateful Dead
Year: 1970
The unalloyed hippie ethos in a rare chart single.

UNDER A RAGING MOON

Artist: Roger Daltrey
Written by: John Parr, Julia Downes
From the album: *Under a Raging Moon*
Label: Atlantic
Year: 1985
Dedicated to his former Who bandmate, the late Keith Moon.

UNDER ASSISTANT WEST COAST PROMO MAN

Artist: The Rolling Stones
Written by: Mick Jagger, Keith Richards
From the album: *Out of Our Heads*
Label: London
Produced by: Andrew Loog-Oldham
Year: 1965
B-side of "Satisfaction." The rare Stonesian sense of humor, tweaking the music business.

UNDER MY THUMB

Artist: The Rolling Stones
Written by: Mick Jagger, Keith Richards
From the album: *Aftermath*
Label: London
Produced by: Andrew Loog-Oldham
Year: 1966
Played during the fatal stabbing at Altamont. Covered by Del Shannon (Liberty, '66).

UNDER PRESSURE

Artist: Queen and David Bowie
Written by: David Bowie, Queen
From the album: *Queen's Greatest Hits*
Label: Elektra
Produced by: David Bowie, Queen
Year: 1982
Techno rock landmark collaboration, largely for its costly video. Suggested segue: "Ice Ice Baby" by Vanilla Ice.

UNDER THE BIG BLACK SUN

Artist: X
Written by: John Doe, Exene Cervenka
From the album: *Under the Big Black Sun*
Label: Elektra
Produced by: Ray Manzarek
Year: 1982
Suggested segue: "Black Hole Sun" by Soundgarden.

UNDER THE BOARDWALK

Artist: The Drifters
Written by: Artie Resnick, Kenny Young
From the album: *Under the Boardwalk*

Label: Atlantic
Produced by: Bert Berns
Year: 1964
Johnny Moore replaces Rudy Lewis for the vocals on this prime summertime escapist anthem, their fifth and last Top 10 hit. The same songwriting team would also write the follow-up, "I've Got Sand in My Shoes," which stiffed in the fall. Covered by the Rolling Stones (London, '64).

UNDER THE BRIDGE

Artist: Red Hot Chili Peppers
Written by: Anthony Kiedis, Michael Balzary (Flea), John Frusciante, Chad Smith
From the album: *Blood Sugar Sex Magik*
Label: Warner Brothers
Produced by: Rick Rubin
Year: 1991
Reflecting on a drug-soaked youth; written for original guitarist Hillel Slovak who died of a heroin overdose in 1988.

UNDER THE MILKY WAY

Artist: The Church
Written by: Steve Kilbey, Karin Jannson
From the album: *Starfish*
Label: Arista
Produced by: Greg Ladanyi, Waddy Wachtel, the Church
Year: 1988
The '80s jangly ethereal answer to "Daydream" by the Lovin' Spoonful and "Waterloo Sunset" by the Kinks.

UNDER THE MOON OF LOVE

Artist: Curtis Lee
Written by: Tommy Boyce, Curtis Lee
Label: Dunes
Produced by: Phil Spector
Year: 1961
Follow-up to "Pretty Little Angel Eyes." Cover by Showaddywaddy went to #1 in the UK (Bell, '76). A couple of years later they also revived "Pretty Little Angel Eyes."

UNDER YOUR SPELL

Artist: Bob Dylan
Written by: Bob Dylan, Carole Bayer Sager
From the album: *Knocked out Loaded*
Label: Columbia
Year: 1986
Many Dylanologists wish they could have been a fly on the wall at this writing session.

UNDERCOVER ANGEL

Artist: Alan O'Day
Written by: Alan O'Day
From the album: *Appetizers*
Label: Pacific
Produced by: Steve Barri, Michael Omartian
Year: 1977
Was 1977 the worst year ever for #1 singles? True, in addition to this, you had "You Light up My Life"

by Debbie Boone leading the way, and two by Leo Sayer ("You Make Me Feel Like Dancing" and "When I Need You"), but on the other side of the ledger, there was Stevie Wonder's "Sir Duke" and "I Wish," Blinded by the Light" by Manfred Mann, "Rich Girl" by Hall and Oates, and "Hotel California" by the Eagles. The debate rages on.

UNDERCOVER OF THE NIGHT

Artist: The Rolling Stones
Written by: Mick Jagger, Keith Richards
From the album: *Undercover*
Label: Rolling Stones
Produced by: Glimmer Twins, Chris Kimsey
Year: 1983
Closest thing to a protest song since "Sympathy for the Devil."

UNDERGROUND

Artist: Ben Folds Five
Written by: Ben Folds
From the album: *The Ben Folds Five*
Produced by: Caleb Southern
Label: Passenger
Year: 1995
Defining their sound and their turf.

UNDERSTAND YOUR MAN

Artist: Johnny Cash
Written by: Johnny Cash
From the album: *I Walk the Line*
Label: Columbia
Produced by: Don Law, Frank Jones
Year: 1964
#1 country/Top 40 crossover.

UNDONE (THE SWEATER SONG)

Artist: Weezer
Written by: Rivers Cuomo
From the album: *Weezer*
Label: DGC
Produced by: Ric Ocasek
Year: 1994
Suggested segue: "The Sweater" by Meryn Cadell (Warner Brothers, '93).

UNEASY RIDER

Artist: Charlie Daniels
Written by: Charlie Daniels
From the album: *Honey in the Rock*
Label: Kama Sutra
Produced by: Charlie Daniels
Year: 1973
A displaced hippie in the post-*Easy Rider* South.

UNFINISHED SYMPATHY

Artist: Massive Attack
Written by: Robert Del Naja, Grant Marshall, Shara Nelson, Andrew Vowles, Sharp

From the album: *Blue Lines*
Produced by: Johnny Dollar
Label: Virgin
Year: 1991
Their techno dance vibe masterwork.

UNFORGIVEN, THE

Artist: Metallica
Written by: James Hetfield, Lars Ulrich, Kirk Hammett
From the album: *Metallica*
Label: Elektra
Produced by: Bob Rock, James Hetfield, Lars Ulrich
Year: 1991
Heavy stuff.

UNINVITED

Artist: Alanis Morrisette
Written by: Alanis Morrisette
From the album: *City of Angels Soundtrack*
Label: Warner Sunset
Year: 1998
Grammy winner for Rock Song of the Year.

UNION OF THE SNAKE

Artist: Duran Duran
Written by: Duran Duran
From the album: *Seven and the Ragged Tiger*
Label: Capitol
Produced by: Duran Duran, Alex Sadkin, Ian Little
Year: 1983
Closing out their first year on the American charts with their third Top 10 hit.

UNITED WE STAND

Artist: Brotherhood of Man
Written by: Tony Hiller, Peter Simons
From the album: *United We Stand*
Label: Deram
Produced by: Tony Hiller
Year: 1970
Uplifting British soul commentary.

UNIVERSAL SOLDIER, THE

Artist: Buffy Sainte-Marie
Written by: Buffy Sainte-Marie
From the album: *It's My Way*
Label: Vanguard
Produced by: Elmer Jared Gordon
Year: 1964
A far cry from the contemporaneous "Soldier Boy" and "Blue Navy Blue," but one that would be getting stronger in the coming years of folk/rock protest. Covered by Donovan (Hickory, '65).

UNKNOWN SOLDIER

Artist: The Doors
Written by: Jim Morrison, Robbie Krieger, John Densmore, Ray Manzarek
From the album: *Waiting for the Sun*

Label: Elektra
Produced by: Paul Rothchild
Year: 1968
Opus from the poet manqué.

UNPRETTY

Artist: TLC
Written by: Dallas Austin, Tionne Watkins
From the album: *Fan Mail*
Label: LaFace
Produced by: Dallas Austin
Year: 1999
In the waning days of chick hop, a major statement on female beauty. Segue: "Beauty's Only Skin Deep" by the Temptations.

UNSATISFIED

Artist: The Replacements
Written by: Paul Westerberg
From the album: *Let It Be*
Label: Twin Tone
Produced by: Steve Fjelstad, Paul Westerberg, Peter Jesperson
Year: 1984
Their answer to "(I Can't Get No) Satisfaction" by the Rolling Stones.

UNSKINNY BOP

Artist: Poison
Written by: Bobby Dall, C. C. Deville, Brett Michaels, Rikki Rockett
From the album: *Flesh and Blood*
Label: Capitol
Year: 1990
Another from the Kiss school of euphemism. Kiss did it better.

UNTIL IT SLEEPS

Artist: Metallica
Written by: James Hetfield, Lars Ulrich
From the album: *Load*
Label: Elektra
Produced by: Bob Rock, James Hetfield, Lars Ulrich
Year: 1995
Hetfield confronts his father's death.

UNTIL IT'S TIME FOR YOU TO GO

Artist: Buffy Sainte-Marie
Written by: Buffy Sainte-Marie
From the album: *Many a Mile*
Label: Vanguard
Year: 1964
Earth-mothering folk ballad answer to Gale Garnett's "We'll Sing in the Sunshine" that found favor among the more macho of pop rock belters, i.e., Bobby Darin (Atlantic, '67), Neil Diamond (UNI, '70), Elvis Presley (RCA, '72), Willie Nelson (Columbia, '84). Also covered by Cher (Imperial, '66), Helen Reddy (Capitol, '73).

UNTIL YOU COME BACK TO ME (THAT'S WHAT I'M GONNA DO)

Artist: Aretha Franklin
Written by: Stevie Wonder, Clarence Paul, Morris Broadnax
From the album: *Let Me in Your Life*
Label: Atlantic
Produced by: Tom Dowd, Jerry Wexler
Year: 1973
#1 R&B/Top 5 crossover. Written and recorded by Stevie Wonder in '67, but not released on an album of his until '77.

UP ABOVE MY HEAD (I HEAR MUSIC IN THE AIR)

Artist: Sister Rosetta Tharpe and Marie Knight
Written by: Rosetta Tharpe
Label: Decca
Year: 1948
Rousing gospel call and response dents the R&B Top 10.

UP AROUND THE BEND

Artist: Creedence Clearwater Revival
Written by: John C. Fogerty
From the album: *Cosmo's Factory*
Label: Fantasy
Produced by: John C. Fogerty
Year: 1970

UP FOR THE DOWN STROKE

Artist: Parliament
Written by: George Clinton, William "Bootsie" Collins, Bernie Worrell, Fuzzy Haskins
From the album: *Up for the Down Stroke*
Label: Casablanca
Produced by: George Clinton
Year: 1974
Establishing funk as the street beat of the '70s.

UP JUMPS DA BOOGIE

Artist: Timbaland & Magoo
Written by: Melvin Barcliff, Missy Elliott, Tim Mosley
From the album: *Welcome to Our World*
Label: Blackground
Year: 1997
Introducing Missy Elliott as a major new presence on the hip-hop circuit.

UP ON CRIPPLE CREEK

Artist: The Band
Written by: Robbie Robertson
From the album: *The Band*
Label: Capitol
Produced by: John Simon, the Band

Year: 1968
Their biggest hit (and only appearance of the jew's harp) on the pop charts. Under the calming influence of the Band, Bob Dylan would travel up that creek to Nashville, without a paddle (although, of course, he'd already been there, to record *Blonde on Blonde*).

UP ON THE ROOF

Artist: The Drifters
Written by: Gerry Goffin, Carole King
From the album: *Up on the Roof, the Best of the Drifters*
Label: Atlantic
Produced by: Jerry Leiber, Mike Stoller
Year: 1962
The essential city soul classic from a classic Brooklyn candy-store tandem—with Rudy Lewis on vocals; a Top 5 R&B/Top 5 crossover. Unforgettably covered by Laura Nyro (Columbia, '70), who, admittedly, spent more time down in the subway station.

UP THE JUNCTION

Artist: Squeeze
Written by: Chris Difford, Glenn Tilbrook
From the album: *Cool for Cats*
Label: A&M
Produced by: John Wood, Squeeze
Year: 1979
Their most affecting rocker.

UP WHERE WE BELONG

Artist: Joe Cocker and Jennifer Warnes
Written by: Will Jennings, Jack Nitzsche, Buffy Sainte-Marie
From the album: *An Officer and a Gentleman Soundtrack*
Label: Island
Produced by: Stewart Levine
Year: 1982
This #1 ballad from the Richard Gere/Debra Winger movie won the Oscar for Best Song.

UPSIDE DOWN

Artist: The Jesus and Mary Chain
Written by: James Reid, William Reid
Label: Creation
Year: 1984
First indie hit for the Scottish Velvet Underground of the '80s.

UPSIDE DOWN

Artist: Diana Ross
Written by: Nile Rodgers, Bernard Edwards
From the album: *Diana*
Label: Motown
Produced by: Nile Rodgers, Bernard Edwards
Year: 1980
Diana's biggest hit is her first solo #1 R&B/#1 crossover since her remake of "Ain't No Mountain High Enough" in 1970

UPTIGHT (EVERYTHING'S ALRIGHT)

Artist: Stevie Wonder
Written by: Stevie Wonder, Sylvia Moy, Henry Cosby
From the album: *Uptight*
Label: Tamla
Produced by: Henry Cosby, William Stevenson
Year: 1966
His second #1 R&B/Top 10 crossover.

UPTOWN

Artist: The Crystals
Written by: Barry Mann, Cynthia Weil
From the album: *He's a Rebel*
Label: Philles
Produced by: Phil Spector
Year: 1962
For the staff writers at the Brill Building in '62, uptown meant 1650 Broadway, a block to the north, where this and many more of the hits were written.

UPTOWN GIRL

Artist: Billy Joel
Written by: Billy Joel
From the album: *An Innocent Man*
Label: Columbia
Produced by: Phil Ramone
Year: 1983
The perfect Four Seasons song, twenty years later.

UP–UP AND AWAY

Artist: The Fifth Dimension
Written by: Jimmy Webb
From the album: *Up–Up and Away*
Label: Soul City
Produced by: Johnny Rivers
Year: 1967
Flighty pop rock standard introduces one of the '60s most distinctive voices, that of songwriter Jimmy Webb.

URGE FOR GOING

Artist: George Hamilton IV
Written by: Joni Mitchell
From the album: *Folky*
Label: RCA
Produced by: Chet Atkins
Year: 1967
Mitchell crosses over to the country Top 20 with the first song she ever wrote, a landmark ode to rolling with the emotional and seasonal changes. Covered in the definitive folk/rock version by Tom Rush (Elektra, '68), which Hamilton actually heard in prerelease form on a Boston radio station. Recorded by Mitchell as the B-side of "You Turn Me On, I'm a Radio" (Asylum, '73).

URGENT

Artist: Foreigner
Written by: Mick Jones
From the album: *4*
Label: Atlantic
Produced by: Mutt Lange, Mick Jones
Year: 1981
Becoming the Chicago of heavy metal, with Jr. Walker guesting on sax. Michael Bolton was listening.

US AND THEM

Artist: Pink Floyd
Written by: Roger Waters, Rick Wright
From the album: *Dark Side of the Moon*
Label: Harvest
Produced by: Pink Floyd
Year: 1973
Originally written for *Zabriskie Point*. Sax solo by Dick Parry.

USE ME

Artist: Bill Withers
Written by: Bill Withers
From the album: *Still Bill*
Label: Sussex
Produced by: Bill Withers
Year: 1972
#1 R&B/Top 10 crossover follow-up to "Lean on Me."

USE TA BE MY GIRL

Artist: The O'Jays
Written by: Kenny Gamble, Leon Huff
From the album: *So Full of Love*
Label: Philadelphia International
Produced by: Kenny Gamble, Leon Huff
Year: 1977
Memories of doo-wop; their eighth #1 R&B crossover of the '70s.

USUAL, THE

Artist: John Hiatt
Written by: John Hiatt
From the album: *Warming up to the Ice Age*
Label: A&M
Produced by: Norbert Putnam
Year: 1985
Covered by Bob Dylan and Fiona in the film *Hearts on Fire*.

V

V

Artist: Dick and Mimi Fariña
Written by: Richard Fariña
From the album: *Celebrations for a Grey Day*
Label: Vanguard
Year: 1965
Dedicated to Fariña's college buddy Thomas Pynchon's epic novel, *V*. Suggested segue: "The Eyes of a New York Woman" by Insect Trust, from the same book, with lyrics by Pynchon.

V-A-C-A-T-I-O-N

Artist: Connie Francis
Written by: Hank Hunter, Gary Weston, Connie Francis
From the album: *The Very Best of Connie Francis*
Label: MGM
Year: 1962
Returning to the scene of "Where the Boys Are."

VACATION

Artist: The Go-Go's
Written by: Kathy Valentine, Charlotte Caffey, Jane Wiedlin
From the album: *Vacation*
Label: I.R.S.
Produced by: Richard Gottehrer
Year: 1982
Answering Blondie's "In the Sun" with a Busby Berkeleyesque twist on beach movie choreography and a tip of the swim cap to Esther Williams.

VAHEVELA

Artist: Loggins & Messina
Written by: Danny Loggins, Daniel Lottermoser
From the album: *Sittin' In*
Label: Columbia
Produced by: Jim Messina
Year: 1971
Segue: "Witchy Tai To" by Brewer & Shipley.

VALENTINE MELODY

Artist: Tim Buckley
Written by: Tim Buckley
From the album: *Tim Buckley*
Label: Elektra
Produced by: Paul Rothchild, Jac Holzman
Year: 1968
Star-crossed love song.

VALERIE

Artist: Richard Thompson
Written by: Richard Thompson
From the album: *Daring Adventures*
Label: Polydor
Produced by: Mitchell Froom
Year: 1986
Covered by Marshall Crenshaw (Warner Brothers, '89).

VALLERI

Artist: The Monkees
Written by: Tommy Boyce, Bobby Hart
From the album: *The Birds, the Bees, and the Monkees*
Label: Colgems
Produced by: The Monkees
Year: 1968
Their last hit, with a legendary guitar part by Louie Shelton.

VALLEY GIRL

Artist: Frank Zappa and Moon Zappa
Written by: Frank Zappa, Moon Zappa
From the album: *Ship Arriving Too Late to Save a Drowning Witch*
Label: Barking Pumpkin
Produced by: Frank Zappa
Year: 1982
Zappa's penchant if not compulsion for satire is passed to the next generation.

VALLEY ROAD, THE

Artist: Bruce Hornsby and the Range
Written by: Bruce Hornsby, John Hornsby
From the album: *Scenes from the Southside*
Label: RCA
Produced by: Neil Dorfsman, Bruce Hornsby
Year: 1988
Southern-flavored folk/pop strikes a country chord.

VALOTTE

Artist: Julian Lennon
Written by: Julian Lennon, Justin Clayton, Carlton Morales
From the album: *Valotte*
Label: Atlantic
Produced by: Phil Ramone
Year: 1984
His first hit.

VAN HALEN

Artist: Nerf Herder
Written by: Nerf Herder
From the album: *Nerf Herder*
Label: Arista
Produced by: Joey Cepe, Ryan Greene
Year: 1997
The year's most outstanding example of rock criticism.

VANILLA OLAY

Artist: Jackie Deshannon
Written by: Jackie DeShannon
From the album: *Jackie*
Label: Atlantic
Produced by: Tom Dowd, Jerry Wexler, Arif Mardin
Year: 1972
A woman's coming-of-age saga. Covered by Marianne Faithful (Immediate, '77).

VASOLINE

Artist: Stone Temple Pilots
Written by: Robert DeLeo, Scott Weiland, Dean DeLeo, Eric Kretz
From the album: *Purple*
Label: Atlantic
Produced by: Brendan O'Brien
Year: 1994
Their biggest hit.

VAUDEVILLE MAN

Artist: Wendy Waldman
Written by: Wendy Waldman
From the album: *Love Has Got Me*
Label: Warner Brothers
Produced by: Chuck Plotkin
Year: 1973
Infectious folk/rock charmer, covered by Maria Muldaur (Reprise, '73). Waldman went on to success in Nashville as a songwriter/producer.

VEHICLE

Artist: The Ides of March
Written by: James M. Peterik
From the album: *Vehicle*
Label: Warner Brothers
Produced by: Lee Productions
Year: 1970
Peterik would return with Survivor.

VENTURA HIGHWAY

Artist: America
Written by: Lee Bunnell
From the album: *Homecoming*
Label: Warner Brothers
Produced by: America
Year: 1972
Not really a rambling song, more of a Sunday drive to the vineyard.

VENUS

Artist: Frankie Avalon
Written by: Ed Marshall
From the album: *A Whole Lotta Frankie*
Label: Chancellor
Produced by: Bob Marcucci, Pete DeAngelis
Year: 1959
Ode to the Goddess of Love cemented Frankie's position as teen idol and beach movie hunk.

VENUS

Artist: Shocking Blue
Written by: Robbie Van Leeuwen
From the album: *This Is the Shocking Blue*
Label: Colossus
Produced by: Robbie van Leeuwen
Year: 1969
Frantic Dutch crossover went to #1 US. Cover by England's Bananarama (London, '86) also went to #1 US. Segue: "Pinball Wizard" by the Who.

VENUS AS A BOY

Artist: Bjork
Written by: Bjork
From the album: *Debut*
Produced by: Nellee Hooper
Label: Elektra
Year: 1993
Boggles the mind.

VENUS IN BLUE JEANS

Artist: Jimmy Clanton
Written by: Howard Greenfield, Jack Keller
From the album: *Venus in Blue Jeans*

Label: Ace
Produced by: Johnny Vincent
Year: 1961
Updates the legend.

VENUS IN FURS

Artist: The Velvet Underground
Written by: Lou Reed
From the album: *The Velvet Underground and Nico*
Produced by: Andy Warhol, Tom Wilson
Label: Verve
Year: 1967
Conjures the legend as a kinky sex and fashion role model.

VERDI CRIES

Artist: 10,000 Maniacs
Written by: Natalie Merchant
From the album: *In My Tribe*
Label: Elektra
Produced by: Peter Asher
Year: 1987
A summer camp song for the privileged class. Suggested segue: "Menemsha" by Carly Simon.

VERONICA

Artist: Elvis Costello
Written by: Declan McManus (Elvis Costello), Paul McCartney
From the album: *Spike*
Label: Warner Brothers
Produced by: Kevin Killen, T-Bone Burnett
Year: 1989
McCartney finally finds his new Lennon. Then they break up after one perfect single.

VICIOUS

Artist: Lou Reed
Written by: Lou Reed
From the album: *Transformer*
Label: RCA
Produced by: David Bowie
Year: 1972
Putting down the hippies ("You hit me with a flower") with his version of "Positively 4TH Street."

VICTIM OF THE GHETTO

Artist: The College Boyz
Written by: Eric Johnson, Rom, Tony Joseph
From the album: *Radio Fusion Radio*
Label: Virgin
Year: 1992
Rap commentary on urban devastation.

VICTORIA

Artist: The Kinks
Written by: Ray Davies
From the album: *Arthur (or the Decline and Fall of the British Empire)*
Label: Reprise
Produced by: Ray Davies
Year: 1970
From Ray's magnum opus.

VIDEO KILLED THE RADIO STAR

Artist: The Buggles
Written by: Geoffrey Downs, Trevor Horn, Bruce Woolley
From the album: *The Age of Plastic*
Label: Island
Produced by: the Buggles
Year: 1979
This #1 UK techno prophecy was the first video played on MTV in '81; the second was "Time Heals," by Todd Rundgren.

VIENNA

Artist: Ultravox
Written by: Billy Currie, Chris Cross, Warren Cann, Midge Ure
From the album: *Vienna*
Label: Chrysalis
Produced by: Conny Plank
Year: 1980
Their biggest #1 UK hit.

VIETNAM

Artist: Jimmy Cliff
Written by: Jimmy Cliff
From the album: *Wonderful World, Beautiful People*
Label: A&M
Produced by: Jimmy Cliff
Year: 1970
Bob Dylan called this the best protest song he'd ever heard. Paul Simon went to Jamaica and used Cliff's rhythm section to record "Mother and Child Reunion" in '72.

VIEW TO A KILL, A

Artist: Duran Duran
Written by: Duran Duran, John Barry
From the album: *A View to a Kill Soundtrack*
Label: Capitol
Produced by: Bernard Edwards, Duran Duran, J. Corsaro
Year: 1985
Burnishing their image with this theme from the James Bond film.

VINCENT

Artist: Don McLean
Written by: Don McLean
From the album: *American Pie*
Label: United Artists
Produced by: Ed Freeman
Year: 1972
Dedicated to Van Gogh's painting "Starry Night."

VINE STREET

Artist: Van Dyke Parks
Written by: Randy Newman
From the album: *Song Cycle*
Label: Warner Brothers
Produced by: Van Dyke Parks
Year: 1968

Defining the L.A. hippie oeuvre, in one of Randy Newman's earlier gems. Covered by Harry Nilsson (RCA, '70).

VIOLET

Artist: Hole
Written by: Courtney Love, Kristen Pfaff, Eric Erlandson, Patty Schemel
From the album: *Live through This*
Label: DGC
Produced by: Paul Q. Kolderie, Sean Slade
Year: 1994
Suggested segue: "Bruised Violet" by Babes in Toyland.

VIOLETS OF DAWN

Artist: The Blues Project
Written by: Eric Andersen
From the album: *The Blues Project Live at Cafe Au Go Go*
Label: Verve/folkways
Produced by: Jerry Schoenbaum
Year: 1966
Anderson's folkie post-coital or post-acid trip reflection showcases the legendary Greenwich Village Blues Project at their daintiest.

VIRGINIA PLAIN

Artist: Roxy Music
Written by: Bryan Ferry
From the album: *Roxy Music*
Produced by: Peter Sinfield
Label: Reprise
Year: 1972
Debut single for the influential art rock band.

VIRTUAL INSANITY

Artist: Jamiroquai
Written by: Jay Kay, Toby Smith
From the album: *Travelling without Moving*
Label: Work
Year: 1997
Great video.

VISION OF LOVE

Artist: Mariah Carey
Written by: Ben Margulies, Mariah Carey
From the album: *Mariah Carey*
Label: Columbia
Produced by: David Lawrence
Year: 1990
Her first single and first #1 R&B/#1 crossover launches an ethereal new voice; pop soul of the spheres and the marketplace.

VISIONS OF JOHANNA

Artist: Bob Dylan
Written by: Bob Dylan
From the album: *Blonde on Blonde*
Label: Columbia
Produced by: Bob Johnston
Year: 1966

Bob's most tangled urban psychodrama, as directed by Fellini.

VIVA LAS VEGAS

Artist: Elvis Presley
Written by: Doc Pomus, Mort Shuman
From the album: *Viva Las Vegas*
Label: RCA
Year: 1964
Saying hello to his future workplace. Covered by ZZ Top in the film *Honeymoon in Vegas* (Epic Soundtrax, '92).

VOGUE

Artist: Madonna
Written by: Shep Pettibone, Madonna Ciccone
From the album: *Like a Prayer*
Label: Sire
Produced by: Shep Pettibone, Madonna
Year: 1989
Dance groove with a sense of Hollywood history. Suggested segues: "Candle in the Wind" by Elton John, "Celluloid Heroes" by the Kinks.

VOICES CARRY

Artist:'Til Tuesday
Written by: Aimee Mann, Michael Hausman, Robert Holmes, Joseph Pesce
From the album: *Voices Carry*
Label: Epic
Produced by: Mike Thorne
Year: 1985
Introducing Boston's leading candidate in the late-'80s waif-like thrush sweepstakes, Aimee Mann. Thrush she may have been, but it turned out she was no waif.

VOLUNTEERS

Artist: Jefferson Airplane
Written by: Marty Balin, Paul Kantner
From the album: *Volunteers of America*
Label: RCA
Produced by: Al Schmitt
Year: 1969
Doomed anthem of a counterculture, up against the wall.

VOODOO CHILE (SLIGHT RETURN)

Artist: Jimi Hendrix
Written by: Jimi Hendrix
From the album: *Electric Ladyland*
Label: Reprise
Produced by: Jimi Hendrix
Year: 1968
Perhaps his most famous composition, his first posthumous hit went to #1 in the UK in 1970, where they were always more amenable to the extravagant gesture. Covered by Stevie Ray Vaughan (Epic, '84).

VOW

Artist: Garbage

Written by: Butch Vig, Duke Erickson, Shirley Manson, Steve Marker
From the album: *Garbage*
Produced by: Butch Vig
Label: Almo Sounds
Year: 1995

VOW, THE

Artist: The Flamingos
Written by: George Motola, Zeke Carey, Danny Webb
From the album: *The Flamingos*
Label: Checker
Produced by: Leonard Chess
Year: 1956

W

WAH-WATUSI, THE

Artist: The Orlons
Written by: Kal Mann, Dave Appell
From the album: *The Wah-Watusi*
Label: Cameo
Year: 1962
Eighth most popular dance specifically mentioned in the Top 40 of '62. Among them the Popeye (twice), the Cha Cha, the Twist (14 times), the Loco-Motion, the Monster Mash, the Limbo (twice), the Stomp (twice), the Mashed Potato, the Hully Gully, the Push and Kick, the New Continental, the Hula, and a striptease.

WAIT

Artist: Sarah McLachlan
Written by: Sarah McLachlan
From the album: *Fumbling Toward Ecstacy*
Label: Arista
Produced by: Pierre Marchand
Year: 1994

WAIT 'TIL MY BOBBY GETS HOME

Artist: Darlene Love
Written by: Jeff Barry, Ellie Greenwich, Phil Spector
Label: Philles
Produced by: Phil Spector
Year: 1963
Biggest solo hit for the legendary Spector back-up singer.

WAITIN' IN SCHOOL

Artist: Ricky Nelson
Written by: Johnny Burnette, Dorsey Burnette
From the album: *Ricky*
Label: Imperial
Produced by: Ricky Nelson, Jimmy Haskell, Ozzie Nelson
Year: 1957
B-side of "Stood Up," written by two-thirds of the Rockabilly Trio, the Burnette brothers.

WAITING FOR A GIRL LIKE YOU

Artist: Foreigner
Written by: Lou Grammatico (Lou Gramm), Mick Jones
From the album: *4*
Label: Atlantic
Produced by: Mutt Lange, Mick Jones
Year: 1981
Trying to renounce their sexist ways, with ten weeks at #2 as delayed gratification.

WAITING FOR A STAR TO FALL

Artist: Boy Meets Girl
Written by: Gary Merrill, Shannon Rubicam
From the album: *Reel Life*
Label: RCA
Produced by: Arif Mardin
Year: 1988
From the songwriting team that wrote "How Will I Know" for Whitney Houston.

WAITING FOR THE SUN

Artist: The Jayhawks
Written by: Gary Louris, Mark Olson
From the album: *Hollywood Town Hall*
Label: Def American
Produced by: George Drakoulias
Year: 1992
And the chiming guitars and moody harmonies of alt/country shall once again be heard throughout the land.

WAITING ON A FRIEND

Artist: The Rolling Stones
Written by: Mick Jagger, Keith Richards
From the album: *Tattoo You*
Label: Rolling Stones
Produced by: Glimmer Twins
Year: 1981
Featuring Peter Tosh in the video.

WAITING ROOM

Artist: Fugazi
Written by: Ian MacKaye
From the album: *Fugazi*
Label: Dischord
Produced by: John Loder
Year: 1988
Hardcore punk revisited: faster and louder.

WAITING, THE

Artist: Tom Petty and the Heartbreakers
Written by: Tom Petty
From the album: *Hard Promises*
Label: Backstreet
Produced by: Jimmy Iovine, Tom Petty
Year: 1981

Wisdom and redemption for folk/rock's eternal changes. Covered by Linda Ronstadt (Elektra, '95).

WAKE ME UP BEFORE YOU GO-GO

Artist: Wham!
Written by: George Michael
From the album: *Make It Big*
Label: Columbia
Produced by: George Michael
Year: 1984
First American hit for the British disco dandies, a #1 US/#1 UK crossover. In the US, Maurice Starr was listening on behalf of the New Kids on the Block.

WAKE ME, SHAKE ME

Artist: The Blues Project
Written by: Al Kooper
From the album: *Projections*
Label: Verve/Forecast
Produced by: Tom Wilson
Year: 1967
Rousing gospel crossover, also known as "Don't Let Me Sleep Too Long," as covered by the Myddle Class (Kama Sutra, '67) and produced by Carole King.

WAKE UP EVERYBODY, PART ONE

Artist: Harold Melvin and the Bluenotes
Written by: Gene McFadden, John Whitehead, Vic Carstarphen
From the album: *Wake up Everybody*
Label: Philadelphia International
Produced by: Kenny Gamble, Leon Huff
Year: 1975
#1 R&B/Top 20 crossover. McFadden and Whitehead would go on to "Ain't No Stoppin' Us Now." Pendergrass would go on to heartthrob status.

WAKE UP, LITTLE SUSIE

Artist: The Everly Brothers
Written by: Boudleaux Bryant, Felice Bryant
From the album: *The Everly Brothers*
Label: Cadence
Produced by: Archie Bleyer
Year: 1957
#1 country/#1 crossover with subject matter that was regarded as risque for Nashville. Chet Atkins on guitar.

WALK A MILE IN MY SHOES

Artist: Joe South
Written by: Joe South
From the album: *Don't It Make You Want to Go Home*
Label: Capitol
Produced by: Joe South
Year: 1970

A landmark country soul gospel-protest song, and a country crossover. Covered by R&B singer Willie Hightower (Fame, '70), Elvis Presley (RCA, '70).

WALK AWAY FROM LOVE

Artist: David Ruffin
Written by: Charles Kipps Jr.
From the album: *Who I Am*
Label: Motown
Produced by: Van McCoy
Year: 1975
#1 R&B/Top 10 crossover was a comeback hit for the former Temptations lead singer.

WALK AWAY RENEE

Artist: The Left Banke
Written by: Michael Brown, Bob Calilli, Tony Sansone
From the album: *Walk Away Renee/Pretty Ballerina*
Label: Smash
Produced by: Harry Lookofsky, Steve Jerome, Bill Jerome
Year: 1966
A New York City post-Brill Building valentine with Stephen Tyler (then of the Chain Reaction) on backup vocals. Covered by the Four Tops (Motown, '68), Orpheus (MGM, '68), Rickie Lee Jones (Warner Brothers, '83).

WALK DON'T RUN

Artist: Chet Atkins
Written by: John H. Smith Jr.
From the album: *Hi-Fi in Focus*
Label: RCA
Produced by: Chet Atkins
Year: 1957
Legendary instrumental was turned into a twangy surf classic by the West coast group the Ventures (Dolton, '60).

WALK LIKE A MAN

Artist: The Four Seasons
Written by: Bob Gaudio, Bob Crewe
From the album: *Big Girls Don't Cry and Twelve Others*
Label: Vee Jay
Produced by: Bob Crewe
Year: 1963
Their third #1. Suggested segue: "Mama Said" by the Shirelles, "Father and Son" by Cat Stevens.

WALK LIKE A MAN

Artist: Bruce Springsteen
Written by: Bruce Springsteen
From the album: *Tunnel of Love*
Label: Columbia
Produced by: Jon Landau, Bruce Springsteen, Chuck Plotkin
Year: 1985
Poignant vision of adulthood. Suggested segue: "Uptown Girl" by Billy Joel.

WALK LIKE AN EGYPTIAN

Artist: Bangles
Written by: Liam Sternberg
From the album: *Different Light*
Label: Columbia
Produced by: David Kahne
Year: 1986
The paisley underground of San Francisco meets the collegiate funk of Athens, Georgia, as the Bangles temporarily out-kitsch the B-52's for their first #1. Later parodied as "Walk with an Erection."

WALK ON

Artist: U2
Written by: Bono, U2
From the album: *All That You Can't Leave Behind*
Label: Island
Produced by: Eno, Julian Gallagher, Mike Hedges, Steve Lillywhite
Year: 2000
Record of the Year Grammy, about a Nobel Prize winning Burmese peace activist.

WALK ON BY

Artist: Leroy Van Dyke
Written by: Burt Bacharach, Hal David
Label: Mercury
Year: 1961
One of the biggest country hits of the last thirty years; a #1 country/Top 10 crossover. Covered by Dionne Warwick (Scepter, '64).

WALK ON THE WILD SIDE

Artist: Lou Reed
Written by: Lou Reed
From the album: *Transformer*
Label: RCA
Produced by: David Bowie, Lou Reed, Mick Ronson
Year: 1972
The vocal version of Andy Warhol's mock documentary *Chelsea Girls*, gives Lou Reed a brief commercial viability. He would move on from there to become the weathered voice of a lost generation.

WALK RIGHT BACK

Artist: The Everly Brothers
Written by: Sonny Curtis
From the album: *Golden Hits of the Everly Brothers*
Label: Warner Brothers
Produced by: Wesley Rose
Year: 1960
Great rocker by the man who wrote "I Fought the Law."

WALK RIGHT IN

Artist: The Rooftop Singers
Written by: Gus Cannon, Harry Woods
From the album: *Walk Right In*
Label: Vanguard
Produced by: Erik Darling, Bill Svanoe
Year: 1963

American jug band classic kicks off the Greenwich Village folk scare on the record charts. Originated by Gus Cannon's Jug Stompers (Victor, '28).

WALK THE DINOSAUR

Artist: Was (Not Was)
Written by: David Weiss (David Was), Donald Fagenson (Don Was), Randall Jacobs
From the album: *What up, Dog*
Label: Chrysalis
Produced by: Don Was, David Was
Year: 1988
Their biggest hit, a dance-hall fave, especially in rooms with rubber walls.

WALK THIS WAY

Artist: Aerosmith
Written by: Steven Tyler, Joe Perry
From the album: *Toys in the Attic*
Label: Columbia
Produced by: Jack Douglas
Year: 1973
Considered semilewd in its day, this ode to the Three Stooges and high school making out eventually crossed over from the arena to the radio. By this time, Tyler was bankrupt—emotionally if not financially, or vice-versa—and the band was kaput. Covered by Run-D.M.C. in 1986, with guest appearances by the writers, the song was a precursor of the move from rock to rap, providing new commercial visibility for the veteran rappers from Queens, as well as a platform for a repentant return to the charts for the previous bad boys from Boston.

WALKIN' BACK TO HAPPINESS

Artist: Helen Shapiro
Written by: Michael Hawker, John Schroeder
Produced by: Norrie Parmaor
Label: EMI
Year: 1961
Biggest UK hit for the deep-voiced teenage British thrush made #100 here.

WALKIN' ON THE SUN

Artist: Smash Mouth
Written by: Robert Delevante
From the album: *Fush Yu Mang*
Label: Interscope
Year: 1997
All-inclusive rant reflects on the history and mystery of rock and roll.

WALKING AFTER MIDNIGHT

Artist: Patsy Cline
Written by: Don Hecht, Alan Block
From the album: *Patsy Cline Showcase*
Label: Decca
Produced by: Owen Bradley

Year: 1956
First country crossover hit for the legendary warbler.

WALKING ALONG

Artist: The Solitaires
Written by: Willie Winston, Hy Weiss
Label: Argo
Produced by: Sam Phillips
Year: 1957
Doo-wop classic.

WALKING DOWN MADISON

Artist: Kirsty MacColl
Written by: Kirsty MacColl, Johnny Marr
From the album: *Electric Landlady*
Label: Charisma
Produced by: Steve Lillywhite
Year: 1991
One of the best New York Cityscapes since her own ineffable "Fairytale of New York," with the Pogues.

WALKING IN MEMPHIS

Artist: Marc Cohn
Written by: Marc Cohn
From the album: *Marc Cohn*
Label: Atlantic
Produced by: Marc Cohn, Ben Wisch
Year: 1991
Bruce Hornsbyesque folk/jazz tribute to the ghost of Elvis Presley, inspired by an Al Green sermon. Crossed over to the country chart.

WALKING IN THE RAIN

Artist: The Ronettes
Written by: Barry Mann, Cynthia Weil, Phil Spector
From the album: *… introducing the fabulous Ronettes featuring Ronnie*
Label: Philles
Produced by: Phil Spector
Year: 1964
And into the sunset, with only one Top 10 hit in the books ("Be My Baby"), belying their enormous stylistic impact.

WALKING MY CAT NAMED DOG

Artist: Norma Tanega
Written by: Norma Tanega
From the album: *Walking My Cat Named Dog*
Label: New Voice
Produced by: Bob Crewe
Year: 1966
Classic Greenwich Village coffee house doggerel.

WALKING ON BROKEN GLASS

Artist: Annie Lennox
Written by: Annie Lennox

From the album: *Diva*
Label: Arista
Produced by: Stephen Lipson
Year: 1992
The former Eurythmic exhibits prime dance-hall pipes.

WALKING ON SUNSHINE

Artist: Eddy Grant
Written by: Kimberly Rew
From the album: *Walking on Sunshine*
Label: Epic
Produced by: Eddy Grant
Year: 1979
Legendary UK production, covered by Rockers Revenge (London, '82) and Rew's band, Katrina and the Waves (Capitol, '85).

WALKING ON THE MOON

Artist: The Police
Written by: Gordon Sumner (Sting)
From the album: *Regatta De Blanc*
Label: A&M
Produced by: Nigel Gray, the Police
Year: 1979
#1 UK follow-up to "Message in a Bottle."

WALKING ON THIN ICE

Artist: Yoko Ono
Written by: Yoko Ono
Label: Geffen
Produced by: John Lennon, Yoko Ono
Year: 1981
Reportedly, Yoko and John were working on this track the day he was shot. Later, its eerie and affecting video would earn Yoko more critical respect in rock circles than she'd previously ever had.

WALKING THE DOG

Artist: Rufus Thomas
Written by: Rufus Thomas
From the album: *Walking the Dog*
Label: Stax
Year: 1963
After l'affaire de "Bear Cat," in which he was sued for copying "Hound Dog," you would think Rufus would have gotten over his dog fixation. But in '63 it returned. While "the Dog" was just a middling R&B/crossover, this follow-up became his defining number, a Top 10 R&B/Top 10 crossover. Unsated, he was back in '64 with "Can Your Monkey Do the Dog," followed a month later by "Somebody Stole My Dog."

WALKING TO NEW ORLEANS

Artist: Fats Domino
Written by: Fats Domino, Dave Bartholomew, Robert Guidry (Sonny Charles)
From the album: *Million Sellers by Fats*
Label: Imperial

Produced by: Dave Bartholomew
Year: 1960
Capitalizing on the attention drawn to his rockin' headquarters that year, Fats has his last and biggest hit of the '60s.

WALL OF DEATH

Artist: Richard and Linda Thompson
Written by: Richard Thompson
From the album: *Shoot out the Lights*
Label: Hannibal
Produced by: Joe Boyd
Year: 1982
Hail and farewell to their omnipresent death motif. Covered by R.E.M. (Capitol, '94).

WANDERER, THE

Artist: Dion
Written by: Ernest Maresca
From the album: *Runaround Sue*
Label: Laurie
Produced by: Gene Schwartz
Year: 1962
No longer a teenager, no longer in love; perhaps his most famous number.

WANDERER, THE

Artist: Donna Summer
Written by: Giorgio Moroder, Donna Summer
From the album: *The Wanderer*
Label: Geffen
Produced by: Giorgio Moroder, Pete Bellotte
Year: 1980
Donna does rock.

WANDERER, THE

Artist: U2
Written by: U2
From the album: *Zooropa*
Label: Island
Produced by: Brian Eno, Flood
Year: 1993
Vocal by Johnny Cash.

WANGO TANGO

Artist: Ted Nugent
Written by: Ted Nugent
From the album: *Scream Dream*
Label: Epic
Produced by: Cliff Davies
Year: 1980
His defining wang-bar moment. Later, he would cash in on the charts through Damn Yankees.

WANNA BE STARTIN' SOMETHING

Artist: Michael Jackson
Written by: Michael Jackson
From the album: *Thriller*
Label: Epic
Produced by: Quincy Jones, Michael Jackson

Year: 1983
Fourth of six Top 10 hits from the monster album.

WANNABE

Artist: Spice Girls
Written by: Melanie Brown, Geraldine Halliwell, Victoria Adams, Melanie Chisholm, Emma Lee Burton, Richard Stannard, Matt Rowe
From the album: *Spice*
Label: Virgin
Produced by: Richard Stannard, Matt Rowe
Year: 1997
Wannabe Madonna clones times five start a profitable year on the American charts.

WANT-ADS

Artist: The Honey Cone
Written by: General Johnson, Greg S. Perry, Barney Perkins
From the album: *Sweet Replies*
Label: Hot Wax
Produced by: Greg S. Perry
Year: 1971
This "Stick Up" rewrite stiffed for Glass House and Freda Payne, before the Honey Cone (featuring Darlene Love's sister) made it a #1 R&B/#1 crossover.

WANTED DEAD OR ALIVE

Artist: Bon Jovi
Written by: Jon Bon Jovi, Richie Sambora
From the album: *Slippery When Wet*
Label: Polygram
Produced by: Bruce Fairbairn
Year: 1987
Mining the rock-star-as-gunslinger motif originated by Bo Diddley.

WANTED MAN

Artist: Johnny Cash
Written by: Bob Dylan
From the album: *Johnny Cash at San Quentin*
Label: Columbia
Produced by: Bob Johnston
Year: 1969
Perfect match of singer, songwriter, song, and venue.

WAR

Artist: Temptations
Written by: Norman Whitfield, Barrett Strong
From the album: *Psychedelic Shack*
Label: Gordy
Produced by: Norman Whitfield
Year: 1970
In the R&B protest mode. Cover by Edwin Starr (Gordy, '70) was a Top 10 R&B/#1 crossover. Covered by Bruce Springsteen (Columbia, '86).

WAR IN PEACE

Artist: Skip Spence
Written by: Skip Spence
From the album: *OAR*

Label: Columbia
Year: 1969
Solo track from the lost Moby Grape founder.

WARMTH OF THE SUN, THE

Artist: The Beach Boys
Written by: Brian Wilson, Mike Love
From the album: *Shut Down (Vol. II)*
Label: Capitol
Produced by: Brian Wilson
Year: 1964
Written a few hours after John F. Kennedy was assassinated.

WARRIOR, THE

Artist: Scandal
Written by: Holly Knight, Nick Gilder
From the album: *The Warrior*
Label: Columbia
Produced by: Mike Chapman
Year: 1984
Only Top 10 hit for the former funky punk princess Patty Smyth.

WASTED

Artist: Black Flag
Written by: Greg Ginn, Keith Morris
From the album: *Nervous Breakdown*
Label: SST
Year: 1978
L.A. punk evergreen. Covered by Camper Van Beethoven (Independent Project, '85).

WASTED ON THE WAY

Artist: Crosby, Stills & Nash
Written by: Graham Nash
From the album: *Daylight Again*
Label: Atlantic
Produced by: Crosby, Stills & Nash, Stanley Johnson, Steve Gursky
Year: 1982
Summing up the faded hopes and dashed dreams of the generation that made them famous. Suggested segue: "Before the Deluge" by Jackson Browne.

WATCH ME ROCK, I'M OVER THIRTY

Artist: Loudon Wainwright III
Written by: Loudon Wainwright III
From the album: *Final Exam*
Label: Arista
Year: 1978
As age begins to creep into his comic's mug, Wainwright deflects it with a joke. A few years later, he'd be a lot more bitter, in "How Old Are You" (Columbia, '85) and "Harry's Wall" (Silvertone, '89).

WATCHING THE DETECTIVES

Artist: Elvis Costello
Written by: Declan McManus (Elvis Costello)

From the album: *My Aim Is True*
Label: Columbia
Produced by: Nick Lowe
Year: 1977
First UK hit for the noted perturbed wordsmith.

WATCHING THE RIVER FLOW

Artist: Bob Dylan
Written by: Bob Dylan
From the album: *Bob Dylan's Greatest Hits (Vol. II)*
Label: Columbia
Produced by: Leon Russell
Year: 1971
Celebrating the inevitable ennui of the living legend. Spiritual cousin to "Watching the Wheels" by John Lennon.

WATCHING THE WHEELS

Artist: John Lennon
Written by: John Lennon
From the album: *Double Fantasy*
Label: Geffen
Produced by: John Lennon, Yoko Ono, Jack Douglas
Year: 1981
Achieving peace at last. His first posthumous release.

WATERFALLS

Artist: TLC
Written by: Lisa Lopes, Organized Noize, Marqueese Ethridge
From the album: *Crazysexycool*
Label: LaFace
Produced by: Dallas Austin
Year: 1994
Shedding their neo-Supremes image with a masterful cautionary streetwise tale, a Top 10 R&B/#1 crossover.

WATERLOO

Artist: Abba
Written by: Benny Andersson, Bjorn Ulvaeus, Stig Anderson
From the album: *Waterloo*
Label: Atlantic
Produced by: Benny Andersson, Bjorn Ulvaeus
Year: 1974
Winner of the Eurovision international song contest, this peppy pop concoction hit #1 UK/ Top 10 US, introducing the world to Sweden's answer to the Mamas & the Papas.

WATERLOO

Artist: Stonewall Jackson
Written by: John D. Loudermilk, Marijohn Wilkins
Label: Columbia
Year: 1959
#1 country/Top 10 crossover.

WATERLOO SUNSET

Artist: The Kinks
Written by: Ray Davies
From the album: *Something Else by the Kinks*
Label: Reprise
Produced by: Shel Talmy
Year: 1967
Originally called "Liverpool Sunset." One of his loveliest watercolors; tranquil, spacious, translucent.

WAY DOWN

Artist: Elvis Presley
Written by: Layng Martine
From the album: *Moody Blue*
Label: RCA
Produced by: Felton Jarvis, Elvis Presley
Year: 1975
Last big hit for the King: #1 country/Top 20 crossover.

WAY DOWN YONDER IN NEW ORLEANS

Artist: Freddy Cannon
Written by: Henry Creamer, Turner Layton
From the album: *Solid Gold Hits*
Label: Swan
Year: 1960
Initiating the year's belated salute to New Orleans. Introduced in '22 by the writers.

WAY I AM, THE

Artist: Eminem
Written by: Marshall (Eminem) Mathers
From the album: *The Marshall Mathers LP*
Label: Interscope
Produced by: Dr. Dre
Year: 2000
The misunderstood white rapper attempts to explain his bad self.

WAY I WALK, THE

Artist: Jack Scott
Written by: Jack Scott
Label: Carlton
Produced by: Ed Carlton
Year: 1959
Future rockabilly classic that barely made Top 40. Covered by Dave Edmunds (Swan Song, '77), Robert Gordon (Private Stock, '78), the Cramps (IRS, '79).

WAY IT IS, THE

Artist: Bruce Hornsby and the Range
Written by: Bruce Hornsby
From the album: *The Way It Is*
Label: RCA
Produced by: Bruce Hornsby
Year: 1986
Anthemic post-civil rights era jazz/rock dirge went to #1.

WAY OVER THERE

Artist: The Miracles
Written by: Smokey Robinson, Berry Gordy Jr.
From the album: *Hi, We're the Miracles*
Label: Tamla
Produced by: Berry Gordy Jr.
Year: 1960
Their first release on Tamla, clocking in at #94.

WAY OVER YONDER IN THE MINOR KEY

Artist: Billy Bragg and Natalie Merchant
Written by: Billy Bragg, Woody Guthrie
From the album: *Mermaid Avenue*
Label: Elektra
Produced by: Grant Showbiz, Milo
Year: 1998
The British folkie gets a chance to harmonize on some newfound Guthrie material.

WAY, THE

Artist: Fastball
Written by: Tony Scalzo
From the album: *All the Pain That Money Can Buy*
Label: Hollywood
Year: 1998
Hard rock philosophizing.

WAY TO BLUE

Artist: Nick Drake
Written by: Nick Drake
From the album: *Five Leaves Left*
Label: Hannibal
Produced by: Joe Boyd
Year: 1969
Big track from the quintessentially depressive English singer/songwriter.

WAY YOU DO THE THINGS YOU DO, THE

Artist: The Temptations
Written by: Smokey Robinson, Bobby Rogers
From the album: *Temptations Sing Smokey*
Label: Gordy
Produced by: Smokey Robinson
Year: 1964
Covered as part of a medley with "My Girl" by Daryl Hall & John Oates with David Ruffin and Eddie Kendricks (RCA, '85).

WAY YOU LOVE ME, THE

Artist: Karyn White
Written by: Kenny Edmunds (Babyface), Antonio Reed (L. A. Reid), Daryl Simmons
From the album: *Karyn White*
Label: Warner Brothers
Produced by: Babyface, L. A. Reid
Year: 1988
#1 R&B/Top 10 crossover for the year's most successful debut artist.

WAY YOU MAKE ME FEEL, THE

Artist: Michael Jackson
Written by: Michael Jackson
From the album: *Bad*
Label: Epic
Produced by: Quincy Jones
Year: 1987
#1 R&B/#1 crossover.

WAYS TO BE WICKED

Artist: Lone Justice
Written by: Tom Petty, Mike Campbell
From the album: *Lone Justice*
Label: Geffen
Produced by: Jimmy Iovine
Year: 1985
Maria McKee's breakout vehicle, which stalled in the passing lane.

WE AIN'T GOT NOTHING YET

Artist: The Blues Magoos
Written by: Emil Thielhelm, Michael Esposito, Ralph Scala, Ronald Gilbert
From the album: *Psychedelic Lollipop*
Label: Mercury
Produced by: Wyld & Polhemus
Year: 1966
Elucidating the garage punk agenda.

WE ALMOST LOST DETROIT

Artist: Gil Scott-Heron
Written by: Gil Scott-Heron
From the album: *Bridges*
Label: Arista
Year: 1977
Former Last Poet envisions nuclear holocaust.

WE ARE FAMILY

Artist: Sister Sledge
Written by: Bernard Edwards, Nile Rodgers
From the album: *We Are Family*
Label: Cotillion
Produced by: Bernard Edwards, Nile Rodgers
Year: 1978
This #1 R&B/Top 10 crossover for the Philly group was adopted by the Pittsburgh Pirates as the anthem of their last championship season. Covered by Babes in Toyland (Reprise, '95), used in the hilarious finale of *The Birdcage* ('96).

WE ARE THE CHAMPIONS

Artist: Queen
Written by: Freddie Mercury
From the album: *News of the World*
Label: Elektra
Produced by: Queen
Year: 1977

Conquring an arena of a different sort, this quintessential anthem, especially in its medley form with "We Will Rock You," was adopted in soccer and football stadiums all around the world as a form of taunting the opposition after a victory.

WE ARE THE NORMAL

Artist: Goo Goo Dolls
Written by: Paul Westerberg, John Rzeznick, Robert Takac, George Tususka
From the album: *Superstar Carwash*
Label: Metal Blade
Produced by: Gavin MacKillop
Year: 1993
Written with one of their idols/influences, Paul Westerberg of the Replacements, a hard-core rocker from the days before they had a "name."

WE ARE THE ROAD CREW

Artist: Motorhead
Written by: Ian Kilmeister (Lemmy), Philthy Taylor, (Fast) Eddie Clarke
From the album: *Ace of Spades*
Label: Mercury
Produced by: Vic Maile
Year: 1980
And a scruffy lot they were.

WE ARE THE WORLD

Artist: USA For Africa
Written by: Michael Jackson, Lionel Richie Jr.
From the album: *We Are the World*
Label: Columbia
Produced by: Quincy Jones
Year: 1985
Worldwide all-star charity sing-along was a #1 R&B/#1 crossover.

WE BELONG

Artist: Pat Benatar
Written by: David Lowen, Daniel Navarro
From the album: *Tropico*
Label: Chrysalis
Produced by: Peter Coleman, Neil Giraldo
Year: 1984
Arena anthem is one of her biggest hits.

WE BELONG TOGETHER

Artist: Rickie Lee Jones
Written by: Rickie Lee Jones
From the album: *Pirates*
Label: Warner Brothers
Produced by: Rickie Lee Jones, Russ Titelman
Year: 1981
Street theatrics from the throwback beatnik chanteuse.

WE BELONG TOGETHER

Artist: Robert and Johnny
Written by: Johnny Mitchell, Robert Carr, Sam Weiss

Label: Old Town
Produced by: Russ Titelman, Lenny Waronker
Year: 1958
Early classic doo-wop/R&B crossover.

WE BUILT THIS CITY

Artist: Starship
Written by: Peter Wolf, Bernie Taupin
From the album: *Knee Deep in the Hoopla*
Label: Grunt
Produced by: Dennis Lambert
Year: 1985
Tribute to San Francisco tweaks corporate rock and benefits from it at the same time, giving the legendary San Francisco band its first #1.

WE CAN BE TOGETHER

Artist: Jefferson Airplane
Written by: Marty Balin, Paul Kantner
From the album: *Volunteers of America*
Label: RCA
Produced by: Al Schmitt
Year: 1969
Hopeful eulogy as the Summer of Love meets a dying fall. B-side of "Volunteers."

WE CAN CHANGE THE WORLD

Artist: Graham Nash
Written by: Graham Nash
From the album: *Songs for Beginners*
Label: Atlantic
Produced by: Graham Nash
Year: 1971
Voicing sentiments that would remain popular until the McGovern debacle of '72.

WE CAN WORK IT OUT

Artist: The Beatles
Written by: John Lennon, Paul McCartney
From the album: *Yesterday and Today*
Label: Capitol
Produced by: George Martin
Year: 1965
Closing out '65 on a more hopeful note than much of the year's and their own output. Covered by Stevie Wonder (Tamla, '70).

WE DIDN'T START THE FIRE

Artist: Billy Joel
Written by: Billy Joel
From the album: *Storm Front*
Label: Columbia
Produced by: Mick Jones, Billy Joel
Year: 1989
The three-minute MTV version of Pop Culture 101. Suggested segues: "It's the End of the World as We Know It (and I Feel Fine)" by R.E.M., "Subterranean Homesick Blues" by Bob Dylan.

WE DON'T HAVE TO TAKE OUR CLOTHES OFF

Artist: Jermaine Stewart
Written by: Preston Glass, Narada Michael Walden
From the album: *Frantic Romantic*
Label: Arista
Produced by: Narada Michael Walden
Year: 1986
Top 10 US/UK ballad bucks the prevailing moral zeitgeist.

WE DON'T NEED ANOTHER HERO (THUNDERDOME)

Artist: Tina Turner
Written by: Terry Britten, Graham Lyle
From the album: *Mad Max Beyond Thunderdome Soundtrack*
Label: Capitol
Produced by: Terry Britten
Year: 1985
The voice of Mel Gibson's post-apocalyptic vision.

WE DON'T TALK ANYMORE

Artist: Cliff Richard
Written by: Al Tarney
From the album: *We Don't Talk Anymore*
Label: EMI-American
Produced by: Bruce Welch
Year: 1979
Second of his three US hits; in the UK he had 59.

WE GET ILL

Artist: Schooly D
Written by: Jessie Weaver
From the album: *Saturday Night (The Album)*
Label: Schooly D
Year: 1987
In your face rap from Philadelphia that reportedly influenced the Beastie Boys.

WE GOT THE BEAT

Artist: The Go-Go's
Written by: Charlotte Caffey
From the album: *Beauty and the Beat*
Label: I.R.S.
Produced by: Richard Gottehrer
Year: 1982
First hit for the edgy girl-group from L.A.

WE GOTTA GET OUTA THIS PLACE

Artist: The Animals
Written by: Barry Mann, Cynthia Weil
From the album: *Animal Tricks*
Label: MGM
Produced by: Mickie Most
Year: 1965
Versatile working-class folk/rock anthem of escape written by one of rock's most contented couples. When covered by Katrina & the Waves on the soundtrack of the Vietnam-era TV series, *China Beach*, it took on a whole new meaning.

WE GOTTA GET YOU A WOMAN

Artist: Runt
Written by: Todd Rundgren
From the album: *Runt*
Label: Ampex
Produced by: Todd Rundgren
Year: 1970
Disarming streetcorner jazz/rock from Rundgren in his formative days.

WE HATE IT WHEN OUR FRIENDS BECOME SUCCESSFUL

Artist: Morrissey
Written by: Stephen Morrissey, Alain Whyte
From the album: *Your Arsenal*
Label: Sire
Produced by: Mick Ronson
Year: 1992
First US chart hit for the poet laureate of mope.

WE HAVE THE TECHNOLOGY

Artist: Pere Ubu
Written by: Pere Ubu
From the album: *The Tenement Year*
Label: Enigma
Produced by: Ken Hamann, Pere Ubu
Year: 1988
The warped voice of the computer age, a decade ahead of its time.

WE JUST DISAGREE

Artist: Dave Mason
Written by: Jim Krueger
From the album: *Let It Flow*
Label: Columbia
Produced by: Jim Kreuger
Year: 1977
Mellow rocker was his biggest hit.

WE LIVE SO FAST

Artist: Heaven 17
Written by: Glenn Gregory, Ian Craig Marsh, Martyn Ware
From the album: *The Luxury Gap*
Label: Sire
Produced by: Greg Walsh, B.E.F.
Year: 1982
Frenetic synth driven thing. Ware and Marsh had cofounded the Human League.

WE LOVE YOU

Artist: The Rolling Stones
Written by: Mick Jagger, Keith Richards
From the album: *More Hot Rocks (Big Hits and Fazed Cookies)*
Label: London
Produced by: Andrew Loog-Oldham
Year: 1967
B-side of "Dandelion." When taken as a whole single, arguably their creative nadir.

WE3

Artist: Dave Pirner
Written by: Dave Pirner
Year: 1996
Over the closing credits of the classic movie *Chasing Amy*, for which Soul Asylum's Pirner selected the songs.

WE WILL ROCK YOU

Artist: Queen
Written by: Brian May
From the album: *News of the World*
Label: Elektra
Produced by: Queen
Year: 1977
Separately or together with "We Are the Champions," their biggest hit of the '70s.

WE'LL BE TOGETHER

Artist: Sting
Written by: Gordon Sumner (Sting)
From the album: *Nothing Like the Sun*
Label: A&M
Produced by: Hugh Padgham, Sting
Year: 1987
Heading toward the middle of the new age road.

WE'LL SING IN THE SUNSHINE

Artist: Gale Garnett
Written by: Gale Garnett
From the album: *My Kind of Folk Songs*
Label: RCA Victor
Produced by: Andy Wiswell
Year: 1964
Advancing the decidedly un-girl-group notion of serial monogamy and winning a Grammy for Folk Song of the Year in the process. Around the corner was emancipation, liberation, the topless bathing suit, Carole Doda, group sex, Janis Joplin. Gale Garnett, meanwhile, returned to Canada, later to reemerge in a cabaret performance of the songs of Leonard Cohen.

WE'RE A WINNER

Artist: The Impressions
Written by: Curtis Mayfield
From the album: *We're a Winner*
Label: ABC
Produced by: Johnny Pate
Year: 1967
#1 R&B/Top 20 crossover.

WE'RE ALL ALONE

Artist: Boz Scaggs
Written by: Boz Scaggs
From the album: *Silk Degrees*
Label: Columbia
Produced by: Joe Wissert
Year: 1976
His breakout barroom ballad. Covered by Rita Coolidge (A&M, '77).

WE'RE AN AMERICAN BAND

Artist: Grand Funk Railroad
Written by: Don Brewer
From the album: *We're an American Band*
Label: Capitol
Produced by: Todd Rundgren
Year: 1973
Their first of two #1 hits.

WE'RE DESPERATE

Artist: X
Written by: John Doe, Exene Cervenka
From the album: *Wild Gift*
Label: Slash
Produced by: Ray Manzarek
Year: 1981
Groundbreaking rockabilly/punk track from L.A., featured in the '81 documentary *The Decline of Western Civilization*.

WE'RE GONNA MAKE IT (AFTER ALL)

Artist: Ellie Greenwich
Written by: Ellie Greenwich
From the album: *Leader of the Pack*
Label: Elektra/Asylum
Year: 1985
Preceding Leiber & Stoller and Goffin & King but not Leonard Cohen to the cabaret showcase arena, brilliant Brill Building songwriter (Barry & Greenwich) sings a tribute to herself.

(WE'RE GONNA) ROCK AROUND THE CLOCK

Artist: Bill Haley and His Comets
Written by: Max C. Freedman, Jimmy Myers (Jimmy DeKnight)
From the album: *Rock around the Clock*
Label: Decca
Produced by: Milt Gabler
Year: 1953
Perhaps the most significant career move of early rock and roll history occurred when Jimmy De-Knight was appointed music director of the movie *Blackboard Jungle*. In his first official act, he ordered "Rock around the Clock," the Bill Haley B-side ("Thirteen Women" was the A-side) he'd written that had already flopped twice (once for Bill, once for its originator, Sunny Dae [Impact, '52]), to be used behind the opening credits. Thus, when the movie opened and the single hit #1 in 1955, rock and roll, as a song and an image, officially crossed over into mainstream America. It's too bad Danny Cedrone, who took the quintessential rockabilly guitar solo, never lived to see it, having died in a fall sometime shortly after the record's original release.

WE'RE GONNA ROCK THIS JOINT

Artist: The Jackson Brothers
Written by: Wilfred Jackson
Label: RCA
Year: 1952
Prescient R&B.

WE'RE GONNA ROCK, WE'RE GONNA ROLL

Artist: Wild Bill Moore
Written by: Teddy Reig, Bill Moore
Label: Savoy
Produced by: Teddy Reig
Year: 1947
Sax-driven, Illinois Jacquet-influenced boogie was a model for Twists to come.

WE'RE NOT GONNA TAKE IT

Artist: Twisted Sister
Written by: Dee Snider
From the album: *Stay Hungry*
Label: Atlantic
Produced by: Tom Werman
Year: 1984
Rock's hungriest New York Dolls wannabes, finally achieve their brief moment.

WE'RE NOT GONNA TAKE IT

Artist: The Who
Written by: Pete Townshend
From the album: *Tommy*
Label: Decca
Produced by: Kit Lambert
Year: 1969
Tommy's FM radio anthem.

WE'RE READY

Artist: Boston
Written by: Tom Scholz
From the album: *Third Stage*
Label: MCA
Produced by: Tom Scholz
Year: 1986
Fourth and last Top 10 hit.

WE'VE COME TOO FAR TO END IT NOW

Artist: The Miracles
Written by: David Jones, Wade Brown Jr., Johnny Bristol
From the album: *Flying High Together*
Label: Tamla
Produced by: Johnny Bristol
Year: 1972
But clearly the Miracles' incredible run was over, as this peaked at #46.

WE'VE GOT TONIGHT

Artist: Bob Seger
Written by: Bob Seger
From the album: *Stranger in Town*
Label: Capitol
Produced by: Bob Seger, Muscle Shoals Rhythm Section
Year: 1979
Cover by Kenny Rogers and Kim Carnes was a #1 country/Top 10 crossover (Liberty, '83).

WE'VE ONLY JUST BEGUN

Artist: Carpenters
Written by: Paul Williams, Roger Nichols
From the album: *Close to You*
Label: A&M
Produced by: Jack Daugherty
Year: 1970
All white lace and promises unkept, the voice of Karen Carpenter inherits the bittersweet, suburban legacy of Brian Wilson.

WEAK

Artist: SWV
Written by: Brian Alexander Morgan
From the album: *It's About Time*
Label: RCA
Produced by: B. A. Morgan
Year: 1993
Celebrating their lack of resistance the chick hop group peaks with a #1 R&B/#1 crossover.

WEAR MY RING

Artist: Gene Vincent
Written by: Don Kirshner, Bobby Darin
Label: Capitol
Produced by: Ken Nelson
Year: 1957
B-side of "Lotta Lovin'." Darin and Kirshner would go on to greater things, but not together.

WEAR MY RING (AROUND YOUR NECK)

Artist: Elvis Presley
Written by: Bert Carroll, Russell Moody
From the album: *50,000,000 Elvis Fans Can't Be Wrong: Elvis' Gold Records (Vol. II)*
Label: RCA
Produced by: Steve Sholes
Year: 1958
Gone and virtually forgotten in Germany, Elvis's teen fashion/commitment commentary languished at a paltry #7 R&B/#3 country/#2 pop.

WEAR YOUR LOVE LIKE HEAVEN

Artist: Donovan
Written by: Donovan Leitch
From the album: *Gift from a Flower to a Garden*
Label: Epic
Produced by: Mickie Most
Year: 1967
In which Donovan becomes the original flower child; Melanie was listening.

WEDDING BELL BLUES

Artist: Laura Nyro
Written by: Laura Nyro
From the album: *More Than a New Discovery*
Label: Verve/Forecast
Produced by: Milt Okun
Year: 1967
Effusive echoes of subway girl-groups and unrequited high-school passions. Covered by the Fifth Dimension (Soul City, '69).

WEDDING SONG, THE (THERE IS LOVE)

Artist: Paul Stookey
Written by: Noel Paul Stookey
From the album: *Paul and*
Label: Warner Brothers
Produced by: Jim Mason, Ed Mottau
Year: 1971
Post-'60s/pre-new age take on the wedding vows.

WEDGE, THE

Artist: Phish
Written by: Trey Anastasio, Tom Marshall
From the album: *Rift*
Produced by: Barry Beckett
Label: Elektra
Year: 1993
The previously unheard sound of the great Northeast.

WEDNESDAY WEEK

Artist: The Undertones
Written by: John O'Neill, Damien O'Neill
From the album: *Hypnotized*
Label: Sire
Produced by: Roger Bechirian
Year: 1980
Covered by Elvis Costello (Columbia, '80).

WEE WEE HOURS

Artist: Chuck Berry
Written by: Chuck Berry
From the album: *After School Sessions*
Label: Chess
Produced by: Leonard Chess, Phil Chess
Year: 1957
A slow blues from his original demo tape, which also contained "Maybellene," became its B-side.

WEIGHT, THE

Artist: The Band
Written by: Robbie Robertson
From the album: *The Band*
Label: Capitol
Produced by: John Simon, the Band
Year: 1968
Their most famous song and a roots rock anthem. Covered by Aretha Franklin (Atlantic, '69). Used in the classic counterculture film *Easy Rider*.

WEIRD SCIENCE

Artist: Oingo Boingo
Written by: Danny Elfman
From the album: *Dead Man's Party*
Label: MCA
Year: 1985
Elfman would move on to scoring pop cultural landmarks like the movie *Batman Returns* and the TV series *The Simpsons*.

WEIRDO

Artist: Charlatans UK
Written by: Charlatans UK
From the album: *Between 10th and 11th*
Label: Beggar's Banquet
Year: 1992
English new rave band takes on a timeless theme.

WELCOME BACK

Artist: John Sebastian
Written by: John Sebastian
From the album: *Welcome Back*
Label: Reprise
Produced by: John Sebastian, Steve Barri
Year: 1976
Former Lovin' Spoonful front man funds his jug band future with the theme for the TV series *Welcome Back, Kotter*.

WELCOME HOME (SANITARIUM)

Artist: Metallica
Written by: Kirk Hammett, Lars Ulrich, James Hetfield
From the album: *Master of Puppets*
Produced by: Fleming Rasmussen, Metallica
Label: Elektra
Year: 1986
Monster metal showpiece is Metallica at its heaviest.

WELCOME TO MY NIGHTMARE

Artist: Alice Cooper
Written by: Vincent Furnier (Alice Cooper), Dick Wagner
From the album: *Welcome to My Nightmare*
Label: Atlantic
Produced by: Bob Ezrin

Year: 1975
I dreamed I was in a mock theatrical heavy metal band and didn't have any time off to play golf.

WELCOME TO PARADISE

Artist: Green Day
Written by: Billie Joe Armstrong, Green Day
From the album: *Ker-Plunk*
Label: Lookout
Produced by: Andy Ernst, Green Day
Year: 1992
Espousing the new slacker style of power punk. Rereleased on their breakthrough album *Dookie* (Reprise, '94).

WELCOME TO THE BOOMTOWN

Artist: David & David
Written by: David Baerwald, David Ricketts
From the album: *Boomtown*
Label: A&M
Produced by: Davitt Sigerson
Year: 1986
'80s L.A. antimellow singer/songwriting answer to Steely Dan.

WELCOME TO THE JUNGLE

Artist: Guns N' Roses
Written by: Guns N' Roses
From the album: *Appetite for Destruction*
Label: Geffen
Produced by: Mike Clink
Year: 1987
Defining arena rock's last bombastic '80s gasp. Featured in the movie *The Dead Pool*.

WELCOME TO THE PLEASURE DOME

Artist: Frankie Goes to Hollywood
Written by: Peter Gill, William Johnson, Mark O'Toole, Brian Nash
From the album: *Welcome to the Pleasure Dome*
Label: Island
Produced by: Trevor Hom
Year: 1984
These supposedly decadent British pleasures were lost on the US audience, though almost everything else with an accent and a synthesizer achieved unprecedented chart success during this period.

WELCOME TO THE WORKING WEEK

Artist: Elvis Costello
Written by: Declan McManus (Elvis Costello)
From the album: *My Aim Is True*
Label: Columbia
Produced by: Nick Lowe
Year: 1977
Leaving his job in computers.

WELL

Artist: Captain Beefheart
Written by: Van Don Vliet
From the album: *Trout Mask Replica*
Label: Straight
Produced by: Frank Zappa
Year: 1969
Eerie and hypnotic poetry from the edge introduced on a revered cult album.

WELL ALL RIGHT

Artist: Buddy Holly
Written by: Buddy Holly, Norman Petty, Jerry Allison, Joe B. Mauldin
From the album: *The Buddy Holly Story*
Label: Coral
Produced by: Norman Petty
Year: 1958
B-side of "Heartbeat."

WELL-RESPECTED MAN, A

Artist: The Kinks
Written by: Ray Davies
From the album: *Kinks Kinkdom*
Label: Reprise
Produced by: Shel Talmy
Year: 1966
Revealing a Dickensian curmudgeon beneath the Music Hall shell.

WENDY

Artist: The Beach Boys
Written by: Brian Wilson
From the album: *All Summer Long*
Label: Capitol
Produced by: Brian Wilson
Year: 1964
Originally in the EP *Four by the Beach Boys*.

WENT TO SEE THE GYPSY

Artist: Bob Dylan
Written by: Bob Dylan
From the album: *New Morning*
Label: Columbia
Produced by: Bob Johnston
Year: 1970
Reputedly about a meeting with Elvis Presley.

WEREWOLF

Artist: The Holy Modal Rounders
Written by: Michael Hurley
From the album: *Moray Eels Eat the Holy Modal Rounders*
Label: Elektra
Year: 1965
Exemplary backwoods howl. Warren Zevon was listening. Covered by Michael Hurley (Raccoon, '71).

WEREWOLVES OF LONDON

Artist: Warren Zevon

Written by: Warren Zevon, Robert Wachtel, Leroy Marinell
From the album: *Excitable Boy*
Label: Asylum
Produced by: Jackson Browne, Waddy Wachtel
Year: 1978
His signature Hollywood name-dropping anthem, costarring James Taylor, Jackson Browne, and Brian De Palma. Featured in the '86 movie *The Color of Money* and sung on his appearance on *The Larry Sanders Show* in '93.

WEST END GIRLS

Artist: Pet Shop Boys
Written by: Neil Tennant, Chris Lowe
From the album: *Please*
Label: EMI-American
Produced by: Stephen Hague
Year: 1986
Trans-Atlantic #1 crossover flopped when first released in '84.

WESTERN MOVIES

Artist: The Olympics
Written by: Fred Smith, Cliff Goldsmith
From the album: *Doin' the Hully Gully*
Label: Demon
Produced by: Fred Smith, Cliff Goldsmith
Year: 1958
In the novelty mode of the Coasters.

WESTERN UNION

Artist: The Five Americans
Written by: Mike Rabon, Norman Ezell, John Durrill
From the album: *Western Union*
Label: Abnak
Produced by: Dale Hawkins
Year: 1967

WHAM, THE

Artist: Lonnie Mack
Written by: Lonnie Mack
From the album: *The Wham of That Memphis Man*
Label: Fraternity
Year: 1963
Scintillating guitar track, coveted and covered by Stevie Ray Vaughan (Epic, '91).

WHAT A DIFF'RENCE A DAY MAKES

Artist: Dinah Washington
Written by: Stanley Adams, Maria Grever
From the album: *What a Diff'rence a Day Makes*
Label: Mercury
Year: 1959
Dinah's biggest hit; a Top 5 R&B/Top 10 crossover, was introduced by the Dorsey Brothers Orchestra (Decca, '34), with Bob Crosby singing vocals.

WHAT A FOOL BELIEVES

Artist: Kenny Loggins

Written by: Michael McDonald, Kenny Loggins
From the album: *Nightwatch*
Label: Epic
Year: 1978
A double dose of mellow. Cover by the Doobie Brothers (Warner Brothers, '79) was a double Grammy winner.

WHAT A GIRL WANTS

Artist: Christina Aguilera
Written by: Shelly Peiken, Guy Roche
From the album: *Christina Aguilera*
Produced by: Guy Roche
Label: RCA
Year: 1999
Not quite a vixen, not yet a vamp.

(WHAT A) WONDERFUL WORLD

Artist: Sam Cooke
Written by: Barbara Campbell, Herb Alpert, Lou Adler
Label: Keen
Year: 1960
Covered by Herman's Hermits (MGM, '65), Art Garfunkel, James Taylor and Paul Simon (Columbia, '78). Theme song of slackers everywhere.

WHAT ABOUT LOVE?

Artist: Heart
Written by: Sheron Alton, Jim Vallance, Brian Allan
From the album: *Heart*
Label: Capitol
Produced by: Ron Nevison
Year: 1985

WHAT ABOUT ME

Artist: Quicksilver Messenger Service
Written by: Dino Valenti (Chester Powers)
From the album: *What About Me*
Label: Capitol
Produced by: Quicksilver Messenger Service
Year: 1971
Activist anthem from San Francisco. Covered by Richie Havens (Stormy Forest, '71).

WHAT ABOUT US

Artist: The Coasters
Written by: Jerry Leiber, Mike Stoller
From the album: *Coast Along with the Coasters*
Label: Atco
Produced by: Jerry Leiber, Mike Stoller
Year: 1959
Couched in their usual humor, a rare note of real outrage.

WHAT ABOUT YOUR FRIENDS

Artist: TLC
Written by: Dallas Austin, Lisa Lopes

From the album: *Ooooooohhh ... on the TLC Tip*
Label: LaFace
Produced by: Dallas Austin
Year: 1992
Top 10 R&B/Top 10 crossover.

WHAT AM I LIVING FOR

Artist: Chuck Willis
Written by: Chuck Willis
Label: Atlantic
Produced by: Zenas "Big Daddy" Sears
Year: 1958
His biggest hit, a Top 10 R&B/Top 10 crossover, was released two weeks after he died.

WHAT BECOMES OF THE BROKENHEARTED

Artist: Jimmy Ruffin
Written by: James Dean, Paul Riser, William Weatherspoon
From the album: *Top Ten*
Label: Soul
Produced by: Mickey Stevenson, William Weatherspoon
Year: 1966
His first and biggest hit.

WHAT DIFFERENCE DOES IT MAKE

Artist: The Smiths
Written by: Stephen Morrissey, Johnny Marr
From the album: *The Smiths*
Label: Sire
Produced by: John Porter
Year: 1984

WHAT DO ALL THE PEOPLE KNOW

Artist: The Monroes
Written by: Robert Davis
From the album: *The Monroes*
Label: Alfa
Produced by: Bruce Botnick
Year: 1982
Leftfield one-shot track and band.

WHAT DOES IT TAKE (TO WIN YOUR LOVE)

Artist: Jr. Walker & the All-Stars
Written by: Johnny Bristol, Harvey Fuqua, Vernon Bullock
From the album: *Home Cookin'*
Label: Soul
Produced by: Harvey Fuqua, Johnny Bristol
Year: 1969
#1 R&B/Top 10 crossover.

WHAT GOOD CAN DRINKING DO?

Artist: Janis Joplin

Written by: Janis Joplin
Label: Sony Legacy
Produced by: John Riney
Year: 1962
Just sitting around the house with some friends in Texas, sipping Southern Comfort, Janis Joplin realized she could sing. This was an early demo, collected on a posthumous anthology.

WHAT HAVE I DONE TO DESERVE THIS?

Artist: Pet Shop Boys with Dusty Springfield
Written by: Neil Tennant, Chris Lowe, Allee Willis
From the album: *Actually*
Label: EMI
Produced by: Stephen Hague
Year: 1987
Dusty's biggest US hit, second biggest for the Pet Shop Boys.

WHAT HAVE THEY DONE TO MY SONG, MA

Artist: Melanie
Written by: Melanie Safka
From the album: *Candles in the Rain*
Label: Buddah
Produced by: Peter Schekeryk
Year: 1970
Her response to having been typecast as a waif and a flower child, when she wanted to be thought of as a poet and a singer/songwriter. Covered by the New Seekers (Elektra, '70), Ray Charles (ABC, '72).

WHAT HAVE THEY DONE TO THE RAIN

Artist: The Searchers
Written by: Malvina Reynolds
From the album: *The New Searchers LP*
Label: Kapp
Year: 1964
Malvina Reynolds' antinuke lament hits the Top 40 as folk/rock.

WHAT HAVE YOU DONE FOR ME LATELY

Artist: Janet Jackson
Written by: James Harris III, Terry Lewis
From the album: *Control*
Label: A&M
Produced by: Jimmy Jam, Terry Lewis
Year: 1986
Her first #1 R&B/Top 10 crossover establishes Jackson's controlling persona.

WHAT I AM

Artist: Edie Brickell and New Bohemians
Written by: Edie Brickell, Kenny Withrow
From the album: *Shooting Rubberbands at the Stars*
Label: Geffen

Produced by: Pat Moran
Year: 1988
Austin-based post-hippie dogma.

WHAT I GOT

Artist: Sublime
Written by: Bradley Nowell, Eric Wilson, Floyd Gaugh
From the album: *What I Got*
Label: Gasoline Alley
Year: 1996
Red-hot rocker.

WHAT I LIKE ABOUT YOU

Artist: The Romantics
Written by: Jimmy Marinos, Wally Palmar, Mike Skill
From the album: *National Breakout*
Label: Nemperor
Produced by: Pete Solley
Year: 1980
Latter-day frat rock anthem.

WHAT IF I CAME KNOCKING

Artist: John (Cougar) Mellencamp
Written by: John Mellencamp
From the album: *Human Wheels*
Label: Mercury
Produced by: John Mellencamp, Malcolm Burn, David Leonard, Mike Wanchic
Year: 1993
Dropping Cougar at last, he writes one of his best songs in years.

WHAT IN THE WORLD'S COME OVER YOU

Artist: Jack Scott
Written by: Jack Scott
From the album: *What in the World's Come over You*
Label: Top Rank
Produced by: Ed Carlton
Year: 1959
Wonderful rockabilly crooning.

WHAT IS LIFE?

Artist: George Harrison
Written by: George Harrison
From the album: *All Things Must Pass*
Label: Apple
Produced by: Phil Spector
Year: 1970
More of George's eternal quest for meaning.

WHAT IS LOVE

Artist: The Playmates
Written by: Lee Pockriss, Paul Vance
From the album: *At Play with the Playmates*
Label: Roulette
Produced by: Hugo and Luigi
Year: 1959

Celebrating the ponytail as the object of teenage male lust. The authors would next take on the bikini.

WHAT IS LOVE?

Artist: Haddaway
Written by: Dee Dee Halligan, Junior Torello
From the album: *Haddaway*
Label: Arista
Produced by: Dee Dee Halligan, Junior Torello
Year: 1993
New Euro-disco sound and attitude.

WHAT IT TAKES

Artist: Aerosmith
Written by: Steven Tyler, Joe Perry, Desmond Child
From the album: *Pump*
Label: Geffen
Produced by: Bruce Fairbairn
Year: 1989
Heavy metal country, a genre with few takers. Segue: "Dead Flowers," by the Rolling Stones, "When the Levee Breaks," by Led Zeppelin.

WHAT IT'S LIKE

Artist: Everlast
Written by: Everlast Shrody
From the album: *Whitey Ford Sings the Blues*
Label: Tommy Boy
Year: 1998
Empathetic urban ode.

WHAT KIND OF MAN WOULD I BE

Artist: Chicago
Written by: Bobby Caldwell, Charles Sandford, Jason Scheff
From the album: *Greatest Hits 1982–1989*
Label: Reprise
Produced by: Ron Nevison
Year: 1989
The end of a golden era of wedding band schmaltz, consisting of 19 Top 10 hits, before this one.

WHAT MADE MILWAUKEE FAMOUS (MADE A LOSER OUT OF ME)

Artist: Jerry Lee Lewis
Written by: Glenn Sutton
From the album: *Another Place, Another Time*
Label: Smash
Produced by: Jerry Kennedy
Year: 1968
The Killer returns to the country charts for redemption.

WHAT THE WORLD NEEDS NOW IS LOVE

Artist: Jackie DeShannon
Written by: Burt Bacharach, Hal David
From the album: *This Is Jackie DeShannon*
Label: Imperial
Produced by: Burt Bacharach, Hal David
Year: 1965
Jackie does Dionne. Dionne would cover it two years later (Scepter, '67).

WHAT THEY DO

Artist: The Roots
Written by: Tarik Collins, Tahmir Thompson, Leonard Hubbard, Jimmy Grey, Rafael Saadiq
From the album: *Iladelph Half Life*
Label: Geffen
Year: 1997
Powerful rap fusion.

WHAT TIME IS IT

Artist: The Jive Five
Written by: Bob Feldman, Jerry Goldstein, Richard Gottehrer
Label: Beltone
Produced by: Les Cahan, Joe Rene
Year: 1962
This classic doo-wop track was rescued from obscurity when it played during a key moment in an episode of *The Sopranos*.

WHAT WAS IT YOU WANTED

Artist: Bob Dylan
Written by: Bob Dylan
From the album: *Oh Mercy*
Label: Columbia
Produced by: Daniel Lanois
Year: 1987
Answering his own "Wanted Man" 18 years later.

WHAT WOULD YOU SAY

Artist: Dave Matthews Band
Written by: Dave Matthews
From the album: *Under the Table and Dreaming*
Label: RCA
Produced by: Steve Lillywhite
Year: 1994
Helping to define the new collegiate sensibility with a loping post-modern Deadhead drawl.

WHAT YOU NEED

Artist: Inxs
Written by: Andrew Farriss, Michael Hutchence
From the album: *Listen Like Thieves*
Label: Atlantic
Produced by: Chris Thomas
Year: 1986
First big hit for the Australian modern rockers.

WHAT YOU SEE IS WHAT YOU GET

Artist: Stoney and Meat Loaf
Written by: Michael Valvo
From the album: *Stoney & Meat Loaf*
Label: Rare Earth
Year: 1971
May be the great lost Stoney Reese last seen auditioning for a Tom O'Horgan musical version of *Sgt. Pepper's Lonely Hearts Club Band* in 1974 Then again, it might not.

WHAT YOU WON'T DO FOR LOVE

Artist: Bobby Caldwell
Written by: Bobby Caldwell, Al Kettner
From the album: *Bobby Caldwell*
Label: Clouds
Year: 1978
Mellow soul classic.

WHAT'D I SAY

Artist: Ray Charles
Written by: Ray Charles
From the album: *What'd I Say*
Label: Atlantic
Produced by: Ahmet Ertegun, Jerry Wexler
Year: 1959
Ultimate merger of soul and raunch, street and gospel, making it a rock and roll classic, and Ray's biggest hit of the '50s (his first #1 R&B/Top 10 crossover). Covered by the Beatles with Tony Sheridan (Polydor, '60), Jerry Lee Lewis (Sun, '61), Bobby Darin (Atco, '62), Elvis Presley (RCA, '64, and in the film *Viva Las Vegas*), Etta James (Argo, '64), the Righteous Brothers (Philles, '65).

WHAT'S A MATTER BABY (IS IT HURTING YOU)

Artist: Timi Yuro
Written by: Clyde Otis
Label: Liberty
Year: 1962
One of the more aggressive female voices of the pre-Joplin '60s.

WHAT'S GOIN' ON

Artist: Marvin Gaye
Written by: Al Cleveland, Marvin Gaye, Renauldo Benson
From the album: *What's Goin' On*
Label: Tamla
Produced by: Marvin Gaye
Year: 1971
First of three straight #1 R&B/Top 10 crossovers in '71, detailing Marvin's new aware stance. Covered by Cyndi Lauper (Portrait, '86).

WHAT'S GOOD

Artist: Lou Reed
Written by: Lou Reed, Mike Rathke
From the album: *Magic and Loss*
Label: Sire
Produced by: Lou Reed, Mike Rathke
Year: 1991

One of the most life-affirming death songs; dedicated to the memory of Doc Pomus.

WHAT'S HE BUILDING

Artist: Tom Waits
Written by: Tom Waits
From the album: *Mule Variations*
Label: Epitaph
Produced by: Tom Waits, Kathleen Brennan
Year: 1999
One of his more intelligible recent efforts.

WHAT'S LOVE GOT TO DO WITH IT

Artist: Tina Turner
Written by: Terry Britten, Graham Lyle
From the album: *Private Dancer*
Label: Capitol
Produced by: Terry Britten
Year: 1984
Her defining anthem and only #1 single, later the title of her biopic.

WHAT'S MY NAME

Artist: DMX
Written by: Hinson, Irving Lorenzo, Earl (DMX) Simmons
From the album: *And Then There Was X*
Label: Def Jam
Year: 2000
Powerful calling card.

WHAT'S MY NAME?

Artist: Snoop Doggy Dogg
Written by: Calvin Broadus (Snoop Doggy Dogg)
From the album: *Doggy Style*
Label: Death Row
Produced by: Dr. Dre
Year: 1993
Gangsta rap personified, with a rap sheet to boot.

WHAT'S MY SCENE

Artist: The Hoodoo Gurus
Written by: Dave Faulkner
From the album: *Blow Your Cool*
Label: Elektra
Produced by: Mark Opitz, Hoodoo Gurus
Year: 1987
Aussie power pop with a vengeance.

WHAT'S ON YOUR MIND (PURE ENERGY)

Artist: Information Society
Written by: Paul Robb, Kurt Valaquen
From the album: *Information Society*
Label: Tommy Boy
Produced by: F. Maher
Year: 1988
Techno dance groove.

(WHAT'S SO FUNNY 'BOUT) PEACE, LOVE, AND UNDERSTANDING

Artist: Brinzley Schwarz
Written by: Nick Lowe
From the album: *New Favourites of Brinzley Schwarz*
Label: United Artists
Year: 1974
Future pure-pop peacenik classic, covered by Elvis Costello (Columbia, '79).

WHAT'S THE FREQUENCY, KENNETH

Artist: R.E.M.
Written by: Michael Stipe, Peter Buck, Bill Berry, Mike Mills
From the album: *Monster*
Label: Warner Brothers
Produced by: Scott Litt, R.E.M.
Year: 1994
Based on a phrase from the weird character who attacked newsman Dan Rather. Rather himself reprised this song with R.E.M. on *The David Letterman Show*.

WHAT'S THE MATTER HERE

Artist: 10,000 Maniacs
Written by: Natalie Merchant
From the album: *In My Tribe*
Label: Elektra
Produced by: Peter Asher
Year: 1987
Commentary on child abuse. Suggested segues: "Luka" by Suzanne Vega, "Dear Mr. Jesus" by Powersource.

WHAT'S THIS LIFE FOR

Artist: Creed
Written by: Scott Stapp, Mark Tremonti
From the album: *My Own Prison*
Label: Wind up
Year: 1997
Asking the big question.

WHAT'S UP

Artist: 4 Non Blondes
Written by: Linda Perry
From the album: *Bigger, Better, Faster, More!*
Label: Interscope
Produced by: David Tickle
Year: 1993
The Angry Young Woman of art rock arrives from Seattle. She would be followed by Courtney Love, P. J. Harvey, Liz Phair, and Alanis Morissette.

WHAT'S UP DOC? (CAN WE ROCK)

Artist: Fu-Schnickens with Shaquille O'Neal
Written by: Kevin KcKenzie, Shaquille O'Neal, R. Roachford, J. Jones, L. Maturine
From the album: *Shaq Deisel*
Label: Jive
Produced by: K-Cut
Year: 1993
As a rapper (and actor), Shaq was smart enough not to give up his night job. As far as Fu-Schnickens, they crumbled like the Orlando Magic.

WHAT'S YOUR NAME

Artist: Lynyrd Skynyrd
Written by: Ronnie Van Zant, Gary Rossington
From the album: *Street Survivors*
Label: MCA
Produced by: Lynyrd Skynyrd
Year: 1977
First single following the deaths of Ronnie Van Zant, and Steve and Cassie Gaines. Suggested segues: "Stray Cat" by the Rolling Stones, "Hot Blooded" by Foreigner.

WHAT'S YOUR NAME?

Artist: Don and Juan
Written by: Claude (Juan) Johnson
Label: Big Top
Produced by: Embee Productions
Year: 1961
Former Genies pop the existential doo-wop question.

WHATCHA GONNA DO

Artist: The Drifters
Written by: Ahmet Ertegun
From the album: *Their Greatest Recordings—The Early Years*
Label: Atlantic
Produced by: Ahmet Ertegun, Jerry Wexler
Year: 1953
Their last hit with Clyde McPhatter as lead singer. Suggested segues: "The Twist," by Hank Ballard or Chubby Checker.

WHATEVER GETS YOU THRU THE NIGHT

Artist: John Lennon
Written by: John Lennon
From the album: *Walls and Bridges*
Label: Apple
Produced by: John Lennon
Year: 1974
His first solo #1 single.

WHATTA MAN

Artist: Salt-n-Pepa
Written by: Herb Azor, David Crawford, Cheryl James
From the album: *Very Necessary*
Label: Next Plateau
Produced by: Mark Sparks, Cheryl James
Year: 1993
The temporary supergroup of Salt-n-Pepa and En Vogue depicts the Sensitive New Age Black Guy.

WHEEL IN THE SKY

Artist: Journey
Written by: Neal Schon, Robert Fleischman, Diane Valory
From the album: *Infinity*
Label: Columbia
Produced by: Roy Thomas Baker
Year: 1978
Steve Perry's second vocal with the band lands them in chart territory.

WHEEL OF FORTUNE

Artist: The Four Flames
Written by: Bennie Benjamin, George Weiss
Label: Specialty
Produced by: Art Rupe
Year: 1952
Covered by the Cardinals (Atlantic, '52), Kay Starr (Capitol, '52).

WHEELS

Artist: The Stringalongs
Written by: Jimmy Torres, Richard Stephens
Label: Warwick
Year: 1961
Guitar instrumental.

WHEN

Artist: Kalin Twins
Written by: Paul Evans
From the album: *Kalin Twins*
Label: Decca
Year: 1958
Irresistible calypso-flavored ditty.

WHEN A MAN LOVES A WOMAN

Artist: Percy Sledge
Written by: Cameron Lewis, Andrew Wright
From the album: *When a Man Loves a Woman*
Label: Atlantic
Produced by: Quin Ivy, Marlin Greene
Year: 1966
One-song definition of soul; #1 R&B/#1 crossover. Sledge would never top it, although "It Tears Me Up" came close.

WHEN CAN I SEE YOU

Artist: Babyface
Written by: Kenny Edmunds (Babyface)
From the album: *For the Cool in You*
Label: Epic
Produced by: Babyface
Year: 1994
His biggest hit.

WHEN DOVES CRY

Artist: Prince and the Revolution
Written by: Prince Rogers Nelson
From the album: *Purple Rain Soundtrack*
Label: Warner Brothers
Produced by: Prince
Year: 1984
Showing his sensitive, dysfunctional-relationship side, Prince takes over '84 with the #1 R&B/#1 crossover of the year.

WHEN I COME AROUND

Artist: Green Day
Written by: Billy Joe Armstrong, Green Day
From the album: *Dookie*
Label: Reprise
Produced by: Rob Cavallo, Green Day
Year: 1994
Influencing a nation of dorks in v-neck sweaters.

WHEN I DREAM

Artist: The Teardrop Explodes
Written by: Julian Cope, Gary Dwyer, Michael Finkler
From the album: *Kilimanjaro*
Label: Mercury
Produced by: Mike Howlett
Year: 1980
Previewing psychedelic Liverpool of the '80s.

WHEN I GET TO THE BORDER

Artist: Richard and Linda Thompson
Written by: Richard Thompson
From the album: *I Want to See the Bright Lights Tonight*
Label: Island
Produced by: Richard Thompson, John Wood
Year: 1974
Previewing their death motif.

WHEN I GROW UP TO BE A MAN

Artist: The Beach Boys
Written by: Brian Wilson, Roger Christian
From the album: *Beach Boys Today*
Label: Capitol
Produced by: Brian Wilson
Year: 1964
The B-side of "Dance, Dance, Dance." Suggested segue: "Sugar Mountain" by Neil Young.

WHEN I NEED YOU

Artist: Leo Sayer
Written by: Carole Bayer Sager, Albert Hammond
From the album: *Endless Flight*
Label: Warner Brothers
Produced by: Richard Perry
Year: 1977
His biggest hit, here and in England.

WHEN I PAINT MY MASTERPIECE

Artist: Bob Dylan
Written by: Bob Dylan
From the album: *Bob Dylan's Greatest Hits (Vol. II)*
Label: Columbia
Produced by: Leon Russell
Year: 1971
Yet another side of Bob Dylan: self-mocking humor. Recorded by the Band (Capitol, '71).

WHEN I SAW YOU

Artist: The Ronettes
Written by: Phil Spector
From the album: *... introducing the fabulous Ronettes featuring Ronnie*
Label: Philles
Produced by: Phil Spector
Year: 1964
Phil's ode to Ronnie, his best since his ode to his father, "To Know Him Is to Love Him."

WHEN I SEE YOU SMILE

Artist: Bad English
Written by: Diane Warren
From the album: *Bad English*
Label: Epic
Produced by: Ritchie Zito
Year: 1989
Inheriting the mantle from Carole King, Warren dispensed hits throughout the '80s and '90s to a variety of deserving and undeserving clients—from Cher to Bon Jovi to Michael Bolton to these post-Journey offshoots, who benefited with an instant #1.

WHEN I THINK OF YOU

Artist: Janet Jackson
Written by: James Harris III, Terry Lewis, Janet Jackson
From the album: *Control*
Label: A&M
Produced by: Jimmy Jam, Terry Lewis
Year: 1986
Her first #1 R&B/#1 crossover.

WHEN I WIN THE LOTTERY

Artist: Camper Van Beethoven
Written by: David Lowery, Victor Krummenacher, Greg Lisher, Chris Pedersen
From the album: *Key Lime Pie*
Label: Virgin
Produced by: Dennis Herring
Year: 1989
Sassy essay on trailer-park culture features a killer rock fiddle part.

WHEN I'M SIXTY-FOUR

Artist: The Beatles
Written by: John Lennon, Paul McCartney
From the album: *Sgt. Pepper's Lonely Hearts Club Band*
Label: Capitol
Produced by: George Martin
Year: 1967
Amiable Baby Boom fable, written by a fifteen-year-old McCartney, for his father.

WHEN I'M WITH YOU

Artist: Sheriff
Written by: Arnold Lanni
From the album: *Sheriff*
Label: Capitol
Year: 1983
The ultimate one-hit wonder, went to #1 five
years after the band broke up.

WHEN IT'S LOVE

Artist: Van Halen
Written by: Eddie Van Halen, Alex Van Halen,
Michael Anthony, Sammy Hagar
From the album: *OU812*
Label: Warner Brothers
Produced by: Van Halen, Don Landee
Year: 1988
Their third Top 10 hit.

(WHEN SHE WANTS GOOD LOVIN') MY BABY COMES TO ME

Artist: The Coasters
Written by: Jerry Leiber, Mike Stoller
From the album: *The Coasters*
Label: Atco
Produced by: Jerry Leiber, Mike Stoller
Year: 1957
Covered by Tom Rush (Elektra, '65). Suggested
segue: "Good Lovin' " by the Clovers.

WHEN SHE WAS MY GIRL

Artist: The Four Tops
Written by: Marc Blatte, Larry Gottlieb
From the album: *Tonight*
Label: Casablanca
Year: 1981
#1 R&B/Top 15 crossover.

WHEN SMOKEY SINGS

Artist: ABC
Written by: Martin Fry, Mark White
From the album: *Alphabet City*
Label: Mercury
Produced by: Martin Rushent
Year: 1987
Blue-eyed studio soul from England.

WHEN SOMETHING IS WRONG WITH MY BABY

Artist: Sam and Dave
Written by: Isaac Hayes, David Porter
From the album: *Double Dynamite*
Label: Stax
Produced by: Jim Stewart
Year: 1966
Suggested segue: "It Hurts Me Too" by Junior
Wells.

WHEN THE CHILDREN CRY

Artist: White Lion
Written by: Vito Bratta, Mike Tramp
From the album: *Pride*
Label: Atlantic
Produced by: Michael Wagener
Year: 1987
Arena ballad.

WHEN THE GOING GETS TOUGH THE TOUGH GET GOING

Artist: Billy Ocean
Written by: Barry Eastmond, Billy Ocean, Robert
John "Mutt" Lange, Wayne Braithwaite
From the album: *Love Zone*
Label: Jive
Produced by: Mutt Lange
Year: 1986
#1 R&B/Top 10 crossover from the movie *The
Jewel of the Nile*. Suggested segue: "Ballad of the
Green Berets" by Sgt. Barry Sadier.

WHEN THE LEVEE BREAKS

Artist: Led Zeppelin
Written by: Jimmy Page, Robert Plant, John Paul
Jones, John Bonham, Memphis Minnie
From the album: *Led Zeppelin IV (Untitled)*
Label: Atlantic
Produced by: Jimmy Page
Year: 1971
Successfully transmogrifying country blues, with a
credit for the source, Memphis Minnie.

WHEN THE MUSIC'S OVER

Artist: The Doors
Written by: Jim Morrison, Robbie Krieger, John
Densmore
From the album: *Strange Days*
Label: Elektra
Produced by: Paul Rothchild
Year: 1967
Another stentorian tone poem that left nothing on
the cutting room floor.

WHEN THE SHIP COMES IN

Artist: Bob Dylan
Written by: Bob Dylan
From the album: *The Times They Are A-Changin'*
Label: Columbia
Produced by: Tom Wilson
Year: 1964
Talking about a revolution, metaphorically speak-
ing, the genesis of which is admirably detailed in his
book, *Chronicles*. Covered by Peter, Paul and Mary
(Warner Brothers, '65).

WHEN THE SPELL IS BROKEN

Artist: Richard Thompson
Written by: Richard Thompson
From the album: *Across a Crowded Room*
Label: Polygram
Produced by: Joe Boyd
Year: 1985
A moody and laconic lament.

WHEN WE WAS FAB

Artist: George Harrison
Written by: George Harrison, Jeff Lynne
From the album: *Cloud Nine*
Label: Dark Horse
Produced by: Jeff Lynne, George Harrison
Year: 1987
Another career summation, presaging his future
collaboration with Lynne in the Traveling Wil-
burys, and in the mid-'90s, on several 3/4 of the
Beatles reunion tunes.

WHEN WILL I BE LOVED

Artist: The Everly Brothers
Written by: Phil Everly
From the album: *The Fabulous Style of the Everly
Brothers*
Label: Cadence
Produced by: Archie Bleyer
Year: 1960
Their ultimate bluegrass gospel harmony ballad.
Covered by Dave Edmunds and the Stray Cats in
the '74 film *Stardust,* Linda Ronstadt (Capitol, '75).

WHEN WILL I SEE YOU AGAIN

Artist: The Three Degrees
Written by: Kenny Gamble, Leon Huff
From the album: *The Three Degrees*
Label: Philadelphia International
Produced by: Kenny Gamble, Leon Huff
Year: 1974
#1 UK/Top 10 US for the Richard Barrett
discoveries.

WHEN YOU DANCE

Artist: The Turbans
Written by: Andrew Jones, Leroy Kirkland
Label: Herald
Year: 1955
Major doo-wop crossover (in which, possibly for
the first time on record, the words "doo-wop" are
actually intoned), instigating, or at least benefitting
from, the year's parallel mambo craze. Suggested
segues: "Mambo Baby" by Ruth Brown, "Papa
Loves Mambo" by Perry Como, "Mambo Rock" by
Bill Haley.

WHEN YOU DANCE (I CAN REALLY LOVE)

Artist: Neil Young
Written by: Neil Young
From the album: *After the Gold Rush*
Label: Reprise
Produced by: David Briggs, Neil Young, Kendall
Pacios

Year: 1970
Hard to picture Young dancing.

WHEN YOU GONNA WAKE UP

Artist: Bob Dylan
Written by: Bob Dylan
From the album: *Slow Train Coming*
Label: Columbia
Produced by: Bob Dylan, Chuck Plotkin
Year: 1979
The wrath of Bob.

WHEN YOU SLEEP

Artist: My Bloody Valentine
Written by: Kevin Shields
From the album: *Loveless*
Label: Sire
Produced by: Kevin Shields
Year: 1991
The droning sound of dream pop arrives; the Cocteau Twins, the Cowboy Junkies, and the Jesus and Mary Chain were all in the same bed.

WHEN YOU WALK IN THE ROOM

Artist: Jackie DeShannon
Written by: Jackie DeShannon
From the album: *Breaking It up on the Beatles' Tour*
Label: Liberty
Produced by: Jack Nitzsche, Jackie DeShannon
Year: 1964
The essence of Beatlesesque songwriting. Covered by the Searchers (Kapp, '64).

WHEN YOU WERE MINE

Artist: Prince
Written by: Prince Rogers Nelson
From the album: *Dirty Mind*
Label: Warner Brothers
Produced by: Prince
Year: 1980
Introducing an important Prince subtheme, the dysfunctional and/or unconventional man-woman relationship, Prince adds poignance and pathos to his quest for a more perfect union. Cross-gender cover by Cyndi Lauper (Portrait, '84) was even more amazing.

WHEN YOU'RE HOT, YOU'RE HOT

Artist: Jerry Reed
Written by: Jerry Reed
From the album: *When You're Hot, You're Hot*
Label: RCA
Produced by: Chet Atkins
Year: 1971
On a roll, with a rollicking #1 country/Top 10 crossover. Reed would also write one of the great country titles, "She Got the Goldmine, I Got the Shaft."

WHEN YOUR HEART IS WEAK

Artist: Cock Robin
Written by: Peter Kingsbery
From the album: *Cock Robin*
Label: Columbia
Produced by: Steve Hillage
Year: 1985
Lush art-rock ballad.

WHENEVER A TEENAGER CRIES

Artist: Reparata and the Delrons
Written by: Ernie Maresca
From the album: *Whenever a Teenager Cries*
Label: World Artists
Produced by: Bill Jerome, Steve Jerome
Year: 1964
Low-rent version of the Shangri-Las. Written by the Shadow Morton of the Bronx.

WHENEVER I CALL YOU "FRIEND"

Artist: Kenny Loggins and Melissa Manchester
Written by: Kenny Loggins, Melissa Manchester
From the album: *Nightwatch*
Label: Columbia
Produced by: Bob James
Year: 1978
Adult but not contemporary.

WHENEVER YOU'RE ON MY MIND

Artist: Marshall Crenshaw
Written by: Marshall Crenshaw, Bill Teeley
From the album: *Field Day*
Label: Warner Brothers
Produced by: Steve Lillywhite
Year: 1983
America's finest pure pop of the '80s was created in New York; in the heartland and in England, the notion of alt/rock was born.

WHERE ARE YOU TONIGHT

Artist: Bob Dylan
Written by: Bob Dylan
From the album: *Street Legal*
Label: Columbia
Produced by: Don DeVito
Year: 1978
Song to his lost '60s audience.

WHERE DID ALL THE GIRLS COME FROM

Artist: James Blood Ulmer
Written by: James Blood Ulmer
From the album: *Free Lancing*
Label: Columbia
Year: 1982
No wave sax god momentarily descends to earth.

WHERE DID OUR LOVE GO

Artist: The Supremes
Written by: Eddie Holland, Lamont Dozier, Brian Holland
From the album: *Where Did Our Love Go*
Label: Motown
Produced by: Brian Holland, Lamont Dozier
Year: 1964
Originally offered to the Marvelettes. The Supremes first #1 after ten tries. A hot streak of mythic proportions would ensue, thereby delaying the Shirelles' entry into the Hall of Fame by a good five years.

WHERE DID YOU SLEEP LAST NIGHT (BLACK GIRL)

Artist: Nirvana
Written by: Traditional
From the album: *MTV Unplugged*
Produced by: Scott Litt, Nirvana
Label: DGC
Year: 1994
A late convert to their parents' blues hero, Hudie Ledbetter (Leadbelly), who performed this classic in the '40s.

WHERE DO THE CHILDREN GO

Artist: Hooters
Written by: Rob Hyman, Eric Bazilian
From the album: *Nervous Night*
Label: Columbia
Produced by: Rick Chertoff
Year: 1985
Introducing the melodica into the folk/rock canon. Distinguished by the throaty moan of Patty Smyth at her most scandalous. Hyman collaborated with Cyndi Lauper on "Time after Time" and later wrote Joan Osborne's "One of Us."

WHERE DO YOU GO

Artist: No Mercy
Written by: Franz Reuther, Peter Bischof-Fallenstein
From the album: *No Mercy*
Label: Arista
Produced by: FMP
Year: 1996
Euro trance.

WHERE HAVE ALL THE FLOWERS GONE

Artist: Pete Seeger
Written by: Pete Seeger
From the album: *The Bitter & the Sweet*
Label: Columbia
Produced by: John Hammond
Year: 1962
Seeger's classic antiwar song, adapted from the Russian novel *And Quietly Flows the Don*. Covered by the Kingston Trio (Capitol, '62), Peter, Paul and

Mary (Warner Brothers, '62), Johnny Rivers (Imperial, '65).

WHERE I'M FROM

Artist: Digable Planets
Written by: Digable Planets
From the album: *Reachin' (a New Refutation of Time and Space)*
Label: Pendulum
Produced by: Butterfly
Year: 1993
Be-bop hip hop, the jazz poetry of the '90s.

WHERE IS THE LOVE

Artist: Roberta Flack and Donny Hathaway
Written by: Ralph MacDonald, William Slater
From the album: *Roberta Flack and Donny Hathaway*
Label: Atlantic
Produced by: Joel Dorn
Year: 1972
#1 R&B/Top 10 crossover ballad.

WHERE IT'S AT

Artist: Beck
Written by: Beck Hanson, Michael Simpson, John King
From the album: *Odelay*
Label: DGC
Produced by: Dust Brothers
Year: 1996
Just hanging around in the alley behind the record store, searching for scraps, organ parts, jazz touches.

WHERE OR WHEN

Artist: Dion and the Belmonts
Written by: Richard Rodgers, Lorenz Hart
From the album: *Dion Sings His Greatest Hits*
Label: Laurie
Produced by: Gene Schwartz
Year: 1960
For all their rebellious bravado, this tune from the '37 musical *Babes in Arms* was their biggest hit.

WHERE THE BOYS ARE

Artist: Connie Francis
Written by: Howard Greenfield, Neil Sedaka
From the album: *More Greatest Hits*
Label: MGM
Year: 1961
Haunting theme from Connie's beach movie. But she was no Annette.

WHERE THE RIVER FLOWS

Artist: Collective Soul
Written by: Ed Roland
From the album: *Collective Soul*
Label: Atlantic
Produced by: Ed Roland, Matt Serletic
Year: 1995

WHERE THE STREETS HAVE NO NAMES

Artist: U2
Written by: Paul Hewson (Bono), Dave Evans (Edge), Adam Clayton, Larry Mullen
From the album: *The Joshua Tree*
Label: Island
Produced by: Brian Eno, Daniel Lanois
Year: 1987
Advancing their stature as the first arena protest band with a song about Ethiopia.

WHERE WERE YOU ON OUR WEDDING DAY

Artist: Lloyd Price
Written by: Lloyd Price, Harold Logan, John Patton
From the album: *Exciting Lloyd Price*
Label: ABC Paramount
Year: 1959
Though it seems Price should have released this tune immediately after (or at least on the flip side of) "I'm Gonna Get Married," it actually came out five months before it.

WHERE'S THE PARTY

Artist: Madonna
Written by: Steve Bray, Madonna Ciccone, Patrick Leonard
From the album: *True Blue*
Label: Sire
Produced by: Steve Bray, Madonna
Year: 1986
Breezin' in from Hollywood, looking for the action.

WHICH WAY YOU GOIN' BILLY

Artist: The Poppy Family
Written by: Terry Jacks
From the album: *Which Way You Goin' Billy*
Label: London
Produced by: Terry Jacks
Year: 1969
An antiwar bubblegum hit. Suggested segue: "Toy Soldiers" by Martika.

WHICH WILL

Artist: Nick Drake
Written by: Nick Drake
From the album: *Pink Moon*
Label: Island
Produced by: John Wood
Year: 1972
Covered by Lucinda Williams (Chameleon, '92).

WHILE MY GUITAR GENTLY WEEPS

Artist: The Beatles
Written by: George Harrison
From the album: *The Beatles*
Label: Apple
Produced by: George Martin
Year: 1968
Essential George philosophy, magical Eric Clapton guitar.

WHILE YOU SEE A CHANCE

Artist: Steve Winwood
Written by: Steve Winwood, Will Jennings
From the album: *Arc of a Diver*
Label: Island
Produced by: Steve Winwood
Year: 1981
Former Spencer Davis Group and Traffic leader returns to the singles charts with an adult ballad.

WHIP IT

Artist: Devo
Written by: Mark Mothersbaugh, Gerald Casale
From the album: *Freedom of Choice*
Label: Warner Brothers
Produced by: Devo
Year: 1980
Devo takes on disco and positive thinking, with help from Thomas Pynchon.

WHIP SMART

Artist: Liz Phair
Written by: Liz Phair
From the album: *Whip Smart*
Produced by: Brad Wood
Label: Matador
Year: 1994
Taut classic from the *Exile in Guyville* follow-up. But if she was so smart, how come she'd wind up seeking teen pop approval eight years later?

WHIPPING POST

Artist: Allman Brothers
Written by: Greg Allman
From the album: *The Allman Brothers Band*
Label: Atco
Produced by: Adrian Barber
Year: 1970
Hoarse and weary arena classic that eventually became the wounded battle cry of 1001 Fillmore requests (undoubtedly by the same hoarse and weary and always denied fan).

WHISKEY AND WOMEN AND MONEY TO BURN

Artist: Joe Ely
Written by: Joe Ely
From the album: *Chippy Original Cast Album*
Label: Hollywood
Year: 1994
From the legendary Austin horse opera.

WHISPERING BELLS

Artist: The Dell Vikings
Written by: C. E. Quick

From the album: *Come Go with the Dell Vikings*
Label: Dot
Produced by: Joe Averbach
Year: 1957
Second and last Top 10 R&B/Top 10 crossover for the interracial doo-wop group.

WHISPERING/CHERCHEZ LA FEMME/C'EST SI BON

Artist: Dr. Buzzard's Original Savannah Band
Written by: John Schonberger, Richard Coburn, Vincent Rose, August Darnell, Stoney Browder Jr., Henri Betti, Andy Horvez, Jerry Seleen.
From the album: *Dr. Buzzard's Original Savannah Band*
Label: RCA
Produced by: Tommy Motolla
Year: 1976
Disco standard is a medley comprised of a couple of pop classics, attached to a Darnell original.

WHISTLE DOWN THE WIND

Artist: Tom Waits
Written by: Tom Waits
From the album: *Bone Machine*
Label: Island
Produced by: Tom Waits
Year: 1992
Dedicated to the memory of singer/songwriter Tom Jans.

WHITE BIRD

Artist: David La Flamme
Written by: David La Flamme, Linda La Flamme
From the album: *White Bird*
Label: Amherst
Produced by: David La Flame
Year: 1976
Violin-driven progressive rock perennial.

WHITE GIRL

Artist: X
Written by: John Doe, Exene Cervenka
From the album: *Los Angeles*
Label: Slash
Produced by: Ray Manzarek
Year: 1980
Lawrence Ferlinghetti's *Coney Island of the Mind* goes to Los Angeles.

WHITE LIGHT/WHITE HEAT

Artist: The Velvet Underground
Written by: Lou Reed
From the album: *White Light/White Heat*
Label: Verve
Produced by: Andy Warhol
Year: 1968
Embracing the dark side.

WHITE LIGHTNING

Artist: George Jones
Written by: J. P. Richardson
Label: Mercury
Year: 1959
First pop hit for the former rockabilly singer turned archetypal country crooner is a #1 country/Bottom 40 crossover, written by the Big Bopper.

WHITE LINES (DON'T DO IT)

Artist: Grandmaster Flash and Melle Mel
Written by: Sylvia Robinson, Melvin Glover
Label: Sugar Hill
Produced by: Melle Mel, Sylvia Robinson, Joey Robinson Jr.
Year: 1983
A rap treatise on cocaine.

WHITE MAN IN HAMMERSMITH PALAIS

Artist: The Clash
Written by: John Mellor (Joe Strummer), Mick Jones
From the album: *The Clash*
Label: Epic
Produced by: The Clash
Year: 1978
This UK single (with "I Fought the Law") was added to the US album called by many the best of the year.

WHITE PUNKS ON DOPE

Artist: The Tubes
Written by: Michael Evans, William Spooner, Roger Steen
From the album: *The Tubes*
Label: A&M
Produced by: Al Kooper
Year: 1975
San Francisco in the decade after the Summer of Love.

WHITE RABBIT

Artist: The Great Society
Written by: Grace Slick
From the album: *Conspicuous Only in Its Absence*
Label: Columbia
Year: 1965
Talk about being ahead of your time. The Great Society's version of this tune, written in '65, wouldn't be released until '68, by which time Jefferson Airplane would be the heirs apparent to psychedelia's fortune, with Society's Grace and her song joining the band on their second album (RCA, '67). Covered by the Muffs (MCA, '95).

WHITE RHYTHM AND BLUES

Artist: Linda Ronstadt
Written by: John David Souther

From the album: *Living in the USA*
Label: Asylum
Produced by: Peter Asher
Year: 1978
Covered by J. D. Souther (Columbia, '79).

WHITE RIOT

Artist: The Clash
Written by: John Mellor (Joe Strummer), Mick Jones
From the album: *The Clash*
Label: Epic
Produced by: Mickey Foote
Year: 1977
Their first single became one of the key songs in establishing punk rock as a vital movement and moment in Britian and throughout the world; its elemental heat and anger helped the original LP become the biggest selling import album in US history.

WHITE ROOM

Artist: Cream
Written by: Jack Bruce, Pete Brown
From the album: *Wheels of Fire*
Label: Atco
Produced by: Felix Pappalardi
Year: 1968
Their second and last Top 10 hit.

WHITE SPORT COAT (AND A PINK CARNATION), A

Artist: Marty Robbins
Written by: Marty Robbins
From the album: *Rock N Roll N Robbins*
Label: Columbia
Produced by: Don Law
Year: 1957
#1 country/Top 10 crossover and as close to rockabilly as he'd ever come.

WHITE SUMMER

Artist: The Yardbirds
Written by: Jimmy Page
From the album: *Little Games*
Label: Epic
Produced by: Mickie Most
Year: 1968
Suggested segues: "She Moves through the Fair" by Davey Graham; "Black Mountain Side" by Led Zeppelin.

WHITE WEDDING

Artist: Billy Idol
Written by: William Broad (Billy Idol)
From the album: *Billy Idol*
Label: Chrysalis
Produced by: Keith Forsey
Year: 1983
Powerful postmodern dirge. Suggested segue: "Love Stinks" by the J. Geils Band.

WHITER SHADE OF PALE, A

Artist: Procol Harum
Written by: Gary Brooker, Keith Reid
From the album: *A Whiter Shade of Pale*
Label: A&M
Produced by: Denny Cordell
Year: 1967
Early Bach and roll, a precursor of the classical Euro-metal sound of progressive rock that would dominate the early '70s.

WHO ARE THE BRAIN POLICE

Artist: The Mothers of Invention
Written by: Frank Zappa
From the album: *Freak Out*
Label: Verve
Produced by: Tom Wilson
Year: 1966
Symphonic, electronic protest song.

WHO ARE YOU

Artist: The Who
Written by: Pete Townshend
From the album: *Who Are You*
Label: MCA
Produced by: Glyn Johns, Jon Astley
Year: 1978
One of his angriest performances.

WHO CAN IT BE NOW

Artist: Men at Work
Written by: Colin Hay
From the album: *Business as Usual*
Label: Columbia
Produced by: Peter Mclan
Year: 1982
Paranoid follow-up to "Down Under."

WHO DO YOU LOVE?

Artist: Bo Diddley
Written by: Ellas McDaniel (Bo Diddley)
From the album: *Bo Diddley's a Twister*
Label: Checker
Produced by: Willie Dixon
Year: 1955
Primordial boasting taken to grandiose extremes. Covered by John Hammond Jr., (Vanguard, '63), the Blues Project (MCA, '66), Quicksilver Messenger Service (Capitol, '69), Tom Ruth (Elektra, '71), George Thorogood (MCA, '78), Santana (Columbia, '83), and the Jesus and Mary Chain in the '89 movie *Earth Girls Are Easy*.

WHO DOES LISA LIKE

Artist: Rachel Sweet
Written by: Liam Sternberg
From the album: *Fool Around*
Label: Stiff
Produced by: Liam Sternberg
Year: 1979

Brenda Lee as a wasted Midwestern roots rocker; produced and directed by the author of "Walk Like an Egyptian."

WHO KNOWS WHERE THE TIME GOES

Artist: Fairport Convention
Written by: Sandy Denny
From the album: *Unhalfbricking*
Label: A&M
Produced by: Joe Boyd, Simon Nicol
Year: 1969
Spotlighting Sandy Denny, a striking new singer/songwriter in the traditional English folk mold. Covered by Judy Collins (Elektra, '69). Featured in the movie *The Subject Was Roses*.

WHO LET THE DOGS OUT

Artist: Baha Men
Written by: Anselm Douglas
From the album: *Who Let the Dogs Out*
Label: Artemis
Produced by: Mike Mangini, Steve Greenburg
Year: 2000
Rousing reggae arena track, popular at dance halls and soccer stadiums. The dog still rules!

WHO LOVES YOU

Artist: The Four Seasons
Written by: Bob Gaudio, Judy Parker
From the album: *Who Loves You*
Label: Warner Brothers
Produced by: Bob Crewe
Year: 1975
Singles-bar anthem, based on a Telly Savalas catch phrase from the TV show *Kojak*.

WHO MADE WHO

Artist: AC/DC
Written by: Angus Young, Malcolm Young, Brian Johnson
From the album: *Who Made Who*
Label: Atlantic
Produced by: Mutt Lange, Harry Vanda, George Young, Malcolm Young
Year: 1986
Appeared in the Stephen King horror movie *Maximum Overdrive*.

WHO NEEDS THE PEACE CORPS

Artist: The Mothers of Invention
Written by: Frank Zappa
From the album: *We're Only in It for the Money*
Label: Verve
Produced by: Frank Zappa
Year: 1968
Hippie-bashing second only to the Velvet Underground.

WHO PUT THE BOMP (IN THE BOMP BA BOMP BA BOMP)

Artist: Barry Mann
Written by: Barry Mann, Gerry Goffin
From the album: *Who Put the Bomp (in the Bomp Ba Bomp Ba Bomp)*
Label: ABC Paramount
Produced by: Al Nevins, Don Kirshner
Year: 1961
The veteran songwriter's only solo hit. But he would have traded it for ten more sales of "The Princess and the Punk" (Arista, '76).

WHO THE CAP FITS

Artist: Shinehead
Written by: Edmund Aiken
From the album: *Rough and Rugged*
Label: African Love Music
Produced by: Claude Evans
Year: 1986
Roots-rock reggae rap, influenced by Bob Marley.

WHO WAS IN MY ROOM LAST NIGHT

Artist: Butthole Surfers
Written by: Butthole Surfers
From the album: *Independent Worm Saloon*
Label: Capitol
Produced by: John Paul Jones, Butthole Surfers
Year: 1993

WHO WILL SAVE YOUR SOUL

Artist: Jewel
Written by: Jewel Kilcher
From the album: *Pieces of You*
Label: Atlantic
Produced by: Peter Collins
Year: 1996
A new acoustic folk/rocker emerges from Alaska.

WHO YOU ARE

Artist: Pearl Jam
Written by: Eddie Vedder, Stone Gossard, Jack Irons
From the album: *No Code*
Label: Epic
Produced by: Brenden O'Brien
Year: 1996

WHO'D SHE COO

Artist: Ohio Players
Written by: Leroy Bonner, Ralph Middlebrooks, Marshall Jones, William Beck, Marvin Pierce, Jim Williams, Clarence Satchell
From the album: *Contradiction*
Label: Mercury
Produced by: Ohio Players
Year: 1976
#1 R&B/Top 20 crossover.

WHO'LL BE THE NEXT IN LINE

Artist: The Kinks
Written by: Ray Davies
From the album: *Kinks Kinkdom*
Label: Reprise
Produced by: Shel Talmy
Year: 1965
One of Ray's fiercest rockers.

WHO'LL STOP THE RAIN

Artist: Creedence Clearwater Revival
Written by: John C. Fogerty
From the album: *Cosmo's Factory*
Label: Fantasy
Produced by: John C. Fogerty
Year: 1970
A rocking companion piece to "Blowin' in the Wind."

WHO'S CRYING NOW

Artist: Journey
Written by: Steve Perry, Jonathan Cain
From the album: *Escape*
Label: Columbia
Produced by: Mike Stone, Kevin Elson
Year: 1981
Their first big hit, on the strength of new vocalist Steve Perry's soaring voice.

WHO'S GONNA TAKE THE BLAME

Artist: The Miracles
Written by: Nick Ashford, Valerie Simpson
From the album: *Pocketful of Miracles*
Label: Tamla
Produced by: Nick Ashford, Valerie Simpson
Year: 1970
Smokey's strongest statement, but one that he was unable to write himself. Even singing it was almost too much for his fragile nonjudgmental persona. A year later he came out with "I Don't Blame You at All."

WHO'S HOLDING DONNA NOW

Artist: Debarge
Written by: David Foster, Jay Graydon, Randy Goodrum
From the album: *Rhythm of the Night*
Label: Motown
Produced by: Jay Graydon
Year: 1985
Middle-of-the-road R&B.

WHO'S JOHNNY (SHORT CIRCUIT THEME)

Artist: El Debarge
Written by: Peter Wolf, Ina Wolf
Label: Motown.

Produced by: Peter Wolf
Year: 86
Biggest hit by the leader of Debarge is from the movie.

WHO'S MAKING LOVE

Artist: Johnnie Taylor
Written by: Don Davis, Homer Banks, Bettye Crutcher, Raymond Jackson
From the album: *Who's Making Love*
Label: Stax
Produced by: Don Davis
Year: 1968
First #1 R&B/Top 10 crossover for the Arkansas soul stirrer.

WHO'S SORRY NOW?

Artist: Connie Francis
Written by: Bert Kalmer, Harry Ruby, Ted Snyder
From the album: *Connie's Greatest Hits*
Label: MGM
Year: 1958
Connie's first hit. Introduced by the Original Memphis Five (Victor, '23).

WHO'S THAT GIRL

Artist: Madonna
Written by: Patrick Leonard, Madonna Ciccone
From the album: *Who's That Girl? Soundtrack*
Label: Sire
Produced by: Patrick Leonard, Madonna
Year: 1987
Her sixth #1.

WHO'S ZOOMIN' WHO?

Artist: Aretha Franklin
Written by: Narada Michael Walden, Preston Glass, Aretha Franklin
From the album: *Who's Zoomin' Who?*
Label: Arista
Produced by: Narada Michael Walden
Year: 1985
Top 10 R&B/Top 10 crossover follows up "Freeway of Love."

WHOLE LOTTA LOVE

Artist: Led Zeppelin
Written by: Jimmy Page, Robert Plant, John Paul Jones, John Bonham
From the album: *Led Zeppelin II*
Label: Atlantic
Produced by: Jimmy Page
Year: 1969
Their only Top 10 single. Suggested segues: "You Need Love" by Muddy Waters (Chess, '62), "You Need Loving" by Small Faces (Deram, '66).

WHOLE LOTTA LOVING

Artist: Fats Domino
Written by: Fats Domino, Dave Bartholomew
Label: Imperial

Produced by: Dave Bartholomew
Year: 1958
Top 10 R&B/Top 10 crossover.

WHOLE LOTTA ROSIE

Artist: AC/DC
Written by: Angus Young, Malcolm Young
From the album: *Let There Be Rock*
Label: Atco
Produced by: Harry Vanda, George Young
Year: 1977
Dedicated to Bon Scott's 266-lb. goddess of love (42-39-56). Voted Song of the Year in the British heavy metal magazine *Kerrang*.

WHOLE LOTTA SHAKIN' GOIN' ON

Artist: Big Maybelle
Written by: Dave Williams, Sunny David (Roy Hall)
Label: Okeh
Produced by: Quincy Jones
Year: 1955
Big Maybelle's biggest B-side. Jerry Lee Lewis' #1 country/#1 R&B/Top 5 triple crossover cover marked his histrionic entrance into rock and roll, with one foot on the keyboard and one foot in the Hall of Fame.

WHOLE OF THE MOON

Artist: The Waterboys
Written by: Mike Scott
From the album: *This Is the Sea*
Label: Chrysalis
Produced by: Mike Scott
Year: 1985
Bouyant tale of discovery is an Irish rock anthem. Covered by Jennifer Warnes (Private, '94).

WHOLE WIDE WORLD

Artist: Wreckless Eric
Written by: Eric Goulden (Wreckless Eric)
From the album: *Wreckless Eric*
Label: Stiff
Produced by: Lowe, Nick
Year: 1978
Legendary Stiff single, stifled.

WHOOMP! (THERE IT IS)

Artist: Tag Team
Written by: Tag Team
From the album: *Whootmp (There It Is)*
Label: Life
Produced by: Tag Team
Year: 1993
The arena chant of the year, as omnipresent as the Wave, spending nearly a year on the charts; a #1 R&B/#2 crossover. Not to be confused with "Whoot, There It Is" by 95 South (Wrap, '93), another arena chant, restricted to the crowd in the parking lot, waiting for the losers to board their bus home.

WHY

Artist: Frankie Avalon
Written by: Pete DeAngelis, Bob Marcucci
From the album: *A Whole Lotta Frankie*
Label: Chancellor
Produced by: Pete DeAngelis, Bob Marcucci
Year: 1959
His second #1 of '59. Covered by Donny Osmond (MMG, '72).

WHY

Artist: Annie Lennox
Written by: Annie Lennox
From the album: *Diva*
Produced by: Stephen Lipson
Label: Arista
Year: 1992
Her most powerful ballad.

WHY CAN'T I BE YOU

Artist: The Cure
Written by: Robert Smith, Laurence Tolhurst, Simon Gallup, Purl Thompson, Boris Williams
From the album: *Kiss Me, Kiss Me, Kiss Me*
Label: Elektra
Produced by: Robert Smith, Dave Allen
Year: 1987
A sort of love song.

WHY CAN'T THIS BE LOVE

Artist: Van Halen
Written by: Eddie Van Halen, Alex Van Halen, Michael Anthony, Sammy Hagar
From the album: *5150*
Label: Warner Brothers
Produced by: Van Halen, Don Landee, Mick Jones
Year: 1986
Their biggest hit after "Jump."

WHY CAN'T WE BE FRIENDS

Artist: War
Written by: Sylvester Allen, Lee Oscar Levitin, Morris Dickerson, Leroy "Lonnie" Jordan, Howard Scott, Charles W. Miller, Harold R. Brown, Gerald Goldstein
From the album: *Why Can't We Be Friends*
Label: United Artists
Produced by: Jerry Goldstein
Year: 1975

WHY CAN'T WE LIVE TOGETHER

Artist: Timmy Thomas
Written by: Tim Thomas
From the album: *Why Can't We Live Together*
Label: Glades
Produced by: Steve Alaimo
Year: 1973
#1 R&B/Top 10 crossover.

WHY DO FOOLS FALL IN LOVE

Artist: Frankie Lymon and the Teenagers
Written by: Frankie Lymon, George Goldner, Herman Santiago
From the album: *The Teenagers*
Label: Gee
Produced by: George Goldner
Year: 1956
#1 R&B/Top 10 crossover doo-wop classic that marked the thirteen-year-old Lymon's meteoric rise to falsetto fame. Covered by the Diamonds (Mercury, '56), Gale Storm (Dot, '56), Diana Ross (RCA, '81).

WHY DO LOVERS BREAK EACH OTHER'S HEARTS

Artist: Bob B. Soxx and the Blue Jeans
Written by: Tony Powers, Ellie Greenwich, Phil Spector
Label: Philles
Produced by: Phil Spector
Year: 1963
Wall of sound one-shot, featuring Darlene Love.

WHY DOES LOVE GOT TO BE SO SAD

Artist: Derek and the Dominoes
Written by: Eric Clapton, Bobby Whitlock
From the album: *Layla*
Label: Atco
Produced by: Tom Dowd, Derek and the Dominoes
Year: 1970
Blues guitar highlight.

WHY DON'T WE DO IT IN THE ROAD?

Artist: The Beatles
Written by: John Lennon, Paul McCartney
From the album: *The Beatles*
Label: Apple
Produced by: George Martin
Year: 1968
John's favorite Paul doing John song.

WHY DON'T YOU WRITE ME

Artist: The Jacks
Written by: Laura Hollins
From the album: *Jumpin' with the Jacks*
Label: RPM
Year: 1955

WHY MUST I ALWAYS EXPLAIN

Artist: Van Morrison
Written by: Van Morrison
From the album: *Hymns to the Silence*
Label: Polydor
Produced by: Van Morrison
Year: 1991
Van mocks his notorious penchant for complaining.

WHY WORRY

Artist: Dire Straits
Written by: Mark Knopfler
From the album: *Brothers in Arms*
Label: Warner Brothers
Produced by: Neil Dorfsman, Mark Knopfler
Year: 1985
Acoustic lament. Covered by the Everly Brothers (Mercury, '85).

WICHITA LINEMAN

Artist: Glen Campbell
Written by: Jimmy Webb
From the album: *Wichita Lineman*
Label: Capitol
Produced by: Al DeLory
Year: 1968
First of two Webb-authored #1 country/Top 10 crossovers for Campbell. The other was "Galveston."

WICKED GAME

Artist: Chris Isaak
Written by: Chris Isaak
From the album: *Heart Shaped World*
Label: Reprise
Produced by: Erik Jacobsen
Year: 1989
From the film *Wild at Heart*.

WILD BILLY'S CIRCUS STORY

Artist: Bruce Springsteen
Written by: Bruce Springsteen
From the album: *The Wild, the Innocent and the E Street Shuffle*
Label: Columbia
Produced by: Jim Cretecos, Mike Appel
Year: 1973
Introducing Danny Federici on accordion, Garry Tallent on tuba.

WILD BOYS, THE

Artist: Duran Duran
Written by: Duran Duran
From the album: *Arena*
Label: Capitol
Produced by: Nile Rodgers, Duran Duran
Year: 1984

WILD CHILD

Artist: Lou Reed
Written by: Lou Reed
From the album: *Lou Reed*
Label: RCA
Produced by: Lou Reed, Richard Robinson
Year: 1972

Lou's answer to Dylan's "Visions of Johanna," a beat street meeting and conversation.

WILD HONEY PIE

Artist: The Beatles
Written by: John Lennon, Paul McCartney
From the album: *The Beatles*
Label: Apple
Produced by: George Martin
Year: 1968
Jamming at the Mahareeshi's.

WILD HORSES

Artist: The Rolling Stones
Written by: Mick Jagger, Keith Richards
From the album: *Sticky Fingers*
Label: Rolling Stones
Produced by: Jimmy Miller
Year: 1971
Their finest acoustic country rocker. Covered by the Flying Burrito Brothers (Warner Brothers, '74), Melanie (Neighborhood, '74), the Sundays (DGC, '92).

WILD IN THE STREET

Artist: Garland Jeffreys
Written by: Garland Jeffreys
From the album: *Ghost Writer*
Label: A&M
Produced by: David Spinozza, Garland Jeffreys
Year: 1977
R&b on the edge of punk/rock.

WILD LIFE

Artist: Captain Beefheart
Written by: Van Don Vliet
From the album: *Trout Mask Replica*
Label: Straight
Produced by: Frank Zappa
Year: 1969
Defining the new underground. Dave Thomas of Pere Ubu was listening.

WILD NIGHT

Artist: Van Morrison
Written by: Van Morrison
From the album: *Tupelo Honey*
Label: Warner Brothers
Produced by: Van Morrison, Ted Templeman
Year: 1971
A Van standard describing the mating habits of the current crop of street habitues, circa downtown L.A. in the '70s. Featured in the '91 movie *Thelma and Louise*. Covered by John Cougar Mellencamp and Me'shell NdegéOcello (Mercury, '94).

WILD ONE

Artist: Bobby Rydell
Written by: Kal Mann, Bernie Lowe, Dave Appell
From the album: *Bobby's Biggest Hits*
Label: Cameo

Year: 1960
His biggest hit. But has nothing to do with the Marlon Brando leather motorcycle epic, in which his co-star Lee Marvin leads a rival gang called "The Beetles," thus giving John Lennon, watching in a movie theatre in England in 1954, a bright idea.

WILD THING

Artist: Tone Loc
Written by: Marvin Young (Young MC), Michael Ross, Matt Dike, Anthony Smith
From the album: *Loc-ed after Dark*
Label: Delicious Vinyl
Produced by: Michael Ross, Matt Dike
Year: 1989
Rap goes national, with one of the biggest selling singles of all time.

WILD THING

Artist: The Troggs
Written by: Chip Taylor
From the album: *Wild Thing*
Label: Fontana
Produced by: Larry Page
Year: 1966
In the frat rock all-time Top 10. Covered by the Jimi Hendrix Experience in a career- and rock-defining moment at the *Monterey Rock and Pop Festival* in '67, released to theaters in '68, and on the album of the event (Warner Brothers, '70). Also covered by Senator Bobby (Parkway, '67).

WILD WILD WEST

Artist: Kool Moe Dee
Written by: Mo Dewese
From the album: *How Ya Like Me Now*
Label: Jive
Produced by: Pete Q. Harris, Chuck New, Lavaba, Moe Dewese
Year: 1987
Updated for use as the title song of the Will Smith film.

WILD WORLD

Artist: Cat Stevens
Written by: Cat Stevens
From the album: *Tea for the Tillerman*
Label: A&M
Produced by: Paul Samwell-Smith
Year: 1971
Matthew and daughter. Covered by Jimmy Cliff (Island, '76), Maxi Priest (Virgin, '88), Mr. Big (Atlantic, '93).

WILD, WILD LIFE

Artist: Talking Heads
Written by: David Byrne, Chris Frantz, Tina Weymouth, Jerry Harrison
From the album: *True Stories*
Label: Sire
Produced by: Talking Heads
Year: 1986
Nerd/rock takes on worldbeat.

WILD, WILD WEST

Artist: The Escape Club
Written by: The Escape Club
From the album: *Wild, Wild West*
Label: Atlantic
Produced by: Chris Kimsey
Year: 1988
Big '80s dance groove.

WILD, WILD YOUNG MEN

Artist: Ruth Brown
Written by: Ahmet Ertegun
Label: Atlantic
Year: 1955
Another big R&B hit for the Broadway Babe.

WILDFIRE

Artist: Michael Murphey
Written by: Michael Murphey, Larry Cansler
From the album: *Blue Sky—Night Thunder*
Label: Epic
Produced by: Bob Johnston
Year: 1975
Country/rocker but no country crossover for Murphey until a year later, with different material, after he stopped trying to be a rocker.

WILDFLOWER

Artist: Skylark
Written by: David Richardson, Doug Edwards
From the album: *Skylark*
Label: Capitol
Year: 1973
Gorgeous Canadian one-shot ballad from the band that featured David Foster. Covered by New Birth (RCA, '73).

WILL IT GO ROUND IN CIRCLES

Artist: Billy Preston
Written by: Billy Preston, Bruce Fisher
From the album: *Music Is My Life*
Label: A&M
Produced by: Billy Preston
Year: 1973
His first #1.

WILL THE WOLF SURVIVE

Artist: Los Lobos
Written by: David Hidalgo, Louie Perez
From the album: *Will the Wolf Survive*
Label: Slash
Produced by: T-Bone Burnette, Steve Berlin
Year: 1985
East L.A. rockabilly with an ecological and philosophical perspective.

WILL YOU BE THERE

Artist: Michael Jackson
Written by: Michael Jackson
From the album: *Dangerous*

Label: Epic
Produced by: Michael Jackson, Bill Bottrell
Year: 1991
Used in the film *Free Willy* in '93.

(WILL YOU) COME BACK MY LOVE

Artist: The Wrens
Written by: Bobby Mansfield
Label: Rama
Produced by: George Goldner
Year: 1955
Seminal classic of the doo-wop era. Covered by the Cardinals (Atlantic, '55).

WILL YOU LOVE ME TOMORROW

Artist: The Shirelles
Written by: Gerry Goffin, Carole King
From the album: *Greatest Hits*
Label: Scepter
Produced by: Luther Dixon
Year: 1960
First of the Shirelles' two #1 hits; they had no #1 R&B crossovers, but four #2 R&Bs. Also first #1 for Goffin & King. Covered by the Four Seasons (Philips, '68), Linda Ronstadt (Capitol, '70), Melanie (Neighborhood, '73).

WILL YOU STILL LOVE ME

Artist: Chicago
Written by: David Foster, Tom Keane, Richard Baskin
From the album: *Chicago 18*
Label: Warner Brothers
Produced by: David Foster
Year: 1986
Moving to a new label, but not losing their spot on the charts.

WILLIE AND THE HAND JIVE

Artist: Johnny Otis
Written by: Johnny Otis
From the album: *The Johnny Otis Show*
Label: Capitol
Year: 1958
His most famous single.

WILLIE THE PIMP (PARTS I AND II)

Artist: Frank Zappa
Written by: Frank Zappa
From the album: *Hot Rats*
Label: Bizarre
Produced by: Frank Zappa
Year: 1969
Zappa in Beelheart territory. Tom Waits was eavesdropping.

WILLIN'

Artist: Little Feat
Written by: Lowell George
From the album: *Little Feat*
Label: Warner Brothers
Produced by: Russ Titelman
Year: 1970
Their most famous downtown Atlanta classic. Covered by the Byrds (Columbia, '70), Linda Ronstadt (Capitol, "74), Commander Cody & the Lost Planet Airmen (Warner Brothers, '75).

WIMOWEH (THE LION SLEEPS TONIGHT)

Artist: The Weavers
Written by: The Weavers (Paul Campell), Solomon Linda, Roy Ilene, Hugo Perretti, Luigi Creatore, George Weiss, Albert Stanton
Label: Decca
Produced by: Milt Gabler
Year: 1951
Adapted from traditional material made famous by the South African group Solomon Linda. New version entitled "The Lion Sleeps Tonight" became a folk pop hit by the Tokens (RCA, '61).

WIN YOUR LOVE FOR ME

Artist: Sam Cooke
Written by: Sam Cooke (Charles Cooke)
Label: Keen
Produced by: Bumps Blackwell
Year: 1958

WINCHESTER CATHEDRAL

Artist: The New Vaudeville Band
Written by: Geoff Stephens
From the album: *Winchester Cathedral*
Label: Fontana
Produced by: Geoff Stephens
Year: 1966
High-camp one-shot.

WIND

Artist: Circus Maximus
Written by: Jerry Jeff Walker
From the album: *Circus Maximus*
Label: Vanguard
Year: 1967
Early FM radio art rocker, by the house band at the Electric Circus just before the Velvet Underground moved in. Jerry Jeff Walker would become famous for "Mr. Bojangles."

WIND, THE

Artist: The Diablos
Written by: Nolan Strong, Quentin Eubank, Willie Hunter, Juan Guiterriez, Bob Edwards
Label: Fortune
Produced by: Jack Brown, DeVora Brown
Year: 1954
Might be the most chilling doo-wop song in history, especially the recitation. Frankie Lymon was listening. So was Nolan's cousin Barrett, who went onto a lucrative songwriting career at Motown. But ethereal Nolan disappeared in the wind.

WIND CRIES MARY, THE

Artist: Jimi Hendrix
Written by: Jimi Hendrix
From the album: *Are You Experienced?*
Label: Reprise
Produced by: Chas Chandler
Year: 1967
For those who have always thought Jimi's lyrics in this song needed work, it has come to light that this particular lyric was written soon after Jimi had been hit on the head with a frying pan by a girlfriend.

WIND OF CHANGE

Artist: Scorpions
Written by: Klaus Meine
From the album: *Crazy World*
Label: Mercury
Produced by: Keith Olson
Year: 1990
Their biggest hit, inspired by the razing of the Berlin wall (and their signature riff).

WINDY

Artist: The Association
Written by: Ruthann Friedman
From the album: *Insight Out*
Label: Warner Brothers
Produced by: Bones Howe
Year: 1967
Creating the '60s folk/rock female stereotype: breezy, blowsy, a little spaced out, but definitely into free love. Suggested segues: "Ruby Tuesday" by the Rolling Stones, "We'll Sing in the Sunshine" by Gale Garnett, "Angel of the Morning" by Merilee Rush, "Arizona" by Mark Lindsay.

WINTER

Artist: Tori Amos
Written by: Tori Amos
From the album: *Little Earthquakes*
Label: Atlantic
Produced by: Davitt Sigerson
Year: 1992
Haunting song about fathers and daughters is a confessional high point she's yet to top.

WINTER IN AMERICA

Artist: Gil Scott-Heron
Written by: Gil Scott-Heron
From the album: *The First Minute of a New Day*
Label: Arista
Year: 1975

WINTER LADY

Artist: Leonard Cohen
Written by: Leonard Cohen
From the album: *Songs of Leonard Cohen*

Label: Columbia
Produced by: John Simon
Year: 1968
Trancelike doom and gloom by the master of the genre, from the movie *McCabe and Mrs. Miller*.

WIPE OUT

Artist: The Surfaris
Written by: Ron Wilson, Robert Berryhill, James Fuller, Patrick Connolly
From the album: *Wipe Out*
Label: Dot
Produced by: Dale Smallin
Year: 1963
Best demented laugh in the history of rock and roll, provided by the group's manager. Featured in the movie *The Wanderers*. Suggested segue: "Delicious" by Jim Backus.

WISH SOMEONE WOULD CARE

Artist: Irma Thomas
Written by: Irma Thomas
From the album: *Wish Someone Would Care*
Label: Imperial
Produced by: H.B. Barnum
Year: 1964
Her biggest R&B hit. B-side of her next single was "Time Is on My Side."

WISH YOU WERE HERE

Artist: Pink Floyd
Written by: Roger Waters, David Gilmour
From the album: *Wish You Were Here*
Label: Columbia
Produced by: Pink Floyd
Year: 1975
Dedicated to their fallen friend Syd Barrett.

WISHFUL, SINFUL

Artist: The Doors
Written by: Jim Morrison, Robbie Krieger, John Densmore, Ray Manzarek
From the album: *The Soft Parade*
Label: Elektra
Produced by: Paul Rothchild
Year: 1969
Follow-up to "Touch Me."

WISHIN' AND HOPIN'

Artist: Dionne Warwick
Written by: Burt Bacharach, Hal David
From the album: *Make Way for Dionne Warwick*
Label: Scepter
Produced by: Burt Bacharach, Hal David
Year: 1963
Covered by Dusty Springfield (Philips, '64).

WISHING ON A STAR

Artist: Rose Royce
Written by: Billy Calvin

From the album: *Rose Royce II / In Full Bloom*
Label: Whitfield
Produced by: Norman Whitfield
Year: 1977
Covered by the Cover Girls (Epic, '92).

WISHING WELL

Artist: Terence Trent D'Arby
Written by: Terence Trent D'Arby, Sean Oliver
From the album: *The Hardline According to Terence Trent D'Arby*
Label: Columbia
Produced by: Martyn Ware
Year: 1987
#1 /R&B/Top 10 UK breakthrough British-influenced pop soul single.

WITCH DOCTOR

Artist: David Seville
Written by: Ross Bagdasarian
Label: Liberty
Produced by: Ross Bagdasarian
Year: 1958
Wholesome family fun with a tape recorder, predating the Chipmunks by about six months.

WITCH, THE

Artist: The Sonics
Written by: Gerry Roslie
From the album: *Here Are the Sonics*
Produced by: Buck Ormsby, Kent Morrill
Label: Etiquette
Year: 1965
Making a racket in the Northwest, aided by Tacoma keyboard legend Kent Morrill, from the (American) Wailers ("Tall Cool One").

WITCHI-TAI-TO

Artist: Everything Is Everything
Written by: Jim Pepper
Label: Vanguard Apostolic
Produced by: Danny Weiss
Year: 1969
3,000-year-old Indian peace chant, covered by Brewer and Shipley in their first album, *Weeds* (Kama Sutra, '70).

WITCHY WOMAN

Artist: Eagles
Written by: Don Henley, Bernie Leadon
From the album: *The Eagles*
Label: Asylum
Produced by: Glyn Johns
Year: 1972
Stating their attitude about the opposite sex.

WITH A LITTLE HELP FROM MY FRIENDS

Artist: The Beatles
Written by: John Lennon, Paul McCartney

From the album: *Sgt. Pepper's Lonely Hearts Club Band*
Label: Capitol
Produced by: George Martin
Year: 1967
All-time communal anthem. Covered by Joe Cocker (A&M, '69).

WITH A LITTLE LUCK

Artist: Paul McCartney and Wings
Written by: Paul McCartney, Linda McCartney
From the album: *London Town*
Label: Capitol
Produced by: Paul McCartney
Year: 1976
His fifth and last solo #1 single.

WITH ARMS WIDE OPEN

Artist: Creed
Written by: Scott Stapp, Mark Tremonti
From the album: *Human Clay*
Label: Wind-Up
Year: 1999
Expectant fatherhood. Grammy winner.

WITH GOD ON OUR SIDE

Artist: Bob Dylan
Written by: Bob Dylan
From the album: *The Freewheelin' Bob Dylan*
Label: Columbia
Produced by: John Hammond
Year: 1963
Antiwar polemic, based on "The Patriot Game," by Dominic Behan.

WITH OR WITHOUT YOU

Artist: U2
Written by: Paul Hewson (Bono), Dave Evans (Edge), Adam Clayton, Larry Mullen, Brian Eno
From the album: *The Joshua Tree*
Label: Island
Produced by: Brian Eno, Daniel Lanois
Year: 1987
Their first #1 and biggest hit.

WITH YOU I'M BORN AGAIN

Artist: Billy Preston and Syreeta
Written by: David Shire, Carol Connor
From the album: *Fast Break Soundtrack*
Label: Motown
Year: 1979
Duet with the ex-Mrs. Wonder, for whom Stevie wrote "Cause We've Ended as Lovers."

WITHIN YOU, WITHOUT YOU

Artist: The Beatles
Written by: George Harrison
From the album: *Sgt. Pepper's Lonely Hearts Club Band*

Label: Capitol
Produced by: George Martin
Year: 1967
Mystical mirror gazing.

WITHOUT HER

Artist: Nilsson
Written by: Harry Nilsson
From the album: *Pandemonium Shadow Show*
Label: RCA
Produced by: Rick Jarrard
Year: 1967
Covered by Blood, Sweat & Tears (Columbia, '68).

WITHOUT LOVE (THERE IS NOTHING)

Artist: Clyde McPhatter
Written by: Danny Small
Label: Atlantic
Produced by: Ahmet Ertegun, Jerry Wexler
Year: 1957
At his soulful best, a Top 10 R&B/Top 20 crossover. Covered by Ray Charles (ABC, '63), Tom Jones (Parrot, '70).

WITHOUT YOU

Artist: Badfinger
From the album: *No Vice*
Label: Apple
Produced by: Paul McCartney
Year: 1970
Cover by Nilsson was #1 US/UK (RCA, '71). Covered by Mariah Carey (Columbia, '94).

WIZARD, THE

Artist: Black Sabbath
Written by: John "Ozzy" Osborne, Tony Iommi, Geezer Butler, Bill Ward
From the album: *Black Sabbath*
Label: Warner Brothers
Produced by: Rodger Bain, Geezer Butler, Tony Iommi
Year: 1970
B-side of "Paranoid." With John "Ozzy" Osbourne, the original behemoth of heavy metal, arising from the moors of Birmingham, England, on harmonica, and four-fingered Tony Iommi on guitar.

WOKE UP THIS MORNING

Artist: A3
Written by: Larry Love, Spirit
From the album: *The Sopranos Soundtrack*
Label: Columbia
Year: 1999
Theme for the gangsta TV series, *The Sopranos*.

WOMAN

Artist: John Lennon
Written by: John Lennon
From the album: *Double Fantasy*
Label: Geffen

Produced by: John Lennon, Yoko Ono, John Douglas
Year: 1981
Reached #1 in the UK two months after Lennon was killed, along with "Imagine" and "(Just Like) Starting Over."

WOMAN

Artist: Peter and Gordon
Written by: Paul McCartney (Bernard Webb)
From the album: *Woman*
Label: Capitol
Produced by: John Burgess
Year: 1966

WOMAN FROM TOKYO

Artist: Deep Purple
Written by: Ritchie Blackmore, Ian Gillan, Roger Glover, Jon Lord, Ian Paice
From the album: *Who Do You Think We Are?*
Label: Warner Brothers
Produced by: Deep Purple
Year: 1973
Segue: "China Girl" by David Bowie, "Turning Japanese" by the Vapors.

WOMAN NEEDS LOVE (JUST LIKE YOU DO), A

Artist: Ray Parker Jr. & Raydio
Written by: Ray Parker Jr.
From the album: *A Woman Needs Love*
Label: Arista
Produced by: Ray Parker Jr.
Year: 1981
Ray Parker steps out as a new soul man of the '80s.

WOMAN OF HEART AND MIND

Artist: Joni Mitchell
Written by: Joni Mitchell
From the album: *For the Roses*
Label: Asylum
Produced by: Joni Mitchell
Year: 1972
Achieving self-definition.

WOMAN TO WOMAN

Artist: Shirley Brown
Written by: Homer Banks, Fred Marvin, Bobby Thigpen
From the album: *Woman to Woman*
Label: Truth
Produced by: Al Jackson
Year: 1974
#1 R&B/Top 25 crossover from the point of view of the other woman. Suggested segue: "From His Woman to You" by Barbara Mason.

WOMAN, A LOVER, A FRIEND, A

Artist: Jackie Wilson

Written by: Sid Wyche
Label: Brunswick
Produced by: Dick Jacobs, Nat Tarnopol
Year: 1960
#1 R&B/Top 20 crossover.

WOMAN, WOMAN

Artist: Gary Puckett and the Union Gap
Written by: James W. Glaser, James O. Payne
From the album: *The Union Gap*
Label: Columbia
Produced by: Jerry Fuller
Year: 1967
First hit for the Paul Revere and the Raiders wannabes.

WOMAN'S GOT SOUL

Artist: The Impressions
Written by: Curtis Mayfield
From the album: *People Get Ready*
Label: ABC Paramount
Produced by: Curtis Mayfield
Year: 1965

WOMAN'S GOTTA HAVE IT

Artist: Bobby Womack
Written by: Bobby Womack, Linda Cooke, Darryl Carter
From the album: *Understanding*
Label: United Artists
Produced by: Bobby Womack
Year: 1972
R&B journeyman's biggest post-Valentinos hit; #1 R&B/Bottom 40 crossover, written with his wife, the daughter of Sam Cooke.

WOMEN IS LOSERS

Artist: Big Brother & the Holding Company
Written by: Janis Joplin
From the album: *Big Brother & the Holding Company*
Label: Mainstream
Produced by: Bob Shad
Year: 1968
The twisted roots of Joplin's upbringing.

WOMEN'S LOVE RIGHTS

Artist: Laura Lee
Written by: Angelo Bond, William Weatherspoon
From the album: *Women's Love Rights*
Label: Hot Wax
Produced by: William Weatherspoon
Year: 1971
Feisty feminist dance-hall diatribe.

WON'T GET FOOLED AGAIN

Artist: The Who
Written by: Pete Townshend
From the album: *Who's Next*
Label: Decca

Produced by: The Who
Year: 1971
Arena anthem was a youth culture rallying cry. Scream was one of Daltrey's finest.

WON'T YOU TRY/ SATURDAY AFTERNOON

Artist: Jefferson Airplane
Written by: Paul Kantner
From the album: *After Bathing at Baxter's*
Label: RCA
Produced by: Al Schmitt
Year: 1968
Conjuring a perfect San Francisco weekend in the late '60s, complete with acid, incense, and balloons. Pyschedelic optimism almost impossible to contemplate in retrospect.

WONDER

Artist: Natalie Merchant
Written by: Natalie Merchant
From the album: *Tigerlily*
Label: Elektra
Year: 1995

WONDER OF YOU, THE

Artist: Ray Peterson
Written by: Baker Knight
From the album: *Tell Laura I Love Her*
Label: RCA
Produced by: Dick Pierce
Year: 1959
Covered by Elvis Presley (RCA, '70).

WONDERFUL LAND

Artist: The Shadows
Written by: Jerry Lordan
From the album: *The Shadows Greatest Hits*
Label: Columbia
Year: 1962
Second of five #1 UK hits and the biggest for the influential guitar band.

WONDERFUL REMARK

Artist: Van Morrison
Written by: Van Morrison
From the album: *King of Comedy Soundtrack*
Produced by: Robbie Robertson
Label: Warner Brothers
Year: 1983
Wistful Van is the highlight of a great soundtrack.

WONDERFUL TONIGHT

Artist: Eric Clapton
Written by: Eric Clapton
From the album: *Slowhand*
Label: RSO
Produced by: Glyn Johns
Year: 1977
Clapton's most affecting and enduring love song.

WONDERFUL WORLD, BEAUTIFUL PEOPLE

Artist: Jimmy Cliff
Written by: Jimmy Cliff
From the album: *Wonderful World, Beautiful People*
Label: A&M
Produced by: Jimmy Cliff
Year: 1970
His first big reggae hit.

WONDERFUL, WONDERFUL

Artist: Johnny Mathis
Written by: Ben Raleigh, Sherman Edwards
From the album: *Johnny Mathis' Greatest Hits*
Label: Columbia
Year: 1957
One of the top make-out ballads of the rock and roll era, and a good reason why his greatest hits album lasted on the charts for about eight years.

WONDERING WHERE THE LIONS ARE

Artist: Bruce Cockburn
Written by: Bruce Cockburn
From the album: *Dancing in the Dragon's Jaw*
Label: Millennium
Produced by: Gene Martynec
Year: 1979
Canadian acoustic singer/songwriter's most popular effort.

WONDERWALL

Artist: Oasis
Written by: Noel Gallagher
From the album: *What's the Story, Morning Glory*
Label: Epic
Produced by: D. Morris, Noel Gallagher
Year: 1995
Waterloo sunset on Penny Lane.

WOOD BEEZ (PRAY LIKE ARETHA FRANKLIN)

Artist: Scritti Politti
Written by: Green Gartside
From the album: *Cupid and Psyche '85*
Produced by: Arif Mardin
Label: Atlantic
Year: 1984
First UK Top 10 hit for the politically-oriented soul group.

WOODEN HEART

Artist: Elvis Presley
Written by: Fred Wise, Ben Weisman, Kay Twomey, Bert Kaempfert
From the album: *G.I. Blues*
Label: RCA
Produced by: Steve Sholes
Year: 1960
One of the more positive results of Elvis' experience in Germany. From the movie *G.I. Blues*. Covered by Joe Dowell (Smash, '61).

WOODEN SHIPS

Artist: Crosby, Stills & Nash
Written by: David Crosby, Stephen Stills, Paul Kantner
From the album: *Crosby, Stills & Nash*
Label: Atlantic
Produced by: Crosby, Stills & Nash
Year: 1969
Sci-fi brain-child of future Starship pilot Kantner, this was covered by Jefferson Airplane (RCA, '69) a few months later.

WOODSTOCK

Artist: Crosby, Stills, Nash & Young
Written by: Joni Mitchell
From the album: *Deja Vu*
Label: Atlantic
Produced by: Crosby, Stills, Nash & Young
Year: 1970
Idealized title tune for the countercultural commencement concert written by someone who was three thousand miles away at the time, and, all considered, pretty glad to be there. Covered by Mitchell on the B-side of "Big Yellow Taxi" (Reprise, '70), Matthews Southern Comfort (Decca, '71).

WOO-HOO

Artist: The Rock-a-Teens
Written by: George Donald McGraw
From the album: *Woo-Hoo*
Label: Roulette
Year: 1959
Fifth biggest guitar instrumental hit of '59.

WOOLY BULLY

Artist: Sam the Sham and the Pharaohs
Written by: Domingo Samudio
From the album: *Wooly Bully*
Label: MGM
Produced by: Stan Kesler
Year: 1965
Tex-Mex on rye.

WORD TO THE BADD

Artist: Jermaine Jackson
Written by: Kenny Edmunds (Babyface), Antonio Reid (L. A. Reid), Daryl Simmons, Jermaine Jackson, Lisa Lopes
From the album: *You Said*
Label: LaFace
Produced by: Babyface, L. A. Reid
Year: 1991
Exploiting the Michael madness of the early '90s, an older brother clocks in.

WORD, THE

Artist: The Beatles
Written by: John Lennon, Paul McCartney
From the album: *Rubber Soul*
Label: Capitol
Produced by: George Martin
Year: 1965
The Mahareeshi was listening.

WORD UP

Artist: Cameo
Written by: Larry Blackmon, Tomi Jenkins
From the album: *Word Up*
Label: Atlanta Artists
Produced by: Larry Blackmon
Year: 1986
Glomming onto one of the decade's catch-phrases Blackmon's troupe gains their funky peak with a #1 R&B/Top 10 crossover.

WORDS

Artist: Missing Persons
Written by: Dale Bozzio, Warren Cuccurrillo
From the album: *Missing Persons*
Label: Capitol
Produced by: Ken Scott
Year: 1982
Peroxide Blondie.

WORDS OF LOVE

Artist: Buddy Holly
Written by: Buddy Holly
From the album: *Buddy Holly*
Label: Coral
Produced by: Norman Petty
Year: 1958
Covered by the Beatles (Capitol, '65).

WORDS OF LOVE

Artist: The Mamas & the Papas
Written by: John Phillips
From the album: *The Mamas & the Papas*
Label: Dunhill
Produced by: Lou Adler
Year: 1966
Answering Buddy Holly's more idealistic sentiments.

WORDY RAPPINGHOOD

Artist: Tom Tom Club
Written by: Tina Weymouth, Chris Frantz, Steven Stanley, Maria Weymouth, Adrian Belew
From the album: *Tom Tom Club*
Label: Sire
Produced by: Tom Tom Club
Year: 1981
Geek rap.

WORK FOR FOOD

Artist: Dramarama
Written by: Jon Easdale
From the album: *Hi-Fi Sci-Fi*
Label: Chameleon
Produced by: Chris Carter, Jon Easdale
Year: 1993
A rollicking rock and roll alternative to grunge despair.

WORK TO DO

Artist: The Isley Brothers
Written by: Ronald Isley, Rudolph Isley, O'Kelly Isley
From the album: *Brother, Brother, Brother*
Label: T-Neck
Produced by: Isley Brothers
Year: 1972
Suggested segue: "Take a Letter Maria" by R. B. Greaves.

WORK WITH ME, ANNIE

Artist: The Midnighters
Written by: Hank Ballard
From the album: *The Midnighters*
Label: Federal
Produced by: Henry Glover
Year: 1954
Based on the earlier "Get It," which was banned as too dirty for radio, this nominally cleaner saga of Annie hit #1 R&B and launched about a dozen responses.

WORKIN' MY WAY BACK TO YOU

Artist: The Four Seasons
Written by: Sandy Linzer, Denny Randell
From the album: *Workin' My Way Back to You*
Label: Philips
Produced by: Bob Crewe
Year: 1966
Covered by the Spinners (Atlantic, '80).

WORKING CLASS HERO

Artist: John Lennon
Written by: John Lennon
From the album: *John Lennon/Plastic Ono Band*
Label: Apple
Produced by: John Lennon, Yoko Ono, Phil Spector
Year: 1970
One of his most searching, searing gems. Covered by Marianne Faithfull (Island, '79).

WORKING FOR THE WEEKEND

Artist: Loverboy
Written by: Paul Dean, Mike Reno, Matthew Frenette
From the album: *Get Lucky*
Label: Columbia
Produced by: Bruce Fairbairn, Paul Dean
Year: 1982
Arena anthem for the working-class. Suggested segue: "Friday on My Mind" by the Easybeats.

WORKING IN THE COAL MINE

Artist: Lee Dorsey
Written by: Allen Toussaint
From the album: *The New Lee Dorsey*
Label: Amy
Produced by: Allen Toussaint
Year: 1965
Segue: "Chain Gang" by Sam Cooke.

WORLD CLASS FAD

Artist: Paul Westerberg
Written by: Paul Westerberg
From the album: *14 Songs*
Label: Sire
Produced by: Matt Wallace, Paul Westerberg
Year: 1993
Reestablishing his alt presence with a fierce rocker.

WORLD I KNOW, THE

Artist: Collective Soul
Written by: Ed Roland
From the album: *Collective Soul*
Label: Atlantic
Produced by: Ed Roland, Matt Serletic
Year: 1995

WORLD IS A GHETTO, THE

Artist: War
Written by: Sylvester Allen, Lee Oscar Levitin, Morris Dickerson, Leroy "Lonnie" Jordan, Howard Scott, Charles W. Miller, Harold R. Brown
From the album: *The World Is a Ghetto*
Label: United Artists
Produced by: Jerry Goldstein
Year: 1972
Hard-hitting protest is their first big hit.

WORLD WITHOUT HEROES, A

Artist: Kiss with Lou Reed
Written by: Stanley Elsen (Paul Stanley), Gene Simmons, Bob Ezrin, Lou Reed
From the album: *Music from the Elder*
Label: Casablanca
Produced by: Bob Ezrin
Year: 1982
Lou Reed's guiltiest collaboration since Bowie.

WORLD WITHOUT LOVE, A

Artist: Peter and Gordon
Written by: John Lennon, Paul McCartney
From the album: *A World without Love*
Label: Cameo
Produced by: Norman Newell
Year: 1964
The Beatles' philosophy, cloned. Covered by Bobby Rydell (Cameo, '64).

WORST THAT COULD HAPPEN

Artist: The Fifth Dimension
Written by: Jimmy Webb
From the album: *Magic Garden*
Label: soul City
Produced by: Bones Howe
Year: 1967
Doo-wop redux. Covered by the Brooklyn Bridge (Buddah, '69).

WOULD

Artist: Alice in Chains
Written by: Jerry Cantrell
From the album: *Dirt*
Label: Columbia
Produced by: Alice in Chains
Year: 1992
Dedicated to late Mother Love Bone guitarist Andrew Wood. Featured in the movie *Singles* (Epic, '92).

WOULD I LIE TO YOU

Artist: Eurythmics
Written by: Annie Lennox, Dave Stewart
From the album: *Be Yourself Tonight*
Label: RCA
Produced by: Dave Stewart
Year: 1985

WOULDN'T IT BE NICE

Artist: The Beach Boys
Written by: Brian Wilson, Tony Asher
From the album: *Pet Sounds*
Label: Capitol
Produced by: Brian Wilson
Year: 1966
Brian visits Fantasyland, never leaves. Used in the '75 film *Shampoo*.

WOW

Artist: Kate Bush
Written by: Kate Bush
From the album: *Lionheart*
Label: EMI-America
Produced by: Andrew Powell
Year: 1980
Unbelievable burst of girlish glee.

WPLJ

Artist: The Four Deuces
Written by: Ray Dobard
Label: Music City
Produced by: Luther McDaniel
Year: 1955
Covered by Frank Zappa (Bizarre, '70). Stands for White Port and Lemon Juice. Later became the call letters of a New York rock radio station.

WRAP IT UP

Artist: Sam and Dave
Written by: Isaac Hayes, David Porter
From the album: *I Thank You*
Label: Atlantic
Produced by: Isaac Hayes, David Porter
Year: 1968
Covered by the Archie Bell & the Drells (Atlantic '70), the Fabulous Thunderbirds (Epic, '86).

WRAP YOUR TROUBLES IN DREAMS

Artist: Nico

Written by: Lou Reed
From the album: *Chelsea Girl*
Label: Verve
Produced by: Tom Wilson
Year: 1967
Classic high-fashion emoting.

WRAPPED AROUND YOUR FINGER

Artist: The Police
Written by: Gordon Sumner (Sting)
From the album: *Synchronicity*
Label: A&M
Produced by: Hugh Padgham, the Police
Year: 1983
Sixth and last Top 10 hit.

WRATHCHILD

Artist: Iron Maiden
Written by: Steve Harris
From the album: *Killers*
Label: Harvest
Produced by: Martin Birch
Year: 1981
Launching the new wave of British heavy metal. Diamond Head was tuning up. Metallica was listening. Judas Priest was oiling their gears. But Def Leppard would get all the girls.

WRECK OF THE EDMUND FITZGERALD, THE

Artist: Gordon Lightfoot
Written by: Gordon Lightfoot
From the album: *Summertime Dream*
Label: Reprise
Produced by: Lenny Waronker, Gordon Lightfoot
Year: 1976
Historically based tale of a 1975 shipwreck on Lake Superior.

WRECK OF THE JOHN B.

Artist: The Weavers
Written by: Traditional
Label: Decca
Produced by: Milt Gabler
Year: 1950
B-side of "The Roving Kind." Covered by the Beach Boys as "The Sloop John B." (Capitol, '66).

WRECKING BALL

Artist: Neil Young
Written by: Neil Young
From the album: *Freedom*
Produced by: Neil Young, Nico Bolas
Label: Reprise
Year: 1989
Covered by Emmylou Harris (Reprise, '95).

WRITTEN ALL OVER YOUR FACE

Artist: The Rude Boys

Written by: Larry Marcus
From the album: *Rude Awakenings*
Label: Atlantic
Year: 1990
Top rap track of the year; #1 R&B/Top 20 crossover.

WRONG 'EM BOYO

Artist: The Clash
Written by: John Mellor (Joe Strummer), Mick Jones
From the album: *London Calling*
Label: Epic
Produced by: Guy Stevens
Year: 1979

WRONG SIDE OF THE ROAD

Artist: Tom Waits
Written by: Tom Waits
From the album: *Blue Valentine*
Label: Elektra
Produced by: Bones Howe
Year: 1978

WUTHERING HEIGHTS

Artist: Kate Bush
Written by: Kate Bush
From the album: *The Kick Inside*
Label: EMI-America
Produced by: Andrew Powell
Year: 1978
Dense and mysterious as the moors, the child-woman with the witchy voice who both wrote and sang this classic story-song (based on Emily Bronte's novel) was the first female to top the UK charts with a self-penned tune. A post-Joni Mitchell generation, led by Tori Amos and Sarah McLachlan, were listening. But only Pat Benatar covered it (Chrysalis, '80).

X

XANADU

Artist: Olivia Newton-John with ELO
Written by: Jeff Lynne
From the album: *Xanadu Soundtrack*
Label: MCA
Produced by: Jeff Lynne
Year: 1980
Her third #1 UK, ELO's first, courtesy of the movie *Xanadu*.

X-OFFENDER

Artist: Blondie
Written by: Deborah Harry, Gary Valentine
From the album: *Blondie*
Label: Private Stock
Produced by: Richard Gottehrer, Craig Leon
Year: 1976
Their first single.

Y

Y.M.C.A.

Artist: The Village People
Written by: Henri Belolo, Jacques Morali, Victor Willis
From the album: *Cruisin'*
Label: Casablanca
Produced by: Jacques Morali
Year: 1979
The one-joke band becomes immortal on the dance floors of middle America.

YA YA

Artist: Lee Dorsey
Written by: Lee Dorsey, Morgan Robinson, Clarence Lewis
From the album: *Ya Ya*
Label: Fury
Produced by: Allen Toussaint
Year: 1961
Easy New Orleans listening is his only #1 R&B/Top 10 crossover.

YAKETY YAK

Artist: The Coasters
Written by: Jerry Leiber, Mike Stoller
From the album: *The Coasters*
Label: Atco
Produced by: Jerry Leiber, Mike Stoller
Year: 1958
Expressing the teenage condition in a comic book fashion so you could laugh at as well as dance to it, the Coasters gain their only #1 R&B/#1 crossover.

YANK ME, CRANK ME

Artist: Ted Nugent
Written by: Ted Nugent
From the album: *Double Live Gonzo*
Label: Epic
Produced by: Tom Werman, Lew Futterman
Year: 1978
Essential arena euphemisms.

YANKEE LADY

Artist: Jesse Winchester
Written by: Jessie Winchester
From the album: *Jesse Winchester*
Label: Ampex
Produced by: Robbie Robertson
Year: 1971
Covered by Brewer & Shipley (Kama Sutra, '73).

YEAR OF THE CAT

Artist: Al Stewart
Written by: Al Stewart, Peter Wood
From the album: *Year of the Cat*
Label: Janus
Produced by: Alan Parsons
Year: 1977
Cat Stevens with a Ph.D.

YELLOW

Artist: Coldplay
Written by: Gerry Berryman, Jon Buckland, Will Champion, Chris Martin
From the album: *Parachutes*
Produced by: Ken Nelson, Coldplay
Label: Capitol
Year: 2000
Passionate emoting from a clever new arena favorite from England.

YELLOW BRICK ROAD

Artist: Captain Beefheart
Written by: Don Van Vliet, Herb Bermann
From the album: *Safe as Milk*
Label: Buddah
Produced by: Bob Krasnow, Richard Perry
Year: 1966
His first single release after the failed "Diddy Wah Diddy" on A&M is a psychedelic bubblegum trifle for which his label was famous. The Captain would move into another psychedelic dimension entirely.

YELLOW LEDBETTER

Artist: Pearl Jam
Written by: Pearl Jam
Label: Epic
Produced by: Brendan O'Brien, Pearl Jam
Year: 1994
Legendary concert-closing B-side of "Jeremy" is an antiwar song for an old friend.

YELLOW SUBMARINE

Artist: The Beatles
Written by: John Lennon, Paul McCartney
From the album: *Yellow Submarine*
Label: Capitol
Produced by: George Martin
Year: 1966
Future Saturday morning cartoon.

YER BLUES

Artist: The Beatles
Written by: John Lennon, Paul McCartney
From the album: *The Beatles*
Label: Apple
Produced by: George Martin
Year: 1968
Heavy metalesque.

YES, I'M READY

Artist: Barbara Mason
Written by: Barbara Mason
From the album: *Yes, I'm Ready*
Label: Arctic
Produced by: Weldon MacDougal
Year: 1965
The girl-group sound, deflowered. Covered by Teri DeSario with K. C. (TK, '80).

YES IT IS

Artist: The Beatles
Written by: John Lennon, Paul McCartney
From the album: *Beatles VI*
Label: Capitol
Produced by: George Martin
Year: 1965
The B-side of "Ticket to Ride."

YES, TONIGHT JOSEPHINE

Artist: Johnny Ray
Written by: Winfield Scott, Dorothy Goodman
Label: Okeh
Year: 1955
Up there with Gloria in the rock honor roll of girl's names (along with Annie and Sara). Ray's last hit was #1 in the UK, where Jimmy Page might have been listening. The last Yardbirds single was entitled "Goodnight Sweet Josephine." Fats Domino also liked the lady, charting in '60 with "My Girl Josephine."

YES WE CAN CAN

Artist: Pointer Sisters
Written by: Allen Toussaint
From the album: *The Pointer Sisters*
Label: Blue Thumb
Produced by: Richard Perry
Year: 1973
Sisters strut to New Orleans for their first hit.

YESTERDAY

Artist: The Beatles
Written by: John Lennon, Paul McCartney
From the album: *Yesterday and Today*
Label: Capitol
Produced by: George Martin
Year: 1965
Blinking in the face of an uncertain future, a solo Paul McCartney writes their most covered classic, spawning nearly 1,000 superfluous covers.

YESTER-ME YESTER-YOU YESTERDAY

Artist: Stevie Wonder
Written by: Ronald Miller, Bryan Wells
From the album: *My Cherie Amour*
Label: Tamla
Produced by: Johnny Bristol
Year: 1969
Middle-of-the-soul road.

YOGI

Artist: The Ivy Three
Written by: Lou Stallman, Sid Jacobson
Label: Shell
Produced by: Lou Stallman, Sid Jacobson, Charles Koppelman
Year: 1960
Celebrating neither Berra nor the Mahareeshi, the Huckleberry Hound co-star Yogi Bear earns this one-shot rock and roll asterisk.

YOU AIN'T GOIN' NOWHERE

Artist: The Byrds
Written by: Bob Dylan
From the album: *Sweetheart of the Rodeo*
Label: Columbia
Produced by: Gary Usher
Year: 1968
Out of traction and longing to be back in action, Dylan turns to country/rock and his best clients for release.

YOU AIN'T SEEN NOTHIN' YET

Artist: Bachman Turner Overdrive
Written by: Randy Bachman
From the album: *Not Fragile*
Label: Mercury
Produced by: Randy Bachman
Year: 1974
Epitomizing the bravado of the big guitar bands of the '70s. Covered by a solo Burton Cummings (Portrait, '76). Suggested stuttering segue: "My Generation" by the Who.

YOU AND I

Artist: Rick James
Written by: James Johnson Jr. (Rick James)
From the album: *Come Get It!*
Label: Gordy
Produced by: Rick James, Art Stewart
Year: 1978
Launching an influential funk career with a #1 R&B/Top 20 crossover, his biggest hit.

YOU AND ME

Artist: Alice Cooper
Written by: Vincent Furnier (Alice Cooper), Dick Wagner
From the album: *Lace and Whiskey*
Label: Warner Brothers
Produced by: Bob Ezrin
Year: 1977
A new mellow Alice lights out for barroom country territory and achieves his biggest hit since "School's Out" in '72.

YOU AND ME AND THE BOTTLE MAKE THREE TONIGHT

Artist: Big Bad Voodoo Daddy
Written by: Scotty Morris
From the album: *Swing This, Baby*
Label: Slimstyle
Year: 1996
From the great indie comedy *Swingers*, this tune launched a mini-revival of Big Band music among swinging youth. Brian Setzer's Gap commercial with Louis Prima's "Jump, Jive an' Wail" didn't hurt either.

YOU ANGEL YOU

Artist: Bob Dylan
Written by: Bob Dylan
From the album: *Planet Waves*
Label: Asylum
Produced by: Bob Dylan
Year: 1974
B-side of "On a Night Like This."

YOU ARE EVERYTHING

Artist: The Stylistics
Written by: Thom Bell, Linda Creed
From the album: *The Stylistics*
Label: Avco
Produced by: Thom Bell
Year: 1971
Introducing a new Philly soul interracial songwriting team, with a Top 10 R&B/Top 10 crossover.

YOU ARE MY LADY

Artist: Freddie Jackson
Written by: Barry Eastmond
From the album: *Rock Me Tonight*
Label: Capitol
Produced by: Barry Eastmond
Year: 1985
The '80s R&B bedroom ballad at its smoothest.

YOU ARE SO BEAUTIFUL

Artist: Billy Preston
Written by: Billy Preston, Bruce Fischer
From the album: *The Kids and Me*
Label: A&M
Produced by: Billy Preston
Year: 1974
B-side of "Nothing from Nothing." Covered by Joe Cocker (A&M, '75).

YOU ARE THE SUNSHINE OF MY LIFE

Artist: Stevie Wonder
Written by: Stevie Wonder
From the album: *Talking Book*
Label: Tamla
Produced by: Stevie Wonder
Year: 1972
Stevie takes a page from the Smokey songbook for his third #1 hit.

YOU ARE THE WOMAN

Artist: Firefall
Written by: Rick Roberts
From the album: *Firefall*
Label: Atlantic
Produced by: Jim Mason
Year: 1976

YOU BEAT ME TO THE PUNCH

Artist: Mary Wells
Written by: Smokey Robinson, Ronald White

From the album: *One Who Really Loves You*
Label: Motown
Produced by: Smokey Robinson
Year: 1962
As Dionne was to Bacharach & David, Mary becomes Smokey's perfect voice with her first #1 R&B/Top 10 crossover.

YOU BELONG TO ME

Artist: The Doobie Brothers
Written by: Michael McDonald, Carly Simon
From the album: *Livin' on the Fault Line*
Label: Warner Brothers
Produced by: Ted Templeman
Year: 1977
Covered by Carly Simon (Elektra, '78).

YOU BELONG TO THE CITY

Artist: Glenn Frey
Written by: Glenn Frey
From the album: *Miami Vice Soundtrack*
Label: MCA
Produced by: Glenn Frey
Year: 1985
Cementing his multimedia comeback with a song that opened an entire season of *Miami Vice*. A decade later Frey's multimedia comeback would achieve its ultimate fruition and devastation, when he would star in the series *Miami Heat*, which was cancelled after one show.

YOU BETTER KNOW IT

Artist: Jackie Wilson
Written by: Jackie Wilson, Norm Henry
Label: Brunswick
Produced by: Dick Jacobs, Nat Tarnopol
Year: 1959
#1 R&B/Top 40 crossover.

YOU BETTER MOVE ON

Artist: Arthur Alexander
Written by: Arthur Alexander
From the album: *You Better Move On*
Label: Dot
Produced by: Rick Hall
Year: 1962
Having already provided the Beatles with several of their more authentic numbers, this dirty soul masterpiece found its way into the repertoire of the Rolling Stones (London, '65).

YOU BETTER SIT DOWN KIDS

Artist: Cher
Written by: Sonny Bono
From the album: *With Love*
Label: Imperial
Produced by: Sonny Bono
Year: 1967
Preparing for the divorce, seven years early. Segue: "Daddy Don't You Walk So Fast," by Wayne Newton.

YOU BETTER THINK TWICE

Artist: Poco
Written by: Jim Messina
From the album: *Poco*
Label: Epic
Produced by: Jim Messina
Year: 1970
Making the move from folk/rock to country/rock.

YOU BETTER, YOU BET

Artist: The Who
Written by: Pete Townshend
From the album: *Face Dances*
Label: Warner Brothers
Produced by: Bill Szymczyk
Year: 1981

YOU BROUGHT THE SUNSHINE

Artist: The Clark Sisters
Written by: Twinkie Clark-Terrell
From the album: *You Brought the Sunshine*
Label: Sounds of Gospel
Year: 1990
Gospel invades the dance-hall in this joyous track.

YOU CAN ALL JOIN IN

Artist: Traffic
Written by: David Mason
From the album: *Traffic*
Label: United Artists
Produced by: Jimmy Miller
Year: 1968

YOU CAN CALL ME AL

Artist: Paul Simon
Written by: Paul Simon
From the album: *Graceland*
Label: Warner Brothers
Produced by: Paul Simon
Year: 1986
A shot of Top 40 redemption, with the bass solo of the year by Baghiti Kumalo. Droll video contained a photo opportunity for Chevy Chase, which was his last and best TV performance before becoming a cartoon in a cartoon graveyard.

YOU CAN GET IT IF YOU REALLY WANT

Artist: Desmond Dekker and the Aces
Written by: Jimmy Cliff
Label: Trojan
Year: 1970
Reggae classic was a smash in England. Covered by Jimmy Cliff on the soundtrack to *The Harder They Come* (Mango, '72). Suggested segues: "You Can't Always Get What You Want" by the Rolling Stones, "You Can't Get What You Want Until You Know What You Want" by Joe Jackson.

YOU CAN HAVE HER

Artist: Roy Hamilton
Written by: Bill Cook
Label: Epic
Year: 1961
His last big crossover hit.

YOU CAN LEAVE YOUR HAT ON

Artist: Randy Newman
Written by: Randy Newman
From the album: *Sail Away*
Label: Warner Brothers
Produced by: Russ Titelman, Lenny Waronker
Year: 1972
A sexual charade, with Newman as Woody Allen. Covered by Three Dog Night (ABC, '75). Also covered in its entirety by Joe Cocker during the steamiest moments of the '86 Kim Basinger/Mickey Rourke steambath, *9 1/2 Weeks*, one of the most sardonic uses of a song in the history of rock in cinema. This led, quite understandably, to a cover by Tom Jones in the movie version of *The Full Monty* (RCA, '97).

YOU CAN'T ALWAYS GET WHAT YOU WANT

Artist: The Rolling Stones
Written by: Mick Jagger, Keith Richards
From the album: *Let It Bleed*
Label: London
Produced by: Jimmy Miller
Year: 1969
B-side of "Honky Tonk Women," the Stones at their rational, antiflower peak. Featured in the funeral scene in *The Big Chill*.

YOU CAN'T CATCH ME

Artist: Chuck Berry
Written by: Chuck Berry
From the album: *Chuck Berry's Golden Decade*
Label: Chess
Produced by: Leonard Chess, Phil Chess
Year: 1967
Car classic—classic car: the Airmobile (named Maybellene). Performed by Chuck in the '57 movie *Rock, Rock, Rock.* Covered by the Rolling Stones (London, '65), the Blues Project (Verve Forecast, '67).

YOU CAN'T CHANGE THAT

Artist: Raydio
Written by: Ray Parker Jr.
From the album: *Rock On*
Label: Arista
Produced by: Ray Parker Jr.
Year: 1979
Top 10 R&B/Top 10 crossover.

YOU CAN'T DENY IT

Artist: Lisa Stansfield
Written by: Lisa Stansfield, Ian Devaney, Andy Morris

From the album: *Affection*
Label: Arista
Produced by: Ian Devaney, Andy Morris
Year: 1990
The UK soul stylist's second #1 R&B/Top 20 crossover.

YOU CAN'T DO THAT

Artist: The Beatles
Written by: John Lennon, Paul McCartney
From the album: *The Beatles' Second Album*
Label: Capitol
Produced by: George Martin
Year: 1964
B-side of "Can't Buy Me Love." George on 12-string.

YOU CAN'T GET WHAT YOU WANT (TILL YOU KNOW WHAT YOU WANT)

Artist: Joe Jackson
Written by: Joe Jackson
From the album: *Body and Soul*
Label: A&M
Produced by: Joe Jackson, David Kershenbaum
Year: 1984
One of his best theses.

YOU CAN'T HURRY LOVE

Artist: The Supremes
Written by: Eddie Holland, Lamont Dozier, Brian Holland
From the album: *Supremes a Go-Go*
Label: Motown
Produced by: Brian Holland, Lamont Dozier
Year: 1966
Their second #1 R&B/#1 crossover. Cover by Phil Collins (Atlantic, '82) hit #1 UK.

YOU CAN'T JUDGE A BOOK BY LOOKING AT THE COVER

Artist: Bo Diddley
Written by: Ellas McDaniel (Bo Diddley)
From the album: *Bo Diddley*
Label: Chess
Produced by: Willie Dixon
Year: 1955
Not merely a man in eternal search of respect, love, and lost royalties, Bo is a down home philosopher of the first rank. This was a R&B crossover in '62. Covered by Stevie Wonder (Tamla, '70), Wilson Pickett (Atlantic, '71).

YOU CAN'T TURN ME OFF (IN THE MIDDLE OF TURNING ME ON)

Artist: High Inergy
Written by: Marilyn McLeod, Pam Sawyer
From the album: *Turnin' On*

Label: Gordy
Year: 1977
Top 10 R&B/Top 20 crossover.

YOU CHEATED

Artist: The Slades
Written by: Don Burch
Label: Domino
Year: 1958
The Little Anthony and the Imperials sound transferred to the West Coast. Covered by Jesse Belvin's one-off supergroup, the Shields (Tender, '58).

YOU DIDN'T HAVE TO BE SO NICE

Artist: The Lovin' Spoonful
Written by: John Sebastian, Steve Boone
From the album: *Daydream*
Label: Kama Sutra
Produced by: Erik Jacobsen
Year: 1966
As infernally joyful as good time folk/rock gets.

YOU DIDN'T TRY TO CALL ME

Artist: The Mothers of Invention
Written by: Frank Zappa
From the album: *Freak Out*
Label: Verve
Produced by: Tom Wilson
Year: 1966
Zappa's parody/homage to his first love, doo-wop. Covered by Zappa as Rueben and the Jets (Verve, '68).

YOU DON'T HAVE TO BE A STAR (TO BE IN MY SHOW)

Artist: Marilyn McCoo and Billy Davis Jr.
Written by: James Dean, John Glover
From the album: *I Hope We Get to Love in Time*
Label: ABC
Produced by: Don Davis
Year: 1976
Uplifting #1 R&B/#1 crossover was the biggest hit for the former 5TH Dimension stalwarts, powered by a great bassline from Motown sideman supreme James Jamerson.

YOU DON'T HAVE TO GO HOME TONIGHT

Artist: The Triplets
Written by: Eric Lowen, David Navarro, Diana Villegas, Sylvia Villegas, Vicki Villegas
From the album: *Thicker Than Water*
Label: Mercury
Produced by: Steve Barri, Tony Peluso
Year: 1991
Updated Ronettes, without the attitude. On the other hand, unlike the Righteous Brothers or the Thompson Twins, the MTV discoveries were really related.

YOU DON'T HAVE TO SAY YOU LOVE ME

Artist: Dusty Springfield
Written by: Vicki Wickham, Simon Napier-Bell, V. Pallavicini, P. Donaggio
From the album: *You Don't Have to Say You Love Me*
Label: Philips
Produced by: John Franz
Year: 1966
Italian soul ballad is her biggest hit. Covered by Elvis Presley (RCA, '70).

YOU DON'T KNOW

Artist: Helen Shapiro
Written by: Michael Hawker, John Schroeder
Produced by: Norrie Paramor
Label: EMI
Year: 1961
First #1 for the UK singer was an international million seller, about twelve of those copies bought in the US.

YOU DON'T KNOW LIKE I KNOW

Artist: Sam and Dave
Written by: Isaac Hayes, David Porter
From the album: *Hold on I'm Comin'*
Label: Stax
Produced by: Jim Stewart
Year: 1966
First R&B crossover for a couple of soul music's more legendary and prolific couples: Sam and Dave, David and Isaac.

YOU DON'T KNOW ME

Artist: Ray Charles
Written by: Cindy Walker, Eddy Arnold
From the album: *Modern Sounds in Country and Western Music*
Label: ABC Paramount
Produced by: Sid Feller
Year: 1962
Ray's Top 5 R&B/Top 5 crossover was introduced as a Top 10 country hit by Eddy Arnold (RCA, '56) and covered by Jerry Vale (Columbia, '56). Also covered by Lenny Welch (Cadence, '60), Elvis Presley (RCA, '67).

YOU DON'T KNOW WHAT YOU'VE GOT

Artist: Ral Donner
Written by: Paul Hampton, George Burton
Label: Gone
Year: 1961
Inspired Elvis imitation was his biggest hit.

YOU DON'T LOVE ME

Artist: Al Kooper
Written by: W. Cobbs
From the album: *Supersession*
Label: Columbia

Year: 1968
All-purpose blues track featured in Al Kooper's super one-off with guitarist Mike Bloomfield and Stephen Stills. Covered by Booker T. (Stax, '68), Kaleidoscope (Epic, '68), the Allman Brothers (Capricorn, '71).

YOU DON'T MESS AROUND WITH JIM

Artist: Jim Croce
Written by: Jim Croce
From the album: *You Don't Mess around with Jim*
Label: ABC
Produced by: Terry Cashman, Tommy West
Year: 1972
First hit for the prototypical '70s singer/songwriter.

YOU DON'T MISS YOUR WATER

Artist: William Bell
Written by: William Bell
From the album: *The Soul of a Bell*
Label: Stax
Produced by: Chips Moman
Year: 1962
Soul essential.

YOU DON'T OWN ME

Artist: Lesley Gore
Written by: John Madara, Dave White
From the album: *Lesley Gore Sings of Mixed up Hearts*
Label: Mercury
Produced by: Quincy Jones
Year: 1963
By the end of a tortuous '63, in which she'd been raked over the emotional coals by assorted boyfriends and girlfriends, Lesley finally finds herself a relationship (as well as an anthem). Written by the authors of "At the Hop" and "The Dawn of Correction." Covered by Blow Monkeys in *Dirty Dancing* (RCA, '87). Segue: "Don't Make Me Over" by Jennifer Warnes.

YOU ENJOY MYSELF

Artist: Phish
Written by: Trey Anastasio
From the album: *Junta*
Label: Elektra
Year: 1988
Early jam band opus and the best use of a trampoline since the movie *Big*, also in '88.

YOU GET WHAT YOU GIVE

Artist: New Radicals
Written by: Greg Alexander, Rick Nowels
From the album: *Maybe You've Been Brainwashed Too*
Label: MCA
Year: 1998
Stonesy rallying cry, but no one showed up for the rally.

YOU GIVE GOOD LOVE

Artist: Whitney Houston
Written by: LaForest (La La) Cope
From the album: *Whitney Houston*
Label: Arista
Produced by: Narada Michael Walden
Year: 1985
Her first hit is a #1 R&B/Top 5 crossover.

YOU GIVE LOVE A BAD NAME

Artist: Bon Jovi
Written by: Jon Bon Jovi, Richie Sambora, Desmond Child
From the album: *Slippery When Wet*
Label: Polygram
Produced by: Bruce Fairbairn
Year: 1986
Song-doctor Child tweaks his magic twanger.

YOU GOT IT

Artist: Roy Orbison
Written by: Jeff Lynne, Roy Orbison, Tom Petty
From the album: *Mystery Girl*
Label: Virgin
Produced by: Jeff Lynne
Year: 1989
Going out on a high note, Roy died while in the midst of a comeback, both solo and with the Traveling Wilburys. Covered by Bonnie Raitt in the film *Boys on the Side* (Arista, '95).

YOU GOT IT ALL

Artist: The Jets
Written by: Rupert Holmes, D. Rivkin
From the album: *The Jets*
Label: MCA
Produced by: Dan Powell
Year: 1987
The author's best pop rocker since "Escape (The Piña Colada Song)." Covered by Britney Spears (Jive, '98).

YOU GOT IT (KEEP IT OUTTA MY FACE)

Artist: Mudhoney
Written by: Mudhoney
From the album: *Superfuzz Bigmuff*
Label: Sub Pop
Produced by: Jack Endino
Year: 1989
Classic grunge track and attitude from Seattle.

YOU GOT IT (THE RIGHT STUFF)

Artist: New Kids on the Block
Written by: Larry Johnson (Maurice Starr)
From the album: *Hangin' Tough*
Label: Columbia
Produced by: Maurice Starr, Michael Jonzun

Year: 1988
Second hit in the US is their only hit in England.

YOU GOT LUCKY

Artist: Tom Petty and the Heartbreakers
Written by: Tom Petty, Mike Campbell
From the album: *Long after Dark*
Label: Backstreet
Produced by: Jimmy Iovine
Year: 1983
Folk/rock with a vengeance.

YOU GOT ME

Artist: The Roots featuring Erykah Badu
Written by: Tarik Trotter, Ahmir Thompson, Jill Scott, Scott Storch
From the album: *Things Fall Apart*
Label: MCA
Year: 1999
Heavy hip hop critics' band.

YOU GOT ME DIZZY

Artist: Jimmy Reed
Written by: Jimmy Reed, Ewart Abner Jr.
Label: Vee-Jay
Year: 1956

YOU GOT ME FLOATIN'

Artist: Jimi Hendrix
Written by: Jimi Hendrix
From the album: *Axis: Bold as Love*
Label: Reprise
Produced by: Chas Chandler
Year: 1968
Wah-wah heaven.

YOU GOT ME HUMMIN'

Artist: Sam and Dave
Written by: Isaac Hayes, David Porter
From the album: *Double Dynamite*
Label: Stax
Produced by: Isaac Hayes, David Porter
Year: 1966
Big in rock circles east and west. Covered by Billy Joel & the Hassles (Vanguard, '67), Lydia Pense and Cold Blood (San Francisco, '70).

YOU GOT ME ROCKIN'

Artist: The Rolling Stones
Written by: Mick Jagger, Keith Richards
From the album: *Voodoo Lounge*
Label: Virgin
Produced by: Don Was, Glimmer Twins
Year: 1994
With a new British invasion afoot, the originals out-rock the baby bands, most of whom preferred to be the Beatles.

YOU GOT THAT RIGHT

Artist: Lynyrd Skynyrd
Written by: Ronnie Van Zant, Steve Gaines

From the album: *Street Survivors*
Label: MCA
Produced by: Lynyrd Skynyrd
Year: 1977
Southern street smarts.

YOU GOT THE LOVE

Artist: Frankie Knuckles
Written by: Jamie Principle
Produced by: Frankie Knuckles
Label: Trax
Year: 1985
Important house music track links disco and dance.

YOU GOT THE LOVE

Artist: Rufus
Written by: Ray Parker Jr., Chaka Khan
From the album: *Rags to Rufus*
Label: ABC
Produced by: Rufus, Bob Monaco
Year: 1974
#1 R&B/Top 20 crossover introduces the future soul superstar Chaka Khan.

YOU GOT THE SILVER

Artist: The Rolling Stones
Written by: Mick Jagger, Keith Richards
From the album: *Let It Bleed*
Label: London
Produced by: Jimmy Miller
Year: 1968
Keith on vocals gives the Stones' answer to the acoustic side of Led Zeppelin, before the question was even asked. Brian Jones on autoharp. Featured in the '70 movie *Zabriskie Point*.

YOU GOT WHAT IT TAKES

Artist: Marv Johnson
Written by: Berry Gordy Jr., Roquel Davis (Tyran Carlo), Gwen Gordy
From the album: *Marvelous Marv Johnson*
Label: United Artists
Year: 1969
Swinging past Motown straight into soul, with a Top 10 R&B/crossover.

YOU GOTTA BE

Artist: Des'ree
Written by: Ashley Ingram, Des'ree
From the album: *I Ain't Movin'*
Label: 550 Music
Produced by: Ashley Ingram, Des'ree
Year: 1994
Lilting pop R&B anthem of affirmations.

(YOU GOTTA) FIGHT FOR YOUR RIGHT (TO PARTY)

Artist: Beastie Boys
Written by: Adam Horovitz, Adam Yauch, Michael Diamond, Rick Rubin

From the album: *Licensed to III*
Label: Def Jam
Produced by: Rick Rubin
Year: 1986
After getting tossed off the Madonna tour, the white rappers translate it into Top 10 success.

YOU HAD TIME

Artist: Ani Difranco
Written by: Ani Difranco
From the album: *Out of Range*
Produced by: Ani Difranco
Label: Righteous Babe
Year: 1994
Bravura keyboard piece by the feminist rocker is one of author Nick Hornby's (*High Fidelity*) favorite songs.

YOU HAVEN'T DONE NOTHIN'

Artist: Stevie Wonder
Written by: Stevie Wonder
From the album: *Fulfillingness First Finale*
Label: Tamla
Produced by: Stevie Wonder
Year: 1974
His fourth #1 R&B/#1 crossover.

YOU JUST HAVEN'T EARNED IT YET, BABY

Artist: The Smiths
Written by: Stephen Morrissey, Johnny Marr
From the album: *Louder Than Bombs*
Label: Sire
Produced by: Stephen Morrissey, Johnny Marr
Year: 1987
Covered by Kirsty MacColl (Charisma, '90).

YOU KEEP ME HANGIN' ON

Artist: The Supremes
Written by: Eddie Holland, Lamont Dozier, Brian Holland
From the album: *Sing Holland-Dozier-Holland*
Label: Motown
Produced by: Brian Holland, Lamont Dozier
Year: 1966
Third #1 R&B/#1 crossover. Covered by the Vanilla Fudge (Acto, '67), Kim Wilde (MCA, '87).

YOU KNOW I LOVE YOU

Artist: B. B. King
Written by: B. B. King, Jules Taub (Jules Bihari)
Label: RPM
Year: 1952
His second straight #1 R&B hit.

YOU LEARN

Artist: Alanis Morissette
Written by: Alanis Morissette
From the album: *Jagged Little Pill*
Label: Maverick

Produced by: Glen Ballard
Year: 1995
Fourth hit from the album of the year among angry young women.

YOU LEFT THE WATER RUNNING

Artist: Barbara Lynn
Written by: Dan Penn, Rick Hall, Oscar Franks
Label: Tribe
Year: 1966
Memphis soul classic, covered by Otis Redding (Stax, '67), Wilson Pickett (Atlantic, '67).

YOU MAKE LOVING FUN

Artist: Fleetwood Mac
Written by: Christine McVie
From the album: *Rumours*
Label: Warner Brothers
Produced by: Richard Dashut, Ken Caillat, Fleetwood Mac
Year: 1977
An ironic face on the intramural coed skirmishes within.

YOU MAKE ME FEEL BRAND NEW

Artist: The Stylistics
Written by: Thom Bell, Linda Creed
From the album: *Rockin' Roll Baby*
Label: Avco
Produced by: Thom Bell
Year: 1973
Their biggest hit, Top 5 R&B/Top 5 crossover.

YOU MAKE ME FEEL LIKE DANCING

Artist: Leo Sayer
Written by: Vini Poncia, Leo Sayer
From the album: *Endless Flight*
Label: Warner Brothers
Produced by: Richard Perry
Year: 1976
Disco-flavored pop rock.

(YOU MAKE ME FEEL LIKE) A NATURAL WOMAN

Artist: Aretha Franklin
Written by: Gerry Goffin, Carole King, Jerry Wexler
From the album: *Lady Soul*
Label: Atlantic
Produced by: Jerry Wexler
Year: 1967
Definitive star performance, a Top 10 R&B/Top 10 crossover. Covered by Carole King (Ode, '71).

YOU MAKE ME WANNA

Artist: Usher
Written by: Jermaine Dupri, Manuel Seal, Usher Raymond

From the album: *My Way*
Label: LaFace
Produced by: Jermaine Dupri
Year: 1997
Launching a pop soul career on the hip hop tip with a #1 R&B/#2 crossover.

YOU MAKE MY DREAMS

Artist: Daryl Hall & John Oates
Written by: Daryl Hall, John Oates, Sara Allen
From the album: *Voices*
Label: RCA
Produced by: Hall & Oates
Year: 1982
At their grooviest.

YOU MAY BE RIGHT

Artist: Billy Joel
Written by: Billy Joel
From the album: *Glass Houses*
Label: Columbia
Produced by: Phil Ramone
Year: 1980
Entering a rocking phase, rocks in hand.

YOU MIGHT THINK

Artist: The Cars
Written by: Ric Ocasek
From the album: *Heartbreak City*
Label: Elektra
Produced by: Mutt Lange
Year: 1984
Their best video, winning the first MTV Video award, over "Thriller."

YOU NEEDED ME

Artist: Anne Murray
Written by: Randy Goodrum
From the album: *Let's Keep It That Way*
Label: Capitol
Produced by: Jim Ed Norman
Year: 1975
#1 country/Top 10 crossover ballad.

YOU NEVER EVEN CALLED ME BY MY NAME

Artist: Steve Goodman
Written by: Steve Goodman, John Prine
From the album: *Somebody Else's Troubles*
Label: Buddah
Produced by: Arif Mardin
Year: 1970
Classic spoof of country form and function. Covered by David Allen Coe (Epic, '73), Doug Kershaw (Mercury, '94).

YOU NEVER GIVE ME YOUR MONEY

Artist: The Beatles
Written by: John Lennon, Paul McCartney
From the album: *Abbey Road*
Label: Apple

Produced by: George Martin
Year: 1969
Segue: "Taxman," by the Beatles.

YOU OUGHTA BE WITH ME

Artist: Al Green
Written by: Al Green, Willie Mitchell, Al Jackson
From the album: *Call Me*
Label: Hi
Produced by: Willie Mitchell
Year: 1972
His third #1 R&B/Top 10 crossover of the year.

YOU OUGHTA KNOW

Artist: Alanis Morissette
Written by: Glen Ballard, Alanis Morissette
From the album: *Jagged Little Pill*
Label: Maverick
Produced by: Glen Ballard
Year: 1995
Taking up where even Tori Amos dared not go, the former child star launches an adult career with two Grammys. Segue: "Miracles" by Jefferson Starship.

YOU REALLY GOT ME

Artist: The Kinks
Written by: Ray Davies
From the album: *You Really Got Me*
Label: Reprise
Produced by: Shel Talmy
Year: 1964
Their second biggest hit. Covered by Van Halen (Warner Brothers, '78) as their first single.

YOU REMIND ME

Artist: Mary J. Blige
Written by: Dave Hall, Eric Militeer
From the album: *Strictly Business Soundtrack*
Label: Uptown
Year: 1992
A major new soul diva emerges with a #1 R&B/Top 30 crossover.

YOU SAY YOU DON'T LOVE ME

Artist: The Buzzcocks
Written by: Pete Shelley
From the album: *A Different Kind of Tension*
Label: IRS
Produced by: Martin Rushent
Year: 1979
Shelley at his Byronic best.

YOU SEND ME

Artist: Sam Cooke
Written by: Sam Cooke (Charles Cooke)
Label: Keen
Produced by: Art Rupe
Year: 1957
Groundbreaking merger of pop, R&B and gospel was the first #1 R&B/#1 crossover by a black solo artist. Marked turning point in Cooke's career,

toward the secular and away from the church. Otis Redding, Marvin Gaye, Al Green were all listening. Little Richard was preparing to go in the opposite direction.

YOU SET THE SCENE

Artist: Love
Written by: Arthur Lee
From the album: *Forever Changes*
Label: Elektra
Produced by: Bruce Botnick, Arthur Love
Year: 1967
Classic psychedelia.

YOU SEXY THING

Artist: Hot Chocolate
Written by: Errol Brown, Anthony Wilson
From the album: *Hot Chocolate*
Label: Big Tree
Produced by: Mickie Most
Year: 1975
Only big stateside hit; in the UK they had thirteen.

YOU SHOOK ME

Artist: Muddy Waters
Written by: Willie Dixon, J.B. Lenoir
Label: Chess
Year: 1962
Essential primordial blues primer. Covered by the Jeff Beck Group (Epic, '68), Led Zeppelin (Atlantic, '69).

YOU SHOOK ME ALL NIGHT LONG

Artist: AC/DC
Written by: Angus Young, Malcolm Young, Brian Johnson
From the album: *Back in Black*
Label: Atlantic
Produced by: Mutt Lange
Year: 1980
Essential metal anthem is their first US Top 40 hit, introducing new lead singer Brian Johnson.

YOU SHOULD BE DANCING

Artist: Bee Gees
Written by: Barry Gibb, Robin Gibb, Maurice Gibb
From the album: *Main Course*
Label: RSO
Produced by: Arif Mardin
Year: 1976
Their first and biggest R&B crossover. Featured in the legendary John Travolta dance scene in *Saturday Night Fever*.

YOU SHOULD HEAR HOW SHE TALKS ABOUT YOU

Artist: Melissa Manchester
Written by: Tom Snow, Dean Pitchford
From the album: *Hey Ricky*
Label: Arista
Produced by: Arif Mardin

Year: 1982
Nightclub rocker was her biggest hit.

YOU SHOWED ME

Artist: The Byrds
Written by: Gene Clark, Jim McGuinn
From the album: *PreFlyte*
Label: Together
Produced by: Jim Dickson
Year: 1969
Recorded by the Byrds in '64 but not released for five years. Covered by the Turtles (White Whale, '69).

YOU SPIN ME ROUND (LIKE A RECORD)

Artist: Dead or Alive
Written by: Peter Burns, Michael Percy, Timothy Lever, Steven Coy
From the album: *Youthquake*
Label: Epic
Produced by: Peter Waterman
Year: 1985
US Dance record of the year; #1 UK.

YOU TALK TOO MUCH

Artist: Joe Jones
Written by: Joe Jones, Reginald Hall
From the album: *You Talk Too Much*
Label: Roulette
Produced by: Harold Battiste
Year: 1960
Top 10 R&B/Top 10 crossover from New Orleans.

YOU TURN ME ON, I'M A RADIO

Artist: Joni Mitchell
Written by: Joni Mitchell
From the album: *For the Roses*
Label: Asylum
Produced by: Joni Mitchell
Year: 1972
Her third Top 40 hit. B-side is the ineffable "Urge for Going."

YOU TURN ME ON (THE TURN ON SONG)

Artist: Ian Whitcomb
Written by: Ian Whitcomb
From the album: *You Turn Me On*
Label: Tower
Produced by: Jerry Dennon
Year: 1965
Paving the way for Gilbert O'Sullivan.

YOU UPSET ME, BABY

Artist: B. B. King
Written by: Maxwell Davis, Joe Josea
From the album: *Live at the Regal*
Label: RPM
Year: 1954

Classic cut from one of the most important electric guitar albums of the era, revered a decade later by Jerry Garcia, Jimi Hendrix, Michael Bloomfield, and a generation of scruffy Englishmen.

YOU WANT THIS

Artist: Janet Jackson
Written by: James Harris III, Terry Lewis, Janet Jackson
From the album: *janet*
Label: Virgin
Produced by: James Harris III, Terry Lewis, Janet Jackson
Year: 1993
#1 R&B/Top 10 crossover. Jackson has the most #1 R&B hits of any solo female performer aside from Aretha Franklin with 13.

YOU WEAR IT WELL

Artist: Rod Stewart
Written by: Rod Stewart, Martin Quittenton
From the album: *Never a Dull Moment*
Label: Mercury
Produced by: Rod Stewart
Year: 1972
Rod displays his sensitive side.

YOU WERE MEANT FOR ME

Artist: Jewel
Written by: Jewel Kilcher, Steve Poltz
From the album: *Pieces of You*
Label: Atlantic
Produced by: Peter Collins
Year: 1996
Melanie's evil twin scores with a folk/rock ballad.

YOU WERE ON MY MIND

Artist: Ian and Sylvia
Written by: Sylvia Fricker
From the album: *Northern Journey*
Label: Vanguard
Year: 1964
Folk/rock harmony standard. Covered by We Five (A&M, '65).

YOU WERE WRONG

Artist: Z.Z. Hill
Written by: Z.Z. Hill
Label: United Artists
Year: 1964
Soul gem from the bluesy belter.

YOU WILL KNOW

Artist: Stevie Wonder
Written by: Stevie Wonder
From the album: *Characters*
Label: Motown
Produced by: Stevie Wonder
Year: 1987
His sixteenth #1 R&B hit.

YOU WON'T SEE ME

Artist: The Beatles
Written by: John Lennon, Paul McCartney
From the album: *Rubber Soul*
Label: Capitol
Produced by: George Martin
Year: 1965
Covered by Anne Murray (Capitol, '74).

YOU'LL LOSE A GOOD THING

Artist: Barbara Lynn
Written by: Barbara Lynn Ozen
From the album: *You'll Lose a Good Thing*
Label: Jamie
Produced by: Huey Meaux
Year: 1962
Simmering New Orleans soul.

YOU'RE A BETTER MAN THAN I

Artist: The Yardbirds
Written by: Brian Hugg, Michael Hug
From the album: *Having a Rave up with the Yardbirds*
Label: Epic
Produced by: Sam Phillips
Year: 1965
Recorded in Memphis at the same session that produced their immortal rendition of "Train Kept a-Rollin'," this track features Jeff Beck's landmark use of a variety of electric guitar effects that would become standard to the guitar hero repertoire in the years to come.

YOU'RE A BIG BOY NOW

Artist: The Lovin' Spoonful
Written by: John Sebastian
From the album: *You're a Big Boy Now*
Label: Kama Sutra
Produced by: Erik Jacobsen
Year: 1966
Title tune from the movie. After writing "She's a Lady" for the theatre (*Jimmy Shine*), Sebastian's next hit would be for TV (*Welcome Back, Kotter*).

YOU'RE A VERY LOVELY WOMAN

Artist: Merry-Go-Round
Written by: Emitt Rhodes
From the album: *The Merry-Go-Round*
Label: A&M
Produced by: Larry Marks
Year: 1967
Hauntingly McCartneyesque folk/rock ballad. Covered by Linda Ronstadt (Capitol, '71). Rhodes also wrote "Live," which was covered by the Bangles.

YOU'RE A WONDERFUL ONE

Artist: Marvin Gaye

Written by: Eddie Holland, Lamont Dozier, Brian Holland
From the album: *Marvin Gaye/Greatest Hits*
Label: Tamla
Produced by: Brian Holland, Lamont Dozier
Year: 1964
Gaye swings. Hits another home run.

YOU'RE ALL I NEED TO GET BY

Artist: Marvin Gaye and Tammi Terrell
Written by: Nick Ashford, Valerie Simpson
From the album: *You're All I Need*
Label: Tamla
Produced by: Nick Ashford, Valerie Simpson
Year: 1968
Second straight #1 R&B/Top 10 crossover for both couples.

YOU'RE ALL I'VE GOT TONIGHT

Artist: The Cars
Written by: Ric Ocasek
From the album: *The Cars*
Label: Elektra
Produced by: Roy Thomas Baker
Year: 1978

YOU'RE BREAKING MY HEART

Artist: Nilsson
Written by: Harry Nilsson
From the album: *Son of Schmilsson*
Label: RCA
Produced by: Richard Perry
Year: 1971
Terse and to the point.

YOU'RE GONNA GET WHAT'S COMIN'

Artist: Robert Palmer
Written by: Robert Palmer
From the album: *Double Fun*
Label: Island
Year: 1978
Covered by Bonnie Raitt (Warner Brothers, '79).

YOU'RE GONNA GET YOURS

Artist: Public Enemy
Written by: Carlton Ridenhour, Hank Shocklee
From the album: *Yo Bum Rush the Show*
Label: Def Jam
Year: 1987
Early major statement from the politcal rap group.

YOU'RE GONNA LOSE THAT GIRL

Artist: The Beatles
Written by: John Lennon, Paul McCartney

From the album: *Help!*
Label: Capitol
Produced by: George Martin
Year: 1965
Comparing the Beatles' movie songs to Elvis' movie songs might be an interesting endeavor, if the Beatles had made upwards of thirty movies, and if all of Elvis' movie songs were written by Leiber and Stoller.

YOU'RE GONNA MAKE ME CRY

Artist: O.V. Wright
Written by: Deadric Malone
From the album: *O.V. Wright*
Label: Back Beat
Produced by: Willie Mitchell
Year: 1965
First R&B hit for the Memphis link between Otis Redding and Al Green. Covered by the Staple Singers (Stax, '70).

YOU'RE GONNA MISS ME

Artist: Thirteenth Floor Elevators
Written by: Roky Erickson
From the album: *Best Of the Thirteenth Floor Elevators*
Label: International Artists
Produced by: Gorbyn Productions
Year: 1966
Classic Texas garage band nugget, written by a certified '60s casualty. Covered by Sir Douglas (Tacoma, '81).

YOU'RE IN LOVE

Artist: Wilson Phillips
Written by: Glen Ballard, Wilson Phillips
From the album: *Wilson Phillips*
Label: SBK
Produced by: Glen Ballard
Year: 1990
The amazing fourth #1 from album. Ace of Base would soon arrive to fill this slot.

YOU'RE IN MY HEART (THE FINAL ACCLAIM)

Artist: Rod Stewart
Written by: Rod Stewart
From the album: *Footloose and Fancy Free*
Label: Warner Brothers
Produced by: Tom Dowd
Year: 1977
Rod's tribute to (and divorce settlement for) Britt Ekland.

YOU'RE LIVING ALL OVER ME

Artist: Dinosaur Jr.
Written by: Joseph Mascis
From the album: *You're Living All over Me*
Label: SST
Produced by: J. Mascis
Year: 1987

Influential alt/rock classic from the East-coast bohemian scene that launched the Lemonheads, Throwing Muses, Sebadoh, Belly, the Pixies, and the Breeders.

YOU'RE MAKING ME HIGH

Artist: Toni Braxton
Written by: Bryce Wilson, Kenny (Babyface) Edmunds
From the album: *Secrets*
Label: LaFace
Produced by: Babyface, Bryce Wilson
Year: 1995
Her only #1 R&B/#1 crossover.

YOU'RE MY BEST FRIEND

Artist: Queen
Written by: John Deacon
From the album: *A Night at the Opera*
Label: Elektra
Produced by: Roy Thomas Baker, Queen
Year: 1975
Having conquered opera, Queen move to the music hall.

YOU'RE MY EVERYTHING

Artist: The Temptations
Written by: Norman Whitfield, Roger Penzabene, Cornelius Grant
From the album: *With a Lot o Soul*
Label: Gordy
Produced by: Norman Whitfield
Year: 1967
Top 5 R&B/Top 10 crossover.

YOU'RE MY FAVORITE WASTE OF TIME

Artist: Marshall Crenshaw with the Handsome, Ruthless and Stupid Band
Written by: Marshall Crenshaw
From the album: *Marshall Crenshaw*
Label: Warner Brothers
Produced by: Marshall Crenshaw, Will Schillinger
Year: 1982
Initial attention-getter for the man who played John Lennon in *Beatlemania*, the movie, and "Sorry (I Ran All the Way Home)" in *Peggy Sue Got Married*. Covered by Bette Midler (Atlantic, '83).

YOU'RE MY LOVE INTEREST

Artist: John Hiatt
Written by: John Hiatt
From the album: *Slug Line*
Label: MCA
Produced by: Denny Bruce
Year: 1979

(YOU'RE MY) SOUL AND INSPIRATION

Artist: The Righteous Brothers
Written by: Barry Mann, Cynthia Weil

From the album: *Soul and Inspiration*
Label: Verve
Produced by: Bill Medley
Year: 1966
Kicking off '66 with their biggest hit; Brill Building songwriters Mann and Weil went on a hot streak as well.

YOU'RE NO GOOD

Artist: Betty Everett
Written by: Clint Ballard Jr.
Label: Vee Jay
Year: 1963
First hit for the Jerry Butler protégé. Cover by Linda Ronstadt (Capitol, '75) was her biggest hit.

YOU'RE ONLY LONELY

Artist: J. D. Souther
Written by: John David Souther
From the album: *You're Only Lonely*
Label: Columbia
Produced by: John David Souther
Year: 1979
A triumph of the laid-back, L.A. singer/songwriter syndrome just-post the heyday of punk and new wave rage.

YOU'RE PROBABLY WONDERING WHY I'M HERE

Artist: The Mothers of Invention
Written by: Frank Zappa
From the album: *Freak Out*
Label: Verve
Produced by: Tom Wilson
Year: 1966
Protest of a personal sort, complete with one of the great rock and roll screams.

YOU'RE SIXTEEN, YOU'RE BEAUTIFUL, AND YOU'RE MINE

Artist: Johnny Burnette
Written by: Dick Sherman, Bob Sherman
From the album: *Johnny Burnette*
Label: Liberty
Produced by: Snuff Garrett
Year: 1960
The Disney version of young love (rumored to have once been entitled "You're 13," perhaps for a Hayley Mills movie). Covered by Ringo Starr (Apple, '74).

YOU'RE SO FINE

Artist: The Falcons
Written by: Lance Finney, Willie Schofield
Label: Unart
Produced by: Bob West
Year: 1959

From the Detroit school of R&B, prefiguring the later '60s emanations of Motown and soul. Group included future stalwarts, Mack Rice, Wilson Pickett and Eddie Floyd.

(YOU'RE SO SQUARE) BABY I DON'T CARE

Artist: Elvis Presley
Written by: Jerry Leiber, Mike Stoller
From the album: *A Date with Elvis*
Label: RCA
Produced by: Steve Sholes
Year: 1957
One of Elvis's most swinging performances. Featured in the movie *Jailhouse Rock*. Covered by Joni Mitchell (Geffen, '82).

YOU'RE SO VAIN

Artist: Carly Simon
Written by: Carly Simon
From the album: *No Secrets*
Label: Elektra
Produced by: Richard Perry
Year: 1972
The year's best pop gossip and her biggest hit. Who was the vain main character of the lyric? Backup singer Mick Jagger? Hubbie James Taylor? Longshot Warren Beatty? Producer Richard Perry? Carly herself? The identity in question remains the rock and roll version of Watergate's Deep Throat.

YOU'RE STILL MY BABY

Artist: Chuck Willis
Written by: Chuck Willis
Label: Okeh
Produced by: Zenas "Big Daddy" Sears
Year: 1954

YOU'RE THE BOSS

Artist: LaVern Baker and Jimmy Ricks
Written by: Jerry Leiber, Mike Stoller
Label: Atlantic
Produced by: Jerry Leiber, Mike Stoller
Year: 1961
Classic call and response. Later used in the Elvis Presley film *Viva Las Vegas* (RCA, '63). Segue: "Love Is Strange" by Mickey & Sylvia.

(YOU'RE THE) DEVIL IN DISGUISE

Artist: Elvis Presley
Written by: Bill Giant, Florence Kaye, Bernie Baum
From the album: *Elvis' Golden Records (Vol. IV)*
Label: RCA
Produced by: Steve Sholes
Year: 1963
The forgotten man of '63, with a mere two Top 10 hits, and one of them was "Bossa Nova Baby." Luckily he had his movies (*It Happened at the World's Fair, Fun in Acapulco*) to keep him preoccupied.

YOU'RE THE FIRST, THE LAST, MY EVERYTHING

Artist: Barry White
Written by: Barry White, Tony Sepe, Peter Radcliffe
From the album: *Can't Get Enough*
Label: 20th Century
Produced by: Barry White
Year: 1974
His third #1 R&B/Top 10 crossover is his most impassioned vocal.

YOU'RE THE INSPIRATION

Artist: Chicago
Written by: Peter Cetera, David Foster
From the album: *17*
Label: Full Moon
Produced by: David Foster
Year: 1985

YOU'RE THE ONE

Artist: SWV
Written by: Allen Gordon, Tamara Johnson, Cheryl Gamble, Andrea Martin, Ivan Matias
From the album: *New Beginning*
Label: RCA
Produced by: Allen Gordon
Year: 1996
Their third #1 R&B/Top 10 crossover.

YOU'RE THE ONE THAT I WANT

Artist: Olivia Newton-John and John Travolta
Written by: John Farrar
From the album: *Grease (Soundtrack)*
Label: RSO
Produced by: John Farrar
Year: 1978
Winsome duet was one of the UK's biggest all-time hits.

YOU'RE THE ONLY ONE

Artist: The J. Geils Band
Written by: Seth Justman, Peter Wolf
From the album: *Monkey Island*
Label: Atlantic
Produced by: J. Geils Band
Year: 1977
Gin-soaked, harp-driven R&B gem.

YOU'RE THE REASON I'M LIVING

Artist: Bobby Darin
Written by: Bobby Darin
From the album: *You're the Reason I'm Living*
Label: Capitol
Year: 1963

(YOU'VE CAUGHT ME) SMILIN'

Artist: Sly & the Family Stone

Written by: Sylvester Stewart
From the album: *There's a Riot Goin' On*
Label: Epic
Produced by: Sly Stone
Year: 1971
A rare light moment from a grim album.

YOU'VE GOT A FRIEND

Artist: Carole King
Written by: Carole King
From the album: *Tapestry*
Label: Ode
Produced by: Lou Adler
Year: 1971
Covered by James Taylor (Warner Brothers, '71). The laid-back mellow L.A. singer/songwriter middle-of-the-dirt-road folk/rock sound of the '70s, defined by a couple of nasal East coast transplants. The payback for "Woodstock."

YOU'VE GOT ANOTHER THING COMIN'

Artist: Judas Priest
Written by: Rob Halford, Kenneth Downing, Glenn Tipton
From the album: *Screaming for Vengeance*
Label: Columbia
Produced by: Tom Allom
Year: 1981
Their metal anthem.

(YOU'VE GOT) THE MAGIC TOUCH

Artist: The Platters
Written by: Buck Ram
From the album: *Encore of Golden Hits*
Label: Mercury
Produced by: Buck Ram
Year: 1956
Top 5 R&B/Top 5 crossover.

YOU'VE GOT TO HIDE YOUR LOVE AWAY

Artist: The Beatles
Written by: John Lennon, Paul McCartney
From the album: *Help!*
Label: Capitol
Produced by: George Martin
Year: 1965
Perhaps about Lennon's relationship with Brian Epstein. Covered by the Silkie (Fontana, '65), produced by Lennon and McCartney.

YOU'VE GOT YOUR TROUBLES

Artist: The Fortunes
Written by: Roger Greenaway, Roger Cook
From the album: *The Fortunes*
Label: Press

Produced by: Roger Greenaway, Roger Cook
Year: 1965
The British garage band sound.

YOU'VE LOST THAT LOVIN' FEELIN'

Artist: The Righteous Brothers
Written by: Barry Mann, Cynthia Weil, Phil Spector
From the album: *You've Lost That Lovin' Feelin'*
Label: Philles
Produced by: Phil Spector
Year: 1964
Phil's epic, tumultuous Dear John letter to Ronnie Spector and the music business was the Righteous Brothers' defining number, a #1 UK/#3 R&B/#1 crossover.

YOU'VE MADE ME SO VERY HAPPY

Artist: Brenda Holloway
Written by: Frank Wilson, Berry Gordy Jr., Brenda Holloway, Patrice Holloway
Label: Tamla
Produced by: Berry Gordy Jr.
Year: 1967
Top 40 R&B/crossover. Covered by Blood, Sweat, & Tears (Columbia, '69).

YOU'VE REALLY GOT A HOLD ON ME

Artist: The Miracles
Written by: Smokey Robinson
From the album: *The Fabulous Miracles*
Label: Tamla
Produced by: Smokey Robinson
Year: 1963
Their second #1 R&B/Top 10 crossover. The generally refined Smokey at his fiercest: "I don't like you … but I love you."

YOUNG AMERICANS

Artist: David Bowie
Written by: David Bowie
From the album: *Young Americans*
Label: RCA
Produced by: Harry Maslin, David Bowie
Year: 1975
Bowie records in and is inspired by Philadelphia. David Sanborn on sax.

YOUNG BLOOD

Artist: The Coasters
Written by: Jerry Leiber, Mike Stoller, Doc Pomus
From the album: *The Coasters*
Label: Atco
Produced by: Jerry Leiber, Mike Stoller
Year: 1957
Early R&B-flavored effort by Doc Pomus, one of the most beloved figures in rock and roll songwriting history, was the B-side of "Searchin'."

YOUNG GIRL

Artist: Gary Puckett and the Union Gap
Written by: Jerry Fuller
From the album: *Young Girl*
Label: Columbia
Produced by: Jerry Fuller
Year: 1968
The mainstream male ego strikes back. Segue: "Don't Stand So Close to Me" by the Police.

YOUNG GUNS (GO FOR IT)

Artist: Wham UK!
Written by: George Michael
From the album: *Fantastic*
Produced by: George Michael, Steve Brown
Label: Columbia
Year: 1982
Their first hit, but only in England.

YOUNG HEARTS RUN FREE

Artist: Candi Staton
Written by: Dave Crawford
From the album: *Young Hearts Run Free*
Label: Warner Brothers
Year: 1976
#1 R&B/#1 UK/Top 20 crossover.

YOUNG LOVE

Artist: Sonny James
Written by: Ric Cartey, Carole Joyner
Label: Capitol
Produced by: Ken Nelson
Year: 1956
Originally released by cowriter Ric Cartey (RCA, '56). James' version was a #1 country/#1 crossover. Covered by Tab Hunter (Dot, '56).

YOUNG MAN BLUES

Artist: Mose Allison
Written by: Mose Allison
From the album: *Back Country Suite*
Produced by: Rudy Van Gelder
Label: Atlantic
Year: 1957
A droll "Summertime Blues" for the over-21 set from the quirky blues singer. Covered by the Yardbirds (Epic, '65), the Who (Decca, 70).

YOUNG ONES, THE

Artist: Cliff Richard
Written by: Brian Bennett, Sid Tepper
From the album: *The Young Ones Soundtrack*
Label: EMI
Year: 1962
1st single to enter British charts at #1.

YOUNG TURKS

Artist: Rod Stewart
Written by: Rod Stewart
From the album: *Tonight I'm Yours*

Label: Warner Brothers
Produced by: Rod Stewart, Jim Cregan
Year: 1981
Joining the MTV-era for a career-boosting video.

YOUNGER GENERATION

Artist: The Lovin' Spoonful
Written by: John Sebastian
From the album: *Everything's Playing*
Label: Kama Sutra
Produced by: Joe Wissert, the Lovin' Spoonful
Year: 1966
The anxieties of expectant fatherhood.

YOUNGER GIRL

Artist: The Lovin' Spoonful
Written by: John Sebastian
From the album: *Do You Believe in Magic*
Label: Kama Sutra
Produced by: Erik Jacobson
Year: 1965
A West Village anthem (all the other rock groups lived in the East Village). Covered by the Critters, who came from New Jersey (Kapp, '65).

YOUNGSTOWN

Artist: Bruce Springsteen
Written by: Bruce Springsteen
From the album: *The Ghost of Tom Joad*
Label: Columbia
Produced by: Bruce Springsteen, Chuck Plotkin
Year: 1995
Entering his second Woody Guthrie phase. Suggested segue: "Allentown" by Billy Joel.

YOUR CASH AIN'T NOTHIN' BUT TRASH

Artist: The Clovers
Written by: Jesse Stone (Charles Calhoun)
Label: Atlantic
Produced by: Ahmet Ertegun, Jerry Wexler
Year: 1954
Their fiercest commentary; covered by the Steve Miller Band (Capitol, '74).

YOUR CHEATIN' HEART

Artist: Hank Williams
Written by: Hank Williams
Label: MGM
Produced by: Fred Rose
Year: 1952
Inspired or caused by his divorce from Audrey. Covered by Ray Charles (ABC Paramount, '62).

YOUR FAVORITE THING

Artist: Sugar
Written by: Bob Mould
From the album: *File under Easy Listening*
Label: Rykodisc
Year: 1994
The Hüsker Dü guitar man finds a new groove.

YOUR GENERATION

Artist: Generation X
Written by: William Broad (Billy Idol), Tony James
From the album: *Generation X*
Label: Chrysalis
Year: 1978
Early punk single by the archetype Idol.

YOUR HEART BELONGS TO ME

Artist: The Supremes
Written by: Smokey Robinson
From the album: *Meet the Supremes*
Label: Motown
Produced by: Smokey Robinson
Year: 1962
A legendary career opens with a solid stiff.

YOUR LITTLE SECRET

Artist: Melissa Etheridge
Written by: Melissa Etheridge
From the album: *Your Little Secret*
Label: Island
Produced by: Melissa Etheridge, Hugh Padgham
Year: 1995
Only David Crosby knew for sure.

YOUR LOVE IS DRIVING ME CRAZY

Artist: Sammy Hagar
Written by: Sammy Hagar
From the album: *Three-Lock Box*
Label: Geffen
Produced by: Keith Olsen
Year: 1983
Biggest hit for the former Red Rocker and future Van Halen frontman.

(YOUR LOVE KEEPS LIFTING ME) HIGHER AND HIGHER

Artist: Jackie Wilson
Written by: Gary L. Jackson, Carl Smith, Raynard Miner, Roquel Davis (Tyran Carlo)
From the album: *Higher and Higher*
Label: Brunswick
Produced by: Carl Davis
Year: 1967
The definitive, enduring Jackie. His first #1 R&B/Top 10 crossover in four years and his last.

YOUR MA SAID YOU CRIED IN YOUR SLEEP LAST NIGHT

Artist: Kenny Dino
Written by: Steve Schlaks, Robert Glaser
Label: Musicor
Year: 1961
Covered by Robert Plant (Es Peranza, '90).

YOUR MAMA DON'T DANCE

Artist: Loggins and Messina
Written by: Kenny Loggins, Jim Messina
From the album: *Loggins and Messina*
Label: Columbia
Produced by: Jim Messina
Year: 1972
Essential folk/rocker. Covered by Poison (Enigma, '88).

YOUR MOTHER SHOULD KNOW

Artist: The Beatles
Written by: John Lennon, Paul McCartney
From the album: *Magical Mystery Tour*
Label: Capitol
Produced by: George Martin
Year: 1967
Suggested segue: "Stray Cat Blues" by the Rolling Stones.

YOUR OWN BACK YARD

Artist: Dion
Written by: Dion DiMucci, Tony Fasce
Label: Warner Brothers
Year: 1970
Dion's soul-baring antidrug anthem. Covered by Mott the Hoople (Columbia, '74).

YOUR OWN SPECIAL WAY

Artist: Genesis
Written by: Mike Rutherford
From the album: *Wind and Wuthering*
Label: Atco
Produced by: Hugh Padgham
Year: 1977
A progessive rock breakthrough Bottom 40 single.

YOUR PRECIOUS LOVE

Artist: Marvin Gaye and Tammi Terrell
Written by: Nick Ashford, Valerie Simpson
Label: Tamla
Produced by: Johnny Bristol, Harvey Fuqua
Year: 1967
Their biggest hit together.

YOUR RACIST FRIEND

Artist: They Might Be Giants
Written by: John Flansburgh, John Linnell
From the album: *Flood*
Label: Elektra
Produced by: Clive Langer, Alan Winstanley, They Might Be Giants
Year: 1990
Their best protest song other than their cover of "One More Parade" by Phil Ochs (Elektra, '90).

YOUR SMILING FACE

Artist: James Taylor
Written by: James Taylor
From the album: *JT*
Label: Columbia
Produced by: Peter Asher
Year: 1977
At the peak of his mellowness.

YOUR SONG

Artist: Elton John
Written by: Elton John, Bernie Taupin
From the album: *Elton John*
Label: MCA
Produced by: Gus Dudgeon
Year: 1970
Written three years earlier and originally released as the B-side of "Take Me to the Pilot." Launches their career and collaboration, with a perfect take on American diction ("Anyway, the thing is … what I really mean….")

YOUR TRUE LOVE

Artist: Carl Perkins
Written by: Carl Perkins
Label: Sun
Produced by: Sam Phillips
Year: 1957
His biggest crossover hit after "Blue Suede Shoes," Top 20 country/Bottom 40.

YOUR WILDEST DREAMS

Artist: The Moody Blues
Written by: Justin Hayward
From the album: *The Other Side of Life*
Label: Polygram
Produced by: Tony Visconti
Year: 1986
Their biggest hit since "Nights in White Satin."

YOURS IS NO DISGRACE

Artist: Yes
Written by: Jon Anderson, Chris Squire, Bill Bruford, Steve Howe, Tony Kaye
From the album: *The Yes Album*
Label: Atlantic
Produced by: Eddie Offord, Yes
Year: 1971
The epitome of British progressive rock, with Steve Howe doing the guitar honors.

YO-YO

Artist: The Osmonds
Written by: Joe South
From the album: *Phase III*
Label: MGM
Produced by: Rick Hall
Year: 1971
Sunny L.A. state-of-the-art-of-'70s studio-craft. Covered by the Hollies (Epic, '74).

YUMMY, YUMMY, YUMMY

Artist: Ohio Express
Written by: Artle Resnick, Joey Levine
From the album: *Yummy, Yummy, Yummy*

Label: Westbound
Produced by: Jerry Kazenetz, Jeff Katz
Year: 1968
Bubblegum standard featuring the voice of Joey Levine, who would be heard from again. And again.

YYZ

Artist: Rush
Written by: Gary Lee Weinrib (Geddy Lee), Alex Zivojinovich (Alex Lifeson), Neil Peart
From the album: *Moving Pictures*
Label: Mercury
Produced by: Terry Brown, Rush
Year: 1981
Geddy Lee at his best. Derived from Morse code.

Z

ZANZ CAN'T DANCE (VANZ CAN'T DANCE)

Artist: John Fogerty
Written by: John C. Fogerty
From the album: *Centerfield*
Label: Warner Brothers
Produced by: John C. Fogerty
Year: 1985
Sparked a lawsuit from the owner of Fogerty's then-disputed previous copyrights, the coincidentally named Saul Zaentz.

ZAZ TURNED BLUE

Artist: Was (Not Was) featuring Mel Torme
Written by: David Weiss (David Was), Donald Fagenson (Don Was)
From the album: *Born to Laugh at Tornadoes*
Label: Warner Brothers
Produced by: Don Was, David Was
Year: 1983
A twisted story-song.

ZIGGY STARDUST

Artist: David Bowie
Written by: David Bowie
From the album: *The Rise and Fall of Ziggy Stardust and the Spiders from Mars*
Label: RCA
Produced by: David Bowie, Ken Scott
Year: 1972
Launching his favorite persona and glam rock in the process.

ZIP-A-DEE-DOO-DAH

Artist: Bob B. Soxx and the Blue Jeans
Written by: Ray Gilbert, Allie Wrubel
From the album: *Zip-A-Dee-Doo-Dah*
Label: Philles
Produced by: Phil Spector
Year: 1962

From the '45 movie *Song of the South*. Sung by Darlene Love, another Spectorian extravaganza gains a Top 10 R&B/Top 10 crossover.

ZOMBIE

Artist: The Cranberries
Written by: Noel Hogan, Dolores O'Riordan
From the album: *No Need to Agree*
Label: Island
Produced by: Stephen Street
Year: 1994
Leaving their pristine image behind, with a strong antiwar message.

ARTIST INDEX

A

AALIYAH
1994   Back & Forth

ABBA
1974   Waterloo
1977   Dancing Queen
1977   Take a Chance on Me

ABBOTT, GREGORY
1986   Shake You Down

ABC
1982   Look of Love (Part One), The
1985   Be Near Me
1987   When Smokey Sings

ABDUL, PAULA
1988   Cold-Hearted
1988   Forever Your Girl
1988   (It's Just) The Way That You Love Me
1988   Opposites Attract
1988   Straight Up
1991   Promise of a New Day
1991   Rush, Rush

ABRAMS COLONEL
1984   Music Is the Answer

AC/DC
1976   It's a Long Way to the Top (If You Want to Rock and Roll)
1977   Whole Lotta Rosie
1979   Highway to Hell
1980   Back in Black
1980   Hell's Bells
1980   You Shook Me All Night Long
1981   Dirty Deeds Done Dirt Cheap
1981   For Those About to Rock (We Salute You)
1986   Who Made Who
1990   Moneytalks
1995   Hard as a Rock

ACE
1975   How Long

ACE OF BASE
1993   All That She Wants
1993   Sign, The

ACE, JOHNNY
1952   My Song
1953   Clock, The
1954   Pledging My Love

ACKLES, DAVID
1968   Down River
1968   Road to Cairo

ACKLIN, BARBARA
1968   Love Makes a Woman

ADAM ANT
1982   Goody Two Shoes

ADAMS, BRYAN
1983   Cuts Like a Knife
1984   Heaven
1984   Run to You
1984   Summer of '69
1991   Can't Stop This Thing We Started
1991   (Everything I Do) I Do It for You

ADAMS, BRYAN, ROD STEWART, AND STING
1993   All for Love

ADAMS, FAYE
1953   Shake a Hand
1954   Hurts Me to My Heart
1954   I'll Be True

ADAMS, JOHNNY
1991   Prisoner of Life

ADAMS, MARIE
1952   I'm Gonna Play the Honky Tonks

ADAMS, OLETA
1991   Get Here

ADKINS, HASIL
1957   She Said

AEROSMITH
1973   Dream On
1973   Mama Kin
1973   Walk This Way
1974   Seasons of Wither
1975   Sweet Emotion
1976   Back in the Saddle
1976   Last Child
1987   Angel
1987   Cryin'
1987   Dude (Looks Like a Lady)
1987   Rag Doll
1989   Janie's Got a Gun
1989   Love in an Elevator
1989   What It Takes
1993   Amazing
1993   Livin' on the Edge
1997   Pink
1998   I Don't Want to Miss a Thing

AFTER 7
1989   Can't Stop
1989   Ready or Not

AFTER THE FIRE
1983   Der Kommissar

AGUILERA, CHRISTINA
1999   Come on Over (All I Want Is You)
1999   Genie in a Bottle
1999   What a Girl Wants

AHA
1985   Take on Me

AHMAD
1994   Back in the Day

AIR SUPPLY
1983   Making Love out of Nothing at All

AKENS, JEWEL
1960   Birds and the Bees, The

ALARM, THE
1989   Sold Me down the River

ALCATRAZZ
1984   Evil Eye

ALEXANDER, ARTHUR
1962   Shot of Rhythm and Blues, A
1962   Soldier of Love

1962   You Better Move On
1963   Anna (Go to Him)

ALIAS

1990   More Than Words Can Say

ALICE IN CHAINS

1992   Rooster
1992   Would
1994   No Excuses

ALL

1988   Just Perfect

ALL SAINTS

1998   Never Ever

ALL-4-ONE

1994   I Swear
1996   I Turn to You

ALLEN, ANNISTEEN

1955   Fujiyama Mama

ALLEN, TONY

1955   Nite Owl

ALLISON, MOSE

1957   Young Man Blues
1958   Parchman Farm
1958   Seventh Son
1964   I'm Not Talking

ALLMAN BROTHERS

1970   In Memory of Elizabeth Reed
1970   Midnight Rider
1970   Whipping Post
1972   Ain't Wastin' Time No More
1972   Blue Sky
1972   Little Martha
1972   Melissa
1973   Jessica
1973   Ramblin' Man

ALTERED IMAGES

1981   Happy Birthday

ALVIN, DAVE

1987   Fourth of July

AMBOY DUKES, THE

1968   Journey to the Center of the
          Mind

AMBROSIA

1975   Nice, Nice, Very Nice
1978   How Much I Feel
1980   Biggest Part of Me, The

AMERICA

1972   Horse with No Name, A
1972   Ventura Highway
1974   Lonely People
1974   Tin Man
1975   Sister Golden Hair

AMERICAN BREED

1967   Bend Me, Shape Me

AMOS, TORI

1992   Crucify
1992   Me and a Gun
1992   Silent All These Years
1992   Winter

ANDERSEN, ERIC

1968   Tin Can Alley

ANDERSON, LAURIE

1982   O Superman
1984   Sharkey's Day

ANDREWS, LEE AND THE HEARTS

1957   Long Lonely Nights
1957   Teardrops

ANGELS, THE

1963   My Boyfriend's Back

ANGRY SAMOANS

1980   Right Side of My Brain

ANIMALS, THE

1965   Don't Let Me Be Misunderstood
1965   It's My Life
1965   We Gotta Get Outa This Place
1966   Don't Bring Me Down
1966   Mama Told Me Not to Come
1967   Monterey
1967   San Franciscan Nights
1968   Sky Pilot

ANKA, PAUL

1957   Diana
1959   Lonely Boy
1959   Put Your Head on My Shoulder
1960   Puppy Love
1960   It's Time to Cry

ANNETTE

1959   Tall Paul
1960   It's Really Love
1960   O Dio Mio

ANOTHER BAD CREATION

1991   Iesha
1991   Playground

ANTHONY, MARC

1999   I Need to Know

ANTHRAX

1986   A.D.I./The Horror of It All
1987   Caught in a Mosh

APHEX TWIN

1992   Digeridoo

APPLE, FIONA

1997   Criminal
1999   Fast as You Can
1999   Paper Bag

AQUA

1997   Barbie Girl

ARCHIES, THE

1969   Sugar Sugar

ARGENT

1972   Hold Your Head Up
1973   God Gave Rock and Roll to You

ARMATRADING, JOAN

1976   Love and Affection

ARMSTRONG, LOUIS

1956   Mack the Knife

ARRESTED DEVELOPMENT

1992   Mr. Wendall
1992   People Everyday
1992   Revolution
1992   Tennessee

ART OF NOISE

1984   Moments in Love

ARTISTS UNITED AGAINST APARTHEID

1985   Sun City

ASH, DANIEL

(See Love & Rockets)

1992   Get out of Control

ASHFORD & SIMPSON

1984   Solid

ASIA

1982   Heat of the Moment, The

ASSOCIATION, THE

1966   Along Comes Mary
1966   Cherish
1967   Never My Love
1967   Windy

ASTLEY, RICK

1987   Never Gonna Give You Up
1988   Together Forever

A3

1999   Woke up This Morning

ATKINS, CHET

1957   Walk, Don't Run
1959   Let It Be Me

ATLANTA RHYTHM SECTION

1976   So into You
1978   Imaginary Lover

ATLANTIC STARR

1986   Secret Lovers
1992   Masterpiece

AVALON, FRANKIE

1958   Dede Dinah
1959   Bobby Sox to Stockings
1959   Venus
1959   Why

AVERAGE WHITE BAND, THE

1974   Pick up the Pieces

AZTEC TWO-STEP

1972   Persecution and Restoration of Dean
        Moriarity, The (On the Road)

B

B.G.

1999   Bling Bling

B.T. EXPRESS

1974   Do It ('Til You're Satisfied)
1974   Express

B-52s

1979   Dance This Mess Around
1979   Rock Lobster
1980   Party out of Bounds
1980   Private Idaho
1983   Song for a Future Generation
1989   Love Shack
1989   Roam

BABE RUTH

1972   Mexican, The

BABES IN TOYLAND

1990   Bruised Violet

BABYFACE

1989   It's No Crime
1989   Tender Lover
1994   When Can I See You

BACHMAN TURNER OVERDRIVE

1973   Takin' Care of Business
1974   You Ain't Seen Nothin' Yet

BACKSTREET BOYS

1997   Everybody (Backstreet's Back)
1997   Quit Playing Games (with My Heart)
1999   I Want It That Way
1999   Shape of My Heart
1999   Show Me the Meaning of Being Lonely

BAD BRAINS

1980   Pay to Cum
1986   Intro

BAD COMPANY

1974   Can't Get Enough
1975   Feel Like Making Love
1979   Rock 'n' Roll Fantasy

BAD ENGLISH

1989   When I See You Smile

BAD RELIGION

1994   21st Century Digital Boy

BADFINGER

1969   Come and Get It
1971   Day after Day

BADU, ERYKAH

1996   On & On

BAEZ, JOAN

1962   Babe I'm Gonna Leave You
1964   Birmingham Sunday
1965   Farewell Angelina
1967   Love Is Just a Four-Letter Word
1967   Saigon Bride
1975   Diamonds and Rust
1992   Stones in the Road

BAHA MEN

2000   Who Let the Dogs Out

BAILEY, PHILIP

(See Earth, Wind & Fire)

1985   Easy Lover

BAINBRIDGE, MERRIL

1996   Mouth

BAKER, ANITA

1986   Sweet Love
1988   Giving You the Best That I Got

BAKER, LAVERN

1953   Soul on Fire
1954   Tweedlee Dee
1955   Bop-Ting-a-Ling
1957   Jim Dandy
1957   Jim Dandy Got Married
1959   I Cried a Tear
1961   Saved

BAKER, LAVERN AND JIMMY RICKS

1961   You're the Boss

BALDRY, LONG JOHN

1971   Don't Try to Lay No Boogie Woogie
        on the King of Rock and Roll

BALIN, MARTY

(See Jefferson Airplane, Jefferson Starship)

1981   Hearts

BALTIMORA

1986   Tarzan Boy

BAMBAATAA, AFRIKA AND SOULSONIC FORCE

1982   Planet Rock
1986   Looking for the Perfect Beat

BANANARAMA

1984   Cruel Summer
1987   I Heard a Rumour

BAND, THE

1968	Across the Great Divide
1968	Chest Fever
1968	I Shall Be Released
1968	King Harvest (Has Surely Come)
1968	Night They Drove Old Dixie Down, The
1968	Rag, Mama, Rag
1968	Tears of Rage
1968	This Wheel's on Fire
1968	To Kingdom Come
1968	Up on Cripple Creek
1968	Weight, The
1969	Jemima Surrender
1970	Shape I'm In, The
1970	Stage Fright
1971	Life Is a Carnival
1975	Ophelia

BAND-AID

| 1984 | Do They Know It's Christmas |

BANGLES

1984	Goin' down to Liverpool
1984	James
1986	If She Knew What She Wants
1986	Manic Monday
1986	Walk Like an Egyptian
1988	In Your Room
1989	Eternal Flame

BANGS, LESTER

| 1981 | Let It Blurt |

BANKS, BESSIE

| 1963 | Go Now |

BARBARIANS, THE

| 1965 | Are You a Boy or Are You a Girl? |
| 1966 | Moulty |

BARBUSTERS, THE

| 1987 | Light of Day, The |

BARE, BOBBY

| 1963 | Detroit City |

BARENAKED LADIES

1992	Be My Yoko Ono
1992	Brian Wilson
1998	One Week

BARRETT, SYD

| 1974 | Terrapin |

BARRY, LEN

| 1965 | One, Two, Three (1-2-3) |

BARTHOLEMEW, DAVE

| 1952 | My Ding a Ling |

BASE, ROB AND DJ E-Z ROCK

| 1988 | It Takes Two |

BASIL, TONI

| 1982 | Mickey |

BASS, FONTELLA

| 1965 | Rescue Me |

BAUHAUS

| 1979 | Bela Legosi's Dead |
| 1981 | Kick in the Eye |

BAY CITY ROLLERS

| 1975 | Saturday Night |

BEACH BOYS, THE

1961	Surfin'
1962	409
1962	Surfin' Safari
1963	Be True to Your School
1963	Farmer's Daughter
1963	In My Room
1963	Shut Down
1963	Surfer Girl
1963	Surfin' USA
1964	All Summer Long
1964	California Saga (Big Sur)
1964	Dance, Dance, Dance
1964	Don't Worry Baby
1964	Fun Fun Fun
1964	I Get Around
1964	Warmth of the Sun, The
1964	Wendy
1964	When I Grow Up to Be a Man
1965	California Girls
1965	Help Me, Rhonda
1965	Please Let Me Wonder
1966	Caroline No
1966	Don't Talk (Put Your Head on My Shoulder)
1966	God Only Knows
1966	Good Vibrations
1966	Hang on to Your Ego
1966	I Just Wasn't Made for These Times
1966	Wouldn't It Be Nice
1967	Do It Again
1967	Heroes and Villains
1970	Add Some Music to Your Day
1973	Sail on Sailor
1988	Kokomo

BEASTIE BOYS

1985	She's on It
1986	Hey Ladies
1986	No Sleep Till Brooklyn
1986	Paul Revere
1986	(You Gotta) Fight for Your Right (to Party)
1989	Shake Your Rump
1992	Pass the Mic
1992	So What'cha Want

BEAT HAPPENING

| 1988 | Indian Summer |

BEATLES, THE

1963	Do You Want to Know a Secret?
1963	From Me to You
1963	I Saw Her Standing There
1963	I Want to Hold Your Hand
1963	I'll Get You
1963	Love Me Do
1963	(P.S.) I Love You
1963	Please Please Me
1963	She Loves You
1963	Thank You Girl
1963	There's a Place
1964	All My Loving
1964	And I Love Her
1964	Any Time at All
1964	Can't Buy Me Love
1964	Don't Bother Me
1964	Hard Day's Night, A
1964	I Feel Fine
1964	I Should Have Known Better
1964	If I Fell
1964	I'll Cry Instead
1964	I'm Happy Just to Dance with You
1964	It Won't Be Long
1964	She's a Woman
1964	Tell Me Why
1964	Things We Said Today
1964	This Boy (Ringo's Theme)
1964	You Can't Do That
1965	And Your Bird Can Sing
1965	Another Girl
1965	Baby's in Black
1965	Day Tripper
1965	Drive My Car
1965	Eight Days a Week
1965	Every Little Thing
1965	Girl
1965	Help!
1965	I Don't Want to Spoil the Party
1965	I Need You
1965	If I Needed Someone
1965	I'll Follow the Sun
1965	I'm a Loser
1965	I'm Looking through You
1965	In My Life
1965	It's Only Love
1965	I've Just Seen a Face
1965	Michelle
1965	Night Before, The
1965	Norwegian Wood (This Bird Has Flown)
1965	Nowhere Man
1965	Run for Your Life
1965	Think for Yourself
1965	Ticket to Ride

1965   We Can Work It Out
1965   Word, The
1965   Yes It Is
1965   Yesterday
1965   You Won't See Me
1965   You're Gonna Lose That Girl
1965   You've Got to Hide Your Love Away
1966   Eleanor Rigby
1966   For No One
1966   Good Day Sunshine
1966   Got to Get You into My Life
1966   Here, There and Everywhere
1966   I Want to Tell You
1966   Paperback Writer
1966   Rain
1966   Taxman
1966   Tomorrow Never Knows
1966   Yellow Submarine
1967   All You Need Is Love
1967   Baby, You're a Rich Man
1967   Being for the Benefit of Mr. Kite
1967   Blue Jay Way
1967   Day in the Life, A
1967   Fixing a Hole
1967   Fool on the Hill, The
1967   Getting Better
1967   Good Morning, Good Morning
1967   Hello, Goodbye
1967   I Am the Walrus
1967   Lovely Rita
1967   Lucy in the Sky with Diamonds
1967   Magical Mystery Tour
1967   Penny Lane
1967   Sgt. Pepper's Lonely Hearts Club
         Band
1967   She's Leaving Home
1967   Strawberry Fields Forever
1967   When I'm Sixty-Four
1967   With a Little Help from My Friends
1967   Within You, without You
1967   Your Mother Should Know
1968   All Together Now
1968   Birthday
1968   Blackbird
1968   Continuing Story of Bungalow Bill,
         The
1968   Cry Baby Cry
1968   Dear Prudence
1968   Don't Pass Me By
1968   Everybody's Got Something to Hide
         except Me and My Monkey
1968   Glass Onion
1968   Happiness Is a Warm Gun
1968   Helter Skelter
1968   Hey Jude
1968   Honey Pie
1968   I Will
1968   Inner Light, The
1968   Julia
1968   Lady
1968   Martha My Dear
1968   Mother Nature's Son
1968   Ob-La-Di, Ob-La-Da
1968   Piggies
1968   Revolution (Revolution 1)
1968   Revolution 9
1968   Rocky Racoon
1968   Savoy Truffle

1968   Sexy Sadie
1968   While My Guitar Gently Weeps
1968   Why Don't We Do It in the Road
1968   Wild Honey Pie
1968   Yer Blues
1969   Ballad of John and Yoko, The
1969   Because
1969   Carry That Weight
1969   Come Together
1969   Don't Let Me Down
1969   End, The
1969   Get Back
1969   Golden Slumbers
1969   Here Comes the Sun
1969   Hey Bulldog
1969   I Want You (She's So Heavy)
1969   It's All Too Much
1969   Maxwell's Silver Hammer
1969   Mean Mr. Mustard
1969   Octopus's Garden
1969   Oh! Darling
1969   Polythene Pam
1969   She Came in through the Bathroom
         Window
1969   Something
1969   You Never Give Me Your Money
1970   For You Blue
1970   Let It Be
1970   Long and Winding Road, The
1970   Two of Us, The
1995   Free as a Bird
1996   Real Love

BEAU BRUMMELS, THE

1964   Laugh, Laugh
1965   Just a Little

BEAVIS AND BUTT-HEAD

1993   Come to Butt-Head

BECK

1993   Loser
1994   Rowboat
1996   Devil's Haircut
1996   Nobody's Fault but My Own
1996   Where It's At
1997   New Pollution, The

JEFF BECK GROUP

(See The Yardbirds)
1968   Beck's Bolero
1968   Plynth (Water down the Drain)
1968   Rock My Plimsoul
1973   Freeway Jam

BECK, JEFF

1976   Goodbye Pork Pie Hat

BEE GEES

1967   New York Mining Disaster 1941
         (Have You Seen My Wife
         Mr. Jones)

1967   (The Lights Went out In)
         Massachusetts
1967   To Love Somebody
1968   I Started a Joke
1968   I've Got to Get a Message to You
1970   Lonely Days
1971   How Can You Mend a Broken
         Heart
1975   Jive Talkin'
1975   Nights on Broadway
1976   Love So Right
1976   You Should Be Dancing
1977   How Deep Is Your Love
1977   Night Fever
1977   Stayin' Alive
1978   Too Much Heaven
1978   Tragedy
1979   Love You inside Out

BELL, ARCHIE & THE DRELLS

1968   Tighten Up

BELL, WILLIAM

1962   You Don't Miss Your Water
1968   I Forgot to Be Your Lover
1968   Tribute to a King
1977   Tryin' to Love Two

BELL BIV DEVOE

1990   Do Me!
1990   Poison

BELL NOTES

1958   I've Had It

BELLE AND SEBASTIAN

1996   Stars of Track and Field
1998   Seymour Stein

BELLS

1971   Stay Awhile

BELLY

1993   Feed the Tree

BELVIN, JESSE

1951   Goodnight My Love

BENATAR, PAT

1980   Hit Me with Your Best Shot
1983   Love Is a Battlefield
1984   We Belong

BENNETT, BOYD

1957   Black Slacks

BENNETT, JOE & THE SPARKLETONES

1955   Seventeen

BENSON, GEORGE

1977   Greatest Love of All, The
1980   Give Me the Night

BENTON, BROOK

1959   It's Just a Matter of Time
1963   Hotel Happiness
1970   Rainy Night in Georgia, A

BENTON, BROOK AND DINAH WASHINGTON

1959   Thank You, Pretty Baby
1960   Baby (You've Got What It Takes)

BERLIN

1986   Take My Breath Away (Love Theme from Top Gun)
1983   Sex (I'm A)

BERN, DAN

1997   Marilyn
1998   Tiger Woods

BERRY, CHUCK

1955   Maybellene
1955   Thirty Days
1957   Brown Eyed Handsome Man
1957   No Money Down
1957   Rock and Roll Music
1957   School Day
1957   Too Much Monkey Business
1957   Wee Wee Hours
1958   Beautiful Delilah
1958   Carol
1958   Johnny B. Goode
1958   Reelin' and Rockin'
1958   Sweet Little Sixteen
1959   Almost Grown
1959   Around and Around
1959   Back in the U.S.A.
1959   Jo Jo Gunne
1959   Little Queenie
1959   Memphis
1959   Roll over Beethoven
1959   Sweet Little Rock and Roller
1960   Bye Bye Johnny
1960   Let It Rock
1960   Too Pooped to Pop
1961   Come On
1961   I'm Talking about You
1961   13 Question Method
1964   C'est La Vie (You Never Can Tell)
1964   Little Marie
1964   Liverpool Drive
1964   Nadine (Is It You?)
1964   No Particular Place to Go

1964   Promised Land
1967   You Can't Catch Me
1970   Have Mercy Judge
1970   Tulane

BERRY, DAVE

1965   Crying Game, The

BERRY, RICHARD

1954   Big Break, The
1956   Louie, Louie

BETTER THAN EZRA

1995   Good

BIG AUDIO DYNAMITE

1991   Rush

BIG BAD VOO DOO DADDY

1996   You and Me and the Bottle Make Three Tonight

BIG BLACK

1986   Kerosene

BIG BOPPER, THE

1958   Chantilly Lace

BIG BROTHER AND THE HOLDING COMPANY

1968   All Is Loneliness
1968   Ball and Chain
1968   Bye Bye Baby
1968   Combination of the Two
1968   Coo Coo
1968   Down on Me
1968   Farewell Song
1968   Women Is Losers

BIG COUNTRY

1983   In a Big Country

BIG FUN

1989   Teenage Suicide (Don't Do It)

BIG MAYBELLE

1954   One Monkey Don't Stop No Show
1955   Whole Lotta Shakin' Goin' On

BIG PUNISHER

1998   Still Not a Player

BIG STAR

1972   Don't Lie to Me
1972   In the Street
1974   Back of a Car

1974   September Gurls
1978   Holocaust

BIKINI KILL

1992   Double Dare Ya

BILL BLACK'S COMBO

1959   Smokie—Part 2

BILLY & THE BEATERS

1981   At This Moment

BIRKIN, JANE AND SERGE GAINSBOURG

1970   Je T'Aime … Moi Non Plus

BISHOP, ELVIN

1976   Fooled around and Fell in Love

BISHOP, STEPHEN

1982   It Might Be You

BIZ MARKIE

1989   Just a Friend

BJORK

1993   Big Time Sensuality
1993   Human Behaviour
1993   Venus as a Boy
1995   Army of Me

BLACK, CILLA

1964   It's for You

BLACK BOX

1989   Ride on Time
1990   Everybody Everybody
1990   Strike It Up

BLACK CROWES, THE

1980   Thorn in My Pride
1990   She Talks to Angels
1992   Remedy

BLACK FLAG

1978   Wasted
1981   Rise Above
1981   TV Party

BLACK SABBATH

1970   Paranoid
1970   Wizard, The
1971   Black Sabbath
1971   Children of the Grave
1971   Iron Man

BLACKSTREET

1994   Before I Let You Go
1996   No Diggity

BLACKWELL, OTIS

1953   Daddy Rolling Stone

BLAND, BILLY

1961   Let the Little Girl Dance

BLAND, BOBBY

1957   Farther up the Road
1960   I'll Take Care of You
1961   I Pity the Fool
1961   Turn on Your Love Light
1963   That's the Way Love Is
1964   Ain't Nothin' You Can Do

BLANE, MARCIE

1962   Bobby's Girl

BLASSIE, FREDDIE

1977   Pencil Neck Geek

BLASTERS, THE

1980   American Music
1980   Marie Marie
1981   Border Radio
1983   Long White Cadillac
1985   Common Man

BLIGE, MARY J.

1992   Real Love
1992   You Remind Me
1994   My Life
1996   Not Gon' Cry

BLIND FAITH

1969   Can't Find My Way Home
1969   Presence of the Lord

BLIND MELON

1993   No Rain

BLINK 182

1999   All the Small Things

BLONDIE

1976   X-Offender
1977   In the Sun
1978   Heart of Glass
1978   One Way or Another
1979   Dreaming
1979   Sunday Girl
1980   Call Me
1981   Rapture

BLOOD, SWEAT & TEARS

1968   I Can't Quit Her
1968   I Love You More Than You'll Ever
        Know
1969   Spinning Wheel

BLOTTO

1980   I Wanna Be a Lifeguard

BLOW, KURTIS

1980   Breaks, The

BLOW, KURTIS AND BOB DYLAN

1986   Street Rock

BLUE, DAVID

1968   These 23 Days in September

BLUE ANGEL

1980   Maybe He'll Know

BLUE MAGIC

1974   Sideshow

BLUE OYSTER CULT

1972   Cities on Flame with Rock and
        Roll
1972   She's as Beautiful as a Foot
1976   (Don't Fear) Reaper, The
1977   Godzilla
1979   In Thee
1981   Burnin' for You
1981   Joan Crawford

BLUE ZONE U.K.

1988   Jackie

BLUES IMAGE

1970   Ride Captain Ride

BLUES MAGOOS, THE

1966   We Ain't Got Nothing Yet

BLUES PROJECT, THE

1966   Violets of Dawn
1967   No Time Like the Right Time
1967   Wake Me, Shake Me

BLUES TRAVELER

1991   But Anyway
1994   Hook
1994   Run Around

BLUR

1994   Girls and Boys
1997   Song 2

BOB AND EARL

1964   Harlem Shuffle

BOBBETTES, THE

1957   Mr. Lee

BODEANS, THE

1987   Forever Young (The Wild Ones)

BODY COUNT

1992   Cop Killer

BOLTON, MICHAEL

1990   How Can We Be Lovers
1991   Love Is a Wonderful Thing

BON JOVI

1984   Runaway
1986   You Give Love a Bad Name
1987   Livin' on a Prayer
1987   Wanted Dead or Alive
1988   Bad Medicine
1989   Born to Be My Baby
1989   I'll Be There for You
1992   Bed of Roses
1994   Always

BON JOVI, JON

1990   Blaze of Glory

BOND, JOHNNY

1955   Hot Rod Lincoln

BONDS, GARY U.S.

1961   Dear Lady Twist
1961   Quarter to Three
1961   School Is Out
1981   This Little Girl
1982   Out of Work

BONE THUGS-N-HARMONY

1996   Crossroads, Tha
1997   Look into My Eyes

BONHAM, TRACY

1996   Mother, Mother

BONOFF, KARLA

1977   I Can't Hold On
1977   If He's Ever Near

BONZO DOG DOO DAH BAND

1968   I'm the Urban Spaceman

BOOGIE BOYS, THE

1985   Fly Girl, A

BOOGIE DOWN PRODUCTIONS

1988   Stop the Violence

BOOKER T. & THE MG'S

1962   Green Onions
1968   Hang Em High
1969   Time Is Tight

BOOMTOWN RATS, THE

1979   I Don't Like Mondays

BOONE, PAT

1956   Don't Forbid Me
1961   Moody River

BOOTSY'S RUBBER BAND

(See Parliament, Funkadelic)
1978   Bootzilla

BOSTON

1976   Long Time
1976   More Than a Feeling
1978   Don't Look Back
1986   Amanda
1986   We're Ready

BOW WOW WOW

1980   Louis Quatorze

BOWIE, DAVID

1968   Space Oddity
1970   Man Who Sold the World, The
1971   Changes
1972   Five Years
1972   Jean Genie
1972   Suffragette City
1972   Ziggy Stardust
1973   Aladdin Sane
1973   Panic in Detroit
1974   Rebel Rebel
1975   Fame
1975   Young Americans
1976   Golden Years
1976   TVC 15
1977   Heroes
1980   Ashes to Ashes
1980   Fashion

1983   Let's Dance
1983   Modern Love
1984   Blue Jean
1986   Absolute Beginners
1987   Day In—Day Out

BOX TOPS, THE

1967   Break My Mind
1967   Letter, The
1967   Neon Rainbow
1968   Cry Like a Baby
1968   I Met Her in Church
1969   Soul Deep

BOY MEETS GIRL

1988   Waiting for a Star to Fall

BOYCE & HART

1967   I Wonder What She's Doing Tonight?

BOYD, EDDIE

1952   Five Long Years

BOYS, THE

1988   Dial My Heart
1990   Crazy

BOYZ II MEN

1991   It's So Hard to Say Goodbye to Yesterday
1991   Motownphilly
1992   End of the Road, The
1994   I'll Make Love to You
1994   On Bended Knee
1997   Four Seasons of Loneliness

BRADLEY, JAN

1963   Mama Didn't Lie

BRAGG, BILLY

1983   New England, A
1991   Sexuality

BRAGG, BILLY AND WILCO

1998   Way over Yonder in the Minor Key

BRAINS, THE

1980   Money Changes Everything

BRANDY

1994   I Wanna Be Down
1996   Sittin' up in My Room

BRANDY AND MONICA

1998   Boy Is Mine, The

BRANIGAN, LAURA

1982   Gloria
1984   Self Control

BRAXTON, TONI

1993   Breathe Again
1996   You're Making Me High

BREAD

1970   Make It with You
1971   Baby I'm-a-Want You
1971   If
1972   Everything I Own

BREAKFAST CLUB, THE

1987   Right on Track

BREATHE

1986   Don't Tell Me Lies
1988   Hands to Heaven
1988   How Can I Fall

BREEDERS, THE

1990   Opened
1993   Cannonball
1993   Saints

BRENSTON, JACKIE & HIS DELTA CATS

1951   Rocket 88

BREWER AND SHIPLEY

1971   One Toke over the Line

BRICK

1977   Dazz

BRICKEL, EDIE & NEW BOHEMIANS

1988   What I Am

BRIDGES, ALICIA

1977   I Love the Nightlife (Disco Round)

BRIGGS, LILLIAN

1956   I Want You to Be My Baby

BRIGHT EYES

(See Commander Venus)
1998   If Winter Ends
2000   Perfect Sonnet, A

BRINZLEY SCHWARZ

1974   (What's So Funny 'Bout) Peace, Love and Understanding

BRISTOL, JOHNNY

1974   Hang on in There Baby

BRONSKI BEAT

1985   Small Town Boy

BROOKS, HADDA

1945   Swingin' the Boogie

BROOKS, MEREDITH

1997   Bitch

BROTHER CANE

1995   And Fools Shine On
1998   I Lie in the Bed I Make

BROTHERS FOUR, THE

1960   Greenfields

BROTHERS JOHNSON, THE

1976   I'll Be Good to You
1979   Stomp

BROWN, ARTHUR (THE CRAZY WORLD OF)

1968   Fire!

BROWN, BOBBY

1986   Girlfriend
1988   Don't Be Cruel
1988   My Prerogative
1988   Rock Wit'cha
1989   Every Little Step
1989   On Our Own (From Ghostbusters II)
1989   Roni
1992   Good Enough
1992   Humpin' Around

BROWN, BUSTER

1960   Fannie Mae

BROWN, CHARLES

1947   Gloria
1949   Trouble Blues
1951   Black Night

BROWN, JAMES

1969   Give It up or Turnit a Loose
1969   Mother Popcorn (You Got to Have a Mother for Me) (Part 1)
1969   Popcorn, The
1970   Sex Machine (Get up I Feel Like Being a Sex Machine)
1970   Super Bad
1971   Hot Pants (She Got to Use What She Got to Get What She Wants)
1971   Make It Funky (Part 1)

1972   Get on the Good Foot, Part 1
1972   Talking Loud & Sayin' Nothing, Part II
1973   Payback, The
1974   My Thang
1974   Papa Don't Take No Mess
1986   Living in America

BROWN, JAMES AND THE FAMOUS FLAMES

1956   Please, Please, Please
1958   Lost Someone
1958   Try Me
1963   Prisoner of Love
1965   I Got You (I Feel Good)
1965   Papa's Got a Brand New Bag
1966   Don't Be a Drop-Out
1966   It's a Man's, Man's, Man's World (but....)
1967   Cold Sweat
1968   I Got the Feelin'
1968   Say It Loud—I'm Black and I'm Proud

BROWN, JULIE

1987   Homecoming Queen's Got a Gun, The

BROWN, MAXINE

1964   Oh! No Not My Baby

BROWN, PETER AND BETTY WRIGHT

1977   Dance with Me

BROWN, ROY

1947   Good Rockin' Tonight
1949   Rockin' at Midnight
1957   Let the Four Winds Blow

BROWN, RUTH

1950   Teardrops from My Eyes
1952   5-10-15 Hours
1953   Mama (He Treats Your Daughter Mean)
1954   Mambo Baby
1954   Oh What a Dream
1955   Wild, Wild Young Men
1957   Lucky Lips
1958   This Little Girl's Gone Rockin'

BROWN, SHIRLEY

1974   Woman to Woman

BROWNE, JACKSON

1972   Doctor My Eyes
1972   My Opening Farewell
1972   Rock Me on the Water
1972   Song for Adam
1973   For Everyman
1973   Ready or Not
1973   Redneck Friend

1974   Before the Deluge
1974   For a Dancer
1974   Fountain of Sorrow
1976   Here Come Those Tears Again
1977   Load Out, The
1977   Pretender, The
1977   Running on Empty
1983   Lawyers in Love
1986   Lives in the Balance

BROWNE, TOM

1980   Funkin' for Jamaica

BROWNS, THE

1959   Three Bells

BROWNSVILLE STATION

1973   Smokin' in the Boys Room

BUCHANON, ROY

1972   Messiah Will Come Again, The

BUCKCHERRY

1999   Lit Up

BUCKINGHAMS, THE

1966   Kind of a Drag, The

BUCKLEY, JEFF

1994   Grace
1994   Last Goodbye

BUCKLEY, TIM

1967   Goodbye and Hello
1967   Once I Was
1968   Valentine Melody
1969   Buzzin' Fly
1969   Strange Feeling

BUFFALO SPRINGFIELD

1967   Bluebird
1967   Broken Arrow
1967   Expecting to Fly
1967   For What It's Worth
1967   Mr. Soul
1967   Nowadays Clancy Can't Even Sing
1967   Rock and Roll Woman
1968   Four Days Gone
1968   I Am a Child
1968   Kind Woman
1968   On the Way Home

BUFFALO TOM

1994   I'm Allowed

BUFFETT, JIMMY

1974   Come Monday
1975   Pirate Looks at Forty

| 1977 | Margaritaville |
| 1978 | Cheeseburger in Paradise |

BUGGLES, THE

| 1979 | Video Killed the Radio Star |

BULLENS, CINDY

| 1999 | Better Than I've Ever Been |

BUOYS, THE

| 1971 | Timothy |

BURKE, SOLOMON

1961	Cry to Me
1961	Just out of Reach (Of My Two Open Arms)
1964	Everybody Needs Somebody to Love
1965	Got to Get You off My Mind
1965	Tonight's the Night
1967	Take Me (Just as I Am)
(The Soul Clan)	
1968	Soul Meeting

BURNETTE, JOHNNY

| 1960 | Dreamin' |
| 1960 | You're Sixteen, You're Beautiful and You're Mine |

BURNETTE, JOHNNY AND THE ROCK 'N' ROLL TRIO

1956	Rockabilly Boogie
1956	Tear It Up
1956	Train Kept a-Rollin'
1956	Rock Therapy

BURNETTE, ROCKY

| 1980 | Tired of Toein' the Line |

BURNETTE, T-BONE

| 1983 | Baby Fall Down |

BUSH

| 1993 | Everything Zen |
| 1999 | Chemicals between Us, The |

BUSH TETRAS

| 1981 | Too Many Creeps |

BUSH, KATE

1978	Man with the Child in His Eyes, The
1978	Them Heavy People
1978	Wuthering Heights
1980	Babooshka
1980	Breathing
1980	Oh England My Lionheart
1980	Wow
1982	Dreaming
1982	Sat in Your Lap
1982	Suspended in Gaffa
1985	Big Sky
1985	Cloudbusting
1985	Running up That Hill
1989	Love and Anger
1989	This Woman's Work
1993	Red Shoes, The
1993	Rubberband Girl

BUTLER, JERRY

1960	He Will Break Your Heart
1961	Moon River
1962	Make It Easy on Yourself
1967	Mr. Dream Merchant
1968	Hey, Mr. Western Union Man
1969	Only the Strong Survive

BUTLER, JERRY & THE IMPRESSIONS

| 1958 | For Your Precious Love |

BUTTERFIELD BLUES BAND, THE PAUL

1965	Born in Chicago
1965	Shake Your Money Maker
1966	East West

BUTTERFIELD'S BETTER DAYS, PAUL

| 1973 | Small Town Talk |

BUTTHOLE SURFERS

1983	Shah Sleeps in Lee Harvey Oswald's Grave, The
1993	Who Was in My Room Last Night
1996	Pepper

BUZZCOCKS, THE

1977	Orgasm Addict
1978	Breakdown
1978	Ever Fallen in Love (With Someone You Shouldn't Have Fallen in Love With)
1979	Everybody's Happy Nowadays
1979	I Believe
1979	You Say You Don't Love Me

BYRD, DONALD

| 1963 | Christo Redemptor |

BYRDS, THE

1965	Bells of Rhymney
1965	I'll Feel a Whole Lot Better
1965	It Won't Be Wrong
1965	Set You Free This Time
1966	Eight Miles High
1966	Five "D" (Fifth Dimension)
1966	Have You Seen Her Face
1966	Mr. Spaceman
1967	Everybody's Been Burned
1967	So You Wanna Be a Rock and Roll Star
1967	Triad
1968	Hickory Wind
1968	I Wasn't Born to Follow
1968	Lady Friend
1968	Nothing Was Delivered
1968	You Ain't Goin' Nowhere
1969	Ballad of Easy Rider
1969	Drug Store Truck Drivin' Man
1969	You Showed Me
1970	Chestnut Mare
1970	Jesus Is Just Alright

BYRNE, DAVID AND CELIA CRUZ

| 1986 | Loco de Amor (Crazy for Love) |

BYRNE, JERRY

| 1958 | Lights Out |

BYRNES, EDWARD AND CONNIE STEVENS

| 1959 | Kookie, Kookie (Lend Me Your Comb) |

C

C COMPANY FEATURING TERRY NELSON

| 1971 | Battle Hymn of Lieutenant Calley |

C&C MUSIC FACTORY

| 1991 | Gonna Make You Sweat |
| 1991 | Here We Go |

C&C MUSIC FACTORY FEATURING FREEDOM WILLIAMS

| 1991 | Things That Make You Go Hmmmm |

CADELL, MERYN

| 1992 | Sweater, The |

CADETS, THE

| 1956 | Stranded in the Jungle |

CADILLACS, THE

| 1954 | Gloria |
| 1955 | Speedoo |

CAFFERTY, JOHN AND THE BEAVER BROWN BAND

| 1984 | On the Dark Side |

CAKE

1996   Distance, The
1998   Never There

CALDWELL, BOBBY

1978   What You Won't Do for Love

CALE, J.J.

1972   Call Me the Breeze
1972   Crazy Mama
1976   Cocaine

CALE, JOHN

(See Velvet Underground)
1974   Fear Is a Man's Best Friend

CALLIER, TERRY

1972   Ordinary Joe
1972   Trance on Sedgewick Street

CALLOWAY

1990   I Wanna Be Rich

CAMEO

1985   Single Life, The
1986   Word Up

CAMPBELL, GLEN

1967   By the Time I Get to Phoenix
1968   Wichita Lineman
1969   Galveston

CAMPBELL, JO ANN

1957   Come on, Baby
1957   Mama, Can I Go out Tonight
1960   Kookie Little Paradise
1963   Mother, Please

CAMPBELL, TEVIN

1993   Can We Talk

CAMPER VAN BEETHOVEN

1985   Bad Trip
1985   Take the Skinheads Bowling
1986   History of Utah
1986   Joe Stalin's Cadillac
1988   Eye of Fatima (Parts 1 and 2)
1989   All Her Favorite Fruit
1989   Borderline
1989   When I Win the Lottery

CANDLEBOX

1993   Far Behind

CANDYMAN

1990   Knockin' Boots

CANNED HEAT

1968   Going up the Country
1968   On the Road Again

CANNON, ACE

1961   Tuff

CANNON, FREDDY

1959   Way down Yonder in New Orleans
1960   Tallahassee Lassie
1962   Palisades Park

CAPITOLS, THE

1966   Cool Jerk

CAPRIS, THE

1961   There's a Moon out Tonight

CAPTAIN & TENNILLE, THE

1975   Love Will Keep Us Together
1975   I Write the Songs

CAPTAIN BEEFHEART

1966   Yellow Brick Road
1969   Well
1969   Wild Life
1972   Big Eyed Beans from Venus
1982   Ice Cream for Crow

CARA, IRENE

1980   Fame
1983   Flashdance…What a Feeling

CARDINALS, THE

1955   Door Is Still Open to My Heart, The

CAREY, MARIAH

1990   Love Takes Time
1990   Vision of Love
1991   Emotions
1993   Hero
1995   Always Be My Baby
1995   Fantasy
1999   Thank God I Found You

CAREY, MARIAH AND BOYZ II MEN

1995   One Sweet Day

CAREY, TONY

1984   Fine Fine Day, A

CARLISLE, BELINDA

1986   Mad about You
1987   Heaven Is a Place on Earth
1988   I Get Weak

CARLTON, CARL

1981   She's a Bad Mama Jama

CARMEN, ERIC

(See the Raspberries)
1975   All By Myself
1987   Hungry Eyes
1988   Make Me Lose Control

CARPENTERS

1970   We've Only Just Begun
1971   For All We Know
1971   Rainy Days and Mondays
1971   Superstar
1973   Top of the World

CARR, JAMES

1967   Dark End of the Street, The

CARRADINE, KEITH

1975   I'm Easy

CARROLL BAND, JIM

1980   People Who Died

CARS, THE

1978   Good Times Roll
1978   Just What I Needed
1978   My Best Friend's Girl
1978   You're All I've Got Tonight
1979   Let's Go
1982   Shake It Up
1982   Since You're Gone
1984   Drive
1984   You Might Think
1985   Tonight She Comes

CARTER, CLARENCE

1967   Slip Away
1969   Snatching It Back
1969   Too Weak to Fight

CASCADES, THE

1963   Rhythm of the Rain, The

CASH, JOHNNY

1956   Folsom Prison Blues
1956   Get Rhythm
1956   I Walk the Line
1958   Ballad of a Teenage Queen
1958   Guess Things Happen That Way
1958   Hey Porter
1959   Five Feet High and Rising
1961   Tennessee Flat-Top Box
1963   Busted

1963   Ring of Fire
1964   Ballad of Ira Hayes
1964   Understand Your Man
1969   Wanted Man

CASH, ROSANNE

1981   Seven Year Ache

CASHMAN AND WEST

1972   American City Suite

CASINOS, THE

1967   Then You Can Tell Me Goodbye

CASS, MAMA

(See The Mamas & Papas)
1970   New World Coming

CASSIDY, SHAUN

1977   That's Rock N Roll
1978   Hey Deannie

CASTAWAYS, THE

1965   Liar, Liar

CAST OF

Hair
1967   Frank Mills *(Shelly Plympton)*
1969   Aquarius/Let the Sun Shine In
1969   Easy to Be Hard
1969   Good Morning Starshine
1969   Hair
Salvation
1970   If You Let Me Make Love to You
          (Why Can't I Touch You) *(Ronnie
          Dyson)*
Godspell
1971   Day by Day
Don't Play Us Cheap
1971   Tenth and Greenwich *(Beatrice Winde)*
Grease
1972   Beauty School Dropout *(Alan Paul)*
1972   Summer Nights *(Carole Demas and Barry
          Bostwick)*
Lemmings
1973   Lonely at the Bottom *(John Belushi)*
Lemmings
1973   Colorado *(Chevy Chase)*
Lemmings
1973   Highway Toes *(Christopher Guess)*
Rocky Horror Picture Show
1974   Hot Patootie—Bless My Soul *(Meat Loaf)*
Rocky Horror Picture Show
1974   Science Fiction Double Feature
1974   Time Warp
1974   Touch-a-Touch-a-Touch Me *(Susan
          Sarandon)*
Dreamgirls
1982   And I'm Telling You I'm Not Going
          (Jennifer Holliday)

Jesus Christ Superstar
1970   Jesus Christ Superstar *(Murray Head)*
1971   Everything's Alright *(Yvonne Elliman)*
1971   I Don't Know How to Love Him
          (Yvonne Elliman)
Little Shop of Horrors
1982   Suddenly Seymour *(Ellen Greene and
          Lee Wilkoff)*
Tommy
1993   I Believe My Own Eyes *(Marcia
          Mitzman and Jonathan Dokuchitz)*
Rent
1997   One Song Glory *(Norbert Leo Butz)*
1997   Seasons of Love
Hedwig & The Angry Inch
1998   Origin of Love

CASTRO, BERNADETTE

1964   His Lips Got in the Way

CASTRO, VINCE

1958   Bong Bong I Love You Madly

CAT MOTHER & THE ALL NIGHT NEWSBOYS

1969   Good Old Rock and Roll

CATHY JEAN AND THE ROOMMATES

1961   Please Love Me Forever

CETERA, PETER

(See Chicago)
1986   Glory of Love (Theme from *The Karate
          Kid)*
1988   One Good Woman

CETERA, PETER AND AMY GRANT

1986   Next Time I Fall

CHAD AND JEREMY

1966   Summer Song, A

CHAIRMEN OF THE BOARD, THE

1970   Give Me Just a Little More Time
1970   Patches (I'm Depending on You)

CHAMBERS, KASEY

2000   Cry Like a Baby

CHAMBERS BROTHERS, THE

1967   Time Has Come Today

CHAMPS, THE

1958   Tequila
1962   Limbo Rock

CHANCE, JAMES

1979   Contort Yourself

CHANDLER, GENE

1961   Duke of Earl

CHANGIN' TIMES

1965   Pied Piper, The

CHANGING FACES

1994   Stroke You Up

CHANNEL, BRUCE

1962   Hey! Baby

CHANNELS, THE

1956   Closer You Are, The

CHANTAYS, THE

1963   Pipeline

CHANTELS, THE

1957   He's Gone
1957   If You Try
1957   Plea, The
1958   I Love You So
1958   Maybe
1961   Look in My Eyes

CHAPIN, HARRY

1972   Taxi
1974   Cat's in the Cradle

CHAPMAN, TRACY

1988   Behind the Wall
1988   Fast Car
1988   Mountains o' Things
1995   Give Me One Reason

CHARLATANS U.K., THE

1992   Weirdo

CHARLES, BOBBY

1955   See You Later, Alligator

CHARLES, JIMMY

1960   Million to One, A

CHARLES, RAY

1952 Roll with Me Baby
1952 Sinner's Prayer
1954 Come Back Baby
1954 Don't You Know
1954 It Should Have Been Me
1954 Losing Hand
1955 Fool for You, A
1955 I Got a Woman (I Got a Sweetie)
1955 This Little Girl of Mine
1956 Drown in My Tears
1956 Hallelujah, I Love Her So
1956 Lonely Avenue
1958 (Night Time Is the) Right Time, The
1958 Sweet Sixteen Bars
1959 What'd I Say
1960 Georgia on My Mind
1960 Unchain My Heart
1961 Hit the Road, Jack
1962 You Don't Know Me
1966 I Don't Need No Doctor
1966 Let's Go Get Stoned

CHARLES, SONNY & THE CHECKMATES

1969 Black Pearl

CHARMS, THE

1954 Hearts of Stone

CHARTS, THE

1957 Deserie

CHEAP TRICK

1976 Surrender
1977 I Want You to Want Me
1988 Flame, The

CHECKER, CHUBBY

1961 Let's Twist Again

CHECKER, CHUBBY AND DEE DEE SHARPE

1962 Slow Twistin'

CHEERS, THE

1955 Black Denim Trousers and Motorcycle Boots

CHEMICAL BROTHERS, THE

1997 Block Rockin' Beats
1997 Setting Sun

CHER

(See Sonny & Cher)
1966 Bang Bang (My Baby Shot Me Down)
1967 You Better Sit down Kids

1971 Gypsies, Tramps and Thieves
1973 Half-Breed
1974 Dark Lady
1989 If I Could Turn Back Time
1989 Just Like Jesse James
1999 Believe

CHERRELLE

1984 I Didn't Mean to Turn You On
1988 Everything I Miss at Home

CHERRY, EAGLE EYE

1998 Save Tonight

CHERRY, NENEH

1989 Buffalo Stance

CHESNUTT, VIC

1990 Isadora Duncan
1991 Guilty by Association
1995 Gravity of the Situation
1996 Myrtle

CHIC

1977 Dance, Dance, Dance (Yowsah, Yowsah, Yowsah)
1978 Le Freak
1979 Good Times

CHICAGO

1969 Beginnings
1970 Make Me Smile
1970 25 or 6 to 4
1972 Saturday in the Park
1973 Just You 'n' Me
1975 Old Days
1976 If You Leave Me Now
1977 Baby, What a Big Surprise
1982 Hard to Say I'm Sorry
1984 Hard Habit to Break
1985 You're the Inspiration
1987 Will You Still Love Me?
1988 I Don't Wanna Live without Your Love
1988 Look Away
1989 What Kind of Man Would I Be

CHIFFONS, THE

1963 He's So Fine
1963 One Fine Day

CHILD, JANE

1990 Don't Wanna Fall in Love

CHI-LITES, THE

1971 (For God's Sake) Give More Power to the People
1971 Have You Seen Her
1972 Oh Girl

CHILLS, THE

1990 Efflouresce and Deliquesce

CHILTON, ALEX

(See The Box Tops, Big Star)
1985 Thank You John

CHIPS, THE

1956 Rubber Biscuit

CHOCOLATE WATCHBAND

1966 Let's Talk about Girls

CHORDS, THE

1954 Sh-Boom (Life Could Be a Dream)

CHRISTIAN, CHARLIE

1944 Solo Flight

CHRISTIAN, FRANK

1988 Three Flights Up

CHRISTIANS, THE

1988 Ideal World

CHRISTIE, LOU

1963 Two Faces Have I
1966 Lightnin' Strikes

CHUMBAWAMBA

1997 Tubthumping

CHURCH, EUGENE

1959 Pretty Girls Everywhere

CHURCH, THE

1988 Reptile
1988 Under the Milky Way

CIRCLE JERKS, THE

1980 Group Sex

CIRCUS MAXIMUS

1967 Wind

CITY, THE

1968 Snow Queen
1968 That Old Sweet Roll

CLANTON, JIMMY

1958 Just a Dream
1959 Go Jimmy Go

1959   Ship on a Stormy Sea
1961   Venus in Blue Jeans

CLAPTON, ERIC

(See Cream, Derek & the Dominoes, The Yardbirds)

1970   After Midnight
1970   Let It Rain
1977   Lay Down Sally
1977   Wonderful Tonight
1978   Promises
1978   Tulsa Time
1980   Blues Power
1981   I Can't Stand It
1983   I've Got a Rock and Roll Heart
1985   Forever Man
1986   It's in the Way You Use It
1989   Bad Love
1991   Tears in Heaven
1992   It's Probably Me
1996   Change the World

CLARK, CLAUDINE

1962   Party Lights

CLARK, DAVE FIVE

1964   Because
1964   Bits and Pieces
1964   Can't You See That She's Mine
1964   Glad All Over
1965   Catch Us if You Can

CLARK, DEE

1961   Raindrops

CLARK, PETULA

1964   Downtown
1965   I Know a Place

CLARK, SANFORD

1977   Fool, The

CLARK SISTERS, THE

1983   You Brought the Sunshine

CLARKE, JOHN COOPER

1980   Beasley Street

CLASH, THE

1977   Clash City Rockers
1977   Complete Control
1977   I'm So Bored with the USA
1977   London's Burning
1977   1977
1977   White Man in Hammersmith Palais
1977   White Riot
1978   Julie's in the Drug Squad
1978   Safe European Home
1978   Stay Free

1978   Tommy Gun
1979   Death or Glory
1979   Lost in the Supermarket
1979   London Calling
1979   Train in Vain (Stand by Me)
1979   Wrong 'Em Boyo
1980   Bank Robber
1982   Rock the Casbah
1982   Should I Stay or Should I Go

CLASSICS IV, THE

1968   Spooky
1968   Stormy
1969   Traces

CLAY, OTIS

1972   Trying to Live My Life without You

CLEFTONES, THE

1956   Can't We Be Sweethearts
1956   Little Girl of Mine
1961   Heart and Soul

CLIFF, JIMMY

1970   Many Rivers to Cross
1970   Viet Nam
1970   Wonderful World, Beautiful People
1972   Harder They Come, The
1972   Sitting in Limbo

CLIMAX

1972   Precious and Few
1981   I Love You

CLIMAX BLUES BAND

1977   Couldn't Get It Right

CLINE, PATSY

1956   Walking after Midnight
1961   Crazy
1961   I Fall to Pieces
1962   She's Got You

CLINTON, GEORGE

(See Parliament, Funkadelic)

1983   Atomic Dog
1986   Do Fries Go with That Shake

CLIQUE, THE

1968   Superman

CLOVERS, THE

1951   Don't You Know I Love You
1951   Fool, Fool, Fool
1952   One Mint Julep
1952   Ting-a-Ling
1953   Good Lovin'

1954   Your Cash Ain't Nothin' But Trash
1955   Blue Velvet
1955   Devil or Angel
1955   Lovey Dovey
1956   Love, Love, Love
1959   Love Potion Number Nine

COASTERS, THE

1956   Down in Mexico
1956   One Kiss Led to Another
1957   Searchin'
1957   (When She Wants Good Lovin)
         My Baby Comes to Me
1957   Young Blood
1958   Yakety Yak
1959   Along Came Jones
1959   Charlie Brown
1959   Poison Ivy
1959   That Is Rock and Roll
1959   What about Us
1961   Little Egypt
1960   Shopping for Clothes

COCHRAN, EDDIE

1956   Pink Pegged Slacks
1956   Twenty Flight Rock
1957   Drive-In Show
1957   Sittin' in the Balcony
1958   C'mon Everybody
1958   Cut Across Shorty
1958   Summertime Blues
1959   Somethin' Else
1959   Teenage Heaven
1959   Three Stars
1960   Three Steps to Heaven
1961   Nervous Breakdown

COCHRAN, WAYNE

1961   Last Kiss

COCHRANE, TOM

1992   Life Is a Highway

COCK ROBIN

1985   When Your Heart Is Weak

COCKBURN, BRUCE

1979   Wondering Where the Lions Are

COCKER, JOE

1969   Delta Lady
1971   High Time We Went
1976   Catfish
1976   Jealous Kind

COCKER, JOE AND JENNIFER WARNES

1982   Up Where We Belong

COCTEAU TWINS

1990   Cherry-Coloured Funk

COHEN, LEONARD

1968   Hey, That's No Way to Say
        Goodbye
1968   So Long, Marianne
1968   Stranger Song
1968   Winter Lady
1969   Seems So Long Ago, Nancy
1971   Famous Blue Raincoat
1974   Chelsea Hotel #2
1974   Take This Longing
1977   Don't Go Home with Your Hard On
1979   Humbled in Love
1985   Hallelujah
1988   Everybody Knows
1988   I'm Your Man
1988   Tower of Song
1992   Closing Time

COHN, MARC

1991   Walking in Memphis

COLDPLAY

2000   Yellow

COLE, COZY

1958   Topsy, Part II

COLE TRIO, NAT

1944   Gee Baby, Ain't I Good to You
1944   Straighten up and Fly Right

COLE, NAT KING

1946   (Get Your Kicks) On Route 66
1947   (I Love You) For Sentimental Reasons
1948   Nature Boy
1950   Mona Lisa

COLE, NATALIE

1975   This Will Be (an Everlasting Love)
1976   I Got Love on My Mind
1989   Miss You Like Crazy

COLE, PAULA

1997   I Don't Want to Wait

COLLECTIVE SOUL

1994   Shine
1995   Where the River Flows
1995   World I Know, The
1997   Listen
1997   Precious Declaration

COLLEGE BOYZ, THE

1992   Victim of the Ghetto

COLLINS, JUDY

1965   Carry It On
1965   Early Morning Rain
1965   Rambling Boy
1965   Thirsty Boots
1966   Dress Rehearsal Rag
1966   I Think It's Gonna Rain Today
1966   Suzanne
1968   Bird on the Wire
1968   Both Sides Now
1968   My Father
1968   Sisters of Mercy
1975   Moon Is a Harsh Mistress, The

COLLINS, PHIL

(See Genesis)
1981   In the Air Tonight
1982   I Don't Care Anymore
1984   Against All Odds (Take a Look at Me
        Now)
1985   Don't Lose My Number
1985   One More Night
1985   Sussudio
1988   Two Hearts
1989   Another Day in Paradise
1989   I Wish It Would Rain Down
1989   Something Happened on the Way to
        Heaven
1990   Do You Remember

COLLINS, PHIL AND MARILYN MICHAELS

1985   Separate Lives (Love Theme from
        White Nights)

COLOR ME BADD

1991   All 4 Love
1991   I Adore Mi Amor
1991   I Wanna Sex You Up

COLVIN, SHAWN

1997   Sunny Came Home

COMMANDER VENUS

1997   Jean's TV

COMMODORES

1974   Machine Gun
1975   Slippery When Wet
1975   Sweet Love
1976   Just to Be Close to You
1977   Brick House
1977   Easy
1978   Three Times a Lady
1979   Sail On
1979   Still
1981   Oh No
1985   Nightshift

COMPTON'S MOST WANTED

1991   Growin' up in the Hood

CON FUNK SHUN

1977   Ffun

CONLEY, ARTHUR

1967   Sweet Soul Music

CONTOURS, THE

1962   Do You Love Me?
1965   First I Look at the Purse

COOKE, SAM

1957   I'll Come Running Back to You
1957   Lonely Island
1957   You Send Me
1958   Win Your Love for Me
1959   Only Sixteen
1960   Chain Gang
1960   (What a) Wonderful World
1961   Cupid
1962   Bring It on Home to Me
1962   Having a Party
1962   Twistin' the Night Away
1964   Another Saturday Night
1964   Change Is Gonna Come, A
1964   Good Times
1965   Shake

COOKIES, THE

1962   Chains
1963   Don't Say Nothin' Bad (About My
        Baby)

COOLIO

1995   Gangsta's Paradise
1995   1,2,3,4 (Sumpin' New)
1997   C U When You Get There

COOPER, ALICE

1971   Eighteen
1972   Elected
1972   School's Out
1974   No More Mr. Nice Guy
1975   Only Women (Bleed)
1975   Welcome to My Nightmare
1976   I Never Cry
1977   You and Me
1989   Poison

CORNELIUS BROTHERS AND SISTER ROSE, THE

1971   Treat Her Like a Lady
1972   Too Late to Turn Back Now

CORNERSHOP

1997   Brimful of Asha

CORREIA, AMY

2000   Fallen out of Love

CORSAIRS, THE

1961   Smokey Places

CORTEZ, DAVE "BABY"

1959   Happy Organ

COSTELLO, ELVIS

1977   Alison
1977   (Angels Wanna Wear My) Red Shoes
1977   Less Than Zero
1977   Watching the Detectives
1977   Welcome to the Working Week
1978   Lipstick Vogue
1978   Pump It Up
1978   Radio Radio
1979   Accidents Will Happen
1979   Oliver's Army
1980   Girls Talk
1980   Hoover Factory
1980   (I Don't Want to Go to) Chelsea
1980   New Amsterdam
1980   Talking in the Dark
1982   Boy with a Problem
1982   Kid about It
1982   Long Honeymoon
1983   Every Day I Write the Book
1983   Shipbuilding
1984   Only Flame in Town, The
1984   Peace in Our Time
1986   Home Is Anywhere You Hang Your
        Head
1986   Lovable
1989   Baby Plays Around
1989   Deep Dark Truthful Mirror
1989   God's Comic
1989   Veronica
1991   Other Side of Summer, The
1994   Just about Glad
1994   Thirteen Steps Lead Down
1996   All This Useless Beauty

COSTELLO, ELVIS AND THE BRODSKY QUARTET

1993   I Almost Had a Weakness

COTTON, JOSIE

1981   Johnny Are You Queer

COUNT FIVE, THE

1966   Psychotic Reaction

COUNTING CROWS

1993   Mr. Jones
1993   Round Here
1994   Einstein on the Beach (for an Eggman)
1994   Rain King
1996   Angels of the Silences
1996   Long December, A
1999   Hanginaround

COUNTRY JOE AND THE FISH

1967   I-Feel-Like-I'm-Fixin'-to-Die Rag
1967   Janis
1967   Not So Sweet Martha Lorraine

COVAY, DON

1961   Pony Time
1965   Seesaw

COVERDALE, DAVID AND JIMMY PAGE

1993   Pride and Joy

COWBOY JUNKIES

1988   Misguided Angel

COWSILLS, THE

1967   Rain, the Park and Other Things, The

CRACKER

1991   Teen Angst (What the World
        Needs Now)

CRAMPS, THE

1979   Human Fly
1980   TV Set
1981   Goo Goo Muck

CRANBERRIES, THE

1993   Dreams
1993   Linger
1995   Zombie
1996   Salvation

CRASH TEST DUMMIES

1994   Mmm Mmm Mmm Mmm

CRAY, ROBERT

1983   Bad Influence
1987   Smoking Gun

CRAZY HORSE

1971   Beggar's Day
1971   I Don't Want to Talk about It

CREAM

1967   I Feel Free
1967   I'm So Glad
1967   Strange Brew
1967   Toad
1968   Crossroads
1968   Politician
1968   Sunshine of Your Love
1968   Tales of Brave Ulysses
1968   White Room
1969   Badge

CREED

1997   My Own Prison
1997   What's This Life For
1997   With Arms Wide Open
1999   Higher

CREEDENCE CLEARWATER REVIVAL

1969   Bad Moon Rising
1969   Born on the Bayou
1969   Down on the Corner
1969   Effigy
1969   Fortunate Son
1969   Green River
1969   It Came out of the Sky
1969   Lodi
1969   Proud Mary
1970   Have You Ever Seen the Rain
1970   Long as I Can See the Light
1970   Lookin' out My Back Door
1970   Run through the Jungle
1970   Travelin' Band
1970   Up around the Bend
1970   Who'll Stop the Rain
1971   Sweet Hitch-Hiker
1972   Someday Never Comes

CRENSHAW, MARSHALL

1982   Cynical Girl
1982   Whenever You're on My Mind
1982   You're My Favorite Waste of Time
1985   I'm Sorry (But So Is Brenda Lee)
1985   Little Wild One (No. 5)
1985   Terrifying Love
1989   She Hates to Go Home
1989   Someplace Where Love Can't Find
        Me

CRESCENDOS, THE

1958   Oh Julie

CRESTS, THE

1957   My Juanita
1959   Angels Listened In, The
1959   Six Nights a Week
1959   16 Candles
1960   Step by Step

CRICKETS, THE

1957   I'm Looking for Someone to Love
1957   Maybe Baby
1957   Not Fade Away
1957   Oh Boy

1957	That'll Be the Day
1958	It's So Easy
1958	Think It Over
1958	Well All Right
1959	I Fought the Law
1959	Love's Made a Fool of You
1960	More Than I Can Say
1960	Peggy Sue Got Married

CROCE, JIM

1972	Time in a Bottle
1972	You Don't Mess around with Jim
1973	Bad, Bad Leroy Brown
1973	I Got a Name
1973	I'll Have to Say I Love You in a Song

CROSBY, STILLS & NASH

1969	Marrakesh Express
1969	Suite: Judy Blue Eyes
1969	Wooden Ships
1969	Long Time Gone
1977	Just a Song before I Go
1982	Southern Cross
1982	Wasted on the Way

CROSBY, STILLS, NASH & YOUNG

1970	Carry On
1970	4 + 20
1970	Helpless
1970	Our House
1970	Teach Your Children
1970	Woodstock
1971	Find the Cost of Freedom
1971	Ohio

CROSS, CHRISTOPHER

1979	Ride Like the Wind
1980	Sailing
1981	Arthur's Theme (The Best That You Can Do)

CROW, SHERYL

1994	All I Wanna Do
1994	Leaving Las Vegas
1995	Strong Enough
1996	Everyday Is a Winding Road
1996	If It Makes You Happy
1998	Mississippi

CROWDED HOUSE

1987	Don't Dream It's Over
1987	Something So Strong

CROWS, THE

1954	Gee!

CRUDUP, ARTHUR BIG BOY

1947	That's All Right, Mama
1950	My Baby Left Me

CRUISE, JULEE

1990	Falling

CRYSTAL METHOD

1997	Busy Child

CRYSTALS, THE

1961	There's No Other
1962	He's a Rebel
1962	He's Sure the Boy I Love
1962	Uptown
1963	Da Doo Ron Ron
1963	He Hit Me (And It Felt Like a Kiss)
1963	Then He Kissed Me
1964	All Grown Up

CUCUMBERS, THE

1983	My Boyfriend
1987	My Town

CUFF LINKS, THE

1969	Tracy

CULT, THE

1985	She Sells Sanctuary

CULTURE BEAT

1993	Mr. Vain

CULTURE CLUB

1983	Do You Really Want to Hurt Me
1983	Karma Chameleon
1983	Time (Clock of the Heart)
1984	Miss Me Blind

CUMMINGS, BURTON

(See The Guess Who)

1976	Stand Tall

CURE, THE

1979	Boys Don't Cry
1979	Jumping Someone Else's Train
1979	Killing an Arab
1983	Let's Go to Bed
1985	In Between Days (without You)
1987	Just Like Heaven
1987	Why Can't I Be You
1989	Love Song
1989	Lullabye
1992	Friday I'm in Love

CURRY, TIM

1979	I Do the Rock

CUTTING CREW

1987	(I Just) Died in Your Arms

CYPRESS HILL

1993	I Ain't Goin' out Like That
1993	Insane in the Brain

CYRCLE, THE

1966	Red Rubber Ball

D

D.J. JAZZY JEFF AND THE FRESH PRINCE

1988	I Think I Can Beat Mike Tyson
1988	Nightmare on My Street
1988	Parents Just Don't Understand
1991	Summertime

D.R.S.

1993	Gangsta Lean

DA BRAT

1994	Funkdafied

DALE, DICK

1964	Surfer's Holiday

DALE, DICK AND THE DELTONES

1961	Let's Go Tripping
1961	Miserlou

DALTREY, ROGER

(See The Who)

1973	Giving It All Away
1985	Under a Raging Moon

DAMN YANKEES

1990	High Enough

DAMNED, THE

1976	New Rose
1977	Neat Neat Neat
1979	Love Song

D'ANGELO

1995	Brown Sugar
1995	Lady

DANIELS, CHARLIE BAND

1973	Uneasy Rider
1979	Devil Went down to Georgia
1982	Still in Saigon

DANLEERS, THE

1958	One Summer Night

DANNY AND DUSTY

1985   Song for the Dreamers

DANNY & THE JUNIORS

1957   At the Hop
1957   Sometimes (When I'm
           All Alone)
1958   Rock and Roll Is Here to Stay

DANZIG

1988   Mother

D'ARBY, TERENCE TRENT

1987   Dance Little Sister
1987   Sign Your Name
1987   Wishing Well

DARIN, BOBBY

1958   Queen of the Hop
1958   Splish Splash
1959   Dream Lover
1962   Things
1963   You're the Reason I'm Living

DARREN, JAMES

1963   Goodbye Cruel World

DAVID & DAVID

1986   Welcome to the Boomtown

DAVIS, MAC

1972   Baby Don't Get Hooked on Me

DAVIS, MILES

1959   So What
1970   Miles Runs the Voodoo Down

DAVIS, SKEETER

1963   End of the World, The

DAVIS GROUP, SPENCER

1967   Gimme Some Lovin'
1967   I'm a Man

DAVIS, TYRONE

1968   Can I Change My Mind?
1970   Turn Back the Hands of Time

DAWN

1970   Candida

DAY, BOBBY

1957   Little Bitty Pretty One
1958   Rockin' Robin

DAY, MORRIS

1988   Fishnet

DAYS OF THE NEW

1997   Touch, Peel and Stand
1998   Down Town, The

DAZZ BAND, THE

1982   Let It Whip

DBS, THE

1981   Living a Lie

DE LA SOUL

1989   Me Myself and I

DE VAUGHN, WILLIAM

1974   Be Thankful for What You Got

DEAD BOYS, THE

1977   All This and More
1977   Sonic Reducer
1978   Ain't It Fun

DEAD KENNEDYS, THE

1980   California Uber Alles
1980   Holiday in Cambodia

DEAD MILKMEN

1989   Punk Rock Girl

DEAD OR ALIVE

1985   You Spin Me Round (Like a Record)

DEADEYE DICK

1994   New Age Girl

DEAN, JIMMY

1961   Big Bad John

DEBARGE

1985   Rhythm of the Night
1985   Who's Holding Donna Now

DEBARGE, EL

1986   Who's Johnny

DEBURGH, CHRIS

1986   Lady in Red, The

DEE, JOEY & THE STARLITERS

1961   Peppermint Twist

DEE, KIKI

1974   I've Got the Music in Me

DEE, KOOL MOE

1987   Go See the Doctor
1987   Wild Wild West
1989   Knowledge Is King
1989   They Want Money

DEEE-LITE

1990   Groove Is in the Heart

DEELE, THE

1987   Two Occasions

DEEP BLUE SOMETHING

1995   Breakfast at Tiffanys

DEEP FOREST

1994   Sweet Lullabye

DEEP PURPLE

1972   Highway Star
1972   Smoke on the Water
1972   Space Truckin'
1973   Woman from Tokyo
1974   Burn
1985   Knocking at Your Back Door

DEF LEPPARD

1981   Bringin' on the Heartbreak
1983   Foolin'
1983   Photograph
1983   Rock of Ages
1987   Armegeddon It
1987   Hysteria
1987   Love Bites
1988   Pour Some Sugar on Me

DEFRANCO FAMILY, THE

1973   Heartbeat—It's a Lovebeat

DEKKER, DESMOND

1969   Israelites
1970   You Can Get It If You Really Want

DEL AMITRI

1990   Kiss This Thing Goodbye

DEL FUEGOS, THE

1985   Don't Run Wild

DEL LORDS, THE

1988   Cheyenne

DEL VIKINGS, THE

1957   Come Go with Me
1957   Whispering Bells

DELANEY & BONNIE

1970   Free the People
1971   Never Ending Song of Love

DELFONICS, THE

1968   La La La (Means I Love You)
1970   Didn't I (Blow Your Mind
       This Time)

DELLS, THE

1956   Oh What a Night
1965   Stay in My Corner

DEMENT, IRIS

1994   My Life
1994   No Time to Cry

DENNY, SANDY

(See Fairport Convention)
1974   Solo

DENVER, JOHN

1971   Take Me Home, Country Road
1973   Rocky Mountain High
1974   Annie's Song
1974   Back Home Again
1974   Sunshine on My Shoulders
1974   Thank God I'm a Country Boy
1975   I'm Sorry

DEPECHE MODE

1981   Just Can't Get Enough
1981   New Life
1984   People Are People
1985   Master and Servant
1990   Enjoy the Silence
1990   Personal Jesus
1990   Policy of Truth

DEREK & THE DOMINOES

1970   Bell Bottom Blues
1970   Layla
1970   Why Does Love Got to Be
       So Sad

DES'REE

1995   You Gotta Be

DESHANNON, JACKIE

1963   Needles and Pins
1964   When You Walk in the Room
1965   Splendor in the Grass
1965   What the World Needs Now Is
       Love

1969   Put a Little Love in Your Heart
1972   Vanilla Olay
1975   Bette Davis Eyes

DESTINY'S CHILD

1998   No No No, Part 2
1999   Bills, Bills, Bills
1999   Jumpin' Jumpin'
1999   Say My Name
2000   Independent Woman

DEVO

1978   Mongoloid
1980   Whip It
1981   Through Being Cool

DEVONSQUARE

1992   Raining down on Bleecker Street

DEXY'S MIDNIGHT RUNNERS

1983   Come on Eileen

DIABLOS, THE

1954   Wind, The

DIAMOND, NEIL

1966   Cherry, Cherry
1966   Solitary Man
1967   Girl, You'll Be a Woman Soon
1967   Kentucky Woman
1967   Red Red Wine
1969   Sweet Caroline
1970   Cracklin' Rosie
1971   I Am … I Said
1972   Songs Sung Blue
1974   Longfellow Serenade
1981   Love on the Rocks

DIAMOND HEAD

1982   Am I Evil
1982   Helpless
1982   Prince, The

DIAMONDS, THE

1957   Stroll, The

DICK AND DEEDEE

1961   Mountain's High, The

DICKIES, THE

1979   Banana Splits (Tra La Song)

DICTATORS, THE

1975   I Live for Cars and Girls
1975.   Two Tub Man

DIDDLEY, BO

1955   Bo Diddley
1955   Diddley Daddy
1955   Here 'Tis
1955   I'm a Man
1955   Who Do You Love
1956   You Can't Judge a Book by Looking at
       the Cover
1957   Before You Accuse Me
1957   Diddy Wah Diddy
1957   Hey Bo Diddley
1957   Mona
1958   Pretty Thing
1959   Crackin' Up
1959   Say Man

DIDJETS

1990   Killboy Powerhead

DIDO

1999   Thank You

DIFRANCO, ANI

1989   Lost Woman Song
1991   Gratitude
1994   You Had Time
1995   32 Flavors
1998   Swan Dive

DIGABLE PLANETS

1993   Rebirth of Slick (Cool Like Dat)
1993   Where I'm From

DIGITAL UNDERGROUND

1990   Humpty Dance, The

DINNING, MARK

1959   Teen Angel

DINO, KENNY

1961   Your Ma Said You Cried in Your Sleep
       Last Night

DINOSAUR JR.

1987   Freak Scene
1987   You're Living All over Me
1994   Feel the Pain
1994   I Don't Think So

DIO

1983   Rainbow in the Dark
1984   Last in Line, The

DION

1963   Donna the Prima Donna
1960   Lonely Teenager
1961   Runaround Sue
1961   Take Good Care of My Baby
1962   Little Diane

1962   Love Came to Me
1962   Lovers Who Wander
1962   Wanderer, The
1968   Abraham, Martin and John
1970   Your Own Back Yard
1989   King of the New York Streets

DION & THE BELMONTS

1958   I Wonder Why
1958   No One Knows
1959   Teenager in Love, A

DIRE STRAITS

1979   Sultans of Swing
1980   Romeo and Juliet
1980   Tunnel of Love
1985   Brothers in Arms
1985   Money for Nothing
1985   Why Worry

DISCO TEX & THE SEX-O-LETTES

1974   Get Dancin'

DISHWALLA

1995   Counting Blue Cars

DISPOSABLE HEROES OF HIPHOPRISY

1992   Language of Violence

DIVINYLS

1991   I Touch Myself

DIXIE CUPS, THE

1964   Chapel of Love
1965   Iko Iko

DIXIE DREGS, THE

1980   Twiggs Approved

DIXIEBELLES, THE

1963   (Down at) Poppa Joe's

DJ SHADOW

1996   Midnight in a Perfect World

DMX

1998   Get at Me Dog
1999   Party Up (Up in Here)
1999   What's My Name

DOBKINS JR., CARL

1957   My Heart Is an Open Book

DOBSON, BONNIE

1963   Morning Dew

DOGG, SNOOP DOGGY

1993   Gin & Juice
1993   What's My Name
1995   Murder Was the Case
1998   Still a G Thang

DOGGETT, BILL

1956   Honky Tonk

DOG'S EYE VIEW

1996   Everything Falls Apart

DOKKEN

1987   Mr. Scary

DOLBY, THOMAS

1983   She Blinded Me with Science

DOMINO

1993   Getto Jam

DOMINO, FATS

1950   Fat Man
1952   Goin' Home
1953   Goin' to the River
1955   Ain't It a Shame
1956   Blueberry Hill
1956   I'm in Love Again
1957   Blue Monday
1957   I'm Walkin'
1958   Big Beat, The
1958   Whole Lotta Loving, A
1959   Be My Guest
1959   I Want to Walk You Home
1959   I'm Gonna Be a Wheel Someday
1959   I'm Ready
1960   Walking to New Orleans

DOMINOES, THE

1950   Do Something for Me
1951   Sixty Minute Man
1952   Have Mercy Baby

DON AND DEWEY

1957   I'm Leaving It up to You
1958   Justine
1958   Koko Joe
1958   Letter, The
1959   Big Boy Pete
1959   Farmer John

DON AND JUAN

1961   What's Your Name?

DONALDSON, BO & THE HEYWOODS

1974   Billy, Don't Be a Hero

DONALDSON, ERIC

1971   Cherry Oh Baby

DONAYS, THE

1962   Devil in His Heart

DONEGAN, LONNIE

1959   Does Your Chewing Gum Lose
         Its Flavor on the Bedpost
         Overnight

DONNER, RAL

1961   You Don't Know What You've Got
         (Until You Lose It)

DONOVAN

1965   Catch the Wind
1965   Season of the Witch
1965   Sunny Goodge Street
1965   To Sing for You
1966   Mellow Yellow
1966   Sunshine Superman
1966   Turquoise
1967   There Is a Mountain
1967   Wear Your Love Like Heaven
1968   Hurdy Gurdy Man
1969   Atlantis

DOO, DICKEY & THE DON'TS

1959   Teardrops Will Fall

DOOBIE BROTHERS, THE

1972   Listen to the Music
1973   China Grove
1973   Long Train Running
1974   Black Water
1976   Takin' It to the Streets
1977   Echoes of Love
1977   You Belong to Me
1980   Real Love

DOOBIE BROTHERS, THE, JOHN HALL AND JAMES TAYLOR

1979   Power

DOORS, THE

1967   Break on Through
1967   Crystal Ship
1967   End, The
1967   Light My Fire
1967   Love Me Two Times

1967 Moonlight Drive
1967 People Are Strange
1967 20TH Century Fox
1967 When the Music's Over
1968 Five to One
1968 Hello, I Love You
1968 Unknown Soldier
1969 Touch Me
1969 Wishful, Sinful
1970 Roadhouse Blues
1971 L.A. Woman
1971 Love Her Madly
1971 Riders on the Storm

DORSEY, LEE

1961 Ya Ya
1965 Get out of My Life Woman
1965 Ride Your Pony
1965 Working in the Coal Mine

DOUBLE DEE AND STEINSKI

1985 Payoff Mix

DOUGLAS, CARL

1974 Kung Fu Fighting

DOVELLS, THE

1961 Bristol Stomp, The

DOZIER, LAMONT

1974 Trying to Hold on to My Woman

DR. DRE

1992 Dre Day
1993 Let Me Ride
1993 Nuthin' but a "G" Thang

DR. DRE FEATURING EMINEM

1999 Forgot about Dre

DR. BUZZARD'S ORIGINAL SAVANNAH BAND

1976 Whispering/Cherchez La Femme/ C'est Si Bon

DR. HOOK

1972 Sylvia's Mother
1973 Cover of the Rolling Stone
1979 Sexy Eyes

DR. JOHN

1968 I Walk on Gilded Splinters
1973 Right Place Wrong Time

DR. WEST'S MEDICINE SHOW AND JUNK BAND

1966 Egg Plant (That Ate Chicago), The

DRAKE, NICK

1970 Northern Sky
1969 Way to Blue
1970 Hazey Jane II
1972 Pink Moon
1972 Which Will

DRAMARAMA

1994 Work for Food

DRAMATICS, THE

1971 In the Rain

DRAPER, RUSTY

1957 Freight Train

DREAM

2000 He Loves U Not

DREAM ACADEMY, THE

1985 Life in a Northern Town

DREAM SYNDICATE

1982 Days of Wine and Roses

DRIFTERS, THE

1953 Money Honey
1953 Whatcha Gonna Do
1954 Honey Love
1954 Such a Night
1955 Adorable
1956 Ruby Baby
1957 Fools Fall in Love
1958 Drip Drop
1959 Dance with Me
1959 There Goes My Baby
1960 Save the Last Dance for Me
1960 This Magic Moment
1961 I Count the Tears
1961 Some Kind a Wonderful
1961 Sweets for My Sweet
1962 Up on the Roof
1963 On Broadway
1964 Under the Boardwalk

DRU HILL

1996 In My Bed
1996 Never Make a Promise

DU DROPPERS, THE

1954 Boot Em Up

DUBS, THE

1957 Could This Be Magic
1957 Don't Ask Me to Be Lonely

DUCKS DELUXE

1974 Don't Mind Rockin' Tonight

DUDLEY, DAVE

1963 Six Days on the Road

DUKE, PATTY

1964 Don't Just Stand There (What's on Your Mind)

DUPREE, ROBBIE

1980 Hot Rod Hearts

DURAN DURAN

1981 Girls on Film
1983 Hungry Like the Wolf
1983 Is There Something I Should Know
1983 Reflex
1983 Rio
1983 Union of the Snake
1984 Wild Boys
1985 View to a Kill, A
1986 Notorious
1988 I Don't Want Your Love
1993 Ordinary World

DURY, IAN & THE BLOCKHEADS

1977 Sex and Drugs and Rock 'n' Roll
1977 Sweet Gene Vincent
1979 Hit Me with Your Rhythm Stick

DYKE & THE BLAZERS

1967 Funky Broadway (Part 1)

DYLAN, BOB

(See The Traveling Wilburys)
1962 Baby Let Me Follow You Down
1962 Song to Woody
1962 Tomorrow Is a Long Time
1963 Blowing in the Wind
1963 Boots of Spanish Leather
1963 Don't Think Twice It's All Right
1963 Girl from the North Country
1963 Hard Rain's a-Gonna Fall, A
1963 He Was a Friend of Mine
1963 Let Me Die in My Footsteps
1963 Masters of War
1963 Playboys and Playgirls
1963 With God on Our Side
1964 All I Really Want to Do
1964 Chimes of Freedom
1964 I Don't Believe You (She Acts Like We Never Have Met)

1964	It Ain't Me, Babe
1964	Lay down Your Weary Tune
1964	Mama You Been on My Mind
1964	My Back Pages (I'm Younger Than That Now)
1964	One Too Many Mornings
1964	Only a Pawn in Their Game
1964	Paths of Victory
1964	Spanish Harlem Incident
1964	Times They Are A-Changin', The
1964	When the Ship Comes In
1965	Ballad of a Thin Man
1965	Can You Please Crawl out Your Window?
1965	Desolation Row
1965	From a Buick 6
1965	Gates of Eden
1965	Highway 61 Revisited
1965	It Takes a Lot to Laugh, It Takes a Train to Cry
1965	It's All over Now, Baby Blue
1965	It's Alright, Ma (I'm Only Bleeding)
1965	Just Like Tom Thumb's Blues
1965	Like a Rolling Stone
1965	Love Minus Zero/No Limit
1965	Maggie's Farm
1965	Mr. Tambourine Man
1965	Positively 4th Street
1965	Queen Jane Approximately
1965	She Belongs to Me
1965	Subterranean Homesick Blues
1966	I Want You
1966	I'll Keep It with Mine
1966	Just Like a Woman
1966	Leopard-Skin Pill-Box Hat
1966	Most Likely You Go Your Way (and I'll Go Mine)
1966	One of us Must Know (Sooner or Later)
1966	Rainy Day Women #12 & 35
1966	Sad-Eyed Lady of the Lowlands
1966	Stuck inside of Mobile with the Memphis Blues Again
1966	Visions of Johanna
1968	All Along the Watchtower
1968	Dear Landlord
1968	I'll Be Your Baby Tonight
1968	John Wesley Harding
1969	Lay, Lady, Lay
1969	Tonight I'll Be Staying Here with You
1970	Day of the Locusts
1970	If Not for You
1970	New Morning
1970	Sign on the Window
1970	Time Passes Slowly
1970	Went to See the Gypsy
1971	Watching the River Flow
1971	When I Paint My Masterpiece
1972	Down in the Flood
1973	Forever Young
1973	Knockin' on Heaven's Door
1975	Idiot Wind
1975	Million Dollar Bash
1975	Shelter from the Storm
1975	Simple Twist of Fate
1975	Tangled up in Blue
1975	You Angel You
1976	Hurricane (Part I)

1976	Joey
1976	Sara
1978	Baby Stop Crying
1978	Where Are You Tonight
1979	Gotta Serve Somebody
1979	When You Gonna Wake Up
1981	Every Grain of Sand
1981	Groom's Still Waiting at the Altar, The
1981	Lenny Bruce
1983	Don't Fall Apart on Me Tonight
1983	Jokerman
1985	Emotionally Yours
1985	Tight Connection to My Heart (Has Anybody Seen My Love)
1986	Brownsville Girl
1986	Under Your Spell
1988	Silvio
1989	Everything Is Broken
1991	Series of Dreams
1992	What Was It You Wanted
1995	Dignity
1997	Highlands
1997	Not Dark Yet
1997	To Make You Feel My Love
2000	Things Have Changed

E

E.U.

1988	Da Butt

EAGLES

1972	Peaceful Easy Feeling
1972	Take It Easy
1972	Witchy Woman
1973	Desperado
1973	Tequila Sunrise
1974	Already Gone
1974	Best of My Love
1974	James Dean
1975	Lyin' Eyes
1975	One of These Nights
1976	Take It to the Limit
1977	Hotel California
1977	Life in the Fast Lane
1977	New Kid in Town
1979	Heartache Tonight
1979	I Can't Tell You Why

EARLE, STEVE

1986	Guitar Town
1988	Copperhead Road
1996	Telephone Road

EARL-JEAN

1964	I'm into Something Good

EARLS, THE

1962	Remember Then

EARTH OPERA

1969	Redsox Are Winning, The

EARTH, WIND & FIRE

1981	Let's Groove
1975	Reasons
1975	Shining Star
1975	Singasong
1975	That's the Way of the World
1976	Getaway
1977	Serpentine Fire
1979	After the Love Has Gone
1979	September
1979	Boogie Wonderland

EASTON, SHEENA

1981	For Your Eyes Only
1981	Morning Train
1984	Sugar Walls

EASYBEATS, THE

1966	Friday on My Mind

ECHO & THE BUNNYMEN

1980	All That Jazz

ECHOES, THE

1961	Baby Blue

EDDY, DUANE

1958	Movin' 'N Groovin'
1958	Rebel Rouser
1959	Forty Miles of Bad Road
1960	Because They're Young

EDISON LIGHTHOUSE

1970	Love Grows (Where My Rosemary Goes)

EDMUNDS, DAVE

(See Rockpile)

1979	Queen of Hearts
1982	From Small Things (Big Things One Day Come)
1985	High School Nights

EDSELS, THE

1958	Rama Lama Ding Dong (Lama Rama Ding Dong)

EDWARD BEAR

1973	Last Song

EDWARDS, JONATHAN

1972	Sunshine

EDWARDS, TOMMY

1951	It's All in the Game

EELS

1996	Novocaine for the Soul

EGAN, WALTER

1977   Magnet and Steel

808 STATE

1989   Pacific

EL DORADOS, THE

1955   At My Front Door (Crazy Little Mama Song)

ELECTRIC FLAG

1968   Groovin' Is Easy

ELECTRIC LIGHT ORCHESTRA

1974   Can't Get It out of My Head
1975   Evil Woman
1975   Strange Magic
1976   Livin' Thing
1976   Telephone Line
1977   Sweet Talkin' Woman
1979   Don't Bring Me Down
1979   Shine a Little Love
1981   Hold on Tight
1983   Rock 'n' Roll Is King

ELECTRIC LIGHT ORCHESTRA WITH OLIVIA NEWTON JOHN

1980   Xanadu

ELECTRIC PRUNES

1967   I Had Too Much to Dream (Last Night)

ELEGANTS, THE

1958   Little Star

ELLIMAN, YVONNE

1971   Everything's Alright
1971   I Don't Know How to Love Him
1977   If I Can't Have You

ELLIOT, RAMBLING JACK

1957   Pretty Boy Floyd

ELLIOT, MISSY

1997   Rain (Supa Dupa Fly), The
1997   Sock It 2 Me
1999   Hot Boyz

ELLIS, SHIRLEY

1963   Nitty Gritty, The
1964   Name Game, The

ELLISON, LORRAINE

1966   Stay with Me

ELY, JOE

(See The Flatlanders)
1977   If You Were a Bluebird
1978   Boxcars
1978   Honky Tonk Masquerade
1981   Musta Notta Gotta Lotta

EMERSON, LAKE & PALMER

1971   Lucky Man
1972   From the Beginning
1973   Karn Evil 9 (1ST Impression, Part 2)
1973   Still …You Turn Me On

EMF

1991   Unbelievable

EMINEM

1999   My Name Is
2000   Real Slim Shady, The
2000   Stan
2000   Way I Am, The

EMOTIONS, THE

1977   Best of My Love

EN VOGUE

1990   Hold On
1992   Free Your Mind
1992   My Lovin' (You're Never Gonna Get It)
1997   Don't Let Go (Love)

ENGLAND DAN & JOHN FORD COLEY

1975   I'd Really Love to See You Tonight

ENGLISH, SCOTT

1972   Brandy (Mandy)

ENGLISH BEAT

1980   Twist and Crawl
1982   Save It for Later

ENIGMA

1991   Sadeness, Part 1
1994   Return to Innocence

ENO, BRIAN

1974   Cindy Tells Me

ENYA

1988   Orinoco Flow (Sail Away)

EPPS, PRESTON

1959   Bongo Rock

ERASURE

1988   Chains of Love

ERIC B. & RAKIM

1987   Eric B. Is President
1987   Paid in Full

ERICKSON, ROKY & THE ALIENS

1982   Don't Shake Me Lucifer

ESCAPE CLUB, THE

1988   Wild, Wild West

ESSEX, DAVID

1973   Rock On

ESSEX, THE

1963   Easier Said Than Done

ESTUS, DEON

1989   Heaven Help Me

ETERNALS, THE

1959   Babalu's Wedding Day

ETHEL AND THE SHAMELESS HUSSIES

1988   One Nite Stan

ETHERIDGE, MELISSA

1993   Come to My Window
1993   I'm the Only One
1995   Your Little Secret
1996   I Want to Come Over

EUROPE

1986   Final Countdown

EURYTHMICS

1983   Sweet Dreams (Are Made of This)
1984   Here Comes the Rain Again
1985   Would I Lie to You?
1986   Missionary Man

EURYTHMICS WITH ARETHA FRANKLIN

1985   Sisters Are Doin' It for Themselves

EVANS, PAUL

1959 Seven Little Girls (Sitting in the Back Seat)
1960 Happy Go Lucky Me

EVE 6

1998 Inside Out

EVERCLEAR

1996 Santa Monica
1997 Everything to Everyone
1997 Father of Mine
1998 Real World

EVERETT, BETTY

1963 You're No Good
1964 Shoop Shoop Song (It's in His Kiss), The

EVERLAST

1998 What It's Like

EVERLY BROTHERS, THE

1957 Bye Bye Love
1957 I Wonder If I Care as Much
1957 Wake up, Little Susie
1958 All I Have to Do Is Dream
1958 Bird Dog
1958 Devoted to You
1958 Leave My Woman Alone
1958 Problems
1958 Should We Tell Him
1959 Take a Message to Mary
1959 'Til I Kissed You
1960 Love Hurts
1960 Cathy's Clown
1960 Like Strangers
1960 Walk Right Back
1960 When Will I Be Loved
1960 So Sad (To Watch Good Love Go Bad)
1961 Ebony Eyes
1962 Crying in the Rain
1962 Don't Ask Me to Be Friends
1962 How Can I Meet Her?
1962 That's Old Fashioned
1965 Price of Love
1968 Sing Me Back Home
1972 Stories We Could Tell, The
1984 On the Wings of a Nightingale

EVERYTHING BUT THE GIRL

1996 Missing

EVERYTHING IS EVERYTHING

1969 Witchi-Tai-To

EXCELLENTS, THE

1962 Coney Island Baby

EXCITERS, THE

1963 Do Wah Diddy
1963 Tell Him

EXILE

1978 Kiss You All Over

EXPOSÉ

1987 Come Go with Me
1987 Point of No Return
1987 Seasons Change

EXTREME

1990 Hole Hearted
1990 More Than Words
1992 Rest in Peace

F

FABARES, SHELLEY

1962 Johnny Angel

FABIAN

1958 I'm a Man
1959 Tiger

FABRIC, BENT

1962 Alley Cat

FABULOUS THUNDERBIRDS, THE

1986 Tuff Enuff

FACENDA, TOMMY

1959 High School U.S.A.

FACES, THE

1972 Stay with Me
1973 Cindy Incidentally

FAGEN, DONALD

(See Steely Dan)
1982 I.G.Y. (What a Beautiful World)

FAIRPORT CONVENTION

1968 Meet on the Ledge
1969 Crazy Man Michael
1969 Percy's Song
1969 Who Knows Where the Time Goes?
1970 Sloth

FAITH NO MORE

1990 Epic
1992 Midlife Crisis

FAITHFULL, MARIANNE

1964 As Tears Go By
1965 Come and Stay with Me
1965 This Little Bird
1980 Ballad of Lucy Jordan
1980 Broken English
1986 Hawk (El Gavilan)
1987 Hello Stranger
1987 Strange Weather

FALCO

1986 Rock Me Amadeus

FALCONS, THE

1959 You're So Fine
1962 I Found a Love

FALL, THE

1977 Repetition

FAME, GEORGIE

1968 Ballad of Bonnie and Clyde

FAMILY, THE

1985 Nothing Compares 2 U

FAMILY STAND, THE

1990 Ghetto Heaven

FANNY

1971 Charity Ball

FANTASTIC JOHNNY C.

1967 Boogaloo down Broadway

FARDON, DON

1968 (The Lament of the Cherokee) Indian Reservation

FARINA, DICK AND MIMI

1965 Michael, Andrew and James
1965 Pack up Your Sorrows
1965 Reno, Nevada
1965 V
1966 Hard Lovin' Loser
1966 Mainline Prosperity Blues

FARLOWE, CHRIS

1966 Out of Time

FASTBALL

1998 Way, The

FAT BOYS, THE

1985   Jailhouse Rap

FATBACK

1979   King Tim III (Personality Jock)

FATBOY SLIM

1998   Rockafella Skank, The
1999   Praise You

FEAR

1982   Let's Have a War

FEATHERS, CHARLIE

1955   Defrost Your Heart

FEELIES, THE

1988   Away

FENDERMEN, THE

1960   Mule Skinner Blues (Blue Yodel #9)

FERGUSON, JAY

1977   Thunder Island

FERRON

1990   Stand Up

FERRY, BRYAN

(See Roxy Music)
1985   Slave to Love

FEVER TREE

1968   San Francisco Girls (The Return of the Native)

FIESTAS, THE

1959   So Fine

5TH DIMENSION, THE

1967   Up—Up and Away
1967   Worst That Could Happen

FIFTY CENT

2000   How to Rob

FILTER

1995   Hey Man, Nice Shot
1999   Take a Picture

FINE YOUNG CANNIBALS

1989   Don't Look Back
1989   Good Thing
1989   She Drives Me Crazy

FINNEGAN, LARRY

1962   Dear One

FIREFALL

1976   You Are the Woman

fIREHOSE

1986   Things Could Turn Around
1991   Flyin' the Flannel

FIREHOUSE

1991   Love of a Lifetime

FIRETOWN

1987   Heart Country

FIRM, THE

1986   All the King's Horses

FISCHER, MISS TONI

1959   Big Hurt, The

FITZGERALD, ELLA WITH LOUIS JORDAN

1946   Stone Cold Dead in the Market (He Had It Coming)

FIVE AMERICANS, THE

1967   Western Union

FIVE CHINESE BROTHERS

1992   Baltimore

FIVE KEYS, THE

1951   Glory of Love
1954   Ling Ting Tong
1955   Close Your Eyes

FIVE MAN ELECTRICAL BAND

1971   Signs

5 NON BLONDES

1993   What's Up

5 ROYALES, THE

1953   Baby Don't Do It
1953   Help Me Somebody
1957   Tell the Truth
1957   Think
1958   Dedicated to the One I Love

FIVE SATINS, THE

1956   I'll Remember (In the Still of the Night)
1957   To the Aisle

FIVE SCAMPS, THE

1949   Red Hot

FIVE STAIRSTEPS, THE

1970   O-o-h Child

FIXX, THE

1982   Stand or Fall
1983   One Thing Leads to Another

FLACK, ROBERTA AND DONNIE HATHAWAY

1972   Where Is the Love
1974   Feel Like Makin' Love

FLAMIN' GROOVIES

1971   Teenage Head
1972   Slow Death
1976   Shake Some Action

FLAMING LIPS, THE

1987   One Million Billionth of a Millisecond on a Sunday Morning
1995   She Don't Use Jelly

FLAMINGOS, THE

1956   I'll Be Home
1956   Vow, The
1959   I Only Have Eyes for You
1959   Lovers Never Say Goodbye
1970   Buffalo Soldier

FLEETWOOD MAC

1968   Got to Move
1969   Albatross
1969   Black Magic Woman
1969   Love That Burns
1969   Green Manilishi (With the Two-Pronged Crown)
1969   Oh Well—Part 1
1969   Rattlesnake Shake
1972   Sentimental Lady
1975   Landslide
1975   Over My Head
1975   Rhiannon (Will You Ever Win)
1975   Say You Love Me
1977   Chain, The
1977   Don't Stop
1977   Dreams
1977   Go Your Own Way
1977   Silver Springs
1977   You Make Loving Fun
1979   Sara
1979   Tusk

1982   Gypsy
1982   Hold Me
1987   Big Love
1987   Little Lies

FLEETWOODS, THE

1959   Come Softly to Me
1959   Mr. Blue

FLESH FOR LULU

1987   I Go Crazy

FLESHTONES, THE

1979   American Beat

FLETCHER, DUSTY

1946   Open the Door, Richard

FLIPPER

1980   Sex Bomb

FLO AND EDDIE

1971   Marmendy Mill

FLOATERS, THE

1977   Float On

FLOCK OF SEAGULLS, A

1982   I Ran (So Far Away)

FLOYD, EDDIE

1966   Knock on Wood

FLYING BURRITO BROTHERS, THE

1969   Hot Burrito #1
1969   Sin City
1971   Colorado

FOCUS

1973   Hocus Pocus

FOGELBERG, DAN

1980   Same Old Lang Syne
1981   Leader of the Band
1975   Part of the Plan
1979   Longer

FOGERTY, JOHN

(See Creedence Clearwater Revival)
1975   Almost Saturday Night
1975   Rockin' All over the World

1985   Big Train from Memphis
1985   Centerfield
1985   Old Man down the Road
1985   Rock and Roll Girls
1985   Zanz Can't Dance (Vanz Can't
           Dance)

FOGHAT

1975   Fool for the City
1976   Slow Ride

FOLDS FIVE, BEN

1995   Boxing
1995   Jackson's Cannery
1995   Underground
1997   Brick
1999   Army

FOLK IMPLOSION, THE

1995   Natural One, The

FONTANA, WAYNE AND THE MINDBENDERS

1964   Game of Love, The

FOO FIGHTERS

1995   I'll Stick Around
1995   This Is a Call
1996   Big Me
1997   Everlong
2000   Breakout

FORBERT, STEVE

1979   Romeo's Tune

FORCE MD'S

1985   Tender Love

FORD, FRANKIE

1959   Sea Cruise

FORD, LITA

1988   Kiss Me Deadly

FORD, LITA (WITH OZZY OSBOURNE)

1989   Close My Eyes Forever

FOREIGNER

1977   Cold as Ice
1977   Feels Like the First Time
1978   Double Vision
1978   Hot Blooded
1981   Urgent
1981   Waiting for a Girl Like You
1982   Juke Box Hero
1984   I Want to Know What Love Is

FORREST, JIMMY

1952   Night Train

FORTUNES, THE

1965   You've Got Your Troubles

FOUNDATIONS, THE

1967   Baby, Now That I've Found You
1969   Build Me up, Buttercup

FOUNTAINS OF WAYNE

1996   Radiation Vibe
1999   Troubled Times

FOUR DEUCES

1955   WPLJ

FOUR FLAMES, THE

1952   Wheel of Fortune

FOUR FRESHMEN, THE

1956   Graduation Day

FOUR PREPS, THE

1958   Big Man
1958   26 Miles

FOUR SEASONS, THE

1962   Big Girls Don't Cry
1962   Sherry
1963   Candy Girl
1963   Walk Like a Man
1964   Big Man in Town
1964   Dawn (Go Away)
1964   Rag Doll
1964   Save It for Me
1965   Bye Bye Baby
1965   Let's Hang On (to What We've
           Got)
1966   Working My Way Back to You
1967   C'mon Marianne
1975   December 1963 (Oh What a Night)
1975   Who Loves You

FOUR TOPS, THE

1964   Baby I Need Your Loving
1965   I Can't Help Myself (Sugar Pie, Honey
           Bunch)
1965   It's the Same Old Song
1966   Reach out, I'll Be There
1966   Shake Me, Wake Me (When It's
           Over)
1966   Standing in the Shadows of Love
1967   Bernadette
1967   Seven Rooms of Gloom
1972   Keeper of the Castle
1973   Ain't No Woman (Like the One
           I Got)
1981   When She Was My Girl

FOUR TUNES, THE

1954 I Understand Just How You Feel

FOWLEY, KIM

1969 Bubblegum

FOX, NORMAN & THE ROB ROYS

1957 Tell Me Why

FOX, SAMANTHA

1987 Touch Me (I Want Your Body)
1988 Naughty Girls Need Love Too
1989 I Wanna Have Some Fun

FOXX, INEX AND CHARLIE

1963 Mockingbird

FOXY

1978 Get Off

FRAMPTON, PETER

1975 Baby I Love Your Way
1975 Show Me the Way
1976 Do You Feel Like We Do
1977 I'm in You

FRANCIS, CONNIE

1958 Stupid Cupid
1958 Who's Sorry Now
1959 Lipstick on Your Collar
1959 My Happiness
1960 Everybody's Somebody's Fool
1960 My Heart Has a Mind of Its Own
1961 Where the Boys Are
1962 Don't Break the Heart That Loves You
1962 Second Hand Love
1962 Vacation

FRANKIE GOES TO HOLLYWOOD

1984 Relax
1984 Two Tribes
1985 Welcome to the Pleasure Dome

FRANKLIN, ARETHA

1967 Ain't No Way
1967 Baby I Love You
1967 Chain of Fools
1967 Do Right Woman, Do Right Man
1967 I Never Loved a Man (The Way I Love You)
1967 (Sweet, Sweet Baby) Since You've Been Gone
1967 (You Make Me Feel Like) A Natural Woman

1968 House That Jack Built, The
1968 Think
1969 Call Me
1969 Share Your Love with Me
1970 Spirit in the Dark
1971 Rock Steady
1972 Day Dreaming
1973 Angel
1973 Until You Come Back to Me (That's What I'm Gonna Do)
1976 Something He Can Feel
1977 Break It to Me Gently
1982 Jump to It
1983 Get It Right
1985 Freeway of Love
1985 Who's Zoomin' Who
1998 Rose Is Still a Rose, A

FRANKLIN, ARETHA AND ELTON JOHN

1989 Through the Storm

FRANKLIN, ARETHA AND GEORGE MICHAEL

1987 I Knew You Were Waiting (for Me)

FRANKLIN, ARETHA AND JAMES BROWN

1989 Gimme Your Love

FRATERNITY OF MAN

1968 Don't Bogart Me

FREAK NASTY

1997 Da Dip

FRED, JOHN & HIS PLAYBOY BAND

1967 Judy in Disguise (with Glasses)

FREDDIE & THE DREAMERS

1965 I'm Telling You Now

FREE

1970 All Right Now

FREE MOVEMENT

1971 I've Found Someone of My Own

FREEMAN, BOBBY

1958 Do You Want to Dance?
1964 C'mon and Swim

FREHLEY, ACE

(See Kiss)
1979 New York Groove

FRENCH FRITH KAISER THOMPSON

1990 Now That I Am Dead

FRESH, DOUG E. AND THE GET FRESH CREW

1985 Show, The

FREY, GLENN

(See the Eagles)
1985 Heat Is On, The
1985 Smuggler's Blues
1985 You Belong to the City

FRIEDMAN, DEAN

1977 Ariel

FRIEDMAN, KINKY

1973 Sold American
1976 Men's Room L.A.

FRIEND AND LOVER

1968 Reach out of the Darkness

FUEL

1998 Shimmer
2000 Hemorrhage (In My Hands)

FUGAZI

1988 Waiting Room
1990 Repeater

FUGEES

1995 Fu Gee La

FUGS, THE

1965 Boobs a Lot
1965 Coca Cola Douche
1965 Frenzy
1965 I Couldn't Get High
1965 I Saw the Best Minds of My Generation Rot
1965 Kill for Peace
1965 Morning Morning
1965 Saran Wrap
1965 Slum Goddess
1965 Supergirl
1968 Exorcising the Evil Spirits from the Pentagon, Oct. 21, 1967

FULLER, JESSE

1954 San Francisco Bay Blues

FULLER, JOHNNY

1959 Haunted House

FULSON, LOWELL

1948   3 O'Clock Blues
1950   Blue Shadows
1950   Every Day I Have the Blues
1954   Reconsider Baby
1967   Tramp

FUN BOY THREE

1983   Farm Yard Connection

FUNKADELIC

(See Parliament)
1970   Free Your Mind (and Your Ass Will
        Follow)
1971   Maggot Brain
1973   Cosmic Slop
1978   One Nation under a Groove
1979   (Not Just) Knee Deep

FUNKY FOUR + TWO

1981   That's the Joint

FUNKY KINGS, THE

1975   Slow Dancing

FURY, BILLY

1959   Maybe Tomorrow

FUTURE SOUND OF LONDON

1991   Papua, New Guinea

FU-SCHNICKENS WITH SHAQUILLE O'NEAL

1993   What's up Doc? (Can We Rock)

G

GABRIEL, PETER

(See Genesis)
1977   Solsbury Hill
1980   Biko
1980   Games without Frontiers
1982   Shock the Monkey
1986   Big Time
1986   In Your Eyes (Theme from "Say
        Anything")
1986   Mercy Street
1986   Red Rain
1986   Sledgehammer
1992   Digging the Dirt
1992   Steam

GABRIEL, PETER AND KATE BUSH

1986   Don't Give Up

GAINES, REG E.

1993   Please Don't Take My Air Jordans

GALLERY

1972   Nice to Be with You

GAMBLERS, THE

1959   Moon Dawg

GANG OF FOUR

1980   Anthrax
1980   I Found That Essence Rare
1982   To Hell with Poverty

GANG STARR

1990   Jazz Thing, A

GAP BAND, THE

1982   Early in the Morning
1982   Outstanding

GARBAGE

1995   Vow
1996   Stupid Girl
1997   #1 Crush
1998   I Think I'm Paranoid
1998   Special

GARCIA, JERRY

(See the Grateful Dead)
1972   Sugaree

GARFUNKEL, ART

(See Simon and Garfunkel)
1973   All I Know

GARNETT, GALE

1964   We'll Sing in the Sunshine

GARRETT, LEIF

1979   I Was Made for Dancin'

GAYE, MARVIN

1962   Stubborn Kind of Fellow
1963   Can I Get a Witness
1963   Pride and Joy
1964   Hitch Hike
1964   How Sweet It Is (To Be Loved by You)
1964   You're a Wonderful One
1965   Ain't That Peculiar?
1965   I'll Be Doggone
1968   I Heard It through the Grapevine
1969   That's the Way Love Is
1969   Too Busy Thinking about My Baby
1971   Inner City Blues (Make Me Wanna
        Holler)
1971   Mercy Mercy Me (The Ecology)
1971   What's Goin' On
1972   Theme from Trouble Man
1973   Let's Get It On
1976   I Want You
1977   Got to Give It Up (Part 1)
1982   Sexual Healing
1985   Sanctified Lady

GAYE, MARVIN AND KIM WESTON

1967   It Takes Two

GAYE, MARVIN AND TAMMI TERRELL

1967   Ain't No Mountain High Enough
1967   If I Could Build My Whole World
        around You
1967   Your Precious Love
1968   Ain't Nothing Like the Real Thing
1968   You're All I Need to Get By
1969   Good Lovin' Ain't Easy to Come By

GAYLE, CRYSTAL

1977   Don't It Make My Brown Eyes Blue

GAYLES, BILLY WITH IKE TURNER'S RHYTHM ROCKERS

1956   I'm Tore Up

GAYNOR, GLORIA

1978   I Will Survive

GEILS J. BAND, THE

1973   Give It to Me
1975   Must of Got Lost
1977   You're the Only One
1979   Love Stinks
1982   Centerfold
1982   Freeze-Frame

GENE AND EUNICE

1955   Ko Ko Mo (I Love You So)

GENERATION X

1978   Your Generation

GENESIS

1972   Supper's Ready
1973   Cinema Show
1974   Lamb Lies down on Broadway, The
1977   Your Own Special Way
1978   Follow You Follow Me
1980   Misunderstanding
1981   Abacab
1983   That's All
1986   In Too Deep

1986 Invisible Touch
1986 Land of Confusion
1986 Throwing It All Away
1987 Tonight, Tonight, Tonight
1991 I Can't Dance
1991 No Son of Mine

GENTRY, BOBBIE

1967 Ode to Billie Joe

GENTRYS, THE

1965 Keep on Dancing

GEORGE, BARBARA

1961 I Know (You Don't Love Me No More)

GEORGIA SATELLITES

1986 Keep Your Hands to Yourself

GERARDO

1991 Rico Suave

GERMS, THE

1980 Manimal

GERRY & THE PACEMAKERS

1964 Don't Let the Sun Catch You Crying
1964 Ferry Cross the Mersey

GIBB, ANDY

1977 I Just Want to Be Your Everything
1978 An Everlasting Love
1978 Shadow Dancing
1979 (Love Is) Thicker Than Water

GIBSON, DEBBIE

1987 Foolish Beat
1987 Only in My Dreams
1987 Out of the Blue
1987 Shake Your Love
1989 Lost in Your Eyes

GIBSON, DON

1958 I Can't Stop Loving You
1958 Oh Lonesome Me
1960 Sweet Dreams

GILDER, NICK

1978 Hot Child in the City

GILL, JOHNNY

1990 My My My
1990 Rub You the Right Way

GILMER, JIMMY AND THE FIREBALLS

1963 Sugar Shack

GILMORE, JIMMIE DALE & THE FLATLANDERS

1972 Tonight I Think I'm Gonna Go Downtown

GIN BLOSSOMS

1992 Found out about You
1992 Hey Jealousy
1995 Til I Hear It from You
1996 Follow You Down

GINUINE

1996 Pony

GLADIOLAS, THE

1957 Little Darlin'

GLASS TIGER

1986 Don't Forget Me (When I'm Gone)

GLITTER, GARY

1972 Rock and Roll (Part II)
1973 Do You Wanna Touch Me

GODFATHERS, THE

1988 Birth, School, Work, Death

GOFFIN, GERRY

1973 It's Not the Spotlight
1993 Masquerade

GO-GO'S, THE

1981 Our Lips Are Sealed
1982 Vacation
1982 We Got the Beat

GOLD, ANDREW

1977 Lonely Boy
1978 Thank You for Being a Friend

GOLDEN EARRING

1974 Radar Love
1983 Twilight Zone

GOLDIE

1995 Timeless

GOLDSBORO, BOBBY

1968 Honey

GOO GOO DOLLS

1993 We Are the Normal
1995 Name
1998 Iris
1998 Slide

GOOD CHARLOTTE

2000 Little Things

GOODMAN, DICKIE

1956 Flying Saucer

GOODMAN, STEVE

1970 You Never Even Called Me by My Name
1971 City of New Orleans, The

GORDON, ROBERT

1978 Fire
1981 Someday, Someway

GORE, LESLEY

1963 It's My Party
1963 Judy's Turn to Cry
1963 She's a Fool
1963 You Don't Own Me
1964 Look of Love, The
1964 Maybe I Know

GORKA, JOHN

1992 Gypsy Life, The

GQ

1979 Disco Nights (Rock Freak)

GRACIE, CHARLIE

1957 Butterfly

GRAHAM, DAVY

1963 Anji

GRAHAM LARRY

1980 One in a Million You

GRAMM, LOU

(See Foreigner)
1987 Midnight Blue

GRANAHAN GERRY

1958 No Chemise, Please!

GRAND FUNK RAILROAD

1970 Closer to Home
1973 We're an American Band
1975 Bad Time

GRANDMASTER FLASH

1980   Adventures of Grandmaster Flash on
        the Wheels of Steel
1982   Message, The
1983   New York, New York
1983   White Lines (Don't Do It)

GRANDMASTER FLASH & THE FURIOUS 5 WITH MR. NESS AND COWBOY

1984   Beatstreet

GRANT, EDDY

1979   Walking on Sunshine
1983   Electric Avenue

GRASS ROOTS

1967   Let's Live for Today
1967   Midnight Confessions
1971   Sooner or Later

GRATEFUL DEAD

1967   Good Morning, Little School Girl
1967   New New Minglewood Blues
1968   Dark Star
1969   China Cat Sunflower
1969   St. Stephen
1970   Attics of My Life
1970   Box of Rain
1970   Casey Jones
1970   Friend of the Devil
1970   Ripple
1970   Sugar Magnolia
1970   Truckin'
1970   Uncle John's Band
1974   U.S. Blues
1975   Franklin's Tower
1987   Touch of Grey
1995   Days Between

GRAY, DAVID

2000   Babylon

GRAY, DOBIE

1964   In Crowd, The
1973   Drift Away

GRAY, MACY

1999   I Try

GREAT SOCIETY, THE

1965   Someone to Love (Somebody to Love)
1965   White Rabbit

GREAVES, R.B.

1969   Take a Letter, Maria

GRECCO, CYNDI

1976   Making Our Dreams Come True

GREEN, AL

1967   Back up, Train
1971   Tired of Being Alone
1972   I'm Still in Love with You
1972   Let's Stay Together
1972   Look What You Done for Me
1972   Love and Happiness
1972   You Oughta Be with Me
1973   Call Me (Come Back Home)
1973   Here I Am (Come and Take Me)
1973   Livin' for You
1973   Take Me to the River
1974   Sha-La-La (Make Me Happy)
1975   Full of Fire
1975   L-O-V-E (Love)

GREEN DAY

1991   Green Day
1992   Welcome to Paradise
1994   Basket Case
1994   Longview
1994   When I Come Around
1995   Brain Stew
1995   J.A.R.
1997   Good Riddance (Time of Your
        Life)
2000   Minority

GREEN RIVER

1985   Swallow My Pride
1985   10,000 Things

GREENBAUM, NORMAN

1970   Spirit in the Sky

GREENWICH, ELLIE

1985   We're Gonna Make It (After All)

GRIFFIN, PATTI

1998   Let Him Fly
1998   One Big Love

GRIFFITH, NANCI

1987   From a Distance

GROSS, HENRY

1976   Shannon

GUARALDI, VINCE TRIO

1962   Cast Your Fate to the Wind

GUESS WHO, THE

1969   Laughing
1969   No Time
1969   These Eyes
1970   American Woman
1970   Share the Land
1974   Clap for the Wolfman

GUIDED BY VOICES

1987   Captain's Dead
1993   Shocker in Gloomtown
1994   I Am a Scientist
1996   Beneath a Festering Moon

GUNS N' ROSES

1987   Patience
1987   Welcome to the Jungle
1988   Sweet Child o' Mine
1989   Paradise City
1991   Civil War
1991   Don't Cry
1991   November Rain

GUNTER, ARTHUR

1954   Baby Let's Play House

GUNTER, HARDROCK & THE PEBBLES

1950   Birmingham Bounce

GUNTER, SHIRLEY & THE QUEENS

1954   Oop Shoop

GUTHRIE, ARLO

1967   Alice's Restaurant
1969   Coming into Los Angeles
1969   Deportees (The Plane Wreck at
        Los Gatos)

GUTHRIE, GWEN

1986   Ain't Nothin' Goin' on But the Rent

GUY

1988   I Like
1988   My Fantasy

H

HADDAWAY

1993   What Is Love

HAGAR, SAMMY

(See Van Halen)
1982   Fast Times at Ridgemont High
1983   Your Love Is Driving Me Crazy
1984   I Can't Drive 55

HALEY, BILL AND HIS COMETS

1952 Rock a-Beating Boogie
1953 Crazy Man, Crazy
1953 (We're Gonna) Rock around the Clock
1954 Dim, Dim the Lights (I Want Some Atmosphere)
1955 Burn That Candle
1958 Skinny Minnie

HALF JAPANESE

1984 Secret Sharer

HALL, DARYL

1986 Dreamtime

HALL, DARYL & JOHN OATES

1974 She's Gone
1975 Camellia
1975 Sara Smile
1976 Rich Girl
1981 Did It in a Minute
1981 I Can't Go for That (No Can Do)
1981 Kiss on My List
1981 Private Eyes
1981 You Make My Dreams
1982 Maneater
1983 Family Man
1983 One on One
1983 Say It Isn't So
1984 Adult Education
1984 Out of Touch
1985 Every Time You Go Away
1985 Method of Modern Love
1988 Everything Your Heart Desires

HAMILTON IV, GEORGE

1956 Rose and a Baby Ruth, A
1967 Urge for Going

HAMILTON, JOE FRANK & REYNOLDS

1971 Don't Pull Your Love
1975 Fallin' in Love (Again)

HAMILTON, ROY

1954 Ebb Tide
1954 Hurt
1955 Unchained Melody
1958 Don't Let Go
1961 You Can Have Her

HAMMER, JAN

1985 Miami Vice Theme

HAMMER, M.C.

1990 Pray
1990 U Can't Touch This
1991 2 Legit to Quit

HAMMOND, ALBERT

1972 Air That I Breathe, The
1972 It Never Rains in Southern California

HANCOCK, HERBIE

1983 Rockit

HANSON

1997 Mmmm Bop

HARDCASTLE, PAUL

1985 19

HARDIN, TIM

1966 Reason to Believe
1967 If I Were a Carpenter

HARPER, BEN

1993 I'll Rise

HARPER'S BIZARRE

1966 Come to the Sunshine
1967 Biggest Night of Her Life, The
1967 High Coin
1967 Simon Smith & His Amazing Dancing Bear

HARPO, SLIM

1957 I'm a King Bee
1966 Baby, Scratch My Back

HARPTONES, THE

1953 Sunday Kind of Love, A
1954 Life Is But a Dream

HARRIS, BARBARA

1975 It Don't Worry Me

HARRIS, EMMYLOU

1975 Boulder to Birmingham
1995 Goodbye

HARRIS, MAJOR

1975 Love Won't Let Me Wait

HARRIS, PEPPERMINT

1951 I Got Loaded

HARRIS, RICHARD

1968 MacArthur Park

HARRIS, WYNONIE

1945 Around the Clock
1949 All She Wants to Do Is Rock

HARRISON, GEORGE

(See The Beatles)
1970 Isn't It a Pity
1970 My Sweet Lord
1970 What Is Life
1971 Bangla-Desh
1973 Give Me Love (Give Me Peace on Earth)
1976 Crackerbox Palace
1976 This Song
1981 All Those Years Ago
1987 When We Was Fab

HARRISON, WILBERT

1969 Let's Work Together

HART, COREY

1985 Never Surrender

HARTFORD, JOHN

1967 Gentle on My Mind

HARVEY, PJ

1992 Dress
1992 Sheela-Na-Gig
1993 Rid of Me
1995 Down by the Water

HATFIELD THREE, JULIANA

1993 My Sister

HATHAWAY, DONNIE

1973 Someday We'll All Be Free

HAVENS, RICHIE

1967 Follow
1967 Handsome Johnny
1968 Klan, The
1969 Freedom

HAWKINS, DALE

1957 Susie Q

HAWKINS, RONNIE

1959 Forty Days

HAWKINS, SCREAMING JAY

1956 I Put a Spell on You

HAWKINS SINGERS, EDWIN

1969 Oh Happy Day

HAWKINS, SOPHIE B.

1992 Damn, I Wish I Was Your Lover

HAWKWIND

1972 Silver Machine
1974 Lost Johnny

HAYES, ISAAC

1971 Theme from Shaft (Who Shaft Where)

HAZARD, ROBERT

1982 Girls Just Want to Have Fun

HAZEL, EDDIE

1977 Frantic Moment

HEAD, ROY

1965 Treat Her Right

HEALEY BAND, JEFF

1989 Angel Eyes
1992 Cruel Little Number

HEAR'N'AID

1986 Stars

HEART

1976 Crazy on You
1976 Magic Man
1977 Barracuda
1978 Straight On
1980 Even It Up
1985 Never
1985 What about Love?
1986 These Dreams
1987 Alone
1990 All I Wanna Do Is Make Love to You

HEARTBEATS, THE

1956 Thousand Miles Away, A

HEARTBREAKERS, THE

1977 Born to Lose
1977 Chinese Rocks

HEARTS, THE

1955 Lonely Nights

HEATWAVE

1977 Boogie Nights

HEAVEN 17

1982 Temptation
1982 We Live So Fast

HEAVY D & THE BOYS

1994 Got Me Waiting
1994 Nuttin' But Love

HEBB, BOBBY

1966 Sunny

HEIGHTS, THE

1992 How Do You Talk to an Angel

HELL, RICHARD

1982 Destiny Street

HELL, RICHARD AND THE VOIDOIDS

1976 Blank Generation

HELMS, BOBBY

1957 My Special Angel

HENDERSON, JOE

1962 Snap Your Fingers

HENDRIX, JIMI

1967 Are You Experienced?
1967 Fire
1967 Foxy Lady
1967 I Don't Live Today
1967 Manic Depression
1967 May This Be Love
1967 Purple Haze
1967 Wind Cries Mary, The
1968 Castles Made of Sand
1968 Crosstown Traffic
1968 If 6 Was 9
1968 Little Wing
1968 Stone Free
1968 Voodoo Chile (Slight Return)
1968 You Got Me Floatin'
1969 Red House
1970 Machine Gun
1971 Dolly Dagger
1971 Freedom
1971 Hear My Train a-Coming
1971 Night Bird Flying
1971 Room Full of Mirrors

HENLEY, DON

(See the Eagles)
1982 Dirty Laundry
1985 Boys of Summer, The
1989 End of the Innocence, The
1989 Heart of the Matter, The

HENRY, CLARENCE "FROGMAN"

1956 Ain't Got No Home
1960 But I Do

HENRY, JOE

1992 Short Man's Room

HENSKE, JUDY

1964 High Flying Bird

HERMAN'S HERMITS

1965 Can't You Hear My Heartbeat?
1965 I'm Henry VIII, I Am
1965 Mrs. Brown, You've Got a Lovely Daughter
1965 Must to Avoid, A
1966 Dandy
1966 Listen People
1967 There's a Kind of Hush

HIATT, JOHN

1979 Pink Bedroom
1979 You're My Love Interest
1983 Riding with the King
1983 She Loves the Jerk
1985 She Said the Same Things to Me
1985 Usual, The
1987 Learning How to Love You
1987 Thing Called Love
1988 Drive South
1990 Through Your Hands
1994 Shredding the Document

HI-FIVE

1990 I Like the Way (The Kissing Game)
1991 I Can't Wait Another Minute
1992 She's Playing Hard to Get

HIGGINS, BERTIE

1982 Key Largo

HIGH INERGY

1977 You Can't Turn Me Off (In the Middle of Turning Me On)

HIGHWAYMEN, THE

1961 Cottonfields

HILL, DAN

1977 Sometimes When We Touch

HILL, JESSIE

1960 Ooh Poo Pah Doo (Part One)

HILL, LAURYN

1998 Doo Wop (That Thing)
1999 To Zion

HILL, Z.Z.

1964 You Were Wrong
1982 Cheating in the Next Room

HITCHCOCK, ROBYN & THE EGYPTIANS

(See The Soft Boys)
1988   Balloon Man
1989   Madonna of the Wasps

HOLE

1991   Babydoll
1991   Pretty on the Inside
1994   Doll Parts
1994   Miss World
1994   Violet
1998   Celebrity Skin

HOLLAND, EDDIE

1961   Jamie

HOLLIES, THE

1966   Bus Stop
1967   Carrie-Anne
1967   On a Carousel
1970   He Ain't Heavy, He's My Brother
1972   Long Cool Woman (In a Black Dress)

HOLLOWAY, BRENDA

1964   When I'm Gone
1967   You've Made Me So Very Happy

HOLLY, BUDDY

(See The Crickets)
1956   Rock around with Ollie Vee
1957   Peggy Sue
1958   Everyday
1958   Heartbeat
1958   I'm Gonna Love You Too
1958   Rave On
1958   True Love Ways
1958   Words of Love
1959   It Doesn't Matter Any More
1959   Raining in My Heart

HOLLY & THE ITALIANS

1981   Tell That Girl to Shut Up

HOLLYWOOD ARGYLES, THE

1960   Alley Oop

HOLLYWOOD FLAMES, THE

1957   Buzz Buzz Buzz

HOLMES, CLINT

1973   Playground in My Mind

HOLMES, RUPERT

1979   Escape (The Piña Colada Song)
1979   Him

HOLT, WILL

1957   M.T.A.

HOLY MODAL ROUNDERS, THE

1965   Half a Mind
1965   If You Wanna Be a Bird
1965   Werewolf
1967   Euphoria

HOMBRES, THE

1967   Let It Out (Let It All Hang Out)

HONDELLS, THE

1964   Little Honda

HONEY BEARS

1954   One Bad Stud

HONEY CONE, THE

1971   Stick Up
1971   Want-Ads

HONEYCOMBS, THE

1965   Have I the Right?

HOODOO GURUS, THE

1987   What's My Scene

HOODOO RHYTHM DEVILS

1972   Still Alive and Well

HOOKER, JOHN LEE

1949   Boogie Chillen
1951   I'm in the Mood
1962   Boom Boom

HOOTERS

1985   Where Do the Children Go

HOOTIE AND THE BLOWFISH

1994   Hold My Hand
1994   Let Her Cry

HORNSBY, BRUCE AND THE RANGE

1986   Every Little Kiss
1986   Mandolin Rain
1986   Way It Is
1988   Valley Road, The

HORTON, JOHNNY

1959   Battle of New Orleans, The
1960   North to Alaska
1960   Sink the Bismarck

HOT CHOCOLATE

1973   Brother Louie
1975   You Sexy Thing
1979   Every 1's a Winner

HOT TUNA

1978   Genesis

HOUSE OF PAIN

1992   Jump Around

HOUSEMARTINS, THE

1986   Happy Hour

HOUSTON, THELMA

1977   Don't Leave Me This Way

HOUSTON, WHITNEY

1985   How Will I Know
1985   You Give Good Love
1987   I Wanna Dance with Somebody (Who Loves Me)
1990   I'm Your Baby Tonight
1995   Exhale (The Shoop Shoop Song)

HOWLING WOLF

1950   Down in the Bottom
1950   Moanin' at Midnight
1951   How Many More Years
1954   Evil
1956   Smokestack Lightning
1960   Spoonful
1961   Little Red Rooster
1962   I Ain't Superstitious
1966   Killing Floor

H-TOWN

1993   Knockin' Da Boots

HUES CORPORATION, THE

1974   Rock the Boat

HUGHES, JIMMY

1964   Steal Away

HUMAN LEAGUE

1982   Don't You Want Me
1983   (Keep Feeling) Fascination
1986   Human

HUMBLE PIE

1971 Stone Cold Fever
1972 Hot N' Nasty

HUNTER, IAN

(See Mott the Hoople)
1975 Once Bitten, Twice Shy
1979 Cleveland Rocks
1979 Ships

HUNTER, IVORY JOE

1950 I Almost Lost My Mind
1956 Since I Met You Baby I
1957 Empty Arms

HÜSKER DÜ

1984 Turn on the News
1985 Celebrated Summer
1985 Girl Who Lives on Heaven Hill
1986 Sorry Somehow
1987 No Reservations

HUTTON, DANNY

(See Three Dog Night)
1966 Beach Baby

HYLAND, BRIAN

1960 Itsy Bitsy Teenie Weenie Yellow
        Polkadot Bikini
1962 Sealed with a Kiss
1963 Save Your Heart for Me

I

IAN, JANIS

1967 Society's Child (Baby, I've Been
        Thinking)
1975 At Seventeen

IAN AND SYLVIA

1964 Four Strong Winds
1964 Someday Soon
1964 You Were on My Mind

ICE CUBE

(See NWA)
1993 Check Yo Self
1993 It Was a Good Day

ICE-T

1988 Colors
1989 Freedom of Speech
1991 New Jack Hustler (Nino's Theme)

IDES OF MARCH, THE

1970 Vehicle

IDOL, BILLY

(See Generation X)
1981 Dancing with Myself
1982 Hot in the City
1983 White Wedding
1984 Eyes without a Face
1984 Rebel Yell
1990 Cradle of Love

IFIELD, FRANK

1962 I Remember You

IKETTES, THE

1961 I'm Blue (The Gong Gong Song)

IMBRUGLIA, NATALIE

1998 Torn

IMMATURE

1994 Never Lie

IMPALAS, THE

1959 Sorry, I Ran All the Way Home

IMPRESSIONS, THE

1961 Gypsy Woman
1963 It's All Right!
1964 Amen
1964 I'm So Proud
1964 Keep on Pushing
1965 People Get Ready
1965 Woman's Got Soul
1967 We're a Winner
1968 This Is My Country
1969 Choice of Colors
1974 Finally Got Myself Together
        (I'm a Changed Man)

INCREDIBLE STRING BAND, THE

1967 First Girl I Loved, The

INCUBUS

1998 Stellar

INDIGO GIRLS

1989 Closer to Fine
1992 Galileo
1994 Power of Two

INFORMATION SOCIETY

1988 What's on Your Mind
        (Pure Energy)

INGRAM, JAMES

1990 I Don't Have the Heart

INGRAM, LUTHER

1971 If Loving You Is Wrong I Don't Want
        to Be Right

INK SPOTS, THE

1946 Gypsy, The

INK SPOTS, THE WITH ELLA FITZGERALD

1945 Into Each Life Some Rain Must Fall

INNER CIRCLE

1993 Bad Boys

INSECT TRUST

1970 Eyes of a New York Woman

INSPIRAL CARPETS

1990 Commercial Rain

INTRUDERS, THE

1968 Cowboys to Girls
1973 I'll Always Love My Mama

INXS

1986 What You Need
1987 Devil Inside
1987 Need You Tonight
1987 New Sensation
1990 Disappear
1990 Suicide Blonde

IRON BUTTERFLY

1968 In-a-gadda-da-vida

IRON CITY HOUSE ROCKERS, THE

1980 Junior's Bar

IRON MAIDEN

1981 Wrathchild
1982 Number of the Beast, The
1982 Run to the Hills
1983 Trooper, The
1988 Can I Play with Madness

ISAAK, CHRIS

1987 Blue Hotel
1989 Wicked Game

ISLEY BROTHERS, THE

1959 Shout (Part 1)
1962 Twist and Shout
1963 Nobody but Me

1964	Who's That Lady
1966	This Old Heart of Mine (Is Weak for You)
1969	It's Your Thing
1972	Work to Do
1975	Fight the Power, Part 1
1976	At Your Best (You Are Love)
1980	Don't Say Goodnight (It's Time for Love)—Parts 1 & 2

ISLEY BROTHERS, THE AND JIMI HENDRIX

| 1971 | Move over Let Me Dance |

ISLEY/JASPER/ISLEY

| 1985 | Caravan of Love |

IVAN (JERRY ALLISON)

| 1958 | Real Wild Child |

IVY THREE, THE

| 1960 | Yogi |

J

JACKS, THE

| 1955 | Why Don't You Write Me |

JACKSON, CHUCK

| 1962 | Any Day Now |
| 1962 | I Keep Forgettin' (Every Time You're Near) |

JACKSON, FREDDIE

| 1985 | You Are My Lady |

JACKSON, JANET

(See The Jackson 5)

1986	Let's Wait Awhile
1986	Nasty
1986	Pleasure Principle
1986	What Have You Done for Me Lately
1986	When I Think of You
1989	Alright
1989	Black Cat
1989	Come Back to Me
1989	Escapade
1989	Love Will Never Do without You
1989	Miss You Much
1989	Rhythm Nation
1992	Best Things in Life Are Free, The
1993	Again
1993	Anytime, Any Place
1993	If
1993	That's the Way Love Goes
1994	You Want This
1998	Together Again
2000	Doesn't Really Matter

JACKSON, JERMAINE

(See The Jackson 5)

| 1980 | Let's Get Serious |
| 1991 | Word to the Badd |

JACKSON, JOE

1979	Is She Really Going out with Him?
1982	Steppin' Out
1984	You Can't Get What You Want (Till You Know What You Want)

JACKSON, MICHAEL

(See The Jackson 5)

1971	Got to Be There
1972	Ben
1979	Don't Stop 'Til You Get Enough
1979	Off the Wall
1979	Rock with You
1979	She's out of My Life
1982	Girl Is Mine, The
1983	Beat It
1983	Billie Jean
1983	Human Nature
1983	P.Y.T. (Pretty Young Thing)
1983	Thriller
1983	Wanna Be Startin' Something
1987	Another Part of Me
1987	Bad
1987	Dirty Diana
1987	I Just Can't Stop Loving You
1987	Man in the Mirror
1987	Smooth Criminal
1987	Way You Make Me Feel, The
1991	Black or White
1991	In the Closet
1991	Remember the Time
1991	Will You Be There
1995	Childhood

JACKSON, MILLIE

| 1973 | Hurts So Good |

JACKSON, STONEWALL

| 1959 | Waterloo |

JACKSON, WANDA

1956	Hot Dog, That Made Him Mad
1956	I Gotta Know
1958	Let's Have a Party
1961	In the Middle of a Heartache
1961	Right or Wrong

JACKSON 5, THE

1967	Michael the Lover
1969	I Want You Back
1970	ABC
1970	I'll Be There
1970	Love You Save, The
1970	Mama's Pearl
1970	Never Can Say Goodbye
1971	Sugar Daddy
1974	Dancing Machine

JACKSON BROTHERS, THE

| 1952 | We're Gonna Rock This Joint |

JACKSONS, THE

(See The Jackson 5)

1976	Enjoy Yourself
1978	Shake Your Body (Down to the Ground)
1980	Heartbreak Hotel
1984	State of Shock

JADE

| 1993 | Don't Walk Away |

JAGGER, MICK

(See The Rolling Stones)

| 1970 | Memo from Turner |
| 1985 | Just Another Night |

JAGGERZ, THE

| 1970 | Rapper, The |

JAM, THE

1977	In the City
1978	Down in the Tube Station at Midnight
1979	Eton Rifles
1979	Going Underground
1982	Beat Surrender
1982	Bitterest Pill (I Ever Had to Swallow), The

JAMES

| 1994 | Laid |

JAMES, ELMORE

| 1952 | I Believe I'll Dust My Broom |
| 1960 | Sky Is Crying, The |

JAMES, ETTA

1955	Dance with Me Henry (The Wallflower)
1960	All I Could Do Was Cry
1960	My Dearest Darling
1961	At Last
1962	Something's Got a Hold on Me
1963	Pushover
1967	Tell Mama
1969	I'd Rather Go Blind

JAMES GANG, THE

| 1970 | Funk #49 |

JAMES, RICK

1978	Mary Jane
1978	You and I
1981	Fire and Desire (With Teena Marie)

1981   Give It to Me Baby
1981   Super Freak (Part 1)
1983   Cold Blooded
1988   Loosey's Rap

JAMES, SONNY

1956   Young Love

JAMES, TOMMY

1971   Draggin' the Line

JAMES, TOMMY AND THE SHONDELLS

1967   I Think We're Alone Now
1968   Mony Mony
1969   Crimson and Clover
1969   Crystal Blue Persuasion

JAMIES, THE

1958   Summertime, Summertime

JAMIROQUAI

1997   Virtual Insanity

JAN & ARNIE

1958   Jenny-Lee

JAN & DEAN

1958   Baby Talk
1963   Drag City
1963   Surf City
1964   Dead Man's Curve
1964   Little Old Lady (From Pasadena), The
1964   New Girl in School, The
1964   Ride the Wild Surf
1965   (Here They Come) From All over the World

JANE'S ADDICTION

1990   Been Caught Stealing
1990   Three Days

JARMELS, THE

1961   Little Bit of Soap, A

JAY & THE AMERICANS

1962   She Cried
1963   Only in America
1964   Come a Little Bit Closer
1965   Cara Mia

JAY AND THE TECHNIQUES

1967   Apples, Peaches, Pumpkin Pie (Ready or Not)

JAY Z

1996   Ain't No Nigga
1998   Hard Knock Life
2000   Big Pimpin'

JAYHAWKS

1992   Waiting for the Sun

JAYNETTES, THE

1963   Sally Go 'round the Roses

JB'S

1973   Doin' It to Death

JEAN, WYCLEF

1997   Gone till November

JEFFERSON, MARSHALL

1986   Move Your Body

JEFFERSON AIRPLANE

1966   It's No Secret
1967   Embryonic Journey
1967   Spare Chaynge
1967   Today
1968   Greasy Heart
1968   Lather
1968   Won't You Try/Saturday Afternoon
1969   Have You Seen the Saucers
1969   Mexico
1969   We Can Be Together
1969   Volunteers
1971   Third Week at the Chelsea

JEFFERSON STARSHIP

(See Starship)
1975   Miracles
1978   Count on Me
1980   Jane

JEFFREYS, GARLAND

1977   Wild in the Streets
1991   Hail, Hail Rock 'n' Roll

JELLY BEANS, THE

1964   I Wanna Love Him So Bad

JELLYBEAN

1986   Sidewalk Talk

JENNINGS, WAYLON

1967   Chokin' Kind, The

JESUS AND MARY CHAIN, THE

1984   Upside Down

JESUS JONES

1991   Real Real Real
1991   Right Here, Right Now

JETHRO TULL

1971   Aqualung
1971   Cross-Eyed Mary
1972   Living in the Past
1972   Thick as a Brick
1974   Bungle in the Jungle
1976   Too Old to Rock 'n' Roll (Too Young to Die)

JETS, THE

1986   Crush on You
1987   Make It Real
1987   You Got It All

JETT, JOAN

1980   Bad Reputation

JETT, JOAN & THE BLACKHEARTS

1982   I Love Rock and Roll
1988   I Hate Myself for Loving You

JEWEL

1996   Who Will Save Your Soul
1996   You Were Meant For Me

JIGSAW

1975   Sky High

JIVE FIVE, THE

1961   My True Story
1962   What Time Is It
1965   I'm a Happy Man

JODECI

1991   Come and Talk to Me

JOE

2000   I Wanna Know

JOE PUBLIC

1992   Live and Learn

JOEL, BILLY

1971   Captain Jack
1974   Entertainer, The
1974   Piano Man
1976   Miami 2017 (Seen the Lights Go out on Broadway)
1976   New York State of Mind

1976 Say Goodbye to Hollywood
1977 Moving Out (Anthony's Song)
1977 Only the Good Die Young
1977 Scenes from an Italian
Restaurant
1977 She's Always a Woman
1978 Big Shot
1978 Just the Way You Are
1978 My Life
1980 It's Still Rock and Roll to Me
1980 You May Be Right
1982 Allentown
1982 Goodnight Saigon
1983 An Innocent Man
1983 Longest Time, The
1983 Tell Her About It
1983 Uptown Girl
1986 Big Man on Mulberry Street
1986 Matter of Trust, A
1986 Modern Woman (From *Ruthless People*)
1986 This Is the Time
1989 I Go to Extremes
1989 Leningrad
1989 We Didn't Start the Fire
1993 River of Dreams

JOHANSEN, DAVID

1977 Frenchette
1977 Funky But Chic
1978 Cool Metro

JOHN, ELTON

1970 Border Song (Holy Moses)
1970 Take Me to the Pilot
1970 Your Song
1971 Levon
1972 Daniel
1972 Honky Cat
1972 Rocket Man (I Think It's Gonna Be a Long Long Time)
1972 Saturday Night's Alright (For Fighting)
1973 Bennie and the Jets
1973 Candle in the Wind
1973 Crocodile Rock
1973 Goodbye Yellow Brick Road
1973 Love Lies Bleeding
1974 Bitch Is Back, The
1974 Don't Let the Sun Go down on Me
1975 Island Girl
1975 Philadelphia Freedom
1975 Someone Saved My Life Tonight
1976 Don't Go Breaking My Heart
1976 I Feel Like a Bullet (In the Gun of Robert Ford)
1976 Sorry Seems to Be the Hardest Word
1977 Mama Can't Buy You Love
1980 Little Jeannie
1982 Empty Garden (Hey Hey Johnny)
1983 I Guess That's Why They Call It the Blues
1983 I'm Still Standing
1984 Sad Songs (Say So Much)

1986 Nikita
1988 I Don't Wanna Go on with You Like That
1992 One, The
1997 Something About the Way You Look Tonight

JOHN, LITTLE WILLIE

1956 Fever
1956 Let Them Talk
1956 Need Your Love So Bad
1958 Talk to Me, Talk to Me
1958 There Is Someone in This World for Me
1959 Leave My Kitten Alone
1960 Sleep

JOHN, ROBERT

1979 Sad Eyes

JOHNNIE AND JACKEY

1961 Someday We'll Be Together

JOHNNIE AND JOE

1957 Over the Mountain, across the Sea

JOHNNY & THE HURRICANES

1959 Red River Rock

JOHNNY HATES JAZZ

1988 Shattered Dreams

JOHNS, SAMMY

1975 Chevy Van

JOHNSON, BUDDY

1949 Did You See Jackie Robinson Hit That Ball

JOHNSON, ERIC

1991 Cliffs of Dover

JOHNSON, KEVIN

1973 (Rock 'n' Roll I Gave You) The Best Years of My Life

JOHNSON, LONNIE

1948 Tomorrow Night

JOHNSON, LOU

1964 Kentucky Bluebird
1964 (There's) Always Something There to Remind Me

JOHNSON, MARV

1958 Come to Me
1959 You Got What It Takes
1960 I Love the Way You Love

JOHNSTON, FREEDY

1994 Bad Reputation

JONES, EDDIE "GUITAR SLIM"

1954 Things That I Used to Do

JONES, ETTA

1947 I Sold My Heart to the Junkman

JONES, GEORGE

1959 White Lightning

JONES, GLORIA

1964 Tainted Love

JONES, GRACE

1981 Pull up to the Bumper

JONES, HOWARD

1985 Things Can Only Get Better
1986 No One Is to Blame

JONES, JIMMY

1960 Good Timin'
1960 Handy Man

JONES, JOE

1960 You Talk Too Much
1961 California Sun

JONES, ORAN 'JUICE'

1986 Rain, The

JONES, PAUL

1967 Privilege (Set Me Free)

JONES, RICKIE LEE

1979 Chuck E.'s in Love
1981 We Belong Together
1982 Living It Up
1989 Horses

JONES, TOM

1965 It's Not Unusual

JOPLIN, JANIS

(See Big Brother & the Holding Company)
1962   What Good Can Drinking Do
1969   Kosmic Blues
1970   Half Moon
1970   Mercedes Benz
1970   Move Over

JORDAN, LOUIS AND HIS TYMPANI FIVE

1944   G.I. Jive
1946   Ain't Nobody Here But Us Chickens
1946   Choo Choo Ch'Boogie
1946   Let the Good Times Roll
1947   Jack You're Dead
1949   Ain't That Just Like a Woman
1949   Saturday Night Fish Fry

JORDAN, MONTEL

1995   This Is How We Do It

JOURNEY

1978   Wheel in the Sky
1980   Any Way You Want It
1981   Don't Stop Believin'
1981   Who's Crying Now
1982   Open Arms
1983   Separate Ways (World's Apart)

JOY DIVISION

1980   Love Will Tear Us Apart

JUDAS PRIEST

1980   Living after Midnight
1981   You've Got Another Thing Comin'

JUMP 'N' THE SADDLE

1983   Curly Shuffle, The

JUSTIS, BILL

1957   Raunchy

K

K., TONIO

1986   Perfect World

K.C. AND THE SUNSHINE BAND

1975   Get down Tonight
1975   That's the Way (I Like It)
1976   (Shake, Shake, Shake) Shake Your Booty
1977   I'm Your Boogie Man
1977   Keep It Comin, Love
1979   Please Don't Go

KADISON, JOSHUA

1993   Jessie

KAHN, BRENDA

1992   Mint Juleps and Needles
1992   She's in Love

KAJAGOOGOO

1983   Too Shy

KALEIDOSCOPE

1968   Beacon from Mars

KALIN TWINS

1958   When

KAMOSE, INI

1994   Here Comes the Hotstepper

KANE, BIG DADDY

1988   Long Live the Kane

KANSAS

1976   Carry on Wayward Son
1977   Dust in the Wind

KAYE, THOMAS JEFFERSON

1974   American Lovers

K-DOE, ERNIE

1961   Certain Girl, A
1961   Mother-in-Law

KEITH

1966   98.6

KELLY, R.

1992   Slow Dance (Hey Mr. DJ)
1994   Bump and Grind
1995   Down Low (Nobody Has to Know)
1996   I Believe I Can Fly
1997   Gotham City

KEMP, JOHNNY

1988   Just Got Paid

KEMP, TARA

1991   Hold You Tight

KENDRICKS, EDDIE

1972   Girl You Need a Change of Mind (Part 1)
1973   Keep on Truckin'

1974   Boogie Down
1975   Shoeshine Boy

KENNER, CHRIS

1957   Sick and Tired
1961   I Like It Like That
1963   Land of a Thousand Dances

KHAN, CHAKA

1978   I'm Every Woman

KID 'N PLAY

1990   Funhouse

KID CREOLE & THE COCONUTS

1981   In the Jungle
1982   Annie, He's Not Your Daddy

KID ROCK

1999   Cowboy

KIDD, JOHNNY & THE PIRATES

1960   Shakin' All Over

KIHN BAND, GREG

1983   Jeopardy
1987   Breakup Song (They Don't Write 'Em)

KILLING JOKE

1985   Love Like Blood

KIM, ANDY

1974   Rock Me Gently

KING, ALBERT

1967   Born under a Bad Sign
1969   As the Years Go Passing By

KING, B.B.

1952   Be Careful with a Fool
1952   You Know I Love You
1953   Please Love Me
1954   You Upset Me, Baby
1961   Sweet Sixteen
1962   How Blue Can You Get
1964   Rock Me Baby
1969   Thrill Is Gone, The

KING, BEN E.

(See The Drifters)
1961   Spanish Harlem
1961   Stand by Me

1962 Don't Play That Song (You Lied)
1963 I (Who Have Nothing)
1975 Supernatural Thing—Part 1

KING, CAROLE

1962 It Might as Well Rain until September
1963 He's a Bad Boy
1971 Child of Mine
1971 I Feel the Earth Move
1971 It's Too Late
1971 So Far Away
1971 Sweet Seasons
1971 Tapestry
1971 You've Got a Friend
1974 Jazzman
1975 Really Rosie

KING, EVELYN CHAMPAGNE

1978 Shame
1982 Love Come Down

KING, FREDDIE

1961 Hide Away
1961 I'm Tore Down
1962 Have You Ever Loved a Woman

KING CRIMSON

1969 Court of the Crimson King
1969 21ST Century Schizoid Man

KING CURTIS

1962 Soul Twist

KING FLOYD

1970 Groove Me Baby

KING HARVEST

1973 Dancing in the Moonlight

KINGSMEN, THE

1965 Jolly Green Giant

KINGSTON TRIO, THE

1958 Tom Dooley
1961 Pastures of Plenty
1963 Greenback Dollar
1963 Reverend Mr. Black, The
1963 Seasons in the Sun

KINKS, THE

1964 All Day and All of the Night
1964 Stop Your Sobbing
1964 You Really Got Me
1965 Tired of Waiting for You
1965 Well-Respected Man, A
1965 Who'll Be the Next in Line
1966 Dedicated Follower of Fashion
1966 I'm Not Like Everybody Else
1966 See My Friends
1966 Sunny Afternoon
1967 Dead End Street
1967 Waterloo Sunset
1968 David Watts
1970 Apeman
1970 Victoria
1971 Lola
1972 Celluloid Heroes
1977 Rock 'n Roll Fantasy, A
1981 Better Things
1981 Destroyer
1983 Come Dancing

KISS

1974 Black Diamond
1974 Deuce
1974 Strutter
1975 Rock and Roll All Night
1976 Beth
1976 Calling Dr. Love
1976 Detroit Rock City
1976 Hard Luck Woman
1977 Christine Sixteen
1977 Love Gun
1979 I Was Made for Loving You
1982 World without Heroes, A
1983 Lick It Up
1989 Forever
1998 Psycho Circus

KLAATU

1977 Calling Occupants of Interplanetary Craft

KLF, THE

1991 Justified and Ancient
1991 3 A.M. Eternal

KLYMAXX

1985 I Miss You

KNACK, THE

1979 My Sharona

KNICKERBOCKERS, THE

1965 Lies (Are Breakin' My Heart)

KNIGHT, GLADYS & THE PIPS

1962 Letter Full of Tears
1970 If I Were Your Woman
1971 I Don't Want to Do Wrong
1971 Make Me the Woman That You Come Home To
1973 Best Thing That Ever Happened to Me, The
1973 I've Got to Use My Imagination
1973 Neither One of Us (Wants to Be the First to Say Goodbye)
1974 On and On

KNIGHT, JEAN

1971 Mr. Big Stuff
1985 My Toot Toot

KNIGHT, ROBERT

1967 Everlasting Love

KNOPFLER, MARK

(See Dire Straits and James Taylor)
2000 Sailing to Philadelphia

KNOX, BUDDY

1957 Party Doll

KNUCKLES, FRANKIE

1985 You Got the Love

KOOL & THE GANG

1973 Hollywood Swinging
1973 Jungle Boogie
1975 Spirit of the Boogie
1979 Ladies Night
1979 Too Hot
1980 Celebration
1983 Joanna
1984 Cherish
1984 Fresh

KOOPER, AL

(See Blood, Sweat & Tears)
1968 You Don't Love Me
1971 New York City (You're a Woman)

KORN

1998 Blind

KOTTKE, LEO

1989 Jack Gets Up

KRAFTWERK

1975 Autobahn
1977 Trans Europe Express
1982 Computer Love

KRAMER, BILLY J. & THE DAKOTAS

1963 Bad to Me
1964 Little Children

KRAVITZ, LENNY

1991   It Ain't over till It's Over
1993   Are You Gonna Go My Way
1998   Fly Away

KRISS KROSS

1992   Jump

KRISTOFFERSON, KRIS

1969   For the Good Times
1969   Help Me Make It through the Night
1969   Sunday Mornin' Coming Down

KROKUS

1983   Eat the Rich

KWESKIN, JIM & THE JUG BAND, FEATURING MARIA MULDAUR

1965   I'm a Woman

KYLIE MINOGUE

1988   I Should Be So Lucky

L

L.T.D.

1977   (Every Time I Turn Around) Back in Love Again

LA FLAMME, DAVID

1976   White Bird

LA TOUR

1991   People Are Still Having Sex

LA'S, THE

1991   There She Goes

LABELLE, PATTI AND MICHAEL MCDONALD

1986   On My Own

LABELLE

1974   Lady Marmelade

LAKESIDE

1981   Fantastic Voyage

LANCE, MAJOR

1963   Monkey Time, The
1963   Um Um Um Um Um Um

LANG, K.D.

1992   Constant Craving

LARKIN, PATTY

1991   Metal Drums

LARKS, THE

1964   Jerk, The

LASALLE, DENISE

1971   Now Run and Tell That
1971   Trapped by a Thing Called Love

LAST POETS, THE

1971   Revolution Will Not Be Televised, The

LATIMORE

1974   Let's Straighten It Out

LAUPER, CYNDI

1984   She Bop
1984   Time After Time
1986   Change of Heart
1986   True Colors

LAURIE, ANNIE

1947   Since I Fell for You

LAURIE, LINDA

1959   Ambrose, Part V.

LAVIN, CHRISTINE

1990   Sensitive New Age Guys

LAWRENCE, VICKIE

1973   Night the Lights Went out in Georgia, The

LEAVES, THE

1965   Hey Joe

LED ZEPPELIN

1969   Black Mountain Side
1969   Dazed and Confused
1969   Good Times, Bad Times
1969   Heartbreaker
1969   How Many More Times
1969   Lemon Song, The
1969   Living Loving Maid (She's Just a Woman)
1969   Traveling Riverside Blues
1969   Whole Lotta Love
1970   Bron Y' Aur Stomp
1970   Gallows Pole
1970   Immigrant Song
1970   Tangerine
1971   Black Dog
1971   Going to California
1971   Rock and Roll
1971   Stairway to Heaven
1971   When the Levee Breaks
1973   Crunge, The
1973   Dancing Days
1973   D'Yer Maker
1973   No Quarter
1973   Ocean, The
1973   Over the Hills and Far Away
1973   Song Remains the Same, The
1975   Kashmir
1975   Trampled under Foot
1976   Achilles Last Stand
1979   All My Love
1979   Fool in the Rain

LEE, BRENDA

1956   Bigelow 6-200
1957   Dynamite
1957   One Step at a Time
1960   I Want to Be Wanted
1960   I'm Sorry
1960   Sweet Nothin's
1960   That's All You Gotta Do
1961   Break It to Me Gently
1961   Dum Dum
1961   Emotions
1961   Fool Number 1
1962   All Alone Am I
1966   Coming on Strong

LEE, CURTIS

1961   Pretty Little Angel Eyes
1961   Under the Moon of Love

LEE, DICKEY

1962   Patches

LEE, JOHNNY

1980   Looking for Love

LEE, LAURA

1971   Women's Love Rights
1972   Rip Off, The

LEE, PEGGY

1989   Is That All There Is

LEFT BANKE, THE

1966   Walk Away Renee
1967   Pretty Ballerina

LEMON PIPERS, THE

1967   Green Tambourine

LEMONHEADS, THE

1992   It's a Shame about Ray

LENNON, JOHN

(See The Beatles)

1970	Instant Karma (We All Shine On)
1970	Power to the People
1971	Crippled Inside
1971	Gimme Some Truth
1971	How Do You Sleep
1971	Imagine
1971	Jealous Guy
1971	Oh Yoko
1973	Mind Games
1974	#9 Dream
1974	Whatever Gets You thru the Night
1980	(Just Like) Starting Over
1980	Watching the Wheels
1980	Woman
1984	I'm Stepping Out
1984	Nobody Told Me
1988	Real Love

LENNON, JOHN & PLASTIC ONO BAND

1969	Cold Turkey
1969	Give Peace a Chance
1970	God
1970	Mother
1970	Working Class Hero

LENNON, JULIAN

1984	Valotte
1985	Too Late for Goodbyes

LENNOX, ANNIE

(See the Eurythmics)

1992	Walking on Broken Glass
1992	Why

LESTER, KETTY

1962	Love Letters

LET'S ACTIVE

1988	Every Dog Has His Day

LEVERT

1987	Casanova

LEWIS, BARBARA

1963	Hello Stranger

LEWIS, BOBBY

1961	Tossin' and Turnin'

LEWIS, DONNA

1996	I Love You Always Forever

LEWIS, GARY AND THE PLAYBOYS

1964	This Diamond Ring
1965	Count Me In
1965	She's Just My Style

LEWIS, HUEY AND THE NEWS

1982	Do You Believe in Love
1984	Heart of Rock and Roll
1984	I Want a New Drug
1985	Power of Love, The
1986	Hip to Be Square
1986	Jacob's Ladder
1986	Stuck with You
1988	Perfect World

LEWIS, JERRY LEE

1957	Great Balls of Fire
1958	Breathless
1958	High School Confidential
1970	She Even Woke Me up to Say Goodbye

LEWIS, SMILEY

1955	I Hear You Knocking
1955	One Night (of Sin)

LEYTON, JOHN

1961	Johnny Remember Me

LFO

1999	Summer Girls

LIEBERMAN, LORI

1972	Killing Me Softly with His Song

LIFEHOUSE

2000	Hanging by a Moment

LIGGINS, JOE

1945	Honeydripper, The

LIGHTFOOT, GORDON

1970	If You Could Read My Mind
1974	Carefree Highway
1974	Sundown
1976	Wreck of the Edmund Fitzgerald, The

LIL KIM

1996	No Time
1996	Not Tonight

LIMELITERS, THE

1962	Those Were the Days

LIMP BIZKIT

1999	Break Stuff
1999	Re-arranged

LIND, BOB

1965	Elusive Butterfly

LINEAR

1990	Sending All My Love

LINHART, BUZZY

1970	Friends

LINKIN PARK

2000	One Step Closer

LIPPS INC.

1979	Funkytown

LISA LISA & CULT JAM

1985	All Cried Out
1985	I Wonder If I Take You Home
1987	Head to Toe
1987	Lost in Emotion
1991	Let the Beat Him 'Em

LITTLE, DEETTA AND NELSON PIGFORD

1976	Gonna Fly Now (Theme from *Rocky*)

LITTLE ANTHONY AND THE IMPERIALS

1958	Tears on My Pillow
1959	Shimmy, Shimmy Ko-Ko Bop
1964	Goin' out of My Head

LITTLE CAESAR AND THE ROMANS

1961	Those Oldies But Goodies Remind Me of You

LITTLE EVA

1962	Keep Your Hands off My Baby
1962	Loco-Motion, The

LITTLE FEAT

1970	Willing
1974	Oh Atlanta
1977	Rocket in My Pocket
1978	All That You Dream
1988	Hangin' on to the Good Times

LITTLE JOE & THE THRILLERS

1957	Peanuts

LITTLE JUNIOR PARKER

1961   Driving Wheel

LITTLE RICHARD

1951   Taxi Blues
1955   True Fine Mama
1955   Tutti Frutti
1956   Girl Can't Help It, The
1956   Heeby Jeebies
1956   Jenny Jenny
1956   Long Tall Sally
1956   Ready Teddy
1956   Rip It Up
1956   Slippin' and Slidin'
1957   Keep A-Knockin'
1957   Lucille
1957   Miss Ann
1957   Oooh! My Soul
1957   Send Me Some Lovin'
1958   Good Golly, Miss Molly
1965   I Don't Know What You've Got (But
         It's Got Me)
1986   Great Gosh a Mighty

LITTLE RIVER BAND

1978   Reminiscing
1979   Cool Change

LITTLE ROGER & THE GOOSEBUMPS

1978   Stairway to Gilligan's Island

LITTLE STEVEN & THE DISCIPLES OF SOUL

1984   I Am a Patriot

LITTLE WALTER & HIS NITECATS

1952   Juke
1955   My Babe

LITTLEFIELD, LITTLE WILLIE

1952   K.C. Lovin'

LIVE

1994   I Alone
1994   Lightning Crashes
1994   Selling the Drama

LIVING COLOUR

1988   Glamour Boys
1989   Cult of Personality
1990   Elvis Is Dead

LL COOL J

1985   I Can't Live without My Radio
1985   I Want You
1985   Rock the Bells
1987   Going Back to Cali
1987   I Need Love
1989   I'm That Type of Guy
1990   Around the Way Girl
1991   Mama Said Knock You Out
1996   Loungin'
1997   Father

LOBO

1971   Me and You and a Dog Named Boo
1972   I'd Love You to Want Me

LOCKLIN, HANK

1960   Please Help Me I'm Falling

LOEB, LISA & NINE STORIES

1994   Stay (I Missed You)

LOFGREN, NILS

1977   I Came to Dance

LOGGINS, DAVE

1974   Please Come to Boston

LOGGINS, KENNY

1978   What a Fool Believes
1978   Whenever I Call You 'Friend'
1980   I'm Alright
1984   Footloose
1986   Danger Zone

LOGGINS & MESSINA

1971   Danny's Song
1971   Vahevela
1972   Angry Eyes
1972   Your Mama Don't Dance

LOLITA

1960   Sailor (Your Home Is the Sea)

LONDON, LAURIE

1957   He's Got the Whole World in His
         Hands

LONDONBEAT

1991   I've Been Thinking about You

LONE JUSTICE

1985   Ways to Be Wicked

LONESOME VAL

1990   To Be Young

LONG, SHORTY

1964   Devil with a Blue Dress On
1968   Here Comes the Judge

LOOKING GLASS

1972   Brandy (You're a Fine Girl)

LOPEZ, JENNIFER

1999   If You Had My Love

LOS BRAVOS

1966   Black Is Black

LOS DEL RIO

1995   Macarena

LOS LOBOS

1985   Will the Wolf Survive
1987   Hardest Time, The
1987   One Time One Night

LOVE, DARLENE

(See The Crystals, Bob E. Soxx & the Bluejeans)
1963   Fine Fine Boy, A
1963   Today I Met the Boy I'm Gonna Marry
1963   Wait 'til My Bobby Gets Home

LOVE

1966   S7 and 7 Is
1967   Alone Again Or
1967   She Comes in Colors
1967   You Set the Scene

LOVE AND KISSES

1978   Thank God It's Friday

LOVE AND ROCKETS

1985   If There's a Heaven Above
1989   So Alive

LOVE SCULPTURE

1969   Sabre Dance

LOVE UNLIMITED ORCHESTRA

1973   Love's Theme

LOVECRAFT, H.P.

1967   I've Been Wrong Before

LOVERBOY

1982   Working for the Weekend
1983   Hot Girls in Love
1985   Lovin' Every Minute of It

LOVETT, LYLE

1987   L.A. County
1987   She's No Lady

LOVICH, LENE

1979   Lucky Number

LOVIN' SPOONFUL, THE

1965   Did You Ever Have to Make up Your
        Mind
1965   Do You Believe in Magic
1965   Other Side of This Life, The
1965   Younger Girl, A
1966   Coconut Grove
1966   Daydream
1966   Nashville Cats
1966   Summer in the City
1966   You Didn't Have to Be So Nice
1967   You're a Big Boy Now
1968   Younger Generation

LOWE, JIM

1956   Green Door, The

LOWE, NICK

(See Rockpile)
1978   Cruel to Be Kind
1978   Heart of the City
1978   (I Love the Sound of) Breaking Glass
1985   I Knew the Bride When She Used to
        Rock and Roll

LSG

1997   My Body

LUHRMAN, BAZ

1999   Everybody's Free (To Wear Sunscreen)

LUKE, ROBIN

1958   Susie Darlin

LULU

1964   Here Comes the Night
1967   To Sir, with Love
1970   Oh Me Oh My (I'm a Fool for You,
        Baby)

LUNDBERG, VICTOR

1967   An Open Letter to My Teenage Son

LYMON, FRANKIE AND THE TEENAGERS

1956   A.B.C.'s of Love, The
1956   I Want You to Be My Girl
1956   Why Do Fools Fall in Love
1957   Goody Goody
1957   I'm Not a Juvenile Delinquent

LYNN, BARBARA

1962   You'll Lose a Good Thing
1966   You Left the Water Running

LYNN, CHERYL

1978   Got to Be Real

LYNYRD SKYNYRD

1973   Free Bird
1973   Gimme Three Steps
1974   Sweet Home Alabama
1975   Saturday Night Special
1977   I Know a Little
1977   That Smell
1977   What's Your Name
1977   You Got That Right

LYTE, MC

1989   Cappucino
1993   Ruffneck
1996   Cold Rock a Party

M

M

1979   Pop Muzik

M.A.R.R.S.

1988   Pump up the Volume

MABON, WILLIE

1952   I Don't Know
1953   I'm Mad

MACCOLL, KIRSTY

1979   They Don't Know
1981   There's a Guy Works down the Chip
        Shop Swears He's Elvis
1991   Walking down Madison

MACGREGGOR, MARY

1977   Torn between Two Lovers

MACK, LONNIE

1963   Wham, The

MADNESS

1983   Our House

MADONNA

1983   Borderline
1983   Holiday
1983   Lucky Star
1984   Angel
1984   Dress You Up
1984   Like a Virgin
1984   Material Girl
1985   Crazy for You
1986   Into the Groove
1986   La Isla Bonita
1986   Live to Tell
1986   Open Your Heart
1986   Papa Don't Preach
1986   True Blue
1986   Where's the Party
1987   Causing a Commotion
1987   Who's That Girl
1989   Cherish
1989   Express Yourself
1989   Keep It Together
1989   Like a Prayer
1989   Vogue
1990   Hanky Panky
1990   Justify My Love
1990   Rescue Me
1990   Sooner or Later (I Always Get My
        Man)
1992   Deeper and Deeper
1992   Erotica
1992   This Used to Be My Playground
1994   Goodbye to Innocence
1994   I'll Remember
1994   Secret
1994   Take a Bow
1998   Frozen
1998   Power of Goodbye, The
1998   Ray of Light
2000   Don't Tell Me
2000   Music

MAGAZINE

1979   Shot by Both Sides

MAGICIANS, THE

1966   Invitation to Cry

MAHAVISHNU ORCHESTRA

1971   Noonward Race, The

MAIN INGREDIENT, THE

1972   Everybody Plays the Fool

MALMSTEEN, YNGWIE

1985   Black Star

MALO

1972   Suavecito

MAMAS & THE PAPAS, THE

1966   California Dreamin'
1966   Go Where You Wanna Go
1966   I Saw Her Again Last Night
1966   Monday, Monday
1966   Words of Love

1967   Creeque Alley
1967   Twelve-Thirty (Young Girls Are
         Coming to the Canyon)

MANCHESTER, MELISSA

1978   Don't Cry out Loud
1982   You Should Hear How She Talks about
         You

MANHATTANS, THE

1976   Kiss and Say Goodbye
1980   Shining Star

MANILOW, BARRY

1976   Looks Like We Made It
1977   Copacabana (At the Copa)

MANN, AIMEE

(See Voices Carry)

1993   Put Me on Top
1995   That's Just What You Are
1999   Save Me

MANN, BARRY

1961   Who Put the Bomp (In the Bomp Ba
         Bomp Ba Bomp)

MANN, MANFRED

1965   Come Tomorrow
1965   If You Gotta Go, Go Now (Or Else
         You Got to Stay All Night
1965   My Little Red Book (All I Do Is Talk
         about You)
1966   Pretty Flamingo
1968   Mighty Quinn (Quinn, the Eskimo),
         The

MANSON, MARILYN

1996   Beautiful People, The
1996   Tourniquet

MARATHONS, THE

1961   Peanut Butter

MARCELS, THE

1961   Blue Moon

MARCH, LITTLE PEGGY

1963   I Will Follow Him (Chariot)

MARCY PLAYGROUND

1997   Sex and Candy

MARDONES, BENNY

1980   Into the Night

MARESCA, ERNIE

1962   Shout! Shout! Knock Yourself Out!

MARK, MARKY AND THE FUNKY BUNCH

1991   Good Vibrations

MARKETTS, THE

1962   Surfer's Stomp
1963   Out of Limits
1966   Theme from Batman

MAR-KEYS

1961   Last Night

MARLEY, BOB AND THE WAILERS

1963   Exodus
1963   Judge Not
1964   Simmer Down
1965   One Love
1966   Rude Boy
1968   Stir It Up
1969   Four Hundred Years
1971   Stop That Train
1971   Trenchtown Rock
1972   Concrete Jungle
1972   Lively up Yourself
1973   Get up Stand Up
1973   I Shot the Sheriff
1974   No Woman, No Cry
1976   Roots, Rock, Reggae
1977   Jamming
1977   Three Little Birds
1978   Is This Love
1980   Could You Be Loved
1980   Redemption Song

MARLEY, ZIGGY

1988   Tumbling Down

MARSHALL TUCKER BAND, THE

1977   Heard It in a Love Song

MARTHA & THE VANDELLAS

1963   Come and Get These Memories
1963   Heat Wave
1963   Quicksand
1964   Dancing in the Street
1965   Nowhere to Run
1966   I'm Ready for Love
1967   Jimmy Mack

MARTIKA

1989   Toy Soldiers

MARTIN, DEAN

1953   That's Amore

MARTIN, JANIS

1956   Drugstore Rock and Roll
1956   My Boy Elvis

MARTIN, RICKY

1998   Cup of Life, The
1999   Livin' la Vida Loca
1999   She's All I Ever Had

MARTIN, STEVE AND THE TOOTS UNCOMMONS

1978   King Tut

MARTIN AND NEIL

1965   I Know You Rider

MARVELETTES, THE

1961   Please Mr. Postman
1962   Beechwood 4-5789
1962   Playboy
1962   Strange I Know
1963   Locking up My Heart
1967   Hunter Gets Captured by the Game,
         The
1967   My Baby Must Be a Magician

MARVELOWS, THE

1965   I Do

MARVIN AND JOHNNY

1954   Cherry Pie

MARX, RICHARD

1987   Don't Mean Nothin'
1987   Should've Known Better
1988   Endless Summer Nights
1988   Hold on to the Nights
1989   Angelia
1989   Right Here Waiting
1989   Satisfied

MARY JANE GIRLS

1985   In My House

MASE

1997   Feel So Good

MASEKELA, HUGH

1968   Grazing in the Grass

MASON, BARBARA

1965   Yes, I'm Ready

MASON, BONNIE JO

1964   Ringo I Love You

MASON, DAVE

(See Traffic)
1970   Only You Know and I Know
1970   Shouldn't Have Took More Than You
       Gave
1977   We Just Disagree

MASSIVE ATTACK

1991   Unfinished Sympathy

MASTER P

1996   Mr. Ice Cream Man
1997   I Miss My Homies
1998   Goodbye to My Homies
1998   I Got the Hook Up
1998   Make Em Say Uhh

MATCHBOX TWENTY

1997   Push
1997   Real World
1997   3AM
2000   Bent

MATHIS, JOHNNY

1957   Wonderful, Wonderful

MATTHEWS BAND, DAVE

1994   Ants Marching
1994   What Would You Say
1996   Crash into Me
1996   So Much to Say
1996   Too Much
1996   Two Step
1997   Tripping Billies
1998   Crush

MAXI PRIEST

1990   Close to You

MAXWELL

1996   Ascenscion

MAYALL, JOHN

1969   Room to Move
1967   Have You Heard

MAYALL'S, JOHN BLUESBREAKERS

1967   Steppin' Out

MAYFIELD, CURTIS

(See The Impressions)
1970   Don't Worry (If There's a Hell below
       We're All Gonna Go)
1972   Freddy's Dead (Theme from *Superfly*)
1972   Pusherman
1972   Superfly

MAYFIELD, PERCY

1951   Please Send Me Someone to Love

MC5, THE

1969   Kick out the Jams

MCCAIN, EDWIN

1998   I'll Be

MCCALL, C.W.

1975   Convoy

MCCANN, LES AND EDDIE HARRIS

1970   Compared to What

MCCANN, PETER

1977   Do You Wanna Make Love

MCCARTNEY, PAUL

(See The Beatles)
1971   Maybe I'm Amazed
1980   Coming Up
1982   Here Today
1982   Take It Away
1984   No More Lonely Nights
1986   Spies Like Us
1993   Off the Ground

MCCARTNEY, PAUL AND LINDA

1983   Say Say Say

MCCARTNEY, PAUL AND STEVIE WONDER

1982   Ebony and Ivory

MCCARTNEY, PAUL AND WINGS

1971   Another Day
1971   Monkberry Moon Delight
1971   Uncle Albert/Admiral Halsey
1972   Hi Hi Hi
1973   Helen Wheels
1973   Live and Let Die
1973   My Love
1974   Band on the Run
1974   Jet
1974   Junior's Farm
1975   Listen to What the Man Said
1976   Let 'Em In
1976   Mull of Kintyre
1976   Silly Love Songs
1978   With a Little Luck
1979   Goodnight Tonight

MCCOO, MARILYN AND BILLY DAVIS

(See The 5th Dimension)
1976   You Don't Have to Be a Star (to Be in
       My Show)
1985   Saving All My Love for You

MCCOY, VAN

1975   Hustle, The

MCCRAE, GEORGE

1974   Rock Your Baby
1975   Rockin' Chair

MCCULLOUGH, IAN

(See Echo & the Bunnymen)
1989   Proud to Fall

MCDANIEL, GENE

1961   Hundred Pounds of Clay, A
1961   Tower of Strength

MCFADDEN & WHITEHEAD

1979   Ain't No Stoppin' Us Now

MCFERRIN, BOBBY

1987   Don't Worry, Be Happy

MCGARRIGLE, KATE AND ANNA

1975   (Talk to Me of) Mendocino
1990   Heartbeats Accelerating

MCGHEE, STICK

1949   Drinking Wine Spo-Dee O-Dee

MCGUINN, ROGER

(See The Byrds)
1990   King of the Hill

MCGUIRE, BARRY

1965   Eve of Destruction

MCKENZIE, BOB AND DOUG

1982   Take Off

MCKENZIE, SCOTT

1967   San Francisco (Be Sure to Wear Some
       Flowers in Your Hair)

MCLACHLAN, SARAH

1992	Into the Fire
1994	Possession
1994	Wait
1995	I Will Remember You
1997	Adia
1997	Angel
1997	Building a Mystery
1997	Sweet Surrender

MCLEAN, DON

| 1971 | American Pie |
| 1972 | Vincent |

MCMURTRY, JAMES

| 1989 | I'm Not from Here |

MCNEELY, BIG JAY

| 1957 | There Is Something on Your Mind |

MCPHATTER, CLYDE

(See The Drifters)

1956	Seven Days
1956	Treasure of Love
1957	Without Love (There Is Nothing)
1958	Lover's Question, A
1961	Lover, Please

MCTELL, RALPH

| 1971 | Streets of London |

MCVIE, CHRISTINE

(See Fleetwood Mac)

| 1984 | Got a Hold on Me |

MEADOWLARKS

| 1955 | Heaven and Paradise |

MEAT LOAF

(See Stoney & Meatloaf)

1977	Paradise by the Dashboard Light
1977	Two out of Three Ain't Bad
1993	I'd Do Anything for Love (But I Won't Do That)

MEAT PUPPETS

| 1982 | Lake of Fire |
| 1991 | Sam |

MECO

| 1977 | *Star Wars* Theme |

MEDALLIONS, THE

| 1954 | Letter, The |

MEDEIROS, GLENN AND BOBBY BROWN

| 1990 | She Ain't Worth It |

MEDLEY, BILL

(See The Righteous Brothers and Jennifer Warnes)

| 1987 | (I've Had) The Time of My Life |

MEGADETH

1988	In My Darkest Hour
1991	Hangar 18
1992	Symphony of Destruction

MEKONS, THE

| 1989 | Empire of the Senseless |

MEL AND TIM

| 1969 | Backfield in Motion |

MELANIE

1969	Beautiful People
1970	Lay Down (Candles in the Rain)
1970	Peace Will Come (According to Plan)
1970	What Have They Done to My Song, Ma
1971	Brand New Key

MELLENCAMP, JOHN COUGAR

1979	I Need a Lover
1981	Ain't Even Done with the Night
1982	Hurts So Good
1982	Jack and Diane
1983	Authority Song
1983	Crumblin' Down
1983	Pink Houses
1985	Lonely Ol' Night
1985	Rock in the U.S.A. (A Salute to 1960s Rock)
1985	Small Town
1987	Cherry Bomb
1987	Paper in Fire
1993	What If I Came Knocking

MELLOW KINGS, THE

| 1957 | Tonite, Tonite |

MELODIANS, THE

| 1970 | Rivers of Babylon |

MELVIN, HAROLD AND THE BLUENOTES

1972	If You Don't Know Me by Now
1973	Love I Lost, The
1975	Wake up Everybody, Part One

MELVINS, THE

| 1985 | Grinding Process |

MEMPHIS SLIM

| 1948 | Rockin' the House |

MEN, THE

| 1992 | Church of Logic, Sin and Love |

MEN AT WORK

1982	Down Under
1982	Who Can It Be Now
1983	Overkill

MEN WITHOUT HATS

| 1983 | Safety Dance |

MERCHANT, NATALIE

(See 10,000 Maniacs)

| 1995 | Carnival |
| 1995 | Wonder |

MERCY

| 1969 | Love (Can Make You Happy) |

MERRY-GO-ROUND

| 1967 | Live |
| 1967 | You're a Very Lovely Woman |

METALLICA

1983	Jump in the Fire
1984	Fade to Black
1984	For Whom the Bell Tolls
1986	Master of Puppets
1986	Welcome Home (Sanitarium)
1988	One
1991	Enter Sandman
1991	Nothing Else Matters
1991	Unforgiven, The
1996	Hero of the Day
1996	Until It Sleeps
1997	Memory Remains, The

METERS, THE

| 1969 | Sophisticated Cissy |

MFSB

| 1973 | TSOP (The Sound of Philadelphia) |

MIAMI SOUND MACHINE

1986	Bad Boy
1986	Conga
1987	Rhythm Is Gonna Get You

MICHAEL, GEORGE

(See Wham!)

1987　Faith
1987　Father Figure
1987　I Want Your Sex
1987　Kissing a Fool
1987　One More Try
1988　Monkey
1990　Freedom
1990　Praying for Time
1992　Too Funky

MICHEL, PRAS

1998　Ghetto Supastar (That Is What You Are)

MICKEY AND SYLVIA

1957　Love Is Strange

MIDLER, BETTE

1972　Delta Dawn
1972　Raspberries, Lilacs and Lime
1979　Rose, The
1983　All I Need to Know (Don't Know Much)

MIDNIGHT OIL

1987　Beds Are Burning

MIDNIGHTERS, THE

1954　Annie Had a Baby
1954　Annie's Aunt Fanny
1954　Sexy Ways
1954　Work with Me Annie
1955　Henry's Got Flat Feet
1959　Teardrops on Your Letter
1959　Twist, The
1960　Finger Poppin' Time
1960　Let's Go, Let's Go, Let's Go
1960　Look at Little Sister

MIGHTY, MIGHTY BOSSTONES, THE

1997　Impression That I Get, The

MIKE & THE MECHANICS

(See Genesis)

1985　All I Need Is a Miracle
1989　Living Years, The

MILBURN, AMOS

1948　Chicken Shack Boogie
1953　One Scotch, One Bourbon, One Beer

MILES, BUDDY

1970　Them Changes

MILLER, ALECK

1951　One Way Out

MILLER, ROGER

1965　King of the Road
1966　My Uncle Used to Love Me But She Died
1967　Me and Bobby McGee

MILLER BAND, STEVE

1968　Children of the Future
1968　Living in the U.S.A.
1969　Mercury Blues
1969　Space Cowboy
1973　Joker, The
1976　Fly Like an Eagle
1976　Rock n' Me
1976　Take the Money and Run
1977　Jet Airliner
1982　Abracadabra
1986　I Want to Make the World Turn Around

MILLI VANILLI

1989　All or Nothing
1989　Baby Don't Forget My Number
1989　Blame It on the Rain
1989　Girl I'm Gonna Miss You
1989　Girl You Know It's True

MILLS, HAYLEY

1962　Let's Get Together

MILLS, STEPHANIE

1980　Never Knew Love Like This Before

MIMMS, GARNET & THE ENCHANTERS

1963　Cry Baby
1963　Get It While You Can
1963　Try (Just a Little Bit Harder)
1967　Piece of My Heart

MINDBENDERS, THE

1966　Groovy Kind of Love, A

MINEO, SAL

1957　Start Movin'

MINISTRY

1988　Land of Rape and Honey
1988　Tonight We Murder
1991　Jesus Built My Hotrod

MINK DEVILLE

1977　Cadillac Walk

MINOR THREAT

1981　Minor Threat

MINUTEMEN, THE

1984　History Lesson (Part Two)

MIRACLES, THE

1958　Got a Job
1959　Bad Girl
1960　Way over There
1961　Shop Around
1963　Love She Can Count On, A
1963　Mickey's Monkey
1963　You've Really Got a Hold on Me
1965　Going to a Go-Go
1965　Ooh Baby Baby
1965　Tracks of My Tears, The
1967　I Second That Emotion
1967　Love I Saw in You Was Just a Mirage, The
1967　More Love
1967　Tears of a Clown, The
1968　If You Can Want
1969　Baby, Baby Don't Cry
1970　Who's Gonna Take the Blame
1972　We've Come Too Far to End It Now
1975　Love Machine (Part 1)

MISFITS, THE

1979　Last Caress
1982　Mommy, Can I Go out and Kill Tonight

MISSING PERSONS

1982　Words

MISSION OF BURMA

1981　That's When I Reach for My Revolver

MITCHELL, JONI

1968　I Had a King
1968　Marcie
1968　Night in the City
1969　Chelsea Morning
1969　Songs to Aging Children Come
1969　That Song about the Midway
1970　Big Yellow Taxi
1971　All I Want
1971　Blue
1971　Carey
1971　Case of You, A
1971　Last Time I Saw Richard, The
1971　River
1972　Blonde in the Bleachers
1972　Cold Blue Steel and Sweet Fire
1972　For the Roses
1972　Woman of Heart and Mind
1972　You Turn Me on, I'm a Radio
1974　Car on a Hill
1974　Free Man in Paris
1974　Help Me

1974   Raised on Robbery
1974   Real Good for Free
1976   Amelia
1991   Come in from the Cold

MOBY

1991   Go
1999   Porcelain
2000   South Side

MOBY GRAPE

1967   Hey Grandma
1967   Omaha

MODERN ENGLISH

1982   I Melt with You

MODERN LOVERS, THE

1970   Pablo Picasso
1971   Astral Plane
1971   Girlfriend
1971   Road Runner
1971   She Cracked
1976   Important in Your Life
1977   Egyptian Reggae
1983   That Summer Feeling

MODEST MOUSE

1997   Jesus Christ Was an Only Child

MODUGNO, DOMENICO

1958   Nel Blu Dipinto Di Blu (Volare)

MOHAWK, ESSRA

1970   Arch Godliness and Purpleful Magic
1970   I Have Been Here Before

MOJO MEN, THE

1966   Sit down I Think I Love You

MOLLY HATCHET

1980   Flirtin' with Disaster

MOMENTS, THE

1970   Love on a Two-Way Street

MONEY, EDDIE

1977   Two Tickets to Paradise
1978   Baby Hold On
1986   Take Me Home Tonight

MONICA

1997   For You I Will
1998   First Night, The
1999   Angel of Mine

MONKEES, THE

1966   I'm a Believer
1966   Last Train to Clarksville
1967   Daydream Believer
1967   Little Bit Me, a Little Bit You, A
1967   Pleasant Valley Sunday
1968   Porpoise Song, The
1968   Valleri

MONOTONES, THE

1957   Book of Love, The

MONROE, BILL

1947   Blue Moon of Kentucky

MONROES, THE

1982   What Do All the People Know

MONTEZ, CHRIS

1962   Let's Dance

MOODSWINGS

1992   Spiritual High (State of Independence)

MOODY BLUES, THE

1968   Nights in White Satin
1968   Ride My See Saw
1968   Tuesday Afternoon (Forever
            Afternoon)
1970   Question
1972   I'm Just a Singer (In a Rock and Roll
            Band)
1972   Isn't Life Strange
1986   Your Wildest Dreams
1988   I Know You're out There
            Somewhere

MOONGLOWS, THE

1955   Sincerely
1957   Ten Commandments of Love, The

MOORE, GARRY

1985   Out in the Fields

MOORE, JACKIE

1978   Personally

MOORE, WILD BILL

1947   We're Gonna Rock, We're Gonna
            Roll
1949   Rock and Roll

MOORE'S THREE BLAZERS, JOHNNY

1946   Driftin' Blues
1950   Rock with It

MORISSETTE, ALANIS

1995   Hand In My Pocket
1995   Ironic
1995   You Learn
1995   You Oughta Know
1998   Uninvited

MORPHINE

1995   Honey White

MORRELLS, THE

1982   Man Who Has Everything, The

MORRISON, MARK

1997   Return of the Mack

MORRISON, VAN

(See Them)
1967   Brown Eyed Girl
1968   Beside You
1969   Caravan
1969   Cypress Avenue
1969   Madamme George
1970   And It Stoned Me
1970   Crazy Love
1970   Domino
1970   Into the Mystic
1970   Moondance
1971   Blue Money
1971   Call Me up in Dreamland
1971   Tupelo Honey
1971   Wild Night
1972   Jackie Wilson Said (I'm in Heaven
            When You Smile)
1972   Listening to the Lions
1983   Wonderful Remark
1986   In the Garden
1989   Have I Told You Lately
1991   Why Must I Always Explain

MORRISSEY

(See The Smiths)
1988   Everyday Is Like Sunday
1988   Suedehead
1989   Interesting Drug
1989   Last of the Famous International
            Playboys
1990   November Spawned a Monster
1991   Driving Your Girlfriend Home
1991   Our Frank
1992   We Hate It When Our Friends
            Become Successful
1993   I Know It's Gonna Happen
1994   More You Ignore Me, the Closer I
            Get, The

MOS DEF

1999   Rock and Roll

MOTELS, THE

1982   Only the Lonely
1983   Suddenly Last Summer

MOTHER EARTH

1968 Down So Low
1968 Mother Earth

MOTHER LOVE BONE

1989 Chloe Dancer/Crown of Thorns

MOTHERS OF INVENTION, THE

1966 Help I'm a Rock
1966 Trouble Comin' Every Day
1966 Who Are the Brain Police
1966 You Didn't Try to Call Me
1966 You're Probably Wondering Why I'm Here
1967 Brown Shoes Don't Make It
1967 Duke of Prunes
1967 Hungry Freaks, Daddy
1967 Son of Suzy Creamcheese
1967 Status Back Baby
1968 Concentration Moon
1968 Who Needs the Peace Corps?
1969 Cruisin' for Burgers
1970 My Guitar Wants to Kill Your Mama
1973 Montana

MOTLEY CRUE

1987 Girls, Girls, Girls
1989 Dr. Feelgood

MOTORHEAD

(See Hawkwind)
1977 Motorhead
1979 Bomber
1979 Overkill
1980 Ace of Spades
1980 We Are the Road Crew
1984 Killed by Death
1986 Deaf Forever
1991 1916

MOTT THE HOOPLE

1972 All the Young Dudes
1973 All the Way from Memphis
1974 Golden Age of Rock 'n' Roll

MOULD, BOB

(See Hüsker Dü Sugar)
1989 See a Little Light

MOUNTAIN

1970 For Yasgur's Farm
1970 Mississippi Queen
1970 Theme for an Imaginary Western

MOUSE

1966 Public Execution, A

MOVE, THE

1969 Blackberry Way
1972 Do Ya

MR. BIG

1992 To Be with You

MR. MISTER

1985 Broken Wings
1986 Kyrie

MUDHONEY

1988 Touch Me I'm Sick
1989 You Got It (Keep It outta My Face)

MULDAUR, MARIA

(See Jim Kweskin Jug Band)
1973 Mad Mad Me
1973 Midnight at the Oasis

MUNGO, JERRY

1970 In the Summertime

MURMAIDS, THE

1963 Popsicles and Icicles

MURPHEY, MICHAEL

1975 Wildfire

MURPHY, EDDIE

1985 Party All the Time

MURPHY, PETER

1990 Cuts You Up
1992 Sweetest Drop, The

MURRAY, ANNE

1970 Put Your Hand in the Hand
1970 Snowbird
1975 You Needed Me

MURVIN, JUNIOR

1976 Police and Thieves

MUSIC EXPLOSION, THE

1965 Little Bit o' Soul

MUSIC MACHINE, THE

1966 Talk, Talk

MUSICAL YOUTH

1983 Pass the Dutchie

MUSIQUE

1978 In the Bush

MY BLOODY VALENTINE

1991 Only Shallow
1991 Soon
1991 When You Sleep

MYLES, ALANNAH

1990 Black Velvet

MYSTICS, THE

1959 Hushabye

N

NADA SURF

1996 Popular

NAILS, THE

1982 88 Lines About 44 Women

NAPOLEON XIV

1966 They're Coming to Take Me away, Ha-Haaa!

NAS

1994 New York State of Mind

NASH, GRAHAM

1971 Chicago
1971 We Can Change the World

NASH, JOHNNY

1968 Hold Me Tight
1972 I Can See Clearly Now

NASHVILLE TEENS, THE

1964 Tobacco Road

NATIONAL LAMPOON

1972 Deteriorata

NATURAL SELECTION

1991 Do Anything

NAUGHTON, DAVID

1979 Makin' It

NAUGHTY BY NATURE

1991 O.P.P.
1993 Hip Hop Hooray

NAZARETH

1975   Hair of the Dog

NAZZ, THE

1968   Open My Eyes
1969   Hello, It's Me

NDEGEOCELLO, ME'SHELL

1993   If That's Your Boyfriend, He Wasn't
         Last Night

NED'S ATOMIC DUSTBIN

1992   Not Sleeping Around

NEIL, FRED

1967   Dolphins, The
1967   Everybody's Talkin'

NELLY

2000   Hot Shit (Country Grammar)

NELSON

1990   (Can't Live without Your) Love and
         Affection

NELSON, RICK

1961   Hello Mary Lou
1961   Travelin' Man
1962   Teenage Idol
1972   Garden Party

NELSON, RICKY

1957   Be Bop Baby
1957   If You Can't Rock Me
1957   Stood Up
1957   Teenager's Romance
1957   Waitin' in School
1958   Believe What You Say
1958   I Got a Feeling
1958   Lonesome Town
1958   Poor Little Fool
1958   Restless Kid
1959   It's Late

NELSON, SANDY

1959   Teen Beat
1961   Let There Be Drums

NELSON, TRACY

(See Mother Earth)
1971   Seven Bridges Road

NELSON, WILLIE

1980   On the Road Again

NELSON

1990   After the Rain

NENA

1984   99 Luftbalons (99 Red Balloons)

NERF HERDER

1997   Van Halen

NERVES, THE

1976   Hanging on the Telephone

NERVOUS NORVUS

1956   Transfusion

NEVIL, ROBBIE

1987   C'est la Vie

NEVILLE, AARON

1966   Tell It Like It Is

NEW EDITION

1983   Candy Girl
1984   Cool It Now
1984   Mr. Telephone Man
1988   Boys to Men

NEW KIDS ON THE BLOCK

1988   Cover Girl
1988   Hangin' Tough
1988   I'll Be Loving You (Forever)
1988   You Got It (The Right Stuff)
1989   Step by Step

NEW ORDER

1982   Temptation
1983   Blue Monday
1985   Age of Consent
1985   Perfect Kiss
1986   Bizarre Love Triangle
1993   Regret

NEW RADICALS

1998   You Get What You Give

NEW RIDERS OF THE PURPLE SAGE

1973   Panama Red

NEW VAUDEVILLE BAND, THE

1966   Winchester Cathedral

NEW YORK DOLLS

1973   Looking for a Kiss
1973   Personality Crisis
1973   Trash
1974   Human Being

NEWBEATS, THE

1964   Bread and Butter

NEWCLEUS

1984   Jam on It

NEWMAN, RANDY

1968   Cowboy
1968   Davy the Fat Boy
1968   Living without You
1968   So Long Dad
1970   Gone Dead Train
1970   Have You Seen My Baby
1971   Lonely at the Top
1971   Maybe I'm Doing It Wrong
1972   Burn on, Big River
1972   God's Song (That's Why I Love
         Mankind)
1972   He Gives Us All His Love
1972   Political Science
1972   Sail Away
1972   You Can Leave Your Hat On
1974   Louisiana, 1927
1977   Short People
1983   I Love L.A.
1983   My Life Is Good
1988   It's Money That Matters

NEWTON, JUICE

1975   Sweetest Thing I've Ever Known, The

NEWTON-JOHN, OLIVIA

1974   I Honestly Love You
1974   If You Love Me (Let Me Know)
1975   Have You Never Been Mellow
1975   Please Mr. Please
1978   Hopelessly Devoted to You
1979   Little More Love, A
1980   Magic
1981   Heart Attack
1981   Make a Move on Me
1981   Physical
1983   Twist of Fate

NEWTON-JOHN, OLIVIA AND JOHN TRAVOLTA

1978   You're the One That I Want

NEXT

1997   Butta Love
1997   Too Close

NICHOLAS, PAUL

1977   Heaven on the Seventh Floor

NICKS, STEVIE

(See Fleetwood Mac)
1982   Edge of Seventeen
1983   Stand Back
1986   Talk to Me

NICKS, STEVIE AND DON HENLEY

1981   Leather and Lace

NICKS, STEVIE AND TOM PETTY

1981   Stop Draggin' My Heart Around

NICO

(See Velvet Underground)
1965   Last Mile, The
1967   Chelsea Girl
1967   Eulogy to Lenny Bruce
1967   Little Sister
1967   Somewhere There's a Feather
1967   These Days
1967   Wrap Your Troubles in Dreams

NICOLE

1998   Make It Hot

NIGHT RANGER

1984   Sister Christian

NIGHTINGALE, MAXINE

1976   Right Back Where We Started From
1979   Lead Me On

NILSSON

1967   Without Her
1969   (I Guess) The Lord Must Be in
         New York City
1968   One
1970   Dayton, Ohio 1903
1971   Coconut
1971   Me and My Arrow
1971   Without You
1972   You're Breaking My Heart

NINE INCH NAILS

1990   Head Like a Hole
1994   Closer
1995   Hurt

1910 FRUITGUM COMPANY

1968   1,2,3, Red Light
1968   Simon Says
1969   Indian Giver

98 DEGREES

1998   Because of You
2000   Give Me Just One Night

NIRVANA

1988   Pay to Play
1991   About a Girl

1991   Come as You Are
1991   Drain You
1991   Lithium
1991   Smells Like Teen Spirit
1993   All Apologies
1993   Dumb
1993   Heart Shaped Box
1993   Pennyroyal Tea
1993   Rape Me
1994   Where Did You Sleep Last Night

NITTY GRITTY DIRT BAND

1970   House at Pooh Corner

NITZSCHE, JACK

1963   Lonely Surfer, The

NIXON, MOJO AND SKID ROPER

1987   Elvis Is Everywhere

NO DOUBT

1995   Don't Speak
1995   Spiderwebs

NO MERCY

1996   Where Do You Go

NOBLES & CO., CLIFF

1968   Horse, The

NOLAN, KENNY

1977   I Like Dreaming

NOTORIOUS B.I.G.

1994   Big Poppa
1994   Juicy
1997   Hypnotize
1997   Mo Money Mo Problems

NRBQ

1974   Get That Gasoline Blues

*NSYNC

1998   I Want You Back
2000   Bye Bye Bye
2000   It's Gonna Be Me
2000   This I Promise You

NU SHOOZ

1986   I Can't Wait

NUGENT, TED

(See Amboy Dukes)
1980   Wango Tango
1975   Stranglehold

1977   Cat Scratch Fever
1978   Yank Me, Crank Me

NUMAN, GARY

1980   Cars
1979   Are Friends Electric

NUTMEGS, THE

1955   Story Untold

NWA

1988   Fuck Tha Police
1988   Straight outta Compton

NYRO, LAURA

1967   And When I Die
1967   Stoney End
1967   Wedding Bell Blues
1968   Confession, The
1968   Eli's Coming
1968   Stoned Soul Picnic
1968   Sweet Blindness
1969   Captain for Dark Mornings
1969   Save the Country
1969   Time and Love
1971   Been on a Train
1976   Stormy Love
1978   American Dreamer

O

O'CONNOR, SINEAD

1988   Troy
1990   Emporer's New Clothes

O'DAY, ALAN

1977   Undercover Angel

O'JAYS, THE

1972   Back Stabbers
1972   Love Train
1973   For the Love of Money
1973   Now That We Found Love
1975   I Love Music (Part 1)
1975   Livin' for the Weekend
1977   Use ta Be My Girl

O'KAYSIONS, THE

1968   Girl Watcher

O'KEEFE, DANNY

1972   Good Time Charlie's Got the
         Blues
1972   Road, The

O'NEAL, ALEXANDER

1987   Fake

O'NEAL, SHAQUILLE

1993   (I Know I Got) Skillz

O'SULLIVAN, GILBERT

1972   Alone Again (Naturally)
1972   Clair

OASIS

1994   Live Forever
1994   Supersonic
1995   Champagne Supernova
1995   Don't Look Back in Anger
1995   Wonderwall

OCEAN, BILLY

1984   Caribbean Queen (No More Love on
        the Run)
1984   Loverboy
1984   Suddenly
1985   Love Zone
1985   There'll Be Sad Songs (To Make You
        Cry)
1985   When the Going Gets Tough the
        Tough Get Going
1988   Get outa My Dreams (Get into My
        Car)

OCHS, PHIL

1963   Power and the Glory, The
1964   Bound for Glory
1964   Here's to the State of Mississippi
1964   I Ain't Marchin' Anymore
1964   There but for Fortune
1966   Changes
1966   Love Me, I'm a Liberal
1967   Outside of a Small Circle of
        Friends

OCTOBER PROJECT

1993   Bury My Lovely

OFFSPRING

1994   Come out and Play
1994   Self Esteem
1997   Gone Away
1998   Pretty Fly for a White Guy

OHIO EXPRESS

1968   Yummy, Yummy, Yummy

OHIO PLAYERS

1973   Funky Worm
1974   Fire
1975   Love Rollercoaster
1975   Sweet Sticky Thing
1976   Who'd She Coo

OINGO BOINGO

1985   Weird Science

OLDFIELD, MIKE

1974   Tubular Bells

OLIVER

1967   Jean

OLLIE AND JERRY

1984   Breakin' … There's No Stopping Us

OLYMPICS, THE

1958   Western Movies
1965   Good Lovin'

OMC

1997   How Bizarre

ONLY ONES, THE

1979   Another Girl, Another Planet

ONO, YOKO

1981   Walking on Thin Ice

ONYX

1993   Slam

ORBISON, ROY

(See The Traveling Wilburys)
1956   Ooby Dooby
1958   Claudette
1958   Sweet and Innocent
1960   Blue Angel
1960   Only the Lonely (Know the Way I
        Feel)
1961   Candy Man
1961   Crying
1961   Running Scared
1962   Dream Baby How Long Must I
        Dream?
1963   Blue Bayou
1963   In Dreams
1964   It's Over
1964   Oh Pretty Woman
1989   You Got It

ORCHESTRAL MANOEUVRES IN THE DARK

1986   If You Leave

ORIGINALS, THE

1969   Baby, I'm for Real

ORIOLES, THE

1948   It's Too Soon to Know
1949   Tell Me So
1953   Crying in the Chapel

ORLANDO, TONY

1961   Bless You

ORLANDO, TONY & DAWN

(See Dawn)
1973   Say, Has Anybody Seen My Sweet
        Gypsy Rose
1973   Tie a Yellow Ribbon round the Old
        Oak Tree

ORLEANS

1976   Still the One

ORLONS, THE

1962   Wah-Watusi
1963   Don't Hang Up
1963   South Street

ORTON, BETH

1999   Central Reservation
1999   Stolen Car

OSBORNE, JOAN

1995   One of Us
1995   Pensacola
1995   St. Theresa

OSBOURNE, OZZY

1981   Crazy Train
1981   Flying High Again
1981   Mr. Crowley
1981   Suicide Solution
1986   Shot in the Dark, A

OSMOND, DONNY

1989   Soldier of Love

OSMONDS, THE

1971   One Bad Apple (Don't Spoil the
        Whole Bunch)
1971   Yo-Yo
1972   Down by the Lazy River

OTIS, JOHNNY

1946   Harlem Nocturne
1950   Cupid's Boogie
1950   Double-Crossin' Blues
1950   Mistrustin' Blues
1958   Willie and the Hand Jive

OTIS, SHUGGIE

1971   Strawberry Letter 23

OUTKAST

1996   Elevators (Me and You)
1997   Jazzy Belle

2000 B.O.B.
2000 Ms. Jackson

OUTLAWS

1975 Green Grass and High Tides

OUTSIDERS, THE

1966 Time Won't Let Me

OWENS, BUCK

1963 Act Naturally
1965 Crying Time

OZARK MOUNTAIN DAREDEVILS, THE

1975 Jackie Blue

P

P.M. DAWN

1991 Set Adrift on Memory Bliss
1992 I'd Die without You
1993 Looking through Patient Eyes

PABLO CRUISE

1978 Love Will Find a Way

PACIFIC GAS & ELECTRIC

1970 Are You Ready

PAGE, JIMMY

(See Led Zeppelin, The Yardbirds)
1988 Only One, The

PAGE, MARTIN

1994 In the House of Stone and Light

PAGE, TOMMY

1990 I'll Be Your Everything

PAGE AND PLANT

(See Led Zeppelin)
1998 Most High

PALMER, CLARENCE & THE JIVE BOMBERS

1956 Bad Boy

PALMER, ROBERT

1978 You're Gonna Get What's Comin'
1979 Bad Case of Lovin' You
1986 Addicted to Love
1988 Simply Irresistible

PANTERA

1992 Mouth for War

PAPA ROACH

2000 Last Resort

PAPER LACE

1974 Night Chicago Died, The

PARADONS, THE

1960 Diamonds and Pearls

PARAGONS, THE

1957 Florence
1963 Tide Is High, The

PARIS SISTERS, THE

1961 I Love How You Love Me

PARKER, GRAHAM

1976 Fool's Gold
1976 Hold Back the Night
1976 Pourin' It All Out
1976 Turned up Too Late
1979 Local Girls
1989 Soul Corruption

PARKER, JUNIOR

1953 Mystery Train
1953 Feelin' Good

PARKER, RAY JR.

(See Raydio)
1982 Other Woman, The
1984 Ghostbusters

PARKER, ROBERT

1966 Barefootin'

PARKS, VAN DYKE

1968 Vine Street

PARLIAMENT

(See Funkadelic)
1967 (I Wanna) Testify
1974 Up for the down Stroke
1976 Mothership Connection
1976 Tear the Roof off the Sucker (Give up the Funk)
1977 Bop Gun (Endangered Species)
1977 Flashlight
1978 Aqua Boogie

PARR, JOHN

1985 St. Elmo's Fire (Man in Motion)

PARSONS, ALAN PROJECT

1982 Eye in the Sky

PARSONS, BILL

(See Bobby Bare)
1958 All-American Boy

PARSONS, GRAM

(See The Byrds, Flying Burrito Brothers)
1971 She
1974 Return of the Grievous Angel

PARTON, DOLLY

1974 I Will Always Love You
1981 9 to 5

PARTRIDGE FAMILY, THE

1970 I Think I Love You
1971 Doesn't Somebody Want to Be Wanted
1971 I'll Meet You Halfway

PASSIONS, THE

1959 Just to Be with You
1960 I Only Want You

PATIENCE AND PRUDENCE

1956 Tonight You Belong to Me

PATTY & THE EMBLEMS

1964 Mixed up Shook up Girl

PAUL, BILLY

1972 Me and Mrs. Jones

PAUL, LES AND MARY FORD

1951 How High the Moon
1953 I'm Sittin' on Top of the World

PAUL AND PAULA

1962 Hey, Paula

PAVEMENT

1992 Summer Babe
1994 Cut Your Hair
1997 Fin
1999 Major Leagues

PAXTON, TOM

1963 Bottle of Wine
1964 Last Thing on My Mind, The

PAYNE, FREDA

1970   Band of Gold
1971   Bring the Boys Home

PEACHES AND HERB

1978   Reunited
1978   Shake Your Groove Thing

PEARL JAM

1991   Alive
1991   Black
1991   Even Flow
1991   Jeremy
1992   State of Love and Trust
1993   Animal
1993   Daughter
1993   Dissident
1993   Go
1994   Better Man
1994   Spin the Black Circle
1995   Yellow Ledbetter
1996   Who You Are
1998   Given to Fly

PEARLS BEFORE SWINE

1967   Playmate

PEBBLES

1988   Girlfriend
1988   Mercedes Boy
1990   Giving You the Benefit
1990   Love Makes Things Happen

PEEBLES, ANN

1972   I Feel Like Breaking up Somebody's
          Home Tonight
1972   I'm Gonna Tear Your Playhouse
          Down
1973   I Can't Stand the Rain

PEECH BOYS

1983   Don't Make Me Wait

PENDERGRASS, TEDDY

(See Harold Melvin & the Bluenotes)
1978   Close the Door

PENGUINS, THE

1954   Earth Angel (Will You Be Mine)
1963   Memories of El Monte

PENN, MICHAEL

1989   No Myth

PENNISTON, CE CE

1991   Finally

PENTANGLE

1968   Let No Man Steal Your Thyme

PERE UBU

1976   Final Solution
1978   Codex
1978   Modern Dance, The
1978   30 Seconds over Tokyo
1981   Birdies
1988   We Have the Technology
1991   Oh Catherine

PERKINS, CARL

1955   Honey Don't
1956   Blue Suede Shoes
1956   Boppin' the Blues
1956   Dixie Fried
1957   Everybody's Trying to Be My
          Baby
1957   Matchbox
1957   Your True Love

PERRY, STEVE

(See Journey)
1984   Oh, Sherrie

PERSUADERS, THE

1971   Thin Line between Love and
          Hate
1973   Some Guys Have All the Luck

PERSUASIONS, THE

1977   Looking for an Echo

PET SHOP BOYS

1986   Opportunities (Let's Make Lots of
          Money)
1986   West End Girls
1987   It's a Sin
1987   What Have I Done to Deserve This
          (With Dusty Springfield)
1991   DJ Culture

PETER AND GORDON

1964   World without Love, A
1966   Woman

PETER, PAUL & MARY

1961   Lemon Tree
1963   Puff (The Magic Dragon)
1964   For Lovin' Me
1967   Great Mandella, The
1967   Leaving on a Jet Plane
1967   Too Much of Nothing

PETERSON, PAUL

1962   My Dad

PETERSON, RAY

1959   Wonder of You, The
1960   Tell Laura I Love Her
1963   Give Us Your Blessing

PETTY, TOM AND THE HEARTBREAKERS

(See The Traveling Wilburys)
1977   American Girl
1977   Breakdown
1977   Listen to Her Heart
1979   Don't Do Me Like That
1979   Even the Losers
1979   Here Comes My Girl
1979   Refugee
1981   Waiting, The
1983   You Got Lucky
1987   Jammin' Me
1989   Free Fallin'
1989   I Won't Back Down
1989   Runnin' down a Dream
1991   Into the Great Wide Open
1991   Learning to Fly
1993   Mary Jane's Last Dance

PHAIR, LIZ

1993   Flower
1993   Glory
1993   Help Me, Mary
1993   6'1"
1994   Super Nova
1994   Whip Smart

PHILLIPS, ESTHER

1965   Release Me
1972   Home Is Where the Hatred
          Is

PHILLIPS, PHIL

1959   Sea of Love

PHILLIPS, SAM

1991   Raised on Promises

PHISH

1988   You Enjoy Myself
1993   Wedge, The
1994   Down with Disease
1995   Curtain, The
1996   Free
2000   Farm House

PHRANC

1991   M.A.R.T.I.N.A.

PHUTURE

1987   Acid Trax

PICKETT, BOBBY "BORIS" AND THE CRYPT KICKERS

1962   Monster Mash

PICKETT, WILSON

(See The Falcons)
1963   If You Need Me
1965   In the Midnight Hour
1966   99 and a Half
1966   634-5789
1967   I'm in Love
1970   Don't Let the Green Grass Fool You
1970   Engine Number 9 (Get Me Back on Time)
1971   Don't Knock My Love

PILOT

1975   Magic

PINK

2000   Most Girls
2000   There You Go

PINK FAERIES

1971   Do It

PINK FLOYD

1967   Arnold Layne
1967   Interstellar Overdrive
1968   See Emily Play
1968   Set the Controls for the Heart of the Sun
1969   Come in Number-51, Your Time Is Up
1970   Astronomy Domine
1973   Brain Damage
1973   Great Gig in the Sky, The
1973   Money
1973   Time
1973   Us and Them
1975   Have a Cigar
1975   Shine on, You Crazy Diamond
1975   Wish You Were Here
1977   Pigs on the Wing, Part 1
1979   Another Brick in the Wall
1979   Comfortably Numb
1979   Run Like Hell
1987   On the Turning Away
1994   Keep Talking

PIPKINS

1970   Gimme Dat Ding

PIRNER, DAVE

1997   We3

PITNEY, GENE

1961   Every Breath I Take
1961   Town without Pity

1962   Man Who Shot Liberty Valance, The
1962   Only Love Can Break a Heart
1964   I'm Gonna Be Strong
1964   It Hurts to Be in Love
1964   That Girl Belongs to Yesterday
1966   Just One Smile

PIXIES, THE

1988   Bone Machine
1989   Debaser
1989   Here Comes Your Man
1989   Monkey Gone to Heaven

PLACE, MARY KAY

1976   Baby Boy

PLANT, ROBERT

(See Led Zeppelin)
1982   Burning down One Side
1983   Big Log
1985   Little by Little
1988   Tall Cool One
1990   Hurting Kind (I've Got My Eyes on You)
1993   Calling to You

PLASMATICS, THE

1981   Sex Junkie

PLASTIC BERTRAND

1978   Ca Plane Pour Moi

PLATTERS, THE

1955   Great Pretender, The
1955   Only You
1956   My Prayer
1956   (You've Got) Magic Touch, The
1958   Smoke Gets in Your Eyes
1958   Twilight Time

PLAYER

1978   Baby Come Back

PLAYMATES, THE

1958   Beep, Beep
1959   What Is Love?

PLIMSOULS, THE

1981   Million Miles Away, A

POCO

1969   Pickin' up the Pieces
1970   You Better Think Twice

POGUES, THE

1985   Pair of Brown Eyes, A
1988   Fairytale of New York

POINDEXTER, BUSTER

1987   Hot! Hot! Hot!

POINTER SISTERS

1973   Yes We Can Can
1975   How Long (Betcha' Got a Chick on the Side)
1980   He's So Shy
1981   Slow Hand
1982   I'm So Excited
1984   Automatic
1984   Jump (For My Love)

POISON

1990   Something to Believe In
1990   Unskinny Bop
1987   Talk Dirty to Me
1988   Every Rose Has Its Thorn

POLICE, THE

1978   Can't Stand Losing You
1978   Roxanne
1978   So Lonely
1979   Message in a Bottle
1979   Walking on the Moon
1980   De Do Do Do, De Da Da Da
1980   Don't Stand So Close to Me
1980   Driven to Tears
1981   Every Little Thing She Does Is Magic
1981   Invisible Sun
1982   Spirits in the Material World
1983   Every Breath You Take
1983   King of Pain
1983   Wrapped around Your Finger

PONI TAILS, THE

1958   Born Too Late

POP, IGGY

(See The Stooges)
1977   China Girl
1997   Lust for Life
1977   Passenger, The

POPPY FAMILY, THE

1969   Which Way You Goin' Billy

PORNO FOR PYROS

1993   Pets

PORTISHEAD

1994   Sour Times

POSITIVE K

1993   I Got a Man

POWER STATION, THE

1985   Some Like It Hot

PRATT, ANDY

1973   Avenging Annie

PRATT AND MCLAIN

1976   Happy Days

PREFAB SPROUT

1985   Appetite

PRESLEY, ELVIS

1955   I Forgot to Remember to Forget
1955   Milkcow Blues Boogie
1955   Trying to Get to You
1956   Any Way You Want Me (That's How I Will Be)
1956   Don't Be Cruel (To a Heart That's True)
1956   Heartbreak Hotel
1956   I Want You, I Need You, I Love You
1956   I Was the One
1956   Love Me Tender
1956   Paralyzed
1957   All Shook Up
1957   Danny
1957   Jailhouse Rock
1957   (Let Me Be Your) Teddy Bear
1957   Loving You
1957   Mean Woman Blues
1957   Too Much
1957   Treat Me Nice
1957   (You're So Square) Baby I Don't Care
1958   Doncha' Think It's Time
1958   Don't
1958   Hard-Headed Woman
1958   I Beg of You
1958   I Got Stung
1958   Wear My Ring (Around Your Neck)
1959   Big Hunk o' Love, A
1959   I Need Your Love Tonight
1959   My Wish Came True
1960   Are You Lonesome Tonight
1960   Dirty Dirty Feeling
1960   Fame and Fortune
1960   Girl of My Best Friend
1960   I Gotta Know
1960   It's Now or Never
1960   Mess o' Blues, A
1960   Stuck on You
1960   Wooden Heart
1961   Can't Help Falling in Love
1961   Little Sister
1961   (Marie's the Name) His Latest Flame
1961   Surrender
1962   Anything That's Part of You
1962   Good Luck Charm
1962   Return to Sender
1962   She's Not You
1962   Suspicion
1963   (You're the) Devil in Disguise
1964   Viva Las Vegas
1965   (Such an) Easy Question
1968   If I Can Dream
1968   Little Less Conversation, A

1968   Memories
1968   Rubberneckin'
1969   Burning Love
1969   Don't Cry Daddy
1969   In the Ghetto (The Vicious Circle)
1969   Suspicious Minds
1970   Always on My Mind
1970   Kentucky Rain
1970   Separate Ways
1975   Moody Blue
1977   Way Down

PRESTON, BILLY

1971   Outa-Space
1973   Space Race
1973   Will It Go Round in Circles
1974   Nothing from Nothing
1974   You Are So Beautiful

PRESTON, BILLY AND SYREETA

1979   With You I'm Born Again

PRESTON, JOHNNY

1959   Running Bear

PRETENDERS, THE

1980   Brass in Pocket (I'm Special)
1980   Kid
1980   Mystery Achievement
1982   Message of Love
1982   Talk of the Town
1984   Back on the Chain Gang
1984   Middle of the Road
1984   My City Was Gone
1984   Show Me
1984   2000 Miles
1984   Time the Avenger
1986   Don't Get Me Wrong
1986   My Baby
1990   Sense of Purpose
1994   I'll Stand by You
1994   Night in My Veins

PRETTY THINGS, THE

1964   Rosalyn
1964   Don't Bring Me Down
1969   S.F. Sorrow Is Born

PRICE, ALAN

(See The Animals)
1973   O Lucky Man

PRICE, LLOYD

1952   Lawdy Miss Clawdy
1957   Just Because
1958   Stagger Lee
1959   I'm Gonna Get Married
1959   Personality
1959   Where Were You on Our Wedding Day

PRIMITIVE RADIO GODS

1996   Standing outside of a Broken Phone Booth with Money in My Hand

PRIMUS

1991   Jerry Was a Race Car Driver

PRINCE

1976   Soft and Wet
1979   I Feel for You
1979   I Wanna Be Your Lover
1980   Partyup
1980   When You Were Mine
1982   Delirious
1982   Little Red Corvette
1982   1999
1984   I Would Die 4 U
1984   Let's Go Crazy
1984   Purple Rain
1984   When Doves Cry
1985   Pop Life
1985   Raspberry Beret
1986   Kiss
1987   If I Was Your Girlfriend
1987   Sign 'o' the Times
1987   U Got the Look
1988   Alphabet Street
1988   I Could Never Take the Place of Your Man
1989   Batdance (From *Batman*)
1989   Partyman
1990   Thieves in the Temple
1991   Cream
1991   Diamonds and Pearls
1993   Pink Cashmere
1993   7
1994   Most Beautiful Girl in the World, The

PRINE, JOHN

1971   Angel from Montgomery
1971   Hello in There
1971   Sam Stone
1973   Dear Abby

PRISONAIRES, THE

1953   Just Walking in the Rain

PROBY, P.J.

1966   Niki Hoeky

PROCLAIMERS, THE

1989   I'm Gonna Be (500 Miles)

PROCOL HARUM

1967   Conquistador
1967   Salty Dog, A
1967   Whiter Shade of Pale, A
1968   Shine on Brightly

PRODIGY

1997   Firestarter

PROFESSOR LONGHAIR

1950   Bald Head
1954   Tipitina

PSYCHEDELIC FURS, THE

1981   Pretty in Pink
1984   Love My Way
1987   Heartbreak Beat

PUBLIC ENEMY

1987   You're Gonna Get Yours
1988   Black Steel in the Hour of Chaos
1988   Bring the Noise
1988   Don't Believe the Hype
1988   Party for Your Right to Fight
1988   Security of the 1st World
1989   Fight the Power
1990   Brothers Gonna Work It Out
1990   Fear of a Black Planet
1990   911 Is a Joke
1991   Can't Truss It
1991   How to Kill a Radio Consultant
1991   Shut 'Em Down
1994   Give It Up

PUBLIC IMAGE LTD

1979   Suit, The
1983   This Is Not a Love Song
1989   Disappointed

PUCKETT, GARY & THE UNION GAP

1967   Woman, Woman
1968   Lady Willpower
1968   Young Girl
1969   This Girl Is a Woman Now

PUFF DADDY

1997   Can't Nobody Hold Me Down
1997   I'll Be Missing You
1998   Been around the World
1998   Come with Me
1998   It's All about the Benjamins

PULP

1995   Common People

PURE PRAIRIE LEAGUE

1975   Amie

PURIFY, JAMES AND BOBBY

1966   I'm Your Puppet

PURSUIT OF HAPPINESS

1988   I'm an Adult Now

PYLON

1980   Cool

PYRAMIDS, THE

1964   Bikini Drag
1964   Penetration

Q

? AND THE MYSTERIANS

1966   96 Tears

QUAD CITY DJS

1996   C'mon Ride It (The Train)

QUARTERFLASH

1981   Harden My Heart

QUATRO, SUZI

1973   Can the Can
1974   Devil Gate Drive

QUATRO, SUZI AND CHRIS NORMAN

1978   Stumblin' In

QUEEN

1973   Keep Yourself Alive
1974   Killer Queen
1974   Stone Cold Crazy
1975   Bohemian Rhapsody
1975   You're My Best Friend
1976   Somebody to Love
1977   Sheer Heart Attack
1977   We Are the Champions
1977   We Will Rock You
1978   Bicycle Race
1980   Another One Bites the Dust
1980   Crazy Little Thing Called Love

QUEEN AND DAVID BOWIE

1982   Under Pressure

QUEEN LATIFAH

1989   Evil That Men Do, The
1989   Ladies First
1991   Latifah's Had It up to Here
1993   U.N.I.T.Y.

QUEENSRYCHE

1988   Eyes of a Stranger
1988   Operation: Mindcrime

1991   Jet City Woman
1991   Silent Lucidity

QUICKSILVER MESSENGER SERVICE

1968   Pride of Man
1970   Fresh Air
1971   What about Me

QUINTONES, THE

1958   Down the Aisle of Love

QUOTATIONS, THE

1961   Imagination

R

R.E.M.

1981   Radio Free Europe
1983   (Don't Go Back to) Rockville
1983   South Central Rain
1985   Can't Get There from Here
1985   Driver 8
1985   Fall on Me
1986   Cuyahoga
1986   Finest Worksong
1986   It's the End of the World as We Know It (And I Feel Fine)
1986   One I Love, The
1988   Orange Crush
1988   Stand
1991   Losing My Religion
1991   Shiny Happy People
1993   Everybody Hurts
1993   Man on the Moon
1994   Bang and Blame
1994   What's the Frequency, Kenneth
1999   Great Beyond, The

RABBITT, EDDIE

1980   Driving My Life Away
1980   I Love a Rainy Night
1981   Step by Step

RADIOHEAD

1993   Creep
1995   Bends, The
1995   Fake Plastic Trees
1995   Street Spirit
1996   High and Dry
1997   Karma Police
2000   National Anthem, The

RADNER, GILDA

1979   Honey (Touch Me with My Clothes On)

RAFFERTY, GERRY

1978   Baker Street

RAGE AGAINST THE MACHINE

1992   Killing in the Name Of

RAINBOW

1982   Stone Cold

RAINCOATS, THE

1981   Only Loved at Night

RAINDROPS, THE

1963   Hanky Panky
1963   Kind of Boy You Can't Forget,
        The

RAITT, BONNIE

1972   Love Has No Pride
1972   Love Me Like a Man
1973   Guilty
1973   I Feel the Same
1975   Good Enough
1975   Sugar Mama
1976   I Could Have Been Your Best Old
        Friend
1977   Louise
1982   Me and the Boys
1991   Something to Talk About

RAMBEAU, EDDIE

1965   Concrete and Clay

RAMONES, THE

1976   Beat on the Brat
1976   Blitzkrieg Bop
1976   I Wanna Be Your Boyfriend
1976   Teenage Lobotomy
1977   Carbona Not Glue
1977   Gimme Gimme Shock Treatment
1977   Pinhead
1977   Rockaway Beach
1977   Sheena Is a Punk Rocker
1978   I Wanna Be Sedated
1978   I Wanted Everything
1978   I'm against It
1979   Do You Remember Rock and Roll
        Radio
1986   My Brain Is Hanging upside Down
        (Bonzo Goes to Bitburg)

RANDAZZO, TEDDY

1957   Kiddio

RANDY & THE RAINBOWS

1963   Denise

RANK AND FILE

1984   Long Gone Dead

RANKIN, KENNY

1972   Peaceful

RARE EARTH

1971   I Just Want to Celebrate

RASCALS, THE

1965   I Ain't Gonna Eat out My Heart
        Anymore
1967   Groovin'
1967   How Can I Be Sure?
1967   I've Been Lonely Too Long
1968   Beautiful Morning, A
1968   People Got to Be Free

RASPBERRIES

1972   Go All the Way
1974   Overnight Sensation (Hit Record)

RAVAN, GENYA

1978   Jerry's Pigeons

RAVENS, THE

1947   Old Man River
1950   Count Every Star
1952   Rock Me All Night Long

RAY, JAMES

1962   Got My Mind Set on You
1962   If You Gotta Make a Fool of
        Somebody

RAY, JOHNNY

1951   Cry
1955   Yes Tonight, Josephine

RAY, GOODMAN & BROWN

1979   Special Lady

RAYDIO

1977   Jack and Jill
1979   You Can't Change That
1981   Woman Needs Love (Just Like You
        Do), A

RAYS, THE

1957   Silhouettes

REA, CHRIS

1977   Fool (If You Think It's Over)

READY FOR THE WORLD

1985   Oh Sheila
1986   Love You Down

REAL McCOY

1994   Another Night
1995   Run Away

RED CROSS

1980   Annette's Got the Hits
1980   I Hate My School
1982   Cease to Exist

RED KROSS

1990   Bubblegum Factory

RED HOT CHILI PEPPERS

1985   Catholic School Girls Rule
1991   Give It Away
1991   Under the Bridge
1993   Soul to Squeeze
1995   My Friends
1999   Scar Tissue
2000   Californication
2000   Otherside

REDBONE

1974   Come and Get Your Love

REDDING, OTIS

1963   These Arms of Mine
1964   Security
1965   I Can't Turn You Loose
1965   I've Been Loving You Too
        Long
1965   Mr. Pitiful
1965   Respect
1965   That's How Strong My Love Is
1966   Fa-Fa-Fa-Fa-Fa (Sad Song)
1966   Try a Little Tenderness
1968   Hard to Handle
1968   I've Got Dreams to Remember
1968   Ole Man Trouble
1968   (Sittin' on) The Dock of the Bay

REDDY, HELEN

1972   I Am Woman
1973   Leave Me Alone (Ruby Red Dress)
1974   Angie Baby

REED, JERRY

1967   Guitar Man
1967   U.S. Male
1971   Amos Moses
1971   When You're Hot You're Hot

REED, JIMMY

1955   Ain't That Lovin' You Baby
1956   You Got Me Dizzy
1957   Honest I Do
1960   Baby, What You Want Me to
        Do

1961 Big Boss Man
1961 Bright Lights Big City

REED, LOU

(See Velvet Underground)
1972 Perfect Day
1972 Satellite of Love
1972 Vicious
1972 Walk on the Wild Side
1972 Wild Child
1973 Berlin
1974 Kill Your Sons
1974 Sally Can't Dance
1976 Coney Island Baby
1978 Dirt
1978 I Wanna Be Black
1979 Bells, The
1986 No Money Down
1989 Dirty Boulevard
1989 Hold On
1991 What's Good

REED, LOU AND JOHN CALE

1989 Hello, It's Me

REESE, DELLA

1959 Don't You Know

REEVES, JIM

1959 He'll Have to Go

REFLECTIONS, THE

1964 (Just Like) Romeo and Juliet

REFUSED

1998 New Noise

REGENTS, THE

1961 Barbara Ann

REMBRANDTS, THE

1995 I'll Be There for You

RENAISSANCE

1973 Ashes Are Burning

RENO, MIKE AND ANN WILSON

1984 Almost Paradise (Love Theme from *Footloose*)

REO SPEEDWAGON

1978 Time for Me to Fly
1980 Keep on Loving You
1980 Take It on the Run

1982 Keep the Fire Burnin'
1985 Can't Fight This Feeling

REPARATA AND THE DELRONS

1964 Whenever a Teenager Cries

REPLACEMENTS, THE

1984 Hootenanny
1984 I Will Dare
1984 Sixteen Blue
1984 Unsatisfied
1985 Here Comes a Regular
1985 Kiss Me on the Bus
1985 Swingin' Party
1987 Alex Chilton
1987 Can't Hardly Wait
1989 Achin' to Be
1989 I'll Be You
1989 Talent Show
1990 Merry Go Round

RESIDENTS, THE

1986 Hello Skinny

REUNION

1974 Life Is a Rock (But the Radio Rolled Me)

REVERE, PAUL AND THE RAIDERS

1966 Hungry
1966 (I'm Not Your) Steppin' Stone
1966 Kicks
1967 Good Thing
1967 Him or Me, What's It Gonna Be

REYNOLDS, DEBBIE

1957 Tammy

REYNOLDS, JODY

1958 Endless Sleep

RHYMES, BUSTA

1997 Put Your Hands Where My Eyes Could See
1998 Dangerous

RHYTHM HERITAGE

1975 Theme from S.W.A.T.

RHYTHM SYNDICATE

1991 P.A.S.S.I.O.N.

RICE, SIR MACK

1965 Mustang Sally

RICH, CHARLIE

1960 Lonely Weekends
1965 Mohair Sam
1973 Most Beautiful Girl, The

RICH PROJECT, THE TONY

1996 Nobody Knows

RICHARD, CLIFF

1959 Living Doll
1962 Young Ones, The
1976 Devil Woman
1979 We Don't Talk Anymore

RICHARDS, KEITH

(See The Rolling Stones)
1988 Take It So Hard

RICHIE, LIONEL

(See the Commodores)
1983 All Night Long (All Night)
1983 Hello
1985 Dancing on the Ceiling
1985 Say You, Say Me

RICHIE, LIONEL AND DIANA ROSS

1981 Endless Love

RICHMAN, JONATHAN

(See The Modern Lovers)
1998 Let Her Go into Darkness

RIDGWAY. STAN

(See Wall of Voodoo)
1989 Mission in Life

RIGHT SAID FRED

1992 I'm Too Sexy

RIGHTEOUS BROTHERS, THE

1963 Little Latin Lupe Lu
1964 You've Lost That Lovin' Feelin'
1965 Hung on You
1965 Just Once in My Life
1966 (You're My) Soul and Inspiration
1973 Rock 'n' Roll Heaven

RILEY, CHERYL "PEPSI"

1988 Thanks for My Child

RILEY, JEANNIE C.

1968 Harper Valley PTA, The

RINKY DINKS, THE

1958   Early in the Morning

RIP CHORDS, THE

1963   Hey Little Cobra

RIPPERTON, MINNIE

1974   Lovin' You

RITCHIE FAMILY, THE

1976   Best Disco in Town, The

RIVERS, JOHNNY

1966   Poor Side of Town
1966   Secret Agent Man
1968   Summer Rain

RIVILERS, THE

1956   Thousand Stars, A

RIVINGTONS, THE

1962   Papa-Oom-Mow-Mow
1963   Bird Is the Word, The

ROBBINS, MARTY

1955   Singing the Blues
1957   White Sport Coat (And a Pink
            Carnation), A
1959   El Paso
1961   Don't Worry

ROBERT AND JOHNNY

1958   We Belong Together

ROBERTSON, ROBBIE

(See The Band)
1983   Between Trains
1987   Broken Arrow
1987   Somewhere down the Crazy River

ROBIN S.

1993   Show Me Love

ROBINS, THE

1951   Rockin'
1954   Framed
1954   Riot in Cell Block #9
1955   Smokey Joe's Cafe

ROBINSON, ALVIN

1964   Down Home Girl
1964   Something You Got

ROBINSON, FENTON

1967   Somebody Loan Me a Dime

ROBINSON, SMOKEY

(See The Miracles)
1973   Sweet Harmony
1976   Quiet Storm
1979   Cruisin'
1981   Being with You

ROBINSON, TOM

1978   Glad to Be Gay
1978   2-4-6-8 Motorway

ROBINSON, VICKIE SUE

1976   Turn the Beat around (Love to Hear
            Percussion)

ROCHES, THE

1979   Hammond Song
1979   Married Men, The
1979   Troubles, The
1982   On the Road to Fairfax County
1985   Love Radiates Around
1989   Everyone Is Good

ROCK FOLLIES

1977   O.K.

ROCK-A-TEENS, THE

1959   Woo-Hoo

ROCKPILE

1980   Teacher, Teacher

ROCKWELL

1984   Somebody's Watching Me

RODGERS, JIMMIE

1957   Honeycomb

ROE, TOMMY

1962   Sheila
1963   Everybody
1966   Sweet Pea
1969   Dizzy

ROGER

1987   I Want to Be Your Man

ROGERS, KENNY

1968   Just Dropped In (To See What
            Condition My Condition Was In)
1976   Lucille
1977   Gambler, The

ROGERS, KENNY AND DOLLY PARTON

1983   Islands in the Stream

ROLLING STONES, THE

1964   I Wanna Be Your Man
1964   Tell Me (You're Coming Back)
1965   Get off of My Cloud
1965   Heart of Stone
1965   (I Can't Get No) Satisfaction
1965   I'm Free
1965   Last Time, The
1965   Mother's Little Helper
1965   Play with Fire
1965   Under Assistant West Coast Promo
            Man
1966   Have You Seen Your Mother, Baby,
            Standing in the Shadow?
1966   Lady Jane
1966   19TH Nervous Breakdown
1966   Paint It Black
1966   Under My Thumb
1967   Back Street Girl
1967   Dandelion
1967   Let's Spend the Night Together
1967   Ruby Tuesday
1967   She's a Rainbow
1967   Something Happened to Me
            Yesterday
1967   2,000 Light Years from Home
1967   We Love You
1968   Factory Girl
1968   Jumpin' Jack Flash
1968   No Expectations
1968   Salt of the Earth, The
1968   Stray Cat Blues
1968   Street Fighting Man
1968   Sympathy for the Devil
1968   You Got the Silver
1969   Gimme Shelter
1969   Honky Tonk Women
1969   Let It Bleed
1969   Love in Vain
1969   Midnight Rambler
1969   You Can't Always Get What You
            Want
1971   Bitch
1971   Brown Sugar
1971   Dead Flowers
1971   Sister Morphine
1971   Wild Horses
1972   Happy
1972   Rocks Off
1972   Tumbling Dice
1973   Angie
1973   Star Star
1974   It's Only Rock 'n' Roll (But I Like
            It)
1976   Fool to Cry
1978   Beast of Burden
1978   Miss You
1978   Shattered
1980   Emotional Rescue
1981   Start Me Up
1981   Waiting on a Friend
1983   Undercover of the Night
1984   She Was Hot
1989   Mixed Emotions
1989   Rock and a Hard Place, A
1994   Out of Tears
1994   You Got Me Rockin'

ROLLINS BAND, HENRY

1991 Low Self Opinion
1994 Liar

ROMANTICS, THE

1980 What I Like about You
1983 Talking in Your Sleep

ROMEO VOID

1984 Girl in Trouble (Is a Temporary Thing), A

ROMERO, CHAN

1959 Hippy Hippy Shake

RONETTES, THE

1963 Baby I Love You
1963 Be My Baby
1964 Walking in the Rain
1964 When I Saw You
1966 I Can Hear Music

RONNY AND THE DAYTONAS

1964 G.T.O.

RONSTADT, LINDA

(See The Stone Poneys)

1970 Long Long Time
1974 Heart Like a Wheel
1975 Love Is a Rose
1976 Someone to Lay down beside Me
1977 How Do I Make You
1978 White Rhythm and Blues
1989 Cry Like a Rainstorm

ROOFTOP SINGERS, THE

1963 Walk Right In

ROOTS, THE

1996 What They Do
1999 You Got Me

ROSIE & THE ORIGINALS

1960 Angel Baby

ROSS, ANNIE

1953 Twisted

ROSS, DIANA

(See The Supremes)

1970 Reach out and Touch (Somebody's Hand)
1975 Do You Know Where You're Going To (Theme from *Mahogany*)

1976 Love Hangover
1980 I'm Coming Out
1980 Upside Down
1981 It's My Turn
1984 Missing You

ROXETTE

1989 Listen to Your Heart
1989 Look, The
1990 Dangerous
1990 It Must Have Been Love
1991 Fading Like a Flower
1991 Joyride

ROXY MUSIC

1972 Virginia Plain
1973 Do the Strand
1973 In Every Dream Home a Heartache
1974 Thrill of It All, The
1976 Love Is the Drug
1979 Dance Away
1982 Avalon
1982 More Than This

ROYAL, BILLY JOE

1965 Down in the Boondocks
1967 Hush

ROYAL GUARDSMEN, THE

1966 Snoopy versus the Red Baron

ROYAL TEENS

1957 Short Shorts
1959 Believe Me

ROYALETTES, THE

1965 It's Gonna Take a Miracle

ROYALS, THE

1952 Every Beat of My Heart

ROYCE, ROSE

1977 Car Wash
1977 Wishing on a Star

RUBY & THE ROMANTICS

1963 Hey There Lonely Boy
1963 Our Day Will Come
1965 Hurting Each Other

RUDE BOYS

1990 Written All over Your Face

RUFFIN, DAVID

(See The Temptations)

1969 My Whole World Ended (The Moment You Left Me)
1975 Walk Away from Love

RUFFIN, JIMMY

(See The Temptations)

1966 What Becomes of the Brokenhearted?

RUFUS

1974 Tell Me Something Good

RUFUS FEATURING CHAKA KHAN

1975 Once You Get Started
1975 Sweet Thing
1983 Ain't Nobody

RUNAWAYS, THE

1976 Cherry Bomb

RUN-D.M.C.

1984 It's Like That
1984 Rock Box
1984 Sucker MC's (Krush Groove)
1985 King of Rock
1986 It's Tricky
1986 Peter Piper
1993 Down with the King

RUNDGREN, TODD

(See Runt)

1972 I Saw the Light
1978 Can We Still Be Friends
1983 Bang the Drum All Day
1989 Parallel Lines

RUNT

1970 We Got to Get You a Woman

RUSH

1976 2112
1977 Closer to the Heart
1978 La Villa Strangiata
1980 Freewill
1980 Spirit of Radio
1981 Limelight
1981 Tom Sawyer
1981 YYZ
1982 New World Man
1991 Roll the Bones
1996 Test For Echo

RUSH, MERRILEE & THE TURNABOUTS

1967 Angel of the Morning

RUSH, TOM

1968 No Regrets
1968 Something in the Way She Moves
1973 Desperados Waiting for a Train

RUSSELL, BRENDA

1988   Piano in the Dark

RUSSELL, LEON

1970   Roll Away the Stone
1970   Song for You, A
1972   This Masquerade
1972   Tight Rope

RUSTED ROOT

1995   Send Me on My Way

RYDELL, BOBBY

1959   Kissin' Time
1960   Swingin' School
1960   Wild One
1964   Forget Him

RYDER, MITCH AND THE DETROIT WHEELS

1967   Sock It to Me, Baby

S

S.O.S. BAND, THE

1980   Take Your Time (Do It Right)
          Part 1

SADE

1985   Sally
1985   Smooth Operator, The
1986   Sweetest Tabu
1988   Paradise
1992   No Ordinary Love

SADLER, S/SGT. BARRY

1966   Ballad of the Green Berets, The

SAFARIS

1960   Image of a Girl

SAINTE-MARIE, BUFFY

1963   Universal Soldier
1964   Cod'ine
1964   Until It's Time for You to Go
1967   Circle Game, The
1992   Bury My Heart at Wounded Knee

SAINTS, THE

1987   Just Like Fire Would

SAKAMOTO, KYU

1963   Sukiyaki (My First Lonely Night)

SALT-N-PEPA

1988   Push It
1991   Let's Talk about Sex
1993   None of Your Business
1993   Shoop

SALT-N-PEPA FEATURING EN VOGUE

1993   Whatta Man

SAM AND DAVE

1966   Hold on, I'm Comin'
1966   I Take What I Want
1966   When Something Is Wrong with My
          Baby
1966   You Don't Know Like I Know
1966   You Got Me Hummin'
1967   Soul Man
1968   I Thank You
1968   Soul Sister, Brown Sugar
1968   Wrap It Up

SAM THE SHAM AND THE PHARAOHS

1965   Wooly Bully
1966   Lil Red Riding Hood

SANDALS, THE

1964   Theme from Endless Summer

SANDS, TOMMY

1957   Teen Age Crush

SANFORD TOWNSHEND BAND

1976   Smoke from a Distant Fire

SAMANTHA SANG

1977   Emotion

SANTANA

1969   Evil Ways
1969   Soul Sacrifice
1971   Oye Como Va (Listen How It Goes)

SANTANA, CARLOS

1999   Maria Maria

SANTANA, CARLOS AND ROB THOMAS

1999   Smooth

SANTO AND JOHNNY

1959   Sleep Walk

SATRIANI, JOE

1987   Always with Me, Always with
          You

SAVAGE GARDEN

1997   I Want You
1997   Truly, Madly, Deeply
1999   I Knew I Loved You

SAYER, LEO

1976   You Make Me Feel Like Dancing
1977   When I Need You

SCAGGS, BOZ

1976   Lido Shuffle
1976   Lowdown
1976   We're All Alone

SCANDAL

1983   Goodbye to You
1983   Love's Got a Line on You
1984   Only the Young
1984   Warrior, The

SCARBURY, JOEY

1981   Theme from the Greatest American
          Hero (Believe It or Not)

SCHENKER GROUP, MICHAEL

1980   Into the Arena

SCHILLING, PETER

1983   Major Tom (Coming Home)

SCHMIDT, CLAUDIA

1983   Hard Love

SCHOOLBOYS, THE

1957   Please Say You Want Me

SCHOOLY D

1987   We Get Ill

SCORPIONS

1975   Sails of Charon, The
1979   Holiday
1982   No One Like You
1984   Rock You Like a Hurricane
1984   Still Loving You
1990   Wind of Change

SCOTT, BOBBY

1956   Chain Gang
1960   Taste of Honey, A

SCOTT, FREDDIE

1963   Hey, Girl

SCOTT, JACK

1958   My True Love
1959   Way I Walk, The
1959   What in the World's Come over You
1960   Burning Bridges

SCOTT, LINDA

1961   I've Told Every Little Star

SCOTT-HERON, GIL

(See The Last Poets)
1975   Bottle, The
1975   Johannesburg
1975   Winter in America
1977   We Almost Lost Detroit

SCRITTI POLITTI

1984   Wood Beez (Pray Like Aretha
       Franklin)
1985   Perfect Way

SEAL

1991   Crazy
1994   Prayer for the Dying
1995   Kiss from a Rose

SEALS AND CROFTS

1971   Summer Breeze
1973   Diamond Girl
1976   Get Closer

SEARCHERS, THE

1964   What Have They Done to the Rain?

SEBADOH

1991   Freed Pig
1991   Gimme Indie Rock
1993   Together or Alone

SEBASTIAN, JOHN

(See The Lovin' Spoonful)
1969   She's a Lady
1976   Welcome Back

SEDAKA, NEIL

1958   Diary, The
1959   Oh Carol
1960   Stairway to Heaven
1961   Calendar Girl
1962   Breaking up Is Hard to Do
1962   Happy Birthday, Sweet Sixteen
1962   Next Door to an Angel
1974   Laughter in the Rain
1975   Bad Blood

SEDAKA, NEIL AND DARA

1980   Should've Never Let You Go

SEDUCTION

1989   Two to Make It Right

SEEDS, THE

1967   Can't Seem to Make You Mine
1967   Pushin' Too Hard

SEEGER, PEGGY

1962   First Time Ever I Saw Your Face, The

SEEGER, PETE

1962   Turn! Turn! Turn! (To Everything
       There Is a Season)
1962   Where Have All the Flowers
       Gone?
1964   Little Boxes

SEEKERS, THE

1965   I'll Never Find Another You
1966   Georgy Girl

SEGER, BOB

1969   Ramblin' Gamblin' Man
1972   Turn the Page
1975   Beautiful Loser
1976   Fire Down Below
1976   Mainstreet
1976   Night Moves
1976   Rock and Roll Never Forgets
1977   Hollywood Nights
1977   Old Time Rock and Roll
1977   Still the Same
1977   We've Got Tonight
1980   Against the Wind
1980   Fire Lake
1982   Shame on the Moon
1983   Makin' Thunderbirds
1986   Like a Rock
1987   Shakedown

SELECTER, THE

1979   On My Radio

SELENA

1995   Dreaming of You

SEMBELLO, MICHAEL

1983   Maniac

SEMISONIC

1998   Closing Time

SENSATIONS, THE

1962   Let Me In

SERENDIPITY SINGERS, THE

1964   Don't Let the Rain Come Down
       (Crooked Little Man)

SEVEN MARY THREE

1995   Cumbersome

SEVILLE, DAVID

1958   Witch Doctor

SEX PISTOLS, THE

1977   Anarchy in the U.K.
1977   God Save the Queen
1977   Holidays in the Sun
1977   Pretty Vacant

SHABBA RANKS

1992   Mr. Loverman

SHADOWS, THE

1960   Apache
1960   Man of Mystery
1962   Wonderful Land
1963   Dance On
1963   Foot Tapper

SHAGGS, THE

1969   My Pal Foot Foot

SHAI

1992   If I Ever Fall in Love

SHAKESPEARE'S SISTER

1992   Stay

SHALAMAR

1979   Second Time Around, The

SHA-NA-NA

1971   Top Forty of the Lord, The

SHANGRI-LAS, THE

1964   Give Him a Great Big Kiss
1964   Leader of the Pack
1964   Remember Walking in the Sand
1965   I Can Never Go Home Anymore
1966   Long Live Our Love
1966   Out in the Streets

SHANICE

1991   I Love Your Smile
1992   Saving Forever for You

SHANNON

1984   Let the Music Play

SHANNON, DEL

1961   Hats off to Larry
1961   Little Town Flirt
1961   Runaway
1964   I Go to Pieces
1964   Keep Searchin' (We'll Follow the
        Sun)
1965   Stranger in Town

SHAPIRO, HELEN

1961   Walkin' Back to Happiness
1961   You Don't Know

SHARKEY, FEARGAL

(See The Undertones)
1985   Good Heart, A

SHARP, DEE DEE

1962   Mashed Potato Time
1962   Ride

SHAW, SANDIE

1965   Girl Don't Come
1967   Puppet on a String

SHEILA E.

1984   Glamorous Life, The
1986   Love Bizarre, A

SHELLEY, PETE

1982   Homosapien

SHELLS, THE

1957   Baby Oh Baby

SHEP & THE LIMELITES

1961   Daddy's Home

SHEPHERD, KENNY WAYNE

1998   Blue on Black

SHERIFF

1983   When I'm with You

SHERMAN, BOBBY

1969   Little Woman
1970   Julie, Do Ya Love Me

SHINDELL, RICHARD

1992   Are You Happy Now

SHINEHEAD

1986   Who the Cap Fits

SHIRELLES, THE

1958   I Met Him on a Sunday
1960   Boys
1960   Tonight's the Night
1960   Will You Love Me Tomorrow
1961   Baby It's You
1961   Mama Said
1961   Soldier Boy
1962   Putty in Your Hands
1963   Foolish Little Girl
1964   Sha-La-La

SHIRLEY AND COMPANY

1974   Shame, Shame, Shame

SHIRLEY AND LEE

1956   Let the Good Times Roll

SHOCKED, MICHELLE

1988   Anchorage

SHOCKING BLUE

1969   Love Buzz
1969   Venus

SHOES, THE

1979   Tomorrow Night

SHONDELL, TROY

1961   This Time

SHONEN KNIFE

1990   Ice Cream City

SHOW STOPPERS

1968   (Ain't Nothing But a) House Party

SHOWMEN, THE

1961   It Will Stand

SIBERRY, JANE

1993   Love Is Everything

SIEBEL, PAUL

1978   Then Came the Children

SILENCERS, THE

1990   Blues for Buddah, A

SILHOUETTES, THE

1957   Get a Job

SILK

1992   Freak Me

SILVER CONVENTION

1975   Fly, Robin, Fly
1976   Get up and Boogie

SILVERCHAIR

1995   Tomorrow

SILVERSTEIN, SHEL

1962   Boa Constrictor
1969   Boy Named Sue, A
1973   I Got Stoned and I Missed It

SIMON, CARLY

1971   Anticipation
1971   Long Term Physical Effects
1971   That's the Way I've Always Heard It
        Should Be
1972   You're So Vain
1974   Haven't Got Time for the Pain
1977   Nobody Does It Better
1986   Coming around Again
1989   Let the River Run

SIMON, JOE

1971   Drowning in the Sea of Love
1975   Get down Get down (Get on the
        Floor)

SIMON AND GARFUNKEL

1964   Bleecker Street
1964   He Was My Brother
1964   Sounds of Silence, The
1966   Cloudy
1966   Dangling Conversation, The
1966   59TH Street Bridge Song (Feelin'
        Groovy), The
1966   For Emily (Wherever I May Find
        Her)
1966   Homeward Bound
1966   I Am a Rock
1966   Patterns
1966   7:00 News/Silent Night
1966   Scarborough Fair—Canticle
1968   America
1968   Hazy Shade of Winter, A
1968   Mrs. Robinson
1969   Boxer, The
1969   Bridge over Troubled Water
1969   Cecilia
1982   Late Great Johnny Ace, The

SIMON, PAUL

1972   Me and Julio down by the School Yard
1972   Mother and Child Reunion
1972   Peace Like a River
1973   American Tune
1973   Kodachrome
1973   Loves Me Like a Rock

1973 One Man's Ceiling Is Another Man's Floor
1973 Something So Right
1975 Fifty Ways to Leave Your Lover
1975 Gone at Last
1975 My Little Town
1975 Still Crazy after All These Years
1977 Slip Slidin Away
1980 Late in the Evening
1983 Allergies
1983 Rene and Georgette Magritte with Their Dog after the War
1986 Boy in the Bubble, The
1986 Diamonds on the Soles of Her Shoes
1986 Graceland
1986 You Can Call Me Al
1990 Born at the Right Time
1997 Bernadette

SIMONE, NINA

1966 I Wish I Knew (How It Would Feel to Be Free)
1969 To Be Young, Gifted and Black

SIMPLE MINDS

1981 Themes for Great Cities
1985 Alive and Kicking
1985 Don't You (Forget about Me)

SIMPLY RED

1986 Holding Back the Years

SIMPSON, BART

1990 Deep Deep Trouble

SINATRA, FRANK

1955 Learning the Blues

SINATRA, NANCY

1966 These Boots Are Made for Walking

SINGING NUN, THE

1963 Dominique

SIOUXSIE AND THE BANSHEES

1978 Hong Kong Garden
1988 Peek-A-Boo
1991 Kiss Them for Me

SIR DOUGLAS QUINTET, THE

1965 She's about a Mover
1969 Mendocino

SIR MIX-A-LOT

1992 Baby Got Back

SISQO

1999 Incomplete
1999 Thong Song

SISTER SLEDGE

1978 He's the Greatest Dancer
1978 We Are Family
1982 All the Man I Need

SISTERS OF MERCY

1987 This Corrosion

SIX TEENS, THE

1956 Casual Look, A

SIXPENCE NONE THE RICHER

1998 Kiss Me

SIZE, RONI & REPRAZENT

1997 New Forms

SKID ROW

1989 Eighteen and Life
1990 I Remember You

SKIP AND FLIP

1959 It Was I

SKYLARK

1973 Wildflower

SKYLINERS, THE

1959 Since I Don't Have You
1959 This I Swear

SLACK, FREDDIE AND ELLA MAE MORSE

1946 House of Blue Lights, The

SLADE

1972 Mama We're All Crazee Now
1973 Cum on Feel the Noize
1973 Gudbye t'Jane

SLADES, THE

1959 You Cheated

SLAYER

1986 Angel of Death

SLEATER-KINNEY

1996 I Wanna Be Your Joey Ramone
1999 Start Together

SLEDGE, PERCY

1966 It Tears Me Up
1966 When a Man Loves a Woman
1968 Take Time to Know Her

SLICKERS, THE

1972 Johnny Too Bad

SLINT

1991 Good Morning Captain

SLITS, THE

1979 Typical Girls

SLY & THE FAMILY STONE

1968 Dance to the Music
1969 Don't Call Me Nigger, Whitey
1969 Everyday People
1969 Hot Fun in the Summertime
1969 I Want to Take You Higher
1969 Stand!
1970 Everybody Is a Star
1970 Thank You (Falettingme Be Mice Elf Agin)
1971 Family Affair
1971 Runnin' Away
1971 (You've Caught Me) Smilin'
1973 If You Want Me to Stay

SMALL, MILLIE

1964 My Boy Lollipop

SMALL FACES, THE

1966 All or Nothing
1967 Itchycoo Park

SMASH MOUTH

1997 Walkin' on the Sun
1999 All Star

SMASHING PUMPKINS

1991 I Am One
1993 Today
1995 1979
1995 Tonight, Tonight

SMITH, ARTHUR & HIS CRACKERJACKS

1946 Guitar Boogie Shuffle

SMITH, ELLIOT

1997 Angeles
1997 Miss Misery

SMITH, FRANKIE

1981 Double Dutch Bus

SMITH, HUEY

1957   Rockin' Pneumonia & the Boogie
       Woogie Flu
1958   Don't You Just Know It

SMITH, HURRICANE

1973   Oh Babe, What Would You Say

SMITH, O.C.

1968   Little Green Apples

SMITH, PATTI

1974   Piss Factory
1976   Gloria (In Excelsius)
1978   Because the Night
1988   Paths That Cross
1988   People Have the Power
1996   About a Boy

SMITH, WARREN

1956   Ubangi Stomp
1957   So Long I'm Gone
1973   Red Cadillac and a Black Moustache, A

SMITH, WILL

1998   Gettin' Jiggy Wit It

SMITHER, CHRIS

1993   Happier Blue

SMITHEREENS, THE

1982   Beauty & Sadness
1986   Behind the Wall of Sleep
1986   Blood and Roses
1988   Something New

SMITHS, THE

1984   Hand in Glove
1984   Heaven Knows I'm Miserable Now
1984   This Charming Man
1984   What Difference Does It Make
1985   How Soon Is Now
1986   Bigmouth Strikes Again
1986   I Know It's Over
1986   Queen Is Dead, The
1986   There Is a Light That Never Goes Out
1987   Girlfriend in a Coma
1987   Shoplifters of the World Unite
1987   You Just Haven't Earned It Yet

SMYTH, PATTY AND DON HENLEY

1992   Sometimes Love Just Ain't Enough

SNAP

1990   Power, The
1992   Rhythm Is a Dancer

SNIDER, TODD

1994   My Generation, Part Two

SNOW

1993   Informer

SNOW, HANK

1950   I'm Movin' On
1952   (Now and Then There's) a Fool Such
       As I

SNOW, PHOEBE

1973   Poetry Man

SOBULE, JILL

1995   I Kissed a Girl

SOFT BOYS, THE

1980   Kingdom of Love

SOFT MACHINE, THE

1970   Moon in June

SOLITAIRES, THE

1957   Walking Along

SON VOLT

1996   Drown

SONIC YOUTH

1986   Evol
1986   Expressway to Yr Skull
1987   Master Dik
1988   Silver Rocket
1988   Sprawl
1988   Teen-Age Riot
1990   Cinderella's Big Score
1992   100%

SONICS, THE

1965   Strychnine
1965   Witch, The

SONNY

1965   Laugh at Me

SONNY & CHER

1964   Baby Don't Go
1965   I Got You Babe
1967   Beat Goes On, The
1971   All I Ever Need Is You

SOUL, DAVID

1977   Don't Give up on Us

SOUL, JIMMY

1963   If You Wanna Be Happy

SOUL ASYLUM

1988   Endless Farewell
1992   Runaway Train
1992   Somebody to Shove
1993   Black Gold
1995   Misery

SOUL BROTHERS SIX

1967   (She's) Some Kind of Wonderful

SOUL STIRRERS, THE

1956   Touch the Hem of His Garment

SOUL SURVIVORS, THE

1967   Expressway to Your Heart

SOUL II SOUL

1989   Back to Life
1989   Keep on Movin'

SOUNDGARDEN

1985   Tears to Forget
1991   Rusty Cage
1994   Black Hole Sun
1994   Spoonman
1996   Blow up the Outside World
1996   Burden in My Hand

SOUTH, JOE

1969   Don't It Make You Wanna Go Home
1969   (I Never Promised You a) Rose
       Garden
1970   Walk a Mile in My Shoes

SOUTHER, J.D.

1972   Run Like a Thief
1979   You're Only Lonely

SOUTHSIDE JOHNNY & THE ASBURY JUKES

1976   He's Got the Fever
1976   I Don't Want to Go Home
1991   It's Been a Long Time

SOXX, BOB E. & THE BLUE JEANS

1962   Zip-a-Dee-Doo-Dah
1963   Why Do Lovers Break Each Other's
       Hearts?

SPACEHOG

1996   In the Meantime

SPANDAU BALLET

1983   True

SPANIELS, THE

1954   Goodnight Sweatheart
1958   Rockin' Good Way (To Mess Around
           and Fall in Love), A

SPANKY & OUR GANG

1967   Sunday Will Never Be the Same

SPARKS

1974   This Town Ain't Big Enough for the
           Both of Us

SPARKS AND JANE WIEDLIN

1983   Cool Places

SPEARS, BRITNEY

1998   Baby One More Time

SPECIAL AKA

1985   Free Nelson Mandela

SPECIALS, THE

1979   Gangsters
1979   Message to You Rudy
1979   Too Much Too Young
1981   Ghost Town

SPELLMAN, BENNIE

1962   Lipstick Traces (On a Cigarette)

SPENCE, SKIP

(See Moby Grape)
1969   War in Peace

SPENCER BLUES EXPLOSION, JON

1993   Afro

SPENCER, TRACIE

1991   This House

SPICE GIRLS

1997   Say You'll Be There
1997   2 Become 1
1997   Wannabe

SPIN DOCTORS, THE

1991   Little Miss Can't Be Wrong
1992   Two Princes

SPINAL TAP

1984   Big Bottom

SPINNERS

1970   It's a Shame
1972   Could It Be I'm Falling in Love
1972   I'll Be Around
1972   One of a Kind (Love Affair)
1973   Mighty Love, A
1976   Rubberband Man, The

SPIRIT

1968   Fresh Garbage
1969   I Got a Line on You
1970   Nature's Way

SPLIT ENZ

1980   I Got You

SPOKESMEN, THE

1965   Dawn of Correction

SPONGE

1995   Molly (Sixteen Candles)

SPOOKY TOOTH

1969   Better by You, Better Than Me

SPRINGFIELD, DUSTY

1964   I Only Want to Be with You
1966   Goin' Back
1966   You Don't Have to Say You Love Me
1969   No Easy Way Down
1969   Son of a Preacher Man
1989   Nothing Has Been Proved

SPRINGFIELD, RICK

1981   Jessie's Girl
1982   Don't Talk to Strangers
1983   Affair of the Heart
1984   Love Somebody

SPRINGSTEEN, BRUCE

1973   Blinded by the Light
1973   4TH of July, Asbury Park (Sandy)
1973   For You
1973   Growin' Up
1973   Incident on 57TH Street
1973   Lost in the Flood
1973   Rosalita (Come out Tonight)
1973   Spirit in the Night
1973   Thundercrack
1973   Wild Billy's Circus Story
1975   Backstreets
1975   Born to Run
1975   Jungleland
1975   Tenth Avenue Freeze Out
1975   Thunder Road
1978   Badlands

1978   Darkness on the Edge of Town
1978   Prove It All Night
1980   Hungry Heart
1980   Independence Day
1980   River, The
1980   Stolen Car
1982   Atlantic City
1982   Johnny 99
1983   Pink Cadillac
1984   Bobby Jean
1984   Born in the U.S.A.
1984   Cover Me
1984   Dancing in the Dark
1984   Glory Days
1984   I'm Goin' Down
1984   I'm on Fire
1984   My Home Town
1985   Seeds
1987   Brilliant Disguise
1987   One Step Up
1987   Tunnel of Love
1987   Walk Like a Man
1992   Human Touch
1992   My Beautiful Reward
1993   Streets of Philadelphia
1995   Dead Man Walking
1995   Ghost of Tom Joad, The
1995   Secret Garden
1995   Youngstown
1998   If I Should Fall Behind
1999   Promise, The

SQUEEZE

1979   Cool for Cats
1979   Up the Junction
1980   Another Nail in My Heart
1980   Pulling Mussels (From the Shell)
1981   In Quintessence
1981   Tempted
1982   Black Coffee in Bed
1987   Hourglass

SQUIER, BILLY

1981   Stroke, The
1982   Everybody Wants You
1984   Rock Me Tonite

SQUIRREL NUT ZIPPERS

1997   Hell

STACEY Q

1986   Two of Hearts

STAFFORD, JIM

1973   Spiders and Snakes

STANDELLS, THE

1965   Dirty Water

STANSFIELD, LISA

1990   All Around the World
1990   You Can't Deny It
1991   All Woman

STAPLE SINGERS, THE

1971   Respect Yourself
1972   I'll Take You There
1973   If You're Ready (Come Go with Me)
1975   Let's Do It Again

STARBUCK

1975   Moonlight Feels Right

STARLAND VOCAL BAND

1976   Afternoon Delight

STARR, RINGO

1970   Early 1970
1971   It Don't Come Easy
1972   Back off Boogaloo
1973   Photograph
1974   It's All down to Goodnight Vienna
1974   No No Song
1974   Oh My My

STARSHIP

(See Jefferson Airplane, Jefferson Starship)
1985   Sara
1985   We Built This City
1987   It's Not Over ('Til It's Over)
1987   Nothing's Gonna Stop Us Now

STATON, CANDI

1976   Young Hearts Run Free

STATUS QUO

1968   Pictures of Matchstick Men

STEALER'S WHEEL

1973   Stuck in the Middle with You

STEAM

1969   Na Na, Hey, Hey, Kiss Him
        Goodbye

STEELY DAN

1972   Dirty Work
1972   Do It Again
1972   Reeling in the Years
1973   Bodhisattva
1973   Pearl of the Quarter
1973   Show Biz Kids
1974   Any Major Dude Will Tell You
1974   Charlie Freak
1974   Rikki Don't Lose That Number
1975   Any World (That I'm Welcome To)
1975   Bad Sneakers
1975   Black Friday
1975   Dr. Wu
1976   Kid Charlemagne
1977   Deacon Blues
1977   Peg
1980   Hey Nineteen

1980   Time out of Mind
2000   Cousin Dupree

STEINMAN, JIM

1981   Rock and Roll Dreams Come
        Through

STEPPENWOLF

1968   Born to Be Wild
1968   Magic Carpet Ride
1968   Pusher, The
1969   Rock Me

STEREO MCS

1993   Connected

STEVENS, CAT

1967   First Cut Is the Deepest, The
1967   Matthew and Son
1970   Lady D'Arbanville
1971   Father and Son
1971   Into White
1971   Katmandu
1971   Morning Has Broken
1971   Peace Train
1971   Wild World
1974   Oh Very Young

STEVENS, CONNIE

1960   Sixteen Reasons (Why I Love You)

STEVENS, DODIE

1958   Pink Shoelaces

STEVENS, RAY

1962   Ahab the Arab
1970   Everything Is Beautiful
1974   Streak, The

STEVENSON, B.W.

1973   My Maria
1973   Shambala

STEVIE B.

1990   Because I Love You

STEWART, AL

1977   Year of the Cat
1978   Time Passages

STEWART, BILLY

1966   Summertime

STEWART, GARY

1975   Quits

STEWART, JERMAINE

1986   We Don't Have to Take Our Clothes
        Off

STEWART, JOHN

(See Kingston Trio)
1979   Gold

STEWART, ROD

(See Small Faces)
1969   Dirty Old Town
1969   Handbags and Gladrags
1971   Every Picture Tells a Story
1971   Maggie May
1971   Mandolin Wind
1972   You Wear It Well
1976   Tonight's the Night (Gonna Be All
        Right)
1977   Hot Legs
1977   Killing of Georgie (Part 1 & 2), The
1977   You're in My Heart (The Final
        Acclaim)
1979   Do Ya Think I'm Sexy
1980   Passion
1981   Young Turks
1982   That's What Friends Are For
1983   Baby Jane
1984   Infatuation
1988   Forever Young
1988   My Heart Can't Tell You No
1991   Motown Song, The
1991   Rhythm of My Heart

STILLS, STEPHEN

(See Crosby, Stills, Nash & Young)
1971   Love the One You're With

STING

(See The Police)
1985   Fortress around Your Heart
1985   If You Love Somebody Set Them
        Free
1987   They Dance Alone
1987   We'll Be Together
1991   All This Time
1993   If I Ever Lose My Faith in You

STONE PONEYS, THE

1965   Different Drum

STONE ROSES, THE

1989   Fool's Gold
1989   I Wanna Be Adored
1989   She Bangs the Drums
1994   Love Spreads

STONE TEMPLE PILOTS

1993   Plush
1994   Big Empty
1994   Interstate Love Song

1994　Vasoline
1996　Big Bang Baby
1996　Trippin' on a Hole in a Paper Heart

STONEY & MEATLOAF

1971　What You See Is What You Get

STOOGES, THE

1969　I Wanna Be Your Dog
1969　No Fun
1970　L.A. Blues
1970　TV Eye
1973　Raw Power
1973　Search and Destroy

STOOKEY, PAUL

(See Peter, Paul & Mary)
1971　Wedding Song, The

STOP THE VIOLENCE

1989　Self Destruction

STRANGELOVES, THE

1965　I Want Candy

STRANGLERS, THE

1987　Always the Sun

STRAWBERRY ALARM CLOCK

1967　Incense and Peppermints

STRAWBS, THE

1973　Part of the Union

STRAY CATS

1981　Runaway Boys
1982　Rock This Town
1982　Stray Cat Strut
1983　(She's) Sexy & 17

STRING CHEESE INCIDENT, THE

1997　Born on the Wrong Planet

STRINGALONGS, THE

1961　Wheels

STRONG, BARRETT

1960　Money (That's What I Want)

STUDENTS, THE

1958　I'm So Young

STYLE COUNCIL, THE

1984　My Ever Changing Moods

STYLISTICS, THE

1971　Betcha by Golly Wow
1971　You Are Everything
1972　Break up to Make Up
1972　I'm Stone in Love with You
1973　Rockin' Roll Baby
1973　You Make Me Feel Brand New

STYX

1974　Lady
1977　Come Sail Away
1979　Babe
1981　Best of Times, The
1981　Too Much Time on My Hands
1983　Mr. Roboto
1991　Show Me the Way

SUBLIME

1996　What I Got
1997　Santeria

SUGAR

1995　Your Favorite Thing

SUGAR HILL GANG, THE

1979　Rapper's Delight

SUGAR RAY

1997　Fly
1998　Every Morning

SUGARCUBES

1988　Birthday

SUGARLOAF

1970　Green Eyed Lady

SUICIDAL TENDENCIES

1983　Institutionalized

SUICIDE

1977　Cheree

SUMMER, DONNA

1976　Love to Love You Baby
1977　I Feel Love
1978　Heaven Knows
1978　Last Dance, The
1979　Bad Girls
1979　Dim All the Lights
1979　Hot Stuff
1979　On the Radio
1980　Wanderer, The

1982　Love Is in Control (Finger on the Trigger)
1983　She Works Hard for the Money

SUMMER, DONNA AND BARBRA STREISAND

1979　No More Tears (Enough Is Enough)

SUNDAYS, THE

1990　Here's Where the Story Ends

SUPERCHUNK

1992　Swallow That

SUPERTRAMP

1979　Logical Song, The
1979　Take the Long Way Home

SUPREMES, THE

1962　Your Heart Belongs to Me
1964　Baby Love
1964　Come See about Me
1964　Where Did Our Love Go
1965　Back in My Arms Again
1965　I Hear a Symphony
1965　Nothing But Heartaches
1965　Stop! In the Name of Love
1966　Love Is Like an Itching in My Heart
1966　My World Is Empty without You
1966　You Can't Hurry Love
1966　You Keep Me Hangin' On
1967　Happening, The
1967　Love Is Here and Now You're Gone
1967　Reflections
1968　Love Child
1969　I'm Livin' in Shame
1970　Stoned Love

SURE, AL B.

1988　Nite and Day
1988　Off on Your Own (Girl)
1992　Right Now

SURFACE

1988　Shower Me with Your Love
1990　First Time, The

SURFARIS, THE

1963　Surfer Joe
1963　Wipe Out

SURVIVOR

1982　Eye of the Tiger (The Theme from *Rocky III*)
1984　High on You
1984　Search Is Over, The
1985　Burning Heart

SUTHERLAND BROTHERS AND QUIVER, THE
1976   Arms of Mary
1973   Sailing

SWAN, BILLY
1974   I Can Help

SWANS, THE
1987   Children of God

SWAYZE, PATRICK WITH WENDY FRASER
1987   She's Like the Wind

SWEAT, KEITH
1988   I Want Her
1990   I'll Give All My Love to You
1990   Make You Sweat
1996   Nobody

SWEET, MATTHEW
1991   Girlfriend
1991   I've Been Waiting

SWEET, RACHEL
1979   Stranger in the House
1979   Who Does Lisa Like
1988   Hairspray

SWEET
1973   Blockbuster
1973   Little Willy
1975   Ballroom Blitz
1975   Fox on the Run
1977   Love Is Like Oxygen

SWEET SENSATION
1990   If Wishes Came True

SWINGING MEDALLIONS, THE
1966   Double Shot (Of My Baby's Love)

SWV
1992   Right Here
1993   I'm So into You
1993   Weak
1996   You're the One

SYLVERS, THE
1976   Boogie Fever
1977   Hot Line

SYLVESTER
1978   Dance (Disco Heat)

SYLVIA
1973   Pillow Talk

SYNDICATE OF SOUND, THE
1966   Little Girl

SYREETA
1974   Cause We've Ended as Lovers

SYSTEM, THE
1987   Don't Disturb This Groove

T

T., TIMMY
1991   One More Try

T. REX
1971   Get It On (Bang a Gong)
1971   Hot Love
1971   Ride a White Swan
1972   Children of the Revolution
1972   Telegram Sam

TACO
1983   Puttin' on the Ritz

TAG TEAM
1994   Whoomp! (There It Is)

TAKE THAT
1995   Back for Good

TALKING HEADS
1977   Psycho Killer
1979   Life During Wartime
1979   Memories Can't Wait
1981   Once in a Lifetime
1983   Burning down the House
1985   And She Was
1985   Road to Nowhere
1985   Stay up Late
1986   Wild, Wild Life
1988   Mommy Daddy You and I
1988   Nothing But Flowers

TANEGA, NORMA
1966   Walking My Cat Named Dog

TARRIERS, THE
1957   Banana Boat Song, The

TASTE OF HONEY, A
1978   Boogie Oogie Oogie

TATE, HOWARD
1966   Ain't Nobody Home
1967   Look at Granny Run Run

TAVARES
1975   It Only Takes a Minute

TAYLOR, JAMES
1969   Carolina in My Mind
1969   Knockin' around the Zoo
1969   Rainy Day Man
1969   Sunshine, Sunshine
1970   Country Road
1970   Fire and Rain
1970   Steamroller Blues
1970   Sweet Baby James
1973   Don't Let Me Be Lonely Tonight
1976   Shower the People
1977   Your Smiling Face
1981   Her Town Too
1986   Only One, The
1988   Never Die Young
1991   Copperline

TAYLOR, JOHNNIE
1968   Who's Making Love?
1973   I Believe in You (You Believe in Me)
1976   Disco Lady

TAYLOR, LITTLE JOHNNY
1963   Part Time Love

TAYLOR, R. DEAN
1970   Indiana Wants Me

T-BONES, THE
1965   No Matter What Shape (Your Stomach's In)

TEARDROP EXPLODES, THE
1980   When I Dream

TEARS FOR FEARS
1982   Mad World
1985   Everybody Wants to Rule the World
1985   Head over Heels
1985   Shout
1989   Sowing the Seeds of Love
1993   Break It down Again

TECHNOTRONIC

1989   Get Up! (Before the Night Is Over)
1989   Pump up the Jam
1992   Move This

TEDDY BEARS, THE

1958   To Know Him Is to Love Him

TEDESCHI, SUSAN

1998   It Hurts So Bad

TEEGARDEN AND VAN WINKLE

1970   God, Love and Rock 'n' Roll

TEENA MARIE

1985   Lovergirl
1988   Ooo La La La

TEENAGE JESUS AND THE JERKS

1979   Orphans

TEEN-QUEENS, THE

1956   Eddie, My Love

TELEVISION

1974   Little Johnny Jewel
1977   Marquee Moon

TEMPO, NINO AND APRIL STEVENS

1963   Deep Purple

TEMPOS, THE

1959   See You in September

TEMPTATIONS, THE

1964   Way You Do the Things You Do, The
1965   My Girl
1966   Ain't Too Proud to Beg
1966   Beauty Is Only Skin Deep
1966   Get Ready
1966   (I Know) I'm Losing You
1967   All I Need
1967   You're My Everything
1968   Cloud Nine
1968   I Could Never Love Another (After Loving You)
1968   I Wish It Would Rain
1969   Don't Let the Joneses Get You Down
1969   I Can't Get Next to You
1969   Psychedelic Shack
1969   Runaway Child, Running Wild
1970   Ball of Confusion (That's What the World Is Today)
1970   War

1971   Just My Imagination (Running Away with Me)
1971   Superstar Remember How You Got Where You Are
1972   Papa Was a Rollin' Stone
1973   Masterpiece
1974   Happy People

10 C.C.

1973   Rubber Bullets
1975   I'm Not in Love
1977   Things We Do for Love, The

10,000 MANIACS

1985   My Mother the War
1987   Hey Jack Kerouac
1987   Like the Weather
1987   Verdi Cries
1987   What's the Matter Here
1989   Trouble Me
1992   These Are Days
1993   Candy Everybody Wants

TEN YEARS AFTER

1968   I'm Goin' Home
1971   I'd Love to Change the World

TEX, JOE

1964   Hold What You've Got
1966   Papa Was Too
1967   Skinny Legs and All
1968   Men Are Gettin' Scarce
1972   I Gotcha

THARPE, SISTER ROSETTA

1947   (Everybody's Gonna Have) a Wonderful Time up There (Gospel Boogie)
1948   Up above My Head, I Hear Music in the Air

THE THE

1989   Beat(en) Generation, The

THEM

1965   Gloria
1965   Mystic Eyes

THEY MIGHT BE GIANTS

1986   Don't Let's Start
1988   Ana Ng
1988   Kiss Me, Son of God
1988   Purple Toupee
1990   Birdhouse in Your Soul
1990   Particle Man
1990   Your Racist Friend

THIN LIZZY

1976   Boys Are Back in Town, The
1976   Jailbreak

THIRD EYE BLIND

1997   Semi-Charmed Life

THIRTEENTH FLOOR ELEVATORS

1966   Fire Engine
1966   You're Gonna Miss Me

38 SPECIAL

1982   Caught up in You
1981   Hold on Loosely
1983   If I'd Been the One

THOMAS, B.J.

1968   Hooked on a Feeling
1970   Raindrops Keep Fallin' on My Head
1975   (Hey Won't You Play) Another Somebody Done Somebody Wrong

THOMAS, CARLA

1961   Gee Whiz! (Look at His Eyes)
1966   B-A-B-Y

THOMAS, IRMA

1962   It's Raining
1964   Time Is on My Side
1964   Wish Someone Would Care

THOMAS, RUFUS

1953   Bear Cat
1963   Walking the Dog
1970   Do the Push & Pull, Part 1

THOMAS, TIMMY

1973   Why Can't We Live Together

THOMPSON, LINDA

1985   Telling Me Lies

THOMPSON, RICHARD

1983   Hand of Kindness
1983   Tear Stained Letter
1985   She Twists the Knife Again
1985   When the Spell Is Broken
1986   Nearly in Love
1986   Valerie
1991   I Feel So Good
1991   I Misunderstood
1991   1952 Vincent Black Lightning
1993   Beeswing

THOMPSON, RICHARD AND LINDA

1974   Heart Needs a Home, A
1974   I Want to See the Bright Lights Tonight

1974	When I Get to the Border
1975	Beat the Retreat
1975	Dimming of the Day, The
1982	Just the Motion
1982	Man in Need, A
1982	Shoot out the Lights
1982	Wall of Death

THOMPSON, SUE

1961	Sad Movies Always Make Me Cry
1962	Norman

THOMPSON TWINS, THE

1983	Love on Your Side
1984	Hold Me Now
1985	Lay Your Hands on Me

THORNTON, BIG MAMA

1953	Hound Dog

THOROGOOD, GEORGE

1982	Bad to the Bone
1985	I Drink Alone

THREE DEGREES, THE

1974	When Will I See You Again

THREE DOG NIGHT

1969	Celebrate
1971	Joy to the World
1971	Never Been to Spain
1971	Old Fashioned Love Song, An
1972	Black & White
1974	Sure as I'm Sittin' Here

3 DOORS DOWN

2000	Kryptonite

THREE FRIENDS, THE

1956	Blanche

THREE O'CLOCK, THE

1985	Mrs. Green

THROWING MUSES

1986	Green
1991	Not Too Soon

THUNDER, JOHNNY

1963	Loop De Loop

THUNDERCLAP NEWMAN

1969	Something in the Air

TICO & THE TRIUMPHS

1961	Motorcycle

TIFFANY

1987	Could've Been

TIL TUESDAY

1985	Voices Carry

TILLOTSON, JOHNNY

1960	Poetry in Motion
1962	It Keeps Right on a-Hurtin'

TIMBALAND & MAGOO

1997	Up Jumps Da Boogie

TIMBUK 3

1986	Future's So Bright, I Gotta Wear Shades, The

TIME, THE

1990	Jerk Out

TIMELORDS, THE

1988	Doctorin' the Tardis

TIMEX SOCIAL CLUB

1986	Rumors

TIN HUEY

1979	I Could Rule the World If I Could Only Get the Parts

TINY TIM

1968	Tip Toe through the Tulips

TLC

1992	Baby Baby Baby
1992	What about Your Friends
1994	Creep
1994	Waterfalls
1999	No Scrubs
1999	Unpretty

TOAD THE WET SPROCKET

1992	All I Want

TOM AND JERRY

1958	Hey, Schoolgirl

TOM TOM CLUB

1981	Genius of Love
1981	Wordy Rappinghood

TOMMY TUTONE

1982	867-5309/Jenny

TONE LOC

1989	Funky Cold Medina
1989	Wild Thing

TONIC

1997	If You Could Only See

TONY! TONI! TONE!

1990	Feels Good
1988	Little Walter

TOOL

1996	Stinkfist

TOOTS & THE MAYTALS

1970	Pressure Drop
1972	54-46 (Was My Number)
1975	Funky Kingston

TORNADOES, THE

1962	Telstar

TOTO

1978	Hold the Line
1982	Africa
1982	Rosanna

TOUSSAINT, ALLEN

1975	Southern Nights

TOWER OF POWER

1973	So Very Hard to Go

TOWNSEND, ED

1958	For Your Love

TOWNSHEND, PETE

(See The Who)

1972	Pure and Easy
1977	My Baby Gives It Away
1977	Street in the City
1980	Let My Love Open the Door
1980	Little Is Enough, A
1980	Rough Boys
1985	After the Fire
1985	Face the Face

TOYS, THE

1965	Lover's Concerto, A

T'PAU

1987   Heart and Soul

TRAFFIC

1967   Paper Sun
1968   Dear Mr. Fantasy
1968   Feelin' Alright?
1968   Forty Thousand Headmen
1968   You Can All Join In
1969   Shanghai Noodle Factory
1970   Freedom Rider
1971   Low Spark of High Heeled Boys, The

TRAIN

1999   Meet Virginia

TRAMMPS

1977   Disco Inferno

TRASHMEN, THE

1963   Surfin' Bird

TRAVELING WILBURYS

1988   Handle with Care
1990   Seven Deadly Sins

TRAVIS AND BOB

1959   Tell Him No

TRAVOLTA, JOHN

1976   Let Her In

TREAT HER RIGHT

1986   I Think She Likes Me

TRENIERS, THE

1952   Rockin' Is Our Business

TRESVANT, RALPH

(See New Edition)
1991   Sensitivity

TRIBE CALLED QUEST, A

1990   Bonita Applebum
1990   Can I Kick It
1992   Scenario
1993   Award Tour

TRICKY

1995   Overcome

TRIO

1982   Da Da Da

TRIP SHAKESPEARE

1988   Pearle

TRIPLETS, THE

1991   You Don't Have to Go Home Tonight

TRIUMPH

1981   Magic Power

TROGGS, THE

1966   Wild Thing
1967   Love Is All Around

TROTSKY ICEPICK

1987   Bury Manilow

TROWER, ROBIN

(See Procol Harum)
1974   Bridge of Sighs

TROY, DORIS

1963   Just One Look

TRUDELL, JOHN

1992   Baby Boom Che

TRUE CONNECTION, ANDREA

1976   More, More, More (Part 1)

TUBES, THE

1983   She's a Beauty
1975   White Punks on Dope
1976   Don't Touch Me There

TUCKER, TOMMY

1964   Hi-Heel Sneakers

TUNE WEAVERS, THE

1957   Happy, Happy Birthday Baby

TURBANS, THE

1955   When You Dance

TURNER, IKE AND TINA

1961   It's Gonna Work out Fine
1962   Fool in Love, A
1966   River Deep, Mountain High
1973   Nutbush City Limits

TURNER, TINA

1984   Better Be Good to Me
1984   What's Love Got to Do with It
1985   We Don't Need Another Hero (Thunderdome)
1985   Stronger Than the Wind
1986   Don't Turn Around
1986   Typical Male

TURNER, JOE

1951   Chains of Love
1954   Honey Hush
1954   Shake, Rattle and Roll
1955   Flip, Flop and Fly
1956   Corrine, Corrina

TURNER, SAMMY

1959   Lavender Blue (Dilly Dilly)

TURNER, TITUS

1955   All around the World

TURTLES, THE

1965   Let Me Be
1967   Happy Together
1967   Outside Chance
1967   She'd Rather Be with Me
1968   Elenore
1968   Story of Rock and Roll, The

TWENTY FINGERS

1994   Short Dick Man

TWINTONES, THE

1957   Jo-Ann

TWISTED SISTER

1984   We're Not Gonna Take It

TWITTY, CONWAY

1958   It's Only Make Believe

TWO LIVE CREW

1989   Me So Horny

2PAC

1993   I Get Around
1993   Keep Ya Head Up
1996   California Love
1996   How Do U Want It
1998   Changes

TYLA GANG, THE

1976   Texas Chainsaw Massacre Boogie

TYLER, BONNIE

1977   It's a Heartache
1983   Total Eclipse of the Heart

TYMES, THE

1963 So Much in Love

U

U.S.A. FOR AFRICA

1985 We Are the World

UFO

1977 Lights Out

UGLY KID JOE

1992 Everything About You

ULMER, JAMES BLOOD

1982 Where Did All the Girls Come From

ULTRAVOX

1980 Vienna

UNCLE TUPELO

1993 Anodyne

UNDERTONES, THE

1978 Teenage Kicks
1978 Get over You
1978 Jimmy, Jimmy
1980 My Perfect Cousin
1980 Wednesday Week

UNDERWORLD

1995 Born Slippy (Nuxx)

UNDISPUTED TRUTH

1971 Smiling Faces Sometimes

URGE OVERKILL

1993 Sister Havana

URIAH HEAP

1972 Easy Livin'

USHER

1997 Nice & Slow
1997 You Make Me Wanna

US3

1993 Cantaloop (Flip Fantasia)

UTAH SAINTS, THE

1992 Something Good

UTFO

1985 Roxanne, Roxanne

UTOPIA

1980 Set Me Free

U2

1980 Gloria
1980 Into the Heart
1982 I Will Follow
1983 New Year's Day
1983 Sunday, Bloody Sunday
1983 Two Hearts Beat as One
1984 Pride (In the Name of Love)
1987 Bullet the Blue Sky
1987 I Still Haven't Found What I'm
        Looking For
1987 In God's Country
1987 Running to Stand Still
1987 Where the Streets Have No
        Names
1987 With or Without You
1988 Angel of Harlem
1988 Desire
1991 Even Better Than the Real Thing
1991 Mysterious Ways
1991 One
1993 Wanderer, The
1997 Discotheque
1997 Staring at the Sun
2000 Beautiful Day
2000 Elevation
2000 Walk On

V

VAI, STEVE

1990 Audience Is Listening, The

VALENS, RITCHIE

1958 Come on, Let's Go
1958 Donna
1958 La Bamba

VALENTINOS, THE

1962 Lookin' for a Love
1964 It's All over Now

VALLI, FRANKIE

(See The Four Seasons)
1965 Sun Ain't Gonna Shine Anymore,
        The
1967 Can't Take My Eyes off You
1974 My Eyes Adored You
1978 Grease

VAN DYKE, LEROY

1961 Walk on By

VAN HALEN

1978 Ain't Talkin' 'bout Love
1978 Eruption
1978 Jamie's Cryin'
1978 Runnin' with the Devil
1979 Dance the Night Away
1980 And the Cradle Will Rock
1982 Little Guitars
1984 Hot for Teacher
1984 I'll Wait
1984 Jump
1984 Panama
1986 Dreams
1986 Love Walks In
1986 Why Can't This Be Love
1988 Black and Blue
1988 Finish What Ya Started
1988 When It's Love
1991 Right Now
1991 Top of the World
1996 Humans Being
1996 Me Wise Magic

VAN RONK, DAVE AND THE HUDSON DUSTERS

1968 Romping through the Swamp

VAN WARMER, RANDY

1979 Just When I Needed You Most

VAN ZANDT, TOWNES

1968 Tucumseh Valley
1968 For the Sake of the Song
1972 If I Needed You
1972 Pancho and Lefty
1972 To Live Is to Fly

VANDROSS, LUTHER

1989 Here and Now
1991 Don't Want to Be a Fool
1991 Power of Love/Love Power

VANILLA ICE

1990 Ice Ice Baby

VANITY FAIR

1970 Hitchin' a Ride

VANNELLI, GINO

1978 I Just Wanna Stop

VAPORS, THE

1981 Turning Japanese

VAUGHAN, SARAH

1959 Broken Hearted Melody

VAUGHAN, STEVIE RAY

1983   Love Struck Baby
1983   Pride and Joy
1983   Texas Flood
1984   Couldn't Stand the Weather
1984   Tin Pan Alley

VAUGHAN, STEVIE RAY AND JIMMIE

1990   Brothers

VEE, BOBBY

1960   Night Has a Thousand Eyes, The
1961   Run to Him
1966   Come Back When You Grow Up

VEGA, ALAN AND MARTIN REV

1980   Dream Baby Dream

VEGA, SUZANNE

1985   Marlene on the Wall
1986   Left of Center
1987   Gypsy
1987   Luka
1987   Tom's Diner

VELVELETTES, THE

1965   He Was Really Saying Something

VELVET UNDERGROUND, THE

1967   All Tomorrow's Parties
1967   Black Angel's Death Song
1967   European Son: To Delmore Schwartz
1967   Femme Fatale
1967   Heroin
1967   I'll Be Your Mirror
1967   I'm Waiting for the Man
1967   Sunday Morning
1967   Venus in Furs
1968   I Heard Her Call My Name
1968   Sister Ray
1968   White Light/White Heat
1969   Foggy Notion
1969   Pale Blue Eyes
1970   Rock and Roll
1970   Sweet Jane

VENTURES, THE

1969   Hawaii 5-Oh

VERNE, LARRY

1960   Mister Custer

VERTICAL HORIZON

2000   Everything You Want

VERUCA SALT

1994   Seether

VERVE, THE

1998   Bitter Suite Symphony

VERVE PIPE, THE

1997   Freshmen, The

VIBRATIONS, THE

1964   My Girl Sloopy

VIDEOS, THE

1958   Trickle Trickle

VILLAGE PEOPLE, THE

1977   San Francisco (You've Got Me)
1978   Macho Man
1979   In the Navy
1979   Y.M.C.A.

VINCENT, GENE AND HIS BLUE CAPS

1956   Be-Bop-a-Lula
1956   Bluejean Bop
1956   Race with the Devil
1957   Dance to the Bop
1957   Lotta Lovin'
1957   Wear My Ring

VINTON, BOBBY

1961   Roses Are Red (My Love)

VIOLENT FEMMES, THE

1991   American Music
1982   Blister in the Sun
1982   Kiss Off

VIOVOD

1989   Missing Sequences

VOGUES, THE

1965   Five O'Clock World

W

WAILERS

1959   Tall Cool One

WAINWRIGHT, LOUDON

1970   School Days
1971   Careful There's a Baby in the House
1971   Motel Blues
1972   Dead Skunk
1972   Red Guitar
1973   Swimming Song, The
1978   Watch Me Rock, I'm over Thirty
1987   Back Nine, The
1989   Me and All the Other Mothers

WAINWRIGHT, RUFUS

1998   April Fools

WAITE, JOHN

1984   Missing You

WAITRESSES, THE

1982   I Know What Boys Like
1983   Square Pegs

WAITS, TOM

1973   Ol' 55
1974   New Coat of Paint
1974   San Diego Serenade
1976   Step Right Up
1976   Tom Traubert's Blues
1978   Romeo Is Bleeding
1978   Wrong Side of the Road
1980   Jersey Girl
1980   On the Nickel
1983   Gin-Soaked Boy
1985   Downtown Train
1987   Hang on St. Christopher
1987   Innocent When You Dream (Bar Room)
1992   I Don't Want to Grow Up
1992   Whistle down the Wind
1999   House Where Nobody Lives
1999   What's He Building

WALDMAN, WENDY

1973   Vaudeville Man

WALKER, BILLY

1961   Funny (How Time Slips Away)

WALKER, JERRY JEFF

1968   Mr. Bojangles
1973   L.A. Freeway

WALKER, JR. & THE ALL-STARS

1965   (I'm a) Road Runner
1965   Shotgun
1969   What Does It Take (to Win Your Love)?
1970   Gotta Hold on to This Feeling

WALKER, T-BONE

1947   Call It Stormy Monday

WALL OF VOODOO

1982   Mexican Radio

WALLFLOWERS, THE

1996   Difference, The
1996   One Headlight
1996   6TH Avenue Heartbreak
1996   Three Marlenas

WALSH, JOE

(See The James Gang)
1973   Rocky Mountain Way
1978   Life's Been Good
1981   Life of Illusion, A

WANG CHUNG

1984   Dance Hall Days
1986   Everybody Have Fun Tonight

WAR

1970   Spill the Wine
1972   Cisco Kid
1972   World Is a Ghetto, The
1973   Gypsy Man
1975   Low Rider
1975   Why Can't We Be Friends
1976   Summer

WARD, ANITA

1979   Ring My Bell

WARRANT

1990   Cherry Pie
1989   Heaven

WARREN G.

1994   This D.J.

WARREN G. & NATE DOGG

1994   Regulate

WARWICK, DEE DEE

1967   I'm Gonna Make You Love Me

WARWICK, DIONNE

1963   Don't Make Me Over
1963   (They Long to Be) Close to You
1963   Wishin' and Hopin'

WARWICK, DIONNE AND THE SPINNERS

1974   Then Came You

WAS (NOT WAS)

1981   Out Come the Freaks
1983   Zaz Turned Blue
1988   Dad I'm in Jail
1988   Spy in the House of Love
1988   Walk the Dinosaur

WASHINGTON, DINAH

1949   Baby Get Lost
1959   What a Diff'rence a Day Makes
1960   This Bitter Earth

WASHINGTON, GROVER, JR.

1981   Just the Two of Us

WATERBOYS, THE

1985   Whole of the Moon, The
1988   Fisherman's Blues

WATERS, CRYSTAL

1991   Gypsy Woman (She's Homeless)
1994   100% Pure Love

WATERS, MUDDY

1948   I Can't Be Satisfied
1950   Rollin' Stone
1954   I Just Wanna Make Love to You
1954   I'm Ready
1954   I'm Your Hoochie Coochie Man
1955   Mannish Boy
1956   Got My Mojo Working
1956   Rock Me
1962   You Shook Me
1977   Blues Had a Baby and They Named It Rock and Roll, The

WATERS, ROGER

1987   Radio Waves

WATLEY, JODY

1987   Looking for a New Love
1989   Everything
1989   Real Love

WATSON, JOHNNY GUITAR

1963   Gangster of Love

WAYNE, THOMAS

1959   Tragedy

WE FIVE, THE

1965   Get Together

WEATHER GIRLS, THE

1983   It's Raining Men

WEATHER REPORT

1977   Birdland
1977   Teen Town

WEATHERLY, JIM

1971   Midnight Plane to Houston

WEAVERS, THE

1949   If I Had a Hammer
1949   Rock Island Line
1950   Goodnight Irene
1951   Kisses Sweeter Than Wine
1951   So Long It's Been Good to Know You (Dusty Old Dust)
1951   Wreck of the John B.
1952   Midnight Special
1952   Wimoweh (The Lion Sleeps Tonight)
1956   Michael (Row the Boat Ashore)
1956   This Land Is Your Land
1958   Gotta Travel On (Done Laid Around)
1958   House of the Rising Sun
1963   Guantanamera

WEBB, JIMMY

1970   P.F. Sloan

WEDDING PRESENT, THE

1991   Niagara

WEEN

1993   Push th' Little Daisies

WEEZER

1994   Buddy Holly
1994   My Name Is Jonah
1994   Undone (The Sweater Song)
1996   Good Life, The

WEIR, BOB

(See the Grateful Dead)
1971   Playing in the Band
1972   Cassidy

WEISBERG, ERIC AND STEVE MANDEL

1972   Dueling Banjos

WELCH, GILLIAN

1996   Orphan Girl

WELLS, JUNIOR

1966   It Hurts Me Too

WELLS, KITTY

1952   It Wasn't God Who Made Honky Tonk Angels
1954   Thou Shalt Not Steal

WELLS, MARY

1961   Bye Bye Baby
1962   One Who Really Loves You, The
1962   Two Lovers

1962   You Beat Me to the Punch
1964   My Guy

WESTERBERG, PAUL

(See The Replacements)
1992   Dyslexic Heart
1994   World Class Fad
1996   Good Day

WESTON, KIM

1965   Take Me in Your Arms (Rock Me a Little While)

WET WILLIE

1974   Keep on Smilin'

WHAM!

1982   Young Guns (Go for It)
1984   Careless Whisper
1984   Everything She Wants
1984   Freedom
1984   Wake Me up before You Go-Go
1985   I'm Your Man
1986   Different Corner, A
1986   Edge of Heaven

WHISPERS, THE

1987   Rock Steady

WHITCOMB, IAN

1965   You Turn Me On (The Turn on Song)

WHITE, BARRY

1973   I'm Gonna Love You Just a Little More Babe
1973   Never, Never Gonna Give Ya Up
1974   Can't Get Enough of Your Love, Babe
1974   You're the First, the Last, My Everything
1977   It's Ecstacy When You Lay down Next to Me

WHITE, KARYN

1989   Superwoman
1989   Way You Love Me, The
1991   Romantic

WHITE LION

1987   When the Children Cry

WHITE ZOMBIE

1994   Thunder Kiss

WHITESNAKE

1987   Here I Go Again
1987   Is This Love
1987   Still of the Night

WHO, THE

1965   I Can't Explain
1965   My Generation
1966   Anyway, Anyhow, Anywhere
1966   Kids Are Alright, The
1966   Substitute
1967   Happy Jack
1967   I Can See for Miles
1967   Pictures of Lily
1967   Quick One While He's Away, A
1968   Magic Bus
1969   Acid Queen
1969   Amazing Journey, The
1969   I'm Free
1969   Pinball Wizard
1969   See Me, Feel Me
1969   We're Not Gonna Take It
1971   Baba O'Riley
1971   Bargain
1971   Behind Blue Eyes
1971   Goin' Mobile
1971   I'm a Boy
1971   Seeker, The
1971   Song Is Over, The
1971   Won't Get Fooled Again
1972   Join Together
1972   Love, Reign o'er Me
1973   5:15
1973   Real Me, The
1975   Slip Kid
1975   Squeeze Box
1978   Guitar and Pen
1978   Who Are You
1981   Don't Let Go the Coat
1981   You Better, You Bet

WIDESPREAD PANIC

1999   Climb to Safety

WILCO

1995   I Must Be High
1999   She's a Jar

WILD CHERRY

1976   Play That Funky Music

WILDE, KIM

1982   Kids in America

WILDER, MATTHEW

1983   Break My Stride

WILLIAMS, DAR

1996   As Cool as I Am

WILLIAMS, DENIECE

1984   Let's Hear It for the Boy

WILLIAMS, HANK

1947   Move It on Over
1949   I'm So Lonesome I Could Cry
1949   Lovesick Blues
1951   Cold, Cold Heart
1951   Hey Good Lookin'
1952   I'll Never Get out of This World Alive
1952   Jambalaya (On the Bayou)
1953   Your Cheatin' Heart
1955   Take These Chains from My Heart

WILLIAMS, JERRY

1979   Giving It up for Your Love

WILLIAMS, LARRY

1957   Bony Moronie
1957   Short Fat Fannie
1957   Slow Down
1958   She Said Yeah

WILLIAMS, LUCINDA

1988   Changed the Locks
1988   Passionate Kisses
1993   Sweet Old World
1998   Car Wheels on a Gravel Road
1998   Right in Time

WILLIAMS, MASON

1968   Classical Gas

WILLIAMS, MAURICE AND THE ZODIACS

1960   Stay

WILLIAMS, OTIS & THE CHARMS

1956   Ivory Tower

WILLIAMS, PAUL

1949   Hucklebuck, The

WILLIAMS, VANESSA

1992   Saving the Best for Last

WILLIAMS, VANESSA AND BRIAN MCKNIGHT

1993   Love Is

WILLIAMS, VICTORIA

1990   Summer of Drugs
1994   Crazy Mary

WILLIAMSON, SONNY BOY

1951   Eyesight to the Blind

WILLIE AND RUTH

1954   Love Me

WILLIS, CHUCK

1952	My Story
1954	I Feel So Bad
1954	You're Still My Baby
1956	It's Too Late
1957	C.C. Rider
1958	Betty and Dupree
1958	Hang up My Rock and Roll Shoes
1958	What Am I Living For

WILLOWS, THE

1956	Church Bells May Ring

WILLS, BOB & HIS TEXAS PLAYBOYS

1946	New Spanish Two Step
1947	Ida Red

WILSON, AL

1973	Show and Tell

WILSON, BRIAN

(See The Beach Boys)

1988	Rio Grande

WILSON, JACKIE

1957	Reet Petite
1958	Lonely Teardrops
1958	To Be Loved
1959	I'll Be Satisfied
1959	That's Why
1959	You Better Know It
1960	Alone at Last
1960	Night
1961	My Empty Arms
1962	Doggin' Around
1962	Woman, a Lover, a Friend, A,
1963	Baby Workout
1967	(Your Love Keeps Lifting Me) Higher and Higher

WILSON PHILLIPS

1990	Hold On
1990	Impulsive
1990	Release Me
1990	You're in Love

WINCHESTER, JESSE

1971	Yankee Lady

WINGFIELD, PETE

1975	Eighteen with a Bullet

WINTER GROUP, EDGAR

1972	Frankenstein
1972	Free Ride

WINTER, JOHNNY

1974	Rock and Roll Hoochie Koo

WINWOOD, STEVE

(See Traffic)

1981	While You See a Chance
1986	Back in the High Life Again
1986	Finer Things
1986	Higher Love
1988	Roll with It

WIRE

1977	Fragile
1977	I Am the Fly
1977	106 Beats That
1977	Reuters
1977	Strange

WISH FEATURING FONDA RAE WISH

1985	Touch Me (All Night Long)

WITHERS, BILL

1971	Ain't No Sunshine
1972	Lean on Me
1972	Use Me

WOMACK, BOBBY

(See The Valentinos)

1972	Woman's Gotta Have It

WONDER, STEVIE

1962	Fingertips
1966	Place in the Sun, A
1966	Uptight (Everything's Alright)
1967	I Was Made to Love Her
1968	For Once in My Life
1968	Shoo-Be-Doo-Be-Doo-Day
1969	My Cherie Amour
1969	Yester-me Yester-you Yesterday
1970	Heaven Help Us All
1970	If You Really Love Me
1970	Signed, Sealed, Delivered I'm Yours
1972	Superstition
1972	Superwoman (Where Were You When I Needed You)
1972	You Are the Sunshine of My Life
1973	Don't You Worry 'bout a Thing
1973	Higher Ground
1973	Livin' for the City
1974	Boogie on Reggae Woman
1974	You Haven't Done Nothin'
1976	I Wish
1976	Isn't She Lovely
1976	Pastime Paradise
1976	Sir Duke
1979	Send One Your Love
1980	Lately
1980	Master Blaster (Jammin')
1982	That Girl
1984	I Just Called to Say I Love You
1985	Part-Time Lover
1987	Skeletons
1987	You Will Know
1991	Jungle Fever

WOOD, BRENTON

1967	Gimme Little Sign

WOOLEY, SHEB

1958	Purple People Eater

WORLD PARTY

1986	All Come True

WRAY, LINK

1958	Rumble
1959	Rawhide

WRECKLESS ERIC

1978	Whole Wide World

WRECKX-N-EFFECT

1992	Rump Shaker

WRENS, THE

1955	(Will You) Come Back My Love

WRIGHT, BETTY

1971	Clean up Woman

WRIGHT, GARY

1976	Dream Weaver
1976	Love Is Alive

WRIGHT, O.V.

1965	You're Gonna Make Me Cry
1967	Eight Men and Four Women
1970	Ace of Spades

WU TANG CLAN

1993	C.R.E.A.M.

WYNETTE, TAMMY

1968	Stand by Your Man

XYZ

X

1980	Los Angeles
1980	We're Desperate
1980	White Girl
1982	Hungry Wolf
1982	Riding with Mary
1982	Under the Big Black Sun

X-RAY SPECS

1977	Oh Bondage, up Yours!

XSCAPE

1993 Just Kickin' It

XTC

1979 This Is Pop
1980 Living through Another Cuba
1982 Making Plans for Nigel
1982 Senses Working Overtime
1987 Dear God
1987 Earn Enough for Us
1987 Summer's Cauldron
1989 Garden of Earthly Delights
1989 Hold Me Daddy
1989 Mayor of Simpleton
1992 Ballad of Peter Pumpkinhead

YARDBIRDS, THE

1964 I Wish You Would
1965 Evil Hearted You
1965 For Your Love
1965 Heart Full of Soul
1965 I Ain't Done Wrong
1965 I'm Not Talking
1965 Still I'm Sad
1965 You're a Better Man Than I
1966 Happenings Ten Years Time Ago
1966 Jeff's Boogie
1966 Over under Sideways Down
1966 Shapes of Things
1967 Little Games
1967 Stroll On
1968 Goodnight Sweet Josephine
1968 White Summer

YAZOO

1982 Only You

YES

1971 Clap, The
1971 Yours Is No Disgrace
1972 And You and I
1972 Close to the Edge
1972 Heart of the Sunrise
1972 Long Distance Runaround
1972 Roundabout
1983 Owner of a Lonely Heart

YO LA TENGO

1993 Nowhere Near

YOUNG, JESSIE COLIN

1964 Four in the Morning

YOUNG, NEIL

(See Crosby, Stills, Nash & Young)
1969 Cowgirl in the Sand
1969 Down by the River
1969 I've Loved Her So Long
1969 Last Trip to Tulsa
1969 Loner, The
1969 Sugar Mountain
1970 After the Goldrush
1970 Cinnamon Girl
1970 Don't Let It Bring You Down
1970 Only Love Can Break Your Heart
1970 Southern Man
1970 When You Dance (I Can Really Love)
1972 Heart of Gold
1972 Needle and the Damage Done, The
1972 Old Man
1975 Cortez the Killer
1977 Like a Hurricane
1978 Comes a Time
1978 Lotta Love
1979 Powerderfinger
1979 Rust Never Sleeps (Hey Hey My My into the Black)
1988 This Note's for You
1989 Rockin' in the Free World
1989 Wrecking Ball
1992 Harvest Moon
1993 Philadelphia
1994 Change Your Mind
1994 Piece of Crap
1994 Sleeps with Angels

YOUNG JESSIE

1955 Mary Lou

YOUNG M.C.

1989 Bust a Move

YOUTH OF TODAY

1988 Flame Still Burns, The

YURO, TIMI

1962 What's a Matter Baby (Is It Hurting You)

ZAGER AND EVANS

1969 In the Year 2525 (Exordium and Terminus)

ZAPPA, FRANK

(See The Mothers of Invention)
1969 Peaches en Regalia
1969 Willie the Pimp, Parts One & Two
1971 Dance of the Rock & Roll Interviewers
1974 Don't Eat the Yellow Snow
1974 Penguin in Bondage
1979 Dancin' Fool
1979 Joe's Garage

ZAPPA, FRANK AND MOON UNIT

1982 Valley Girl

ZEVON, WARREN

1976 Carmelita
1976 Poor Poor Pitiful Me
1978 Excitable Boy
1978 Lawyers, Guns and Money
1978 Werewolves of London
1987 Detox Mansion
1987 Even a Dog Can Shake Hands
1990 Searching for a Heart
1991 Mr. Bad Example
1991 Renegade
2000 Life'll Kill Ya

ZOMBIES, THE

1964 She's Not There
1964 Tell Her No
1967 Time of the Season

ZZ TOP

1973 La Grange
1975 Tush
1983 Gimme All Your Lovin'
1983 Sharp Dressed Man
1984 Legs
1985 Sleeping Bag
1995 Pincushion

THE ROCK YEARS INDEX

1944

Charlie Christian turns the world onto the electric guitar in "Solo Flight."

Louis Jordan shows Chuck Berry how to write a rock and roll song ("Is You Is or Is You Ain't My Baby").

Nat Cole croons his way onto the pop, country and R&B charts with "Gee Baby, Ain't I Good to You."

*Gee Baby, Ain't I Good to You	Nat Cole Trio
Straighten up and Fly Right	Nat Cole Trio
*Solo Flight	Charlie Christian
G.I. Jive	Louis Jordan and His Tympani Five
*Is You Is or Is You Ain't My Baby	Louis Jordan and His Tympani Five

1945

The Ink Spots pave the way for doo-wop.

Swingin' the Boogie	Hadda Brooks
Around the Clock	Wynonie Harris
*Into Each Life Some Rain Must Fall	The Ink Spots and Ella Fitzgerald
Honeydripper, The	Joe Liggins

1946

Johnny Otis puts L.A. on the R&B map with "Harlem Nocturne."

Bob Wills ("New Spanish Two Step") and Freddie Slack ("The House of Blue Lights") bring an edge of country music.

(Get Your Kicks) on Route 66	Nat King Cole
Stone Cold Dead in the Market (He Had It Coming)	Ella Fitzgerald and Louis Jordan
*Open the Door, Richard	Dusty Fletcher
Gypsy, The	The Ink Spots
Ain't Nobody Here But Us Chickens	Louis Jordan and His Tympani Five
Choo Choo Ch'Boogie	Louis Jordan and His Tympani Five
Let the Good Times Roll	Louis Jordan and His Tympani Five
*Driftin' Blues	Johnny Moore's Three Blazers
*Harlem Nocturne	Johnny Otis
*House of Blue Lights, The	Freddie Slack and Ella Mae Morse
Guitar Boogie Shuffle	Arthur Smith & His Crackerjacks
*New Spanish Two Step	Bob Wills & His Texas Playboys

1947

Arthur Big Boy Crudup pens the future Presley classic "That's All Right, Mama."

T-Bone Walker ups the ante on the electric guitar with "Call It Stormy Monday."

Bob Wills' "Ida Red" provides the inspiration for "Maybellene."

Wild Bill Moore ("We're Gonna Rock, We're Gonna Roll") and Roy Brown ("Good Rockin' Tonight") name the beast.

"Move It on Over" signals the arrival of Hank Williams.

One of the year's defining songs.

Gloria   Charles Brown

Good Rockin' Tonight   Roy Brown

(I Love You) for Sentimental Reasons   Nat King Cole

*That's All Right, Mama   Arthur Big Boy Crudup

I Sold My Heart to the Junkman   Etta Jones

Jack You're Dead   Louis Jordan and His Tympani Five

Since I Fell for You   Annie Laurie

Blue Moon of Kentucky   Bill Monroe

We're Gonna Rock, We're Gonna Roll   Wild Bill Moore

*Old Man River   The Ravens

*(Everybody's Gonna Have) A Wonderful Time Up
    There (Gospel Boogie)   Sister Rosetta Tharpe

*Call It Stormy Monday   T-Bone Walker

*Move It on Over   Hank Williams

*Ida Red   Bob Wills & His Texas Playboys

1948

A big year for the blues with Lonnie Johnson, Memphis Slim Muddy Waters and Lowell Fulson.

The Orioles cross over from Baltimore ("It's Too Soon to Know)."

Nature Boy   Nat King Cole

3 O'Clock Blues   Lowell Fulson

*Tomorrow Night   Lonnie Johnson

*Rockin' the House   Memphis Slim

Chicken Shack Boogie   Amos Milburn

* It's Too Soon to Know   The Orioles

Up above My Head, I Hear Music in the Air   Sister Rosetta Tharpe

*I Can't Be Satisfied   Muddy Waters

1949

Louis Jordan hits his peak ("Saturday Night Fish Fry").

Paul Williams starts a new dance craze, "The Hucklebuck."

John Lee Hooker perfects the boogie.

Jackie Robinson breaks in with the Brooklyn Dodgers.

The Weavers bring Leadbelly to the mainstream ("Rock Island Line").

Trouble Blues   Charles Brown

Rockin' at Midnight   Roy Brown

Red Hot   The Five Scamps

All She Wants to Do Is Rock   Wynonie Harris

*Boogie Chillen   John Lee Hooker

Did You See Jackie Robinson Hit That Ball   Buddy Johnson

Ain't That Just Like a Woman   Louis Jordan and His Tympani Five

*Saturday Night Fish Fry   Louis Jordan and His Tympani Five

Drinking Wine Spo-Dee O-Dee   Stick McGhee

Rock and Roll   Wild Bill Moore

Tell Me So   The Orioles

Baby Get Lost   Dinah Washington

If I Had a Hammer	The Weavers
*Rock Island Line	The Weavers
I'm So Lonesome I Could Cry	Hank Williams
Lovesick Blues	Hank Williams
*Hucklebuck, The	Paul Williams

1950

The "Fat Man" arrives in New Orleans.
Howling Wolf arrives in Chicago.
The Dominoes bring sex to Cleveland.
Ruth Brown brings her soul to NYC.
The Ravens battle the Orioles in Baltimore.

*Teardrops from My Eyes	Ruth Brown
Bald Head	Roy Byrds & His Blues Jumpers
Mona Lisa	Nat Cole
My Baby Left Me	Arthur Big Boy Crudup
*Fat Man	Fats Domino
*Do Something for Me	The Dominoes
Blue Shadows	Lowell Fulson
Every Day I Have the Blues	Lowell Fulson
Birmingham Bounce	Hardrock Gunter & the Pebbles
Down in the Bottom	Howling Wolf
*Moanin' at Midnight	Howling Wolf
I Almost Lost My Mind	Ivory Joe Hunter
Rock with It	Johnny Moore's Three Blazers
Cupid's Boogie	Johnny Otis with Mel Walker & Little Esther
Double-Crossin' Blues	Johnny Otis with Mel Walker & Little Esther
Mistrustin' Blues	Johnny Otis with Mel Walker & Little Esther
*Count Every Star	The Ravens
I'm Movin' On	Hank Snow
*Rollin' Stone	Muddy Waters
*Goodnight Irene	The Weavers

1951

Les Paul ("How High the Moon") invents the Les Paul.
Jackie Brenston goes for a ride in a "Rocket 88."
DJ Alan Freed aligns himself with the Dominoes.

Goodnight My Love	Jesse Belvin
*Rocket 88	Jackie Brenston & His Delta Cats
Black Night	Charles Brown
Don't You Know I Love You	The Clovers
Fool, Fool, Fool	The Clovers
*Sixty Minute Man	The Dominoes
It's All in the Game	Tommy Edwards
*Glory of Love	The Five Keys
I Got Loaded	Peppermint Harris

I'm in the Mood	John Lee Hooker
How Many More Years	Howling Wolf
Taxi Blues	Little Richard
Please Send Me Someone to Love	Percy Mayfield
One Way Out	Aleck Miller
*How High the Moon	Les Paul and Mary Ford
*Cry	Johnny Ray
Rockin'	The Robins
Chains of Love	Joe Turner
Kisses Sweeter Than Wine	The Weavers
So Long It's Been Good to Know You	
(Dusty Old Dust)	The Weavers
Wreck of the John B.	The Weavers
Cold, Cold Heart	Hank Williams
Hey Good Lookin'	Hank Williams
Eyesight to the Blind	Sonny Boy Williamson

1952

Lowell Fulson's keyboard player Ray Charles steps out ("Sinner's Prayer").

Bill Haley considers rock and roll.

Elmore James has a slide guitar workout on "I Believe I'll Dust My Broom."

Little Walter has a blues harp workout on "Juke."

My Song	Johnny Ace
I'm Gonna Play the Honky Tonks	Marie Adams
My Ding a Ling	Dave Bartholemew
Five Long Years	Eddie Boyd
5-10-15 Hours	Ruth Brown
*Sinner's Prayer	Ray Charles
One Mint Julep	The Clovers
Ting-a-Ling	The Clovers
Goin' Home	Fats Domino
Have Mercy Baby	The Dominoes
Night Train	Jimmy Forrest
Wheel of Fortune	The Four Flames
*Rock a-Beating Boogie	Bill Haley and His Comets
We're Gonna Rock This Joint	The Jackson Brothers
I Believe I'll Dust My Broom	Elmore James
Be Careful with a Fool	B.B. King
You Know I Love You	B.B. King
*Juke	Little Walter & His Nightcats
K.C. Lovin'	Little Willie Littlefield
I Don't Know	Willie Mabon
Lawdy Miss Clawdy	Lloyd Price
Rock Me All Night Long	The Ravens
Every Beat of My Heart	The Royals
(Now and Then There's) A Fool Such as I	Hank Snow

Rockin' Is Our Business	The Treniers
Midnight Special	The Weavers
Wimoweh (The Lion Sleeps Tonight)	The Weavers
It Wasn't God Who Made Honky Tonk Angels	Kitty Wells
I'll Never Get out of This World Alive	Hank Williams
Jambalaya (on the Bayou)	Hank Williams
Your Cheatin' Heart	Hank Williams
My Story	Chuck Willis

1953

Big Mama Thornton puts a couple of L.A. songwriters on the map with "Hound Dog."

Junior Parker puts Sun Records on the map with "Mystery Train."

Lowman Pauling puts Cincinnati on the map with "Baby Don't Do It."

Dean Martin comes into Elvis' living room every Sunday night on The Colgate Comedy Hour *singing "That's Amore."*

Clock, The	Johnny Ace
Shake a Hand	Faye Adams
Soul on Fire	LaVern Baker
Daddy Rolling Stone	Otis Blackwell
Mama (He Treats Your Daughter Mean)	Ruth Brown
Good Lovin'	The Clovers
Goin' to the River	Fats Domino
Money Honey	The Drifters
Whatcha Gonna Do	The Drifters
*Baby Don't Do It	The 5 Royales
Help Me Somebody	The 5 Royales
Crazy Man, Crazy	Bill Haley and His Comets
*(We're Gonna) Rock around the Clock	Bill Haley and His Comets
Sunday Kind of Love, A	The Harptones
Please Love Me	B.B. King
I'm Mad	Willie Mabon
*That's Amore	Dean Martin
One Scotch, One Bourbon, One Beer	Amos Milburn
Crying in the Chapel	The Orioles
Feelin' Good	Junior Parker
*Mystery Train	Junior Parker
I'm Sittin' on Top of the World	Les Paul and Mary Ford
Just Walking in the Rain	The Prisonaires
Twisted	Annie Ross
Bear Cat	Rufus Thomas
*Hound Dog	Big Mama Thornton
Take These Chains from My Heart	Hank Williams

1954

"Earth Angel" and "Sh-Boom" cross over from R&B to pop.

A big year for big-voiced female R&B singers Faye Adams, LaVern Baker, Big Maybelle, and Ruth Brown.

"Annie" shocks the masses.

Honey Hush	Joe Turner
*Shake Rattle and Roll	Joe Turner
I Just Wanna Make Love to You	Muddy Waters
I'm Ready	Muddy Waters
*I'm Your Hoochie Coochie Man	Muddy Waters
Thou Shalt Not Steal	Kitty Wells
Love Me	Willie and Ruth
I Feel So Bad	Chuck Willis
You're Still My Baby	Chuck Willis

1955

"Rock around the Clock" hits #1 thanks to Blackboard Jungle.
Chuck Berry promotes "Maybellene."
Bo Diddley promotes "Bo Diddley."
Little Richard gives up on the blues.
Frank Sinatra is "Learning the Blues."
Elvis Presley tries his hand at the blues.

Fujiyama Mama	Annisteen Allen
Nite Owl	Tony Allen
Bop-Ting-a-Ling	LaVern Baker
Seventeen	Boyd Bennett
*Maybellene	Chuck Berry
Thirty Days	Chuck Berry
*Whole Lotta Shakin' Goin' On	Big Maybelle
Hot Rod Lincoln	Johnny Bond
Wild, Wild Young Men	Ruth Brown
Speedoo	The Cadillacs
Door Is Still Open to My Heart, The	The Cardinals
See You Later, Alligator	Bobby Charles
Fool for You, A	Ray Charles
*I Got a Woman (I Got a Sweetie)	Ray Charles
This Little Girl of Mine	Ray Charles
Black Denim Trousers and Motorcycle Boots	The Cheers
Blue Velvet	The Clovers
Devil or Angel	The Clovers
Lovey Dovey	The Clovers
*Bo Diddley	Bo Diddley
Diddley Daddy	Bo Diddley
Here 'Tis	Bo Diddley
I'm a Man	Bo Diddley
Who Do You Love	Bo Diddley
Ain't It a Shame	Fats Domino
Adorable	The Drifters
At My Front Door (Crazy Little Mama Song)	The El Dorados
Defrost Your Heart	Charlie Feathers
Close Your Eyes	The Five Keys

WPLJ	Four Deuces
Ko Ko Mo (I Love You So)	Gene and Eunice
Burn That Candle	Bill Haley and His Comets
Unchained Melody	Roy Hamilton
Lonely Nights	The Hearts
Why Don't You Write Me	The Jacks
Dance with Me Henry (The Wallflower)	Etta James
I Hear You Knocking	Smiley Lewis
One Night (Of Sin)	Smiley Lewis
True Fine Mama	Little Richard
*Tutti Frutti	Little Richard
My Babe	Little Walter
Heaven and Paradise	Meadowlarks
Henry's Got Flat Feet	The Midnighters
Sincerely	The Moonglows
Story Untold	The Nutmegs
Honey Don't	Carl Perkins
Great Pretender, The	The Platters
Only You	The Platters
I Forgot to Remember to Forget	Elvis Presley
*Milkcow Blues Boogie	Elvis Presley
Trying to Get to You	Elvis Presley
Yes Tonight, Josephine	Johnny Ray
Ain't That Lovin' You Baby	Jimmy Reed
Singing the Blues	Marty Robbins
Smokey Joe's Cafe	The Robins
Learning the Blues	Frank Sinatra
When You Dance	The Turbans
Flip, Flop and Fly	Joe Turner
All around the World	Titus Turner
Mannish Boy	Muddy Waters
(Will You) Come Back My Love	The Wrens
Mary Lou	Young Jessie

1956

James Brown magically appears in Cincinnati.

Humes High in Memphis produces two stars, Johnny Burnette and Elvis Presley.

The Weavers bring Woody Guthrie to the mainstream ("This Land Is Your Land").

Freddy Paris writes the doo-wop classic "I'll Remember (In the Still of the Night)" in Korea.

Richard Berry writes the garage rock classic "Louie Louie" in L.A.

Wanda Jackson sings "Hot Dog (That Made Him Mad)" in Nashville.

Mack the Knife	Louis Armstrong
*Louie Louie	Richard Berry
Don't Forbid Me	Pat Boone
I Want You to Be My Baby	Lillian Briggs
*Please, Please, Please	James Brown and the Famous Flames

Rock Me	Muddy Waters
Ivory Tower	Otis Williams and the Charms
Michael (Row the Boat Ashore)	The Weavers
*This Land Is Your Land	The Weavers
It's Too Late	Chuck Willis
Church Bells May Ring	The Willows

1957

Buddy Holly meets the Crickets in Clovis, New Mexico ("That'll Be the Day").

Jackie Wilson quits the ring in Detroit ("Reet Petite").

Sam Cooke channels Nat Cole ("You Send Me").

Brenda Lee channels Edith Piaf and Kitty Wells ("Dynamite").

Danny & the Juniors take a writing tip from Dick Clark ("At the Hop").

Rick Nelson makes a TV show.

Elvis Presley makes a movie.

She Said	Hazil Adkins
Parchman Farm	Mose Allison
Young Man Blues	Mose Allison
Long Lonely Nights	Lee Andrews and the Hearts
Teardrops	Lee Andrews and the Hearts
Diana	Paul Anka
Walk, Don't Run	Chet Atkins
Jim Dandy	LaVern Baker
Jim Dandy Got Married	LaVern Baker
Black Slacks	Joe Bennett & the Sparkletones
Brown Eyed Handsome Man	Chuck Berry
No Money Down	Chuck Berry
Rock and Roll Music	Chuck Berry
School Day	Chuck Berry
Too Much Monkey Business	Chuck Berry
Wee Wee Hours	Chuck Berry
Farther up the Road	Bobby Bland
Mr. Lee	The Bobbettes
I'm Sticking with You	Tommy Bowen
Let the Four Winds Blow	Roy Brown
Lucky Lips	Ruth Brown
Come on Baby	Jo Ann Campbell
Mama (Can I Go out Tonight)	Jo Ann Campbell
He's Gone	The Chantels
If You Try	The Chantels
Plea, The	The Chantels
Deserie	The Charts
Searchin'	The Coasters
(When She Wants Good Lovin) My Baby Comes to Me	The Coasters
Young Blood	The Coasters
Drive-In Show	Eddie Cochran

Honeycomb	Jimmie Rodgers
Short Shorts	Royal Teens
Teen Age Crush	Tommy Sands
Please Say You Want Me	The Schoolboys
Baby Oh Baby	The Shells
*Get a Job	The Silhouettes
Rockin' Pneumonia & the Boogie Woogie Flu	Huey Smith
So Long I'm Gone	Warren Smith
Walking Along	The Solitaires
Banana Boat Song, The	The Tarriers
Happy, Happy Birthday Baby	The Tune Weavers
Jo-Ann	The Twintones
Dance to the Bop	Gene Vincent and His Blue Caps
Lotta Lovin'	Gene Vincent and His Blue Caps
Wear My Ring	Gene Vincent and His Blue Caps
Bony Moronie	Larry Williams
Short Fat Fannie	Larry Williams
Slow Down	Larry Williams
C.C. Rider	Chuck Willis
Reet Petite	Jackie Wilson

1958

The Quarrymen record "That'll Be the Day" in England.
Duane Eddy puts Twang into "Rebel Rouser."
Phil Spector mourns his father in "To Know Him Is to Love Him."

Seventh Son, The	Mose Allison
Dede Dinah	Frankie Avalon
I've Had It	Bell Notes
Beautiful Delilah	Chuck Berry
Carol	Chuck Berry
*Johnny B. Goode	Chuck Berry
Reelin' and Rockin'	Chuck Berry
*Sweet Little Sixteen	Chuck Berry
Chantilly Lace	The Big Bopper
Try Me	James Brown and the Famous Flames
This Little Girl's Gone Rockin'	Ruth Brown
For Your Precious Love	Jerry Butler & the Impressions
Lights Out	Jerry Byrne
Ballad of a Teenage Queen	Johnny Cash
Guess Things Happen That Way	Johnny Cash
Hey Porter	Johnny Cash
Bong Bong I Love You Madly	Vince Castro
Tequila	The Champs
I Love You So	The Chantels
*Maybe	The Chantels
Leave My Woman Alone	Ray Charles

*Wear My Ring (Around Your Neck)	Elvis Presley
Stagger Lee	Lloyd Price
Down the Aisle of Love	The Quintones
Endless Sleep	Jody Reynolds
Early in the Morning	The Rinky Dinks
We Belong Together	Robert and Johnny
My True Love	Jack Scott
Diary, The	Neil Sedaka
Witch Doctor	David Seville
*I Met Him on a Sunday	The Shirelles
Don't You Just Know It	Huey Smith
Rockin' Good Way (To Mess Around and	
Fall in Love), A	The Spaniels
Pink Shoelaces	Dodie Stevens
I'm So Young	The Students
*To Know Him Is to Love Him	The Teddy Bears
Hey, Schoolgirl	Tom and Jerry
For Your Love	Ed Townsend
It's Only Make Believe	Conway Twitty
Come on, Let's Go	Ritchie Valens
Donna	Ritchie Valens
La Bamba	Ritchie Valens
Trickle Trickle	The Videos
Gotta Travel On (Done Laid Around)	The Weavers
*House of the Rising Sun	The Weavers
She Said Yeah	Larry Williams
Betty and Dupree	Chuck Willis
Hang up My Rock and Roll Shoes	Chuck Willis
What Am I Living For	Chuck Willis
*Lonely Teardrops	Jackie Wilson
To Be Loved	Jackie Wilson
Purple People Eater	Sheb Wooley
*Rumble	Link Wray

1959

The Miracles "Got a Job" with Berry Gordy's new company in Detroit.
"Moon Dawg" by the Gamblers starts a surf craze in L.A.
The Kingston Trio inaugurates the Great Folk Scare with "Tom Dooley."
Hank Ballard writes "The Twist"; is advised to put it on the B-side.

Lonely Boy	Paul Anka
Put Your Head on My Shoulder	Paul Anka
Tall Paul	Annette
Let It Be Me	Chet Atkins
Bobby Sox to Stockings	Frankie Avalon
Venus	Frankie Avalon
Why	Frankie Avalon

Teen Beat	Sandy Nelson
Just to Be with You	The Passions
Wonder of You, The	Ray Peterson
Sea of Love	Phil Phillips
What Is Love?	The Playmates
Big Hunk o' Love, A	Elvis Presley
I Need Your Love Tonight	Elvis Presley
My Wish Came True	Elvis Presley
Running Bear	Johnny Preston
I'm Gonna Get Married	Lloyd Price
Personality	Lloyd Price
Where Were You on Our Wedding Day	Lloyd Price
Don't You Know	Della Reese
He'll Have to Go	Jim Reeves
Living Doll	Cliff Richard
El Paso	Marty Robbins
Woo-Hoo	The Rock-a-Teens
Hippy Hippy Shake	Chan Romero
Believe Me	Royal Teens
Kissin' Time	Bobby Rydell
*Sleep Walk	Santo and Johnny
Way I Walk, The	Jack Scott
What in the World's Come over You	Jack Scott
*Oh Carol	Neil Sedaka
It Was I	Skip and Flip
Since I Don't Have You	The Skyliners
This I Swear	The Skyliners
You Cheated	The Slades
See You in September	The Tempos
Tell Him No	Travis and Bob
Lavendar Blue (Dilly Dilly)	Sammy Turner
Broken Hearted Melody	Sarah Vaughan
*Tall Cool One	The Wailers
What a Diff'rence a Day Made	Dinah Washington
Tragedy	Thomas Wayne
I'll Be Satisfied	Jackie Wilson
That's Why	Jackie Wilson
You Better Know It	Jackie Wilson
*Rawhide	Link Wray

1960

Phil Spector joins Leiber & Stoller at the Brill Building in NYC.

The Shirelles pick up where the Chantels left off with "Will You Love Me Tomorrow."

The great unknown guitar band the Shadows have a big year in England ("Apache").

Birds and the Bees, The	Jewel Akens
Puppy Love	Paul Anka

1961

Dick Dale ("Lets Go Trippin'") and the Beach Boys ("Surfin'") take up the surf sound.
Chubby Checker ("Let's Twist Again") and Joey Dee ("Peppermint Twist") are still twisting.
Peter, Paul & Mary join the Kingston Trio on the folk circuit with "Lemon Tree."
Howling Wolf's "Little Red Rooster" is heard in England.

Calendar Girl	Neil Sedaka
Hats off to Larry	Del Shannon
Little Town Flirt	Del Shannon
Runaway	Del Shannon
Walkin' Back to Happiness	Helen Shapiro
You Don't Know	Helen Shapiro
Daddy's Home	Shep and the Limelites
Baby It's You	The Shirelles
Mama Said	The Shirelles
Soldier Boy	The Shirelles
This Time	Troy Shondell
It Will Stand	The Showmen
Wheels	The Stringalongs
Gee Whiz! (Look at His Eyes)	Carla Thomas
Sad Movies Always Make Me Cry	Sue Thompson
Motorcycle	Tico & the Triumphs
It's Gonna Work out Fine	Ike and Tina Turner
Walk on By	Leroy Van Dyke
Run to Him	Bobby Vee
Roses Are Red (My Love)	Bobby Vinton
Funny (How Time Slips Away)	Billy Walker
Bye Bye Baby	Mary Wells
My Empty Arms	Jackie Wilson

1962

Joan Baez befriends Bob Dylan.

The Crystals crystallize Phil Spector's Wall of Sound ("He's a Rebel").

Janis Joplin gets drunk with some friends in Texas.

Shot of Rhythm and Blues, A	Arthur Alexander
Soldier of Love	Arthur Alexander
You Better Move On	Arthur Alexander
*Babe I'm Gonna Leave You	Joan Baez
409	The Beach Boys
Surfin' Safari	The Beach Boys
You Don't Miss Your Water	William Bell
Bobby's Girl	Marcie Blane
Green Onions	Booker T. & the MG's
Make It Easy on Yourself	Jerry Butler
Palisades Park	Freddy Cannon
Limbo Rock	The Champs
Hey! Baby	Bruce Channel
You Don't Know Me	Ray Charles
Slow Twistin'	Chubby Checker and Dee Dee Sharpe
Party Lights	Claudine Clark
She's Got You	Patsy Cline
Do You Love Me?	The Contours

Let Me In	The Sensations
Wonderful Land	The Shadows
Mashed Potato Time	Dee Dee Sharp
Ride	Dee Dee Sharp
Putty in Your Hands	The Shirelles
Boa Constrictor	Shel Silverstein
Zip-a-Dee-Doo-Dah	Bob B. Soxx & the Blue Jeans
Lipstick Traces (On a Cigarette)	Bennie Spellman
Ahab the Arab	Ray Stevens
Your Heart Belongs to Me	The Supremes
It's Raining	Irma Thomas
Norman	Sue Thompson
It Keeps Right on a-Hurtin'	Johnny Tillotson
Telstar	The Tornadoes
Fool in Love, A	Ike and Tina Turner
Lookin' for a Love	The Valentinos
You Shook Me	Muddy Waters
One Who Really Loves You, The	Mary Wells
Two Lovers	Mary Wells
You Beat Me to the Punch	Mary Wells
Fingertips	Stevie Wonder
What's a Matter Baby (Is It Hurting You)	Timi Yuro

1963

The Beatles explode with "Love Me Do," "She Loves You," and "(P.S.) I Love You."

Bob Dylan explodes with "Blowing in the Wind," "Masters of War," and "A Hard Rain's Gonna Fall."

The Angels, the Cookies, the Ronettes, Martha & the Vandellas, Darlene Love, the Exciters, and the Chiffons make this year girl-group heaven.

Janis Joplin gets turned on to Garnett Mimms.

Bob Marley and the Wailers get started in Jamaica "Judge Not," "Exodus").

Anna (Go to Him)	Arthur Alexander
*My Boyfriend's Back	The Angels
Go Now	Bessie Banks
Detroit City	Bobby Bare
Be True to Your School	The Beach Boys
Farmer's Daughter	The Beach Boys
In My Room	The Beach Boys
Shut Down	The Beach Boys
Surfer Girl	The Beach Boys
Surfin' USA	The Beach Boys
Do You Want to Know a Secret?	The Beatles
From Me to You	The Beatles
I Saw Her Standing There	The Beatles
*I Want to Hold Your Hand	The Beatles
I'll Get You	The Beatles
*Love Me Do	The Beatles

Don't Make Me Over	Dionne Warwick
(They Long to Be) Close to You	Dionne Warwick
Wishin' and Hopin'	Dionne Warwick
Gangster of Love	Johnny Guitar Watson
Guantanamera	The Weavers
Baby Workout	Jackie Wilson

1964

The Beatles make a movie.

Paul Simon moves to England to become a busker.

The Rolling Stones, the Kinks, and the Yardbirds arrive on the coattails of the Dave Clark Five.

Pete Seeger makes the Top 100 with a Malvina Reynolds' song ("Little Boxes").

The Supremes become Motown's greatest girl-group.

The Shangri-Las are the first punk girl-group.

I'm Not Talking	Mose Allison
*Birmingham Sunday	Joan Baez
All Summer Long	The Beach Boys
California Girls	The Beach Boys
Dance, Dance, Dance	The Beach Boys
Don't Worry Baby	The Beach Boys
Fun Fun Fun	The Beach Boys
I Get Around	The Beach Boys
Warmth of the Sun, The	The Beach Boys
Wendy	The Beach Boys
When I Grow up to Be a Man	The Beach Boys
All My Loving	The Beatles
And I Love Her	The Beatles
Any Time at All	The Beatles
Can't Buy Me Love	The Beatles
Don't Bother Me	The Beatles
*Hard Day's Night, A	The Beatles
I Feel Fine	The Beatles
I Should Have Known Better	The Beatles
I'll Cry Instead	The Beatles
I'm Happy Just to Dance with You	The Beatles
If I Fell	The Beatles
It Won't Be Long	The Beatles
She's a Woman	The Beatles
Tell Me Why	The Beatles
Things We Said Today	The Beatles
This Boy (Ringo's Theme)	The Beatles
You Can't Do That	The Beatles
Laugh, Laugh	The Beau Brummels
C'est la Vie (You Never Can Tell)	Chuck Berry
Little Marie	Chuck Berry
Liverpool Drive	Chuck Berry

Rag Doll	The Four Seasons
Save It for Me	The Four Seasons
Silence Is Golden	The Four Seasons
Baby I Need Your Loving	The Four Tops
C'mon and Swim	Bobby Freeman
We'll Sing in the Sunshine	Gale Garnett
Hitch Hike	Marvin Gaye
How Sweet It Is (To Be Loved by You)	Marvin Gaye
You're a Wonderful One	Marvin Gaye
Don't Let the Sun Catch You Crying	Gerry & the Pacemakers
Ferry Cross the Mersey	Gerry & the Pacemakers
Look of Love, The	Lesley Gore
Maybe I Know	Lesley Gore
In Crowd, The	Dobie Gray
High Flying Bird	Judy Henske
You Were Wrong	Z.Z. Hill
Little Honda	The Hondells
Steal Away	Jimmy Hughes
Four Strong Winds	Ian and Sylvia
Someday Soon	Ian and Sylvia
You Were on My Mind	Ian and Sylvia
Amen	The Impressions
I'm So Proud	The Impressions
Keep on Pushing	The Impressions
Who's That Lady	The Isley Brothers
Dead Man's Curve	Jan & Dean
Little Old Lady (From Pasadena), The	Jan & Dean
New Girl in School, The	Jan & Dean
Ride the Wild Surf	Jan & Dean
Come a Little Bit Closer	Jay & the Americans
I Wanna Love Him So Bad	The Jelly Beans
Kentucky Bluebird	Lou Johnson
(There's) Always Something There to Remind Me	Lou Johnson
Tainted Love	Gloria Jones
Rock Me Baby	B.B. King
*All Day and All of the Night	The Kinks
Stop Your Sobbing	The Kinks
You Really Got Me	The Kinks
Little Children	Billy J. Kramer and the Dakotas
Jerk, The	The Larks
This Diamond Ring	Gary Lewis and the Playboys
Goin' out of My Head	Little Anthony and the Imperials
Devil with a Blue Dress On	Shorty Long
Here Comes the Night	Lulu
Dancing in the Street	Martha & the Vandellas
Ringo I Love You	Bonnie Jo Mason

Baby Don't Go	Sonny and Cher
I Only Want to Be with You	Dusty Springfield
Baby Love	The Supremes
Come See About Me	The Supremes
*Where Did Our Love Go	The Supremes
Way You Do the Things You Do, The	The Temptations
Hold What You've Got	Joe Tex
Time Is on My Side	Irma Thomas
Wish Someone Would Care	Irma Thomas
Hi-Heel Sneakers	Tommy Tucker
It's All over Now	The Valentinos
My Girl Sloopy	The Vibrations
Simmer Down	The Wailers
My Guy	Mary Wells
*I Wish You Would	The Yardbirds
Four in the Morning	Jessie Colin Young
She's Not There	The Zombies
Tell Her No	The Zombies

1965

B.B. King plays the Regal in Harlem.

The Animals, the Lovin' Spoonful, Simon and Garfunkel, Sonny and Cher, and the Byrds create folk/rock.

James Brown, Otis Redding, the Temptations, and the Four Tops create soul.

The Paul Butterfield Blues Band and the Yardbirds create blues/rock.

The Sonics and the Leaves create garage rock.

The Great Society create psychedelic rock, two years before its time.

Don't Let Me Be Misunderstood	The Animals
*It's My Life	The Animals
*We Gotta Get outa This Place	The Animals
Farewell Angelina	Joan Baez
Are You a Boy or Are You a Girl?	The Barbarians
One, Two, Three (1-2-3)	Len Barry
Rescue Me	Fontella Bass
Help Me, Rhonda	The Beach Boys
Please Let Me Wonder	The Beach Boys
And Your Bird Can Sing	The Beatles
Another Girl	The Beatles
Baby's in Black	The Beatles
Day Tripper	The Beatles
Drive My Car	The Beatles
Eight Days a Week	The Beatles
Every Little Thing	The Beatles
Girl	The Beatles
*Help!	The Beatles
I Don't Want to Spoil the Party	The Beatles
I Need You	The Beatles

Dawn of Correction	The Spokesmen
Dirty Water	The Standells
Different Drum	The Stone Poneys
I Want Candy	The Strangeloves
Back in My Arms Again	The Supremes
I Hear a Symphony	The Supremes
Nothing but Heartaches	The Supremes
Stop! In the Name of Love	The Supremes
No Matter What Shape (Your Stomach's In)	The T-Bones
My Girl	The Temptations
*Gloria	Them
Mystic Eyes	Them
Lover's Concerto, A	The Toys
Let Me Be	The Turtles
Sun Ain't Gonna Shine Anymore, The	Frankie Valli
He Was Really Saying Something	The Velvelettes
Five O'Clock World	The Vogues
(I'm a) Road Runner	Jr. Walker & the All-Stars
Shotgun	Jr. Walker & the All-Stars
*Get Together	The We Five
Take Me in Your Arms (Rock Me a Little While)	Kim Weston
You Turn Me On (The Turn on Song)	Ian Whitcomb
I Can't Explain	The Who
*My Generation	The Who
You're Gonna Make Me Cry	O.V. Wright
Evil Hearted You	The Yardbirds
*For Your Love	The Yardbirds
*Heart Full of Soul	The Yardbirds
I Ain't Done Wrong	The Yardbirds
Still I'm Sad	The Yardbirds
You're a Better Man Than I	The Yardbirds

1966

In response to the Beatles, Brian Wilson writes Pet Sounds ("Good Vibrations").

In response to New York City, Bob Dylan goes to Nashville to record Blonde on Blonde ("Visions of Johanna").

In response to the hippie invasion of Los Angeles, Frank Zappa and the Mothers of Invention freak out ("Help, I'm a Rock").

In response to the war in Vietnam, Phil Ochs protests against the protesters ("Love Me, I'm a Liberal").

Don't Bring Me Down	The Animals
*Mama Told Me Not to Come	The Animals
*Along Comes Mary	The Association
Cherish	The Association
*Moulty	The Barbarians
Caroline No	The Beach Boys
Don't Talk (Put Your Head on My Shoulder)	The Beach Boys
God Only Knows	The Beach Boys
*Good Vibrations	The Beach Boys

1967

In San Francisco, Jefferson Airplane and the Grateful Dead put LSD on the map.

Further south, Jimi Hendrix and Janis Joplin light fires at Monterey.

In New York, the Velvet Underground up the ante to heroin.

Further downtown, Hair! The tribal rock opera premieres; it would spawn four Top 10 singles in 1969.

The Beatles release no singles from Sgt. Pepper's Lonely Hearts Club Band.

Eric Clapton leads a new English blues/rock invasion.

Aretha Franklin has her coronation in Memphis.

1968

Dylan and the Band go back to their country roots in Woodstock.
Elvis Presley goes back to his country roots in Memphis.
Jerry Lee Lewis goes back to his barroom roots.
The Stones go back to their working class roots.

David Bowie goes back to his roots on Mars.

The Brill Building goes back to its roots with bubblegum music.

Carole King, Joni Mitchell, Randy Newman, and Laura Nyro create the singer/songwriter niche.

The Beatles split with the Mahareeshi.

The Delfonics bring soul to Philadelphia.

| Goodnight Sweet Josephine | The Yardbirds |
| White Summer | The Yardbirds |

1969

The Beatles approach "The End."

Chicago approach their "Beginnings."

Led Zeppelin turn blues/rock into heavy metal.

King Crimson creates progressive rock.

Sly Stone creates funk.

James Taylor, Neil Young, and Van Morrison go solo.

The Jackson 5 reinvent Frankie Lymon & the Teenagers.

The festivals at Woodstock and Altamont effectively end the Alternate Culture.

Sugar Sugar	The Archies
Come and Get It	Badfinger
Jemima Surrender	The Band
Ballad of John and Yoko, The	The Beatles
Because	The Beatles
Carry That Weight	The Beatles
*Come Together	The Beatles
Don't Let Me Down	The Beatles
End, The	The Beatles
Get Back	The Beatles
Golden Slumbers	The Beatles
Here Comes the Sun	The Beatles
Hey Bulldog	The Beatles
I Want You (She's So Heavy)	The Beatles
It's All Too Much	The Beatles
Maxwell's Silver Hammer	The Beatles
Mean Mr. Mustard	The Beatles
Octopus's Garden	The Beatles
Oh! Darling	The Beatles
Polythene Pam	The Beatles
She Came in through the Bathroom Window	The Beatles
*Something	The Beatles
You Never Give Me Your Money	The Beatles
Can't Find My Way Home	Blind Faith
Presence of the Lord	Blind Faith
Spinning Wheel	Blood, Sweat & Tears
Time Is Tight	Booker T. & the MG's
Soul Deep	The Box Tops
Give It up or Turnit a Loose	James Brown
Mother Popcorn (You Got to Have a Mother for Me) (Part 1)	James Brown
Popcorn, The	James Brown
Buzzin' Fly	Tim Buckley
Strange Feeling	Tim Buckley

I Can't Get Next to You	The Temptations
Psychedelic Shack	The Temptations
*Runaway Child, Running Wild	The Temptations
Celebrate	Three Dog Night
Something in the Air	Thunderclap Newman
Shanghai Noodle Factory	Traffic
Foggy Notion	The Velvet Underground
Pale Blue Eyes	The Velvet Underground
Hawaii 5-Oh	The Ventures
What Does It Take (To Win Your Love)?	Jr. Walker & the All-Stars
Acid Queen	The Who
Amazing Journey	The Who
I'm Free	The Who
*Pinball Wizard	The Who
*See Me, Feel Me	The Who
*We're Not Gonna Take It	The Who
My Cherie Amour	Stevie Wonder
Yester-me Yester-you Yesterday	Stevie Wonder
Cowgirl in the Sand	Neil Young
*Down by the River	Neil Young
I've Loved Her So Long	Neil Young
Last Trip to Tulsa	Neil Young
*Loner, The	Neil Young
*Sugar Mountain	Neil Young
In the Year 2525 (Exordium and Terminus)	Zager and Evans
*Peaches en Regalia	Frank Zappa
Willie the Pimp, Parts One & Two	Frank Zappa

1970

Funkadelic create heavy metal funk.

The Allman Brothers create Southern rock.

Miles Davis creates fusion.

The Stooges create punk.

Jonathan Richman creates lo-fi.

Neil Young creates the guitar solo that inspired grunge.

David Bowie puts on makeup.

Jane Birkin and Serge Gainsbourg have sex at a discotheque in Paris.

In Memory of Elizabeth Reed	The Allman Brothers
Midnight Rider	The Allman Brothers
*Whipping Post	The Allman Brothers
Without You	Badfinger
Shape I'm In, The	The Band
Stage Fright	The Band
Add Some Music to Your Day	The Beach Boys
For You Blue	The Beatles
*Let It Be	The Beatles

1971

Big year for soft rock with Bread, the Carpenters, Elton John, and Carole King.

Al Green and the Chi-Lites put Philly Soul on the map.

John Lennon, Paul McCartney, and George Harrison recover from the Beatles.

*Betcha by Golly Wow	The Stylistics
You Are Everything	The Stylistics
Get It On (Bang a Gong)	T. Rex
Hot Love	T. Rex
Ride a White Swan	T. Rex
Just My Imagination (Running Away with Me)	The Temptations
Superstar Remember How You Got	
Where You Are	The Temptations
I'd Love to Change the World	Ten Years After
Joy to the World	Three Dog Night
Never Been to Spain	Three Dog Night
Old Fashioned Love Song, An	Three Dog Night
Low Spark of High Heeled Boys, The	Traffic
Smiling Faces Sometimes	Undisputed Truth
Careful There's a Baby in the House	Loudon Wainwright
Motel Blues	Loudon Wainwright
Midnight Plane to Houston	Jim Weatherly
Playing in the Band	Bob Weir
Baba O'Riley	The Who
Bargain	The Who
Behind Blue Eyes	The Who
Goin' Mobile	The Who
I'm a Boy	The Who
Seeker, The	The Who
Song Is Over, The	The Who
*Won't Get Fooled Again	The Who
Yankee Lady	Jesse Winchester
Ain't No Sunshine	Bill Withers
Clean up Woman	Betty Wright
Clap, The	Yes
Yours Is No Disgrace	Yes
Dance of the Rock & Roll Interviewers	Frank Zappa

1972

The heyday of the laid-back, mellow singer/songwriter.

Bob Marley, Jimmy Cliff, Toots & the Maytals, and the Slickers ride a reggae wave on the heels of the movie, The Harder They Come.

Grease debuts off-off Broadway

The Eagles perfect country/rock with "Take It Easy."

Ain't Wastin' Time No More	The Allman Brothers
Blue Sky	The Allman Brothers
Little Martha	The Allman Brothers
Melissa	The Allman Brothers
Horse with No Name, A	America
Ventura Highway	America
Hold Your Head Up	Argent

54-46 (Was My Number)	Toots & the Maytals
Pure and Easy	Pete Townshend
Easy Livin'	Uriah Heap
If I Needed You	Townes Van Zandt
*Pancho and Lefty	Townes Van Zandt
To Live Is to Fly	Townes Van Zandt
Dead Skunk	Loudon Wainwright
Red Guitar	Loudon Wainwright
Cisco Kid	War
World Is a Ghetto, The	War
Cassidy	Bob Weir
Dueling Banjos	Eric Weissburg and Eric Mandel
Join Together	The Who
Love, Reign o'er Me	The Who
Frankenstein	Edgar Winter Group
Free Ride	Edgar Winter Group
Lean on Me	Bill Withers
Use Me	Bill Withers
Woman's Gotta Have It	Bobby Womack
Superstition	Stevie Wonder
Superwoman (Where Were You When I Needed You)	Stevie Wonder
*You Are the Sunshine of My Life	Stevie Wonder
And You and I	Yes
Close to the Edge	Yes
Heart of the Sunrise	Yes
Long Distance Runaround	Yes
*Roundabout	Yes
Heart of Gold	Neil Young
*Needle and the Damage Done, The	Neil Young
Old Man	Neil Young

1973

Pink Floyd releases Dark Side of the Moon.

Arena anthems from Aerosmith, Slade, Queen, Led Zeppelin, the Allman Brothers and Lynyrd Skynyrd as well as Pink Floyd, unite the rock guitar troops.

Lemmings *debuts off-off Broadway.*

The New York Dolls make "Trash" hip.

On the coasts, two poets emerge: Tom Waits in L.A., Bruce Springsteen in NJ.

*Dream On	Aerosmith
Mama Kin	Aerosmith
*Walk This Way	Aerosmith
Jessica	The Allman Brothers
*Ramblin' Man	The Allman Brothers
God Gave Rock and Roll to You	Argent
Takin' Care of Business	Bachman Turner Overdrive
Sail on Sailor	The Beach Boys

So Very Hard to Go	Tower of Power
Nutbush City Limits	Ike and Tina Turner
Swimming Song, The	Loudon Wainwright
*Ol' 55	Tom Waits
Vaudeville Man	Wendy Waldman
L.A. Freeway	Jerry Jeff Walker
Rocky Mountain Way	Joe Walsh
Gypsy Man	War
I'm Gonna Love You Just a Little More Babe	Barry White
Never, Never Gonna Give Ya Up	Barry White
5:15	The Who
Real Me, The	The Who
Show and Tell	Al Wilson
Don't You Worry 'bout a Thing	Stevie Wonder
*Higher Ground	Stevie Wonder
*Livin' for the City	Stevie Wonder
La Grange	ZZ Top

1974

Patti Smith and the Talking Heads create a punk rock scene on NY's Lower East Side.
The disco beat hits #1 with "Rock the Boat."
The Rocky Horror Picture Show *starts its cult classic after midnight run.*

Waterloo	Abba
Seasons of Wither	Aerosmith
Lonely People	America
Tin Man	America
Pick up the Pieces	The Average White Band
Do It ('Til You're Satisfied)	B.T. Express
Express	B.T. Express
You Ain't Seen Nothin' Yet	Bachman Turner Overdrive
Can't Get Enough	Bad Company
Terrapin	Syd Barrett
Back of a Car	Big Star
September Gurls	Big Star
Sideshow	Blue Magic
Rebel Rebel	David Bowie
(What's So Funny 'bout) Peace, Love and Understanding	Brinzley Schwarz
Hang on in There Baby	Johnny Bristol
My Thang	James Brown
Papa Don't Take No Mess	James Brown
Woman to Woman	Shirley Brown
*Before the Deluge	Jackson Browne
For a Dancer	Jackson Browne
Fountain of Sorrow	Jackson Browne
Come Monday	Jimmy Buffett

| Don't Eat the Yellow Snow | Frank Zappa |
| Penguin in Bondage | Frank Zappa |

1975

Bob Dylan makes a comeback with Blood on the Tracks.
Joan Baez tells their story in "Diamonds and Rust."
Bruce Springsteen breaks through with "Born to Run."
Simon reunites with Garfunkel on "My Little Town."
Earth, Wind & Fire make a movie.
K.C. and the Sunshine Band hit #1 on the R&B charts ... twice!

How Long	Ace
Sweet Emotion	Aerosmith
Nice, Nice, Very Nice	Ambrosia
Sister Golden Hair	America
Feel Like Making Love	Bad Company
*Diamonds and Rust	Joan Baez
Ophelia	The Band
Saturday Night	Bay City Rollers
Jive Talkin'	Bee Gees
Nights on Broadway	Bee Gees
Fame	David Bowie
Young Americans	David Bowie
Pirate Looks at Forty	Jimmy Buffett
*Love Will Keep Us Together	The Captain and Tennille
*I Write the Songs	The Captain and Tennille
All By Myself	Eric Carmen
I'm Easy	Keith Carradine
Old Days	Chicago
This Will Be (An Everlasting Love)	Natalie Cole
Moon Is a Harsh Mistress, The	Judy Collins
Slippery When Wet	Commodores
Sweet Love	Commodores
Only Women (Bleed)	Alice Cooper
Welcome to My Nightmare	Alice Cooper
I'm Sorry	John Denver
Bette Davis Eyes	Jackie DeShannon
I Live for Cars and Girls	The Dictators
Two Tub Man	The Dictators
*Idiot Wind	Bob Dylan
*Million Dollar Bash	Bob Dylan
*Shelter from the Storm	Bob Dylan
Simple Twist of Fate	Bob Dylan
*Tangled up in Blue	Bob Dylan
You Angel You	Bob Dylan
Lyin' Eyes	Eagles
One of These Nights	Eagles

Johannesburg	Gil Scott-Heron
Winter in America	Gil Scott-Heron
Bad Blood	Neil Sedaka
Beautiful Loser	Bob Seger
Fly, Robin, Fly	Silver Convention
Get Down Get Down (Get on the Floor)	Joe Simon
*Fifty Ways to Leave Your Lover	Paul Simon
Gone at Last	Paul Simon
*Still Crazy after All These Years	Paul Simon
*My Little Town	Paul Simon (with Art Garfunkel)
*Backstreets	Bruce Springsteen
*Born to Run	Bruce Springsteen
*Jungleland	Bruce Springsteen
Tenth Avenue Freeze Out	Bruce Springsteen
Thunder Road	Bruce Springsteen
Let's Do It Again	The Staple Singers
Moonlight Feels Right	Starbuck
Any World (That I'm Welcome To)	Steely Dan
*Bad Sneakers	Steely Dan
Black Friday	Steely Dan
Dr. Wu	Steely Dan
Quits	Gary Stewart
Ballroom Blitz	Sweet
Fox on the Run	Sweet
It Only Takes a Minute	Tavares
*I'm Not in Love	10 c.c.
(Hey Won't You Play) Another Somebody Done Somebody Wrong Song	B.J. Thomas
Beat the Retreat	Richard and Linda Thompson
Dimming of the Day, The	Richard and Linda Thompson
*Funky Kingston	Toots & the Maytals
Southern Nights	Allen Toussaint
White Punks on Dope	The Tubes
Low Rider	War
Why Can't We Be Friends	War
Slip Kid	The Who
Squeeze Box	The Who
Eighteen with a Bullet	Pete Wingfield
Cortez the Killer	Neil Young
Tush	ZZ Top

1976

Disco explodes with Donna Summer, K.C. and the Sunshine Band, Johnny Taylor, and Andrea True.

Punk explodes with the Ramones, Blondie, Pere Ubu, the Damned, and Richard Hell.

Funk explodes with Parliament and Prince.

Arena rock's last stand with AC/DC, Boston, Cheap Trick, Kiss, and Led Zeppelin.

*Love to Love You Baby	Donna Summer
Arms of Mary	The Sutherland Brothers and Quiver
*Boogie Fever	The Sylvers
Shower the People	James Taylor
*Disco Lady	Johnnie Taylor
Boys Are Back in Town, The	Thin Lizzy
Jailbreak	Thin Lizzy
Let Her In	John Travolta
*More, More, More (Part 1)	Andrea True Connection
Don't Touch Me There	The Tubes
Texas Chainsaw Massacre Boogie	The Tyla Gang
Step Right Up	Tom Waits
Tom Traubert's Blues	Tom Waits
Summer	War
Play That Funky Music	Wild Cherry
I Wish	Stevie Wonder
Isn't She Lovely	Stevie Wonder
Pastime Paradise	Stevie Wonder
*Sir Duke	Stevie Wonder
Dream Weaver	Gary Wright
Love Is Alive	Gary Wright
*Carmelita	Warren Zevon
Poor Poor Pitiful Me	Warren Zevon

1977

England takes up the punk rock chalice with the Sex Pistols, the Buzzcocks, Elvis Costello, and the Clash.

Tom Petty takes up the folk/rock chalice with "American Girl."

Weather Report takes up the fusion chalice with "Teen Town."

The Bee Gees suffer from Saturday Night Fever.

Dancing Queen	Abba
Take a Chance on Me	Abba
Whole Lotta Rosie	AC/DC
How Deep Is Your Love	Bee Gees
*Night Fever	Bee Gees
*Stayin' Alive	Bee Gees
Tryin' to Love Two	William Bell
Greatest Love of All, The	George Benson
Pencil Neck Geek	Freddie Blassie
In the Sun	Blondie
Godzilla	Blue Oyster Cult
I Can't Hold On	Karla Bonoff
If He's Ever Near	Karla Bonoff
Heroes	David Bowie
Dazz	Brick
I Love the Nightlife (Disco Round)	Alicia Bridges
Dance with Me	Peter Brown and Betty Wright

Pinhead	The Ramones
*Rockaway Beach	The Ramones
*Sheena Is a Punk Rocker	The Ramones
Jack and Jill	Raydio
Fool (If You Think It's Over)	Chris Rea
O.K.	Rock Follies
Gambler, The	Kenny Rogers
How Do I Make You	Linda Ronstadt
Car Wash	Rose Royce
Wishing on a Star	Rose Royce
Closer to the Heart	Rush
Emotion	Samantha Sang
When I Need You	Leo Sayer
We Almost Lost Detroit	Gil Scott-Heron
Hollywood Nights	Bob Seger
Old Time Rock and Roll	Bob Seger
Still the Same	Bob Seger
We've Got Tonight	Bob Seger
*Anarchy in the U.K.	The Sex Pistols
*God Save the Queen	The Sex Pistols
Holidays in the Sun	The Sex Pistols
Pretty Vacant	The Sex Pistols
Nobody Does It Better	Carly Simon
Slip Slidin' Away	Paul Simon
Don't Give up on Us	David Soul
*Deacon Blues	Steely Dan
Peg	Steely Dan
Year of the Cat	Al Stewart
Hot Legs	Rod Stewart
Killing of Georgie (Part 1 & 2)	Rod Stewart
You're in My Heart (The Final Acclaim)	Rod Stewart
Come Sail Away	Styx
Cheree	Suicide
*I Feel Love	Donna Summer
Love Is Like Oxygen	The Sweet
Hot Line	The Sylvers
*Psycho Killer	Talking Heads
Your Smiling Face	James Taylor
*Marquee Moon	Television
Things We Do for Love, The	10 c.c.
My Baby Gives It Away	Pete Townshend
Street in the City	Pete Townshend
*Disco Inferno	Trammps
It's a Heartache	Bonnie Tyler
Lights Out	UFO
*San Francisco (You've Got Me)	The Village People

Blues Had a Baby and They Named It Rock and Roll,

    The   Muddy Waters

Birdland   Weather Report

*Teen Town   Weather Report

It's Ecstacy When You Lay down Next to Me   Barry White

Fragile   Wire

I Am the Fly   Wire

*106 Beats That   Wire

*Reuters   Wire

Strange   Wire

*Oh Bondage up Yours   X-Ray Specs

Like a Hurricane   Neil Young

1978

Eddie Van Halen reinvents rock guitar with "Eruption."

Black Flag brings punk to L.A. with "Wasted."

Pere Ubu starts a punk scene in Akron with "30 Seconds over Tokyo."

How Much I Feel   Ambrosia

Imaginary Lover   Atlanta Rhythm Section

Too Much Heaven   Bee Gees

Tragedy   Bee Gees

Holocaust   Big Star

*Wasted   Black Flag

Heart of Glass   Blondie

One Way or Another   Blondie

Bootzilla   Bootsy's Rubber Band

Don't Look Back   Boston

Cheeseburger in Paradise   Jimmy Buffett

Man with the Child in His Eyes, The   Kate Bush

Them Heavy People   Kate Bush

*Wuthering Heights   Kate Bush

Breakdown   The Buzzcocks

*Ever Fallen in Love (With Someone

    You Shouldn't Have Fallen in Love With)   The Buzzcocks

What You Won't Do for Love   Bobby Caldwell

Good Times Roll   The Cars

Just What I Needed   The Cars

*My Best Friend's Girl   The Cars

You're All I've Got Tonight   The Cars

Hey Deannie   Shaun Cassidy

*Le Freak   Chic

Promises   Eric Clapton

Tulsa Time   Eric Clapton

Julie's in the Drug Squad   The Clash

Safe European Home   The Clash

*Stay Free   The Clash

He's the Greatest Dancer	Sister Sledge
We Are Family	Sister Sledge
*Because the Night	Patti Smith Group
*Badlands	Bruce Springsteen
Darkness on the Edge of Town	Bruce Springsteen
Prove It All Night	Bruce Springsteen
Time Passages	Al Stewart
Heaven Knows	Donna Summer
Last Dance, The	Donna Summer
Dance (Disco Heat)	Sylvester
Boogie Oogie Oogie	A Taste of Honey
Hold the Line	Toto
*Teenage Kicks	The Undertones
Grease	Frankie Valli
Ain't Talkin' 'bout Love	Van Halen
*Eruption	Van Halen
Jamie's Cryin'	Van Halen
*Runnin' with the Devil	Van Halen
I Just Wanna Stop	Gino Vannelli
Macho Man	The Village People
Watch Me Rock, I'm over Thirty	Loudon Wainwright
Romeo Is Bleeding	Tom Waits
Wrong Side of the Road	Tom Waits
Life's Been Good	Joe Walsh
Guitar and Pen	The Who
Who Are You	The Who
Whole Wide World	Wreckless Eric
Comes a Time	Neil Young
Lotta Love	Neil Young
Excitable Boy	Warren Zevon
Lawyers, Guns and Money	Warren Zevon
*Werewolves of London	Warren Zevon

1979

Dylan gets born again.

Bauhaus ("Bela Lugosi's Dead") and the Cure ("Killing an Arab") create gothic rock.

The B-52's start a scene in Athens, GA with "Rock Lobster."

The first rap song is either "Rapper's Delight" by the Sugarhill Gang or "King Tim III (Personality Jock)" by Fatback.

Highway to Hell	AC/DC
Dance This Mess Around	The B-52's
*Rock Lobster	The B-52's
Rock 'n' Roll Fantasy	Bad Company
*Bela Legosi's Dead	Bauhaus
Love You inside Out	Bee Gees
Dreaming	Blondie
Sunday Girl	Blondie

Bad Girls	Donna Summer
Dim All the Lights	Donna Summer
Hot Stuff	Donna Summer
On the Radio	Donna Summer
No More Tears (Enough Is Enough)	Donna Summer and Barbra Streisand
Logical Song, The	Supertramp
Take the Long Way Home	Supertramp
Stranger in the House	Rachel Sweet
Who Does Lisa Like	Rachel Sweet
*Life During Wartime	Talking Heads
Memories Can't Wait	Talking Heads
Orphans	Teenage Jesus & the Jerks
I Could Rule the World If I Could Only Get the Parts	Tin Huey
*Get over You	The Undertones
*Jimmy, Jimmy	The Undertones
Dance the Night Away	Van Halen
Just When I Needed You Most	Randy Van Warmer
In the Navy	The Village People
*Y.M.C.A.	The Village People
Ring My Bell	Anita Ward
Giving It up for Your Love	Jerry Williams
Send One Your Love	Stevie Wonder
This Is Pop	XTC
Powderfinger	Neil Young
Rust Never Sleeps (Hey Hey My My into the Black)	Neil Young
Dancin' Fool	Frank Zappa
*Joe's Garage	Frank Zappa

1980

A new arena era starts in Ireland with U2.

A new heavy metal era starts in England with Judas Priest.

Punk rock spawns roots rock in Los Angeles with the Blasters and X ("Los Angeles").

Grandmaster Flash channels the Last Poets.

*Back in Black	AC/DC
Hell's Bells	AC/DC
You Shook Me All Night Long	AC/DC
Biggest Part of Me	Ambrosia
*Right Side of My Brain	Angry Samoans
Party out of Bounds	The B-52's
*Private Idaho	The B-52's
Pay to Cum	Bad Brains
Hit Me with Your Best Shot	Pat Benatar
Give Me the Night	George Benson
Thorn in My Pride	The Black Crowes
*American Music	The Blasters
Marie Marie	The Blasters

And the Cradle Will Rock	Van Halen
Dream Baby Dream	Alan Vega and Martin Rev
*Jersey Girl	Tom Waits
On the Nickel	Tom Waits
Lately	Stevie Wonder
Master Blaster (Jammin')	Stevie Wonder
*Los Angeles	X
We're Desperate	X
White Girl	X
Living through Another Cuba	XTC

1981

The MTV era begins, with Rick Springfield ("Jessie's Girl"), Duran Duran
("Girls on Film"), and Talking Heads ("Once in a Lifetime") creating breakthrough videos.
In Athens, GA, R.E.M. prefer to cling to the radio era ("Radio Free Europe").
In Chicago, Tee Scott helps keep the DJ art alive ("Tee's Happy").

Dirty Deeds Done Dirt Cheap	AC/DC
*For Those about to Rock (We Salute You)	AC/DC
Happy Birthday	Altered Images
Hearts	Marty Balin
Let It Blurt	Lester Bangs
Kick in the Eye	Bauhaus
At This Moment	Billy & the Beaters
Rise Above	Black Flag
TV Party	Black Flag
Border Radio	The Blasters
Rapture	Blondie
Burnin' for You	Blue Oyster Cult
Joan Crawford	Blue Oyster Cult
This Little Girl	Gary U.S. Bonds
Too Many Creeps	Bush Tetras
She's a Bad Mama Jama	Carl Carlton
Seven Year Ache	Rosanne Cash
I Can't Stand It	Eric Clapton
I Love You	Climax Blues Band
In the Air Tonight	Phil Collins
Oh No	The Commodores
Johnny Are You Queer	Josie Cotton
*Goo Goo Muck	The Cramps
Arthur's Theme (Best That You Can Do)	Christopher Cross
Living a Lie	The dBs
*Bringin' on the Heartbreak	Def Leppard
Just Can't Get Enough	Depeche Mode
New Life	Depeche Mode
Through Being Cool	Devo
Love on the Rocks	Neil Diamond

Hold on Loosely	38-Special
Genius of Love	Tom Tom Club
Wordy Rappinghood	Tom Tom Club
Magic Power	Triumph
Turning Japanese	The Vapors
Life of Illusion, A	Joe Walsh
Out Come the Freaks	Was (Not Was)
Just the Two of Us	Grover Washington Jr
Set This House Ablaze	Paul Weller
Don't Let Go the Coat	The Who
You Better, You Bet	The Who
While You See a Chance	Steve Winwood

1982

Tears for Fears presage a synth invasion from England with "Mad World."
George Michael and Wham presage a blue-eyed soul invasion from England with "Young Guns (Go for It)."
Richard Thompson delivers the guitar part of the year in "Shoot out the Lights."
Marshall Crenshaw plays John Lennon in Beatlemania, but more nearly recalls Buddy Holly.

Look of Love (Part One), The	ABC
*O Superman	Laurie Anderson
Goody Two Shoes	Adam Ant
Heat of the Moment, The	Asia
Planet Rock	Afrika Bambaataa & Soulsonic Force
Mickey	Toni Basil
It Might Be You	Elvin Bishop
Out of Work	Gary U.S. Bonds
Gloria	Laura Branigan
Dreaming	Kate Bush
Sat in Your Lap	Kate Bush
Suspended in Gaffa	Kate Bush
*Ice Cream for Crow	Captain Beefheart
Shake It Up	The Cars
Since You're Gone	The Cars
Hard to Say I'm Sorry	Chicago
*Rock the Casbah	The Clash
Should I Stay or Should I Go	The Clash
Up Where We Belong	Joe Cocker and Jennifer Warnes
I Don't Care Anymore	Phil Collins
Boy with a Problem	Elvis Costello
Kid about It	Elvis Costello
Long Honeymoon	Elvis Costello
Cynical Girl	Marshall Crenshaw
*Whenever You're on My Mind	Marshall Crenshaw
*You're My Favorite Waste of Time	Marshall Crenshaw
Southern Cross	Crosby, Stills & Nash
Wasted on the Way	Crosby, Stills & Nash

*Still in Saigon

Let It Whip

*Am I Evil

Helpless

Prince, The

*Days of Wine and Roses

And I'm Telling You I'm Not Going

From Small Things (Big Things One Day Come)

Save It for Later

Don't Shake Me Lucifer

I.G.Y. (What a Beautiful World)

Let's Have a War

Stand or Fall

Gypsy

Hold Me

I Ran (So Far Away)

Juke Box Hero

Jump to It

Shock the Monkey

To Hell with Poverty

Early in the Morning

Outstanding

*Sexual Healing

Centerfold

Freeze-Frame

Vacation

*We Got the Beat

*Message, The

Fast Times at Ridgemont High

Maneater

*Girls Just Want to Have Fun

Temptation

We Live So Fast

Destiny Street

Dirty Laundry

Key Largo

Cheating in the Next Room

Don't You Want Me

Hot in the City

*Number of the Beast, The

Run to the Hills

Steppin' Out

Beat Surrender

*Bitterest Pill (I Ever Had to Swallow), The

*I Love Rock and Roll

Allentown

Charlie Daniels Band

The Dazz Band

Diamond Head

Diamond Head

Diamond Head

Dream Syndicate

Dreamgirls

Dave Edmunds

The English Beat

Roky Erickson & the Aliens

Donald Fagen

Fear

The Fixx

Fleetwood Mac

Fleetwood Mac

A Flock of Seagulls

Foreigner

Aretha Franklin

Peter Gabriel

Gang of Four

The Gap Band

The Gap Band

Marvin Gaye

The J. Geils Band

The J. Geils Band

The Go-Go's

The Go-Go's

Grandmaster Flash and the Furious 5

Sammy Hagar

Daryl Hall and John Oates

Robert Hazard

Heaven 17

Heaven 17

Richard Hell

Don Henley

Bertie Higgins

Z.Z. Hill

Human League

Billy Idol

Iron Maiden

Iron Maiden

Joe Jackson

The Jam

The Jam

Joan Jett & the Blackhearts

Billy Joel

| Only You | Yazoo |
| Valley Girl | Frank and Moon Unit Zappa |

1983

MTV's first breakout female star is a Detroit dancer named Madonna Louise Cicconne (second place, Patty Smyth from Scandal).

MTV's first breakout black star is Michael Jackson, with nearly every song from Thriller *(second place, Bobby Brown in New Edition).*

Robert Cray makes the charts with a blues tune "Bad Influence."

The Clark Sisters stir up the dance crowd with a gospel song "You Brought the Sunshine."

The synthesizer rocks.

Cuts Like a Knife	Bryan Adams
Der Kommissar	After the Fire
Making Love out of Nothing at All	Air Supply
Song for a Future Generation	The B-52's
Love Is a Battlefield	Pat Benatar
Sex (I'm A)	Berlin
In a Big Country	Big Country
*Shah Sleeps in Lee Harvey Oswald's Grave, The	Butthole Surfers
*Long White Cadillac	The Blasters
Let's Dance	David Bowie
*Modern Love	David Bowie
*New England, A	Billy Bragg
Lawyers in Love	Jackson Browne
Baby Fall Down	T-Bone Burnette
Flashdance…What a Feeling	Irene Cara
I've Got a Rock and Roll Heart	Eric Clapton
*You Brought the Sunshine	The Clark Sisters
Atomic Dog	George Clinton
*Every Day I Write the Book	Elvis Costello
Shipbuilding	Elvis Costello
*Bad Influence	Robert Cray
*My Boyfriend	The Cucumbers
Do You Really Want to Hurt Me	Culture Club
*Karma Chameleon	Culture Club
Time (Clock of the Heart)	Culture Club
Let's Go to Bed	The Cure
Foolin'	Def Leppard
*Photograph	Def Leppard
Rock of Ages	Def Leppard
Come on Eileen	Dexy's Midnight Runners
Rainbow in the Dark	Dio
*She Blinded Me with Science	Thomas Dolby
*Hungry Like the Wolf	Duran Duran
Is There Something I Should Know	Duran Duran
Reflex	Duran Duran

1984

Springsteen dances with Courtney Cox on MTV in "Dancing in the Dark."

Dylan makes a video for "Don't Fall Apart on Me Tonight."

Rap goes Hollywood with Breakin'.

Prince goes Hollywood with "Purple Rain."

Hollywood goes Hollywood with Footloose *and* Eddie & the Cruisers.

Metallica channels Black Sabbath in San Francisco.

The Bangles channel the Beatles in Los Angeles.

The Minutemen hoist their freak flag in San Pedro.

The Replacements and Hüsker Dü hoist their freak flags in Minneapolis.

The Smiths hoist their hankies in England.

State of Shock	The Jacksons
Upside Down	The Jesus and Mary Chain
Sad Songs (Say So Much)	Elton John
Cherish	Kool & the Gang
Fresh	Kool & the Gang
She Bop	Cyndi Lauper
*Time after Time	Cyndi Lauper
I'm Stepping Out	John Lennon
Nobody Told Me	John Lennon
Valotte	Julian Lennon
Heart of Rock and Roll	Huey Lewis and the News
I Want a New Drug	Huey Lewis and the News
I Am a Patriot	Little Steven and the Disciples of Soul
Footloose	Kenny Loggins
Angel	Madonna
Dress You Up	Madonna
*Like a Virgin	Madonna
*Material Girl	Madonna
No More Lonely Nights	Paul McCartney
Got a Hold on Me	Christine McVie
*Fade to Black	Metallica
*For Whom the Bell Tolls	Metallica
*History Lesson (Part Two)	The Minutemen
Killed by Death	Motorhead
99 Luftbalons (99 Red Balloons)	Nena
Cool It Now	New Edition
Mr. Telephone Man	New Edition
Jam on It	Newcleus
Sister Christian	Night Ranger
Caribbean Queen (No More Love on the Run)	Billy Ocean
Loverboy	Billy Ocean
Suddenly	Billy Ocean
*Breakin'…There's No Stopping Us	Ollie and Jerry
Ghostbusters	Ray Parker Jr.
Oh, Sherrie	Steve Perry
Automatic	Pointer Sisters
Jump (For My Love)	Pointer Sisters
*Back on the Chain Gang	The Pretenders
Middle of the Road	The Pretenders
*My City Was Gone	The Pretenders
Show Me	The Pretenders
Time the Avenger	The Pretenders
2000 Miles	The Pretenders
I Would Die 4 U	Prince
Let's Go Crazy	Prince
*Purple Rain	Prince

Hot for Teacher	Van Halen
I'll Wait	Van Halen
Jump	Van Halen
Panama	Van Halen
*Couldn't Stand the Weather	Stevie Ray Vaughan
Tin Pan Alley	Stevie Ray Vaughan
Missing You	John Waite
Dance Hall Days	Wang Chung
Careless Whisper	Wham!
Everything She Wants	Wham!
Freedom	Wham!
Wake Me up before You Go-Go	Wham!
Let's Hear It for the Boy	Deniece Williams
I Just Called to Say I Love You	Stevie Wonder
Legs	ZZ Top

1985

Social conscience attacks the charts, with "We Are the World" and "Sun City"; "Free Nelson Mandela" by the Specials Stiffs.

In L.A., the Paisley underground flourishes with the Three O'Clock, Danny & Dusty, and Camper Van Beethoven.

In Seattle, the seeds of grunge are planted by Green River, Soundgarden, and the Melvins.

Rapper LL Cool J becomes a pop superstar.

Miami Vice briefly becomes the new MTV.

Be Near Me	ABC
Take on Me	AHa
*Sun City	Artists United Against Apartheid
Easy Lover	Philip Bailey
*She's on It	Beastie Boys
Common Man	The Blasters
*Fly Girl, A	Boogie Boys
Small Town Boy	Bronski Beat
Big Sky	Kate Bush
Cloudbusting	Kate Bush
*Running up That Hill	Kate Bush
Single Life, The	Cameo
Bad Trip	Camper Van Beethoven
*Take the Skinheads Bowling	Camper Van Beethoven
Tonight She Comes	The Cars
You're the Inspiration	Chicago
Thank You John	Alex Chilton
Forever Man	Eric Clapton
When Your Heart Is Weak	Cock Robin
Hallelujah	Leonard Cohen
Don't Lose My Number	Phil Collins
One More Night	Phil Collins
Sussudio	Phil Collins
Separate Lives (Love Theme from White Nights)	Phil Collins and Marilyn Michaels

Stay up Late	Talking Heads
*Everybody Wants to Rule the World	Tears for Fears
Head over Heels	Tears for Fears
Shout	Tears for Fears
Lovergirl	Teena Marie
Telling Me Lies	Linda Thompson
She Twists the Knife Again	Richard Thompson
When the Spell Is Broken	Richard Thompson
Lay Your Hands on Me	The Thompson Twins
I Drink Alone	George Thorogood
*Mrs. Green	The Three O'Clock
Voices Carry	Til Tuesday
After the Fire	Pete Townshend
Face the Face	Pete Townshend
Stronger Than the Wind	Tina Turner
We Don't Need Another Hero (Thunderdome)	Tina Turner
*We Are the World	U.S.A. for Africa
*Roxanne, Roxanne	UTFO
*Marlene on the Wall	Suzanne Vega
Downtown Train	Tom Waits
*Whole of the Moon	The Waterboys
I'm Your Man	Wham!
Touch Me (All Night Long)	Wish featuring Fonda Rae
Part-Time Lover	Stevie Wonder
Sleeping Bag	ZZ Top

1986

Throwing Muses start an indie scene in Boston with "Green."

The Beastie Boys takeoff with their rap takeoffs ("No Sleep til Brooklyn").

Steve Earle invents alt country with "Guitar Town."

Sonic Youth's experiments revitalize NYC ("Expressway to Yr Skull").

The Pet Shop Boys go back to the dance-hall in England ("West End Girls").

Shake You Down	Gregory Abbott
Who Made Who	AC/DC
A.D.I./The Horror of It All	Anthrax
Secret Lovers	Atlantic Starr
Intro	Bad Brains
Sweet Love	Anita Baker
Tarzan Boy	Baltimora
Looking for the Perfect Beat	Afrika Bambaataa & Soulsonic Force
*If She Knew What She Wants	Bangles
*Manic Monday	Bangles
*Walk Like an Egyptian	Bangles
*No Sleep till Brooklyn	Beastie Boys
Paul Revere	Beastie Boys
*(You Gotta) Fight for Your Right (To Party)	Beastie Boys

I Know It's Over	The Smiths
*Queen Is Dead, The	The Smiths
There Is a Light That Never Goes Out	The Smiths
Evol	Sonic Youth
*Expressway to Yr Skull	Sonic Youth
Two of Hearts	Stacey Q
We Don't Have to Take Our Clothes Off	Jermaine Stewart
Wild, Wild Life	Talking Heads
Only One, The	James Taylor
*Don't Let's Start	They Might Be Giants
Nearly in Love	Richard Thompson
Valerie	Richard Thompson
*Green	Throwing Muses
*Future's So Bright, I Gotta Wear Shades, The	Timbuk 3
Rumors	Timex Social Club
I Think She Likes Me	Treat Her Right
Don't Turn Around	Tina Turner
Typical Male	Tina Turner
Dreams	Van Halen
Love Walks In	Van Halen
Why Can't This Be Love	Van Halen
Left of Center	Suzanne Vega
Everybody Have Fun Tonight	Wang Chung
Different Corner, A	Wham!
Edge of Heaven	Wham!
Back in the High Life Again	Steve Winwood
Finer Things	Steve Winwood
Higher Love	Steve Winwood
All Come True	World Party

1987

Aerosmith makes a comeback ("Dude Looks Like a Lady"), but Guns N' Roses rule the arena turf ("Welcome to the Jungle").

Debbie Gibson is the new Carole King ("Only in My Dreams"), but Tiffany rules the mall ("Could've Been").

Eric B. is hailed as the new rap leader ("Eric B. Is President"), but Public Enemy has the all the righteous rage ("You're Gonna Get Yours").

The Replacements become cult heroes by celebrating one ("Alex Chilton") but Guided by Voices are gathering momentum in obscurity ("Captain's Dead").

The greying Grateful Dead finally have a hit single ("Touch of Grey").

When Smokey Sings	ABC
Angel	Aerosmith
Cryin'	Aerosmith
*Dude (Looks Like a Lady)	Aerosmith
Rag Doll	Aerosmith
*Fourth of July	Dave Alvin
*Caught in a Mosh	Anthrax
Never Gonna Give You Up	Rick Astley

1988

Choreography comes to MTV with Paula Adbul ("Straight Up").

Grunge comes to Seattle with Mudhoney ("Touch Me, I'm Sick") and Nirvana ("Pay to Play").

A Jam band called Phish forms in Vermont ("You Enjoy Myself").

NWA ups the anger ante in East L.A. ("Straight outta Compton").

Alt/country poetess Lucinda Williams pens her first anthem ("Passionate Kisses").

Cold-Hearted	Paula Abdul
Forever Your Girl	Paula Abdul
(It's Just) the Way That You Love Me	Paula Abdul
Opposites Attract	Paula Abdul
*Straight Up	Paula Abdul
Just Perfect	All
Together Forever	Rick Astley
Giving You the Best That I Got	Anita Baker
In Your Room	Bangles
*It Takes Two	Rob Base and DJ E-Z Rock
Kokomo	The Beach Boys
Indian Summer	Beat Happening
*Jackie	Blue Zone U.K.
Bad Medicine	Bon Jovi
*Stop the Violence	Boogie Down Productions
Waiting for a Star to Fall	Boy Meets Girl
Dial My Heart	The Boys
Hands to Heaven	Breathe
How Can I Fall	Breathe
What I Am	Edie Brickell and New Bohemians
*Don't Be Cruel	Bobby Brown
My Prerogative	Bobby Brown
Rock Wit'cha	Bobby Brown
*This Woman's Work	Kate Bush
Eye of Fatima (Parts 1 and 2)	Camper Van Beethoven
I Get Weak	Belinda Carlisle
Make Me Lose Control	Eric Carmen
One Good Woman	Peter Cetera
Behind the Wall	Tracy Chapman
*Fast Car	Tracy Chapman
Mountains o' Things	Tracy Chapman
Flame, The	Cheap Trick
Everything I Miss at Home	Cherrelle
I Don't Wanna Live without Your Love	Chicago
Look Away	Chicago
Three Flights Up	Frank Christian
Ideal World	The Christians
Reptile	The Church
Under the Milky Way	The Church
Everybody Knows	Leonard Cohen
I'm Your Man	Leonard Cohen
Tower of Song	Leonard Cohen
Two Hearts	Phil Collins

1989

Madonna is still in "Vogue" but Janet Jackson leads the "Rhythm Nation."

Ani DiFranco ("Lost Woman Song") and the Indigo Girls ("Closer to Fine") represent a new independent woman.

808 State introduce the sound of electronica ("Pacific").

Elvis Costello, the Cure, and Love & Rockets have their chart breakthroughs.

2 Live Crew break down the barriers to profanity in song with "Me So Horny." Dozens cheer.

Love in an Elevator	Aerosmith
Janie's Got a Gun	Aerosmith
What It Takes	Aerosmith
Can't Stop	After 7
Ready or Not	After 7
Sold Me down the River	The Alarm
Love Shack	The B-52's
Roam	The B-52's
It's No Crime	Babyface
Tender Lover	Babyface
When I See You Smile	Bad English
Eternal Flame	Bangles
Hey Ladies	Beastie Boys
Shake Your Rump	Beastie Boys
Teenage Suicide (Don't Do It)	Big Fun
Just a Friend	Biz Markie
Ride on Time	Black Box
Born to Be My Baby	Bon Jovi
I'll Be There for You	Bon Jovi
Every Little Step	Bobby Brown
On Our Own (From *Ghostbusters II*)	Bobby Brown
Roni	Bobby Brown
Love and Anger	Kate Bush
All Her Favorite Fruit	Camper Van Beethoven
Borderline	Camper Van Beethoven
When I Win the Lottery	Camper Van Beethoven
If I Could Turn Back Time	Cher
Just Like Jesse James	Cher
Buffalo Stance	Neneh Cherry
What Kind of Man Would I Be	Chicago
Bad Love	Eric Clapton
Miss You Like Crazy	Natalie Cole
Another Day in Paradise	Phil Collins
I Wish It Would Rain Down	Phil Collins
Something Happened on the Way to Heaven	Phil Collins
Poison	Alice Cooper
Baby Plays Around	Elvis Costello
Deep Dark Truthful Mirror	Elvis Costello
God's Comic	Elvis Costello

1990

A Euro dance explosion features Black Box, Depeche Mode, and Lisa Stansfield.
They call the latest hip hop diva Mariah ("Vision of Love").
A Tribe Called Quest moves hip hop into Afro Bohemia ("Can I Kick It").
Riot Grrrls fester in Minneapolis, led by Babes in Toyland ("Bruised Violet").

Moneytalks	AC/DC
More Than Words Can Say	Alias
*Bruised Violet	Babes in Toyland
Do Me!	Bell Biv Devoe
Poison	Bell Biv Devoe
Everybody Everybody	Black Box
*Strike It Up	Black Box
She Talks to Angels	The Black Crowes
How Can We Be Lovers	Michael Bolton
Blaze of Glory	Jon Bon Jovi
Crazy	The Boys
*Opened	The Breeders
I Wanna Be Rich	Calloway
*Knockin' Boots	Candyman
Love Takes Time	Mariah Carey
*Vision of Love	Mariah Carey
Isadora Duncan	Vic Chestnutt
Don't Wanna Fall in Love	Jane Child
Efflouresce and Deliquesce	The Chills
Cherry-Coloured Funk	Cocteau Twins
Do You Remember	Phil Collins
Falling	Julee Cruise
High Enough	Damn Yankees
Groove Is in the Heart	Deee-Lite
Kiss This Thing Goodbye	Del Amitri
Enjoy the Silence	Depeche Mode
*Personal Jesus	Depeche Mode
Policy of Truth	Depeche Mode
Killboy Powerhead	Didjets
*Humpty Dance, The	Digital Underground
Hold On	En Vogue
Hole Hearted	Extreme
More Than Words	Extreme
Epic	Faith No More
Ghetto Heaven	The Family Stand
Stand Up	Ferron
Now That I Am Dead	French Frith Kaiser Thompson
Repeater	Fugazi
Jazz Thing, A	Gang Starr
My My My	Johnny Gill
Rub You the Right Way	Johnny Gill

1991

Pearl Jam ("Alive") and Soundgarden ("Rusty Cage") emerge in Seattle, but Nirvana creates the breakthrough standard ("Smells Like Teen Spirit").

Moby, Massive Attack, and Future Sound of London join the trance revolution, but shoegazers My Bloody Valentine and Slint rule Brittania.

In the heartland, everyone is still sweating to C&C Music Factory, MC Hammer, Paula Abdul, Salt-n-Pepa, and Lisa Lisa.
A "Green Day" dawns in Southern California, but up North, Metallica has their biggest hit ("Enter Sandman").

All Woman	Lisa Stansfield
Motown Song, The	Rod Stewart
Rhythm of My Heart	Rod Stewart
All This Time	Sting
Show Me the Way	Styx
*Girlfriend	Matthew Sweet
I've Been Waiting	Matthew Sweet
One More Try	Timmy T.
Copperline	James Taylor
I Feel So Good	Richard Thompson
I Misunderstood	Richard Thompson
*Vincent Black Lightning	Richard Thompson
*Not Too Soon	Throwing Muses
Sensitivity	Ralph Tresvant
You Don't Have to Go Home Tonight	The Triplets
Even Better Than the Real Thing	U2
Mysterious Ways	U2
*One	U2
Right Now	Van Halen
Top of the World	Van Halen
Don't Want to Be a Fool	Luther Vandross
Power of Love/Love Power	Luther Vandross
American Music	The Violent Femmes
Gypsy Woman (She's Homeless)	Crystal Waters
Niagara	The Wedding Present
Romantic	Karyn White
Jungle Fever	Stevie Wonder
Mr. Bad Example	Warren Zevon
Renegade	Warren Zevon

1992

A Minneapolis Replacement named Westerberg sings a song in Singles, *Cameron Crowe's movie about Seattle ("Dyslexic Heart").*

The Jayhawks turn folk/rock into Americana ("Waiting for the Sun").

Tori Amos ("Crucify") and PJ Harvey ("Sheela-Na-Gig") bring confessional rock to new depths.

Andre Young (Dr. Dre) leaves NWA for greater fame ("Dre Day").

Rooster	Alice in Chains
Would	Alice in Chains
Crucify	Tori Amos
Me and a Gun	Tori Amos
*Silent All These Years	Tori Amos
*Winter	Tori Amos
*Digeridoo	Aphex Twin
Mr. Wendall	Arrested Development
People Everyday	Arrested Development
Revolution	Arrested Development

Runaway Train	Soul Asylum
Somebody to Shove	Soul Asylum
Two Princes	The Spin Doctors
Human Touch	Bruce Springsteen
If I Should Fall Behind	Bruce Springsteen
My Beautiful Reward	Bruce Springsteen
Swallow That	Superchunk
Right Now	Al B. Sure
Right Here	SWV
Move This	Technotronic
These Are Days	10,000 Maniacs
Baby Baby Baby	TLC
What About Your Friends	TLC
All I Want	Toad the Wet Sprocket
Scenario	A Tribe Called Quest
*Baby Boom Ché	John Trudell
Everything about You	Ugly Kid Joe
*Something Good	The Utah Saints
I Don't Want to Grow Up	Tom Waits
Whistle down the Wind	Tom Waits
*Dyslexic Heart	Paul Westerberg
Saving the Best for Last	Vanessa Williams
Rump Shaker	Wreckx-N-Effect
Ballad of Peter Pumpkinhead	XTC
Harvest Moon	Neil Young

1993

Alt rock emerges with Nirvana and Pearl Jam leading the way, followed by Beck ("Loser"), Counting Crows ("Mr. Jones"), and Blind Melon ("No Rain").

The Goo Goo Dolls, Bjork, Belly, the Breeders, Liz Phair, and Aimee Mann make strong debuts.

But Gangsta rap is offering a stiff challenge for the teen dollar, with Snoop Doggy Dogg ("Gin and Juice"), Tupac Shakur ("Keep Ya Head Up"), and the Wu-Tang Clan ("C.R.E.A.M.") releasing powerful statements and Dr. Dre ("Nothin' but a G Thang"), Cypress Hill ("I Ain't Going out Like That"), DRS ("Gangsta Lean"), Ice Cube ("It Was a Good Day"), and MC Lyte ("Ruffneck") providing colorful commentaries.

All That She Wants	Ace of Base
Sign, The	Ace of Base
All for Love	Bryan Adams, Rod Stewart, Sting
Amazing	Aerosmith
Cryin'	Aerosmith
Livin' on the Edge	Aerosmith
Come to Butt-Head	Beavis and Butt-Head
*Loser	Beck
*Feed the Tree	Belly
*Big Time Sensuality	Bjork
Human Behaviour	Bjork
Venus as a Boy	Bjork

None of Your Business	Salt-n-Pepa
Shoop	Salt-n-Pepa
*Whatta Man	Salt-n-Pepa featuring En Vogue
Love Is Everything	Jane Siberry
Today	Smashing Pumpkins
Happier Blue	Chris Smither
Informer	Snow
Black Gold	Soul Asylum
Afro	Jon Spencer Blues Explosion
Streets of Philadelphia	Bruce Springsteen
Connected	Stereo MCs
If I Ever Lose My Faith in You	Sting
Plush	Stone Temple Pilots
I'm So into You	SWV
Weak	SWV
Candy Everybody Wants	10,000 Maniacs
I Get Around	2Pac
*Keep Ya Head Up	2Pac
Break It down Again	Tears for Fears
Beeswing	Richard Thompson
I Believe My Own Eyes	*Tommy*
Award Tour	A Tribe Called Quest
Wanderer, The	U2
*Anodyne	Uncle Tupelo
Sister Havana	Urge Overkill
*Cantaloop (Flip Fantasia)	US3
Push th' Little Daisies	Ween
Sweet Old World	Lucinda Williams
Love Is	Vanessa Williams and Brian McKnight
*C.R.E.A.M.	Wu Tang Clan
Just Kickin' It	Xscape
*Nowhere Near	Yo La Tengo
Philadelphia	Neil Young

1994

The death of Kurt Cobain speeds up the end of alt rock as we know it for the rest of the decade, but not before Soundgarden and Alice in Chains cash in.

A new British Invasion forms around Oasis, Blur, and Portishead.

Hootie and the Blowfish, the Dave Matthews Band, and Pavement start making noise on the college circuit.

R. Kelly and Aaliyah become an item on the hip hop scene, but the Notorious B.I.G. rules.

Back & Forth	Aaliyah
Back in the Day	Ahmad
No Excuses	Alice in Chains
I Swear	All-4-One
When Can I See You	Babyface
*21st Century Digital Boy	Bad Religion

*Liar	Henry Rollins Band
Prayer for the Dying	Seal
Together or Alone	Sebadoh
My Generation, Part Two	Todd Snider
*Black Hole Sun	Soundgarden
Spoonman	Soundgarden
Love Spreads	The Stone Roses
*Big Empty	Stone Temple Pilots
Interstate Love Song	Stone Temple Pilots
Vasoline	Stone Temple Pilots
Whoot! (There It Is)	Tag Team
Creep	TLC
*Waterfalls	TLC
Short Dick Man	Twenty Fingers
Don't Tell Me What Love Can Do	Van Halen
Seether	Veruca Salt
*Regulate	Warren G. & Nate Dogg
This D.J.	Warren G.
100% Pure Love	Crystal Waters
*Buddy Holly	Weezer
My Name Is Jonas	Weezer
Undone (The Sweater Song)	Weezer
World Class Fad	Paul Westerberg
Thunder Kiss	White Zombie
Crazy Mary	Victoria Williams
Change Your Mind	Neil Young
Piece of Crap	Neil Young
*Sleeps with Angels	Neil Young

1995

Take That revive the Boy Band sound ("Back for Good").

Alanis Morissette emerges as the angriest of the angry young women of rock ("You Oughta Know").

Underworld ("Born Slippy"), Tricky ("Overcome"), and Goldie ("Timeless") keep the midnight dance floors packed.

The murder of Selena ("Dreaming of You") starts a Latin music revival, the chief beneficiary of which is "The Macarena" by Los Del Rio.

A rare Beatles song is found ("Free as a Bird").

Bruce Springsteen enters his Woody Guthrie phase ("The Ghost of Tom Joad").

Hard as a Rock	AC/DC
*Free as a Bird	The Beatles
Good	Better Than Ezra
Army of Me	Bjork
Sittin' up In My Room	Brandy
You're Making Me High	Toni Braxton
And Fools Shine On	Brother Cane
Always Be My Baby	Mariah Carey
Fantasy	Mariah Carey

1996

Sleater-Kinney rekindle the spirit of indie rock.

Steve Earle reclaims the mantle of Americana from Son Volt.

Jacob Dylan's Wallflowers reclaim the folk/rock mantle from daddy Bob.

Erykah Badu remakes Afro Bohemia in her own image.

Master P makes a career move from hoops to hip hop.

"Pepper" and "Popular" share an uneasy moment in the spoken word poetry slam.

The murder of Tupac Shakur brings rap's West Coast–East Coast friction to a boil.

I Turn to You	All-4-One
Criminal	Fiona Apple
*On & On	Erykah Badu
Mouth	Merrill Bainbridge
Devil's Haircut	Beck
New Pollution, The	Beck
*Where It's At	Beck
*Stars of Track and Field	Belle & Sebastian
*You and Me and the Bottle Make Three Tonight	Big Bad Voodoo Daddy
*No Diggity	BlackStreet
*Not Gon' Cry	Mary J. Blige
*Crossroads, Tha	Bone Thugs-n-Harmony
Mother, Mother	Tracy Bonham
*Pepper	Butthole Surfers
Distance, The	Cake
Myrtle	Vic Chesnutt
Change the World	Eric Clapton and Babyface
All This Useless Beauty	Elvis Costello
Everyday Is a Winding Road	Sheryl Crow
If It Makes You Happy	Sheryl Crow
Angels of the Silences	Counting Crows
Long December, A	Counting Crows
Salvation	The Cranberries
Counting Blue Cars	Dishwalla
*Midnight in a Perfect World	DJ Shadow
Everything Falls Apart	Dog's Eye View
*Telephone Road	Steve Earle
Novocaine for the Soul	Eels
I Want to Come Over	Melissa Etheridge
Santa Monica (Watch the World Drown)	Everclear
Missing	Everything But the Girl
Big Me	Foo Fighters
Radiation Vibe	Fountains of Wayne
#1 Crush	Garbage
Stupid Girl	Garbage
Follow You Down	Gin Blossoms
Pony	Ginuine
Every Little Bit	Patti Griffin

Humans Being	Van Halen
Me Wise Magic	Van Halen
Difference, The	The Wallflowers
One Headlight	The Wallflowers
*6TH Avenue Heartbreak	The Wallflowers
*Three Marlenas	The Wallflowers
Good Life, The	Weezer
*Orphan Girl	Gillian Welch
Good Day	Paul Westerberg
As Cool as I Am	Dar Williams

1997

The Boy Band sound of the Backstreet Boys leads to the Girl Power of the Spice Girls.

In the heartland, Commander Venus invents Emo ("Jean's TV") and Modest Mouse refine their indie chops ("Jesus Christ Was an Only Child").

The sitar returns to rock and roll, briefly, in Cornershop's "Brimful of Asha."

Bob Dylan summons the energy to write a new thirteen-minute opus ("Highlands").

Missy Elliot jumps up from Virginia with a reinvention of the Dramatics' "In the Rain."

The Notorious B.I.G. still ruled New York when he was gunned down in the rap wars.

Pink	Aerosmith
Barbie Girl	Aqua
Everybody (Backstreet's Back)	Backstreet Boys
*Quit Playing Games (With My Heart)	Backstreet Boys
*Marilyn	Dan Bern
Song 2	Blur
Look into My Eyes	Bone Thugs-N-Harmony
Four Seasons of Loneliness	Boyz II Men
Bitch	Meredith Brooks
*Block Rockin' Beats	Chemical Brothers
Setting Sun	Chemical Brothers
Tubthumping	Chumbawamba
I Don't Want to Wait	Paula Cole
Listen	Collective Soul
Precious Declaration	Collective Soul
Sunny Came Home	Shawn Colvin
*Jean's TV	Commander Venus
*C U When You Get There	Coolio
*Brimful of Asha	Cornershop
*My Own Prison	Creed
What's This Life For	Creed
With Arms Wide Open	Creed
*Busy Child	Crystal Method
Touch, Peel and Stand	Days of the New
*Highlands	Bob Dylan
Not Dark Yet	Bob Dylan
To Make You Feel My Love	Bob Dylan

*Karma Police	Radiohead
*Put Your Hands Where My Eyes Could See	Busta Rhymes
*What They Do	The Roots
I Want You	Savage Garden
Truly Madly Deeply	Savage Garden
Bernadette	Paul Simon
*New Forms	Roni Size & Reprazent
*Walkin' on the Sun	Smash Mouth
Angeles	Elliot Smith
*Miss Misery	Elliot Smith
Say You'll Be There	Spice Girls
2 Become 1	Spice Girls
*Wannabe	Spice Girls
*Hell	Squirrel Nut Zippers
*Born on the Wrong Planet	The String Cheese Incident
Santeria	Sublime
Fly	Sugar Ray
Semi-Charmed Kind of Life	Third Eye Blind
*Up Jumps Da Boogie	Timbaland and Magoo
If You Could Only See	Tonic
Discotheque	U2
Staring at the Sun	U2
Nice & Slow	Usher
*You Make Me Wanna	Usher
*Freshmen, The	The Verve Pipe

1998

Lost Woody Guthrie manuscripts found in Brooklyn and interpreted by Billy Bragg and Wilco, featuring Natalie Merchant.
"Mississippi" is Bob Dylan's best song since "The Groom's Still Waiting at the Altar" and Sheryl Crow's best performance, period.
Fatboy Slim's "The Rockafella Skank" is the dance mantra of the year.
Lauryn Hill leaves the Fugees to produce a masterpiece "Doo-Wop (That Thing)" and a Queen (Aretha Franklin's "A Rose Is Still a Rose").
Jonathan Richman makes the most of his cameo in There's Something about Mary *("Let Her Go into Darkness").*
*Justin, from the boy band *NSYNC and girl millionaire Britney Spears are the latest hot gossip on MTV.*

I Don't Want to Miss a Thing	Aerosmith
Never Ever	All Saints
One Week	Barenaked Ladies
Nobody's Fault but My Own	Beck
Seymour Stein	Belle & Sebastian
Tiger Woods	Dan Bern
*Still Not a Player	Big Punisher featuring Joe
*Way over Yonder in the Minor Key	Billy Bragg and Natalie Merchant
Boy Is Mine, The	Brandy and Monica
*If Winter Ends	Bright Eyes
I Lie in the Bed I Made	Brother Cane

*Pretty Fly for a White Guy	Offspring
Most High	Jimmy Page and Robert Plant
Given to Fly	Pearl Jam
Been around the World	Puff Daddy
Come with Me	Puff Daddy
*It's All about the Benjamins	Puff Daddy
New Noise	Refused
Dangerous	Busta Rhymes
*Let Her Go into Darkness	Jonathan Richman
*You Got Me	The Roots featuring Erykah Badu
*Closing Time	Semisonic
Blue on Black	Kenny Wayne Shepherd
Kiss Me	Sixpence None the Richer
Gettin' Jiggy wit It	Will Smith
*Baby One More Time	Britney Spears
Every Morning	Sugar Ray
*It Hurts So Bad	Susan Tedeschi
*Changes	2 PAC
*Bitter Suite Symphony	Verve
*April Fools	Rufus Wainwright
*Car Wheels on a Gravel Road	Lucinda Williams
Right in Time	Lucinda Williams

1999

Ricky Martin makes the most of the moment on the Grammy Award telecast to usher in a Latin rock fiesta. A year later Carlos Santana would win seven.

Christina Aguilera plays Debbie Gibson to Britney's Tiffany. A year later it would be vice-versa.

Dr. Dre discovers Detroit's tortured genius Marshall (Eminem) Mathers. A year later Mathers would be suing his wife and mother and vice-versa.

Limp Bizkit advises the crowd at Woodstock '99 to "Break Stuff" and they willingly comply.

*Woke up This Morning	A3
Come on Over (All I Want Is You)	Christina Aguilera
*Genie in a Bottle	Christina Aguilera
What a Girl Wants	Christina Aguilera
*I Need to Know	Marc Anthony
Fast as You Can	Fiona Apple
Paper Bag	Fiona Apple
*I Want It That Way	Backstreet Boys
Show Me the Meaning of Being Lonely	Backstreet Boys
Bling Bling	B.G.
All the Small Things	Blink 182
Lit Up	Buckcherry
Chemicals between Us, The	Bush
Better Than I've Ever Been	Cindy Bullens
Thank God I Found You	Mariah Carey
*Believe	Cher

*Climb to Safety   Widespread Panic
*She's a Jar   Wilco

2000

*Coldplay goes after the chalice of U2 and Radiohead. But U2 ("Beautiful Day") and Radiohead ("The National Anthem")
are not ready to give it up.*

Eminem goes after the chalice of Bob Dylan. But Bob is not ready to give it up ("Things Have Changed").

Fifty Cent is looking to be Rap's next great hope ("How to Rob") but OutKast is already there ("Ms. Jackson").

Unlike "Most Girls," Pink can compete with Christina and Britney.

Steely Dan makes a comeback ("Cousin Dupree").

Bluegrass makes a comeback in the movie O Brother Where Art Thou.

Warren Zevon writes his epitaph ("Life'll Kill Ya").

Shape of My Heart	Backstreet Boys
*Who Let the Dogs Out	Baha Men
Perfect Sonnet, A	Bright Eyes
Cry Like a Baby	Kasey Chambers
*Yellow	Coldplay
Fallen out of Love	Amy Correia
Independent Woman	Destiny's Child
*Jumpin' Jumpin'	Destiny's Child
He Loves U Not	Dream
*Things Have Changed	Bob Dylan
*Real Slim Shady, The	Eminem
*Stan	Eminem
*Way I Am, The	Eminem
*How to Rob	Fifty Cent
Breakout	Foo Fighters
Hemorrhage (In My Hands)	Fuel
Little Things	Good Charlotte
Babylon	David Gray
Minority	Green Day
Doesn't Really Matter	Janet Jackson
Big Pimpin'	Jay Z
I Wanna Know	Joe
*Sailing to Philadelphia	Mark Knopfler and James Taylor
Hanging by a Moment	Lifehouse
*One Step Closer	Linkin Park
Don't Tell Me	Madonna
Music	Madonna
Bent	Matchbox Twenty
South Side	Moby & Gwen Stefani
Hot Shit (Country Grammar)	Nelly
Give Me Just One Night	98 Degrees
*Bye Bye Bye	*NSYNC
It's Gonna Be Me	*NSYNC
This I Promise You	*NSYNC

*B.O.B.	OutKast
*Ms. Jackson	OutKast
Last Resort	Papa Roach
*Farm House	Phish
*Most Girls	Pink
*There You Go	Pink
*National Anthem, The	Radiohead
*Californication	Red Hot Chili Peppers
Otherside	Red Hot Chili Peppers
*Cousin Dupree	Steely Dan
Kryptonite	3 Doors Down
*Beautiful Day	U2
Elevation	U2
Walk On	U2
Everything You Want	Vertical Horizon
*Life'll Kill Ya	Warren Zevon

SELECTED SOURCES FOR THE
ROCK SONG INDEX

ASCAP. *ASCAP Index of Performed Compositions*. New York: American Society of Composers, Authors and Publishers, 1978.

Betrock, Alan. *Girl Groups: The Story of a Sound*. New York: Delilah Press, 1982.

Bronson, Fred. *Billboard Book of Number One Hits*. New York: Billboard Publications, 1985.

Buskin, Richard. *Inside Tracks*. New York: Avon Books, 1999.

Christgau, Robert. *Christgau's Record Guide, the 70s*. New Haven, CT: Ticknor & Fields, 1981.

Christgau, Robert. *Christgau's Record Guide, the 80s*. New York: Pantheon Books, 1990.

Christgau, Robert. *Christgau's Record Guide, the 90s*. New York: St. Martin's Griffin, 2000.

Clark, Al. *The Rock Yearbook, 1984*. New York: St. Martin's Press, 1983.

Coupe, Stuart and Glenn A. Baker. *The New Rock and Roll: The A-Z of Rock in the 80s*. New York: St. Martin's Press, 1983.

Cranna, Ian. *The Rock Yearbook, 1986*. New York: St. Martin's Press, 1985.

Denisoff, R. Serge and Richard Peterson. *The Sounds of Social Change*. Chicago, IL: Rand McNally, 1972.

Crenshaw, Marshall. *Hollywood Rock*. New York: Harper-Perennial, 1994.

Dudley, Bonnie. *Phonolog Reports*. San Diego, CA: Trade Service Corporation.

Ehrenstein, David and Bill Reed. *Rock on Film*. San Francisco: Miller Freeman, 1992.

Erlewine, Michael and Scott Bultman. *The All Music Guide*. San Francisco: Miller Freeman, 2001.

Escott, Colin. *Tattooed on Their Tongues*. New York: Schirmer Books, 1996.

Escott, Colin and Martin Hawkes. *Good Rockin' Tonight: Sun Records and the Birth of Rock and Roll*. New York: St. Martin's Press, 1991.

George, Nelson. *Where Did Our Love Go: The Rise and Fall of the Motown Sound*. New York: St. Martin's Press, 1986.

Gilbert, Bob and Gary Theroux. *The Top Ten, 1956 – Present*. New York: Fireside Books, 1982.

Gillette, Charlie. *The Sound of the City: The Rise of Rock & Roll*. New York: Outerbridge and Dienstfrey, 1970.

Graff, Gary. *Music Hound / Rock: The Essential Album Guide*. Detroit, MI: Visible Ink Press, 1996.

Groia, Phillips. *They All Sang on the Corner*. West Hempstead, NY: Phillie Dee Enterprises Inc., 1983.

Guralnick, Peter. *Feel Like Going Home: Portraits in the Blues and Rock and Roll*. New York: Outerbridge and Dienstfrey, 1971.

Guralnick, Peter. *Sweet Soul Music*. New York: Harper & Row, 1986.

Helander, Brock. *The Rock Who's Who, 2nd ed*. New York: Schirmer Books, 1996.

Hibbert, Tom. *The Rock Yearbook, 1987*. New York: St. Martin's Press, 1986.

Hirshey, Gerry. *Nowhere to Run: The Story of Soul Music*. New York: Times Books, 1984.

Hornby, Nick. *Songbook*. New York: Riverhead Books, 2003.

Jackson, John A. *Big Beat Heat: Alan Freed and the Early Years of Rock and Roll*. New York: Schirmer Books, 1991.

Irvin, Jim. *The Mojo Collection: The Greatest Albums of All Time*. Edinburgh: Mojo Books, 2000.

Jancik, Wayne and Tad Lathrop. *Cult Rockers*. New York: Fireside Books, 1995.

Larson, Glen. *The Guinness Encyclopedia of Popular Music*. London: Guinness, 1995.

Lax, Roger and Frederick Smith. *The Great Song Thesaurus*. New York: Oxford University Press, 1985.

Lethem, Jonathan. *Fortress of Solitude*, New York: Doubleday & Co, Inc., 2002.

Marcus, Griel. *Stranded: Rock and Roll for a Desert Island*. New York: Alfred A. Knopf, 1979.

Marcus, Griel. *Mystery Train*. New York: Plume Books, 1990.

Marsh, Dave. *The Heart of Rock & Soul: The 1001 Best Singles Ever Made*. New York: Plume Books, 1989.

Marsh, Dave and John Swenson. *The Rolling Stone Record Guide*. New York: Random House, 1979.

Marsh, Dave and John Swenson. *The New Rolling Stone Record Guide*. New York: Random House, 1983.

McAleer, Dave. *British and American Hit Singles, 1960-1990*. London and New York: Omnibus, 1990.

Murrels, Joseph. *Million Selling Records from the 1900s to the 1980s*. New York: Arco, 1985.

Nite, Norm N. *Rock On: The Illustrated Encyclopedia of Rock N' Roll*. New York: Popular Library, 1974.

Olson, Eric, Paul Verna, and Carlo Wolff. *The Encyclopedia of Record Producers*. New York: Billboard Books, 1999.

Palmer, Robert. *Baby That Was Rock and Roll: The Legendary Leiber & Stoller*. New York: Harcourt Brace Jovanovich, 1978.

Palmer, Robert. *Deep Blues*. New York: Penguin, 1982.

Pollack, Neil. *Never Mind the Pollacks*. New York: Harper Collins, 2003.

Pollock, Bruce. *In Their Own Words: Lyrics and Lyricists, 1955–1974*. New York: Macmillan, 1975.

Pollock, Bruce. *When Rock Was Young*. New York: Holt, Rinehart & Winston, 1981.

Pollock, Bruce. *When the Music Mattered*. New York: Holt, Rinehart & Winston, 1983.

Pollock, Bruce. *Interviews with Great Songwriters*. Port Chester, NY: Cherry Lane Books, 1986.

Pollock, Bruce. *Hipper Than Our Kids: A Rock & Roll Journal of the Baby Boom Generation*. New York: Schirmer Books, 1993.

Pollock, Bruce. *Working Musicians*. New York: Harper-Collins, 2002.

Pollock, Bruce. *Popular Music: An Annotated Index of American Popular Songs, 1980–1999*. Detroit, MI: Gale Research Co., 1980–2000.

Pollock, Bruce and Nat Shapiro. *Popular Music: An Annotated Index of American Popular Songs, 1920–1979*. Detroit, MI: Gale Research Co., 1983.

Quirin, Jim and Barry Cohen. *Rock 100*. Covington, LA: Chartmaster, 1976.

Recording Industry of America. *Songs of the Century*. New York: Recording Industry of America, 2000.

Robbins, Ira. *Trouser Press Record Guide, 4th ed.* New York: Collier/Macmillan, 1991.

Rock and Roll Hall of Fame. *Rock and Roll Hall of Fame 500.* Cleveland, OH: Rock and Roll Hall of Fame, 1997.

Rhode, H. Kandy. *The Gold of Rock and Roll, 1955–1967.* New York: Arbor House, 1970.

Romanowski, Patricia and Holly George-Warren. *Rolling Stone Encyclopedia of Rock & Roll.* New York: Fireside Press, 1996.

Roxon, Lilian. *Roxon's Rock Encyclopedia.* New York: Workman Publishing, 1976.

Santelli, Robert. *The Sixties: A Listener's Guide.* Chicago, IL: Contemporary Books, 1985.

Shannon, Bob and John Javna. *Behind the Hits.* New York: Warner Books, 1986.

Tosches, Nick. *Unsung Heroes of Rock 'n' Roll.* New York: Harmony Books, 1991.

Various. *Sun Records: The Discography.* Hambergen, Germany: Bear Family Books, 1987.

Various. *Rhinolog.* Los Angeles, CA, 1997.

Various. *The Rolling Stone Record Review.* New York: Pocket Books, 1971.

Various. *Zagat Guide to Rock and Roll.* New York: Zagat, 2003.

Whitburn, Joel. *Bubbling Under, 1959–1981.* Menomenee Falls, WI: Record Research, Inc., 1982.

Whitburn, Joel. *Top Pop Albums, 1955–1999.* Menomenee Falls, WI: Record Research, Inc., 2000.

Whitburn, Joel. *Top Country Hits, 1944–1997.* Menomenee Falls, WI: Record Research, Inc., 1997.

Whitburn, Joel. *Top Pop Singles, 1955–1999.* Menomenee Falls, WI: Record Research, Inc., 2000.

Whitburn, Joel. *Rock Tracks.* Menomenee Falls, WI: Record Research, Inc., 1995.

Whitburn, Joel. *Top R&B Hits, 1941–1999.* Menomenee Falls, WI: Record Research, Inc., 2000.

White, Adam and Fred Bronson. *The Billboard Book of Number One Rhythm and Blues Hits.* New York: Billboard Publications, 1993.

Williams, Paul. *Rock and Roll: The Best 100 Singles.* New York: Carroll & Graf, 1993.

Web Sites

All Music Guide (allmusic.com)
ASCAP.com
BMI.com
Bomp.com
Musicmatch.com
Producer Index (mojavemusic.com)
Songfacts.com
Velvetrope.com

Magazines

Alternative Press
Billboard Magazine
Blender
Cashbox
College Music Journal

Creem
Entertainment Weekly
Guitar for the Practicing Musician
Hit Parader
Hits
Mojo
Musician
Playback
Q
Rock
Rolling Stone
Saturday Review
Spin
Stereo Review
Trouser Press
Village Voice
Viva

Selected Boxed Sets/Liner Notes

The Clash on Broadway. New York: Sony Legacy, 1991.

Cohen, Norm. *Folk Song America.* Washington, DC: Smithsonian Recordings, 1990.

Escott, Colin. *Loud, Fast & Out of Control.* Los Angeles, CA: Rhino Records, 1999.

Escott, Colin. *The King R&B Boxed Set.* Nashville, TN: King Records, 1995.

Guterman, Jimmy. *Sun Records Collection.* Santa Monica, CA: Rhino Records, 1984.

Hyde, Bob. *Doo Wop.* Los Angeles, CA: Rhino Records, 1993.

Jorgensen, Ernst Mikael and Roger Semon. *Elvis, The King of Rock 'N' Roll: The Complete 50's Masters.* New York: BMG Entertainment Co., 1992.

Jorgensen, Ernst Mikael and Roger Semon. *Elvis, Command Performances, Essential 60's Masters II.* New York: BMG Entertainment Co, 1995.

Kaye, Lenny and Gary Stewart. *Nuggets, Original Artyfacts from the First Psychedelic Era.* Los Angeles, CA: Rhino Records, 1972.

Mansfield, Cary and Robert Simms. *Hitsville, USA: The Motown Singles Collection.* Los Angeles: Motown Records, 1992.

Mansfield, Cary. Hitsville, USA: *The Motown Singles Collection Volume Two 1972–1992.* Los Angeles: Motown Records, 1993.

Marshall, James. *The Okeh Rhythm & Blues Story, 1949–1957.* New York: Sony Legacy, 1993.

McNeil, W.K. *The Blues.* Washington, DC: Smithsonian Recordings, 1993.

Myers, Ted. *Washington Square Memoirs.* Los Angeles, CA, Rhino Records, 2001.

Shaw, Greg and Dawn Eden. *The Brill Building Sound.* Plymouth, MN: K-Tel International, 1993.

Stewart, Gary *No Thanks, The Punk Rock Box.* Los Angeles, CA: Rhino Records, 2003.

Various. *Bob Marley: Songs of Freedom.* New York, London: Tuff Gong Records, 1992.

Various. *Cowabunga, the Surf Box.* Los Angeles, CA: Rhino Records, 1996.

Vera, Billy. *The Specialty Story.* Berkeley, CA: Specialty Records, 1994.

ABOUT THE AUTHOR

Pollock is perhaps the most important scholar of American pop music. He also wrote *Hipper Than Our Kids*, one of the best books about the "boomers" and their generation.

—Greg Shaw, *Bomp Bookshelf* (2001)

Working Musicians is a marvelous, compulsively readable book—not only an invaluable resource (and an instant education) for any aspiring musician, but also a treasure trove of good reading and new insights and perspectives for any music lover. Few books about music come so close to the truth about how it really comes into existence.

—Paul Williams, founder of *Crawdaddy* magazine (2001)

Rock Song Index (1st Edition) Succinct and many times excellent comments by Pollock.

—*Library Journal*

Since winning the Jerome Lowell Dejur prize for fiction at City College in 1971, Bruce Pollock has had a highly successful career as a Deems Taylor award-winning journalist and author of a dozen books, and has contributed to such publications as *The New York Times, Saturday Review, TV Guide, Cosmopolitan, Family Weekly, USA Today, Playboy, The Gannett Westchester Newspapers*, and *The Village Voice*. In 1983, he created and served as the first editor in chief of *GUITAR: For the Practicing Musician*, which would go on to become the most popular new music magazine launched in the 1980s. In the early 1990s, he continued to write for *Musician* and *Entertainment Weekly* and edit the annual reference book *Popular Music: An Annotated Index of American Popular Songs* while taking on the job of compilation producer and music historian at Sony BMG Music Entertainment in New York City.

He is married, has two daughters, and lives in Connecticut.